THE PEOPLE'S ARMIES

FRANCE IN 1793
Map from Donald Sutherland,
France 1789–1818 (Collins, 1985).

THE PEOPLE'S ARMIES

The *armées révolutionnaires*:
instrument of the Terror in the departments
April 1793 to Floréal Year II

RICHARD COBB

Translated by
Marianne Elliott

Yale University Press
New Haven and London

Original edition, *Les armées révolutionnaires: instrument de la Terreur dans les départements, avril 1793–floréal an II*, by Richard Cobb, published by Mouton & Co., Paris, in 2 vols: vol. I, 1961; vol. II, 1963

Designed by John Nicoll

Set in Linotron Bembo by Best-set Typesetter Limited, Hong Kong and
printed and bound in Yugoslavia by Papirografika, Ljubljana.

Library of Congress Cataloging-in Publication Data

Cobb, Richard, 1917–
   The people's armies.

   Translation of: Armées révolutionnaires.
   Includes index.
   1. France—History—Revolution, 1793.   I. Title.
DC184.C613   1987   944.04'2   87–10641
ISBN 0-300-02728-1
ISBN 0-300-04042-3 (pbk.)

CONTENTS

BOOK TWO

The Terror in the Village: the
armées révolutionnaires in action

FOREWORD

A quarter of a century ago, when this book was first published in French, I wrote in an Avant-Propos dated 'Paris, September 1960' that I would have wished to dedicate the book to all of my French friends, had they not been so numerous; but had had to content myself with naming many of them in the notes to the work. I owe a large debt to those friends, and to the great cities and bourgs of their country: since 1935, when I first went to Paris, I have been the object of a veritable *conspiration de l'amitié*; and the researches which led up to the original publication of this work gave me above all a marvellous excuse for *promenades* over virtually the whole of France, and were for me the best justification for a study from which I came to know La Croix-Rousse, Marseille, Le Havre, Lille, Toulouse, and the little communes of the Ile-de-France, Haute-Normandie, and the periphery of Paris.

The idea for the work, which I wished to make as comprehensive as possible, was suggested to me by two great historians of the Revolution, Pierre Caron and Georges Lefebvre, my masters and counsellors, sometimes severe, always supportive; General Herlaut and Georges Javogues guided my first steps as a researcher in 1938–9; Albert Soboul and George Rudé, my old companions in the Archives, preceded me, true pioneers, in writing the history of the sans-culottes. Without the friendship and guidance of these and other historians, the courtesy and care of the many archivists and local historians whom I attempted to list in the original preface, and the support of many others, former colleagues, helpers, and friends, named there, *Les armées révolutionnaires* would never have been finished or published. Once again on this occasion I thank them all, living and dead, for their company and their affectionate encouragement; and now add my thanks to Dr Marianne Elliott for her patience and perseverance over the English translation of this large and complex work, and to Yale University Press for making the work available, this many years later, to a new audience.

Richard Cobb
Oxford, November 1986

TRANSLATOR'S PREFACE

Richard Cobb's *Les armées révolutionnaires*, though one of his earliest works, has long been accepted as perhaps his best and, certainly in terms of historical approach, his most characteristic work. For a quarter of a century the absence of a translated version and the density of detail, particularly in the footnotes, has denied access to readers with either no French or a moderate command of it. Having long recommended an English translation of the book, my response on being asked by Richard Cobb to undertake the task combined pleasure that it was at last about to be undertaken and – recognising the sheer enormity of that task – deep reservations about my own role in it. This was in 1980 when I was still completing my own *Partners in Revolution*. That book written, the translation finally got under way in January 1983. Two years later it was completed, having taken a somewhat different form to that at first envisaged.

At an early stage it became quite apparent that the chief merit of *Les armées* – the intricate detail, the deep insight into the minutiae of life among the *petit peuple* – would suffer in a free translation; that the example piled upon example, quotation upon quotation, lists of names, occupations, places, responses, situations, though translating jerkily into English, were nevertheless so much a part of the almost legendary reputation which Richard Cobb's *Les armées* has acquired, that the sacrifice of a more flowing style seemed the smaller price to pay for their retention. The full text appears here in translation, and even though the work in English is shorter than the original French, nothing has been omitted. Indeed many of the original footnotes – particularly the long quotations from original documents – have been incorporated into the text. The remaining notes contain all the original references, even if many have been merged and their contents summarised. While readers therefore will find fuller references than in many other translations from foreign languages, the historical researcher may still wish to check for detail with the original.

Les armées révolutionnaires was originally published in Paris in two volumes, the first in 1961, the second in 1963. The first volume describes the institutional framework of these remarkable bodies; the second, longer, volume contains the bulk of the material for which *Les armées* is deservedly celebrated: the analysis of the *mentalité* of those involved in, and with, the institutions – the benefactors, beneficiaries, and victims alike. The reader will consequently notice a very different 'feel' in the earlier and later parts of the English version. The whole problem of trying to preserve some sense of the original style in a translation is undoubtedly the most intractable one likely to be encountered by any translator. This problem was uppermost in the mind of the present translator, given the unique style of Richard Cobb's works in English. However, Richard Cobb's French style is very different from his English one, dictated as much by the medium as his English style is by the message. I have endeavoured to convey the essential character of his particular approach, without being able entirely to deliver what in any case is the more mature and more highly developed style of the later works. What I hope to have achieved is to have unlocked the appreciable merits of Richard Cobb's most substantial published work to a wider English-speaking readership. The 60-page bibliography of the original is omitted because the wide and diversified range of archival sources is clear from the notes, and researchers can refer to the original if necessary.

The bulk of this translation was completed during an honorary visiting professorship at Iowa State University, and latterly in the Department of History at Liverpool University. To the academic and secretarial staff of both institutions, to Professor Richard Lowitt, Professor Andrejs Plakans and Mrs Audrey Burton of the former, and Suzanne Robinson and Dr Richard Waller of the latter, I owe particular thanks. Dr Peter Jones of Birmingham University read and commented on the final product and Catharine Carver pulled the whole thing together in a quite remarkable feat of copy-editing. My debt to both is immeasurable.

University of Liverpool   Marianne Elliott
March 1985–November 1986

Introduction*

I *Originality of the* armées révolutionnaires

Of the many para-revolutionary and spontaneous institutional creations of the Terror, the *armées révolutionnaires* were among the most original and characteristic. Some were popular armies in outline; most were recruited through truly democratic means; all represented the Terror's solution to the eternal problem of relations between the civil authorities and the armed forces. Above all, the *armées révolutionnaires* were groups of armed civilians, and if some acquired a sense of corporate identity it was that of a privileged political élite. The *armées* never became militarised. They had all the weaknesses of civilian forces and their subordination to the political powers is particularly illustrated by the way in which recruitment was left to the *sociétés populaires* and to the political authorities.

It is true that some of the duties assigned to these *armées* were not original. Peasants have always had to suffer the effects of military quartering and requisitions. But to confide the task of requisitioning grain to those most interested in the supply of the main towns was an original, if not a revolutionary, idea. Equally original was the idea of attaching an armed force, chosen for its political orthodoxy, to the urban 'apostles' sent to preach the revolutionary gospel to the rural populace. These *révolutionnaires*, whose battles were fought within the *sociétés populaires* and in the pulpits of former churches, were no ordinary soldiers. Theirs was a war fought less by cannon and gun-shot than by the word and judicial terror.

---

* *Translator's note:* The author's original 1961 Introduction has been edited and slightly abridged in this translation, to account for a certain amount of obsolescence in its historiographical section. Although no work on the *armées révolutionnaires* of comparable range and depth has appeared since Richard Cobb's second volume was published, in 1963, readers may care to consult the following more recent publications for bibliographies and historiographical accounts covering the intervening years: Martyn Lyons, *Revolution in Toulouse. An Essay in Provincial Terrorism* (New York, 1978); Colin R. Lucas, *The Structure of the Terror* (Oxford, 1973); R. B. Rose, *The Making of the Sans-Culottes: Democratic Ideas and Institutions in Paris, 1789–92* (Manchester, 1982); Morris M. Slavin, *The French Revolution in Miniature: Section Droits-de-l'Homme, 1789–1795* (Princeton, 1984).

'The *armée révolutionnaire* was one of the essential elements of the terrorist system', observes Laukhard, with greater accuracy than was normal for this curious figure. A deserter from the Prussian army and later a Lutheran minister and university professor, he claimed to have enrolled as a 'French sans-culotte' in one of these *armées*. 'In those areas through which it passed, people were terrified to utter anything which might be construed as counter-revolutionary.'[1] It is best to view these *armées* as essential cogs in the administration of the Terror. They represented the Terror on the move, the village Terror. They aroused fear and such was the intention of their creators. They were instruments of vigilance and vengeance, punishing the guilty, terrorising the lukewarm and the indifferent, regenerating public spirit and supplying the urban markets by force. Compared with these, their vision of helping the oppressed sans-culottes, of extending an urban revolutionary hand to their 'fréres de campagne', to the poor and the destitute, was a very secondary one indeed. The *armées révolutionnaires* represent the triumph of violence exalted to a political system and at times becoming an end in itself – hence the originality of the tasks assigned to them and, even more, the manner in which they were executed. The adjective distinguishing these *armées* from other troops was well earned: their soldiers were *révolutionnaires* – it was the name they preferred – and most of their activities sought to 'revolutionise', to overturn, to 'electrify', to change things and people by brusque and violent means, by a violence spectacular and deliberate. They were in fact 'révolutionnaires' both in the extraordinary instruments employed and in the position which they occupied in the hierarchy of revolutionary authorities. Albert Soboul, speaking of the Parisian *armée*, rightly observes: 'Of all the institutions demanded by the ultra-patriots and created through popular pressure, the *armée révolutionnaire* was undoubtedly the one which they held closest to their hearts and in which they placed most hope...'.[2] Like all the sans-culotte institutions, the *armées révolutionnaires* arose out of the administrative anarchy preceding the law of 14 Frimaire, and like the institutions of the Sections, the *armées* tended towards decentralisation, towards a kind of popular Federalism and counter-authority which threatened to break away from the Convention and its Committees altogether.

The *armées révolutionnaires* were original because the Terror was a novel system of government and because they were a fundamental part of that system. Like the Terror, they were extraordinary institutions. In 'normal' times, times of peace, under the rule of law and with courts to uphold it, such institutions are inconceivable. Like the Terror, therefore, their lives would be short. But the months of the *Grande Révolution* cannot be measured like those of calmer times and these *armées* were no less important for their short life-span.

[1] Superscript figures refer to the References at p. 633.

II *The* armées révolutionnaires *and the historians of the Revolution*

Despite their central position in the system of the Terror and in the activities of the popular organisations of the Year II, the *armées révolutionnaires* have attracted little historical attention. Only with the publication in the 1950s of Jacques Godechot's major study of the institutions of the Revolution and Empire were they at last restored to their place as *institutions de liaison* between town and country, between proconsul and village.[3] Until then, those historians who touched upon the *armées* simply recited their misdeeds, their more dramatic acts of destruction and iconoclasm. This may have been the most spectacular aspect of their operations, but it was not the most important. It is not surprising, however, that historians writing about the small communes under the Terror should have been particularly struck by this destructive tendency; religious objects were the first to pay the price and many of these local historians were churchmen.

The 'celebrities' of the *armées* have attracted most historical interest. The rank and file and the institutions themselves have either been left in obscurity or dismissed with summary epithets. Even the accounts of the 'celebrities' are to be found in books dealing with other topics. Thus Herlaut's biography of Ronsin devotes only one chapter to his rise to the command of the Parisian *armée révolutionnaire*. It is rather Ronsin as one-time actor, Ancien Regime soldier, general in the Vendée, member of the so-called 'Hébertist group', apprentice dictator, a second Cromwell, which most interests his biographer. The *armée révolutionnaire* scarcely figures at all, save to support the case that Ronsin sought to use the *armée* to over-throw the Revolutionary Government and assume power himself.[4]

Parein figures in the historiography of the Terror as the president of the Commission des Sept in Lyon, member of the Commission Militaire of Angers, Fouché's protégé in Lyon and later at the Police Ministry – possibly an accurate description of the role of this general of repression, whose involvement with the fate of the *armée*, of which he was second in command, was purely incidental.[5] The Grammonts, father and son, feature in theatrical histories of the period as does that other actor turned military politician, Simon Dufresse, commander-in-chief of the *armée révolutionnaire* of the North, and later general-baron under the Empire.[6] Boulanger, like Parein a *général de brigade* in the Parisian *armée*, finds a niche in the principal works on the Revolution as the friend and protégé of Robespierre and Hanriot, whose fate he shared after 9 Thermidor. But his role on the general staff of the Parisian *armée révolutionnaire* and his activities as spy for the Committees after the crisis of Ventôse–Germinal have been examined in only one article.[7] The local historians of the Oise have looked at the activities of Mazuel in the region and I have devoted an article to his role in the famous 'plot' of Ventôse.[8] But his activities as organiser and recruiting officer for the revolutionary cavalry, of which he was the real, if not the nominal, commander, remain unexplored.

There remain those soldiers of the departmental *armées* who appear as the celebrities, more often as the villains of local histories covering the period of the Terror. Certain groups of commanding officers and second officers have been the subject of separate articles.[9] Then there are those episodic studies of the personnel of the Terror, where no attempt is made to disentangle the revolutionary officers' role in the promotion and implementation of terrorist measures. But the greatest failing of such works is the total absence of anything on the *commissaires*, by far the most important figures in the *armées* after they had been put into active service. Marcellin and Paillardelle are unknown to historians, even though they played a much more important role in the direction of all manner of repressive operations than Clémence and Marchand, subjects of an important thesis by Henri Calvet.[10]

Most historians, then, concentrate on the commanders rather than the men, on the personalities rather than the institutions. For the ordinary soldier and the corps in which he served they reserve the moral epithet or the abusive comment on their social origin. By critic and defender alike the *armées* are judged according to very precise political standards. No other institution of the Terror can lay claim to such a torrent of abuse, much of it plagiarised from the massive literature of the Thermidorean period. Such abuse, however, is a token of the importance of these *armées* as instruments of the Terror and élite institutions in the revolutionary hierarchy, and of the dreadful reputation which they have acquired.

It was Thiers who set the tone. But he was preceded by Father Guillon de Montléon, whose 1824 work was to supply Taine's arsenal many years later. Thiers also may have borrowed from the Lyon priest when he spoke of the *armée* having been recruited 'from all the vagabonds in Paris' and composed of 'adventurers, robbers, *septembriseurs* feigning patriotism, but preferring to plunder the interior rather than travel to the frontiers where life would be poor, difficult and perilous...'. These men, whose courage and revolutionary patriotism he dismisses, are moreover 'petty tyrants' easily identified by their 'moustache and huge sabres'. But Thiers, the politician, is nevertheless more just in his judgements than Taine, and he has some very sensible passages on the importance of the *armées révolutionnaires* in the history of the Terror.[11]

Taine, however, took only the abusive epithets from Thiers, and developed them further. His work takes pride of place in this inventory of slanderous writings. He describes the *armée révolutionnaire* as 'composed almost exclusively of artisans without work, wigmakers without clients, lackeys without positions, wretches incapable of earning a living by honest work'[12] – a foolhardy thesis which reduces all revolutionary zeal to the level of the belly, but one which found favour with the conservative historians of the nineteenth and twentieth centuries, for it allowed them to emphasise the ingratitude of these 'flunkeys' towards their former masters and benefactors. A similar thesis runs through their descriptions of the personnel of the *comités révolutionnaires* and the *comités de surveillance*. Taine then progresses to pure insult: Ronsin's soldiers in Lyon are 'two thousand debauched and bloodthirsty vagabonds', 'proletarians, paid at the rate of 40 sols per day' (a point on which Taine and the socialist historian Daniel Guérin are unlikely bedfellows), and 'ultra-Jacobins' – a strange description for an *armée* only partially recruited from among the Sectionary clubs and rarely from the Jacobins and Cordeliers.[13]

The conservative historians do not have a monopoly on such slander. From quite a different school, Louis Blanc is equally unsympathetic towards men who could be foolish enough to suspect Robespierre. For Blanc they are 'bullies', 'devastating hordes', 'ravenous wolves'. To a military man like the maréchal Gouvion de Saint-Cyr the Haut-Rhin *armée* was composed of 'deserters' – the most common accusation, after that of 'cowardice', leveled at these *révolutionnaires* by historians – 'vagabonds and the scum of the *sociétés populaires*'.[14] Laukhard's account is less stark, and if he insists on the indiscipline of the sans-culotte soldiers and on the extremely varied composition of their units, he does not question the political sincerity and revolutionary enthusiasm of these primitive levellers. In addition, the Saxon pastor has the merit of pointing out that the *armées révolutionnaires* were the marching wing of the *sans-culotterie*, 'the people armed for the people', in the words of the second-in-command of the Lille *armée*. For a full development of this relationship between the urban *sans-culotterie* and the *armées révolutionnaires*, which were in effect its armed extension, we had to wait for the superbly documented work of Albert Soboul.[15]

Most of the conservative historians of the last century accuse the *révolutionnaires* of robbery and pillage. For Taine, they are 'a pack of thorough scoundrels', for Borély, the Le Havre historian, a 'collection of brigands', for Barère, the former *Conventionnel* and himself one of their creators, they are 'one of those bodies represented in the play *Robert chef de brigands*'.[16] All these writers have simply elaborated upon themes popularised by the massive literature of the Thermidorean period, the original source of nearly all such accusations. In the pamphlets of the Year III, for instance, the *armées révolutionnaires* are referred to as 'highwaymen', 'bullies', 'ravenous wolves' 'vagrants', 'adventurers', bankrupts', 'lackeys without employment', 'wigmakers without clients', 'robbers', 'deserters', 'cowards', 'vagabonds', 'wretches', 'vicious, bloodthirsty hooligans', 'myrmidons', 'boors', 'guttersnipes', '*septembriseurs*', 'butchers', 'informers', 'the dregs of the populace', 'proletarians', 'ultra-Jacobins', 'the scum of the *sociétés populaires*' – all those phrases which were to be used in nineteenth-century conservative historiography against a group of men whose principal sin was their terrorisation of the 'honnêtes gens'. It is perhaps a reflection on the popular composition of the *armées* that these historians did not likewise condemn the conduct of the young scamps in the Muscadin gangs of the Year III. Indeed for Taine and Thiers the main crime of the *armées révolutionnaires* lay in their popular origin, and from this Taine developed a complete theory to explain all their actions – the theory of social jealousy. Thus he sees these 'thankless wretches' overjoyed at their new ability 'to throw their former superiors into the gutter and to strut haughtily in their place, proving by their arrogance that they too could be princes . . .'.[17]

All these theories of envy, base self-interest or cowardice are repeated in the only work devoted exclusively to the *armées révolutionnaires*: that of Antoine Hadengue, Action Française militant.[18] Writing in 1930, Hadengue could draw for comparison on a number of recent situations unavailable to his nineteenth-century predecessors, and to the epithets used by Taine he adds that of 'red guards', the precursor of the workers' militia in the civil war which followed the Russian Revolution. Thus Hadengue's otherwise valuable work differs little from the rest in its attack on the idea of a popular army, and that nightmare of the French bourgeoisie, the people in arms.

What conclusions can we draw from such unanimously unfavourable accounts? Take first of all the idea that the *armées révolutionnaires* were recruited from the ranks of the unemployed, particularly those who had been in service or employed in the luxury trades before the emigration. It is a claim which supplies in effect a complete treatise to explain terrorist behaviour in terms of envy and primitive vengeance, and allows someone like Taine to jibe at the ingratitude of the *révolutionnaires*. Such moral judgements tell us more of a certain kind of bourgeois mentality than of the *révolutionnaires* themselves, whose true identity remains hidden behind such oversimplified and tendentious epithets. Nor did the *armées révolutionnaires* find a defender among the republican historians of the last century. As we have seen, Louis Blanc simply emulated Taine. Michelet, Cabet and later Jaurès showed no more interest than the conservative historians, commenting only on the political complexion of the Parisian *armée*,[19] and in general there is an over-concentration on the problem of its participation in the so-called 'military plot' of Ventôse Year II – when the Parisian *armée* reputedly sought to replace the Revolutionary Government with a military dictatorship.

None of the main historians of the revolutionary period have examined the social composition of the *armées révolutionnaires*. Kropotkin alone looks at the problem of their effectiveness from an economic point of view, concluding nevertheless that they were ineffective in this sphere and even contributed to the deterioration of relations between Paris and the provinces.[20] All the other historians have confined themselves to matters of purely political interest: the relationship between the *armées* – particularly the Parisian one – and the so-called 'parti hébertiste'; and, once again, the role of the Parisian *armée* in the 'plot' of Ventôse, a dramatic, if secondary, incident in the political history of the Revolution. Apart from the usual summary judgements on the personal defects of the *révolutionnaires* and on the collective morality of the *armées*, these works provide no clear idea of the social class of the political soldiers and have considerably tarnished the reputation, without appreciably increasing our understanding, of these popular armies.

As for the local historians, they have concentrated on the most spectacular and destructive aspects of these instruments of the Terror: the *révolutionnaires'* verbal abuse of the 'tièdes' or 'fanatiques', their brutal destruction of religious objects, their drunken orgies in presbyteries and the houses of rich suspects, the arrests, the use of violence to inspire a 'terreur salutaire' among the people, the arson, the pillage, the rape. Typical of this genre are the works of canons Charrier, Bidoux, Eugène Sol and Louis Chaumont, which concentrate on the religious life of the Nièvre, Seine-et-Marne, Lot and Saône-et-Loire.[21] They are devoted exclusively to descriptions of the religious persecution, the afflictions of the priests and the faithful, the kidnappings, the acts of iconoclasm, the sacrilegious processions and the blasphemous sermons. All of this, however, represents only a fraction of the activities of these *armées*, and usually the more unusual. No local history has examined their economic activities, their part in the repression, their role in the dissemination of urban news and ideas, the trials and tribulations of the *Père Duchesne* and its numerous imitators in the departments. Finally, like the national histories of the Revolution, such works provide only summary and partial views of the behaviour of the revolutionary soldiers and of the composition of their companies and battalions. We are left as little informed as before about their conditions of service, their recruitment, their equipment, their pay and, finally, their disbandment.

Until now Hadengue's is the only attempt to compile a complete list of the *armées révolutionnaires*. But his list is incomplete and he makes no clear distinction between 'active' *armées* and those which remained incomplete at the time of the law of 14 Frimaire. These inadequacies derive from Hadengue's use of central archival sources alone. Local archives have been entirely neglected, with the result that the author has been unable to follow the activities of the *armées* in the departments. Furthermore, despite his original research in the Paris archives, Hadengue's extreme, partial and polemical tone colours his judgements.

It seems strange that Communard historians like Gustave Tridon should have been completely ignorant of the existence of these *armées*, despite their favourable treatment of Hébertism and the view of contemporary conservative or Robespierrist historians that the *armées* were its instruments. It is not until the article of Edmond Leleu in the *Revue du Nord* for 1920 that we find any serious social analysis of a departmental *armée*.[22] Mathiez was the first to point to their importance in the execution of requisitions, the protection of grain supplies and the application of the Maximum.[23] We have an abundance of information on the campaign in favour of the Paris *armée* after 31 May 1793 and on the reasons for its defeat, but Soboul's work on the *mouvement sectionnaire* does not extend either to the composition of the *armée* or to the activities of the second Parisian *armée* after the companies had left the Sections to take up service in the countryside. In the 1951 edition of his history of the Revolution, Georges Lefebvre analyses the orders of certain *représentants en mission*, like Châles, Isoré, Taillefer, Baudot, Paganel, Isabeau and Tallien, who set up the *armées* in the departments, and he puts forward the idea that these institutions supplied the needs of the unemployed and calmed fears of public disturbances by removing potential sources of trouble from the cities.[24] Finally, the work of Pichois and Dautrey contains extremely useful information on the Lille *armée*, on Châles's role and on his conflict with the Lille authorities.[25]

Only one work deals exclusively with the activities of an *armée révolutionnaire* in the departments, that of Axel Duboul on the tour of duty by the Toulouse *armée* in Beaumont and Grenade. But this has been overtaken by P. Gérard's exemplary article, the first work to provide an exhaustive study of the organisation, administration and composition of a departmental *armée*.[26] General Herlaut also has articles on the Lille *armée* and the uncompleted *armée* at Versailles, though the latter says nothing of the composition of the *armée* raised in this former royal capital of France.[27] Yet this is an important topic, for a large proportion of the Versailles population was unemployed at the time of recruitment, which makes Versailles an admirable case in which to examine the numbers of unemployed or ex-servants in the *armée*. Alfred Gernoux, who has undertaken the difficult task of rehabilitating Carrier, has devoted an article to the Compagnie Marat, whose origins have been erroneously attributed to this unfortunate man from the Auvergne.[28] In an old Alsatian review there is a brief section on the people who presided over the fate of the small *armée* of the Bas-Rhin, while Emile Dard in his biography of Hérault de Séchelles supplies some information on the formation and disbanding of the Haut-Rhin *armée*.[29]

The attitude of the Revolutionary Government towards the *armées* which proliferated in the provinces, despite government efforts to prevent it, is never very clear. Marcel Reinhard's note on Carnot, who played such an important part in formulating the Committee of Public Safety's policy towards the *armées*, provides an invaluable insight.[30] The initial hostility of Robert Lindet emerges from the biography by Armand Montier, the *notaire* from Les Andelys.[31] But we know little about the views of the other members of the Committee. Robespierre's attitude is particularly contradictory, and his championship of the *armée* between April and September 1793 had changed to bitter opposition by the following spring.[32] Barère's *Mémoires* of 1841 give an extremely inaccurate account of his own role in the establishment of the Parisian *armée*. The attitudes of the members of the Committee of General Security towards these instruments of the Terror, first used by its own agents, are even more obscure, despite the fact that Moïse Bayle was the prime mover behind the Parisian *armée* and Vadier had a force set up in his home department, the Ariège. So even in the sphere of central government policy the history of the *armées* has yet to be written.

In two books and in a series of articles I have attempted to supply some of these deficiencies and to outline possible areas of future research. These are but fragmentary pieces, dealing with the local activities of certain companies in a district, a department, or a collection of departments in the south of the country, and the information they contain is insufficient for any general assessment.[33] I wanted rather to present some typical examples of the activities of a detachment in a department or district and the suggested hypotheses are valid for the south-west of France alone. Furthermore, the articles and the work on Lyon concentrated on the personnel of the general staff of the *armées* and on the detachment commanders. The 'military plot' of Ventôse Year II and the relationship between the revolutionary general staff in the rue de Choiseul and the Jacobin party was examined in three articles published in the 1950s,[34] while several further articles investigated the former *révolutionnaires* as members of a proscribed group, the object of a series of repressive measures against former terrorists passed between 1795 and 1816.[35]

III   *Sources used for this history of the* armées révolutionnaires

For a work covering all 40 or so *armées révolutionnaires* active throughout nearly half of France, not to mention those left uncompleted, both the Paris archives and scattered holdings of the numerous departmental and municipal archives have been used. The latter in particular proved a rich source of information on the activities of the *armées* in the various bourgs and villages. For the organisation and administration of the Parisian *armée* and the main provincial ones, the Archives Historiques de la Guerre at Vincennes and the papers of the *Comité militaire* of the Convention and of the *représentants en mission* were a readily accessible source. For the other *armées* I have relied principally on the departmental and municipal archives, on the registers of the *sociétés populaires*, the *comités de surveillance*, the communal *conseils généraux* and the district directories. Having discussed the anarchical and illegal origins of many of these *armées* and the small number of effectives in some, I cannot claim to have produced an exhaustive list. But an intensive search has been made in some 50 departmental archives, with negative results in only one, that of the Somme. No search was made in the archives of the western departments, the Charente, Charente-Inférieure, Deux-Sèvres, the Vendée and the Dordogne, because there is no sign of any *armée populaire* ever having existed in any of those regions. Likewise the Mont-Terrible was left uninvestigated. Elsewhere a simple investigation was followed up by more extensive research when the existence of an *armée* in a district or department was revealed.

Investigation into the composition of the *armées* presented far greater problems. For some officers there are individual dossiers at Vincennes, either in the general classification of the Archives Administratives de la Guerre or in the *Pension militaire* series. But both deal exclusively with career soldiers; the officers of the *armées révolutionnaires*, who had previously been civilians or had served only in the National Guard, have no dossiers. There are however dossiers for *commissaires des guerres* and for some *commissaires civils*. This source, therefore, supplies information on only a small portion of the officers of the *armées révolutionnaires*, even though valuable for information on their earlier careers. But the Archives de la Guerre are silent on the humble soldier; only those who had served as second officers in certain Ancien Regime regiments have left any trace in the regimental muster rolls.[36] This want of information is due to the political origin of these civilian companies and to the way in which they were enrolled.

On the other hand, the papers of the Committee of General Security, notably those of the famous alphabetical series F7 in the Archives Nationales, which I have used extensively, supply all kinds of information on the political background and social position of many Parisian *révolutionnaires* (over 400 out of a total of 6,000), and sometimes on the soldiers of the provincial *armées* as well. Other papers of the Paris Sections can sometimes provide collective information from enrolment lists, or personal details from letters denouncing certain individuals in the Parisian *armée*. Ultimately one is forced to make personal evaluations, for the archives contain no complete enrolment lists, or details of civilian status before enrolment, for any of the *armées* except those of Versailles and Lille. For both these *armées* the lists provide an immense amount of detailed information on more than a third of their effective strength. Statistical calculations with any degree of accuracy are possible, then, in the case of those two *armées* only. For the other *armées* we have to rely on fragmentary information. We can, nevertheless, reconstruct representative biographies and present the *révolutionnaires* as living beings in action, rather than rigid figures confined by their roles as political soldiers. The statistical lists therefore are no loss, for, given the social mobility of the ordinary people at the end of the eighteenth century – particularly during the disruption of the revolutionary period – such lists are of doubtful value. They are of little assistance, for example, in estimating the number of shoemakers in a certain company, for many would have been relative newcomers to the trade, and even very accurate documentation would not facilitate a reliable assessment of the number of small tradesmen involved. The restrictions imposed by the nature of the documentation make any positive conclusions on the social composition of the *armées* impossible; indeed it is often easier to discover what the *armées* were not than what they actually were. But this book is about men rather than statistics and lists of occupations, and one can only be thankful that such insufficiencies have dictated a more lively, more humane approach than might otherwise have been the case.

The problem of sources is particularly acute for a study of the activities of so many companies spread over half the French countryside. Here the problem is not one of scarcity, but one of selection from sources which tend to become richer as one moves down the administrative hierarchy. At government level information is sparse; at district level it is already starting to fill out; but it is in the municipal archives, in the registers of municipal deliberations, the minutes of the *sociétés populaires*, the papers of the *juges de paix*, that one must look for information on the daily operations of the detachments. As central sources we have the correspondence of the two Committees with the *représentants* and with their agents in the departments; the reports sent to the Committee of General Security by the districts and by the *comités de surveillance*, as well as its vast army of appointed *commissaires* throughout the country; the correspondence of ministerial *commissaires* with the ministers, particularly the Minister of War, and at another level with the Cordeliers club, of which most of the *commissaires* were members. Then there are the military sources, particularly those in the Archives Historiques de la Guerre, the correspondence between the general staffs of the different front-line Armies and the Minister, the *ordres du jour* of the various garrison commanders, the *régistres d'ordre* of certain *armées révolutionnaires*.

Government sources offer but a superficial view of such operations. The *représentants* could not be everywhere at once; they were ill informed and the Committees equally so through them. Some relied entirely on their *délégués*, others were outwitted by the existing authorities, particularly the district directories. Then there were the *délégués* of the *représentants* and the whole group of 'hommes de liaison' – *commissaires* of all kinds, 'apostles' of the urban clubs – who were the best informed of all (their letters are far more interesting than those of the *représentants*, who simply received information at second or third hand). From the correspondence of the *représentants* and the different general staffs it has been possible to estimate the number of 'active' *armées*. But central sources were most useful for setting limits, providing guidelines for the more detailed research in the local archives. Hadengue's work is a prime example of the pitfalls involved in using central documentation alone; its weaknesses reflect those of a government unable to keep abreast of all the minor details of life in the departments under the Terror.

The judicial archives are another important source. From Floréal Year II, and particularly during the Thermidorean period, former soldiers and commanders of the *armées révolutionnaires* were prosecuted by the district and departmental criminal tribunals for pillage, abuses of power, arbitrary arrests, attacks on property, cruelty and wilful arson. These trial briefs – some of which can be found in the departmental archives or among the papers of the Convention's *Comité de législation* in the Archives Nationales – contain detailed information on the missions of the *révolutionnaires* in the departments. Their trials were not simple criminal prosecutions, but political trials conducted in a climate of hate, where vengeance and passion had free rein. They were designed to discredit one of the most characteristic institutions of the Terror, and the documentation on them, provided one

remembers its bias, can supply some valuable information. After the spring
of 1794 – the height of Robespierre's dictatorship – the criminal tribunals
had their full powers restored and were charged with bringing the former
ultra-revolutionary institutions to trial. The process was intensified in the
Year III when the Thermidorean reaction restored bourgeois justice,
devoted to the protection of property. The records of these trials must be
used with caution; one must remember that the *révolutionnaires* were not
themselves permitted to testify, and all those who had felt insecure in the
Year II took delight in avenging themselves on men whose greatest crime
had been to make them feel afraid. Their vigorously anti-terrorist language
is reminiscent of the Thermidorean pamphlets, and has been used in
particular by local historians preoccupied with the history of religion under
the Terror.

It is to the communal archives that the researcher who wants to discover
every side of the activities of the *armées* must direct his attention, particularly to the minutes and correspondence of the communes, the *sociétés
populaires*, and the *comités de surveillance*. In the present work, these have
supplied the main body of information on the economic, political and
religious activities of these political soldiers.

Finally, since the *armées révolutionnaires* were above all instruments of
repression, the papers of the main repressive bodies of the period are particularly informative. Firstly, there are the dossiers of the great extraordinary
commissions: the Commission Temporaire of Lyon, the Military Commissions of Feurs and Mâcon, the revolutionary tribunal of Brest. From
the records of these bodies, which frequently directed the operations of the
armées révolutionnaires and of which the latter were themselves a part, it is
possible to assess the role of the *armées* in the general work of repression.
The papers of the revolutionary tribunal in Paris – before which accuser and
accused, the victims of the *armées* and their commanders, appeared in rapid
succession – have also been used. Fouquier-Tinville's private papers contain
a huge number of accusations made by individuals against the *armées*, and
by the *armées* against inhabitants of the areas to which they had been sent on
mission. This daily exchange of recriminations offers a useful, if repugnant,
mine of information to anyone willing to plough through the labyrinth of
its partially completed catalogue.

For the behaviour of the ordinary Paris soldier after his return, the papers
of the *commissaires de police* of the Paris Sections (Archives de la Police, quai
des Orfèvres) have been used. The papers of the *tribunaux de commerce*
(Archives de la Seine) concerning bankrupts have also been investigated,
but they supplied little information and, as with similar provincial sources,
were in consequence not followed up. Neither have the judicial archives of
the Ancien Regime been investigated for details on the background of those
noted for their violence, brutality and enthusiasm under the Terror. For any
criminal antecedents I have remained satisfied with the chance revelations of
documents like those in the personnel dossiers of the Committee of General

Security. The numbers involved in these *armées* made any systematic search through the judicial records of the Ancien Regime impossible, though future researchers may wish to take up a task which I was forced to abandon.

Contemporary newspapers were of marginal use, except in the case of the Parisian *armée*, which received wide press coverage from the outset. On the whole the *armées* took little care over their public image and all had a bad press. Only one paper, the *Journal révolutionnaire de Toulouse*, had anything interesting to offer on the operations of the Haute-Garonne *armée* in the Toulouse area and of the Lot *armée* in the Aveyron and in the Lozére. Most papers simply reported the various fêtes in which the troops participated and the speeches made on such occasions. The Lyon newspapers imitating the *Père Duchesne* did carry information on the public activities of the Parisian *révolutionnaires* and the repressive tendencies which the indifference, pride, slyness and hostility of the Lyonnais awakened in them. Only the Thermidorean press, however, in its witch-hunt against former terrorists and their favourite institutions, devoted much attention to the *armées*; many local papers carried accounts by their victims in the Year II. In some Thermidorean papers, in Toulouse for example – not to mention the 'Fréronist' press in Paris – articles were published which enquired into the 'excesses' and the 'brigandage' of these 'buveurs de sang'.[37] Such accounts formed part of the general campaign of denigration and hatred against the *armées*; they were biased and their terminology deliberately extreme, but they sometimes provoked useful rejoinders from those under attack.

Personal accounts by these *révolutionnaires* are rare; they were rough, uneducated, illiterate men who did not keep diaries. All that remains are the uniform 'pocket biographies' set out in the petitions and letters sent by former *révolutionnaires* in detention to the Committee of General Security, to the *comités civils* of their Sections, to the *Comité de législation* or to the Convention. It is rather their enemies, the victims of the *armées*, who write memoirs, and we see these 'hommes à moustache' from the wrong side of the courtroom bench or military commission table. The dreadful judges in plumed hats, Parein, Corchand and Marcellin, left no memoirs other than their courageous declarations of republicanism, which they in turn were to make before other judges in the Years IV and IX. Laukhard's *Souvenirs*, in other respects suspect because of the good pastor's mythomania, never-theless provide the only account by a 'sans-culotte révolutionnaire' of his life as a *révolutionnaire*. On their return to civilian life most authentic *révolutionnaires* had but one desire: to seek in obscurity immunity from Robespier-rist or Thermidorean reprisals. We are left then with the semi-official and extremely orthodox administrative record; and with the odd letter of some sans-culotte soldier to his Section, expressing a certain moral and revolutionary orthodoxy rather than his intimate feelings. It is difficult there-fore to discover the private person behind the too-regular features of this 'perfect sans-culotte révolutionnaire'. This is the drawback of all official sources; even the letters of *révolutionnaires* to their Sections, expressing a pitiless and inhuman repressive zeal, are deceptive, for we learn even from hostile witnesses that these artisans from Paris and Nevers were moved by the sight of the defeated populace of Lyon and their attitude softened in consequence (an incident which must have been repeated in other regions). Nothing of this appears in their letters, which are of a uniform orthodoxy and dullness, as if they sensed the watchful eye of comrades and the presence of the 'peuple vengeur' of which they were a part.[38]

IV   *Aims of the book*

Although other works in the field have looked at individual *armées*, none have examined the *armées révolutionnaires* in general. The present study is designed to remedy that defect as far as possible within the limits of the sources available. The principal aim has been to assess the place of the *armées* in the history of the Terror and the popular movement of the Year II, and to stress their character as primordial, violent institutions, which were short-lived and sometimes quite ineffective.

The book will examine the origins of these *armées*, their common points of organisation, and the thorny problem of their composition: the kind of men these *révolutionnaires* were and their reasons for enrolling. It is as important to study the dominant traits of their temperament and behaviour, as systematically to analyse their social origins, and since a purely statistical approach is impossible, it has been supplemented here by 'impressionistic' portraits of the typical *révolutionnaire*. But it is with their activities rather than the institutions and the men themselves, that the main body of the book will be concerned, and these will be examined in a number of spheres. I shall then try to analyse the place of the *armées* in the system of the Terror and their relationship with the Jacobin dictatorship, the local authorities, and the 'parallel hierarchies' of the ultra-revolutionary powers.

There are two crucial landmarks through which the complex problem of the *armées*' relationship with central government can be examined: the law of 14 Frimaire and the crisis of Ventôse Year II. But to evaluate the constantly changing nuances of government attitudes, we must first of all analyse the activities of the *armées*, including that of Paris, for it was by their works that they were judged by the Jacobin dictatorship, and their spontaneous intervention in public life was what eventually alienated it. I am thinking here in particular of the *armées*' attack on religion, the anarchic quality of some of their operations, the development of the doctrine of popular sovereignty, the pillage and 'taxes révolutionnaires' which so terrified property owners, the violence of their methods and government fears of a 'systéme militaire', to which their proliferation and their disregard of the civil authorities gave rise.

These considerations, and the need to analyse the activities of the *révolutionnaires* before discussing their relations with the established authorities in the countryside, did not lend itself to a straightforward chronological approach. Moreover, the Parisian *armée* and three others continued their activities for over three months after the promulgation of the law of 14 Frimaire. The book closes with the history of the individual corps of these *armées populaires,* following the fate of certain militants who became the victims of successive proscriptions of ex-terrorists, or those suspected of being such, between 1793 and 1816. Certain former *révolutionnaires* were the automatic focus of those purges, and their trials form part of the history of the *armées,* to which they had the misfortune to belong during the Terror.

The book is entitled 'The People's Armies (*Les Armées révolutionnaires*)', that is to say the Parisian *armée* and any others known to have been active. It could be argued that the Paris *armée,* because of its importance and its legal character, should be distinguished from the others and studied separately. Such objections are valid: without the Paris *armée,* the movement in favour of other similar corps would not have been so vociferous (Lille and Toulouse could scarcely have been refused something already granted to Paris). The Parisian *armée* did differ from the others in many ways: firstly in its origins as a legal *armée,* created by the decree of the Convention; secondly in its organisation, which gave it an assured place in the application of the Terror; thirdly in the fact that it was less anarchical than those of the departments; and finally in the part attributed to it in the so-called 'military plot' of Ventôse–Germinal, which, although a minor episode in its history, has attracted the attention of almost every historian of the Revolution, because of its exploitation for political ends and because it forms part of national history.

I have not, however, chosen to concentrate on the Parisian *armée,* but while respecting its separate identity, I have been able to point to the similarities between it and the numerous corps fashioned in its image, which were violent caricatures of this the first of the *armées.* To make a rigid distinction between the Parisian *armée* and those of the departments and communes would be to deny the national character of this phenomenon of proliferating corps. It would also be a repetition of the same work, for all these *armées* belonged to the same family. They were produced by the same climate of opinion, activated by the same concerns, recruited under the same orders, were all more or less democratic, and owed their existence to pressure from the *sociétés populaires.* There were differences between them, but of detail only, and if the Parisian *armée* is treated apart, we risk distorting the true picture and failing to understand the other corps. Besides, the indiscretions, violence, crimes and excesses of some *armées* reflected upon and compromised all the others, and the most anarchical and disorderly corps set the tone. Contemporary opinion was not mistaken in thinking the violence, the banditry, the anarchy, the enthusiasm part of a single phenomenon. For the 'honnêtes gens', all the *armées* represented bloodshed and pillage. For the sans-culottes, they were simply scattered parts of the same *armée populaire*, which they would have liked to see established on a national basis.

Certain distinctions, however, have been made between the Parisian *armée* and the other corps. The composition of the former has been examined separately. Moreover, its economic and repressive activities were carried out under conditions and for ends quite different from those of the other *armées*; the provisioning of the capital for instance was the responsibility of this one legal *armée*, and in consequence separate chapters have been devoted to it. On the other hand, the interference of all these *armées* in religious matters, their social and political activities, the accusations of banditry levelled against them all, justifies a general approach to bring out common characteristics. Nevertheless, I have devoted the last two chapters exclusively to the Paris *armée*, excepting only the debris of the three departmental *armées* attached to it after the 14 Frimaire.

Despite the individual character of each of these *armées*, all belong to the same institutional family; all are 'révolutionnaire', almost all act 'révolutionnairement' and all their soldiers are 'révolutionnaires'. I have therefore given the book the title, 'The People's Armies. The *armées révolutionnaires*: instrument of the Terror in the departments, April 1793 to Floréal Year II'. It is not a book about the Armies of the Republic, the military corps, and none of these *armées*, not even the Parisian one, was active in the capital – rather they were the 'instrument of the Terror in the departments'. The terminal dates, April 1793 to Floréal Year II, mark the period from the first mention of the term 'armée révolutionnaire' to the return to civilian life of the last members of the Parisian *armée* after its disbandment.

BOOK ONE

The Institutions and the Men:
structure and composition of
the *armées révolutionnaires*

But of the marchings and retreatings of these Six Thousand no Xenophon exists. Nothing, but an inarticulate hum, of cursing and sooty frenzy, surviving dubious in the memory of ages! They scour the country round Paris; seeking Prisoners; raising Requisitions; seeing that Edicts are executed, that the Farmers have thrashed sufficiently, lowering Church-bells or metallic Virgins. Detachments shoot forth dim towards remote parts of France; nay new Provincial Revolutionary Armies rise dim, here and there, as Carrier's Company of Marat, as Tallien's Bourdeaux Troop; like sympathetic clouds in an atmosphere all electric.... One sees them drawn up in market-places; travel-splashed rough-bearded... Pipe in cheek, sabre on thigh; in *carmagnole complète*!

Such things have been; and may again be. Charles Second sent out his Highland Host over the Western Scotch Whigs: Jamaica Planters got Dogs from the Spanish Main to hunt their Maroons with: France too is bescoured with a Devil's Pack, the baying of which, at this distance of half a century, still sounds in the mind's ear.

Thomas Carlyle, *The French Revolution,*
vol. III: *The Guillotine* (1837), 319–20

CHAPTER 1

The Campaign For and Against (April–October 1793)

I *Organised campaign or spontaneous movement?*

In the first days of April 1793, the revolutionary authorities in several regions outlined plans for the formation of a people's national army or several regional armies. They were to watch over internal security, be recruited from among orthodox republicans, and financed out of massive taxes levied on the rich and the 'malevolent' (*malveillants*). It was in that month also that the expression '*armée révolutionnaire*' was used for the first time. The expression was novel; but the idea had been germinating in certain patriotic circles from the beginning of the winter of 1792. The Légion des Sans-culottes de Bruxelles, established in December 1792 by the French garrison commanders there, and composed of members of the *société populaire*, provided the prototype in composition, action and parentage.[1] That it served as the model for other similar legions seems likely, since after the battle of Neerwinden its creators were forced to withdraw from the Belgian provinces to Lille, where by October 1793 they had come to occupy the most important positions in the town's *société révolutionnaire*. It was upon their initiative that the Lille *armée révolutionnaire* was formed.

In April 1793, several *sociétés* and municipalities outlined plans for *armées révolutionnaires* in petitions to the Convention or to the Jacobins. The campaign had been launched. In May, Lyon went on to pass the necessary measures for arming and equipping the *révolutionnaires*, and the popular army was on the point of formation when the *journée* of 29 May took place. In Paris the *journées* of 31 May and 2 June pushed the creation of an *armée révolutionnaire* to the fore of Sectionary demands, and the Convention felt obliged to agree to it in principle, in its decree of 4 June. But the decree evoked considerable opposition, which was intensified by the alliance of several companies of cannoneers with the moderate Sections. Recruiting did begin in some Sections. But on the whole the June decree remained a dead letter. In the following months the questions of the formation of an *armée révolutionnaire* and of the appointment of Hanriot or Raffet to its command, became touchstones of political opinion in the Sections. Both questions, in fact, became part of the problem of who would control the Parisian *armée*, and the formation of an *armée révolutionnaire* in Paris was to fortify the sans-culotte minorities which sought to capture control of the Sections.

In August, there was some respite in the Paris conflict. But it flared up again in the departments, and was so successful that the Federalist authorities denounced *armées révolutionnaires* and *comités révolutionnaires* alike, as instruments of Parisian terrorism – a condemnation which would prove advantageous to the *armées* after the defeat of Federalism. The campaign in the departments assumed a semi-official character in September, after the decree of the 5th, which had been forced from the Convention by the Paris Commune. At the same time the movement lost its spontaneity, when the *sociétés populaires* joined in large regional assemblies and remained in continuous correspondence to give effective weight to their demands for such forces.

The arguments invoked in support of these demands had themselves altered between April–May and September. In April–May the internal threat from centres of rebellion was the main concern; by the end of August the accent was no longer on internal defence – even if Bordeaux and Lyon still resisted, and Toulon had been handed over to the English – but on the selfishness of the farmers. The *armées révolutionnaires* were beginning to emerge as the weapon of the economic interests of the urban sans-culottes, and the campaign was the expression of their fears and their punitive attitude towards internal political enemies and economic fraud. September also revealed the most disquieting element in the campaign: encroaching municipalisation[2] – one of the many manifestations of that extreme administrative and institutional decentralisation of which Soboul has spoken.[3] With each urban *société populaire* demanding its own *armée*, France was to be reduced to a series of autonomous communes, or, to borrow Jaurès's partisan phrase, to so many 'petites Polognes démagogiques'. To combat this danger, some *sociétés* and *représentants* proposed forming large regional *armées*, to be drawn from several departments. The urban *sociétés* wanted a national *armée révolutionnaire* established under their control, and the Légion des Montagnards, formed in September from the union of some 70 *sociétés* in the South, was the prototype. But such a project held its own dangers, for it threatened to provide those *sociétés*, which were already establishing themselves as some kind of counter-power in the name of direct democracy, with a huge armed force composed of their own members. Sooner or later the central government would become uneasy at such a prospect.

After September, with the campaign officially sanctioned by decree, revolutionary conformism also contributed to its progress. *Armées révolutionnaires* became fashionable, and the request for an *armée* in a particular area became the hallmark of that area's orthodoxy and revolutionary zeal. From the time of Boisset's declaration in favour of these *armées*, such demands became entirely respectable. The campaign continued throughout the autumn, with the desire for an *armée* bringing about their immediate creation in many areas. But although opposition had been defeated in the Paris Sections in August, and compromised in the departments by Federalism, it remained strong even among good patriots, who condemned this use of force against the rural population. The administrators of the Commission des Subsistances pointed to the dangers of trying to ensure food supplies through force. Lindet shared their fears. Others recalled the detested Ancien Regime practices of garrisoning and billeting. At the beginning of the autumn such voices were few; it was only after October that opposition became organised, particularly in the Parisian press.

Amidst such conflicting ideas, the attitude of the central government remained unclear. Lindet was openly hostile; Robespierre was a tenacious supporter of the *armées* and the Committee of Public Safety was favourably disposed, if reticent, on the progress of the campaign. The success of the campaign and the number of decrees setting up these anarchical *armées* were themselves symptoms of a growing administrative anarchy, which sought to replace the established authorities with spontaneous revolutionary institutions claiming popular sovereignty. Thus was the close union established between the *armées révolutionnaires* and the *sociétés populaires*, from which they had grown.

II   *Measures taken in the Hérault and Rhône-et-Loire, and Robespierre's first intervention in the Jacobins (3 April–29 May 1793)*

The expression 'armée révolutionnaire' first appears in the documentation in April 1793, in a debate in the Jacobins, in some proceedings in Lyon, and in a decision of the department of the Hérault. In the Jacobins on 3 April Robespierre declared: 'We must raise an *armée révolutionnaire* composed of every patriot and sans-culotte and its main strength should come from the faubourgs.' 'This is not to say', he added, 'that we should sharpen our swords and kill priest-followers; as enemies they are too contemptible.'[4] Where did Robespierre take this expression from, this idea of arming the faubourgs and forming a popular army? He certainly did not invent it. The ideas must already have been in circulation, for someone as sensitive to the political atmosphere as Robespierre to give them such powerful public expression. With the treason of the generals, and the 'patriots' away fighting on the frontiers, the atmosphere of April was dominated by fears of counter-revolution. The bourgeois-dominated National Guard seemed unreliable, and like all the principal measures of that spring, the *armées révolutionnaires* were born of fear, rather than any desire to punish or to avenge the martyrs of liberty.

Robespierre's idea was even more revolutionary than it was to prove in practice, for in proposing the arming of the faubourgs, he was proposing the creation of a truly sans-culotte army. We must not of course read too much into this reference to the faubourgs, and it would be wrong to think that Robespierre envisaged a scheme to provide work for the less well-off republicans. Certainly they would have to be remunerated, for they could not 'wield a trowel and a gun at the same time'; but he was not proposing charity. Robespierre looked to the inhabitants of the faubourgs because they were veterans of the great *journées*, because they had proved themselves, and because they were the 'pauvres', that is to say the virtuous producers who worked with their hands. Let them defend the regime against its internal enemies! Robespierre's reference to the faubourgs was a rhetorical device, calculated to evoke images of the taking of the Bastille. Nevertheless it was the sans-culottes as a body, the revolutionary populace, of which he was thinking, a point which comes out clearly in his interventions of May and June, when he insisted again on the need to form an *armée révolutionnaire*, an *armée* of sans-culottes: '...I have asked for an army to be established in the heart of Paris, not that of Dumouriez, but a people's army, continuously under arms and able to impose its will on Feuillants and moderates. *This army should be composed of paid sans-culottes* and enough money should be set aside *to arm the artisans, all good patriots.*' Note his interpretation of the word 'artisan', which for Robespierre did not simply denote a social category: '...Let me recapitulate: I want the Sections to raise an army large enough to form the nucleus of an *armée révolutionnaire*, an army which will exterminate rebels and which will be composed of all the sans-culottes of the departments; and secondly I want a sans-culotte army formed in Paris to restrain the aristocracy...'. Thus was Robespierre the first, and thereafter the most persistent, champion of the Sections' demands for the creation of a popular army on a national basis, with that in Paris forming the nucleus. But he thought of it in terms of a reserve army, subject to military laws and training, and not autonomous in itself. He would never have championed 'special armies', or suggested that they should be accompanied by judges and guillotines.[5]

On 19 April, two weeks after Robespierre's first intervention, a group calling itself the 'patriots of the Hérault department' presented to the Convention the draft of a law to establish in the Hérault '*an armed and paid force* of five thousand men...which would guard important places in the department or march to help the northern part of the Republic'. 'This force will not be recruited through normal channels but by selection, that is to say by personal summonses to those citizens recognised as the most patriotic...'; and its costs were to be met out of a forced loan of 5,000,000 levied upon the rich.[6] The Convention gave a favourable hearing to this address and instructed the Committee of Public Safety to draw up an order embodying its suggestions right away. The Hérault's proposal had arisen from a decision of the Montpellier *société populaire* on 10 April: Chauvet, president of the district tribunal, had demanded a force capable of resisting tyranny if it should triumph in the North – a demand prompted by fears of a counter-revolutionary attack on Paris.[7]

On 9 April, apparently quite independently of Montpellier, the Lyon Jacobins urged their General Council to raise an '*armée révolutionnaire*'. The municipal authorities complied and set to work. But it was only on 3 May that the Rhône-et-Loire department issued an order announcing the enrolment of an *armée révolutionnaire* in that arrondissement.[8] The *sociétés populaires* in the Sections opened enrolment registers the very next day. Throughout May the Sections received registrations and the municipality pressed ahead with the organisation and equipment of the companies.[9] In these first days of May, Chalier went through the streets of Lyon reading from a proclamation in his hand: 'You are invited to form an *armée révolutionnaire* immediately; the time has come to suspend clemency; the sword of justice must strike down every guilty head without exception'.[10] It was the first sign of that repressive urge which was to characterise the *armées*. The Lyon *armée* was not simply designed to preserve the fragile sans-culotte minority in the town; it had proclaimed itself the instrument of a pitiless repression. On 5 May the correspondence committee of the Lyon *société populaire* made the first attempt at co-ordination, in a letter taken by Leclerc to the Paris Jacobins: 'This is indeed an important measure, long desired by all the friends of the Republic,' it read; 'but it will be incomplete without the addition of a revolutionary tribunal. This is what we ask for and this is what you must ask for us....'.[11] This call, as we shall see, was to be echoed by the assemblies of the Paris Sections. But first let us look more closely at this plan for the first *armée révolutionnaire* as outlined by the Lyonnais.

The organisation of the companies continued throughout May in accordance with an order of 12–13 May, fixing the effective strength of the *armée* at 6,400, in 8 battalions of 750 men. By 28 May, Fillion, *procureur* of Lyon, was able to point to a nucleus of 750 men already clothed, equipped and formed into companies.[12] On the following day – the very day of those tragic events which would result in the expulsion of Lyon from the Republic – a member of the *société populaire* of the Bellecordière Section 'extended a fraternal invitation to all its members and citizens to enrol in the *armée* without delay'. The invitation was debated and the members enrolled accordingly. Later, in Floréal and Prairial Year II, bills for cloth and uniforms were presented to the General Council and paid without question.[13] It was yet another sign that organisation of the *armée* was well advanced when the Federalist revolt brought to a bloody end the projects of Chalier, Bertrand, Gaillard and the Jacobin minority in Lyon, whose survivors would return to the fold of the republican *armée* in the autumn amidst the ruins of their city. Indeed, Lyon just missed being the first town to establish such a popular army by a day or two. The advanced state of preparations may even have precipitated the crisis of 29 May – the National Guard and the moderate Sections fearing possible seizure by the sans-culotte minority which dominated the *société*, and which, despite its unpopularity, would have controlled the armed strength of the town once the *armée* had been organised.

These efforts by the Lyon sans-culottes to raise an *armée révolutionnaire*, and the reason put forward in justification, prefigured the campaign, during the summer and autumn of 1793, for the creation of a huge *armée révolutionnaire*. In their letter to the Jacobins, the Lyon *sociétaires* had demanded a roving commission of popular justice to follow the detachments – a demand which would be echoed by the Paris Sections and by the provincial *sociétés populaires* in the following months. Chalier had emphasised the punitive desires of the Lyonnais. On 3 May another speaker to the Bellecordière *société* (possibly Chalier again) recommended adopting the measures proposed by the Hérault authorities, 'for the *patrie* is in danger... and the troubles in the Vendée and in the neighbouring departments are a striking example of the harm brought about by discontent, priestly fanaticism and the myth-making of the nobility'. On the same day the department declared an *armée révolutionnaire* to be the only means of overturning 'the foul mass of counter-revolution, apathy and selfishness'. The recruitment and payment procedures adopted by Lyon would be taken up elsewhere, with the *sociétés populaires* supervising enrolment, checking on the political orthodoxy of the recruits, and levying 'revolutionary taxes on the rich', which supplied the funds for so many *armées révolutionnaires*.[14]

III   *Measures taken at Châteauroux and Bellac (May)*

In the first days of May, therefore, the project had already been discussed at the bar of the Convention and at the Jacobins in Paris, as well as in Lyon and Montpellier. The campaign was gathering strength. The member of the *société populaire* of Châteauroux – a town threatened by the movement of the Chouans towards Poitiers – must surely have read the news from Paris when on 12 May he put forward 'several projects for the public safety of the department'. He urged 'the creation of an armed force of 600 men divided into 7 companies, one to be placed on permanent duty in each district *cheflieu* to facilitate its dispatch to areas where its services were required', and suggested 'that the cost of such a force should be met from a graduated contribution levied on the rich...'. The suggestion was not taken up, and does not reappear in the registers of the *société* until 16 September, when, under quite different circumstances, a proposal for the establishment of an *armée révolutionnaire* for the Indre was discussed.[15] However, the motives behind the proposal of 12 May, and the method suggested for financing it, remained unchanged in the September campaign, and the administrative framework already outlined in May was quickly adopted.

On 20 May the Bellac district, in the neighbouring department of Haute-Vienne, decided to form 'a paid company of national guard, in view of the position of the district with respect to the troubles in the Vendée'. The company would be composed of 65 citizens 'known for their *civisme* and morality...'.[16] Was this a recommendation simply to extend the National Guard, or to create a completely new force? The constantly changing terminology used in the summer of 1793 does not permit any clear

distinction between the two. Nevertheless, the Bellac district did impose a
political qualification for joining the new company – the hallmark of the
future *armées*.

It is impossible to discover if danger from insurgents provoked similar
measures in the other districts of the Haute-Vienne and in the neighbouring
departments of the Vienne, the Indre-et-Loire and the Cher, all in turn
threatened by 'brigands'. In Montpellier, Lyon, Châteauroux, Bellac and in
Paris itself, the emphasis was always on measures for internal defence. It
was the extension of the counter-revolution, particularly in the North, that
was most feared, and the authorities in Montpellier even contemplated
coming to the defence of liberty threatened there. No one seemed to foresee
that it was the Midi which would prove the real bastion of Federalism.

IV *The debate in the Paris Sections and the first* armée révolutionnaire *(May–July)*

Between 8 May (when one Paris Section adopted a programme of republican
defence which included the formation of an *armée révolutionnaire*), and
12 July (when the moderate Sections won their last political success by
burying the decree forced from the Convention on 13 May), the question of
the creation of an *armée révolutionnaire* became the focus of the struggle
within the Paris Sections and was the principal point dividing sans-culotte
from moderate Sections. Albert Soboul has examined in detail the vicis-
situdes of the struggle,[17] and we need only concern ourselves here with the
broad outlines of the conflict. A few zealous Sections went as far as completing the enrolment lists in the first half of June, but the organisation of
this abortive *armée* stopped there.

On 8 May the sans-culottes of the Contrat-Social Section presented a
programme of revolutionary defence to the Convention. It proposed: 'the
extermination of all known conspirators, the immediate arrest of all suspects, the formation of an *armée révolutionnaire* and a tribunal to legalise its
activities, and the confiscation of the goods of known conspirators to finance
payment of a lifetime annuity of 150 livres to every armed *révolutionnaire*...'. It was the Lyon programme to the letter, of which by then they
must have been completely informed. On 18 May it was the turn of the
volunteers of the faubourg Saint-Antoine, about to leave for the Vendée, to
demand protection for Paris 'from the horrors of civil war' and the
immediate formation of 'a defending force of sans-culottes...' – doubtless a
reference to Robespierre's promises in his speeches of 3 April and 8 May.[18]
Thus was the creation of an *armée révolutionnaire* put to the fore of the sans-
culottes' programme; but it was the popular *journées* which allowed them to
impose that programme on the Convention.

Already by 30 May the Marchés Section – a bastion of the *sans-culotterie*[19]
– had nominated commissioners to present a petition to the Evêché *comité*,
calling for 'the formation of an *armée révolutionnaire* of paid sans-culottes, *as*

you have decreed....'.[20] The outcome was the first overture by the Evêché *comité* to the Convention, in an address which survives in draft form. After a second request from the *comité*, the Convention deferred, in principle, to popular pressure. The levy of an *armée révolutionnaire* was voted on 2 June, and with the decree of the 4th, its organisation commenced. It looked now as if nothing could stop the progress of an *armée* which only a minority in the Sections had been clamouring for. Several Sections went ahead with the organisation of such a force without waiting to complete enrolment formalities. The Pont-Neuf Section did not even wait for the decree before opening its register on 31 May, and it was able to send a complete list to the department of Paris by 4 June.[21] The Panthéon Section commenced enrolment that day, after a delay caused by a changeover of officials and the need to clarify certain procedural details not outlined by the decree. The neighbouring Finistère Section began enrolling almost immediately, and on 9 June its *comité révolutionnaire* asked the general assembly if it could enrol also the numerous candidates coming forward from the neighbouring communes of Ivry, Gentilly, Villejuif and Choisy. The *comité* was also responsible for checking on the recruits' political orthodoxy and for the issue of certificates of *civisme*; but the final scrutiny and weeding-out process was the assembly's responsibility. The *comité* of the Observatoire Section also sent its list of recruits to the general assembly for scrutiny on 9 June.[22] The Sectionary organisations were anxious not to lose control of the new *armée*, which above all would be an *armée* of *purs*. This is all we know of the enrolment procedure, the fragmentary documentation permitting investigation only of the three Left-Bank Sections and that of the Ile de la Cité.

On 9 June opposition, muted at first, began to grow rapidly as the decree was carried into effect. It was exacerbated by the undoubtedly intentional vagueness of the decree, which glossed over such important issues as effective numbers, conditions of service, minimum age of recruits, etc. Such lack of clarity also gave the moderate Sections an excuse to drag their heels over the organisation of an *armée* of which they were essentially afraid. The western Sections were still under moderate control, despite the *journées* of 31 May and 2 June, and another two months' struggle was required before the sans-culotte minorities were able to reverse the balance of power in these Sections. On 8 June the Mail Section circulated a notice to the 47 other Sections, replying to the criticism of the faubourg Saint-Antoine: 'according to our enemies, the Mail Section is composed only of the rich and therefore of those hostile to the Revolution.... They forget that the rich man is upstanding, the soul of commerce, the father of the worker, the friend and support of the poor; they do not seem to recognise that just as well-supplied shops are guarantees against dearth, so in the hands of the humane and sensitive rich man wealth is held only in trust'.[23]

Such arguments were scarcely calculated to placate those sans-culottes who were clamouring for the immediate organisation of an *armée révolutionnaire* to use against these self-same rich. Indeed, from 31 May the addresses of the Sections were calling on the sans-culotte *armée* not only to crush the 'malveillant' and 'strike terror into' the intriguer, but also to pursue the 'égoïste', in other words the big farmer and the merchant. Such a programme could not fail to terrify the inhabitants of the Mail Section and the many moderates holding important positions in Sections near the centre such as the Piques and Butte-des-Moulins. But, as Soboul has shown, even the popular Sections were divided on the issue, and the first open demonstration against the implementation of the decree of 4 June came actually from the Sans-Culottes Section. At its session of 10 June it opposed the formation of the *armée révolutionnaire*, claiming that it wanted no privileged corps of 'janissaries' or praetorian guards, as the *armées* were to be called by their opponents. The attitude of this Section was clearly unrepresentative, for the motion had been passed in the presence of Hanriot, commander of the Parisian National Guard. Son of a Nanterre servant, this sans-culotte general saw the *armée* as a possible rival to the National Guard, and was accordingly one of its most bitter opponents. In view of Hanriot's fixed hostility to Ronsin and the general staff of the *armée révolutionnaire* after the formation of the second *armée* in September, it seems likely that his opposition was already manifest in June and that the stand taken against the *armée* in June and July by the companies of cannoneers under his command was with his encouragement.

From 10 June the forces of opposition began to assert themselves. On the 11th some companies of cannoneers appeared before the Convention to protest against the decree. That same day the Marchés Section, the most important Paris Section, and one which had been to the fore of the campaign for the *armée révolutionnaire* in May, reaffirmed its support; but it acted alone. On the 12th the Réunion and Piques Sections expressed their hostility to the new *armée*, the former after pressure from a company of cannoneers under the leadership of their lieutenant, Féline. Féline was already suspect for his opposition to the *journée* of 31 May,[24] and his influence behind the cannoneers throws quite a different light on their supposed collective protest to the Convention on the 11th. As a moderate, Féline was totally opposed to a measure which threatened to place at the disposal of the most popular Sections, an armed force officially appointed as the scourge of the moderates. The opposition of the cannoneers was consequently being used by those who dreaded the consequences of the two *journées*.

But there were signs of opposition even within those Sections known for their total commitment to the *journées*. In the Poissonnière Section, Louis Huet, employed in the *administration des domaines*, and André Fossey, a tax officer, were accused of having opposed the formation of the *armée révolutionnaire* after 31 May by supporting Jacquemier, a jeweller and a leading moderate. Fossey denied the charge; Huet admitted his opposition and invoked the usual argument about the dangers of 'military government'. 'I am a true revolutionary soldier', he claimed at one of the sessions in early June which discussed the affair. 'People of Paris, be wary of the daring and ambitious intriguer who might corrupt this proposed army and use it to promote the counter-revolution.' He later claimed that although he was jeered at and threatened by seven or eight citizens, he was enthusias-tically applauded by all the rest.[25] As for Jacquemier, he was the leader of the moderate group at the heart of the general assembly, author of a petition in favour of Dumouriez, and, as an opponent of the events of 31 May, was later accused of having 'thwarted the desire of the patriots for the formation of an *armée révolutionnaire*'.[26] Indeed the Poissonnière Section joined forces with that of the Picques by placing itself at the head of the opposition movement after 12 June. Now if the Poissonnière *sectionnaires* could be 'deceived' by such men, it is clear that they were still uncertain how to react towards an *armée* which they were told might become the plaything of a 'dictator'. The success of the campaign against the Parisian *armée*, therefore, owed as much to the hesitations and irresolution of the sans-culottes themselves, as to the determination of the moderates.

It was the Piques Section which led the moderate attack, and sometime before 12 June it circularised the 47 other Sections, proposing a meeting of representatives to prepare a petition for the repeal of the decree of 4 June.[27] The circular contains all the usual moderate protests against a 'praetorian guard' and the dangers of 'military government' – though in reality it was the prospect of a popular army, placing guns in the hands of the most determined sans-culottes, which most terrified them. But the authors of the address had another, more sinister argument, one which would be revived with frightening results after the creation of the second Parisian *armée*. 'How will the defenders of your frontiers view such a force', they asked, 'which earns three times as much as they for doing scarcely anything.' Thus were the soldiers on the frontiers being appealed to against these political soldiers, the pampered élite in the interior. Every opponent of the *armées* was to revert to this argument, and in many garrison towns it provoked scuffles between regular soldiers and *révolutionnaires*. The Piques address also referred to the excessive expense (more than 6,000,000) involved in creating such a force, and, affecting to believe that the main purpose of the measure was to employ and help deserving sans-culottes, it asked if there was not a better way of doing this than by creating a force of 6,000 idlers. But, one may well ask, if this *armée* was to remain idle, why then were the moderate Piques *sectionnaires* so frightened by the prospect?

This address was signed by the members of the general assembly's committee; but it had been promoted by two men in particular, the former marquis de Sade and Jean-Baptiste Pyron. Pyron was a former steward of the comte d'Artois, a speculator closely attached to Calonne, and in 1793 was living off his wife's *rentes* – fine parentage for a moderate address. At this time Pyron was president of the general assembly. He was a cautious man and waited until Germinal Year II before explaining his role in these events. 'It was I who presided over the assembly of deputies from the 48 Sections in June 1793, when it demanded the suppression of the *armée révolutionnaire...*', he claimed on 15 Germinal after the Parisian *armée* had been disbanded.[28] In Messidor Year II Sade laid claim to a more modest achievement, that of having drawn up the petition in the first place: 'As a literary man, I was usually asked to draft and read my Section's petitions to the Convention and at the bar of the Convention I read one from the 48 Sections which spoke of the dangers of establishing an *armée révolution-naire...*'. Sade's claim is supported by the account of his political conduct drawn up by the *comité révolutionnaire* of his Section, and it looks as if Pyron and Sade were indeed the moving forces behind the moderate reaction of 12 and 14 June.[29]

How many Sections joined the movement or supported the address which was subsequently presented to the Convention? The figure of 48 given by Pyron and Sade is certainly exaggerated, for we know that some Sections refused to be associated with the petition, and after 15 June came to the defence of the *armée révolutionnaire*. On the 15th the Droits-de-l'Homme Section, for instance, following the example set by the Chalier (Beaurepaire) Section some days previously, revoked its decision to take part in the movement initiated by the Piques Section, and instead proclaimed its support for the creation of the *armée*.[30] The Invalides Section, with the Ecole Militaire in its arrondissement, was particularly afraid of political armies and the dangers 'of assembling 6,000 men in the same place who might be used by a Lafayette or a Dumouriez, if a commander as treacherous as those scoundrels were found...'. It opposed the *armée révolutionnaire* in June and again in September–October and was certainly among the Sections supporting the Piques address. Soboul speaks of 27 Sections having supported the address.[31] So the moderates had attained their goal, even if the Piques Section never in fact delivered its petition to the Convention, or indeed a second petition of 12 July, mentioned by Pyron,[32] for, by demonstrating the strength of opposition from the Sections, they allowed the government to plead majority opinion in abandoning a project which had been accepted reluctantly in the first place. Many of the Sections in the centre must have experienced violent internal conflicts before the moderates eventually prevailed–note for instance the number of persons from the Réunion, Bonne-Nouvelle, Poissonnière and Faubourg-Montmartre Sections who were later denounced for having 'opposed the formation of the *armée révolutionnaire*'. The outcome, however, is indisputable. The moderates would pay dearly for their victory by their expulsion some weeks later from the general assemblies and their committees, and by being arrested during Frimaire and Nivôse. But between July and September the *armée révolutionnaire* was no longer discussed, either in the Sections or in the clubs, and another popular *journée* would be required to force the Convention to re-open the project first legislated for on 4 June.

Was this silence, following a sustained campaign by a vociferous minority in the Sections, a token of popular indifference towards a scheme so dear to the sans-culotte militants? I think not: the indifference was only apparent, and the *armée révolutionnaire* was simply pushed temporarily into the background along with other elements of the popular programme. During July and August the militants of the Sections had other problems to think about, particularly the expulsion of the moderate majorities. Internal revolutions in most Sections during August completely altered the leadership of the formerly moderate Sections.[33] The Piques Section was purged in this way and the Butte-des-Moulins (with its name changed to the Montagne) was to become the citadel of the ultra-revolutionaries who filled the *armées révolutionnaires* and the special Commissions. Even the Tuileries would provide one of the principal recruiting grounds for the revolutionary artillery after September. The success of these 'internal revolutions' was such that even formerly moderate Sections like the Tuileries, Montagne, Champs-Elysées and Lepeletier Sections would supply as many notable figures to the *armée* formed in September as the traditionally sans-culotte Sections. The same transformation can be seen on the Left Bank, where the Invalides Section was to supply some of the principal officers of an *armée* whose formation it had opposed on two previous occasions. There was, then, still considerable support for the project during the summer; it had not been abandoned by the Sections, and in September when the issue was re-opened, the same names were to reappear. Some *sectionnaires* who had won places on the *comités révolutionnaires* or on the committees of the general assemblies because of the events of 31 May or of July–August, were the first to enlist when the *armée* was formed in September.

In Paris, therefore, the campaign had simply been suspended. In the departments, however, it had actually been intensified because of Federalist successes, and the more the *armées* were denounced by the rebel authorities, the more favour they gained with the republicans, particularly with the *société patriote* of Mâcon which was to give the campaign its precise expression. Condemned by Lyon, Marseille, Avallon and in the Eure, the *armée révolutionnaire* became in consequence the symbol of republican aspirations.

V   *'Federalism'* and *'armée révolutionnaire' (May–July 1793)*

The Federalist authorities reserved their most bitter propaganda for this project of a national *armée révolutionnaire* – a potential means of spreading the 'dictatorship' of Paris to the provinces. They saw a Parisian *armée révolutionnaire* as a formidable weapon in the hands of the Paris Commune, the chosen instrument of a sans-culotte social policy, and the channel through which Paris might impose her centralising tendencies on them.

It was the Marseille authorities who took the lead in this campaign. On 10 June, when the moderate campaign in the capital was at its height, most of the arguments against the *armées* were reproduced in resolutions inspired by Boileau and sent to all the departments by the Federalist authorities of Avallon.[34] Article 4 called for 'the suppression of all so-called committees operating under the title "révolutionnaire", of every so-called *armée révolu-*

tionnaire, extraordinary tribunal and all other such instruments of inquisition and anarchy...'. The resolutions sought in particular to dismantle the administrative machinery of the Terror which had been set up in March and April; but if they were well received in Federalist circles, the reaction was quite the contrary among the *sociétés patriotes*, that of Mantes actually ordering the burning of this 'indecent' document and the Le Havre, Fécamp and Sèvres *sociétés* responding with similarly severe condemnations.[35]

In a number of areas, the Federalist authorities took up the sans-culotte project for their own ends and raised special armed forces to defend themselves. Some of these 'departmental' forces shared certain traits with the future *armées révolutionnaires*, notably the high rate of pay and democratic composition. Thus, although the *plumets rouges*, a cavalry corps formed to defend the Jura, was predominantly bourgeois in complexion – all the Federalist *grande bourgeoisie* of Lons-le-Saunier being conspicuous in its ranks[36] – elsewhere these departmental forces were generally open to popular elements. In Bordeaux many would be accepted into the revolutionary battalions three months later.[37] There is nothing surprising about this. The clothing, lodging and pay had no political colour and many of these unfortunates, victims of events which they did not really understand, were untroubled by matters of conscience, even had they been given the choice. Orthodoxy, conformism and prudence dictated enrolment in a Federalist force in Federalist regions during June and July, and in an *armée révolutionnaire* after September. Besides, we must not be under any illusion as to the popular character of these Federalist forces; they were firmly under the control of the *grands bourgeois*, instruments of Federalist decentralisation, weapons of one class only.

The existence of the Federalist forces supplied yet another argument to the opponents of the *armées révolutionnaires*, and many sincere republicans used them to underline the threat posed by such special armies. But the similarities between the Federalist battalions and the revolutionary forces were only superficial, and if one was produced by decentralisation, the other by 'communalisation', the resemblance stops there. The Federalist forces sought to arm the enemies of Paris; the *armées révolutionnaires* in contrast sought to ensure supplies to the capital, and, more particularly, to impose the ideas and aspirations of the Parisian sans-culottes on the provinces. Despite the popular composition of some Federalist forces, they were nevertheless the instrument of social groupings quite opposed to the sans-culottes.

VI *The* sociétés populaires *in the departments organise* (*August–September*)

At the same time as these Federalist forces were being formed, *armées révolutionnaires* began to take shape in the areas which had remained faithful to the Republic. The *armée* of the Lot was the first to become active in September and there are signs that the process may have begun as early as

May in that department.[38] Certainly in August, when Paris was silent, the campaign continued in the provinces. It was predominantly an urban campaign, with the petitions coming primarily from the *sociétés populaires* of district or departmental *chefs-lieux*. After August–September these urban clubs underwent a profound transformation: many leaders compromised in the Federalist revolt were removed, and the *sociétés* took on the aspect they were to retain throughout the Terror – that of associations comprised of small tradesmen, artisans, shopkeepers, clerks, employees, some members of the legal profession, doctors, administrators and officials, former priests, and occasionally foundry or factory workers.

In August and September many *sociétés populaires* sprang up in the rural communes, frequently on the initiative of 'missionaries' from the large urban clubs, which were anxious to guarantee the political complexion of the main grain-growing regions. On the whole such rural *sociétés* remained open to popular elements, to day-labourers and the poorest artisans. Some even became platforms for the village 'enragés' who were common enough in certain populous agricultural districts. More popular, strictly speaking, in their composition than the urban *sociétés*, the village bodies shared all the sans-culotte prejudices against the big farmer, the corn merchant and their traditional allies, the *juge de paix* and the *notaire*. The labourers and artisans who controlled the *sociétés* hounded these men who dominated the municipalities and the districts. From August–September, in the large grain-growing areas such as the 'Pays de France', the Vermandois, the Santerre, the French Vexin, and even more so in the pays de Caux, the Soissonnais or the Lauragais, the political struggles were accompanied by an extremely violent social conflict.[39] If the farmer could count on the *juge de paix* and the district directory, the rural *sociétaire* could look outside the agricultural community for allies in the towns. Thus the campaign for the creation of *armées révolutionnaires* was intensified by quite bitter social antagonism.

After August the renewed petitions asking the Convention to form an *armée révolutionnaire* came for the most part from the *sociétés populaires*. Their language, arguments and timing were so similar, that they must have been the outcome of a concerted strategy. The first general assembly of these *sociétés* took place at Valence in June, to discuss the means of combating Federalism.[40] The outcome was a co-ordinated campaign by the *sociétés* to pressurise the Convention into creating the instruments of internal repression: the *armées*, the revolutionary tribunals, the popular commissions.

The first petition came from the extremely active *société populaire* of Mâcon on 15 August. Two weeks later the campaign took off in the major provincial towns and in Paris, with Claude Royer supporting the Mâcon proposal in the Jacobins.[41] The urban *sociétés*, with their habit of correspondence, their affiliation procedures, their general assemblies, were well equipped to conduct such a campaign. At the beginning of September there was another assembly in Valence, when over 70 *sociétés* from the Midi met to decide on certain 'measures of public safety' and to set the date for another rendezvous at Avignon.[42] It was the Avignon meeting which put forward plans for the formation of a Légion de la Montagne – the 'child' of the *sociétés populaires* which was to be recruited from *sociétés* throughout the Republic.[43] The example of the Valence–Avignon–Marseille assembly was followed elsewhere. The assembly which met at Gap between 20 and 24 Brumaire agreed on the creation of a revolutionary battalion for the Hautes-Alpes. In Le Havre a reunion of *sociétés* in Haute-Normandie, on 15 October, voted to demand from the Convention either the creation of a departmental *armée*, or the dispatch of a Parisian *armée* into the Seine-Inférieure.[44]

Such efforts at co-ordination showed that if the *sociétés* could agree on a regional basis, they could also join forces when it came to a national campaign. A few active men, like François Allier from Valence, had been responsible for arranging the general assembly. But the government agents, the so-called 'hommes de liaison', also played an important role in the campaign for the formation of local *armées*, as they would do later in the debate over sending detachments into the villages. The gatherings were the channels through which the urban *sociétés* forced their views on the Convention and on the Committees, and nearly all produced orders either creating *armées révolutionnaires* or demanding their dispatch into the areas where the special meetings had taken place. In reality, the *sociétés populaires* were in the process of creating an alternative administration which, under the pretence of carrying through 'revolutionary' measures, threatened to set itself up in the place not only of the local authorities, but of the Convention and the very government itself. Hence, even before the organisation of departmental and communal *armées*, the campaign was characterised by administrative anarchy and rivalry between the different powers. It was not difficult to see how these *armées*, which owed their existence to the *sociétés populaires*, might become their most faithful instruments. The departmental *armées* were to become exaggerated versions of the one in Paris: through them the initiatives of the Paris Sections were implemented more completely, and more violently, than in Paris itself. The banding together of the departmental *sociétés* in general assemblies was a much more dangerous version of the *fraternisation* of the Paris Sections to bring pressure on the Jacobin government.[45] Thanks to the affiliation to the Cordeliers which the club granted to many provincial *sociétés*, these assemblies threatened to become both a permanent and a national institution, and the *armées révolutionnaires* were to become the means by which this new and irresponsible power could give to its demands the weight of force. The campaign, therefore, was to have extremely serious consequences.

VII   *The Parisian* journée *of 4 September*

Before we examine the petitioning campaign of the departmental *sociétés* during the autumn months of 1793, let us recall the events in Paris which.

compelled the Convention and the Committees to reactivate the decree of
4 June and commence organisation of the Parisian *armée*. Some assessment
of this new development in the relationship between the Sectionary movement and the Revolutionary Government is crucial for an understanding of
the repercussions of the Paris *journée* on the provinces. The decree of
9 September, produced by this *journée*, recreated the Paris *armée*, and was
the excuse for the provincial *sociétés* to demand its application to the whole
country, either in the form of a huge, national people's army of '100,000
men', or smaller *armées* in every department and every large town. When
they learnt from the newspapers of the September measure, the *sociétés* drew
up addresses which, under the pretext of congratulating the Convention on
its 'salutary decree', demanded a whole series of repressive measures against
'malveillants' and 'égoïstes'. By thus congratulating the Convention and
Committees on their 'volonté punitive', the departmental *sociétés populaires*
sought to push them into adopting a real policy of terror which the *sociétés*
would then direct. In effect a militant minority was turning to its own
advantage repeated popular demands for the punishment of the disloyal
towns and regions: Lyon, Marseille, Toulon, Bordeaux, the Aveyron, the
Lozère and the West.

The *journée* of 4 September had retrieved for Paris the initiative lost to the
country, but it was not unconnected with the Mâcon petition of 15 August.
In the Jacobins on 1 September, Claude Royer declared his support for 'an
address from Mâcon calling for an *armée révolutionnaire* to spread out
through the Republic and eradicate all the germs of Federalism, royalism
and fanaticism with which it is still infected...'. He then put forward his
own thoughts on the idea: 'You have made terror the order of the day; what
better way to ensure its success than to create an army of 30,000 men, divide
it into flying columns and attach a revolutionary tribunal and a guillotine to
administer justice to traitors and conspirators alike?' To Royer, the *armée*
was more an instrument to avenge the regime than one to protect it. 'There
was a time when it would have been dangerous to propose such a force
[because of its possible 'federalisation']; but today, when the Rolandist
faction has been defeated, when the Republic's army is in Marseille, when
Lyon is about to fall and Bordeaux has been won from its errors, there is no
longer any obstacle to our success; liberty must triumph...'. He concluded
by asking the Society to support the Mâcon address in the Convention.[46]

The following day, 2 September, another event took place which would
prove decisive in the campaign for the creation of an *armée révolutionnaire*:
news arrived of the treason of Toulon. The news revived the worst fears of
a counter-revolutionary coup and stimulated the desire for repression. The
Parisian *armée* was the product of Toulon's treason and the reaction was
similar outside the capital.[47] That evening in the Jacobins, Royer's motion,
supported this time by Hébert, was carried, and the Society agreed to take it
in a body to the Convention. On the 4th Royer led the deputation which
consisted of the Jacobin Society and *commissaires* from the 48 Sections.

'Representatives of the people', he declared, 'the danger to the Republic is extreme, the remedy must be likewise.... We demand the establishment of an *armée révolutionnaire*; it should be divided into several sections, and a formidable tribunal and a guillotine should follow each one. Let this *armée* and its tribunals continue to operate until the soil of the Republic is purged of traitors and the last conspirator eliminated....'[48] Royer and his Jacobin supporters thus saw the *armée révolutionnaire* as an extraordinary instrument, intended to remain in existence only as long as the extraordinary crisis which had led to its creation.

It was Chaumette, however, who carried opinion in the Convention on 4 September. Climbing on to a table, he addressed the workers who had invaded the headquarters of the General Council: '...We now have open war between the rich and the poor...so they want to crush us—well, we must stop them—we must crush them ourselves and we have the means at hand! ...I demand that the Convention be asked to establish an *armée révolutionnaire* immediately, an *armée* which can go into the countryside to supervise the requisition of grain, to prevent the manoeuvres of rich *égoïstes* and to deliver them up to the vengeance of the laws'. 'Let the *armée* leave the instant the decree has been passed,' added Hébert; 'but above all each division, each column should be followed by a guillotine....'[49] Royer, Chaumette, Hébert—these were the real creators of this second *armée révolutionnaire*; the members of the Committees and the *Conventionnels,* Moïse Bayle, Billaud-Varenne, Barère, Léonard Bourdon, Danton, were simply giving in to pressure from the Commune when they presented this programme to the Convention and the Jacobins on the 5th.

What were the motives of Chaumette and Hébert? Were they simply seeking their own ends, as Soboul has suggested, trying to channel protest to a political end and thereby distract attention from the more radical social demands of the building workers, of those who had taken part in the *journée* of 4 September and of those militants from the Sans-Culottes Section, who on the 2nd had gone so far as to demand a 'maximum des fortunes' (a statutory restriction on wealth)?[50] The creation of the *armée révolutionnaire*, in other words, was the lesser evil, a bone for the voracious sans-culottes to gnaw upon. Chaumette's programme for this future *armée* did incorporate one of the most frequently voiced demands of the *sectionnaires*, that force should be used against the big farmers and their many allies in the provinces, for the guillotine alone could ensure the application of the Maximum and the adequate supply of Paris.[51] But this was only a small portion of the popular demands, and by yielding on the *armée* issue, Chaumette and the members of the Convention surely hoped to ward off more revolutionary demands. Certainly the *procureur-syndic* and his deputy knew well enough how to exploit popular grievances for their own ends. When on 10 September a deputation from the Marseille-et-Marat Section came to congratulate the Convention on its decree, the gesture was as much a celebration of the political success gained by the Cordelier group as an act of gratitude to the Assembly for having acceded to popular demands. The creation of the Parisian *armée* was in fact a considerable political success for Momoro and the other leaders of this Section. But it was also a popular victory. Soboul is right to stand apart from Mathiez and Hadengue, who see in the success of these demands the triumph of political Hébertism. Rather he sees it as 'a movement which emerged from the very heart of the people'.[52] The militant *sectionnaires* attached so much importance to this *armée révolutionnaire* that, once in power, they pursued everyone who had blocked its creation between June and September: from October, the accusation of having 'opposed the formation of the *armée révolutionnaire*' was sufficient reason for refusing certificates of *civisme* to those concerned. The *armée révolutionnaire* was much more 'the *armée* of the Sections' than 'the *armée* of the Commune', and certain leading Cordeliers were greatly mistaken in thinking that they could make it an instrument of their own ambitions. The crisis of Ventôse–Germinal was to be a bitter disappointment for them.

The *armée révolutionnaire* did indeed represent only a small part of popular demands, most of which remained unsatisfied, despite the *journée* of 4–5 September. It was moreover an emasculated *armée*, 'castrated', lacking the requested back-up of guillotines and popular commissions, its numbers (Chaumette spoke of 30,000) falling far short of the 100,000 demanded by the Sectionary petitions. The Convention and the Committees had conceded the principle, but held back from its realisation. It is nevertheless true to say that the creation of the *armée* represented a striking success for Sectionary propaganda and was an encouragement to the *sociétés populaires* in other large towns. What had already been granted to Paris could scarcely be refused to Lille, Bordeaux, or to any other town, and, with the treason of Toulon, the decree of 9 September injected new life into a campaign which had been in progress since mid-August. There was also the natural tendency to imitate, to conform, particularly noticeable during the revolutionary period, and since the *armée révolutionnaire* could now claim to have the blessing of the Convention, it acquired respectability with the hesitant and the careerist. The treason of Toulon reawakened popular fears and sparked off a whole series of precautionary measures throughout the Midi. Municipalities mounted night guards and patrols at the town gates, *comités de surveillance* redoubled their zeal in checking passports and scrutinising lists of those staying at the *auberges*.

VIII   *Petitions and addresses from departmental* sociétés populaires
       (September)

If the Mâcon *société* was the first to resurrect the campaign which had collapsed during August, its rival town, Châlon-sur-Saône, was the first to congratulate the Convention on its decree of 5 September. In an address of 5 September, entered in the *Bulletin de la Convention* for the 12th, 'the sans-

culottes of the *société* of Châlon-sur-Saône' asked the Convention to pass a
decree establishing 'a mobile *armée révolutionnaire* with a popular tribunal at
its head...'.[53] Popular demands, whether voiced in Châlon or Paris, had
lost none of their sharpness or their repressive desire. On 9 September the
Le Puy *société populaire* expressed the same desire in even plainer terms: 'the
safety of the Republic demands immediate and rigorous action—an *armée*
of 24,000 men should be created and sent to the four corners of the
Republic, each division moving through those departments assigned to it,
followed by a revolutionary tribunal and a guillotine...'.[54] On that date
also the district directory of Arles sounded another note in the campaign
when it supported the demand of the municipality for 'an armed force,
stationed at various points to prevent the secret exportation of grain...'.[55]
The authorities of Arles – situated in the richest grain-producing plain of the
south-east – had adopted a policy of 'immobilism' and hostility to any
export of grain from the region. Everyone, rich or poor, hoped to use the
new *armées* to their own advantage, and if rich areas sought to prohibit grain
exports, the poor towns were just as willing to resort to force to maintain
supply levels.

On 10 September the *sociétés* of Tours and Le Havre were the first to
demand an extension of the decree of 5 September to the entire country,
since only a general measure could ensure safety. The Tours address went
on to voice another, more important, demand, which highlights the long-
term intentions of the *sociétés populaires*. It demanded 'that the *armée révolutionnaire* should be composed only of true republicans *taken from among the
friends of the Constitution*'. The Le Havre address asked the Convention 'to
require the *sociétés populaires* to provide five out of every hundred members
of this *armée*...', thereby giving them control over its recruitment and a
guaranteed number of places in its ranks.[56]

This same concern over numbers and the control of recruitment by the
sociétés populaires can be found in the address of 18 September from the
société of Toulon-sur-Arroux, a small locality in the Charolais: 'The *armée
révolutionnaire* you have wisely decreed shall consist of 100,000 men of the
Republic: but they must be republicans of the most decided patriotism. We
think therefore that *it would be best to select these soldiers from among the sociétés
populaires*, for it is here that you will find true sans-culottes: each *société*
knows its own members and can indicate those known for their patriotism
...'; and this *société*, like the others, wanted the *armée* to march 'with the
instrument of terror', the guillotine.[57] On 29 September, another small-
town *société*, that of Arc-sur-Tille in the Dijon district, composed of
'workers and yeomen farmers', declared, in a picturesquely worded address
– 'in language simple and rough like their occupations' – that all the inhabitants of their commune were ready to form an *armée révolutionnaire*. As in
the petitions of April, May and June, the accent was on the political duties
of these *armées*: 'Soon the sowing time will be over and in winter we
normally hunt boar and other wild beasts; let us instead employ our time

destroying these hordes of slaves whom we detest more than the voracious animals who destroy our crops and our herds. Just say the word, citizen representatives, and we will set out at the first signal, armed with our hunting guns and our pitch forks...their skin is not as tough as that of the boar and wolves, our blows will not be resisted. We are accustomed to the frost and the snow....'.[58]

   This address highlights one of the great weaknesses of the *armées révolutionnaires* in the localities – where would these men, willing to forsake their homes in search of internal enemies, be employed? Did they not, like the men from Arc-sur-Tille, see the *armée* as a kind of hunting party, to be used only in the neighbouring woods and forests? The *sociétaire* was eager enough to take up arms, provided he could do so near his own home, hunting the suspect by day, returning to his fireside at night, to rest his republican gun near his hearth and enjoy the praise and attention of his 'virtuous republican wife' – a service moreover which would be sweetened by the same pay of 40 sols per day accorded to the Parisian *révolutionnaire*. Many in fact viewed the *armée révolutionnaire* as little more than a reinforced National Guard. But when the Dijonnais were asked to go and fight the rebels in the West, they responded with indignant protests and claims that they had enlisted simply to police their own districts. This ambiguity lay at the heart of all the petitions sent to the Convention in the autumn of 1793, and later, when the *armées* saw active service, it was to thwart the efforts of those who wanted to form the scattered forces into one large national body. Finally, the petitioners of Arc-sur-Tille expected such service to be purely half-time, over and above their daily work (a view shared by the Parisian recruits). The enthusiasm of the departmental sans-culottes would rapidly evaporate when they were faced with service requiring more than just the loss of leisure time and removal from their home territory.

   Many of these concerns – in addition to one peculiar to a town so deeply affected by the social changes of the Revolution – were neatly summarised in a decision by the general assembly of the 13th Section in Versailles on 13 September. It was the town's poorest Section, inhabited by grooms, valets, servants and others employed by the royal household or in the luxury trades which had been so badly affected by the emigration. The decision was inspired by the decree of 5 September, and inaugurated an abortive campaign by the *sociétés populaires* and the local authorities for the establishment of an *armée révolutionnaire* in the Versailles and Montagne-Bon-Air (Saint-Germain-en-Laye) districts. 'Given the urgent need for advance preparations to combat the desperation of poverty', the 13th Section had decided to petition the Convention, in association with the other 12 Sections of the town, for permission to levy an *armée* of 400–500 men. After stressing that 'the citizens serving with the *armée* should nevertheless continue to live with their families', its members added the revealing point that 'this organisation...will provide each fusilier with the same pay as the gendarmerie, replacing the salary which many of them had received formerly as grooms in the royal stables...'.[59]

The decision was well received by the other Sections and by the town's two *sociétés populaires*. The Vertu-Sociale *société* – more artisan in composition and more open to Cordelier influence than that of the Amis de la Liberté – adopted all its proposals on the 23rd and approved the demand for a Versailles *armée révolutionnaire* to be commanded by Ronsin, with the proviso that it should never have to serve outside the department. It was a characteristic reservation, highlighting the contradictory aims of the supporters of the *armées*.[60] This resolution, and the adhesion of the Vertu-Sociale *société*, were the point of departure for the department's approach to its deputies in Brumaire.

IX   *The campaign spreads (September – October)*

In September the campaign became more widespread, thanks to the official encouragement given by the decree of 5 September and the force of circumstances (the treason of Toulon and the difficulty of assuring grain supplies after the application of the General Maximum). It was taken up by municipalities, *comités de surveillance*, district directories and by individuals. Among the latter, we find the 'étrangers', the garrison soldiers, who diligently attended the sessions of the local *sociétés*, the 'hommes de liaison', mostly Cordeliers from Paris, government *commissaires, commissaires des guerres, commissaires aux subsistances*, along with local personalities, small-town revolutionaries and village 'enragés'. The municipality of Nesle, for instance, was prompted by its energetic *procureur-syndic* to propose the formation of 'national or departmental legions...recruited from the working masses' – the product of this small town's need to ensure food supplies to the urban markets, despite the ill will of the big farmers.[61] On 26 September, in the wake of a supposed attempt at Abbeville on the life of the *représentant* in the Somme, André Dumont, the commune of Sourdon, in the Montdidier district, proposed that the Convention should 'place a close guard on all *représentants* sent into the departments...to protect them from attack by internal enemies'. On 18 September the Convention heard a novel proposal for recruiting a national *armée révolutionnaire* from among the representatives of the primary assemblies. It came from Pierre Blondel – a former Benedictine and son of a village weaver – himself a delegate from the primary assembly of Frohan-le-Grand in the Doullens district of the Pas-de-Calais department. Such proposals poured in from the departments during September, and many felt, with some justification, that the Committees were dragging their heels over the creation of the *armée* – a sentiment conveyed by the Cordelier journalists in Paris to their friends in the provinces. At the beginning of October the 3rd battalion of the Cantal, serving in the Ile-d'Aix, echoed the press campaign of the *Père Duchesne* and the *Journal Universel* by asking the Convention to accelerate the mobilization of the *armée révolutionnaire*; a month had passed since the decree and 'every delay affords the guilty more time to plan new crimes....'.[62] On 10 October, the Parisian Mourgoin, *commissaire* with the Moselle Army, wrote to Bouchotte from Sarrebruck: 'I cannot stress enough the urgency of sending a detachment of the *armée révolutionnaire* to the Moselle to enforce the law on the price of foodstuffs, which are as dear in Metz as in foreign territories...such a mission is all the more imperative because of the uselessness of the authorities of this department, who try to spare the farmers, to gain their support in the next elections...' – an astute observation on the universal collusion between the district authorities and the farmers. On the 15th Mourgoin took up the charge again in a second letter: 'Even if the *représentants* had the power to raise an *armée révolutionnaire* in this department, they would not find any *révolutionnaires* to fill it...'.[63] Mourgoin, as *commissaire* both of the Ministries and the Committee of General Security, was one of those 'hommes de liaison', the group most favourably disposed towards the *armées*.[64]

Similar opinions were expressed by another Parisian on mission to the Armies. Jean-Jacques Derché was a Jacobin, like Mourgoin, a friend of Rossignol and Boulanger (then commanding the garrison at Caen), and editor-in-chief of the *Journal de l'Armée des Côtes de Cherbourg*. On 13 September he announced the decree of the 5th to the Parisian-dominated Caen *société*, and claimed it as a great victory for public safety. On the 19th he outlined for his readers the advantages of this new institution, and spoke of its organisation on a national basis and of the accompanying revolutionary tribunals and guillotines, as if they were already established facts.[65] On 6 October, Houdbert, an officer in the 6th battalion of the Aube, proposed that the same Caen *société* should 'send an address to the Convention requesting an *armée révolutionnaire*...in every department'. The proposal was seconded by the Swedish-born Parisian sans-culotte Lindberg, from the Bonnet-Rouge Section, in an argument frequently expressed by the Parisian *sectionnaires* who favoured the extension of *armées révolutionnaires* to all parts of the country: 'Before we rush to the frontiers to destroy the satellites of tyranny, let us first destroy the internal traitors by adopting the necessary means to contain them – of these, the *armée révolutionnaire* is the best...'. However, Canby, a local man, disagreed, arguing that an *armée révolutionnaire* was unnecessary, that it was 'the public duty of every citizen to pursue the enemy, and besides, such an *armée* would be a slur on the Caen National Guard...'. Such an argument, which claimed that the existence of the National Guard rendered an *armée révolutionnaire* superfluous, appealed to local loyalties, and was used frequently by opponents in the departments. The debate in the Caen *société* was between the supporters and the opponents of the *armée révolutionnaire*, and it was Lindberg, the Parisian and Cordelier, who replied to Canby, the provincial: 'The National Convention, in creating an *armée révolutionnaire* for Paris, was not trying to dishonour the city: but it knew that there were enemies even in the National Guard.'[66]

X *Geography of the campaign and the motives behind it (October 1793)*

From the beginning of October the campaign began to produce the first local decrees setting up such revolutionary bodies. The campaign continued as long as the *armées* themselves, and new battalions were still being called for when the law of 14 Frimaire brought the brief existence of these *armées* to a close. In October 1793 most of the large towns – municipalities and *sociétés populaires* alike – took part in the campaign. At the same time its tone changed: increasingly it sought to enforce the Maximum, ensure supplies and execute requisitions.

Complaints mounted from all parts of the country about the slow organisation of the Parisian *armée*, and were themselves responses to the insistence of its generals, Ronsin, Parein and Boulanger. 'You must hasten the organisation of the *armées révolutionnaires*', wrote the Sarlat *société* to the Convention on 4 October. 'The *armée révolutionnaire* should be launched', urged the small *société* of Conches on 1 Brumaire, 'and soon the plots hatched by despots and supported by our internal enemies will founder.'[67] 'Where will it be organised? When will monopolists cease to exist?'[68] The Varennes *société populaire* expressed its impatience to participate in 'the military tour of the departments by the *armée révolutionnaire*'.[69] The powerful sans–culotte-dominated *société* of Rouen voiced the anxieties of the large towns about the declining stocks in the markets, and recommended a departmental *armée révolutionnaire*, composed of sans–culottes from Rouen, which would march against recalcitrant farmers and oblige them to enforce requisitions in favour of the Rouen market.[70]

As such demands became more insistent, municipalities started to pass firm resolutions, without waiting for permission from the Convention. Nor was the movement confined to the large towns like Lille, Rouen, Le Havre, Metz, Nantes, Chaumont, Châlons-sur-Marne or Troyes,[71] but extended to small towns and district or cantonal *chefs-lieux*, places like Charlieu in the Loire, La Clayette, Paray-le-Monial and Charolles in the Saône-et-Loire, Lisieux (which sent a particularly eloquent appeal), Versailles, Saint-Germain and many small communes in the Centre and the Midi, the Cantal and the Basses-Pyrénées.[72] In the Basses-Alpes, the campaign was organised by a general assembly of the *sociétés populaires* meeting in Marseille.[73] In the Vaucluse it was the public prosecutor of the department's criminal tribunal who organised the campaign.[74] The motive most frequently invoked by these urban *sociétés populaires* and municipalities was the necessity of using force to implement requisitions and end the complicity of the rural municipalities. Without an *armée révolutionnaire*, they claimed, the law of the Maximum was a dead letter. Less frequently they invoked the necessity of crushing royalists and counter-revolutionaries.

The order of priorities, therefore, had changed since the summer, and in October economic problems took precedence everywhere. Yet the areas putting forward such demands were not the traditional large grain markets, and among those towns demanding the creation of instruments of economic terror one will search in vain for names like Provins, Dammartin, Bray-sur-Seine, Noyon and Pont L'Evêque, Pont-Saint-Maxence, Pontoise and Beaumont, Montdidier, Péronne, Soissons, Langres, Saint-Jean-de-Losne, Rozoy-en-Brie, Janville or Chartres, all those regional centres of the grain-producing areas which supplied the enormous needs of Paris. Nor will we find the names of Tôtes or of the market centres of the Cauchois plateau, which supplied Rouen and Le Havre, or Castelnaudary and the villages of the Lauragais, which supplied Toulouse; and if Arles is represented, it is for reasons quite opposed to those put forward by the other towns: to prevent grain leaving a rich district, rather than to facilitate its entry into a poor one.

Almost all the localities taking part in this campaign were situated in areas poor in grain, but with large populations to support. In this respect the very large centres, almost all the *chef-lieu* of a department or a district – places like Rouen, Amiens, Toulouse, Lille or Bordeaux – had less to complain of than those smaller centres without means of coercing the rural communes which supplied their markets, or of seeking grain supplies further afield in another canton or district.[75] This is why we find so many municipalities and small communes among those demanding the formation of revolutionary battalions, or the dispatch of detachments from Paris. For the same reason, the Parisian *armée* would have a poor reception in grain-rich towns such as Pontoise, Noyon, Chartres, Provins and all the other places which had remained conspicuously silent during the autumn campaign. The campaign, therefore, highlighted the fundamental divergence of interests between the town and the cereal plains, and the conflict was intensified after the General Maximum of 29 September and the law of 18 Vendémiaire granting the older market centres the right to draw requisitions on villages which had normally supplied them before the Revolution.

The conflict between town and country was accompanied by a social struggle within each town and village. The members of their *sociétés populaires* had no means of acquiring flour themselves, and were dependent on the bakers for bread. They had already put forward the policy of cheap bread, eventually embodied in the General Maximum, and had a personal stake in its success. But there was another class in each village or town (the corn merchants and the farmers, large and small), which sought to defend its interests by immobilising and stock-piling supplies, or by diverting them from controlled markets to secret destinations. In the hands of the artisans and small merchants of the towns, the *armée révolutionnaire* was the ideal instrument of an economic policy which favoured the small consumer.

Finally, the change in emphasis in the campaign was caused by the change in season. In April, May and June, fear of the aristocratic plot was uppermost; in September, Toulon again raised the spectre of treason. But although Toulon was not retaken until Frimaire, by October Lyon, Marseille and Bordeaux had already been restored to the Republic and a good harvest had been gathered in. Now, those who lived in the country and in the small market towns had to make provision for the long autumn and winter evenings. They had time not only to take part in the impassioned sessions of the *sociétés populaires*, which by now they had come to dominate, but also to play at being soldiers, so long as they did not have to move far from their own homes. Such service held an additional attraction in the prospect of financial compensation – a useful supplement in this period of seasonal unemployment.

Like all new institutions, the *armées* excited the appetites of all those involved, and many a clerk behind the counter abandoned the corner grocery for the promise held out by a uniform, epaulettes and gold braid. Such sentiments enhanced the power of the *sociétés* as employment agencies and distributors of favours; hence their eagerness to speed up the organisation of these bizarre *armées*.[76]

There remains the attitude of the established authorities and the Revolutionary Government itself to these *armées*. The municipal authorities of the large towns were not averse to the creation of an instrument which could be used in support of their own policy of maintaining supplies. Carnot likewise recognised the utility of the *armées* in ensuring supplies to the Army and the war zones, even though he was hostile in principle to special armies, particularly popular ones. As for the local authorities, particularly in the districts, they were glad of the opportunity to offload unpopular requisitioning duties on to these 'étrangers'. Likewise many *représentants* were eager to spare the regular Armies the onerous duties associated with the gathering in of the harvest, the requisitioning of agricultural labour, etc. But this is to run ahead of ourselves. We shall return to central government attitudes when discussing the enrolment and organisation of the *armées révolutionnaires*. In fact the campaign developed quite apart from the central government, and if it did nothing to oppose it, neither did it offer any official encouragement.[77]

Such was the state of affairs just before winter set in. The popular *armées* were taking shape in every corner of the Republic. The Parisian *armée* was being organised with official blessing, before leaving to 'frapper le grand coup', as expected by its adherents and by men in high places such as Collot-d'Herbois.[78] It was the end product of an enthusiastic, if self-interested campaign, of which the *sociétés populaires* of the towns and bourgs were the leading supporters. The campaign had attracted support from those departments poor in grain and from the lower orders in the countryside. Its success was the product both of the real needs which had inspired it and of flimsier motives such as the desire to 'flow with the revolutionary tide' or to follow the latest fashion. The attitude of the local authorities varied according to the degree to which they expected to use this new instrument to their own advantage, and to the disadvantage of their neighbour. Above all the *armées* were products of circumstance, means produced to deal with an exceptional situation which did not allow for deeply laid plans or solutions.

The *armées* had the faults of any extraordinary institution: despite the range of petitions from all over the country, none had put forward any definite plans, and there was no clear idea on whether the *armée* should be one national body or a series of regional ones. Proposals for effective numbers ranged from 24,000 to 100,000, with the *sociétés populaires* favouring the larger figures; and although every petition restricted enrolment to true revolutionaries, none laid down precise procedures, except to insist on the need for some kind of political check by the *sociétés*. The proposals asked for high rates of pay, but said nothing of conditions of service, and the question of whether the men would serve on home territory or elsewhere was left unanswered. All these points were raised without being resolved. It was suggested that the volunteers' pay could be levied as revolutionary taxes on the rich – a scheme particularly popular with the supporters of the *armées*, as it would make their victims also their paymasters. But methods of pay were left unresolved, and methods of finance unprovided for. Furthermore, nothing was said about the command structure. Would the *armées* be autonomous bodies, each under its own commander, or would they be placed at the disposition of the local authorities, under existing garrison commanders? In almost every petition the *armées* were seen in the same light, as institutions of terror and repression, to be accompanied by guillotines and commissions of popular justice. Yet such a demand was never granted, and was still being made by the Parisian sans-culottes in Ventôse, only a few weeks before the last of the *armées* was suppressed.

All in all, the supporters of these popular forces had grandiose visions, and they hoped that the *armées* would be endowed with equally grand powers to 'frapper de Terreur' the 'malveillants' and 'égoïstes'. As for their opponents, most remained prudently silent after September, and the powerful, while appearing to yield to popular pressure on the principle, in reality took active measures to undermine the *armées*. But if they succeeded in emasculating the Parisian *armée*, those in the departments were less susceptible to such sabotage, and they prospered under the shelter of widespread disorder.

CHAPTER 2

The Organisation of the Parisian *Armée révolutionnaire* and its General Headquarters in the rue de Choiseul

PART I   ADMINISTRATIVE MACHINERY

The *armée révolutionnaire* had a disproportionately large bureaucratic structure: its officer complement was excessive for a body of less than 7,000 men, and its general staff was particularly cumbersome and complicated. Its three divisions of infantry, cavalry and artillery were headed by a high command, *l'état-major général révolutionnaire*, based in the rue de Choiseul in Paris. In addition, the infantry and cavalry each had its own general staff composed of the superior officers. The artillery, in contrast, had no officer above the rank of company captain; each company of cannoneers remained autonomous under its own commander, and all attempts to superimpose a commander-general failed. The control of the general staff over the artillery of the Parisian *armée* was consequently uncertain and was challenged by Hanriot as commander-general of the Parisian armed forces.

Such anomalies will dominate our account of the facts. First of all we will need to look at the formation of this complicated administrative machinery whose powers were as ill defined as the numbers involved. At the time of its dissolution the organisation of the Parisian *armée* was still incomplete, and organisational confusion undermined its effectiveness. Then we will present the individuals who held positions on the general staff, the men with apparent control over this new instrument of the Terror; the *chefs de bataillon* and *chefs d'escadron*, more important than the men in the rue de Choiseul by virtue of their daily contact with their detachments; and finally the artillery, lacking a high command, will be discussed, with the cannoneer officers, in Chapter 3. The removal of the latter to a separate chapter should not be taken as an attempt to reduce its historical importance, for the artillery officers were the most politically aware element of the entire body.

When the *armée révolutionnaire* is spoken of, it is first and foremost in terms of people like Ronsin, Boulanger, Parein, Mazuel, the Grammonts and the host of young officers who followed them; perhaps too of the *commissaires civils* (though these were as little known to their contemporaries as they are to historians). Sited in Paris, the general staff at headquarters was constantly under the gaze and frequently under the attack of the sans-culottes, and by attacking this one element of the new corps which remained visible to the Parisians, its enemies sought to undermine the entire *armée*.

The general staff were widely considered the political leaders of the *armée*, and the entire institution was judged by the conduct of its chiefs and their entourage in Paris. Historical judgement has followed the same pattern by making the Parisian *armée* the instrument of a political clique which 'colonised' the general staff and through them tried to establish control over the entire body.

Studies of armies usually start at the top with the commanders. But there is another reason for treating the general staff separately. It is often the case with political armies – organised hastily and amidst confusion – that the general staff, physically and morally removed from the detachments and unfamiliar with the duties they have to undertake, is compelled to work in something of a void, and has little influence over the activities of the detachments. At the same time the social position and political affiliations of its members set the general staff apart from the bulk of the officers and men. In the case of the Parisian *armée*, the men were certainly aware of this division and complained of the improper and unrepublican conduct of the best known figures in the rue de Choiseul. They felt themselves compromised by their general staff, and they were right.

They lived in separate worlds: the general staff in the public glare, their rivalries, quarrels and extravagances fuelling café gossip and forming part of the political climate of revolutionary Paris. It is too easy, however, to paint a black picture by forgetting that the general staff was neither a single body nor in the service of any particular political group; and if collectively the group in the rue de Choiseul appears removed from the concerns of the rank and file, certain of its members, *commissaires civils, commissaires des guerres, chefs d'escadron* or *de bataillon*, remained in contact with the *armée* properly speaking.

In any case – and it is this which explains the discontent of the *révolutionnaires* – superiors and soldiers, general staff and detachments formed but one homogeneous whole in the eyes of contemporaries and historians alike. Thus Ronsin (who scarcely ever saw the soldiers of 'his' *armée*) and Grammont (who only left his office to go to the theatre or a café, or to shut himself up in his own house) personally influenced the destiny of these corps. And finally, even if it is true that the general staff could not know everything about the activities of the detachments, it did transmit the orders of the government Committees and in this respect acted as a restraint on the most revolutionary initiatives. The general staff of the *armée* was in the service of the government, particularly the Committee of Public Safety, and not of a single man or party, and they did influence the direction of government policy, even if in a limited fashion. Undoubtedly the real history of the *armée révolutionnaire* lies with the detachments and their struggles with the local authorities, in the performance of their thankless and unpopular missions. But even when left without orders, the detachments were not autonomous bodies; they were linked to their Sections, with whom they preferred to deal, and with their general staff, on whom they depended for their administrative and material needs. The *armée* was a political body, and the concerns of its superiors were ultimately those also of the entire *armée*. The 50-plus membership of the general staff was extremely varied: talented soldiers, genuine revolutionaries and diligent administrators rubbed shoulders with frivolous young men and jumped-up officers who had experienced over-rapid promotion. Above all it was not a homogeneous body, and its influence over the detachments varied according to the honesty or roguery, frivolity or seriousness of its members. It is important therefore to understand these men who so influenced the destiny of the Parisian *armée*, sometimes in spite of themselves.

I Origins of the revolutionary cavalry

From the moment of its creation, the new *armée* was attached to troops already in action – it was a case of dealing immediately with the most urgent problems, and the only entirely original part of this popular *armée* was the infantry. The artillery was formed by the simple administrative device of converting half the companies of cannoneers in Paris into units of the revolutionary artillery for a period of three months, after which time the 24 companies would be replaced by the remaining 24. In this manner all the companies would see some service in the *armée révolutionnaire*, and any favouritism or division between the different Sections would be avoided. The cavalry was largely formed from the extraordinary levies in the departments of Paris, Seine-et-Oise and Oise[1] during the month of August, with the result that young men from the first requisition were reaching the ranks of the *armée révolutionnaire* from the outset. Another consequence of this kind of 'amalgamation' – whereby young conscripts, in service simply because they were the right age and height, were joined to a political corps composed of men chosen for their service to the Revolution and to their Sections – was that the revolutionary cavalry was not uniformly an élite political corps. Its officers on the whole were former career soldiers, hussars and dragoons whose advancement was due solely to the revolutionary war, its troopers young men of the required height but not necessarily of the right political principles. This confusion would be further aggravated by recruiting methods reminiscent of the Ancien Regime (touting and impressment included), which the new *chefs d'escadron* adopted in the weeks before the *armée* went into service.

In terms both of composition and dates of creation, then, the Parisian *armée révolutionnaire* comprised three quite distinct parts, each of which would develop its own individual characteristics. The artillery, composed of the cannoneers of the Sections, whose guns had been the deciding element in the popular *journées*, represented the political élite of the *sans-culotterie*. To them went the key positions not only in the Sectionary institutions, but also the political posts which devolved on the Parisians in the course of their operations in the provinces. Recruitment to the infantry followed the same political pattern, with the fusilier officer class often composed of the same kind of Sectionary personalities as that of the artillery. But the political sympathies of the cavalry were less certain, and patriots rubbed shoulders with rich young men, shirkers, adventurers and counter-revolutionaries.

The Parisian *armée* therefore was not entirely recruited from the sans-culottes and the Sections; indeed the cavalry was not even recruited uniquely from Paris, but had drawn as many men from the neighbouring departments. Here is one distortion of the image of the *armée* as presented by the petitions from the country that summer and autumn. There were to be many others, not only of the *armée*'s composition, but of the principle itself, for the image presented was of an autonomous and repressive body, enjoying extraordinary powers and accompanied by guillotines. Were such distortions perhaps an early manifestation of a deliberate policy on the part of the Committee of Public Safety to 'depoliticise' this new *armée*? I think not. The 'amalgamation' was above all dictated by the need to move quickly, by the urgent demands of the sans-culottes who wanted to see these detachments put into action without delay, and above all by the difficulties of implementing the Maximum in the countryside (particularly in the area which supplied Paris). The Committee simply made the most of what it had, and attached to the political force the cavalry which was already at hand.

This cavalry was formed by a decision of the Committee of Public Safety on 4 August, ordering a special levy of six squadrons in the departments of Paris, Seine-et-Marne, Seine-et-Oise and Oise; and a document of 15 August in Bouchotte's hand lists its future commanders, including the famous Mazuel, the gendarme Payot, and the former soldiers, hussars and dragoons, Gury, Fischer, Bernard, Bussy, Bresch, Koening, Picard, Bastien and Delmotte.[2] From 23 August elections took place of officers and non-commissioned officers for the first companies of Mazuel's squadron, composed largely of recruits from the Oise.[3] New elections took place and further recruits were raised at Beauvais on 13, 14 and 15 September, after the decree on the *armée révolutionnaire*. Even before this decree the command structure of the revolutionary cavalry had been decided, and if the later practice of electing the officers by the men was not adopted, it was because many of the latter had no *certificats de civisme* and fewer were in the twenty-five-to-forty age group of the second requisition.

II   *Establishment of the administrative machinery: decree of 5 September, decision of the 9th. Laws and regulations*

On 5 September Chaumette appeared before the Convention at the head of a large deputation of Jacobins, *sectionnaires* and common people. 'Legislators', proclaimed the *procureur* of the Commune, 'the huge assembly of citizens gathered yesterday and this morning outside the Commune's headquarters were of one opinion, and we have been instructed to lay it before you; this is it: subsistences, and to secure them *force à la loi* [which would become the slogan of the Parisian *armée* and appear on its banners and in its official pronouncements]. We have been instructed to demand the formation of the *armée révolutionnaire* which you have already decreed [4 June] but which intrigue and the fears of the guilty have frustrated...the nucleus of this *armée* must be formed immediately in Paris.' The deputation received the honours of the session and Moïse Bayle, a member of the Committee of General Security, laid before the Convention a motion stating the demands of the Sections. He was supported by Raffron, Billaud-Varenne, Léonard Bourdon, Gaston, Danton, and of course Drouet, who had inspired the address from the commune of Varennes. On behalf of the Committee of Public Safety, Jeanbon Saint-André promised a report 'after which measures would be proposed to meet the demands of the people'. Barère presented the Committee's report in the course of the same session, and after describing the general situation of the Republic, he asked, 'What will put a stop to all these crimes and plots? An *armée révolutionnaire* to sweep away the conspirators.' After this intervention, 'having heard the Committee of Public Safety's report', the Convention decreed:

1. That an armed force, financed by the national treasury, and consisting of 6,000 men and 1,200 cannoneers, be established in Paris to suppress counter-revolution, to execute revolutionary laws and public safety measures decreed by the National Convention, and to protect supplies.
2. This armed force will be organised this very day following the terms laid down by the law. The municipality of Paris and the commander-general will join with the members of the Committee of Public Safety to arrange its formation.
3. The pay of this 'revolutionary' force will be the same as that of the national gendarmerie of Paris.[4]

The Parisian *armée* had then a distinguished set of sponsors. Robespierre was the first to propose it to the Jacobin Club, and it had been supported not only by Chaumette, Hébert and Royer, but also by Léonard Bourdon. In the Convention the initiative had been taken by a member of the Committee of General Security, Moïse Bayle, with the support of Billaud, who that same day was to become a member of the Committee of Public Safety. As for Barère, his part is undeniable, however much he tried in 1842 to depict his role as restricted to presenting the decree, and then trying to limit its scope – a version of the facts designed to shift the blame on to Danton and Robespierre. He is closer to the truth in claiming that it was Carnot in particular who succeeded in limiting the effects of the decree, by putting the future *armée* under the control of the military authorities.[5]

The following day, 6 September, Bouchotte ordered the adjoint in the 6th Division of the War Ministry to prepare to carry out the decree. Hanriot too was active during this period, for the commander-general was anxious to establish his control over the new force while he still had no rival at the head of the general staff. He consequently assumed responsibility for recruitment, announcing in his order of 6 September that 'Following the decree establishing the *armée révolutionnaire*, all patriotic citizens should present themselves for enrolment with their Sections; each day the *commissaires* of these committees should submit two lists of those enrolled, one to the *mairie* and one to the commander-general, which will be subjected to scrutiny by the commissions of the Commune and the department; they should enrol upstanding and honest men, capable of restoring peace, calm and plenty to Paris'.[6] Thus had Hanriot already closely associated the Sections with the formation of the *armée*: the general assemblies and most of all the *comités révolutionnaires* would examine the *civisme* of candidates; the General Council (victor of the *journée* of 4 September and soon to claim credit for the creation of the *armée révolutionnaire*), the departmental *comité de surveillance* and the commander-general himself would control its operations. Moreover, Hanriot himself was being considered as possible commander for the new *armée*, and between 6 and 15 September he issued a series of orders settling the details of these measures and urging sluggish Sections to put them into effect and to send him the enrolment lists.[7]

Several authorities were thus already associated with the recruitment of the *armée* and the Jacobins too must be included because of an overture from Mazuel's 'dragoons'.[8] Everything indicates a desire in high places to prevent exclusive control of the new popular force falling to any one authority: the Sections were shadowed by the General Council, this in turn by the department and by Hanriot, and over all stood the Military Affairs Commission of the Committee of Public Safety. This Commission reported in the form of a decree on 9 September, and the order on which it was based was entirely the work of Carnot. This new decree rehearsed the arrangements already announced by Hanriot for the inspection of candidates by the *comités révolutionnaires* (Article 1), ordered the attachment to the *armée* of squadrons already formed by the extraordinary levy of August (Article 4), fixed the number of infantry (Article 5) and artillery (Article 3), and laid down rules for the appointment of officers and members of the general staff (Articles 6, 7, 8, 9 and 10).[9]

The order-decree of 9 September marks the birth of the Parisian *armée révolutionnaire*, and bears all the hallmarks of the person who composed it, Carnot. But if he was accepted as the official creator of this popular force, he was also the one member of the Committee of Public Safety who, from the outset, tried to limit its scope in terms of numbers, action and powers. The *armée* as it emerged from this order was already far removed from that large *force populaire* (of 25,000 or 100,000 sans-culottes), whose commanders were to have been elected by the *sociétés* and by the Sections at their general assemblies, and whose detachments were to have been accompanied by a formidable machinery of repression. At every step the Committee of Public

Safety watched over its organisation; and although it was the Executive Council's task to appoint *chefs de bataillon* or members of the general staff, their names still had to be submitted for approval to the Jacobins and ultimately to the Committee of Public Safety. As for the Sections and the *sociétés*, they were by-passed in the election of the commanders; the Parisian Sections might comment on the officers and men, but the *sociétés* were not directly involved in these elections. Undoubtedly considerable influence was still exercised by the Executive Council, i.e. the War Ministry, and by Cordelier circles, but the Jacobins and the Committee had the final say. Moreover, it was the Committee that designated the companies of cannoneers and controlled the movements of the detachments, and from the outset it made every effort to prevent any autonomous action by the new *armée*.

The moderating role of Carnot becomes even more clear if the order of the 9th is compared with one projected by the unfortunate *Conventionnel*, Hérault de Séchelles. Article 2 of the latter proposes: '*the establishment of two military commissions to follow this* armée, *each with four judges and a president, and two revolutionary units*'.[10] In Carnot's order there is no question whatsoever of these. In addition it fixes the number of effectives at 6,000, plus 1,200 cannoneers, with no possibility of augmentation; and there is no mention of recruitment in the departments. If the final article seemed to suggest a life-span of some years for the new *armée*, it was but a paltry consolation for those who had dreamed of a huge popular force and instead found themselves left with a tiny and powerless *armée*. Carnot was not, however, averse to employing methods of force or terror; as his biographer claims with much accuracy, 'he was a *révolutionnaire*...hence his part in creating such a terrible instrument; but he wanted to control its use'. Above all he dreaded the extension of a popular army, and when delegates from the *société* at Le Havre came to request his permission to raise an *armée révolutionnaire* in the department of Seine-Inférieure, he told them that the *armée révolutionnaire* was 'only an army like any other' and they might just as well use the gendarmerie.[11]

The order of the 9th also left many unresolved questions. Which Sections would supply the 24 companies? Who would choose them? Would the Committee do so? Certain artillery companies, which were not formed until the second half of September or even later, would indeed be formed in the image of the Paris populace, for they would be drawn from every quartier of the city: 3 companies from the western Sections, 15 from the very active central Sections, 2 from the faubourg Saint-Antoine, 5 companies (or rather fractions of companies) from the Sections of the Left Bank – some 28 Sections in all, half those in the capital, furnished companies or parts of companies for the Parisian artillery, thereby exceeding the projected limit of 24. Others were added to the list later.[12] We can simply report without being able to explain this discrepancy between the numbers of the revolutionary artillery as outlined in the order and the final figure as it worked out in reality.

It only remained now to determine the relationship between the new popular army and the local authorities, as well as military personnel like the garrison commanders and the *commissaires des guerres*. Would the local authorities have power to call out the *armée*, or would it remain entirely autonomous, subject only to the orders of the *représentants en mission*, to their *délégués* and to the representatives of the various authorities in Paris? Would it be subject, as the troops of the line were, to the rules of military discipline, despite the stipulations of the decree of the 4th that it was to be used only against 'internal enemies'? And how were these to be defined? If the *armée* were to be put under military control, there was nothing to stop the generals and local commanders using it both for military operations against the 'brigands' in the West, and indeed against external enemies. Now in their call to the sans-culottes the *comités révolutionnaires* in the Sections had laid great emphasis on the fact that the services required of volunteers would be confined to the interior of France, and even to the Paris region. In addition, because prospective volunteers were told that their primary task would be to enforce the laws of the Maximum and to combat 'malveillance', they were given the impression that they had full authority to act without having to consult the local authorities – a particular source of future misunderstanding.

Subsequent orders and decrees would try to set out strict guidelines on these issues, usually designed to limit the autonomy of this army. But on one point popular opinion was triumphant, and that was the extension of the area of recruitment to the entire nation. On 29 Vendémiaire, following a request from the officers and men of the Rhine Army to be allowed to join this new force, Bouchotte decided that any citizen from the departments would be eligible to join, provided he could produce a *certificat de civisme*. Following this order, recruits for the *armée révolutionnaire* were raised not only in the departments around Paris, the Oise, Seine-et-Oise and Seine-et-Marne, but even in Lyon and far-off Lozère.[13] Ronsin took advantage of this, and invited the *sociétés populaires* of the Paris and Seine-et-Oise departments to put forward suggestions which they thought would be of use to the general staff and to the formation of the *armée*.[14]

This was to be the only occasion on which Sectionary wishes were actually consulted. Other matters were settled in a fashion directly opposed to popular opinion. For example, a Committee of Public Safety order of 3 Brumaire (undoubtedly Carnot's work, even though Barère claimed to have been its co-author) put the *armée révolutionnaire* under regular military control, making it answerable to the garrison commanders and to the generals in the war zones. Thus was the *armée révolutionnaire* stripped of all autonomy even before it started to function. The result was to curtail any effective action against internal enemies, for, on the whole, the military authorities and the troops they commanded were to prove extremely hostile towards these political soldiers and their 'luxury' army.[15]

The attention of the commanders of the various detachments was recalled to this order by a series of reminders from the Minister that they were to be subject at all times to the authority of the municipalities and the district directories. 'It is of the utmost importance', declared the Committee of Public Safety, 'that this public force submits to, rather than usurps, the authority of the civil powers; it must obey orders, not issue them, ...and take no spontaneous action against the people or the established authorities.' Now the *armée révolutionnaire* was by very definition a political instrument, designed to strike terror into recalcitrant farmers and the local authorities who protected them; to insist that the *armée* must submit at all times to those authorities was to deprive it of any power to take effective action. Nor did the Committee stop there, but eagerly took up every complaint from the municipalities about the conduct of these *révolutionnaires*, and readily agreed to requests for the removal of these burdensome detachments which had been foisted upon them from Paris. Ronsin was right to lament the fate of 'this *armée* whose principle of formation had been defective'.[16]

So an *armée révolutionnaire* had been legislated for; but that was the only satisfaction allowed to Chaumette, to those employed in the workshops of the rue du Temple and the rue Sainte-Avoye, and to the deputations from the Arsenal, Cité and Gravilliers Sections – the main participants in the *journée* of 4 September. The *armée* was 'castrated' before it started functioning, and the Committee of Public Safety and, following its lead, the War Ministry and general staff of the *armée* sought to appease the districts and municipalities. Was it worth the effort to have created an *armée révolutionnaire*, to be reduced to this? This was the question asked by two notable *révolutionnaires* in Paris, Champeaux and Dumez (administrators of the Commission des Subsistances), on 18 September, shortly after the creation of the *armée*. They expressed their thoughts on this matter to Antoine Descombes, the Paris Commune's *commissaire des subsistances* in Provins (a future victim of Robespierre's dictatorship after the Hébertist *journée*), when he asked for a detachment of the new *armée* to help levy requisitions in a department which was prosperous, but particularly ill disposed towards the interests of Paris:

We wanted and were given an *armée révolutionnaire* to ensure the supply of Paris. You ask for a detachment of this *armée* to defend your operations.... But have you weighed the advantages of using the *armée* for this task? The country population consists entirely of farmers, and whoever is not one in his own right works for others who are...everyone in the hamlet depends...upon the yeoman farmer.... Hence when he states publicly: 'Friends, a Parisian army is coming to take all our corn and we shall die of hunger. It brings a gallows with it to punish those who oppose its designs...', nothing will force hunger on people who so fear it, hunger destroys all, and risings propelled by the fear of it have never bowed to force.... On news of the arrival of these Parisians in an *armée révolutionnaire* the first question of these countrymen will be: 'How many are there?' 'But a few...', will be the answer of the *malveillants* who will eagerly snatch at this point to undermine them; 'But a few', because we have had to split up the detachments and send them to a hundred different places at once....[17]

They would simply succeed in rousing the countryside against Paris, added the two administrators, 'that arrogant town which now lords it over us', without instilling any fear, for 6,000 fusiliers and cavalry, and 1,200 cannoneers could scarcely succeed against the hundreds of thousands of farmers in the huge area of eight departments or more which supplied Paris. They had in fact put their finger on the other main weakness of this *armée*: its numerical inferiority. Not only had it no right to independent action; it did not have enough men to carry out any effective action whatsoever. There is no policy worse than that of vain threats.

From September the *armée* commanders asked the Committee to increase its numbers to those outlined in the decree. What could be achieved, they asked, with an army of less than 8,000 men? But the Committee turned a deaf ear to these appeals and even refused Ronsin permission to enrol an auxiliary company of cannoneers, despite the demands of the cannoneers themselves and the *comité* of their Section. Later the Committee was to remove two non-commissioned officers from the Parisian *armée* as in excess of a company's quota.[18]

In the Jacobins on 28 September Robespierre stressed the urgency of organising the general staff of the *armée révolutionnaire* so that it might commence operations: 'it is time we pushed forward with this and hastened the implementation of requisitions – the farmers are emboldened by the immunity they are enjoying'.[19] Despite his pleas, nothing was done during the first weeks of October. The *commissaires des guerres* were left without orders, clothing, arms and money, and they did not even know how to reply to those offering their services because the law had not specified the age-limit of volunteers.[20] It was not generally the Sections who were responsible for this foot-dragging; on the contrary they were anxious to accelerate the election of officers and NCOs.[21] The *sectionnaires*, with the revolutionary press such as the *Père Duchesne*, the *Journal Universel* and, even more, departmental papers like that published at Caen by the Jacobin, Derché, were all growing impatient at these delays and the possible loss of the decree's psychological effect in the countryside when the early noise and fuss about using measures of 'Terror' were not followed up. Such shiftings and shufflings, with the severe limitation on numbers, enfeebled the *armée révolutionnaire* from the outset. Had this in fact been the intention of the Revolutionary Government? Many *sectionnaires* were asking themselves this very question in October.

In Brumaire many crucial problems remained unresolved. The Committee of Public Safety had assimilated the *armée révolutionnaire* to the Paris gendarmerie for purposes of payment. Did this mean that it too, like garrison troops, would be paid in instalments when away on service? And would the *armée* be provisioned by the military administrators or by the municipalities? Would the soldiers be placed on the same footing as those on garrison duty, each receiving 24 ounces of bread for which 32 deniers would be deducted from pay; or would they, like those on active service, receive an additional 4 ounces of bread, half a pound of meat and an ounce of rice free of charge? Both the military authorities and the municipalities would try to shift responsibility for these decisions on to the other, at the same time accusing the *révolutionnaires* of making claims as incessant as they were excessive; all of which contributed to the unpopularity of these demanding Parisians in the eyes of authorities already overwhelmed by work, and of the people in the small towns who took a dim view of the privileged status of the Parisians in matters of food supplies. Although the most common form of disagreement between different branches of the military was over pay (and also the more delicate matter of wives), nothing was more calculated to rouse the ire of an underfed populace than the spectacle of soldiers in receipt of superabundant rations. These problems, however, were only finally resolved by two decrees of the Executive Council on 17 and 21 Brumaire. The first put the *armée révolutionnaire* on the same footing as troops on active service, which allowed them to receive supplementary rations without any loss of pay. While on the move they would be provisioned by the military authorities; but 'in those places where the authorities have no stores, the company will furnish its own supplies (buying at current market prices) and be indemnified for any loss incurred by the high price of provisions...'.[22] One can but imagine the deals and abuses which arose from the various interpretations of this article.

In principle the *armée révolutionnaire* was designed to operate not in garrison towns and large military centres, but in the villages and market towns. How would the men be accommodated? In general there was no question of housing them in barracks, for barracks were almost as scarce in revolutionary France as they had been under the Ancien Regime. Sometimes it did happen that the *révolutionnaires* were quartered, despite their complaints, in the damp living conditions of secularised religious houses. But more often these Parisians were billeted on the local inhabitants, which proved a source of innumerable disputes and incidents. In certain areas the revolutionary authorities used this as a way of punishing the *riches égoïstes* with whom the Parisians were lodged as a matter of course; 'billeting of troops' was, in effect, a kind of tax or duty, as it had been under the Ancien Regime, and in the circumstances of 1793 it was reserved predominantly for the rich and the suspect. Lyon in particular had the *révolutionnaires* billeted on its inhabitants and the abbé Guillon de Montléon, followed by Taine, wrote at length of the manner in which these Parisians were supposed to have acted towards the *haute bourgeoisie* of Lyon: '...Dare I mention those officers of the *armée révolutionnaire* who had husbands murdered in order to take their wives. . .'.[23] It cannot be denied that here, as elsewhere, the *armée* did take advantage of its privileged situation as an occupation force among 'internal enemies'. But the obverse is equally true: the Parisians made friends among the country people, which in turn weakened their vigilance. Their commanders and the *commissaires civils* had feared this, for if the soldiers were to carry out the duties assigned to them, it was important that they should not be swayed by personal considerations, and also, as the rue de Choiseul insisted, that they should not remain too long in the same locality. When all is said and done it was more likely that the country girls corrupted the *révolutionnaires* than the reverse, for the ferocious political soldiers were not insensible to these rustic beauties, and many ended up by marrying and settling in the countryside. Moreover, the Parisians did not much care for barracks life, preferring rich houses and well-stocked cellars to the damp austerity of national properties. But the municipal authorities bowed to public complaints and sought to rid themselves of the soldiers by sending them off to convents and former religious houses. The problem was all the more acute since the Committee of Public Safety and the Commune (who had been responsible for the creation of the *armée*) left such matters to improvisation.

Thus, despite three months having elapsed between the June decree and that of September, everything continued to progress in a disorderly fashion and with the characteristic slowness of an improvised administration. Armament, clothing, pay, rations, lodging, and as many more problems again, were only gradually resolved. Thanks to the Committee and Hanriot, it was thus a thoroughly disorganised *armée* which was taking shape.

III   *Organisation of the general headquarters*

The order of 9 September left to the provisional Executive Council – in other words to Bouchotte, Vincent and the heads of the various Divisions in the War Ministry – the task of suggesting candidates for the new *armée*'s general staff; and yet not only had the order said nothing about the effective size of the general staff, but details of numbers and qualifications for aides-de-camp and adjoints had to await a further order of the Committee of Public Safety on 13 Brumaire. This authorised the Minister to accept NCOs as aides-de-camp to the three revolutionary generals, and as adjoints to the three adjutants-general; in addition it provided for four sappers to be attached to each battalion and to receive the same rate of pay as the gendarmerie.[24]

The provisional list, which the Executive Council was to submit, was in turn to be scrutinised and purged by the Jacobins and then approved by the Committee of Public Safety and the General Council of the Commune. On 17 September the Executive Council submitted its recommendations for appointment to the general staff: Ronsin as commander-in-chief of the *armée*, Boulanger and Parein, *généraux de brigade*, and Mazuel, Houssaye and Maubant, adjutants-general; *chefs de bataillon*, Mollin, Theurel, Halm, Lemaire, Delorme and Cordier, adjutants-major, Bréard, Bernard (or Benard), Thomasset, Gondrecourt, Du Hommier and Tolède; quartermasters, Ducastel, Fromant, Lacour, Jaillet, Gachet and Liébaut de la Neuville.[25] This list would undergo several further modifications before the general staff and upper echelons of the Parisian *armée* were finally completed. Candidates had to be approved by the Jacobins: some would fail to pass the test; others would reject the positions offered them on personal grounds; and even after scrutiny by the Jacobins, the reduced list was altered yet again following interventions by the Sections or by revolutionary personalities.

On 25 September when Dufourney asked the Jacobins to see the list, it was not yet ready and only on the 27th did the Jacobins get around to scrutinising the candidates. At this session Ronsin, Parein and Boulanger were accepted without any difficulty. David extolled the merits of the former – the artist paying homage to the actor whom he had known for ten years and whose revolutionary patriotism he could vouch for. The revolutionary general owed much to his literary acquaintances, who had now raised him to the pinnacle of the politico-military hierarchy, having already secured him work in the years before the Revolution. David had other protégés whom he successfully placed in the new *armée*.

At this session Mazuel declined the position of adjutant-general on grounds of inexperience; his modesty was applauded, and he allowed himself to be cajoled into accepting a place as *chef d'escadron* in the revolutionary cavalry.[26] It was not so much lack of military experience that persuaded him to decline the first position, as the thought of using the less elevated one of *chef d'escadron* as a springboard to higher things and ultimately to overall control of the revolutionary cavalry. In an *armée* with pretensions already to administrative and military autonomy, Mazuel wanted to turn the cavalry into a still more autonomous corps. Jean Tolède had the same scruples about his appointment as *chef de bataillon*, citing, like Mazuel, his lack of military experience. But the Jacobins were not convinced: Tolède was a good patriot, so his name was approved and in the end he accepted a place as adjutant-major.

Another candidate, the restaurateur Lemaire, was objected to as having spoken against Marat, who had abused him in *L'Ami du Peuple*. But his past sins were overlooked after his vindication by the Montagne Section, whose armed force he commanded, and who recalled his services to the Section 'in the *partie des jeux*'. Lemaire was to become one of the leading spokesmen for the ex-*révolutionnaires* during their years of proscription. Others were also objected to: Maubant, for instance, was confused by the Jacobins with the Federalist of the same name – though when his identity was established, this former soldier and wigmaker from the Faubourg-du-Nord Section was confirmed in the rank of adjutant-general.

The Jacobin purge of the list continued the following day (28 September):

Cordier, nominated as *chef de bataillon*, was removed after an unfavourable report on him from the Faubourg-Montmartre Section (though he was accepted as captain of a company of fusiliers). The Jacobins also wanted to set aside the names of other candidates, like Thomasset, Ducastel and Theurel, as being unfamiliar to them; but once again Robespierre intervened and demanded a speedier conclusion to the business. It was imperative to activate this *armée* quickly, he argued, for the *malveillants* were the only beneficiaries of the delays which had already occurred in its organisation. His intervention barely saved the former soldier Houssaye, called 'Pas-de-Bon-Dieu', who was known to spend his time propping up the bars of the Palais-Royal and whose morality was objected to by several members. All the other names were passed *en bloc* and Bouchotte had the task of awarding commissions to those nominated.

The final list of the general staff was sent by the Minister to the Committee of Public Safety on 22 Vendémiaire and adopted at its next session. It differed appreciably from that presented by the Executive Council on 17 September: Ronsin, *général de division* and commander-in-chief; Boulanger and Parein, *généraux de brigade*; Grammont, Houssaye and Maubant, adjutants-general and *chefs de brigade*; Halm, Lemaire, Theurel, Vézien, Donville and Buard, commandants and *chefs de bataillon*; Thomasset, Gondrecourt, Tolède, Ducastel, Renault and Bernard, adjutants-major; Fromant, Lacour, Jaillet, Liébault, Gachet and Mutelé, quartermasters of the 1st, 6th, 5th, 4th, 2nd and 3rd battalions respectively. The nomination of the three generals was confirmed by an order of the Committee on 1 October, signed by Carnot, C. A. Prieur, Billaud-Varennes and Hérault.[27]

This list underwent only a few changes during the lifetime of the Parisian *armée*. As early as 7 Brumaire Houssaye was suspended, having had no opportunity to exercise his functions except in the cafés, and this likewise resulted in the suspension of his adjoint, Collard-Dutrône. Grammont's commission was revoked on 26 Pluviôse, with that of his son, who acted as his adjoint. He was replaced as overall head of the general staff by his colleague, Maubant, while Berthaud, second-in-command of the Tuileries Section, was appointed adjutant-general two days later on 29 Pluviôse, in place of Clémence who had resigned, apparently without ever taking up his post.[28] Finally, on 3 Ventôse, Bernard was raised from the rank of adjutant-major to that of adjutant-general to replace Maubant in Lyon.[29] These mutations in the higher echelons of the *armée* necessarily led to changes lower down the command structure of this already numerous general staff. In the first place there was a host of aides-de-camp and adjoints, mostly young men, owing their appointments to the political generals and revolutionary personalities who decided the fate of the *armée*; they were political appointments usually granted as a favour to *Conventionnels* and other political figures, and reflecting a high degree of nepotism. Grammont for instance secured a post for his own son, as well as for his theatrical cronies. The positions of aide-de-camp and adjoint were filled by protégés and self-important young men justifiably considered by sans-culotte opinion to be remnants of another regime based on favour, nepotism and privilege, and as such to be unworthy of such positions.

In addition, we must take account of the commanders of the revolutionary artillery (the captains of the companies of cannoneers, for the artillery never had an overall commander, despite the insistence of Ronsin on this point),˙the *chefs d'escadron* and the two *commissaires des guerres*, who held particularly important positions in such a political army, and finally the two *commissaires civils*, who, even more than Ronsin and the officers of the general staff, were the real leaders of this political force.

Let us first of all calculate the number of aides-de-camp. Attached to Ronsin we know of six: Allais, Rocher, Gaillard, Krems, Dorchy and Benoît (a shoemaker who would eventually pass into Maubant's service). Parein's aides were Corchand, Pagès and Puech, and we know Benoît and Piette to have been aides-de-camp to Boulanger. Grammont's adjoints were Berger, the younger Grammont, Puech, Lavault and Folleville; Maubant's were Dobigny (at first attached to the adjutant-general, Clémence, but retrieved by Maubant after Clémence's resignation), Grasset, Mathieu and Rigaud. In his fleeting career as adjutant-general, Houssaye had his companion in debauchery, Collard-Dutrône, as adjoint, and possibly a second called Teinturier. Berthaud's adjoints were to be Vincent and Vallière.[30] How can we explain such a multiplicity of people, when under the terms approved by the Committee of Public Safety Ronsin was only entitled to three aides-de-camp, the two *généraux de brigade* to two each, and each adjutant-general to two adjoints? Indeed, though Ronsin may have failed in his efforts to increase the effective numbers of the *armée*, its general staff far surpassed the numerical limits set down by the orders of the Committee of Public Safety. Five adjoints were attached to Grammont alone, when he was entitled to only two. But all of these would not have functioned at the same time, and as with all general staffs that of the rue de Choiseul experienced various mutations. Of all the positions dependent on the favour of *les grands*, none was more unstable than that of an aide-de-camp, who might pass frequently from one 'protector' to another; the commanders exchanged adjoints in much the same manner as *grand seigneurs* used their valets as stakes at cards. And since the aides-de-camp and adjoints shared the fate of suspended generals, one may well ask whether these 22 appointees (Collard being the only one not to receive a brevet because of the disgrace of his master) were placemen or military personnel? The Committee of Public Safety had permitted the commanders of the Parisian *armée* to recruit their aides-de-camp and adjoints from among the non-commissioned officers, the ordinary soldiers, and indeed the civilian population, and many profited from such freedom by appointing from all three areas. Rocher was a sapper, Dobigny a sergeant from the Queen's regiment, Pagès a former grenadier, Allais an ordinary soldier, Folleville and Gaillard civilian employees in the

War Ministry. It was thus a general staff flexible in number and recruitable from every political milieu.

Moving now to the organisation of the cavalry command, the *chefs d'escadron* – both permanent and provisional – were Mazuel, Noël and Dugrand (1st squadron), Payot (2nd), Fischer (3rd), Gury, Bastien and Bussy (4th), Bresch and Blanquet (5th), and Durand, known as Dugrand, and Dupré (6th).[31] Officially simply leader of the 1st squadron, Mazuel nevertheless occupied a special position in the revolutionary cavalry. As former aide-de-camp to the Minister, charged with the extraordinary levy for the Army of the Nord, he continued to meddle in the cavalry's recruitment and organisation to the extent of visiting barracks and extracting his own recruits from among the young men of the first requisition, much in the manner of an Ancien Regime captain raising his personal company; and the complaints against Mazuel and his officers for having 'almost totally forgotten the sacred rights of man' in thus enrolling these volunteers, were to be the subject of a police inquiry in September 1793.[32] Until his arrest in Ventôse, such was the irregularity of Mazuel's position as virtual commander of the entire cavalry, that Payot, his chief opponent and the only *chef d'escadron* to stand up to him, likened him to an ancient Persian despot. Mazuel epitomised that anarchy of individualism at the heart of a most unmilitary general staff, and his position as effective commander of a cavalry whose function remained ambiguous and ill-defined caused the Parisian *armée* to acquire that dubious reputation which attaches to any institution not subject to strict guidelines. His example was to furnish its detractors with their most effective argument against the *armée*: the spectre of military government.

But if Ronsin had little confidence in Mazuel and opposed the attempts of this ambitious silk-embroiderer to make the cavalry an autonomous corps, the commander-general was guilty of trying to establish a similar command post in the artillery for his cousin, Leclercq, like Ronsin a native of Soissons and a former non-commissioned officer in the Army of the Nord. The Committee of Public Safety, however, stood by its original order on the organisation of the general staff, and Ronsin had to remain satisfied with the position of adjutant-general which he obtained *in extremis* for his cousin in Ventôse; though, on the eve of his own arrest, Ronsin's support had become a liability.[33]

Under the Committee's order, each artillery company was to be commanded by its own captain and retain its Sectionary character. Only in Lyon does there appear to have been any attempt at grouping the different companies, after the serious disturbances of Frimaire. But this seems to have been a purely local initiative, the product of the Parisians' sense of isolation amidst the hostility alike of the populace and the military garrison. The Committee of Public Safety had good reason for insisting on such autonomy and for preventing any grouping of companies under one man (indeed it was such autonomy which prevented the Paris artillery from acting collectively, and saved the Convention on the night of 9 Thermidor).[34] On this issue it had the support of the Sections, which likewise feared the establishment of a personal power base. Ronsin himself enjoyed only nominal control over the different companies whch formed the revolutionary artillery; each was autonomous, subject to the orders of its captain, and above all to the wishes of its Section, with which it corresponded when detached for duty outside Paris.

The initial organisation of the general staff did not allow for any *commissaires civils*. But once it was formed, a chief ordnance officer, Boissay (who secured an adjoint, Rayot, after his arrival in Lyon), and two *commissaires des guerres*, Paris and Martin, were attached to the Parisian *armée*. These were appointed, by an order of the Committee of Public Safety of 14 Brumaire, to act as the Committee's representatives both with the detachments destined for Lyon, and, more importantly, with the *réprésentants* there – two Jacobins, Marcellin and Paillardelle, who had been recommended by Ronsin and Parein.[35]

An administrative council was appointed to regulate the affairs of each battalion, to rule on differences between the men and their officers, and to examine cases of serious indiscipline. The principal function of such councils was to ensure contact between the companies of fusiliers and the Parisian Sections, and as such they reflected every aspect of Sectionary opinion. One of these leading Sectionaries was Scévola Sandoz, a dealer in engravings in the rue de Buci, a member of the *comité révolutionnaire* of the l'Unité Section, a lieutenant in the cannoneers of his Section, and an influential member of the Cordeliers club.[36] The general staff of the *armée* also included several secretaries who had been nominated by Grammont and his successor Maubant – notably two health officers, Pascal and Poisson, who were continually being asked to pronounce on requests for sick-leave from *révolutionnaires* threatened with dispatch to Lyon.[37] The inclusion of elderly men, notably doctors, in the Parisian *armée* was a useful precaution.

Despite such an extensive general staff, the work of its officers was always poorly carried out. There were too many aides-de-camp and adjoints, too many young swaggerers with no precise function, but not enough clerks. The *commissaire des guerres*, Paris, charged with the practical details of the *armée's* organisation, was overburdened, and correspondence with the widely scattered detachments fell behind. Maubant was to blame Grammont for this. But the very organisation of the central administration, which precluded any sustained correspondence with the detachments sent into the countryside, was in itself defective, and to judge by the *régistre d'ordre*, Grammont did his best to eliminate delays, a task beyond the ability of even the most zealous official. The result was that commanders, left without orders, and spurred on by revolutionary zeal, followed their own initiative and caused all manner of disputes with the local authorities. Maubant's replacement of Grammont towards the end of Pluviôse brought a reduction of such incidents, a regularisation of correspondence between the detachments and headquarters, and more effective control of the former by the central and local authorities.

I   *The chiefs of the Parisian* armée

(i) GENERALS AND ADJUTANTS–GENERAL

The names of Ronsin and his fellow officers, who already held important positions in public life, were widely known before their appointment to the general staff of the *armée révolutionnaire*. Such was not the case with the officers of the infantry, cavalry and artillery, nor of the secondary personnel in the rue de Choiseul. Before looking at the general staff as a group, therefore, it is necessary to examine briefly the dossiers of these 40 or so figures, for in such a political army, scattered in small detachments through a number of regions, the role of the men who presided over the actions of the *révolutionnaires* in Paris, and even more so in their departmental 'fiefs', was considerable.

Charles-Philippe Ronsin is too well known a figure in revolutionary iconography for us to linger on his political and professional past. He was the son of comfortably-placed artisans, his father a master cooper at Soissons, his godfather a master tailor.[38] Born at Soissons on 1 December 1751, he served as a soldier in the Aunis regiment from 1768 to 1772, rising to the rank of corporal. It was his only military experience, as with many other generals of the Revolution and Empire who served only a few years in the armies of the Ancien Regime and emerged as non-commissioned officers. From 1772 to 1789 this former soldier launched himself into the world of letters, and while his performance was mediocre, he made some useful and faithful acquaintances in the world of the theatre and the arts. In 1783 he met David, who watched over him and encouraged him in the years before the Revolution. In 1785–6, still swamped by financial difficulties, he published a collection of plays with funds donated by the Protestant community in Nîmes (doubtless at the instigation of some protector), which even secured him a position as private tutor in the house of a wealthy co-religionist. The pastor Rabaut was among those who took an interest in Ronsin's theatrical works at this time.[39] He continued to receive help from such Protestant circles in the first years of the Revolution, and in 1788 or 1789 secured a position with the duc de Chartres through the influence of Pieyre, a Protestant notable. His life then was that of a late-eighteenth-century man of letters or journalist without fortune, who needed protectors and positions of favour with the great. Under the Revolution, particularly in 1794, however, such a life-style might be deemed dishonourable.

In 1789 Ronsin was already a well-known figure in Parisian life. From

11 July, this former corporal, tutor and man of letters was made a captain in the Saint-Roch National Guard. In 1790 his play *La Fête de la Liberté*, glorifying Lafayette, was staged at the Théâtre de la rue de Richelieu, and in the years following, the flow of his 'pièces patriotiques' accelerated: *La ligue des fanatiques et des tyrans*, a tragedy staged in 1791; *Arétaphile, ou la révolution de Grèce* (another tragedy) and *L' Oraison funèbre des citoyens morts à la journée du 10 août*, both staged in 1792; and a play *Mucius-Scévola*, staged in December 1792 at the Théâtre de la Nation, by which date he had already left the theatre world. In April 1792 he took up residence in the rue des Grands Augustins, Marat Section, where his association with Momoro and the other Cordeliers seems to have begun, and where he resided until his nomination to the *armée révolutionnaire*. He then moved his antique furniture and large collection of theatrical books into a small apartment in the boulevard Montmartre (Mont-Blanc Section), to be nearer the headquarters in the rue de Choiseul.

In 1792 he was a 'patriot' of some repute. That summer Roland sent him on three missions into the departments as Ministry *commissaire*, in which he acquitted himself so well and with such zeal that in November Pache appointed him to the important post of *commissaire-ordonnateur* with Dumouriez's army in Belgium. He established his headquarters at Liège, with his future father-in-law, Lequesne, as one of the employees. Ronsin was a good administrator, issuing clear and well-written reports, and – rarer still in such positions – he was honest. That was his ruin, for in denouncing the dilapidations carried out in the unfortunate 'Belgian provinces', he became embroiled with the powerful army contractors, and protégés of Dumouriez, Malus and Petitjean, who had all but institutionalised pillage. The latter protested to the Minister and demanded the recall of this troublesome observer.[40]

Ronsin, however, retained Pache's confidence, and for several months after his return from Liège he combined the functions of Minister's aide-de-camp with that of employee at the War Ministry. Such was his career up to July 1793, when his fortunes took a dramatic turn for the better. Indeed, on 1 July he was promoted at a stroke from the rank of captain of chasseurs to that of *chef d'escadron*; two days later he was elevated to adjutant-general, and on the 5th to *général de brigade* in the Army of the Côtes de La Rochelle – thereby clearing all the grades from captain to general in less than a week. A dramatic advancement indeed, which, as his biographer General Herlaut maintains, undoubtedly owed more to political pull than to professional competence (for Ronsin was the chosen representative of the Cordeliers, the War Ministry and the Marat Section).[41] But Herlaut's low opinion of Ronsin's military abilities does little justice to his administrative acumen, and such rapid promotion was fairly common at a time when there was a particular need for generals of the correct political hue.

Was Ronsin's generalship in the Vendée disastrous and did his tactical errors help prolong that terrible war? We will leave that to the military historians to decide, noting, however, their tendency towards severity in the case of a man who committed the sin of being a 'civilian general'. Perhaps Ronsin did make mistakes, but he was not the only one to do so and the Vendée was a veritable graveyard of military reputations. His passage through the Vendée is particularly interesting for two reasons which have nothing to do with military history: it was during this mission that Ronsin collected that group of protégés who were to be found later at the head-quarters of the *armée révolutionnaire* – Grammont, Folleville, Corchand, Fusil, Saint-Félix, the young non-commissioned officers of his personal general staff in the Army of the Côtes de La Rochelle.[42] In the second place, Ronsin's military competence was already under attack before he became commander of the new army, in the bitter dispute between Philippeaux's supporters from the Le Mans *société* and the War Ministry.

Temperamentally, Ronsin was not the man to disarm his critics: violent, quick-tempered, possessed of enormous physical and moral courage and a revolutionary sentiment tinged with simplicity, he lacked cunning, and his verbal violence was to be his downfall. Straightforward, sensuous, relishing the delights of the table, the hunt and female company, he certainly had not the makings of a great military leader. But, despite his violence and rages, he was not the hysterical crank depicted in the works of Tissot, Thiers, Blanc, Louis Blanc and even Jaurès. An excellent administrator in Belgium, an assiduous correspondent as commander of the *armée révolutionnaire*, he never gave the Committee of Public Safety any cause for complaint. His reports were always clear, level-headed and well-written. Politically he was no fool, and should not be confused with his companion in misfortune, Vincent, a real pathological case of the 'wild young man'. Ronsin was capable of seeing beyond the 'massacres' and 'grand coups', and in Ventôse it was he alone among the Cordelier leaders who proposed an *entente* be-tween the republican factions, which might have healed the rift between Cordeliers and Jacobins if the intransigence of the Robespierrists had not negated every effort at compromise. He was too genuine a republican to have had dictatorial ambitions, even if his inherent courage made him capable of contemplating a political coup, particularly if he felt that the Revolution was slowing down, gripped by the 'new moderantism'.

Did he have any 'political philosophy'? To claim that he did would be to flatter him; with Ronsin temperament was uppermost. He was an anti-parliamentarian, not on principle but because he disliked most of the *Con-ventionnels* and had few friends among them. His programme was simplicity itself: to combat *malveillance* and *moderantisme*, to purify the Convention, strengthening the repressive means at the government's disposal, and, if necessary, to set up *commissions populaires* and clear the prisons (those sources of 'plots' and disaffection) in a 'new 2 September'. It was a purely negative programme, one of revolutionary defence. Ronsin's thinking was simple and naïve: he believed in 'unlimited liberty' and was convinced that it would eventually succeed in triumphing over factionalism, even if at the outset it devoured its most faithful adherents along with its bitterest enemies. 'Liberty cannot be destroyed', he was to say to Hébert; 'the party which sends us to our death will follow us in turn'.[43] Such honest and laudable convictions were to give him the strength to die with courage and cheerfulness. The means of attaining this 'unlimited liberty' were left unspecified, but they lay neither with the Revolutionary Government nor with the Convention.

Was he ambitious? Historians and contemporaries alike have depicted him as a man whose sole ambition was to attain power, and who, after he and his supporters were expelled from the Convention and the Committees, demanded the restoration of the Assembly and the end of the Revolutionary Government and viewed the *armée* he commanded as the instrument for achieving this. This at least was what was said and written of him. But Ronsin was always obedient to the Committee's orders and we will show just how flimsy is the basis for this standard thesis of a 'military plot'.

The former soldier who had been dubbed with the military surname of 'Darius', was neither a great military leader nor a political luminary; but he was a courageous and a frank man, a good administrator and still something of a disciple of Rousseau. He was a cultured man, and after his arrest his library was found to contain not only maps and plans but works on the theatre, the sale of which would fetch 2,152 livres in *assignats*. These, with the abandoned child he had adopted in 1793, were his only worldly assets. He did not profit from the Revolution and died poor.[44]

Servais-Baudoin Boulanger, the second leading figure in the Parisian *armée*, was born at Liège around 1756. In April 1793 he said that he had lived in Paris for 21 years – so like many eighteen-year-old artisans from Liège, he had come as an apprentice. Domiciled in the Saint-Eustache quartier, with other famous men like the Swiss Sépher, Reukin, the jeweller and future Ministry *commissaire*, and the shoemaker Wendling, Boulanger was in 1790 already listed among the active citizens of Place-Louis XIV Section. In December 1793 he was a member of the Jacobins. His military career started before his political one, with service first in the National Guard of the Saint-Eustache district after 1789, then successively as an ordinary soldier, cannoneer, lieutenant and captain (second in command) of the Halle-au-Bled Section's armed force.[45] On 17 May 1793 he was nominated provisional commander-general of the Parisian armed force by the General Council of the Commune, and the following morning he appeared amidst cheers to take his oath. But his nomination met with lively opposition from certain moderate-controlled Sections, such as the Arsenal and Panthéon, which invoked the autonomy of the Sections to forestall this attempted imposition of a commander by the Commune, and Boulanger withdrew his candidacy.[46] But his turn was to come the following month, and his advancement would be almost as rapid as that of Ronsin. Appointed adjutant-general *chef de brigade* in the Army of the Côtes de Cherbourg on 5 July, he was promoted to *général de brigade* on the 22nd.[47] His commander was his

Parisian neighbour, Charles Sépher, while another neighbour, Michel
Wendling, originally from Wislheim in Alsace, was adjutant-general in the
same Army. At the time of the formation of the *armée révolutionnaire* in
September, Boulanger was temporary commander of the garrison at Caen,
and one of the leading figures of its *société populaire*, which was dominated
by the garrison soldiers, most of them Parisians. At Caen he was in the
confidence of the *réprésentants* and of their secretary Derché, a Jacobin and
emissary of the Committee of Public Safety.[48]

Boulanger was a very different man from Ronsin, possessing neither his
fiery temper nor his frankness. This artisan from Liège was prudent, and
handled with equal tact his Section, whose support he never lost, the
Jacobins, of which he was a long-standing member (another factor setting
him apart from Ronsin), the Committee of Public Safety, where he was
respected by the Robespierrist clan, the Committee of General Security,
where he could count on the support of Le Bas, and finally Hanriot and the
general command of the Parisian armed forces. Boulanger was important
only in terms of whom he knew; as a personality in his own right he scarcely existed, even if occasionally he repaid the support he received from the
government by becoming its spy. He was typical of those who cut a figure
in the Revolution largely because of the support of their Section, and
because he assiduously attended the general assembly of the Halle-au-Bled
Section, he was one of the few from the general staff of the *armée révolutionnaire* to retain the favour of the Section's institutions. In social terms too he
remained close to the sans-culotte militants; at his death he was still an
apprentice jeweller. He was poor in 1789, and remained so.[49]

But although Boulanger had followed the orthodox path of the *sectionnaire*, his appointment to the general staff seems to have been imposed by
Robespierre and the Committee. His presence near Ronsin would be a
guarantee against any autonomous tendencies within the *armée* which might
reflect unfavourably on the Revolutionary Government. As a Jacobin he
would counteract the overwhelming influence of the Cordeliers and the
War Ministry, and Hanriot, who never abandoned his designs on the new
Parisian armed force, could count on him. Boulanger was to be rewarded
for such services at the final reckoning to which his commander and many
of his colleagues fell victim. Later, under Hanriot at the general command,
he would again prove useful to the government as agent in charge of executions in the *bureau de surveillance* (the instrument of Robespierre's and Saint-
Just's foul deeds), for this former apprentice jeweller was a policeman as
well as a spy in his spare time.[50]

Like Ronsin and Boulanger, Parein was also in his prime in 1793. Pierre-
Mathieu Parein was born on 13 December 1755 at Le Mesnil-Aubry, a
village in the 'pays de France' on the main route between Paris and Flanders,
a rest station and military camp where one met regularly with 'gens de
guerre'. His father, Jean Parein, was a master saddler, and among those
assisting at his baptism we find a merchant and several farmers. His brother,

Louis, himself a farmer, married Marie-Anne Perreau, daughter of the principal farmer of the town.[51] The Pareins were not 'poor village artisans', as Parein's detractors later claimed, in order to emphasise his apparently rapid social rise and undeniable accession to wealth. In fact, they were a family of artisans intermixed with land-owning farmers. So he came from a propertied family; he did not start at the bottom, and he was far removed from the apprentice silversmith from Liège and the impecunious playwright.

Parein qualified as an 'homme de loi' in 1789 and his career in that field was unremarkable. His revolutionary career started early; and like many members of the revolutionary general staff, he was a 'Vainqueur de la Bastille'.[52] By virtue of this title he joined the Bastille volunteer company as quartermaster in September 1789 – it was to be the nucleus of the famous 35th division of gendarmerie. But at the beginning of 1792 Parein discovered his true vocation as a political policeman when he was congratulated by the Interior Minister for uncovering a cache of false *assignats*. Like Ronsin he performed several missions in the departments that summer as Ministry *commissaire*, accompanied by André Corchand.[53] From there he moved into the War Ministry and in May 1793 was sent as *commissaire* into the Vendée. It was here that his true aptitude as a public prosecutor was revealed for the first time.

On 10 July 1793, Ronsin created the Military Commission in Angers (to be known later as the Commission Parein-Félix). It was composed of five judges and was empowered to pass summary judgement on rebels and suspects. In August the Commission set itself up in Saumur, where Parein remained until his appointment to the general staff in September, and on 29 July he was also appointed *commissaire des guerres*.[54] His term on the Angers–Saumur Commission determined his revolutionary career as judiciary general. But the Commission Parein certainly did not merit its reputation as the sanguinary instrument of the Terror; under Parein's presidency it was moderate and clement in its judgements, and it was only after October that it acquired the image of a pitiless tribunal, whose severity instilled terror into the Vendéeans. It was Parein's first experience of political justice, however; he was to draw his methods and some of his personnel from it, and the famous revolutionary Commission -- the 'Commission des Sept', over which he presided in Lyon – was simply a replica of this first commission which inaugurated the reign of those extraordinary tribunals. Henceforth Parein reigned as the specialist in political and judicial repression.

Parein's progress in his military career was as rapid as that of his two colleagues: as *commissaire des guerres* he performed only civil functions in the Vendée. However, from his service in a salaried company of Vainqueurs he had retained the rank of lieutenant in the Parisian National Guard. On 2 October he rocketed from the rank of lieutenant to that of *général de brigade*, a promotion which he owed to the influence of Ronsin, who had known him in the Vendée and who, like all the Cordeliers, held him in high esteem.

If Boulanger was the candidate of the 'government men', there is no disputing the fact that Parein, the friend and correspondent of Vincent, had the backing of the Cordeliers, the War Ministry and of Ronsin himself.[55]

Parein was the most intelligent of the revolutionary generals and knew how to utilise his connections. At Lyon in particular he made some extremely useful ones. Fouché appreciated the jurist in him, the calm, methodical specialist in repression, the model functionary, and when the former became Minister of Police he was to utilise the special gifts of this singular general. Parein may have looked after his own interests – he was later to draw upon the secret funds of the Ministry, was classed a rich landowner on his death in 1831, and left behind a son who was a wholesaler in Paris and a daughter married to a notary from Sarcelles.[56] But if Parein was more cunning than his two colleagues whom he survived, his revolutionary convictions seem nevertheless to have been sincere. He was hated by the royalists and was particularly noted for his 'detestable' opinions and his 'plebeian' haunts by the royalist gendarmerie instructed to watch him in his Mesnil-Aubry retreat from 1815 to 1830. His 'ferocity' has been much talked about, particularly in his role as president of the 'Commission des Sept'. He was undoubtedly a severe judge and a particular enemy of priests; but this little man who tried to give himself military airs, to intimidate his victims no doubt, was no brutal executioner. He used the violent language of the *Père Duchesne*, as did most of the Cordeliers and men of the War Ministry, but he did not have the fiery temperament of his chief. He was, all told, the most complex character of the general staff.[57]

The adjutants-general were not men accustomed to terror and repressive measures like Ronsin and Parein. None had carried out missions as Ministry *commissaires* under the first Terror; none had served on the extraordinary commissions sitting in the Vendée to speed up the sentencing of the rebels. Grammont had indeed accompanied Ronsin to the Army of the Côtes de La Rochelle, but his colleagues were former soldiers or Parisian artisans, whose service with the *armée révolutionnaire* was to be their first repressive mission. Setting aside Maubant, the *armée* was poorly served by its adjutants-general: Grammont, the actor, was a playboy, Houssaye an adventurer, Berthaud a drunkard, and none had any deep convictions.

Guillaume-Antoine Nourry, known by his theatrical name of Grammont, was born in La Rochelle on 10 June 1750, making him forty-three when he became head of the general staff of the *armée révolutionnaire*. A well-known actor who had started his career at the Théâtre-Français in 1779, he specialised in tragic roles, and was celebrated in particular for his performance as Don Carlos. He was expelled from the Théâtre-Français after his proud and quarrelsome temperament had led to a violent disagreement; but as a result of the patronage of Marie-Antoinette, who held him in particular esteem, he returned to the stage that same year, and on the eve of the Revolution was part of the Montansier troupe which was playing at Versailles. Until then his career had been that of a talented and highly rated actor. The Revolution opened to him a new career as politician and soldier, into which he eagerly threw himself after 1789, 'out of ambition' and 'personal interest', claims Hérissay, who never forgavè Grammont his 'ingratitude' towards his ostensible patroness, Marie-Antoinette. After July 1789 he served as an officer in the *garde bourgeoise* of his district, Saint-André-des-Arts, rising quickly to the rank of lieutenant-colonel.[58] The only action he saw was in the attack on the Tuileries of 10 August.

In July 1793, while serving in a volunteer battalion from Paris with the Army of the Côtes de La Rochelle, he met Ronsin, whom he must have known before the Revolution in the masonic-like world of the theatre. Ronsin appointed him, along with other actors from the Théâtre Montansier, to his general staff at Saumur. But Grammont had other powerful supporters, and his appointment as head of the general staff of the *armée révolutionnaire* cannot be attributed to Ronsin alone. He had a close connection with Hérault, a long-standing acquaintance, who, as one of the founders of the *armée révolutionnaire*, certainly wanted to place his friends in it. The friendship between Grammont and Hérault played an enduring role in the 'politicisation' of the *armée révolutionnaire*. Each time Grammont ran into difficulties with his colleagues, with the Committee or with Hanriot, he turned to Hérault, and the correspondence registers of the rue de Choiseul bear witness to the frequency with which the adjutant-general asked to see the *Conventionnel* 'to discuss urgent business'. Since he also frequented the offices of Danton and the other Aube deputy, Ludot, his political affiliation was with the Dantonists rather than the Cordeliers. On the general staff Grammont was isolated: Ronsin seems not to have had any great confidence in him; Boulanger watched him; Mazuel detested him and denounced him frequently to Bouchotte; Maubant was to complain of his laziness and the disorderly state of his office's correspondence. His isolation in the last days of Pluviôse was a political event representing the defeat of the Dantonist element within the general staff, and a triumph both for the Cordeliers and the 'government men', Maubant and Boulanger. Grammont's removal also constituted a moral revolution.

In addition to his illegitimate son, whom he made his first adjoint, Grammont brought with him an entire troupe of actors: Folleville, Gaillard and Lavault, former colleagues at the Montansier and République theatres; Berger, his last adjoint, was the only one who was not a theatrical associate. In the end the offices in the rue de Choiseul took on the appearance of a theatre backstage, with attractive girls coming in at all hours of the day to visit these moustached and dandified young officers. One can but imagine the hopes generated among the frivolous and spendthrift frequenters of the theatrical world by the appointment of men of their own kind to positions which gave them power to dispense rewards and emoluments. The headquarters of the *armée* was besieged by such men and by pretty women demanding places for their lovers or husbands. Grammont had the open-handed nature of those of his profession and wanted to gratify everyone; he was moreover extremely susceptible to feminine wiles. The former tragic actor and his protégés therefore brought to the headquarters in the rue de Choiseul an atmosphere very far removed from the world of the sans-culottes. Gentlemen of leisure in Paris in the final years of the Ancien Regime, they had a life-style to maintain and they had debts. The younger Grammont was a love-child, and the father signed IOUs for needy actors, several of whom were also members of the general staff.[59]

The general headquarters soon acquired the reputation of an exclusive club with the sans-culottes, quick to shock at the best of times. This was possibly too severe a judgement, but under Grammont the command of this 'popular' *armée* cut a poor appearance. Nor could the presence of well-dressed women in the building at all hours of the day be explained away as essential to its service. Grammont was a compromising extravagance for the *armée*. Moreover, as soon as any difficulty arose, his colleagues would attach the blame to him as head of the general staff. And yet, to judge by the correspondence contained in the *régistre d'ordre*, the former actor carried out his duties with zeal, regularly transmitting the commands and reprimands of the Committee of Public Safety, struggling with the difficulties created by lack of personnel, premises and finance. Above all Grammont fell victim to the poor reputation of the acting profession in popular circles and even within the Revolutionary Government; it was easy enough to condemn the personnel of the general staff by referring to them pejoratively as a troupe of actors, but there is nothing to suggest that men like Folleville and Gaillard were poor officers or dishonest assistants. Grammont certainly had no very profound revolutionary convictions – for him the Revolution was above all a great adventure, into which he threw himself wholeheartedly, more from a love of challenge than from interest. His only gain from holding this important, thankless and highly exposed position would be the favours of women he had been able to oblige, and the hostility of a greater number of people he had been obliged to rebuff. His attitude towards the Revolution resembled that of his amiable and gentle friend, Hérault. Having met each crisis in the *armée* with a shrug, he met death with courage and set an example by his serene dignity. Grammont, the talented actor, the gambler, distinguished, light-hearted and charming, was out of place at the head of an *armée* in which the *sectionnaires* placed all their hopes. Grammont smacked too much of the Ancien Regime; and this, in a word, was his greatest sin.

The second adjutant-general, Joseph Houssaye, otherwise known as 'la Violette', or 'Pas-de-Bon-Dieu', spent only a short term in the Parisian *armée*. This twenty-one-year-old jeweller had, like Boulanger, won his position on the battlefields of Belgium; a volunteer in the Bataillon des Lombards from the time of its formation in September 1792, he rose rapidly to the rank of corporal and then sergeant. Dumouriez himself had promoted him to the rank of captain on the field of Jemappes, where Houssaye had shown exceptional courage. General Lavalette, who, like Brune, had known him in Belgium, described him as' something of a reveller..., his giddiness needs watching, but never his heart, nor his patriotism...'.[60] An impressive soldier under arms, Houssaye's sojourns in Paris were characterised by unfortunately spectacular sessions of revelry in the gambling dens of the Palais-Royal, the scene of battle of his Parisian activities. In August 1793, while on sick leave, he escaped from the military hospital of Gros Caillou and quickly became a source of scandal by picking a quarrel with some volunteers and biribiri players in a tavern in the Palais Egalité, Montagne Section. Goaded to it, he passed himself off as aide-de-camp to a general in the Army of the Nord. He liked to fantasise: this was not the first occasion on which he had given himself grades and braids to which he was not entitled, and the cafés frequently saw him attired in the uniform of an adjutant-general or *chef d'escadron*. Appointed adjutant-general for real in the Ardennes Army, on the recommendation of Danton, who admired his courage and youthful ardour, Houssaye was transferred to the *armée révolutionnaire* before he could regain his frontier posting. But on 7 Brumaire, after reports about his rakish past were received from the *comité révolutionnaire* of his Section (Lombards), he was suspended before he could exercise his new functions.

Despite his repeated requests to rejoin his army on the frontier (particularly since Paris was out of bounds to him as a suspended officer), he was left in a state of inactivity which was to prove fatal. Denounced as having uttered counter-revolutionary words, insulted the *comité* and authorities of his Section and usurped certain military grades, he was arrested a second time in Pluviôse. He remained in detention in his Section for only a few days, and on his release he renewed his efforts to get a new military posting, with no more success. On 15 Germinal he was arrested once again after a much more serious offence. With suicidal hardiness, he denounced the judges of the revolutionary tribunal as 'scoundrels' for their judgement against his patron Danton. The incident would have been forgotten, or put down to the effects of drink, had he not been detained by the *comité* of the Lombards Section, at last in possession of its victim. The list of accusations against him – protégé of Dumouriez and Danton, one-time adjutant-general of the *armée révolutionnaire*, who had been drunk and disorderly and attacked the sacrosanct tribunal – would have been incriminating at any time, let alone at the height of the crisis of Germinal. His *comité* sent him to the *maison d'arrêt;* on 30 Floréal poor La Violette was transferred to the Conciergerie and the following day, 1 Prairial, appeared before the tribunal to hear himself condemned to death as 'the accomplice of Ronsin', 'agent of Dumouriez', and for having spread false rumours, and 'vilified' the public functionaries.[61] Fouquier had a tendency to 'confuse the charges'.

This young man did not deserve such a cruel fate. Had he been given military employment, he would have made an excellent soldier (one of the witnesses against him agreed that he had a reputation for valour with his battalion, even if his actions had lacked discipline) and it was the worst kind of disservice both to him and to the *armée révolutionnaire*, which could not afford the luxury of someone so open to attack, to have raised him to such a high position in a political force. The importance of his functions, which he was never able to exercise, went to his head; his posturing in the cafés did the rest.

Houssaye's death also dragged down the man who had shared his brief and dangerous spell of glory. But Thomas Bernardin Collard-Dutrône could not plead youth as an excuse. He was born at Caen on 4 May 1756, the son of Thomas Collard a master joiner; he had the years but not the wisdom of Boulanger. The name of Dutrône he had taken from some land belonging to his father in the Caen region. As courageous as his young patron, this former sergeant with the Halle-au-Bled Section cannoneers distinguished himself at the taking of the Tuileries on 10 August, not only by his courage, but by an act of honesty when he discovered and surrendered 1,500 louis and jewels found in Marie-Antoinette's rooms, which won for him the praise of the Assembly.[62] Initially a volunteer with the infantry of his Section, then with its cannoneers, Collard too was singled out by Dumouriez for his bravery on the field of battle at Jemappes. Unfortunately it was Dumouriez personally who issued Collard's brevet as captain in the legion based in the Ardennes (to become the '2nd bataillon franc'), and requested Pache to confirm him in this grade. But the *représentants* sent to the Ardennes Army later tore up the brevet, and in March 1793 Collard left for Paris in the hope of having this grade confirmed to which he considered his courage had fully entitled him.[63] As in the case of Houssaye, his stay in Paris did him nothing but harm.

Collard in fact was typical of the gamblers and drinkers who hung around the cafés. He never had a regular job, or trade, or home of his own, and after his arrival from Rouen a few months before the Revolution he moved from one set of furnished rooms to another in a Paris full of risk and excitement. What was his background in Rouen and had he not been condemned by the Parlement there? He claimed to have been involved in the cloth trade in the Norman capital, and though he had spent three days in prison, he explained disingenuously it was because he had 'stayed too late at a friend's'. But had he not been handed over to the Châtelet for some criminal offence? He denied it, though a neighbour claimed that he 'never saw him except in gambling and drinking dens', and that he had been involved in criminal affairs in Rouen and in Paris, where he was detained in the Châtelet. 'In a word', added this witness, 'he is an intriguer who used all manner of trickery and deception against the Rouen merchants and he is unable to prove by what means he subsists. . . .' The 'governing body' of the Guillaume-Tell Section was to adopt *in toto* this unfavourable opinion of a man whose lack of regular domicile, dissipated life-style, showy attire, in short everything about him, offended their revolutionary puritanism.[64] Collard was further compromised by the portable gaming set bearing the royal emblem that was found in his pocket, and by various prizes from his campaigns discovered at his lodgings, including three miniatures of the Queen and her two brothers taken from Marie-Antoinette's secretaire, and an Austrian sabre bearing the imperial crown which he had won on the battlefield in Belgium. In such a moral portrait, Fouquier had already more than enough for a most damning indictment, but Collard aggravated his case by wearing his officer's uniform, to which, with his chief suspended, he no longer had the right. He was, however, permitted to remain in Paris, and even had a vague kind of mission to search for army deserters there, a mission which the chief of military police had ridiculously entrusted to his light-hearted companion.

Collard had spent only a few weeks in the *armée révolutionnaire*. He had certainly assisted at the review of the entire *armée* on the Champ de la Fédération. But his 'service' stopped there and the *armée* was quick to rid itself of two members whose presence on the general staff might give the entire corps a bad reputation. Arrested on a charge of counter-revolution on 12 Nivôse, Collard preceded his young master and fellow reveller to the Conciergerie. For several months he languished there and was only called before the revolutionary tribunal on 1 Messidor, after foolishly drawing attention to himself in a petition to Fouquier-Tinville: 'I have been incarcerated in the Conciergerie for five months now without knowing the cause of my detention. I can assure you that I am a good patriot who took part in the major events of the Revolution and fought in the Belgian campaign and I am now without either money or linen. . .', and he pleaded for permission to secure both from his lodgings. The charges against this cheerful Norman, whose only crime was an excessive fondness for gambling, adventure and wine, were even more ridiculous than those which had sent 'Pas-de-Bon-Dieu' to his death. Collard was accused of being a counter-revolutionary on the basis of the trinkets and souvenirs retained from his various exploits, and he was condemned to death that same day.[65]

But the man whose prudent and conciliatory personality made an impact, even greater than Ronsin and Grammont, on the *armée révolutionnaire* during its short history was the third adjutant-general, Etienne-Quentin Maubant. He was a Parisian, born in the parish of Saint-Roch on 9 February 1754 (making him almost the same age as Parein and Boulanger), son of a wig-maker, Etienne Maubant, whose trade he was to follow (one of the few wigmakers among the revolutionary officers, contrary to what Taine says). He joined the company Godeau of the Chartres-Infanterie on 10 October 1772, when he took the military surname 'Monte-au-Ciel', and rose to the rank of corporal in 1778 and sergeant in 1780, taking then the name 'Bien-aimé' (expressive perhaps of a plan of action, or homage to years already well spent).[66] He retired in 1783 after ten years of service. Having returned to his old quartier in Paris, he seems to have resumed the trade of wig-maker; but shortly afterwards was engaged as a clerk in the office of the elder Tripier, attorney to the Parlement of Paris. At the time of the Revolution Maubant's past military career brought him to the attention of his fellow citizens. 'On 14 July 1789', he wrote, 'I was in command of the citizens of my quartier; but when I realised that I was serving the interests of one man [Lafayette] rather than those of the people, I withdrew [from the salaried National Guard] and embarked on a more useful career....'[67] What did he do in the years 1790–1? We do not know, and on that subject he always maintained a discreet silence. His enemies were to claim that he was in the service of the duc d'Orléans – a common accusation at the time, used by moderates to cast doubt on the reputations of many *révolutionnaires*, and we need pay little attention to it. He reappears after 10 August as a member of the first *société fraternelle* and of the *comité révolutionnaire* of the Faubourg-du-Nord Section, in which he had been residing since the first months of the Revolution. In 1792 and again the following year he and Léonard Bourdon were sent on a mission by the Commune to secure provisions from the area around Paris. Finally, in May 1793, he joined the 6th Division of the War Ministry under Xavier Audouin, having had the doubtful honour of being recommended by the famous royalist agent, Dossonville.[68]

Was it this relationship which now caused such hostility towards him in his Section, particularly within the *comité révolutionnaire*? Or was it, as he himself claimed, the product of pure jealousy? 'Till then', he later wrote, 'I had no position. I was offered one in the *armée révolutionnaire*...which I accepted, and my appointment was approved unanimously by the Jacobins' (it was not, as we have seen above, entirely unopposed). 'My enemies were furious', he went on. 'But they were to become more so when I was promoted from a simple fusilier to a higher rank.'[69] Maubant's version of events seems plausible, for, from September until the Year III, his *comité révolutionnaire* lost no opportunity of harassing this man whose only error had been his over-rapid promotion. The animosity had another source: Léonard Bourdon and his brother Marc-Antoine had considered appointing one of their own protégés to the position of adjutant-general, the porcelain sculptor Guillaume Constant, himself a member of the *comité révolutionnaire*. In the event Constant had to remain satisfied with the position of captain of a company of fusiliers in this Section, but neither the *comité* nor Bourdon ever forgave Maubant for having done better than their candidate.[70]

Fortunately the new adjutant-general also had protectors in Collot-d'Herbois, Boulanger and Hanriot. Like Boulanger Maubant was a 'government man', and at the same time as being associated with Parein and with the Cordelier group (of which Ronsin himself was a member), he successfully preserved his own independence and prevented the general staff from becoming too 'Hébertist' in sympathy. Above all this former soldier was an extremely prudent politician and the best administrator in the entire *armée*.

Leclercq had little time to fulfil his duties with the *armée révolutionnaire* and

Colette was ineffectual. That leaves Berthaud, appointed towards the middle of Pluviôse to replace Grammont, and arrested the following month on the same day as Ronsin, 24 Ventôse. This former commander-in-chief of the armed force of the Tuileries Section, an engraver by profession, possessed few of the qualities needed for high command in such a revolutionary institution. His *comité révolutionnaire* said as much in accusing him '...of having on the 9 August proposed to the citizen guarding the château that he dine with two Swiss sergeants', of having signed the petition of 8,000, of having been one of the warmest supporters of Lafayette, and finally of having petitioned the duc de Brissac for a position on the military establishment of the Court. And, leaving nothing to chance, the *comité* added: 'in addition he is in a state of perpetual drunkenness...and whilst in this condition...he has expressed contradictory views on the revolution to those who would have taken them as his considered opinion'.[71] That same day Berthaud was taken off to the Bourbe prison.

These then, with Mazuel who will be discussed in the section dealing with the cavalry command, were the men who would command the new *armée*. Boulanger, Maubant and, when he chose to apply himself to his work, Grammont, were the most important, because the most effective. Their daily work was closely concerned with the *armée* and Parein was overwhelmed with the duties of repression. As for Ronsin, he applied himself assiduously to his duties in the rue de Choiseul and his signature can be seen on numerous letters until the very eve of his final arrest. But his importance was political; he paid only one visit to the detachments, was removed from the scene by a six-week imprisonment, and exercised a very limited influence over the daily life of the *armée*. Houssaye and Berthaud had no influence whatever, but through their personal lives they gave the *armée* the worst of reputations during the short period of their association with it.

Boulanger and Maubant were 'government men', attentive to the least directive of the Committees. In their hands the Paris *armée* would never have slipped away from central government control. If Ronsin had some individualist notions, his colleagues were out-and-out conformists, whose principal concern was to retain the good will of the Committee of Public Safety and to prevent any embarrassing initiative which might compromise the *armée* in the eyes of the government. Doubtless Boulanger, Parein and Maubant shared with Ronsin the desire to increase the number and powers of their *armée*, but as prudent men they confined themselves to respectful suggestions to the Committee of Public Safety, and were careful to stand aside from the campaign launched by Ronsin in the Cordeliers and in the Sections, to force the hand of the Committees by appealing over their heads to the sans-culottes. Maubant took prudence even further by constantly seeking to moderate the zeal of the detachment commanders in the departments, always preaching obedience to the legally constituted authorities. At the same time this former wigmaker, who felt himself close to the *révolutionnaires*, always sought to excuse their acts of indiscipline to the Committee by recalling their qualities as fathers and sans-culotte *sectionnaires*.

Ronsin then was quite alone. Boulanger no doubt liked him, and after the crisis of Ventôse Maubant was courageous enough to claim that he had always considered him a republican and a patriot. But they accepted that they might have been deceived, and neither ever had any intention of following him. Like Parein they were the docile instruments of the Committees and of the *représentants*. They were in fact honest men and it would take a major flight of fancy to imagine them as 'brigands' and 'ruffians'. They were, above all, administrators. As for their military talent, that is of no importance. The Committee knew their men and could depend on them as chiefs of an *armée* which had no military attributes apart from the name.

(ii)   *CHEFS DE BATAILLON*
The rue de Choiseul was the political centre of the Parisian *armée* and the adjutants-general, aides-de-camp, adjoints, *commissaires des guerres* who worked there, near the source of all favours, enjoyed considerable political influence over an indebted 'clientele'. One has but to look at the enormous correspondence of Mazuel, consisting largely of petitions from friends and relatives, to recognise the importance of headquarters as a sort of labour exchange. Ronsin, Boulanger, Grammont, Maubant, not to mention Mazuel, in charge of the cavalry, were bombarded by incessant requests from all the leading figures of the revolutionary regime, *Conventionnels*, jurors on the revolutionary tribunal, ministers, highly placed officials, Jacobins, Cordeliers, departmental *sociétaires* – all the world seemed to want some position. During the life-span of the Parisian *armée*, the members of its general staff were among the most sought-after dinner guests in the city; but they had to earn their invitations through time devoted to the interests of their hosts. The dispensation of favours was the price they paid for their political power.

Moreover the general staff had little power to enforce the guidelines laid down by the Committee of Public Safety for those officers on detached duty away from Paris; since the execution of those guidelines – and the manner of their execution mattered more than their general direction – was left entirely to the officers in the localities and in daily contact with the authorities there. So if the general staff owed its influence to its political contacts with the 'great' in Paris, the real leaders of the *armée* were the *chefs de bataillon*, the *chefs d'escadron*, the adjutants-major, the *commissaires civils*, in sum those officers of the three sections of the *armée* in command of companies sent out of Paris. It was they who wielded this new instrument of the Terror, they who had the task of putting into operation the major economic and repressive measures for which the *armée révolutionnaire* had been expressly created. The man who enforced the Terror at bayonet point, therefore, was the detachment commander. If he was violent, the action taken by the detachment would be also; if he was level-headed, everything would be conducted calmly, and conflict with the local authorities avoided.

The *chefs de bataillon* held a higher position in the command hierarchy than the adjutants-major.[72] With the two *commissaires civils* and the two captains of the cannoneers, they were the most important people in the entire *armée*. The younger members of the general staff were in touch with the detachments by correspondence only, and visits were rare;[73] the *chefs de bataillon*, on the other hand, both saw their troops in the localities and remained in touch with Paris. Three of these officers in particular, Lemaire, Buard and Donville, were to play key roles in the departments, and although Halm remained most of the time in Paris, his visits to the detachments in the Eure were to have important political repercussions. Only Theurel and Vézien remained in the background, operating in the shadow of Parein, Maubant and the extraordinary commissions established in Lyon.

The shrewd and intelligent Julien Buard, formerly a soldier in the service of Spain and commander of the 1st battalion of the *armée révolutionnaire*, is discussed elsewhere,[74] and a brief outline of his picturesque career will suffice. He was born in Le Mans on 5 April 1743 and joined the Royal-Marine regiment at an early age. 'After having sailed as a volunteer to the Malvinas on board the frigate *La Boudeuse*', he wrote in 1793, 'I passed into Spanish service on the surrender of the islands, arrived at Buenos Aires and was employed by don Francisque Buracelley, Captain-general of Paraguay, in the expulsion of the Jesuits from almost the whole continent of South America. I received a lance wound in the forehead in combat with the savages of *las pampas*, and on the way back to Europe I was wounded by an axe when we were boarded by pirates just north of the Canaries, and our ship was wrecked entering the Bay of Cadiz; in all, eight years of service....'

On his return to France the warrior of *las pampas* set about looking for employment. But he was to remain strangely reticent as to its nature, and malicious gossips would later claim that it was as *maître d'hôtel* with the maréchal de Biron and Marie-Antoinette's friend, the duchesse de Polignac.[75] Buard himself would lend credence to these rumours by talking of mysterious 'reverses' experienced under the Ancien Regime, and by making frequent references to 'royal ingratitude'. A man who knew how to show himself off to best advantage, this former soldier of fortune found that the Revolution provided the ideal opportunity to exercise his remarkable talent for self-assertion. Having spent the first four years of the Revolution in the Parisian National Guard, he mobilised useful friends, and his overtures to Bouchotte to secure a position as *commissaire des guerres* succeeded in winning the favour of three *Conventionnels*, David, Massieu and Laignelot, as well as the Minister of Contributions, Destournelles. 'After having served in most of the Spanish empire, and having a fairly good knowledge of the Castilian language, your petitioner thinks that he might be of use to his native country.' But despite his efforts, his suit was unsuccessful.

In August 1793, however, he was elected commander of the armed force of the Montagne Section, a position which reflected favourably on his candidacy for the *armée révolutionnaire* the following month. His name was on the list presented to the Jacobins by Bouchotte, but by some oversight was omitted from that which emerged from the *scrutin épuratoire*. Abandoned after having got so far, Buard was incensed, because for someone who had never been in permanent employment, a position in the *armée révolutionnaire* was particularly desirable. Once again he mobilised the support of Destournelles, David and his other influential friends, and through their intervention his appointment as commander of the 1st battalion was confirmed early in Brumaire, 'a position which I felt obliged to accept from my devotion to the public interest and lack of fortune', he later claimed. For someone forced to accept, he took it eagerly enough. Now that Buard had found a position, he was to do everything in his power to keep it and to avoid offending the Revolutionary Government, and in his relations with the local authorities he was prudent in the extreme. On such a man the Committee could count implicitly.

Lemaire, a violent and heedless character, was a friend of Buard, an inhabitant likewise of the Montagne Section, and commander of the 4th battalion. Like Buard he had suffered many reverses in fortune, but this was their only similarity and in Lemaire's case, such reverses were actually produced by the Revolution, for he was a restaurateur. 'Seeing his career as a caterer declining steadily', wrote a hostile witness in the Year III, 'Lemaire thought he might recoup his fortunes through the Revolution. He threw himself on to the side of the anarchists and was quickly recognised as useful by the agents of the Terror. This is how he secured the command of one of the battalions in the *armée révolutionnaire...*' – a simplistic explanation similar to the 'ingratitude' thesis. But the vocation of a *révolutionnaire* cannot be explained merely by the crisis in the luxury trades, and Lemaire differed from Buard in being an exalted revolutionary. 'I went to live in the Section in '87', he claimed, 'where I acquired a catering establishment known as the Hôtel de Malthe from citizen Arnée for 25,000 livres rent, which I always paid promptly.... I owed not a sou to anyone, and if I ever neglected it, this was because of my preoccupation with the public interest. When the Revolution occurred I tried to do the duty of an honest man by honouring it, and I have no regrets in view of all the injustices which were committed under the Ancien Regime. Perhaps I may have made some mistakes in pursuing this devotion with rather too much fervour, but you know, we have no say in the way our character is made, and mine is a spirited one....'

A corporal in the National Guard from 1789, Lemaire was made a lieutenant after the 10 August, then captain of a company formed by the residents of the rue Traversière, and finally second-in-command of the Montagne Section force under Buard. Then came his appointment to the command of the 4th battalion of the *armée révolutionnaire* – 'the greatest of my mistakes...', avowed Lemaire in the Year III, 'but one which I had not asked for. My prudence and carefulness was as pronounced as my ardour, considering the feebleness of my military talent while on mission'. In fact

Lemaire did show himself to be one of the Committee's most discreet agents. But he was also capable of taking the initiative himself: he turned accuser in Paris and in the Coulommiers region made arrests on his own authority, though he did inform the Committee of General Security after the event. A 'Jacobin since '89 without interruption', he claimed never to have consorted with the politicians nor held any position on the *comités*, and according to his *comité civil* he was a 'hard...and extraordinarily narrow-minded' man.[76] From these various appraisals we can draw a picture of a simple and undoubtedly brutal man, who had neither the subtlety nor the prudence of Buard.

The commander of the 6th battalion, Guillaume-Xavier Donville, was a former soldier of the same age as Maubant, Parein and Boulanger. Born 1 August 1756, in the parish of Saint-Benoît in Paris, he served in the Ile-de-France-Colonies regiment, fought as a sergeant in the West Indies under Dupleix, and declared that he 'knew the ropes tolerably well' thereafter. On his return from the West Indies he took up residence in Saint-Denis, of whose National Guard his co-residents invited him to take command. In 1793 he was also a member of the *comité de surveillance*. 'Familiar with the handling of arms and troop manoeuvres', this war-wounded soldier became the watchdog of the *armée révolutionnaire*. To the Parisian artisans whom he commanded, and for whom he affected the greatest contempt (complaining incessantly of their dirtiness, indiscipline and drunkenness), he tried to communicate his enthusiasm for expert manoeuvres on the Champ de Mars, and was to apply for a position as instructor at the Camp des Sablons after the dissolution of the *armée*.[77] One wonders how such a man could ever have drifted into the *armée révolutionnaire*.

The commander of the 3rd battalion, Mathias Halm, likewise suffered material loss through the Revolution, and in a more direct manner than Lemaire. A drawing master in the faubourg Saint-Germain (rue des Saint-Pères), he was a Rhinelander born in Koblenz on 14 April 1745; he moved to Paris around 1775 and married a French girl the same year. An elector in 1791 and a determined opponent of Lafayette and the Sainte-Chapelle club, he was commanding the forces of the Fontaine-de-Grenelle Section on 13 October 1793, at the time of his nomination to the *armée révolutionnaire*. Under his calm exterior Halm was a zealous revolutionary – subscribing in the Year III to Lebois's newspaper – and an active dechristianiser. A sincere republican and influential *sectionnaire* who presided over the Section's general assembly in Messidor Year II, he had no time for the Cordeliers, and far from having a sense of attachment to his commander, he was actually to lodge a complaint against him at the time of the 'Hébertist' trials.[78] His action on this occasion cannot simply be explained by a desire to flow with the general tide of opinion, for in the Year III, when hounded as a former terrorist, he did nothing to placate his Thermidorean adversaries.[79] He was the only *chef de bataillon* to remain in Paris for the entire short life-span of the *armée révolutionnaire*, leaving only once, for his brief, but dramatic, mission to the Eure. To him would fall the thankless task of maintaining discipline among the idle *révolutionnaires* left behind at the Ecole Militaire, who avenged themselves by denouncing him as a foreigner, 'an Austrian', and – unsuccessfully as it turned out – by demanding his replacement.[80]

The commanders of the 2nd and 5th battalions, Theurel and Vézien, were both former soldiers. Jean-Baptiste Theurel was only twenty-six, born in Strasbourg on 2 April 1767, an Alsatian, like many career soldiers under the Ancien Regime. He combined a taste for the arts and letters with recognised military ability and during his battalion's campaign of repression in Lyon he wrote in lyrical tone to Joguet, a friend from his Section (l'Homme-Armé) and one-time secretary to Louis XVI: 'We are all become Romans now; all we need is bread, circuses, music, poetry, painters and fine actions.'[81] His companion, Jean-Baptiste Vézien, known as 'Belle-Rose', or as 'Brin-d'Amour', was more prosaically occupied, as befitted his situation and the circumstances, and the *représentants* in Lyon would complain of his idleness and drunkenness (each *révolutionnaire* having his own way of offsetting the atmosphere of melancholy and hatred which enveloped this huge disgraced city). A native of Poligny (Côte-d'Or), Vézien enlisted on 4 April 1765, at the age of sixteen, in the Chartres-Infanterie regiment. The following year, as 'Brin-d'Amour', he transferred to the Saint-Victor grenadiers, and received his discharge on 31 July 1769. But despite his reputation, Vézien was not just a drunken soldier: in Thermidor Year II, on the occasion of his nomination to the *comité révolutionnaire* of his Section (Invalides), he was described as 'a Jacobin since the foundation of this society'.[82] In Nivôse Year IX, when he was accused of having been a former 'terrorist' and friend of the 'Septembriseur', Julien Richard – another leading figure of the Invalides Section – the description of Vézien was expanded to include 'secretary-general of the Jacobins, in charge of transmitting information to the Editor of the Society's journal'.[83] This is a portrait far removed from that of the 'drunken and idle soldier' painted by Parein and Boissay. Vézien had sufficient political experience to be recognised by his co-*sectionnaires*, and if, in the Year IX, he was employed in the library of the Institute, he was surely as well qualified as his young and enthusiastic colleague, Theurel.

Both Theurel and Vézien, however, played very secondary roles in the *armée révolutionnaire*. The former was completely dominated by Parein and Maubant and there is no sign of his ever having taken any personal initiative in the whole of his long stay in Lyon. Vézien remained for most of the time in the Paris region; and during his tours of inspection in Saint-Germain and Montereau, he was noted for his moderation, his good sense and his attention to the wishes of the local authorities, even if they were against the real interests of the detachments. In Ventôse he replaced Maubant in Lyon.

The *chefs de bataillon* were 'government men', almost all Jacobins; and though Lemaire, Buard, Halm and Vézien were also leading *sectionnaires*, none was a member of the Cordeliers. The battalions were therefore firmly in the hands of men on whom the Revolutionary Government could count completely and who would never permit any autonomous action which might displease the Committee. They had no connection whatsoever with the 'parti hébertiste'; their relations were with the Jacobins, the *représentants* and the *comités* of their Sections, themselves instruments of central government.

(iii)　ADJUTANTS–MAJOR

The adjutants-major came from similar backgrounds: former soldiers, leading *sectionnaires*, members of the Jacobin club, likewise having no connection with the Cordeliers; Ducastel alone came via the War Ministry, the channel through which the influence of Vincent's and Ronsin's group was normally brought to bear. Inferior in grade to the *chefs de bataillon*, two of the adjutants-major, Jean Tolède and Renault, would nevertheless play an important political role in Lyon during the life-span of the *armée révolutionnaire*. The others were men of secondary importance.

The adjutant-major of the 1st battalion, François Thomasset, born 23 February 1722, was undoubtedly the oldest member of an institution which contained many old and infirm men. This veteran soldier figured on the list of the Vainqueurs de la Bastille and by this token he entered the 35th gendarmerie division with the rank of brigadier 1st class. In 1789 he was living in the cul-de-sac des Jacobins-Saint-Honoré and like Maubant served in the Saint-Roch battalion. Like Donville, this old war horse attached great importance to military manoeuvres and despised the civilians who made up the bulk of the *armée révolutionnaire*. The Terror, with its cult of the old, wanted to reward this veteran for his long years of service and his role as Vainqueur.[84]

Of Gondrecourt we know nothing save that he was a member of the *comité insurrectionnel* of 10 August. His name was on the first list for the general staff, but does not seem to have been retained, and was undoubtedly removed for political reasons during the *scrutin épuratoire* by the Jacobins or the Commune. After that we hear no more of him in the ranks of the *armée révolutionnaire*.[85]

The adjutants-major of the 2nd and 5th battalions, Renault and Tolède, were among those leading *sectionnaires* who had no military experience and owed their appointments solely to their political activity in the Sections. Renault was a stationer in the rue Saint-Honoré and a neighbour of Boulanger, who seemingly had him appointed to his new position. Before entering the *armée révolutionnaire* he had been a member of the *comité révolutionnaire* of the Halle-au-Bled Section; he was a Jacobin and had served in the salaried National Guard since 1789. A prosperous businessman, he became in 1790 an active citizen.[86]

Jean Tolède had lost his clientele with the emigration; having been a decorator in the rue du faubourg Saint-Denis, he became a member of the *comité révolutionnaire* of the Faubourg-du-Nord Section, which was also Maubant's Section. On his return from Lyon, where he had been personal secretary to Collot, Tolède returned to his place on the *comité*.[87]

Ducastel and Bernard were, on the other hand, former soldiers. Jean-Nicolas Ducastel was born at Corbeil on 27 March 1764, the son of a master mason there. He served for seven years in the Marine artillery, Brest division, and, as a *Vainqueur de la Bastille*, spent two years (July 1791–July 1793) in the 2nd Paris battalion. In between he was successively clerk to a *notaire*, clerk to a *procureur*, a surveyor and a printer, and before entering the *armée révolutionnaire*, he spent a short time in the War Ministry (*commissaires des guerres* division). Ducastel, 'who was never rich except in patriotism', undoubtedly owed his nomination to the fact of having been a Vainqueur.[88] The sixth adjutant-major, Jean Bernard, served for several years in the Swiss Guards, gaining his discharge in 1788 at the age of twenty-six. At the time of his nomination to the *armée révolutionnaire* he was commander-in-chief of the armed force of the Popincourt Section.[89]

Thus we find the same mixture of military men and artisans from the luxury trades among the adjutants-major as mong the *chefs de bataillon*, but in both cases the first category predominated.

(iv)   THE SUBORDINATE PERSONNEL OF THE GENERAL STAFF: AIDES-DE-CAMP,
        ADJOINTS AND 'ÉPAULETIERS'

The *armée révolutionnaire* was poorly served by the crowd of aides-de-camp and adjoints who hung around the leading figures in the rue de Choiseul and gave the entire body a bad name by their spectacular escapades and blatant idleness. These 'gentlemen of the *état-major gramonicide*', as one contemporary observer labelled them, sinned by being too much in the public view, moving from *cabaret* to *cabaret*, wearing gold-braided uniforms and linking arms with pretty, young and non-republican women in the theatre foyers. Sans-culotte opinion was scandalised by the frivolity of these youths whom they thought would have been better employed on the frontiers, and those remaining in the capital blackened the *armée* even in the eyes of its most enthusiastic and disinterested supporters. In the departments the behaviour of those few aides-de-camp and adjoints who left the delights of Paris was even more compromising, and their insolence and their drunkenness did not pass unnoticed in small towns like Villefranche-sur-Saône.

In practical terms the aides-de-camp and the adjoints served little purpose in the *armée* except when occasionally sent on mission to detachments which had been denounced by the local authorities.[90] In other respects their main function was to add by their numbers to the importance of their chiefs and protectors, and the existence of such a group allowed Ronsin and his colleagues to extend further their circle of obligation; *représentants* and other key government figures did not scoff at a popular *armée* which allowed them to bring a son, a relative, or the child of a friend back from service on the frontiers. Among their number were to be found also some veterans of the revolutionary movement and some genuine sans-culottes who saw in it their reward for long devotion to the public interest.

Ronsin was unfortunate in his choice of aides-de-camp. The first, Allais, appeared inoffensive enough, but it was said of him that he had been the servant of the comte d'Artois, which was scarcely calculated to recommend him to the sans-culottes. A former aide-de-camp to Santerre, Allais had accompanied Ronsin in the Vendée and he was closely attached to him and to the people in the War Ministry. He was, in other words, the archetypal representative of the 'Hébertist group' on the general staff.[91] Ronsin's second aide-de-camp was a disastrous choice: Pierre Rocher, '*sapeur* in the Saint-Lazare battalion', 'keeper of Capet in the Temple', then sub-lieutenant in the 11th regiment of hussars in the Vendée, where he joined Ronsin's following and brought opprobrium and scandal on the *armée révolutionnaire* and its commander alike. Having been suspended by Ronsin for indiscipline, he took his revenge by putting up notices around Paris addressed: 'Le sapeur Rocher à ses concitoyens', in which he had the bad taste to accuse Ronsin's wife of having stolen underwear and bedclothes – accusations which were the delight of the Indulgents and a source of considerable mirth to the idle onlookers. The *affaire de l'affiche* also had political repercussions, for Ronsin accused Grammont of being behind it in his personal vendetta against him.[92] In his choice of a third aide-de-camp, Gaillard, Ronsin further contributed to the reputation of the *armée* as a haven for out-of-work actors, or those whose age exposed them to possible service on the frontiers – for Gaillard was the son of the stage manager of the République theatre. Since his father had put on the mediocre plays of Ronsin, he in turn felt obliged to help the son,[93] just as Grammont did Grasset, stage manager of the Montansier.

If the majority of this group were little more than 'obligés', young men given positions to gratify the politically powerful, or military men being rewarded for long service, André Corchand, aide-de-camp and confidant of Parein, belonged to quite a different category. He was the most interesting among the aides-de-camp, owing his position to considerable services he had already rendered the new regime since its inauguration. Originally from Rodez, Corchand like many of his compatriots came to Paris in search of work some years before the Revolution. A Vainqueur de la Bastille, he qualified as a *fondeur-mécanicien* about this time and was living in the house of a 'bourgeois', Renouard, in the rue Saint-Jacques.[94] He was still practicing this trade when in August 1792 he was named in the first group of Ministry *commissaires*, along with Parein, Ronsin, Momoro, Bourdon and several others. Through the missions which he undertook in the Oise, Seine-Inférieure and Somme departments in the autumn of 1792, Corchand was already closely connected with Parein, and it was with him that he took his first steps as political and bureaucratic missionary of the Terror.[95] Still a young man – about twenty-eight in 1792 – he enlisted in the 14th Paris battalion, was elected captain, and left for the Vendée. Now attached to

Ronsin's general staff, he was wounded in the Chemillé affair and returned on sick-leave to Paris that September. At this time he called himself a haberdasher, and with the change for the better in his social position which accompanied his rapidly rising political fortune, he seems also to have changed his living quarters, for when he was named aide-de-camp to Parein in the new *armée* he was living in the Montagne Section.[96]

In the *armée révolutionnaire* Corchand's career was to follow the same pattern as that of Parein: shortly after his arrival in Lyon he had himself nominated to the revolutionary Commission and soon acquired a reputation for harshness and severity. 'Corchand, a Parisian like Parrein [*sic*]', noted (erroneously) a Lyonnais who had appeared before the tribunal, 'lodged with the latter, was animated, stormy and severe in character and condemned almost without exception...'. He recognised in Corchand, however, the qualities of an artist and a certain indulgence towards those of similar disposition,[97] for this *fondeur-mécanicien* and haberdasher seems also to have been an engraver.

Corchand's attachment to the *armée révolutionnaire* was only incidental. His real place was on the Commission des Sept, and like his friend and master, Parein, he showed himself a specialist in repression. As to his revolutionary convictions, they were beyond question, and few leading *révolutionnaires* were persecuted so bitterly as he in the years of proscription between 1795 and 1802. Indeed, after his deportation by the Sénatus-Consulte in Nivôse Year IX, he died of fever in Zanzibar in 1801 or 1802.[98]

With his appointment to the Commission, Corchand was replaced as aide-de-camp to the general staff at Lyon by a former soldier, Pagès, known as 'la Fleur'; a grenadier with the 78th infantry regiment, he would remain attached to Parein until the *armée révolutionnaire* was disbanded. The orders governing the organisation of the general staff had in effect anticipated this appointment of simple soldiers, civilians and even non-commissioned officers to the posts of aide-de-camp and adjoint.[99]

Benoît was aide-de-camp to Boulanger, a neighbour from the Halle-au-Bled Section. A former soldier who had served ten years in the Royal-Roussillon regiment and fought in the West Indies under Dupleix, he received his discharge in 1783, set himself up as a shoemaker in Paris, and was still working as such in the first years of the Revolution. He also claimed to have served as Ministry *commissaire* in the autumn of 1792, at the time of the first Terror, but I have found no trace of his involvement in this group.[100] He was elected captain in the 23rd regiment of foot chasseurs in June 1793, took part in the Vendée campaign (clearly the main point of entry to the politico-military positions of the new *armée*), and became adjoint to adjutant-general Colette, great friend and admirer of Ronsin, who at one stage considered Benoît for a position as adjutant-general in the *armée révolutionnaire*.[101] In his new position Benoît showed himself to be a shrewd politician, always remaining close to Boulanger, who was to retain him in his service after the dissolution of the *armée* and recommend him to

Hanriot – ultimately to prove a mixed blessing: Benoît did not long survive the death of his two protectors, committing suicide on 11 Thermidor, at the age of forty, before he could be interrogated by the Committee of General Security.[102]

André Krems, who served as fourth or fifth aide-de-camp to Ronsin, and Barthélémy Piette, second aide-de-camp to Boulanger, were, like Pagès, former soldiers who had served in the Vendée or on the Rhine, and like many other soldiers, even officers, they did not consider it beneath them to accept choice positions in this political army.[103]

Following Grammont, the acting fraternity – the younger Grammont, Lavault, Folleville – were firmly installed as adjoints in the rue de Choiseul. Noël Folleville, like Grammont, had been in the Montansier troupe at Versailles and Paris.[104] Other actors, like Armand Vertheuil and Vallière, had imprecise functions in this '*état-major gramonicide*', while Grasset, stage manager of the Montansier theatre, became Maubant's aide-de-camp. He had served as second lieutenant in the 11th regiment of hussars in the Vendée, where he was one of those Hérissay calls 'stage puppets' in Ronsin's and Boulanger's circle.[105] So here already we have six actors placed. It is easy to see why sans-culotte opinion should have taken offence at this theatrical monopoly of the plum positions in a supposedly popular *armée*. Such criticism was not entirely justified, for these actors were not all bad officers, nor simply men pushing themselves in new careers created by revolutionary circumstances. But sans-culotte opinion being what it was, the existence of theatrical people at the head of this new *armée* incontestably blackened the reputation of the entire institution in the eyes of the *sectionnaires*.[106]

However, even Grammont's entourage did not consist entirely of actors. Berger, who seems particularly to have enjoyed the confidence of Ronsin and Grammont, and who was sent by them on several important missions to the detachments, was a former soldier with eight years' service in the Royal-Auvergne regiment, and as his aide-de-camp Grammont secured for him a commission in the revolutionary cavalry. Puech, adjoint also to Maubant, had served in the 11th hussars regiment in the Vendée, where he joined Ronsin's general staff.[107] The hussar regiments, almost equally with the National Guard or the 35th gendarmerie division, were among the principal channels through which young officers or non-commissioned officers secured places on the general staff. However, once organised, the *armée révolutionnaire* would have few enemies as bitter as these hussars and dragoons.

Besides Grasset, sent back to Paris for his pursuit of young Lyonnaises, Maubant's adjoints were Rigaud, a young Jacobin recommended by his Section, and Mathieu, a young man from a comfortable Marseilles family, and previously adjoint to adjutant-general Reynier. Rigaud was to show signs of real administrative ability during his attachment to Maubant, which he would use in the world of commerce after leaving the *armée révolutionnaire*.[108]

The final adjoint, Edouard Dobigny, was a muddle-headed young man in comfortable circumstances – his father being a *fabricant* in the faubourg Saint-Hilaire, Rouen – and as dissolute in conduct as Grasset. A soldier in the Queen's Regiment under the Ancien Regime, this twenty-five-year-old had served in the 8th regiment of hussars in the Vendée during the summer of 1793, as aide-de-camp to General Rossignol. After the formation of the Parisian general staff, he was adjoint to Clémence until the latter's resignation, and was then inherited by Maubant. An unfortunate legacy, for a person less suited to this prudent adjutant-general, who was always careful to maintain good relations with the government and the local authorities, can scarcely be imagined. Dobigny was in reality that caricature of the revolutionary officer as presented by the Indulgents press: drunken, insolent, loud-mouthed, a womaniser, who accumulated excesses and indiscretions, quarrelled with all the authorities in Villefranche-sur-Saône, however republican and patriotic they might have been, declared the town a centre of counter-revolution, and crowned it all by getting drunk and becoming infatuated with the daughter of a gentleman, himself in detention as a suspect. But Dobigny had many relatives in Paris; Maubant and the Lyon commanders had not heard the last of him, and the relief of the latter at his recall to Paris was cut short by the return of this troublesome young man, who lost little time before again embroiling the *armée* with the local authorities. That was the last straw. Maubant intervened with Collot and had the amorous and heedless young man finally recalled to Paris, where he was accused of having been Ronsin's 'accomplice'. He spent many months in detention because of these escapades, but thanks to his relatives was liberated in the Year IV, and shortly afterwards got himself elected to the new municipal administration in Rouen.[109] Dobigny's extravagant behaviour, however, had done immense harm to the *armée révolutionnaire*.

(v)   THE COMMANDERS OF THE REVOLUTIONARY CAVALRY

The individual character of the revolutionary cavalry was reflected even at command level. With the exception of Mazuel it was a homogeneous command, and the exception is important, for all the *chefs d'escadron* were career soldiers, with many years of service in the Ancien Regime cavalry behind them. This was true in the case of Jean-Baptiste Payot, a native of Rethel, where his father was mayor. Born in 1756, he was the same age as Boulanger and Maubant, and had served in the cavalry of the Scots Guard from 1783 to 1788, rising to the rank of second lieutenant. In June 1791 he joined the national gendarmerie and was commanding the Rethel division when nominated to the 2nd squadron of the revolutionary cavalry. He brought to it the habits and the mind of a gendarme officer, crossing swords with Mazuel, whose civilian background and exaggerated pretensions he despised, and alienating the men in his squadron by his disciplinarianism.[110]

Melchior Bastien joined the revolutionary cavalry from the 13th infantry regiment, before which he had served for more than 20 years in the hussars. Jean-Nicolas Gury, a farmer and farmer's son from the Vosges, had an even longer military career: born 27 May 1739, he served without interruption from 1756 to 1788 (in the Royal-Piedmont regiment from 1771 to 1779). He rejoined the cavalry in 1791, and was made a captain the following year. He was fifty-two at the time of his nomination to the Parisian cavalry.[111]

Jean Bussy, who would command the 4th squadron after Bastien and Gury, had a similar career: he served in the cavalry from 1770 to 1786, and was second lieutenant at the time of his discharge. He became lieutenant in June 1792, captain the following September, and *chef d'escadron* in the new levy of 15 August 1793. The Alsatian Jean Bresch enlisted as a hussar in the Nassau regiment in 1776, moving to the Esterhazy regiment the same year, where, after ten years of service, he was promoted to squadron sergeant in 1786. He left this regiment only in 1792, for a captaincy in the 16th cavalry regiment, was made *chef d'escadron* on 30 August 1793 and in Brumaire was commanding the 5th squadron, a position which he eventually ceded to Blanquet. Bresch was a rather limited and undistinguished soldier.[112]

Silvestre Blanquet, Bresch's successor, who was in command of the 4th squadron when the *armée* was disbanded, did not join the army until after the Revolution, in 1790, when he became a lieutenant in the gendarmerie of his native town, Marvejols. Promoted to captain in July 1793, he was made a *chef d'escadron* only on 30 Ventôse, a few days before the *armée* was disbanded. He subsequently became one of Napoleon's aides-de-camp, and this former officer in Ronsin's *armée* got himself killed in Russia while crossing the Beresina with the Grand Army in 1812.[113]

The commander of the 6th squadron, formed somewhat late in the day, was the former cannoneer Durand, or Dugrand. He appears to have been one of Grammont's protégés, installed by Bouchotte without the knowledge of Mazuel, who would do everything possible to undermine his position when he was sent to Lyon.[114] The 1st squadron had no real commander, since Mazuel, its nominal commander, had no wish to accompany it to Lyon. Effective command was therefore exercised by the first captain, Noël.[115] That leaves only Fischer, commander of the 3rd squadron, first at Beauvais, then at Nantes. At the time of his nomination Fischer was a lieutenant in the 16th cavalry regiment, the same in which Bresch served as captain.[116] We know no more of his previous career, though like Bresch he was undoubtedly a non-commissioned officer under the Ancien Regime.

Albert Mazuel was not content to remain a simple *chef d'escadron* like his five colleagues. From September he claimed the right to oversee the entire corps by virtue of his rank as *chef de brigade*, which he maintained had been granted him at the time of the general staff's organisation, but which in fact had never been officially confirmed. Mazuel sought in particular to act as inter-

mediary between his colleagues and headquarters, requiring all correspondence concerning the individual squadrons to pass through him. The
Minister and Ronsin sought in vain to oppose his pretensions, which they
considered unfounded. Until the time of his final arrest, Mazuel persisted
in his claims, and even succeeded in establishing effective control over 'his'
cavalry, at least in terms of recruitment and appointments.[117] Contemporary opinion was right in viewing him as the real commander of the cavalry,
and if he failed to impress his wishes on Payot and the other *chefs d'escadron*,
he nevertheless controlled the cavalry in terms of appointments, even
holding his own, if the need arose, against the general staff, against
Grammont and even against Ronsin himself.

Mazuel was one of the strongest political figures of the Parisian *armée*.
He claimed to come from the people ('born a plebeian I shall die as one');
but he had been in the luxury trade and from his correspondence with
his family seems to have been tolerably well off. He was a former silk-
embroiderer from La Croix-Rousse, and in 1793 he still had family there,
including a brother-in-law, a well-established silk merchant. Mazuel himself left Lyon for Montpellier some years before the Revolution, to open
an embroidery business with his sister, who ran it in the absence of this
fédéré captain. There was also a Mazuel (a cousin perhaps) who was a master
jeweller in the arcades of the Palais-Royal. The Mazuels may have been
plebeians, but they had a solid footing in the luxury trade which even the
events of the Revolution did not greatly upset, and as soon as Lyon was
retaken the brother-in-law returned to his business there. In Montpellier,
however much of an artisan he might have been, Mazuel was closely
acquainted with the bourgeoisie, and the young men from Montpellier for
whom he found lieutenancies in 'his' cavalry were not sans-culottes.

Mazuel liked to invoke his popular origins, but he was also at home in
better society, particularly among its female members. To judge from the
vast number of love letters he received he certainly derived full benefit from
his military glories, exchanging frivolous letters in semi-military language
with his mistresses, and receiving requests for favours from a host of young
women in terms of such tenderness that success was guaranteed. His
reputation as a womaniser was so well established that it even reached his
wife, though he had taken the precaution of leaving her and their child
behind in Beauvais, so that he might be free to pursue his life as a gallant.
On the occasion of his final arrest in Ventôse, he was taken while riding in
the park with two young Parisiennes who had travelled to Versailles to see
him. Mazuel revelled in the life of a handsome cavalry officer, and the
splendour of his wardrobe, the only possessions left at his lodgings after his
execution, testifies to his self-image as the dandy *révolutionnaire*. He was just
as frivolous in his flights of passion and in his over-fondness for drawing his
sword, and he was well known for the tragi-comic scenes he provoked in
public places in Paris when he felt his honour, and that of 'his' cavalry, was
being called into question.[118]

However Mazuel was not simply a womaniser and a stage soldier. He was courageous, knew how to command in the field, and despite his fits of anger and his frivolity, he was ambitious, had political know-how and was an expert in utilising his friendships. He was neither a fool nor a pure demagogue. He did have some revolutionary convictions, and however difficult they are to discover behind his grandiloquent manner, they were, it seems, sincere. But above all Mazuel was the young provincial who had come up to Paris, thrown himself eagerly into revolutionary society, and quickly became known to the leaders of the day. His brief revolutionary career in fact was a study in success.

As for so many others, the National Guard was Mazuel's road to advancement and political contacts. He very soon joined the Montpellier *garde bourgeoise* (was he an 'active citizen'?), becoming conspicuous in the popular party. 'It was I who suffered and sacrificed myself at the time of the Nîmes massacres and was at the fore in combating the spread of fanaticism in Montpellier and in the Cévennes...', he proclaimed with that want of modesty so typical in the leading *révolutionnaires*. Mazuel shared the prejudices of the sans-culottes of Nîmes and Montpellier against the Protestants, whom he considered representatives of a patrician bourgeoisie. We know nothing of his life in Montpellier, but Aigoin, friend of Robespierre and future juror on the revolutionary tribunal, found it praiseworthy. Mazuel, he said, always took the part of the patriots in the Midi, and was persecuted by the moderate authorities for doing so.[119] Aigoin remained on friendly terms with Mazuel right to the end, and to this confidant of Robespierre, Mazuel, who would later join the Cordeliers camp and be labelled a 'Hébertist', was a true *patriote révolutionnaire*. By June 1792 Mazuel's reputation had been established; he was elected to head the company of *fédérés* which the capital of the Hérault was sending to the Fête de la Fédération, and the road to Paris was thereby opened to him. He owed this success to those patriot circles which in April 1793 would sponsor the famous decision of the 'Hérault authorities', recommending the creation of an *armée révolutionnaire*.

By the time of his arrival in Paris Mazuel was also in command of the first company of *fédérés* from the Côte d'Or, who had joined him after their journey to Dijon. All this added to his importance and the *journée* of 10 August provided an opportunity for displaying his courage and sang-froid: at the attack on the Tuileries he distinguished himself so brilliantly in the exercise of his dual command, that the general assembly of the *fédérés*, which had played such a vital part in the preparation and success of the attack, raised him to its presidency.[120] Mazuel was to use this strategic position and the prestige of the victorious *fédérés* to advantage as a springboard for his political career in Paris. In fact the *fédérés* expected to follow up their victory by departing for the frontier; but their leader had other plans. Having acquired a taste for political activity, he lingered in Paris with 'his' troops (he was in effect the commander of what amounted to a private

army), long enough to cause concern with a section of Parisian opinion. It
was only in the autumn that Mazuel agreed to leave with his *fédérés* from the
Midi and the West, and thereafter they became attached to the Army of the
Rhine. He would later claim to have taken part in the winter campaign
there: 'I...have just taken part in the Trèves campaign during the winter
season,' stated the handsome soldier, indignant at 'seeing himself insulted
by the pacifist command of the National Guard [in Versailles]', which had
complained about the conduct of his cavalry. *La gloire* had carried him
away, and the young *fédéré* captain thought of himself as a seasoned warrior.
He had indeed taken part in the campaign for the Palatinate; but neither had
he neglected the opportunity to forward his own political ambitions, and in
the *société populaire* of Nancy his numerous interventions soon won him a
reputation as an assiduous *sociétaire* and an energetic proposer of motions.[121]
The 'campaign during the winter season' had clearly left him time for other
diversions.

Mazuel did not stay long in the East, but he brought back with him all the
pretensions of the practised soldier and was keen to assert his superiority
over the civilian population – which augured ill for his relations with the
civil authorities during his spell of service in the *armée révolutionnaire*. He
returned to Paris in April 1793,[122] shortly after the dismissal of Beurnon-
ville, and became aide-de-camp to the new Minister, Bouchotte. He put his
appointment to good use, dispensing positions in the vast military machinery to relatives and friends from Lyon and Montpellier, thereby creating
even this early a following of 'obligés'. His family was proud of the success
of this young silk-embroiderer, and it is not difficult to imagine what it
meant to the artisans and small traders of Lyon and Montpellier to have a
brother-in-law or a cousin or simply a friend go up to Paris and become
aide-de-camp to the War Minister. It is scarcely surprising that the people of
La Croix-Rousse thought this 'enfant du pays' capable of anything when his
family boasted so loudly of his success. In the numerous congratulations
which Mazuel received from friends and relatives after March 1793, hopes
of preferment are barely disguised by expressions of affection. 'I would very
much like to visit Paris,' wrote his brother-in-law Louis Roujon from Lyon;
'tell me if you advise it, or if you could place me in some *bureau de subsistance*
until business picks up again'.[123] Another friend in Lyon asked him to
intervene in the case of some embroidered waistcoats bound for Switzerland, and seized by the customs at Carouge. From the spring onwards
Mazuel was effectively administering a bureau for processing requests and
distributing positions, and through him friends in Montpellier secured
positions in the military hospitals, in the *bureaux des subsistances*, or as
lieutenants in the new levy. He even succeeded in having an old friend
appointed to command a garrison in the Midi.

After having taken part in the *journée* of 31 May, only service in the
Vendée was wanting in his list of necessary qualifications for admission to
the general staff of the *armée révolutionnaire*. He did conduct a vague kind of
mission to the Army of the Côtes de La Rochelle, becoming acquainted

with Rossignol and Ronsin, and making an excellent impression on them. He returned to Paris at the end of July and through the support he enjoyed in the War Ministry, notably from the powerful Secretary-General, Vincent, he was entrusted by Bouchotte with the task of organising the new levy of the squadrons established in August 1793. Hoping to make the new cavalry 'his', as with the *fédérés*, Mazuel had already paid considerable attention to matters of personnel in his capacity as Bouchotte's aide-de-camp, and since he had control of nominations to all grades below that of *chef d'escadron*, he took advantage of this power to place even more of his Lyon and Montpellier friends in lieutenancies. Indeed there existed in the cavalry what amounted to a clan of 'amis de Mazuel', Séran from Lyon, and Delpêche, Fayet, Hurault, Colombel and Duplessis, all from Montpellier, all of whom were rewarded with lieutenancies or second lieutenancies. He also had an important clientele in Paris, and was much solicited by the powers of the day. Such liberality, however, put Mazuel in direct competition with the rival 'amis de Grammont', who also had friends to place, and however friendly Folleville might appear towards him, there was a running battle between the two groups.

Could Mazuel have counted on the support of his personal following in the cavalry in the event of a 'coup'? We can only offer hypotheses on this matter. One thing is certain, however: Mazuel could not dispose of the cavalry as he wished; at best he had authority over two squadrons only, those in Versailles. The *chefs d'escadron* acted without consulting him, even those who were friendly towards him. When he was arrested in Pluviôse the officers and non-commissioned officers of the squadrons made favourable overtures to Fouquier-Tinville on his behalf, and congratulated him on his release. But too much cannot be read into this, for in Ventôse the same signatures were to be found on the address of congratulation to the Convention for having 'unmasked' the 'conspiracy' of which Mazuel was to have been one of the leaders. The 'amis de Mazuel' proved as quick to disassociate themselves from their former leader then, as they had been eager to defend him only weeks earlier.

Mazuel was undoubtedly popular with his group; but he was a long way from being the prestigious head of a military junta. His friends from Montpellier profited from the favour he enjoyed with the Minister; but when he was definitely condemned by the Revolutionary Government, the Huraults, Penels, Sérans – his 'best friends' – pretended not to know him. Mazuel, however, was undoubtedly the most dangerous man in the *armée révolutionnaire* from the government's viewpoint, for it was he who had the most friends and clients, and gave the impression of manipulating the cavalry as a private army, stocked with henchmen. He himself had contributed to this impression by his unorthodox practice of enrolling indiscriminately and showing a positive preference for 'mauvais sujets' and suspects – as if he felt they would be easier to dominate because of their past. His recruiting procedure was indeed that of a brigand chief.

It was not ambition that Mazuel lacked, but prudence. He instantly crossed swords with Grammont who would not tolerate his attempt to use the cavalry for his own ends, and the two men attacked one another as intriguers. 'I am not at all surprised at your actions,' wrote Mazuel to Grammont, just before the latter's removal; 'I have seen a letter from you to Jourdeuil of 14 Pluviôse in which you claim that I am intriguing in Paris; it would grieve me thus to resemble you. . . .'[124] But he also alienated Payot, the former gendarme and *chef d'escadron*, who objected to being lorded over by this insolent young man; while Maubant, Grammont's successor, was soon irritated by his incessant complaints, his indiscipline, his escapades in the cafés, and above all by his refusal to rejoin his post at Lyon. Even Ronsin eventually found him an encumbrance, and Collot-d'Herbois, constantly canvassed by Mazuel, declared that this young man was in danger of compromising the entire corps in the eyes of the sans-culottes, while adding formidable ammunition to the arsenal of the Indulgents.

Mazuel in fact rarely stayed in one place, leaving his lawful wife with his trunks in the departmental capital of the Oise, and entertaining his mistresses either in Paris or in the Cadran Bleu, the *auberge* in which he established his cheerful and frivolous headquarters in Versailles. Was it ambition or pleasure which kept him so near to Paris? His refusal to leave for Lyon would be used against him, at the time of the mock-trial of the 'Hébertists', when it was claimed that he wanted to remain at Versailles to use 'his' squadrons in a military coup against Paris. But Mazuel had not in fact wanted to remain in Versailles, and on several occasions had requested a posting with the Army of the Midi, on the grounds that local knowledge would render him of more use to the Republic there than in Paris.[125] A complex personality, he was not simply an ambitious climber, and it does appear that his conscience was bothered by this long period of inactivity in Versailles. His arrest in Nivôse, following a scene provoked by him in a theatre, succeeded in finally discrediting the cavalry. While under arrest he tried to exonerate himself with his own troops, with the Sections and with the Cordeliers, claiming to be a victim of his revolutionary patriotism, when he was simply paying the penalty for his violence, his insolence as the dashing cavalry officer, and his intemperance.[126]

Mazuel was an unstable and excitable character; and though by his good sense and administrative and revolutionary zeal he had won the praise of the Oise authorities, he argued with those of Versailles, whom he accused of having 'insulted' the cavalrymen of 'his' army. Like so many *révolutionnaires* he could not abide the Versaillais, whom he considered remnants of the old order of things, and in character he resembled his friend Vincent, the wild young man of the Revolution. He was the most imprudent of the Cordeliers group in the War secretariat. Vincent at twenty-seven, Mazuel at twenty-eight, both possessed the recklessness of youth and in choosing Mazuel as the target for attack, the 'philippotins' had gone straight for the weakest point in the revolutionary command.

A womaniser, an ambitious careerist, a courageous soldier, a handsome

and dashing cavalry officer,[127] unstable, violent, domineering and impatient
– is this the complete portrait of the man who figured so prominently in the
history of the *armée révolutionnaire*? Can he be credited with any revolutionary sincerity or political thinking? Mazuel's politics were somewhat
improvised and it is difficult to detect any political philosophy in the drafts
of speeches which reveal, above all, an astonishing verbal violence and, as in
nearly all the *révolutionnaires*, a taste for grandiloquence. The words 'sans-
culotte' and 'bonheur de la patrie' appear frequently. But can we go so far as
to draw from this a real political programme and the means of attaining it?
Besides these 'stylistic exercises' the most we can speak of confidently in
this connection is the favour which Mazuel always showed towards the
sociétés populaires, and in this he shared his friend Vincent's belief that these
assemblies were the legitimate representatives of popular sovereignty. 'The
Sovereign Body of the People is excellent, pure and vigorous in nearly
every corner of the Republic,' the young Secretary-General for War wrote
to him, with the recommendation: 'Multiply the *sociétés populaires*; then
every trace of intrigue will disappear and the popular system will triumph.
Vive les sans-culottes...'.[128] This was the kind of direct democracy of which
Soboul speaks as the central aim of all sans-culotte political action. Mazuel
attended the clubs and *sociétés* wherever he went, in Montpellier, Nancy,
Beauvais and finally in Paris, where he was an assiduous member of the
Cordeliers and had even attended the Jacobins in September and in
Ventôse.[129] Like nearly all the leading members of the general staff, he
saw in these popular assemblies the natural allies of the new *armée*, whose
creation had owed so much to their activities; and in the wild impatience
which the obstruction by the local authorities evoked in him, and that
soldier's insolence which dominated his relations with civilians, we find the
anti-government prejudice of an ultra-revolutionary.

Finally, Mazuel shared the violent anticlericalism of most *révolutionnaires*,
at least in his public utterances. In such an ambitious man it is difficult to tell
whether he was sincere in this respect or whether he was simply subscribing
to the orthodoxy of the day. 'Brave companions in arms,' he wrote in the
draft of a speech, 'we are marchinig against the enemy, against fanaticism
and superstition...danger is all around us... deceitful priests, who trick us
with their lying teachings, and their empty missions, whose empire rests on
the credulity of women, the feebleness of men and the ignorance of peoples
– these then are our enemies....' And – spoken like a true revolutionary
patriot – 'The world is watching us, everywhere there are *philosophes*, wise
men, men born for liberty...It is to the Republicans of France that the
world owes the return of peace and happiness...'.[130]

We have lingered for some time on the personality of Mazuel, not only
because the young *chef d'escadron* played an extremely important role at the
head of the revolutionary cavalry, but because he is the only commander of
the *armée* almost all of whose personal and administrative papers have
survived.[131] Mazuel's personal failings weighed heavily on the *armée*. His

bad reputation, and the whiff of scandal which always attached to him, spread to the cavalry as a whole; and the haste with which he raised the corps by indiscriminate recruiting from among the young men of the first requisition (even from among prisoners-of-war), accepting the first comer, be he a deserter, counter-revolutionary, former noble or adventurer, only served to sink the reputation of the entire force.

Mazuel then was quite a specimen: a true revolutionary, violent and courageous, but at the same time a self-seeking and ambitious careerist. A spell in Paris did such a man no good whatsoever, and after permitting him such rapid advancement in that frontier zone between political and military life, so favourable to the careers of such 'hommes de liaison', it destroyed him. It would have been better for everyone – for his colleagues, for his army, for his cavalry, and most of all for himself – if Mazuel had secured his transfer to the Midi. His continued presence in Paris and in Versailles supplied him with too many opportunities to compromise the *armée révolutionnaire* in the eyes of the Committee, the Convention, the Parisian press, and above all the local authorities.

(vi)   POLITICAL LEADERS: *COMMISSAIRES CIVILS* AND *COMMISSAIRES DES GUERRES*

The subordination of the new *armée* to the supreme political authority, i.e. the Committee of Public Safety, was assured by the existence of two *commissaires civils*. These in effect were political *commissaires*, delegates from the Committee, entrusted with a number of missions against suspects in the Paris region, then dispatched to Lyon to watch over the activities of the most important of the detachments. However, the Committee did not appoint from agents already in its service, but accepted the two men recommended by Ronsin and Parein: the Jacobins, Marcellin and Paillardelle.

The most prominent of the two was François-Julien Marcellin, the inspector of police in Paris under the Ancien Regime, a calling to which he would again return in the difficult years following Thermidor. We know nothing of his revolutionary career until this date, except that he was a *commissaire* of the Paris Commune in the Vendée, from whence he moved to the Sénar Commission in Tours, and was replaced there by Millier. Shortly afterwards we find him on the Commission Parein-Félix in Angers, which he left on 1 Brumaire to take up his new post as *commissaire civil* in Paris.[132] Marcellin, therefore, started with the double advantage of already knowing Parein at the time of the general staff's organisation, and of having served on a political tribunal charged with the repression of a rebellious region. He almost certainly owed his nomination to Parein rather than to Ronsin, and on the journey from Paris to Lyon it would have been abundantly clear that Marcellin was no novice in political action. In Lyon and its environs he was to be the most important political representative of the general staff; next to the *réprésentants* it was he who exercised most power, and Maubant had to rest satisfied with the implementation of orders transmitted through him.[133]

His colleague, Paillardelle, played a lesser role, and if Marcellin continued to be an important figure in the republican opposition until his arrest and exile to Bordeaux in the Year XII, we hear scarcely anything further of Paillardelle after the completion of his mission to Lyon. A French merchant in Cadiz, who had been ruined by the war with Spain, he was expelled after his refusal to take the oath required from the French colony against the new French Constitution. In Cadiz he had married a rich Spanish lady; but her fortune remained tied up in Spain. Before entering the world of commerce he had held several positions in the naval offices of Marseille, Toulon and Brest, where he profited from his knowledge of Castilian and Italian. In the *armée révolutionnaire* he remained in the shadow of the energetic Marcellin, and Parein dismissed him as a drunkard and a sluggard. In the last days of the Jacobins he seems to have been the Society's secretary, and at the session of 5 Brumaire he recommended Lebois's paper, *L'Ami du Peuple*, to its members.[134] He had thus remained faithful to his convictions as a former terrorist.

Marcellin and Paillardelle were the only *commissaires civils* to be attached to the Parisian *armée*, and their appointment testifies to the importance which the Revolutionary Government attached to the operation in Lyon. Similar functions were performed with other detachments by a host of *commissaires* acting in the name of various Parisian authorities. But whatever the source of their authority – whether the Committee of General Security, the *comité de surveillance* of the Paris department, the Commission des Subsistances, the *comités révolutionnaires* in the Sections, or the Executive Council – these 'hommes de liaison' exercised effective command over the revolutionary troops, directing their activities and dictating the missions to be undertaken. At the time of its first mission, the Parisian *armée* was effectively commanded by two *commissaires* of the departmental *comité de surveillance*, Clémence and Marchand, commissioned on this occasion by the Committee of Public Safety and entitled *commissaires civils de l'armée révolutionnaire* for the duration of the operation.[135] Elsewhere the Parisian detachments operated under the orders of *commissaires* appointed by the Committee of General Security. But Marcellin, Paillardelle, Clémence and Marchand were the only ones to hold the title *commissaire civil*. In the departmental and communal *armées* this subordination of the military to the civil authority was still more pronounced, with each *armée* subject to one of these officials.

In the Parisian *armée* the role of the *commissaires des guerres* was both political and administrative and owed more to the personalities than to the position of the men who exercised it. The two men who fulfilled the function, Jean-Charles Boissay and Pierre-François Paris, the former as *commissaire-ordonnateur*, the latter as *commissaire des guerres* of the *armée révolutionnaire*, did not remain satisfied with the simple exercise of their administrative duties. Boissay, son of a shopkeeper in Alencon, and a compatriot of Hébert, was thirty-three in 1793. He was an old friend of the founder of the *Père Duchesne*, whom he had known since his youth, and.

associated with since the Revolution – it was Hébert who had signed his *certificat de civisme*. A long-standing member of the Cordeliers, he was also a close friend of Vincent and Momoro, and commanded the respect of the *représentant* Laplanche. It was thanks to these connections that he secured his first position as *commissaire des guerres* in Pache's ministry.[136] In March he was sent to Moulins, the main town of the 21st military division. From then until October his political career took off in the Allier, and through his revolutionary energy and the violence of his pronouncements he soon attracted the attention of Fouché. In the departments of the Allier and the Nièvre, Boissay served his apprenticeship as an ultra-revolutionary, and from April 1793 was Fouché's 'viceroy' in Moulins. To him Fouché confided the task of levying taxes on the rich, forming an *armée révolutionnaire*, clearing the churches of their statues and silver, purging the Moulins *société*, creating a *comité de surveillance* there, and *comités* and *sociétés* in the other towns and villages of the department. No other member of the Parisian *armée* had such direct and varied experience of revolutionary action. Of all the general staff Boissay was the closest to the Cordelier group and the War Ministry, a true Hébertist, come to the *armée révolutionnaire* with a reputation already established as an accomplished terrorist. At the time of his nomination on 27 September, he was again deeply involved in the repression of the Allier. Fouché secured his release from duties there, and again at Fouché's request he was sent to Lyon. From there he would maintain almost daily contact with his friends in Paris.[137]

Another political man through his revolutionary past and his Cordelier contacts, Pierre-François Paris, the principal *commissaire des guerres* of the Parisian *armée*, was the same age as Boissay, born 'with a republican soul' at Porrentruy in the Jura on 7 September 1759. His military career had started in the Parisian National Guard, where he was appointed captain and assistant medical officer on 1 September 1789. In 1791 he passed briefly into the 102nd infantry regiment, then in 1792 he rejoined the 36th division of gendarmerie, which, like the famous '35th', was a refuge for Vainqueurs de la Bastille. In September 1792 he was appointed *commissaire des guerres*, second level.

A republican by birth – 'I was not surprised by the French Revolution, and its progress kept pace with my own' – this child 'of the free people of the Jura' was indeed as advanced in revolutionary temperament as he was lacking in modesty. In his first posting at Thionville he clashed immediately with the municipality, which he accused of weakness towards the farming and commercial community. His proposal to use armed force against the farmers to secure the supply of this important town, caused the municipality to complain that he was the leader of 'a faction of disorder' determined to 'create total disorder in the town by substituting the most complete anarchy in the place of our most sanctified laws designed to protect persons and property'. This 'faction of disorder', led by Paris, had expelled 'the most honest and judicious citizens' (for which read the richest) from the *société populaire* and would have seized control of it to effect their 'anarchical plans'. More serious still, the municipality accused Paris of having 'concerted a plan to destroy all discipline in the garrison', by telling the soldiers and non-commissioned officers 'that for too long they had been the slaves of their officers'. He was reproached for his 'cowardly condescension towards the military, his pretence of going arm-in-arm with the soldiers...'.[138] Here then was the confirmed and authentic *révolutionnaire*, who would become the principal organiser of the *armée révolutionnaire* in Paris.

Paris's adjoint, the *commissaire des guerres* Martin, was *commissaire* of the Réunion Section *comité révolutionnaire*. After the departure of his chief for Germany, to effect the exchange of the Mainz prisoners, Martin would assume responsibility for matters such as pay, permissions, leave and payment of debts incurred by the *armée révolutionnaire*. Boissay's adjoint was a young Rouen man named Rayot. 'At thirty', wrote the latter, 'I had already spent 15 years in offices of various businesses and was about to reap the fruits of my youthful labours in the foundation of my own establishment, when the war destroyed my hopes.... I supported the war without hesitation....' After serving in the Rouen National Guard, he left for the Ardennes Army where he served as adjoint and secretary to an adjutant-general.

Mathieu Fromant, quartermaster and treasurer of the 1st battalion, was an inhabitant of the Théâtre-Français Section, a member of the Jacobins and of the Société des Hommes-Libres, and had been in charge of correspondence in the secretariat of the Paris Commune. His colleague and quartermaster of the 2nd battalion from 23 Vendémiaire was Charles Gachet of the Montagne Section. His revolutionary career had got off to a bad start following the denunciation by the Saint-Florentin *comité de surveillance* of a namesake, the son of a former provost in the Ile-de-France *maréchaussée*.[139] We have no information on the other four quartermasters.

The administrative Councils, of which there were to be one per battalion, were not permanent bodies. They only sat on exceptional occasions to pronounce in cases of conflict between officers and men, or on other disciplinary or political questions. Thus the Council of the 2nd battalion convened to pronounce on the fate of Gachet after his denunciation, that of the 4th to decide the issue between Lecourtier, commander of the Laon detachment, and his officers and men who complained of his harshness. Sometimes issues were decided without convening the Councils, as when the wigmaker, Lassagne, was expelled from the Bonne-Nouvelle Section company for having signed the petition of the 20,000, the company captain Réaume having simply called a general assembly of the company, which voted the expulsion of this 'unworthy' soldier.[140] Above all the administrative Councils, composed as they were of officers, non-commissioned officers, soldiers and Sectionary authorities, underline the democratic and civilian nature of this Parisian *armée*. Their existence was a guarantee against the eventual militarisation of this political body.

What conclusions can be drawn from this series of individual biographies about the political and social composition of the command structure of the *armée révolutionnaire*? One thing is abundantly apparent: the general staff was above all else composed of soldiers. Out of the 45 whose previous careers we know something about, 23 served as officers, or more often as non-commissioned officers and soldiers, in the regiments of the Ancien Regime – less common were those whose military careers dated only from the time of the Revolution. Some of these 23 can also be classed under other categories: Ronsin, for instance, was more a member of the theatrical than of the military profession. But what about Maubant? Should he be classified with the former soldiers, with the artisans employed in the luxury trade (since he was, like his father, a wigmaker), or with the legal fraternity, given his employment as clerk to a *procureur*? He was in addition a *fonctionnaire*, for he moved on to work for the War Ministry. There are other cases of such social mobility. Gury, for instance, who served for many years in the Ancien Regime cavalry, was also a yeoman farmer. Dobigny, the son of a manufacturer, who despite his service in the Queen's Regiment and then in the Rouen National Guard, was a manufacturer for all that, and soon followed in his father's footsteps. Given these reservations, nearly half the general staff was still composed of former soldiers. Was the *armée révolutionnaire* then more military and less civilian and political in character than is commonly supposed? Too much must not be read into these figures: they pay excessive attention to the cavalry, which was indeed composed largely of military men, they do not include the artillery officers, they disguise the fact that the cannoneers did not have a general staff, and that, as we shall see, the artillery was distinctly civilian in composition.

Service on the revolutionary general staff, particularly as *chef d'escadron* and even more as *chef de bataillon* or adjutant-major, aide-de-camp or adjoint, was little more than an episode in a long military career. It was, nevertheless, a profitable episode, bringing with it lightning advancement; and if the officers who experienced such rapid promotion in this political army preferred to remain silent about their service in a popular army, in the years to come, they had no scruples about retaining the rank acquired there. A cavalry officer who ended up as Napoleon's aide-de-camp would not want his revolutionary service remembered; but the few months spent in Ronsin's *armée* would have launched him in every sense. The military men used this army, in which promotion was so easy, to gain their stripes, even if they later denounced it as a 'despicable corps'. Few could equal the opportunism and raw ambition of these career soldiers.

Some members of the general staff had been employed in the luxury trades and were left high and dry by the circumstances of the Revolution: they included an assistant to a silversmith (Boulanger), a jeweller's assistant (Houssaye), a decorator (Tolède), a drawing master (Halm), a restaurateur (Lemaire), a silk-embroiderer (Mazuel), as well as two former servants, or reputedly so (Allais and Buard; the latter also being a soldier of fortune), and a wigmaker (Maubant). In a similar category, but having profited rather than suffered because of the Revolution, were the actors and members of the theatrical profession, six in all – a high proportion due largely to Grammont's influence and to the existence of a group of 'amis de Grammont', in this '*état-major gramonicide*'. Ronsin also surrounded himself with theatre people, as did the engraver Corchand, a protégé of Parein (who also prided himself on being something of a playwright).

There were only four who might be collectively described as merchants or businessmen, two of whom, Paillardelle and Rayot, had their business careers interrupted by the declaration of war. There were two shopkeepers, a stationer (Renault) and a haberdasher (Corchand again). Artisans were an equally rare category: there was a shoemaker (Benoît), and a fireman (Rocher). There was in addition a man of the law (Parein), a policeman (Marcellin), a clerk (Fromant) and an ex-convict (Collard-Dutrône).

In its political make-up the general staff possessed as little unity as in its social. No preponderant influence can be traced, and it would be inaccurate to describe it as predominantly Hébertist, Jacobin, ultra-revolutionary or 'governmental'. To take the veterans first: the 'Hercules' of the Revolution were rewarded and the general staff included four Vainqueurs de la Bastille (Parein, Corchand, Thomasset and Ducastel). There were also several heroes of 10 August, Grammont and Mazuel among them. We know of no Septembriseurs, though they can be found in the departmental *armées*. The Jacobins seem to have outnumbered the Cordeliers, and those like Paris, Boissay and Parein who belonged to a little group centred on the War Ministry, the Cordeliers club, and the general assembly of the Marat Section, were but a minority. The 'government men', like the Jacobins, were more numerous: four were members of the *comités révolutionnaires* of Paris Sections, Renault, Tolède, Vézien and Martin, and there were several leading *sectionnaires* such as Halm (Fontaine-de-Grenelle), Lemaire (Montagne), Tolède (Faubourg-Montmartre). The *chefs de bataillon* were Jacobins, men on whom the government could entirely rely. As for the cavalry commanders, they were career soldiers and since most were neither Parisians nor *sectionnaires*, they were unknown to both Jacobins and Cordeliers. The government had nothing to fear from such a general staff and could command almost complete obedience from a body of men who were career-conscious and sincere but orthodox revolutionaries. Real *révolutionnaires*, men like Paris, violent, anarchical and independently-minded men, were rare.

The general staff reflected the Parisian *armée* it was supposed to command in neither political nor social terms. Simple *révolutionnaires* were scandalised by the morals, the ambitions and the frivolity of the young actors whose eccentricities lent an air of insubstantiality to the entire *armée*. The general staff was not sans-culotte; the *armée* was. The former was composed of men younger than the rank and file, men of the twenty-five-to-thirty-five age group who had barely escaped the first requisition. Fathers and married men were less numerous in the rue de Choiseul than in the companies. All sans-culottes were prejudiced against bachelors, and this was another grudge of the *révolutionnaires* against the general staff. Finally, the preponderance of military men on the staff was quite exceptional and declines as one descends through the ranks.

What then decided the choice of these 50 or so men? Was it *civisme*? Services rendered to the Revolution? Military talent? All of these undoubtedly counted for something, and the election process had inbuilt guarantees of *civisme* and morality. On the other hand certain names were passed by the Jacobins simply because they were known, and the members of the Society must have been poorly informed indeed if they could confuse the name of Maubant with that of the notorious Federalist Mauban. All of which leads to the conclusion that the *épuration* by the Jacobins was a mere formality, and the final choice had already been made when the lists were drawn up for presentation to the club. The Jacobins were simply being offered a pack of cards which had already been shuffled.

The really decisive factors were personal relationships and political friendships. Boissay was not alone in playing politics with friendships. Only consider the way in which Mazuel filled the ranks of the revolutionary cavalry, Grammont recruited his personal general staff, or Ronsin, Parein and Boulanger chose their closest collaborators. The only rule was that of acquaintance, the only bond that of obligation and favour. Grammont had his own son as adjoint, the generals approached those whom they had known in the Vendée. There was the 'clan de Grammont', and 'the amis de Mazuel' – southerners for the most part – the 'groupe de Boulanger', which was likewise that of Hanriot and of the friends of Robespierre and Le Bas, the protégés of Fouché and those of Collot-d'Herbois, the friends of Hérault de Séchelles and those recommended by David. Doubtless the favour of the War Ministry was still the decisive element, since it was the Executive Council which supplied the initial list; but the composition of the general staff did not emerge full-blown from the offices of Jourdeuil, Audouin, Vincent and Sijas, or even those of the Cordeliers in the rue de Thionville. The composition of the *armée* was too complex to lend itself to such simple analyses. Ultimately the men of the War Ministry and the Cordeliers were a long way from controlling all the places on the general staff, with power to install their own candidates. Its composition represented a compromise among a multitude of elements, just as the creation of the Parisian *armée* was the outcome of a compromise between the Revolutionary Government and the Sectionary movement. It was a product of lengthy haggling, and as such reflected all manner of tendencies, with no dominant influence readily recognisable.

Was this outcome the result of forward planning to prevent the *armée* from falling under the control of one person, or was it produced by the chance combination of different personal relationships? This is a question with no ready answer. But the net result was that the general staff did not fall under the exclusive control of any one person or any single political grouping. Politically it was not a united force, socially too it was composed of extremely diverse categories. It was far removed from anything resembling a corps of janissaries or a praetorian guard, and its very composition protected it against adventurers and personal ambition. Those who dreaded the hatching of any *pouvoir militaire* had nothing to fear from this quarrelsome group, riven by disputes, torn by clan rivalries, and its lack of homogeneity preserved the *armée révolutionnaire* from harmful associations and over-politicisation in favour of any one group. Such a general staff would serve the ambitions of no one, except perhaps those military men anxious to rush through all the stages up the ladder of promotion.

Technically, then, what can we say of the *armée* general staff and of the men who worked in it or pretended to do so? The general staff, like the *armée* itself, was formed in haste, its organisation improvised amidst disorder. But Ronsin was a good general and above all the general staff had at its head a government man, a man anxious to fulfil the commands of the Committee of Public Safety. In this sense it might be described simply as a liaising element, through which the Committee could transmit its orders to the different revolutionary detachments.

CHAPTER 3

The Officers and Men of the Parisian *Armée*

The unknowns of this popular army were the officers, the company or detachment commanders, and the *révolutionnaires* themselves. The few historians who have looked into this most under-investigated institution of the Terror have concentrated exclusively on its general staff. However, the *armée révolutionnaire* was created not to stroll the streets of Paris, or to add to the prestige of certain figures in the rue de Choiseul, but to support a necessarily unpopular programme with threats and terror. It was the task of the artillery and infantry officers as well as the cannoneers and the fusiliers to implement this programme, and the cavalry officers remained apart from the other branches in this respect, as they did also in origin, age, and above all in behaviour. Those other branches were composed of *sectionnaires*; the cavalry for the most part was not.

The Parisian *armée* was an egalitarian force. Little distinguished officer from fusilier or cannoneer, and they were often neighbours with the same social background. The division of the present chapter into two parts reflects, therefore, not a social hierarchy, of which the members of the *armée* would have been unaware, but the different nature of the documentation. Thanks to an abundance of personal dossiers it is possible to construct biographical studies of the officers; for the *révolutionnaires* we can only build a composite portrait from the fragments of rudimentary material.

The *armée révolutionnaire* was not a homogeneous force and possessed little *esprit de corps* in the military sense. It was an army of civilians, whose hero was the *révolutionnaire*, whose rallying point was the Section, and whose essential unity rested on the Sectionary companies. But the absence of complete lists of these companies prohibits any study (usually artificial and impersonal in any case) of its social structure. This chapter therefore is devoted to the individual officers and men of the Parisian *armée*.

PART I   THE REVOLUTIONARY OFFICER

I   *Cannoneer officers*

The revolutionary artillery was the élite corps of this popular army. A Parisian and above all a Sectionary corps, its basis was the autonomous company which remained in close contact with the Section in which it had originated. The cannoneers were in the service of their Sections; they were on loan to the *armée révolutionnaire*, and paid little attention to Ronsin and his general staff, whose control over them was weak and transient. They criticised the *réprésentants* freely, denounced the local authorities at will, and were compliant only towards the *commissaires* of the Committee of General Security, who were frequently members also of the *comités révolutionnaires* in the Sections; for the artillery was not only a Sectionary force, it was linked as well to the *comités révolutionnaires*.

With no superior artillery command, the cannoneer captain was his own master, and his position at the head of a company was much more important than that of a fusilier captain under orders from his *chef de bataillon* and the general staff. Later, during the great crises of Thermidor Year II and Germinal and Prairial Year III, the attitude of each company would depend above all on that of its captain. As a leading figure in the Section, known to his men as a military commander and even more as a neighbour, owing his elected position to the confidence of his fellow citizens and his acute sense of political reality, his powers of action were considerable. Babeuf, Buonarroti, Germain, Félix Lepeletier and the Police Minister Cochon, all in their different ways experts on these *révolutionnaires*, agreed in according the company captains, as well as the officers and simple cannoneers, a particular importance. They were given by these conspirators a special place in the list of 'men capable of commanding' not only because of their technical expertise, but above all because, as leading *sectionnaires*, they still in the Year IV exercised a very real influence over their fellow citizens, who had often served under them in the Parisian terrorist élite. Cochon was to honour these men with a particularly severe surveillance.

They had gained their position in the hierarchy of terror for a number of reasons: they were mature, averaging thirty-five years of age,[1] civilians like the men they commanded, and had a solid footing among the tradespeople and artisans of Paris. Military men were rare in this corps; its members were formed in the image of the militant minority which directed the Sectionary movement, and shopkeepers (often comfortably-off ones), tradesmen and artisans predominated.[2] The cannoneer officers were Parisians and political men, and everything pointed to them as commanders of a political army and directors of the revolutionary operation in the departments. In the execution of their duties they were to show themselves worthy of the confidence placed in them by their fellow *sectionnaires*, and the conduct of certain artillery captains testified to the sincerity and firmness of their convictions.

If these officers were so important politically, it was not only because of their activities in connection with a particular instrument of the Terror, whose life was even shorter than that of the regime and the political atmosphere which had produced it; they had further claims to be considered notable *révolutionnaires* and their term in the Parisian *armée* was but one episode in a longer political life. We must also resist the temptation to view these leading *sectionnaires* as typical representatives of the *armée révolutionnaire*; they may have formed a political élite within it, but they were never entirely a part of it. For these experienced terrorists, this spell in the Parisian *armée* represented the period of their greatest revolutionary activity. But it would convey a false impression of the political understanding of the normal revolutionary officer to take the lives of certain artillery commanders as representative: the infantry provides more typical examples of the average officer, while the fusiliers were the Parisian *armée*, strictly speaking, and their existence terminated with it. The typical Parisian officer like the typical revolutionary soldier was a fusilier, the 'sans-culotte' of Laukhard's account.

Despite their political importance the cannoneer officers have left little documentary evidence. Civilians for the most part, they do not figure in the military archives. Those who played a notable role in Sectionary activity before Thermidor, or participated in the opposition movement after the Year III, may appear in the documentation for the Sections and in the police records on which it is based. But they were a tiny minority. The 28 companies had more than 80 officers who took part in the activities of the *armée révolutionnaire*; but for only 15 of those officers do we know more than the name and Section – an insufficient body of evidence to permit reliable generalisations for the whole group. But since this selection was the product of circumstances as well as police surveillance, we can assume that these 15 supplied that active and militant minority which came to dominate and direct every revolutionary institution. Two were notable *révolutionnaires* whose political careers continued long after the Terror: Jean-Louis Eude, captain of the Droits-de-l'Homme Section company, and Jean-Baptiste-Antoine Lefranc, who commanded that of the Tuileries. The others need not detain us, except where the chance word or accusation of terrorism tells something of the scope of their actions or their social position.

Eude, the youngest of these cannoneer officers, was born at Saint-Ouen near Paris on 26 August 1768. A master clockmaker, like many artisans involved in the luxury trades he threw himself at an early stage into the revolutionary movement. His brother was a member of the Paris Commune and was to fall victim to the proscription after Thermidor. The two were leading figures in the Droits-de-l'Homme Section, the same Section as Varlet, and one which had a rather unusual social composition because of the number of lodging-houses, with their ragged population of carpenter's apprentices.[3] The Eude brothers did not belong to this class, and politically were far removed from both Varlet and Descombes, another leader of the Section, who was a *commissaire* for subsistences in the Pontoise district and future victim of the Hébertist trials. The younger Eude brother, Jean-Louis, was elected company captain on 1 September 1793, before the formation of the Parisian *armée*. We know nothing of this independent artisan's activities in the *armée*, and it was not until after Thermidor, and even more so after

Prairial Year III, that his resolutely hostile attitude to the new order won him both a place of honour on the list of Babouvists and the attention of the Police Minister, Cochon. Eude was a republican, but it was only in the period of proscription that we find proof of this. Under the Terror he was 'a government man', a 'Robespierrist' *sectionnaire* like his brother, and one whom Soboul places with the Jacobins rather than the sans-culottes. However, September 1793 was an important date for this Paris clockmaker; having found a salaried position in the revolutionary institutions he would not return to his trade until after 1814, following a long career in semi-civil, semi-military posts in France and in those parts of Europe occupied by the imperial armies, sometimes as commander of a prisoner-of-war camp, sometimes as a supply officer. For Eude, still a young man in 1793, the *armée révolutionnaire* opened the door on a new career, one quite different from his own, and if he gave good service to the Revolution, the Revolution in turn made a personality of him.[4]

Lefranc was a much more important figure than this modest clockmaker, and after a long career in military administration he became commander of a prison camp. A native of Paris, this thirty-one-year-old captain of the Tuileries company was a rich man who called himself a carpenter simply to conform to current taste. He had 'sans-culottised' himself in much the same way as Duplay. But this 'carpenter' was a building contractor and an architect, who carried out important commissions on behalf of the Republic, including the construction of the new powder magazine at Saint-Germain-en-Laye, the conversion of the Ursuline grain warehouse at Saint-Denis, and the repair of the University buildings. It was no simple carpenter to whom Collot and Fouché entrusted the work of rebuilding France's second city, where Lefranc found himself with his company and was made head of public works and member of the General Council by the municipality. At the time of his arrest in the Year III he owed 10,000 livres in pay – a token of the numbers in his employ.[5]

But if he was undoubtedly the richest man in the *armée révolutionnaire*, Lefranc's convictions were also the most sincere, his service as a militant *révolutionnaire* the longest and most impressive, and like most energetic *révolutionnaires*, he remained entirely faithful to the Convention after Thermidor.[6] In its service he lost his fortune and liberty, and from the Year III until 1816 there was scarcely any republican conspiracy or anti-terrorist proscription in which his name did not figure. In electing him to command their company in October 1793, the sans-culottes of the Tuileries Section undoubtedly recognised the kind of man they were dealing with, and from the time of his departure for Lyon onward, Lefranc distinguished himself during long years of service as a masterful administrator of the Terror. Although he never exercised any political function in his Section, apart from commanding its cannoneers, he was to use the methods of an accomplished terrorist en route to Lyon, 'electrifying' the *sociétés populaires*, stimulating the municipalities to pursue economic frauds and 'malveillants', denouncing weakness and negligence where necessary, and commanding the *comités de surveillance* to be more vigilant. He even seems to have instilled this renewed vigilance into the members of his company, chosen out of all the revolutionary units to act as adjoint *commissaires*, to assist – and to watch – the Lyonnais on the *comités révolutionnaires* of the 32 Sections.

Not only was Lefranc an exceptional *révolutionnaire* who turned his company into a school for the Terror. Exceptional too was his revolutionary temperament: a well-off man, a Jacobin rather than a sans-culotte, he was to become in the Year IV an inept and imprudent conspirator; and a conspirator he would remain for the rest of his active life. In the Year XII, having just returned from Cayenne, sick and without money, he wrote to Bonaparte from the château of Brest, 'at all events the fever of delirium has gone for ever...'. But 'the fever of delirium' took hold of him again in 1816; he became involved in a republican conspiracy and was incarcerated on Mont Saint-Michel.[7] *Révolutionnaire*, French patriot, conspirator, Lefranc was indeed very different from the others, and his experience in repression during the missions of the Year II scarcely prepared him for the role of secret conspirator. Given the particular circumstances of the Parisian *armée*, the importance of his career derived not only from his pure temperament and unshakeable fidelity, but even more from the fact that this building contractor was captain of a company of cannoneers. This position, more than his personality, would draw him to the attention of Babeuf, Germain and Buonarroti. Finally, the personal role of Lefranc in the Parisian *armée* was considerable and this militant communicated his zeal, his 'delirium' to all around him. No other member of the *armée* had as great a personal influence on the course of events.

Louis David Sandoz, known as 'Scévola' Sandoz, somewhat resembled Lefranc in his revolutionary service. As a printer and engraver with a shop in the rue de Buci, l'Unité Section, he was, like many militant *sectionnaires*, involved in the luxury trade. He was also a foreigner, born in Geneva. A lieutenant in the l'Unité company of cannoneers, Sandoz remained in Paris when the company was sent to Toulon, occupied with the concerns of his Section, as member of the *comité révolutionnaire* and the Cordeliers, whose sessions he presided over during the crisis of Ventôse–Germinal. He was also the proposer of a motion in favour of mobile guillotines. Like Lefranc and Eude he was part of the republican opposition in the Year III, appeared on Babeuf's lists, and was the object of surveillance and arrest on several occasions. On 24 Fructidor Year IV he was arrested near the camp of Grenelle, brought before the military commission of the Temple, condemned to death on 6 Vendémiaire Year V, and was shot the same day on the plain of Grenelle. If Sandoz does not quite fit into the category of cannoneer officers, he was nevertheless closely associated with the organisation and administration of the *armée révolutionnaire*; he remained one of its most resolute supporters, and his exemplary career as a militant *sectionnaire* deserves a mention among those of the political chiefs of the artillery.[8]

Beside Lefranc, the revolutionary Gil Blas, all the other officers of the
revolutionary artillery seem dull. Several were closely involved in the
journées of the Year III, in the Babeuf affair, and in the proscription of the
Year IX. But during their term in the *armée révolutionnaire* they also distinguished themselves in ways other than as political militants, by their background, by certain attitudes which brought them near the mass of the
sectionnaires, and by their problems as civilians and fathers. Thus the lieutenant of the Bonne-Nouvelle company[9] was more a leading *sectionnaire*
than an artillery officer at a time when relations were deteriorating between
the Sectionary movement and the republican government. Jean-Baptiste
Coppin was forty-seven, a Belgian in origin from Ypres who ran a shoe-
mending business. As president of his Section's *société populaire* in Pluviôse
Year II, he demanded the use of the *armée révolutionnaire* against the butchers,
whom he accused of favouritism in the distribution of the meagre meat
rations. The Jacobin government, always acutely sensitive on matters of
food supply, especially meat which was particularly scarce in the spring of
1794, accused him of being 'a disturber of the public peace'. The Bonne-
Nouvelle *comité révolutionnaire* for its part, acting as agent for the Committees, and confining him to prison, denounced that 'coalition' and that 'esprit
de corps' which 'undermined the position of the established authorities' – a
condemnation of the claims of a cannoneer company to act independently,
by invoking the subsistence laws in favour of the consumer.[10] For the
comité Coppin's initiative raised the spectre of an independent artillery
which might completely escape government control and provide the Sectionary movement with a military wing; and when a cannoneer officer was
simultaneously president of the Section's *société*, with his company inactive
in Paris and on hand for possible use, such fears were not without foundation. It was only with the disbandment of the *armée* and the return of the
cannoneer companies to Paris, that similar examples appear in other
Sections of conflict between cannoneers and *commissaires* of the *comités
révolutionnaires*.

Delacroix and Dauphinot, captain and lieutenant respectively of the Bon-
Conseil company, participated in the first mission of the *armée* to the Gonesse
district in September. There, Jean-Louis Delacroix, a fifty-two-year-old
basket-maker of the rue Montorgeuil, and a native of Conflans-Sainte-
Honorine, distinguished himself by his enthusiastic participation in blasphemous processions. He was accused of having decked himself out in a
chasuble and of having conducted 'mocking benedictions in the squares', to
which he replied: 'I admit that I put on a chasuble, but I don't believe I committed a sacrilege, yes I will say with satisfaction that I watched the baubles
of superstition transformed into gold ingots in the republican crucible...'.
He spent only a short time at the head of this company, obtaining his leave
in Brumaire 'to be free to deal with his business affairs'.

Delacroix was replaced by his first lieutenant, Denis Dauphinot, an active
sans-culotte and *sectionnaire*, and the unflattering portrait of him by the

Thermidorean authorities was in effect a tribute to his activities as a *révolutionnaire*. Accused of having deserted a dragoon regiment some years before the Revolution, by 1789 Dauphinot had set himself up as a café-owner in the rue Pavé, his café becoming the haunt of 'libertines and disreputable characters, to whom he served drinks almost all night long in defiance of police rulings...'.[11] The Thermidorean mythology in which every *révolutionnaire* was a drunkard and a bad lot merits closer examination. Dauphinot was certainly not as violent as depicted, but his occupation as café-owner lent itself to accusations of this nature. Café-owners and innkeepers occupy a special place in the history of the Terror; they were propagators of revolutionary ideas and at the same time had links with the secret and violent world of crime. A man might derive considerable political importance from such an occupation, since the café-owner was not only in contact with the sans-culottes, but also with the floating and wretched population of the garrets, and it was among the latter that someone with political ambitions like Dauphinot might organise a following. This is why the *comités civils* of the Year III, and even more the Robespierrist authorities of 1794, so feared the café-owning class.

We know little about the other cannoneer officers. Chevalier, commander of the Section des Marchés company, kept a toy shop in the rue Saint-Denis. Mera, lieutenant in the Gardes-Françaises company, was a haberdasher and draper, and like Delacroix was to request his discharge to look after his business.[12] Louis Vallantin, captain of the Guillaume-Tell company, born in 1755, the son of a farmer in the Berry, is one of the few to have a dossier in the Archives de la Guerre, for he remained in the army and had a long career in the artillery. His lieutenant, Jean-Michel Suicre, was thirty-four years of age and though a native of Württemberg had lived in Paris since 1775. He is described as an 'artiste' or 'worker', but he must have been a goldsmith, jeweller or clockmaker because he was considered useful in the manufacture of arms and thus escaped the laws against foreigners.[13] He belonged to that same group of foreign artisans working in the luxury trades from which the second-in-command of the Parisian *armée*, Boulanger, and the *chef de bataillon*, Halm, had come.

The commander of the Arcis company, Pierre Poupart, a thirty-six-year-old goldsmith, was denounced in Frimaire by one of his men for having squandered the company's effects. The Arcis *comité* attributed this accusation to personal spite and retained him in his command. But new accusations of a political nature woud be made against him in Thermidor when several witnesses claimed to have seen him about to shake the hand of General Hanriot on the night of 9 Thermidor. He was arrested on the 14th, but the *comité révolutionnaire* came to his defence, claiming that he had mistaken the intentions of the commander-general, and he was released in Fructidor Year II.[14] Potemont, a master locksmith, was captain of the Montreuil company and an important *sectionnaire* of the faubourg and with many other cannoneers he would figure on Babeuf's lists as a possible leader in his conspiracy.[15] The brothers Monvoisin, captain and lieutenant respectively of the Luxembourg company, notable agitators in their Section, and leaders of the republican opposition between 1795 and 1800, were from the same social grouping – one qualifying as an engraver in 1793, the other appearing in police records in the Year IX as a clockmaker.[16] The captain of the Arsenal company, Petit, was a tapestry-maker. His name appears on Babeuf's lists (though he is sometimes confused with two others of the same name), and police reports of the Year IX credited him with an active role in the *journée* of 31 May.[17]

Jean Mirau, an officer of the Brutus Section cannoneers, belonged to a completely different social group from most of the artillery officers. At the time of his election he was destitute; the *armée révolutionnaire* was a life-line for him, and thanks to the support of his Section's *société*, of which he was a member, he secured a position as a checker in the National Treasury's *bureau de comptabilité* on his discharge. He was one of the few *commis* among the officers and was also a member of the administrative Council of the 4th battalion. He too would figure in the Babeuf conspiracy.[18] Finally Jean-Louis Hardy, second lieutenant in the Guillaume-Tell company (born at Chantilly in 1765), and Pascal Diacre, commander of the Contrat-Social company, were former soldiers and generally considered as different in this civilian force.[19]

Did these men belong to any 'party'? Can they be described as 'government men' or sans-culotte *sectionnaires*? Eude and Lefranc belonged to the Jacobin world; Lefranc was even well off, and the 'carpenter' of the rue Thomas-du-Louvre resembles the 'joiner' Duplay of the rue Honoré. But the resemblance stops there; Lefranc would not become a member of the Jacobins until Vendémiaire Year III,[20] and far from being a Robespierrist, he gloried in his loyalty to the Convention and was even Thermidorean in outlook. His attitude was that of most of the cannoneer officers, who were attached to the Convention rather than to a man or a particular grouping; Eude alone might be considered a Robespierrist, his brother being a member of the General Council of the Commune. Nor were the others Hébertists, and though Lefranc later became a member of the Jacobins, there are no known Cordeliers in this group. Coppin, the brothers Monvoisin and Mirau were *sociétaires* who figured prominently in the Sectionary movement, the first by encroaching on the subsistence area, and alienating the Revolutionary Government in the process, the Monvoisins, with their company at Alençon, displaying all the grievances of the Parisians against the 'égoïstes' and 'fanatiques' of the departments. Potemont, the faubourg man, and Petit emerge from political obscurity simply by virtue of their appearance on the lists of the Babouvists and their proscription in the Years VII and IX. Vallantin, in behaviour a government man, organised everyone else during his missions. Delacroix was anti-clerical, but no Hébertist for all that.

The War Ministry was not able to place its people in the artillery command, and the decisive influence in the choice of officers was that of the *comités révolutionnaires*. They could err in recommending men like Coppin, who were to prove undisciplined *sectionnaires*, but on the whole they succeeded in gaining the acceptance of popular personalities who were also submissive to the authority of central government. If the need arose – as in the case of Poupart's rescue by the Arcis *comité révolutionnaire* – the *comités* would come to the assistance of protégés under attack from the cannoneers or the general body of *sectionnaires*.

The artillery officers were above all men of independent spirit, conscious of their privileged position and feeling themselves superior to their colleagues in the infantry. What is more, they succeeded in establishing this opinion with their own men, with the authorities, and with most of their contemporaries. The artillery officer considered himself the accredited defender of the regime: and expected its gratitude in return.

II   *The fusilier officers*

We know more of the fusilier officer than his undoubtedly more important colleague in the cannoneers. Since military men were more numerous in the infantry than in the artillery, we have abundant documentation on them in the form of individual dossiers. But such an abundance carries its own dangers, for if it informs us of the military careers of many of these officers, it can also give the appearance of a greater preponderance of military men in this corps than existed in reality. The 'civilian' documentation is also misleading, for it concentrates on 'mauvais sujets' and counter-revolutionaries, or those accused as such, particularly in pre-Thermidorean documentation. This is the drawback of all police-initiated material, for the officer or fusilier who leaves behind a dossier is usually the one who has become embroiled with the police, the *comités révolutionnaires*, or the Committee of General Security. The range widens after Thermidor when all the officers become suspect in the eyes of the authorities of the Year III. Always allowing for the style of Thermidorean pronouncements on anything concerning the personnel of the *armée révolutionnaire*, the documentation of the period is nevertheless a rich source of information on the occupations and revolutionary lives of many of the civilians at the head of fusilier companies. The military men on the other hand do not appear in this type of document, for they remained in the army and thus escaped the attention of the *comités civils* and of those responsible for the proscription of these former terrorist units.

Despite these gaps in documentation and the consequent distortions, this material provides information on nearly half the infantry officers (40 out of a total of 81),[21] 24 of whom are military men, the rest civilians. Like the artillery officers they are nearly all aged between thirty and fifty; 5 are over fifty, 3 are less than thirty.[22] While never a veteran corps, the infantry command was nevertheless composed of older men than those on the extraordinary Commissions in the departments. They were the same age as the members of the *comités révolutionnaires* and the militant minority in the Sections, to which most of these officers had belonged. If this sample devotes too much attention to the military men to be truly representative of the corps as a whole, it nevertheless incorporates a wide selection from the Paris Sections (34 out of 48).[23]

(i)   THE MILITARY MEN

This group accounted for a number of detachment commanders, some of the most violent. François Briois, lieutenant of the Loude company from the l'Indivisibilité Section, is one example, who, after having served in the Colonial regiment from 1768 to 1790, took part in the repression at Lyon. François Bouveron, captain of the 1st company of the 1st battalion (Sans-culottes?) was a more level-headed person than Briois, with a history of military service just as long, having served continuously from 1773 to 1792. Chuine, another military man, whom Bouveron replaced at Chauny, was to be denounced by his company for his harshness.[24]

The case of Jean-Baptiste Carteron is more complex, because like many second officers under the Ancien Regime this former officer had abandoned his military career to follow one under the Revolution. He was born at Coiffy (Haute-Marne) in 1754, enrolled in the Vintimille regiment in 1771, and transferred in 1776 to the Berry regiment, which he deserted on the significant date of 13 July 1789. The same day he was elected corporal in the Hulin company of the Parisian *garde bourgeoise*, and the following day took part in the capture of the Bastille. As a Vainqueur de la Bastille his revolutionary career was assured, and he quickly passed through all the grades in the National Guard back in his own department. Commencing as commander of the Jussey National Guard in 1792, he was elected sergeant in the grenadiers of the Haute-Saône, 4th battalion, then a gendarme in the 35th division, and his absence without leave in December 1792 still did not prevent his promotion to lieutenant in the 36th demi-brigade. Finding himself once more in Paris – again probably without leave – this man who flitted in and out of public notice was now, in Frimaire Year II, elected captain of the Lepeletier Section fusiliers.[25]

Carteron's activities, however, were not limited to the exercise of his command. As an inhabitant of one of the most counter-revolutionary Sections of the capital, he was connected with Fouquier-Tinville and the underground police world. In September 1793, by hiding in a cupboard, he became police informer in a shady case of false non-emigration certificates. On his discharge from the *armée* in Floréal he joined Maillard's hit-men and as a member of the police force of the Parisian general staff carried out a number of arrests in Paris and surrounding areas on behalf of Hanriot.[26] The following month he was again of service to Fouquier as a prison spy in the Burlandeux-Pigasse affair, a complicated business involving both royalists and Hébertists (such as the police agent Lafosse) in an attempt to release Marie-Antoinette. Carteron got himself mixed up in the affair, acting from the cover of Mme Bourgoin's house in the rue Grange-Batelière, and finding himself in prison he wrote on 28 Nivôse Year II to his patron Fouquier: 'I have just now learnt of your search for those involved in the plan to rescue Capet's widow. I wanted you to know that I discovered this infamous plot and the conspirators had me thrown in prison in order to silence me...if you grant me an audience you will be astonished at my revelations...'.[27] An inmate of the Ecole Militaire at the time, this hit-man turned informer was a thoroughly nasty piece of work.

Jean Gasson and François Langlois of the revolutionary infantry were also former military men with political associations. The first, at only twenty-five years of age, was the youngest member of this corps; when elected captain of Marat Section company he might even have fallen within the age-range of the first requisition. But he had the backing of the War Ministry, which had a body of supporters in the Section. Gasson was a native of Bordeaux and had served in the Languedoc regiment from 1784 to 1791. He was a volunteer in the 3rd Gironde battalion, and after the destruction of his former company in the Vendée transferred to the 4th regiment of *chasseurs-carabiniers*. Arriving in Paris as a sergeant-major in this corps, he secured permission from the military police to join the *armée révolutionnaire*, and was chosen to command the Marat company. The Marat Section had thus selected someone with all the enthusiasm and imprudence of youth, who would involve his detachment in serious conflict with the local authorities.[28]

Langlois entered the Parisian National Guard in November 1789, after three years in the Lorraine-Infanterie regiment, and at the same time pursued an active revolutionary career in the Marchés Section. At the time of his election as lieutenant in the Marchés company he was a 'herbalist', occasionally a doctor, and a member of the Section's *comité révolutionnaire*. He was an active dechristianiser and would later be one of the hard core of ex-terrorists in the Years VIII and IX.[29]

François Dumany, who was to command the Melun detachment, possessed all the prudence and calmness in which young Gasson was lacking. Born in Paris in 1742, he was over fifty, and after service of twenty years (1760–80) in the Neustrie regiment, he returned to live near the Louvre in Paris. The Revolution gave him the opportunity of a new military career and he quickly advanced through all the promotion stages in the National Guard of his district, then of his Section, and was second-in-command of the Muséum Section armed force when the *armée révolutionnaire* was formed. Another protégé of David, he became captain of the Muséum fusiliers, and remained with his detachment in the Melun district throughout the existence of the *armée révolutionnaire*. The Melun authorities had so much confidence in the good sense of this Parisian soldier, who knew how to restrain the untimely enterprises of his officers and men, that they appointed him to the *comité de surveillance* of their commune. He was admitted to the Invalides when he came out of the *armée révolutionnaire*, and in the

Year IV was back in service again in the company of Meaux veterans.[30]

André Chamot, commander of the detachment sent to Montereau and to the Nemours district, was not destined to have the same success as Dumany in his relations with the local authorities. Born in 1749, he too was a former military man, who had served under the surname 'Sans-Souci' in the Chartres-Infanterie regiment from 1768 to 1776. This son of a *charcutier* in Neuilly-lès-Beaune, on the outskirts of Pontoise, set himself up in the rue Montholon in Paris when he left the army. At the time of his arrest at the Grenelle camp in the Year IV he was described as a second-hand dealer, a trade which he seems to have pursued from the time of his discharge in 1776 to that of his election as captain of the Faubourg-Montmartre company (the 2nd company, 4th battalion) on 24 Vendémiaire Year II.[31] Like many of these former soldiers, Chamot was a militant *sectionnaire* whose loyalty to revolutionary principles explains his involvement in the Grenelle affair.

Charles Loude, captain of the l'Indivisibilité Section company, and later commander of an advance detachment in the Coulommiers region, had spent a decade in the Swiss Guards. His friend Jean Edme, born in 1753, served in the Beaujolais regiment from 1773 to 1790, then in the Parisian National Guard until 1792, and passed into the 102nd infantry regiment on its formation, becoming a lieutenant that same year. Loude and Edme had all the impatience of military men when faced with obstacles raised by the civil authorities, and in the Pontoise district they were to act in a particularly arbitrary manner.[32]

Like Maubant, Dumany, Chamot, and, it seems, Loude, Laurent Macquart served for five years in the Chartres-Infanterie regiment before transferring to the National Guard, from which he purchased his discharge after eight years of service. Born at Bar-le-Duc in 1757, the son of a tapestry-maker working in Paris, Macquart also set himself up in Paris in 1786 as a toy dealer and would later take part in the repression of Lyon.[33] Isidore Ruide, captain of the l'Unité Section company (6th of the 3rd battalion), served for two years in the Vexin regiment, secured his discharge in 1783, and took up residence in the rue de Seine in Paris, where he was still living in the Year III. This former soldier was a member of the *société populaire* in the l'Unité Section.[34] The final military man of this group was Huel, otherwise known as 'Désiré'. After having served from 1764 to 1777 in the Viennois regiment, he was appointed lieutenant of the l'Homme-Armé company (7th in the 5th battalion) on the formation of the Parisian *armée*. He moved to Lyon with his company and was elected member of the Military Commission and *commissaire* on the *comité de présentation* of the *société populaire*.[35]

The former military men, therefore, these second officers from the Royal Infantry regiments, occupied a very important place in the command structure of the revolutionary infantry. Paradoxical as it may seem, they owed this position not to their technical expertise gained in the Ancien Regime armies or in the officer class of the National Guard, but to the service which they had already rendered the Revolution. Several were important *sectionnaires* or political personalities, all were well known in their quartiers, some as members of their *sociétés sectionnaires*, and Langlois in addition was *commissaire* of his Section's *comité révolutionnaire*. Gasson was supported by the Cordeliers and the Hébertist group in the Marat Section; Dumany was also a protégé of David, who placed many such men in the new *armée*. All these military men, therefore, had a solid base in the small-business and artisan world of Paris, whether as toy dealer, herbalist, or tapestry-maker, for all had established themselves there after buying their way out of the army. Most had experienced several years of civilian life before the outbreak of the Revolution. The younger ones still serving in the Royal armies at the time of the Revolution, took advantage of the event to desert and throw in their lot with the new military authority, the urban National Guard, which was anxious to acquire these former soldiers with their valuable infantry experience.

These military men in fact owed a great deal to the Revolution and on the whole showed themselves grateful to a regime which had offered them so much. The departmental authorities were to find them just as capable of 'revolutionising' as the civilians. Furthermore, they were responsible for many of the most flagrant abuses of authority such as the arrest of an entire municipal body about to go into session, and the armed invasion of the premises of a *comité de surveillance*. Such acts of authoritarianism, which would so damage the reputation of the Parisian *armée* and incur the displeasure of the Committee of Public Safety, were committed by men who, from their years of service with the King of France, had retained a sense of contempt for civilians and a lack of respect for elected authorities. Whether arranging military quarters in the name of the King or revolutionising in the name of the Paris Commune and Sections, their mode of action savoured of military despotism. Such brutality might also be directed against the *révolutionnaires*, and to the officers who manhandled the local authorities as though conducting a campaign of military repression, revolutionary style, must be added those who acted like *chiens de quartier* towards their own troops, subjecting them to excessively harsh discipline.

(ii)   THE CIVILIANS

Some civilians among the infantry officers played an important part in the history of the Parisian *armée*. Cardinaux, Thunot, Boisgirault of the Panthéon-Français Section; Réaume, Bonne-Nouvelle Section; Chaumont and Martin, Bondy Section; Grossin, Montagne Section; Gary, Champs-Elysées; Collin and Keller, Gardes-Françaises; Fauveau of the Invalides Section: these were the principal organisers of the infantry's revolutionary action in the departments and the main targets of criticism from local authorities. Some were active for only a short period, but Cardinaux, Réaume and Fauveau were seasoned *révolutionnaires* and belonged to the small number of militant terrorists who sought to maintain some cohesion after the disappearance of the Sectionary institutions. Their period in the *armée révolutionnaire* was to be as important for them as for the military men like Lefranc and Eude in the cannoneers, for not only did it leave its mark in terrorist experience gained at first hand, but it reinforced their political leanings and convictions by exposing them to Thermidorean proscription.

In this respect the most instructive career is undoubtedly that of Pierre Cardinaux, lieutenant in the Panthéon company. It was a Section which accounted for three notable personalities in the revolutionary infantry – a reflection of its advanced political consciousness, rather than an accident of documentation. Cardinaux was another of those foreign artisans who had come as young men to seek their fortune in Paris. A native of Neuchâtel in Switzerland, he had been living in the Sainte-Geneviève quartier since 1770, and had set himself up in business as a caterer-restaurateur some years before the Revolution. An active citizen and an elector of 1792, who had been chosen to carry the flag for his Section's armed force the same year, Cardinaux was made a member of the Panthéon-Français *comité révolution-naire* on its formation in March 1793. With Hû and Jumillard, he quickly established himself as a leading personality in the general assembly and in the *société fraternelle*, playing an active role as the representative of his Section in the *journées* of 31 May and 2 June, and participating in the June–July conflict over plans for the first *armée révolutionnaire*. However, if his career continued into the republican opposition of the years 1795–1801, the cause lay not with Cardinaux himself, an uncultivated and unintelligent man, but in the fact of his wife's acquisition of restaurant premises in a former Génovéfien convent, now national property, during his absence with the *armée*. It was a perilous enterprise at any time, and in Floréal Year II a sure road to bankruptcy for Cardinaux, lately returned to civilian life. Despite this setback, however, the restaurateur borrowed the money to open a new establishment on the place de l'Estrapade. The Bal Cardinaux, as it became known, soon acquired a certain notoriety as the meeting place of 'éxclusifs' and Babouvists (members of the so-called 'club du Panthéon'), where a number of republican conspiracies were hatched, and in consequence was closely watched by the police authorities. Cardinaux himself was only a poor café-owner, who according to contemporary accounts had succumbed to the occupational hazard of the bottle. Too limited ever to make an effective political leader, he nevertheless found himself at the centre of every plot, from his acquaintance with former terrorists who preferred to drink in his establishment – the watering-hole for every republican malcontent. As he explained to Fouché on 8 Pluviôse Year IX, after his sentence of deportation: 'It is true that I proclaimed myself in favour of the republic...to the detriment of my family I acquired some sort of reputation, not out of natural talent, with which I am ill-endowed, and I was never a speaker at any political or public assembly. But I had the misfortune to run a large establishment, where, in conformity with the laws of the time, people gathered to form a political society – my only concern, however, was to sell wine...'. Cardinaux seems to have been popular with his Section – 'a good republican', as he was described by the guards of the Panthéon in a police spy's report – and since he was recommended by Parein it does look as if he may have worked for the political police.[36]

The two officers of the Bondy Section company, Chaumont and Martin, come to our attention rather as detachment commanders. Zealous sans-culottes, excellent officers, and highly regarded by their men, these Parisian artisans were to become scapegoats, sops to rural vengeance for having acted in a revolutionary manner against the authorities in their anxiety to implement requisitions in the capital's favour. Adrien-Josse Chaumont, captain of the Bondy company, was thirty-six at the time of his election. He was a native of Roigny (Eure), a father of six and a master jeweller at 52, rue du Faubourg-Saint-Martin. His lieutenant, Nicolas Martin, was a forty-eight-year-old Parisian and a market porter. Like Cardinaux, they were the object of quite ridiculous accusations; they were paying the penalty of the excesses committed by the Parisian detachments in the countryside, and even more so for the very principle of supplying the towns through force.[37]

Jean-Etienne Réaume, a native of Acy (Oise), captain of the Bonne-Nouvelle company, was one of the most intelligent and consistent of the militant *sectionnaires* in the *armée*. In 1778, after eight years' service in the Queen's regiment, he set himself up as a toymaker in the rue Saint-Denis, the quartier in which Hébert lived. He was thirty-nine at the time of the Revolution and that December he enrolled in the National Guard. In July 1792 he was made second-in-command of the Section's armed force and in June 1793 became postal *commissaire*. A prime example of the militant *sectionnaire*, this former soldier turned tradesman commanded his company in Lyon, and the almost daily correspondence which he maintained with the *comité révolutionnaire* of the Bonne-Nouvelle Section is particularly instructive on the mentality of a revolutionary officer who had come up from the Sections. Repression he entirely supported, and he adopted all the cruel expressions of his neighbour Hébert to mock Lyonnais condemned to the firing squad and the guillotine. Learning of the arrest of Hébert – one of the celebrities of his Section – and of his chief, Ronsin, Réaume expressed no sense of surprise: 'We must beware of all men', he observed philosophically, 'and attach ourselves to principles only.'

In his conformism and his severity towards the Lyonnais, Réaume is a good example of a certain type of revolutionary mentality which reflected something of 'Terror bureaucracy'.[38] He had, for example, a tendency towards denunciation, Dossonville, the royalist police agent, who would later take his own revenge, being one of his victims. But he was no coward: a *sociétaire* of the Year II, in possession of a membership card from the former Bonne-Nouvelle *société* at the time of his arrest, he was to remain faithful to his convictions; he subscribed to Babeuf's paper, and got himself expelled from the Section's guard in the Year III by the Muscadins who detested this prototype terrorist, this 'hero of the Revolution', as one informer called him derisively. He could also be a conspirator when he wanted and would be arrested near the Soleil-d'Or on the night of the Grenelle affair. On this occasion his sentence by the Commission Militaire to three years' detention was reversed because he was not a soldier and not subject to military justice. In Lyon he brought the violence and truculence of the former soldier to the normal activities of this civilian force, and in the Year IV his wife initiated divorce proceedings 'on the grounds of cruelty, mistreatment and serious injury'. Another aspect which identifies him with the militant *sectionnaires* was his economic position as a comfortable shop-owner, and despite his reputation as a terrorist, he was chosen by his fellow citizens in the Year IV as *commissaire* to assist in the estimates and sale of *biens nationaux*. With the full force of his personality as a militant terrorist, Réaume dominated the officers of his company.[39]

Collin, captain of the Gardes-Françaises company, was a glazier. His lieutenant, Keller, was a zealous denouncer and would later appear on Babeuf's lists as a militant *sectionnaire*. He was detested by the Laon authorities for his provocative insistence on pointing out their every infraction of the Maximum, and in the Year III he was himself denounced as a 'terrorist' by his Section. Toussaint Fouques, captain of the Droits-de-l'Homme fusiliers, was a saddler with a large family. On his discharge from the army he was represented as being unemployed and living in the greatest poverty.[40] Nor had the captain and lieutenant of the Contrat-Social company, Henry and Lallemant respectively, any fixed employment; they were unemployed at the time of their election, and recognised the *armée révolutionnaire* as a way out of their misery, a door on to better times. In Lyon their conduct was so scandalous that they were denounced by their men to the *comité* and *société* of their Section. According to the fusiliers, they were constantly drunk, pursued women and played cards. After their return from such an enjoyable mission the two found themselves again out of work and applied to their Section for employment in the postal service.[41]

Henry and Lallemant were not the only men of this type in the *armée*; their colleagues in the Finistère company, the captain, Doré (aptly so-called), and his lieutenant and acolyte in pleasure, Masson, were of the same breed. We know nothing of the civilian life of the fun-loving Doré. In the *armée* he and Masson devoted themselves entirely to women, cards and cafés, in the limited measure that a small town like Honfleur could accommodate the demands of these two Parisian revellers. Like the two officers from the Contrat-Social Section, Doré and Masson were so little concerned about their men and their military and political duties, that in Germinal they abandoned their company on the road and made their own way back to Paris. They were not *sectionnaires* like their men, and when denounced by the latter to the Lazowski *société populaire* for having preferred the gaming table to the affairs of their company at Honfleur, they simply replied that they had better things to do than listen to constant denunciations and that the Lazowski *société* could 'bugger off'.[42]

There are some officers whose civilian occupations we know, but the information adds little to our understanding of their personalities. The captain of the Montagne company, Grossin, had private means and during his stay in the Compiègne district his men denounced him for his softness towards the farmers. Unlike them he did not seem to see these 'blood-suckers' of the people as the enemies of Paris and the Revolution, seeking rather to spare them the experience of requisitions by force. Despite such accusations, which Grossin claimed to be the retaliatory action of certain *révolutionnaires* whom he punished for indiscipline, he was able to secure a position as instructor at the Ecole de Mars, Sablons camp, when he left the *armée*.[43] Davril, second lieutenant in the 3rd company, 3rd battalion, was also detested by his men. This young tailor's assistant, like many provisional officers taken from civilian life, had been intoxicated by over-rapid promotion and made himself detestable to his men by his brutality and his pretensions.[44]

Finally, let us look briefly at those other officers whose occupations we know. Constant, captain of the Faubourg-du-Nord company, was a porcelain sculptor, a protégé of Léonard Bourdon, and a member of this Section's *comité révolutionnaire* in Thermidor; as such he played an active part in rallying his Section to the side of the Convention.[45] As a friend of Bourdon's, Constant was a 'government man' by inclination and personal connections. Dufour, first lieutenant of the Quinze-Vingts company, and one of the few faubourg officers of whom we know something, was a day-labourer at the time of his election. Dumany's lieutenant in the Muséum company, Leconte, was a cutler in the rue de l'Arbre-sec.[46] Antoine Pudepièce, at sixty the oldest officer of the corps, was second lieutenant of the l'Homme-Armé Section company and a saddler with his own carriage-hire business in the rue de Braque. On news of his dispatch to Lyon, 'I obtained leave after a month to put my affairs in order, to sell my carriages and lease my house...'. His business must have prospered, for he was able to live off the proceeds of the sale and the income from his creditors until his arrest as a former terrorist in 1799. He died in prison in 1800, a delayed retribution for his part in the Lyon expedition.[47] In the Year III the former officers and soldiers of the *armée révolutionnaire* were called 'Septembriseurs', but in the Year IV, at the time of the mammoth trial of so-called 'massacreurs', only one former officer was named: René Joly, a twenty-seven-year-old shoe-mender, a former gendarme and lieutenant in the Arsenal company.[48]

(iii) THE POLITICAL MEN

For most of the detachment leaders there is no information either on their occupations or on any previous service. Such is the case with Jean Thunot, captain of the Panthéon-Français company, and his lieutenant, Boisgirault, two officers who were much talked about during their mission to Compiègne. There were two Thunots in this Section, one described as a pedlar, the other as a joiner, and our captain was undoubtedly one of them. We know that in June 1793 he was a member of his Section's commission for *certificats de civisme*. Like Boisgirault he was a political militant, and on several occasions denounced reputed suspects and political adversaries like the *juge de paix* Hû (one of the most controversial personalities in the Panthéon-Français Section) to the *comités révolutionnaires* of the Panthéon-Français and Finistère Sections.[49]

Pierre Fauveau, captain of the Invalides company, is another officer with political leanings whose position in civilian life we know nothing about. A friend of Vézien and Marcellin, he is known to us only by virtue of the many occasions on which he was arrested. He was taken into custody for the first time in Prairial Year II under the Robespierrist dictatorship, again as a former terrorist in the Year III,[50] and his name was on Babeuf's lists in the Year IV. A native of Melun, he was twenty-eight years of age at the time of his election to the *armée révolutionnaire*. But what of the occupations of Lecourtier, captain of the Halle-au-Bled company and such a stern disciplinarian that his men demanded his replacement;[51] or of those known to us only by name, or because of accusations which resulted in their recall to Paris: men like Michel Chaussepied, commander of the Arcis company; Louis Du Mans, captain, Mutius-Scévola company; Edmond, captain, Sans-Culottes company;[52] Queneuille, commander of the Poissonnière company;[53] Gary, who led the Champs-Elysées company to Cluny and Lyon;[54] Bourgoin, commander of the Tuileries armed force, and then captain of its company in the *armée*;[55] Coste, commander of the Réunion company; Surbled, commanding that of Chalier;[56] Villedieu, lieutenant in the Amis-de-la-Patrie company[57]? These unknowns were clearly neither former soldiers nor leading *sectionnaires*, and the denunciations of the Year III, though methodical, did not mention them.

This group of fusilier officers then included leading *sectionnaires*, authentic revolutionaries, disciplinarians from among the former military men, men who spent all their time in the gambling dens, and above all obscure men known only through their declarations of domicile. Nothing distinguishes the latter from the great mass of people in the Sections, whose support had temporarily elevated them to higher things. However, if they forgot their origins and as infantry officers flew their own standard, their men soon recalled them to reality in the Year II. Lecourtier was stripped of his command because his disciplinarianism had alienated his entire company. Chuine, a career soldier in command of a detachment sent to Provins, then to Chauny, found himself the object of similar complaints from his men, and on 22 Ventôse Maubant tried to remind him of the realities of such a political command: 'Comrade, after close examination of your claims and those of citizens Tétu, corporal, Prieur, Pierre Seran and the letter signed by the entire company, it seems clear that there is some animosity between you and them. *Since you are a good soldier, and they are also*, these kinds of quarrels must stop between republicans. . . . You as captain must be a father to these soldiers. When a *révolutionnaire* fails you, you do have a right to punish him...But to become involved in personal quarrels is beneath the dignity of a true republican...This affair is not worth all the fuss it has aroused...'.[58] Grossin too was denounced to his Section for having forgotten that the object of the *armée* was to feed the Parisian sans-culottes and his men considered his indulgence towards the big farmers as some form of criminal *lèse-sans-culotterie*.

These then were the men who – more than the *chefs de bataillon*, few in number and immobilised in garrison towns, more than the artillery commanders whose companies were grouped in the great centres of repression like Lyon and Brest – found themselves in daily contact with the local authorities in the towns and villages. And when one examines the activities of the Parisian *armée* these men, who scarcely figure in the history of the Parisian Sectionary movement, take on new importance. To them fell the task of making this instrument of the Terror effective in the area for which it was created; they also had to shoulder the responsibilities and frequently the risks which this involved.

III   *The cavalry officers*

The peculiar, not to say scandalous, character of the revolutionary cavalry was even more pronounced in its officer corps than in its high command. If most of the *chefs d'escadron* were military men with respectable service records and regular positions in the *armée*, such was not the case with the captains, lieutenants and second lieutenants. Here Mazuel's hasty methods of raising a force made up of all and sundry, and totally dependent on himself, had the most pernicious effects. The officer corps of the cavalry was peopled by favourites over whom Mazuel – the 'Baladin des Brotteaux', as a former friend wickedly called him – had complete control. Mazuel's power derived from the distribution of lieutenancies and second-lieutenancies in 'his' cavalry, and he prided himself on being able to secure confirmation from the War Ministry of all the provisional commissions which he distributed with such abandon to those recommended by the leading figures of the day. 'I was aware...that the treacherous Mazuel, unable to tolerate anyone who knew all his villainies, sought my undoing', Borcsat reported to the Committee of General Security; '...on his private initiative he appointed officers, despite the protests of the Corps...in defiance of the decree which required the appointment of officers from the *scrutin épuratoire*....'[59]

His recruitment methods were a public scandal. Everyone knew that many young men, often within the age-group of the first requisition, found refuge in this corps as lieutenants or second lieutenants.[60] There were also as many deserters in the officer class as in the ranks, and Mazuel gave lieutenancies to foreigners, and well-off young men, whose relatives made pressing requests on their behalf, were also gratified. In this corps Parisians, sans-culottes and *sectionnaires* were rare, while men from the provinces, particularly from the South, abounded. In short, the officer class of the cavalry was a caricature of the entire body. 'As far as I can see', wrote one lieutenant to Mazuel, 'the first squadron is composed of a large number of Prussian deserters and even French deserters from Spain....'[61]

The accuracy of this unfavourable judgement is all too clear from innumerable case histories. Take the French deserters, for example: Romain Richard, a native of Dourdan who was appointed second lieutenant, 1st company 1st squadron, was a twenty-one-year-old deserter from a corps of dragoons.[62] Jean-Baptiste Orhand, the same who had written to Mazuel about the 1st squadron, was a former soldier in the Gardes-Françaises, who had become a fencing master after his discharge, and enlisted in the Beauvais cavalry after having deserted from a corps of chasseurs.[63] Nicolas-Josué Steenhouwer, a Dutch refugee, was also given a position at the request of Cloots. Born in Amsterdam on 7 October 1763, he was a former student cadet in the Dutch navy, who had subsequently transferred to the Hessian Legion. A lieutenant in the Salm cavalry, Steenhouwer had sought refuge in France in 1792 or 1793 and joined the Free Foreign Legion. On his own personal authority Mazuel had him appointed lieutenant in the 1st company of the 4th squadron. It is true that Steenhouwer was soon removed from the corps on Ministerial orders, the law on the organisation of the *armée révolutionnaire* prohibiting the admission of foreigners, but he was the only foreign officer so expelled.[64] Mazuel respected neither law nor minister and simply recruited as he saw fit. Aigoin wrote to him on behalf of 'a dashing young revolutionary', a Belgian in whom Bastide and Goguet were interested. Clearly this 'dashing young revolutionary' was also furnished with a commission, for Mazuel could refuse nothing to his Montpellier friends.[65] Everyone in the *armée* knew that foreigners could easily secure commissions in the new cavalry, as testified by the letters of request to Mazuel from people like Belair, captain of the 3rd Belgian regiment; from Bouquet, lieutenant in the 1st Hainaut battalion; and from 'Georgius Kenessey', writing in Latin, 'houzard hungarus natus bonus Respublicanus', a deserter 'well-educated, unhappy at the military treatment of his country...with a liking for the French Republic'.[66]

Hippolyte Bourgeois falls into the second category of well-off young men who, thanks to influential relatives, found positions in a cavalry destined for service in the interior. A lieutenant at little more than twenty years of age in the 2nd company of the 6th squadron, he was the son of a *Conventionnel*, to oblige whom Mazuel kept the young Hippolyte near him, sharing with him the comfortable existence of a *chef d'escadron*, and installing him in the Cadran Bleu *auberge* near the park of Versailles. But such favours held their own dangers, and young Bourgeois, with a protector become conspirator and *persona non grata* overnight, was himself arrested along with the two young ladies and the carriage-driver who had accompanied them on their outings to the Trianon. The young Bourgeois paid the price of his gilded existence with several weeks in prison, before his father's pleas to

Fouquier-Tinville, the two Committees and to his own colleagues, secured his release. Mazuel was likewise petitioned by Louis Lépine, director of public works with the Paris municipality, to spare his son the horrors of the first requisition.[67]

The case of Pierre-Louis Borcsat is somewhat similar. This twenty-nine-year-old was also a well-off young man. His father was president of the criminal tribunal of the Gex district and a wealthy *notaire* in Ferney-Voltaire, where in 1793 his brother presided over the *société populaire*, in itself a family affair, founded by Jean-Louis. They were all known to Gouly and to Jagot, a member of the Committee of General Security. Borcsat himself joined the light cavalry, but was expelled by the other officers for his attempts to 'republicanise' the ordinary soldiers. Borcsat took his complaint of their 'counter-revolutionary' leanings to the Minister in Paris, and won the ear of the Jacobins, who sent Audouin and Sijas to investigate. Audouin secured Borcsat a lieutenancy in the revolutionary cavalry. In this he did Mazuel a disservice, for Borcsat turned out to be a viper in the nest. He found intolerable the insolence and authoritarian spirit of Mazuel, whom he had known for some time, and quarrelled with him from the outset. An element of jealousy undoubtedly underlay the conflict, for the two men were almost the same age; but the republican of Ferney-Voltaire felt he had better revolutionary claims than the silk-embroiderer and play-boy from La Croix-Rousse. Mazuel in turn found Borcsat an unwelcome witness to his intrigues, and had him arrested and removed on the pretext of indiscipline. Borcsat remained in detention until the *armée* was disbanded, but triumphed eventually when his old enemy was condemned.[68]

Mazuel's Montpellier friends were the first to commend themselves to the good will of their old acquaintance. The former soldier and bailiff from Montpellier, Louis Séran, called 'Mucius', rushed to Paris on learning of the position occupied by his old companion in misfortune – in 1792 they had been imprisoned together in Montpellier as suspected Maratists. While waiting in the antechamber of his powerful friend's office, Séran scribbled this disconcertingly frank note to him: 'I need a little money to survive for another fortnight [in Paris]'. Before that fortnight was up Séran found himself a second lieutenant with the 1st squadron at Beauvais, where he quickly assumed a political role. 'I am going to the *société populaire* with *commissaire* Girard', he wrote to Mazuel, 'and will do all in my power to fire their patriotism – they need it, for there are no more than 50 Montagnard patriots here, that is to say 50 *révolutionnaires*....' An intriguer and an ambitiously political soldier, Séran presided over the *société populaire* when sent to Lyon, and was denounced by the Lyonnais after Thermidor as a terrorist and agent of the repression.[69] Almost the only cavalry officer to find himself in this position, Séran soon attached to himself a group of other young men from Montpellier, attracted to Paris by the same good news: 'Junius' Fayet, Colombel, Laurent Delpêche (Mazuel's brother-in-law), all alike appointed to second-lieutenancies through their friend's favour.

Besides deserters and 'friends', this corps was composed largely of military men – but military men of a different breed from those who dominated the infantry. The cavalry officers were young men serving in the hussars or the dragoons who had secured their transfer to Mazuel's force thanks to connections in the War Ministry or in the political world. There were also some long-serving soldiers like Paul Péré, a captain in the 2nd squadron, who had served in the Gardes-Françaises from 1777 to 1785, then as an army surgeon in the line infantry.[70] Louis Menu was an even more remarkable case – one of those rare veterans with uninterrupted service since 1756, including 22 years as adjutant with the Ile-de-France regiment. He was also one of the few cavalry officers to be disarmed and denounced as a terrorist in the Year III, by the *comité civil* of the Bonne-Nouvelle Section, which places him with the political *sectionnaires* so common among the fusilier and cannoneer officers, but virtually non-existent in the cavalry.[71] But the most typical example of this group was young Hurault from the Contrat-Social Section, who left the Charenton workshops to join the 27th cavalry regiment, moving on to a lieutenancy in the 1st squadron. He was a thankless character who would later denounce Sijas and Mazuel, the two men to whom he owed his new position.[72] In the same way the twenty-one-year-old Jacques Roman moved straight from the 1st regiment of chasseurs to a second-lieutenancy in the 4th squadron, on the recommendation of Xavier Audouin. Roman had arrived in Paris from Grenoble in July 1793. He was soon in trouble with the Guillaume-Tell *comité révolutionnaire*, which suspected him of trying to evade conscription and accused him of scandalous behaviour in his relationship with the wife of a Beauvais *notaire*. On this occasion he was helped by his compatriot, who vouched for his *civisme*.[73] Michel Martin left the dragoons for a second-lieutenancy in the same squadron as Roman, while Chomez made a similar transfer, thanks to help from Duverger, *chef de division* at the War Ministry. Chomez was another of those rare political militants in the cavalry, a member of the Cordeliers club who claimed to have participated in the capture of the Bastille, and a soldier of long standing, having served since the age of eleven both in the Indies and in Europe.[74]

Guignard, a captain in the 1st squadron, had urgent personal reasons for leaving his old corps to seek refuge in the revolutionary cavalry. This former soldier, a native of the Beaujolais, had served under the Ancien Regime in the Gérardmer cavalry. After the Revolution he was appointed to a commission in the Tuileries battalion of the National Guard, moving then to a lieutenant-colonelcy in the 19th infantry regiment. He was well versed in the military practices of the Ancien Regime, and in July 1793 he was denounced by one of his soldiers to the *société populaire* of Mantes 'for shirking his duties' and for having 'cheated the Republic by charging for the clothing of deserters, ... and his soldiers, by taking money from the letters addressed to them...'. Guignard took advantage of the August levy to leave his regiment and have himself appointed to the Beauvais cavalry, where he stayed for several months. But even Mazuel's cavalry sometimes had to defer to the wishes of the sans-culottes in matters of morality. The Mantes *société* had correspondents in the Lyon *société*: Guignard, unmasked, abandoned by his colleagues, and in every way in an unenviable position, was summoned to explain himself and obliged to tender his resignation. Claiming a plot against him, he retired to his village in the Saône-et-Loire.[75]

What was the attraction of this new force for these young men? The chance of rapid promotion perhaps? The hope certainly of a milder discipline than in the dragoon corps and less risk than in the light cavalry. Finally, there was the attraction exercised by all newly-formed corps whose cadres had just been organised. A cavalry which was not 'like any other corps' offered perspectives as dazzling as they were vague and roused the ambitions of young officers languishing in dreary and dangerous cantonments far from Paris. Such ambitions were all the more active when candidates were told that they might by-pass the *scrutin épuratoire* and election by the company, if supported by someone in the War Ministry, by a *Conventionnel*, by Mazuel or by a juror on the revolutionary tribunal.

In such conditions it is not surprising that civilians and *sectionnaires* were rare. There were nevertheless some: Charles Pérony, a captain in the 5th squadron, also appointed on the recommendation of Prosper Sijas, was a thirty-five-year-old stonecutter living in the Halle-au-Bled Section. This man, who undoubtedly owed much to Mazuel, and would join the other squadron officers in Versailles in signing petitions in support of their commander as a 'persecuted patriot', was nevertheless to give evidence against him which would provide Fouquier-Tinville with the basis for his 'military plot' thesis at the time of the Hébertist trials.[76] Mazuel had put together a clientele of 'amis' for nothing. On the day of his arrest these young officers could not dissociate themselves from him quickly enough, and they signed an address congratulating the Convention on its vigilance in having unmasked this 'conspirator' who had succeeded in raising himself to the command of their corps. The 'grandeur mazueliste' (as one 'ami' called it),[77] the personal ascendancy which he exercised over 'his' cavalry, faded with his loss of favour.

But if Pérony thus appears to be an authentic *sectionnaire* in the mould of Bernard Caperon, a lieutenant in the same squadron, there are still some uncertainties about this and a service note of 10 Germinal describes him as being 'an ex-guard of Capet'.[78] As for Delgas, a former adjutant of the Bonne-Nouvelle Section's armed force, then company captain in the revolutionary cavalry, he was highly regarded by the Thermidorean authorities, and would be recommended by his Section to a position on the newly-formed *comités de surveillance* of the arrondissement, to which sans-culottes were not admitted.[79] Finally, Nicolas Thévenin owed his second-lieutenancy to the recommendation of Brisse, president of the *société populaire* of Nancy and a great friend of Mazuel. Thévenin, who had been a clerk attached to the Moselle Legion, was an active member of his *société*.[80] In contrast, one of the few leading *sectionnaires* in this corps, the forty-six-year-old Jean-Baptiste Edme Machard – first captain of the 1st squadron, formerly second-in-command of the Tuileries Section armed force – seems, like Borcsat, to have been a victim of the despotism of Mazuel, who had him arrested at Beauvais on 21 Vendémiaire Year II, and detained in the Sainte-Pélagie. Machard alerted his Section, which rushed to his defence, and denounced Mazuel to the Minister. On 11 Nivôse he was liberated on orders from the Committee of General Security. It was a major defeat for Mazuel, who was already in difficulties by this date. But despite repeated pleas from his Section, Machard never regained his position at the head of the 1st squadron, nor his arrears in pay. He was disarmed at the time of the Thermidorean reaction, but rearmed on 16 Thermidor Year III at the request of the *comité civil* of the Tuileries Section, which praised his moderation. With Delgas, Machard had the rare talent among former *révolutionnaires* of being able to please the Thermidorean authorities.[81]

The officers of the revolutionary cavalry, then, had little to recommend them and the corps fully deserved its poor reputation. Parisian opinion was right in thinking it a refuge for adventurers, deserters and suspects, while the Versailles authorities were scandalised by the insolence and drunkenness of these young officers who imitated the scorn their commander had for the civil authorities. They had an *esprit de corps*, these cavalry officers, and it was a detestable one – the basis of a 'military system' in an army which was intended to be democratic, civilian and Sectionary. Nor did these officers have anything to recommend them in their personal behaviour, and the shady dealings of Guignard were not an isolated case. There was also a scandal in the 6th squadron which had extensive ramifications and compromised several officers.[82] Those who remained idle at Versailles had plenty of time to find yet more ways of discrediting the corps.

It is impossible to arrive at any reliable statistical analysis of the social composition of the officer class and the general staff of the Parisian *armée*. In view of the defective nature of the documentary sources, the military men appear more important than they were in reality. Yet, from the tone of those general orders which have survived, the artillery must certainly have been commanded primarily by civilians. The same was probably true for the fusiliers and it was only the cavalry which had an officer corps composed of true military men.

Out of a total of 117 officers from all divisions, for whom we possess occupational information, there were 60 former soldiers, 15 artisans (4 shoe-makers, 1 stone-cutter, 1 glazier, 1 market porter, 1 harness-maker, 1 basket-maker, 1 cutler, 1 engraver, 1 apprentice mason, 1 assistant to a tailor, 1 clockmaker, and a fireman); 10 were linked in some way or other with the luxury trades (1 fencing master, 1 drawing master, 1 assistant to a silversmith, 2 assistants to jewellers, 1 porcelain sculptor, 1 decorator, 1 fan merchant, 2 caterer-restaurateurs); 3 or 4 had been in service (2 house servants and a wigmaker); 11 were shop-owners or retailers (2 toyshop-owners, 1 herbalist, 1 stationer, 1 haberdasher-clothier, 1 saddle-seller, 1 second-hand dealer, 1 Rouen 'manufacturer', 2 'merchants', 1 café-owner); there was 1 architect–building contractor (Lefranc), and the actors accounted for 7 (6 of them on the general staff). There were 6 known foreigners, 5 of them in the cavalry (2 Belgians, 1 Dutch, 3 'Germans'), 5 deserters from the cavalry, 2 farmers, 1 day-labourer, 2 clerks or office workers, 2 'without occupation', several 'rich young men', a bailiff, and a man of the law (Parein). The civilian element dominated in the artillery, and undoubtedly, though to a lesser extent, the infantry – though the division between civilian and soldier in the artisan and small-trade world is somewhat artificial, since former soldiers tended to return to such trades after leaving the army. A typical career would be that of the son of an artisan, tradesman or farmer, who joined the army at the outbreak of the Seven Years War, bought his discharge around 1780 and set himself up in a small business in Paris, or, more rarely, as a government clerk. With the Revolution, this former soldier, already well integrated into the life of his quartier, had an advantage over his fellow citizens, and with the formation of the bourgeois National Guard would secure a rank superior to that he held when discharged from the army. In some cases he would have been appointed an officer as early as 1789 or 1790 in virtue of his military expertise, and if promotion came too slowly in the Parisian National Guard, he could always join that of the smaller towns. In any event, the former soldier had been well launched on his new revolutionary career, where, for the less known, a commission in the Parisian artillery or infantry represented the pinnacle of achievement.

Another means of access was by way of the Sectionary institutions, comités, sociétés, or as reward for participation in the great journées. Married men of more mature age tended to dominate the artillery and infantry; the cavalry officers were generally younger and unmarried, and in the eyes of the sectionnaires, bachelors in uniform were birds of prey, and objects of scandal.

The motives which lay behind the enrolment of the cavalry officers in the new armée are outlined in the foregoing group study. For the artillery and infantry the reasons for joining were the same for the officers as for the men, and will be discussed later. However, there is no doubt that vanity played a greater role in the motives of the former. Election to a captaincy, lieutenancy or second-lieutenancy was not only a kind of political apotheosis, but gave a sense of sweet victory to these small tradesmen, and even more to the former non-commissioned officers, whose wildest dreams were suddenly realised. Commissions were bitterly sought after in the artillery and infantry, and some of those elected succumbed to the temptation to abuse an authority which was more apparent than real. The cavalry was a different case entirely and lieutenancies could be won, without the preliminary of the scrutin épuratoire, through personal contacts; and far from being a proof of one's civisme, a commission in this branch was more likely to be a cause for suspicion.

These marked political and social differences between the cavalry and the other two branches of the *armée* were reflected also in the behaviour of the different officers. The cavalry officer behaved almost as badly as his men; the cannoneer officer had a political conscience as sharp as that of his men; the fusilier officer held himself apart in an attempt to impose a sense of military values on these civilians – in which attempt he would fail completely.

PART II   THE REVOLUTIONARY SOLDIER

In such a political army the soldier was more important than the officer. The officer was elected and could also be broken by the soldier; the latter considered military hierarchy and military discipline for slaves only, and since he and the officer he elected came from the same social milieu, the haberdasher fusilier addressing his butcher or master-shoemaker neighbour, who happened also to be his captain, did not consider the phrase 'ton égal en droit' ('your rightful equal'), with which the sans-culottes liked to conclude letters, an empty formula. He was indeed his officer's equal and if that officer tried to pull rank or impose discipline, he was quickly called to task by the administrative Council, or more likely by the *comité* or *société* of the Section. The *révolutionnaire* had no respect for rank; he was prepared to follow the orders of his officer voluntarily, if that officer seemed to act like a 'revolutionary patriot', but at no time would he abandon his rights as a *sectionnaire*.

It is important to get to know this man, the fusilier or cannoneer, for in the last analysis he *was* the *armée révolutionnaire*. This egalitarian army was not a disciplined force and when the *révolutionnaire* left Paris, the instructions and flattery of the *comités révolutionnaires* would still be ringing in his ears. It was his duty to keep a watchful eye on the 'malveillant', an ear pealed for the malicious word, and above all, 'to watch over the grain supply', and ensure food supplies for his family and his friends. *Force à la loi* was the motto inscribed on his flag, but of that law he was the guardian and interpreter, and if the authorities, however constitutionally established, chose to contest his actions, it was a sign of their ill will towards Paris. In the eyes of the unaccommodating and totally humourless *révolutionnaire*, all opposition to his mission was deemed an act of counter-revolution. Such an attitude augured ill for relations between the detachments and the local authorities, and for the maintenance of even the most elementary discipline.

It is hard to imagine a man as full of his own importance, as touchy and as suspicious as the *révolutionnaire* Conscious also of the urgency of his mission, and like all sans-culottes relentless in its pursuit, his attitude towards the country people, made up of distrust, fear, pride and the desire to punish, was an important element in the conduct of operations. To the country people these Parisians seemed intolerable, which indeed they were. But there were also 'frères' in the departments, less well instructed, less schooled in the Revolution, because not fortunate enough to be Parisians, but sans-culottes like himself nevertheless, who must be helped and instructed. Pathologically distrustful of the farmers, Ronsin's soldier was naïve enough to credit the wildest accusations against them, when made by those shrewd enough to represent themselves – often a mere pose – as his rural 'frères'.

The behaviour of the individual was rendered more important by the scattering of the *révolutionnaires* in tiny detachments. It was rare for the *armée* to arrive in force in any given region, save in the case of major missions to suppress revolts. On the whole its image for the country people was that presented by a half-dozen moustached and unkempt men, who swore heartily all the curses and damnations of the *Père Duchesne*, but who were, on the whole, easygoing, unless provoked or fired by the discovery of keys to wine cellars. Above all they were not warlike and were visibly inept in the use of arms. But the countryside was filled with real ex-soldiers, and one can but imagine the cynicism of these 'veterans', obliged to watch the clumsy manoeuvres of these artisans and Paris shopkeepers, disguised as soldiers in their blue and red uniforms. A group of a dozen or so *révolutionnaires* were not at risk when they tried to instil fear into the countryside. But sometimes groups of two or three were sent alone into an area, and it is not surprising that their pose as masters in revolution sometimes exposed them to unfortunate consequences. These faithful apostles of Parisian doctrines, so sure of themselves when they left the metropolis, would be thrashed and half-killed by the villagers leaving church after mass, for having dared to preach the gospel according to *Père Duchesne* to these Thiérache villagers, hostile to innovation and baffled by the presentation of St. Joseph as simply an old man. The village on the edge of the wood was not the Sectionary assembly, and traditional religious imagery was far more acceptable than that of the *marchand de fourneaux* – the *Père Duchesne's* glorification of *sans-culotterie*. The isolated *révolutionnaire* was wrong to place so much confidence in his pipe and moustache; the peasant was not that easily impressed. Thus was the poor Parisian delivered over to the rural populace. Sometimes he was overcome by panic and deserted his post, taking refuge with the nearest *comité de surveillance*; sometimes, prudently, he allowed himself to be 'contaminated'.

The revolutionary soldier has been the subject of so many legends that it is difficult to discover the truth. For some he was simply a brigand in differ-ent clothing, one of a 'bande à la Cartouche';[83] for others he was the proto-type proletarian, a member of the workers' militia, a man from the fau-bourgs animated by a sense of class. What kind of man was he in reality? Why did he enrol in the Parisian *armée*? What was his family situation? Was he violent, a man of blood? Before examining him at work, we must first try to understand the man himself. We will try to isolate some characteris-tics common to the entire corps by studying the individual amidst his fears and suspicions, certainly no longer the pure and flawless *révolutionnaire* of legend, but a small Paris shopkeeper or artisan, thrown into a hostile and dangerous world of small courtyards and vines, of fields and presbyteries with cellars all too well stocked, an expansive countryside, dotted with church steeples and wayside crosses, all alike provocations in his eyes. We must explain rather than judge the man – a task worth the effort, for Ronsin's soldier is a little-understood figure, and yet one whose very ubiquity brought the humbler side of the Paris revolution into many different parts of France. This section we have entitled 'the revolutionary soldier', though he himself would have preferred the term '*révolutionnaire*' or 'sans-culotte', and one thing he would not have tolerated was being called a 'soldier'.

I *Portrait of the* révolutionnaire

The *révolutionnaire* may have sported the moustache, pipe and sabre of Thermidorean imagery, but the resemblance between the real man and the traditional portrait of a Terrorist stops there.[84] Even if the moustache did constitute part of the *révolutionnaire's* attire, it was considered more a sign of virility than anything else, and did not necessarily transform its wearer into a violent brigand. Indeed some authorities made the moustache obligatory, the order of the Limoges *comité de surveillance* for the levy of the Haute-Vienne battalion, for example, referring to the 'moustache, hair worn loose and unpowdered...' and the 'sans-culotte uniform' as compulsory attire.[85] 'Nothing equals the frightening display staged for the accused', wrote Prudhomme of the *révolutionnaires* on duty with the revolutionary tribunal in Brest, 'placed between two gendarmes with sabres unsheathed, before them a soldier of the *armée révolutionnaire* flamboyantly rattling his sword, his face topped by an enormous mat of hair and darkened by a heavy moustache, his bloodthirsty and sparkling eyes barely perceptible...'.[86] The moustache was clearly intended as a ferocious accessory, to strike fear into the peasantry. There can be no doubt that they were alarmed by the very sight of these moustached soldiers, whom they considered plunderers and precursors of the *chauffeurs*, to the extent that the country people around Meaux called one leader of a group of *révolutionnaires* 'General Moustache'. For the orthodox *sectionnaire* in the fusiliers or cannoneers, the moustache identified him with the figure from Parisian legend who appeared on the title-page of Hébert's journal. For the country people the same trait symbolised the brigand and the mercenary. The Lyonnais who appeared before the terrible Commission des Sept were struck by the 'ferocious appearance' of Parein, Corchand and their colleagues, sinister Punch-like figures with their moustaches and huge plumed judge's hats. Likewise the farmers and their wives, roused in the middle of the night by detachments making domiciliary visits, and still half asleep, were terrified by the sight of these strangers with their huge bushy moustaches, rifling the drawers and cupboards.

It was, however, an external ferocity, and far from being a man of war the *révolutionnaire* was simply a family man, of mature years and from a peaceful, small-trading background. Most of Ronsin's soldiers – the cavalry excepted – were, like the officers, aged between thirty and forty-five, a few being fifty to seventy, and some really infirm.[87] Indeed, the *commissaire des guerres* in Paris lamented 'the sexagenarians' among these soldiers 'showing all the decrepitude of their age', and 'others who were so sickly that common sense ought to dictate their non-admission'.[88] Maubant recommended the discharge of one soldier, Mouret (known as 'Sans Dents') 'who is deaf and incontinent'; and the health officers granted leave to many because of hernias, a widespread condition among these middle-aged artisans. But the greatest weakness of these second-rate soldiers was their drunkenness. Old Mouret's case was not an isolated one, and *chef de bataillon* Donville attributed 'the clumsiness of some soldiers in the handling of their arms' largely to their 'drunkenness and slovenliness...'.[89] So well established was this reputation of the *révolutionnaire* as a drunkard, that when the *commissaires* of the Finistère Section arrived in a village of the Yonne, at the head of a small detachment, their first act was to seize the key to the *auberge* to prevent the soldiers from ensconcing themselves in it.[90]

In this respect the *révolutionnaires* quickly acquired the habits of real soldiers throughout the ages: those of eating and drinking without paying. Laukhard describes the descent of a detachment bound for Lyon into the Saône valley between Mâcon and Villefranche, a land of plenty the like of which these Parisians had never before seen: 'On several occasions we went into bourgeois homes where people supplied us with free drink, knowing that the sans-culotte was not fond of paying'. Further on, having somehow or other got past Mâcon, 'we stopped for at least half an hour at every *auberge* en route, drinking heartily, paying rarely...'.[91] A wigmaker's assistant from the Quinze-Vingts Section announced his intention of joining the *armée révolutionnaire* to a client whom he was about to shave, adding candidly 'that he expected quite a spree drinking the farmers' wine and eating their chickens' -- a remarkably agreeable method of 'revolutionising' the countryside and one which the *révolutionnaires* sought to apply in many areas. At Saint-Brice, in the Gonesse district, they 'allowed themselves to be wined and dined, and consumed about two-thirds of a *demie* [?] of *vin de pays*'. At Clairoix, near Compiègne, a detachment took two casks of wine from the mayor's house and did not pay at the *cabarets* for their drinks.[92] Drunkenness, in fact, was the cause of most of the incidents between these political soldiers and the regular troops, and the authorities everywhere ordered the closure of the *auberges* after 9 p.m. to put an end to such disputes. It also explains much of the throw-away language employed by the Parisians when talking with the local authorities. Furthermore, in such remote villages, the sans-culottes had little to relieve their boredom in the evening but the *société populaire*, which met only two or three times a *décade*, the bed of an obliging *paysanne*, of whom there were insufficient to go around, or the saloon. Most opted for the latter. These thirty- or forty-year-olds were long accustomed to supplementing insufficient diets with vile Choisy wine. And anyway, one could drink more on a tour of duty than at home: for most *révolutionnaires* such a mission was a picnic in the countryside (a *partie de campagne*), and later they would tell of the good time they had then. In the café these bored and nostalgic Parisians would become more and more violent in their verbal, and often their physical attacks on a populace which they considered hostile.[93] Then woe betide those saints in their grottoes and those wayside crosses.

The *révolutionnaire* was usually a family man,[94] with a son at the frontier – which made him more than ever conscious of his privileges as a defender of the regime. He had no desire to be used on garrison duty – he had better things to do than march up and down on guard – and when it was proposed to assign them to the defence of the Channel coasts, these Paris shopkeepers refused to leave their cantonments on the grounds that it would constitute 'foreign service'. Their dispatch to Lyon aroused bitter resentment: they had been deceived, they claimed, for they had enlisted on the express condition of serving only near Paris. The *commissaires des guerres* and officers were incensed by this assertive tendency, and if, according to Boissay, the *armée* was 'in general worthy of its name', he had to admit to the Minister that there were 'some individuals who spend more time looking for ways of protesting than concentrating on their duties. I am overwhelmed with these complaints from morning till evening...every day I have 200 or 300 to reply to, which leaves me scarcely any time to do my work...'.[95] The 'barrack-room advocate' was a particularly pervasive character in this civilian army. The Parisians intended to derive the maximum benefit from their enrolment and to get everything they considered their due. In the departments they demanded lodging with the locals – preferably the richest – and privileged treatment, with a butcher and baker assigned exclusively to their needs in each locality; as defenders of the regime they had to have white bread. Already overpaid, they demanded, in addition, supplementary wages for serving more than two miles from their cantonments, claiming as justification the right of the gendarmes to such payment. Sometimes they had the audacity to make their victims pay for their services by levying 'revolutionary taxes' and pocketing the receipts. Overpaid soldiers, making intolerable demands – the municipalities thought the Republic far too generous.

Moreover, they were full of their own importance. 'I am from the *armée révolutionnaire*, no *commissaire* controls me,' one fusilier from the Réunion company claimed when a member of a *comité révolutionnaire* raised objections to his employment.[96] This happened in Paris. In the provinces the soldiers were worse, and as soon as they arrived in a village they would rush to the tribune of the *sociéte populaire*, uttering threats against the 'malveillants' and words of protection and encouragement for their poor 'frères'. Artisan or small shopkeeper in Paris, launderer, wine-grower, day-labourer, gardener or porter from the city's outlying communes, the *révolutionnaire* shared all the prejudices of the *sectionnaire* against 'les gros': merchants, farmers, corn-factors, entrepreneurs, men of the law. For the merchant, particularly those involved in supplying food, he held a particular hatred. Coppin's attitude towards the butchers of Bonne-Nouvelle was replicated throughout the fusilier and cannoneer corps, not only when they were on mission, but even more in Paris. A *charcutier* in the rue de la Vannerie, Arcis Section, lodged a complaint with the police commissioner against an individual 'in national uniform who claimed to be in the *armée révolution-naire*', and who, after buying a saveloy costing five sols, 'complained that it was too dear and that all traders were vagabonds and scoundrels who should be guillotined, and if he had any say in it they would all be guillo-tined on the spot'.[97] Words in the wind, but representative of a feeling widespread among these soldiers.

In the small towns they harassed the *comités de surveillance* – torn between fears of appearing lukewarm and a desire to spare their fellow citizens – with daily denunciations against infractions of the Maximum. The *révolution-naires* were not beyond reproach themselves in this respect, and some took advantage of their stay in the country to go from farm to farm buying eggs and butter at giveaway prices. Indeed one butcher from the Tuileries Section actually sent entire carcasses back to his shop there, though this was probably an exceptional case. But always the soldier shared the small con-sumer's prejudices against the dealer in foodstuffs, small and large alike. Prejudices already well developed in Paris increased apace as they moved away from the capital and these Parisians were convinced that all the mer-chants in the departments were in league to defraud them.

Suspicious of the merchants and 'les gros', they eagerly received the complaints of the 'poor sans-culottes', whether they were comfortable innkeepers or purchasers of *biens nationaux*. The Tuileries cannoneers told Laukhard that nearly all 'the local population [of Mâcon and Lyon] were contemptible merchants who brazenly fleeced the poor craftsmen, workers and labourers of their wages'. 'Those kind of people have nothing better to do than flaunt their wealth and assume airs and graces and don't give a damn for the poverty and distress of the poor devils who toil and sweat for them. . . .'[98] Laukhard, writing in the nineteenth century, was undoubtedly ascribing a sense of class to these *révolutionnaires* which they were far from possessing; nevertheless one recognises in these words the egalitarianism and puritanism, the moral condemnation of luxury and idleness, which was the essence of sans-culotte 'thought', something behavioural rather than doctrinal. It was their mission then to assist the 'poor craftsmen', and in Normandy, in the Gonesse district, in the Yonne and in the Soissonnais, they lent a willing ear to the complaints of the agricultural labourers, the village artisans, the fishermen's wives, the raftsmen, who came to seek their protection against the big farmers, the men of the law, the moderates. The Parisian's self-esteem was flattered by this role as redresser of wrongs, defender of the poor, and he saw himself as something of a sans-culotte St.

Louis. Seated, not under an oak, but in the *auberge*, he listened eagerly to the *aubergiste*, a self-styled 'Mère Duchesne', complaining about 'les gros' of her village. Taking little account of his own ignorance of the people and the ways of the country, the somewhat summary and naïve concern of the *révolutionnaire* for social justice frequently led him to interfere in protracted village disputes.

The 'sixteen commandments of the patriot' stressed vigilance above everything else.[99] The *révolutionnaire* took his instructions about internal enemies extremely seriously, and in village and town was a zealous denouncer, not only of economic offences, but sometimes also of 'mauvais' words. In Lyon one of the victims of the cannoneers' 'denunciation' was a young girl with the charming name of Fanchette, who was courageous enough to say in their presence that she had brought food every day to 'the brave men of Lyon' during the siege, and would do it again if she had to.[100] This was an extreme case, for Fanchette, like so many Lyon people, did not conceal her hatred for the Parisians. The *révolutionnaires* were also quick to condemn any criticism of the regime; they denounced one Vernon man for having stuck his tongue out each time he heard the word 'Republic' uttered in his presence,[101] and pointed 'in horror' to those expressing the peculiar desire to 'shit on the Republic' or to 'bugger the nation'. In Paris someone was arrested for having called the *armée révolutionnaire* 'nothing but a pack of informers'.[102] Informers they were not, and as denouncers they were less zealous and certainly less dangerous than the practised experts – the country people, the embittered wives, the concierges, the 'crows' – but like all sansculottes, they attached immense importance to words, and since they were totally lacking in any sense of humour (irony and wit being the prerogative of the former privileged classes), they made no allowances for the linguistic excesses of the ordinary people, particularly the housewife infuriated by the difficulties of everyday life under a beleaguered republic. For them it was all a matter of visible orthodoxy, and they affected an often ridiculous zeal in their effort to locate signs of the Ancien Regime or of 'superstition'. Just as the electors of the Bon-Conseil Section preferred to eat off the table at a fraternal banquet, after having broken some 50 plates bearing the fleurs-de-lis, so the members of the Vernon contingent – and these were the 'purs' – caused considerable anxiety to a cost-conscious municipality by complaining of the floor covering of the Maison-Commune which bore the pattern of the cursed flower.[103] Few local authorities shed any tears over the departure of these wearisome Arguses of the Revolution.

Their iconoclasm, the childish pleasure they took in the destruction of religious objects, were all part of the need to stress a fundamental orthodoxy, and at the same time it symbolised the anticlericalism, even the entrenched anti-Catholicism, of the Parisian *petit peuple*. It would be wrong to think of them as militant atheists; their intervention in religious matters was entirely negative and destructive, as will be seen when the dechristianising activities of the *armées révolutionnaires* are examined more fully.

The *révolutionnaires* were citizens rather than soldiers; each was conscious of himself as part of the national sovereignty, and when one is a member of the sovereign people, the nagging by commanders is more difficult to endure. 'They called themselves by this name [of sans-culottes] or *révolutionnaires*, but they would not be called soldiers or even volunteers', remarks Laukhard. 'Military discipline meant little to them, and they repeatedly threatened to smash any officer who commanded them to do anything other than march against the aristocrats'.[104] In conflicts with their officers, whom they frequently denounced for brutal conduct reminiscent of the Ancien Regime, or even more for having slept with Lyonnaises, they mobilised not only their own Sections, but the departmental *comités* and *sociétés*. The Lyon sans-culottes, who detested all Parisians, were delighted at the opportunities thus offered of throwing oil on the fire by actively taking up the defence of some soldiers in the revolutionary garrison, victims of their commanders' 'despotism'. Grammont tried in vain to rally the captain of the detachment at Provins, who was detested and completely outflanked by his men. 'Without discipline, there can be no strength,' he urged. While Maubant reminded his own troops: 'You cannot be good soldiers if you do not submit to military procedures . . . You have elected your commanders . . . You also owe them obedience. Certainly you and they are equals outside the service, but while that service lasts discipline and the most perfect obedience must guide you . . .'.[105] Such efforts were lost on these Parisians. They did not want to listen. If they did not win their cases against the officers they still had the right to resign, and the cannoneers in particular used this way out more and more frequently, citing family or business reasons. If they were refused leave, they took it anyway.

The *révolutionnaires* also found additional reasons in their service records for this ready insolence towards their officers. Survivors of the Champ de Mars, combatants of 10 August, strategists of 31 May did not need to be forced to serve, and Maubant reminded the local authorities that the Parisian soldiers were 'veterans' of the revolutionary movement. It was a way of explaining, if not excusing, their often intolerably arrogant conduct.

As civilians these strange soldiers were not primitive animals. Certainly they wholeheartedly approved of the pitiless repression directed against all the Lyonnais, regardless of their social origin; some soldiers played a direct role in it, others were spectators or guards at the executions. In letters to their Sections, they complacently totted up the daily toll of victims, noting with satisfaction the acceleration of the carnage in vulgar language reminiscent of the black humour of the *Père Duchesne*'s account of the *petite fenêtre* (the guillotine). In this cruel imagery shooting the Lyonnais is translated, 'making the people of this vile town dance the *carmagnole* to the tune of the garrison commander'. But the *révolutionnaire* was no butcher. His violence was largely verbal, part and parcel of the revolutionary orthodoxy, and too much importance must not be attached to it. Indeed there was a kind of demagoguery of verbal violence, with the commanders in particular outdoing each other in its usage and setting the example for the ordinary *révolutionnaires*.[106] But more remarkable perhaps were the number of officers and men in Lyon who pitied the fate of the crucified population to the extent even of protesting against the repression. According to the statements of the Lyonnais in the Year III there were some *révolutionnaires* who, at the risk of being condemned as counter-revolutionaries, were prepared to go beyond protests to help the people hide or escape that plagued city.

Conformist rather than naturally cruel, most of these Parisians were honest fellows. And even though temptation was frequently put in their way, particularly when instructed to guard sequestrated property, misappropriation of the caches of money and silver was rare, and these usually ended up in the national crucible after careful inventorying. The soldier had fewer scruples, however, when it came to wine, eau-de-vie and chicken. Everything drinkable and edible was fair game, a kind of *taxe de guerre*, a duty on *incivisme*.

Some cannoneers en route through Avallon proclaimed the doctrine that in 'times of revolution there were no laws, only the people, which was sovereign'. It was occasioned by their report to the *société populaire* of a decision taken by a *juge de paix*.[107] A similar claim appears in the document which Chaumont prepared for his defence before the Aisne tribunal; in times of revolution, he argued, it is not always possible to act within the law, and since the *armée révolutionnaire* was instructed to take action against the internal enemies by every means possible, it could not always follow laws proclaimed in calmer times. Instead he invoked an alternative law: that of 'revolutionary necessity'. Do these two examples indicate a consciousness of popular sovereignty exercised through the *sociétés populaires* as assemblies of the people? This is perhaps making too much of the tendency of the *révolutionnaire* to favour the local *société* wherever he went, which was largely due to his need to seek allies among the militant minorities in a generally hostile countryside. The *carte de visite* was the Parisian soldier's diploma from his Section's *société populaire*, and his first action on arrival in a new locality was to deposit it with the local *société*. Indeed he would be annoyed if none existed; its absence spoke ill of the patriotic sentiments of the populace, for in his mind, if one was free and republican, one joined a people's organisation to read the laws. When a *société* existed the Parisian became a member, and could then leave two diplomas at his next posting, a double testimonial to his *civisme*.

But all this did not amount to any desire for direct democracy or the replacement of the Revolutionary Government and Convention with a new hierarchy of *sociétés*. Such an idea did not occur to the majority of Ronsin's soldiers, who, in their lack of respect for the local authorities, made attachment to the Convention a veritable cult, and the device, *Force à la loi*, an article of faith. Nor was this 'loi' that of the criminal tribunals or the magistrates; it was, rather, the decrees of the Convention, itself the organ of the popular will. When the Convention spoke, the *révolutionnaire* obeyed. In

Germinal when it decreed that it no longer needed the *armée révolutionnaire*, the soldiers rushed to resign before the official disbandment, as a sign of their voluntary submission. At no time did they consider resisting a decree of the Convention. 'We are your children, we exist only through you, we will cease to exist on your command,' proclaimed the soldiers in Lyon; and their acceptance of the official version of the 'crimes' of their commanders is one example of such submission. If the Convention said that Ronsin, Mazuel and the Grammonts were conspirators, then it must be true. This was not simply inertia on the soldiers' part, nor even orthodoxy or ignorance; the *révolutionnaire* believed in the Convention.

II   *Motives for enrolment*

The portrait sketched above will help explain why more than 6,000 men in their prime, mostly from Paris or its outskirts, enlisted in the revolutionary artillery or infantry. The extreme case is that of the Quinze-Vingts wigmaker who hoped to 'have a spree' at the expense of the peasantry; belonging to an endangered profession, he had nothing to lose by enlisting and everything to gain from such a highly paid service. Unemployment or under-employment, high wages, the promise of gastronomic spoils, and undoubtedly for the wigmaker the thought of all those farm girls – this was the range of attractions outlined in the account by Taine and indeed in those of many contemporaries. Many sans-culottes, scandalised by the gilded idleness of the soldiers left in the Ecole Militaire, asked what purpose this *armée* served except as a leisure pursuit for the idle, the drunken and all the riff-raff attracted by the promise of food and lodging.

These explanations cannot be entirely set aside, but it would be wrong to accept them as generally applicable. Merchants, sometimes well-off ones, or artisans in prosperous trades, did not enlist to escape starvation, but for a number of different motives, which included revolutionary enthusiasm, a taste for adventure, and the vanity of the civilian attracted by a uniform. There was a Tartarin in many of these shopkeepers who dreamed of setting off to impose the law on the provincials. Others thought they could help supply Paris by threatening the greedy farmer with force if he did not send grain voluntarily – an understandable pattern of reasoning when the crisis seemed to have been brought about by the selfishness of the farmers. Then there are the imponderables – such as the violent temperament of some who viewed this instrument of the Terror as an excellent opportunity for action.

These were the stated motives. But the regular soldiers detested the *armée révolutionnaire*, not only because of its high pay, but above all because they considered the *révolutionnaires* cowards, who were afraid of being sent to serve on the frontiers. The laws governing the organisation of the Parisian *armée* made it difficult for such men to enlist; but there were ways of evading the law, especially if you were rich and powerful, and several young men subject to conscription managed to gain places in this army designed for domestic service only. But they were the exception; the revolutionary authorities were on the watch for such cases, and most of those of conscription age were eventually ferreted out. It was a question of the honour – and thereby the efficacity – of the new corps. The presence of well-off young men in its ranks, once it was known to Sectionary opinion, could act as a worm in the fruit. Chance also played its part, for the *armée* recruited wherever it went, and a chance encounter in an *auberge*, a conversation in a barber's shop, might provide an opportunity for the unattached, the itinerant, the pedlar to join. Some of these men who had become attached to the life of the road were former soldiers, and could not fail to be attracted by service in an *armée* which satisfied the desire to be constantly on the move.

'In times of revolution the extremes meet' is a theory of government held by *ultras* and *citras* alike, a way of justifying repression and human sacrifice by the principle of revolution, a theory which has always found favour with 'centralisers' and bureaucrats – a Robespierrist theory, in other words. The theory has some validity when applied to the Parisian *armée*; there were certainly authentic counter-revolutionaries in it, princes and returned émigrés badly in need of documents to prove their *civisme*, servants who had accompanied their masters into the Belgian provinces or into Germany, been abandoned by them without pay and made their way back to France clandestinely. Where better to shelter than in the heart of a para-revolutionary institution? Nothing could have been easier. The cavalry was there at Versailles to receive them. Some suspects even managed to get into the infantry. But we only know of those who were discovered. In the disordered state of France in the Year II, others must have found a safe shelter far from the eyes of the Sectionary *comités* and the municipalities of their places of origin.

Certain trades were subject to requisition for war work: shoemakers and locksmiths, for example, could be obliged to work for wages set by the Maximum to supply the needs of the armies. Despite rulings excluding workers in these categories from the *armée révolutionnaire*, many did join, and it took several months – the life-span of the *armée* in fact – to get the locksmiths, shoemakers, iron-workers and engravers out again.

Finally there were the criminals, the bandits, patrons of every new institution. An *armée* whose main task was to make domiciliary visits to peasant households was an excellent screen for banditry, and a number of bandit chiefs operating in the Seine-et-Oise region gained valuable experience there.

But the best way of discovering motives for enrolling is to ask the *révolutionnaires* themselves, always taking into account the date of their explanations. Until Germinal Year II they still gloried in what was, until then, seen as a patriotic action. After the disbandment of the *armée*, however, the tone changed and they instead sought excuses for having entered a body already seen as suspect. After Thermidor every explanation was coloured by the need to apologise. It was no longer something to be boasted about, and in the Year III the former *révolutionnaires* stressed need above all else; with a large family, they had not thought they could afford to refuse such employment. This was indeed the explanation preferred by their adversaries; yet before Thermidor every *révolutionnaire* had tried to refute the idea that he had been attracted by the high pay.

The explanation put forward by Pierre Prévost of the Contrat-Social Section was undoubtedly that preferred by the *révolutionnaires* and that which they would have liked to see accepted by their fellow citizens. Aged thirty-seven, Prévost was a former soldier, who had served from the age of sixteen to thirty, then worked as a ferryman. He wanted to enrol in the Muséum Section's fusiliers and wrote to the Section's *comité révolutionnaire*: 'Citizen president, wishing to be of use to my country, and with no sense of strain on either my heart or soul, I thought I would present myself to you ...my decision to join this corps comes not from the pay which is higher than any other force...but because it will allow me to serve my country – ...I will go to serve in any department to which I might be sent without asking a sou extra...the desire to join this corps came only after self-examination, and I said to myself: only known and honest citizens are taken, and that is the truth...'. Fine words! But though he may have been an honest fellow, Prévost was clearly carried away by his new authority. Admitted as a fusilier in the Muséum company, he was arrested on 6 Ventôse by the Contrat-Social *comité* for having posed as a police inspector of lodging-houses, and having arrested two women whom he accused of sleeping around. The *comité* accepted his excuse of having acted out of revolutionary patriotism.[108]

Former soldiers jumped at every opportunity for re-enlistment: even the constitutional priest from the Gonesse district, Pontian Gillet – invalided out of the Couronne regiment, and in 1793 acting as curé and public official in Vauderland – petitioned Clémence and Marchand for a place in the new *armée*, assuring them that 'the Republic, protected by the Supreme Being, would be victorious [over] its enemies'.[109] We do not know if the Parisian *armée* took up this offer of service from the padre, with its guarantee of protection by the Supreme Being.

The motives outlined by Pierre Antoine Boudringuin, a locksmith's assistant in the Lepeletier Section, were equally respectable: 'After serving 13 months in the 2nd Paris battalion and having been wounded near Menin on 27 August 1793, by a *biscayen* in my right thigh, I was moved from hospital to hospital...finally to one in Paris. On my discharge, 28 Brumaire, the *conseil de santé* gave me living costs for a fortnight. On 14 Frimaire I enrolled in the *armée révolutionnaire* of the Lepeletier Section in the hope of being of use on the arms maintenance side. I was not to be disappointed and was indeed employed in this capacity...'.[110] Though only a locksmith's assistant, he was nevertheless liable to requisition, and such enrolment seems to have been a way of avoiding it. Chance too played a part, and one almanach-seller and travelling pedlar in the Eure 'was brought by chance into the *armée révolutionnaire*, then crossing the department'.[111]

Some enrolments were clearly products of unemployment. Louis Haumann, a seventy-year-old Alsatian living in the rue du Chantre, Gardes-Françaises Section, 'had been a wigmaker until the loss of his acquaintances [the emigration of his clientele], because of the Revolution, forced him to leave, and since then [he] has been serving as a volunteer in the 2nd battalion of the *armée révolutionnaire*'. His was a case of extreme need, and on 13 Messidor he wrote to the Committee explaining that since the disbanding of the *armée* he had been without funds or occupation and asking for relief or work 'that he might be able to supply the needs of his advanced years...'.[112] The same reason for enrolling applied to three volunteers from the Tuileries Section, Dubesy, Laporte and Duperret, the first 'a former hairdresser', the other two waiters. Two lieutenants from the Cambrai chasseurs, Berny and Mathon, petitioned the same *comité* on 3 October: 'finding themselves unemployed with the disbandment of their corps', they asked to be allowed into the *armée révolutionnaire* in consideration of 'their former services'.[113] Such cases are multiplied over and over, and despite his proud protestations – 'with our arms we have sworn to crush all the aristocratic, royalist and fanatical vermin which infest the republic' – Hauplond, a volunteer from the Bon-Conseil Section, was also motivated by necessity. When he found himself again unemployed on leaving the *armée* he sought employment in a munitions workshop.[114]

One curious individual, Louis Reguex, a clockmaker's assistant who got himself dismissed from the army for ill conduct, was quite a vagabond, but fairly typical of most *révolutionnaires*. Listen to the recital of his misfortunes: 'My enemies claimed that I was fond of drink, and it is true that it is a weakness, but one can be a drinker without being any the less a republican, so I was dismissed from the Corps on indefinite leave, but I was not discontented, for I could still be useful', and since his service with the *armée* had left him 'disgusted at being in a Corps which seemed more burdensome then useful to the Republic.... I returned to my home, and worked at my trade...even when in the Brie I discovered some false tobacco [this Argus claimed also to have uncovered a cache of silver].... Now I ask you if such a subject can be a counter-revolutionary...no, citizens, there is not a Parisian who has a heart like mine and who since the Revolution has not ceased to be vigilant, that is why my enemies worked to secure my dismissal.... They claimed to have heard me say that I had a position with the Sûreté [Committee of General Security, the great police Committee]; but that's a lie for I had had too much to drink, and I can assure you that I probably said to them I had written to the Committee of Public Safety to ask for work...'. But the Marchés *comité* was not convinced; it described Reguex as 'un mauvais sujet, errant et vagabond', and had him arrested one morning in a café for having passed himself off as an agent of the revolutionary tribunal, and having cursed the traders as thieves and bloodsuckers. His case was aggravated by his desertion from his detachment in the Brie and return to Paris, and he was imprisoned in Thermidor by the revolutionary tribunal.[115] Reguex's story provides a composite portrait of the average Parisian *révolutionnaire*, with his drunkenness, his pride, his desire to return to Paris, and his suspicious nature which caused him to see treasure hidden everywhere. Reguex was above all the unstable wanderer of the *comité*'s portrait. He was bored with his work and sought a change by enrolling in the *armée révolutionnaire*. But when he was sent to the Brie he found service equally boring and granted himself leave to return to Paris. He was not the only soldier to be something of a mythomaniac, with imaginary duties – another product of that intoxicating taste for power so widespread among these Parisian artisans.

Let us move on now to those whose motives are less easy to ascertain. Young Barrau, for instance, a banker's son, a conscript from the Muséum Section, who 'prior to the levy was a shop assistant, then a clerk at the War Ministry, forced into barracks with our young men he soon found means of joining the National Guard: finally, having been sent back from this corps, he thought he could avoid the levy by concealing himself in the cavalry of the *armée révolutionnaire* at Versailles...'. But he was soon excluded from this also because he did not meet the height requirements. 'He returned to us therefore and declared that he had been a printer's assistant. A declaration,' observed the Muséum *comité*, 'which we considered ludicrous, since we knew Barrau to have an income of 15,000 to 20,000 livres...'.[116] The *armée révolutionnaire* therefore had not worked for this well-off young man. Others were more fortunate: Louis-Hyacinthe Lafrété, for example, a young man of twenty-five, son of the former receiver-general of Lorraine, a banker with correspondents in Madrid, living off his property. Young Lafrété also had been included in the first levy and had taken refuge in Mazuel's cavalry at Beauvais, 'after he had read a decree permitting citizens between the ages of eighteen and forty to join the cavalry of the *armée révolutionnaire*'. But he was reluctant to say much about it to the *comité révolutionnaire* of his Section, which released him from arrest and sent him back to his battalion. His father, who had also been arrested for trying to remove his son from the levy, was named president of the *comité de bienfaisance* of the Mont-Blanc Section in Messidor Year II. The reign of the sans-culottes was over.[117]

More astonishing still was the case of Jules Guéthenoc, prince of Rohan-Rochefort, who successfully got himself engaged by the cavalry by simply turning up at the gates of the Palace of Versailles. He might, nevertheless, have made an excellent *révolutionnaire*, had he not been discovered the following day talking to a former servant who called him 'Monseigneur' out of habit.[118] The marquis de Baudelaire was more fortunate and remained unnoticed in a squadron for the entire existence of the cavalry. In Ventôse three ex-nobles and two ecclesiastics were expelled from the 6th squadron alone.[119] Indeed, enrolment in the cavalry was the best means for a noble of escaping the attention of the *comités révolutionnaires*.

A similar category was that of servants of émigrés who had returned secretly to France. Barré, a cannoneer of the République Section, was a footman who had accompanied his master to Belgium, then left his service in March 1793 when refused a wage rise, and returned through enemy lines to hide himself in the revolutionary artillery.[120] But his case pales into insignificance beside that of Jacques Berteau. This Frenchman living in London, and serving with the English army, had deserted from the Duke of York's forces in Belgium to the French lines near Lille. Having returned to his home town of Boulogne-sur-Mer, and possessing no *certificat de civisme*, he joined an infantry regiment to escape the vigilance of the *comités de surveillance* in the areas through which he passed. Hospitalised in Saint-Denis (where he claimed to have uncovered a royalist plot) he eventually found his way into the *armée révolutionnaire* in Compiègne. No one asked any questions, and it was only after the disbandment of the *armée*, and his necessary reintegration into civilian life – with all its dangers for one without papers – that his secret was discovered. 'With the *armée révolutionnaire* now disbanded', he wrote to Fouquier on 2 Floréal, 'I will happily accept the most dangerous posting, for I have long chafed at the inaction of this corps...'. Fouquier was to condemn him to permanent inaction by sending him to the guillotine.[121]

A similar case was that of the twenty-five-year-old Prégaux, a former servant and a native of Chaillot, who had served for six years in the Neustrie regiment, deserting in 1790 to enter the service of the marquis de Saint-Clair, colonel of the Belsunce cavalry in Mannheim. After a year he took his leave of the marquis at Breda and entered the service of a Dutchman. On his way through Brussels he became orderly to an officer with the Lille garrison, spent a short time in Paris, returned to Lille, and eventually came to grief as a repairer with a bootmaker in Châlons-sur-Marne. On 30 Brumaire he presented himself to the Champs-Elysées *comité* for enrolment with its company. But instead of accepting this poor illiterate victim of the Revolution, the *comité* had him sent to the Mairie as a returned émigré.[122]

There were also less admissable personal motives for joining the *armée*. Nobles, servants of émigrés, French cooks in London were all victims of the Revolution. Dourlans, a bankrupt jeweller-enameller, was overjoyed, unlike most of his colleagues, to be sent to Lyon, hoping thereby to place a comfortable distance between himself and his creditors in Paris. Then there is the curious case of the former monk Chandèze, administrator of the Hôpital de la Charité and seducer of a seamstress, who succeeded in having himself elected to head the l'Unité company, doubtless to flee the responsibilities of paternity and the consequences of his amourousness. At the end of September he wrote to his mistress, Victoire Rogay, that he had accepted a captaincy (!) in the *armée révolutionnaire*, claiming to have done so in the belief that she no longer wanted to see him: 'adieu, my heartless love, you are sending me to my death...'. But Victoire was having none of this ruse, and on the 28th she wrote to the l'Unité *comité révolutionnaire*: 'I appeal to the law..., I am a young woman who allowed myself to be abused by a man unworthy of my friendship.... But I do not know what to do to rid myself of him; he has threatened to blow my brains out or slit me open if I ever leave him.... Furthermore he is a former monk from the Charité.... I am a seamstress and my father gives me a small allowance...'.[123]

Finally there is the case of François Maillet, a paper-hanger, rue Bourg-l'Abbé, Amis-de-la-Patrie Section, whose motives seem to fit into all the categories cited above: prudent demagogy, need, and patriotism. His Section's *comité révolutionnaire* had him arrested on 29 Brumaire as a suspect, who had defended Lafayette and who had 'tried to assume a mask of patriotism by joining the *armée révolutionnaire*'. His wife, a meat-trader, gave another motive for his thwarted attempt to enrol, in her petition to the Committee of General Security: 'Slackness in his trade and the need to support his wife and children brought about his decision; but he abandoned the attempt and instead accepted a position at 31 sols per day...', a more plausible explanation. Maillet himself gave a third: 'Far from having tried to join the *armée révolutionnaire* on his own initiative, he was brought to it by his fellow citizens who knew his zeal; he thought he could refuse it without compromising the Republic, and accept a situation which would also permit him to support his large family...'.[124]

There is abundant information on these kinds of men and on the unemployed who approached their Sections or the Committee of Public Safety in an effort to find work again after leaving the *armée*. As always, however, this documentation gives a blighted view of the motives for enrolment, for the small shopkeeper or trader who enrolled on patriotic grounds does not appear. We can conclude that despite the *scrutins épuratoires*, suspects were able to conceal themselves in the *armée révolutionnaire*, particularly if they joined outside Paris. But surveillance by the *comités* did not cease after enrolment and throughout its existence the *armée*, and the cavalry in particular, underwent repeated purges. Take the case of the former wigmaker Lassagne, appointed sergeant of the Bonne-Nouvelle company in October, denounced by his wife as having lived off immoral earnings, and expelled from his company and forced to return to Paris even after he had left for Lyon.[125]

For some, motives were extremely mixed, vanity or material gain, the desire to ensure food supplies to their families, or to undermine 'malveillance', all playing a part. Service in this *armée* was not a vocation, but a privileged position, and the *révolutionnaire* expected respect and reward alike from it. Most had dwelt too long in obscurity not to feel a desire to avenge past humiliations, and in some respects Taine was right to see these humble mortals, having graduated to such heights, imitating their former masters. Under the Terror the shopkeeper was king and with such men vanity always played a greater part than thought of material gain.

III   *Social and political composition of the Parisian* armée: *general characteristics*

In spite of its name the *armée révolutionnaire* was not exclusively Parisi... .
The cavalry in particular recruited on a first-come, first-served basis with
its most dubious recruits coming from the Versailles population of ᵢ ᵢrmer
wigmakers, 'supernumeraries', footmen and coachmen. One squadron was
almost entirely composed of farmers, day-labourers and artisans from the
Beauvaisis, and if the artillery seemed typically Parisian, recr its from
the surrounding communes were attached to the fusilier companies from
the outset. All the *sociétés* in the Paris department were circularised by
Ronsin and invited to nominate candidates worthy of forming the 'nucleus'
of the patriotic army. Some *sociétés* did respond to the invitation, and as
early as June the Finistère Section was assailed with demands from the
people of Ivry, Gentilly and Choisy. Socially inferior to the Parisians, and
worse affected by the food shortages, the people of these communes flocked
to take advantage of an institution which offered such desirable employment. Launderers and laundresses from Vaugirard and Vanves came, wine-
growers and wine merchants from Issy, Clamart and Meudon, bargemen
and dock-workers from Charenton and Carrières, gardeners, market
gardeners and small farmers from the Pré-Saint-Gervais and Saint-Mandé,
tannery-workers from Saint-Denis, wagoners and 'journeymen workers of
every description who pass briefly through our commune' (Montrouge),
rabbit breeders from Ivry – in other words a mobile and unstable population
camped outside the gates of the capital.[126] It is impossible to calculate the
importance of these numbers coming from the area surrounding Paris. The
comités révolutionnaires in the Sections naturally tended to prefer their fellow
citizens, and those from outside Paris had to wait their turn. But the rural
or semi-rural element in this urban army does seem to have come from the
surrounding communes rather than from the few Sections, such as Bondy,
possessing rural populations of their own.[127]

Moreover, once a detachment had been sent out of Paris it continued to
recruit from among the local people or those passing through the area.
Take, for example, the pedlar enrolled in the Eure, or the weaver by the
detachment in Montereau.[128] Others were recruited in Compiègne, and
even the detachment sent to Lyon recruited en route. Ronsin's circular was
read to the *société populaire* of Mende; and the Auvergne, which sent so
many poor rabbit-skin dealers, impoverished water-carriers and low-wage-
earners to Paris, was justly represented in this Parisian *armée* whose composition reflected the diversity of the French population.[129] The cavalry,
which contained the most suspect elements of the *armée*, also recruited from
among the most poor: *commissionnaires* from Savoy, water-carriers from the
Auvergne, lettuce-sellers from the Basse-Normandie, day-labourers and
petit peuple from the countryside of the Beauvaisis. However, one must
not exaggerate the importance of these recruits from the surrounding

communes or from the lodging-houses of the most densely populated Sections. The *armée révolutionnaire* was above all a sans-culotte institution, and such country people as found their way into it did so only by accident. In no way was it a charity designed to help the floating population of the capital.

We have very few general guidelines on the social composition of the *armée*. Most of the documentation concentrates rather on the individual and consists largely of police or Committee of General Security papers, and while such individual dossiers may supply a living picture of the persons concerned, and help trace their social mobility, they do not permit any overall statistical analysis. Moreover, it serves no purpose to know that there were a dozen or so shoemakers in the Parisian *armée*, if we cannot discover the total enrolment figure for this trade; and even if that could be established, we would still have to distinguish between master craftsmen and assistants or apprentices. Finally, the recruit described as a shoemaker at the time of his enrolment may very well have followed another trade, or several trades, some years previously.

Such then are the limitations of individual documentation. But it can be supplemented by other sources providing almost complete figures for certain specific groupings: military men, workers in war industries, farmers and weavers, and most of all the 'undesirables'. For administrative reasons, these categories occupy a place in the documentation out of all proportion to their numerical importance in the *armée* itself.

First of all let us examine the snippets of general information available on the overall composition of the artillery and infantry. The detachment in Lyon accounted for more than a third of the effective strength of the entire *armée* and two-thirds of the artillery, and the correspondence of Maubant and the other commanders consequently supplies some valuable insights into the *armée* as a whole. Their letters, for example, refer to the cannoneers' belief that they should be permitted the same privileges in matters of debts owed as any other soldier under arms, particularly since 'they were for the most part small businessmen who had not had sufficient time to put their affairs in order before their sudden departure [from Paris]'. In another letter concerning the ever-growing number of requests for leave, Maubant estimated the number of family men, businessmen or shopkeepers in the Lyon artillery at more than 600. Since there were just over 600 cannoneers altogether in Lyon (627 in Pluviôse if their officers are included), nearly all were small businessmen, if Maubant's figures can be credited.[130] Further-more, despite the vagueness of this assertion it is confirmed by what we know of the individuals. In the fusiliers the artisan element rivalled that of small business (dominant in the artillery) for pride of place. Both elements tended towards political independence – a point to which we will return. But there was also the matter of individual temperaments, and while one shoemaker might be a militant *sectionnaire*, a born revolutionary, another would never rise above the obscurity of his shop. Finally the farmers, day-labourers, gardeners and weavers held a place of such importance among the fusiliers, that a reminder was issued from headquarters to the effect that since those categories were not subject to requisition for war work, they ought not to be liberated from the *armée*.[131]

Everybody agreed that the composition of the cavalry was pretty inferior.[132] Besides the 'rural people', the 'seasonal' workers such as the water-carriers,[133] and the domestic servants (and among this group was a black man, a former valet in one of the big houses), its ranks were filled with deserters, French and foreign alike, well-off young men, thoroughly disreputable characters, and even some nobles and former priests. *Sectionnaires* and former soldiers were rare.

Did the *révolutionnaires* belong to any identifiable political groupings? This is largely a question of education, something always very difficult to determine. But the survival of individual dossiers allows us to recognise one fusilier as illiterate, another able to write in phonetic French, and others able to write tolerably well. The cavalry was full of illiterates; some fusiliers could sign congratulatory addresses with a cross; but the majority of the infantry could sign their names. The cannoneers undoubtedly came from a higher social category. Most were members of Sectionary *sociétés populaires*, which required a minimum level of education; as such they were a privileged minority,[134] and if at Lyon it was from the cannoneers that the *commissaires* were chosen for attachment to the 32 *comités révolutionnaires*, it was surely because more could read and write than among the infantry. The political militants were the *sociétaires* who were frequently the largest grouping in the artillery, but insufficiently numerous to form a recognisable entity in the fusiliers.

Distinct political groupings such as the Jacobins or Cordeliers were equally rare. In the Contrat-Social company of fusiliers the four Jacobins stand out as an isolated and privileged group, insupportable to their colleagues, and subjected to all kinds of harassment by them.[135] Despite its demagogic pose and opposition to government policy, the Cordeliers was a club exclusively for the officer and the *commissaire civil*. The *révolutionnaires* were too lowly to be admitted (except for the privileged few), and when they denounced their officers to the club, it invariably took the latter's part. Indeed some members even reminded the soldiers to respect their betters. The soldiers soon learnt not to direct their petitions to the Cordeliers, who were allies of the clan in the rue de Choiseul.[136] It might be argued that the best-educated of the *révolutionnaires*, like the *sectionnaires* in nearly all the towns, were eager readers of the *Père Duchesne* and would communicate to their less well-educated colleagues the joys and angers of the *marchand de fourneaux* with whom they liked to identify. Indeed such was their passion for Hébert's paper that at Lyon all their own journals were expressly modelled on it. Admittedly Hébert was a talented journalist who knew how to capture the sans-culotte audience. But the reader of the *Père Duchesne* in Paris and Lyon was as indifferent to Hébert himself as he was to his own

General – both unfamiliar figures – and showed no trace of *hébertisme* as such.

In sum, the political minority consisted of *sociétaires* with a certain amount of education, who were probably more numerous in the cannoneers than in the infantry. Finally, the royalists formed another political minority which spanned as many social levels as the 'patriots', and *révolutionnaires* condemned to death for counter-revolutionary language were on the whole of humble origin: former servants, wigmakers,[137] and even some artisans with all the social attributes of the sans-culottes.

(i) 'ACTIVE MINORITIES': MILITANT *SECTIONNAIRES* AND COUNTER-
    REVOLUTIONARIES

As with the officer corps, certain leading *sectionnaires* can be singled out among the *révolutionnaires*: on the one hand members of the *comités révolutionnaires* and other specialists in repression; on the other, ringleaders of the *sociétés populaires*, often accused by the Jacobin authorities of being ultra-revolutionaries. One fusilier volunteer belonging to both categories was Louis Mathieu Potel, a joiner and member of the Contrat-Social *comité* who enrolled in the first and in the second *armée révolutionnaire*, in June and September. This artisan spent but a short time in the *armée*, for in Floréal he was accused of Hébertism, and recalled by his *comité*. In the same category, even if 'a government man', was the fifty-year-old marble-cutter, Jean Laurent, member of the Quinze-Vingts Section *comité révolutionnaire*, who remained in the *armée* until its disbandment. He then rejoined the *comité* and in the Year III was described as one of those responsible for the *journées* of Germinal and Prairial in the faubourg. Parant, a carpenter, Bourse, an engraver, and Baradelle, a bookseller's assistant, all from the Pont-Neuf Section, were members of the Société des Hommes Libres, of which Baradelle was a founding member. Like Potel this young man had already been a candidate for the *armée* in June, while Bourse was a cannoneer.[138]

Combas and Dessirié, sergeant-major and corporal respectively of the Cité Section cannoneers, were both leading *sectionnaires* and specialists in repression in the departments. These two artisans from the Notre-Dame quartier (Dessiré a foreman printer of some 30 years' standing – Combas's occupation we know nothing of)were appointed, with Fourrier, their lieutenant, as temporary jurors on the revolutionary tribunal of Brest, which had been established in Pluviôse Year II by an order of the *représentants* in the Finistère. Dessirié was also appointed to the *comité de surveillance* at Brest by an order of Jeanbon Saint-André in Ventôse Year II. Combas continued to be involved in republican opposition circles, and in the Year IV was a subscriber to Babeuf's paper.[139]

Another specialist in repression was the concierge, Louis, called 'Brutus', a sapper in the Lepeletier Section cannoneers. After serving in Lyon, he moved on to Marseille, where Barras and Fréron, in whom he was to find powerful protectors, appointed him president of the Military Commission.[140] Despite his republican convictions (he was reported in Floréal Year IV to have had frequent meetings with Parein and Corchand), Barras's support saved him from arrest on several occasions in the Year IV, when he served as his secretary. But his turn came eventually in the Year IX, when he was deported to Cayenne to die with many other former terrorists.[141]

The forty-six-year-old Pierre Fontaine was another cannoneer who, if the surveillance of the Thermidorean police is anything to go by, must have been a formidably militant *sectionnaire*. He was a goldsmith in the Arcis Section with a workshop employing several assistants near the port Saint-Paul. Suspected of having participated in the September massacres of prisoners between Orléans and Versailles, this independent artisan, like many other Sectionary leaders, was to be accused of 'corrupting' his apprentices with his 'anarchist' ideas. Fontaine seems to have been a 'revolutionary by temperament' whose workshop, like Cardinaux's dance hall, was a school for conspiracy. He too had his place on Babeuf's lists and was another object of police surveillance in the Year IV. He too would be deported in the Year IX, to die in the Seychelles.[142]

Another cannoneer and leading *sectionnaire*, notably through family connections, was the thirty-eight-year-old shoemaker, Nicolas Duval, brother-in-law to Laurent Burloy, one of the 'ringleaders' of the l'Homme-Armé Section. An inhabitant of the rue des Blancs-Manteaux – departure point for the Chevalier-Desforges conspiracy of the Year IX – Duval was one of those 'hommes de liaison' acting as a link between the Parisian Sectionary movement and terrorist circles in the departments. Through his brother-in-law he was connected with the artisan and small-business world of Auxerre and Vermenton, two areas in which the cannoneers of the *armée révolutionnaire* played an important role, and during the years of proscription the police of Cochon and Fouché represented Duval as in contact with the 'anarchists' of the Yonne, a department in which the terrorists remained extremely active.[143]

Julien Hubert, a master carpenter of the Arsenal Section and a fusilier, was a member of the Administrative Council of the Parisian *armée*. With the master mason, Anne Grelêt, and the basket-maker Varet, he was to be accused in the Year III of having been one of the main 'proposers of motions' in the Section, while Varet was denounced as an agent of the former *comité révolutionnaire*.[144] These three artisans were consequently both militant *sectionnaires* and leading figures within the *armée*. Bourdin, a fusilier and gaslighter in the rue Mouffetard, Finistère Section, attracted the attention of Babeuf and his friends as a revolutionary patriot who commanded the support of the faubourg Marceau workers.[145] Like Fontaine he also employed assistants in his own right.

Petit, a cannoneer and ribbon-maker of the Gravilliers Section, Fouques, a fusilier and fruiterer from the Droits-de-l'Homme Section, Brabant, a box-maker, and Charles Sormois, a former joiner, then jailer at La Grande Force (the last two, cannoneers of the Eude Section company), were likewise leading *sectionnaires* sufficiently well known to figure on Babeuf's lists.[146] The 'Equals' were above all interested in *sectionnaires* who had remained in touch with their colleagues in the terrorist institutions and who had sufficient influence to bring their own adherents with them. Sormois, after a decade and a half of persecution, was to end in 1814 by 'throwing himself at the foot of the throne', this veteran of the Sectionary movement proclaiming his undying loyalty to the Bourbon dynasty![147]

Vainqueurs de la Bastille are not to be found among the rank and file of the *armée*, for their veteran status entitled them to commissions. There were undoubtedly numerous combatants of 10 August, and a former fusilier was to be tried in the Year IV as a Septembriseur. Of the former we know litttle, but two *révolutionnaires* figured on the lists of those wounded during that *journée* and in receipt of pensions from the Republic: these were Joseph Deloutte, a mason from the Gravilliers Section and a witness at the trial of Osselin, and Antoine Guy, a shoemaker from the l'Unité Section. According to Maubant, many more of these soldiers may have taken part in the capture of the Tuileries.[148] The reputed Septembriseur was a locksmith's assistant from the Droits-de-l'Homme Section, François-Baptiste Joachim Bertrand, a young man of twenty-three and a drum-major of the Parisian *armée*.[149]

There were also some leading terrorists who did not belong to the world of the Sections: Brault, a cavalryman in the *armée révolutionnaire*, was one of the permanent agents of the Committee of General Security.[150] The starch-dealer Massé was a Jacobin, aide-de-camp to General Hanriot,[151] and considered the leader of the Saint-Denis ultra-revolutionaries. As early as Brumaire Year II the municipal *comité* of this commune denounced him as the author of 'disorganising proposals' tending to promote civil war between the inhabitants of the commune and those of Paris.[152] Finally, on 4 September, Massé proposed to the Franciade *société* 'cutting the throats of all the inmates of the commune's prisons'.[153] That was the date of the Paris *journée*, which, in its demand for the pitiless pursuit of internal enemies, led to the creation of the Parisian *armée*. Massé was certainly thoroughly informed of the movement which was preparing in the capital. He was later accused of being the instigator of the *journée* of 3 Prairial Year III, which broke out in Saint-Denis following the popular risings in Paris.[154] This is not the last we shall hear of this violent and authentic revolutionary, who was in the same mould as the *commissaire des guerres*, Paris. An anonymous note of the Year IX to the prefect of police was to point to him as someone worth watching: '...in the *armée révolutionnaire* he committed every possible outrage as a terrorist, anarchist and fanatical Jacobin...'. It was Massé who expressed most forcibly those cherished aspirations of the less privileged popular circles, and he had all the qualities necessary to make himself detestable to the conformists of the Jacobin dictatorship.[155]

The turbulent Etienne Jourdan, protégé of Ronsin and drum-major of the *armée révolutionnaire*, should be placed in the same category. He was thirty-eight years old and had spent sixteen of them in the army. A native of Alès in the Gard, he was to claim relationship with the celebrated 'Coupe-Tête' during the Terror, only to deny it later when it became compromising. In May 1793, while serving in the Vendée with his battalion, despite his illiteracy, he was employed by Ronsin as his aide-de-camp. Even at this date his drunken habits were getting him into trouble with the Tours *comité révolutionnaire*, which demanded his removal after he had caused a number of brawls in the cafés. But despite his bad reputation, Ronsin remembered him when the Parisian *armée* was organised, and secured for him his position of drum-major in the Guillaume-Tell company. On detachment to Le Havre he got into more mischief. When he left the *armée* he lived in straitened circumstances and filled in as a replacement in the guard of his Section. In Frimaire Year III he was again arrested following disturbances in a café and in the Year IV police reports refer to him as at the head of a clandestine meeting of terrorist leaders at the château de Bercy. Jourdan was a primitive, violent and drunken individual; always quick to draw his sword, he had more of the career soldier in him than the militant terrorist of Massé's type, though the two types are frequently found together. But can anyone so completely illiterate really be considered a political militant?[156]

The *armée* did include among its poorest elements, a minority of employees and artisans, who, before their enlistment, or more often after their discharge, took part in the social agitation caused by government policy on wages. Delamare, a cannoneer and innkeeper from the Droits-de-l'Homme Section, was accused of having taken part in the pillage of the grocery shops after the troubles of February-March 1792; the activities of Chaufourier, a thirty-eight-year-old fusilier from the Mont-Blanc Section, ranged over a wider field. Successively a carter, coalman and navvy in the Rodin quarry, he was arrested in Floréal Year II for having taken part in a demonstration of tobacco shredders at the Longueville town hall. At the time of his arrest his destitute wife was requesting relief from the *comité de bienfaisance* of the Section. A similar case is that of Faroux, a cloth-worker and finisher and former fusilier in the Montagne company. On his return from the *armée révolutionnaire* he entered a workshop in the Sans-Culottes Section for the manufacture of bayonets and was arrested during the winter of 1794 'for having been one of the leading participants in the workers' movement'.[157] But such cases were rare for the good reason that the *armée* contained only a small number of wage-earners capable of taking part in any agitation which condemned the *sectionnaires*. The *armée révolutionnaire* itself was charged with the repression of similar movements among the bargemen, raftsmen and workers on the waterways.

Finally, as with all revolutionary institutions, the *armée* contained a minority which opposed the regime, poor miserable wretches, whose sole crime was their open expression of their attachment to the old order of things and to the Catholic religion. With the exception of the journalist Groslay, secretary of the general staff at Lyon and editor of the paper the

Soirée des Campagnes, none of these unfortunates could be considered as militant royalist supporters.[158] Royalists aside, this militant élite was distributed between the artillery and the infantry. In the cavalry only Brault would qualify for inclusion.

Of the 280 soldiers whose occupations we know, only about 40 were described specifically by the authorities of the Years II or III as 'ringleaders', 'notorious terrorists', leading figures of the *sociétés sectionnaires* or even, by the same token, 'men capable of commanding' in the lists of Buonarotti and Charles Germain. The smallness of the number is not simply due to lack of sources, for the dossiers of the Committee of General Security are in fact a kind of dictionary of the sans-culotte élites, and once again they reveal the minority aspect of the Sectionary movement: in the Parisian *armée* as in the wider domain of the Parisian Sections, a distinction must be made between the leader and the general mass. The militants formed but a tiny minority and for the most part Ronsin's soldiers were obscure individuals, content to follow the tide, and above all anxious not to draw attention to themselves; their political life was coextensive with the terrorist institutions to which they were attached for several months. The militants were less numerous: but each was known to the shopkeepers and artisans of his Section, and their restricted number was not necessarily a sign of weakness. Each of these men could command support from six to ten others, often drawn from among their own employees.

(ii)   UNEMPLOYMENT, BANKRUPTCIES AND OCCUPATIONAL CHANGES

The drawback of making any analysis of occupations on the basis of statistical documentation – lists of enrolments by company, for example, or of the special categories of requisitioned workers – is that such documentation disguises a major social phenomenon, accentuated after 1792, and more so after 1793, by scarcity, the cessation of the exportation and circulation of goods, and the loss of a wealthy clientele. This was the general trend towards salaried employment in the revolutionary administration of people involved in the luxury, food and clothing trades, and to a lesser extent of those artisans most affected by the scarcity of raw materials. Often service in the Parisian *armée* was but the first step towards such a salaried status, artisans, shopkeepers, former *révolutionnaires* seeking positions on their discharge as guards of sequestrated property, clerks, employees in public transportation (the great refuge of shopkeepers and wigmakers short of work), court clerks or prison warders – this last a form of administration which under the Terror experienced a sinister expansion.[159] It is rather in the individual dossier that this phenomenon, so important in the lives of the artisan and shopkeeper under the Terror, can be detected. There we can find examples of the bureaucratisation of the artisan and small-business class, a process which restricted the political independence of the sans-culottes and at the same time encouraged the trend towards orthodoxy and conformism. An independent shopkeeper might be a 'ringleader', but a guard of sequestrated property or a prison warder was constantly obliged to think of his superiors and the government.

A further disadvantage of such 'lists' is that they fail to distinguish between the small businessman who was still prospering at the time of his enrolment, and those who sought a solution to actual unemployment. Many who claimed involvement in a trade or business when enrolling in the *armée*, were declaring themselves unemployed by the time of its disbandment, seeking relief for their families and salaried positions for themselves. The number of actual unemployed enrolled in this army was consequently much higher than suggested by the incomplete statistical accounts.

Then we have the related problem of the numbers of shopkeepers and small businessmen who enrolled to escape their creditors. In principle, bankrupts were debarred from public office, and especially from such a privileged institution as the *armée révolutionnaire*; they came under the heading of 'proscribed groups', as did *parlementaires, fermiers-généraux,* nobles, ecclesiastics and lottery officials, and one of the aims of the *scrutins épuratoires* was to weed them out. However, this precaution was insufficient: bankrupts still succeeded in joining, some even remaining until the end, while others were expelled after two or three months of service at the insistence of their Sections.

Occupational instability, unemployment, bankruptcy – these were typical problems of the period, with the more striking examples being found in the departmental and communal *armées*, notably those of Versailles, Lille and Bordeaux. The social composition of the Parisian *armée* seems to have been on a higher level. We will return to this question when we open the dossiers of the departmental soldiers. But the papers of the Committee of General Security provide a number of examples from the Paris *armée*. Galand, a fusilier in the l'Homme-Armé company, a tailor and porter on his enrolment, was asking his *comité révolutionnaire* for a position as a guard of sequestrated property in Floréal.[160] The case of Charles Duser is even more clear-cut: a cabinet-maker in the Gardes-Françaises Section, he had been unemployed since the first years of the Revolution. His enrolment only just saved him from destitution and in his absence his wife had to seek help from the Section. After his discharge, he approached the *comité de bienfaisance* for temporary assistance to provide for his wife and children while he sought employment.[161]

Hachet, a forty-three-year-old fruiterer from the Tuileries Section, was without work when he left the *armée* and requested a position in the transportation service. Had his business collapsed in his absence, or had he been obliged to sell up even before his enrolment? This we do not know. Gaillard of the Gardes-Françaises Section ran a lodging-house and café in October 1793; in Floréal he was forced to sell up at a loss to avoid bankruptcy and proceeded to seek employment with the police. The forty-two-year-old paper merchant Bacot, from the Marchés Section, joined the *armée révolutionnaire* but was back at his trade in Floréal. A year later, however, he had abandoned it and tried to enter the gendarmerie, only to be rejected because of accusations that he had spoken against the Thermidorean Convention.[162] In such cases it is difficult to determine whether these small businessmen were victims of revolutionary patriotism which had caused them to enrol and neglect their businesses, left under temporary management or in the care of their wives, or whether they sought to forestall threatened bankruptcy and avert the catastrophe of unemployment (all were married with large families) by eagerly accepting the first salaried employment to present itself. There is evidence to support both hypotheses: in Germinal a number of fusiliers would try to have themselves accepted into the artillery,[163] in order to remain in the *armée*; but in the Year II, and even more so in the Year III, many cannoneers would ask for leave to return to Paris in order to help their wives maintain their shops. A particularly revealing example of this is the case of André-François Dupuis, who enlisted in the fusiliers because he was out of work, and in Germinal succeeded in transferring to the Popincourt company of cannoneers. In Pluviôse Year III his wife was demanding his return: '...with work of every description difficult to find', she explained, 'the working class sought to support their families, and my husband...decided therefore...as much from republicanism as love of his family [to enrol in his Section's company of fusiliers]....after its disbandment...wishing still to be of use to his country, he enrolled in the cannoneers on pay of 42 sols per day...'. Having been assured that the pay would remain the same when they were away, he and his colleagues left Paris, 'content in the knowledge that they would be able to continue to support their families'. But the family could not live on the sum of 15 sols to which his pay was reduced, and the wife requested his return to Paris from Tours, where his company was serving.[164] This letter gives an admirable account of the combination of self-interest and patriotism which pushed these artisans and family men to enrol in the highly paid new *armée* and then to abandon the cannoneers at the time of the reform of the Year III (a reform which in fact was designed to rid the artillery of that very popular element which they represented and which was so suspect to the Thermidorean authorities).

For the wigmaker, the hairdresser, the servants, coachmen and cooks of the great houses, service in the *armée révolutionnaire* offered a deferment of that unemployment which they so dreaded, and on their discharge they once more went in quest of salaried employment. Floquet, former servant to the marquis de Sillery, was doubly fortunate: profiting from his privileged position as a *révolutionnaire*, he denounced his wife as a royalist, had her imprisoned, and having rid himself of her he managed on his discharge from the *armée* to secure a position with military transport. For the seventy-year-old former wigmaker, Haumann, the *armée révolutionnaire* was a happy interlude. The jeweller-enameller Dourlans was declared insolvent both in 1788 and again in Lyon, where he was living with the wife of an émigré, to the scandal of his colleagues who denounced his conduct to the *comité révolutionnaire* of his Section. He would be denounced again in the Year III, but this time as a terrorist.[165]

Finally, there was the problem of unemployment among those formerly employed in administrations which no longer existed. Jean Ferrant, a thirty-eight-year-old fusilier sergeant, had been employed for 11 years with the Ferme Générale. In Messidor, two months after his departure from the *armée révolutionnaire* and still out of work, he asked for a position as assistant in the record office of the Plessis prison. Lavigne, also one of the General Farm's employees and a fusilier from the Guillaume-Tell Section, declared that he was without work at the time of his enrolment. Finally, the fifty-eight-year-old François Guillaume, a sergeant of fusiliers in the Maison-Commune company, and employed with the royal lottery before the Revolution, was again unemployed when he left prison in Messidor Year II.[166]

The short and violent career of Claude Nicolas, a fusilier in the Bonnet-Rouge company, underlines the social mobility of those in certain marginal trades – the thin line dividing the honest artisan from the shady dealer – and reminds us of the danger of trusting in appearances. Nicolas, a twenty-five-year-old native of Flavigny, in the Nancy region, posed as a dealer in second-hand goods, a trade which prospered in such times of scarcity. But at the time of enrolment he declared himself to be a launderer. Both trades were in fact screens, for he belonged instead to the world of theft and banditry; his connections were with an itinerant group of horse- and vegetable dealers, pedlars and laundresses in the suburbs, whose real occupation was crime. Nicolas did not remain long in the *armée révolutionnaire*, but he retained its uniform and promoted himself bandit chief of a fictitious *armée révolutionnaire*, which, under pretext of requisitioning, pillaged the isolated farms of the Montfort district. This real bandit would be executed in the public square of Versailles with other members of his band in Floréal Year II.[167]

(iii)   THE CRIMINAL ELEMENT

Claude Nicolas was the only real bandit of this *armée*, one of the only *révolutionnaires* whom we know for certain to have belonged to the criminal underworld. Undoubtedly other criminal elements may have entered by subterfuge and escaped the vigilance of the revolutionary authorities. But this seems unlikely given the multiple means of checking available to the *comités révolutionnaires*. Revolutionary vigilance was the order of the day; the police of the Year III were very well organised, and along with political suspects and counter-revolutionaries, common criminals were likewise their victims. At no time in the eighteenth century was prostitution attacked with such rigour as during the reign of the virtuous sans-culottes, and with Lyon swept of dangerous persons by the municipality and *comités section-naires*, the Parisian soldiers there were the first victims of that rigour, and they showed little gratitude for this excessive concern for their virtue.[168] In the interests of virtue and the war effort, Sectionary opinion pursued 'loose women' and men living off immoral earnings with the same severity. Despite the *scrutins*, two or three such men did manage to enter the *armée*, but these were rare cases.[169] It was more common for the *révolutionnaires* sent on detachment to take along their wives or female companions, referred to as 'lady friends' by the prudish rural *comités révolutionnaires*, or 'hussies' by Taine. On the other hand there was at least one receiver of stolen goods, the wine merchant Busserole, a sergeant in the Gardes-Françaises fusiliers; and when police searched the furnished house of which he was either owner or manager, they found over 30 wallets in the lavatory.[170]

Nicolas and Busserole were the real criminals within the *armée*. Other unsavoury elements were only semi-criminals or criminals by accident, taking advantage of their new situation to make unauthorised requisitions. Beauchant, for example, simply filled out requisition forms on his own behalf and went round the farms in the Compiègne district; for this he was sentenced to two years' detention, in Nivôse Year II.[171] Others pretended to be police inspectors and threatened those with guilty consciences[172] – though it is difficult to discover whether this was a form of blackmail, or a product of the kind of mythomania from which Houssaye suffered, and which certainly existed in all the revolutionary institutions. Then there were the former soldiers who continued the unsavoury practices of the Ancien Regime army, notably that of claiming false stops en route and of misappropriating the company's effects; almost all were sergeants in the cavalry or infantry – a thoroughly dishonest lot in every epoch, without being downright criminals.[173] Finally, there was a small percentage of poor devils found guilty of petty thefts and punished with a pitiless severity out of all proportion to the crime: men like the fusilier Defresne, condemned to four years in irons for having stolen a pistol from a gunsmith's in Provins, or the cavalryman, Rabot, condemned to five years in irons for theft.[174] In Lyon in particular the Military Commission, comprised of officers and non-commissioned officers from the revolutionary garrison, punished the smallest theft with a harsh sentence of six to ten years, as if the reputation of this sans-culotte *armée* required such pitiless justice. The Lyon terrorists and *révolutionnaires* alike complained of this severity as reminiscent of the dreadful military code of the Ancien Regime army.[175]

Given the nature of the documentation, it is likely that most cases of soldiers found guilty of crimes or offences have been recorded. If so, the numbers are very small: 2 cases of men with indisputable criminal pasts, about 20 of crooked dealings in military supply, 3 or 4 of multiple swindle, in the style of Vidocq, and facilitated by the incredible confusion of the revolutionary and military government, and finally 20 or so charged with petty thefts, largely of clothing, occasioned by extreme poverty. It is difficult to accept Taine's argument, therefore, that the Parisian *armée* was composed largely of anti-social elements, former galley slaves, convicts and members of the mysterious Paris underworld. The civilians who made up the bulk of the *armée* were respectable citizens; Ronsin's *armée* was not a criminal one, and the unsavoury elements came almost entirely from among the former soldiers.

(iv) OCCUPATIONAL ANALYSIS

Of the 280 *révolutionnaires* on whose occupations we have details at the time of their enrolment or the disbandment of the *armée*, there were 118 artisans, 80 small businessmen, 19 soldiers, 11 employees, 10 countrymen, 5 'intellectuals' and 53 'undesirables'. Incomplete as this list may be, it is sufficient to underline the marked differences between the men and the officers. Among the former the military element is less important, and if artisans outnumber small businessmen it is simply an accident of documentation. Within these separate groupings the occupations which recur most frequently are shoemakers, carpenters, locksmiths, café-owners and wigmakers. The figures for the locksmiths are probably complete, thereby giving them a disproportionate importance in the group under consideration. Among the artisans the most important group (22 in all) is that associated with the furniture or building trades: 8 joiners, 2 masons, 2 stone-cutters, a carpenter, a cabinet-maker, a toymaker, a layer of wooden floors, a marble-cutter, a navvy, a glazier, a mattress-maker and a boxmaker.[176] Second in importance are those in the clothing trades: 8 shoemakers, 3 tailors, 2 hatters, a button-maker and a ribbon-maker. Shoemakers, threatened with requisition to make shoes for the army, flocked to take up positions in the various revolutionary bodies. Fifty artisans were involved in trades useful to the war effort: 11 locksmiths, 4 blacksmiths, 4 engravers, 4 clockmakers, 2 assistant metal-casters, 2 boiler-makers, 2 wheelwrights, a metal-gilder, a turner, a gunsmith and 27 'workers in iron' whose precise trades are unspecified. Miscellaneous trades included a journeyman saddler, a fan merchant, a clay-potter and, among the seasonal workers, 5 water-carriers from the Aveyron, 2 *commissionaires*, 2 casual workers. In addition there was a 'machinist' and 3 unspecified 'workers'.

Of the merchants and shopkeepers the food trade accounts for most, and of the 13 soldiers (all cannoneers or fusiliers) 6 were café-owners or wine-merchants, 3 fruiterers, 2 caterers, one a seller of roast meats, and one a confectioner. Domestic service also furnishes an important group, 20 in all: 7 wigmakers, 6 former servants (domestic staff, footmen, coachmen), 4 apprentice jewellers and a cook. In the book trade we have a bookshop assistant, two apprentice printers and the foreman of a composing room. Related to these are an instructor, a journalist, a public letter-writer and an actor. From the country come wine-growers, day-labourers, gardeners and market gardeners, all from Paris or its suburbs, 10 in all. Eleven are described as employees: 7 clerks from Parisian government offices, 4 formerly employed with the Fermes Généraux or the lotteries. Of the 19 former soldiers, 12 were NCOs in the Ancien Regime army and 5 gendarmes. Deserters from the first requisition or from foreign armies have not been included in this category, nor those who had been soldiers only since the Revolution.

Fifty-three are listed as 'undesirables' – an impressive figure, seemingly confirming Taine's thesis. Closer examination of the figures, however, shows his exultation to have been unjustified. In the first place this list is certainly more complete than the scraps existing for other groupings and includes all or almost all of those considered 'undesirable' by the authorities of the Year II: criminals and degenerates certainly, but even more so those whose origins or previous occupations rendered them suspect. So if the list includes 14 accused of theft, larceny, receiving or embezzling – and most of these were only occasional rather than professional criminals – 2 procurers, 2 adventurers, 2 swindlers, 1 or 2 highway robbers and a blackmailer, there are also 11 deserters from the first levy, 5 or 6 foreign deserters, 6 former nobles, 5 ex-ecclesiastics, 4 well-off young men and 2 who can only be described as inveterate drunkards. Two-thirds of these 'undesirables' were in the cavalry; very few were in the infantry and artillery.[177]

The fragmentary lists nevertheless underline the extreme diversity in the composition of this popular force. It was a diversity reflecting that of the Parisian populace, the *sans-culotterie*, the *menu peuple*, socially so difficult to define because of the fluidity of the line dividing the revolutionary élite and the mass of the *sectionnaires* from the 'Jacobin bourgeoisie'. The Parisian *armée* can be described as sans-culotte, but it is difficult to be precise about a social group which brought together an entrepreneur and a master joiner, employing between four assistants and fourteen – and such employers were generally to be found in the ranks[178] – with impoverished and unemployed wigmakers, water-carriers, clerks and even joiners' assistants living in furnished accommodation. It is necessary to add, however, that the latter, the flotsam and jetsam of the Parisian population, were only a tiny percentage of this Sectionary *armée*. Such homeless individuals were unknown to their fellow citizens, who in the elections naturally tended to choose acquaintances, people who frequented the same shops and cafés. It was an *armée* of *sectionnaires*, which meant resident citizens, and it was more difficult for a stranger to enter the ranks of the infantry and artillery than to secure a place on the general staff.[179] To find any large representation from the lodging-houses in an *armée révolutionnaire* one must look instead to the departmental forces outside Paris, notably to that of Lille.

What then is the conclusion of this long chapter? Socially, officers and men of the *armée* came principally from the small-business and the artisan world, a world composed above all of resident citizens of several years' standing, known for their *civisme*, their sound morals and their honesty. In addition the infantry command contained a number of former soldiers, who themselves had become artisans or small businessmen and been quickly absorbed into the life of the Parisian districts. The composition of the cavalry was noticeably different, which goes a long way to explaining its behaviour and political indifference, and its obvious defects compromised the entire *armée* in 'patriot' opinion.

The same distinctions can be found in the political affiliations of the three branches. Because of its political indifference, the cavalry might have become a praetorian guard if its squadron leaders had been ambitious: but as prudent men and good soldiers, they avoided such dangers. The artillery was a Sectionary élite, the creature of the Sections and, in the last resort, of the Convention; it would never have risked falling under the control of any one man or group. The state of mind among the infantry was similar, though political consciousness was less developed among the fusiliers and had not reached the same level of instruction as among the cannoneers. As with the fusiliers, however, there was a militant minority among the infantry officers. But despite their independent spirit the fusiliers and cannoneers remained faithful to the Convention, and anyone seeking to use the Parisian *armée* against the Convention or the Revolutionary Government, even to replace it with a new system based on the *sociétés populaires*, could not have counted on the support of the officers and men of the revolutionary artillery or infantry.

One could go on indefinitely about the motives which pushed these men to enrol in a political, privileged and grossly overpaid army. Undoubtedly the decisive motives were vanity and material gain. Most of the cannoneers and fusiliers could have done without this new employment and were not dependent on the *armée* for a livelihood. Such relative independence explains their attitude towards a service for which they were not prepared to make too many sacrifices; they expected to remain near Paris and considered their enlistment as some kind of part-time employment.

It was an army of civilians, of shopkeepers and artisans, the marching wing, in the departments, of the Sectionary movement. But if the Sectionary element preserved it from the play of personal ambitions, it was the principal cause of its military weakness. A force of *sectionnaires* constantly looking back to their civilian life, to their shops or workshops, was ill prepared to implement the tasks assigned to them. They were fine when that task was the pursuit of hoarders or concealed grain, the destruction of religious objects or the application of the Maximum; but ask them to go and conduct the repression of Lyon, Brest or Avranches, and they rebelled, the cannoneers in particular, and the *armée* was bled by increasing requests for leave and by resignations. Throughout its stay in Lyon, 5 to 10 per cent of its effective numbers were absent at any given time, on leave or in hospital rather than in detention,[180] for the sick far outnumbered the unruly and some companies presented a spectacle reminiscent of the Cour des Miracles; and when these cannoneer or fusilier shop- or workshop owners were denied leave to return to Paris, they took it anyway.[181]

All of this went side by side with a lack of respect for the officers and an inaptitude for military exercise and discipline. Former soldiers, in command of the infantry battalions, despaired of such men: the captain was at the mercy of the *révolutionnaires*, negotiating with, rather than commanding, them. There was no sign of any *esprit de corps* developing beyond the auton- omy of the Sections, and unity was achieved only at company level. Assisted by time and their distance from Paris (particularly in the case of the huge detachment in Lyon), the loss of the more independent elements through leave, resignation and desertion, the process of proper militarisation within the *armée* had unquestionably begun at the time of its disbandment. But it was a temporary development and there was never any question of making real soldiers out of these civilians. The Parisian *armée* was a provisional institution, formed to deal with an exceptional situation. The *révolution- naires* could be brought to make certain sacrifices if their patriotism was appealed to; but their enthusiasm did not survive the passage of time. After three months, the cannoneers, claiming that they had been 'deceived', called for their return to Paris and were followed in this demand by many of the fusiliers. Only the cavalrymen grew accustomed to extended service, because all had good reasons for wanting to remain in the squadrons: the young men to avoid service at the frontiers; the ex-nobles and those deprived of certificates of *civisme* or of non-emigration, to avoid prison or the guillotine; the sergeants, former hussars or dragoons, because of the opportunity the marches provided for fraudulent practices; the deserters and foreigners because they found it easier than service with the 'tyrants'.

Here then was an institution which cost the Republic dear, whose mem- bers, with their independent and unaccommodating spirit, were sometimes quite intolerable, but who were nevertheless the privileged élite of the regime. The *révolutionnaires* knew how to sell their services dearly; they had precise ideas about their rights and duties and would reject in advance any service which did not fit into the narrow category of the struggle against the 'enemies of the interior'. The Revolutionary Government was accused of having emasculated this instrument of the Terror at the outset. But it was the revolutionary soldier himself who was the main cause of weakness in an institution which ought to have been terrifying, and miracles could not have been expected of an *armée* composed largely of Parisian *sectionnaires* who prided themselves precisely on the fact that they were not soldiers.

CHAPTER 4

Enrolment of the Departmental and Communal
Armées révolutionnaires (September 1793 to Frimaire Year II)

In the autumn and winter of 1793 the enrolment of *armées révolutionnaires* was a national phenomenon. In half the departments, companies, battalions and some real armies, raised on the Paris model, commenced activities often amidst disorder, and forces were planned in at least 20 other departments. This efflorescence offers a typical example of the kind of administrative anarchy and revolutionary emulation which led to such novel experiments in pre-Nivôse France.

The forces were more numerous than the departments which spawned them, but despite considerable variation in their effective numbers, in no area were those numbers large. Their importance, however, cannot be measured by a head count, for the terror unleashed in their passage bore no relation to their modest numbers and means. It was not a question of hordes with extensive powers of intervention, but of small groups under the command of a privileged few. Two-thirds of these forces saw action, the organisation of the remainder was cut short. Some were little more than private armies, others were criminal bands disguised by a title giving them the right of widespread interference. Simple enumeration, therefore, is misleading.

The *armée révolutionnaire*, as an institution, was in fashion. Despite the variation in their effective numbers, all the 'respectable' *armées* had certain traits in common: methods of recruiting, political qualifications for admission, high pay, links with the *sociétés populaires*, their largely urban and artisanal composition, imprecise origins and administrative status. Revolutionary emulation ensured that such common traits were more numerous than those peculiar to an individual corps; spontaneity was absent. These instruments of the Terror exercised a powerful attraction; the *armées* were all created about the same time, with each one anxious to imitate its neighbour, each seeking revolutionary apotheosis.

However, it would be wrong to see in all this a campaign orchestrated by Paris. For once, sans-culottes and Paris Jacobins agreed in condemning this multiplication of departmental forces, which they correctly saw as a triumph for local autonomy and the beginnings of popular Federalism. There were undoubtedly some Parisian *commissaires*, Cordeliers or Jacobins sent on mission to the departments, who favoured such initiatives to the point of actually suggesting them to the ignorant, hesitant or prudent local authorities, but these 'hommes de liaison' were militants who had the support neither of the clubs of which they were members nor of the Ministers whom they represented in the departments. At no time did the organs of Parisian opinion – newspapers, assemblies, Sectionary *sociétés*, clubs – lend their weight to measures which most Parisians considered disquieting.

Thanks to the administrative anarchy caused by distance and the indecision of central government, the departments managed to push ahead with these revolutionary experiments. Ultra-revolutionaries of every kind, muzzled in Paris, reigned as masters in the bourgs and villages as in the large towns down-graded because of their Federalism. But sincere emulation or prudence was not the main reason for the support such initiatives received from the militants, and even from the unrevolutionary municipalities. Rather the creation of departmental or communal armies was a response to pressing problems and had very definite aims: the need to supply the urban markets and to ensure the circulation of provisions, merchandise and people; the suppression of subversive machinations; the defence of local interests; municipal and regional rivalries; the 'communalisation' and fractionalisation of power. The desire to help the unemployed, or more often to send them away from the towns, may also have been a consideration.

Born in anarchy, many of these *armées* remained anarchical. On what authorities did they depend? Who commanded them? In whose name and in whose interest would they act? Were they the instruments of the regular authorities, were they subject to the orders of the garrison commanders, or were they in danger of falling into the hands of irresponsible persons or illegal institutions? The administrative status of these disturbing *armées* was itself equivocal, and in such a jungle the most daring initiatives were possible.

The enrolment of departmental and communal forces is just one more episode in the administrative history of the Terror in the departments. It raised in a particularly urgent manner the problem which lay at the centre of the entire history of the Revolution, that of government and authority. Who was in charge? What limits should be set to revolutionary activity? What place did the *sociétés populaires* occupy? Where was the revolutionary movement going? Should priority be given to the war effort or to the realisation of a revolutionary programme in the interior? The history of the departmental *armées* occurred at a time when the central government, whether through silence or indecision, was incapable of setting out precise limits of action for the local militants or of imposing a clear definition of administrative responsibility. On the day when it decided to do so, the *armées* disappeared.

I *The balance sheet*

Since most departments had participated in the campaign in favour of local *armées révolutionnaires* or a national *armée*, the decree of 5 September produced a rapid succession of orders, from all kinds of authorities, across two-thirds of the nation. Although these orders borrowed certain disposi-tions from the Convention's decree – regarding pay for these élite soldiers, conditions governing the *civisme* of candidates, their uniforms, the devices inscribed on their flags, etc. – they followed no general rule as to age limit, effective numbers, and administrative responsibilities. While some com-panies consisted of only 30–50 men – with some amounting to no more than 10 – others might number from 100 to 1,200 or 1,500. The various *armées* sent to the Aveyron and the Lozère seem even to have exceeded 6,000 in number, the total for the entire Parisian *armée*. If only those *armées* which had completed their organisation and been active before the law of 14 Frimaire are taken into account, some 30,000 men would have assumed the sans-culotte uniform in the autumn and early winter months: if the Parisian *armée* is included, 36,000–40,000 *révolutionnaires* would have been under arms throughout France in Frimaire. A force insufficiently numerous per-haps to mount a *coup d'état*, to act as an instrument of anarchy, or to terrify the *honnêtes gens*; but this was just a beginning, and the movement was rapidly expanding when interrupted by the law of 14 Frimaire.

It would be wrong then to judge the real importance of these little *armées* by their numbers, the modesty of which was undoubtedly an element of relative weakness. Their political effectiveness did not depend on numbers alone, for the *révolutionnaires* in the departments were also among the most privileged citizens and in many regions their battalions and companies en-joyed a monopoly of armed force. Their ubiquitous nature must also be taken into account, for if the total number of political soldiers under arms did not surpass 40,000, they were active in 40 departments throughout the nation, stretching from Flanders to the Atlantic coast, from the Alps to the Pyrenees; and in 20 other departments similar forces were being organised. Sixty-six departments in all experienced the phenomenon of the *armées révolutionnaires*, with only 20 departments remaining outside the move-ment. Over 45 '*armées*', battalions or companies saw active service, 20 more were in the process of organisation at the time of the decree of 14 Frimaire, and there were perhaps a dozen bogus *armées révolutionnaires* or criminal bands operating also in widely scattered areas.

Such communal and departmental forces, while rare within a hundred-mile radius of Paris, achieved their maximum strength in the centre and south-west of the country. In former Federalist areas the extraordinary commissions simply acted as they pleased, and the 'map' of 'active' *armées* was more than anything that of the great 'proconsulates' and the para-revolutionary administrations. The Midi, the Centre and above all the departments of what was once Languedoc seem to have been the election grounds for these anarchic forces. They were also numerous in frontier areas like the Loire valley, or the Lyon area, and their absence from the Paris region can be explained by the proximity of the Committee of Public Safety and the fact that the Parisian *armée* fulfilled many of the functions which were assigned to departmental and communal companies elsewhere. Apart from exceptional cases like that of the Lyon region, it was unusual for Parisian detachments and local forces to coexist in the same area.

Almost all these *armées*, with the exception of those recruited in a group of departments, originated in towns which were having difficulty supplying their markets: Lille, Metz, Evreux, Nantes, Orléans, Tours, Nevers, Clamecy, Moulins, Mâcon, Saint-Etienne, Montbrison, Roanne, Charlieu, Besançon, Grenoble, Bordeaux, Agen, Toulouse, Montauban, Cahors, Moissac, Pau, Tarbes, Montpellier, Aix, Marseille, Valence, Orange, Digne, Gap, Serres, Briançon.* Many of these towns had also participated in the campaign of September–October, when the orders creating the *armées* had achieved their desired end: the defence of the interests of the small urban consumer. Above all the map of active *armées* corresponds with areas in which crises of circulation and arrival of foodstuffs usually occurred.

Why were certain departments absent from this truly national movement? For Corsica and the Vendée the reason is evident: they were areas torn by civil war, their people, suspect in the eyes of the revolutionary authorities, appeared unworthy to bear arms, and it would indeed have been imprudent to enrol companies in disaffected areas. Besides, as in the Var, the repression of counter-revolutionary intrigues in the interior had assumed the proportions of a full-scale military campaign, and was beyond the capabilities of small political companies of poorly led civilians. Thus the conscripted troops were renamed for the occasion 'armée révolutionnaire de Toulon', or 'armée révolutionnaire du Midi',[1] just as the army which recaptured Bordeaux was entitled 'armée révolutionnaire de l'Ouest'.[2] The nature of the task justified the title. It is more difficult, however, to explain why the Somme and Pas-de-Calais, populous departments experiencing difficulty supplying their urban centres, escaped the experience of neighbouring departments – the Nord for instance having its own *armée* of the North, the Oise and Seine-Inférieure being visited by that of Paris. The explanation can probably be found in the personalities of the *représentants* sent on mission to these departments, and if André Dumont was typical of the demagogue who took spectacular initiatives, the Robespierrist, Le Bon, and his colleague, Laurent, disapproved of the actions of their colleagues in Lille in raising a departmental *armée*.

While not entirely relevant to our examination of real *armées révolutionnaires* as instruments of the Terror, 'private' *armées* in the service of particular groups, and bogus *armées* – criminal bands which assumed this imposing title – nevertheless deserve to be included, since their existence was in itself a kind of homage, albeit a compromising one, to the institution whose name they usurped so readily.[3] They also command attention for

* For the geographical distribution of 'active' and 'ephemeral' *armées*, see Appendix A, Tables 1 and 2.

another reason: acting under a borrowed name, they succeeded in casting doubt upon the activities of the legitimate *armées*. Five armed bands caused commotion in the area around Paris, two were active in the Lyon region and many at the gates of towns or more often in the brigands' paradise of the Lozère, Ardèche, Aveyron and particularly in the Forez. Other such bands proliferated in the vicinity of large towns or more often in regions where legitimate companies of *révolutionnaires* were active, as if some kind of bastard relationship existed between them and the legal or semi-legal forces from which they claimed to derive their powers, and sometimes even their emblems and uniforms. The large farmers never tried to distinguish between real and bogus *armées*; for them the relationship was self-evident.

In addition to such bandits, deserters reduced to living in the woods and fugitives from Federalism hiding in the mountains of the Beaujolais and the Forez – the chief recruiting ground for the bogus *armées révolutionnaires* – there were 'private' *armées*, formed in one place by a *société populaire*, in another by two or three local dignitaries to bolster their contested authority and reduce all opposition to the tyranny of the cantonal *chef-lieu*. The little 'armée' of Lassay, in the Mayenne, falls into this category; it was an instrument of the partisan passions of three or four notables, violent men, using their band of 'heavies' to thrash their opponents in the streets. Of the same breed was the Dax company, a pressure tool in the hands of the clan which dominated the *société populaire* and which held the municipality and *comité révolutionnaire* in its grip. The company was composed of those who propped up the bars in the little town; they were entirely devoted to their masters, who funded their gilded idleness, paid for their drinking bouts, and who could count on them in the *société populaire* and in the streets.[4] In Sedan a group of advanced but patriotic revolutionaries – treated as Hébertists under the Robespierrist dictatorship – were surrounded by a body of soldiers in charge of prisoners and bearing the strange title of 'armée révolutionnaire du Mont-Dieu'.[5] At a time when revolutionary forces proliferated under a multitude of names, it was tempting for ambitious, eager or unscrupulous men to acquire such a malleable instrument by arming hired hands or simpletons for their own purposes – an initiative all the more attractive when it cost them nothing. The small 'band' of Lassay lived off fines and 'taxes' which its leaders extracted from the rich and the 'fanatical'.[6] The Dax company was paid for by the commune; the Sedan guard was subsidised by the prisoners, obliged to pay the costs of their detention. It is not difficult to see where all this could lead, and the transition from the 'private' army to one of extortion was easily made. After Thermidor it was said of the Sedan 'armée' that its masters intended using it to extort money from wealthy inhabitants under threat of arrest. It is true that such abuses existed also in the real *armées* – the Viton soldiers acted in a similar manner in the Aveyron – but since these forces were controlled by a number of different authorities, it was much more difficult for such practices to take hold.

The commanders of the 'legal' *armées* (if such an adjective can be applied to institutions produced by a revolutionary crisis and a confusion of authority) were the first to recognise the dangers of such 'competition'. At their request large detachments from the Paris and Moselle *armées* were sent to crush these brigand groups by depriving them of their titles, and if public order was better preserved on the roads and in the woods during that winter than it was in the Year III, and particularly in the Year IV, much of the credit must go to the *armées révolutionnaires*. The existence of such 'bands' and 'private' *armées* reflected on the honour and therefore on the effectiveness of the real ones and furnished the opponents of the *armées révolutionnaires* with their most effective arguments against their existence.

All these *armées*, however, whether 'legal', 'private' or bogus, were still part of the same family, even if they did not always serve the same ends. The former served a *société*, a town, a district or a department, the others reinforced the personal ambitions of a handful of men or gave themselves over to banditry; but all were tainted with illegality from the outset. The Parisian *armée* might pride itself on its statutory basis; the departmental and communal *armées*, however, were begat in questionable circumstances and amidst disorder. The peasantry was right to consider them 'anarchical forces', because administratively they owed their existence to anarchy. This is true in particular of the small companies, formed in the shadow of the large *armées* and worming themselves into existence unnoticed by the *représentants* and the superior authorities. They were also the most disorderly in their activities, as if to compensate for material weakness by deliberately brutal behaviour. Born in anarchy, the small forces in particular were to act out their existence in confusion and violence.

II   *The administrative status of the departmental and communal* armées

(i)   A CENTRAL *ARMÉE* OR LOCAL *ARMÉES*?

The petitioning campaign of September–October and the decree of 5 September left the choice open between the formation of a central *armée révolutionnaire* and the multiplication of local *armées* at department, district or local level. The former supposed an enormous expansion of the Parisian *armée*, with recruitment open to the whole of France. This is not only what Ronsin and his colleagues asked for, because of its obvious advantages, but what Sectionary opinion too, and even certain Jacobin circles, would have liked. For once *sectionnaires* and militant Jacobins were in agreement in recommending a centralised solution which, in giving priority to Paris, would avert all danger of 'Federalism'.[7] Even the Parisian sans-culottes who in their demands as in their political methods were champions of decentralised autonomy, opposed such autonomy when it benefited the sans-culottes and *sociétés* of the departments rather than Paris and its Sections.

The second solution, in contrast, was that which most pleased the departmental revolutionaries, anxious to protect that local autonomy which would guarantee their special institutions and innovatory initiatives. The large assemblies of the *sociétés populaires*, initially confined to the South-East, favoured the establishment of a force enrolled from several departments, viewing it perhaps as a way of perpetuating their own influence by bolstering it with an inter-departmental, even national, armed force. At the same time these assemblies, which were extraordinary and short-lived unions of local *sociétés populaires*, were trying to turn themselves into permanent institutions through the creation of 'delegations' and permanent offices. The Légion de la Montagne, whose enrolment had been decided at Valence in September, though recruiting exclusively from *sociétaires* in Frimaire, later at Marseille was willing to accept candidates from all over the country, provided they had certificates or diplomas from their *sociétés populaires*. The enrolment of this Legion, necessitating the formation of a general staff as excessive in number as that of the rue de Choiseul, with offices for correspondence and enrolment in the rue Libertas in Marseille, permitted the principal delegates from the assembly also to remain active, travelling through the neighbouring departments, raising recruits for the departmental forces as well as for the Légion and organising repressive measures. Here then was an *armée*, an administration and a general staff under the control of the *sociétés populaires*, a 'federal' *armée* already in existence and on its way to becoming the kind of national *armée* of which the sans-culottes dreamed. In Pluviôse when this 'child' of the *sociétés populaires* lost its autonomy and was joined to the military corps, volunteers flocked to Marseille from every corner of the Republic.[8]

The enrolment of the Légion de la Montagne, and its recruitment from all over the Republic, was the only concrete result of the efforts of the south-eastern *sociétés populaires* to establish 'federal' *armées*. It was indeed a spectacular result, but one from which the *sociétés* could derive little benefit, since the Légion was to be incorporated into the armies of the Republic prior to their dispatch to fight the Spanish. By the same stroke the Légion became a harmless institution, a 'governmental' body like the 'Jacobin cavaliers', themselves the product of *société* initiative.

The example of Valence–Marseille was repeated at Gap. The *armée* created by the popular assembly of the Hautes-Alpes was recruited exclusively from this department. But the assembly delegates aspired to a more extensive recruitment, dreaming also of a 'federal' *armée* whose example might be followed by the other departments, and while the order of 21 Brumaire envisaged the formation of a revolutionary battalion of 200 men, 50 from each district, the door was left open for further extension. 'Let this example find many imitators!' proclaimed the Hautes-Alpes assembly; 'such unions of true sans-culottes are the only means of giving that hatred, which every Republican feels for Federalists, tyrants, and traitors, the revolutionary energy which circumstances demand...'.[9] In this way, from one assembly to another, France would soon have been covered with a network of 'federal' institutions and inter-departmental *armées* loyal to them. But there was no sequel to the Gap assembly, for it was the last of these gatherings which so disturbed the Committee of Public Safety and even sans-culotte opinion, because of the concrete form they gave to the spectre of a new, popular and armed 'federalism'.

Some *représentants* in the South-West and East also favoured an 'inter-departmental' solution, although for quite different reasons, for they saw in such a combination a way of preventing the pre-eminence of any one department. Paganel opted for federal recruitment in the case of the so-called 'armée de la Haute-Garonne' in order to prevent the departmental administration, and even more the Toulouse authorities, from using it in the exclusive interest of their citizens. His effort was wasted, for this *armée*, despite the fact that elements from other departments, already on garrison duty in Toulouse, were incorporated, nevertheless did become the instrument of the Toulouse authorities.[10]

In the East, on the other hand, initially at least, this method was more successful, with two cases of *armées* recruited from a group of departments. On 24 Vendémiaire the *représentants* to the Rhine and Moselle Armies (Mallarmé, Lacoste, Guyardin, Ehrmann, Milhaud, Ruamps, Borie, Miou, Richard and Soubrany) ordered the enrolment of two large 'regional' *armées*: the *armée révolutionnaire* of the Moselle (called 'armée révolutionnaire de l'Est'[11] or 'armée révolutionnaire de Metz'), and that of the Bas-Rhin (called 'armée révolutionnaire de Strasbourg').[12] Encouraged no doubt by the Strasbourg example, three other groups of *représentants*, in a series of somewhat contradictory orders, also proceeded to enrol 'inter-departmental' *armées*. On 9 Brumaire the *représentants* to the Army of the Alps, then in Lyon–Couthon, Maignet, Sébastien Delaporte, Châteauneuf-Randon and Albitte – announced the formation of an *armée* of 1,000 men in the departments of the Ain, Jura, Côte-d'Or, Haute-Saône, Saône-et-Loire, Rhône, Loire, Isère, Mont-Blanc and Drôme. On the very same day, however, the *représentants* at Chambéry (Simond and Dumas) also announced the enrolment of a revolutionary battalion for Mont-Blanc, to be composed of 9 companies of 130 men each, and recruited from this department alone.[13] The authorities of the Loire were quick to point out to the *représentants* in Lyon that their department already possessed a departmental *armée révolutionnaire*, created by an order of Javogues and Bassal on 20 October,[14] and which was already being organised at the time of the collective order of 9 Brumaire. But there was more: at Besançon, Bassal, in the absence of his colleague Bernard de Saintes, issued an order for the formation of a large *armée* of 24 companies, each of 100 men, 4 or 5 companies to come from each of 6 departments: the Doubs, Jura, Côte-d'Or, Haute-Saône, Ain and Mont-Terrible – in other words almost the same area covered by the Lyon order[15] – an excellent example of the administrative disorder of the period, with the multiplication of *armées* created by rival *représentants*.

The large 'collective' forces were above all intended to accelerate the process of supplying the Armies at the front, ensuring that the grain harvest was threshed, watching over the routes to the frontiers and preventing exportation to Switzerland or Piedmont, gathering horses, carriages and harness, and generally keeping the peace in the rear of the troops fighting the allied forces – tasks which went beyond the exclusive interests of any one town or department. Indeed Delaporte and his colleagues ensured against local interests prevailing by specifying in their collective order that the *armées* formed by the group of 10 departments should operate outside their departments of origin and under *commissaires* who were themselves strangers to the departments in which their operations took place. It was laid down, for example, that the *armée* of the Haute-Saône would 'revolutionise' the Côte-d'Or, that of the Loire, the Rhône, and so on. It was not simply a question of removing the departmental grip on these *armées*,[16] but of ensuring that supplies requisitioned in this group of departments would reach the regular Armies of the Alps, Rhine and Moselle, away fighting the enemy at the frontier. 'Our external enemies act in concert with those of the interior', claimed the order, '...to starve our armies...it is essential that a military force be assigned to act constantly and exclusively to procure for the Armies of the Rhine and Moselle everything they need...'.[17]

The intentions of the *représentants*, however, were far from clear and some local administrations, overwhelmed with work and grappling with a succession of contradictory orders, wondered quite what was expected of them. Ought they to send the volunteers to Metz or to Strasbourg, to swell the forces being raised there? Or was it simply a case of raising battalions for service in their own or in neighbouring departments?[18] In the departments of Mont-Blanc, Marne and Haute-Marne the authorities were indeed recruiting for the Strasbourg or Metz *armées*.[19] But simultaneously this group of departments, behind the military zone from the Marne to the Isère, were raising departmental battalions. All was done amidst incredible confusion, largely produced by this succession of contradictory orders, with the lower administrations repeatedly asking the district or department what steps they ought to take. Right until the end some *comités* and *sociétés populaires* had no fixed destination for the battalions whose organisation they were nevertheless doing everything to accelerate. Preparations were sufficiently advanced, by the time of the law of 14 Frimaire, that the volunteers had been enrolled and some had already been paid and received their uniforms. At Mâcon and, it seems, at Besançon[20] district companies were already active, while the large *armées* of the East and of Alsace were covering the frontier zones. But as late as Frimaire many districts were still asking where these companies and battalions were to serve, and in the Marcigny district the *commissaires* firmly declared that they were to protect local supplies.[21] Thus, even if these areas participated in the formation of two 'inter-departmental' *armées* on the frontiers, the orders of Bassal and his colleagues produced a simultaneous proliferation of companies which never got beyond the planning stage in more than 20 districts. Once again the outcome was the kind of fractionalisation which this recruiting method had specifically sought to avoid.

Besides, the *représentants* were not unanimous in recommending an 'inter-departmental' solution; most creators of such forces were content to limit their efforts to a single department. For Maure, of Auxerre, for instance, the question was quite simply one of ensuring food supplies for his electors in the Yonne. As for the large urban *sociétés populaires* or those of the bourgs, they preferred *armées* which would remain exclusively under their control and insisted on the creation of departmental or communal forces. Only rarely did anyone oppose such measures.[22] The *comités de surveillance* and the municipalities also preferred a system which in their eyes had the merit of assuring them practical control of the new *armées*.

In this 'debate' between the supporters of a central *armée* and those of a series of inter-departmental or of innumerable local *armées*, the Revolutionary Government intervened in only a negative fashion: by closing the door on any further expansion of the Parisian *armée*, it condemned the solution favoured by Sectionary opinion, by the *Père Duchesne*, and by certain Jacobins. By this action it cleared the way for local experiment, for if the Committee turned a deaf ear to Ronsin and the Sections, it remained silent for a long time in the face of the *fait accompli* presented by the proliferation of orders at departmental, district and communal level. Undoubtedly the Committee did not yet want to disavow the work of some of its most active disciples, and perhaps it was divided within itself: Couthon, Hérault and Jeanbon had certainly contributed to the formation of departmental or inter-departmental *armées*, while some of their colleagues in the Committee of General Security looked favourably on orders of which they were sometimes themselves the authors. In a symbolic gesture of 30 September, the Committee of Public Safety provided an insight into the private opinions of some of its members by ordering Bouchotte to have the so-called 'armée révolutionnaire de l'Ouest' debaptised, adding: 'there are no individual armies in a republic'. For the Committee the Parisian *armée* alone had the right to call itself 'révolutionnaire' inasmuch as it was the '*armée* of the Convention'. But no one seems to have paid much attention to such weak signs of disapproval, and the Committee's attitude remained equivocal and even contradictory. If Ronsin's *armée* was in its eyes the only legal revolutionary force, it did not sanction the reinforcement of that body, and for a long time its silence facilitated the flow of orders creating departmental forces. It did not even speak out on an issue of such national importance as the enrolment of the Légion de la Montagne, and left the responsibility for its legitimisation to the *représentants* at Marseille.[23] That silence was to be interpreted as positive encouragement, and many *représentants* thought they could proceed on their own initiative. It was not until the last days of Brumaire that the Committee forsook its reticence.[24] Until then the initiative remained with those on the spot: *représentants* and their *délégués*, Ministry *commissaires*, assemblies of the *sociétés populaires*, individual *sociétés*, municipalities, *comités de surveillance*, urban 'disciples', country revolution-aries from the violent and ambitious world of the bourg and the village, *commissaires des guerres*, sincere patriots, demagogic ultras, administrators struggling with the immobility and the ill will of the rural population.

(ii) THE CREATORS OF THE DEPARTMENTAL *ARMÉES*

The creation of the departmental and communal *armées* posed administra-tive problems of formidable proportions, but thanks to central govern-ment's abandonment of responsibility and the absence of any precise rules, these problems were overcome so well that it is difficult to identify the authorities responsible for the initial creation of the *armées*. Most corps claimed that they had originated with an order from one of the *représen-tants en mission*, which, in the absence of any indisputably legal existence, gave them some sort of respectability in the doubtful hierarchy of terrorist institutions. Others, products of decisions by the urban *sociétés populaires*, were legitimised by the *représentants* who assumed their parenthood. But there were others, in no way 'respectable', which owed their origin to the inspiration of one man, acting sometimes on his own initiative, sometimes on that of a *société populaire,* a *comité révolutionnaire* or a municipality. These corps had no order of formation to define their areas of competence, and they were often the most violent, the most undisciplined, the most 'révolu-tionnaire'.

In the South-West, the creators of the *armées révolutionnaires* were general-ly the *représentants*, those great proconsuls who, far from Paris, and pro-tected as personal emissaries of the Committee of Public Safety, lorded over vast areas covering several departments. For them the battalions and com-panies were simply a modest cog of enforcement in a huge terrorist machine which they were putting together with the assistance of some henchmen noted for the violence of their language, the ardour of their convictions and their zeal for 'revolutionising'. These were the secretaries and *délégués* of the *représentants*, the *commissaires civils*, the members of central *comités de surveil-lance*, the district administrators, and the *commissaires* sent on circuit by the extraordinary commissions. The most prolific creators of *armées* were Paganel, Taillefer, Baudot, Chaudron-Rousseau, Dartigoëyte, Monestier (from the Puy-de-Dôme), Boisset and Reynaud, *Conventionnels* who divided between them all of Languedoc, the Pyrenees to the Massif Central, and the Rhône valley.

In the South-east, scene of the general assemblies and choice territory for the small communal companies, the *représentants* who assumed responsi-bility for such creations were Barras, Fréron, Pomme, Charbonnier, Moïse Bayle in the Bouches-du-Rhône, Maignet in the Vaucluse, d'Herbez-Latour and Beauchamp in the Hautes- and Basses-Alpes.

Tallien and Isabeau created the revolutionary forces of the Gironde, their zeal even causing them to 'revolutionise' the title of the army which laid siege to Bordeaux. In the Centre the originators of these forces were, above all, Javogues and Bassal (who created two *armées*), Fouché and Laplanche, Delaporte, Albitte, Maignet, Châteauneuf-Randon and Couthon; and in the Alps, Simond and Dumas. The large *armées* of the East and of Alsace owed their existence primarily to Mallarmé, Lacoste, Guyardin, Richaud, Soubrany, Ehrmann and Baudot; Hérault de Séchelles created a small *armée* in the Haut-Rhin,[25] and Châles and Isoré gave their blessing to the Lille *armée*. Finally, in the West, Carrier, Hentz, Francastel and Jeanbon Saint-André signed orders creating revolutionary forces, while nearer to Paris, the timid Maure made plans for an *armée* in the Yonne.

At first sight, therefore, the *représentants* seem to have been solely responsible for this profusion of individual *armées*. But this is an over-simplified picture; these men did not form a unified body. Only a minority were convinced terrorists: others changed with the wind, conforming to the current revolutionary trend; others again were real fanatics who took advantage of their immense powers to 'revolutionise' at an accelerated pace. Boisset in the Hérault was one of the weathervanes who, after having been a vociferous supporter of the new forces, given his blessing to the Légion de la Montagne, and consented to the creation of another battalion at Montpellier (whose praises he sang), was quick to condemn them when he sensed the changing wind. Tallien and Isabeau, Barras and Fréron sought to avert suspicion of their own purity of principle by particularly spectacular and violent measures, orders couched in pitiless terms, and by the creation of military commissions; violence with them was a cloak for embezzlement and fraudulence. The creation of an *armée* allowed a weakling or a villain to pass for a hardened Montagnard, a 'Brutus' for a public-spirited republican. Barras too should be singled out from the other three *Conventionnels*; an authentic terrorist in his time, he was able to use his influence after the Year III to protect his former subordinates in terrorism.

The case of men like Paganel and Dartigoëyte is more complicated. Seeking to imitate their neighbours – and in the South-West it was the doctor, Taillefer, who sought to drive the 'revolutionary chariot' at an almost demonic pace – subject also to intense pressure from local zealots, they had no wish to remain idle. They nevertheless had their doubts, for these terrorists were also men of order who found the excesses of anarchy repugnant, and their *armées* were hedged about by all kinds of restrictive and frequently contradictory rulings, in the same vein as those of the Committee of Public Safety when on 9 September it imposed rigid restrictions on the free development of the Parisian *armée*. Paganel feared the 'federalisation' of these forces; unsure of himself, he maintained a voluminous correspondence with the Committee of Public Safety in the hope of receiving some directives. These were a long time in coming. The position of those pursuing such a 'wait-and-see' policy was not easy, for the government said nothing, and the actions of their colleagues furnished the local revolutionaries with powerful arguments.

Let us move on now to those who were determined supporters of the new *armées* and all the major repressive measures. They were not all furious men like Taillefer who 'revolutionised' in the Lot, Aveyron, Cantal and Lozére, or like Claude Javogues, a noble-hearted and courageous man, a genuine revolutionary and patriot, who terrorised the moderates and former Federalists of the Loire. Some were government men, like Vadier and Bayle, Couthon, Hérault and Jeanbon; others were energetic Montagnards, but without the violence and drive of a Taillefer or a Javogues. For them these *armées* were necessary instruments of the Terror, designed to ensure supplies and effect measures of repression. In creating them they in no way deferred to pressure from the *sociétés populaires*; they never intended placing them in the hands of an irresponsible power, but sought to use them as instruments of government. The leading figures behind the departmental *armées* were Fouché in the Nièvre and the Allier, Laplanche in the Loiret – the two proconsuls who initiated the movement, their orders providing the model for many others – Châles and Isoré in the Nord, Mallarmé, Lacoste and Baudot in the East, Baudot again, Monestier, Dartigoëyte and Chaudron-Rousseau in the departments of the South-West, Carrier and Francastel in the Loire-Inférieure and Morbihan, Simond in the Alps, Reynaud in the Puy-de-Dôme and the Loire,[26] Bassal in Burgundy, Franche-Comté and the Loire. Some were responsible for the creation of two or three *armées* in different departments as they moved from one region to another: Baudot enrolled *armées* in the South-West before going to the East, Bassal created an *armée* in the Loire, then, at a much later date, another at Besançon. Thus the same names can be found at the bottom of orders issued in the Midi and in the East, and the personal influence of these *Conventionnels* was an essential element in the extension of the forces via their proconsulates. 'Governmental' terrorists, some were also convinced dechristianisers, and if former ecclesiastics like Bassal, Laplanche, Châles and Fouché were among the most resolute supporters of the *armées*, it was because, as we shall see, they saw in them instruments of an anti-religious policy based on force which they had only dreamed about until then.

Conformism and revolutionary emulation favoured the course adopted by this group of determined and energetic men, and their actions ended the hesitation of other proconsuls, who took advantage of the same bitter administrative conflicts. Their colleagues were to accuse these men of having sought to use 'private' armies, 'praetorian guards', 'janissaries' to invade departments not covered by their orders. In fact territorial boundaries had been poorly drawn by the Committee and missions overlapped within the same departments. In Brittany two groups of *représentants* opposed each other over the creation of revolutionary battalions: Carrier, Hentz, Francastel and Pocholle on one side, Tréhouard and Laignelot on the other, with the latter two accusing Carrier of having 'invaded' their jurisdictional area of Morbihan on behalf of an *armée* formed in the Redon district of the neighbouring department.[27] Likewise Gouly, on mission to his native region, denounced Javogues to the Committee for having encroached upon his territory by sending revolutionary forces from the Loire, Rhône and Saône-et-Loire to the Ain department. The result was a bitter dispute between the two *représentants* which the Committee terminated by recalling both to Paris.[28] In the Nord, Laurent and Le Bon, on mission in the Pas-de-Calais, anxiously watched the energetic activities of the Montagnards Châles and Isoré at Lille, and the *armée révolutionnaire* of the North, created by the latter two, became the focus of the controversy which resulted in the recall of the two *représentants* at Lille, and their replacement by Florent Guiot and Duhem.[29] In the South-West, Fabre and Gaston, on mission to the Army of the Pyrénées-Orientales, were voicing as early as October their misgivings about the consequences of the revolutionary measures initiated by their colleagues Baudot and Chaudron-Rousseau in the neighbouring departments.[30] And on hearing of Maure's order for the formation of a departmental *armée révolutionnaire* in the Yonne, Garnier, on mission in the Aube, alerted his colleague to the consequences of such a dangerous measure; Maure prudently abandoned his project, at the same time complaining to the Committee of Garnier's interference in the affairs of Tonnerre.[31] These conflicts were above all personal affairs, with the revolutionary-minded Montagnards pitted against temporisers and moderates anxious to shield their electors from terrorist measures such as a visit from these revolutionary forces. (Tréhouard was a Breton, Gouly was from Bourg and Garnier from Troyes.) But the explanation lies also in the administrative anarchy caused by the Committee itself in sending multiple missions to the same regions. More serious was the exposure of departments bordering on those with revolutionary forces to the danger of forced revolutionisation by an outside battalion. Thus at the highest levels, and in the absence of central government direction, such measures only increased the disorder by making certain *représentants* veritable warlords, with forces all the more devoted to them because of gratitude for their high pay and employment in a privileged corps. Undoubtedly these Montagnards never considered using the *armées* to promote their personal ambitions. That was not the danger. But in multiplying the companies and battalions they made the administrative imbroglio more delicate and certainly more explosive.

The *représentants* were far from being the only creators of *armées révolutionnaires*. Even in the cases cited it was often a matter of responsibility shared among *représentants, sociétés populaires* and *comités de surveillance*, even of 'legitimising' measures already taken by revolutionary authorities which had no administrative competence, particularly in the regulation of armed forces. Knowing their powerlessness in this respect, *sociétés populaires* and *comités révolutionnaires* sought to cover themselves by seeking approval of their decisions and projects from the *représentants*. Proconsuls such as Fouché,[32] Laplanche[33] and Monestier,[34] who took sole responsibility for raising battalions in their territory, were in a minority. The situation is not so clearly drawn in the other departments. Carrier, for instance, although a great supporter of the *armées révolutionnaires*, simply confirmed the existence of the Marat battalion at Nantes, which was created when he was still at Rennes by the *comité révolutionnaire* or the Vincent-la-Montagne *société*, or both together. On his arrival at Nantes, Carrier accepted the *fait accompli* and his contribution was simply to give the battalion legal status and to change its name from 'compagnie révolutionnaire' to 'bataillon Marat'.[35]

In the Nord a project to organise 2,000 men under the denomination 'Armée révolutionnaire' was submitted to the *représentants* by the *société révolutionnaire*. The president of the *société* was Dufresse, and its administration was totally dominated by a group of Parisians, all soldiers from the Panthéon-Français Section or civilians like Decrosne, president of the *comité de surveillance*, a Cordelier and Ministry *commissaire*. Three days later, the *représentants* Châles and Isoré agreed to the suggestion, and the 'armée révolutionnaire du Nord' was formed by an order of 5 Brumaire which followed the recommendations of the *société* almost to the letter. The final stage came when Decrosne, in the name of the *société* and with the blessing of the *représentants*, launched the recruiting campaign.[36] At a later date Isoré would take responsibility for the creation of 'his' *armée*, but the real creators were Dufresse, Lavalette and Decrosne.[37] The two *représentants* had been away in Brussels that winter, where they raised the Brussels Légion des Sans-culottes, and were consequently not around for the early stages of the project.[38] The role of Châles and Isoré was minimal, and after having approved the *armée révolutionnaire* in principle, the *représentants* confided the business of raising it to the administrative council.[39]

Thanks to the conflict between Dufresse and Decrosne, Châles and Isoré, and their colleagues (and enemies) on mission to Arras, plus the proceedings instituted against Dufresse in the Year III, we have an abundance of information on the circumstances leading to the creation and organisation of the Lille *armée*. The main conclusion we can draw is that no one man was responsible for this measure. The garrison soldiers and the Parisian leaders of the *société populaire* were the first to conceive of such a popular *armée*, but the decisive step came when the *représentants* took the matter in hand. This *armée* therefore had a multiple parentage and the case does not seem to have been an unusual one. In other areas too the role of the *représentants* was limited to one of approving projects presented by the *sociétés* or by the *comités*. Even the initiatives taken by the spirited Javogues probably owed much to pressing requests from the extremely active *société* of Charlieu,[40] and in Taillefer's proconsulate the *armées révolutionnaires* were already a live topic long before his arrival.[41] This Montagnard was to be quickly surpassed by the actions of his numerous *délégués*. At Moissac the *comité de surveillance* on its own initiative ordered the enrolment of a tiny, if none the less violent, *armée*, destined to ensure it a very dubious authority over the entire district of Lauzerte, when its official powers covered only Moissac and its canton. Having made this decision the *comité* took the opportunity of Taillefer's arrival to have it confirmed.[42]

In Montauban too, the *comité* took the initiative, writing to Baudot on 21

September to announce the formation of a revolutionary battalion: 'we send the enclosed order which we thought we should draw up to secure authorisation for its prompt formation'. Baudot was not offended by such cavalier action and on receipt of the letter he took measures to confirm the step taken by the *comité*. The *comité* received this 'official' order, dated 22 September, on the 27th and proceeded immediately to organise the battalion.[43] In the Hautes- and Basses-Alpes, the *représentants* simply countersigned the orders issued by the general assembly of Gap and by the delegates from Marseille and the Drôme sent by the Valence–Marseille assembly as 'disciples' into these two departments.[44] In Montpellier, Delbret and Boisset acceded to repeated entreaties from the *société populaire*, in which the 'agitators', friends of Mazuel, had been authors of the initial project of April 1793. Boisset also agreed to proposals for the enrolment of the Légion de la Montagne addressed to him by the general assembly of Valence.[45] If Monestier was ahead of the local authorities in the Hautes-Pyrénées, in the neighbouring department the first proposals in favour of a departmental force came from the *sociétés* of Pau and Morlaas, on 25 September and 19 Vendémiaire.[46] In Limoges the *comité* and *société* decided upon the creation of a revolutionary battalion without contacting anyone; later Brival and Lanot took up the project, which they hastened to render inoffensive.[47]

Did Maure then decide on his own initiative to raise an *armée* in the Yonne? This seems unlikely, particularly since the Auxerre *société* included an active minority of notable terrorists, who were on close terms with the 'agitators' of the l'Homme-Armé and Finistère Sections in Paris.[48] In the East, Mallarmé was undoubtedly primarily responsible for the creation of the Moselle *armée*, but the influence of the two *commissaires civils*, Gobert and Delteil, the former an important personality at Metz, the latter a Parisian and 'homme de liaison', was dominant in all issues concerning the organisation and enrolment of this *armée*. Once again it would be no exaggeration to speak of it as a collective product.[49] In the Jura too, if its local historian is to be credited, Bassal simply acceded to the entreaties of the local terrorists.[50]

Most *représentants* were strangers to the departments when they arrived – those who were not, Gouly and Tréhouard, for example, were hostile to the creation of the *armées* – and from the time of their arrival they simply yielded to pressure from the local *sociétés* and from those already on the scene: *commissaires* of the Ministries, garrison soldiers, country revolutionaries. Isolated as they were in regions where the enemies of the Revolution predominated, and dependent on revolutionary minorities to execute their orders and for information on the local situation, the *représentants* were in no position to resist. It would have taken considerable courage and determination for a *représentant* to set his face against the militants in the departments, who would not have hesitated to denounce him as 'lukewarm' had he opposed the implementation of these major revolutionary measures. The result was that in many areas the role of *représentant* was purely a formal one, with his signature giving an appearance of legality to measures already decided upon, and sometimes partially implemented. No one, at least in the Year II, contested the right of the *représentants* to authorise the enrolment of political armies. It was simply a matter, therefore, of 'hommes de liaison', the *sociétaires* and other local revolutionaries getting the proconsuls to accept administrative responsibility for measures already decided upon by a select group in the *sociétés* or by the *comités de surveillance*.[51] Everyone felt properly covered once the order was signed and thereafter it was difficult to contest the legality of these measures by accusing the local authorities of having acted beyond their powers. The participation of the *représentants*, whether active or passive, was therefore indispensable. In some regions, though this happened rarely, the local authorities, not content with this guarantee, sought the approval also of the Convention or the Committee of Public Safety. Carrier, a more prudent man than is generally thought, wondered if the agreement of the Convention or the Committee of Public Safety was necessary for the enrolment of revolutionary battalions in Brittany; but his hesitation was fleeting, and he proceeded without it. The Vertu-Sociale *société* at Versailles, and the general assembly of *sociétés* in Gap did expect some recourse to the Convention, while the *société* at Ornans, though enthusiastically in favour of the formation of an *armée* in the Doubs, was overcome by doubts: 'we ought to refer it to the Convention which will tell us the method and the manner'.[52] But in the Hautes-Alpes Beauchamp did not wait for a signal from the Assembly to activate the battalion,[53] and elsewhere people were content to have such measures confirmed by the *représentants*.

The importance of the proconsuls to such creations becomes all the more evident in departments where they were sufficiently strong to oppose them. In the Seine-Inférieure Louchet and Delacroix brutally terminated the projects put forward by the *sociétés* of Rouen, Le Havre and neighbouring towns in favour of a departmental *armée*.[54] At Perpignan, Gaston and Fabre were hostile to all large-scale terrorist measures, but more importantly they were furious at the way their authority was held up to ridicule by the *société populaire* and by the Ministry *commissaire*, Hardy, and moved quickly to crush any project for a Pyrénées-Orientales *armée révolutionnaire* at the outset. It was not simply a matter of *amour-propre*, but one of fear, a fear shared by many more *représentants*, that the *sociétés populaires*, the 'hommes de liaison' (at Perpignan the shoemaker Hardy and a local terrorist, Chambon)[55] and the *commissaire des guerres* would replace them once these last had an armed force at their disposal.[56] In the Seine-et-Oise the response of the *représentants* to demands which ultimately were supported by all the local authorities of Versailles and Saint-Germain was more qualified. Levasseur de la Sarthe, an energetic Montagnard, certainly supported them. But the *armées révolutionnaires*, particularly that of Paris, had no opponent more bitter than Delacroix, on mission in this department in Brumaire, when the Versailles Sections were attempting to put their projects into effect.[57] As for Crassous, a subtle, prudent colonial, by turns a relentless terrorist and a moderate, it is difficult to see quite what game he was playing. But as far as one can tell, most *représentants* in this department, Delacroix excluded, were content to transmit the wishes of the Versailles authorities to the Convention or the Committee without themselves commenting on the subject. In sum, the negative influence of the *représentants* was probably more important than any favourable intervention on their part.[58]

Forty of the 54 battalions or companies activated were thus guaranteed, if not actually created, by orders signed by the *représentants en mission*, even if the initiative had come originally from a *société populaire* or a *comité de surveillance*. In terms of administration, the participation of the *représentants* was of the utmost importance, which will be all the more apparent when we examine the origin of the 20 *armées* which were prevented from ever functioning by the law of 14 Frimaire.[59] At least 12 of these 'ephemeral' forces owed their initial organisation to joint orders of the *représentants* in a group of departments.*

There remain about a dozen *armées* which enjoyed no support from the *représentants* but owed their existence to departmental, municipal or district decisions, to the intervention of 'hommes de liaison' from the major towns or local revolutionaries, to *commissaires* of all kinds from Paris or the other major communes, to delegates from the general assemblies or agents from the great extraordinary commissions – men who united in themselves those political and judicial functions which Sectionary opinion in Paris and the terrorist minorities in the departments wished to see entrusted to the *armées révolutionnaires*.[60] Many, like the *représentants*, were 'outsiders', but because of extended residence in a region, they had an influence which was real. Unlike the proconsuls, constantly on the move within their areas of jurisdiction, their influence intermittent, these men acted as political counsellors to the departmental terrorists and were often highly esteemed by them. They knew the local militants, were informed about personal conflicts, and held commanding positions in the *sociétés*. In this respect, the situation at Lille, where the *société révolutionnaire* was truly 'colonised' by such outsiders, notably by Parisians, was simply a broader version of what happened in many other localities, particularly those which also had important garrisons.

The other main element behind the creation of the *armées* were the *sociétés populaires* in towns or bourgs with markets to supply; and although in some large towns or military posts these *sociétés* fell into the hands of outsiders, they were on the whole instruments of active minorities and clusters of local revolutionaries. More than half the *armées*, both 'active' and 'ephemeral', were first announced in motions and orders by the popular assemblies. The others owed their existence to decisions by the *comités de surveillance*, which

* See Appendix A, Table 3, for a chronological list of these orders.

were as important as the *sociétés* in terms of setting the whole process in motion, and much more so in terms of translating hopes into actions, organising the battalions and putting them into operation.[61] Two *armées* were created by departmental administration, the Meurthe *armée* and the Cher cavalry, and one by a district directory (Clamecy), whose personal guard it later became.

In origin therefore the departmental and communal *armées* were linked above all to the *sociétés populaires* and the *comités de surveillance*. Only at Versailles, Lille and Bordeaux can we talk in terms of an *armée* of *sectionnaires*, and Versailles was certainly the only town in France outside Paris where the initial demand for a sans-culotte *armée* had come from the Sectionary assembly.

In the departments, even more than in Paris, the *sociétés* and even the *comités* were outside the control of the legal authorities, remaining instead the preferred instruments of small groups of 'agitators'. The situation developing at Dax repeated itself elsewhere, and it was with good reason that the worried Jacobins christened the Bas-Rhin *armée* the 'guard of honour' of Euloge Schneider.[62] The *armées* of Vauquoy and Contamin did indeed belong to these two men; in the Corbigny district the local militant and *commissaire civil*, Chaix, spoke of 'his' sans-culottes, while Mazuel likewise referred to 'his' cavaliers. It might be argued that these are extreme cases and that most companies and battalions remained the docile and obedient instruments of the *comités* and the established authorities. But the danger of such 'personalisation' was ever present, particularly in small towns and bourgs where the revolutionary institutions could easily be taken over and used in the interests of a few militant revolutionaries or interested individuals. It was not mere chance that the most violent and most undisciplined *armées* were also the smallest; only the very large *armées*, raised in several departments, escaped the grip of such 'agitators' or the *sociétés* which gave them their power.

The *sociétés populaires* sought to derive maximum benefit from the situation, and frequently complained of the delays caused by some local authorities in the organisation and equipment of the new forces. If the great urban *sociétés* had had full control of proceedings, France would almost certainly have been completely covered by these political troops. But the *sociétés* had to work with the elected authorities who were less enthusiastic about unleashing such urban guards upon their electors, and could do little more than nag and entreat.[63] One must also distinguish between the town *sociétés* and those of the country, whose zeal was often feebler than that of the local authorities. In the Trévoux district, it was the directory which complained of the tardiness of the *sociétés* of the arrondissement in opening enrolment lists.[64]

The creators of the departmental *armées* were therefore the *représentants*, the 'hommes de liaison' who were generally not native to the region in which they operated,[65] and the local 'agitators' who led the *sociétés popu-*

laires.[66] In a few cases the influence of a district, a department or a Section can be detected. Some *armées* were created by *comités de surveillance*. But it was not enough just to create an *armée*, it had to be organised too and set in motion, and this involved the participation of many different authorities. Even when the *sociétés populaires* were closely associated with the creation of an *armée* and succeeded in retaining some hold over its recruitment, they did not generally succeed in directing operations once the battalion had been organised. Their victory was an empty one, for the instrument of force, which they had been largely responsible for forging, was in the hands of other authorities.

(iii)   THE ADMINISTRATIVE CONTROL OF THE NEW *ARMÉES*

The most characteristic aspect of all the departmental and communal *armées* was undoubtedly the strict control which the *sociétés populaires* and the *comités de surveillance* exercised over the choice of these future soldiers. Most orders of formation specified that candidates must possess certificates of *civisme* and undergo the *scrutin épuratoire* of the *sociétés* – some went further in specifying that they must also be *sociétaires* in possession of diplomas as such. In the East, in Franche-Comté and in Burgundy, the *représentants* also involved the *sociétés* in the next stage of the enrolment and organisation of the companies and battalions by ordering them to form 'nuclei' – small groups of a dozen or so men, all *sociétaires*, who would assume responsibility for recruitment. Most *représentants* therefore agreed in officially associating the *sociétés* with the recruitment process, thus recognising the composition of the *armées* as their particular area of concern, while dangling before them the prospect of also directing the future activities of these forces. Of course in the orders issued by the other authorities, the task of guaranteeing the political orthodoxy of candidates was also reserved to the *sociétés.*[67]

The choice of candidates was not, however, the monopoly of the *sociétés.* In the groups of departments covered by the orders of the *représentants* at Lyon and of Bassal, the *comités de surveillance* and the departmental and district administrations were also invited to participate in the formation of the small organisational nuclei.[68] In general the *comités révolutionnaires* had the final say. Everywhere candidates had to possess clean record sheets from them, and in some departments they were also responsible for recruitment and for all the stages of organisation without any involvement from the *sociétés.*[69] Such *comités*, while less 'governmental' than those of the Paris Sections, nevertheless avoided falling under the exclusive influence of the *sociétés* with which they were frequently in conflict.[70] Here then was one barrier to the exclusive control of the recruiting process by the *sociétés.*

In large towns such as Bordeaux, Lille, Metz, Toulouse and even medium-sized towns like Nevers and Moulins, and important bourgs like Salins, the Sections were also involved in this process. In Bordeaux, the general assemblies of the Sections joined to nominate candidates,[71] whose names were then submitted to an initial scrutiny by the *comités révolution-*

naires of the Sections. This was only the first stage. The final lists, drawn up by the Sections in agreement with their *comités*, were sent both to the *comité de surveillance* of the Bordeaux district and to the national club. The *comité* vetoed some candidates, but at this stage the *scrutin épuratoire* was little more than a formality, and the club accepted most of those on the list.[72] One can see why: the Sectionary assemblies acted from sound knowledge, recommending known citizens who were resident in the Section – Bordeaux and Lille prepared lists of candidates according to the streets in which they lived[73] – and the *comités révolutionnaires*, operating also at the level of the Section, had the same advantage. At club and district level they were dealing with unknowns. There it was only a matter of discarding those whose origin or occupation placed them automatically in the suspect category. There was a delay of four to six weeks between the time of compilation of the initial lists by the Sections and the scrutiny at national club level – hence the slowness of organisation of the *armées* in certain towns.

At Lille, where everything was done with greater rapidity than in Bordeaux, the *société* and the six Sections co-operated closely in drawing up the lists. A register was opened in each of the six Sections and remained in the possession of a *sociétaire*; each candidate had to possess a certificate testifying to his republican integrity, and be approved by a recognised patriot. Lists would be read out daily to the *société populaire*, the *scrutin épuratoire* applied to each individual, and no candidate was admitted without the approval of the *société*.[74] But the decisive factor in the choice of a candidate seems to have been the recommendation of a leading *sectionnaire*, a member of the *société* known to the inhabitants of his street.[75] The Lille *armée* was recruited in this fashion by small groups of militants, who used the general assemblies as recruiting grounds. Indeed, despite the many different stages (lists were submitted to the *comité de surveillance* after the *société*), elections were conducted rapidly in Lille, with the *scrutins épuratoires* completed in two weeks, 15–30 Brumaire, and most of the candidates accepted before the 22nd. This *armée*, though a Sectionary force, had also numerous links with the *société* which supplied its recruits.

At Versailles too recruitment was carried out by the Sections, and we have no evidence of the lists presented by the 13 Sections having been submitted to the two *sociétés*.[76] In Moulins the elections took place in the Sectionary assemblies, under the direction of *commissaires* from the *comité de surveillance*; and in the little towns of the Jura, Doubs and Saône-et-Loire, the *comités de surveillance* drew up the initial lists before presenting them to the *sociétés*.[77] At Gap, even though it was specified that the *armée* should be chosen from among the *sociétés* of the Hautes-Alpes, the election of candidates proceeded in an original manner, with the assembled National Guard being asked to nominate them.[78] At Nantes the *comité révolutionnaire* chose the members of the future company, and it was only in very small towns like Dax that a *société* managed to fill an entire company with recruits of its own choosing.[79]

The *sociétés populaires* then were being asked to organise a preliminary or, more often, a secondary sifting of candidates. *Armées* composed entirely of *sociétaires* were not normally the object, though the *sociétés* were asked to review those candidates nominated by their Sections, and they could exclude individuals by the refusal of a *certificat de civisme*. Of course in the smaller towns which tried to avoid any conflict between the Sections, the *sociètaires* took the first steps in forming a 'nucleus', the leading personalities of the popular assemblies placing their own names at the head of the list.[80] But this method was not adopted everywhere, and in some towns the enrolment registers were held by the *comités de surveillance* or even by the municipalities.

The participation of the *sociétés* above all supposed a voluntary service and every order insisted that candidates should be volunteers. But some *représentants* were less optimistic than their colleagues about the attractiveness of the new *armées* and foresaw the possibility of volunteers being insufficient to fill the ranks; in that case obligatory service would be considered, with district administrations instructed to nominate citizens from the second requisition. In general the lists were easily filled and there are only a few cases where the authorities had to resort to compulsion. At Pau, for instance, enrolment was more or less forced, for volunteers had been few in number. Briançon had a similar experience. But most departmental and communal *armées*, like that of Paris, were largely composed of volunteers, even if, at times, they had to be persuaded. This fact is important for an understanding of the independent spirit displayed by most of these political soldiers.[81] The *armées révolutionnaires* were never normal military forces composed of conscripts; thanks to the methods of recruitment their character as a voluntary force and a political élite was maintained.

As in Paris, the recruiting process was hedged about by all manner of political safeguards. This is why the *sociétés populaires* and the *comités de surveillance* were associated in the process. But once the choice of candidates had been made the role of the sociétés was considerably reduced, and details of the enrolment, organisation and equipping of the companies fell to the *comités*, the municipalities, the district directories and the *commissaires des guerres* – the influence of the *sociétés* only making itself felt thereafter through individual *sociétaires* who had succeeded in raising themselves to important positions in the new *armées*. Those who had been members of the original 'nucleus' sought to secure the rank of captain or lieutenant for themselves; but more often than not the key positions escaped them. The *commissaire civil*, though nearly always a member of a *société*, had links also with other authorities. Sometimes he was a member of the *comité de surveillance* in the departmental or district *chef-lieu*; often as an outsider, sometimes a Parisian, he belonged to a *société* other than that which had presided over the recruitment of the local company. It was the *commissaire civil* who was in charge; the military commanders were his subordinates, to the point where in certain *armées* they were powerless figures, 'parade horses', taken seriously by nobody.[82] In some towns positions of military command were given to old soldiers, beyond the age of actual campaigning, as a reward for past services and revolutionary loyalty. The *armée* of the North excepted, all the departmental forces were under civilian authority, either in the person of the *commissaire civil*, or through the *comités de surveillance*, the municipalities and the districts.[83] In several localities, the *commissaires civils* were members of departmental or district administrations; more often they were already *commissaires* of a *comité de surveillance*. Their existence therefore was not simply a guarantee against the 'militarisation' of these companies; it also proportionately reduced the influence of the *sociétés*, by placing the new forces under the control of men who were strangers to the region, who held a mandate from the departmental authorities or had come from another department entirely, as *délégués* of the *représentants en mission*.

Once the 'nucleus' had been formed, control of operations slipped away from the *sociétés*. The *comités de surveillance* or the local authorities were responsible for the pay of this group, once it started work.[84] The *sociétés populaires* had no public funds at their disposal, and these privileged *armées* were extremely expensive; the municipalities and districts had to assume the costs of raising the forces, which allowed them to take full administrative control. Certain *sociétés* sensed this danger and tried to equip the companies themselves by opening subscriptions among their members. But such gestures, while permitting some fine flights of oratory, were insufficient to ensure the *sociétés'* financial control over the new institutions.[85] As soon as public funds were involved, the paymaster had the final word. This provided the authorities with their main opening, and from the outset the organisation of the companies became part of the routine work of the public administrations. In these terms, the companies were no longer revolutionary, having been integrated into the general system of district or departmental administration.

Thus even at the organisational stage, many different bodies were involved in the enrolment of these *armées*: *sociétés*, *comités de surveillance*, municipal and district administrations, paymasters-general, and, since it was necessary to arm and equip the *révolutionnaires*,[86] certain military authorities such as *commissaires des guerres* and garrison commanders. The departmental *armées*, in contrast to that of Paris, were never autonomous forces, those of Lille, Toulouse and the Lot being the only ones to have *commissaires des guerres* attached exclusively to serve them.[87] The military authorities, jealous of the political *armées*, tried to profit from this situation to establish their dominance over them – the source sometimes of bitter conflict between the garrison commanders and the civil authorities. These conflicts were complicated in certain departments where *commissaires civils*, appointed by the *représentants* to undertake the organisation of such battalions, were themselves also *commissaires des guerres*.[88]

Even in skeleton form, the new *armées* posed enormous administrative problems. Many authorities were involved in their organisation, but few wanted to pay the costs. The result was that even the municipalities and district directories, which did not normally favour major revolutionary initiatives, did support 'revolutionary taxes on the rich' and duties on *incivisme* as a way of financing the new *armées*. In this way the enrolment of the *armées révolutionnaires* accentuated the move towards innovatory measures. But these administrative questions were nothing compared to the problems of command. When it came to putting the battalions into action, there was no shortage of people wishing to assume control. Everyone was agreed on one point: the revolutionary officers should not be left to command operations; instead, they should be watched, and the primacy of the civil authority maintained. But which civil authority precisely? And on whom would that civil power depend? The *représentants*, perhaps? But they were constantly on the move, rarely in a position to watch over such expeditions, and even if the *commissaire civil* was responsible to them he would be left master of his own particular territory, with powers as extensive as those of the *représentant* himself. The *comités de surveillance*, then? This was a more viable solution, and the one most frequently adopted; the departmental *armées*, designed for repressive duties, accordingly became the chosen instruments of the *comités* and gave them a monopoly of economic and political repression. Would the *commissaire civil* receive his instructions from the municipalities? The municipalities sought to use the companies to make forced requisitions from the villages of their arrondissement, thereby leaving the door open for communal anarchy. Another possibility was that the *commissaire* would receive his missions from the *sociétés*. The *sociétés* could not have asked for more, for they saw the companies as a way of protecting the 'disciples' they had sent through the countryside, and who were often in need of protection against the anger of the peasants. A last solution had the companies depending on the districts. The directories were as eager as the municipalities to secure such armed backing, for they were responsible for enforcing requisitions and all the other major revolutionary measures.

In the last analysis the final word rested with the *commissaire civil* himself. With unimpeded administrative and police powers, he had more authority than a commander-in-chief, took little notice of the orders sent by the municipalities, districts and *comités de surveillance*, and acted autonomously in the name of the invisible and far-off *représentants*. To these men, possessed of all the violence, passion and imprudence of the revolutionary temperament, were given powers as formidable as they were undefined. The result was a man who paraded the countryside at the head of an armed force, a violent personage wearing a plumed hat and a tricolour sash and calling himself the *délégué* of the *représentant* or the extraordinary commission.[89] Here was revolutionary action reduced to its most elementary level.

The origin of such administrative anarchy lay with the delegation of powers, against which the established authorities had protested in vain. In nearly every department the *représentants* appointed such *délégués*, with complete authority over persons, goods and administration. *They* were the real *représentants en mission*, and some even assumed the title. When the *représentant* left, the *délégués* remained behind and there was nothing to prevent them from appointing *délégués* of their own, who operated at the level of the canton and the commune. When Fouché left the Allier and the Nièvre to go to Lyon, his *délégués* remained behind, though they derived their authority from a *représentant* who no longer had any mission in the region. On 25 Brumaire an inhabitant of the Decize district complained to the Committee of Public Safety: 'The *délégués* sent by citizen Fouché into the Decize district have continued their activities although this *représentant* has moved on to another department.... They have liberated suspects, incarcerated patriots, replaced the public functionaries...', and he asked that their measures be declared void.[90] The established authorities everywhere complained about these 'delegations', and the Committee of Public Safety responded with the law of 14 Frimaire, one of its clauses forbidding such erosion of sovereign authority.

The dangers of autonomous action by the *commissaires civils*, some veritable bandit chiefs, were increased in several regions where normal administration had been suspended to make way for the great extraordinary commissions, which united in themselves administrative as well as judicial powers and which ruled over areas sometimes comprising several departments. These commissions possessing sovereign power offered the new *armées* ideal conditions for revolutionary action. Several *commissaires civils* who were also members of the commissions found themselves at one and the same time, judges, 'apostles', administrators and police agents, wielding the might of republican vengeance while dispensing the good word of the civic preacher. If in some departments the *armées* acted in an ultra-revolutionary manner, it was usually because of the presence of one of these persons, members of repressive bodies like the Commission Temporaire of Lyon,[91] the Commission Militaire of Bordeaux,[92] the Commission Départemental of the Jura,[93] the Commission Militaire of Feurs,[94] the Commission 'Civile-Révolutionnaire' of the Aveyron,[95] and even members of central *comités de surveillance* such as those of the Allier or the Nièvre.[96] It was a case of a substitution of powers and the subjugation of the established, elected and legal authorities to an extraordinary, revolutionary, repressive, and unrepresentative one.

The companies and battalions were subjected to extremely tight recruitment rules. Everything it seemed had been thought of – everything, that is, except the most essential point: who would be responsible for these instruments of the Terror? Who would give them their orders? Who would direct their operations?

III   *Aims behind the enrolment of such forces*

The grand strategy outlined in September by the *sociétés* and by certain departmental authorities sheds some light on the primary aims behind the emergence of the *armées révolutionnaires*. Even before the *armées* commenced operations, economic considerations were uppermost: the circulation of foodstuffs, the supply of the urban markets, the implementation of requisitions, the acceleration of the threshing process and the application of the Maximum. But repression was of a piece with this, and in reading the orders it is difficult to draw a clear line between economic, political and religious considerations. In the controlled economy which accompanies a war, the execution of economic measures entails persistent problems of public order, while supply is as much a political as a technical problem. The struggle against the hoarder cannot be separated from that against the hidden counter-revolutionary and enemy of the regime; meanwhile the refractory priest was fishing in troubled waters, calling on the peasants to rebel against the Maximum and against recruitment, urging them to combat the Revolution by hiding their grain and withdrawing their sons from military service. In time of civil war the 'enemy within' assumes a thousand faces, and a repressive instrument *par excellence* such as the *armée révolution-naire* had to pursue the struggle on several fronts simultaneously.

But the perspective changes according to the authority involved. A municipality, a *comité de surveillance* or a small-town *société* scarcely looked beyond the need to supply their own markets, and for them the 'enemy within' was above all the one who hindered this process. But the *représentant* and his *délégué*, strangers to the departments in which they found themselves, saw things from the level of an Army, a military region, or a group of departments. The result was that in municipal orders, the accent was above all on problems of food supply, the creators of the small communal *armées* thinking first and foremost of their electors. In those of the *représentants*, however, the aims were both more varied and larger in scale: getting in the harvest, or requisitioning supplies for the Armies. It was only a question of emphasis, but the difference of vision also disguised differences in interests. The municipalities were concerned with their own needs, the *représentants* with those of the armies.

Rather than listing all the orders, which are sometimes identical in terminology, it is better to select a few and extract the main preoccupations of their authors: the desire to punish, an element of threat,[97] the struggle against the enemies within, the extirpation of 'fanaticism', the menace of summary and pitiless justice, the circulation and arrival of grain and supplies, the expediting of requisitions in favour of the Armies and the large towns, the application of the Maximum, the search for specie and silver, the tearing down of church bells, the fight against desertion (the scourge of the countryside) and its ally, banditry, the encouragement of the *sociétés populaires* and the support of the sans-culotte minorities in the countryside. Occasionally one finds another kind of concern: the suppression of workers' combinations (a more unusual aspect of the fight against monopolisers), the search for vagrants, the elimination of forestry offences, the struggle against smugglers and exports. These popular *armées* were therefore destined to carry out extremely unpopular tasks, for smuggling, forestry offences, desertion and vagabondage were above all activities of the poorer people, and many *armées* took on the aspect of a rural gendarmerie and customs police rolled into one. Now and again there are signs of a certain class element in the concern of these documents with supplies, social order, problems of unemployment, and the use of such expressions as 'army of the poor'.[98] Take also the example of one of the very first documents, dated 9 September, in which the *représentant* Laplanche announced the creation of the *armée* of the Loiret, promising also a mobile guillotine to satisfy popular demand for summary and 'terrible' justice.[99] But was this rhetoric not perhaps a way of avoiding further massacres without committing the *représentant* to anything? In the Nord, for instance, a *commission de justice* and a mobile guillotine – the apparatus of popular vengeance – were likewise called for to accompany the new *armée*, and in default of the latter the commander of the Lille *armée* had to rest content with a symbolic wax guillotine on wheels, engraved on the seal of the *armée* and on the cartouches of the Lille sans-culottes.[100] If such a paper guillotine hardly posed a threat to the 'malveillants', it nevertheless provided some harmless satisfaction to popular demands for pitiless justice.[101]

Two resolutions, one of a Section, the other of a *société* in Versailles, express both the characteristic sans–culotte interpretation of the cause of the subsistence crisis and their deep-seated mistrust of merchants and farmers. In the resolution of the 13th Section, the inhabitants of this extremely poor quartier affirmed: 'it is malice alone which has caused this scarcity in basic necessities, a scarcity which has existed only since the National Convention struck out against these people with vigorous laws, which they have brought on themselves by holding food back from the people'. And their analysis of the evil: 'The town is suffering from lack of foodstuffs... caused by cupidity and selfishness as much as the malevolence which treacherously encourages the country people into one error after another'. And the remedy: 'Only an armed force, constantly in action, can allow consumers to enjoy the benefits of the decree which has fixed the price of foodstuffs....'.[102] If this resolution offers a very clear exposition of a policy of force in favour of the small consumer, that of the Vertu-Sociale *société* underlines the social character of the new instrument being created. Although the Versailles *sociétaires* did not betray any 'class–consciousness' as such, they did at least insist on the necessity of confiding the execution of this urban policy to those interested in its success: 'the *commissaires* who accompany the detachment [of the Versailles *armée*] should not be taken from the merchant class or from among relatives and friends of the farmers, for the old proverb states that wolves do not eat each other...'.[103] It was a reminder that the *armées révolutionnaires* should not simply be some kind of supplementary gendarmerie, or instrument of the police; the sans–culottes expected them to solve the subsistence crisis through a policy of constraint paid for by the well-off farmers.

Two Breton documents repeat the insistence of the *représentants* on the unity of the repression. On 9 Brumaire, Carrier and Francastel gave the commander of the Marat company of Nantes 'the right of surveillance over all suspect citizens in Nantes, and strangers entering the town, ...over monopolisers of every description, and all those who seek to withdraw, or fraudulently conceal, subsistences, merchandise and basic foodstuffs...', while the younger Jullien wrote to the Committee of Public Safety: 'We must have a detachment of the *armée révolutionnaire* in the Morbihan to round up all those former priests and nobles spread over the countryside where risings are a daily occurrence...'.[104]

Most *représentants*, struggling with the difficulties of ensuring supplies, with the political disorders provoked by conscription and with the battle against Catholicism, still insisted, like Carrier and Francastel, on the duality of their task, even if economic measures were a priority. 'Such is the timidity of the town of Toulouse', Paganel wrote to the Committee, 'that it seems as if it is surrounded by an enemy army, with basic necessities no longer getting through and the country people coming in only to empty the shops; everywhere people are grimly holding on to supplies'. Paganel ordered the Haute-Garonne *armée* 'to ensure the re-establishment of the traffic in grain and necessary foodstuffs, and to collect any surplus so that others might enjoy it...to place in the hands of the nation all luxury objects of any use...to support the good sans-culotte citizens and protect them from aristocratic harassment...to place in custody all men who oppose the progress of the revolution...'.[105] This, along with Fouché's orders for the formation of the Nièvre and Allier battalions, is the most complete expression of the economic, political and egalitarian aims (the egalitarianism of a war economy) behind the formation of these *armées*, aims which would be implemented through force.[106]

Fouché was in fact thundering against the rich 'égoïste', the suspect, the fanatic, thereby giving the measures to be implemented by these battalions, and paid for by the wealthy suspects, an egalitarian appearance. 'I am astonished, citizens, at your predicament', he told the Moulins *comité*. 'You lack flour: take it from the rich aristocrats, they have it; you lack corn: raise your *armée révolutionnaire* and bring those farmers and proprietors to the scaffold who resist your requisitions; you lack lodging: take the mansions belonging to your prisoners, you can return them after the peace; you lack beds: demand them from the rich, they have thousands which are of no use to them...'.[107] But he also insisted on economic measures. Like Contamin, the Crémieu locksmith, Fouché readily affected a popular manner of speech; but it would certainly be wrong to read into his thundering threats – intended for the ears of the comfortable inhabitants of the Nièvre and the Allier – the outline of a real social programme. Even in the case of Contamin, the future Babouvist and protégé of Félix Lepeletier, the exigencies of a war economy and the need to ensure a more logical distribution of the surplus were uppermost. There is no need to read any 'programme' into the empiricism of the practical revolutionary; it was simply a case of seeing to first things first. If sheets, mattresses and metal were needed, it was the rich who would supply them.[108]

In the East the overriding issue was the needs of the Armies, and in the order of 24 Vendémiaire, as we have seen, the *représentants* stressed the necessity of hastening the harvest and the requisition of animal fodder.[109] The orders issued by the *représentants* in the Pyrenees and the Nord were preoccupied with the same issues. Behind the frontiers the new *armées* sought to maintain internal peace and ensure the transportation of food to the Armies.[110] In such regions, facing the threat of invasion and vacated by most of the young men and many ardent revolutionaries, the old spectre of counter-revolution was also present in some of these orders. Thus in the suburbs of Lille, the Brétecque commune invited its fellow citizens to enrol in the Lille *armée*: 'At a time when our warriors have gone to fight our external enemies, to guard against any attempt by our secret internal enemies, the representatives of the people, your Magistrates, the *société populaire* wish to inform you that they are about to raise an *Armée révolutionnaire* in Lille...'.[111]

In Lille, it was also a question of combating 'fanaticism', and the *représentants* (Châles being a former canon) adopted a moralising tone: 'Convinced that there exist...vile, black and corrupt hearts, palpitating with a desire to undermine reason and the laws of man, that the prejudices created by a legion of ambitious charlatans who, hiding under a cloak of hypocrisy, preaching chastity and sobriety, furtively nurture their desires to sow superstition in ignorance and cultivate a terror in feeble hearts which shames Heaven itself, and in an effort to make the declaration of the rights of man, which is the foundation stone of the French Republic, the only revolutionary book of Religion and Government', they ordered the formation of the Lille *armée*.[112]

There remain the hidden considerations, undisclosed and undisclosable: personal ambition, a taste for domination, or even the more respectable one of supplying good sans-culottes with work. There can be no doubt that the overriding aim of the creators of the Dax 'salaried guard' was to ensure that their 'janissaries' had control of all the authorities of the little town.[113] The little Sedan '*armée*' is more complex, because this force did stand for something.[114] As for the attempt to provide unemployed sans-culottes with paid employment, such hopes, if held by the *représentants* or the other originating authorities, were not openly stated. However, in Versailles the petition from the 13th Section was clearly motivated by the desire to create employment for the many grooms and employees of the local stables; and if Monestier is to be credited, the Dax guard was to have been composed 'of workers and artisans, family men, young and old alike', receiving a wage of thirty sols per day 'since none will be able to attend to their trades...'.[115] Far from solving the problem of unemployment, however, this company simply deprived the workshops of labour. It was the same at Aix and at

Moulins, for many expected still to exercise their trades, going out with the *armée* only when necessary.[116] The Bourg *société* at its session of 4 Frimaire drew up a list of 'the most patriotic' citizens, but also of 'the most needy' to form the *armée révolutionnaire*.[117]

To support this theory of unemployment as a reason for creating such forces, the high pay of the *révolutionnaires* and the insistence on 'sans-culottes and family men' as recruits, are the points usually invoked.[118] But this only shows, as the *représentants* had intended, that these privileged *armées* were meant to reward deserving citizens. It was also a case of simple good sense: in popular *armées* formed to implement an economic policy opposed to the interests of the wealthy, it was wise to approach those who had a personal interest in the success of that policy. But one did not have to be poor to find a place in the *armées*. It was enough simply to have acted as a good patriot, in other words as a sans-culotte.[119] The companies were élite forces and the smallness of the numbers involved could have made little impact on the unemployment problem. If sans-culottes were given preference, it was because to the men of the Year II moral worth and social need were complementary. We know of only one order which stated specifically that candidates should be poor, and that was the illegal one setting up the small *armée* of Crémieu.[120]

Artisans, employees and a certain number of derelicts undoubtedly did succeed in entering the companies, but in general they were seeking supplementary employment rather than a solution to unemployment, and many of those in other salaried revolutionary institutions had done likewise.[121] The contrary would have been more surprising and a place in a company was not something to be dismissed.

The emphasis on this quality of 'sans-culottism', a political and moral quality as much as a social one, can therefore be explained by the requirements of a policy undertaken in favour of the small urban consumer and against the rural population. Other considerations probably came into play as well, but we can only offer hypotheses on this matter. An 'army of the poor' would certainly have placed malleable instruments in the hands of ambitious men and it is more than likely that demagogues like Marc Dolle, a revolutionary 'ultra' from La Guillotière and *commissaire civil* with the tiny Crémieu *armée*, or the Dax 'agitators', may have chosen the poorest elements of the rural and urban populace to establish their control over these 'bands'. The men of Chaix were also particularly devoted to their commander, for securing employment and other favours for them.[122] We do not know if the Lormes *juge de paix* selected his soldiers from among the poorest artisans for this reason. But such a danger did exist, and the proof can be found in the Year III, when the former soldiers of the Allier battalion caused a minor riot by demanding the return of their 'benefactor', the former mayor Delan.[123]

The time of year also played a part and most orders for the formation of *armées* were issued in the autumn-to-early-winter period when the main consideration was the need to push ahead with the threshing process and set in motion the winter and spring requisitions for the towns and Armies. After the campaign in favour of a central *armée* had begun in April, the main consideration was the threat to the regime. From September onwards, it was the application of the Maximum, for the passage of this law had caused the traffic in foodstuffs to cease, and the flow of supplies to the official markets to dry up. The municipal administrations were also stripping the urban markets. Everyone looked to the new formations to end the opposition of the country people, and the overriding consideration behind all the orders establishing them was the struggle against rural 'selfishness'.

Many of these orders were also instruments of propaganda, and chilling threats of the imminent arrival of justice commissions and mobile guillotines on the heels of the new *armées* were included for the benefit of the rural populace. In this threat in advance of the use of force, the countryside was being warned of the imminence of a revolutionary doomsday. There was an element of bluff in such language,[124] and those *représentants* most averse to the use of force against their fellow citizens, even in the countryside, were also the most violent in their language; by frightening the farmers they might avoid more extreme methods, the threat itself sufficing to make them release their grain. In this they were proved wrong, for the peasant was not so impressionable; he gave little credence to the unseen guillotine on wheels, and felt that he would still have time to conceal his stocks when the terrible *armées* were announced in the countryside. In this he was right, for the orders sounded more terrifying than they were in reality. Most of the threatened commissions of popular justice failed to materialise from the wishful thinking of the sans-culottes and the Montagnard *représentants*, and were scarcely seen outside the Bas-Rhin districts and the area around Lyon. If the *représentants* thought they could 'strike terror' into the rural population by announcing terrible measures with the maximum of publicity, using public notices and drums (as in the case of the address *Aux habitants des campagnes* of Gobert and Delteil) they were mistaken. But did they themselves believe in the thunderbolt they brandished?

Very often it was a case rather of the deliberately spectacular pronouncement, designed to disarm the adversary, the countryman, along with his allies, ·the rich 'égoïste', the 'fanatical priest', the counter-revolutionary and the Federalist of the countryside. The unity of repression was never lost sight of. But in addition to the enemies of the regime, the creators of these *armées* were also thinking of their rural 'frères' whom they wished to help, since the town had to seek allies in the village among the sans-culotte minorities. The orders therefore devoted some space – admittedly not very much – to this mission to the countryside.[125] In military regions the main concern was with more immediate needs, and in the East it was said of the soldiers that they would have to know how to thresh grain[126] – perhaps the only task not associated with repression or political apostleship. All of this was summed up by the phrase: *Force à la Loi*. The *armées* were designed to ensure that the revolutionary laws were applied in the face of opposition from the countryside and from the *honnêtes gens* – an eminently disagreeable, dangerous and difficult task.

IV   *Chronology of the orders*

In general the departmental and communal *armées* took a long time to organise. The orders were spread over a period of three months, from the second *décade* of September to the last *décade* of Frimaire, and, for the departments furthest away from Paris, to the first *décade* of Nivôse. (See Appendix A, Table 3.) This time-lag is explained in part by the slow circulation of government laws and decisions to all levels of local authority. Furthermore the orders were rarely implemented quickly and the organisational measures, sometimes involving considerable administrative difficulties, dragged on even when their realisation was not slowed down artificially by the ill will or the caution of the local authorities. However, if the authorities, central and local alike, were to be presented with a *fait accompli* in the form of battalions and companies spread over the whole of France, speed was of the essence.[127] It was easy enough to terminate the existence of these *armées* when they were still in the process of organisation; but to do so after they were already in operation presented serious difficulties. The delays therefore proved fatal to the departmental and communal *armées*, permitting the Revolutionary Government to retake the initiative and impose its wishes on the hesitant and perplexed local authorities.

As early as 9 September Laplanche had announced the enrolment of the Loiret companies at Orléans; on the same day the Légion de la Montagne began organisation at Valence, while the Châteauroux *société*, spurred on no doubt by Volland, showed itself ready to follow the example of the capital.[128] Still a rarity in September, the orders multiplied in October to reach their maximum number in Brumaire, the month in which all the major revolutionary initiatives were taken in the departments. In Frimaire *armées révolutionnaires* continued to be created, and all over France companies and battalions started 'revolutionising'. If Brumaire then was the period of initiatives, Frimaire was that of action, and in Nivôse – one month after the law on revolutionary government – the Midi was still in the process of organising these forces. Certain *armées* in the South-West and the South-East, with imprecise titles such as 'gardes soldées', 'gardes civiques', 'bataillon des sans-culottes,' were still in existence as late as Pluviôse and even Ventôse, because by chance they had not adopted the compromising adjective 'révolutionnaire'. In some departments the *armées* were formed in several stages. Sometimes it was a matter of a single formation, initiated by a *société* and later sanctioned by a definitive order of a *représentant*. Elsewhere there were many different *armées* formed by several *représentants* together, or by rival authorities.

Between the initial steps – often little more than simple avowals or declarations of principle – and serious organisation, there was a delay of anywhere between ten days and six weeks.[129] The organisation of the revolutionary battalion of Bordeaux, created by an order of the *représentants* on 27 Vendémiaire, started well, with the Bon-Accord Section opening enrolment lists as early as the 29th. But it was only between 15 Brumaire and 15 Frimaire that the national club got round to the *scrutin épuratoire* of the officers and soldiers, which was scarcely completed when overtaken by the announcement in Bordeaux of the law of 14 Frimaire. The delays were caused by the multiplicity of authorities called upon to participate in the process, whereas in Lille the different stages had been completed in a third of the time.

The entire group of *armées* included in the collective order of 9 Brumaire was organised extremely slowly, and the local authorities were torn between this first order and a later one (the precise date of which we do not know) of Bassal. In the Côte-d'Or, Doubs and Haute-Saône, for example, the communal authorities seem to have been unsure of the precise *armée* for which they were enrolling candidates, the Lyon group, or the *armée* of Bassal; and they often took the precaution of implementing both orders at the same time to avoid offending the powerful proconsuls. Another cause of delay were the numerous stages through which the recruiting process had to pass. The departments instructed the districts to supply lists of those composing the 'nuclei', the directories then wrote to the *société* of the *chef-lieu*, which in turn had to consult the *sociétés* or, in the absence of any, the municipalities, of all the communes in the district. The small rural *sociétés populaires* were slow in returning their lists and all this took time. These delays were to prove fatal to the *armées* of Burgundy and Franche-Comté. In the Côte-d'Or the *société* stage was reached only on 8 Frimaire in Dijon and Nuits-Saint-Georges, and on 20 Frimaire in Montbard.[130] At Jussey and Gray operations dragged on from 19 and 21 Brumaire to 24 and 27 Frimaire respectively.[131] If in the Saône-et-Loire Mâcon succeeded in mounting a battalion by the middle of Frimaire, in Marcigny enrolment registers were only opened in the *sociétés* and *comités* on 26 Brumaire, and at Paray and La Clayette they were still waiting for lists of names on 7 Frimaire.[132]

The Ain witnessed the same delays, with the Trévoux district, on 6 Frimaire, trying to stimulate the zeal of the *sociétés* in its arrondissement which were taking a long time to draw up their lists: 'we cannot stress too much the importance of submitting these lists, for the *armées révolutionnaires* are intended to hasten the tempo of the Revolution...'.[133] But the appeal seems to have had little effect, for we hear nothing more of these measures in this district. In the district of Bourg the *société* delayed circularising the local *sociétés* until 4 Frimaire; on the 11th it abruptly suspended all recruiting operations.[134] The Montluel district did not instruct the Pérouges *société* on what steps to take until 2 Frimaire; after that date, there is no further mention of a departmental *armée*.[135] The Ain perhaps is a special case; Gouly's influence was hostile to the organisation of these *armées*, and he was undoubtedly aware of the sudden decision of the Bourg authorities to cease all operations three days prior to the law of 14 Frimaire. But there were similar delays in the Mont-Blanc, where the situation was even more confused following the two orders of 9 Brumaire, one concerning the enrolment of a departmental contingent for the inter-departmental *armée*, the other, issued by Simond and Dumas, envisaging the creation of a purely departmental force for the Mont-Blanc area alone. At its session of 16 Brumaire the Thonon *société* greeted the announcements of these major terrorist measures with enthusiasm; ten days later a departmental administrator opened the enrolment lists, and candidates registered daily from 26 Brumaire to 19 Frimaire. This was undoubtedly Simond's *armée*. At Chambéry too the district took the first steps on 16 Brumaire, and further decisions were made on 19, 26 and 28 Brumaire and 5, 6, 15 and 26 Frimaire, the date on which the cessation of operations was announced.[136]

In the Isère, a department included in the collective order of 9 Brumaire, the organisation of the *armée* was extremely slow. After an initial proclamation of 15 Brumaire, the department waited until the 23rd before sending precise details to the districts and the municipalities.[137] At Vienne the municipality did not announce the opening of lists until its session of 14 Frimaire, the very day on which the Convention in Paris was ordering the suppression of the *armées révolutionnaires*.[138] At Grenoble the authorities moved with greater speed to implement the order; on 16 Brumaire, the national agent for the commune ordered the commander of the National Guard to place 300 men at the department's disposition the following day, 'to form a permanent armed force until the organisation of the *armée révolutionnaire* is completed'.[139] But the *armée* never saw the light of day. In contrast the enrolment of 100 men for the Grenoble company was quickly achieved. On 28 Brumaire the municipality communicated the departmental order of the 26th to the *société*, instructing it 'to take immediate steps to have 100 men ready to leave by tomorrow'. The *société* complied, and as early as 12 Frimaire this company was operating in the area around Grenoble.[140]

In the Basses-Alpes operations lasted from 17 October until 27 Brumaire – a delay largely explained by the fact that after the companies had been raised with the utmost speed, those responsible began to organise a battalion.[141] In the neighbouring department the process was brisk: the formation of the Hautes-Alpes *armée* was decided on 21 Brumaire, the order setting it up issued on the 24th; on 3 Frimaire the Gap *société*, in conjunction with the municipality, made preparations for elections the following day, and by the end of the month a revolutionary company was in action in the Serres district.[142]

In the Nièvre we are faced with two *armées révolutionnaires*. In the Clamecy district the enrolment of a revolutionary legion was being discussed as early as 6 September, by virtue of a commission from the *commissaires civils* dated 21 August.[143] But the order of Fouché, announcing the formation of the battalions of the Nièvre and the Allier, was only issued on 30 September.[144]

These two battalions, the 'official' *armées*, were organised quickly: in Moulins the *commissaires* were appointed by the Sections as early as 1 October, the elections took place 2–5 October, and the battalion was detached to the districts of the department as early as the first *décade* of that month.[145]

In Lille the *armée* was ready to march 15 days after the second order of Châles and Isoré. The Lille revolutionaries and their Paris friends were in a hurry and in ten days 400 Lille artisans were on a military footing. At Cambrai and Douai, on the other hand, scarcely anything had been done when, on 21 Frimaire, the law on revolutionary government was announced.[146] The *armée* of the North was consequently a Lille one. In Metz, the Moselle *armée* was in action by the second *décade* of Brumaire; it had taken only 15 days to organise it.[147] In Nantes, also, no time had been wasted.[148] In Toulouse little time elapsed between the official organisation of the *armée révolutionnaire* on 5 Brumaire and the commencement of its activities at Grenade, where the *commissaires civils* arrived on the 14th.[149] The large *armées* of the Lot and the Cantal were also raised virtually overnight;[150] the former returned to Cahors on 3 Frimaire, having completed its operations, only to be disbanded on the 5th on instructions from the *comité* of this town.[151] But these *armées* of the South-West did not follow the same recruitment pattern as those of other regions, for they took young men of conscription age and from companies already organised for the army of the line; at Toulouse some of the garrison troops were even incorporated.[152] They made the most of what was at hand, and in this region the *représentants* and local revolutionaries were too anxious for action to worry about the choice of candidates. None of these *armées* were recruited exclusively from among the *sociétés* or even from the urban artisans.

In the Loire the *armée* was almost ready by the middle of Frimaire, despite the slowness of its organisation. The order of Javogues and Bassal was dated 20 October; the districts started organising around 16 Brumaire, following a circular from the Roanne district to the municipalities within its jurisdiction.[153] On this date the municipality of Saint-Bonnet wrote to the *comité révolutionnaire* of Montbrison, the departmental *chef-lieu*: 'We are still awaiting your orders on the revolutionary force'. In Montbrison itself the company was in action as early as the first days of Frimaire.[154] But at Charlieu nothing had been done by the 10th when the *société* received a letter from the Marcigny district dated the 6th, inviting them 'to accelerate measures for the formation of the *armée révolutionnaire*'.[155] At Saint-Rambert the organisation of the company was not entirely completed by 12 Frimaire, when its captain was lamenting its inability to depart because of a lack of officers.[156] Despite these delays, however, the Loire *armée* was complete by 15 Frimaire, when a general review was held at Feurs of the 11 companies of Roanne, Saint-Etienne, Montbrison and Saint-Rambert, with a total force of 1,148 men.[157] If the organisational process had thus been brought to a successful conclusion, despite the delays, credit must go to

Javogues, to his *délégués* and to energetic revolutionary officers like Civeton and Archimbaud.

What were the causes of these delays? In places where the future *armées* were obliged to recruit in small country communes as well as in the towns, the main reason was ignorance rather than ill will on the part of the municipalities and the *comités de surveillance*. The cautiousness and hostility to change of the country people was also a factor. But administrative causes predominated, for the creation of the *armées révolutionnaires* was not the task of central government and it was left to individual *représentants*, to *délégués*, or more often to the departmental administrations to decide on procedure. Each had a different method, but more often than not the absence of any clear directive meant that the local authorities had to improvise. In general the *armées* were organised slowly and amidst confusion. Everything depended on local conditions, and the presence of some zealous men at the head of a *comité de surveillance*, a district directory or a *société* could change everything. Problems tended to fade before the vigour of a Vauquoy, a Gobert or a Decrosne, and the speed or slowness with which these operations were conducted was an effective barometer of the revolutionary temperature of a particular locality. In areas with groups of determined men, battalions or companies were successfully organised, while in the group of departments included in the order of 9 Brumaire, progress was so slow that the law of 14 Frimaire and the disbandment of the *armées* became intermingled with the final stages of recruiting.[158] A third of the revolutionary forces were still in the process of organisation when surprised by the decree; the Revolutionary Government had acted quicker than the local authorities. However efficacious these *armées* might have been, speed was of the essence. To drag out the organisation was to give all the forces of opposition time to manifest themselves and bring pressure to bear on the more timorous *représentants*. The departmental *armées* were above all vehicles of terror; but the 'exterminatory sword' could not be suspended indefinitely over the heads of the 'malveillants' and the 'égoïstes'. After threatening the country people with the arrival of the terrible *armées*, the act had to follow the threat; but delay a month or six weeks and the effect evaporated. Once the Revolutionary Government had re-found its feet – and the resolution and unanimity absent between October and Frimaire – and discovered that a large number of the *armées* existed only in outline, it was easy to sign away these paper battalions with the stroke of a pen.

V   *Chief organisational features of the departmental and communal* armées

Three features were common to nearly all the departmental *armées*: the high pay, the relatively advanced age requirement for volunteers, and their modest numbers. Each of these had important consequences for the future action of the *armées* when formed. The high pay was a source of friction between the political and the regular soldiers, while the local administrations were ill disposed towards such a costly institution when they had to pay the bill. The age requirement for volunteers reduced the *armées'* military effectiveness by giving pride of place to mature family men, men almost old in the conditions of the eighteenth century, who were difficult to discipline, made excessive demands and were frequently drunk. On the other hand if these rules were departed from and young men in the age range of the first requisition were admitted, the *armées* became militarised and lost their special character as political *armées*. Finally, the paucity of their numbers, while removing any danger of the establishment of a military power, considerably limited their effectiveness and increased the importance of certain individuals, notably the *commissaires civils*. It required only a few men as energetic as these to terrorise and 'revolutionise' an entire district.

The revolutionary battalions and companies were the pampered children of the regime – but the cost was high. With the exception of the Evreux company, whose members were not paid, all these *armées* received pay four times as great as that of the conscripted troops.[159] In general the *représentants* set the same standard of pay as that of the Parisian *armée*: 40 sols per day, in itself extremely generous. But in some departments they went to 100 or 120 sols per day, which was a scandalous extravagance. To this were added many allowances. The soldiers of the Lot-et-Garonne received 6 livres per day, those of Montauban 5, the *armées* of the Nièvre and the Allier, of Limoges and Crémieu, 3 livres. The battalions of Montpellier and Pau, the Lille *armée*, the groups of the East and the South-East, those projected for the Yonne and Versailles, received the same pay as the Parisian *armée*. Only the *armée* of the Marne and the Dax 'guard' had to rest content with a lower wage of 30 sols per day. Thus not only was the Parisian *armée* imitated in this respect, but in more than half the departments it was surpassed, with pay sometimes two or three times as great. It was a case of the departments 'outbidding' the capital, and when Parisian revolutionary measures were applied in the departments they were always 'exaggerated'.*

To finance these costly *armées*, most orders permitted recourse to 'revolutionary taxes' on the rich and the suspect,[160] a kind of tax on *incivisme*, which the *représentants* thought would be sufficient to finance pay, arms, equipment and clothing for the volunteers. In this they badly miscalculated, for despite the heavy 'taxes' in kind and in money levied by the *commissaires civils* during their missions,[161] the cost of maintaining the new *armées* soon fell back upon local finances. One can see why these luxury *armées* were unpopular with the regular armies and certain *comités de surveillance*.[162] Nor did their repeated claims for their wives and children and travel expenses and displacement allowances for themselves do anything to increase the popularity of the soldiers.[163] Many municipal authorities greeted the law of 14 Frimaire with obvious satisfaction, for it released them from the

---

* See Appendix A, Table 1, the General Table of Departmental and Communal *Armées*.

obligation of footing the bill for these costly soldiers and their frequently numerous families.[164]

The *révolutionnaire* himself was often the main victim of such an excessively high wage, for it isolated him from other soldiers and from the local authorities and discredited him with a portion of patriot opinion which could not believe that such highly paid people could be disinterested revolutionaries. The pay, in effect, gave rise to charges of avarice against the soldiers and provided their numerous enemies with convincing evidence for their claims that the sans-culottes were little more than vulgar hired hands.[165] It was a mistake to overpay such a force, service in which was deemed to be a privilege, an honour, a consecration of political and social virtues.

The high pay had another consequence, which in the long run proved disastrous for the country's war economy. It threatened to denude the workshops by placing the *armées révolutionnaires* in direct competition for manpower with the war industries. At Dax, Moulins, Aix-en-Provence, and doubtless elsewhere, shoemakers, hatters' assistants and foundry workers enrolled in large numbers, attracted both by the high pay and by the allowances for their wives. The high pay, the allowances, the promise of 'travel expenses' and payment in cash, and the real, if unavowed, possibility of getting money for the release of prisoners, threatened to entice workers away from the manufacture of war materials and clothing for the troops, where the daily rate of pay was subject to the Maximum.[166]

These ill effects were so obvious that one may well ask what caused the *représentants* to award such exorbitant wages to volunteers everywhere. The main reason was undoubtedly the requirement, expressed in so many orders, for candidates to be 'sans-culotte family men'. A price had to be paid for such a sans-culotte composition, for most of these urban artisans, winegrowers, small farmers or agricultural labourers could not afford the luxury of unpaid patriotic gestures. If unpaid volunteers were to be depended upon, as in Evreux, a 'bourgeois guard', like the 'companies of the centre' raised in April during the Federalist crisis, rather than a 'sans-culotte' army, 'an army of the poor', would be the outcome. All the *sociétés populaires* were in agreement in their demand for high pay, seeing it as a way of attracting men of their own kind into the battalions; and besides, *they* did not have to pay for it.

In the opinion of the *représentants*, service in the *armées révolutionnaires* would not be half-time service, and they foresaw the case of the *armées* serving outside their areas of origin. Thus the same misunderstanding existed in the departments as in Paris between the Committee of Public Safety and the *comités sectionnaires*, for the departmental sans-culottes, while anxious to enrol in the new *armées*, would do so only on condition that they remained at home and could work part of each day at their civilian employment.[167] At Moulins the counter-revolutionaries tried to discourage volunteers from enrolling by saying that they would surely be sent to Lyon, to Toulon, or perhaps even further away. The *comité de surveillance*, well attuned to the way the artisan volunteers thought, was the first to recognise the threat to the recruiting campaign posed by such 'treacherous suggestions'. Ruthless measures were taken against those propagating the alarms and an immediate proclamation issued, outlining the conditions of service in the battalion.[168] Most soldiers had enrolled with a fixed determination to remain at least within their district, whereas for the *représentants* it was a question of 'full' service; consequently the sans-culottes had to be guaranteed a compensatory wage. In reality, however, the pay was so generous that it was more than compensatory, and many artisans earned more in the companies than if they had stayed at home.

Finally, there was the conception of revolutionary service as an honour and a privilege. The sans-culottes were no ordinary soldiers, but accredited protectors of the regime. By paying them well the Republic was rewarding its most meritorious children for past services. This evaluation of revolutionary patriotism in monetary terms, however, was dangerous, and threatened to produce a totally opposite result by attracting the dregs of the towns and countryside into the companies. We will see if it did so when we examine their composition; but here we can at least marvel at the fact that despite the high pay the departmental *armées* should have included in their ranks many honest and even well-off artisans, notables and small businessmen, for whom the pay was not the main attraction.

Most orders simply followed the example of the Paris *armée* in setting the same age-limit of twenty-five to forty as the second class of the military conscription. Fouché's order for the Nièvre fixed narrower age-limits of thirty to forty.[169] The Montluel district interpreted the collective order of 9 Brumaire in the way it saw fit, though claiming to restrict entrance to candidates between twenty-five and thirty-five years of age, while the Dijon district declared that candidates should be over thirty. The Briançon district invited the municipalities to choose men between the ages of thirty-five and fifty; in the Avallon district, the ages of candidates ranged from twenty-five to forty.[170] Lémare's circular to the districts of the Jura appealed to 'republicans, heads of families', and the Toulouse *société* had also a word for the 'family men' in its address opening the lists for the Haute-Garonne *armée*.[171] Despite such variations and lack of precision the aim of these orders was to recruit men between the ages of thirty and forty to forty-five.

This emphasis on the age-limit of candidates was to exclude the young men of the first requisition (eighteen to twenty-five) and the old, whose age rendered them unsuitable for service, even in these 'civilian' *armées*. The *représentants* and the *sociétés* had no intention of making corps of veterans out of these *armées*, and in some cases took the precaution of fixing a maximum age. At Lille the 2nd Section declared that it would not accept candidates over forty-eight years of age; at Nuits-Saint-Georges a sixty-year-old volunteer was rejected, though his patriotism was applauded; while a sixty-nine-year-old was turned down by the 1st Section of Versailles.[172] But such precautions seem to have been ineffective, for even at Lille the 6th Section accepted men of sixty-seven, fifty-eight, fifty-seven and fifty years of age,[173] while at Versailles, 26 candidates accepted by the Sections – a quarter of the entire force – were in their fifties, 3 were in their sixties, 22 in their forties, and another 26 in their thirties. More than half the Versailles *armée* was therefore over forty.[174] The Jussey *société* accepted a sixty-year-old as one of its 'nucleus', while that in Châteauroux proposed admitting candidates up to that age.[175] There were consequently many old men in the departmental *armées*, though most recruits were in the thirty to fifty age range, and the artisans and shopkeepers of the Marat company of Nantes were aged between thirty and forty.[176]

Nor were very young men of eighteen and under turned away. The Légion de la Montagne accepted volunteers below the age of the first requisition,[177] and adolescents of fifteen to seventeen were to be found in the *armées* of the North and of Versailles.[178] Nearly every battalion had a drummer, a position often reserved for children, who were frequently also given decorative roles as colour-bearers.

In three *armées* – and it is a factor distinguishing them from the others – the rules forbidding entry to young men of the first requisition were disregarded. A special order of Châles and Isoré allowed members of the Lille National Guard, regardless of age, and young men from the conscripted troops, to enlist in the *armée révolutionnaire* of the North.[179] Many volunteers in the Lille and Amiens battalions, quartered at Lille, were to take advantage of this to have themselves accepted into companies already purged by the Sectionary assemblies,[180] and it was not without reason that Denis Bourdon, brother of the *Conventionnel* Léonard Bourdon, *commissaire des guerres* at Lille and enemy of Dufresse and Châles, should have accused the creators of the Lille *armée* of having 'denuded' the frontier of hussars and dragoons by attracting them into this 'useless' and overpaid force.[181] How can such a departure by the *représentants* from a rule which they themselves had established be explained? Did they not realise that in admitting young men from the first requisition into their *armée révolutionnaire* they were harming it at the very outset by attaching to it the suspicion of harbouring deserters or of underhand recruiting methods? If Châles and Isoré, after weighing up these arguments, carried on regardless, it was because they were in a hurry. Had recruitment in the Sections not fulfilled their expectations? The two Montagnards, anxious to put the new instrument of the Terror into action right away, took the easiest way out by applying to the garrison troops.[182]

The same situation was repeated at Toulouse, Paganel gathering into his *armée* volunteers from the battalions of several departments then in the town. At one stroke the Toulouse *armée* acquired a military character which distinguished it from all the others.[183] In the Lot also the eighteen-to-twenty-five age group was approached when the repressive expedition to the Gourdon district was being prepared.[184] Here too it was a matter of putting into immediate action an assorted force, composed of whatever elements were at hand, to deal with an urgent situation. The crisis passed and the young men who had been 'on loan' to the new *armées* returned to their battalions.

The cases of Lille, Toulouse and the Lot were exceptional. But even within these three *armées* young men were in a minority. In the Lille *armée* the majority were artisans and workers in the thirties age group; in the Toulouse *armée*, most were artisans and shopkeepers in the thirty-to-forty age range;[185] while the Lot *armée* was dominated by rural wine-growers and artisans from Cahors, all over the age of twenty-five.[186] These cases, how-ever, caught the attention of contemporary opinion and supplied dangerous arguments to the ever-watchful enemies of these popular institutions. The frontiers were being denuded to supply a 'personal guard' for some ambi-tious men, they claimed; the soldiers of the Republic were being 'corrupted' by such easy service, and those remaining at the frontier 'demoralised' by the temptation of idle service in the interior. It was indeed a dangerous argument which demagogues of Denis Bourdon's type could develop with ease. Such exceptional cases were, therefore, of immense propaganda value and were skilfully exploited to discredit these *armées* whose high pay was already a subject of scandal and envy.

In reality, if the departmental *révolutionnaires* were men who had already proved themselves in the revolutionary movement, they were also men who were physically worn out and could not be relied upon for long night marches or bivouacking in the open air. Instead these forty- and fifty-year-old artisans sought out feather beds and solid roofs in the homes of 'rich suspects'. They might have been able to thresh grain, but there was no point expecting military competence of them, or any ability to withstand the hard life of an army on the march. The creators of the *armées* had wanted 'family men', and that is exactly what they got. If the volunteers were 'well endowed with patriotism', they were in no hurry to leave their homes, particularly to go and fight the Spaniards, the Austrians or the English on the frontiers. The age of the *révolutionnaires* accentuated the civilian charac-ter of these *armées*,[187] reducing their means of action and even their prestige as terrorist institutions. Old men (as these were by eighteenth-century standards) inspire no terror, and they were either laughed at or their excesses considered irritating. These then were the 'frères' of the Parisian soldiers, these 'farcical cavaliers', these 'butter and cheese soldiers'.

The third feature common to nearly all these '*armées*', most of which were only companies or battalions – and to call them even this is to compliment them – was the smallness of their effective numbers. Of the active *armées*, only those of the Lot and the Cantal together exceeded 1,000 in number, calculations of their effective numbers ranging from over 3,000 to 6,000 men.[188] But this case was quite exceptional, as were the circumstances dic-tating its rapid organisation and immediate intervention. The collective *armée* created by Bassal and Bernard de Saintes was, it is true, to have amounted to 2,400 men; but this figure was to cover six departments, with each supplying only 300 to 400, or at most 600 men each.[189] Most *armées* never surpassed 1,000[190] – the projected figure for the *armée* of the North, which nevertheless only reached 400 or 500, all recruited from Lille. Did the *armées* of the East, whose numbers were likewise fixed at 1,000, ever achieve their full complement?[191] Even taking into account the estimates in the orders of formation – nearly all of which were excessively optimistic – only nine departmental *armées* were destined to reach 1,000 (that of the Loire even reached 1,300).[192] The average number of effectives was 300 to 500, with only the Toulouse and Redon *armées* reaching between 600 and 750.[193] The Nièvre and Allier battalions, subject of so many legends, their activities so feared by the *honnêtes gens* of these departments, consisted of only 350 *révolutionnaires* at the most. (See Appendix A, Table 1.) However, in their organisation and composition, in the orders received from Fouché and above all in the character of the operations assigned to them, they represented the prototype of the *armées révolutionnaires*.

In the Midi effective numbers decreased as the *'armées'* multiplied. The companies of the little southern towns never reached the 500 of those at Montauban or Montpellier; the average was 100 or 120 men and there were many more urban companies, like that of Agen, which could number only 25 sans-culottes. In the Bouches-du-Rhône, as at Nantes, the salaried guards and these sans-culotte companies mustered no more than some 40 to 60 artisans and shopkeepers.

Moreover, these little *'armées'* rarely operated in large detachments and only very occasionally was their full complement gathered together for one expedition. On the contrary, they were scattered over the countryside and at town gates in groups of 10, 25 or 50 men. The 'malveillants' had to deal with a political gendarmerie rather than the 'great popular army' of 100,000 patriots envisaged by Hébert and the sans-culottes.[194] The total number of effectives in all the active *armées* barely reached 30,000, dispersed over 40 or so departments. Those who feared the dawn of military government could rest assured. Such minuscule companies were not forces capable of effecting a *coup d'état* and at best might serve the ambitions of some small-town 'enragés', or dominant figures in cantonal *chefs-lieux*, by lending armed support to the deliberations of a *société populaire* or a *comité de surveillance*. Recognising their weakness, the revolutionary soldiers in the departments were docile in the hands of their masters: the districts, *comités*, municipalities or the *commissaires civils*. But this did not stop them from acting with considerable violence, especially when commanded by energetic *commissaires*.

However, too much importance should not be attached to this question of numbers.[195] There was never any question of reversing the established order, even if certain *commissaires civils* were foolish enough momentarily to dream of replacing the Revolutionary Government by a direct democracy based on the *sociétés populaires* and their armed extensions. The enemy was not distinguished by number either, but by its ruses, by the thousand faces it could adopt and by the complicity, both open and concealed, which it enjoyed with the greater part of the rural population. In the implementation of repressive measures, therefore, quality counted more than numbers. By offering such high pay – a mistake – by inviting the *sociétés* and *comités* to participate in the recruitment, the intention was to arm the sans-culotte élite, whose strength lay in its purity of principle rather than in its numbers.[196] In these *armées* the soldiers were not anonymous roll-numbers, but conscious republicans. In the *armées révolutionnaires* the individual counted for everything, which is perhaps the best commentary on their unmilitary character.

Paucity in numbers, therefore, was compensated for, not only by the importance of individuals, by the political qualities of the soldiers, mostly volunteers – even if the voluntary element was at times a little forced, a product of conformism and reluctance to be labelled 'lukewarm'– but also by the greater liberty of action enjoyed by the *commissaires civils* who led these forces than by their equivalents in the Parisian *armée*. In the hands of a Chaix or a Vauquoy, a cluster of 20 men was not a negligible force, particularly when they were dealing with disarmed and cautious peasants. It was very rare in fact for such detachments to meet with any armed resistance from the country people. Everything therefore depended on the character of the *commissaire* or officer, and among the latter there were many authentic revolutionaires, 'hommes de liaison', or 'village *enragés*', who could 'revolutionise at will', because of the absence of any restraint by the local authorities. We must also remember the fourth feature common to nearly all the *armées* – excepting those in Burgundy and Franche-Comté, which never got beyond the planning stage – and that is their urban composition. The revolutionary soldiers were men of the town and the bourg, and the departmental and communal *armées* were instruments of the towns against the countryside. In most regions, therefore, they provided the towns with the means of dictating their wishes to the countryside.

So even if the final total fell far short of expectations, and the revolution-ary mountain gave birth to a mouse in a red bonnet, we still come out with a total of 30,000 men under arms; and the extension of these urban and egalitarian *armées* over two-thirds of the nation's departments represents a major success in principle for the revolutionary authorities and particularly for the *sociétés populaires*.[197] The Committee of Public Safety was not the only sovereign authority in the republic when *sociétés*, *commissaires*, and municipalities could use such an armed force at will, even if it was minus-cule in proportion. In Brumaire and Frimaire these authorities outside the established hierarchy, the *sociétés*, the extraordinary commissions, the *délégués*, and many more, had once again to be taken into account, for they constituted in effect an ultra-revolutionary power network. With such armed forces on hand, the men of this new, unregulated and dangerous power could 'revolutionise' at will. It was indeed a major victory of principle.

VI   *The bogus* armées révolutionnaires

The proliferation of communal and departmental *armées* in the autumn of 1793 was the result of an administrative anarchy, which increased as one descended the hierarchy of territorial divisions: *sociétés populaires*, extraordinary commissions, men with undefined powers but violent temperaments, profited by the absence of central government control to raise forces for their own ends. The way was clear for the determined *commissaire*, unhindered by jurisdictional scruples or clearly defined powers, to 'revolutionise' in any way he thought fit, assisted by this new armed force. Others followed his example, using the pretext of 'revolutionising' for pillage and banditry pure and simple. In the region around Paris the Parisian *armée* gave rise to a whole host of 'bands' acting under its name, and in the departments the creation of 'legal' *armées* was accompanied by the activities of groups of deserters, survivors from Federalism, and simple bandits. Many *armées*, therefore, cast disquieting and compromising shadows.

Little was needed – a few centimetres of tricoloured ribbon, a plumed hat and the all-encompassing title of 'commissaire civil' – to transform a band of pillagers into zealous revolutionary soldiers. The farmer, wakened in the middle of the night by blows on his door and the command: 'Open in the name of the law', and presented with false requisition orders, was unable to distinguish between a real and a bogus *armée révolutionnaire*. The bandits also took over from the *armées* the device *'Force à la loi'* in order to pillage isolated farms undeterred. Some even had the temerity, not only to utilise the distinctive insignia of the Parisian or departmental *armées*, but even the flags carrying the most characteristic revolutionary legend: *Guerre aux châteaux, Paix aux chaumières*. But such sanguinary and pitiless men did not bring peace; rather they were *chauffeurs* disguised as *révolutionnaires*.

The criminal elements were not the only ones to capitalise on a situation which lent itself to all manner of deception. Groups of deserters, and even soldiers still in service, would form themselves into 'armées révolutionnaires' to get food from the peasantry and 'live off the countryside'. In Frimaire the municipality of Saint-Rambert-Ile-Barbe complained to the department of the Rhône about volunteers from the Aude battalion 'calling themselves soldiers from the Paris *armée révolutionnaire*, and claiming by this title the right to make domiciliary visits and take away arms and goods...'.[198] Not far from there, in the Beaujolais hills at Denicé, a man was arrested in Frimaire, also accused of having terrorised the farmers of the area by claiming that he was from the *armée révolutionnaire* and 'that 600 of the *armée* had arrived at Villefranche, that they had brought a guillotine with them and that by midday they were to be at Montmélas...that they were going to Revolet to cut the head off the big-wig Mathieu...that they would go through all the parishes as far as Montbrison and then move on to the Loire to cut the heads off all the inhabitants...'.[199] On this occasion the culprit was a soldier from the garrison at Villefranche. In the Seine-et-Marne also at the village of Thieux in the Meaux district, some of General Hanriot's aides-de-camp and officers of the Parisian National Guard – claiming to be part of the Parisian *armée* – requisitioned horses and silver and metalware from the farmers. This occurred in the first *décade* of Brumaire, at a time when Ronsin's *armée* was no longer active. On the 9th of the same month 'a detachment of this bogus force of 25 or so men, a kind of advance guard wearing the national uniform, ...was noticed entering the home of citizen Gilbon, a yeoman farmer of Saint-Géry, near Corbeil, at seven o'clock in the evening...'.[200] Such cases were not isolated ones, and in Prairial Year II the public prosecutor of the Seine-et-Oise alluded to 'these bands which scour the countryside in fake patrols of the *armée révolutionnaire*, opening doors in the name of the law which they have usurped, its sacred name sullied by rape, brigandage and murder'. 'Many farms have been pillaged by these bands, several farmers have had the soles of their feet roasted with burning charcoal to make them reveal their treasures.'[201]

Such then was the situation around Paris, where the *armée* of Ronsin, legally created by a decree of the Convention, became the screen for banditry pure and simple. In the departments, where every revolutionary phenomenon took an exaggerated turn, the situation was worse and the expansion of political *armées* opened the way for military banditry. In the East the *commissaires civils*, Gobert and Delteil, put the farmers on their guard against such impostors. 'Informed that some soldiers have abused the name of this *armée* [of the Moselle] to harass the country people, and convinced that such conduct is totally criminal, and can only serve the designs of the enemies of the Republic', they ordered that 'any soldier or citizen whatsoever who uses the name of the *armée révolutionnaire*, the dress of the *commissaires civils* or judges of this *armée*, who in any manner whatsoever commits violence against persons or property, will be arrested at once and brought before the tribunal of the *armée révolutionnaire*...'.[202] If these two *commissaires* felt it necessary to warn the country people against such impostors in a printed notice, circulated through all the departments within the military region of the Armies of the Rhine and Moselle, we can be sure that such abuses were not isolated cases. Besides, the administrative anarchy, by opening the way for all kinds of innovations, offered an obvious opportunity for men 'decked out in red bonnets, with black moustaches and dirty clothes',[203] to operate within the jungle of marginal institutions.

The appearance of bogus *armées*, led by fake *commissaires civils*,[204] possessing fake requisition orders, is perhaps the most dramatic example of the deterioration of established authority. From the moment when a small-town *société*, a *comité de surveillance* or a 'village *enragé*' could legally arm men of his own choice for his own ends, there was nothing to prevent simple bandits, some of whom were deserters from real *armées révolutionnaires*, from doing the same thing in the name of 'revolutionary law' and 'public safety'. Banditry was the logical outcome of the tendency towards decentralisation, towards the substitution of powers, during the September–November 1793 period, under the aegis of which numerous 'legal', 'marginal' or 'private' *armées* proliferated. These 'bands' or fake *armées révolutionnaires* were simply more anarchic caricatures of the real *armées*, from which they took their violence and disorder, along with their devices, emblems, and even their uniforms.

The creation of departmental and communal *armées* was a response to two opposing trends. In the eyes of the *représentants* and even more of all the authorities responsible for the needs of the Armies fighting at the frontiers, the *armées* were simply secondary instruments in the war economy. Designed to 'put the revolutionary laws into operation', they found themselves assigned the repressive role of a political gendarmerie. But the *représentants* had not reckoned on their subordinates, those men who had presided over the creation of the *armées* and who would take charge of the detachments sent out to implement repressive measures. These men, *délégués, commissaires civils*, leaders of the *sociétés populaires*, 'hommes de liaison', were not content simply to give the device '*Force à la loi*' a concrete expression. They also wanted to 'revolutionise', to take terror and implacable and summary justice into the most remote villages; to use an '*armée* of the poor' to make war on the 'rich *égoïstes*' and bring help to the san-culotte minorities isolated in the countryside and exposed to the joint attack of the farmers and the men of the law; to help the towns – especially their *sociétés* and privileged minorities – dictate the law to the *plat pays*.

These aims were not entirely contradictory since the results were the same. Requisitions for the Armies could only be implemented by violent means because of the opposition they aroused among the farmers, and violence breeds excess and exaggeration in language and action. The *commissaires civils* assigned to secure supplies for the Grand Armies fighting on the frontiers were no less violent than their colleagues operating in the interior.

But there were serious misunderstandings at the time of the creation of the *armées*. The orders of formation fixed pay, numbers, conditions of service and method of recruitment, and the organisation of these *armées* was simply another duty added to the workload of local administration. But the problem of command remained unresolved, and as long as the *armées* occupied no specified place in the administrative hierarchy, they were not subject to strict control by the established authorities. This would have posed no problem if there had not been men ready to profit from this power vacuum to use the armed force for their own ends. The *sociétés populaires*, with certain *commissaires civils*, had definite views about how to use these institutions which had only to be given orders. The problem of command, which was an administrative one, became more pronounced when the *commissaire civil* was a determined revolutionary, who saw beyond the simple task of lending *force à la loi*. The *commissaire civil* was master in his own territory, more important than the revolutionary officer, who was generally little more than a supernumerary, and significantly more important than the soldier of the departmental *armées*, a humble being, infinitely pliable in the hands of someone energetic. This then is the man whom we must get to know.[205]

CHAPTER 5

Officers and Men of the Departmental *Armées*

There were around 40,000 revolutionary soldiers under arms or being enrolled in the departments. What of their origins, occupations, ages, behaviour? Can we compose a picture of them, even an impressionistic one? The documentation does not permit an exhaustive study in the manner adopted for the Parisian *armée*. At the level of the individual the very most we can do is to comment on those in positions of command. In addition we do have several enrolment lists which sometime give the age and occupation of candidates and we will select a dozen or so *armées* which possess such lists, have certain characteristics in common, and which for one reason or another merit attention. These are modest aims with solutions which are more often than not negative. But it is always useful to be able to say what the *armées* were not, particularly when they have been discussed so often in the blackest of terms.

Since the effective command of most of these small formations rested with the *commissaires civils*, we will commence with these dramatic and mysterious figures. How many of them were there throughout France, revolutionising at the head of their 'bands'? Can we accept the Thermidorean figure of 50,000 of these 'roaring lions' – which would mean virtually one *commissaire civil* for every soldier? Such figures are extremely exaggerated and one must be careful to distinguish between the *commissaires civils* and the numerous *délégués* of the *représentants* who fulfilled similar functions. Should the fake *commissaires* also be included? They were certainly more numerous and infinitely more picturesque than the real ones. And who were these celebrated 'hommes de liaison', these scourges of the country people? Were they of humble origin? Did they possess a social doctrine or hold egalitarian ideas? Did they belong to any distinct political category – were they Hébertists, ultra-revolutionaries, anarchists? What meaning can we read into the expressions attributed to, or claimed by them? Were they *exagérés*, mad or violent men? Or were they just common pillagers, criminals, degenerates? 'Godless men', were they agents of a sect, or the 'Sect' (Protestantism and Freemasonry), as many rural dwellers believed? How many were foreigners or secret agents of the counter-revolution? These are the questions we must ask about these men who gave the revolutionary detachments their particular style and outrageous character.

The creators of the *armées révolutionnaires* wanted to form élite forces composed of men who were morally and politically sound. In the preceding chapter we saw the different administrative means used to achieve this end. But did the reality live up to the expectations of the *sociétaires* and the other political circles which favoured such privileged troops? And did the composition of the departmental *armées* follow the same social pattern as that of the Parisian *armée*? If in fact the local battalions and companies were stocked from more modest and less independent social milieus than those supplying the Paris *armée*, one can see how they might become more malleable instruments, capable both of greater militarisation and of greater subservience, in the hands of ambitious men.

Many contemporaries had no hesitation in claiming that the departmental *armées* were recruited from the dregs of urban society, from among criminals, rapists and draft-dodgers. With formations which varied enormously in terms of numbers and recruits, it would be difficult to comment accurately on such claims, as trenchant as they are simplistic. We know that recruitment was not restricted to the towns – and here already we have a deviation from the standard picture. To detect other differences the best method is to choose individual *armées* for particular attention: the Lille *armée* because of its excellent documentation; that of Versailles, because it suggests a concern with unemployment among the creators of the *armées*; the battalions of the Allier and Nièvre, because they are the closest to the Paris model; the famous Marat company of Nantes, a terrifying, and possibly also a criminal company; the *armées* of the Yonne, Haute-Saône, Jura and Basses–Alpes as examples of rural recruitment; the Crémieu *armée* as a 'social' *armée* composed of the poor; that of the Haute-Garonne as a mixed *armée* composed of artisans and peasants, civilians and soldiers; and the Gironde battalion, as a Sectionary force with very individual characteristics, notably its foreign element.

Such a method, dictated by a documentation full in places, but decidedly deficient in general, has two advantages. First of all, by emphasising the tremendous social, political and moral diversity of personnel gathéred from such divergent regions and social milieus, we can quickly dispose of the simplistic picture which has the *révolutionnaires* recruited entirely from among criminals, deserters and the dregs of the towns. The second advantage of this method is more problematic: we have seen that there are certain characteristics common to all the *armées révolutionnaires* – conditions of recruitment, the high pay, the age of candidates, the voluntary aspect, the election of officers and NCOs. We now have to seek other points of resemblance in the social origins and moral and political attitudes of the men. These *armées* were original, even unique institutions, in terms of organisation; were they also unique in their composition?

I   *A political and moral élite*

The institution of the *armées révolutionnaires* reflected a notion of privilege
clearly expressed in most of the orders establishing them. The intention was
to arm a political and moral élite drawn from the *sociétés populaires* themselves, or from other platforms reserved for 'frères' of more modest standing than the militant minorities. In some cases it was even claimed that they
were establishing sans-culotte *armées* from which certain political and social
categories, like suspects and bourgeois, would be barred. Automatic exclusions on the basis of social origin or profession, however, were rarely
expressed in the orders of formation and even more rarely applied, and the
main concern was rather with the establishment of a political and moral
élite. Above all one had to be a good sans-culotte, a pure patriot, a good
family man to be accepted; these were political and moral requirements
which paid little attention to the candidates' financial or occupational
standing.

The revolutionary soldier, declared the famous cartouche of the Lille
armée, 'must be pure in conduct, frank, firm and republican'. Drunkenness,
acts of violence, and any act which 'sullies the dignity of the People, will
result in the instant expulsion of the offender and mark as suspect the sans-
culotte who could thus shock the religion of his brothers; the *scrutin
épuratoire* shall be the order of the day for everyone'.[1] The final phrase in
particular has echoes of Cromwell addressing his soldiers. But there are also
traces of a threat; privileges carry dangers as well, and woe betide the
recruit, accepted into the *armées*, who proved unworthy of the honour
shown him! Access to the revolutionary institutions was relatively easy, exit
was not, and expulsion could lead directly to imprisonment or to the
scaffold. The few soldiers from the Parisian *armée* accused of using royalist
expressions did not long await the services of Sanson. This threat hung over
all the personnel of the revolutionary institutions and in the Year III former
soldiers, defending themselves against their attackers, were to plead the
extreme danger involved in leaving positions so exposed to the public
glare. Thermidorean opinion was to accept the validity of this argument. In
the eyes of the soldier, his family and his neighbours, to serve in a
revolutionary formation was indeed a privilege, but a privilege that one
paid dearly for.

The ideal then was that proposed by the Vitry *société* to that of Châlons-
sur-Marne: 'Fellow citizens, have you not considered, like us, that when
you have enrolled the Jacobin cavaliers...they will form legions like the
Montagnard Legion organising in the Midi? Such well-organised legions,
composed primarily of Jacobins pledging themselves voluntarily, will help
bring the war of Liberty against Tyranny to a successful conclusion....'.[2]
The ideal soldier was a member of a *société populaire*, or an assiduous
attender at the popular club, preferably of modest means (though the

definition of a good sans-culotte was extremely flexible),[3] and in addition had to possess a sobriety and probity capable of withstanding any test.

A soldier who was too perfect was being sought, and such moral requirements were soon shown to be too ambitious. In particular one would search for a long time to find a sober soldier, though those of probity were less rare than most historians have claimed. On the other hand, in some *armées* the notion of a political élite drawn from the *sociétés* was translated into reality. The best example is the Légion des Montagnards. But there were also real *armées révolutionnaires* whose command structure at least was taken over by influential members of the clubs, and in many places they were responsible for organising the recruiting process.

In Lille in particular the *sociétaires* had a veritable monopoly of command positions in the new *armée*; and this was not all, for influential members on their committees also succeeded in placing protégés, relatives and neighbours in the subordinate ranks. If we take the senior positions first of all, they were held by the Rossignols, father and son, manufacturers in the rue des Etaques; Buisine, a municipal official, who had made his money as a second-hand dealer out of the poverty of the mill-workers; Dorez, an unemployed launderer who had become commissioner of police; Dubrusle, a shopkeeper and notable; Cuigniez, a member of the *comité de surveillance* and a sculptor; Menteur, a porcelain painter; Fleur, a furrier.[4] The positions they held in the *société* entitled them to appointment to the more interesting positions in the new *armée*: Dorez became legion commander, Dubrusle, quartermaster, Buisine, Fleur and Menteur members of the administrative council; the elder Rossignol, appointed an officer, took advantage of his position to bring a dozen of his friends and employees into the *armée*. The other Lille members of the *société* committees acted likewise in the general assemblies of their Sections.

But the Lille members were not the main beneficiaries. The best places on the general staff were snatched by the Parisian soldiers of the garrison who had advanced in the entourage of Lavalette and Dufresse, their noisy presence dominating the *société* of this frontier town as they had already dominated the Jacobin society in Brussels the previous year. Thus young Calmet-Beauvoisins, son of a well-off Parisian family, former aide-de-camp to Lamarlière, then to Lavalette (he easily survived them both), owed his election to the position of adjutant-general, second-in-command of the Lille *armée*,[5] as much to the fact that he was secretary of the *société* as to the support of the general-marquis. Defferrez, cannoneer captain of the Panthéon-Français Section and a member of one of the committees of the *société*, was elected at its request to command the revolutionary artillery.[6] The other figures of the new general staff – Agut and Adhémar, adjutants-general, d'Hollande, *chef de bataillon*, Christol, captain, Braëmt, captain, Griois, *commissaire des guerres*[7] – owed their places, like Dufresse, their commander-in-chief and president of the *société*, to the fact that in Brumaire they were part of the clan which dominated this club. As men from quite different social categories – the Rossignols, Buisine, Fleur and Calmet were men of some wealth, while Dorez and Menteur were only poor sans-culottes – this was their only link. The soldiers were mostly NCOs from the army of the Ancien Regime and men of modest means. Defferrez was the exception: twenty years before the Revolution he had married the daughter of a Lille sugar merchant; he was an educated man who taught topography and drawing at the Bureau des Plans. As for Adhémar, before entering the *armée* he had been first secretary to the department of the Charente-Inférieure. These men who formed the command of the Lille *armée* were not part of the *sans-culotterie* or indeed of any distinct social milieu. They were simply *sociétaires*, militants of the Lille club.

Lille is undoubtedly an extreme example of the grip of a *sociéte* on the command of a revolutionary force. In Bordeaux the militants of the Sectionary assemblies and the national club shared the places. In the Bordeaux Sections the *commissaires*, presidents, and members of the committees of the general assemblies were given priority. Among the candidates accepted by the assembly in the Bon-Accord Section was Bonfin, its president in September, Caillavet, secretary before the Federalist period, Benoît, member of the subsistence committee,[8] and Laclaverie, its secretary in October. The other candidates accepted – Malleville, Coblentz, Chapus, Martin – had with Benoît and Caillavet been members of the committee of 12 nominated in October to elect the new *comité révolutionnaire* of the Section, while Castera was appointed *commissaire* to the bakeries on 21 Brumaire.[9] The story was the same in the Parfaite-Union Section: Simon, a joiner elected captain of the company of this Section, had been one of the *commissaires* appointed by the Section on 4 September to go before the *représentants* at La Réole.[10] This Simon was an important personality, having also been appointed a member of the new *comité révolutionnaire* formed on 28 September. Two other *commissaires* of this *comité*, Latour who presided over the Sectionary assembly after 27 August, and Prosper, a wagoner, were also elected to the company, though in October Prosper was to be denounced as unpatriotic for having withdrawn his candidacy. Béchade, appointed a member of the inscriptions committee on 21 October, profited shamelessly from this strategic position to have himself placed first on the list, followed by several of his colleagues. At Bordeaux, as at Lille, the militant minority of a Section utilised the Sectionary institutions to reserve the best places in the companies for themselves, whilst retaining their positions in the assemblies and committees. We have information on these two Sections alone, but the Sectionary officers were in such a hurry to profit from this new privileged institution that a similar situation must have occurred in the other Sections. In Bordeaux, more than anywhere else, admission to a revolutionary battalion was a kind of consecration of republican patriotism and most of those referred to above had distinguished themselves among the anti-Federalist minority. Besides, it was dangerous to refuse these honours.

One of the captains of the Nièvre battalion, de Goy, a printer–stationer from Nevers, was a member of the committee of the *société populaire*.[11] Civeton, a bourgeois of Roanne and captain of the town company, had been a *délégué* of Javogues to this district, charged with purging its *société*.[12] In him were united nearly all the attributes of an 'homme de liaison', for he held both a military command and the post of *délégué* of a *représentant* to a district and a *société populaire*. The *commissaires civils* for the Allier battalion, as well as Baldy, second in command, were personalities of the Moulins *société*, over which Grimaud had presided several times, and it was from this *société* that Boissay and the Moulins *comité révolutionnaire* recruited the political leaders of this force.[13] The *armées* formed at Toulouse, Montpellier, at Montauban and Aix were also led by the members of *société* committees, and the Aix battalion borrowed its title from the Société des Anti-Politiques.[14] The small *armée* planned by the Perpignan *société* had a general staff of *sociétaires*.[15] In the Marne the *commissaires civils* attached to the revolutionary force were leading members of the Châlons, Reims, Sainte-Ménehould and Sézanne *sociétés*: Alfonce, from Paris, former broker to a banker there, now employed in military supply; Tessier, a dancing-master and former *valet de pied*; Capitaine, a *rentier*; Le Maître, a carpenter; Depoix, a ropemaker; Villers, also a Parisian and employed with military transport – all were from the Châlons *société*; Belliart, a former teacher, was a leading agitator in the Reims *société*; Gambet and Leclerc were former priests and *sociétaires* of Sainte-Ménehould; Belpêche, a botanist and herbalist, was president of the Sézanne *société*.[16] Here again we have a socially disparate group whose common denominator was an influential position in a *société*.

Of Chaix, the revolutionary *commissaire* in the Corbigny district, we can say that he manipulated the small Lormes *société* as he pleased.[17] In the Côte-d'Or, Haute-Saône and Doubs, the *sociétés* all reserved the plum positions on the projected general staffs for themselves. At Pontarlier, for example, the *société* having opened a register, 'eighteen of its members put their names down, among them the two constitutional priests of Pontarlier...'.[18] At Carcassonne, when the *société* started to organise the *armée révolutionnaire* of the Aude, it sent one of its members, Lacroix, *procureur* of the commune, to Toulouse to find out about procedure from the leaders of the *société* there.[19] In the Haute-Loire, according to a hostile observer, one of the *commissaires* of the revolutionary detachments was also a leading light of the Rozières *société*, the *juge de paix* Galavelle.[20]

This grip of the *sociétés populaires* on the command of the *armées* was a natural consequence of the place given to them in the forces' organisation and choice of personnel. But their grip rarely went beyond the command. The *commissaires civils*, officers and NCOs were *sociétaires*, members of the militant élite; but many of the soldiers were recruited outside the *sociétés*, undoubtedly, as Descrosne had urged, from 'the men of the tribunes', or more so, from people recommended by influential *sociétaires* in the Sections. At the head of most of these *armées* we find men as different in origin as they were in temperament, whose only common tie was their membership of an active minority in an urban *société populaire*.

It is not among the command, therefore, that we should look for the ideal of a political and moral élite, an ideal of a revolutionary élite from which the military chiefs and most of the officers were far removed. The Parisian *armée* itself, although an *armée* of *sectionnaires*, was nevertheless used by many militants as a means of spectacular advancement. The departmental *armées*–apart from those of the large towns, which had fewer links to the Sections–put up less resistance to colonisation by these invading military men. But such colonisation had little importance for the *armées*' future activities, since effective command was in the hands of civilians.

II   *The political command*

Article X of the collective order issued by the *représentants* at Lyon on 9 Brumaire declared that the *commissaires civils* 'will lead the *armée révolution-naire* and it will implement their orders...'; while in Hérault de Séchelles's *Instruction* to the *commissaires civils* of the Haut-Rhin *armée*, they were to 'lead the *armées révolutionnaires* to points on the frontier...'.[21] This much then is clear: responsibility for directing the operations of the *armées* lay with the *commissaires civils*; the military commanders were their subordinates. 'These *commissaires civils*', a Toulouse historian accurately observes, 'were the political cog-wheels without which the *armée revolutionnaire* could not have functioned...'.[22] 'The whole system of Terror was supported by swarms of commissaries and agents, with unlimited powers, who went through the whole of France...', claimed William Playfair.[23] At a higher level military power was subordinated to the *représentants*, and the picture painted by a Bordeaux prisoner in the château de la Réole is one of the *représentant* galloping on ahead, followed at a respectful distance by the revolutionary general and his aides-de-camp.[24] The same was true even at a lower level, for the *commissaires civils*, acting under mandate from the *représentants*, issued orders to the revolutionary generals. In the Morbihan the adjutant-general Avril was under orders from the cook Le Batteux, a *délégué* of Carrier; in the Aveyron, General Marbot obeyed, with ill grace, the wigmaker Viton. In the area around Lyon, we know the names of the *commissaires* who led operations, but the officers were so obscure that even the Thermidorean denouncers did not trouble to cite their names. In the Moselle and the neighbouring departments, the names of Gobert and Delteil are often heard, but we do not know the name of a single officer in the Metz *armée*. Some commanders of the Toulouse *armée* would be denounced at the same time as the *commissaires civils*, but they were considered very subordinate by their denouncers. The *commissaire civil* then *was* the departmental or communal *armée révolutionnaire*, the personification of revolutionary action. The personal importance of these men was so obvious to contemporaries that they went to the lengths of giving them their own special personalities and physiognomies. If observers are to be believed, the *commissaires civils* were almost a race apart, of revolutionary, furious, violent men, recognisable even by their external appearance.

How many belonged to this bizarre new race of men? Playfair, using Thermidorean sources, speaks of a horde of over 50,000.[25] But this is pure fantasy, even if we add to the real *commissaires* a more numerous group of imitators. A more accurate calculation would be in the order of 500, which would already give us around 10 for each active *armée*. It is difficult to reach more precise figures, because of the nature of their often extremely fanciful functions. Their very title was equivocal, and the Thermidorean authorities were right to refer to them as 'these so-called *commissaires civils*' or 'men calling themselves *commissaires révolutionnaires*'.[26] Often one was a *commissaire civil* only for the duration of one expedition, and there were 50 or more members of the *comités révolutionnaires* in the Paris Sections who could claim the title because of missions conducted with detachments from Paris, on behalf of the Committee of General Security. In the Nièvre, 20 persons – members of the Nevers *comité de surveillance, sociétaires* of the town, functionaries of the district or departmental administrations – enjoyed this title at one time or another, while leading a revolutionary battalion into the districts of the department or the environs of Lyon. In the Allier we know the names of 11 *commissaires civils* active in the districts or around Lyon. In the same way, in the area of activity of the Toulouse *armée*, there were 15 persons who held the position in the Haute-Garonne or the Ariège. The great expedition to the Lot, Aveyron, and Lozère mobilised 14 or 15 *commissaires civils*, drawn from the Cantal, the Lot or the local area. In the East likewise we know of 10 or more, and the department of the Marne alone produced 8. Not only was their function often short-lived, but sometimes it was necessary also to send *commissaires des guerres*, who then adopted the title, quite rightly, for men like Griois at Lille, Seigneur at Nevers and Peyrend-d'Herval at Bordeaux certainly exercised the functions of a *commissaire civil*. There were also the *délégués* of the *représentants*, and circulating judges, who were frequently confused with the *commissaires civils*. While it is impossible to arrive at any precise figure, therefore, it would not be an exaggeration to speak of hundreds of *commissaires civils* for the whole of France.[27]

That was already a lot for an élite. The *commissaires civils*, however, like the tiny *armées* they commanded, were impressive not so much because of their numbers, but because of their violence and the fear they aroused. Relatively few in number, they were nevertheless so talked about that the peasant imagination, with its tendency to inflate everything, saw one at every turn of the road. Their terrifying appearance also owed much to the vividness of popular imagination. There were undoubtedly villainous-looking men and there is much talk of black hair, matted and stinking, their moustaches and their accoutrements.[28] Take the description of Belpêche, for example, 'with his *bonnet rouge*, his moustaches and his blood-red sash...'; or the *commissaire* of the Bordeaux battalion 'appropriately decked out in moustaches, large sabre, pistols at his belt and all the tokens and medals of the order...'.[29] It is probably far too black a portrait, for the peasants were trying to justify the terror these men from the towns aroused in them. But there is surely some truth in the descriptions, for the *commissaires* were not placid men and the violence of their gestures, their words, their actions, to which we have abundant testimony, must also have appeared in their eyes, their facial expressions, their gait. In the Year III the Thermidorean authorities searching for the former monk, Commerçon, *commissaire civil* to the Nièvre battalion, described him in these terms: 'He is a man of enormous vivacity, in his speech, bearing and gestures.... Aged around forty-five, he has a black beard, and black hair...'.[30] One wonders if a true *révolutionnaire* could ever have been blond!

Men of such violence and so rebarbative an appearance could only have been foreigners, and it was above all under this guise that they aroused such fear. Riouffe, the Bordeaux Federalist who seems to have been such an accurate observer of things and people of the Terror, claimed that the *commissaires* and their agents in Bordeaux were 'Savoyards, Biscayens and even Germans'[31] – foreigners being numerous in the great port. An historian writing in 1797 sought similar origins for the many *commissaires* active in the South-East, whose violence he attributed, with some contradiction, 'to the hot-headedness of southerners, who exaggerate everything and to whom measure and moderation are alien...'.[32] But to an inhabitant of Quercy, these 'black' men could only have come from Bordeaux.[33] For the peasants all those who were not from their own area were foreigners, and by this token nearly all the *commissaires civils* appeared as such in rural eyes. Belpêche was reproached for being only a recent resident of Sézanne, while the pious inhabitants of Saint-Girons would speak of Picot-Belloc as 'an inhabitant of God knows where'.[34] In the Morvan a *bouquiniste* from Nevers was considered a foreigner because he came from the town, and Parisians and Toulousains, who were particularly numerous among the *commissaires*, were considered 'intruders'. It was rare, as we have seen, for a *commissaire civil* to operate in his native region, and both the *représentants* and the *comités de surveillance* made a deliberate policy of using *commissaires* from districts adjoining those into which they were sent.[35]

In reality nearly all the *commissaires civils* were French, even if some had indeed worked abroad before the Revolution. But this was no crime; indeed in the Year II it was a positive virtue, for many of these refugees had been victims of their republicanism, and Picot-Belloc who had 'worked with his hands' in Spain was unjustly reproached for this by the Saint-Girons clergy.[36] The only real foreigners were Schneider and his acolytes – the *commissaires civils* and travelling judges with the Bas-Rhin *armée* – all refugees from the Palatinate and from Prussia. Indeed in Alsace the struggle between ultra-revolutionaries and Jacobins assumed the form of a conflict between German dechristianisers and the French of the Propagande (the Catholic faction),[37] but this was an exceptional situation. Despite the efforts of Robespierrist and Thermidorean propaganda to depict the *commissaires* as foreign agents, despite the accusations of the peasantry against these 'black men', we can state quite positively that nearly all the known *commissaires* were of French nationality.

The peasants saw these 'godless men' not only as foreigners, but as members also of the 'Sect', in other words the *armées* and the other institutions of the Terror as serving the secret designs of Protestantism and Freemasonry.[38] The *commissaires civils* were thereby incorporated into the system of abbé Barruel. For the peasants, the main victims of the energetic iconoclasm of these men, there was not a shred of doubt about this: the *commissaires civils* like the 'apostles' from the urban *sociétés*, could only be the agents of militant Calvinism.[39] However, even in the South-West, there was no *commissaire civil* of whom we could say with any certainty that he was Protestant.[40] Indeed it is the former Catholic clergy, the priests, curates, monks, lay brothers or seminarians who stand out clearly because of their numbers – the priests finding a kind of revolutionary vocation at the head of detachments, their terrifying processions interspersed with civic sermons. They were, however, sincere converts to the new ideas and they were to die unrepentant. These *curés rouges* and the various kinds of ultra-revolutionaries were a recognised social phenomenon in many areas of the Republic. Doubtless there were *pasteurs rouges* too, but we know of none commanding revolutionary detachments.

The *commissaires civils* belonged to no distinct social category and, given their extremely varied origins, occupations and fortunes, it would be unwise to try to see in this socially disparate group conscious representatives of the sans-culottes or *petit peuple*; the few socially levelling principles that can be attributed to them cannot be explained by any common plebeian origins and still less by class awareness. Undoubtedly there were some real sans-culottes in their ranks, small-town artisans, small businessmen or shopkeepers, some of whom employed assistants – 16 *commissaires* in fact came from this group.[41] But men of the law, *notaires*, attorneys, public prosecutors and *juges de paix* were the most numerous, since we know of 17 definitely.[42] Fifteen *commissaires* belonged to a privileged world far removed from *sans-culotterie*: property-owners, purchasers of national property, merchants, tanners, manufacturers, several of whom were referred to as 'bourgeois' in the lists of *sociétaires*.[43] It was this group which supplied some of the most violent *commissaires*. Domestic service, on the other hand, was poorly represented with three men only.[44] This might appear surprising considering how sought-after these positions were by the economic victims of the new regime. Twelve who had been Catholic clerics before the Revolution became *commissaires*;[45] there were a few employees,[46] two or three farmers – the only country people in this group of townsmen[47] – and a few career soldiers,[48] for whom the move to a political command at the head of an *armée révolutionnaire* was but one episode in their steady advancement through a career in military supply. Finally, there were five doctors, surgeons and health officers,[49] making a total of close to 80 *commissaires civils* whose professions are known.[50]

We must be careful not to attach too much importance to these figures, which have no statistical value, since they account for less than 80 *commissaires*, and of these nearly a third come from the two particularly well-documented departments of the Nièvre and the Allier. They also give a static picture of their professional standing and do not permit any analysis of the characteristic phenomenon of social mobility which we have already seen in the Parisian *armée*. Above all the *commissaires civils* were birds of passage, these positions, like the more numerous ones in military supply, representing short interludes in careers which were constantly moving forward, in search of chance and adventure. Doubtless the majority of these men were not adventurers, but artisans, shopkeepers and men of the law with solid roots in the society of their native villages, and it would be wrong to treat most in this category as *déclassés*.[51] Some were indeed adventurers and we will look at them again in the chapter on morality. But a typical case is that of Alfonce, a currency broker with a Parisian banker before the Revolution, then employed as a simple cannoneer in the Parisian artillery; thanks to political friendships in the War Ministry, he secured a position as inspector of supplies in the 2nd military division at Châlons, where he quickly became one of the personalities in the *société populaire*. In Germinal Year III he declared that his entire fortune consisted of the salary of 650 livres which he had earned as inspector of supplies. The future career of this 'homme de liaison' provides some valuable information on the fate of these men whose task of economic mobilisation carried them through the garrison towns at the rear of the armies. In 1806 Alfonce was supply inspector to the Dalmatian Army; he moved over to the Grand Army that same year, then to the Armée d'Allemagne in 1809, and was finally demobilised the following year, 'his age and infirmities no longer permitting him to follow a military career...'.[52] Like many ex-terrorists, this *commissaire civil* of the *armée révolutionnaire* of the Marne found refuge in the French armies of occupation.

Peyrend d'Herval, *commissaire des guerres* at Bordeaux, and *commissaire civil* of the Gironde battalion, presents a similar case. This former *charitain* monk from Clermont-Ferrand had gone to Paris in the first years of the Revolution, began to frequent the Cordeliers, and in April 1793, thanks to the favour he enjoyed with Vincent, obtained a place as *commissaire des guerres* at Bayonne. From there he went to La Réole, the general head-quarters of the *représentants* conducting the operations against Bordeaux; he entered this town in the baggage train of the republican armies, as secretary to the *représentants*, a position which he joined to that of *commissaire des guerres*. Despite the many denunciations made against him in the Year III, this former monk was able to continue his career as *commissaire des guerres*, both in France and in the armies of occupation.[53]

The move to the *armée révolutionnaire* as *commissaire civil* and *commissaire des guerres* of the Toulouse *armée* also determined the career of Picot-Belloc. He was born in Toulouse in 1754, son of Capitoul, and more than likely a former Garde du Roi. Some years before the Revolution, probably because of financial failure or some kind of shady dealings, he had gone to seek his fortune in Spain, without however finding it, for if he is to be believed he ended up 'working with his hands'. Here, however, we need to take account of the fact that this well-off son of a noble,[54] from old military stock, would naturally wish to pass for a simple sans-culotte in 1793, when he was leading the Toulouse sans-culottes in the Ariège. In any case for Picot, as for Alfonce and Peyrend-d'Herval, the war, and the formation of an immense politico-military machine, opened bright prospects for a new career. Thanks also to connections in the War Ministry, and to the support of the Toulouse *société populaire*, Picot secured a position as *commissaire des guerres* in his native town. After distinguishing himself, in his brief career in the Toulouse *armée révolutionnaire*, by his violence of language and anti-Catholic interventions, this unstable man was able to continue in his new career as *commissaire des guerres* in the South-West until his retirement, in 1812, to some property acquired at Barbaran in the Saint-Gaudens arrondissement.[55]

The career of Gobert, a personality in Metz and *commissaire civil* with the Moselle *armée*, is not dissimilar, in his advancement in military administra-tion and promotion to head a political *armée*. Gobert too had changed his career several times, though he remained in his native region. Having become a legal worthy in the *baillage* of Metz in 1780, he was appointed the town's money-changer in 1784; but at the time of the Revolution he had become a tanner at Moulins-les-Metz. 'Take the example of citizen Gobert of Metz', wrote a journalist in the Year V; 'from being a bankrupt, he becomes president of a revolutionary tribunal. From there it was only one step into the Administration of military supply. In this administration no one worried about his reputation; they knew that he was rich but never doubted his *civisme*...'.[56] That year this *'chevalier* of the Terror' was elected to the Conseil des Anciens; some years later he married the only daughter of Ladoucette, a former *commissaire civil* like himself, who had accompanied him abroad on his missions to ensure military supplies, and who, under the Empire, was to become prefect of the Moselle.[57]

For other *commissaires civils* this transfer to an *armée révolutionnaire* was also a step in their social advancement. Le Batteux, formerly a cook in a monastery, became a postmaster, and by the Year III had an *auberge* of his own at Redon.[58] Men like Belpêche and Villers had come to the departments in search of positions with the revolutionary administrations, while Grimaud, the former teacher in the *collège* of Clermont-Ferrand, after many misadventures in his native town, came to seek his fortune in Moulins, then in Paris, where in the Year III he just managed to secure a position as clerk in the Commission for the Colonies.[59]

The feature common to all these men was their instability. Military administration was particularly congenial to men who had an errant existence, and adventurers of the same mould as Vidocq found it excellent territory for criminal activities. His equal among the *commissaires civils* was the native of Grenoble, Marc Dolle, a great villain for whom the *armée révolutionnaire* of Crémieu, in which he was some kind of 'commissaire', was simply an instrument with which to terrorise his creditors. For the moment let us concentrate, not on the morality of this adventurer, gambler and pillager but on the events in his life. A former merchant from a well-off family, his fortune ruined through gambling, Dolle left Grenoble for Paris, where he succeeded in re-establishing his republican purity, compromised in the Federalist movement in the Dauphiné). His fortune re-established, he moved first to La Guillotière, where he played the part of patron and defender of the sans-culottes, then to the villages of the Isère, where he acquired enough property to permit him to flee back to Paris, before being arrested, first there, then at Marseille, and was finally transferred to the prisons of Bourgoin.[60] Dolle was the archetypal adventurer, a demagogue, gambler and womaniser, and like all his colleagues in this strange world of revolutionary *commissaires*, he was violent and unstable.

A biographical sketch of Vauquoy, Dolle's chief, and principal *commissaire civil* in the Isère, will highlight certain traits shared by Vauquoy and his colleagues and fellow Parisians, Peyrend and Alfonce. Alfonce was broker to a dealer in foreign currency, Vauquoy was a clerk in the administration of the Ferme Générale. Following the Revolution he moved from a political position, as secretary to the Jacobins, through a series of positions with military administration,[61] before being appointed to the Commission Temporaire. He was then coming to the end of his revolutionary career, for he was to be guillotined in Messidor Year II, the first victim of a proscription which touched only one other former *commissaire civil*. This was Jean-François Baby, a former property-owner of Tarascon, who according to his enemies had been guilty of fraudulent bankruptcy – a common accusation in Thermidorean denunciations to which too much credit should not be attached – and was shot on the plain of Grenelle in the Year IV.[62] Nicolas Viton, effective *commissaire* with the Lot *armée*, and its nominal commander, was the person who most resembled Vauquoy, both in terms of his modest origins – Vauquoy having been a clerk with the Ferme Générale, and Viton an assistant wigmaker in the wealthy quartiers of Paris – and in the way in which he advanced himself in a revolutionary career by combining a political position with military missions: he had been secretary to a *représentant*, where Vauquoy was secretary to the Jacobins, and both fulfilled missions in Bouchotte's name. But, more fortunate than Vauquoy, Viton managed to return to military administration when his command terminated. We will speak again of him in the section on military command, though as a type he belongs to that strange race of political *commissaires*.

Among the *commissaires* there was also a category of those who lived irregular lives. But of the 80 of whom we know something, not all followed a life on the roads and in garrisons, and those who took refuge in Paris to escape the violence of the Year III – which far surpassed that committed by these men, whose main failing was rather one of verbal imprudence – formed only a minority of political militants. Far more numerous were those whose roots and possessions in the countryside kept them at home. We have already spoken of Gobert, the tanner and former officer of justice, who had benefited from the Revolution. But what can be said of Lagasquie, *commissaire civil* in the Aveyron, national agent of the Cahors district and a member of the town's *comité de surveillance*? He was a society doctor under the Ancien Regime, was called to Paris in 1786 to treat the duchesse de Bourbon, and was acquainted with his fellow doctor, Jean-Paul Marat, in the Royal Academy of Medicine.[63] Lagasquie, therefore, had not needed the Revolution to become famous, and it seems certain that conviction alone led him into the same group as Vauquoy and Viton, from whom socially he was very far removed.

If these men were thus a race apart, a separate family, what were the links connecting them? It was certainly not social origin or fortune, for while some were landowners with enough resources to retire to their property in time of difficulty, others were employees or artisans, dependent on their occupations for a livelihood. There was no common social denominator linking a Gobert to an Allard, a Dolle to a Grimaud or an Alfonce.

They did not then all lead irregular existences, and one must distinguish between the bachelors – whether Parisians or artisans from Moulins or Toulouse – who did not mind spending their entire lives with the army, even in conquered countries, and family men with a solid base in their native towns. Picot, Vauquoy and Dolle were single men who chased after the innkeeper's daughter, the peasant girl or the lady of the manor, and whose conduct on their missions was flashy and scandalous. But one could never have accused Lagasquie or Gobert, or the many former ecclesiastics, of having taken advantage of their prerogatives to supply themselves with women. Some behaved scandalously, but most followed the path of virtue, and were deficient only in sobriety.

Perhaps it was simply a case of enthusiasm, or youthful passion? But most of these men were not young: 18 were over thirty, 5 alone were around twenty.[64] Wisdom had not come with age, however, and the most passionate and imprudent of this group were also the oldest: Grimaud was fifty-eight when he took detachments from his Allier battalion on their dechristianising mission to the districts of that department.

Nor was it a case of a distinct political group; it would take the imagination of a Fouquier-Tinville to construct a secret web of conspiracy by turning these 'hommes de liaison' into Hébertists. Some certainly owed their positions to friendships in the War Ministry, several were friends of Sijas, Vincent and Vilain d'Aubigny, while nearly all used the slogans and coarse language of the *Père Duchesne* when they went on mission. But any number of agents in the enormous military machine made use of friendship with the head of a division in the War Ministry, while the readers of Hébert's paper amounted to thousands, perhaps ten of thousands. Besides, they were Jacobins rather than Cordeliers, and in any event Parisians were a minority in this group. These men were not emissaries of any party.

They were, on the other hand, ultra-revolutionaries. Their duties demanded as much. In the execution of their missions they showed signs of being primitive social levellers, sometimes going so far as to affirm that they were making war on the rich on behalf of the poor, that one should take from the rich to give to the poor, that the rich had been in place for too long and that it was now the turn of the poor, that they distrusted people with education and intelligence, that a bourgeois could not be a good republican, that the law had been made for the rich, but that popular justice favoured the sans-culottes. This is what the *commissaires* were expected to say when on campaign. But despite all this rhetoric they were not primitive socialists or conscious doctrinarians. They were being charged with the implementation of a brutal programme of war economy for which the rich would pay. If they appeared to be ultra-revolutionaries, it was because they functioned at a level of revolutionary anarchy, and no one asked a *commissaire civil* to respect established hierarchies or private property. Of course they were ultra-revolutionaries, and that by definition. But it is also necessary to distinguish the enthusiasts, the convinced and sincere, from the conformists and the adventurers.

However, one feature above all others distinguished these men from the mass of ordinary mortals, one which, more than their turbulent lives, came to be identified with them in future commentaries, and this was their violence. Nearly all were violent men, and if they all seem to use the same language in their sermons in the countryside, it is because they were uniformly violent in their speech, even if they did not always say the same thing. Nor was such violence confined to words: contemporaries, not all of them hostile witnesses, depict these *commissaires* as fuming with anger, always ready to raise the baton or stick; Grimaud, Chaix, Vauquoy, Picot-Belloc and Peyrend-d'Herval were men of unspeakable violence. There is undoubtedly an element of anti-revolutionary exaggeration in Prud-homme's comment about Peyrend-d'Herval: 'His name was so hated in this commune [Bordeaux], that a pregnant woman aborted when it was mentioned before her...'.[65] But we do know that in Ventôse Year IV, Bompois, former *commissaire* in the Nièvre, broke a huge stick over the head of the president of the Nevers criminal tribunal, whom he had met at the corner of the street, and at a time when he was assessor to a *juge de paix*.[66] Grimaud was not only intemperate in his words, but is represented as being about to attack, in Moulins cathedral, another canon whom he accused of having taken his place. And if he managed to turn the entire *société populaire* against him in Floréal Year II, it was because of his brutal outbursts against the inhabitants of Moulins.[67] Legend has it that Schneider was a sanguinary brute who derived pleasure from the mental torture of his victims.[68] As for Baby, a taste for violent action combined with the solid republican convictions of this former landowner of Tarascon was the departure point leading directly to the execution stake of Grenelle. Baby was not a man made for life in peaceful times.[69] The portrait we have of Commerçon could just as well be that of a Chaix or a Vauquoy, and of so many more of these *commissaires*, simple men of conviction, all hewn from the same stone. If they did not all share the prejudices of a Sadet, who declared that there was no place in a republic for men of intelligence and education,[70] they were nevertheless not men who recognised shades and subtleties. Even educated men like Grimaud, Agar, Gobert or Lagasquie did not think any differently when it came to enemies of the regime: one was for or against the Revolution – it was as simple as that.

Undoubtedly such violence was innate in many cases, though lack of information on the previous careers of these obscure men renders any confident assessment difficult. But the excitement of the moment also played a part. Such men went about their missions with vigour and determination, exposing themselves to the hatred of the rural population. Violence, therefore, may have been a kind of calculated defence mechanism, as it was with certain *représentants* who often preferred the threat to the repressive action itself. The *armées révolutionnaires* were above all designed to 'strike terror', the *commissaires* at least had to adopt a terrifying air, and to judge from the impression made upon the peasants they were entirely successful in their ploy. Much of this verbal violence, however, was simply the characteristically direct and brutal manner of speech of the career soldier. Picot's style of preaching was certainly learnt in the Ancien Regime army, and Delport, the former priest and soldier – who was labelled with the terrifying, though unmerited, name of 'Captain Without Quarter'[71] – had the brusque and frank manner of a soldier, unrivalled even by the *Père Duchesne*.

In short, the *commissaires* belonged neither to any political or religious sect, nor to any distinct social category. Their attitudes were not dictated by class-consciousness, nor by any desire to implement a well-thought-out social programme. It is not always easy to make a distinction between men of conviction and demagogues; but most of these seem to have been extremely sincere men, living in a state of intense and exaggerated excitement, and motivated by a genuine hatred for the enemies of the regime, notably refractory priests and the rural populace. Rather than sanguinary brutes,[72] they were preachers of civic virtue, conscious of their importance, and animated by an intense punitive will, to which vague primitive levelling ideas were sometimes attached. Their violence, particularly in speech, and their state of over-excitement, sometimes lasting for days on end, was very often due to an excess of drink, for in their drunkenness the *commissaires* were unrivalled, even by the men under their orders. In the East people remembered the gastronomic pillaging by the Metz 'band', under the command of Gobert and Delteil; and in Metz itself the excuse given to the Thermidorean authorities for the terrorism of one of Gobert's acolytes was that he was almost always drunk.[73] In the Isère Vauquoy fortified his antichristian zeal with the priests' sometimes quite excellent wine, gulped in great quantity from chalices used for religious services.[74] In the canton of Lormes, Chaix, at the head of his sans-culottes, forced himself on the hospitality of the presbyteries, and, having refreshed himself, started to insult his hosts and to express egalitarian theories.[75] Picot-Belloc also refound his civic eloquence after having dined, and the expedition to the Ariège resembled the best *parties de campagne* of the Parisian *armée*.[76] As for the *aubergiste* Le Batteux, he seemed to suffer from the malady common to his profession and his outburst of fury, when he heard of the promulgation of the law of 14 Frimaire, can only be explained by a drinking bout with his colleagues from Vannes.[77] Not all of these men can have been inveterate drunkards, and their violence was not simply the outcome of too much wine; but their missions lent themselves to such gastronomic abuses and provided the occasion to whip up temperaments not noted for moderation or a sense of proportion at the best of times.

This was their greatest weakness. They were certainly accused of all manner of defects and according to the country people, the Thermidoreans, and historians such as Prudhomme, the artisans among them were frauds and criminals from the very dregs of society, and those from the liberal professions or the propertied classes were *déclassé*. Having thus given them a past made to measure and pigeon-holed them after scarcely any proper investigation, commentators on the morality of these men readily attributed all kinds of violation and pillage to them. In reality they were not quite so base; for the most part they were not politically involved, and a future supporter of Lebois or Babeuf would not have been so captivated by tankards of wine.[78]

Violent and authoritarian they certainly were, treating the established authorities and the military commanders with equal disdain, accusing the former of being accomplices of 'égoïsme' and 'fanatisme', and taking a high tone with the latter, whom they considered mere 'parade horses'. The presence at the head of the detachments of such reckless and fiery men, with little sympathy for moderation, and even less for legality, was to give the activities of the *armées révolutionnaires* their dramatic and anarchic character. This special kind of temperament went with being a *commissaire civil*.

There was no middle way for men possessed of such an exaggerated temperament; the group epitomises all that was best and purest in the Terror, but also all that was most equivocal and most violent. The best were the Chaixes, the Babys and others like them who inspire real sympathy because of their simplicity of behaviour, their optimistic naïvety as dispensers of somewhat primitive justice, the bantering humour with which they brushed aside the complaints of the tight-fisted farmers' wives, threatening to throw open their cupboards and announcing a revolutionary *dime* of a hundred per cent. They *were* educated, not enough to separate them from the more humble, but enough to be of assistance to them. They commanded respect by the dignity and self-denial of revolutionary lives devoted to the cause of equality, particularly during the reaction of the Years III to IX, and were enemies likewise of injustice, privilege and the established order – doubtless even that of the Year II, for the Robespierrist order had no place for men who revolutionised at will. It is difficult to imagine individuals more remote from the 'government men', the prudent high priests of Robespierrism and Jacobinism, content to implement the orders of their superiors, the bureaucrats of the Revolution rather than the revolutionaries.

For a Chaix everything was possible, the revolutionary city was of this world and he began to build it with every means available; defective means, like a few poorly-armed soldiers wanting to return home, compromising means too, for these soldiers did not always possess the ardent sincerity of their political leaders. These leaders, these authentic revolutionaries, were in fact naïve, because they believed in example and thought that by taxing the rich and threatening the fanatical, equality and reason could be established overnight. They were naïve also in their belief that one could pursue the egalitarian aims of the Revolution of the Year II – a levelling revolution – at the same time as the war effort against monarchist Europe. Their error was a generous and humane one, and these men with their varied backgrounds and their very different experience, already fully possessed of hope and a tendency to disorder, were the truest and purest revolutionaries of the great period of the anarchical Terror. Through their optimism they atoned for the baseness of some of their colleagues, such as the Vitons and perhaps the Vauquoys, who saw in the extensive powers they possessed nothing but a favourable opportunity for pillage, despotism, cruelty and sexual excess.

III   *The military leaders*

The military leaders of the *armées révolutionnaires* were colourless men for
the most part, completely dominated by the *commissaires civils*, and little
more than 'parade horses', as a Toulouse journalist put it in the Year III.
The peculiar organisation of the *armées*, assigning control to the civil command, was responsible for this reduction of the military men to places of
secondary importance. They were little more than executors, super-
gendarmes, conveyors of orders. In this group political personalities are
rare, and it is difficult to distinguish any individual characteristics among
these anonymous men, considered so unimportant that their names scarcely
figure in royalist works like the famous *Dictionnaire des Jacobins vivans*[79] and
Prudhomme's study.[80] However, some *armées* had no *commissaire civil*
attached, and in these cases the commander and his subordinates could play
an important role. In the Nord in particular, Dufresse, Calmet, Agut and
Adhémar were military politicians and people of sufficient importance to
have some control over events. In the Lot Viton belonged to the class of
commissaires civils rather than to that of the military commanders, and
effectively united both functions. At Crémieu the locksmith, Contamin,
was the real master of his little *armée*; he was also a leading terrorist and
conspirator. Finally, in the Nièvre Brunière, who for some time commanded the battalion, had as much influence over the conduct of operations
as the *commissaires civils*, of whom there were a great many in this department and to whom he was linked through kinship, background and
temperament. It is only by accident that men such as these four should
figure in a section devoted to the military command, for their role was
virtually identical with that of the *commissaires*, from whom they borrowed
their individual characteristics, their language, passion and their methods.
Because of their individual influence, the four deserve to be examined
separately.

Career soldiers were by far the most numerous among the officers of the
departmental *armées*; though in truth there were soldiers and soldiers,
particularly in the Year II when the former barriers to advancement in the
military hierarchy were breaking down everywhere, producing a stampede
for commissions. It is necessary, therefore, to distinguish between three
main categories of officers: officers and NCOs in the garrisons of fortified
places, notably in frontier areas at the time of the formation of the *armées
révolutionnaires*; those retired from the gendarmerie or *maréchaussée* and
recalled to service in these unwarlike *armées*; and finally, the most important
group numerically, the officers of the urban National Guard, many of
whom took command of revolutionary battalions formed in their native
towns. For the first group, the main issue was promotion; for the second
the end of an onerous retirement; for the third a simple change, satisfying
the *amour-propre* of the self-centred.

For such military men, service in an *armée révolutionnaire* was merely one stage in a career already launched, but an important stage permitting a man to progress from a simple lieutenancy or captaincy at the formation of the force to the rank of major or adjutant-general at the time of its disbandment. These positions and ranks depended on the favour of the *représentants en mission*, the *sociétés populaires* or the War Ministry, and the military men, more than any other profession, had to conform to the requirements of revolutionary orthodoxy. During the existence of the *armées* these newly promoted officers used the language of the *Père Duchesne* in terms as strong as any civilian, and were lavish in their expressions of affection for Vincent, Sijas and the other chiefs in the War Ministry. Their vocabulary soon changed when *Père Duchesne*, in the form of Hébert and Vincent, disappeared, and the *armées révolutionnaires* were disbanded. But they retained the ranks they had gained in the terrorist institutions, and continued in service with succeeding regimes. Several who had led revolutionary detachments into the countryside were to fire on the populace in Germinal and in Prairial Year III, on the royalists in Vendémiaire Year IV, and to throw themselves at the foot of the throne in 1814.

The best example of this use of a political force by military men to further their own careers can be seen in the general staff of the Lille *armée*. Besides Dufresse, the actor general, who despite his extreme terrorism (particularly its verbal side) was to follow a profitable career in the army until the Restoration, and even beyond, we have the three adjutants-general, Adhémar, Agut and Calmet-Beauvoisins, all career soldiers. Adhémar was unlucky, getting himself killed in 1796 – the only member of a revolutionary general staff to fall victim to this kind of occupational hazard.[81] Agut ended an inglorious career in the Year X, when he retired as a lieutenant in the gendarmerie, and set himself up in Paris.[82] Calmet-Beauvoisins, a well-off young man, was not wanting in political *savoir-faire*: as soon as the Lille *armée* was established, he transformed himself into a sans-culotte, took control of the rostrum of the Lille *société révolutionnaire*, and carried on a steady correspondence with his Cordelier friends in Paris. Momentarily compromised in the disgrace of his patron, Lavalette, and the so-called Hébertists of Lille, he quickly withdrew from the affair, by recommending himself to the adjutant-general, Pille, Bouchotte's successor. In Germinal Year III he won the favour of the Thermidorean Convention by helping defend it, on horseback. Later, despite his obvious intention of playing to every regime, he experienced a reverse of fortune. Imprisoned in Egypt, he was brought to Constantinople; there he spent several years in captivity, during which time his family in Paris suffered its first bankruptcy. Exchanged in Nivôse Year X, he returned to Paris; but he had lost the favour of the great, and we hear nothing more of him thereafter.[83] It was the end of a military and political career which had been so full of promise.

The last member of the little group gathered around Dufresse was Louis

Capron. Like Agut he had originated in Lille and was an infantry officer at the time of the formation of the *armée révolutionnaire* of the North. After its dissolution he remained in the army and in the Year IV succeeded in gaining a position as adjoint to the adjutant-general Ducoudray, commander of the fortress at Dunkerque.[84] His move to the Lille *armée* had thus paid dividends.

Most of the junior officers of this *armée* were also career soldiers, if we except the artillery captain Defferrez – an esteemed topographer and representative of those Parisian cannoneers who were justly considered the militant élite of Ronsin's *armée*[85] – and the *commissaire des guerres* Griois, who ended his career as a high official under the Empire.[86] The two *chefs de bataillon*, Dorez and d'Hollande, had been soldiers under the Ancien Regime, although the first had temporarily abandoned the army at the start of the Revolution, to set himself up as a launderer in Lille.[87] In the same way, the company commanders and lieutenants were all officers in the Lille or Somme battalions, or in the gendarmerie,[88] the only exceptions being Buisine, a second-hand clothes dealer, and Braëmt, a dyer, both from Lille.[89] The military men had thus captured every position on the general staff and nearly every officer grade in the *armée* – an extreme example of the military grip on the command of one of these political *armées*. The high percentage of military men in the command of these companies was undoubtedly due to the fact that Lille, as a frontier town, had a large and politically very active garrison, and we can see similar occurrences in other frontier towns in which *armées révolutionnaires* were formed or planned. In Perpignan, for example, the general staff of the *armée révolutionnaire* was taken over entirely by the garrison officers, who also dominated the *société populaire*.[90] At Redon, which in the circumstances of the Year II was a republican stronghold on the outskirts of Chouan territory, the command of the revolutionary force, hastily raised and composed of National Guardsmen and soldiers from the garrison, was given to a career soldier, Jean-Jacques Avril, provisional adjutant-general.[91]

In certain towns in the interior, the officers' ranks seem to have been reserved principally for professional soldiers: in Bordeaux, although we have no information on the background of the commander of the revolutionary battalion, Petit, its lieutenants, Lamarque and Mialhe – the latter a native of Castres and son of a pastor in Le Désert – had served in the armies of the King.[92] At Toulouse the commander-in-chief was Bonnafous, from Saint-Porcquier, a former soldier who, thanks to political friendships, had himself elected commander of the National Guard of the entire district in 1792, which qualified him to command an *armée révolutionnaire*.[93] His second-in-command, the younger Barateau, an embroiderer and former manufacturer of chasubles – according to the Toulouse Thermidoreans, he made a fraudulent declaration of bankruptcy after his business had fallen into difficulty because of the Revolution – only became a soldier in 1792 when he led a battalion of volunteers into the Vendée.[94] The other commanders of this *armée*, Delport and Picot-Belloc, had already acquired military experience, the former in a battalion of the conscripted army, the latter as a soldier in the royal armies; and even Gélas, *feudiste*, surveyor, geometrician and owner of a vineyard in the Toulouse region, had served before the Revolution.[95] In Montpellier, the command of the battalion was given to Chauvet, brother of the president of the criminal tribunal, and himself commander of the coastal fortifications.[96] The Chauvet brothers were also important figures in the *société populaire*. The Bas-Rhin *armée* was commanded by a gendarme from Bouxvillers, Frédéric Pfersdorf, who took as his adjoint a Prussian deserter, Frédéric Bohler.[97]

The Nièvre, where there were two *armées révolutionnaires* and where everything was done amidst confusion and violence, was the choice territory for *commissaires civils*, and at least four people, all soldiers, held the title 'commander of the revolutionary force' at various times and from various authorities. Brunière, who had the best claim to such a title, since he led the Nevers detachment to Lyon, was an officer in the gendarmerie.[98] Pierre Bussière, whose command in the district of Clamecy seems to have been only semi-official, had made his career in the infantry;[99] while Seigneur, a former soldier with an extremely long service record, had successfully raised himself to a position as *commissaire des guerres* at the time of Fouché's order.[100] There was also Porchery, lieutenant-colonel,[101] and Rougette, commander of the portion of the *armée* which remained at Nevers, but of whom we know nothing except his name. Serving under these different commanders were four officers who had come to the *armée* of the North from Nevers: Clément, Maire, Moutoir and Dobeil.[102] If there were some small businessmen or artisans from Nevers among the officers of this formation – de Goy, lieutenant, was a printer and stationer in the municipality, Richard, likewise a lieutenant and brother to a member of the Commission Temporaire, was a joiner[103] – professional soldiers accounted for the majority. As a prototype of all the *armées révolutionnaires* then, this battalion was commanded by professional soldiers, but these in turn were subordinate to the all-powerful *commissaires civils*.

Of the battalion in the neighbouring Allier, we know little: Lavigne, second lieutenant, had served in the Chartres-Infanterie regiment.[104] But the commander and second-in-command, Desprez and Baldy, seem to have been officers from the Moulins National Guard, with no military experience beyond such peacetime service, for on the disbandment of the *armées* they returned their certificates of discharge to the *comité* and *société*. As in the neighbouring *armée*, we do encounter some small businessmen and shopkeepers, notables of Moulins, like the brothers Montluçon, one a stocking manufacturer, the other a shoemaker;[105] but at Moulins also the majority of the officers of this battalion seem to have been professional soldiers. Finally, at Troyes, the so-called 'armée révolutionnaire troyenne' was commanded by two Parisian soldiers, officers in the 1st battalion of the first requisition: Fleury, adjutant-general, and Richard, captain.[106]

So much for the career soldiers. When we move to the other *armées*, particularly to those of the little towns of the Midi, we notice a predominance of local personalities, bourgeois, shopkeepers and artisans from the towns. Thanks to their rank as officers acquired in the National Guard, these tended to move directly to the command of the new formations, which were often little more than a National Guard under a new title, and after their disbandment most of the officers simply returned to command positions in the same National Guard. The Loire *armée révolutionnaire* supplies the best example of this process. Commanded by its organiser, Descombes, it had Jean-Baptiste Civeton, a well-off bourgeois, former *délégué* of Javogues to the district, and commander-in-chief of the Roanne National Guard – a post which he took up again after the disbandment of the revolutionary force[107] – in command of the Roanne company. Fayolle, a bailiff, commanded the Saint-Germain-Laval company, while Archimbault, captain of the Saint-Rambert company, was a former gendarme turned proprietor in the small town. Of the officers of the Montbrison company – Martin, captain; Drouillet and Olagnier, lieutenants; Dubois, second lieutenant; and Phalipon, provisional captain – we know nothing save that they were officers of the National Guard and became so again after their short term at the head of a political *armée*.[108]

As for the command of the famous Marat company of Nantes, it seems to have been artisanal in complexion, like that of its rank and file. Padiolleau and d'Héron, both referred to as commanders, were unknowns,[109] but the quartermaster, the elder of two Naud brothers, was a gunsmith. His brother, Louis Naud – a member of the *comité révolutionnaire* – was a cooper and earthenware dealer, and a militant sans-culotte in the town.[110] Richard, adjutant of the company and its effective commander of repressive operations, was a hatter aged thirty-three, and Joly, or Jolly, his second on these sinister expeditions to the edge of the Loire, was a copper caster.[111] Proust, whose functions in the command structure are unclear, but which included those of *commissaire des guerres* and *commissaire civil*, was a nail-maker.[112]

At Bordeaux also the majority of the battalion officers were artisans, clerks or employees in the large town: Aybec, leader of the revolutionary cavalry, was an officer in the National Guard; the three captains, Albert, Brunet and Dejunca, the last a clerk to the municipality, were *sectionnaires*, as were the lieutenants, Rosseletty, Roux and Viquoi.[113] As for the small urban companies, they were controlled almost exclusively by civilians. The Crémieu dragoons were commanded by an authentic militant, the locksmith Contamin, national agent of the commune, a future Babouvist and protégé of Lepeletier.[114] The officers of the Basses-Alpes companies were personalities of the *sociétés* and *comités de surveillance* of Digne, Castellane, Forcalquier and other bourgs, most having formerly served as officers in the National Guard, to which they returned after the dispersal of the communal companies.[115] As for the Vaucluse *armée*, its commander-in-chief, Jourdan, held a top grade in the gendarmerie, while one of its detachment leaders was a printer from Orange.[116] The battalions of Montpellier and Montauban were commanded by civilians, with the exception of Chauvet,[117] and the *armée* which went to the Aveyron under the orders of the wigmaker Viton – a 'general' at twenty-one years of age and secretary to a *représentant du peuple* after only two years of service[118] – had a general staff and company commanders drawn from the officers of the Cahors National Guard.[119] Finally, commissions in the companies of the Bouches-du-Rhône and in the famous paid company of Dax were also almost totally monopolised by the leading personalities of the local National Guard[120] – a situation not without its dangers, for it placed in the hands of these petty despots of the cantonal *chef-lieu* and district the control of an armed force and the means of pressuring the local authorities and *sociétés*. At Dax the leaders of the company constituted a real military power which at first sought to expel from the town and the *société* all the other troops which had erred in not obeying them, and then the 'foreigners', in other words the people from the neighbouring towns. In this way the domination by former officers of the National Guard 'municipalised' the armed force and all the other popular institutions, and opened the way for local tyranny. The very principle of a command working for the advantage of men from the locality could lead to obvious abuses of power.

The frontier *armées* of the North, Moselle and Bas-Rhin (we have no information on the Haut-Rhin *armée*), and to a lesser extent that of the Haute-Garonne (apart from the small *armées* formed at Pau and Tarbes, of which we know little), were exceptions in terms of their entirely military command structure. Most other battalions and companies were commanded by local personalities, who had usually held some kind of command previously in the paid National Guard or in the gendarmerie – the gendarmes being everywhere the first to take advantage of this unexpected opportunity for advancement (all retaining their new ranks thereafter). These civilians came from all walks of life, and comfortable property-owners, rich *notaires*, esteemed local personalities and well-off young men did not scorn grades coveted alike by artisans and small shopkeepers. It would be futile to speculate on the motives of either group; the interest of the soldiers, like the gendarmes, is understandable. That of the civilians is more complex; undoubtedly the attraction of the epaulettes played a part, as it had with the Parisians, the small-town officers being particularly vain. In Bordeaux, election to the command of a company was one of the surest guarantees of one's civic virtue, a considerable inducement in a town where many needed to clear their names. In this group the 'pures', the enthusiasts, the political militants were rare;[121] they were to be found among the *commissaires civils* or in the ranks. Among the officers dishonesty was rife, notably in the *armée* of the Lot. But if the officer class was lacking ardent republicans or terrorists of high calibre, it included many likeable, fantastic, roguish and picturesque characters, who attracted attention and gave the institutions which had permitted them to rise from obscurity an unmerited radiance.

Dufresse and Viton belonged to the class of adventurers and unprincipled go-getters, the kind of men who successfully ride out great political upheavals, using and betraying each new regime in turn. Dufresse, the man who had a guillotine on wheels engraved on the wax seal of the *armée révolutionnaire* of the North, became general-baron of the Empire, governor of the Deux-Sèvres, and made his way successfully into the services of the restored monarchy by recommending himself to the La Rochejacquelain family. If his words in 1815 can be credited, this general-baron and former actor with the Théâtre Feydeau was a secret royalist in the summer of 1793, when, like so many other future leaders of the *armées révolutionnaires*, he was conducting a mission to the West on behalf of the Ministry. In reality Dufresse was as much a royalist as he was a revolutionary, seeking to build a future by pleasing everyone.[122]

Viton belonged to the same apolitical family. This terrifying 'general' of the Lot and the Aveyron, and protégé of the doctor Taillefer, had the audacity to get himself recommended in 1814 by Choiseul-Praslin, an officer of the Lorraine-Infanterie, to a company in which, as a young wigmaker, Viton had served for several months in 1792. Viton and Dufresse had mounted this assault on the plum positions of the Terror under the same patron, Brune, a man as devoid of principle as his two imitators, and both were to overcome the difficult hurdle of the Restoration with relative ease.[123]

So much for their political conduct. Through their lack of morality these two men attached an aura of scandal to all those around them, as well as to the institutions which gave them the opportunity to affect such airs and graces. The militants of the Lille *société révolutionnaire* had the puritanical outlook of all sincere sans-culottes, and were alarmed at the way the former actor flaunted himself at the theatre and in the cafés, accompanied by a woman of dubious repute who had left the arcades of the Palais-Royal for the military ardours of the frontier.[124] Rumours of scandalous affairs with women, of debts, extortion and revelry followed him. But despite his violent speech and terrifying threats against the rich and the indifferent, Dufresse was a sham terrorist: at Lille he played the part of an implacable revolutionary, but it was all play-acting and no one died on his orders. Indeed it was the Thermidorean authorities who supplied the most convincing proof of his lack of serious revolutionary conviction by acquitting him. He was not a wicked man; but he was a compromising one.[125]

The young Viton, a wigmaker from the Tuileries Section, and son of a shopkeeper of Langres, was intoxicated by his immense power. He too had theatrical qualities and was described by the Montauban *comité* as 'this very young and inexperienced general, adorned in his three-star epaulettes', 'an oriental satrap' both lascivious and cruel. Like Dufresse he tried to give himself a terrifying image, for he too had a seal engraved with the emblem of a mobile guillotine,[126] and like Dufresse also he took advantage of his proconsulate to seduce young girls. But against Viton more serious charges were brought; complaints had already been made against him by a shop-keeper in the Palais-Royal, and he was found guilty of several thefts during his operations in the Aveyron. In the towns through which he passed with his *armée* (Cahors, Figeac, Gourdon, Najac, Séverac, Rodez, Saint-Géniez), he had left behind debts, suppliers angered by his offhandedness (a trait also described as 'oriental'), and the memory of his depredations.[127] Viton was not a terrorist but a professional pillager, and much more of a nuisance than the actor general from the Théâtre Feydeau.

Dufresse and Viton, however, were out on their own, and adventurers and dishonest men were as rare among the officers of the departmental *armées* as political militants of the calibre of a Brunière, a Delport or a Contamin. Their main sin was to have talked too much about themselves and thereby furnished Thermidorean literature with one of its favourite themes: the moral degeneration and natural cruelty of the men of the Terror. The reality was more run-of-the-mill, and most of the officers were distinguished neither by their courage in defending the republican cause in difficult years, nor by major crimes or dramatic brutalities. In the Year III when most of the men of the Terror were being called to account, those whose only wrong was to have been officers in the *armées révolutionnaires* were scarcely touched. Thermidorean opinion had not erred, for these obscure men had been of very little importance in the history of the Terror and in the activity of the *armées*.

IV   The revolutionary troops – their social composition

The Thermidoreans, and the historians after them, were not far wrong in detecting common social origins and characteristics in the soldiers of the departmental *armées*, which set them apart from the *honnêtes gens*. 'To hasten his murderous attempts, Carrier surrounded himself with cut-throats', claimed Prudhomme, clarifying his claim with the assertion that 'all the disreputable and criminal elements of Nantes were incorporated into his corps . . .'. Collectively they were 'a horde of hired assassins, unthinking instruments of a faction'. Of the little *armée* of Tarbes he painted as brutal a picture, 'a troupe of brigands gathered from all over . . .'.[128] They were 'all disreputable characters', as Riouffe wrote of the Bordeaux soldiers.[129] 'What were the elements making up the *armée* of Dufresse?' enquired a more recent historian. 'It is not difficult to imagine. All the patriotic and healthy young men were in the army; one had to look then to the vagrants, the unemployed, always numerous in a large town and attracted by hopes of

guaranteed pay and food...recruits were found therefore among the idle
and the wretched and the patois of Lille was more respected in the companies than political theory...'.[130]

It is pointless to cite more such claims, for they simply reiterate the main
arguments of the Thermidoreans and of those historians who have drawn
on the sources of the Year III. According to these, the *armées* were recruited
from among the unemployed, the criminal, the foreign elements– they
were *armées* therefore of criminals and the unemployed. The *révolutionnaires*
were ignorant, deprived and illiterate men, mere instruments in the hands
of the main culprits, whose orders they executed blindly. Simple executors
of orders, moved by the most sordid of motives, excited by drink and a
taste for pillage and desecration, they were only partly responsible for the
crimes which their cruel masters made them commit.

Such explanations, never based on a systematic examination of the enrolment lists, are clearly suspect. On one point however they merit some
acceptance: their insistence on the role of the soldiers as mere executors of
orders. The departmental soldiers were in fact more humble men than their
brothers in Paris, poorer and more miserable, consequently less independent, less inclined to dispute orders, to denounce their officers, or to take
political initiatives themselves. This is one generalisation which we can
make with confidence. In Paris there were not many men from the cheap
lodging-houses in the ranks of the *armée*; access to these was largely reserved
for the artisan and the shopkeeper, the two pillars of the *sans-culotterie*. Such
was not the case with some departmental *armées*. Into these were recruited
the homeless, the employees, those who worked as apprentices or in the
workshops supplying arms and military clothing for the Republic, indeed
even the dregs of the urban and rural population: the village poor, the
rootless, the day-labourers, vineyard workers, water-carriers, porters,
casual labourers, an entire world of the ragged and needy who, thanks to the
filter system operated in Paris by the Sectionary assemblies and the *comités
révolutionnaires*, rarely progressed beyond the hurdle of the *scrutin épuratoire*.
In short, the departmental *armées*, while still attracting the independent
artisan and small shopkeeper, had a more extensive area of recruitment than
Ronsin's *armée*, penetrating further into the popular milieux, while at the
same time taking in people from the wealthiest circles in the small towns
and in the countryside: men of the law, big farmers, landowners, merchants. The result was a spread of occupations much wider than in the
Parisian *armée*, which was essentially a sans-culotte force, made in the image
of the assemblies and Sectionary *sociétés* of the capital. The departmental
companies and battalions were more popular in composition than the
sociétés which had presided over their creation and organisation. The best
example of this difference between a *société* and an *armée* can be seen in the
Allier battalion, recruited largely from among the hatters' assistants, the
foundry-workers and various employees, elements which scarcely figured

in the *société*, let alone in the public tribunes.[131] The composition of the departmental *armées* was generally poorer and more modest than that of the *sociétés*, whose membership was restricted to the militant élites.

In the departments too one encounters elements unheard of in the Parisian *armée*: rural dwellers of every description, from rich yeomen farmers to day-labourers, cowherds and the most miserable raftsmen; foreigners such as Portuguese and Russian Jews of Bordeaux, German refugees from the Alsatian *armées*, Belgian refugees, numerous in Lille, deserters from the Prussian and Imperial armies, attracted to forces with milder discipline and easier conditions of entry than the *armée* of Ronsin. Sometimes too the young men of the first requisition were accepted, a factor giving the *armées* of Lille, Metz and Toulouse that military character which distinguished them from those battalions with a purely civilian composition.

Such variety makes generalisations like that of the *armées* being composed of 'disreputable characters', wigmakers, valets and criminals, rather dangerous. Domestic servants were often present in large numbers in the ranks; but whereas they undoubtedly constituted an important element in Versailles, they were extremely rare in Lille. In fact, taking together all the *armées* for which we possess some precise occupational information, including that of Versailles, domestic service played a very small role indeed (see the table at p. 684 below).[132] The same applies to the criminal element. In Versailles, Nutin, who was accepted into a Sectionary company, was to be found guilty of murder some years later.[133] But we know of no other case, and it would be foolish to take this one example as proof that the departmental *armées* were criminal ones. In fact we do not know one way or the other, for even more than for the Parisian *révolutionnaires*, personal details are lacking for those of the departments. In matters of the behaviour and occupational background of the individual soldier we have to be content with isolated examples having as little value as that of Nutin. There were, for example, debtors and bankrupts in the Marat company at Nantes and in the Nevers battalion;[134] but their presence is not sufficient proof that the *armées* as a whole were recruited largely from *déclassés* and bankrupts. Moreover, at Nantes, where commerce had been dealt a death blow by the Revolution and the war, it was natural to find in such paid service men who had lost their positions and fortunes through the interruption of colonial trade[135] – there were similar cases in Bordeaux.[136] Nor could the departmental *armées* be said to be composed of *déclassés* because a few bankrupts, deserters or foreign soldiers managed to enter them. And if the Moulins *comité révolutionnaire* received a number of complaints about the drunkenness of the soldiers in its battalion,[137] does it follow necessarily that the soldiers of the departments, like their brothers from Paris, acted like ruffians everywhere?

Variety is also a leading feature in the age-range of the soldiers. If the *armées* of the North, the East and Toulouse undoubtedly contained a majority of young men of the age of the first requisition, most of those of Moulins and Nantes fell within the thirty-to-sixty age-range, forty-to-sixty in Versailles, and thirty-five-to-fifty in the Hautes-Alpes.[138]

But if such variety marked the fortunes, occupations, origins and even the ages of the departmental soldiers, one would be right in thinking that they must have had some political beliefs in common, for was it not a question of arming the people for the people, forming cohorts of sans-culottes of unquestionable republicanism, an *armée* 'composed of all that is most pure in the *sans-culotterie*', according to the hopes expressed by one of the founders of the Lille *armée*?[139] The reality was of course often very far removed from the ideal, despite all the precautions taken by the *sociétés* and the *comités* to sift and sort through the candidates. In all the *armées* there was a minority of active *sociétaires* or *sectionnaires*, notable terrorists in their native towns; but we have seen how, in Lille and elsewhere, ambitious men, anxious to capture the best positions, shunned the inferior ranks.[140] These were consequently often left to less reliable, indeed sometimes highly suspect persons, and the only *armée* composed entirely of seasoned terrorists was the little company of Nantes. The Allier battalion also enjoyed considerable political cohesion, its soldiers being zealous denunciators and making up the principal element of the revolutionary opposition at Moulins during the Thermidorean period. The battalion of the neighbouring Nièvre also seems to have been as well composed as it was commanded.[141]

Elsewhere, however, a mass of poor miserable wretches vegetated alongside the active sans-culottes, more preoccupied with pay than with politics, and politically indifferent or undecided. In Cahors, in Frimaire, when there was a dramatic eruption of religious troubles, the *comité* attributed them to religious enthusiasts among the *révolutionnaires* recently returned from the Lozère and the Aveyron.[142] In Bordeaux, where service in the battalion was the swiftest way to clear oneself of a recent Federalist past, certain soldiers would also have served previously in the departmental forces.[143] One must not expect to find complete orthodoxy in the political composition of these *armées*; the soldiers were not political militants, and in many towns they were recruited from circles which would hardly have been admitted into the *sociétés populaires*. The departmental *armées* were in the hands of active political terrorists, but most of the soldiers were simply their instruments and took only a distant seat at the great conflicts agitating the controlling minorities.

A brief examination of the social composition of the lower echelons of certain *armées* will give a better idea of this diversity. We will start with the Lille *armée*, not because it represented the prototype of an *armée révolutionnaire* – on the contrary, it had quite exceptional characteristics – but because its abundant documentation allows us to risk some precise conclusions. The *armées* of Versailles, Nevers and Moulins undoubtedly come closer to the ideal of an *armée* of pure republicans, and for this reason we ought to linger briefly on them. The Marat company is part of anti-terrorist legend, and few institutions of the Terror so merit the abundant and fanciful literary attention paid them as this one – an abundance of commentary which nevertheless tells us nothing about these 'ferocious men' who serviced the prisons and were the executioners in the *noyades*. We will therefore take a closer look at these 'men of blood', who gave rise to such descriptions and who periodically attempted to explain themselves. The Bordeaux battalion was a Sectionary force with a particularly cosmopolitan and politically heterodox composition, while the little company of Crémieu was a social *armée* because only the poor were recruited. As for the Haute-Garonne *armée*, its character was mixed, for it was composed in more or less equal proportions of military men, conscript soldiers from the garrison at Toulouse, civilians, artisans and merchants from the town, along with farmers and day-labourers from the countryside around Toulouse.

(i) THE LILLE *ARMÉE*

We have lists of enrolment for three of the six Sections in Lille, the 1st, 2nd and 6th, i.e. the poorest Sections of the town, the rue d'Etaques, the faubourg des Malades and the Rivage de Deule, quartiers inhabited above all by spinners and carders from the mills. These figures, therefore, are in danger of artificially accentuating the popular character of this *armée*, and it is probable that the lists of the three other Sections may not have shown such a preponderance of textile workers.

In the three registers preserved, 272 names are listed, 201 accompanied by the age and occupation of the candidate – an excellent piece of statistical evidence covering nearly half the number of recruits for the Lille *armée* (see the table at p. 685 below).[144] Of these 201, 126 were soldiers of the age of the first requisition, most coming from the battalions of Lille and the Somme; 40 worked in mills as spinners, carders, or machinists, or in the clothing trade. The food trade is represented by 7 soldiers, the iron trade by 5, domestic service by 5, the luxury trades by 4, and 15 were artisans employed in various urban or rural occupations. These figures require some explanation. If the crisis in the textile industry had particularly affected Lille, the luxury trades all over the Republic had been dealt a mortal blow by the Revolution. It was the same story, even if not quite so dramatic, in the food and iron trades, both affected by the dearth of staple materials. However, the Lille *armée* does not appear to have been a refuge for the unemployed, for if that had been the case those responsible for its organisation would not have had to appeal to soldiers to fill the places left empty by the unwillingness and the slowness of the civilians to come forward. Yet at Lille, which experienced an economic crisis unrivalled elsewhere – the town being almost in view of the armies and completely cut off from the materials essential to its industry – even the poorest quarters of the town put up no more than 80 candidates for service in an *armée* which was well paid, clothed and shod. After the third or fourth day of enrolment had produced such pitiful numbers, the Sectionary authorities consulted the garrison officers and the *société*, and on their authority proceeded to take the names of young men of the first requisition, who were eager to be accepted into an *armée* which was well paid and destined for service in the interior. They needed little persuading.

Given such evidence, it is difficult to support Leleu and the other historians who see the *armées* as a way of reducing unemployment and providing work. Lille in the middle of a severe economic crisis had difficulty recruiting sans-culotte soldiers, even among the most deprived inhabitants of its poorest quartiers.

(ii) THE VERSAILLES *ARMÉE*

The *armée révolutionnaire* of Versailles never saw the light of day, but the inscription lists for certain Sections of the town have been preserved; we therefore have information on the trades of some of the candidates, as well as their motives for enrolling. If the lists are not sufficiently complete to make the same kind of statistical analysis possible as for the Lille *armée*, we can nevertheless get an idea of what the Versailles *armée* might have been like, and the picture which emerges is one of a projected *armée* which in its compositional variety and motives for enrolling, resembles the two *armées* created by Fouché at Nevers and Moulins.

In this demoted royal seat, the former French capital, now suspect and disgraced, unemployment was extensive, and not surprisingly the enrol- ment lists contain some domestic servants and artisans from the luxury trades: from the 1st Section, 4 former employees of the Princes, a head cook, a café-owner, a launderer and an unemployed man. In the 13th Section the rural element dominates: 7 day-labourers, 4 market gardeners, 2 gardeners; and among the candidates of the 4th Section we have 2 Swiss.[145] These elements, at least in such proportions, are peculiar to Versailles. On the other hand, as elsewhere, we have a large percentage of artisans, shop- keepers, small entrepreneurs, the habitual clientele of the *sociétés* and the Sectionary assemblies and the group active in the Vertu-Social *société*.[146] The Versailles *armée* was therefore composed largely of small tradesmen and master artisans;[147] but as in Paris several richer businessmen also found their way into it, Javon, a master carpenter and wood merchant, for instance, declaring on his enrolment that he had a shop containing 1,200 planks of wood.[148] Dumoustier, a master mason and entrepreneur, and Billiard, an entrepreneur in charge of the town cleaning service, were both wealthy notables from the 1st Section. Ouaine, a captain in the National Guard, a municipal officer and furniture dealer who presented himself in the 4th Section, was not pushed by need to enrol, and Denis, a master locksmith, received by the 1st Section, resigned because two of his workers had left his workshop to seek places in the munitions factories of the capital.[149] Among the candidates received at Saint-Germain, a barrister and a wholesale grocer figured among the normal complement of artisans.[150] The presence of well-off men in the ranks of the *armées* was not peculiar to Versailles or Saint-Germain, since some of the most notable businessmen of Nevers and Moulins enrolled in the battalions of those towns. In thus enrolling, notables of Ouaine's kind sought not gain, but the honour of serving the Revolution and above all the possibility of shining in the eyes of their neighbours.

The *armée* of Versailles, in its mixed composition, was to be the model for most of the departmental *armées*. Comfortable entrepreneurs and rich merchants, who sought to satisfy their *amour-propre* by service in a half-time and undemanding occupation[151] – amounting sometimes to no more than the replacement of billiards or skittles – rubbed shoulders with servants, supernumeraries, wigmakers in want of work, crowds of small tradesmen and independent artisans, the backbone of the Sectionary movement, and even with a strong rural element: market gardeners, gardeners, inhabitants of Montreuil, Porchefontaine and the poor communes on the outskirts of Versailles, who came to seek work in the former capital when they could find none in the fields or gardens. A very mixed composition, in fact, which defies any general definition, any precise political label. Ouaine and his colleagues were certainly not ultra-revolutionaries and in this town the *société populaire*, which was considered Hébertist, was composed principally of artisans and shopkeepers, while the *société* accused by its adversaries of having been 'governmental' and Jacobin, and which had carried the title 'Société des Amis de la Liberté', included numerous servants, former valets, equerries and supernumeraries.[152] The *armée révolutionnaire* was recruited as much from one social category as another, and if it had any political colouring, it was that of a republican rainbow, ranging from the militant dechristianiser to the comfortably-off Jacobin, and including also some village 'enragés' and rural communists. It was no more an *armée* of the poor than it was one of the Jacobin bourgeoisie, it was neither specifically sans-culotte nor entirely urban. Politically it placed the cautious and moderate alongside the wigmaker who read the *Père Duchesne* and corresponded with the Cordeliers. In other words, it had no definable political colour.

The case of the Versailles *armée* was the same as that of the Nevers, Moulins, Montpellier and Montauban battalions, the 'anti-politiques' of Aix and the companies planned for the small towns of the Doubs and the Jura. The Moulins battalion undoubtedly had a more popular composition than that of the other towns, the workers from the Brillantais foundry, the hatter's assistants, the shoemaker's assistants, the labour force of the workshops and some poor wigmakers being among its number.[153] But there were also employers,[154] and in Nevers, whose battalion, according to one hostile witness, was composed of 'a crowd of downright rogues, of vermin', even some leading merchants of the town enrolled.[155] Among the 12 family men over thirty, chosen by the Dijon *société* to form part of the town's company, there were 2 goldsmiths, a tobacconist, a butcher, a distiller, 2 second-hand clothes dealers and a landlord[156] – the usual fan-tail of small tradesmen, artisans and wage-earners. It was the same story at Montbéliard: 2 master shoemakers, a master carpenter, a joiner, a baker, a suit-tailor, a cutler, a wheelwright, a stocking-maker, a weaver, a *cabaret-owner* and a wine-grower.[157] At Salins the mixture was similar, but 3 soldiers were also added.[158] In composition none of these *armées* bore any resemblance to a popular militia, a battalion of indigents, a troupe of unemployed, and since they also contained men of the law, *notaires*, solicitors as well as tanners and entrepreneurs, it would also be inaccurate to call them sans-culotte *armées*. Indeed some of the candidates behaved most unlike sans-culottes: at Salins two members of the company, a gardener and a café-owner, were denounced for having infringed the law of the Maximum, and a third for *incivisme*.[159] For the sans-culottes, infractions of the Maximum and hoarding were counter-revolutionary crimes *par excellence*. When the very soldiers of these privileged *armées* were denounced for such offences – and Salins was not the only company to experience such, for at Agen also the whole company was denounced for having abused its police powers on market day, by ensuring that its own members were served before the public[160] – it was clear that these institutions had failed in their task through defective composition. It was clearly very difficult, despite all the *scrutins épuratoires* and the *certificats de civisme*, to form *armées* of the 'pure'.

(iii)   THE RURAL *ARMÉES*

The *armées révolutionnaires* were above all instruments of urban politics in subsistence matters; to execute such a policy one looked particularly to the town-dwellers. But even in the formations of the large towns, countrymen were recruited from the surrounding areas: market gardeners and gardeners from Wazemmes and the faubourgs of Lille, day-labourers and wine-growers from the Versailles region, just as in Paris Ronsin's *armée* had recruited gardeners from the Bondy Section, day-labourers and wine-growers from Clamart and Issy, market gardeners and rabbit-breeders from Choisy and Montreuil. But they were fairly unimportant minorities at the heart of formations dominated by artisans and small tradesmen from the towns.

However, certain departmental *armées* existed which were almost entirely rural in composition. If the Bordeaux battalion offers the usual mixture of artisans, liberal professions and commerce, the *armée révolutionnaire* formed by the *représentants* in the Lesparre district was composed of soldiers who were 'all peasants', while the *juge de paix* of Cahors and the *représentant* Taillefer spoke of the Lot *armée* as having been composed primarily of small wine-growers and farmers from the area around Cahors.[161] Moreover we know that the rural areas of this department sent volunteers to this force and that far from being composed exclusively of Cahors residents, it seems to have been recruited from all over the department.[162] In the absence of inscription lists it is impossible to be more precise, but it is very possible that in these two *armées* the rural element predominated.

The small companies of the Hautes- and Basses-Alpes, recruited both in the district *chefs-lieux* and the small country localities, seem also to have had a largely rural composition: proprietors, poor farmers, wine-growers, village artisans.[163] In the Doubs, Haute-Saône and Jura, since the companies were recruited from all the communes in the canton, the lists indicate a percentage of rural recruits of one-third to half the effective number. This corresponds with the terms of the orders setting up the companies, which had foreseen that those recruited in Franche-Comté and Burgundy would have to know how to thresh grain, and the same trend is noticeable in the orders setting up the *armées* of the East and Haut-Rhin, which were also undoubtedly largely rural in composition. At Montbard a yeoman farmer from Corcelles was accepted, while the list from the Jussey *société* included a wine-grower from Bousserancourt and a yeoman farmer from Vauvilliers, the other members of this contingent also being inhabitants of the small communes of the canton.[164] At Montbéliard and at Salins some wine-growers and gardeners from the surrounding communes were accepted along with the urban artisans.[165] The Yonne *armée*, which had just started to recruit and organise, seems to have been entirely rural, to judge from the inscription lists which have survived for the Avallon district: of 64 candidates agreed upon by the Avallon authorities, 54 were from the countryside, mostly belonging to the rural proletariat – 15 day-labourers, 6 farm servants – but side by side with these poor people we also find 3 farmers, 2 wine-growers, 2 weavers, as well as a few rural artisans: shoe-makers, clog-makers and blacksmiths.[166] This *armée* of the Yonne therefore was not made up of barefoot peasants, and in every case of major rural participation the more comfortably-off elements of the village are also represented; landowners and yeomen farmers were as prompt to enrol, if not more so, than the poor day-labourers and servants, for whom absence could have had disastrous consequences, reducing their families to beggary. Just as the urban *armées* were not workers' militias, neither were those of the countryside the refuge of the rural proletariat. In both cases their composition fits into no definable category, and both the most deprived and the well-off were caught up in the same process. This is why these rural *armées* were so slow to organise and so ineffective, for the small farmers and wine-growers had no desire to move very far from their own hearths.

(iv)   THE MARAT COMPANY OF NANTES

No revolutionary company had as bad a press as the famous 'Marats' of Nantes. When the members of the *comité révolutionnaire* of this town were tried, one of the main accusations against the leaders was that of having formed this company and filled it with 'the most abject individuals'. 'The *comité*', wrote Phélippes, former president of the criminal tribunal, 'thought it should form a small *armée révolutionnaire*, composed of 60 of the most despised and most despicable of individuals...men with the most tainted of reputations'. They were, affirmed Prudhomme, 'the most abandoned and criminal elements of the Nantes population...'. The only favourable comment comes from the *comité* itself, which remained faithful to an institution it had created and directed, declaring its ethos to have been that of 'pure and pronounced *civisme*...'.[167] Was this company then an '*armée* of crime' and its soldiers criminals?

We have an abundance of information on one-third to half of its members.[168] In terms of social composition it is the normal mixture of small shopkeepers, merchants, artisans and the proletariat of the luxury trades: 4 wigmakers (a number in itself sufficient to discredit the company because of the poor reputation of wigmakers in sans-culotte circles), 3 coopers, 2 shoemakers, 3 nail-makers, a metal-caster, a parasol vendor, 2 shopkeepers, a former arms dealer, a former broker in the colonial trade, a hatter, a dyer, a painter and a jeweller – i.e., a heavy concentration of those involved in the colonial and luxury trades or in service (the wigmakers).

The Marats were not rich men. Some had been, but had lost their fortunes as a result of the Revolution; some had been involved in bad business deals, others had changed their jobs several times before enrolling. Cousin was successively a cooper and a warehouseman; Jomard, a former merchant, subsequently imprisoned in the Vendée, obtained help from the *société* on his return to Nantes. There is little doubt why most of these men enrolled: the desire to secure paid employment was an element, but so also was a desire to avenge the atrocities committed by the Chouans against their companions. Two features distinguished the members of this company from the other revolutionary soldiers. One was that all or nearly all had participated in the campaign against the Chouans, in the battalions of the Nantes National Guard; several had gathered up the mutilated corpses of their comrades, who had fallen into the hands of the peasants, and all lived in fear, knowing the fragility of the situation at Nantes, threatened on all sides by a violently counter-revolutionary countryside. In the second place, nearly all were natives of Nantes. In addition they were uneducated men, most of them declaring their inability to read at the time of Carrier's trial.

We will see later how their fastidiousness in the exercise of their functions was to expose them to formidable temptations; it is indisputable that Joly and Durossier, and many others besides, emptied the pockets of their prisoners, relieving them of watches and jewellery, and that they accepted bribes payable in kind or in favours – Joly in particular is known to have slept with his prisoners. All were possessed of a physical brutality unusual among the *révolutionnaires* of the Year II, and at least one of their number, a young volunteer whose friends had been tortured by the Vendéean peasants, had the courage to admit before the Thermidorean tribunal that he regretted nothing, and that if he had to do it again he would be there to cut off the hands of those trying to cling to the edge of the barges or to deliver blows with the flat of his sabre to the female prisoners. Others, more sensitive, or less honest, wept when the scenes of horror on the transport vessels were recalled. But they were all part of a true proletariat of the repression.

They were, however, neither criminals nor brutes. Circumstances had made them ferocious, and if a parasol vendor or a former *procureur* had reached the point where he could push old men, women and children into the water, it was due to his position as a member of a besieged terrorist minority in a town deeply hostile to the Revolution. There was, it is true, a gangster element among the Marats: the copper-caster Joly, Richard the hatter and Durossier the former broker seem to have belonged in this category. But the Marat company was not a gang of pillagers. The reality is much more complicated: they were limited individuals, made brutal by circumstances, dishonest too, but at the same time sincere revolutionaries who lived in fear. In composition the company resembled all the other urban formations, but in their behaviour its men were very far removed from the easy-going and debonair *révolutionnaire* of the departments. They operated amidst hatred and fear, brutally executing the commands of their superiors. Hardened terrorists, they were nevertheless merely executors; none belonged to the militant ranks of the Vincent-la-Montagne *société populaire*, and in the Year III most were released because they had 'not acted maliciously' but simply followed orders.[169]

(v)   THE REVOLUTIONARY BATTALION OF BORDEAUX

The registers of the national club contain the names of 164 members of the revolutionary battalion, cavaliers, fusiliers, cannoneers, submitted to the *scrutin épuratoire* from the first decade of Frimaire. However, this is a deceptive source, for of the 164 names listed, only 18 give occupation.[170] In terms of Sections the picture is also deceptive: one name accompanied by occupation for the Bon-Accord Section, two for the Parfaite-Union Section, six for the Franklin Section. Thus we possess information on the occupations of only 22 members of the battalion – a mere sample.

It is clear from the lists (see the table at p. 687 below)[171] – that the battalion was composed largely of urban artisans; the Franklin Section, noted for its revolutionary spirit, was above all sans-culotte in composition. But in the other Sections representatives from the world of business and commerce had not disdained such service. In the 10 Août Section, silverware dealers and Jewish businessmen enrolled in large numbers – they were French citizens to whom certificates of hospitality had been granted.[172] One of them, Mardoché Léon, was refused a certificate of *civisme* by the municipality in Prairial on the pretext that he had 'speculated in coin', and another was to be accused of having sold 'bad flour' to the Republic.[173] There were also some foreigners: some of the Jews who enrolled were still subjects of the Russian Empire, while Laurent Walter, a candidate accepted by the Bon-Accord Section, was Swiss.[174] The particular feature of this

Bordeaux force was its incorporation of elements who were politically suspect, former members of the departmental force, and the presence of some substantial merchants, dealers in silver and men of the law – some of whom were extremely wealthy – alongside the usual artisans and shopkeepers. The battalion reflected the population of a major port, and if Riouffe was guilty of exaggeration when he described this institution as having been commanded and stocked by foreigners (Germans, Spanish and others), we do know for certain that the Jewish community was substantially represented. As for the presence of other foreigners, and the level of Protestant representation, we are limited to conjecture. Finally, the Bordeaux battalion is not without some resemblance to the *armée* of Ronsin, particularly in its recruitment by the Sectionary assemblies, which meant that its composition varied according to whether the Section was more or less sans-culotte, more or less commercial, more or less suspect. An urban battalion formed in a great port, it was above all a Sectionary force.

(vi) THE TOULOUSE *ARMÉE*

The Haute-Garonne *armée*, like that of Metz, was mixed in character, and young men already in military service (having come to the Toulouse garrison from the Corrèze battalions) were joined to civilians, mainly from Toulouse and Beaumont. On the composition of the civilian part of this *armée* we have very little information, and the little that we do have suggests the usual mixture. The inclusion of the Beaumont company explains the rural element; there were also two ecclesiastics, a cook, a wigmaker, two tailors, a sock-maker, a carpenter, two joiners, two farmers, a ploughman, a clerk employed with the department, and a surgeon.[175] Shopkeepers and businessmen seem to have been more rare here, though the information is too sparse to be able to speak confidently on that subject.

There is no point examining the cases of the other *armées*, many of their companies from the Midi, because as far as we can establish their composition hardly varied save in the proportions of artisanal to business elements. At Aix and Montpellier, workshop employees and shoemaker's assistants were sufficiently numerous to attract the attention of the *représentants* and the other authorities;[176] it was the same with the Dax company with its largely worker composition.[177] The only exception to the generally mixed quality of these forces is the small *armée* of Crémieu, composed of 30 dragoons, all poor men from the small town and chosen as such – Contamin distrusting both the petit-bourgeois and the artisans as unsound, and judging from the actions of this force he was probably right.

The *commissaires civils*, the officers and men of the departmental *armées* came from the most diverse social backgrounds, ranging from a poor employee in a workshop or one requisitioned for war work, a day-labourer, a farm servant, a former valet, a wigmaker with no clientele, to a businessman or a well-off farmer, an entrepreneur, a workshop overseer, a *notaire* or man of the law, a purchaser of national land, a tanner and a prosperous manufacturer, to former ecclesiastics, a curate or parish priest turned administrator. Among the *commissaires civils* no trace of class-consciousness can be detected, for the good reason that they belonged to no distinct social grouping. The factors uniting these men were the violence of their convictions and temperaments and a certain political naïvety. The military command was drawn from three principal categories: former career soldiers, gendarmes, town and bourg notables raised to the military hierarchy because of service in the paid National Guard and the acclaim of their fellow citizens. As for the rank and file, the worker, employee and rural proletariat element was more pronounced in these *armées* than in that of Paris, while never accounting for a majority, for in all these *armées* there was a percentage of sans-culottes (small businessmen, shopkeepers, independent artisans) as well as some bourgeois, landowners, men of the law and well-off notables.

It is therefore possible to state what these *armées* were not: they were not workers' militias, red guards on the 1917 model, nor gangs consisting largely of former valets and household servants, nor charitable institutions created to help the unemployed. Quite the contrary, some of the very poor sought to escape the honour paid them by their fellow citizens when they were enrolled in these companies, for they feared that their absence would plunge their families into beggary. Neither were they *armées* of crime, even if criminals were enrolled, for adventurers and the disreputable rubbed shoulders with honest revolutionaries. And even if there were some foreigners, these forces were almost entirely composed of Frenchmen, and it is impossible to think of them as foreign instruments. Nor were they *armées* of draft-dodgers or deserters, even if three or four did include young men from the requisitions and deserters in disguise. Old men and those over thirty were far more numerous than the young. If townspeople pre-dominated, these were nevertheless not exclusively urban *armées*, and several recruited heavily among the rural populace. But even these had no class character, for the substantial yeoman farmer was joined by the farm servant and the day-labourer.

Although the *commissaires civils* and some of the officers belonged to the terrorist élite, with the leaders of the *sociétés* reserving the best places for themselves, those who had hoped for sans-culotte *armées*, composed of politically orthodox *sociétaires*, were to be bitterly disappointed. The Lille *armée*, the Marat company and the Nièvre and Allier battalions were largely composed of such 'pure' revolutionaries, but the same cannot be said of that of the Lot, whose soldiers were accused of religious 'fanaticism', or the Bordeaux battalion which included those suspect on political and economic grounds: former members of the departmental forces, dealers in silver, speculators, hoarders – categories also represented in the Franche-Comté *armées*. Whether the *armées* were composed entirely of civilians, or a mixture of civilians and soldiers, the political character of them all was established by the methods of recruitment and organisation, and by the close links between most of the recruits and the *sociétés populaires* of their native towns. However, they were not *armées* of *sociétaires*, as the Légion de la Montagne was, for example; and if the *sociétaires* captured the best positions, the ranks were recruited from among the people of the tribunes, the lodging-house population, the illiterate, as much as from the privileged and militant *sans-culotterie*. For this reason it is difficult to attribute any precise political views to soldiers who were only instruments in the hands of the *commissaires civils* and the officers.

The relationship between the *sociétés populaires* and the companies was a personal rather than a political one. The composition of a company reflected all the opinions and social levels of the *société* which patronised it; but it was a mirror which distorted, at times enlarging, at other times reducing, and giving a greater place to those from the poorest sectors of society than to those from the more wealthy. The companies represented a spread of professions and fortunes as great as that of the *sociétés* themselves, but they penetrated deeper into the lower social levels.

Because of this political and social diversity, it would be foolish to try to see the revolutionary soldiers as instruments of a single political faction or religious grouping. We are extremely ill-informed about the percentage of Protestants in the many companies of the South-West, but of the small group of *commissaires civils* of whom we know something, none was a member of the Reformed Church. On the contrary, it is the former priests who stand out; even if they were a small group, they were distinguished by their education, their intelligence and their violence. However, it would be just as ridiculous to argue from this that the companies were instruments of the violently dechristianising and egalitarian views of the *curés rouges* and the ultra-revolutionaries among the ecclesiastics.

So much for the negative assessment – it could hardly have been otherwise, for the documentation is too fragmentary to permit statistical assertions about the composition of each of these *armées*. But it does allow us at least to brush aside certain oversimplified theories: that of the *armées révolutionnaires* as having been composed of the dregs of society, proletarian forces animated by class-consciousness, or the more flattering argument that they were *armées* of the 'pure', revolutionary knights, or of the unemployed. Nor do they slot easily into the image of moustached men, with pipes and *bonnets rouges*, conscious imitators of the Parisian model and the *Père Duchesne*, as the soldiers of Dufresse are represented. Rather they were middle-aged, often family men, prone to shouting, fond of feasting, dragging their huge sabres with difficulty. Such humble characters hardly fit into the impressionistic picture[178] which has been drawn of the Parisian soldier, a more loquacious, better educated, more independent individual, and certainly more conscious of his role as a politically privileged soldier, than his rural colleague. Only the members of the Marat company had an identity as individuals and they were certainly not typical *révolutionnaires*. Most of the departmental soldiers were more submissive and less demonstrative than the Parisians. Like most of their officers they were simply instruments in the hands of others – family men brought out by the exceptional circumstances of the Year II. The *révolutionnaires par excellence*, by birth or by adoption, the *commissaires civils, commissaires révolutionnaires, chefs de bande,* naïve 'apostles', unyielding, enthusiastic, violent, terrors of the countryside, were to find in their subordinates, auxiliaries who lacked enthusiasm, many having been recruited almost by force, selected rather than having volunteered, anxious not to be sent too far from their families and work places. They were sorry instruments in the hands of this clutch of eager and reckless men.

BOOK TWO

The Terror in the Village:
the *armées révolutionnaires* in action

Preamble

It would be impossible for one historian to give a complete account of the activities of all the *armées révolutionnaires* operating in the different regions of France in the Year II. Instead, I have traced modes of action common to all the *armées*, at the same time emphasising traits peculiar to a given region. Each *armée* operated under very different conditions: some were no more than docile instruments in the hands of *comités de surveillance*, municipalities or districts; others, though fewer in number, were in the hands of 'hommes de liaison', acting sovereignly. In the case of the former, the action was administrative in character; in that of the latter it was revolutionary. In both cases the innovative action came close at times to simple pillage.

For the sake of clarity in a subject with such imprecise limits, certain categories of activity have been singled out: economic action, repression, political intervention (considering also its social significance), dechristiani-sation, pillage and depredation. Such categories are necessarily artificial and in reality there is no clear division between them. Every activity is dominated by the constant struggle between town and country: sometimes the economic aspect is dominant, with the application of a policy of supply that favoured the urban consumer; sometimes it is the religious aspect which dominates, with compulsory dechristianisation being imposed on a universally hostile populace by emissaries from the towns; at other times the political aspect is uppermost, in the assistance brought by the *révolutionnaires* to sans-culotte minorities in the villages and the formation of *sociétés populaires* as channels for expressing and imposing their opinions. Revolutionary action constituted a whole, however, for the application of new economic laws and the mobilisation of the entire nation's resources behind the war effort brought with it repression and, with the removal of bells and silver from the churches, the initial steps of dechristianisation. The *taxes révolutionnaires* levied on the rich, an attempt at an egalitarian programme, were the product of a simplistic war economy which sought to make the rich pay for the defence of the regime. Where then did economic action cease and repression begin? Farmers who opposed requisitions were treated in the same way as avowed counter-revolutionaries, rebels in arms, fanatics, deserters and pillagers; all were considered internal enemies, requiring the attention of the new *armées*. And since these *armées* were above

249

all a force to police the economy and apply the Maximum, their intervention quickly assumed a repressive character. One would like to draw a
distinction between economic repression and repression pure and simple
(arrests, summary executions, the dispatch of victims to the revolutionary
tribunal), but the dividing line is difficult to find. In the last analysis, the
judges of the Years II and III and the rich farmers, from their different
viewpoints, considered these activities as little more than organised pillage,
the *armées* as bands of highwaymen pure and simple and the *révolutionnaires*
as part of a single phenomenon: the Terror in the village.

We will start with the economic activities – with which the *armées* were
primarily concerned. Here it is necessary to distinguish between the activities of the Parisian *armée*, charged exclusively with the supply of the capital,
and the more varied goals of the other *armées*, ranging from that of securing
provisions for the armies on the frontiers, to the attempt of a commune to
extract supplies for its own markets from the surrounding villages. Ronsin's
armée was under orders from the Commission des Subsistances of the Paris
Commune; the other revolutionary forces served the needs of military
provisioning or communal supply. The Parisian and departmental forces
are, in effect, two entirely separate subjects.

The same approach has been adopted for repressive activities. Taking first
the Parisian *armée*, we have tried to calculate the number of arrests made by
the detachments, either on orders from their own commander or from the
Committee of General Security. But the step from repressive action to the
abuse of power is a short one, and our line of investigation will uncover
some bitter conflicts between the Parisian officers and the local authorities.
For the departmental *armées* we will present certain characteristic examples
of their repressive activities: the actual physical repression, the shootings,
the drownings, the atrocities; the mixed operations like those in the Nièvre
and Allier, where arrests were combined with *taxes révolutionnaires*, political
propaganda on behalf of the sans-culottes and the poor, and military
operations – a veritable war against internal enemies; the administrative
operations, above all that of policing the prisons – the *révolutionnaires* acting
as warders; and lastly those repressive activities of an individual and spontaneous nature (denunciations, vigilance, repressive impulses, credulity,
mistrust).

Political action concerned primarily the relations between the companies
and the popular *sociétés* and was largely the preserve of those *commissaires
civils* whose importance as initiators of a certain revolutionary excess has
already been outlined. Since these urban soldiers were obliged to seek allies
in the villages, political action inevitably acquired a social aspect – the
struggle against the rich, the 'egoïste', the moderate, and in favour of the
poor 'classe intéressante du peuple'. Nor was it simply moral support, for
part of what had been taken from the rich was very often distributed to the
poor.

In the eyes of the rich this was little better than administrative pillage.

In the strict legal sense, however, almost all revolutionary action fell into the category of theft, and some officers accused of abuse of power and depredations rightly stressed the contradiction between the law as interpreted by the tribunals and revolutionary law which followed no code but public interest. But there were also true pillagers who did not concern themselves with such niceties. To revolutionise was one thing; to steal for personal profit was quite another.

Book One introduced the *révolutionnaires*, their officers and their political leaders. The reader therefore will not be surprised at their often violent and undisciplined action, nor at their bias against the country people, their simplistic ideas on food supply, their virulent anticlericalism – attitudes which were deeply ingrained in the *sociétés populaires*. Nor will he be surprised to find these men living it up at the expense of the peasant, pursuing everything in petticoats, or sacking presbytery cellars. In a climate of fear and hatred, small shopkeepers and peaceable umbrella vendors can become ferocious brutes who drown and shoot without pity and take macabre pleasure in totting up the toll of their victims.

The *armées révolutionnaires*, however, were but the visible aspect of something much greater. In the eyes of the villagers they represented the concrete expression of the Terror, and a study of their activities in the countryside is ultimately that of the installation of the terrorist regime in the village, the passage through the smallest and most backward communes of the great anarchical wind of this ultra-revolutionary epoch. The villagers themselves were correct in attributing a semi-mythical importance to the sudden incursion of these urban soldiers into the calm of country life, by making the *armées* the favourite theme of popular legends for years to come. In 1848 the exploits of Vauquoy's *bande* were still talked about in certain communes of the Isère; while in the Aveyron of the Restoration the memory of the wigmaker general, Viton, and his 'hommes noirs' vied with the 'lament of Fualdès', himself a notable terrorist who had apparently collaborated with the soldiers visiting Cahors in the Year II. These of course are only legends, exaggerating, distorting the reality. But popular attachment to them is a token of the enormous impression made by the tornado-like sweep of this urban Terror through the villages. This Book will examine the activities of the detachments in the towns as well as in the countryside; but its principal theme will be the effects of the anarchical Terror of autumn 1793 on the tiny communes, slumbering until then under the protection of their crosses, their ignorance, their indifference and the conservatism of their municipalities. True, most communes did not experience the Terror in such a spectacular form. Nevertheless, the area of activity of the *armées révolutionnaires* was extremely wide, encompassing two-thirds of the departments of France, for it took only a few men to upset totally the life of a village. A detachment in one locality became the topic of conversation for miles around, and an entire canton or district would tremble with fear.

In the analysis of these diverse activities we will have occasion to look again, though from a different angle, at the problem of subsistences, so often discussed purely from the point of view of the government. By following the missions of the detachments into the heart of the countryside, and the mechanism by which supplies were moved from the farmers' barns to the urban market halls and to the storehouses in Paris, something of the very complexity of those activities can be established. To evaluate the efficacy of the intervention by the Parisian *armée* in this domain, the entire policy of constraint requires investigation. The Maximum, the requisitions, the economic mobilisation of the nation's resources necessitated resorting to force. But could force succeed against the solidarity of the rural populace? This it would be difficult to answer with any precision and we can only emphasise the main difficulties confronting this necessarily unpopular task. Any discussion of subsistences also requires an account of popular psychology, the fears of the lower orders in the countryside, the urban artisan's mistrust of the peasant, the myths which constantly complicated the task of ensuring supplies. Indeed supply was such an explosive topic that the authorities of the Year II forbade its discussion. Shared prejudices and credulity placed the urban sans-culotte and the countryman in direct confrontation. This then is the main theme of Book Two: the frequently acrimonious relations between the emissary from the town and the peasant or artisan of the countryside.

CHAPTER 1

The Economic Activity of the Parisian *Armée révolutionnaire*

The main duty of the Parisian *armée* was to lend force to the law (*force à la loi*), and in this case the law meant the Maximum. The *armée* was the necessary instrument of an economic policy based on force: it was the *armée* which would apply the requisitions ordered by the Committee of Public Safety for the supply of Paris and certain armies, the *armée* which would protect the transport of grain and other foodstuffs to strategically-placed stores round the capital. To Ronsin's *armée*, in other words, was entrusted the task of supplying the immense Paris population with its daily ration of bread. On its success depended not only the well-being of the sans-culottes and their families, but public order and the very fate of the new regime; for when bread was scarce in the capital, *journées* were the outcome.

This in essence was the task assigned the Parisian *armée*, in contemporary terminology that of policing provisions (*police du ravitaillement*). It also encompassed the protection of secondary supplies: dairy products, poultry, meat, fish, wood for the bakers' ovens and the furnaces of the arms manufactories. Though never in the same league of importance as bread, nevertheless when these items became scarce, the people complained. In the spring of 1794 there was a considerable reduction in these secondary supplies, nothing like a genuine subsistence crisis, but causing sufficient discontent to worry the government and make it shift the blame on to the *armée révolutionnaire*.

The maintenance of food supplies was a matter of public order, and consequently a government affair. But there was also the question of mobilising the country's resources behind the war against the European monarchies. France was scoured for silver, leather and every kind of metal to make cannon, bullets and guns. The new soldiers required clothing; the wounded, medical care – priestly vestments and the surplus wardrobes of the rich would supply the need, and the Parisian *armée* would assist in their removal.

No problem has given rise to so many myths as that of subsistences, and both the simplistic mentality of the *révolutionnaires* and the prejudices of the country people need to be considered when discussing such an explosive question. The principal difficulty was not a technical matter; it was not a failure in production, but rather a human one – the fear of going short.

The Revolution had undoubtedly aggravated the problem. But the

253

supply of Paris was also subject to certain constants in economic geography, which had scarcely varied for the last two or three decades of the Ancien Regime. This will be our starting point.

I   The geography of Parisian supply

Throughout the eighteenth century, and with more reason during the Revolution, the problem of supplying Paris had been one of the government's major preoccupations. More than anything else it was a question of public order and one that tested the effectiveness of any regime. Added to the material difficulties hindering the circulation and distribution of grain and other foodstuffs at any time, was the more serious human one inspired by fear and rumour. In times of revolution in particular, fear, suspicion, and credulity inflate rumours, and suddenly the problem becomes more acute. In a letter dated Germinal, the administrators of the Pont-Châlier (Pont-Audemer) district in the Eure warned the Committee of Public Safety about the activities of the refractory clergy: 'The problem of subsistences in particular gives them free range, and the naturally uneasy country people become alarmed and angry when such a delicate chord is touched upon by the person they consider the oracle and the divinity...'.[1] It is at this point that the problems of subsistence and dechristianisation meet. They went hand in hand, and Isoré underlined the connection when he announced his intention of sending the Parisian soldiers to his native department, the Oise, 'to the districts where mistaken beliefs harm agriculture...'.[2] By attacking 'superstition' the *commissaires* of the Paris Commune sought to curb the driving force behind other popular myths exacerbating an already difficult problem – the entrenched belief that grain was being exported outside the country, for example, or even to the rebellious departments within the country. 'Such panic fears', observed the administrators of Basse-Normandie, 'use the pretext of requisitions to retard the supply of the towns and totally alter any pattern of circulation...'.[3] In attacking the very root of such superstition, religion itself, the *révolutionnaires* only aggravated the situation by making the country people believe that they were out to deprive them not only of their grain (for export abroad), but of their God as well (which caused some to claim that the Parisian *commissaires* were emissaries of both Pitt and the devil. Of the numerous difficulties besetting the supply of the towns, the psychological one was undoubtedly the most serious and the least amenable to resolution.

The obstacles to the circulation of grain and the supply of the large urban markets lay in distribution rather than production; the weak point in the supply system throughout the eighteenth century was in the transport of grain from one place to another. This is what contemporaries aptly called the 'problème des arrivages'. There were a thousand ways of hindering *arrivages*: the pillage of grain boats when they were vulnerable, during delays at the various locks and during the unloading process (the fixed itinerary of water transport leaving them more exposed to such dangers than in transport by land); the nocturnal transport of grain, usually on men's backs, to secret destinations (which in any case were not the official markets); farmers holding back their grain and selling it on the spot, or in the *auberges* at the town gates; retailers going ahead of the convoys and the travelling dealers and intercepting supplies at the entrance to towns. In addition combinations were often organised among the turbulent transport workers: bargemen, dock loaders and unloaders, carters and wagoners, all alike quick to revolt against the daily wage rates fixed by the Maximum or by the barge masters. The Revolution and the war in particular caused further problems: horses were in short supply, the army required enormous numbers and they disappeared entirely from the roads in certain regions. Large quantities of carts were also required for military transport, basic materials were used up and there was no iron for the most essential repairs. Added to all this were the constant problem of poor roads, the inadequate maintenance of waterways and canals, and worst of all the seasonal hazards: droughts affecting the waterways, ice blocking the rivers and making the roads unusable, spring thaws turning the latter into muddy torrents. These constant difficulties were aggravated – and with them popular fears – by the particular circumstances of the Revolution; the virtual autonomy of each district under the new administrative structure permitted the district directories to prevent the departure of grain, thereby removing it from the official markets and creating an atmosphere of panic and suspicion.

It was above all the distribution problem which caused the national authorities to resort to force, in the form of the *armées révolutionnaires*. The main duty of the Parisian *armée* would be to protect grain convoys, watching over every stage of their journey and accelerating the progress of the *arrivages* towards the capital or the designated stores. Even supporters of *laissez-faire* policies in the grain trade were ready to see the *armée* assume this function, so convinced were they that only force would ensure the movement of grain towards the official markets.[4] The priority given to this task is particularly evident when one examines the geography of *armée* activities in the Paris supply zone. Certain geographical constants governed the supply of Paris: the network of roads and waterways dictated the positioning of milling centres and grain stores (most mills were located along rivers, most storage places within reach of the main grain-growing areas). To facilitate distribution the zone supplying Paris was divided in the Year II into four administrative districts (arrondissements) each with a subsistence officer appointed to watch over the stores. (See Table A in References, p. 688.)[5]

Of the 63 localities having grain stores, chosen because of their situation along the rivers and major roads between the wheat-growing areas and Paris, some 40 were to have more or less permanent garrisons of the *armée révolutionnaire*,[6] while a further 6 would see detachments passing through.[7] These were crucial points in the Paris supply system, with natural facilities which made them ideal storage stations (and more than a third possessed water-mills operating to supply Paris), as well as being on busy traffic routes. Predictably the temptations for their sometimes numerous and usually hungry populations were enormous. Moreover, such a parcelling out of detachments was already a well-known practice and would be used again by the Thermidorean authorities in Floréal Year III, just days before the major riots of Prairial, during that period of seasonal troubles between harvests. Some 90 communes figured on the list of those to which garrisons of hussars and dragoons were sent to escort the convoys in Floréal Year III; of these, some 60 had revolutionary garrisons in the Year II (see Table B in References, p. 689).[8] To the list of 90 communes garrisoned in the Year III must be added the ports of Le Havre and Honfleur where detachments were stationed, as they were in the Year II, for the protection of the Paris stores. Other places in addition – Reims, Sézanne, Epernay – had the Marne *armée révolutionnaire* pass through.

But not all these towns were of equal importance in the Paris supply system. In a vast zone extending from the sea to the Orléans and Champagne regions, certain towns, traditional market and milling centres, were particularly important in terms both of the volume of their traffic and the high risk of pillage. In this respect the waterways and river ports were the first concern of the authorities, for although water transport was cheaper and required less manpower, it nevertheless had the disadvantage of being more prone to pillage, and cargoes were less easy to unload. It is surely no coincidence that the two points where the troubles of May 1775 started were Beaumont and Lagny, or that the ports of the Oise, Marne and the lower reaches of the Seine saw constant stoppages in the first years of the Revolution.[9] In the ranking of hazardous places, the Oise ports – Pont-l'Evêque (port of Noyon), Pont-Saint-Maxence, Beaumont, and above all Pontoise, the point of collection for grain from the Vexin, the Soissonnais region and Santerre – had acquired particularly bad reputations because of their disorderly inhabitants and their strategic positioning on the map of *arrivages*. For similar reasons Meaux, Lagny and the other ports of the Marne, which channelled the grain of the Château-Thierry region and some of that from the Brie and the Goële, were also considered weak links requiring particular surveillance.[10]

Besides these major waterways, three roads were key elements in the geography of Parisian supply: those from the Nord, traversing the Pays de France by Senlis, La Chapelle-en-Serval, Louvres, Gonesse and Le Bourget, or by Chantilly, Chaumontel, Luzarches, Le Mesnil-Aubry, Ecouen, Villiers-le-Bel and Saint-Denis – roads which were doubly important because they served both the main supply arteries bringing grain to Paris from the Soissonais, and grain, bread and flour from the Gonesse district – and the military road linking the capital to the Army of the Nord.[11] The Brie route served the great markets of Provins and Rozoy, through Nangis, Mormant, Brie-Comte-Robert (the scene of frequent disorders), Boissy-

Saint-Léger, and the bulk of the Brie region's immense output tended to travel along this route rather than by the more distant rivers Seine and Marne.

It is important to emphasise the importance of the Gonesse district to the supply of Paris, because of its position on the two major northern routes, its production (it was the wheat-growing area closest to Paris), and the particular composition of this huge populace at the very gates of the capital. 'This district', wrote its administration in September 1793, 'is in general inhabited by two classes of men, on the one hand cultivators, landowners or farmers, on the other, workers, day-labourers and carters – both alike concerned with the cultivation of the land. It would be dangerous to permit troubles and disorders to spread among these peaceable men, who in one way or another are the providers for Paris...'.[12] This district in fact was to be the theatre of a particularly violent political and social struggle between these two classes, necessitating the intervention and permanent presence of the Parisian *armée*.

As for the Brie route, not only did the Provins authorities threaten the success of the requisitions by their reluctance to implement the orders of the Parisian *commissaires* (one, the unfortunate Descombes, even getting himself guillotined, accused of having sent grain abroad to the Austrians) but the road was beset with danger, notably in the Brie itself and the small towns on the outskirts of Paris.

The southern routes are less important in the period under consideration. The route from the Orléans region, passing through Etampes, Etréchy, Arpajon, Montlhéry, Longjumeau, Montrouge – a particularly turbulent town, with its shifting and violent population of wagoners, rabbit-skin dealers and genuine criminals – and Gentilly,[13] loses its importance when the Loiret department, and certain districts of the Eure-et-Loire, were detached from the zone supplying Paris and assigned to the needs of the Army of the West. Etampes nevertheless remained a leading centre for gathering grain from Beauce, and with more than 20 mills along the Juisne, it was the principal milling centre for the Janville district.[14] It was also the route by which Paris was supplied with cheese products, dried vegetables, eggs and honey, and the scene of a number of stoppages, the main victims of which were the poultry and dairy merchants of the intervening towns of Etréchy and Méréville, which acquired a particularly unsavoury reputation as a result.[15]

Under the Ancien Regime the three great routes from the west, leading from the Beauce plain to Paris, starting out from Chartres, Epernon and Dreux, were, with the roads from the Brie, the main supply channels for Paris. But it was a particularly exposed channel, for it passed through the bottleneck of Versailles, a dangerous town because of its large population and lack of resources.[16] Versailles, in fact, was a place as notorious for its stoppages and pillage as the Brie and Lagny and the great ports on the Oise. But, as stated, with three-quarters of the Beauce grain production going to feed the armies in the West, the great roads from the Beauce to Paris lost their importance in 1793–4. Only the Chartres, Janville and Dreux districts remained within the Parisian supply zone, leaving the last short and obliging it to seek its own stocks from the neighbouring districts.[17] Versailles remained an important point of passage for food supplies to Paris; but the Parisians mistrusted the Versailles authorities and frequently accused them of hindering the supply of dairy produce to the capital, by arresting the dealers sent from Paris to secure them. In spring 1794 the fear of going short radiated out from Versailles to the poor neighbouring communes, which found survival difficult in the shadow of Paris.[18]

There remains only the great waterway of the Seine. The upper Seine, with the Yonne, carried the bulk of the firewood destined for the workshops and homes of Paris (hence the importance of Montereau in the system of *arrivages*).[19] It also carried a portion of the Brie grain – some going to Corbeil, the main milling centre of the Paris region. But the Seine only served the outskirts of the Brie region and part of the Gâtinais, which included the region of Nemours and Château-Landon, Malesherbes and Pithiviers, and had been subject to requisitions for Paris for several months. The Nemours district was the poorest in the Seine-et-Marne department and its inhabitants, like those of Montereau and Moret, suffered shortages throughout the life-span of the *armée révolutionnaire*. Pithiviers was in a better position, but its produce was disputed by a horde of *commissaires* from Paris, Orléans and the armies in the West, and output fell in 1793.[20] The Aube department was excluded from requisitioning for Paris (which did not deter the Parisian *commissaires* from encroaching on this supply zone for Troyes, by taking grain from the Nogent-sur-Seine district),[21] and the Seine downstream from Montereau scarcely figured in the *arrivage* system, except as a secondary route for grain from the Brie gathered at the Provins market and embarked at the port of Bray.[22]

The lower Seine on the other hand was the capital's safety line, particularly in times of dearth between harvests, when grain from the north – the Polish and Pomeranian grain purchased in Wismar, Altona, Hamburg and Copenhagen, and landed at Le Havre, Honfleur and Fécamp – helped Paris through the difficult hiatus. From its mouth to Saint-Germain, the river was lined with stores and warehouses belonging to the Commune of Paris, flour mills and biscuit factories of the Republic: important grain stores at Le Havre, Honfleur, Harfleur, Rouen, Les Andelys, a flour mill at Vernonnet, biscuit factories at Honfleur, more grain warehouses at Vernon, Meulan, Poissy (with Sceaux the main livestock mart supplying fresh meat to Paris),[23] Mantes, Conflans, a salting plant at Le Pecq, depots at Saint-Denis and Ile-Saint-Denis, the port for La Grenouillère. In addition to its importance as the main supply route for grain from the north and wood from the forest of the Brotonne, the lower Seine also brought the grain from the Eure assigned to the two rural districts of the Paris department.[24] Nearly all the river communes had an abominable reputation with the Rouen and Paris authorities, since stoppages and pillage were extremely frequent through the whole period.

Two other routes from the east – Meaux to Paris, through Claye and Villeparisis, and Coulommiers to Paris by Crécy, Lagny and Vincennes – were used to transfer large consignments of grain and wood to be transported on the Marne. They were not particularly important to the supply of Paris, and if the routes from Couilly, Condé, Coupvray and Lagny are discussed in some detail, it is because of their situation as river ports. A third route of which we hear little, but which seems to have enjoyed a unique tranquillity, was that of Hurepoix, linking Dourdan to Arpajon. And yet the Dourdan district fell within the requisition area for Paris. Perhaps this district, with that of Crépy-en-Valois, much praised for its zeal and celerity, was the exception in a picture of general ill will, chaos, administrative disorder, popular violence and, very often, real dearth.

Such a vast system of *arrivages* necessitated the dispersal of detachments from the tiny Parisian *armée* all over a zone with so many trouble spots. The whole system required controlling: hence the division of the *armée* into hundreds of tiny droplets on the landscape, rather than the stationing of large detachments at the main assembly points, to report any suspicious happenings on the rivers or the roads. Almost every port on the Oise, from Chauny to the confluence, had its detachment: Pont-l'Evêque, Sempigny, Chiry, Saint-Léger-aux-Bois, Montmacq, Le Plessis-Brion, Choisy-au-Bac, Clairoix, Compiègne, Pont-Saint-Maxence, Creil, Saint-Leu-Esserent, Précy-sur-Oise, Boron, Royaumont, Asnières, Parmain, L'Isle-Adam, Mériel, Auvers, Méry, Pontoise (with Chauny, Noyon and Compiègne, the centres possessing the most important revolutionary garrisons), Eragny, Vauréal and Fin-d'Oise. There were very few localities which did not have a landing stage, a lock and a population of sailors and fishermen. Detachments were more numerous near rivers than in the interior of this region and it is clear that their primary duty was the surveillance of river traffic.

The same imperatives explain the distribution of detachments among the communes of the important Gonesse district. This time the placements were dictated by the road network, and there were garrisons at Chantilly, Chaumontel, Luzarches, Le Mesnil-Aubry, Villiers-le-Bel, on the Chantilly –Paris road; at Senlis, Louvres, Gonesse and Le Bourget, on the Senlis– Paris road; and at Dammartin and Roissy-en-France on the Goële–Paris road. Other garrisons were positioned in the isolated villages situated between the two great northern routes, at Jagny (the scene of endless disorders), Marly-la-Ville, and Mareil-en-France; but in this case it was to suppress disorders unconnected with the geography of supply. Villages situated on military routes bore most of the burden of such detachments, and it was a burden all the more difficult to endure when troops were moving through almost incessantly. It is not difficult to see why the local authorities of a place like Luzarches should not have relished the dispatch of a detachment there.[25]

There would be fewer detachments stationed on the routes through the Brie, with the exception of that from Provins to Paris. They were scattered in particular on the outskirts of Brie-Comte-Robert, at Solers, Coubert, Suisnes, Grisy, Servon, Boissy-Saint-Léger and their hinterland (Combes-la-Ville, Soignolles, Grégy, Evry-les-Châteaux, Moissy, Fourches, Limoges, Lésigny). On the Sézanne route garrisons were placed at La Ferté-Gaucher and Coulommiers, but they were there for repressive purposes. On the parallel route through Tournan, detachments were placed at Beton-Bazoches, Jouy-le-Châtel, an important source of butter and eggs for Paris, and Rozoy-en-Brie, location of a granary serving Paris.[26] On the Gâtinais route garrisons followed the line traced by the valley of the Loing; from Montargis (which had a detachment from the Loiret *bataillon révolutionnaire*),[27] through Nemours to Moret (both these towns having detachments of the Parisian *armée*), then to Fontainebleau, Melun and Corbeil. It was likewise to protect the Brie convoys coming down from Provins to the mills at Corbeil, that garrisons were stationed along the route from Guigues to Corbeil, at the communes of Limoges and Moissy.

As for the routes from the west, it was deemed sufficient to post garrisons at the departure points for the grain coming from Beauce: at Chartres, Dreux and on the important route through Versailles. For a while a detachment was stationed at Houdan, but it was considered unnecessary to protect the convoys at other points on this route. Nor do we know of any garrisons having been placed between Etampes and Paris on the route from the Orléans region, apart from those in the Etampes district itself: at Boissy, Saint-Cyr, Fontaine, Abbéville, Estouches, Blandy, Roinvilliers, Sainte-Croix, La Forêt and Marolles. But their principal function here was to implement requisitions in the villages along the roads from Etampes to Pithiviers, rather than to protect the convoys from Etampes to Paris.[28]

The importance of the lower Seine artery is underscored by the number of detachments of the Parisian *armée* cantoned in the river localities, from the mouth of the river to the villages of the Montagne-Bon-Air district (Saint-Germain-en-Laye), situated in the shadow of the capital. Important divisions were also stationed at Le Havre and Honfleur, with their huge Parisian and naval stores, and where the discontent of workers requisitioned for naval work caused fears of interruption in the supplies to Paris and pillage of the stocks stored at the port.[29] Detachments of more modest proportions were sent to the most exposed areas along the river: to Pont-de-l'Arche (where the municipality was frequently accused by the Rouen authorities of having delayed the progress of grain shipments between Rouen and Paris),[30] to Les Andelys, Port-Mort, Notre-Dame-de-l'Isle, Pressagny, Vernonnet, Giverny, on the right bank, and to Saint-Pierre and Vernon on the left bank.[31] If the ports of the Mantes district have no revolutionary garrisons – permanent ones at least – such garrisons reappear after Meulan and Les Mureaux, at Poissy, Conflans, Saint-Germain, Le Pecq, and at Sèvres, the very gates of Paris.[32] The northern route from Paris to Le Havre through the Vexin was also protected by garrisons at Harfleur, Saint-Romain-de-Colbosc and Bolbec, and, to the south of Rouen, at Ecouis, Frenelle, Boisemont, Suzay, Villers-en-Vexin, Thémericourt, Vigny, Pontoise and at Saint-Ouen-l'Aumône.[33] These same considerations dictated the choice of postings in the riverside villages of the Aisne, from Chauny as far as the confluence with the Oise at Choisy-au-Bac, and passing through Soissons, Couloisy, Lamotte, Attichy, Berneuil-sur-Aisne, Rothondes and Le Francport.[34]

In thus distributing detachments along the rivers and roads rather than in the heart of corn-producing areas, the Parisian authorities responsible for supplying the capital showed that they considered the problems involved in the distribution and circulation of grain to be far more urgent than those of its production. It is true that detachments could be found in the villages of the hinterland, searching for grain in farmers' barns, but these were conducting special missions rather than performing garrison duties, and they departed once the requisitions had been secured. The protection of the *arrivages*, on the other hand, required the presence of a permanent garrison on through routes and at embarkation points.

Apart from the mission to Lyon – an exceptional affair – the main concern of the Parisian *armée* was the protection of *arrivages*. This stands out quite clearly in the account given of the *armée* on 20 Ventôse (see Table C in References, p. 692).[35] Though it was already late in the day and a time when, with the requisitions for Paris nearly completed, the order of priorities had moved towards political operations, nevertheless, the same towns figure in the list of places at which detachments were stationed.

The important detachments sent to Laon (380 fusiliers, a company of artillery), Le Havre (375) and Honfleur (234), in particular, highlights the government's preoccupation with grain shipments from the Baltic and the Aisne region – a valuable secondary source of Parisian food supplies throughout the eighteenth century.[36] But a statement of positions for Brumaire and Frimaire would also show the presence of strong detachments in the communes of the Gonesse district, as well as at Saint-Germain, Le Pecq, Poissy and Conflans. A total of over 3,000 fusiliers would thus have been involved in the protection of *arrivages* and the implementation of requisitions. In addition many of the 1,200 fusiliers sent to Lyon were also used to ensure supplies to the Lyon market, as witnessed by the squads sent into the communes of the La Tour-du-Pin district – notably to Saint-Priest and to Mions –[37] and the expeditions into the Campagne district.[38] The fusiliers were the economic wing of the *armée*, the cavalry its police. Though an artillery company was used for economic missions into the Soissons district, cannoneer involvement in matters of *arrivages* was rare.[39]

The distribution of garrisons accordingly follows the map of *arrivages*, with relatively permanent squads assigned to strategic points. But within this map one must ask why the *armée révolutionnaire* conducted missions into some communes rather than into others. To answer this, another map, a more complicated one, would need to be drawn, showing the villages which had customarily supplied the large urban markets on the eve of the Revolution, and whose produce in 1793 was requisitioned for this purpose by the law of 18 Vendémiaire. Such a task would be extremely complicated and would go beyond the limits of a study devoted to the economic action of the *armées révolutionnaires* in the interest of Parisian supply. An additional difficulty arises from the way in which the new administrative divisions split the economic unity of many regions and cut certain towns off from the countryside which normally supplied their markets (the unfortunate commune of Alençon being an extreme example).[40] The result was an endless series of disputes between neighbouring districts over their respective supply zones. The map of requisitions sketched from details of missions conducted by the detachments into the districts and cantons is neither an ideal nor a very natural one. The Parisian *commissaires* who led such missions were in a hurry and had little time to investigate the competing claims of districts and towns over supply areas. In general they adopted the most obvious geographical solution, assigning to each important commune the nearest villages within the relevant canton – a sensible solution, in a wheat-producing region, but tragic when the hinterland consisted of woods, vines, moors and marshes. It was not, however, in the poorest regions that requisitioning encountered most difficulties, but in the corn belts such as the Soissonnais, the Pays de Caux and the Brie region.

Besides, the map of the economic missions conducted by the Parisian *armée* corresponds not with that of areas which traditionally supplied the major markets, but with the map of ill will, covering recalcitrant communes only. In wealthy areas these were in the majority; but in some districts, even rich ones like Crépy-en-Valois and Chartres, the *armée* had to be used against isolated villages. On this map, therefore, the number of missions represents the barometer of good or ill will in the rural municipalities, and of the energy or complicity of the district administrations. It is thus the map of economic patriotism and revolutionary fraternity.

The case history of the Les Andelys district in the Eure provides some idea of the way in which these detachments were divided out among the farmers, and of how they functioned. It was an area which the Parisian authorities considered wealthy. 'Despite the low figures submitted by you', wrote the Franciade district threateningly, 'we are not ignorant of the fact that you have considerable resources remaining, that much of the corn from the harvest before last remains in your arrondissement, that this year's harvest has been abundant and that in the last analysis you have the wherewithal to help with our requisitions'.[41] But the area also included three poor, wooded cantons: Lyons-la-Forêt, Charleval and Mainneville, 'which have grain to supply the needs of their inhabitants for no more than six or seven months of the year, since most of their terrain consists of forest and grassland...'. This district also had to contribute to the needs of the Vernon market on the other side of the Seine, whose lands were also wooded and poor in grain.[42] Furthermore, in addition to supplying grain to the rural districts of the department of Paris and to the Vernon market, each farmer in this district – with the exception of the three poor cantons – had also to provide 4 hundredweight per ploughland to the Rouen market. Besides these external obligations the area also had to supply the Les Andelys, Etrepagny, Ecouis, Lyons and Giverny markets.

When the detachment of the Parisian *armée* arrived the Les Andelys communes were arguing among themselves about levying their own requisitions on the communes of their cantons. In the first place the authorities of Les Andelys asked the *révolutionnaires* to implement the requisition of supplies for their own market in the communes of Hennezis, La Bucaille, Guiseniers, Guitry, Mouflaires, Harqueny, Harquency, Fontenay, Cantiers, Corny, Noyers, Cuverville, Boucherolles, Longuemare, Paix, Suzay, and Bacqueville. All were neighbouring communes, but not all were in the canton. At the same time the municipality of Ecouis, spurred on by an extremely enterprising and sans-culotte-dominated *société populaire*, was using the small detachment there to levy requisitions on communes over which it had no authority: Boisemont, Bacqueville and others. In the north of the district the Lyons municipality had sent detachments to Puchay, Mesnil-Verclives, Morgny and Bezu-la-Forêt to expedite requisitions for its own market, which was threatened with a permanent shortage; while the municipality of Etrepagny acted likewise towards the communes in its canton: Provemont, Le Thil, Saint-Martin, Heudicourt, Bezu-Saint-Etienne (these last already under requisition to the district). Elsewhere, the Giverny municipality had also sent a detachment to impose requisitions on the commune of La-Chapelle-Saint-Ouen.[43]

Thus in one district alone, the directory and seven of the municipalities sent detachments against the communes supposed to form part of their supply zones. Some of these communes were requisitioned to supply several markets at the same time, those of Les Andelys, Vernon and Ecouis for example, those of Ecouis and Lyons, or those of Giverny and Vernon. Externally this district had to supply the markets of the Paris department, and those of Rouen and Bernay, not to mention the district of Evreux with its centre at Vernon. This is a not untypical example of what was happening within each district at a time when requisitions were being forced on all parts of the country, and when the *chef-lieu* of each district and canton was in competition with the neighbouring commune to snatch the maximum number of wheat-producing communes for its own needs. The map of requisitions was above all that of administrative anarchy and of malfunction in the system of controlled supply. Certain communes had to endure double, even triple, requisitions, while municipalities were in competition with directories in the deployment of the armed detachments. Each municipality, each district, lied, exaggerating its own difficulties and painting a glowing picture of the resources of neighbouring districts and municipalities. In the final analysis, although the Parisian *armée* carried the device '*Force à la Loi*' on its flags, its utilisation followed the rule of '*La Loi est la Force*', since the positioning of detachments was often dictated by the desires of an energetic municipality, determined to use that force to extend its own supply zone. And here we return to the problem referred to earlier, that of a hierarchy of powers controlling the armed force.

II   *Administrative disorder and jurisdiction of the various authorities in economic missions*

The district directories bore initial responsibility for the execution of missions to supply the city and department of Paris. But these in turn were subordinate to Isoré, the *représentant* charged by the Committee of Public Safety with the implementation of requisitions. Isoré then delegated his almost sovereign powers to subordinates, mostly *commissaires* from the Commission des Subsistances of the Commune of Paris, 'hommes de liaison' representing the great municipal fief. At the same time, when it was a question of requisitions of fodder, the army requisitioners had a say, and the *commissaires* charged with supplying the Nord Army had the same authority to issue orders to the Parisian detachments as Isoré's emissaries. Such orders were often contradictory and in the last analysis it was the strongest who disposed of the armed force.

The picture is even more complicated at lower levels. In the Les Andelys district detachments were requested by municipalities, some of which were not even cantonal *chefs-lieux*. Elsewhere detachments marched on orders from a *comité de surveillance* or a *société populaire*. Sometimes economic missions were ordered by the *commissaires* of a Parisian *comité révolution-naire*, sometimes by agents of the Committee of General Security; while *commissaires* from the Commission des Subsistances in Paris, not content with interfering in requisitions, also ordered the closure of churches and the arrest of priests. Since requisitions affected subsistences and thereby public order, everyone interfered, whether authorised to do so or not.

The result of all this was that although in theory the *armée révolutionnaire* remained subject to the established authorities, it could find itself at the disposal of a multitude of successive and often competing powers. Such imprecision lent itself to administrative and personal rivalries, as well as to abuses of power by the subsistence *commissaires* and the detachment com-manders. It was not so much a matter of intentional as unintentional abuse of authority stemming from this administrative confusion. Even when revolutionary officers took it upon themselves to arrest mayors, municipal officers, or members of a *comité de surveillance*, they thought they acted within their rights because of orders emanating from the revolutionary general staff, the Commune of Paris or one of the government Committees.

It is therefore difficult to trace the precise limits of competence of the different authorities, and even more difficult to assign initial responsibility for the different economic missions. All proceeded amidst the greatest confusion. It is nevertheless possible to list the different authorities involved in the economic activities of the Parisian *armée*: districts, *comités de surveill- ance*, municipalities, *sociétés populaires*, Parisian *commissaires*, the Committees of Public Safety and of General Security, *comités révolutionnaires* of the Paris Sections, *commissaires civils* of the Parisian *armée*.

The most common mission was one ordered by a district, usually invol- ving the protection of *arrivages* or the implementation of requisitions. But when such missions required some form of repressive action, notably in the search for silverware and the discovery of infractions of the Maximum, it was the *comités de surveillance* which assumed the direction of operations. Often there was a kind of complicity between these *comités* and the Parisian *armée*, in areas of conflict with the municipalities or the districts – a kind of solidarity between revolutionary authorities whose fate was connected. Moreover, sans-culottes were more numerous in the *comités de surveillance* than on the district and municipal authorities, and the composition of the *comités* made them natural supporters of the economic policy which the Parisian *armée* was supposed to implement and less inclined than the district authorities to favour the interests of the farmers, the grain dealers and the merchants.

Relations were more difficult with the municipalities, which were re- sponsible for policing the markets. But their jurisdiction extended beyond the gates of the towns and in the Eure they were to be seen ordering mis- sions and detachments into the communes. The result was that, far from being universally opposed to the Parisians, as they would have everyone believe after Ventôse, many municipalities, having requested the dispatch of a detachment, used it shamelessly for its own supply needs.

In the Oise and the Seine-et-Marne the responsibility for economic operations fell to the *commissaires* of the Paris Commune's Commission des Subsistances. They were ardent and in general upright men, close to the Cordeliers in terms of political outlook, and entirely committed to the needs of Parisian supply and the policy of regulation. These men, Parisians for the most part, and often *sectionnaires*, used the Parisian *armée* to imple- ment requisitions, to protect *arrivages* and to suppress combinations and monopolies. They took little account of the local authorities, who com- plained bitterly about the *commissaires'* tendency to order out the armed force, often without consulting them. Their role can thus be compared to that of the *commissaires civils* with the departmental *armées*, and in the region adjacent to the capital they were the real initiators of all the economic acti- vity of the *armée révolutionnaire*. They were to be the principal targets of the local authorities, unable to forget their independence of action or their haughty attitude.

Gaulthier, for example, *commissaire* of the Commission des Subsistances in the Compiègne district, used detachments as he saw fit, consulting neither district nor municipality, *comité de surveillance* nor *société populaire*. On the pretext of levying requisitions, he dabbled in everything, ordering the Parisian *armée* out on purely repressive missions and dechristianising crusades. 'For some time now', declared the Compiègne *comité*, 'Gaulthier has usurped every power, taking upon himself the task of making arrests, confiscating silverware and many more operations irrelevant to the commisson with which he is specially and uniquely charged...'.[44] On the same day the combined authorities wrote to the mayor of Paris denouncing 'this madman, or rather this delirious old man of only twenty-seven, for he is in the last stages of syphilis, the ravages and pain having undoubtedly led him to commit such shocking excesses'.[45] Perhaps Gaulthier was violent, and syphilitic too – a possible explanation for revolutionary excess encountered in so many *commissaires civils* – and he was certainly imprudent. But which party was in the right in these frequent conflicts? Undoubtedly the local authorities had the right to be consulted about the movement of detachments in areas under their jurisdiction, but the *commissaires aux subsistances* were equally free to act as they saw fit to accelerate supplies to Paris and to take action against defaulters. Gaulthier, for instance, was criticised for having made arbitrary arrests, but he had arrested only farmers and municipal officers accused of having opposed requisitions for Paris, despite numerous summonses.

The case of Gaulthier was not an isolated one, and even if he was guilty of indiscretions, surely all his colleagues who encountered the same difficulties and accusations of despotism in their relations with the districts and municipalities cannot also have been guilty. At Provins the unfortunate Descombes would be accused of having caused an artificial shortage by sending grain from the district abroad, and at Lagny the *comité* and municipality were to denounce Ballardelle for having obstructed the supplies for Paris and for being an accomplice of Hébert.[46] In both cases the only crime of these Parisians had been their excessive zeal in implementing the requisitions and pursuing defaulting authorities. But the real fault of these Gaulthiers, Ballardelles, Descombes and their Parisian colleagues sent on mission into the departments, was that they were not of the *pays*. They were outsiders, scapegoats for a policy necessarily unpopular with the country people. By shifting all the blame on to these Parisians, the local authorities could disguise their own responsibility and direct all the hatred caused by such forced measures towards Paris. Most of the conflicts between the local bodies and the outsiders had their origin in this unspoken solidarity between the district administrators, the municipal officers and their electors, the country populace. It was all too easy to shift the unpopularity for measures, otherwise recognised as necessary, on to the Parisians. The motives of the *commissaires* and *révolutionnaires* were accordingly being put on trial.

III   *Seasonal conditions governing the economic missions*

The first mission of the Parisian *armée* was to the Gonesse district and the communes bordering the forest of Chantilly, where the first detachments arrived around 20 September. The other missions did not start until early October, and some later still, at the close of winter, in Pluviôse and Ventôse. Although the primary aim of these missions remained that of implementing requisitions, some of the secondary duties of the *armée* were dictated by the seasonal cycle. Thus the initial concern of the higher authorities was to accelerate the grain-threshing process and to see that the farmers could not invoke a manpower shortage as an excuse for failing to fulfil their obligations towards the Commune of Paris. Some authorities attributed the food shortages to threshing difficulties, the municipality of Louvres, in the Pays de France and situated on one of the main northern roads, claiming on 8 September 'that threshing difficulties were causing shortages in the parish...that the difficulty seemed to come from the failure of farmers and threshers to agree on wage rates, that a large body of the said threshers came before the assembly and complained that, whereas citizen Thérouenne had agreed a rate with his threshers of around 40 sols per *septier*, a number of them [the farmers] had already reduced it to 36 sols...'.[47] Similar scenes took place in most of the wheat-growing areas, the demands of the threshers supplying the farmers with a pretext for stopping work and failing to fulfil their agreement with the Commune of Paris. Elsewhere the farmers invoked the impossibility of finding farm hands. The intervention of the Parisian *armée* was consequently designed to compel the threshers to work for the rate fixed by the authorities, to prevent the formation of workers' combinations among them, and to see that the farmers did not try to stop work on some trumped-up pretext. It was a thankless task, which exposed the *révolutionnaires* to the hatred of the rural population and which many found repellent. In the Vexin, one soldier, from the Pontoise detachment, abandoned his post after the threshers threatened to beat him to death.[48] In other areas also the soldiers found themselves as unwelcome with the country work force as with the farmers. In Frimaire Boisgirault took a detachment through the villages of the canton of Pierrefonds to examine the barns and stimulate the zeal of the threshers. He wrote to the Parisian authorities denouncing all those guilty of interrupting work and of demanding pay rates which this Parisian shoemaker considered excessive. '...We took ourselves with the citizen *révolutionnaires*...into the barn of the said Desmoulins...there we found some 1,500 sheaves of old corn still unthreshed...and the new corn piled on top of it. Of the threshed corn which we examined, the only fault we could find was in the *pontrains*, the threshers present telling us that it could not be threshed any better, since no price had been agreed. Our reply to this was to call the threshers in the commune to assemble before us...the following day...to agree on rates...and to invite them to complete their

task with exactitude and without supervision from us. An estimated 17,000
[sheaves] of corn and rye remained to be threshed...'.[49] Threshing continued throughout the winter, but after Nivôse the *armée révolutionnaire* was
no longer involved.[50]

During the winter the *armée* was given no cause for intervention against
the transport workers – that turbulent and independent group. But with the
reopening of communications after the thaw,[51] the bargemen and wagoners
began to complain about the derisory wage rates fixed by the Maximum –
which were considerably below those of the contracts agreed upon with the
district administrations – and the high costs of rigging and harness. They
also complained of difficulties in securing supplies of bread in the towns
through which they passed.[52] In the first days of spring a series of combinations were formed among the river workers and in Ventôse the Parisian
armée was set in motion to suppress a movement whose extension threatened to paralyse supplies of grain and wood to Paris.

The grievances of the transport workers spread to those in the ports as
well as to the woodcutters of the Yonne who floated the logs downstream.
In Ventôse the Committee of Public Safety sent the *armée* against the Yonne
raftsmen. On the 3rd the weighers employed in the important Paris
storehouse at Provins refused to work, declaring 'that it was because a
soldier from the *armée révolutionnaire* had been assigned to them, and they
wanted none of these outsiders [*étrangers*] involved in their work...'.[53]
Geoffroy, the *commissaire* from Paris, had to intervene to put an end to this
stoppage. On the 4th Salmon, master of the Le Pecq bridge, denounced a
boatman from the lower Seine to the municipality for having stationed his
boatload of provisions in the port, thereby blocking 'the progress of a great
number of other boats carrying supplies to Paris, which will result in a
shortage in Paris of those goods [mainly firewood] with which they are
loaded'. The Le Pecq municipality threatened to bring in the *armée* if the
boatman continued to linger in port, instead of using the horses which the
commune had placed at his disposition to pull his boat to Chatou. There
were several more incidents like this in the course of that month,[54]
incidents, seemingly minor, but which, by exposing the municipalities to
the dreaded charge – particularly in Ventôse – of having hindered supplies
to munitions works, could quickly become an affair of state. Carnot himself
was responsible for the missions of the Parisian *armée* in Pluviôse and
Ventôse against such combinations. In Pluviôse a large detachment was sent
to Le Havre, following a stoppage of work by the carpenters and caulkers
requisitioned for the naval workshops.[55] This real social crisis, taking the
form of a series of claims by the work force in wartime industries and
transport, was not a seasonal one like that of the threshers in the autumn;
rather it was provoked by the application of the Maximum to the daily
wage rates.[56]

The final task of the Parisian *armée*, therefore, that of suppressing
combinations, was essentially an anti-popular one. At the same time the last

months of its existence witnessed a relaxation in its intervention in the countryside. After Pluviôse garrisons stationed with reluctant farmers began to be withdrawn. In Ventôse the main requisitions had been filled, and only those in secondary regions like the districts of Nemours, Breteuil and Compiègne continued in force. On the eve of its disappearance the *armée révolutionnaire* had fulfilled its main goal – that of assuring bread supplies to Paris. Its final missions were concerned rather with military needs, and in Pluviôse and Ventôse when normal traffic resumed on the rivers and the roads, everything was subordinated to preparations for the new campaign. The supply of Paris, a governmental and public-order problem, took second place to the requirements of the military situation and the enormous needs of the armies preparing for action in the North and East.

The bulk of the military activities by the Parisian *armée* took place in the winter, often in rigorous conditions, and at night, to achieve the maximum effect on the rural inhabitants. Domiciliary visits, often between midnight and 2 a.m., struck terror into these villagers rudely awakened by armed men frightening in appearance. 'In the dead of night, in the stormiest weather, it [the *armée*] was ordered out, even without outdoor clothes, horses or arms, at the first bugle call...and marched all night through side roads, woods and swamps, soaked by freezing rain...'.[57] Such were the conditions in which missions in Brumaire were carried out.

The economic action of the Parisian *armée* was as we have seen conditioned by seasonal demands, by the state of the roads and by the preparations for the spring campaign. If the implementation of requisitions remained its most important task, after Pluviôse–Ventôse, when the corn-growing regions had already supplied their quotas, the resumption of traffic after the spring thaw, and the attendant increase in the risk of interruptions in that traffic, required a stricter watch over wagoners and workers on the waterways. Pluviôse and Ventôse were always the months of circulation problems, and what is referred to as *la crise des subsistances* of Ventôse Year II was above all a crisis in *arrivages*. Fouquier-Tinville was to make it the *pièce de resistance* of his extraordinary 'Act of Accusation' against the Hébertists, including the unfortunate Descombes, former *commissaire* of the Commission des Subsistances at Provins and the main denouncer of the *égoïsme* and *malveillance* of the authorities in this grain-rich district.

IV   *The* révolutionnaires *and the supply of Paris*

The *révolutionnaires* were fully convinced of the importance of their economic mission, and like all urban sans-culottes they felt that the ill will of the country people, the farmers and the grain merchants could only be ended by force. In this they found themselves in agreement with some district authorities.[58] They were intensely mistrustful of the farmers and ever ready to accuse the local authorities of a lack of energy towards and even of complicity with them. 'There are, as citizen Hébert states in his paper', one *sectionnaire* told his comrades, 'farmers who seek only the destruction of sans-culottes. They leave a vast quantity of kernels harmful to health in their corn, removing hardly any of the dust so as to increase its weight, thinking only of their personal interest...'.[59] This opinion, a common one with the Parisians, was expressed again in the complaints of one *révolutionnaire* garrisoned at Laon, which were directed against the municipality as much as the Laonnois in general. 'The townspeople', wrote Mouchain to his Section, 'have forbidden us to implement *our laws* relative to the Maximum, since the municipality of Laon has allowed them to make their own...' – in fact his main grievance against them was the high price they charged for wine.[60] But his phrase 'our laws relative to the Maximum' was a much-used one among the *révolutionnaires*, a reflection of their quasi-religious esteem for the General Maximum, which caused them constantly to denounce not only *aubergistes* and farmers for their infractions of this 'sacred law', but those who even spoke against it or criticised its principles.[61]

Such zeal did not easily adjust to the inevitable administrative delays, and the watchfulness of many municipalities, and the *révolutionnaires* became increasingly impatient with the long periods of inactivity which all soldiers have to endure between campaigns. 'For more than three months now we have been asking to be permitted to use our powers of surveillance', complained the fusiliers on detachment in the Pontoise district, to the Observatoire Section; 'our requests have proved in vain, our *frères* are in want of everything...we have requested domiciliary visits, but they are either not made at all, or made half-heartedly...'.[62] From the fusiliers stationed in the Pont-Châlier district (Pont-l'Evêque) we hear the same refrain: 'In all the communes in which we have found ourselves, we have asked in vain to be put into action...to protect...supplies to Paris and to the other departmental towns...'. This company also complained of having to spend entire days 'in their rooms', inactive, 'while the rich in the towns and in the countryside enjoy an abundance of foodstuffs...'.[63] Finally, on 24 Ventôse, the Committee of General Security acknowledged receipt of a 'letter from the detachment of the *armée révolutionnaire* stationed at Jouy, complaining of their inactivity and their inability to prevent the violation of the laws, which they see at every turn...'.[64] These complaints date from the final months of the existence of the *armée*, when the *révolutionnaires* felt discouraged and bitter in the face of the impunity of the farmers and merchants. It was a genuine sense of disappointment on the part of the sans-culottes, who had expected so much of an *armée* now seen to be powerless.

The men were equally zealous in their denunciation of all inaction which might delay the *arrivages* or jeopardise the interests of the Paris consumer, the millers, the wine-growers, the *aubergistes* and the bakers coming in for particular criticism. Thus, on 5 Brumaire, the general assembly of the Sans-

Culottes Section received a complaint from two members of its company concerning 'the inactivity of the mills on the river Hières and abuses in the storage of grain and flour at Corbeil. . .'.[65] There are many more examples of this kind of punctiliousness which so infuriated the local authorities. Moreover, the Parisian soldiers were quick to credit the most fantastic rumours, the most simplistic explanations for shortages, and the word of any sans-culotte who accused a municipality of trying to starve the poor in order to turn them against the Revolution. At Vermenton, on the Paris –Lyon road, Gachot, a member of the *comité de surveillance* of this large village of raftsmen and woodcutters, tried to incite the people against their magistrates, 'notably when the *armée révolutionnaire* was passing through, when, during an assembly of the General Council, and in the presence of the people and some soldiers from the *armée révolutionnaire*, he reproached the magistrates for having done nothing about subsistences, and for biased distribution, leaving most of the inhabitants to live off unripe corn and bran. . .'.[66] The Parisians, much impressed by this, were quick to denounce the Vermenton municipality to their Sections, to the Cordeliers and to the Commune of Paris, for having tried to reduce the poor people to starvation. At Trouville, in the district of Pont-Châlier, the cannoneers from the Bon-Conseil Section were just as eager to credit the complaints of the inhabitants of this port, fishermen and their wives, against their mayor 'who seeks to deprive the inhabitants of food by holding back supplies'. One woman even told the cannoneer captain that when she asked this unworthy mayor for bread for her children and for herself, he replied 'that if she had none, she could eat unripe corn'.[67] Petit, the officer in question, reported her words to the *comité de surveillance* at Honfleur.

This readiness of the *révolutionnaires* to give a political and social complexion to difficulties of supply, and to read counter-revolutionary intentions into what was often no more than incompetence, or inability to improve a difficult situation, was symptomatic of the sans-culotte tendency to adopt simplistic explanations for problems of which they could usually see only one aspect. Ronsin's soldiers tended to bring everything back to the Maximum and to its non-execution, but they also accepted as true the most extravagant rumours about exports to the enemy and stocks hidden away in the bowels of the earth.[68] The traces of sheaves and kernels discovered in farmyard manure owed less to the fanciful explanations of the *révolution-naires* than to the simple fact that it cost the farmers less to feed the grain to their animals than to sell it at the official markets.

All of this explains the profound mistrust of the Parisians for the municipal authorities in the small wheat-producing towns, so convinced were they of some kind of pact between the municipal officers and *les gros*: men of the law, farmers, grain dealers, millers and *aubergistes*. 'We wish to let you know', wrote one Parisian *commissaire* to the Bonnet-Rouge Section, 'that the members of the directory [of the district] of Pontoise are all hoarders, men of the law, priests and agents of former nobles'[69]; while at

Rozoy-en-Brie the cavalrymen 'replied by insulting the municipal officers, calling them rascals and declaring that, if they could not have justice, they would f...g well get it for themselves...'.[70] Most of the incidents which occurred between the Parisian soldiers and the municipalities originated in this kind of defiance, and in the conviction of the *révolutionnaires* that the local authorities were trying to thwart their rights as privileged soldiers, by refusing to lodge them with the inhabitants or by skimping on travel expenses. It was an attitude at once defiant and demanding, belligerent and insolent, guaranteed to rouse rural opinion against them and to weaken their position *vis-à-vis* the local authorities in conflicts between the soldiers and the municipalities.

V   *The* révolutionnaires *as seen by the peasants*

On 19 Brumaire Hardy and Robert, two Parisian *sectionnaires*, Cordeliers and Ministry *commissaires*, en route through Lyon to re-assume their posts with the Pyrénées-Orientales Army, wrote to the Minister, Bouchotte: 'At Avallon our carriage was surrounded by sans-culottes shouting demands for "Justice against the hoarders, justice against the aristocracy of merchants and farmers, and the prompt arrival of the *Armée révolutionnaire*..." '.[71] There are many such accounts indicating the impatience of popular circles in the small towns and in the countryside for the arrival of this *armée*, which they expected to solve all the ills caused by the shortages. All along the route from Paris to Lyon, the small-town *sociétés populaires* saw these Parisians as dispensers of justice, redressers of wrongs, tribunes of the *petit peuple* – in Joigny,[72] Vermenton,[73] Avallon,[74] Mâcon, Cluny,[75] and Sennecey-le-Grand,[76] their reception was delirious, their arrival greeted with streamers, *arcs de triomphe*, and open-air fraternal banquets. There may have been an element of prudence, of conformism in all this, the local authorities seeking to mollify these ferocious soldiers with fine words and even more so with laden tables under trees of liberty. But there was also genuine enthusiasm and revolutionary emulation on the part of the *sociétaires* of these little towns, and the kind of welcome given the Parisians undoubtedly reflected genuine feelings which persisted in many localities throughout the Parisians' stay. In fact, to the municipalities of places like Tonnerre and Troyes, which had requested the dispatch of detachments,[77] must be added a greater number which demanded the retention or return of the *armée* after the initial experience. On 24 Frimaire, for example, the *représentants en mission* in the Seine-et-Oise department were told 'that the presence of the detachment of the *armée révolutionnaire*, now stationed at Meulan, ...was essential to the maintenance of tranquillity in the markets and the protection of supplies to the said commune...', and the commander of the detachment was requested to remain there for another month.[78] On 6 Pluviôse the *comité* of Lisieux expressed its satisfaction at the news of 'the arrival of 23 *bons bougres* to bring hoarders and *égoïstes* to heel', and a month later the municipality of this little town, which experienced constant difficulty supplying its market, was still expressing its satisfaction at the presence of the detachment.[79]

As for the extremely energetic *société* of Ecouis, it could scarcely contain its enthusiasm. The detachment, it declared, 'has been constantly on hand to help us in the urgent surveillance of the large proprietors and rich *égoïstes* of our canton, and in our struggle against the farming and mercantile aristocracy, and those offenders in the national forests which surround us', and it lamented the 'sudden departure, occasioned by the unexpected recall of the said detachment, which is irreplaceable as the surest means of helping us with the revolutionary measures which the authorities of this commune situated on the major route [Paris to Rouen] must ceaselessly employ'.[80] In Honfleur too the *comité* paid homage to the energy and efficacity of the detachment at the time of its departure for Alençon,[81] while the Le Havre authorities expressed their satisfaction with the conduct of the Parisians at the time of their disbandment in Germinal.[82]

In the cities the most flattering accounts come from the sans-culotte elements. Like those in Rouen, they had expected so much from the arrival of this avenging *armée* which would 'make the counter-revolutionaries pale with fear'[83] and put an end to the intrigues of the big farmers and merchants. All this reflects a predictable social alignment and it was present even at the level of the district and municipal authorities, some of whom also expressed their satisfaction at the results obtained by the presence of the detachments. In the Oise, the Chaumont district wanted to recall the cavalrymen who had just returned to Beauvais;[84] and even that of Noyon, which had complained ceaselessly about the *armée révolutionnaire* and its commanders, still recognised that 'we have often had to employ the armed force to extract from the municipalities, what patriotism and the desire to assist their brothers in Paris ought to have produced spontaneously...'.[85] The Compiègne authorities, equally ill disposed towards the detachments, were later to admit that 'the *armée révolutionnaire*...was received with friendship and considerable enthusiasm....'.[86]

If the sans-culottes were overjoyed at the coming of this instrument of a supply policy conceived in the interests of the small consumer, the districts and municipalities were not, at the outset, hostile to the use of force, and showed no hesitation in utilising the detachments against the farmers. Their attitudes changed at a later date, but it was a change caused by the political situation in Paris, when the arrest of Ronsin caused the local authorities to think the days of the *armée* numbered.[87] In the final analysis the detachments attracted as many testimonials of satisfaction as complaints from the municipal officers.[88]

The most harmful opinion held by many municipalities about the *armée révolutionnaire* was that the presence of these Parisians was somehow a slur on their town, a mark of distrust of the patriotism of its administrators. How often do we come across municipalities protesting about the calumnies of the Parisian *commissaires* against their towns as centres of counter-revolution, Federalism or hoarding.[89] Their fears were justified, for the *révolutionnaires* were not being sent as friends, and measures were taken to prevent the development of friendly relations between the Parisians and the locals, which might dull the former's zeal.[90]

However, one way of avoiding the kind of discredit which attached to the presence of a detachment was to use the gendarmerie or the conscripted troops to implement requisitions and the laws on subsistences. Thus the authorities of Mantes,[91] Crépy-en-Valois, Janville and probably Dourdan were able to avoid the use of the *armée révolutionnaire* by taking advance measures to render its presence unnecessary. In the very nature of things the Parisian *armée* had scarcely any dealings with those authorities who were most 'patriotic' and most favourably disposed towards Paris, and, unfortunately for its officers and soldiers, the 'map of good will' rarely corresponded with that of its activities. The dispatch of a detachment was the final resort, when persuasion and threat had proved futile.

It follows, therefore, that in many towns relations were bad from the outset. There were many reasons for this, some purely personal: the harshness of some of the officers, the drunkenness and indiscipline of some of the men because of poor command. Some municipalities transferred to the detachments all the hatred they felt for the 'greedy' Commune of Paris, which sought to deprive them of food and remove any margin of profit from their administrations. The authorities of Laon, Noyon and above all of the small town of Vernon were in particularly bad odour with the rue de Choiseul,[92] and Vernon had had a bad reputation with the Parisian *commissaires* for some time because of the persistent hindrance of cargoes of grain, wine, iron, pig-iron and wood passing through its port en route for Paris or Rouen. The complaints of the commanders of detachments in Compiègne and Provins[93] about the complicity of the notables and the farmers in efforts to prevent requisitions and the application of the laws of the Maximum, were added to a long series of complaints from agents employed in the supply of Paris about the selfishness of these towns. In Noyon, Provins, Rozoy-en-Brie, Pontoise, Beaumont, Vernon, Montereau,[94] Etampes,[95] and Lagny[96] – all important centres of passage or of *arrivages*, the first four also being situated in the middle of rich wheat-growing regions – the stay of the Parisian *armée* was to give rise to a whole series of mutual recriminations. The map of ill will did not correspond with that of deprivation. Quite the contrary: communes which were rich in grain were the most opposed to the Parisians and to all form of regulation, while impoverished communes were the most 'patriotic' when it came to helping their 'frères' in Paris. In Compiègne and Noyon, and undoubtedly in Pontoise and Provins also, it did look as if the district administrators – men of the law for the most part – were in league with the large farmers and the prosperous grain dealers. To both these Parisians were intruders. Accusers are never liked, particularly when they are right, and the zeal with which the *révolutionnaires* denounced the municipalities' want of energy, and pointed to the smallest infraction of the Maximum, was a particular grievance to those who had bad consciences.

The authorities were also overworked. Those in district *chefs-lieux* were faced with enormous difficulties, and needed all their wits to fulfil a host of requisitions, while they were hard put to discover the real resources of communes in whose interest it was to plead famine. Not knowing which way to turn, confronted by the silent hostility of the rural communes on the one hand, and the incessant demands of innumerable Parisian *commissaires* on the other, and having to face up to speculators and the demagogy of refractory priests who fanned the flames, the administrators found the pernickety surveillance of the *révolutionnaires* insupportable, particularly when these men also wasted a considerable amount of their time with petty quibbles over the high price of wine in the inns, or lard sold above the price set by the Maximum.

Above all there was a lack of confidence on both sides. The Parisians, seeing the hand of the rich *égoïste*, the *malveillant* – the enemy of their city – behind everything, refused to admit the possibility of a real shortage, caused by a succession of requisitions beyond the resources of certain regions to fulfil. The municipal officers, for their part, considered the presence of these Parisians as proof of an unjustified suspicion of their patriotism on the part of the Parisian authorities. One spied on the other and accused the other of hindering the supply of Paris – a serious charge in time of foreign war and domestic revolution.

In short, if the *sociétés populaires* were generally better disposed towards the *révolutionnaires* and more ready to recommend their use in implementing economic policies than the municipalities, the attitudes of the latter varied according to the resources of the commune, the social composition of the municipal institutions, and personal conflicts. There was no common ground between the attitude of ultra-revolutionary municipalities like Presles and Taverny in the district of Pontoise,[97] Jagny, in that of Gonesse, Ecouis and Lyons-la-Forêt in that of Les Andelys, which favoured violent action against the farmers, and the kind of complicity between municipalities and farmers which existed in Pontoise, Provins, Noyon or Compiègne. Most of the sans-culotte municipalities administered communes which were extremely poor in grain, situated in the middle of woods or on the edge of rivers: Taverny, Presles, Ecouis, Lyons, Meulan, L'Isle-Adam (whose *société* asked the teacher to use the children to gather acorns in the forest)[98] were close to famine. The situation of these places bore no resemblance to the great traditional market centres of the wheat-growing regions, places like Pontoise, through which the grain of the Vexin and the Soissonnais flowed, like Noyon, market for the Santerre and Vermandois regions, or Provins and Rozoy, the two great markets for the Brie region, in all of which subsistences were in abundant supply. Yet this fundamental difference does not explain why some communes experiencing shortages,

like Vernon, Compiègne and Montereau, were notable for their opposition
to the detachments. It must also be remembered that these detachments
were intended to ensure supplies for the Paris stores alone and not for those
of the communes or districts in which they were stationed. Such stores
could be found in Vernonnet, Provins, Montereau and Noyon, and for the
authorities of these towns the armée révolutionnaire was no more than an
instrument of Parisian subsistence policy. In small towns which had no such
stores, the soldiers might be employed in the interests of the citizens against
the farmers of neighbouring communes. This is what happened at Lisieux,
Honfleur, Ecouis and Lyons, and it was natural that these municipalities
should wish to retain such useful instruments. Practically no one questioned
the need for force; disagreement arose only when it came to deciding who
would dispose of that force and to what ends.

Such was the general acceptance of the need for force, that even the grain
and poultry dealers and the dairymen requested the protection of the armée
against the dangers attending the transport of their goods to market.[99] The
instinct for immobilisme, which reappeared during every shortage, was on
the part of the country people rather than the farmers and the grain dealers.
Even if the latter did not wish to take their grain to the official markets, they
still wanted it to circulate, for the highest bidder was also often the most
distant. The armée révolutionnaire was the guarantor of such traffic, and in
this role it was hailed by everyone, town and country people alike, who
wanted bread to reach the markets.

Ranged against the armée were the millers and all those with an interest in
directing grain towards more profitable outlets and whose operations were
threatened by the arrival of the révolutionnaires. We have thus returned to the
fundamental distinction made by Hardy, and remarked upon by so many
contemporary observers, between 'the farming and mercantile aristocracy'
and the sans-culottes. The attitude of the local authorities would be
conditioned by their leaning towards one group or the other. Every farmer
was not an aristocrat, nor every cultivator a vile 'égoïste'; revolutionary
patriotism was not always absent from the large farms. But little remained
when most of the farmers were obliged to oppose a policy conceived in the
interest of the town, and they found willing allies among many administrators and the poorer inhabitants who were anxious to prevent the exit of
grain. It was, therefore, an extremely wide alliance, and its victims were
these soldiers, these 'étrangers', who had come to take away the grain for
dispatch to unknown destinations.

VI   Policing the food supplies

The economic action of the armée révolutionnaire can be described as that of
policing food supplies. But this loose description covers a wide range of
activities, having little in common except the intent to supply Paris, the
armies or the war industries. The activities of the force ranged from the

production of that bread which supplied the staple diet of Paris (watching over the threshing and grinding of grain or the baking of bread), to its distribution (protection of *arrivages,* regulation of sales at official markets, suppression of workers' combinations). But if the *armée* was primarily concerned with grain and bread-related problems, its mission also included supervising the production, transport and distribution of other staple products (wood, dairy produce, vegetables, poultry, meat), the protection of national forests, the repression of economic offences (infractions of the Maximum, hoarding), the collection of silverware, precious metal and pig-iron, surveillance of the Channel fishermen,' and generally the repression of any disorder which might compromise the flow of food supplies.

The collective action of the *armée,* under the direction of the municipalities or the districts in which it was operating (the implementation of requisitions, the protection of convoys, the surveillance of illicit traffic), can also be distinguished from the action of individual *révolutionnaires.* This last took the form primarily of denunciations particularly of the numerous infractions of the Maximum. In effect, even when they were not on duty, the Parisians were constantly 'on the job', going before *comités de surveillance* even in the dead of night to tell of economic offences.

(i) IMPLEMENTATION OF REQUISITIONS AND PROTECTION OF *ARRIVAGES*
Intervention by the Parisian *armée* fell into two main categories: the accompaniment of grain from the fields to the urban markets, even to the very ovens in the bakeries, and the application of the Maximum on bread. The operation was usually initiated by reports of farmers dragging their feet over requisitions or the threshing of grain. The next step was to prod the often reluctant municipalities into investigating the resources of the recalcitrant farmers and to stimulate the zeal of those *juges de paix* who were reluctant to institute proceedings against village notables. When requisitions had been completed in a village or canton, a further step was to ensure the transport of grain to the nearest store for Paris, with all the human and natural hurdles which that involved: popular opposition to the removal of grain, the ill will of transport workers, the condition of the roads, the activity of retailers at town gates. Once the grain had been stored, difficulties of another order arose: a portion of the grain had to be sold locally, for the needs of the commune, following a strict ruling designed to prevent out-of-market transactions and permit the workers and inhabitants to purchase before the grain dealers and outsiders from the surrounding villages stocked up at the main market in the *chef-lieu.*

Even without pillage, grain disappeared mysteriously in transit. Popular imagination saw clandestine warehouses, stores and stock-piled grain everywhere. One Parisian woman declared that underground passages ran all along the right bank of the Seine from Meulan to the sea, taking grain abroad.[100] Further grain reserves disappeared in the mills, without the equivalent in flour emerging from the other end. Cargo certificates and bills of loading were inadequate deterrents to fraud, and false destinations and quantities were simply inserted. At every stage there were loopholes through which grain and flour could find its way to unknown destinations. It was the same with other foodstuffs, transported often on men's backs and in women's baskets, and if the large grain convoys travelling by road and river were easy enough to keep track of, there was no way of following every poulterer, dairyman or farmer who took his eggs or butter to market on foot, sometimes as far as 10 or 20 miles. The *comités de surveillance* of roadside and riverside communes were sufficiently zealous to require cargo certificates; but such zeal was sometimes counter-productive, turning merchants away from the main routes, and some *comités* used this pretext to confiscate for their own use food supplies and merchandise destined for Paris.[101] Even in a society as heavily policed as that of revolutionary France in the Year II, with vigilant and inquisitive *comités de surveillance* in every commune, it proved impossible to exercise any kind of close control over the movement of foodstuffs along routes which were often little more than animal tracks through the grassland of the Pays d'Auge, across the Seine at the bridge of Mantes, to the great market of Poissy. The *armée révolutionnaire*, scattered in tiny detachments and in 'garrisons' billeted on the farmers, could not cope with everything at once. At best its intervention was limited to the supervision of important *arrivages* at the stores in the major towns, and the movement of secondary foodstuffs almost completely escaped effective control.[102]

Let us examine one revolutionary detachment at work, from the time of its arrival in a commune to stimulate the faltering zeal of the village authorities and hasten the application of requisitions in favour of the large towns. Proceedings opened with an address, in which calls to patriotism were mingled with threats. Here's how Marcellin, *commissaire civil* of the Parisian *armée* detached to Lyon, introduced himself to a specially convened general assembly in the little commune of Mions, just outside Lyon:

> after having outlined his powers, he told us that he had come with a detachment of cavalry of the *armée révolutionnaire*...and we were required to lodge and feed these 20 cavaliers and their horses...citizen Marcelin [*sic*] also told us that in nearly every commune, foodstuffs like butter, eggs, vegetables etc. were no longer getting to the markets of the large towns as in the past, and he attributed this falling off to the ill will of many farmers who did not wish to sell at prices laid down by the Maximum; that he was determined to see the laws executed and he warned those who were accustomed to taking their foodstuffs to the markets, that they did so under pain of being treated as suspects according to the law, and finally he told us to write to him at the headquarters of the *armée révolutionnaire* in Ville-Affranchie stating the result of the present requisition, warning us that just as he acted

fraternally at this moment, so he would act severely if he was forced to return. . . .

Leaving his cavalrymen in Mions, to drive home the underlying threat of his words, the *commissaire civil* then moved on to Saint-Priest, where he spoke in the same vein: 'He said he was astonished that since the law of the Maximum the country people no longer brought their goods to the markets as in the past'. 'To this', wrote the municipal officers, 'we replied that our commune produced very little of the foodstuffs he spoke about, that's to say butter, cheese, eggs, etc., and as for grain we could assure him that we had furnished Commune-Affranchie with all we could spare. . .'.[103]

Here Marcellin was using threats rather than the *armée* to ensure the application of requisitions. In this case, however, his action was out of line, since traders were free to take second-level foodstuffs like butter, eggs and cheese to whatever market they pleased.[104] It was only cereals and wood which were subject to stricter controls, because of the requisitions in favour of large units like the Commune of Paris and the armies. At a later date, less important towns were authorised themselves to requisition the communes which had supplied them prior to 1789, and some very large towns like Lyon, Marseille and Bordeaux were put on a par with the armies and given more extensive powers of requisitioning. It was this kind of secondary requisitioning which was the major preoccupation of many of the *armées*.

But if threats proved ineffective, then action was the next stage, and garrisons were stationed with farmers who were behind with their requisitions. This practice, which dated from the Ancien Regime, was particularly dreaded by the peasantry, thus obliged to lodge and feed for an undetermined period, soldiers who profited from the situation to demand a diet fit for a king, and a daily allowance of 30 or 40 sols, or even 2 to 3 livres, depending on their rank. Such 'pranks' must have been hard to take by the farmers who bore the brunt of such totally illegal 'taxes'.[105]

Let us now turn to the way in which a detachment was used to secure requisitions for the market of a small town. Again our example is Vernon, provisional *chef-lieu* of the district of Evreux, a riverside commune surrounded by woods and bog, and obliged to feed its populace with grain from communes on the right bank of the Seine. These communes, in the district of Les Andelys–Tilly, Mezières, Civières, Fours, Hennezis, Forêt, La Chapelle-Saint-Ouen, Guiseniers, Surcy, Heubécourt, Fontenay, Corby, Panilleuse, Guitry, Cahaignes, Haricourt and Bois-Jérôme – according to the Vernon authorities had 'always, since time immemorial, supplied the bulk of supplies to the Vernon market'. 'Considering that the law of 18 Vendémiaire has maintained the markets as they existed before 1789', the district, at its session of 29 Pluviôse, passed the following resolution:

Article 1: The municipality of Vernon is authorised to require the commander of the *armée révolutionnaire*, or any other commander of the armed forces at Vernon, to place at its disposal the number of men it requires. . . .*Article 3:* It will appoint two or three *commissaires* from the commune; these *commissaires*, accompanied by the armed force, will take with them [the] number of threshers considered necessary by the municipality. *Article 4*: Armed with powers delegated to them by the municipal officers of Vernon, these *commissaires* will go immediately to the communes of Tilly [followed the list of the aforementioned communes]. *Article 5*: When they have discovered the *égoïstes* and the guilty among the farmers, they will place with them a requisite number of threshers, the expense to be borne by the offender. . . .[106]

When these measures proved to be ineffective, force was resorted to. Even before this, on the outskirts of Vernon, a detachment of 25 men had been ordered out to arrest the recalcitrant farmers and bring them to the *chef-lieu*. On 14 Pluviôse, 'The *sieur* Dumerle, a farmer accused of failing to bring to the granary the amount of grain required of him by his commune', was brought in by five *révolutionnaires*. On the 26th François Aubry and Robert Léjart, farmers from Saint-Germain-Fresney and Boisset-le-Prévaucher, were brought in, accused of having failed to supply quotas of 69 and 98 hundredweight of corn respectively. In these two cases the district sent the culprits to prisons in Vernon or Evreux, but elsewhere the outcome was less brutal, and garrisons were simply placed with such farmers until the requisitions had been implemented in their entirety.

These measures appear to have had the desired effect, the district directory observing at its session of 24 Germinal that fear alone was enough to make indifferent farmers act patriotically. This was such a well-accepted truth that every administration tried to secure the attachment of an armed force; the net effect was that every district and town was placed in competition with every other over requisitions. The Vernon municipality, for example, complained 'that the armed force of the commune of Les Andelys marched into the communes assigned to our supply and took away all the grain. . .such measures can only lead to famine in our canton. . .'.[107] But in the neighbouring district similar abuses occurred. On 20 October, the commune of Boisemont denounced a blatant act of force against it by Ecouis, the cantonal *chef-lieu*: 'An armed force from outside has today, the 17th, been deployed in our commune. . . . A band of 60 to 80 persons appeared, armed with rifles and pikes and led by municipal officers in their sashes of office. . . . Imagine our surprise when we learnt that this armed force had come from Ecouis and that the municipality of the said Ecouis, without any authorisation from you [the district] was leading this troop. . . . It wanted to place the commune of Boisemont under requisition for its market because we are in its canton. . .'.[108] But Boisemont was already under requisition to supply the market of Les Andelys.

Examples of similar abuse of the armed forces are legion and amidst such anarchy each commune was exposed to pressure from the district and cantonal *chefs-lieux* alike. Faced with double, often triple, requisitions, the farmers had ample pretext for evading their obligations. Though defective in many other respects, the Parisian *armée* at least had the virtue of remaining relatively free from such municipalisation, since it was not in the exclusive service of any commune besides that of Paris. For this reason the district authorities preferred to use it rather than the National Guard, which was too wedded to local interests.

Thanks to the garrisons and to the arrest of the most stubborn farmers, the district administrators and the *commissaires aux subsistances* of the *chefs-lieux* were relatively successful in the implementation of requisitions in favour of Paris and its department. But even with the aid of armed force, these measures were not executed with the speed required by the Parisian supply agents. They were in a hurry, and this very urgency was undoubtedly a further obstacle to the smooth implementation of the requisitions, the farmers complaining of being left no food stocks to tide them over till the next harvest. The Parisians were deaf to such arguments and pushed on regardless, sometimes completely denuding the country granaries of corn and intensifying popular fears. Isoré made only one concession to demands from the wheat-growing areas that requisitions should be spread over the year; and that was to divide the supply districts into two groups, the first to provide supplies only during the period Brumaire to Ventôse. That was small consolation to this first group, which watched its resources dwindle from the first days of winter. Besides, given the haste with which calculations were drawn up, the application of requisitions did not always correspond to the actual resources of each district, and some bore an unfair burden.[109]

But the use of garrisons did accelerate the application of requisitions by weeks, if not months – an important outcome for a government anxious to ensure supplies of grain and fodder by a certain date. There were still considerable delays, despite the existence of the *armée*; but they were nothing by comparison with those of the period from May to September. By the spring of 1794, Isoré could declare that the main requisitions for Paris had been secured.

But the levy of requisitions was only part of the story; the grain still had to be brought to the markets and the Parisian granaries, and the *révolutionnaires* spent a considerable amount of time on the roads or in the river ports where boats were loaded with grain. This was a difficult operation to organise, because of the agility of carters and boatmen in eluding the vigilance of the revolutionary authorities. On 23 Ventôse, the municipality of the important way-station of Brie-Comte-Robert declared that, 'in view of the repeated complaints from the soldiers of the detachment of the *armée révolutionnaire* escorting the convoys of corn for Paris from the stores of this commune to Corbeil, that the carters...refuse to travel together,...making it impossible to escort and protect them...', the convoys should in future leave at fixed times, one or two per day.[110] But the carriers could detour grain from

official destinations in other ways, and the weakest link in the chain of distribution from the farmer's granary to the market hall was the transport
service. All the authorities of the Year II complained of the greed and ill will
of the carters attached to the *armée*, some of whom were draft-dodgers,
counter-revolutionaries, well-off young men and wigmakers.[111] The
reputation of the civilian carriers was little better: they were restive about
the requisitions, reluctant to work at rates fixed by the districts, and refused
to leave unless these were increased. The *armée révolutionnaire* was to be used
against them also.[112]

To such human frailties were added practical difficulties: farmers hid their
horses, knowing well that those requisitioned to draw the military wagons
or those bound for Paris would be returned not at all or in a state fit only for
the abattoir. In the Aisne farmers were arrested by the detachment for
trying to remove their horses and harness from the requisitions for the
Nord Army, and in the Pontoise and Etampes regions the Parisians were
used to break down this resistance to the levy of horses in the countryside.
At Etampes two revolutionary soldiers caused panic among the peasantry
by spreading the rumour that *all* their horses would be requisitioned for the
needs of Paris.[113] Such rumours gained all the more credit when requisitions
fell so hard on the countryside that some regions complained of having no
horses at all left for agricultural purposes.

But it was the waterways traffic rather than the convoys by road which
were most exposed to interruption and pillage. The riverside dwellers lived
amidst vines, woods or marshes and were more often the victims of
shortages than the people of the plains;[114] the river workers belonging to a
powerfully organised corporation, were always ready to take advantage of a
difficult situation to demand increased wages and rations, and unless the
authorities were prepared to use force against them, they had to agree to
their demands. The Revolutionary Government had no such reservations
and sent the Parisian detachments to force requisition orders upon the
recalcitrant bargemen. This use of the detachments, particularly in the Oise
valley, ensured the regular movement of food supplies. But it was only a
temporary solution to a more deep-seated problem, brought about by the
government's economic policy, which penalised the work force by fixing
excessively low daily wage rates.[115] Revolutionary soldiers could not be
placed on every boat; the bargemen and their employees remained masters
of their schedules and even if they succumbed to force, they did so
unenthusiastically, and at every opportunity invoked equipment problems
to delay transport. Night traffic on the waterways was forbidden, and
the bargemen could find all manner of pretexts to linger in port, knowing
well that their services were indispensable. The occupation of bargeman and
rope-drawer, like that of raftsman, was highly specialised, and the *révolutionnaires*, these small shopkeepers and artisans from Paris, would have been
as inept in this field as they were at threshing.

Finally, there were the retailers, those people who could be seen on market days on the outskirts of towns and bourgs, barring the route of the merchants and dairymen and trying to take their produce, either by force or by offering a price above that of the Maximum. If they succeeded, they would then take the supplies to one of the *auberges* – the distribution centres for such clandestine traffic. From there they would be sold from door to door to the well-off, who were willing to pay dearly for supplies, thereby placing them beyond the reach of the sans-culottes. The activities of these retailers were the main cause of the shortage in secondary foodstuffs. To put an end to it, the municipal authorities responsible for policing the markets stationed small night patrols of *révolutionnaires* at the approaches to the town; there they would be in position at dawn, when the merchants arrived at the end of their exhausting journey. Such precautions were adopted at Honfleur with the desired result,[116] likewise at Le Havre, at the gates of Lyon, in the commune of Châlier (Croix-Rousse), at Saint-Just,[117] on the routes from the Ain and the Isère, as well as at Compiègne, Laon and Noyon.

The retailers tried to get the highest price for their foodstuffs by selling them within the towns. Every *comité* was able to point to certain houses as the outlets for this clandestine trade, and many instructed detachments to make domiciliary visits to the homes of the rich and the merchants.[118] At the same time they stationed soldiers in the market hall to apply every detail of the rulings on market procedure, particularly that guaranteeing precedence to the local inhabitants over the merchants and the surrounding villagers.[119] Nor did the duties of the soldiers stop at that, for they were also empowered to search villagers and merchants leaving town after their purchases, to prevent them from taking away goods whose export was forbidden. The Parisians, therefore, were the successors to those Ancien Regime troops charged with policing the markets.

(ii) ECONOMIC MOBILISATION AND RURAL POLICE

The *armée révolutionnaire* was not simply the instrument ensuring supplies to Paris; it was also assigned an important duty in the economic mobilisation of the nation's resources for the war effort. Indeed this *armée* of the people was the victim of an unjust fate, for it was made the instrument of extremely unpopular tasks such as the confiscation of church silver – which turned the bulk of the rural populace against it – and even more, the repression of forestry offences. By a curious twist of fate these Parisian artisans had replaced the former gamekeepers – many of whom had emigrated with their masters – hounding the poor country people who cut down trees or took dead wood from the forests.

The confiscation of silverware from the churches was partly an economic operation, but the symbolism of this attack on the externals of religion was part and parcel of revolutionary propaganda, and bordered on dechristiani-sation. The two *commissaires*, Marcellin and Paillardelle, instructed the members of the Joigny *comité* 'to have all remnants of fanaticism and feudalism destroyed, and to send to the National Convention all the gold, silver, copper, etc, from the temples, leaving nothing but a bell to call all the citizens of the commune together'. They did the same at Avallon where they had 'two members of the *comité* announce, that at the roll of the drum all good citizens should bring their gold, silver and silverware, needed by the Republic, to be exchanged for *assignats*, on pain of being regarded as suspects and arrested. . . '.[120]

The search for gold and the confiscation of religious objects was a popular duty with the *révolutionnaires*, for in it they could satisfy at one and the same time their fundamental egalitarianism, their destructive anticlericalism and their simplistic views on economic problems. They therefore brought a zeal to it which antagonised the local authorities, [121] and terrified the country people, often woken and searched in the middle of the night.[122] Even the battalion commanders did not shrink from such searches, which they considered a patriotic duty.[123] In Poissy the Parisians carried their zeal so far as to present the municipality with 'the metal remnants of a symbol of fanaticism found at the end of the bridge in the commune of Carrières'.[124] The passion with which they went about destroying crosses and saints will be seen again when we look at the dechristianising activities of the *armées révolutionnaires*. The aspect which concerns us here is that of national defence;[125] for the soldiers of Ronsin and their officers undertook this task with particular pleasure as symbolising more than any other the destruction of the former regime and the spectacular affirmation of revolutionary patriotism. Moreover, the violent and foolishly zealous way in which these measures were executed created many of the difficulties encountered by the *commissaires* entrusted with this economic mission.

During the autumn and winter of 1793–4 the national woods and forests created from sequestrated estates underwent such systematic pillage that it reached the level of a national disaster. The culprits were not content to carry off dead wood, as the poor were permitted by the authorities to do in the wooded districts of the Oise; trees were also cut down at night-time, wood stored in the river ports was stolen and the woodcutters themselves collaborated, with stolen wood finding its way into practically all the houses of the villages situated on the Yonne. The widespread nature of such offences was the result of the removal of traps and wardens from the forests, and they were particularly serious in the wooded area around Paris. Throughout this region the municipalities turned to the Parisians for help in repressing these offences and searching for stolen wood. The detachments sent to Moret and Château-Landon watched over the cutting and sale of wood;[126] in the forest of Compiègne they pursued pillagers night and day; in the Breteuil district the cavalrymen denounced the peasants' destruction of the woods of Aussanvillers and Bouvillers, and in the neighbouring district of Grandvilliers, they carried out searches for stolen wood.[127] The Pontoise district sent a small detachment to Ennery to put an end to a movement which was bringing about the destruction of the forests,[128] while the Committee of Public Safety sent the Montereau detachment against both the woodcutters and the raft workers of the Yonne, who were threatening a stoppage of work to secure an increase of wages.

The surveillance of the Channel fishermen by detachments sent to Le Havre and Honfleur forms quite a separate chapter in the history of the *armée révolutionnaire*. The Parisians were instructed to board fishing boats as they put to sea, to prevent them selling fresh vegetables to the English fleet in return for payment in specie. These Parisian artisans, no doubt recalling the misfortune which had befallen the National Guardsmen sent on a similar mission – the fishermen claiming that they had fallen overboard – mutinied, on the grounds that they had enrolled for service in the interior. Faced with such insubordination, the authorities of Le Havre and Honfleur seem to have taken little action, other than reporting the refusal to the rue de Choiseul. In the end no *révolutionnaire* had to undertake any seafaring mission and none ended up in the prisons or the hulks of His Majesty.[129]

No, it was a more banal and certainly less dangerous task which occupied the attentions of the *armée*: that of policing butchering, suppressing illicit slaughter of livestock and searching for home-produced meat. Such abuses were common, for a weak government had tried to placate the graziers and livestock dealers by exempting livestock from the Maximum, whilst imposing it on dead meat.[130] The *révolutionnaires*, who found it difficult to ensure their own supplies, were particularly vigorous in their harassment of the butchers and infuriated some authorities by their incessant interference.

(iii) INDIVIDUAL ACTIVITIES

We have already referred to the pernickety zeal of the Parisians in their denunciation of infractions of the Maximum or of any criticism of this sacrosanct law. Ronsin himself set the example at the time of his famous outing to Vincennes, when he listened attentively to accusations against the commune's monopolies *commissaire*, made by a butcher with undoubtedly very good reasons for wanting to avenge himself on such a conscientious official.[131] If the *armée* achieved anything, it was this establishment of respect for the Maximum through the fear which the detachments inspired in the traders.[132] Already charged with missions which were naturally unpopular with the mass of the rural population, the soldiers also succeeded in making themselves hated by the inhabitants of the small towns and by the local authorities, placed in a difficult position by incessant denunciations which required some semblance of punishment. In Ventôse the authorities were able to turn the tables on the Parisians by accusing them of sabotaging the famous law by their own involvement in the traffic in foodstuffs.

But the Parisians and their wives were not the only ones to take advantage of a privileged position to sell eggs and butter to the farmers at prices above the Maximum, and it required considerable hypocrisy to accuse them of causing the worsening shortage in secondary foodstuffs in the spring of 1794. Several communes even drew up charges against the

Parisians on this account, however, and in the scrupulously detailed indict-
ments prepared by the municipalities of Pontoise, Chantilly, Beaumont,
Noyon and Provins,[133] one senses a determination to exaggerate a traffic
which in reality involved only a small number of items and a few individuals. Moreover, those dishonest soldiers who had profited from their stay
in the country to supply their families in Paris or to set themselves up as
'retailers' in the small towns were severely punished by their own officers.
But the harm was already done, and hostile municipalities succeeded in
attaching an aura of shameful venality and shady dealings to the *armée
révolutionnaire*. So successful was the campaign that once the impression had
gained ground of the *révolutionnaires* themselves having sacrilegiously
violated the holy law of the Maximum which they had been appointed to
defend, even a portion of sans-culotte opinion in Paris accepted without
regret the disappearance of the popular *armée* in which they had once placed
so much hope. The *armée révolutionnaire* was to lose its reputation unjustly
because of a few baskets of eggs diverted by 10 or 20 soldiers for the use of
their families. In reality the whole business was little more than a vulgar
settling of scores by those municipalities who had been persistently singled
out for their reluctance to assist in the supply of Paris. Far more numerous
were those communes who did not take advantage of the vulnerability of
these poor wretches at the time of their disbandment, but instead praised
their economic effectiveness and their purity of conduct. The Parisian *armée*
had no part in the subsistence crisis of Ventôse–Germinal and since it
affected only secondary foodstuffs, it was a crisis which aroused no fears of
popular commotion.[134]

At the time of the formation of the Parisian *armée* in September 1793, the
supplies experts were not optimistic about its success. We have already
referred to the reservations expressed by two members of the Commission
des Subsistances in Paris, Champeaux and Dumez – both energetic Jacobins,
with considerable experience of supply problems, after missions that
summer to the corn-growing region round Paris. The *armée* was too small
to impose its will on the country people, they said, and the net effect would
simply be to turn them against Paris and to sharpen their opposition to
measures of compulsion: 'Your battalions cannot be on permanent duty
everywhere. The terror they will inspire might extract something, when
they are on the spot; but people give as little as possible to those who
demand it by force. Once your bayonets have disappeared, you will receive
nothing further. . . . It has been proved that the use of the *armée révolutionnaire* would ill serve the supply of Paris, that it would even be impolitic and
dangerous to liberty. On the other hand, it has also been proved that
without this *armée* freedom of commerce is still incapable of ensuring
supplies, because the combination of ill will and cupidity is as active today
as it has always been, and it has been found necessary to pass the law of 4
May to end this freedom of commerce which pushed the price of grain to
unprecedented levels. . . '.[135]

Such then were the predictions of two experts who were well informed on peasant attitudes. Condemning free commerce in grain as ineffective, because it went against the country people's instinct towards immobility, they accepted the need for force, but considered an army of 4,000 men – 2,000 of whom would be garrisoned at Lyon and thereby removed from economic service – as inadequate to inspire the terror necessary for success. They might, certainly, be able to protect the *arrivages* by escorting convoys from the grain-growing regions to Paris or to the stores, but in this they would simply be fulfilling the same function as the *maréchaussée* of the Ancien Regime, or the hussars and dragoons of 1792. That had indeed always been a job for troops. But should we also subscribe to the pessimism of the two administrators in dismissing Ronsin's *armée* as an unsuitable agent of such an economic programme? Only an appraisal of the results can answer this question.

As far as *arrivages* were concerned the contribution was positive. It is true that after Pluviôse there would be a resurgence of stoppages and troubles in the movement of supplies throughout the Paris supply zone.[136] But such problems were normal at that time of year and only affected secondary foodstuffs, notably butter, eggs and meat. In Fouquier's enquiry in the third *décade* of Ventôse, grain and bread were not mentioned. By all accounts it proved impossible to combat the kind of traffic which was usually transported on human backs and in very small quantities. But when it came to protecting the large grain convoys, the *armée* did well by Paris, ensuring a regular ration of reasonably-priced bread to its inhabitants. In this respect there is no comparison between Ventôse Year II and the catastrophic situation of the terrible spring of 1795. The *armée révolutionnaire* did count for something, even if it is impossible to reach a precise evaluation of its role in an area where the government of the Year II scored its most notable success. Nor was the *armée* entirely ineffective in suppressing the activities of the 'retailers', even if its successes in this field were only local and temporary in nature, confined entirely to the time when the detachments were on the spot.

The Parisian *armée* was particularly effective in the major requisitions of grain and fodder for Paris and the Army of the Nord. In Ventôse, the period of major requisitions came to an end, and their success was such that Isoré was able to release the corn-growing regions from their obligations – a breathing space in the draconian economics of the Year II. Indeed the *armée* had succeeded almost too well, and once the requisitions had been achieved, its existence no longer seemed necessary in the eyes of the government men charged with the supply of Paris and the armies.

In two other areas the *armée's* intervention also proved effective. In the first place it allowed the *commissaires* to confiscate bells and silverware from the churches, despite the fury of the villagers. In the second, the workers' combinations were easily dispersed because their local nature meant that the detachments could deal with them one at a time. In these two fields the *armée* proved a useful auxiliary to the war effort, by facilitating the supply of wood and metal to the arms manufactories.

These successes are important, and should not be lost sight of when considering areas where the intervention of the *armée* was not crowned with success. Denunciations against infractions of the Maximum, for example, proved fruitless; their very repetition is the best indication of the failure of the Maximum in foodstuffs other than grain, and they simply irritated the country people and the local authorities. As for forestry offences, it would have been unrealistic to expect an *armée* of 4,000 to put an end to a practice in which almost the entire rural population was involved. Nor could force bring meat back to the market, when the shortage was caused by a fundamental flaw in the government's economic policy, which, while submitting dead meat to the Maximum, left the graziers to sell live animals as they wished.

In the final analysis a controlled economy necessitated a resort to force. Everyone, or nearly everyone, in the Year II was agreed on this, and no one could claim that the peasantry might be brought round by persuasion or by appeals to a revolutionary patriotism of which they were totally devoid. Besides, even in the Year III a government which was well disposed towards the farmers had to send huge detachments of cavalry into the countryside. The use of force was widely accepted by urban opinion as necessary.[137] What was not so readily accepted was that it should be popular. However, the best testimony to the economic effectiveness of the Parisian *armée* was the explosion of joy in the countryside on news of its disbandment. It was a cause for reflection by many moderate Jacobins with no love of ultra-revolutionary measures. If the farmers so detested the soldiers of Ronsin, they said to themselves, these soldiers must then have been of some use; and sans-culotte opinion in general viewed with some anxiety the jubilation which greeted the abandonment of the experiment in controlled economy.

The *armée révolutionnaire* had served the Commune of Paris well: by helping supply its vast population with bread, it had spared the government of the Year II the dangers of a popular *journée* provoked by shortage. It could thus prepare for the military campaign of that summer without fear of trouble in Paris. This service to the Jacobin dictatorship can be measured more effectively against the events of a similar period in the Year III. Thus, from the economic point of view, the *armée révolutionnaire*, in serving the interests of Parisian supply, had been a faithful instrument of the Revolutionary Government, and Saint-Just recognised as much.

CHAPTER 2

National Defence and Urban Supply:
The Economic Action of the Departmental and Communal
Forces

Like that of Paris, the departmental *armées* were intended to implement by force and threat the new economic laws, particularly that of the Maximum.[1] They were to combat hoarding, which was a crime against equality and national security, and was therefore counter-revolutionary. The hoarder was possibly even more of a threat than the distributor of false *assignats*, because almost everyone was a hoarder at times, and the country people always were.[2]

The Parisian *armée* was predominantly concerned with the supply of the capital. The departmental *armées* did not have the advantage of such unity of purpose. Rather, in their concern with military supply, they were economic adjuncts to the Grand Armies fighting on the frontiers. Everything was subordinated to this end, and its effective realisation depended on the drawing up of inventories, the implementation of requisitions of grain, fodder, horses and harness, the acceleration of threshing, the confiscation of precious metal, the protection of forests, the suppression of smuggling at the frontiers and of combinations among workers in areas of supply and war production.

The supply of the urban markets took second place. Some large towns were, like Paris, assimilated to the armies and supplied militarily. But they were few in number and were only accorded this privilege because of their strategic position, the size of their population and the military stores situated within their boundaries. Most towns had no way of blackmailing the higher authorities with threats of disorder or food riots, and the great bodies of soldiers almost totally bypassed them. There remained the small battalions and companies, the ideal instrument of a communal supply policy.

It is difficult to distinguish between the economic action by the most important of these *armées* in the cause of national defence and the social and egalitarian action common to all the revolutionary formations and designed to help the poor and the sans-culottes. The confiscation of silverware and precious metals was necessitated by the war effort, but it only affected the rich. The laws of the Maximum also followed a certain class policy, for they helped only those who worked, produced and were useful to the mobilisation of the country's economic resources. There would have been little justice, after all, in permitting the rich and the idle to profit from this sacred law by picking up foodstuffs at the same low prices as the sans-culottes, when all along they could afford to pay the high prices for luxury foods that obtained outside the official markets.[3] Such was the reasoning of the sans-culottes of the commune of Nesle, and all their 'frères' thought likewise, for the success of the new laws was vital to the sans-culottes. The political and social undercurrents of the war economy will be discussed in another chapter; the aim here is rather to describe the activities of the departmental forces in the supply of the armies and the arms factories, and secondly to gauge their effectiveness in the provisioning of urban markets.

In many ways the problems presented by military and urban requisitions were the same as those causing so much difficulty for the Parisian *commissaires*. And if the difficulties were the same in the departments, so too were the simplistic solutions put forward by the sans-culottes there.[4] Every department experienced the same stoppages, hindrances and clandestine traffic as in the Paris region. With famine a close acquaintance the poor country people of the Massif Central were obsessed by fears of going short and particularly receptive to the most extravagant of rumours. This nervous chord in popular mentality was especially vibrant among the poor peasants of the Midi and the South-West.[5] As in the Paris region, the effort to supply the armies and the large towns placed country and town in direct competition: and the people of the more arid regions would sometimes take up arms to defend their gods, tighten their grip over their food supplies, and protect their sons from that other, human, form of requisition, conscription. Seasonal difficulties were also more pronounced in these harsh regions, and during the few weeks or months of their activities there, the revolutionary soldiers had to cope with the old enemy to food supplies – the wolf, chased from the forests by the cold, and venturing into the village markets.[6] The Paris region would have to wait until the terrible winter of the Year III to witness similar depredations.

Thus, if the problems in the departments were the same as those faced in the Paris supply zone, they were also generally more marked. The only exception was the coastal region of the Mediterranean from Nice to Marseille, where the constant supply of grain from Genoa spared the inhabitants from the threat of shortages and disturbances. To cope with a situation which was more difficult in almost every respect than that facing Paris, the departmental suppliers had less power and less means than their colleagues in the capital. If the *commissaires* in charge of supplying the armies could follow up threats with the reality of a commission of popular justice – and when the *commissaires* with the Armies of the East and the Bas-Rhin spoke of summary and terrible justice to the farmers of these regions, it was no empty threat – their colleagues, serving only an urban *comité*, could do little more than issue a stern warning or, at best, serve a summons on the recalcitrants. Nevertheless, thanks to their personal energy and their revolutionary temperament, some of these men attained remarkable results by terrorising the rural population with a minimum of means – this was low-cost terror. But miracles could not be expected from often derisively small *armées* confronted with the solidarity of the rural masses.

I Distribution problems

The supply zone for Paris was already enormous; but in the eighteenth century there seemed at times to be a needless criss-crossing of the entire country by grain convoys. Cereals from the north – from Pomerania, Livonia and Courland – landed at Dunkerque, were transported by road and river to Marseille. Much was stolen en route, and the remainder ran the risk of rotting before it reached its destination. Grain from the Mediterranean and the Barbary coasts supplied a large portion of the Midi as well as Lyon and its region. Stores of grain were dotted all along the banks of the Rhône, at Marseille, Arles, Beaucaire and Pont-Saint-Esprit, as well as along the Seine, and there were further stores on the Mediterranean at Sète, Toulon and Nice. Lyon had a store at Arles; but the huge town also supplied itself from as far in the other direction, from the Saône valley, from Franche-Comté and Burgundy, and the Lyon merchants had stores and boats in the ports of Gray and Saint-Jean-de-Losne.[7] When the other populous communes of the Lyon and Beaujolais regions could no longer count on requisitions because of a total shortage, they too sent *commissaires* to purchase grain in these other regions.[8] American grain shipped to Bordeaux was sent to Paris and to nearly all the towns of the Garonne valley;[9] while the people of Nîmes and Montpellier tried to find supplies in the Lauraguais, through the canals of the Languedoc and Lunel, and in the markets of Genoa, where *commissaires* from the Midi – Protestants for the most part – argued over the much-contested grain supplies from Sicily, Tunis and the other ports of the Maghreb.[10] In this scenario Toulouse and Marseille were the only major towns to have the advantage of proximity to the two finest granaries in France: the Lauraguais and the plain of Arles. In normal times Toulouse found supplies from the Lauraguais adequate, but in 1793 much of the produce of the Castelnaudary district was consumed by the incessant requisitions for the Pyrénées-Orientales Army.[11]

If grain convoys were made to travel vast distances – 'We must,' said Coupé de l'Oise, 'distribute revolutionary patrols...to Dunkerque, to the mouths of the Somme and the Seine, to Nantes and Bordeaux, and to several other towns'[12] – it was the same with other supplies, including wine. One Saint-Flour carrier took butter, cheese and lard regularly to Paris. Indeed, in a burst of fraternal enthusiasm, the small *société populaire* of Morlaas in the Low Countries, decided to follow the example of Pau in supplying the Parisians with lard and salt pork.[13] The wine merchants of Sceaux, in the shadow of the capital, claimed that they received their wine from Tours, Blois, Orléans, Auxerre, Coulanges and Chablis, as well as from Mâcon, Pouilly, Beaune and the Gâtinais,[14] the same zone which supplied the wine merchants of Paris itself.

The importance of river traffic in the Paris region can be deduced from a statement of the Year II: 'The goods which normally arrive by water are wood, coal and charcoal, some wine, hay, oats, corn, barley, cider, iron and steel...'[15], i.e. all the foodstuffs and merchandise needed to supply the urban consumer, the armies and the arms manufactories. But the same statement could have been made for the whole of France, and the other rivers were as important in the national supply plan as the Seine, the Oise and the Marne were to Paris. The Rhône in particular had large numbers of grain boats moving in both directions, while the Saône supplied Lyon with corn from the Bassigny region and from Franche-Comté. The Midi canal brought the immense riches of the Lauraguais to the sea, to the Gard and to the poor mountain departments, as well as to Toulouse. Further north the Garonne enabled supplies of foreign grain from Bordeaux to reach the towns along its banks. Finally, part of the Lauraguais harvest also went down river to Bordeaux, making the small port of Tonneins an important transit station.[16] Metz was supplied via the Moselle,[17] Châlons by the Marne,[18] Orléans with grain from the Berry and Bourbonnais regions via the Loire, and Nantes with grain from the Centre and wood from the Morvan by the same means.[19]

This virtually total dependence of the supply system on the waterways was one of its major weaknesses, for traffic was interrupted almost altogether by low water in the summer, and then by the autumn rains; while the riverside people, often the first to be affected by shortages, were always ready to plunder. Stoppages multiplied in Brumaire and Frimaire, as in the spring, in Pluviôse and Ventôse, when the thaw allowed the convoys to move again. The small towns of the Garonne valley contested the passage of grain to Bordeaux, and the instances of interruptions and pillage in the towns along the Languedoc canal were countless,[20] to say nothing of natural and seasonal hazards, like drought, flood, and ice, or the demands of the port workers, who were just as turbulent in the Centre and the Midi as in the Paris region. Restif alluded to them in his remark about the 'horrible drawers of floating wood', and 'those boat women, soured by suffering...'.[21]

'France has enough food', wrote Coupé de l'Oise, but it had to be sought in its place of origin and transported to the urban markets past a thousand dangers. 'In the countryside the bakers always make good bread, while in the towns and above all with the armies it is always poor....'[22] The solution put forward to combat weaknesses in the distribution system was to place revolutionary patrols at every point, but above all in the ports, at the mouths of rivers, in the river valleys, from the Flemish coasts to those of the Atlantic. Like his compatriot Isoré, this deputy Coupé was well informed on the whole supply issue, and had put his finger on the main weakness of a system whose lines of distribution were overextended and

above all which denied the frontier regions the chance of supplying themselves from the interior. In fact if the bread was particularly bad in fortified
places and in army zones, the reason lay in the deep-seated fear of exportation among the *petit peuple* of the countryside, and the reluctance of wagoners to penetrate into the military zone for fear of falling foul of the terrible
requisitioners of military transport.[23] The supply of the armies and the
fortified places would thus be one of the most important functions of the
new *armée*, because in addition to the usual difficulties which had dogged
the movement of grain throughout the eighteenth century, the authorities
of the Year II were confronted by a situation which in some respects was
entirely novel. Ancien Regime governments had never been faced with the
need to supply with food, particularly bread, from domestic sources
immense bodies of men, fighting for the most part on national soil; and the
soldier not only ate more bread than the civilian but demanded bread of
higher quality.[24] Even in the Year III the situation was not quite so acute,
for the most important armies, those of the Nord and the Sambre-et-
Meuse, were then able to live off conquered territory, producing shortages
in former Austrian territory in the Low Countries. The total number of
French mouths to feed had not changed with the *levée en masse*, but most of
these soldiers were peasants who would have been able to feed themselves
in times of peace. The problem, therefore, was one of securing enough to
feed such an enormous mass of men at the price fixed by the Maximum. As
always, the main difficulty was one of distribution rather than production,
and the presence of huge armies on the frontiers and in the West completely
disrupted a distribution system which was already precarious and overworked. The armies encroached upon the normal supply zones for the large
towns and the poor departments, and the entire map of *arrivages* had
consequently to be redrawn. At a time when the countryside was already
short of manpower and horses, traffic intensified, and the roads and rivers
witnessed an extraordinary amount of activity. To cope with such an
exceptional situation and to protect the convoys at perilous points – at the
mouths of rivers, during their river passage, near the frontiers, on the lines
of communication with the Grand Armies – hundreds of thousands of
révolutionnaires would have been required. The numbers were to fall far
short of such requirements.

II   *The 'fear of going short' and the human obstacles*

As in the Parisian supply zone, so myths, rumours, and the popular alarm
which they produced, complicated the task of the civil and military
requisitioners, already beset by the difficulties of a poorly organised and
illogical distribution system, which was particularly vulnerable in time of
war when transport was inadequate. 'Fear of going short of food', one
Alpine district noted in Ventôse Year II, 'can obstruct the movement of
grain from one town to another...'.[25] We have seen the effects of this 'fear

of going short' in the Parisian region, even among the inhabitants of the wheat-producing areas. The French peasant lived in constant terror of shortage, a hazard all too real to the eighteenth-century peasant family. Obsessed by this fact, the peasant opposed all movement of grain outside his commune, stopped convoys passing through, and forced the munici- palities to empty the boats and wagons and sell their cargoes on the spot at a price fixed by himself.

The communes most exposed to such millenarian fears were naturally those which witnessed the heaviest traffic – in other words those situated along the great waterways: the rivers Garonne, Saône, Rhône and Loire and the Languedoc canal. This river traffic was the object of particularly close scrutiny by the local *comités*, those revolutionary Arguses who were only too happy to prove their ardour and serve the interests of their fellow citizens by querying the destination of convoys and stopping them on the pretext of combating monopolisers. The *commissaires* of the communes along the Garonne and the Saône found an additional motive for scrupulousness in matters affecting the movement of foodstuffs: possible attempts to supply the 'rebels' of Bordeaux and Lyon. It was an excellent excuse for stopping and unloading shipments at one's own port, and the *commissaires* never failed to use it. Long after the two towns had been retaken, the authorities of Tonneins and Moissac, Villefranche and Chalon-sur-Saône, were still using it to question the destinations of cargoes and subject the unfortunate carriers to endless interrogation.[26] Such zeal was well calculated to discourage the merchants, constantly faced with the possible loss of their cargoes before they reached their destinations, and every large town was to be the victim of similar procedures.[27]

The authorities of these riverside towns were undoubtedly perfectly sincere in their conviction that the rich Bordelais or the big Lyon merchants were trying to starve good republicans, by snapping up all the corn of the Lauraguais and Bassigny regions for export abroad or sale to the rich of these two hated cities. For years the people of a town like Tonneins had endured the insolence of the Bordeaux commercial class; but the tables were turned by the events of summer 1793, which tarred all the Bordelais with the Federalist brush. The inhabitants of the poor communes of the Saône valley were likewise delighted at the opportunity to lay down the law to the proud Lyonnais. So widespread was suspicion of the second city of the Republic, that the *représentants* were obliged to camouflage requisitions for it as food supplies for the Army of the Alps, knowing that the patriotic authorities of the Ain, Côte-d'Or and the Haute-Saône would release supplies for the army, which they would not for the unworthy city.[28]

But the two former capitals of Federalism were not the only victims of such mistrust. The inhabitants of Montauban and Cahors would not accept the needs of Toulouse, which, according to them, was flush with supplies, despite the many requisitions made on its supply zone – the Lauraguais, Tarn and Gers areas – on behalf of the two Pyrenees Armies.[29] It was the same picture everywhere, fear mixed with distrust and considerable ill will; everyone was convinced that his neighbour was lying when he pleaded famine, and if, with Coupé, one was ready to believe in an abundance, or at least a sufficiency in grain somewhere in France, particularly after a harvest which the specialists proclaimed as adequate, no local authority would have been sufficiently imprudent or naïve to admit an excess in corn or other foodstuffs. The requisitioners had to work in the dark, faced with false declarations by district authorities and themselves ignorant of the true resources of the communes under their direction, where lying was a regular practice.

In the Paris region the less well-disposed communes were given cause to reflect by the presence of innumerable *commissaires* from the Commission des Subsistances, who wielded considerable power. In the departments far removed from the capital the *représentants* had little choice but to accept the declarations made by the departments and by the districts. In the final analysis, the communes remained independent, almost autonomous in the assessment and distribution of grain, and in the Midi it proved a positive boost to municipal *égoïsme*. From the time of the first Maximum, quite a separate economy of inter-communal exchange developed, whereby wine-producing communes exchanged their produce with wheat-producing ones.[30] Municipalities were thus concluding effective commercial treaties with each other, certain foodstuffs were being removed from normal circulation, and the large towns and the armies were the principal victims of this closed-circuit economy. It is true that some large towns, such as Marseille or Nantes, had ways of protecting themselves in this jungle, since they had a virtual monopoly over certain colonial products in short supply everywhere else – soap, sugar, oil and coffee – and the municipality of Nantes was to propose to the communes of the Bassigny region the exchange of sugar for grain. The armies, however, had nothing to exchange, and were the main sufferers, since the military requisitioners had a reputation of grabbing everything at the price set by the Maximum.

But the communes were not always content to make reciprocal arrangements. They also used reprisals: one holding back grain and merchandise destined for a neighbouring town, the other responding by forbidding all traffic to the offending town. Real economic wars were in progress, accompanying, and sometimes explaining, political and administrative rivalries between two towns struggling for control of the district or departmental *chef-lieu*. The famous conflict between Beaumont and Grenade placed a small, needy town against a bourg reputed to be rich in grain.[31] Such struggles were reflected in every district and it is not difficult to visualise the use to which the revolutionary force would be put by a commune poor in grain. Thus everything was conspiring to 'freeze' transportation and immobilise subsistences, and to the opposing interests of town and country after the introduction of the Maximum, must be added the life-and-death struggle between rich and poor departments. It is not surprising, therefore, to find the Lot and the Cantal – two of the most deprived departments of France at this time – among the most fervent supporters of the use of the revolutionary force, when their efforts to secure grain in the Corrèze, Tarn, Haute-Garonne and Gers encountered a whole series of obstacles.[32]

At the bottom of all these difficulties lay peasant calculation – the true source of such 'immobilisme'. 'The countryside in general is populated by *égoïstes*', claimed the municipality of Troyes, with considerable justification, when discussing the scarcities experienced by its market at its session of 24 September. 'On the one hand we have the moans of the farmer, on the other the casual labourer is obsessed by the fear of going short this winter. The latter's excessive fears about the future give him a kind of proprietorship over the grain of his commune, to the point where he believes that he alone has the right to dispose of it, and he becomes distressed and unruly when he sees a grain-wagon going through the streets of his village...'.[33] There could be no clearer exposition of this instinct for *immobilisme* among the *petit peuple* of the countryside, an instinct roused as much against the town as against the rich yeoman farmer, whose interest was served by the free movement of grain. But the Maximum restored rural solidarity, for then the yeoman farmer himself had little interest in supplying the urban markets, preferring instead to keep his grain stored in his barns until prices rose.

Faced with such closed ranks, the townspeople cried out for the use of force against these rural *égoïstes*. All France was affected by the struggle between town and country, not simply the communes supplying Paris. 'Citizens', Gobert and Delteil proclaimed in their address to the peasants of the departments in the East, 'your brothers in the towns have good cause to complain about you since the law of the Maximum; you came to them and received their goods at prices fixed by the law; since then the markets have remained empty and you have shown little concern about thus exposing them to the most dreadful shortages...'.[34] On 15 Brumaire, the day following the publication of this printed proclamation, the mayor of Vougy was denounced to the *comité de surveillance* of Charlieu, in the Loire, for having spoken, during a casual conversation in the *auberge*, of a civil war erupting between town and country.[35] Another token of this 'civil war' – which was none the less real for not having been declared, since it existed in the heart-felt hatred of the country people – was the denunciation by a citizen of Troyes, to the *comité révolutionnaire* of the 1st Section of the town on 14 October, of citizen Gauthier, marshal of Montgueux, 'for having uttered sinister words about the town seeking "only to scourge the country"...and that "the laws were biased towards the town" and if there were many more like him the town could go to hell...'.[36]

That 'the laws were biased towards the town' was a truism recognised as much by the towns as by the country. The law of the Maximum was passed in the interests of the poor townsman, the sans-culotte; its application was a matter of life and death to him. The interests of the countryman were scarcely considered, for many of the items he needed, and which could only be obtained in the town, were omitted from the Maximum, while all those he could produce himself were subject to it. The peasant had other ways of protecting himself: 'it would be of considerable benefit to us', declared the small *société* of Monein at its session of 3 Germinal, 'if we could get some milk, but since the cowherds prefer to make it into cheese, which is presumably bought by the rich, the poor are thus deprived of part of their subsistence...'.[37] Listen also to a member of the *comité* of Saint-Geniez in the Aveyron, who claimed at the 28 Ventôse session 'that the walnut harvest has been abundant this year, and yet there is no oil in the shops...I know well that this is not the fault of the wholesalers who have done all they can to procure it; the fault lies squarely with the farmers, who, on the pretext that they are forced to give it up and sell it at the statutory price, have failed to produce their oil at the normal time...'.[38] The peasant held back his produce, expecting prices to rise, or ceased production out of pure spitefulness; he even fed his produce to his cattle if he could not sell secretly to the rich. The policy of the Maximum was a policy of class, and to get round it was effectively to deprive the *petit peuple* of subsistence and to direct them instead to the houses of the rich.[39] The peasant thus showed himself as not only the enemy of the town, but also the ally of the rich. Rural and urban self-interest had joined forces.

The reality of this struggle between town and country, between sans-culotte and peasant (including the poor peasant producing just a little above his own needs, to sell in the markets or at the homes of individuals), was to dominate the economic action of the departmental battalions and communal companies. If we except the few very large *armées* – of the North and the Moselle – concerned primarily with military supply, these forces served the interests of their town of origin, and in general of a single commune. Even the Haute-Garonne *armée*, which, on Paganel's advice, was to be removed from the exclusive control of the Toulouse authorities, was nevertheless used by the town's Commission des Subsistances in the interests of Toulouse supply, and against the communes of the district and those of some neighbouring districts.

As in the Paris region, it was the departments and communes weakest in corn production which were the most eager to use the battalions. The departments of the Loire, Moselle, Rhône, Nièvre, Allier, Aveyron, Cantal, Lot, Gironde, Gard, Ardèche and Hérault, whose line of supply was extremely long, freely resorted to the use of force.[40] The Haute-Garonne was better supplied, but the Toulouse district alone could not supply the *chef-lieu*, which had to go as far afield as the Castelnaudary or Castelsarrasin districts, or even to the Tarn and the Gers for its grain supplies. Certain other towns had the same problem: Cahors, Montauban, Aurillac, Mont-pellier, Bordeaux, Moulins,[41] Nevers, Lille, Orléans, Grenoble, and Limoges,[42] as well as some bourgs like Saint-Bonnet-le-Château and Charlieu in the Loire.[43] All these localities recommended the use of the revolutionary force to police the markets and above all to levy requisitions, and they claimed the right to apply such requisitions to the communes under their jurisdiction.

Once again we come up against the eternal problem of administrative jurisdiction. How far did the authority of the municipality extend? All these communes insisted that it extended outside the town walls. 'We demand the authority to require supplies for our granaries from the municipalities in our canton', wrote the municipal body of the Saint-Bonnet-le-Château commune to the *comité* of Montbrison, the district *chef-lieu*. 'In two granaries we have very little or no grain; only consider your own needs.... Give us the necessary authorisation to levy requisitions throughout our canton, for the corn gathered from every corner of this commune is insufficient to provide for a town populated by workers whose only source of supply is here...'.[44] At the other side of the department, the *comité de surveillance* of Charlieu took the following decision without seeking authorisation from the district of Roanne to which it belonged: 'Since the municipalities of this canton', it declared on 25 Vendémiaire, 'are in charge of supervising the threshing of grain... [the *comité*] orders the municipalities...to see that the grain is threshed without delay...and that it is brought regularly and in the proper proportions to the public markets...'.[45] This commune, as we have seen, had been a warm supporter of the formation of revolutionary forces; like Saint-Bonnet, it was populated with poor workers who had no way of procuring foodstuffs but through the public market. The first responsibility of the municipalities was to their poor fellow citizens; it was impossible to feed them by appeals to the fraternal spirit of the countryside, since such a spirit did not exist among the farmers. They could be fed only through measures of compulsion, 'in view of the ill will of those owning stocks of grain [in the canton of Monein] surplus to their own needs', and the *société* of this commune in the Pays Basque decided 'to seek authorisation to raise an *armée révolutionnaire* from among the sans-culottes of Monein to put these requisitions into effect without delay...'.[46]

This *peur de manquer*, then, this fear of going short, was the most dangerous and most persistent obstacle to the movement of grain to the urban markets. It was an irrational, an instinctive, fear which ranged the entire *petit peuple* of the country against the acquisitiveness of the town and paralysed the internal French economy. In vain did the civilian and military requisitioners demonstrate the groundlessness of these fears; no one listened. Indeed, sometimes such fears were justified, for it was impossible to calculate fairly the resources of each department and district. The basic principle behind the major requisitions of 1793 and the Year II was to take only the peasant's surplus produce, leaving him enough to feed his family; but things did not always work out that way. Some districts – even districts that were already poor in grain – were entirely stripped of their stocks, and the poor peasants experienced real distress in the wake of draconian requisitioning. But in corn-growing areas such requisitions were not an insupportable burden, and the urban *commissaires* were correct in claiming that regions like the Lauraguais could support triple, even quadruple, requisitioning and still have stocks left, not only for personal consumption, but also for speculation and clandestine sale.[47]

The belief that grain was being exported was almost as strong as the fear of going short, and was the traditional excuse for *égoïsme* and peasant *immobilisme*. Here again it was a matter of psychology and considerable irrationality, for exportation would have been extremely difficult in the conditions of the Year II. It did however happen where the possibility existed, in frontier regions, and the authorities of such regions were the first to credit such fears. No doubt they exaggerated the extent of the exports, trying to find in such a simplistic explanation the origin of a scarcity which had other causes, sometimes even their own incompetence. It was very easy to explain the denuded markets in terms of wicked manoeuvres by a selfish few.[48] But the important point was that the *petit peuple* in the towns and countryside alike believed it, just as they believed in an artificial shortage and in speculation. The result was that the frontier departments experienced particular difficulty in supplying themselves from the wheat-producing areas in the interior.[49]

Given the persistence of these popular fears, the Maximum could only aggravate an already difficult situation, for it laid bare the reality of this conflict between rich and poor, between town and country, a conflict which determined the actions of all the revolutionary institutions during the autumn and winter of the anarchic Terror. Thus was rural egoism (or quite simply peasant interest) ranged against the town, and both were struggling for survival. If the Maximum was a success, the entire rural population would be penalised; if the statutory price of bread was not applied, the sansculotte and his family went without food.[50]

The Maximum also affected the work force, and events in Paris were reproduced in the departments. In the districts of the Nièvre, the revolutionary authorities had to intervene to stimulate the zeal of workers, who were unenthusiastic about the ten-day week, and to put an end to what they called a spirit for combining among the sailors.[51] Elsewhere too, the revolutionary detachments moved against the workers on the waterways and the wagoners. Such combinations also posed a danger to the movement of supplies in the valleys of the Yonne, the Garonne, the Rhône and the Saône, as well as in those of the Seine and Oise. Everywhere statutory wages and prices penalised the workers in transport, in the fields and in the arms manufactories; at Moulins, the Brillantais foundry workers deserted their workshops in droves to seek other positions in Saint-Etienne, Paris and Lyon.[52]

Against all these human obstacles, the military requisitioners had but one weapon: the threat of force. The needs of the armies were first on the list of priorities when it came to sending the revolutionary force against the farmers.

III *Supplying the armies*

The large, semi-official *armées*, product of collective orders of the *représentants en mission* with the Armies of the Nord, Moselle, Rhine and Alps, were
above all designed to ensure the carrying out of requisitions in favour of the
military stores near the frontiers. Since they were exclusively assigned to
the needs of military supply, they were of little benefit to the communes
responsible for raising them. Indeed, their existence was sometimes
positively harmful to the interests of civil requisitioners in the fortified
towns, since the *armées* were placed at the disposal of the military requisitioners who were the first to go into the countryside. But the military
authorities had to consider the interests of towns like Lille or Strasbourg,
for discontent among the inhabitants at the rear of the armies on the frontiers could jeopardise lines of communication, and it was sound military
policy to keep these places supplied.

All the revolutionary forces contributed to national defence by their
searches for silver, silverware and the precious metals necessary for war
manufacture. This confiscation of metals, one of the principal activities of
the sans-culotte forces, was a war economy measure; but it also had political, religious and social consequences. Most of the *armées* were likewise
involved in the requisitioning of horses. In one way or another, then, all the
revolutionary forces were associated with the economic mobilisation in
preparation for the spring military campaign. In their activities, as well as in
their origins, the departmental and communal *armées* were products of
national defence policy.

In the East in particular, power lay with the military men and with the
requisitioners for the Moselle and Rhine Armies. The commune of Metz
was the first to pay the price for this hierarchy of priorities. 'We are requisitioned by the district [of Metz] to supply its markets', reported the General
Council at its 23 Frimaire session, 'but the commune is already undergoing
military requisitioning; the corn goes to the strongest, to the military agent
who threatens us with the *armée révolutionnaire* and its guillotine, while the
civil administration can only use words and the letter of the law . . .'.[53] It is
certainly true that the *armée révolutionnaire* in the East was used exclusively
to ensure military supply, and even in the Marne, the civil *commissaires*
levied requisitions exclusively for the military warehouses at Châlons and
elsewhere.[54] The entire region would see innumerable conflicts between
civil and military requisitioners; but the latter always had the last word. In
the South-West the situation was more confused, since the military requisitioners were themselves involved in a disastrous contest in the Lauraguais,
with the two Pyrénées armies competing for food supplies in the same
districts.[55] The Pyrénées-Orientales Army had the undoubted advantage,
with the Toulouse *armée révolutionnaire* at its disposition. This was but a
foretaste of the situation which would be reproduced in the Belgian
provinces in 1795.

Gobert and Delteil, *commissaires civils* with the *armée révolutionnaire* of the East, started out by emphasising the needs of the citizens: 'Woe to those who show no eagerness to bring to their brothers in the towns those gifts which they have only been made guardians of by nature', ran their first address. 'The *armée révolutionnaire* will go through the villages and these selfish monsters will be treated as enemies of the fatherland more bitter than the Austrians and the Prussians....'[56] Some days later the Parisian Delteil informed the Minister of War: 'The *armée révolutionnaire* has had the most marvellous effect; every district hastens to supply its quota...'. The same day the two *commissaires* outlined their procedure for calculating and levying requisitions in favour of the military stores at Metz:

> One article [from the order of the *représentants* setting up this *armée* in the East] requires the *commissaires civils* to leave nothing at the disposal of the landowner and the farmer that will not be recognised, after an official hearing before the municipality, as strictly necessary for his own subsistence and that of his family, and for the cultivation of his land; this measure is essential; ... but it must be implemented as soon as possible: you must recognise that we cannot do this ourselves, an entire army would not be sufficient to cover the seven departments required to supply the Moselle Army.... It is necessary that you should appoint at once honest republicans from among yourselves or the popular *sociétés* who will hasten to your different districts.... If assessments and delivery of quotas are not forthcoming, and quickly, and if the *malveillants* hinder your progress, tell us immediately and the *armée révolutionnaire*, accompanied by its tribunal, will set out to come to your assistance....

The procurement of supplies through threats and force seems to have produced rapid results, for on 3 Frimaire the *commissaires* wrote to Bouchotte from Longwy: 'Quotas of grain, oats and fodder are arriving with great speed from all over...'.[57] A month later another Parisian also testified to the effectiveness of these measures. 'The establishment of a commission and an *armée révolutionnaire* has had the best of effects in the Moselle and in surrounding departments, quantities of grain and foodstuffs have poured in, the markets have been supplied, and all has gone smoothly...'.[58] This picture, painted by an ardent supporter of the *armées révolutionnaires*, is perhaps overenthusiastic; but the Moselle Army was supplied in the space of a month, order was maintained on the roads and in the markets, horses were sent to the army depots, and the towns in the rear of the war zone were also supplied. A frontier population thus fed as in normal times was the best guarantee of success for the military requisitions and the arrival of grain and fodder in the military stores.

We have less information on the other revolutionary forces operating in the war zones. The Lille *armée* was responsible for levying requisitions for the stores of the Flemish capital,[59] applying the Maximum in the ports, and searching for herds of cattle abandoned at the border with the Austrian Low

Countries.[60] In the Bas-Rhin department too the *armée* of Schneider was little more than an auxiliary to military requisitions, destined in particular for the military depots of Strasbourg. To achieve this end the *commissaires civils* used threat and terror, and were particularly pitiless in their search for horses, silverware and hidden supplies, and in the application of the Maximum.[61] In Grenoble the tiny company of 100 men was involved in requisitioning for the Army of the Alps which had important stores there.[62]

All the revolutionary forces, therefore, whether on the frontiers or in the interior, were involved in the confiscation of silver and metal, and in the search for caches of coins and jewels. Such measures affected the rich in particular and they had good reason to tremble at the approach of the detachments.[63] Chaix, the famous *commissaire civil* of the Corbigny and Lormes detachment, put it bluntly when he declared that 'the rich had to bear the costs of the war'.[64] In the Cantal a detachment took itself into a country house belonging to a rich inhabitant of Aurillac, 'from which they took away two huge cartloads of copper, pewter, brass, iron; they even took the ploughs... and my shaving mug, razor, scissors...'. Another witness from this department was to write at a later date that 'the detachments were forever taking citizens' purses, jewels, and all their metal objects...'.[65] The Cahors *comité* ordered one detachment of the Lot *armée* to take away all leather, silver and iron objects from religious houses;[66] in the Nièvre, Bussière, commander of one of the Clamecy detachments, took the silverware from presbytery tables and from individuals, and Chaix did the same in his territory of Lormes.[67] Throughout this department, and in the neighbouring Allier, the stern orders of Fouché were executed religiously and zealously by the *commissaires* at the head of their detachments.[68]

In the Aube, the *commissaires* from Troyes, under orders from Rousselin, carried off the bells and silver from the rural communes in the Ervy district,[69] while in the Ariège, the Toulousains were particularly brutal in their execution of these measures, spreading terror through the extremely Catholic frontier population.[70] In the Isère, 'Vauquoy's band', and some of the revolutionary detachments stationed at Lyon, took particular delight in such work, and it was accompanied by mock sermons and wilful destruction.[71] At Marmande, a detachment undoubtedly from Bordeaux seized the jewels, gold and silver of the rich.[72] Wherever they existed the detachments hunted down coins, gold, metal and anything of value. It was the main reason for the hatred they excited among the rich, who accepted with ill grace this kind of 'patriotic contribution' which to them seemed more like theft. Finally, as in the East, some of the *armées* went in search of horses requisitioned for the cavalry and for military transport.[73]

In the overall economic plan, then, all the revolutionary forces, even the smallest, played some role in the massive economic mobilisation represented by the removal of church bells (a measure already in operation before the *armées* were formed) and the collection of metal. The use of force was essential to the implementation of such measures, and in departments without revolutionary formations, troops from the first requisition were used, particularly the urban battalions which proved as zealous in such work as the political soldiers. But in the eyes of the victims it was the latter who were the main instruments of these egalitarian measures.

The protection of the forests and the suppression of forestry offences also formed part of the economic mobilisation, for coal and wood were used to stoke the furnaces of the arms manufactories and some specialised wood was earmarked for the navy, then engaged in an ambitious programme of construction. The Parisian *armée* was actively involved in this kind of forestry policing, to the point of making themselves odious to the poor inhabitants of the wooded regions surrounding the capital. We have less information on the role of the departmental forces in this sort of anti-popular repression. Indeed, in one area, the Nièvre, the *commissaires civils* intervened in favour of poor people detained on orders of the *juge de paix* for damaging the woods and collecting dead wood, notably in the Moulins-Engilbert region, where Paumier, Henriot and their colleagues, undoubtedly from a sense of pity and social justice, ordered the release of these poor wretches.[74] We do not know what happened elsewhere, but in the Aveyron the soldiers of Viton, far from protecting the woods, actually managed to set fire to them in the course of trying to burn villages accused of harbouring bandits and rebels.[75] Since forestry crimes were above all committed by the poor, the *commissaires civils*, some of whom were dedicated egalitarians, were clearly reluctant to pursue people whose actions were dictated by poverty and privation.

In short, some of the large *armées* played an important part in supplying the military stores with grain and fodder and military transport depots with horses and harness. All the departmental forces were zealous participants in the confiscation of silver and useful metals, and in the hunt for hidden stores. In every area they were useful auxiliaries to the military requisitioners and of immense service to the armies, in terms of the movement of supplies to fortified stations and the suppression of peasant discontent behind the combat zone.

IV   The role of the revolutionary forces in the supply of the communes

The *armées révolutionnaires* of the North and the East were of little benefit to Lille and Metz, the communes which had presided over their birth and supplied most of their effective numbers. The Lille district was unable to use the detachments of Dufresse to supply its markets; and although the General Council of Metz may have had the authority to borrow a detachment to police its market and the surrounding roads,[76] it never used the *armée* to levy requisitions on the communes of its district. The *armée* of the East was simply not used for communal supply.

Elsewhere, the hopes placed by the municipalities and *sociétés populaires* in this new instrument of 'communalist' subsistence policies were not entirely disappointed. The *comité révolutionnaire* of Nantes used the Compagnie Marat to pressurise surrounding villages and to protect the peasant women bringing poultry and other supplies to its markets.[77] In Toulouse the municipality and district frequently resorted to the *armée* to provision its market and force the communes of the Toulouse, Beaumont–Grenade and Castelsarrasin districts to implement requisitions in favour of the *chef-lieu*; the great expedition to Grenade in particular was partly dictated by economic considerations. In the final analysis, the Haute-Garonne *armée* was to be as useful to the supply of Toulouse as to that of the military stores.[78] In the Allier the *comité de surveillance* and subsistence commission of Moulins gave extensive power to the *commissaires civils* to levy requisitions throughout the department in favour of the markets of the district *chefs-lieux*,[79] and when the commune of Montluçon requested permission to form a revolutionary company, it was to enable it to follow the example of Moulins and levy requisitions on the communes of its own arrondissement. The departmental *chef-lieu*, anxious to retain the monopoly of an armed force so useful to its own interests, rejected such an initiative, which might have placed the little town in economic competition with itself.[80]

In the Loire too the companies were used to supply the markets of Saint-Etienne, Montbrison, Roanne and Saint-Rambert, while the Grenoble company seemed to limit its action entirely to protecting *arrivages* and policing markets, combating the activities of dealers at city gates in particular.[81] In the Montpellier district the *commissaires civils* and the officers of the revolutionary battalion served warrants for requisitions on recalci-trant farmers, and the revolutionary detachments were assigned to protect convoys of grain coming by river from the Lauraguais. The Aix battalion of 'anti-politiques' concentrated entirely on the internal policing of the markets and the struggle against hoarding. In Marseille the sans-culotte battalion was particularly concerned to prevent the clandestine traffic of goods in the rocky coastal inlets, and was undoubtedly the only revolu-tionary formation to deal with fish supplies.[82] In the Hautes- and Basses-Alpes, the companies played an intermittent role in policing the markets, but their economic action seems to have been minimal.[83] In the Haute-Loire the detachments made life difficult for farmers seeking to evade the regulations fixing the price of foodstuffs, but they did not intervene in support of requisitions for Le Puy or any other commune.[84] The Lot *armée* had no economic role (if the search for silver is excluded); and its inter-vention in the Aveyron, far from improving the plight of a department exceedingly short of food supplies, actually aggravated it, the presence of so many hungry and voracious *révolutionnaires* draining the limited supplies which had existed before this invasion. Finally, the Bordeaux battalion was certainly employed in the region around that great commune, notably watching over river traffic on the Garonne;[85] but we do not know whether it also helped to levy requisitions for its market.

Let us now follow the daily activities of one of these small communal companies. The Agen company has been chosen because we have particularly detailed records of the *comité de surveillance* and *société populaire* of that place. As the departmental *chef-lieu* of the Lot-et-Garonne, Agen is interesting on several accounts: as a river port on the Garonne, it was situated on the supply route for Toulouse and Bordeaux. Carters, sailors, itinerant dealers all passed through it on their way to Toulouse, Bordeaux, the Mediterranean and the Pyrenees; and it possessed a company of 150 fusiliers and 20 or so cavaliers – too small a force to help with requisitions, but sufficient to perform the more modest duties of policing the internal economy of the little town's immediate vicinity.

Fears of hoarding had pushed the Agen *société* into demanding the formation of a revolutionary company. At its session of 25 Vendémiaire the *comité*, 'having received justified complaints...against the merchants and others withholding goods and primary foodstuffs, thereby flouting the law of the Maximum, blatantly cheating the sans-culottes and employing fraud in the sale of these goods...', decided to form a company 'to implement all requisitions required by the *comité de surveillance*'. Two days later, on the 27th, the company was activated and its commander ordered to send six men to Brax to search the house of Ligeard, 'in which it is said that there is a considerable stock of primary produce...'.[86] In the course of that same day the officer seized goods from the homes of several Agen merchants: sail-makers, candle-makers and grocers. The main offenders were imprisoned for 24 hours. On the 28th the *comité* distributed the proceeds of a 100-livre fine to the fusiliers who had taken part in the operation.

On 1 Brumaire, 'two soldiers from the revolutionary company were introduced, one denounced citizen Magens, plasterer, for having hidden essential foodstuffs in a hole behind his bed...the other, finding himself in the cellar of another citizen, whom he didn't name, noticed a gap under his feet and thought that something was concealed in the ground...'. The Agen *révolutionnaires*, like their Parisian 'frères', were obsessed by the idea of hidden stores, and were just as zealous in the denunciation of economic offences.

On 3 Brumaire, the *comité de surveillance* imposed fines of 50 livres (to be paid to the company) on a hoarder of cooking oil and a wine merchant accused of failing to declare two barrels. The same day an innkeeper was called before it, accused of having insulted the company. The following day the *comité* received a letter from the *procureur* of the commune asking for 'six men from the revolutionary company to maintain order at the market and control hoarders'. On the 7th another shopkeeper, Madame Castex, was summoned before the *comité* for having said of the *révolutionnaires* 'that they were nothing but a joke'. She was warned that if she made fun of the citizens in the revolutionary company again, the *comité* would be obliged to place her under arrest. On the 8th the company was used to requisition horses within the commune; on the 14th it was ordered to inspect weights and measures in all the shops. On the 16th this incorruptible *comité* instructed the company to search the home of one of its own officers, Chalmel, squadron leader, suspected of having hidden stocks of grain. On 26 Brumaire, yet another woman – an innkeeper's wife – was denounced for having called the *révolutionnaires* 'pillagers and loud-mouths'. Clearly the company was not very popular with tavern folk.

By the beginning of Frimaire there was a relaxation of economic activity. Calls on the Agen traders and on the farmers in surrounding areas became rarer, whilst outright repressive operations against suspects or those reputed as such multiplied. On 15 Frimaire, however, the commander gave an account of a mission to the miller in Saint-Capraix: they had found wheat husks in the horse droppings. The same day, after the Agen carriers had refused to take corn to the Garonne port at tariffs fixed by the municipality, the *comité* ordered the company to disperse this nascent combination by forcing the protesters to walk to the port. On 22 Frimaire the company was once again looking for caches, on this occasion investigating a mysterious bricked-up door on the property of the émigré from Montpézat. Finally, on the 26th the *comité* sent a detachment to the homes of several inhabitants of Artigues, accused by a village *aubergiste* of having hidden stocks of grain.

Some members of the company, meanwhile, had themselves been denounced for having steered foodstuffs brought to market to their friends and supporters. The president of the *comité*, Mignot, was sufficiently concerned about these accusations to urge the soldiers to act with more propriety, even while showering praise on the institution itself ('the *armées révolutionnaires* are working wonders everywhere, they have the best of intentions, we should therefore sing the praises of all who serve with them'), and he declared that it was only a few individuals who took advantage of their powers to supply themselves first, notably by diverting some baskets of grapes. Like the Parisians, these 'brothers in trickery' were not incorruptible, but their misdeeds were trivial ones, and, after a long enquiry, even the Thermidorean authorities, despite their detestation for this company, as for all terrorist institutions, were only able to accuse three of its members by name.[87]

The economic action of this little company was for the most part limited to ensuring that statutory prices were observed; keeping on the backs of lard dealers, grocers or innkeepers who were reluctant to display the Maximum price-table or who refused to sell at fixed prices; searching for hidden stocks in the town or in surrounding farms; and, on one occasion, intervening against transport workers who refused to work at statutory wage rates. Repression took the anodyne form of fines or 24-hour detentions. Moreover, the company was little more than an instrument in the hands of the *comité de surveillance*, which directed all operations and, if necessary, called officers and soldiers to order. It was Terror in its mildest form. Agen, it is true, was a small peaceable town, virtually untouched by the Federalist crisis; but there were many more like it, and the economic action of this Agen company was representative of that of a dozen others of similar size, acting under orders from the *comités* to ensure observance of the Maximum, to combat hoarding and to police the markets. These were modest ends, barely touching the principal problem of food supply, which involved using force to apply requisitions and to compel the farmers to supply the markets.

This outline of the activities of the Agen company might be applied with equal validity to most of the small formations in the South-West and South-East. Such meagre results were far removed from the heightened expectations of the sans-culottes when the *armées* were formed, and were scarcely calculated 'to restore abundance'. But the conclusion that their limited numbers and means of action rendered the formations economically ineffective does not necessarily follow. They were above all instruments of propaganda and even the least independent and smallest of companies made some impact on the shopkeepers, wholesalers and farmers through the fear they inspired. The very existence of a small company was a major incentive to honour the Maximum, and the hatred which the little Agen company inspired among the *aubergistes* and grocers – usually the prime culprits in the economic fraud – is perhaps the best proof of this. The announcement of these *armées* inspired such fear that the rich landowners hid their specie and jewels on news of their approach. The tiny companies did therefore have some impact in the towns, helping maintain economic order particularly in the markets; but their influence did not extend beyond the urban centres, and only the more important formations penetrated into the countryside.

V   *Economic achievements of the revolutionary forces*

The creation of the *armées révolutionnaires* accentuated the divisions between the sans-culottes and the peasants, and as with the policy of the Maximum, it set most of the rural population against the towns. Was this increased hatred of the peasantry for the large, greedy towns – indeed for the revolutionary regime itself – compensated for by any appreciable achievement, any noticeable improvement in the economic situation, through the intervention, or at the very least, the existence of these new instruments of the Terror? This is the question which must be asked at the end of this chapter, even if no definitive answer can be supplied. We will let others answer it instead: the Thermidorean authorities, for example, were the first to express their conviction that the existence of such 'bands' had actually harmed urban supply, frightening the peasants and causing the farmers to hold back their grain from the markets out of sheer spite. It was said of Chaix, for example, that he had 'so alienated these good farmers from the inhabitants of the barren commune of Lormes, that most of them refused to provision it...'.[88] A plausible explanation, but does it necessarily prove that without such measures the country people might have supplied the markets out of a sense of fraternity or revolutionary patriotism? Under the conditions of the

Maximum such an eventuality was highly unlikely; persuasion and appeals
to patriotism had already been tried during the summer, with pitiful results.
In the final analysis, however, the effectiveness of the *armées* cannot be
calculated statistically, and we must rest content with clues rather than
quantifiable proof.

To take the Maximum first. It was impossible to apply statutory prices
for goods other than corn, wood, and perhaps wine. To have imposed the
Maximum on all merchants would have proved a superhuman task. At
most the existence of a company and the threat it posed to the shopkeepers
instilled a temporary sense of prudence; but the number of contraventions
and fines are a token of the enormity of the task, and most revolutionary
authorities had to accept the total failure of the Maximum as applied to
secondary foodstuffs. At a meeting of the Courthézon *société populaire* on
10 Nivôse, 'one member raised the motion that it was astonishing how the
Maximum, which had been established for the general happiness of the
Republic, was only observed for corn and wine...'.[89] Some months later,
after the disbanding of the popular *armées*, the Saint-Bonnet *comité* in the
Hautes-Alpes observed sadly that 'the Maximum was generally not applied,
either in the case of agricultural wage rates or of primary foodstuffs apart
from grain...'.[90] But even the application of the Maximum to grain was a
considerable achievement, and most of the authorities of the Year II recognised that grain and bread had indeed been sold at statutory prices, not only
in Paris, but throughout France.[91]

The absence of any popular unrest sufficiently widespread to jeopardise
public order must also be attributed to the departmental forces, even if they
were fortunate enough to exist during the traditionally calm season, stoppages usually only starting again in the spring. Grain and wine, transported
in large quantities, usually by water, lent themselves rather more easily to
continuous surveillance than other foodstuffs. Transport of secondary
foodstuffs such as eggs, vegetables, fruit and cheese, however, was operated
on an individual level, as a cottage industry almost, and no force in the
world could have regulated such a multitude of tiny consignments carried
on human backs or in women's baskets. Every revolutionary force played
its part in ensuring the movement of grain and fodder, and perhaps wine
also, since all were assigned at one time or another to the protection of
arrivages, or the struggle against 'dealers'. If disturbances occurred in
Brumaire or Frimaire, the cause was rural attachment to Catholicism rather
than shortages of bread or wine.[92]

That the Maximum was so ineffective where other foodstuffs were concerned was not the fault of the *armées révolutionnaires*, nor did it cast doubt
on the use of force in a controlled economy. Almost the entire country
population had an interest in circumventing the Maximum: the poor
Basque cowherd who converted his milk to cheese for sale to the rich, the
agricultural worker in revolt against Maximum wage rates, the very poor
peasant who somehow or other managed to put aside a few hundredweight

of wheat for sale to the highest bidder. The interest of every countryman –
with the sole exception of some village artisans who, like the sans-culottes,
supplied themselves from the bakers – lay in extending clandestine trade, a
trade which favoured the rich at the expense of the sans-culottes and the
urban markets. Force was therefore essential, but the means employed were
skimped and so many tiny companies could only increase the peasants'
irritation and turn them increasingly towards more furtive means. The
application of the Maximum, even by a strong regime, was probably
impossible in eighteenth-century society and in the face of entrenched local
interest. Even the municipalities tended to ignore infractions of the law for
fear of alienating their rural electors.

Perhaps the greatest achievement of the departmental and communal
armées was their confiscation, often amidst the most violent protest, of
silverware and metal needed for the war manufactories. But such success
carried its own dangers, for it resembled pure pillage too closely not to be
viewed with disquiet by moderate opinion in the towns. It was clearly
impossible to win the rich *égoïstes* over to the side of the egalitarian revolution of the Year II, but by alienating most of the country women as well,
the regime was creating additional, and perhaps unnecessary enemies.

Inside the towns themselves, the small companies did police the markets
effectively, even if some of their members occasionally abused their powers
by placing the interests of themselves or their friends first. They fought the
'dealers' and the clandestine traffic of goods to individual houses, and
thereby made the lot of the worker or the sans-culotte, obliged to buy at the
bakers and in the official markets, more bearable.

This, however, was not the real concern of the *représentants* and the
central authorities. From the latter's point of view the *armées révolutionnaires*
were particularly important because of their considerable assistance in
supplying the Grand Armies of the Nord, Rhine, Moselle and the Alps. The
armée révolutionnaire of the East seems to have been particularly effective.
The authorities had certainly supplied these frontier formations with everything necessary for speedy results, by attaching to them energetic *commissaires civils* and commissions of popular justice; and the methods employed
proved far more effective than those of the requisitioners with the Sambre-
et-Meuse Army in the Belgian provinces in 1795, who were so intensely
unpopular that famine and a peasant war were the outcome.

The *armées* of the Year II only rarely served urban subsistence policy,
except in the struggle against hoarding and in the application of the
Maximum. The farmers did indeed bring their grain to the urban markets
for a few weeks, after pressure from the garrisons, a few symbolic arrests,
and searches made of their barns. But these operations were on too small a
scale and too limited in duration to effect any major change in the difficult
market situation of the small towns. Too many conflicting duties were
heaped upon the *armées*, and Agen was not Paris, nor even Toulouse. The
small communes in the interior could not resort to blackmail; they used

their few advantages to the fullest extent, referring obliquely to the importance of traffic over their roads, and the danger of stoppages and pillage.
But the *représentants* and above all the *comités* were only seriously concerned
about fortified and garrison towns with important military stores.

There is, for example, no disputing the material advantage to Toulouse of
'its' *armée*, whose intervention clearly increased *arrivages* of grain to its
market – Toulouse was better supplied in Frimaire than in September.[93]
The cases of Lille and Metz are more debatable, but by their efforts to
ensure military supply, the two *armées* in the North and East must surely
have brought some relief to the civilian plight as well. According to
Mallarmé and his colleagues, the Bas-Rhin *armée* reopened the stores and re-
established the movement of foodstuffs and merchandise inside the
commune of Strasbourg.[94] The municipality of Grenoble declared itself
satisfied with the work of its company, notably in its protection of convoys
to the gates of the town, and in Puy-de-Dôme the *Conventionnel*, Reynaud,
declared that requisitions and the Maximum were no longer enforced after
the disappearance of the revolutionary forces.[95] In the Moselle also,
according to the Parisian, Mourgoin, the immediate outcome of the
disbandment of the *armée* of the East was a cessation in the movement in
supplies and in the application of requisitions. The municipalities, free from
the attention of the popular commissions, simply turned a blind eye to
infractions of the Maximum and the non-execution of requisitions.[96]

We must be careful, however, not to derive too optimistic a picture of the
effectiveness of these primitive instruments of a brutal economy from the
accounts of former *commissaires* and large municipalities; both the latter had
a vested interest in the retention of such forces. The *armée révolutionnaire* sent
out from Cahors, far from bringing abundance to the Aveyron, a region
deficient in natural resources, actually aggravated the shortage. The arrival
of such a mass of hungry men had the same effect as a cloud of locusts, for
Viton's soldiers were above all concerned with their own needs, and the
departmental communes which were already experiencing difficulties in
supplying their own markets could ill support the additional requisitions.[97]
Elsewhere the men set fire to barns, crops, forests and woods. Everyone
complained of the disastrous effect of the expedition on this already poor
department, and the Lot soldiers found no defenders even among the sans-
culottes of Rodez, Villefranche and Najac.

The small communes were not involved with the *armées*. They were
helpless in the face of the ill will of the farmers, and rarely secured the
assistance of the urban armed force to levy requisitions on the communes of
their cantons which had supplied grain to their markets prior to 1789. The
large towns such as Lyon, Marseille, Bordeaux, Lille, Strasbourg and
Toulouse were privileged enough to be able to link into the network of
military supply. But Vaise, Saint-Just, La Mulatière, Châlier (Croix-
Rousse) and La Guillotière had no requisitioning powers. The requisitioners
for Lyon were preoccupied with its needs, and in the final analysis, the
authorities of these little border towns – even though heavily populated and

obliged to feed a turbulent and mobile populace of carriers and ne'er-do-wells (La Guillotière in particular enjoying the same reputation as Mont-rouge and Gentilly, as the resort for all the dregs of the Lyon region) – had no other recourse than to private trading expeditions into the grain-producing areas of Franche-Comté and Bassigny. In terms of supplies Vaise held the same position *vis-à-vis* Lyon as Ivry, Choisy or Vincennes did to Paris.[98] The *représentants* may have taken some of the resources of communes like Toulouse or Metz for the army. But there was a limit to this kind of withdrawal; these towns contained important military stores and if the people of Toulouse were starving, they knew where to look for grain and flour. The higher authorities were careful to ensure that things did not come to such a pass. Furthermore, it was perfectly lawful for the Toulouse authorities to send detachments to Grenade or to the communes of its own district to enforce requisitions. But no one in high authority cared about the fate of the people of these small communes, or cantonal *chefs-lieux*.[99] In short, the departmental companies did at times serve the interests of a certain communalist policy on subsistences, but only of those communes which were important in terms of their population, their strategic situation or the presence of military stores within their boundaries.

To be of any use to the supply of Paris, its *armée* had to operate in a dozen different departments. Other large towns had to spread their net equally wide to be effective, and the *armée* of the East ranged over seven depart-ments to supply the Moselle Army. This was exceptional; most companies operated within one department, often within one district. But most were scraping the bottom of already empty barrels, and in most cases these small formations only succeeded in exporting urban shortages to the countryside and aggravating relations between sans-culotte and peasant without appre-ciably relieving the plight of the urban dweller. The communal companies operated within sight of their town of origin. The ideal would have been to have had larger *armées* operating in extended areas, like those supplying Paris or the armies on the frontiers. The movement and distribution of foodstuffs was a national problem which required solutions at national level. Simply to multiply small formations and give them restricted powers within restricted areas only aggravated the farmers and country people gratuitously, without effectively solving the problems of the urban dweller.[100] Where large-scale solutions would have been necessary, the problem was tackled only at commune, canton and district level. In poor departments – and in general revolutionary forces existed only in such departments – such a solution could have been little more than an irritant. The departmental *armées* were not an effective instrument of urban supply, because the higher authorities, instead of deciding on a real policy of force, had opted for the worst of compromises – that of rationing force and scattering it in small detachments, large enough to frighten the peasants but too small to tackle the problem at the level of naturally defined economic regions.

The higher authorities were only concerned with supplying the huge armies on the frontiers, and in matters of military supply they showed no squeamishness about employing the utmost force, despite the blatant contradictions involved in a policy which sought to mollify the peasantry in matters of internal supply, but oppressed them when it came to supplying the armies. The armies were supplied with grain and fodder during the autumn and winter, which does represent a tremendous success, and the more important departmental *armées* played a part in that success. More importantly, the regular soldier of the Year II was clothed, paid, and his wounds cared for. His clothing was frequently the product of raids by the *commissaires civils* on the rich; his bandages were secured by the same methods. Moreover, the silver acquired in such raids improved the financial situation of the regime. By such means did the departmental and communal formations contribute to the victory of Fleurus, so crucial to the preservation of the Revolution.

CHAPTER 3

The Parisian *Armée* and Repression

Repression was undoubtedly the most spectacular collective activity of the Parisian *armée* and that on which the attention of contemporaries and local historians has focused above all others. More effort was made to depict the Parisian soldier as an object of terror – with his ferocious moustache, his small bloodshot eyes – a brutal *égorgeur*, an executioner (or a judge, depending on one's point of view), than as a ruffian or a pillager. The official propaganda of the Year II and the terrorist press, which sought to frighten moderates and those of guilty conscience by representing the *révolutionnaire* as the instrument of popular vengeance, was as much responsible as the anti-terrorist writers of the Year III for creating such a misleading and exaggerated portrait.

The repressive activity of the Parisian *armée* was above all that of a political gendarmerie and manifested itself more in terms of arrests than in actual physical repression. The Parisians were rarely executioners or torturers and to call them such is to endow them with greater importance than they possessed in reality. At the very most they were assistant executioners, auxiliary torturers, or guards mounted on guillotines; they were not practitioners of collective murder. Rather their repressive role consisted of serving arrest warrants, escorting prisoners before the extra-ordinary tribunals, flanking the plumed judges of these ardently popular courts, their sabres gleaming, guarding the prisons, or spying upon the rich suspects on whom they were billeted. They resembled the *exempt* (the military policeman) or the archer of the Ancien Regime more closely than the legendary executioner, and their role in repressive missions to disaffected areas was in no way revolutionary, for the use of armed force against supposedly dangerous civilians and rebels was in keeping with the authoritarian methods of the old French monarchy.

However, the Terror was more than a method of repression; it was an entire political system, a way of ruling, one might even say a way of living. For one grew accustomed to the Terror and habit removed its force. To be effective the Terror had to be uncertain, sudden, mysterious; it had to strike with surprise and with speed. In October 1793, however, it became administrative, acquiring a bureaucracy, ministers and an extensive per-sonnel scattered throughout the departments. At the head of this vast

machine was the Committee of General Security, the ministry of arrests and
political death. Immediately under its orders were the revolutionary
tribunal in Paris and the great commissions of popular justice in those areas
recently engulfed by civil war and Federalism. There was in fact a distinct
geographic zone of the Great Repression, a vast region in which popular
judges replaced local authorities, and the administration of the repression at
town, bourg and village level fell to the *comités de surveillance* and the *comités
révolutionnaires* in the Sections. Their tools were the revolutionary soldiers,
who served warrants, carried out domiciliary visits, and on very rare
occasions were entrusted with large-scale combined operations of a military
character. The Parisian *armée révolutionnaire* was simply the instrument of
the official policy of repression. But it was a zealous instrument and official
demands for severity met with an enthusiastic response and a personal
commitment on the part of the *révolutionnaires*.

Indeed, such was the personal zeal of the Parisian officers and soldiers that
occasionally they took it upon themselves to make perfectly arbitrary
arrests without waiting for orders from the Committee of General Security,
from its subsidiary agents, or from the *comités de surveillance*. Sometimes
such abuses of power – and they were regarded as abuses even amidst the
summary justice of the Year II – involved outright swindling, with soldiers
blackmailing victims to extort valuable rewards. But those abuses fall
within the category of pillage rather than repression, and will be discussed
in another chapter. It is rather the disinterested abuse of powers which
concerns us here, the number of people arrested or liberated by the
révolutionnaires on their own initiative – for the Parisian, having assumed
sovereign authority and appropriated judicial powers, was just as likely to
liberate those who had been legally detained as forcibly to detain reputed
suspects, on the pretext that the former were good sans-culottes and victims
of unjust magistrates. It is important therefore to distinguish between
official arrests and arbitrary ones made by the detachments. Though the
latter were few in number, the scandal they caused accentuated the terrorist
reputation of the *armée*. The tally of official arrests (though incomplete, the
number made by the Parisian *armée* in Lyon proving particularly difficult to
calculate) was equally small. The *armée révolutionnaire* was simply 'a
gendarmerie like any other', and as gendarmes the Committee of General
Security had plenty from which to choose.

What distinguished the *révolutionnaire*, the political gendarme, from the
actual gendarme – whom he resembled in uniform and conditions of service
– was his personal commitment to a policy of repression aimed at certain
groups in society: ex-nobles, nuns, refractory priests, men of the law, ex-
parlementaires, *fermiers généraux*, political personages of defeated parties,
Federalists and 'fanatiques', large farmers suspected of having evaded the
Maximum (the *révolutionnaire* was particularly zealous in applying
economic repression against the 'égoïstes' of the countryside), deserters,
distributors of false *assignats*, bandits and *chauffeurs* on the major routes and

in the forests. The Parisian was also extremely accessible to the arguments
of the sans-culottes of the bourg and the village, his brothers in Revolution.
The arrest warrant was by far the most effective political weapon and in the
Year II it was deployed in particular by local revolutionaries, members of
the *comités de surveillance* and the *sociétés populaires* – for the most part in
the minority in their own localities – against *les gros*, or those whom they
claimed to be such. Almost all the repressive operations carried out by the
detachments in the cereal plains stemmed from appeals by village minorities
to the outsiders (i.e. the Parisian authorities), because for the rural sans-
culotte salvation could come only from outside. Sometimes too family
connections lay behind such appeals. One village *commissaire* wrote to his
brother (member of a *comité révolutionnaire* in a Paris Section) about the
disturbing situation in his village, menaced, he claimed, by the intrigues of
'fanatics' and 'moderates'. The brother lost no time in telling the
Committee of General Security and the entire repressive machinery was
activated. Sometimes the appeals came via friends among the Parisian sans-
culottes, who maintained close associations with the countryside. The
Gonesse district in particular, lying in the very shadow of the capital and its
supplier of bread and vegetables, experienced the effects of such constant
personal contact between village revolutionaries and terrorist personalities
in the city. Indeed it was easy for a *commissaire* of a small commune in the
Pays de France to travel to Paris and present himself to a Sectionary *comité*;
he would not even have been obliged to stop overnight. He could find a
thousand pretexts to justify the journey to his naturally suspicious
compatriots, jealous of their recently re-established autonomy. Visiting
Paris to sell his market-garden produce and buy candles, soap, brown and
white sugar and coffee, the villager who was also a zealous revolutionary
would still have had time for a small detour via the nearest Sectionary
comité, after having finished at the market and shaken hands with some
passing acquaintances at the *auberge*. This method left less evidence than
letters of denunciation, and in the northern quartiers of Paris the
Sectionary *comités* were to experience many such incidents – that is why the
Gonesse district figures so prominently in the present chapter.

There is an additional reason for this, which will be examined later when
discussing the political and social action of Ronsin's *armée* in the course of its
missions to the country. The Gonesse district was the theatre of a particularly bitter social struggle by a sizeable rural proletariat against *les gros*:
those men of the law, yeomen farmers and grain dealers who were still
solidly ensconced in the municipalities and in the district directories. For the
sans-culottes of the region, who at best controlled only the *comités de
surveillance* and the *sociétés populaires*, salvation could only come from Paris,
in the form of a repressive mission by *commissaires* from the Sections and
detachments of *révolutionnaires*, sent under the pretext of 're-establishing
internal order', temporarily undermined by incidents whose gravity had
been deliberately exaggerated. The arrests which followed restored the

balance in favour of the sans-culotte minorities, by eliminating their main opponents, who were dispatched to the prisons of Luzarches, Chantilly and Compiègne, or sent before the revolutionary tribunal in Paris.

Such interference was not peculiar to the Gonesse district, though the class-conflict aspect was more pronounced there than in other areas around Paris. But similar interventions occurred in other districts of the Seine-et-Oise and in certain communes of the Oise, Seine-et-Marne, Eure, Calvados and even the Yonne. Generally they can be explained by the accident of family relationships; but in the very interesting case of Vermenton the position of such a large bourg on the main route from Paris to Lyon provoked the intervention of two Parisian officers in inter-clan quarrels which had divided this explosive population of raftsmen, small wine-growers, spinners and rich yeoman farmers from the outset of the Revolution.

Arrest was the most effective repressive weapon. But in Lyon and its region the Parisian *armée* took part in physical repression, summary executions and wilful arson. In the great town on the Rhône, as in Brest, officers and soldiers served the summary justice of the people much more directly by sitting as judges or jurors on the extraordinary tribunals, and even more as adjoints to the *comités révolutionnaires* of the Sections. It was a tribute to their experience as Parisian terrorists.

There remains the sadly banal aspect of repressive administration: the stationing of these Parisians to guard prisons and the homes of individuals too old or too rich to undergo the rigours of detention. In some places the *comités de surveillance* positioned *révolutionnaires* as sentinels in front of the buildings in which they were meeting. But it was rare for these Parisians to be used to guard sequestrated property, which spared them the perilous temptations to which many *gardiateurs* and some soldiers of the departmental *armées* were to succumb.

Above all we must try to distinguish between the different aspects of this repressive activity, which varied as much in the degree of violence employed, the numbers of soldiers and victims involved, as in the administrative back-up – some operations having been ordered by the Revolutionary Government itself, others being the product of personal initiative by local sans-culottes or Parisian officers. All the activities of the popular armies were repressive; but there are different ways of repressing. The most common was by arrest; but even here there are many problems. Who ordered the arrests? How many were arrested by Ronsin's *armée*? To which political and social category did the victims belong? Domiciliary visits, sometimes throughout an entire town, would precede arrests. At the other end of the process the suspect again encountered the *révolutionnaire*, wielding the thunderbolts of popular justice, seated behind the table covered with green cloth, surrounded by dossiers scattered in confusion and overlooked by the empty stare of a painted wooden figure of the Republic.

I *Official instructions, personal attitudes*

'A death-cry went up. The *frères*, consumed by an inextinguishable thirst, decided that, within 24 hours, an *armée révolutionnaire* would be formed, that it would be followed by an incorruptible and fearsome tribunal, and by the fatal instrument. . . .'[1] In the autumn of 1793, this 'thirst' for blood had become a trait of revolutionary orthodoxy and the very programme of government policy. Cries for vengeance rang out from the summit of the Mountain; circulars from the two Committees to the local authorities repeatedly stressed the need to strike, forcefully and pitilessly, at the enemies in the interior. 'Some speak of arresting, transporting the counter-revolutionaries from our midst; *no, we must send them to oblivion. . .*',[2] echoed Collot-d'Herbois. At last, he declared at the announcement of the revolutionary detachment for Lyon, they could achieve '*de grandes choses* and strike a great blow' – *de grandes choses* indeed, the outcome of which would be the extermination of half the population of France's second city.[3] At the time of the formation of the *armée révolutionnaire*, Parein and Boulanger rivalled each other in severity, one demanding a guillotine to accompany each detachment, the other demanding two, and Parein boasting of having sent numerous Federalists to their death when he presided over the Commission at Angers. The words in Derché's journal, published at Caen when the Parisian *armée* first went into action, also come to mind here: 'Before rushing to the frontiers to exterminate the satellites of tyrants', Derché's friend Lindberg, a Parisian of Swedish origin, advised the Caen *société populaire*, 'let us exterminate the traitors in the interior; let us adopt courageous measures to contain them. . .'.[4] When a woman presented to the same *société* a petition for the amnesty of many Caennais detained for having taken part in the Federalist movement, the Jacobin Derché was scandalised by such an impudent demand: 'Is this the moment, when the nation has the greatest outrages to avenge, the greatest measures to take to ward off the dangers threatening liberty, for someone to venture such propositions? *Armées révolutionnaires* have been formed to bring down these enemies in the interior. . .'.[5] It was no time for clemency and unfortunate was the person who dared to express openly ideas of leniency, or re-commendations of pity; those who entertained such sentiments entertained them in private, and even the journalist, Dorfeuille, who had publicly blown the trumpet of popular vengeance by railing against the Lyonnais, showed in his letters to a friend that he was privately horrified by some revolutionary excesses.[6]

Officially at least, the public authorities and the newspapers laid down the path to be followed by the *armée révolutionnaire*, whose very name would strike terror into traitors. But the violence of these public expressions of pitiless severity contained an element of calculation, for this *armée* was above all a psychological instrument of terrorist propaganda. 'Their name alone will suffice to impress the malevolent', wrote Bouchotte optimisti-

cally to General Vialle, announcing the arrival of a detachment; while the
Honfleur authorities gave voice to the same fashionable sentiments: 'You
know that these noble sans-culottes love those like themselves and detest
égoïstes, fanatics and aristocrats of every kind; vengeance is their cry as it is
ours...'.[7]

Official propaganda also sustained the repressive ardour of the Parisians
by cries of hatred and vindications of murder in newspapers produced
specially for them. Thus on 14 Ventôse Millet and Damame, writing in the
Lyon *Père Duchesne de Commune-Affranchie* (a paper whose violence rivalled
that of Hébert's journal, on which it was modelled), gave thanks for the
beneficial effects of the repression, notably the shootings: 'Thanks to the
Revolutionary Commission and the hallowed guillotine we can now
breathe easier.... Ah! Those damned rascals of lace merchants!...how
anxious they are to keep the poor workers down, how greedy for riches....
We will send them more of our dragoons, our cannoneers, our volunteers
and make them dance the *carmagnole* to the tune of the garrison commander,
who will politely have their heads smashed in with gunfire...'.[8]

The Parisians needed little prompting to sustain their instinctive mistrust
of the great Lyon merchants. But did they necessarily support the principle
of the repression? Were they as ferocious as the government spokesmen,
who, having made terror the order of the day, seemed also to have
substituted the words 'gunning down' for 'governing'? It is difficult to
speak with certainty on this matter, for officers and soldiers alike were
eager to express their support for the official policy of severity in letters to
their *sociétés populaires*, knowing that these would be read from the platform
of the *société*, at the Sectionary assembly, or at the session of the *comité
révolutionnaire*. What they wrote to their wives or relatives, we unfortunately do not know. Writing on 26 Frimaire to the Bonne-Nouvelle
Section's *comité*, Réaume, captain of a company of fusiliers from this
Section, added the postscript: 'I told you in my previous letter that each day
the guillotine dispatched some dozens of rebels and as many more were
shot, today I can tell you that we will now be shooting hundreds each day;
in this way we will soon be rid of these scoundrels who would continue to
defy the Republic until they are executed'.[9] Is this not ample confirmation
of the sanguinary ferocity attributed by the Thermidorean historians to the
revolutionary soldiers? And is Réaume not one of those 'buveurs de sang',
like the Parisian soldier whom Prudhomme described as facing the accused
beside the judges of the revolutionary tribunal in Brest: 'His face, topped by
an enormous mat of hair and darkened by his whiskers, his eyes, barely
perceptible, gleaming, blood-thirsty...'?[10] But Réaume, in the same letter,
also expressed his impatience to leave 'this dreadful area', as if the sinister
ballets of the 'dancing master' – Declaye, garrison commander at Lyon – no
longer amused him. Can the repressive sincerity of this shopkeeper of the
rue Saint-Denis then be questioned, despite his militant terrorism, despite
his payment with his life for his faithfulness to the system of the Year II? It

seems not; for Réaume, as for many of his colleagues and the bulk of the men under his command, the Lyonnais were rebels who deserved death for having risen against the indivisibility of the Republic.

These sentiments are faithfully echoed in other letters from the revolutionary officers to their friends in Paris. Thus wrote Junius Fayet to his friend, Mazuel (himself from Lyon), on 2 Pluviôse: 'Every day Saint Guillotine purges this land of liberty of all the Federalists of the Rhône-et-Loire department, always the same activity, and *ça ira...*'. Fayet's satisfaction was shared by two other cavalry officers, who announced complaisantly to their absent chief: 'All continues to go well here, we are guillotining and shooting all the insurgents...and often have to mount horses to conduct these executions...'.[11] More suspect as evidence is the reason put forward in the Year III for disarming a former soldier of the Parisian *armée*, whom the general assembly of the Marchés Section represented as 'having applauded the shootings which took place in Lyon, and reported them with satisfaction...'.[12]

We must not, however, assume too readily a near-unanimous approbation by the Parisian soldiers of the most ferocious form of repression. There was a considerable element of conformism behind the most brutal expressions; severity was a necessary part of the good revolutionary's apparel. We know that at individual level the Parisians tried to shelter some Lyonnais and Lyonnaises, and to lessen the horrors of the repression in various ways. Later, after Thermidor, the Lyon people were to come forward as witnesses to such acts of humanity, when the soldiers were being accused of having been men of blood. Indeed one officer of the Parisian *armée* questioned the very principle of extraordinary political justice. On 16 Frimaire, one member of the Commission Temporaire came to tell his colleagues of the 'scandalous scene' he had witnessed at the *société populaire*. He had just given his support to the 'patriotic motion' of a Lyon *sociétaire*, demanding the proscription of his rebellious compatriots, when, 'all of a sudden, an individual from the *armée révolutionnaire*, said to be called Cotillon and holding the rank of captain or lieutenant, rejected the motion, declaring that *in a Republic there was no proscription*, that the counter-revolutionaries ought to be judged according to normal legal procedures...'.[13] For a moment the meeting was utterly stupefied by the expression of an opinion so contrary to current views; then the *société* went overboard to express its enthusiasm and applaud Cotillon's courageous motion. We are not told whether the applause came from the Parisian or the Lyon members present at this remarkable session.

Few *révolutionnaires* can have felt jurisdictional and humanitarian scruples as explicit as those of Cotillon, clearly a well-educated and an unusual figure. Undoubtedly not all approved of the singular horrors committed at the plaine des Brotteaux, but in some areas officers and soldiers demanded even sterner repression against certain categories of the population, and they were rarely outdone in their denunciation of counter-revolutionary language and infractions of the economic laws. Such was their hatred of nobles, refractory priests, former *parlementaires*, merchants and political personalities of proscribed parties, that they could not but approve of extraordinary laws directed against such categories. On 28 Pluviôse Captain Thunot wrote from the prison in which he was being held: 'Arriving at Compiègne, we were not surprised...to see in the *comités*, apart from the *comité révolutionnaire*, large numbers of priests and above all of nobles. Nor was it in the *comités* alone that suspects were to be found, but also in the Commune and above all in the *société populaire*, which welcomed a former comte as well as Madame la comtesse during the entire course of our stay. I was unable to contain my indignation at this and had the courage to state from the rostrum of the said *société* that it was necessary to crush the men who had always been the scourge of France...'.[14]

The same indignation can be found among the fusiliers of the Finistère Section, who lamented their demoralising inactivity in a country full of nobles and rich farmers: 'We had been told that there were many aristocrats who should be arrested, but if there were such large numbers, we received no orders...'.[15] On another occasion, Thunot, who had sent many before the revolutionary tribunal during his revolutionary career, again gave free rein to his typical sans-culotte hatred for the legal profession, describing the Compiègne authorities as composed entirely of '*procureurs* and Muscadins...'. As for the *comité de surveillance* of the same commune, they were, according to Thunot, nothing but 'a bunch of Feuillants and moderates...'.[16] So much for the new categories which the vigilant joiner would have liked to see added to the list of proscribed.

Personal prejudices, deeply rooted in the unsophisticated egalitarianism of the Parisian soldiers, were further intensified by the desire to avenge those who had fallen victim to the counter-revolutionary rebels and by the soldiers' fear that they too would become victims of the numerous, though hidden, enemies in the politically suspect regions to which they were sent on detachment. 'I have no pity for the enemies of my fatherland', declared one cannoneer from the Bon-Conseil Section, on detachment to Caen; 'because of them the blood of my brothers has flowed and still flows, all cry out for vengeance and all those who have played the part of counter-revolutionaries can play too at hot cockles.... I have just come through the department of Calvados, a department far from being entirely re-publicanised.... There [in the commune of Caen] I thought I saw all the knives of the Corday woman's partisans being sharpened, ready to assassinate the patriots...'.[17] These were groundless fears, for no revolutionary soldier was to be assassinated on mission, but they were none the less deep-seated fears with the Parisians, and were constantly renewed by the example of a Chalier or a Marat. It was a recognised fact that many Parisians leaving Paris to re-establish order in the dissident regions were easily persuaded that they risked martyrdom after facing a thousand perils. (Nor were they alone in such fears; the members of the Committee of

Public Safety were themselves convinced that their names were on hit-lists drawn up by Pitt and Wickham.)

The rich Thermidorean imagery, the royalist pamphlets issuing from Lausanne and Hamburg in the years 1795–9, and the historical literature of the 1820s which derived from them, are three principal sources for certain tendentious simplifications concerning the men and the events of the Great Terror. But they are far from accurate in depicting the soldiers of the Parisian *armée révolutionnaire* as bloodthirsty men, professional torturers, amateur cutthroats, their eyes glinting with cruelty and drunken rage. That is to put the whole group on trial. The *révolutionnaire* was no more cruel than the average urban sans-culotte, raised in the violence of Paris, a city disturbed nightly by beatings carried out by young nobles in the last years of the Ancien Regime. Actual murderers were rare in the ranks of this *armée*; and it was not sadism which prompted these shopkeepers to demand swift and exemplary justice against domestic enemies. They did not consider revolutionary justice cruel. Rather it was meant to be expeditious, and they demanded this exercise of popular vengeance as the best way of preserving the regime, threatened by innumerable plots, and themselves, living constantly as they claimed 'under the threat of assassins' knives'. When it came to repressing political crime and sending before the extraordinary tribunals certain categories of people whose professions or past political action made them suspect, the soldiers proved zealous and enthusiastic auxiliaries and contributed to the swiftness of these repressive measures by their unstinting personal commitment. All approved of the repression against the entire populace of Lyon. But at individual level they were more accommodating than the various *Pères Duchesne* and the bards of pitiless repression. Men and women of Lyon would be denounced by these soldiers, but others would be saved from the holocaust by their personal intervention. In other areas the *révolutionnaires* confined themselves to carrying out arrests, generally acting as auxiliaries of revolutionary justice and showing no signs of personal passion.

II   *The arrests*

The weight of repression was as diverse and unequal as the principle itself was arbitrary. The number of arrests made by the *révolutionnaires* varied considerably from one region to another, and it is often difficult to find, in the tangle of information, a valid explanation for the variation. Sometimes the absence of local authorities, detained as suspect, left the way clear for an extraordinary commission to make a clean sweep – which explains the severity of the repression in regions torn by civil war. Elsewhere the diversity might have stemmed from any number of causes: proximity to Paris, the activities of 'hommes de liaison', social disturbances, excessive intriguing by refractory priests, the frequent passage of soldiers, the presence of an energetic Parisian *commissaire*, fears of the government

Committees, particularly in matters concerning strategically-positioned regions. These, however, are but partial explanations, and from the geographic tally of repression in the autumn, winter and spring of 1793–4 one can state that such diversity existed without coming any nearer to explaining the reasons why. The barometer of arrests no doubt owes its sharp variations to chance, rather than to any fixed or centralised policy. The repression, like the other branches of terrorist administration, was not entirely centralised, but suffered the consequences of a certain communalist anarchy. Our first task therefore will be to describe the geographical area of the repression, .based on the number of arrests in which the Parisian *armée* was involved, either directly or indirectly. The arrest warrant was the most effective tool of the repression: everything else stemmed from it, and the appearance of the prisoner before the revolutionary tribunal, his deportation or summary execution were simply the end products. Through their implementation of arrest warrants, the Parisian *commissaires* and *révolution-naires* effected internal revolutions within the villages, sometimes in favour of the sans-culotte minorities.

Documentary sources do not permit any precise calculation of the arrests made by the Parisian *armée*. An exact tally can be made for the Noyon region, thanks to the existence of some papers of *juges de paix*, and similar statistical evidence survives for some other districts. Elsewhere, however, the most complete obscurity prevails; for example, we do not know of a single arrest made by the substantial Parisian detachment operating in the Egalité-sur-Marne district (Château-Thierry); yet they must have been as numerous there as in the other districts of the Aisne. Indeed even if we could draw up a precise list of the number of arrests made in every region where the Parisian *armée* was responsible for implementing the repression, its value would depend on the existence of similar figures for all those regions not subjected to the presence of revolutionary troops. Until a detailed study is made of the repressive action of the Committee of General Security throughout the Republic, followed by a series of local studies of the execution of the extraordinary laws in every district,[18] we have no basis for determining whether the presence of a revolutionary detachment in a given district necessarily brought about an increase in the number of arrests. We can, nevertheless, put forward a hypothesis: that the presence or absence of the *armée révolutionnaire* made very little difference to the total arrests. Messengers conveying the warrants would never have had any trouble getting some gendarme or other to implement them; the *révolutionnaires* were not indispensable, and in areas without them, just as many arrests were probably made.

It is important, however, to distinguish between arrests made by the Parisians on the orders of competent authorities, and those, less numerous, made upon their own initiative. In the first case the soldiers were merely the docile instruments of the great repressive machinery; in the second they had taken over policing powers and gone beyond their role as simple executants. To make this distinction we have to broach the extremely complicated question of the competence of the different revolutionary authorities in matters of repression.

Who were the principal victims of these arrests? Was the arrest warrant in the hands of a revolutionary *commissaire* or a Parisian officer a class weapon, permitting the sans-culottes to rid themselves of *les gros*, the men of law and their allies in the countryside? These are important questions for any assessment of the social impact of the Terror. At the start of their missions, the Parisians did indeed intend to use the policing powers entrusted to them 'to crush the enemies in the interior', in other words the particular *bêtes noires* of the sans-culottes: the rich *égoïste*, the Federalist, the moderate, the lukewarm, the noble, the man of the law. Let us see what became of these intentions.

(i) GEOGRAPHICAL DISTRIBUTION AND APPROXIMATE NUMBER OF ARRESTS
With the exception of the Lyon region, Finistère, the Loire-Inférieure, as well as the Orne, Sarthe and the Manche,[19] and undoubtedly the Saumur region, where the detachments were used in large-scale repressive operations, the map of arrests corresponds above all to the Paris supply zone, the limits of which have already been outlined. The missions entrusted to the *révolutionnaires* in the Lyon region, the Manche and in the West were quite exceptional; the overriding preoccupation of the Parisian authorities was the maintenance of peace within the area supplying the capital. Thus the two most important missions assigned to Ronsin's *armée* had as their theatre the districts of Gonesse and Rozoy-en-Brie, both of prime importance to the system of *arrivages*. If the Committee of General Security sent detachments to the Honfleur area, the districts of Louviers, Vernon and Les Andelys, as well as the riverside communes of the Haute- and Basse-Seine, the Oise, Marne and Aisne, it was because these places were closely associated with the Paris supply system. The dispatch of a detachment to Le Havre may have been prompted by different concerns, provoked as it was by combinations among those employed in the naval workshops. But once they had arrived in the Montivilliers district, the *révolutionnaires* spent their time tracking down economic crimes,[20] and we have already seen how nearly all the arrests in the canton of Vernon were provoked by infractions of the Maximum or by refusals to carry out requisitions in favour of the rural districts of the Paris department.

Far less numerous were missions, such as those to Livry, Villeblevin, Jagny, and the districts of Breteuil and Chaumont-sur-Oise (where mutinies had occurred among the troops of the first requisition), which were dictated by policing problems rather than those of supply. The *armée révolutionnaire* was above all designed to facilitate *arrivages* and to maintain peace in the communes situated in the wheat-growing regions or along the major roads and waterways converging on Paris. The *révolutionnaires* themselves conceived their goals in the same terms, and when they were assigned tasks bearing no relation to the supply of Paris, or sent to regions of no importance in this respect, they protested vigorously against what they considered, not without reason, to be an abuse of their terms of service. When the cannoneers were sent to the district of Granville, they complained to the Minister against the orders of General Vialle. It was not their role, they wrote, to combat the consequences of *chouannerie* in Normandy and Brittany, since that had no connection with the supply of foodstuffs to the Paris market. Those sent to Lyon felt that they had been betrayed, and ceaselessly demanded their return to the Paris region. Certainly they had no pity for the Lyonnais and called for their exemplary punishment; but they had better things to do than to become embroiled in repression that was above all political.

For how many arrests in Lyon were the Parisian soldiers responsible? The famous list of denouncers published at Lausanne in 1795 does indeed include the names of three or four Parisian soldiers and many more from the Nièvre and Allier battalions. But these are isolated cases beside the denouncers from Lyon itself, the detested *mathevons*, and searches in the *livres des dénonces* of the Lyon Sections and in the papers of the Commission Temporaire, will produce no further fruit. The Parisians account for no more than a dozen or so of these denouncers, as against the hundreds of Lyonnais informing on their compatriots.[21] In all probability the *révolutionnaires* had only a marginal impact on the rate of arrest in this town. As for their role in the Finistère and the other western departments, we have no statistical information whatsoever. The cannoneers, placed at the disposition of the *représentants* and the other revolutionary authorities in the Brest district, were certainly ordered to implement warrants in the rural communes around the port; but we do not know how many arrests they made.

We are, however, on surer ground when it comes to the departments in the Paris supply zone, even though we have no comparative figures, since, with the exception of Honfleur and the canton of Vernon, we do not know the total number of arrests in the area. Within this zone the Parisian *armée* arrested about 360 persons, on orders from the Committee of General Security or the local *comités de surveillance*, and only very occasionally on its own initiative. Of this total, most arrests were made in the Oise department (about 130), the Gonesse district (80–90), and the department of Seine-et-Marne (50–60). The Parisians arrested about 30 in the Eure, about the same number in the environs of Honfleur, 20 or so in the Pontoise district, about 10 in that of Saint-Germain-en-Laye, and the same at Versailles. We do not know the figures for the Aisne; in the Yonne, the soldiers arrested about 30, following unusual incidents, most of them in the two communes of Vermenton and Villeblevin.

Within each of these regions the distribution of the arrests was quite haphazard, depending on the location of repressive missions and village disturbances. Clémence and Marchand claimed that they had arrested about

100 persons during their mission to the Oise, while Mazuel's cavalry arrested 32 inhabitants in the Beauvais district. In the area around Noyon, particularly in the canton of Attichy, the Parisians acted under orders from the Noyon *commissaires*, friends of Decaisne and Gasson, and arrested about 30 people during their stay. In the Compiègne district some 20 arrests can be attributed to them, some of which had been ordered by Gaulthier, *commissaire* of the Commission des Subsistances, unbeknown to the *comité révolutionnaire* of the *chef-lieu*. In the Breteuil and Chaumont districts the cavalrymen arrested about 20 young men, mutineers or deserters, and escorted them to detention centres in the *chefs-lieux*. The detachments in the Oise thus figure most prominently in our calculations, for their number was considerable, and they remained during the entire life span of the *armée*. Another explanation perhaps for the high level of activity in this department was the existence of a main detention centre at Chantilly, to which many persons arrested in the neighbouring departments of the Aisne, Somme, Seine-et-Oise and Eure were brought, either by the detachments or by gendarmes.

Turning to the Gonesse district, here, as in the Oise, it was Clémence and Marchand who were primarily responsible for the volume of arrests which set this district apart from the others in the same department. In fact the two revolutionary *commissaires* arrested some 20 at Luzarches (where most of the suspects from the district were imprisoned), 10 at Jagny, and another 10 at Marly-la-Ville. Further missions under Briois and Sollier, and authorised by the Committee of General Security, would result in the arrests of another 10 from Jagny; while other *commissaires*, at the head of detachments, issued warrants against 20 people from Marly-la-Ville, who were accused of having been partisans of the former *seigneur*, Lallemant de Nantouillet. The expedition which the *commissaires* from the Observatoire Section took to Livry in Ventôse produced 8 or 10 arrests. The *armée révolutionnaire* was to serve a further 3 or 4 warrants in Saint-Brice, 3 in Deuil, and 1 each in the communes of Mareil-en-France, Viarmes, Boran and Royaumont. Ten of those arrested in this district by the *armée révolutionnaire* were finally to be condemned to death by the revolutionary tribunal in Paris.

The reason for the prominence of the Seine-et-Marne department in the hunting ground of the *armée révolutionnaire* was the religious revolt in the canton of Mauperthuis, which brought a widespread and severe repression upon the entire region of Rozoy and Coulommiers. The number of arrests reputedly amounted to some 300, and even if only 20 were finally brought before the revolutionary tribunal in Paris, this mini-'Vendée briarde' could well have produced the hundreds of arrests which were rumoured. The Brie *comité* ordered 10 arrests of inhabitants accused of having caused religious disturbances on former feast days. The Melun *comité*, of which Dumany, captain of the Muséum company, was a member, had 10 men and women from Echoux-Boulain apprehended for similar reasons. The Provins detachment, under Thunot's command, arrested several leading nobles who had been brought to the attention of the *comité révolutionnaire* of the *chef-lieu* by this Paris joiner – a craftsman also in denunciation. Arrests were only marginally fewer in the Nemours district; the Montereau detachment arrested the curé of Cannes and 2 or 3 farmers from the surrounding district, while the Nemours detachment, headed by the *commissaires* from the *comité* of the *chef-lieu*, had 5 or 6 inhabitants of Château-Landon arrested, following a religious disturbance. At Coulommiers the detachment commander, Lemaire, had the members of the Montesquiou family incarcerated on his own initiative, though he took the precaution of informing the Committee of General Security of his action.

In the Eure the *commissaires* of the Vernon *comité* issued 19 warrants against the farmers, for execution by the detachment under Captain Dumont's command. At Vernon, 2 people, one a bailiff, were arrested after denunciations by the Parisian soldiers; and in the neighbouring district of Louviers, it was again in the wake of a religious disturbance that the Parisians made 10 arrests there and in Pont-de-L'Arche. In the district of Les Andelys, several farmers were arrested for having caused delays in the implementation of requisitions for the rural districts of the Paris department. We do not know the precise numbers, but all were ordered by the *commissaires aux subsistances* of Paris or by the local *comités de surveillance*.

There were an estimated 25 arrests at Honfleur, 12 or 13 involving former nuns, apprehended by the two *comités* in the town on the advice of Donville, the local garrison commander and head of the revolutionary detachment. At Trouville Petit's detachment made 2 arrests, one of which was the mayor. But in the whole Pont-l'Evêque district, there were only some 30 arrests, at most, and the detachment complained bitterly about its inactivity, claiming that many nobles and refractory priests were being left at liberty. At Lisieux also, the two Sectionary *comités* called upon the detachment to execute their warrants, though we do not know how many, nor whether the Caen detachment was used to implement them.

Nor did the number of arrests in the Pontoise district exceed 30: 4 inhabitants of Vigny, 4 of Cormeilles-en-Vexin (following the destruction of a tree of liberty), 4 at Presles (on the demand of its sans-culotte minority), 4 at Vauréal, and a few isolated arrests in the communes of Frémencourt, Mériel, Auvers, Avesnes, Béthemont, Nesles and Pontoise.

The *armée révolutionnaire* saw almost no repressive action in Paris itself or in the surrounding communes, the *commissaires* of the Sectionary *comités* executing warrants themselves, or, if the need arose, applying to the National Guard. We know of only 2 persons arrested by the revolutionary soldiers in Paris. Ronsin and Marcellin, seemingly on their own initiative, had 7 inhabitants of Auteuil placed under house arrest by a small detachment. The revolutionary soldiers also arrested 2 persons at Coupvray, 1 at Neuilly-sur-Marne and 1 at Conflans, bringing the total number arrested in the department of Paris to no more than 15.

Following religious disturbances at Fourqueux, in the Saint-Germain district, the *comité* of the *chef-lieu* ordered the arrest of 6 inhabitants, one of whom was the curé, who was to be condemned to death by the revolutionary tribunal in Paris. In Saint-Germain itself, 2 Austrian prisoners-of-war were denounced and arrested by the *révolutionnaires*.

We have little information on the arrests around Le Havre. The revolutionary detachment had a former *parlementaire* brought to Paris, where he was condemned to death by the revolutionary tribunal. In the Yonne the detachment sent to Villeblevin arrested 17 people. At Vermenton, 4 arrests were made after the detachment had left, but they followed accusations made by its captain, Fauveau, to the *comité* of the Popincourt Section.

To judge by the number of arrests, therefore, the repressive action of the *armée révolutionnaire* was extremely moderate, and it does not seem to have been an indispensable instrument of the Terror, at least not in the large Paris region.[22] An energetic *comité de surveillance* could maintain the numbers and pace of arrests without its assistance; while in the Crépy district the authorities made some 60 arrests – more than in any other district in the Oise – without ever calling upon the revolutionary troops.[23] Likewise in the Meaux district, many arrests were made without help from the *armée révolutionnaire*. In places where detachments were stationed, the *comités* used them as far as they could; but there was never any shortage of gendarmes or National Guardsmen to execute their warrants.

(ii) MOTIVES FOR ARRESTS AND THE POLITICAL AND SOCIAL POSITION OF THOSE
      ARRESTED

The reasons for arrests are generally not difficult to establish; even if they are not mentioned in the margin of the warrants, they are self-evident from the status or profession of the person apprehended. If the detainee was a farmer, then nine times out of ten the offence was economic (infractions of the Maximum, delays in the delivery of grain, hoarding); if a woman, she was almost certainly accused of provoking religious disturbances. Certain categories were doomed to almost automatic arrest and proscription by the very nature of their position and their past. Such was the case with refractory priests, former *parlementaires* or *fermiers généraux*, and deposed generals (and in the Year II one had only to be a weak commander to be dismissed). Some figures were so notorious that their family name alone tells us the reason for their arrest: that of the former *parlementaire*, Duval-Déprémesnil, for example, arrested by the detachment at Le Havre and transferred to Paris, or of Bailleul, former deputy in the Legislative Assembly, by the Provins detachment;[24] it explains the dispatch of a squadron to Auvers to serve a warrant against Chéron, another former deputy, while in the Oise the *révolutionnaires* arrested and brought to Paris one Potter, a well-known porcelain manufacturer, doubly suspect as a rich man and a British subject.[25] The first three of these were condemned to death by the revolutionary tribunal. It was the same for certain professional groupings, men of the law for instance, above all former *feudistes* and village *notaires*. Sometimes the authorities responsible for the major repressive operations listed the proscribed categories: thus Fusil and Marcellin, on mission to the Montbrison district, instructed the *comités de surveillance* and the revolutionary officers to search for 'priests, foreigners, nobles and the rich', in particular[26] – a wide spread of candidates and the principal clientele of all these political operations.

However, the most common victim of the Parisian *armée* was the refractory priest, the constitutional curé (though fewer in number), and the former noble who had remained in France. Many priests, refractory and contitutional alike, would appear before the revolutionary tribunal and suffer the death penalty, along with some former nuns, alike the object of warrants executed by the *révolutionnaires*, notably in the Calvados and the Oise. Such was the fate of the curés of Luzarches, Oudaille,[27] of Fourqueux, near Saint-Germain, and Ducastelier, and of a group of Carmelite nuns, arrested in the Oise department and conveyed to prison in Chantilly by the detachments.[28] They also arrested many owners of châteaus, hiding deep in the countryside.[29] The arrest of a priest was rarely an isolated event, for in general it would also involve the arrests of a group of inhabitants, notably women, accused by the local *comités révolutionnaires* of having attended clandestine masses, roused the population against the constitutional clergy, denounced the authorities as godless and caused mobs to cut down trees of Liberty.[30] The protagonists in the affairs of Livry and Vermenton were also priests, but far more dangerous in these two cases because of the tremendous popularity they enjoyed with their flocks and the esteem in which they were held by many of the inhabitants. These arrests sometimes caused considerable commotion, and on many occasions the local or Parisian *commissaires* had to seek the assistance of the *armée révolutionnaire* after they had failed to execute warrants against figures so powerful in the countryside. A notable example was that at Fourqueux, where the *commissaires* of the Saint-Germain *comité* had to beat a retreat in the face of the almost unanimous hostility of the village, and they were only able to return with the support of a veritable army composed of gendarmes, *révolutionnaires* and National Guardsmen.[31] But such measures were the product of public-order considerations rather than determined religious persecution, and if these priests were martyrs to the faith in the eyes of their supporters, to the *commissaires* of the local *comités* they were dangerous agitators, whose ascendancy over the population permitted them to thwart the application of every revolutionary measure. The *commissaires* fought the *réfractaires* as they did the deserters whom the priests protected, and for the same reasons.

Deserters, in fact, figured prominently in the repressive programme of the *armée révolutionnaire*.[32] They were generally young men, hiding out in the secluded villages of the cereal plains, and tracked down by the vigilant members of small rural *comités* whose function was to direct the *révolutionnaires* to their victims. Mutineers were pursued in the same manner.[33] In the wooded regions of the Ile-de-France, and even more to the north of Paris, deserters had joined with others outside the law to form gangs which attacked stage-coaches and pillaged farms. These bandits also figured on the detachments' hit-list, notably in the Compiègne district.[34] Distributors of false *assignats* were also enemies of the regime; the *armée* arrested several in the Oise, Seine-et-Marne, and above all in the Aisne, the department closest to the frontier and to the Belgian forgers.[35] Travellers using false passports were a similar category (a secondary duty of the *révolutionnaires* in many areas being to inspect the passports of through-travellers), and the soldiers seemed particularly eager to arrest foreigners, usually prisoners-of-war like the Austrians of Saint-Germain, sometimes also textile manufacturers and engineers from Yorkshire, a colony of whom existed in the Montivilliers region.[36] At Coupvray and in other communes near Paris, at Taverny, Presles and Mareil, they also arrested émigré agents, former seigneurial bailiffs or intendants, and sometimes men of the law.[37] In the important affair of Marly-la Ville, the Parisian *armée* performed three successive missions to the town, and a detachment was stationed in its château; the main victims of Clémence, Marchand and the other *commissaires* who followed them were accused of having been agents of the former seigneur, either in a legal capacity or as servants in the château.[38] Many arrested under this pretext were undoubtedly victims of vendettas. The Parisians were in no position to decide one way or the other, and the real masters of repression were the village *comités* which furnished them with lists of 'dubious' personages. But the *révolutionnaires* lent a ready ear to such denunciations by the *comités*, particularly when they involved men of the law. At Honfleur, Vernon, Jagny and elsewhere *notaires*, clerks and *juges de paix* were denounced and arrested. The Parisian shared the prejudice of Thunot against 'former attorneys'.

Another category tracked down with equal vigilance by the *armée révolutionnaire* were those accused of speaking against these paladins of the Terror, and in the eyes of the soldier everyone who criticised the *armée* was, by definition, a reactionary. To the country people, as to the Lyonnais, these soldiers were 'super grasses', 'butter and cheese soldiers', and in the communes of the Oise, as at Coupvray, and above all in Lyon, some 20 people were arrested for giving vent to their resentment against the burdensome outsiders.[39]

Was there, then, a class element in these arrests? Many contemporaries said as much. Preslin, *commissaire* of the Observatoire Section and a juror of the revolutionary tribunal, who had taken his detachment to Livry, was accused, for example, of having 'caused the blood of the richest and best citizens of the commune to flow...'.[40] In the same month, Ventôse, the Finistère Section's *commissaires* had 17 people arrested, including '5 of the 7 yeomen farmers in the commune...'; 'the flower of the country...', added the hostile witness. At Jagny too (below, pp. 362 ff.), opponents of the revolutionary measures accused the leading terrorist (a woman) in the commune of being 'a dangerous agitator, who sought to attract the landless and subject them to her will...'. The supporters of this woman, the effervescent Madame Pruneau, also saw a class element behind the campaign: 'the crime of the commune of Jagny', they would later claim, 'was that it pursued with revolutionary fanaticism priests and farmers who spoke out against liberty...'.

The victims of the repression in Luzarches, cantonal *chef-lieu* in that same district of Gonesse, were listed as: 'the baker woman, Noël, a Royalist attached to the former Princes of the Ancien Regime, Brador, an advocate who pines for the Ancien Regime..., La Robignac, wife of a former noble..., the girl Bizet, an edge-tool maker and agent of the clergy, Charles Imbert, a former yeoman farmer and a gangrenous aristocrat... Boucher, one-time agent to the former seigneurs, Trossu, a surveyor [a profession particularly detested by the poor peasants and day-labourers] and an exaggerated aristocrat.... Groguet, master of ceremonies and processions...'.[41] The edge-tool maker was a sans-culotte, but the others were people of some wealth. The Luzarches *comité*, dominated by Hertizy – an extremely active terrorist and friend and correspondent of the young Vincent, Secretary-General for War – seems to have followed the recommendations of Clémence to the letter on his arrival in the commune: 'Give me the names of the rich and I'll have their guts when they're caught...'.[42] An exaggeration, undoubtedly, but one which illustrates perfectly the viewpoint of the *révolutionnaires* and of Clémence himself. The Parisian soldiers made little distinction between the *riche égoïste* and the avowed counter-revolutionary.

Nor were the examples of Jagny and Luzarches unique in this disturbed district. At Deuil, Guigne, Clémence's colleague in the departmental *comité*, accompanied by a detachment of cannoneers from the Brutus Section, arrested a substantial landowner and former district tax collector; 60 cannoneers also tried to take Trenonay, a former keeper of Monsieur's furniture stores, but he had absconded. At Mareil-en-France the detachment arrested Thiboust (or Thibault), the leading proprietor of the commune, while at Marly-la-Ville the main victims of these operations were men of the law and grain merchants.[43] Arrest was not always a class weapon, even in this district, and occasionally it was even used against sans-culotte personalities. The mayor of Viarmes was such a case, the victim of his overzealous application of revolutionary laws, whose personal enemies somehow managed to convince the *révolutionnaires* to make the arrest. The mayor's enemies were sham sans-culottes; but the Parisians were taken in by appearances.[44] On rare occasions the weapon of arrest was even turned against hyperactive officers from Paris, of whom the local authorities wished to be rid. But they were rare occasions, and in the Gonesse district, with its large population of day-labourers, repression, as applied by the Parisian *armée*, was directed primarily against *les gros*, and above all against the yeomen farmers, who in turn were actively protected by their friends in the district directory. In the Year III, Delacroix, who commanded the operations in Marly-la-Ville, was accused of having caused disturbances 'by bringing in citizens bound hand and foot' and 'glorying in the atrocities which were committed...notably in Marly-la-Ville, where he sought the arrest of municipal officers and had them sent, their wrists bound, to the Committee of General Security...'.[45]

The arrests in this district were initiated by the members of the *comités de surveillance*, the *sociétés populaires*, and to a lesser extent by the municipalities, and in September–October 1793, the victims were mostly sans-culottes: village artisans, saddlers, farriers, shoemakers, day-labourers, small proprietors, wine-growers, schoolmasters and former servants.[46] The role of the shoemakers should be emphasised in particular; village revolutionaries, installed in the *mairies* after the popular upsurge of the summer of 1793, they dominated the *comités de surveillance*, which in turn led the sans-culotte minorities in their assault on the positions occupied by *les gros*. Fénin, the celebrated mayor of Villeblevin, whose antics were the cause of the quarrels which disrupted the village, was a shoemaker; so was Brings, the dominant figure of Taverny, who was responsible for bringing in the revolutionary detachment;[47] and shoemakers made up the majority in the lists of 'terrorists to be disarmed', drawn up in the countryside during the Year III. It was an undeniable social phenomenon; like the *aubergistes*, the shoemakers seem to have had a true revolutionary vocation, and the arrival of revolutionary troops and mobilisation of the repressive machinery was very often due to their intervention.

In other regions notable for repressive action, the social character of the arrests was not quite so pronounced. Undoubtedly the arrival of the detachment at Presles and at Taverny, in the Pontoise district, brought about the arrest of the richest inhabitants and a tightening of control by the sans-culotte minorities over local authority – even if they were frowned upon by the majority of inhabitants because of their anti-Catholic initiatives. In Vermenton too, the presence of the detachment gave the advantage, momentarily, to the sans-culotte minority and its clientele of woodcutters and small wine-growers in the neighbouring communes, by locking up former notables, such as the priests, the men of the law, and the yeomen farmers.[48] In Villeblevin, those who brought about the arrival of the detachment had an obvious interest in representing the endless quarrels which had torn apart this village and the Sens district since the 1770s, as a conflict between yeomen farmers and artisans. Certainly the bulk of those arrested in Ventôse were *les gros*, and their opponents were led by a shoemaker; but there were yeomen farmers also in the opposing party, and it was the interests of a clan rather than a class which the *armée révolutionnaire* served in this particular commune.

The case of this village cannot have been unique; appearances can deceive, and all too often personal quarrels were disguised as struggles between sans-culottes and *les riches* in the Year II, or between *honnêtes gens* and *anarchistes* in the Year III. Furthermore, it was quite normal for repression to fall more heavily upon the rich than the poor, since it was in the interests of the former to evade the laws of the Maximum, just as it was in the interest of the latter to see that those laws were rigorously applied. In the area around Paris the repression was above all directed against such evaders, in other words against those who possessed surpluses of grain and other foodstuffs for clandestine sale. The *révolutionnaires* were the first to draw the conclusion that the rich country people could not be good revolutionary patriots.

Arrests on economic charges did tend, therefore, to assume a class character when farmers and dealers in grain and other foodstuffs were their primary target. But in the countryside, particularly in the departments of the Seine-et-Oise, Oise and Seine-et-Marne, just as many victims were accused of *fanatisme*, of being the henchmen of refractory priests; and those who supported the priests were not all rich. Far from it; many of those arrested by the *revolutionnaires* were ordinary women whose main crime was that of having remained too much attached to their religion. Nor were all those who denounced fanaticism, and brought about punitive expeditions by the *révolutionnaires*, sans-culottes; in the Noyon district, Decaisne and Hennon, the two men who directed the repression, along with the revolutionary officer, Gasson, were in fact relatively well off, the first a man of the law, from a very old Noyon family.[49] The repression of religious troubles, therefore, was directed against the lowest levels of the rural populace as much as the yeoman farmer, and most of the unfortunates sent before the revolutionary tribunal after the 'Vendée briarde' were in fact poor village artisans, day-labourers and farm servants.[50]

The picture changes, however, when we move away from the Paris region to the scene of the most severe repression, around Lyon. Here, in the Isère, the Loire, the Ain, and in the Saône-et-Loire, it was the rich above all who were compromised by the Federalist movement, and they who suffered the consequences. It was they whom Fusil and Marcellin had in mind when they issued their commands to the Montbrison *comité*,[51] likewise their colleagues, when they went on mission into the Isère to hunt out the wealthy. In this region, handed over to a para-revolutionary administration and where even the local authorities were powerless to protect their officials, repression assumed a particularly repulsive character unknown in the Paris region. The *décimateurs*, as Vauquoy, Théret and the other members of the Commission Temporaire called themselves during their operations in the country around Lyon, tried to use the arrest warrant as a means of extorting a kind of war contribution from the rich. It would have been futile in this respect to arrest those who did not have the means of buying their freedom, and in the communes of the La Tour-du-Pin district the full weight of the repression fell upon the most rich. The district did indeed provide fertile territory for such operations, with its substantial number of wealthy farmers, known for their avarice and *égoïsme* and proving it by their dilatory response to the supply needs of the Lyonnais.[52] Such abuses were largely confined to the most irregular communal forces, but small detachments of the Parisian *armée* may also have been used occasionally for this kind of expedition. Such was the administrative anarchy which reigned in these areas that it was quite acceptable for a former bankrupt of Grenoble, a wayward young rake who had bought a château out of his winnings at the Parisian gaming tables, to use the *armée révolutionnaire* to threaten his creditors and defaulting tenants with arrest. In the hands of the unscrupulous, and under certain conditions, therefore, the execution of the arrest warrants could become a means of blackmail.

In Lyon itself the Parisians would have liked to make repression a class weapon, with the 'mercantile aristocracy' and the 'lace merchants', whom they considered responsible for the Federalist uprising, the chief objects. Yet, even though such repression was entirely at the whim of the occupier, in the event it was not exercised in any class spirit; the victims of the Commission des Sept were mostly ordinary people and more silk-workers and small manufacturers were shot, mown down, or guillotined than merchants. The Federalist movement had its roots firmly among the people; its social composition, its very means of action – the Sectionary institutions – against the Jacobin municipality, were the same as for those leading the repression: the detested *mathevons*, the Jacobin or sans-culotte minorities, many of whom had returned to Lyon in the baggage train of the republican *armées*.[53] Even the Parisian cannoneers, usually the first to come to the aid of their sans-culotte brothers, denounced the ordinary people of Lyon, the serving-girls, the poor laundresses and small shopkeepers, whose only crime had been to have spoken out against these outsiders and defended the Federalists.[54] Far from being a class instrument, therefore, the repression in Lyon assumed the form of a huge campaign of vengeance against an entire population, accused of having conspired against the indivisibility of the Republic. It was, in effect, a campaign of depopulation.

Arrests were carried out as much in the interests of personal quarrels and village power struggles as in those of the sans-culottes or rural proletariat. The arrests also had social consequences, in that sans-culotte minorities were able to take the place of the more comfortably-off thus removed. But victories scored in such a brutal fashion were short-lived and the penalties were severe. Few of those arrested by the detachments in the countryside were guillotined, and most returned to their villages after only a few months of detention, sworn to vengeance against these sans-culotte minorities who had committed the unpardonable crime of calling upon outsiders from Paris to come to their aid. The dominance over a municipality or *comité de surveillance* which these arrests permitted the village sans-culottes was a precarious one, requiring the constant threat of force and the support of the avenging detachments to maintain it, and becoming untenable after the disappearance of the Parisian *armée* in spring

1794. The Terror and its institutions were transitory, and *les gros* lost nothing by waiting. Even before the fall of Robespierre, some succeeded in ousting the new masters, and everywhere they would be hunted down with cruel passion during the Thermidorean period. It was then that the arrest warrant and the repression were to become real class weapons, as instruments of vengeance in the hands of the *honnêtes gens*. On the pretext that in certain communes the repressive operations of the Year II had been provoked by the poor, by the sans-culottes, the Year III witnessed a real class proscription, and the terms 'poor', 'terrorist', and 'buveur de sang' became interchangeable.[55]

The really class-conscious then were the victors of Thermidor in the countryside, not the village sans-culottes of the Year II, activated as much by revolutionary patriotism as by a desire for social vengeance. It must not be forgotten that the repressive operations of the Year II were military expeditions, frequently dictated by the needs of national defence. The repression of the Year III, on the other hand (carried out without any special armed force, unless the Muscadins and *jeunesse dorée* can be counted as such, and using ordinary tribunals), had no such justification. It was rather a settling of scores, the rural bourgeoisie punishing, collectively, the village sans-culottes who had taken advantage of exceptional and transitory circumstances and used the Parisian soldiers to expel the notables from the *mairies* and install themselves in their place. The arrests of the Year II thus took on retrospectively a clearer class character than they had had in reality.

(iii)   ADMINISTRATIVE RESPONSIBILITY FOR THE ARRESTS: 'LEGAL' AND
        ARBITRARY ARRESTS

The opponents of the *armées révolutionnaires*, among them certain Jacobin patriots, had pointed to the dangers of popular Caesarism and military government developing from the multiplication of separate armed forces. These fears were shared by some members of the Revolutionary Government, whose initial concern was to ensure the strict subordination of the Parisian *armée* to its own agents, and to those in the districts, the *comités de surveillance* and the municipalities. At all cost the *armée* must be prevented from taking the initiative and making arrests on its own authority, in the villages and communes to which it was detached on mission. The danger was a real one, for in the villages the *révolutionnaires* would have the advantage of numbers, if not a monopoly of force. A cluster of men in possession of a cannon could dictate their will to an entire village, and witnesses of the expedition to Livry had good reason for claiming 'that it seemed like a return to the times of the League', the Parisians behaving 'like the armed bands which ravaged our countryside during the Middle Ages'.[56]

Was the *armée révolutionnaire* therefore destined to serve the ambitions of a few hotheaded and energetic officers, a few *commissaires* raging against the country people? Would the municipalities, particularly those composed of farmers and of men ill inclined to accept revolutionary laws, be able to resist the presence of this armed force? And in the event of conflict, which seemed inevitable in the circumstances, would the *révolutionnaires* have the mayor and municipal officers arrested and take over the government of the commune by substituting their own candidates? Such fears were perfectly understandable. But in the event they proved groundless. Only rarely did the Parisian detachments depart from their role as executors or conveyors of warrants, to establish themselves as a sovereign political police force, either in the arrest of public authorities or individuals, or, which was just as important, in liberating them. The few abuses of power of this kind even led to intervention by the Committee of Public Safety and vigorous communications from the revolutionary general staff calling detachment commanders to order. But the events did not justify this uproar, and such arbitrary interventions were consciously exaggerated by opponents of the Parisian *armée* – as was every other terrorist measure – in an effort to frighten the *honnêtes gens*.

In certain circumstances a detachment did occasionally arrest a village mayor, wearing his chain of office, and have him led away to prison under an armed guard. Indeed, in one small town a detachment commander, supported by a sans-culotte minority of the *pays*, had an entire municipality arrested. In another, a captain with his soldiers in arms broke into the meeting hall of a *comité de surveillance*, and forced it to hand over the list of suspects. Finally, in two or three localities, Parisian officers or soldiers liberated prisoners who, according to the local sans-culottes, had been victims of *les gros* and *les modérés*. All these arbitrary and illegal interventions provoked intense reactions from the local authorities, from the *représentants en mission* and from the Committee of Public Safety out of all proportion to the enormity of the crime. The record was, in fact, a modest one; the *armée révolutionnaire* was not a tool of arbitrary action.

There were both personal and administrative reasons for this. On the whole the Parisian soldiers were extremely respectful of the law and eager to obey government agents and local authorities alike. Any arbitrary act on their part was usually the result of a conflict between different local authorities and above all between municipalities and *comités de surveillance*. Besides, the Revolutionary Government had taken precautions and kept a tight rein on this powerful instrument of repression. The Parisian *armée* was above all the instrument of the Committee of General Security, and this Committee, some of whose members had always favoured the multiplication of special armies, was the source for nearly all its repressive missions. It was only in cases considered particularly serious and requiring the intervention of a major force, that the Committee of Public Safety joined with that of General Security to issue orders for such missions: the dispatch to the Gonesse district of a large detachment under Clémence and Marchand, agents of the Committee of Public Safety,[57] the expedition of Mauperthuis [58] and that of Fourqueux,[59] being examples of such joint authorisation. In each of these cases public order was threatened by the outbreak of internal rebellion, and an act of government was involved. The expedition to Lyon also involved an act of government, and was authorised by the Committee of Public Safety alone,[60] as was the dispatch of a detachment to Le Havre (naval construction falling within the jurisdiction of this Committee).[61] In other words the Committee of Public Safety became involved when the affair assumed the proportions of a military expedition or when political decisions were required. Otherwise, all regular operations by the Parisian *armée*, involving little more than its dispatch to a particular commune to arrest persons named in warrants issued in Paris by the Committee of General Security, were performed under its auspices alone. Certainly three-quarters of the total number of arrests carried out by the detachments – with the exception of the detachment sent to Lyon – were the outcome of orders issued by the great police Committee.

To ensure execution of its orders, the Committee of General Security resorted most frequently to the *commissaires* of the *comités révolutionnaires* in the Parisian Sections – institutions which progressively slipped from sans-culotte control to become little more than instruments of the Revolutionary Government.[62] The real leaders of the repressive missions were these Parisian *commissaires*, not the revolutionary officers. All the most spectacular missions, to Livry, Jagny, Villeblevin, were led by them; and in several cases they themselves had alerted the Committee of General Security and bore the main responsibility for initiating the missions. Nor was the intervention of the *commissaires* from the Sections limited to the Paris region alone; it extended much further, even as far as the southern departments, the Committee sending them as far as Nîmes and Perpignan with arrest warrants. One royalist author described Lacombe, a tailor and member of the Tuileries *comité*, as having 'denounced' and 'guillotined', 'during a short spell in the Midi. . .'.[63] The Livry expedition was to be led by Dumoustier, Goust and Bernot, members of the Observatoire *comité*,[64] that of Villeblevin by Moroy, Hardon, Baron and Gency, members of the Finistère *comité*,[65] while Chanorier and Coutelier, of the Guillaume-Tell *comité*, Gaudelot (l'Homme-Armé) and Brault (Brutus), appeared alongside the *révolutionnaires* on several occasions – at Vernon, Evreux and the surrounding areas – to execute arrest warrants.[66] Allmer and Desgault, of the Mont-Blanc *comité*, operated in Provins, Briois, Sollier and Brault again, of the Brutus *comité*, followed Clémence to the Gonesse district,[67] Desmargot (Popincourt) executed warrants in Vermenton, and Petit-Drouet from the Panthéon-Français Section also operated in the Gonesse district, a district criss-crossed by men carrying warrants.[68] Nor is this the final account, for in each case cited, the *commissaires* had asked the *armée révolutionnaire* to accompany them on their circuits – an aggravating factor in the crimes they were later to be accused of, in the proscription of the Year III and succeeding years. In fact, several of these men, all small artisans in Paris, were among the cluster of militants deported under the Consulate – a fitting tribute to the dominant influence these Sectionary *commissaires* had on the repressive missions in the Paris region.

In the execution of warrants, the Parisians came also under the authority of other *commissaires* from Paris: those sent by the Commission des Subsistances, with warrants against farmers guilty of impeding requisitions or of other economic crimes. In the Compiègne district in particular, Gaulthier, under the pretext of pursuing recalcitrant farmers, issued warrants indiscriminately, often with no bearing whatsoever on matters relating to Parisian supply and in complete disregard of the *comité de surveillance* of the *chef-lieu*. The *comité* clearly bore a grudge against this excessively active young man, and undoubtedly exaggerated his repressive role. But it is certain that he did order arrests on his own initiative in the communes of Plailly, Précy, Creil and Saint-Martin-lès-Boran, and that the local *comités* had no idea of the charges. The victims – 15 in all – farmers, men of the law and priests, were then taken by the detachments to the prison at Chantilly.[69] The authorities of the Chaumont district likewise ascribed such initiatives to Gérard (*délégué* of André Dumont), and to Bachod, another *commissaire* from the Commission des Subsistances in Paris.[70]

In the area around Lyon and in half a dozen neighbouring departments, the detachments operated under the orders of 'roving' *commissaires* from the Commission Temporaire, come to serve warrants on those denounced as Federalists. They could be seen at work, these proconsuls of the repression, near the Swiss border, in the Forez and the Beaujolais, and throughout the Rhône valley as far as the Ardèche and the Drôme.[71] Repression in this region was 'autonomous', for the Committee of General Security had effectively ceded its powers to the Commission Temporaire.

The *révolutionnaires*, then, operated either under orders from the different Parisian *commissaires*, serving warrants issued by the Committee of General Security, or from the *comités de surveillance* in the district *chefs-lieux*. However, they were not simple instruments of these *comités*, executing summonses and warrants and making domiciliary visits at their behest. Occasionally they were no more than this, when, for example, they were used by a *comité* to guard its premises. But generally the Parisians and the local *commissaires* collaborated on an equal footing, as representatives of the revolutionary institutions against the local authorities. Undoubtedly soldiers and *commissaires* felt a certain kind of affinity as agents of a repression which was their very *raison d'être*, and as members of the same sans-culotte social milieu. Whatever the reason, very close relationships often developed between the detachments and the *comités* of the bourgs and the villages, through their association in the same task of repression. At Vernon, for example, the captain and his detachment, though in bad odour with the municipality and district directory, could always count on the support of the *comité*, one of whose members, Patin, would later be accused of having been intimate with the Parisians.[72] Moreover, nearly all the arrests made by the detachment in this district were on orders from the Vernon *comité*. Such indeed was the credit of the Parisians with the latter that Halm, the battalion commander, was able to secure a summons from the *comité* against a local personality of doubtful *civisme*, the *juge de paix*, Mordant, likewise the object of a denunciation made by Halm to the Committee of General Security.[73]

In Montereau and the surrounding district, arrests were likewise made on orders from the *comité*, and it was the Nemours *comité de surveillance* which called in the revolutionary detachment to make arrests in the canton of Château-Landon.[74] Around Melun and Brie-Comte-Robert, it was the *comités* again which took the initiative in these operations, and in the departmental *chef-lieu* cooperation assumed a more intimate, more personal character, when the members of the *comité* invited Dumany, the detachment commander, to sit with them as an adviser.[75] The same thing was to happen in Lyon, where the *représentants* attached *commissaires* taken from the ranks of the Parisian *armée*, or from those of the Nièvre or the Allier, to each of the 32 Sectionary *comités* – though here it was not a case of spontaneous collaboration, for the measure had been imposed by Fouché and Collot-d'Herbois against the wish of the *comités*, which were as 'lyonnais' as the municipality.[76] In the Aisne, the municipality of Laon was to accuse the *comité* of being in league with the Parisians, for had they not joined together to oppress the *bons citoyens*?[77] Thunot, in his indictment of the public authorities in Compiègne, excepted several members of the *comité* as good patriots, even while condemning the *comité* collectively. In this district the *comité* issued orders to the detachments to search for refractory priests, bandits and dilatory farmers,[78] and this was the situation in nearly every region in which the detachments carried out repressive missions. At Honfleur, Donville acted as mentor to the Sectionary *comités* in such matters, while they in turn sent a cannoneer captain to Trouville to arrest the mayor and put an end to disturbances there.[79] In Noyon too the detachment advised the *comité* on arrests, by indicating suspects;[80] and the Le Havre detachment spent most of its time executing warrants issued by its energetic *comité de surveillance* in the communes of the Cauchois plateau.[81] Sometimes roles were reversed, and in the Loire in particular, the area of the Great Repression, *commissaires civils* dictated their wishes to the local *comités*.[82] But the *commissaires civils* were the real proconsuls of the repression, much more important than the officers or *révolutionnaires*, and on top of the normal administrative hierarchy in this region was another layer of extraordinary authorities.

We have already seen how two *comités* might co-exist in some communes, a legal one in correspondence with the Committee of General Security, the other quite illegal, formed within the *société populaire*, frequently emerging from the *comité épuratoire* which existed in every *société*. When the *armée révolutionnaire* functioned as the instrument of *comités* thus composed of *sociétaires*, abuses were rife, for it opened up all kinds of possibilities of their lording it over individuals and local authorities alike. In the communes of the canton of Attichy, the detachments followed orders from a group of pseudo-*commissaires*, members of the Noyon *société* who were totally unconnected with the *comité de surveillance* in the district *chef-lieu*. The incidents at Noyon itself, resulting in the illegal removal and arrest of the members of the municipality, likewise stemmed from this kind of collusion between the detachment and the local leaders of the *société*. According to the testimony of the town notables, hostile to Gasson and his friends, the arrests were decided upon in small committee sessions of the *société*, or in assemblies at which the armed Parisian soldiers assisted.[83] Such usurpation of judicial power by a handful of soldiers and local militants had obvious dangers, since it placed in the hands of a totally unrepresentative minority a powerful weapon of blackmail and control, and laid the ground for the development of an anarchical and irresponsible counter-power. We will return to this problem when discussing the political action of the Parisian *armée*, particularly its relations with the local *sociétés*.

In principle, then, the detachments were at the disposition of the agents of the Committee of General Security or the local *comités de surveillance*, which were responsible for indicating those to be arrested and for outlining the repressive measures to be taken. Certainly roles might be reversed, the *révolutionnaires*, more politically aware than the local *commissaires*, signalling suspects and advising the *comités*. The soldiers also had a greater personal stake in the success of these repressive measures, for they considered the presence of large numbers of suspects in the countryside – rich Parisians sheltering in their houses in the country, where supply was easier,[84] refractory priests and deserters – as an important factor aggravating the subsistence crisis in Paris itself. They were strangers in the country and had no need to pander to local susceptibilities, whereas the members of the *comités* had to live with those they had formerly sent to prison. For all these reasons the Parisians were generally more zealous in the task of proscription than the local *commissaires*, indeed even than the *comités de surveillance*. The zeal of the Parisians made them even more unwelcome with the local *commissaires*, for it highlighted their own lack of zeal and became a living reproach to the inaction of the departmental police authorities.

This fundamental difference of approach was the source of most of the conflicts between the detachments and the local authorities. The *révolutionnaires* complained ceaselessly of the timidity and half-heartedness of the municipal officers, who in turn accused the detachments of acting arbitrarily and of overstepping their authority by assuming policing powers. In Noyon, Gasson was irritated by what he considered the 'criminal indulgence' of the *comité de surveillance* towards suspects who, according to his two mentors, Hennon and Decaisne, proliferated in the area. It was, moreover, a district known to possess considerable resources and one already in bad odour with the Parisian authorities. Gasson had no confidence in this *comité* and he denounced its moderation in letters to the revolutionary headquarters, to the Marat Section and to the *représentant*, Dumont.[85] Thunot also lost patience soon after his arrival in Compiègne

with the dilatory policy of the district and municipality, and since the
révolutionnaires had been told often enough before they left Paris of the
countless enemies of the regime, particularly in the countryside, and of their
need to be constantly vigilant, to be true 'Arguses in revolution', this joiner
from the Panthéon-Français Section was convinced of his own rectitude in
declaring war against all authorities, whom he accused of having sabotaged
the repressive laws.[86] Such incidents were commonplace, arising not so
much from a taste for the arbitrary, or a desire by these small shopkeepers
for unaccustomed power, as from revolutionary patriotism and impatience
with the slowness and the waiting game played by the country people.
Since the local authorities did not seem up to the task, the Parisians took it
upon themselves to administer security measures. This was undoubtedly
the reason why some officers overstepped their powers by making arrests
on their own initiative.

The Parisian *armée* however enjoyed no policing powers; it had no right
to make decisions on arrests and still less on the release of prisoners. The
commissaires civils, such as Marchand, Marcellin and Paillardelle, on the
other hand, had full powers from the Committee of Public Safety to
take whatever security measures they considered necessary to fulfil their
duties.[87] The many arrests ordered by the *commissaires civils* were not
arbitrary, at least not in terms of so-called 'revolutionary legality'.
However, some officers and ordinary soldiers imitated these specialists in
repression, and made arrests on their own authority. At Avallon they even
ordered the liberation of prisoners, despite opposition from the *juges de paix*.
The most notorious case of such an abuse of power took place at Noyon,
again, where Gasson, the detachment commander, ordered the removal and
arrest of all the members of the municipality. In this he was supported, and
undoubtedly advised by the small terrorist clan in the *société populaire*, which
was composed largely of artisans, small shopkeepers and petty clerks, and
by a member of the *comité de surveillance* acting on this occasion without
consulting his colleagues. These measures were passed in the *société populaire*
in a tumultuous session and in the presence of the soldiers. To justify such
an act of force, Gasson and his supporters invoked the pathetic excuse that
old requisition orders, bearing the fleur-de-lis and found at the *hôtel de ville*,
proved the monarchist leanings of the municipality.[88] The Committee of
Public Safety acted immediately on receipt of news about this perfectly
arbitrary action; in a letter to Grammont, signed by nearly all its members,
it reminded the chief of the *armée*'s general staff that the armed forces, even
if 'revolutionary', were subordinate to the established authorities, and
ought not to become involved in civil matters.[89] Grammont took
immediate steps to warn the detachment commanders against a repetition of
this kind of abuse of their authority, but such warnings were not entirely
effective and the business at Noyon was not an isolated incident. In
Pontoise, the detachment, led by Edme, its captain, invaded the meeting
place of the *comité de surveillance*, extracted the list of suspects by making

personal threats against *comité* members, and demanded also the arrest of persons indicated by the vigilant Parisians. On this occasion the *comité* protested to the district. But the affair seems to have had no sequel; the government was not informed, and good relations were re-established between the detachment and the *comité*, with the latter sending the Parisians on a number of repressive operations into the French Vexin and the communes of the Oise valley.[90]

The *révolutionnaires* would also be criticised for a number of similar abuses of authority committed above all in rural communes, where they were far from the watchfulness of the *comités* in the *chefs-lieux* and freer to act as they wished. Thus in the Laon region the soldiers arrested a farmer without consulting the *comité* and municipality of the area. These in turn complained to the district, and one of the Parisians seems to have been arrested following this incident.[91] But in this department of the Aisne, it was the Chaourse affair, in the canton of Montcornet, which would have the most important repercussions for relations between the *armée révolutionnaire* and the civil authorities. Two Parisian officers, Chaumont and Martin, were convicted of having unlawfully arrested a village mayor, without a warrant from one of the policing authorities. They were to pay dearly for their initiative; their trial was an event of major importance in the history of the Parisian *armée*, and will be further discussed in Book Three, in the chapter dealing with relations between the *armée* and the Committee of Public Safety. The point at issue was one of arbitrary arrest, and the Laon magistrates sought to punish with exemplary severity this interference of the military in civil matters. The two officers had excellent excuses for their action, having been considerably provoked by a populace notorious for its ill will towards Paris; they were in fact the scapegoats for all the abuses of authority by their colleagues.

However, the initiative taken by Ronsin and the *commissaire civil*, Marcellin, in the first days of the *armée*'s existence, when they went to Auteuil, arrested half a dozen ex-nobles and former *parlementaires* in the village, and placed them in the custody of a group of *révolutionnaires*, does not fall into the category of arbitrary arrest. Marcellin was the direct agent of the Committee of Public Safety, from which he derived considerable powers; the *comité* and municipality, which had not been consulted, protested in vain against these measures and the victims remained in detention throughout the period of the Jacobin dictatorship, recovering their liberty only after the fall of Robespierre.[92] The initiative taken by Lemaire, in arresting members of the Montesquiou family in the Coulommiers region, falls into the same category, for this prudent *chef de bataillon* took the precaution of immediately informing the Committee of General Security of his action, stating his belief in the necessity of keeping a close watch on such notorious suspects. The Committee responded with a retrospective warrant made out in the name of the prisoners.[93]

Elsewhere the *révolutionnaires* were denied their prey. At Pont-de-l'Arche, a detachment broke into a church during the office, to arrest the priest and national agent. But they were forced to retreat before the threatening attitude of the people and the curé was not arrested until the Parisians had left the area.[94] Likewise, at Vernon, the efforts of the detachment to take Godcheut, the court clerk, encountered lengthy opposition from the local authorities. The *révolutionnaires*, however, had the final word, when, following their renewed accusations in the Sectionary *comités* after their return to Paris, the Committee of General Security sent a *commissaire* to the area to arrest this man of the law.[95] Similarly, in Vermenton, Legry was denounced by the officer Fauveau, but was arrested only several months later, by a *commissaire* sent by the Committee from the Popincourt Section.

The arrest warrant could be a double-edged weapon, however, and on occasion might be turned against the Parisians: Thunot's efforts to appropriate police powers and his threats against the established authorities simply set him on the road to prison in Compiègne, and Chaumont and Martin spent several years in prison for similar reasons. In almost every commune officers and soldiers were arrested and imprisoned, on orders from the municipalities or *comités de surveillance*, for acts of insubordination or economic offences.[96] Some *révolutionnaires* even appeared before the revolutionary tribunal, accused of counter-revolutionary crimes, and several were condemned to death as royalists. The so-called 'praetorian guard' could not shelter behind the Terror; they were little more than its lowly instruments, and the civil authorities rarely had trouble reasserting their authority against attempts at military encroachment.

But the arrests made by the *armée* had consequences which were less direct. Few persons were arrested on the sole initiative of the Parisians, and such arrests, being arbitrary, were rarely upheld. We cannot even state with certainty that the arrest warrant was a class weapon of the sans-culottes against the rich. Indeed, the repressive influence of the Parisian *armée* was decisive only when it was bolstered by beleaguered sans-culotte minorities in villages where the local authorities were dominated by *les gros*. By themselves the *révolutionnaires* could achieve little. But with the support of a *société*, a *comité* or a local clan composed of shoemakers, innkeepers, day-labourers, they could sweep away opposition and re-establish the political equilibrium of a commune in favour of the ultra-revolutionaries. Likewise, in many communes, the presence of the *révolutionnaires* accelerated the application of repressive measures and stimulated the zeal of the *comités de surveillance*. Their presence occasioned an increase in the number of arrests made by the local authorities, anxious to win their favour and to avoid being denounced by them for want of energy.

In the final analysis, the attitude of the *comités de surveillance* and the other local repressive bodies was decisive. In districts such as that of Crépy-en-Valois, where the *commissaires* were energetic patriots, the Parisian *armée* was not required. By the same token, when the local authorities were anxious to humour their electors, the presence of a detachment had little effect on the pace of the repression, and the *révolutionnaires* watched with helpless irritation as the law on suspects was sabotaged and former nobles and those evading the economic legislation remained at liberty. Repression was only effective when supported by local notables, by zealous militants or by village 'enragés'. That was the main lesson of the affairs of Vermenton, Villeblevin, Jagny and, in a negative sense, of Compiègne.

III   *Examples of repressive missions*

All the repressive expeditions carried out by the Parisian *armée* in the rural communes had certain things in common. In the first place, they all originated in appeals to Paris from sans-culotte, or self-proclaimed sans-culotte, minorities, and in nearly every case the dispatch of a detachment to a commune followed a request by a mere handful of its inhabitants. Thus a group of 'patriots' from Jagny came to Paris to explain to a Sectionary *comité* the tragic situation of their fellow republicans in this commune, who were threatened with 'counter-revolution'. At Vermenton an innkeeper and several artisans stopped the revolutionary officers on their way to Lyon, declaring that the municipality was controlled by notorious 'Federalists'. The former mayor of Villeblevin directed his complaints to the *comité révolutionnaire* of the Finistère Section, whose members included the brother of one of the village's sans-culotte minority. The Parisians went to Livry after some of its inhabitants had persuaded the *comité* of the Observatoire Section that their opponents in the municipality were dangerous counter-revolutionaries.[97] At Mareil-en-France, Saint-Brice and Marly-la-Ville, the intrigues of the so-called 'counter-revolutionaries' had been brought to the attention of the *comité de surveillance* of the Paris department, by villagers who had travelled expressly to Paris for that purpose.[98] Elsewhere, people from small rural communes, situated far from main thoroughfares, came to the *chefs-lieux* of the canton or district, where detachments were based, to request their intervention. Thus the fishermen and women of Trouville asked Donville's assistance,[99] while a delegation from Epone sought aid from the Meulan detachment against a group of moderates, who were persecuting good republicans.[100] In Avallon, the Parisian soldiers were accosted by some sans-culottes with lists of those to be arrested. The *juge de paix*, they claimed, was an agent of the moderate faction; he had sent 'patriots' to prison, and they called for their prompt release (see below, p. 425). Certainly the Parisian *commissaires* were flattered to find themselves appealed to as arbiters and redressers of wrongs, and were all the more prepared to respond when the suppliants appeared to be sans-culottes, and supported their petitions with bottles of wine.

Examples of calls from within the communes from minorities claiming themselves oppressed, could be multiplied over and over again. Local opinion was to pursue with particular vehemence these 'traitors to their villages', who had brought the vengeance of revolutionary justice upon the heads of their compatriots. Under the Thermidorean reaction, to have 'sought the help of the *armée révolutionnaire*', or 'called upon the revolutionary detachment', was the most frequent reason given for the disarming and arrest of those whose names appeared on the lists of 'buveurs de sang'.

These approaches generally unleashed repressive operations. But the role of the 'patriots' did not stop there: the *révolutionnaires* needed advisers, and more often than not they chose them from within the *sociétés populaires* and *comités révolutionnaires*, and instinctively avoided the municipalities. They conferred with the 'patriots', and asked *them* to draw up the lists of suspects. In reality, therefore, the direction of operations remained in the hands of the country people; the Parisians were little more than instruments or agents of transmission. For example, when soldiers were passing through the region, local sans-culottes, or those claiming to be such, would use them to channel their complaints against the local authorities to Paris, or to the great repressive commission in Lyon. The Parisians very often simply acted as their couriers. An examination of certain noteworthy incidents will bring out some characteristics common to nearly all the repressive missions.

(i) THE *ARMÉE RÉVOLUTIONNAIRE* AND THE VERMENTON AFFAIR

Vermenton was a large village of over 2,000 inhabitants situated on the main route from Paris to Lyon. In consequence, it witnessed the ceaseless passage of troops – the first circumstance permitting the discontented of the village to make their voices heard on high, even in Paris, without having to go through the district of Auxerre or the departmental administration, where their adversaries had friends and supporters. The town also had a shortage of foodstuffs,[101] which served to accentuate the differences between the sans-culottes and the rich, accused of indifference to the subsistence problems of the poor. The municipal officers were *égoïstes*, held responsible by the poorest citizens for their hunger. The same situation existed at Trouville (below, p. 424), which was also prey to clan disputes, dating back to the first years of the Revolution and polarised at the time of the Federalist crisis. Yet these words 'fédéraliste' and 'patriote' were mere fronts, behind which lay the realities of personal hatreds and family rivalries, and many calling themselves patriots simply did so because a hated neighbour had proclaimed himself a Federalist. The same positions were adopted over dechristianisation. The Vermenton affair provides the most typical example of a spontaneous operation caused by the chance passage of a revolutionary detachment. The friends of the former mayor literally ran in front of the *révolutionnaires* when they arrived on the main road from Paris. Indeed at the first word of the prospective passage of the Parisians, the villagers recognised the advantage they could draw from it and had dossiers prepared listing the crimes of the opposing party.

Three men were named by the so-called sans-culottes of Vermenton as being the leaders of the moderate party: Girault, former curé, Legry, former chaplain to Louis XVI's pages,[102] and Souflot, *juge de paix* of the canton. These men were represented as having signed a Federalist address in June 1793, and after some kind of *coup d'état*, as having set up a former Benedictine monk, one Guilbert, a straw man, as mayor and head of the municipality.[103] This 'counter-revolution' of September 1792 had removed Edme Dathé (or Darthé) from the *mairie*. He was a vineyard owner who, according to Legry's friends, had been elected mayor at the beginning of the Revolution through the support of the woodcutters, the bargemen and the poor wine-growers, to whom he had promised 'communal wood-cutting rights'.[104] To the former curé and *juge de paix*, Dathé was nothing but a demagogue; to the poorer elements of the population – with the exception of the women, most of whom supported Legry and Girault – he was an ardent patriot. Since his eviction from office, Dathé had champed at the bit, seeking ways to wreak revenge on his successors, and he can be found behind all the denunciations against the new authorities. An assiduous scribbler, he bombarded all and sundry with letters: the *société* of Auxerre, that of Avallon, the *représentant*, Maure, and even Maximilien Robespierre.[105] Certainly much of this was done out of personal spite, but Dathé also gave very detailed evidence of Souflot and Legry having spoken out against Paris during the Federalist crisis and of having been allied with the leaders of the Federalist party in Avallon. Not all his motives, therefore, were base, and such was his success in this campaign against the muni-cipality that in the autumn of 1793 the Federalist stigma was attached to the entire commune. Its reputation sank accordingly, so that even prior to their arrival at Vermenton the better-informed of the revolutionary officers would have been convinced that they were entering counter-revolutionary territory. Against sustained attacks from the former mayor, Legry and his friends tried to defend themselves by exciting popular passion against Dathé as an 'enemy of our holy religion', and by threatening to arrest those who continued to criticise the municipality.

But Dathé was not alone; he too had a party. His most resolute supporter was a woman, Agathe Devilliers (the widow Duchesne), who kept an *auberge* on the main road, and proclaimed her revolutionary patriotism by calling herself 'mère Duchesne' (a splendid way of introducing herself to these Parisian soldiers). This formidable woman had a daughter, the widow Malguiche, who helped her at the *auberge*, the 'headquarters' of the 'patriots'. Mère Duchesne was constantly in touch with the troops of the first requisition, the hussars and dragoons, whom she tried to rouse against the municipality by saying that it occupied 'a world of aristocrats'. Her *auberge* was the centre for oppressed 'patriots'; their war cry, 'Vive la mère Duchesne', became a rallying call which was repeated to the soldiers in transit, and the soldiers, copiously wined by the two female innkeepers, required little persuading.[106]

The other members of Dathé's party were Labrousse, who won the support of the woodcutters in the neighbouring commune of Jouy, by rousing them against the *égoïsme* of the municipality of Vermenton, which opposed the export of subsistences; Nicolas Gachot, a member of the *comité de surveillance* and the minority *société populaire* (there were two in this unfortunate town), who likewise played upon the sensitive issue of food shortages by accusing the municipality of being responsible 'for the terrifying position of this commune in terms of subsistences' (his brother François, whom he had sent to Paris to purchase provisions for the town, profited from the occasion to denounce the municipality to a *comité sectionnaire*);[107] and finally, Edme Monetot, adjutant of the National Guard, and a man called Pierre Doistot.

Such then were the forces ranged against each other. Legry and his friends held the stage, inasmuch as they were the legal authorities. But this advantage was offset by a major disadvantage: that of being at the head of a municipality in a period of extreme penury. They controlled the official *société populaire*; but the supporters of Dathé, finding themselves in a minority, simply formed their own *société*, which was not recognised by the others in the department. Control of the *comité de surveillance* and part of the National Guard was thereby lost by the municipality. Masters in their own territory, they nevertheless had little power outside it as long as their enemies could find an approving audience in the *sociétés* of Auxerre and Avallon. In Vermenton itself, however, Dathé and his friends were in a minority; the women supported the mayor and Legry, and the former mayor was accused – with some justification – of having spoken ill of the commune to 'outside' authorities. Thus local patriotism – that 'communalism' which was still such an important force in the Year II – worked against Dathé and his group, forcing them to appeal to 'outsiders' and to the people of the surrounding villages. Their story was that of nearly all sans-culotte minorities in the villages: unpopular and deprived of the means of action within their own communities, they further discredited themselves by appealing to outsiders – indeed, worse, by insisting on the Federalist past of many of their fellow villagers, in letters to the Paris and Auxerre authorities, they broke the law of silence; these were *histoires du pays*, not meant for the ears of outsiders. To betray the village group in which one lived was the most unpardonable of offences.

The first detachment of the *armée révolutionnaire* arrived in Vermenton on 25 Brumaire Year II. It included the cannoneer company from the Tuileries Section, commanded by Lefranc, and the fusiliers from Les Invalides, under their captain, Fauveau. Both officers were important Sectionary personalities, much respected by their general assemblies and *comités révolutionnaires*. From the moment of their arrival these two officers and their soldiers were taken over by the two women innkeepers, by Dathé, Labrousse and Gachot. On the very first evening the former mayor presented Lefranc with a copy of the famous Federalist petition. It had been prepared specially for the occasion, for the arrival of the Parisians in the commune had been expected since the time of their stormy passage through Auxerre.[108] Later Dathé would be accused 'of having, on 25 Brumaire, urged the *armée révolutionnaire* to slander the established authorities and murder the mayor and the *juge de paix*, of having used the rallying cry "vive la mère Duchesne", and attached...a civic garland to his door, and of having accompanied those same soldiers in the distribution of similar garlands for the doors of his accomplices'. The other supporters of the mayor were likewise accused of having displayed civic garlands as a means of identifying 'patriot' houses, protecting them from the ravages of the *révolutionnaires*, and by the same token singling out those of the *malveillants*.

As for the widow Duchesne, 'she spent the night with the most villainous [of the Parisians] in a disgusting orgy.... On the 26th, the soldiers, urged on by her, sought out the *juge de paix* to cut his head off...'. Mère Duchesne had been supported by her friend, Madame Boulard, who 'denounced the mayor to the *armée révolutionnaire* as partisan, and as a scoundrel, and citizen Vitry as having been in the service of the nobles...'. Dathé was no less active in trying 'to rouse the people against their magistrates by perfidious and slanderous insinuations, by representing them as bloody villainous rogues...'. Gachot, for his part, cleverly played upon an issue particularly sensitive with the lower classes: '...he reproached the magistrates for having done nothing about subsistences, and for biased distribution, leaving most of the inhabitants to live off unripe corn and bran' – which was not far from the truth in this needy commune.

Such a barrage was well calculated to impress the revolutionary soldiers, harangued for an entire evening by people who represented themselves as oppressed sans-culottes and who, moreover, plied them with drink. Dathé and his supporters were, in effect, working against time, since to achieve their ends they had to take advantage of this providential passage of the Parisian armed force. Knowing their unpopularity with the commune itself, they called a communal assembly for the 26th, before the departure of the Parisians, counting on their presence to silence supporters of the mayor and former curé, and, if the need arose, on their assistance to resist the entry of further supporters into the meeting hall. According to his Thermidorean denouncers, Monetot appears to have directed the operation: he 'urged Dathé on in his denunciations and used the sentinels of the *armée révolutionnaire* in support of Dathé's perfidious scheme...to prevent citizens entering the Maison Commune....he incited these sabre-rattling soldiers to slander the magistrates of the people and assassinate the *juge de paix*, by telling them that Souflot was a scoundrel and by pulling from his portfolio a petition and other papers which he presented to them...'.

The petition undoubtedly concerned the motion for the replacement of the mayor and the municipality, which was put to the assembly in the presence of the Parisians and after the main supporters of Souflot and Legry had been excluded. If this was the intention of the *patriotes*, the scheme backfired; indeed they were hard pressed to protect themselves against the huge crowd which had converged on the Maison Commune and tried to force its way into the assembly. In the final analysis, the presence of the *armée révolutionnaire* only served to rouse the fury of the womenfolk, much attached to the former curé, and to reaffirm village solidarity in the face of these 'étrangers'. Dathé and his friends had to rest content with sending copies of their petition and long denunciations to the department,[109] to the *société* at Auxerre and to the Committee of General Security. Even with the assistance of the Parisians, this minority had been unable to impose its opinions, and once they had gone, it was even more defenceless against its enemies.

The Parisians marched away on the afternoon of the 26th, leaving a rear guard which sent a long report to the Committee of General Security, detailing not only the divisions which had caused such a rift in the *société populaire*, but also the events which followed the departure of the main body of the detachment.[110] It told of how the supporters of the municipality had hastened to convoke a second assembly for that very evening, which might express itself freely in the absence of this outside force. Things changed for the worse for Dathé and his group, guilty above all of having approached the Parisians. They were excluded from the *société*

for having communicated with the cannoneer officers of the 2nd battalion of the *armée révolutionnaire*, for having given one of those same officers a counter-revolutionary document written by the *juge de paix* of Vermenton.... The same day, after the departure of the officers, around eleven in the evening, the people were again called out and formed into a troop in front of the church doors, one of the excluded citizens was then forced from his home by three persons calling themselves envoys of the people, and summoned to the church to preside over the *société populaire*, holding its session that same evening.... Shortly afterwards, several citizens, one after the other, ascended the rostrum with a priest, Le Gris [*sic*]...where they spoke out against the conduct of the said officers and soldiers of this *armée révolutionnaire* in their pursuit of citizen Souflot... against whom various accusations had been made and documents produced, protesting that such searches ought to have been made in the presence of...the members of the municipality and General Council.... These officers were treated like brigands, and the same day a complaint was lodged against them, and information given by the *comité de surveillance* against those who had presented the documents and made the denunciations....

The officers, Lefranc and Fauveau, for their part continued to occupy themselves with the affairs of Vermenton, writing to their Sections, to the Committee of General Security and to the *représentant* Maure, denouncing Legry and Souflot and complaining of the ill treatment they claimed to have received during their stay in the town. Petitioned from all quarters, Maure sent two *commissaires* to Vermenton on 30 Brumaire to investigate. Shortly afterwards, the Auxerre *comité de surveillance*, through the intercession of its president, Bonnard, and its secretary, Bailly, presented its observations on the situation at Vermenton to the Committee of General Security. Its report was overwhelmingly against Legry and Souflot. 'The *comité* formally denounces the priest Legris [*sic*], as suspect because of his form of existence before the Revolution, dangerous because of his intrigues and his deceitfully fanatical behaviour. Public spirit is almost non-existent in Vermenton, the patriots are few in number and this depravity of opinion is largely the work of the priest Legris; he is unworthy in our opinion of enjoying liberty much longer...'. After having stressed the isolation of the patriotic minority at Vermenton, the Auxerre *comité* laid into Souflot, 'author of a vile address to the tyrant, he abuses liberty by victimising the patriots and ought not to enjoy it...'.[111]

Despite such insistence, however, the two leaders of the moderate party were left in their positions and at liberty for some time. But Dathé and his supporters did score one success in securing the resignation of Legry's stooge, Girault, the mayor, in the last decade of Nivôse. The final denouement of the affair came only at the end of Ventôse. On the 3rd, Desmargot, a member of the *comité révolutionnaire* of the Popincourt Section, alerted as early as Brumaire by Fauveau, appeared in the town with a warrant from the Committee of General Security against the national agent.[112] On 5 Prairial, an order of Maure's removed Souflot from his position as *juge de paix*; and finally, on 19 Messidor, two *commissaires*, also from the Popincourt *comité*, came to Vermenton to arrest Legry, Souflot and Girault, and to bring them back to Paris.[113] The delay saved the three men and they were still waiting to appear before the revolutionary tribunal on 9 Thermidor. Legry and Souflot were finally tried and acquitted on 1 and 4 Fructidor; Girault in turn was acquitted by a judgement of 18 Vendémiaire Year III.

On their return to Vermenton, the first thought of these men was of revenge against their accusers. Their task was greatly facilitated by the publication of Courtois's report, in which the name of Dathé appeared repeatedly in letters from the former mayor to Robespierre. Thus was their principal enemy publicly and officially damned as a 'partisan of the former tyrant'. On 23 Pluviôse Year III, the regenerated Vermenton *société* denounced Dathé and Mère Duchesne to the *comité de surveillance* (likewise purged) 'as holding nightly confabulations' – a common accusation at the time – and the latter was also accused of having been 'an intimate and correspondent of the supporters of Ronsin, Hébert, Chaumette and Collot-d'Herbois'. But this was only the beginning: the main attack was launched the following 21 Floréal, during a communal assembly held in the presence of Mailhe. This time Dathé, Labrousse and Madame the *aubergiste* were accused of the crime of having had dealings with the '*égorgeurs de l'armée révolutionnaire*'. As elsewhere, the *journées* of Prairial unleashed a wave of repression against the former terrorist forces, and 48 hours later two gendarmes arrived to arrest the two Duchesnes, mother and daughter. Too late! They had fled, only to be tracked down soon afterwards at Châtel-Censoir. Others accused were disarmed on the spot.[114] But that was not enough. 'The indignation manifested everywhere against supporters of the late tyranny', wrote Mailhe, *procureur-syndic* of the department, on the 13th, 'requires prompt repressive measures. There is a general desire for the right accorded the Parisian Sections, to arrest all friends of the Terror, to be extended to the Departments. Their number here is not great. But their audacity and their insolence dismays all good citizens...'.[115]

After this date we lose sight of Mère Duchesne and her friends, who were the main losers in this complicated and sordid affair, so typical of most village and small-town quarrels. Doubtless, after spending some months in the prisons of Auxerre, they judged it prudent to leave the country, and like many terrorists from the Yonne, to seek anonymity in the Parisian jungle. The real victor was the former abbé Legry, who became mayor of Vermenton at the beginning of the Empire. It was a position which he still held at the time of his death on 15 March 1814,[116] which in turn released the former chaplain to the royal pages from having to make a difficult choice between the Emperor and his long-standing fidelity to the Bourbons. The real moral of this small-town saga is: better to choose your friends from among those already in office than to seek them from outside. The drama of Mère Duchesne and Dathé was that of all the sans-culotte minorities, isolated within rural populations and compelled to look for support to the towns, the *chefs-lieux* and most of all to the poorest elements in their own communes, who were often also the most malleable and impressionable.

(ii)   THE VILLEBLEVIN AFFAIR AND THE EXPEDITION OF VENTÔSE YEAR II

The Villeblevin affair is only indirectly associated with the history of the repressive activities of the Parisian *armée*, whose arrival in this commune simply marked the culmination of a long, recurrent conflict. In this tiny commune of the Sens district – much less important in terms of population and situation than Vermenton – the *armée révolutionnaire* was merely the instrument of a group of Parisian *commissaires*, who took complete control in the name of the Committee of General Security. At Vermenton the revolutionary officers had been in charge of a powerful detachment, bound for Lyon; they had the confidence of the Revolutionary Government, and their intervention was decisive. At Villeblevin, however, a tiny detachment operated during the closing days of the *armée révolutionnaire*; its role was simply that of a gendarmerie, acting under police authority in the person of the *commissaires* from the Finistère Section's *comité révolutionnaire*, who in turn were appointed by the Committee of General Security.

In the Vermenton affair, two groups were involved, roughly corresponding to two political families and two opposing social strata. There could be no mistaking the moderate character of the Legry clan, composed partly of former Federalists; whereas Dathé and Mère Duchesne represented the *petit peuple* and the poor. At Villeblevin the conflict did not fall neatly into one between *gros* and *petits, modérés* and *patriotes*. Yes, it had its village sans-culottes, its shoemaker, its ousted mayor in one group, and large farmers, men of the law, relatives of the national agent of the Sens district and some ecclesiastics in the other. The composition of the latter group was fairly typical of the municipal majorities in rural areas which, with the support of the district directories, managed to neutralise the effects of most of the revolutionary laws. However, it would be quite wrong to explain the dispute in terms of class conflict. The exceptionally bitter character of the affair was due to the presence in this isolated village of certain vindictive personalities and to the long memory of years of hate and discord, penetrating the very heart of family life.

This ferocious affair, though barely touching upon the history proper of the *armée révolutionnaire*, provides an insight into the process whereby sans-culotte minorities – or those claiming to be such – called for help from their 'frères' in Paris. The Committee of General Security would never have been alerted, had one of the supporters of the former mayor not had a brother, a member of the Finistère Section's *comité révolutionnaire*. The abundant documentation permits us to follow at close quarters a quarrel whose origins went far back into the Ancien Regime. It is important to situate such affairs in time, since in Villeblevin – as undoubtedly in many other villages during the Terror – the circumstances of the Year II polarised personal divisions and professional disputes round new political groupings: *fédéralistes* and *patriotes, modérés* and sans-culottes. The Villeblevin affair is above all the story of any village during the Revolution and the Thermidorean reaction. Take the shoemaker, turned patriot because his neighbour (who was also his cousin), with whom he had had a long-standing dispute over the boundary between their respective fields, was compromised with the Federalist group – how often we come across his like in the documentation. Or the small wine-grower, angry at the way the district directory defended the big farming interests, who nevertheless did not stand up for those of the small proprietor, because he had scores to settle with the former sans-culotte mayor. Such polarisations are difficult to trace precisely, but one feels them pulsating below and through the catch-all terms of 'patriote' and 'modéré'. At village level the Revolution provided the occasion for settling old grudges; the intervention of the *armée révolutionnaire* was the final act in a long series of petty quarrels and rural jealousies, and the Parisian soldiers were strangely innocent next to the crafty village politicians who had called them in. Above all the expedition to Villeblevin demonstrates how rural clans used the Terror and its instruments to settle scores with personal enemies.

Finally, in terms of the history of the Terror itself, it is worth noting that even in Ventôse, at a time when government policy was turning in favour of the large farmers, the Committee of General Security did not hesitate to send the armed force into a village in the Yonne to arrest 17 persons, the flower of the countryside, mostly yeomen farmers and men of the law. Thus, on the eve of the disappearance of the Parisian *armée*, the great police committee had in no way abandoned the use of those measures of force demanded by the Sectionary assemblies. On the contrary, in confiding the execution of the warrants, and even the right to arrest whom they wished, to the *commissaires* from the Finistère Section, Vadier and his colleagues were giving in to the repeated demands of one of the most active Sections in the capital in favour of expanding the Terror. In the course of the same month, the Finistère Section continued its campaign by demanding the establishment of commissions of popular justice to follow the detachments. The expedition to Villeblevin was consequently a personal victory for the militants of that Section.[117]

Let us look, first of all, at the personalities involved. On one side was the former curé, Lombard, aged sixty-three in the Year II, and having served the Villeblevin church from 1778 until 5 Ventôse Year II, when it was forcibly closed. Lombard, whose nephew was a grocer in the Guillaume-Tell Section in Paris, came from a comfortable background. His adversaries even claimed him to be a moneyed man, one who would have liked to get rid of his curate, some years before the Revolution, in order to keep the salary for himself. Whether or not this was so, the curate certainly allowed himself to be enlisted into the clan opposed to the curé. Lombard was undoubtedly an intransigent, hot-tempered and violent man, pugnaciously conducting the defence of his ministry and the Catholic religion and wielding immense influence over the feminine population of Villeblevin. Such was the confidence of his fellow citizens in him, that he was made *procureur* of the commune, and his protégé, the former Victorin monk, Duchesne, was made mayor. The two were removed in November 1791, when the shoemaker Fénin, Lombard's principal enemy, was elected mayor – which ensured the artisan of the former curé's undying hatred. Lombard was at the centre of the bitter struggle in the village between the supporters and the opponents of Catholicism, at the time of the particularly ostentatious celebrations of the Fête-Dieu in June 1793, when some 'unknowns' denounced to the Parisian authorities, and to the *comité de surveillance* at Sens, the 'fanatical spirit' of a group of inhabitants of the commune.

The leader of the opposing group, Etienne Fénin, a shoemaker and proprietor, was just as intransigent and hot-tempered as the terrible old priest. Before the Revolution he had been official receiver to the community; in June 1791 he was named an elector to go to Auxerre, and on 13 November was elected mayor. He remained in charge of the municipality until Brumaire Year II, when he was suspended by the district of Sens, following a number of complaints about his management of municipal affairs. He was accused of refusing to submit his accounts as receiver, but most of all of executing the laws against the confraternities with excessive zeal. Fénin was one of those inveterate anticlericals found in many small isolated communities. The circumstances of the Revolution and the war against monarchist Europe favoured his kind, placing the supporters of Catholicism under suspicion of complicity with the enemies of revolutionary France, and accelerating the application of anti-religious measures. Fénin was criticised not so much for having executed the laws suppressing the confraternities, which were immensely popular in this part of the Yonne – indeed, as mayor, it would have been dangerous for him to have avoided their execution – as for having done so with obvious glee. Fénin was devoid of subtlety and certain of his adversaries, some based in the district of Sens, considered him a dangerous rabble-rouser who would have to be removed from the *mairie*. Having already cut himself off from the majority of the inhabitants by his passionate hatred of the confraternities and his denunciations after the Fête-Dieu, Fénin further isolated himself within a community already suffering from subsistence problems,[118] by applying the economic legislation in favour of Paris, and the requisitions in favour of Auxerre, with a rigour unusual in rural authorities. Undoubtedly such zeal won him the plaudits of the Auxerre sans-culottes, the *société populaire* of the *chef-lieu*, and some Parisian *commissaires* who considered Fénin and his few friends 'workers like themselves'.[119] But ultimately such conflicts were decided locally, and the mayor, the municipality and the *comité de surveillance* of Villeblevin were already detested by most of its inhabitants before the events which caused the intervention of the *armée révolutionnaire*.

These then were the two ringleaders, each with his allies inside and outside the village. Lombard, however, was better placed in this respect. In the village he had the support of the richest man in the region, the seventy-year-old Georges Lorillon, a major farmer, whose brother, Nicolas, was administrator of the district of Sens.[120] In September 1793, assisted by the artisan-dominated *comités de surveillance* of Villeblevin and Villeneuve-la-Guyard, Fénin succeeded in having Lorillon arrested. But he was to pay dearly for his victory, for Nicolas secured not only the release of his brother, but the replacement of the two *comités*, for abusing their powers. The great strength of the Lombard and Lorillon party lay in the assistance it could command from the district directory, just as at Jagny the opponents of Madame Pruneau and the sans-culotte party could count on the district of Gonesse. The other leaders of this group were the two Tonnelliers, father and son (the former the brother-in-law of the Lorillons); Cortet, servant of Lombard; Chamarand, a former curé; Régnier, a pensioner of 'Prince Charles', and a man of private means; and Lafollye, a wine-grower and farmer whom his party succeeded in placing at the head of the municipality following the removal of Fénin in Brumaire. These were not on the whole sans-culottes, and such men would hardly approve of the economic measures to supply Auxerre and Paris. However much Lombard claimed 'always to have executed the laws and ensured that his fellow citizens did likewise, by pointing out to them the benefits of the Revolution such as the elimination of the salt tax, the customs duties and feudal rights',[121] the former curé and his friends, the farmers and the well-to-do, did not consider requisitions and quotas among the benefits of the Revolution, and by warning their fellow citizens against the removal of grain, it was easy for them to stir up opinion against the municipality and a *comité de surveillance* composed of sans-culottes.

By summer 1793 Fénin and his group were already in a precarious position and could scarcely show themselves or 'express their opinion without great danger, notably in the primary and communal assemblies...'. They could still count on the police, because of the attachment of the *comité de surveillance*. But this too was lost in September when the *comité* was purged by the district. The armed force was still with them, since the two brothers Rousseau who commanded the National Guard were among the shoemaker's most resolute supporters. But their most effective ally was a wine-grower and farmer in the commune, Etienne Rognon, whose brother was a member of the *comité révolutionnaire* of the Finistère Section. Several inhabitants of the village had influential brothers, and if Lombard and his friends could call on the district of Sens – an authority in bad odour with the Parisians – the sans-culottes of Villeblevin had the ear of one of the most energetic Sections in the capital. Thanks to such family connections this village situated off the main route to Burgundy was to see the arrival of the future Babouvist, Juste Moroy, who controlled the Parisian armed force, and was a colleague of Rognon in the Finistère *comité*.

The mayor and his friends began to find themselves in difficulty after June 1793. The first trouble occurred as early as the 2nd, when the *procureur* of the commune summoned some inhabitants before the General Council 'for having caused a disorder in the church...on Friday during worship of the holy sacrament by displaying the banners and signs...of the suppressed confraternities...'. The principal protesters were sentenced to three days' detention and disarmed (a particularly humiliating punishment). But already the weakness of the municipality was open knowledge and some frightened municipal officers refused to sign the summons and associate themselves with its implementation. At the same time some witnesses to the events in the church – Lombard supporters no doubt – accused the municipality of having provoked this disorder in order to apply the laws 'against religion'. Faced with the shortcomings of some of its members, the majority of the municipality then made the unwise decision of calling upon the directory of the district of Sens. A report on 23 June showed that the situation continued to be alarming, 'with threats on the same issues of disarming some citizens...and abolishing the confraternities', and by 5 July the municipality had surrendered to the pressure and restored the arms to those responsible for the disturbance.

Despite this retreat, the commune continued to live in a state of smothered civil war, fanned assiduously by Lombard and his friends, with threats of renewed disturbance and even physical assault on the municipal officers. The latter, in their 3 August session, accused the former curé of constantly fomenting discord 'in defiance of the public functionaries...'. The already tense situation was exacerbated by a mediocre harvest caused by drought and the municipality felt compelled to make domiciliary visits to the large farmers who had refused to bring their corn to market. A month later, the General Council denounced the elder Tonnellier for refusing to sell his wheat at the price fixed by the Maximum. On 29 September it sent four other farmers before the Villeneuve-la-Guyard *comité de surveillance* on similar charges, and they were later arrested at the same time as Lombard. Fénin had thus had the audacity to raise his hand against the brother-in-law of a district administrator.

The situation in the village became worse after the application of the second Maximum. On 2 October the municipal officers again attacked Lombard, this time for having 'spoken in one of his sermons against the law of 10 June on the division of common lands'. Finally, on 17 Brumaire, the Villeblevin *comité de surveillance* took the campaign into the enemy camp by ordering the arrest of Lombard and a search of his property – measures which should have been taken back in June. This was the last straw, and Lombard's friends had recourse to the normal weapon of village majorities trying to rid themselves of militant sans-culottes, calling a village assembly for the same day – a ploy which had the additional recommendation of giving the women a major say. The assembly decided on the removal of Pierre Rousseau, a member of the *comité*, whom they held responsible for Lombard's arrest. They proceeded to replace the entire *comité* and wrote to the district of Sens, denouncing the mayor of Villeblevin and the *comité* of Villeneuve-la-Guyard for acting beyond their authority. For months the district directory had been waiting for just such an opportunity; at its session of 21 Brumaire it ordered the arrest of Fénin and the removal of all the members of the *comité* of the cantonal *chef-lieu*. The following day Fénin was taken to prison and Lombard and Lorillon, arrested that morning, were set free the same evening. On the 25th the district instructed the criminal tribunal to proceed against three members of the purged *comité*, Chartier, François Rousseau and Claude Cunault, for offences committed at Lombard's home three days previously.[122]

Just as this counter-revolution in Villeblevin and Villeneuve-la-Guyard was ejecting sans-culottes and energetic revolutionaries from positions of influence, the large detachment of the Parisian *armée* was moving through Sens towards Lyon.[123] It looks as though Fénin and his friends may have tried, like the Vermenton sans-culottes, to establish contact with the Parisian officers, but without success – Villeblevin was off the main road, and by the time the detachment passed through Sens, the former mayor was already behind bars. The victory of Lombard and Lorillon seemed complete. But it still depended on the official replacement of Fénin by one of their own men. Fénin, however, was not the kind of man to give in without a struggle, and from his prison he conducted a campaign directed at his still numerous adherents among the agricultural workers, the small wine-growers and the Villeblevin artisans. He still had adherents also within the municipality, and on 25 Brumaire, on receipt of a letter from their mayor, the majority on the General Council proclaimed their confidence in him. Indeed, the municipal officers decided to denounce the arbitrary action of the district to the department and the Committee of General Security.

But once again the force of this decision was largely undermined by the absence of unanimity in the municipality; a minority refused to sanction such measures or to attach their names to the minutes of the session. Their hesitation simply assisted the intrigues of Lombard and his group. Two days later, on the 27th, Robert, *procureur* of the commune, sought to weaken the impact of the municipal decision by declaring himself neutral, alluding to the troubles which beset the village and calling, with questionable sincerity, upon one and all to unite as 'members of the one family, one fraternal body'. *That* was highly unlikely. But in a conciliatory gesture Robert also offered to call in the department *commissaire* to listen to the complaints of both sides. The minority opposed to Fénin would not hear of this, knowing full well that a *commissaire* from sans-culotte-dominated Auxerre would pronounce in favour of the mayor – and they were right, for their only real hope lay with the district. Feeling under pressure, the enemies of the mayor resorted once again to their favourite weapon: the convocation that same day of a village assembly to appoint a new mayor, 'citizen Fénin having lost their confidence'. Those attending proclaimed the removal of Fénin for having promoted divisions among the inhabitants of Villeblevin and the neighbouring parishes, and in his place they elected Lafollye the younger, a substantial farmer and friend of the Lorillons.

But Fénin did not yet consider himself defeated. On 22 Frimaire – he had been freed in the meantime, on a date we cannot discover – he appeared at a session of the municipal body. Four officers, the same ones who had engineered his removal, demanded his withdrawal. He refused, claiming still to be mayor since the *représentants*, Maure and Dubouchet, on mission in the department, had not yet recognised his suspension, which in any event had been proclaimed by an illegal assembly, called without advance notice and in an irregular manner. Faced with his insistence, the municipality agreed to arbitration by the department. But since this would work to the disadvantage of the shoemaker's enemies, they again precipitated events by calling a third assembly, on 23 Nivôse. This meeting not only re-elected Lafollye, but proclaimed the reinstatement of the municipality, from which Fénin's remaining adherents were to be removed. For the moment victory lay with the Lorillons, with Lombard, and most of all with the district of Sens, which was notorious for its delays in implementing revolutionary measures.[124] The new municipality was composed entirely of friends of the curé, and the sans-culottes had been expelled from the *comité de surveillance*.

The supporters of the mayor had no recourse other than to Paris. On 19 Nivôse the brothers Rousseau, 'both farmers from Villeblevin', appeared before the Finistère Section's *comité révolutionnaire* and declared that 'the said Lombard did not adhere to the principles of the Revolution, that on the contrary he had redoubled the zeal and activity with which he perpetuated fanaticism, preparing a catechism for use in the diocese of Sens and celebrating even more feast-days and Sundays than usual, thereby creating such a following that most of the women-folk were ready to do anything to support their curé.... The said Lombard proclaimed against the division of common land, while perpetuating confraternities to different saints, to such àn extent that all the talk in that commune is of murdering those who have espoused the principles of the Revolution, notably citizen Fénin, the former mayor...who was obliged to flee at gun-point...'. The Finistère *comité* was not surprised at the removal of the Rousseau brothers, for it was already well informed of the quarrels in the village through the presence of the committee member Jean-Baptiste Rognon. He told his colleagues that 'having been in his native Villeblevin at the time of the Revolution, 16 July [1789], he had heard the said Lombard say...that the Parisians were scoundrels and fanatics for having taken up arms against their King....'.[125]

Having drawn up a statement about these dénunciations, the *comité* then sent copies to the two government Committees. Clearly they had other things to cope with besides such village squabbles, for the Finistère *comité* was obliged to return to the charge on 2 Pluviôse, stipulating 'that the Committee of General Security should again be written to...to warn it that the said Lombard...had just transferred C. Fénin to the prisons of Sens,[126] that he was thus at the mercy of the clique of the curé [who] wielded a dangerous influence in the said commune and on those attached to it...'. This time the pleadings of the *comité* were successful and we find the denunciations made by the Rousseaus and by Rognon listed in the Committee of General Security's correspondence register under the date of 27 Pluviôse. Besides, by this date the Committee was already aware of the affair, from the correspondence coming from Fénin and his fellow detainees in prison.[127]

This time things started to move. Lombard suddenly became a liability and his friends in the newly purged municipality and *comité de surveillance* began to see the wisdom of disassociating themselves from this priest, now being denounced in high places. On 5 Ventôse the General Council learnt of an address to the Jacobins and the Paris Commune in which the villagers – undoubtedly the Rousseaus – represented the municipality and the *comité* as entirely under the thumb of the pugnacious ecclesiastic. To cut short such accusations the municipality asked Lombard to leave Villeblevin within 24 hours.[128] Lombard lingered for several days in Villeblevin, doubtless in the hope of stirring up support from the women. But nothing of the sort happened and the former curé disconsolately set off for Paris on 8 or 9

Ventôse. In Villeblevin he was still a figure of some note; in Paris he was simply a tired old man, who set himself up with his grocer nephew in the Guillaume-Tell Section.

With Lombard gone, the municipality no doubt felt safe, thus shorn of a compromising ally. But nothing could stop the machinery of repression once it had been set in motion, and the Committee of General Security, having been so assiduously petitioned, at last decided to act. On 15 Ventôse it appointed four *commissaires* from the Finistère Section – Juste Moroy, Jacques Baron, Jean-Nicolas Hardon and Jacques Langlois (called Gency) – to leave immediately on a mission 'to the commune of Villeblevin...to serve an arrest warrant on Lombard, curé, and Chamarand [ex-curé]...to investigate public feeling in the commune and to make such provisional arrests as general security requires...',[129] and to set Fénin at liberty. In a second order the Committee placed at the disposition of the four men the local gendarmerie and the detachment of the *armée révolutionnaire* at Montereau. The Finistère *commissaires* were thus given extensive police powers and were covered by the sovereign authority of the Committee of General Security.

The Committee soon learnt that Lombard was in fact in Paris, and before they set off for Villeblevin, the *commissaires* arrested him at his nephew's, on 16 Ventôse. They left Paris the following day, reached Montereau on the 18th, where they dined with the mayor and the *juge de paix*, leaving with a detachment of 24 men — 13 *révolutionnaires*, 1 captain, undoubtedly Chamot (or Chamault), and 10 gendarmes from Montereau — and arriving finally at Villeblevin at 2 a.m. on the 18th. It was characteristic of these agents of repression to strike at night, surprising their prey in bed, and creating a greater impression with the country people. On arrival, the *commissaires* delivered their authorisations to sleepy municipal officers, roused from their beds to receive them, served drinks to their men and then set about their work – all in the middle of the night. On the 19th they left the *révolutionnaires* in the village and took the gendarmes to Sens to liberate Fénin; they then left for the village of Chaumont – which the Sens *comité* had described as a 'hotbed of fanaticism' – before returning to Villeblevin.

On the first day they arrested only Chamarand. But the following day, the 20th, some 30 persons were arrested, the outcome of old accusations about the commotion at the time of the Fête-Dieu, reiterated by Fénin's supporters: 'Since then', they declared, 'two parties have been formed in the commune, one aristocratic, the other patriotic...and the former the strongest'. The *commissaires* also received individual denunciations from different villagers – one from Claude Cunault, for example, who had been pressurised some days earlier by Lorillon, the national agent of the Sens district, into retracting a statement he had made against the Tonnelliers and other such bigwigs.[130] The presence of the Parisian *commissaires* and the *révolutionnaires* loosened many tongues and instilled courage into the sans-culotte minority, whose very existence was frequently threatened in a village dominated by a clan of large farmers. Cunault was surely not alone in re-finding his voice on this occasion. Nor were the *commissaires* satisfied with testing the disposition of the inhabitants of Villeblevin; they also extended their investigation to Villeneuve-la-Guyard and to the other villages of the canton. At Villeneuve they re-installed the sans-culotte *comité de surveillance*, expelled after Lorillon's show of strength.

It was, however, on the last night of their stay in Villeblevin, 21 Ventôse, immediately after they had received the depositions of the supporters of the former mayor, that the *commissaires* swept the board of anti-Féninists. 'On the night of the third day', noted the municipality in its account of the events, 'they [the *commissaires*] arrested 17 citizens on what charges we know not, among whom were 5 out of the 7 yeomen farmers in the commune and the remainder were wine-growers, farmers and two small *rentiers*...who were of the utmost utility to the commune at a time of sowing and pruning of vines, it being impossible to find anyone else to do their work, owing to the shortage of manpower...'. The responsibility of Fénin and his friends for these arrests cannot be doubted, and in the report of their operations, submitted on 15 Germinal, the four Parisians admitted as much.[131] Clearly, in the absence of their colleague, Rognon, the Parisian *commissaires* were entirely dependent on the advice of the country people in compiling lists of those to be arrested, and from their prison in Paris the victims could point confidently to their accusers: 'a former receiver, the mayor, well known as an intriguer and twice removed from office, assisted by a cabal of some 20 to 30, succeeded in tearing us away from our work...'.[132] As for the municipality, whose partiality towards Lombard and the Lorillons was notorious, it stood aside from the entire operation.

Revolutionary fines to the tune of 2,555 livres, more than the entire cost of the expedition, were also levied on the victims. Chamarand's wife had to pay 200 livres, as well as having to feed the Parisian soldiers for three days; Madame Regnier paid 100 écus, the wives of Claude and Georges Lorillon and Tonnellier, 100, 150 and 200 livres respectively, and those of Michel and Arnaud, 100 écus each. Madame Maréchal, fined 100 livres, was told by the *commissaire* come to arrest her husband at two o'clock in the morning, that 'if the curé were incriminated, it might save her husband'. On 15 Germinal the prisoners wrote again to the president of the Convention: 'Never was there such desolation as at the time of our arrest, the soldiers, some 15 or 16 in number, having eaten at some of our houses...'. The *commissaires* for their part admitted 'that a wine seal was broken, but we took the cellar key away from the *armée révolutionnaire* when we noticed it...'. On the 21st the *commissaires* marched away with the 17 prisoners taken during the night, and on the 23rd they were conducted to the Luxembourg prison in Paris.[133]

The various arrests of Fénin had raised little comment in the country. He was after all but a simple sans-culotte, and his party was composed of modest, poor, 'unenlightened' individuals. But on this occasion *les gros* were involved, and the entire district erupted in protest. The municipality was the first to protest, the day after the arrests. Then on the 23rd the district came to the defence of its colleague, Lorillon: 'We have learnt with the utmost astonishment', it wrote to the Committee of General Security, 'that C. Lorillon, national agent to our district, has been implicated in the inexplicable [!] and unfortunate dispute between the inhabitants of Villeblevin and their ex-mayor, Fénin, who, it is said, has denounced him as the inspirer and instigator of the persecutions which he claims [!] to have experienced at their hands'.[134] On the 27th the acting national agent wrote to Maure: 'Write, I beg of you, to the Committee of Public Safety about the arrest of the good citizens of Villeblevin, who have been taken off to Paris by the *commissaires* of the Committee of General Security of the Paris Commune, which does not seem to have the necessary authority to make such arrests...'.[135] It was a rather crude manoeuvre – this highly placed public official (though we do not know the position of districts in the administrative hierarchy of the Year II) pretending to confuse the great police Committee with the *comité de surveillance* of the Paris department. The mistake was clearly intentional: Lorillon's replacement was trying to play off the Committee of Public Safety against the Committee of General Security at a time when they were at odds, precisely on this question of police powers. But his reasoning went even further, for he was questioning the authority of the Committee of General Security to delegate powers of arrest to its *commissaires*. And as we have seen these *commissaires* had a general mandate to make whatever arrests they considered necessary, both in Villeblevin and throughout the district.

The detainees for their part addressed the Committee of General Security (and *they* made no mistake), as early as 2 Germinal, demanding their release, citing the powerful support they were receiving from the countryside and complaining of the *taxes* they were forced to pay, under threat of 'being declared suspect or deported'.[136] Lombard, the Lorillons, the Tonnelliers and their sort were no fools. As shrewd politicians they were alive to the nuances in the political climate of the capital, and while their friends in Sens tried to play off Maure and the Committee of Public Safety against the Committee of General Security, they quickly recognised the advantage to be derived from the condemnation of the Hébertists and the execution of the commander of the Parisian *armée*. For had they not been arrested by a detachment of this very *armée*? In their second petition, of 8 Germinal, they prefaced an emotional commentary on their own fate with a discreet reference to the recent events: 'We recognise', they wrote, 'that the discovery of serious internal conspiracies must be absorbing all your attention'; then moved on to essentials. 'We are 17 farmers, wine-growers and yeomen, we are family men [even Lombard?] who worked and did not waste our time in the *cabarets*, or adopt that wild, ferocious air which characterises the anti-republicans;[137] to them attaches the folly of rumour-mongering, putting up motions, and trying to enlist support and public

approval...'. Then, after these transparent allusions to the ultra-revolutionary characteristics of their enemies, comes the exordium: 'Citizens,
when you see the earth warmed by the heat of vegetation, nature does not
say to you: forget those workers who are in prison. On the contrary, she
urges you to find them all, to see them, listen to them and reach the swiftest
possible conclusion.... Amongst the 17 here are 6 hale old men of seventy-
four, seventy and sixty-eight.... It will anger you to know that the citizens
charged with bringing us to Paris, aside from their feasting at our homes,
also took 2,560 livres for their own travel expenses, to say nothing of
ours...'.[138]

As this powerful campaign was being mobilised in favour of the 'victims'
of the arbitrariness of the Ancien Regime, the *commissaires* of the Finistère
comité were drawing their repressive mission to a close. On 4 Germinal,
Hardon and Moroy, back in Villeblevin, this time without the *révolutionnaires*, arrested Duchesne, mayor in the first years of the Revolution, against
whom the Committee of General Security had issued a warrant on 29
Ventôse. He was sent off to Paris, accompanied by a denunciation against
him from the same 20 or so villagers who had denounced the other 17
prisoners.[139]

His arrest, however, was the last success scored by the Villeblevin sans-
culottes and their friends from the Finistère Section. The whole business
had taken place at a particularly unfavourable time for such major repressive
measures. The *armée révolutionnaire* was about to disappear, several of the
most active members of the Finistère *comité* were caught up in the
proscription of the Hébertists, and the Committee of General Security was
running out of steam. The prisoners had judged well in making themselves
out to be victims of the ultra-revolutionaries; as long as the latter were
suspect, and every sans-culotte accused of Hébertism, their victims by the
same token became oppressed patriots. The Committee of Public Safety
was particularly susceptible to influences from the districts and one of the
detainees was a national agent. Moreover, most of those arrested claimed to
be farmers, work in the fields demanded their presence, and after a month in
detention an order of the Committee of General Security on 23 Germinal set
them at liberty once again.[140]

The whole affair, therefore, had a predictable ending. Fénin and his
friends paid dearly for their audacity in attacking 'the flower of the
countryside'. After the punishment of the Hébertists, egalitarianism was no
longer in fashion, and the official hierarchies were re-established. On 24
Germinal, the very day after the liberation of his persecutors, Fénin was
summoned before the district to answer a charge of breaking the Maximum
– a common ploy of the moderates to sink the militant sans-culottes in the
esteem of the *petit peuple*.[141] The charge was not upheld, but the district lost
nothing by waiting. In Frimaire Year III the *Comité des finances* ordered an
enquiry on the four *commissaires*, and the following 14 Prairial, the district of
Sens sent Mailhe the claims of the 17, 'containing a statement of the sum

extorted from each by five vile agents of tyranny sent from Paris and backed up by the so-called *garde révolutionnaire* of Montereau'.[142] On 29 Germinal a warrant from Mailhe ordered the disarmament of Fénin, Pierre and Médard Rousseau, Augustin Pommier, Claude Davauderne, the younger Guillaume Rognon (called Barroy), Jacques Dumesnil, Nicolas Robert and Jean Guillain, for having brought to Villeblevin 'all the scum of Montereau'.[143] Finally, on 15 Thermidor Year III, Lombard, now back in the village, told the municipality of his intention of establishing the Catholic religion once again. The victory of his clique seemed complete. But it was not entirely so, for after the revolution of 1830, the younger Guillaume Rognon was appointed to the Orléanist municipality.[144]

The Villeblevin affair is more than just another sordid and petty village quarrel. In its counterposing of interests and play of personalities it is illustrative of certain aspects of the period of the Terror, when sans-culotte minorities attacked notables who were solidly established in control of the municipalities and districts, and ready to defend their patrimony as the domain of the rich and the educated. It was the impudence of Fénin, and of the artisans and small farmers who supported him, in thinking they could run the affairs of the village in place of Lombard and his friends that the latter could not forgive. But the affair also touches upon the history of the repressive action of the Parisian *armée révolutionnaire*, for it illustrates, in the first place, the process whereby an appeal made by a sans-culotte minority to a Paris Section might eventually bring about the active intervention of one of the great Committees of government. Secondly, because of the diversity of interests involved and the unpredictable train of events, it provides a salutary caution against ready-made conclusions that all such village quarrels were part of a class war between sans-culottes and *les gros*. Undoubtedly the line of division usually was that between rich and poor, old and young; but the former curé had the support of many poor women-folk, while the Lorillon family – and it was undoubtedly the very poor who felt themselves victims of the two brothers, these *chefs de clan* – were among the adherents of Fénin. Finally, it shows how costly the dispatch of a revolutionary detachment could be; and the transitory results rarely justified the resort to such means.

(iii)   THE JAGNY EXPEDITIONS AND THE INCONSISTENCIES OF GOVERNMENT
         REPRESSIVE POLICY, SEPTEMBER 1793 – GERMINAL YEAR II

The affair of Jagny, a small village in the Pays de France, just off the two main routes from Paris to Chantilly and Paris to Senlis, brought about the intervention of the *armée révolutionnaire* in a three-stage operation, involving first the two Committees combined, then the Committee of General Security on its own, and finally four *représentants en mission* and a whole swarm of Parisian *commissaires*. It is one of the best illustrations of the incoherence of the Revolutionary Government's repressive policy, shuttled backward and forward between rival groups of *représentants en mission* and acting on conflicting advice from opposing groups of country sans-culottes and district administrators. The case was the same with the *représentants* and the Parisian *commissaires* who succeeded (and sometimes accompanied) them in this embattled region. For Levasseur de la Sarthe, for Clémence and Marchand, the Terror and the use of revolutionary force were above all meant to help the sans-culottes in their struggle against the moderates and *les gros* – both extremely powerful in this region of large-scale farming. But Delacroix, Musset and their subordinates are proof that the Terror could just as well serve the interests of the rich farmers, the men of the law, the merchants and those already in power against the sans-culottes. As for the Parisian *armée*, petitioned from all sides, its action too, like that of the government, was totally incoherent; one moment it was helping to tighten the grip of a sans-culotte group on a village, the next helping to unseat it.

On 20 September 1793, the *comité de surveillance* of the department of Paris (of which Clémence, Marchand and Guigne were members) received a deputation 'from the commune and inhabitants of Jagny...come to express their fears to the committee. They said that a new Vendée was developing, that the municipal officers could not establish their authority, even the gendarmerie refusing their requests to enforce the law, that they could not return to their homes for fear of the aristocrats and armed brigands... falling upon them....'. The following day, 21 September, 'citizen Clémence, charged with accompanying the mayor and a group of inhabitants from Jagny to the Committee of Public Safety,...reported back that the Committees of Public Safety and General Security in united session praised the zeal of the inhabitants, and gave him complete authority to take 300 armed men and two cannon to Jagny and anywhere else that he thought his presence necessary....'.[145] Thus began the famous expedition to Gonesse, the first use of the Parisian *armée* as an instrument of the Terror.

The origins of an affair which overnight brought about the intervention of the two government Committees and the deployment of unusual repressive machinery, were however quite modest. The incessant quarrels of which the village of Jagny had been a victim since the summer of 1792 owed much to the pugnacity of a well-off female landowner, Madame Pruneau, who wielded considerable power over the *petit peuple*.[146]

The detachment led by Clémence arrived in Jagny on 22 September, the day after the order of the two Committees. On the 23rd the *commissaire civil* arrested Boucher, *juge de paix* of the canton of Luzarches, in which Jagny was situated, and a great enemy of the municipality and of Madame Pruneau. A few farmers and men of the law were also arrested. But the toll of repression in this first sortie of the Parisians *armée* was modest, and in their report drawn up in Fructidor, the two *commissaires* claimed to have arrested only 10 or so persons, 'after charges made against them by the local authorities, on whose request and for whose protection we were sent....'.[147] According to a report drawn up in Brumaire, this conflict of the municipality with the legal profession and the large farmers had a distinctly social character: 'everyone [in Jagny]', it read, 'was animated by the purest patriotism, except the farmers, the priests and the agents of the late tyrant, who worked incessantly to obstruct the progress of the Revolution...'. This opinion was repeated by the municipal officers themselves in an address to the Convention explaining the reasons for their appeal to the departmental *comité de surveillance*: 'The crime of the commune of Jagny and of citizen Pruneau lies in the excessive revolutionary passion with which they pursued priests and farmers who expressed opinions contrary to liberty...'.[148]

By going in a body to Paris and addressing the two government Committees directly, the Jagny municipality had stolen a march on their opponents in the town itself, and in the canton and district. The expedition was decided upon within 24 hours and two days later the detachment and *commissaires civils* were in action. It had been enough to raise the spectre of 'a new Vendée' erupting so near to Paris and to the two strategic roads to the Nord. But such a victory, gained through an element of surprise and the audacity of these rural officials, was too suddenly gained to be permanent. Those detained in the prison of Luzarches were not short of counter-weapons and could count on the active support of the directory, which in its turn contacted the Parisian authorities. In response the Committee of General Security revised its opinion, ordering a second mission and a new enquiry under two *commissaires* from the *comité* of the Brutus Section, Briois and Sollier, as well as the famous Maillard. They arrived at Jagny in the first days of Brumaire. Their first action was to release the victims of the previous operation; their second to order the arrest of the sans-culotte municipality and the woman Pruneau. This decision was confirmed by Delacroix and Musset, who had a tendency in their interventions to favour the large farmers and grain merchants rather than the sans-culottes.

But the two *représentants* did not remain sole masters of the district for long. In the first *décade* of Brumaire they were joined by Levasseur de la Sarthe, an energetic Montagnard and protector of sans-culotte minorities. The imprisoned municipality of Jagny was quick to inform Levasseur of their sufferings and he in turn dispatched Parisian *commissaires* to mount yet another investigation in this quarrelsome commune. It was the third such mission since September. The report by these *commissaires*, Mothrée and Vuable, spoke extremely unfavourably of their immediate predecessors: 'We hear nothing but complaints', they wrote, 'against Maillard, Briois and Sollier, their names are never mentioned without horror, they had ten Jagny patriots incarcerated...'. Pulled in all directions by rival groups of *représentants en mission*, the two government Committees changed tack once again, and in a decision taken at a plenary session of the two Committees on 15 Brumaire, and signed by Robespierre, Billaud-Varenne, Jagot, Vadier, Louis (Bas-Rhin) and Dubarran, they ordered the freeing of the municipal officers of Jagny, Madame Pruneau and the others detained on the orders of Briois and Sollier. The two *représentants* were arrested and their successors were ordered by the Committees to bring them to Paris and lodge them in La Force. Maillard too was recalled to Paris to give an account of his conduct, and the powers given him by the Committe of General Security were revoked.[149] For the moment the sans-culottes of Jagny held the advantage, and a fourth *représentant*, Crassous, sent to the district in Ventôse – Germinal to provide a new impulse for repressive measures, left the authorities installed by Levasseur in place.[150] It was not until the Year III that their enemies, the big proprietors, settled the score with these impudent sans-culottes, who, aided by the repressive climate of the Year II, had dared to lay their sacrilegious hands on the *natural* leaders in the countryside.

Throughout the affair the *armée révolutionnaire* and the *commissaires civils* were little more than the uncoordinated instruments of a repressive policy which remained largely local in inspiration. What was the effect on Jagny? On one side was the municipality, which was sans-culotte in composi- tion, but powerless in the face of the covert hostility of the district administrators, who delayed implementation of the repressive laws; on the other were the former notables, temporarily unseated from the municipality but knowing that they had the powerful protection of the district and of the *juge de paix* in the canton, and the support of the women-folk in the commune. The result: impasse. The powerful of yesterday had nothing to fear from the district directory; the municipality, isolated in the country, had no recourse other than to outside intervention to make its wishes effective. Its task was facilitated by the proximity of Paris. Certainly it was the government Committees and their agents, the *commissaires*, who then assumed direction of the operation; but it was the municipality of Jagny which decided on the arrests and the names of those to be arrested.[151]

(iv)   THE ARREST OF THUNOT AND BOISGIRAULT IN COMPIÈGNE

The intervention of the *armée révolutionnaire* did not, then, directly affect repressive policy except at Vermenton, Avallon, Vernon and several communes in the Seine-et-Oise. At Villeblevin the detachment was simply the instrument of the Parisian *commissaires*, themselves in the service of a village sans-culotte minority. At Jagny too the local militants called the tune, with such success that they repeatedly caused the Revolutionary Government itself to intervene in the obscure affairs of their commune. At Viarmes, finally, the Parisian *armée* served the interests of the moderates, trying to rid themselves of a troublesome and over-zealous sans-culotte mayor. But this *armée*, so detested by the districts and certain moderate municipalities, was not itself immune from a repression which could just as well be turned against the revolutionary institutions themselves. Most localities had to wait until the crisis of Ventôse-Germinal provided the occasion for attacking these officers and men, whose greatest crime had been that of arousing fear. Everywhere people knew that the days of the Parisian *armée* were numbered and that its members no longer enjoyed any immunity as priests of the repression. However, in one locality the unanimity of the authorities allowed it to take action earlier, in Nivôse, and the excessively zealous detachment commander and his adjoint, thus isolated in hostile territory, were arrested and transferred to prison in Paris.

The place was Compiègne, which had a bad reputation with the Parisian authorities; the victims were the joiner Thunot, captain of the Panthéon-Français company, and his lieutenant, Boisgirault.[152] Thunot was the archetypal sans-culotte militant and expert denouncer; before leaving with his company for Provins, he was already well known in Paris for reporting royalist or counter-revolutionary words overheard in the *auberges* to the Panthéon-Français and Finistère *comités*. In Provins he pursued the enemies of the Revolution, real or imaginary, with similar zeal. In letters, addressed with exemplary regularity to the *comité* and *société* of his Section, he affected the phonetic spelling and naïve style used by market porters and stall-keepers in their denunciations to Fouquier-Tinville.

The brave Thunot quickly convinced himself in Provins that he was in counter-revolutionary territory – even the local *société populaire* was suspect. Not only did he express his fears in letters to the Sectionary assembly, but he did so publicly, at the tribune of the *société*, and in the cafés, lashing out at all the local authorities and causing them to join together in common opposition to the Parisian *armée* and the revolutionary laws. There was no sans-culotte minority in Compiègne – or if there was it never had a chance of expressing itself – and it was easy for Thunot to feel himself confronted by a coalition of every local interest. So united were the authorities in their opposition to the Parisians, that as early as Brumaire and Frimaire some members of the *société* could even query the usefulness of the *armée révolutionnaire* altogether, an *armée* which they felt could be better used on the frontiers. There was no fear of the Parisians in Compiègne; the authorities sought to restrain the progress of the Terror and ignored the complaints of Thunot and his colleagues. It was a case of playing off country solidarity against these 'outsiders', and in the persons of the two officers, the entire *armée révolutionnaire* was being put on trial.

Thunot and Boisgirault were arrested on 26 Nivôse, on the order of the municipality, the district and the *comité de surveillance*. The same day the district informed the Committee of Public Safety: 'we considered it imperative to detain these two citizens until we received your orders and instructions and we beg of you to send them as quickly as possible. More than once there have been murmurs by the country people against some individuals in this *armée*, but fear has restrained them and until now nothing positive has been done...'. At the same time the directory assured headquarters in the rue de Choiseul that 'it has vexed us greatly to have to act harshly against the misdeeds of two individuals belonging to a corps which has rendered immense public service in so many ways...'. Finally, in a third letter, addressed to the Committee of General Security, it was implied that the two officers' only crime was their violent speech: to slander the local authorities and bring them into disrepute, would have been a crime in any event. The Compiègne district was trying to convince the Parisian authorities that the *armée* itself was not on trial, despite all the evidence to the contrary, and some days later, 11 Pluviôse, the district sought to elaborate on this thesis of established authority having been brought into disrepute, this time in a letter to the two government Committees. 'Two officers of the Parisian *armée* have uttered the most offensive, the most slanderous words against the municipality and the established authorities', it stated. 'If it had been only a matter of vague and ill-considered words uttered indiscreetly, we would have left them to fade by themselves, and spared our hearts any additional wound; but the complaints were so loud, so unjustified, and the crime so serious in itself, so potentially dangerous, that the accused have been placed under arrest...'. What were these complaints, these crimes? The district did not elaborate, and the information laid before the *société* at its session of 10 Pluviôse was equally scanty. But as if it felt that a charge of uttering 'injurious and slanderous words against the authorities and citizens of this commune' was insufficient justification for the arrest of the two officers, the *société* added another, equally vague: 'Moreover, they sometimes acted and often threatened to act beyond their authority...'. That was hardly a serious crime, threats being one of the few weapons which the *révolutionnaires* had against the local authorities. To strengthen its case, the *société* added some inconsequential details concerning Thunot's drunkenness and violence, the fact that he had beaten his wife in the street and his scandalous debauchery. But on 13 Pluviôse, after the *société* had heard a report from the *commissaires* – the *représentant*, Isoré, was present, though he took no part in the debate – it abandoned these minor charges against the two Parisians, retaining only that of injurious words against the authorities.

Despite the fragility of the accusations the Compiègne authorities managed to satisfy the two Committees and the General Council of the Paris Commune, the latter even writing on 20 Pluviôse to congratulate the municipality 'on the measures taken against Thunot and Boisgirault'.[153] Its action thus sanctioned, the *société populaire* somewhat softened towards the two prisoners and asked that they be transferred to Paris, so that the case could be examined with all speed. Accordingly, on 23 Pluviôse, they were taken to the Bourbe prison in Paris. From there Thunot bombarded his Sectionary *comité* with a series of self-exculpatory memoirs. He was a true sans-culotte, he wrote on 28 Pluviôse, known to his Section since 1782, arrested without warrant or interrogation 'for having spoken too freely at the rostrum of the fraternal *société*'. 'The citizens under my command called out for justice, every comrade demanded to know the charge, but were refused...'. Finally, Ronsin, the officers' commander-in-chief, wrote to the municipality on 23 Pluviôse, asking the reasons for their arrest, 'general headquarters having received no information on the subject'. 'I must observe', he added timidly, 'that such arrests should not be made until the *armée* commanders have been forewarned'.[154]

It was not, however, the best of times for undertaking the defence of a

revolutionary officer, and the Compiègne authorities were assisted by the
favourable coincidence of Ronsin's arrest and the onset of 'moderantism'.
With the former's removal, Thunot and Boisgirault gained little more than
the transfer to Paris, and, notwithstanding a constant campaign by their
Sectionary authorities, they remained in prison throughout the
Robespierrist dictatorship, only finally regaining their liberty on 30
Vendémiaire Year IV.[155]

IV   The Great Repression: the case of Lyon

The main case against the Parisian armée révolutionnaire was to rest on its role
in 'la Grande Répression' against the population of France's second city,
Lyon. Many witnesses who were silent on its role in the war effort or in the
supply of the large towns, showed no such restraint in accusing the armée of
having been the principal, if not the sole, agent in the shootings and the
many other atrocities to which thousands of Lyonnais, from every walk of
life, fell victim. When the men of the institutions of the Great Terror were
brought to trial in the Year III, the example of Lyon bulked as large in the
case against Ronsin's armée as that of the noyades in Nantes did in the case of
the famous Bataillon Marat; and nothing was as damaging to the reputation
of the Parisian soldiers as this picture of them as apprentice-assassins and
executioners of unarmed citizens. Contemporary opinion on this count has
dictated the views of most historians. The two authors of a strongly
counter-revolutionary account of the events of this period were to refer
contemptuously to 'this new breed of battalion, whose only act of courage
was to murder...and to charge against unarmed people...'. Following
their lead, the first historians of the Revolution accepted the image of the
révolutionnaires as 'bragging cowards, who took their courage from their
long moustaches, their cocked hats and the blasphemies which they
constantly regurgitated' – sinister and sanguinary braggarts, then, whose
only victory was that gained over an unarmed populace, the dismal blood-
stained plaine des Brotteaux their glorious battleground. The reputation of
these men, seemingly devoid of even the saving virtue of courage, could not
have been more effectively destroyed.[156]

Those initially responsible for such deplorable publicity were not the
moderate press, the supporters of clemency, nor even the Lyonnais
historians and chroniclers who had survived the massacre. Rather it was the
Revolutionary Government itself, which in ordering the représentants in
Lyon to strike at this 'guilty populace' without pity had promised them the
support of the armée révolutionnaire. The Committees sent to Lyon the
strongest detachment of the Parisian armée ever brought together, with one
clear aim: to accelerate the measures of repression.[157] Collot-d'Herbois well
recognised such intentions when he wrote thanking the Committee of
Public Safety for assistance which would permit him to 'faire de grandes
choses'. In Lyon the armée révolutionnaire was simply an instrument of

government, in its policy of punishing an entire population harshly, pitilessly. Later, in the Thermidorean period, when the officers and NCOs charged with having participated in the shootings and the other atrocities committed at Lyon were unable to deny it, they would invoke in mitigation superior orders and above all official instructions for pitiless severity. The Committees may never actually have proposed the firing squad as a way of accelerating this 'regenerative' repression. But they gave the *représentants carte blanche* to act as they saw fit, and moral responsibility for the shootings lies first and foremost with Robespierre and his colleagues in the Committee of Public Safety. At a later date Robespierre lent a sympathetic ear to Gravier and to the other Lyon Jacobins who came to Paris to plead the cause of their city, and he spoke out against the blind repression of an entire populace, when Collot and Fouché remained enthusiastic participants in the 'grand bal' organised there. But Collot and Fouché were more honest than Robespierre, who combined a short memory with an extremely flexible conscience. Robespierre never condemned the principle of repression itself, and until his death could order the summary execution of the enemies of the Revolution (particularly those unfortunate enough to question his policies) without batting an eyelid. His was a sensibility which demanded killings without show, death with discretion; the mass shootings shocked him.

After the government, responsibility falls on the two proconsuls, the archangels of the repression, who never troubled to hide their satisfaction in reporting the progress of their 'purifying' mission. The various Lyon journalists for their part blew the *Père Duchesne* trumpet, giving maximum publicity to this pitiless policy and associating it with revolutionary patriotism. Proclamations of support for the repression were a sort of badge of political orthodoxy, and the *révolutionnaires* who took satisfaction in setting out the daily toll of massacres in letters to their Sections, were simply giving public expression to the sanguinary appetites of the Millets, Dorfeuilles/Damames and the other apologists of the atrocities. Ronsin himself set the example for his men when, after his visit to Lyon during the first round of executions, he gleefully plastered the walls of Paris with a letter, intended for the Cordeliers, boasting of the swift accomplishment of this slaughter. Thus, at the time, everyone tried to claim personal responsibility for the summary executions, as a badge of their revolutionary patriotism. The main aim, according to the sans-culotte papers of Lyon and the letters of the revolutionary officers, was to act quickly, to accelerate the depopulation. The repression should not be dragged out.

Were Ronsin's soldiers truly the *mitrailleurs*, the *égorgeurs* of Lyonnais iconography? It is difficult to say. But we can state unequivocally that they did perform a duty every bit as revolting as that of actually carrying out the executions and physical atrocities: that of mounting guard at the guillotine. Even before the repression gathered speed in Frimaire-Nivôse, the instrument of republican vengeance in the place des Terreaux was flanked by *révolutionnaires*, as were the accused and their judges at the Commission Révolutionnaire. In Lyon, therefore, they served both as gendarmes at the trials, and as assistants to the executioner. As for their participation in the massacres themselves, opinion differed according to who was asked: individuals denied personal responsibility, but left the collective responsibility of their corps an open issue. Thus the fusiliers claimed no direct role in the executions, while letting it be understood that this was not the case with the cavalry or cannoneers. The cavaliers observed that firing cannon was not one of the duties of a mounted company, while the cannoneers, who were more directly implicated, pleaded their lack of ability to fire cannon. According to their accounts, the mass shootings must have been the work of artillerymen, better trained in the use of such equipment than these Paris shopkeepers: in other words the regular troops of the first requisition. Certainly the testimony of those who escaped from the plaine des Brotteaux depicted Ronsin's cavalry as preparing to carry out the most odious of all tasks: the pursuit on horseback of fleeing victims, to cut them down with sabres like the terrible red horsemen in Breughel's paintings.

The first account by one of those involved comes from a sergeant-major in the Droits-de-l'Homme Section fusiliers, Charles-François Prou, denounced in Prairial Year III as 'a terrorist, an agitator, and as co-operating in the shootings in Lyon'. 'It is well known', replied Prou, in a petition to the Committee of General Security, 'that no one from the former *armée révolutionnaire* was in command at the fusillade, it is therefore a scandalous untruth on the part of the accuser to say that your petitioner was involved at Lyon, for supposing that it were as true as it is false, the rank of sergeant-major, which he then held, would have exempted him from this kind of service'.[158] Prou, as we can see, took the precaution of using a double alibi. Renault, adjutant-major and an officer in the fusiliers, was more specific. 'Through sheer spitefulness', he wrote around the same time, 'my enemies are trying to pin on me some of the responsibilities for the dreadful shootings at Lyon. They pretend ignorance of the fact that the shootings were carried out by the artillery, while I was only an infantry officer, and I enclose a certificate to that effect from citizen Theurel, my superior...'.[159] A third argument was that used by Réaume, a fusilier captain, when he was accused by his Section of being a former terrorist and *mitrailleur*: 'my enemies mean by that', he wrote in Floréal Year III, 'that I co-operated with the executions which took place in that town. The truth is that when I arrived in Lyon I was appointed storekeeper-captain to the 2nd and 3rd battalions...the duties involved in this position dispensing me from any military service.... I never held a commission there, and could not have participated in the executions which took place...'.[160] These denials ring rather false in view of the fact that Réaume had been an enthusiastic supporter of the repression in the autumn of the Year II (pp. 318–19) and was certainly a member of the Commission Militaire set up in Lyon to judge soldiers accused of indiscipline, pillaging and other crimes; though it is also true that this Commission was never involved in the repression directed against the civilian population.

Unfortunately we have no testimonial from the cannoneers about their role in the shootings, and must rest content with snippets of indirect information. Thus on 28 Frimaire the general from Liège, Declaye, commander of the garrison and organiser of the massacres, issued the following order to Lefranc, cannoneer captain from the Tuileries Section: 'Tomorrow, 29 Frimaire, at 5 a.m. precisely, you will be at the Commission Temporaire with 32 sans-culottes, intended to accelerate the agreed measures'. What did he mean by these disturbing words? It may have been nothing more than a routine police operation; but the previous day he had asked Lefranc to select soldiers 'to lead a republican operation....'.[161] Might this not have been a mere euphemism for some vast measure of summary justice, a huge legalised massacre? As we have already seen, the sans-culottes showed considerable prudery in their reluctance to call things by their correct name, particularly if it involved blood-letting, and the adjective 'republican' frequently had a very specific meaning. Certainly, some weeks later the cannoneer companies from Paris were the only artillery elements in the Lyon garrison.[162] What we need to discover is whether there were any other artillerymen under orders from Declaye during Frimaire-Nivôse – the period of the shootings. Unfortunately in the absence of a chart plotting the stations of the garrison for this period, we can say nothing concrete one way or another. At the same time, if other cannoneers were present in Lyon in Frimaire, it is likely that they would have been employed rather than the Parisians, who were unused to handling artillery, At least this is what was implied by a writer not particularly well disposed towards the *armée révolutionnaire*, the abbé Guillon de Montléon, who spoke of the presence of dragoons and volunteers at the time of the great massacres.[163] But not everybody accepted this viewpoint, and in an article of 11 Pluviôse Year III, cited later by the writer Maton de la Varenne, a Thermidorean journalist saw the *armée révolutionnaire* as the chief culprit, and the troops of the first requisition in a rather better light. 'To carry out [the shootings]', he wrote, 'a battalion of the first requisition was brought forward; but so frightened was it by what it had to do, that it discharged its muskets hesitantly and killed only 15 to 20 people. It was then withdrawn and replaced by a battalion of the Parisian *armée révolutionnaire*, which fired without flinching, but did not kill everyone; some of these unfortunates remained standing...the cannibals then rushed upon them, dispatching them as they could, by sabre, pistol and axe...'.[164] This was to endow the revolutionary artillery with a sense of assurance and command which it was far from possessing, and we do know that in fact it played but a secondary role in the shootings – as Prudhomme said, taking up a claim made by the writer in the *Courrier Républicain*, the *révolutionnaires* only delivered the *coup de grâce* to many unfortunates who had not been killed by the first volley; which in fact was just as repugnant.[165]

If the *révolutionnaires* were not the real executors of this physical repression, however, they served the repression in many other equally effective ways. They were used in particular in preliminary operations which supplied the Commission des Sept with its daily batch of victims. The Parisians were specialists in domiciliary visits, vast, spectacular operations engulfing the entire town, terrorising the Lyonnais as much as the great massacres and leaving the same red blots on local memory. The Parisians were the heralds of death: 'fear marched ahead of them, people trembled at sight of them and fled at their approach', but 'the process was carefully orchestrated; the soldiers of the *armée révolutionnaire* spread out through all the homes; they seized people in their homes, arrested them in the streets. . . .'.[166] Nor was this picture of the systematic 'combing' of the labyrinths of this dark and secretive city exaggerated. The *révolutionnaires*, however, as strangers to the town, were less terrifying than the local *mathevons*, the *commissaires* of the Sectionary *comités*, who led the operations, knew the guilty ones, and who indicated which heads were to fall.[167] Indeed, during these domiciliary visits, or even more when they were placed on guard over prisoners too ill to be transported to the Maison de Roanne, the Parisian soldiers sometimes hid suspects and saved them from revolutionary justice. Later, in the Year III, some of these people were to express their gratitude. According to the Lyonnais, the fusiliers and cannoneers were less inhuman than the universally detested cavalrymen. The reason no doubt was the peculiar composition of the cavalry, filled with undesirables and opinionated young men. Sometimes, these domiciliary visits went beyond the limits of the town to take in the communes of the La Campagne district – the refuge of many escaping from the 'siege'.[168] Other soldiers accompanied Fusil, Marcellin and Lefranc on their repressive circuit through the communes of Le Forez.[169]

V   *Revolutionary justice*

The *armée révolutionnaire* as a corps was above all an instrument of the repression, and its officers and soldiers were considered as specialists in Terror. As Parisians they were ultra-revolutionary patriots, in tune with the current political climate, and above all accustomed to purges and denunciations. Wherever they went they immediately took over from the local terrorists the task of enforcing the various laws against suspects and of administering summary political justice. In areas where civil war had been waged, and in the absence of local sans-culottes on whom they could lean, the *représentants* and the members of the extraordinary commissions used these Parisians out of preference, and derived precious support from their presence. Even in those departments where normal administration still operated, the *comités de surveillance* and the municipalities frequently sought advice from the officers and soldiers on how to interpret certain of the extraordinary laws.

In Lyon, some *révolutionnaires* became the real masters of the repressive machine: Parein, Corchand and Armé were members of the Commission des Sept, Marcellin and Lefranc formed part of the roving commissions sent into the surrounding departments by the Commission Temporaire, Tolède became the secretary of Collot-d'Herbois, while 62 members of the detachment – 49 of them cannoneers – were appointed assistant *commissaires* to the *comités révolutionnaires* in each of the 32 Sections of the town (6 soldiers from the Allier revolutionary battalion and 1 from that of the Nièvre also worked with them).[170] Another way in which the Parisians were able to control the repressive machinery was through the places they occupied on the admittance committee of the *société révolutionnaire*, over which a cavalry officer, a friend of Mazuel, presided in Pluviôse Year II.[171]

At Mâcon four of the judges of the *commission populaire* set up by Javogues seem to have been members of the Parisian detachment: Armand, a carter, Henry, a day-labourer, Rollet de Lavau, a tailor, and Bonnefond, a toymaker – all from the Invalides Section.[172] The revolutionary tribunal set up in Brest likewise included among the jurors three revolutionary cannoneers from the Cité Section, and one was also a member of the *comité de surveillance* of the same commune.[173] We have already emphasised the role of advisers on repression filled by such men as Donville at Honfleur and Dumany at Melun. Parisian cannoneers may also have sat on the Military Commission at Granville, while that of Saumur was the breeding ground for the masters of repression in Lyon.[174] Thus it was, that in areas lacking their own bodies of militants, the Parisians, some of whom had already served on *comités révolutionnaires* in their Sections before joining the *armée révolutionnaire*,[175] zealously fulfilled the functions of judges, juries or *commissaires* in the service of that popular and summary justice so often called for by the militant sans-culottes of the Sectionary *sociétés* in the capital.

However, to judge by its repressive activity, the Parisian *armée* was scarcely a very effective instrument of the Terror. Above all it did not merit the sinister reputation it acquired from the writings of the survivors of the plaine des Brotteaux, or of the Lyon refugees at Lausanne. Designed to *frapper de grands coups* and to strike fear into the enemies of the Revolution, its means never quite matched up to its official mission. Only in Lyon was it able to operate independently of the local authorities, and even here it was simply an instrument of the great proconsuls. It is even doubtful whether it played any active part in the *mitraillades* – its role seeming to have been one of guardian of the apparatus of execution rather than actual executioner. In any case the operation in Lyon was exceptional, and the Parisian *armée* there was simply the tool of government policy. To put Ronsin's *armée* on trial for the happenings there is to put the policy of the Committee of Public Safety towards the rebellious town on trial.

Elsewhere the toll of repression was negligible. The detachments, operating almost always on orders from superior authorities, arrested only a few relatively unimportant people. Of these a mere handful made their way to the revolutionary tribunals or mounted the steps of the scaffold. As for the arbitrary arrests made on the orders of the Parisian officers alone, these were so rare that they occupy but one page of the dossier prepared by the Committee of Public Safety on the misdeeds of this undisciplined army; their significance was artificially inflated by the civil authorities' fear of a *pouvoir militaire* in embryo. The handful of abuses of this kind were products of an excess of zeal and revolutionary patriotism rather than any desire to humiliate the civil authorities; the officers acted as revolutionaries rather than as ambitious soldiers.

Any autonomous action by the Parisian *armée* in the area of repression was both unimportant and uncoordinated; it had marked political and social consequences only when it was inspired by sans-culotte minorities or by those 'hommes de liaison', the Parisian *commissaires*, who had some clear idea of the desired outcome. Only then did arrest become the most effective weapon of the political terror: carefully deployed, an arrest warrant could be the most convincing of arguments. But the Parisian *armée* alone could not effect village revolutions.

As individuals, however, their intervention was sometimes more decisive. They were readily used as specialists in repression and in troubled regions, the *représentants* resorted to them to fill the commissions of popular justice. They were not, however, *égorgeurs*, eager to spill the blood of their compatriots, and the Parisian soldier who had no pity for internal enemies was acting in self-defence. It was ony a few cavaliers who showed signs of a pikeman mentality.

In short, the existence of this *armée* contributed little to the march of the Terror, contrary to the intentions of its creators. The number of victims of the Terror was greater in regions where the *armée* did not operate, than in those where it did. The propaganda which preceded the detachments, and which was indeed intended to frighten the public and spread panic, succeeded all too well. The *révolutionnaires* themselves completed the picture by their consciously terrifying appearance, their verbal violence, their finger on the trigger. The country people remembered most of all the spectacle of the famous *promenades vengeresses*; the legend was born and became more and more inflated with its removal in time from events which in reality had claimed few victims. In terms of the repression generally, the *armée* was a costly luxury, created amidst disorder and difficulty, inspiring dispro-portionate fear and accomplishing little. Champeaux and Dumez cannot have been the only ones to complain that the results scarcely justified the trouble and cost of raising this particular instrument of the Terror. Above all the Revolutionary Government itself distrusted the popular *armée*, and clearly intended it to have little effectiveness in an area where it might threaten civil liberties and the very existence of the regime.

CHAPTER 4

The Repressive Action of the Departmental and Communal *Armées*

The repressive activity of the departmental and communal forces consisted of a few spectacular episodes, which made such an impression on public opinion that all the *armées*, great and small alike, gained terrorist reputations which few merited. The violence and brutality of two or three notorious bodies like the Bataillon Marat or the Lot *armée* reflected upon all the rest. But those responsible for the *armées* also contributed to this reputation by their dramatic antics, announcing the completion of their missions to the Convention in terms which exaggerated their importance by depicting them as full-scale campaigns. Each address assumed the qualities of a military dispatch or a war communiqué: such-and-such an area had been subdued, such-and-such a populace brought to obedience, order and peace restored in the countryside, the *malveillants* overwhelmed, the refractory priests arrested, rebels awaiting judgement, the lukewarm gone to ground – the sans-culotte *armée* had performed miracles and the 'méchants' trembled at its approach. The officers, civilians for the most part, affected military terminology; they too wanted their victory bulletins. But the campaigns which they spoke of with such grandiloquence, the great victories which they announced with such savage joy, in true Hébertist style, were above all literary exercises. Repression assumed greater ferocity in the written word.

In September, at the same time as the Parisian *armée* was completing its first tour of duty north of the capital, that of the Lot went on mission into the Gourdon district. In October, swollen by elements from the Cantal and the Tarn, it moved into the Aveyron and that department was to be the theatre of the most important repressive operation undertaken by any departmental *armée*. Likewise in October, as if in response to some general order, the battalions from the Nièvre and Allier started to fan out through these departments of the Centre, giving their officers, from Nevers, Clamecy, Moulins and Montluçon, their first experience of political repression. It would stand them in good stead in Lyon and the surrounding area some weeks later. The excursions through the Nièvre and the Allier were in effect apprenticeships in repression and formed the model for future operations, both north and south of the Loire. In Brumaire the Toulouse *armée* went to teach the law to the Grenadins, and before the close of that month the *armée* of the Lot was back at Cahors. The great military and anarchic repression had, it seemed, started to run out of steam; everything would now return to normal, said the peasants; the worst had passed.

But it had not. For if Frimaire witnessed a certain relaxation in repressive activity in the Midi and the Centre, the country north of the Loire was experiencing a vigorous burst of punitive measures. In Frimaire the terrible *noyades* of Nantes took place; in the second half of the month, the troops from Redon, commanded by Avril and Le Batteux, passed through the Morbihan, leaving a trail of burning farms and churches and dead behind them, as if they wanted to out-distance the Committee of Public Safety by keeping just ahead of the law of 14 Frimaire, which reached them at Vannes. The Redon cook was thus arrested in full terrorist flight, as he was about to enter in triumph and punish this guilty town on the orders of Carrier. He could scarcely contain his anger, arrested the two messengers who had brought such unwelcome news, and hoped to continue on the course mapped out by the *représentant* at Nantes. This produced his own arrest, on orders from another *représentant en mission* to the Breton departments; his *armée* returned quietly to Redon, and the Morbihan became calm again. The defeat of Le Batteux marked the end of large-scale violent repression, and although companies remained active in the South-East and South-West, the heart had already gone out of the campaign and such continuing activities can only be explained in terms of the isolation of these regions and the inevitable time lapse in the implementation of government decisions throughout the Republic. The main repressive action by the *armées* took place between the expedition to Gourdon and the crossing of the Morbihan, the two spectacular actions which marked their birth and their demise.

It was a period notable for its rumours and the spread of the most exaggerated fears through the countryside – a kind of *grande peur* such as that which gripped the people of Paris and its suburbs in the spring of 1794. The great operations of October took place against a backdrop of false information which reinforced the instinctive distrust, the gut dislike of the country people for their nearest neighbours, and the repression very soon became a weapon in the rivalries between towns or neighbouring villages.

The position of republicans in this region, the home of treason and armed revolt, was much more dangerous than that of the rural sans-culottes around Paris, and the sans-culotte minorities came to view the repression as their best safeguard amidst hostile populations. It was they who repeatedly asked for more detachments and for *grands moyens*, and they were encouraged by the pitiless orders issued by the civil and military authorities, by the *représentants*, the generals and the garrison commanders. Civilians and soldiers rivalled each other in brutality and reminded their agents, the *commissaires civils* and *comités de surveillance*, that they must strike without pity.

Despite the spectacular nature of some expeditions, however, the repressive activity of these *armées* was incoherent and ineffectual. Their operations were even more disorderly than those of the Parisian *armée*; it was a fitful repression reflecting administrative disorder and confusion of powers. Violence turned into anarchy and such visible anarchy made contemporaries forget the more normal activity of companies whose officers were content to serve as docile instruments of the *comités de surveillance*. These 'normal' activities consisted of implementing arrest warrants, conducting prisoners to detention centres and guarding them there, mounting guard over the *comités*, visiting *auberges*, inspecting passports, and making domiciliary visits. The *grands moyens* were the exception, autonomous actions as in conquered territory were rare, and if the Parisian *armée* was above all the arm of the Committee of Security General, the small communal companies were for the most part simply extensions of the *comités de surveillance*.

I   *Anarchy and repression*

Whereas the Parisian *armée* had to devote most of its efforts to problems of supply, the protection of *arrivages* and to garrison service in fortified places, the companies and battalions in the departments were above all instruments of repression. It was in these activities that the contrast between Parisian and departmental *armées* was greatest. The latter were barely tolerated by the central power and owed their existence to the favour of some *représentant* and all manner of local initiatives; whereas the Parisian *armée* was produced by a decree of the Convention, a decision by the Committee of Public Safety, and endowed with full legal status. If the Parisian *armée* was on the whole simply the docile instrument of official repression, certain departmental *armées* concentrated almost entirely on repression and their activities were so violent and so wide-ranging that they often had no official sanction whatsoever. Some *armées* gave themselves over to full-scale war operations, such as the expeditions to the Aveyron and the mission of the Toulouse *armée* to the Ariège. Some *armées* specialised in punitive expeditions, which resembled certain sorties by the Parisian *armée* (Livry, Montcornet), and which tended to take on a kind of uniformity, as if some unknown hand had traced a pattern of repression stretching from the Pyrenees to the Loire, from the Gironde to the Rhine. The formula was essentially the same in Corbigny and Montmarault, in the villages of the Isère, and in the communes of Alsace and of the Toulouse region; only the men were different. Cannon would be placed at each corner of the main square, the local authorities and populace would be assembled and harangued menacingly. The little groups of 'patriots', who would already have been pointed out, would then be asked to draw up lists of proscription – on the basis of which arrest warrants would be issued and *taxes révolutionnaires* imposed – and lists of those to replace the 'tièdes', the 'égoïstes', the 'modérés' on the municipalities and the *comités de surveillance*. Then the church would be closed, with or without the consent of the curé – though in general his voluntary withdrawal and a declaration approving the conversion of the church into a temple of Reason was sought before any force was employed. Having thus levied and registered the *taxes*, distributed the income from the illegal revenue to the poor sans-culottes, closed the church or diverted it to other uses, and arrested or defrocked the priest, the next stage was to take prisoners – not many: half a dozen, 20, 30 at most – to be locked up in the *maison d'arrêt* of the *chef-lieu*. This was the normal pattern of operations, conducted usually by *commissaires civils*, whose unlimited powers gave them more freedom to act than the most powerful *commissaires civils* of the Parisian *armée*.

In the Allier, the Nièvre, the Loire, the Ain, the Isère and some Breton departments, in the South-West, the Massif Central and in Alsace, these revolutionary forces reigned momentarily as masters, conducting themselves as in a conquered country, dismissing, arresting, liberating, replacing and sweeping away established authorities and jurisdictional objections alike. Some *représentants* approved, indeed encouraged all this; but most were more prudent, letting it happen, but informing the Committee of Public Safety of their concern about such contempt for the local authorities. Everything the most ardent Parisian *révolutionnaires* would have liked to do, the *commissaires* actually did in some departments. Violence and excess were part and parcel of provincial life, and contemporaries were to claim that Hébertism, as the manifestation of a certain kind of revolutionary temperament, was likewise a product of the departments.

If it is an exaggeration to accuse the Parisian *armée* of atrocities like the *mitraillades* of Lyon, in which they seem to have played only an indirect part, atrocities were not unknown in the 'feats' of certain departmental forces, even though their brutality and importance was later inflated by interested parties. The famous *armée* of the North, for instance, in no way merited the emblem of a mobile guillotine which its leader, in a flight of optimism, had engraved on its official seal. On the other hand, the *armée* commanded by General Marbot, adjutant-general Lamarque and Viton, even if it was only partially *révolutionnaire* (with equal numbers taken from the battalions of the first requisition in the Tarn and Haute-Garonne), effectively ravaged several districts in the Aveyron, burning farms and houses, sometimes even forests and wheat fields. It was a way of clearing the mountain region to make it uninhabitable for Charrier's supporters, still hiding out there with the complicity of the inhabitants. In the Morbihan too, Le Batteux burnt houses and had villagers shot on his own authority. In the Nièvre and Allier, even if things did not assume the same terrible proportions, the *commissaires civils*, at the head of their columns, likewise spread terror through the rural districts.

Not that these revolutionary *bandes* actually killed many people. But at Nantes they participated directly in the *noyades*. In the Allier the battalion sent some 30 inhabitants of Moulins to the guillotine; in the Loire the *armée* created by Javogues was to be the principal supplier of the Military Commissions of Feurs and Lyon; and the Bas-Rhin *armée* supplied a host of unfortunates to the tribunal of Schneider. The revolutionary battalions, instruments of the *commissaires civils* and *juges populaires*, thus filled the antechambers of these extraordinary commissions which enjoyed a disturbing florescence in the Centre, the West, the South-West and in the frontier areas. In most of these areas the hierarchy of power had been reversed, and with normal restraint by regularly established authorities removed, the field was left clear for the extraordinary authorities.

Can we accept the conclusions of Restif de la Bretonne and the other Thermidorean authors, attributing this increased violence, this revolutionary excess to mysterious influences of environment and temperament? The Méridionaux, the *hommes noirs* who figure so prominently among Restif's shady *canaille* (he even goes so far as to claim that the September *massacreurs* did not have a Parisian accent, that they were *étrangers*, Savoyards or Auvergnats in other words),[1] and in the writings of Méhée and Riouffe, were they then more violent, more brutal than the Parisians? This was not always the opinion of contemporaries. Quite the contrary: the Parisian *commissaires*, for instance, the principal activators of the revolutionary battalions, sent to the South-East and elsewhere, complained of the idleness and spinelessness of the men of the South, whom they considered scarcely worthy of the name 'republican'. 'In this country', wrote Pierre Chartrey, *commissaire des guerres* from Montpellier, 'there is no one to confide in, the men are different from those elsewhere in France, they are deceitful, proud and very selfish....'.[2] To explain the variations in the level of repression from one department to another, it is necessary to go back several months, for violence begets violence and the battalions were to act more licentiously in regions torn by civil war. In a peaceable area such as the Agenais, the company was content to fulfil the duties of a supplementary gendarmerie. If the Compagnie Marat was so brutal, one must remember that the Nantes sans-culottes lived in constant fear of a concerted attack by the brigands who dominated the surrounding countryside, while their friends and relatives crammed the town's prisons. The notion of a prison plot was a real threat for these sans-culotte artisans, outsiders and a minority in the community in which they lived. In the same way the Toulousains were particularly ferocious towards the frontier people of the Ariège, whom they suspected, not without reason, of appealing to Charles IV to deliver them from these 'atheistic' republicans. Charrier's *bande*, even if its size was exaggerated, was a threat to public tranquillity so long as its leaders remained at large, hidden in the caverns of that savage countryside or retreating into the most inaccessible parts of the Lozère. The level of revolutionary brutality measured up to that of royalist violence.

This brings us to another general point concerning the repressive activities of the small companies and revolutionary battalions. If the Parisians distrusted the inhabitants of the departments, how much more important in the play of repression were the traditional enmities between neighbouring towns or provinces, how much more ferocious were old quarrels, which for generations had pitted those *en haut* against those *en bas*. And what more perfect instrument for appeasing these almost legendary hatreds than a company or battalion formed by the inhabitants of a small town and entirely in the service of municipal policy. Note the satisfaction of the populace of Cahors, marching to impose the law on the Rouergois, and the latter's sense of grievance against this invasion of outsiders: 'from all parts', wrote the administrators of the Saint-Geniez district, 'we receive complaints about the various detachments of the Gourdon battalion forcing all kinds of contributions from the people...'.[3] Such were the hatreds which divided the people of the two departments, that at Gourdon, shortly after the departure of the *armée* for Rodez, even the words of a stranger could command credence – he was 'a young man wearing a check shirt and carrying a jacket under his arm' (what admirable precision), an 'homme noir', thought to be from Bordeaux, who claimed that 'the *armée révolutionnaire* had had so many men killed that the Rouergois could build walls with the corpses...'. One good woman, likewise encountered on the road, claimed for her part to have heard that '400 of our volunteers [at Rodez] had been given poison in their bread...'.[4] Some said these rumours had originated with a peasant claiming to be 'from the Haute Causse'. They showed that, long before the Fualdès affair, the inhabitants of Rodez had assumed a singularly ferocious character in the eyes of their neighbours.

Assisted by the revolutionary battalions, tiny communal formations, repression, like authority, became 'federalised' and assumed all the violence, all the passion of people who knew each other. The repression gave free rein to local hatreds in their most dreadful, their most venomous form, and it is scarcely surprising that central government viewed with anguish this proliferation of instruments of fratricidal violence. In the national train of events it could foresee a time when each village in the Midi would have its own company ready to combat that of the neighbouring town. Nor were such fears groundless, for in the Cantal, the two towns of Aurillac and Saint-Flour, which had been in competition since the first days of the Revolution to become *chef-lieu* of the department, did indeed form separate revolutionary companies, paid for by each municipality.[5] These initiatives opened up all kinds of dangerous prospects of the repression degenerating into a sordid settling of old scores between rival localities. The Parisian *armée* had at least the advantage of being dependent upon central authority.

Possessing greater liberty of action than the *armée* of Paris, some of the local battalions were able to go further not only with purely repressive action, but with the propaganda and political and social initiatives which often accompanied it. The repression usually had a double aspect: it punished with one hand, rewarded with the other, *taxes révolutionnaires* were balanced by hand-outs to poor sans-culottes, arrests and purges, by the appointment of 'patriotes sûrs'. In the record of repression by the Parisian *armée*, cases such as those of Jagny and Villeblevin were rare; but in that of the Centre and the South-West there were many Jagnys.

The dramatic aspect of some of these repressive missions, however, should not blind us to the many calm areas, much greater in number than those subjected to violent repression. In most districts where companies were deployed, they remained firmly under the control of the revolutionary or the regular authorities (districts/municipalities, *comités de surveillance/ sociétés populaires*), and their services consisted entirely of policing duties and guarding the prisons. In the Hautes- and Basses-Alpes, in the Hérault and Lot-et-Garonne, to cite but a few cases, the soldiers implemented arrest warrants issued by the *comités de surveillance* and brought suspects to detention centres or before the extraordinary tribunals. These peaceable companies have no history, but their behaviour was just as much the norm as that of the formations of the Allier, the Nièvre, the Haute-Garonne or the Lot, which were so talked about because of their violence and reputed crimes. Repressive action was not necessarily brutal and anarchic. Indeed nothing could have been less spectacular than the daily routine of the small company of Agen or of all the tiny municipal formations in the towns of the Basses-Alpes. The *armée* of the North, which was large by revolutionary standards, deliberately tried to be dramatic and imposing (it was, after all, commanded by an actor), in order to arouse fear – hence the famous seal, the blusterings of Dufresse, the compulsory pipes and *bonnets rouges* of his soldiers. But such play-acting had little effect upon the population, judging by the attitude of the people of Cambrai and Douai, who were unimpressed by such artificial ferocity. As for the *armée* of the East, it was largely concerned with military supply, using repression only when disturbances in the rear of the large armies threatened the *arrivages* of grain, fodder and horses for the military zones. Their usual victims were deserters, swindlers – always numerous in the shady world of military transport – authorities who were slow to implement requisitions, and wagoners and drivers who refused to work for wages agreed upon with the *commissaires des guerres*. The soldiers under the orders of the two *commissaires civils* were, in effect, military policemen rather than agents of political terror. On arrival at Longwy on 3 Frimaire, the *armée* commanders, Gobert and Delteil, wrote to Bouchotte: 'The guillotine, mounted on its cart, was placed in the middle of the square. We suppressed a small insurrection in a battalion which would have had unfortunate consequences.... Several officers were denounced for attempting to disorganise and excite insurrections...'.[6] The only feature shared by these modest *armées*, these small companies in peaceful towns, auxiliaries of the gendarmerie or of the military police, and the undisciplined hordes, bursting with zeal and ready to overturn everything, was their name.

Though only one revolutionary tribunal existed in the capital, there were several in the West, the Centre and the Midi. Their procedures were more expeditious than that of the capital, their daily quota of victims much greater. Their powers extended over several departments at the same time, and, as commissions of revolutionary justice, they were involved in all branches of administration. Each day small groups of suspects were marched into Lyon, Feurs, Bordeaux and Rodez for summary judgement – which for most meant certain death.

It is difficult to draw distinctions which can be applied equally to all these battalions and companies. On the whole the Parisian *armée* adhered to certain rules laid down by the superior authorities, upon whose orders they acted. The Committee of Public Safety followed a set pattern of procedure almost everywhere, with the result that the intervention of Ronsin's *armée* varied little from one place to another. Such was not the case with the departmental and communal companies, whose activities varied enormously. Certainly one can detect a kind of regular pattern in the operations in the Allier, the Nièvre, the Loire and the Isère. But such operations bore no resemblance to great expeditions like that of the Aveyron, nor to the humdrum activities of the small administrative companies of the Alps and the Agenais. The latter remained under the control of a municipality or a *comité*; the former knew no restraint but the violent desires of an all-powerful *commissaire civil* , which in effect were no restraint at all.

In the departments everything depended upon the attitudes of those responsible for repressive measures: *représentants, commissaires civils*, and, in rare cases, revolutionary officers. The ordinary soldiers had no say and hardly ever took the initiative. Like the Parisians they were zealous denouncers of those making uncivic remarks. But those denunciations were much rarer and certainly less dangerous than those made by the local inhabitants; the views of the soldiers were of secondary importance only, and they were even somewhat despised by the revolutionary authorities themselves. They were less sharp, less proud than the stormy Parisians; but this made them even more dangerous in the hands of an adventurer like Viton or a fanatic such as Vauquoy. No one in the Compagnie Marat was to question the legality of the *noyades*, or – under a republican regime which prided itself on having substituted more humane and decent methods for the barbarous cruelties of the Ancien Regime – the recourse to such atrocities; they did their drowning with zeal and said nothing. Some undoubtedly did pity the victims of these massacres – the old, the women and children – and tried to save them from the waves and bring them to the bank once the operation had finished. But they were the exception, and their humanity only accentuates the brutal indifference of most of their comrades, content to do as they were told, without reflection. Nor did the 'dragoons' of Contamin protest at the burning of a farm or the rape of a serving-girl; and the artisans of Cahors and the peasants of the Lot, formed into battalions to go to the Aveyron, acted unquestioningly when ordered by their *commissaires* to set fire to a forest, a field of wheat or a thatched roof. They were again on hand to *chauffer* the feet of members of a farm family to force them to reveal the hiding place of their savings; and when Viton organised a mock beheading for a similar purpose, his soldiers were happy to act out the role of executioners.

In short, adminstrative anarchy south of the Loire and in the other exceptional regions helped to make an already anarchic and unregulated repression even more violent. In one place the repression could be mild and limited; in another it was ferocious and fickle. Arbitrariness reigned supreme and in these areas repression assumed a host of different forms, depending on chance, individual violence, and general lack of direction. It was an anarchical repression, the most unjust, the most ineffective kind.

II   *Orders to act with severity – the desire to punish*

'We are like soldiers whose general has ordered the sabring of the inhabitants of a besieged town and who are blamed for the deed while the general is not called to account. . .'.[7] Such was the defence of the members of the *comité révolutionnaire* of Nantes and the former Bataillon Marat, in their much publicised trial of Frimaire Year III, arranged by the Thermidorean authorities to discredit the 'régime de sang' of the Year II. Every one of the Nantes artisans who had participated in the *noyades* invoked the orders from the *représentants*, Carrier and Francastel, in their defence. It was they who had ordered an extensive and pitiless repression as the only way of preserving that tiny island of republicanism from a general uprising starting in the prisons. Such a line of defence played right into the hands of the Thermidoreans and the *jeunesse dorée*, who attended the trial and greeted the declarations of Chaux and his co-defendants with repeated cries of 'Carrier! Carrier!'. The former proconsul in the Loire-Inférieure was depicted as the head of Medusa in accordance with the Thermidorean picture of the Terror, and the scene was thus set for his own trial.

Carrier was far from being the only *représentant* to have issued such extremely severe orders to his subordinates; but he was to pay, almost alone, for the consequences of such a policy. With much courage he accepted responsibility in order to clear the military and civil authorities of Nantes and Paimbœuf, even though it was they who had warned him against showing any leniency towards a counter-revolutionary populace, which they represented as being on the verge of revolt. 'They denounced a conspiracy to me', Carrier was to state at his trial; 'they acted in the public good. . . . Some patriots having had wind of a conspiracy. . .came to tell a *représentant* and me, separately, that there was a move to destroy the *représentants* and the administrators and that we must destroy the traitors who amounted to some 6,000'.[8] On his departure for Nantes, Carrier had likewise received orders from the Committee of Public Safety to employ the greatest severity in order to save Nantes from attack by internal enemies. Once he arrived in the town, he would have had no reason to doubt the foundation of the fears expressed by the sans-culotte minority, particularly since they were members of the *société populaire* of Vincent-la-Montagne. It would be futile to try to assign responsibility for a repressive policy which culminated in the terrible *noyades*; but it can at least be stated that Carrier was not the only one involved. His role was above all one of lending official sanction to a policy of brutality which had already been called for – and indeed already put into practice before his arrival, both by the Nantes sans-culottes and the military authorities there. In Nantes, as in Toulouse and the Lot, the civilians were just as vociferous as the soldiers in proclaiming the merits of pitiless measures to save the Republic.

Responsibility for the punitive expedition to the Morbihan and the shootings there is more clear-cut. But Le Batteux and Avril were to shelter behind the orders issued to them by the *représentant* at Nantes. Had not Carrier ordered this former cook, turned postmaster of Redon, 'to have everyone put to death whom he found organising gatherings of rebels against the Republic...'? Le Batteux no doubt interpreted the word 'gathering' (*rassemblement*) somewhat freely when he had people shot coming out of high mass, but he could still say at his own trial, 'his orders [Carrier's] were to shoot aristocrats, nobles, fanatical priests...', even while admitting that 'it was on my orders that they were shot'. The commander of this expedition returned to the charge in another declaration indicating Carrier's responsibility. 'When the authorities denounced some rebels to me, I wrote to Carrier who told me to shoot them...', which he did. He even burnt a chapel at Questembert.[9] This time, however, Carrier made no effort to cover for his subordinates, declaring at his trial when confronted by Le Batteux: 'I cannot be held responsible where Le Batteux and [Avril] exceeded their orders, that concerns them alone...'.[10] Carrier may not in fact have ordered Le Batteux to shoot peasants, men and women alike, leaving church on a Sunday morning. But his injunctions in every letter to his *commissaire* in the Morbihan and to the adjutant-general, Avril, to use *grands moyens* to suppress a revolt which he was told threatened to engulf the entire department, and perhaps also Redon – key to the Vilaine – are incontestable.

Carrier was not alone of his kind. In the most diverse regions, *représentants en mission* recommended unlimited severity in the pursuit of internal enemies of the regime, and their appeals found enthusiastic adherents at every level: *commissaires civils*, garrison commanders, generals and district administrators. Clearly we must be careful not to take such calls for a legalised 'system of depopulation' too literally, and in the Year II we know that threats were used intentionally, as a means of avoiding the act. But in several cases, which we will examine, these instructions from the *représentants* were followed to the letter by the subordinate authorities, and atrocities, shootings and burnings were the result. In regions disturbed by bandits, these instructions were effective *ordres de mission*, outlining the tactics to be adopted.

Take for instance the doctor, Taillefer, the terrible 'Casse-Fer', 'Bras-de-Fer', who ordered his *commissaires* in the district of Villefranche-d'Aveyron to 'Strike, strike hard against these vile seducers who have brought national vengeance down upon their fellow citizens, strike those too who have been seduced...never forgetting that they cannot be won back...'[11] – scarcely a recommendation to leniency. Taillefer having set the tone, his subordinates would go one better: 'Give no quarter to these scoundrels', the garrison commander at Toulouse recommended to General Marbot, in a letter dated 8 Brumaire.[12] Cart, a Parisian, and government *commissaire* at Rodez, spoke in similar terms: 'The physical situation of the country is such', he wrote four days earlier to Bouchotte, 'that an army of 60,000 men would be insufficient to surround the mountains, the only sure way of crushing the rebels would be to destroy all the houses scattered over the mountains...'.[13] When in the Year III Viton was accused of having devastated the Aveyron, he justifiably replied that 'this department being the resort of royalist rebels...my orders were to burn woods, forests and everything which might offer them shelter as I advanced into the country...'.[14] Orders of such severity, two former *commissaires* were to claim later, were 'dictated by the danger in which these scoundrels placed the Republic; the Vendée, the Lozère required strong measures. Verdier [one of the *commissaires*] wanted to stamp out the germ of this fanatical war, nurtured in that area and threatening to spread into the Lozère, which was then in insurrection...'.[15]

Two other *commissaires*, writing shortly after these events, painted an equally alarming picture. 'Brigands infested the department of the Aveyron; they pillaged and murdered patriots, ...they schemed against Rodez, Sévérac and Millau...[and] were encamped with and commanded by experienced leaders...fanatical priests preached murder and arson in the name of God, whose mouthpiece they claimed to be...'.[16] However exaggerated a viewpoint – and the Lozère authorities seem to have adopted a less bleak view[17] – such fears were not the product of an imagination overheated by peasant rumour. Rather a very real royalist army existed in the Aveyron, the Cantal and the Lozère, flexible in numbers, commanded by military officers and enjoying considerable complicity from the villagers. In this region the sans-culotte minorities did indeed live in terror, and it is all too easy to forget the atmosphere of civil war and threat in which they acted, and which would compel even the Thermidorean authorities – scarcely sympathetic towards terrorist measures – to mount full-scale military operations in several departments.

Other *représentants* echoed Carrier and Taillefer, both of whom were natives of the South-West.[18] In the general assembly of Saint-Paterne the former monk, Laplanche, announced the creation of a revolutionary battalion and popular commissions, and sought to assure the patriots that: 'The Guillotine...will not touch the sans-culottes...'. Likewise, Javogues was to recommend 'his *armée révolutionnaire* to shoot former nobles, priests, men of the law and pettifoggers, as they would wild beasts...'.[19] Such invitations to a patriotic hunt did not fall on deaf ears, and we possess many testimonials to the collective approval by the sans-culottes – the members of the revolutionary battalions included – of such recommendations to severity against the enemies, real or supposed, of the regime. 'These scoundrels', the Lille soldiers were to tell a national agent in the Year III, 'spoke only of guillotines, sought only victims, everywhere proclaiming against the rich, against commerce...'.[20]

Individually too, *commissaires civils*, officers and a few soldiers expressed their satisfaction at such measures, with a macabre humour and vulgarity directed at the unfortunate victims. 'Our guillotine is rusting...we shall oil it with your sister', Verd was to reply delicately to one woman come to plead for a relative detained in the prisons of Moulins.[21] Henriot, *commissaire civil* in the neighbouring department, revelled in the same sick humour: 'Have you any money?' he asked a curé from the Corbigny district. 'I have but twelve livres, here they are'; 'that is not worth death, said Henriot, keep them, if we find you have more, you will be guillotined...'.[22] Such black humour was not always translated into action. But what of the words addressed by a member of the Compagnie Marat to one of the destined victims of the *noyades*: 'it's good to drink from a large cup...'?[23]

The Marats did not only joke; they openly approved of the massacre of the inmates of the Gouffay prison. 'You can cry, you bloody cretin', one of the soldiers said to a young prisoner whom he was accompanying to the barges; 'we're short of bread here, you can go to another world'[24] – a remark reminiscent of some attributed to those involved in the September massacres. Not only did the sans-culottes consider the prisoners a threat to stability, but also as *bouches inutiles* (useless mouths). Why should they have to feed the enemies of the regime, when the sans-culottes themselves could scarcely feed their families? Were not the subsistences destined solely for 'bons patriotes'? The counter-revolutionary, the lukewarm, the indifferent, the idle, the fanatical, were not simply dangerous, they were *inutiles*; consequently they had no right to food. This is what the unknown artisan, member of the Nantes battalion, really meant, and many sans-culottes would have supported him. Robin, a twenty-year-old National Guardsman from Nantes who had been wounded fighting the Chouans and had discovered the mutilated bodies of several of his comrades, when invited to participate in the drownings, unhesitatingly said yes. 'I jumped at the chance', he stated in the Year III; 'the horrors I had lived through decided that...'.[25]

For Robin, a pitiless and wide-ranging repression was above all a means of preservation; a means both of avenging those comrades finished off by children with pitchforks, at the edge of fields, and of 'extirpating' (as the sans-culottes liked to term it) those who were not worthy to live in a republic or who refused to make their peace with the regime. Robin and his like were thinking particularly of returned émigrés and their relatives, accomplices and agents, and of refractory priests and the peasants 'fanaticised' by them. In this region repression was given particularly wide limits. Durossier, former clerk of the Marat company, later said that he and his comrades had been given orders to arrest 'all who had an aristocratic air'. The cowardly young men of the Thermidorean *jeunesse dorée* acted no differently in attacking everyone in work clothes and arresting those with callused hands. In the eyes of some of these soldiers the repression was indeed a weapon against the rich. 'That is how to treat, and how we must treat aristocrats, *égoïstes* and moderates', Viton lectured his soldiers from the Lot during a domiciliary visit to a rich man in Moissac, when a hefty *taxe révolutionnaire* was levied.[26]

Several elements made up this approval of the repression: a sense of preservation, a desire to punish, a thirst for vengeance, class hatred, a wish to be rid of non-productive *bouches inutiles*, a hatred of priests, particularly refractory ones,[27] and above all a hatred of the townsman for the countryman. Usually repression took place in areas far removed from one's own and it was easier to use extreme brutality against 'étrangers' than against neighbours. The victims of the *noyades* were only rarely Nantes people; those pursued by Viton's soldiers were rather from the Rouergue. It was the same old story of feuding between the peoples of neighbouring regions.

In short, if one accepts surviving personal testimony – and it must be remembered that in the Year II noisy approval of the most spectacular acts of terror was the most elementary and least costly way of manifesting one's political conformism and revolutionary patriotism – it would seem that even the most ferocious measures had the support of all those responsible for implementing the orders of the *représentants*, the *commissaires civils* and the commanders of the revolutionary battalions. If some felt in their hearts that such atrocities and the quasi-automatic proscription of social categories were unworthy of a republican regime, they maintained a prudent silence. Within the ranks of the departmental companies we will search in vain for someone with the courage of the Parisian captain who protested against the arbitrary and inhuman character of the repression in Lyon.

III   *The arrests*

Like the Parisian *armée*, the main duty of the departmental and communal companies was the fairly mundane one of serving arrest warrants and escorting those arrested to the *maisons de détention* in the departmental and district *chefs-lieux*. In this they followed orders from the different authorities in charge of policing suspects – *représentants*, extraordinary commissions, *délégués* of one or the other members of the *comités de surveillance*. We know of no case of them implementing orders of the Committee of General Security, which seems to have used the Parisian *armée* exclusively.

Most of the arrests effected by the revolutionary forces were ordered by competent authorities. Only rarely was the source a particularly active *société populaire*, which had upset the normal hierarchy of power and taken over the *comité de surveillance*. The detachments themselves were but agents implementing orders; arbitrary arrests on the initiative of revolutionary officers were rare. Nor were the companies indispensable to the running of the repressive machine, and it is unlikely that their existence increased the overall number of arrests in regions where they were active – a negative finding already noted in the repressive action of Ronsin's *armée*.

No, the *commissaires civils* and the members of the *comités de surveillance* were the real power behind operations involving arrests, and the two were often the same persons. Going out at the head of detachments, it was they who ordered the arrest and release of victims. In the archetypal operations of the Nièvre and the Allier, the direction of the repression lay exclusively with the members of the *comités* of Nevers and Moulins. Many of the arrests in these departments were ordered in advance of the departure of the detachments, by the *comités*; but individual *commissaires* on mission were permitted to add names to the lists on their own authority. Grimaud, Desmazures, Marcillat and their colleagues took advantage of this liberty to increase the numbers of arrests in the communes through which they passed. In addition, several of these *commissaires* became members of the Commission Temporaire, and, endowed with even more extensive powers, they led the battalions into areas around Lyon and acted as absolute masters of the repression. Here too the revolutionary soldiers were simply executors of orders.

In the Hautes- and Basses-Alpes, the small companies were tightly controlled by the *comités de surveillance*. 'The famous delegates from the congress of Marseilles were still at Manosque on 24 October', wrote a local historian. 'They had formed a revolutionary battalion in the town. . . . *This troop was unarmed*; also the *comité de surveillance*. . .finding its actions too slow, ordered 200 men from the Forcalquier battalion to maintain order in the town and guard the prisoners. It was then that the real hunt began. Suspects were hunted down and put to the sword. Patrols scoured the town and the countryside.'[28] The same tight control by the *comité* can be seen at Digne, Entrevaux and Sisteron. In the last-mentioned the *comité* used the company against 'a nest of Federalists' within the department, and even offered it to the Hautes-Alpes authorities. Indeed this *comité* even revoked an arrest warrant of the *représentant*. In Sisteron the *comité* was clearly the real master of the repression.[29]

It was the same story in Agen, Moissac, Montpellier and Bordeaux. In Agen the tiny company was sent mostly on economic missions. But it too participated in repressive missions: on 27 Vendémiaire its commander was ordered by the *comité* to search for letters from Spain to certain inhabitants; on 2 Brumaire, he was ordered to make arrests, which he accordingly did, the 4th at La Sauvetat-Savères, the 6th of some deserters, the 8th the brother of an émigré, and on the 15th he was instructed to examine passports and arrest all foreigners among those passing through the *auberge*. Arrests continued in the early days of Frimaire and on the 22nd and 23rd detainees from Monbalen and Artigues were transported to Agen.[30] In the Montpellier district the *comité* likewise controlled the reins of repression. On 17 Brumaire it sent two companies to Mèze, where the municipality had been denounced; 1 Frimaire the company was ordered to make arrests of deserters in the surrounding region; 5 Frimaire it transported Federalists from the Bouches-du-Rhône to Marseille to appear before the Military Commission there, and in the course of that month it was sent to many other small towns to make arrests ordered by the *comité*. Likewise at Bordeaux, the revolutionary battalion of the Gironde made arrests on the authority of the departmental *comité* – a member of which even had a revolutionary officer arrested for questioning his orders.[31] In Grenade, the Toulousain *armée* made some arrests, but responsibility fell to the *commissaires civils* and the judges of the department's criminal tribunal. In most regions where revolutionary companies saw action, therefore, they enjoyed no autonomous repressive role, and these tiny companies were in no way a threat to the liberty of their fellow citizens.

There were, however, several regions in which the civil and military leaders of the revolutionary forces, as well as some officers, exercised authority without reference either to the *comités* or to the *représentants*. These were the Lot, the Aveyron, the Cantal and part of the Lozère, Nantes and its environs, and finally the Morbihan. In all these regions the number of arrests *was* decidedly increased by the existence of revolutionary companies. Yet it is important to distinguish between the different areas of this region of large-scale repression, for in the Lot in particular most of the arrests were made by the *comités de surveillance*.[32] Only in Moissac was Viton reproached for having made arrests arbitrarily without consulting the local *comité*, a *comité* indeed which so distinguished *itself* by its repeated abuse of power, that its members were later to be arrested and brought before the Committee of General Security in Paris.[33] In this department the situation was further complicated by the fact that certain revolutionary officers sat with the *comité* of Cahors when important measures of security and repression were being shaped, and it is difficult to separate their respective roles. Nevertheless, we know of only one case of an arrest having been made on the authority of the *armée révolutionnaire* alone, and even here it may in fact have been ordered by the Cahors *comité*.[34]

In certain areas in the Aveyron there was similar collaboration. But even in a department which witnessed real military repression, the number of arbitrary arrests was few. At Najac, Villefranche-de-Rouergue, Saint-Geniez and Sévérac, *commissaires civils* or members of the local *comités* made all decisions on arrests; the *révolutionnaires* were simply executants, and since they were strangers to the area, they would in any case have been unable to recognise supporters and accomplices of Charrier, who were thick on the ground in the mountain villages.[35] However, the officers from Cahors, on the advice of local patriots, did on occasion order arrests themselves. The worst abuses occurred in Villefranche, according to its *comité*, which accused these soldiers not only of having trafficked in arrest warrants, but also of having acted harshly against *les patriotes*.[36] But the most common abuse in this department seems to have been a kind of 'blackmail of arrest', whereby some members of the *armée* sought to profit from the discretionary power given them by the Military Commission and by Taillefer. When all is said and done, however, it is an extreme exaggeration, even in this zone of civil war, to speak of autonomous action by the *armée révolutionnaire* in terms of arrests. Here, as elsewhere, individual abuses provoked the same kind of protest from the established authorities as they would do later – just one of many indications that, at the time, the *armée révolutionnaire* caused much less fear than its adversaries would have us believe.

The case of Nantes is unique. Here one cannot speak of abuse of powers or arbitrary arrests, since each member of the Compagnie Marat held a *délégation* from Carrier to make arrests, not only in Nantes itself, but even more in the surrounding countryside. The men were not even obliged to refer to the *comité révolutionnaire*, soon to be in conflict with the company on this very issue of 'trespassing' upon its authority.[37] In Nantes, therefore, each 'Marat' possessed a portion of sovereign authority, the most visible aspect being the power to administer justice – one of Carrier's orders even declaring that these soldiers could arrest 'on sight' all who looked aristocratic. The Compagnie Marat was the only body empowered to act with complete autonomy in matters of arrest. It is true that such a position was short-lived, since the *représentant* responded to protests from the *comité révolutionnaire* and the established authorities by revoking such powers and subjecting the company to the control of the *comité*.[38] But for some time the company was able to act as it pleased, and since it was to make some 400–500 arrests within two months, it clearly made full use of such powers.[39]

In the Morbihan, Le Batteux held a *délégation* from Carrier, which he felt gave him the right to arrest, even to shoot, when he thought necessary. On arrival at Vannes, he was even imprudent enough to arrest a Jacobin personality, the pharmacist, Mouquet, from Lorient.[40] Le Batteux bore full responsibility; the officers and soldiers of his *armée* were unimportant, and when the leader was arrested, the subordinates were released. The problem highlighted by the case of Le Batteux was not so much one of arbitrary arrest as that of delegation of power – a problem only finally resolved by the law of 14 Frimaire.

A final assessment of the source of authority for the various arrests shows that the battalions and companies were a long way from being uncontrollable and unregulated agents of repression. Far from arresting 'on sight', abuses of power by the *révolutionnaires* were minimal; the threat of death held over the populace was usually little more than a threat, and they were content to execute the orders of the *comités de surveillance*, without going beyond their role as deliverers of warrants. There was, of course, that 'blackmail of arrest'; but this is a case of swindling rather than abuse of powers, and we know of only the one example of completely autonomous repression. Likewise the number of arrests made on the initiative of the revolutionary officers was not great, except in disturbed regions such as the Aveyron; here the demands of the struggle against well-commanded, well-disciplined and armed bands of rebels gave rise to all manner of excesses, brutalities and ultra-revolutionary measures. In terms of arrests, the role of these new instruments of the Terror differed little from that of the *exempts* of the previous regime.

Where did the weight of this repressive action fall? Was the arrest warrant a weapon in some social struggle by the departmental forces, as it sometimes was in the intervention of the Parisian *armée*? Were those arrested mostly the rich, the *coqs de village*, the most important merchants, the leisured? And did these arrests permit the sans-culottes to take the places of the *honnêtes gens* in the municipalities?

We can best discover the social categories which the *commissaires civils*, the *représentants* and the others responsible for the Terror sought to move against, by examining their orders and the instructions delivered by the *comités de surveillance* to the detachment commanders. The members of the Compagnie Marat, for example, were charged with the surveillance and if need be the arrest of suspect citizens of Nantes, foreigners passing through the port, those who had fled to the town to escape the attention of the *comités* in the localities where they were known, hoarders, *malveillants* and those who frequented literary salons.[41] The span was extensive; a vast clientele was assigned to the Marats, composed of the richest inhabitants of this newly prosperous town, of the shipowners and colonial supply merchants, with their beautiful, newly-erected stone houses on the quays of the île Feydeau. As if to emphasise the social nature of the repression which he was about to undertake, Carrier took up residence on his arrival in Nantes in one of these sumptuous island mansions belonging to an imprisoned slave-trader. From this luxurious residence (which still exists) the *représentant* from the Auvergne began his scourge of the 'riches égoïstes'.[42] The already corrupt soldiers had a direct interest in such a campaign, for in the apartments of the rich they were able to fill their pockets, and when the *comité révolutionnaire* finally learnt of this growing pillage, it intervened to remove the most corrupt elements from the company.

Certainly, throughout its reign, the Compagnie Marat devoted its attention almost exclusively to the shipowners and merchants, so hated by the small artisans and shopkeepers of Nantes.[43] In the Year III the entire company was blamed for having pursued 'the most worthy inhabitants' (Thermidorean terminology) in the town. However, we have little precise information on the 400 or so persons arrested during the two months' existence of the famous company. Nor can any further light be thrown on the matter by the social status of the victims of the *noyades*, most of whom were not native to Nantes. Rather they were peasant women and children, petty noble Chouans,[44] and refractory priests from the Bourbonnais, the Nivernais, the Forez and the Velay. The inhabitants of the île Feydeau seem not to have figured much among the victims of these massacres, though their arrest does lend a social aspect to the repression, under cover of which the sans-culottes were making war on the rich.

Elsewhere the situation is less clear. In the Loire in particular, and in other departments bordering on the Rhône, those in charge of the Terror were primarily concerned with fugitives from the siege of Lyon, hiding in safe houses tucked away in the mountains, after the final withdrawal of the comte de Précy's troops. Nobles, priests, and men of the law were the prey indicated by Javogues to his *armée* (p. 385). Many country nobles (*hobereaux*) were arrested in this department, including the royal body-guards who seem to have assumed an increasingly important position on Précy's general staff as the siege of Lyon became prolonged. In the Campagne and Villefranche districts bordering Lyon, those arrested were mainly small *seigneurs* and lawyers; while in the Ain the revolutionary soldiers arrested relatives of émigrés and large farmers.[45] But most of the arrests made in these three departments should be classed with the repression carried out by the Parisian *armée* or by the battalions from the Nièvre and the Allier. In the Isère, in the district of La Tour-du-Pin, the Parisians were seconded by the dragoons of Vauquoy and Contamin, and used primarily against refractory priests and large farmers – particularly numerous in this region – as well as those who owed money to the notorious Dolle. For his part, Contamin – the son of an artisan and himself an artisan in a wealthy little town[46] – seems to have considered it a point of honour to make things difficult for the yeomen farmers.

In the Allier, the battalion did arrest some poor artisans of Moulins, whose only crime was to have spoken ill of the revolutionary soldiers, and warned against enrolling in a force whose destination was unknown.[47] But this was an exceptional case, and in general the victims of arrest warrants in this department were people from a quite different social category. In Moulins itself, the *comité* had arrested 32 notables, mostly highly placed functionaries and leading personalities of the Ancien Regime: *parlementaires*, financiers, *fermiers généraux*, presidial judges, categories liable to automatic proscription because of their previous positions, as well as certain nobles, kinswomen of émigrés, and priests. All were taken to Lyon by a detachment of the revolutionary battalion, and there guillotined.[48] In the Montmarault district – according to the Thermidorean authorities – *commissaires* from the same *comité*, at the head of a squad of *révolutionnaires*, arrested only 'peaceable yeomen', and en route to Burges-les-Bains (Bourbon-l'Archambault), they had a dozen or so people locked up, all relatives of émigrés, priests and nobles, and municipal officers accused of having sheltered them. On his return to Lyon, Verd (a particular specialist in repression, and one of those responsible for the death of the 32 Moulinois) was accused of having pursued with particular virulence 'the Muscadins, bourgeois and village *messieurs*'[49] – precisely those categories against which the sans-culottes sought to use the full weight of the Terror.

Laplanche (himself a former monk) was to claim with some satisfaction the arrest of 'all the fanatical priests' as among the accomplishments of his *armée* in the districts of the Loiret.[50] Likewise in the districts of the Nièvre, Fouché's *commissaires* concentrated on ecclesiastics and political person-alities accused of having supported the *système fédéraliste*.[51] In both these departments the repression assumed political rather than social overtones, despite the hopes entertained by a man like Chaix that 'his' sans-culottes could be used as a class weapon against *les gros*, and *les bourgeois*.[52]

In the Aveyron the battalions from the Lot, in concert with the *commissaires civils* and the local *comités*, concentrated on the pursuit of Charrier's *bande*, and here, in this region of civil war, the *armées révolutionnaires* came nearest to attaining the goals for which they were created: to combat *les ennemis de l'intérieur*. Here the struggle did assume a military aspect, the 'bandits' sometimes taking up arms to wage real battles in the woods and mountains. In the course of one day, 6 Brumaire, a detachment from the Lot made 13 arrests in the area around Coussergues, on orders from the *comité* of Saint-Geniez-d'Olt. The next day the *comité* ordered it to capture two bandits who had taken refuge in the woods after assassinating some patriots.[53]

Who were the victims of this repression, which at times assumed the proportions of a punitive expedition against entire communities, with the Lot soldiers setting fire to villages and forests? The main victims were *gentilshommes*, former royal guards, like those refugees from Lyon hiding in the hills of the Forez. On 25 Brumaire, Jean-Baptiste Caplat, former royal *commissaire* at the district tribunal of Sévérac, appeared before the Rodez revolutionary Commission – over which Taillefer presided – accused of having directed the rebel encampment at Lapanouse which had terrorised the people of Sévérac.[54] The same camp was cited again some days later when it was announced that the *armée révolutionnaire* had arrested one Bedos, a 'brigand chief, commanding the cavalry of Charrier', and based at this remote camp. At the beginning of winter more than 300 held in the prison of Rodez still awaited judgement; 100 more had already appeared before the revolutionary Commission. But the *commissaires civils* estimated that there were not more than 4 or 5 actual military leaders, out of more than 40 known to be leading the different *bandes* still active in the area, among this number.[55] The repression waged by the *armée* of the Lot and the Cantal, therefore, only managed to catch in its net the rank and file brigands, along with their accomplices. in the mountain villages.[56]

In the Cantal, the revolutionary battalion, under orders from the Aurillac *comité*, managed to arrest at least one of the leaders of the insurrection plaguing part of this department. He was a former royal *procureur*, Louis Deveche, arrested 'as a suspect and denounced as having been at the head of a counter-revolutionary gathering on the Aveyron borders...'[57] – the only important capture that can be ascribed to this battalion. And yet the *comité* of Aurillac made every effort to trace these bands disturbing the border areas of the Aveyron and Lozère. At its session of 14 October, to which the departmental administration was invited, the *comité* ordered 200 men from the *armée révolutionnaire* to Montsalvy, under citizen Fau, and likewise, to the Marvejols area 'as many men raised from the districts of Saint-Flour and Murat, as considered necessary by the *représentants...*'. We do not know whether such a major deployment of force had any more success in the struggle against these royalist guerrillas than the *armée* of the Lot had in the neighbouring department.

There are no further references to arrests of leaders in the proceedings of this *comité* and the other operations assigned to the battalion were mundane in the extreme: on 1 Brumaire it was ordered by the *comité* to arrest Salsac, department administrator, accused of having spoken against Taillefer's *délégué*, Delthil; on the 27th a detachment was ordered to bring before the criminal tribunal of Aurillac a group of noblewomen from the Cantal who had taken refuge with sympathisers in the Puy-de-Dôme, and been tracked down by the Clermont-Ferrand *comité de surveillance* on information furnished by the Aurillac *comité*. Finally, on 13 Frimaire, the *comité* decided to send four revolutionary soldiers with one of its *commissaires* to arrest another man of the law, one Laussert, suspected of complicity with the brigands of the Lozère and Aveyron. All in all a disappointing return for Delthil, who nevertheless 'did not cease to thunder against the aristocracy of the rich and the Muscadins...' in his interventions with the *comité*. On 11 Brumaire he even listed the precise categories which he thought the *comité* ought to have watched and arrested: 'a crowd of scoundrels, fanatical priests, royalists, Federalists, *égoïstes*, Muscadins, moderates, indifferents, and bad citizens of every kind', he declared, 'are trying to seduce the people of the countryside and rouse the inhabitants of the Aveyron against the hallowed principles...'.[58] In the Cantal, therefore, despite the sound of soldiers marching, despite the inflamed spoutings of Delthil, despite the repressive enthusiasm of the Aurillac *comité* (whose members were friends and correspondents of Carrier),[59] the battalion arrested few and never went beyond its role of policing the tribunals. It is true that the main effort of this battalion was concentrated on the Aveyron, where it acted in conjunction with the Lot *armée*.[60]

In the Lot, the troops raised in Cahors and Gourdon were to arrest priests, religious fanatics among the womenfolk, rumour-mongers, Federalist leaders from the Dordogne – whose arrest was called for by the Sarlat *comité* – and a very few country notables whose wealth attracted the attention of men who adopted Viton's advice and made them pay dearly for the privilege of remaining at liberty.[61]

In the Basses-Alpes, the *comités* used the small companies against Federalist fugitives from the Hautes-Alpes, some of whom were accused of being in touch with the Piedmontese; and finally against deserters who, as in so many savage regions, 'took to the maquis', swelling the various troops of brigands and royalists.[62] The repressive operations of the companies from Montpellier, Montauban and Agen were directed towards the same categories, though few arrests were actually made, and their repression was mild. Indeed in Agen the activities of the company were so low keyed that the inhabitants never experienced the full rigours of the Terror.[63] In the Haute-Loire, if Prudhomme is to be believed, the battalion created by Reynaud ruthlessly pursued the poor artisans of the mountain villages, the lacemakers, men and women alike, who had not sworn the oath and had taken refuge with their priests in the woods.[64] At Méthanis in the Vaucluse, an *armée révolutionnaire* of sorts went in pursuit of 'fugitives, scoundrels, fanatics and refractory priests who might seek refuge in our woods and mountains...'.[65] In the Ariège, the Toulouse detachment arrested priests, and a few peasants, denounced for fanaticism or anti-French talk. Those battalions operating near the frontiers were primarily concerned with traitors, enemies of the regime, foreign agents and distributors of false *assignats*. In the Ariège in particular, the sorties of Baby's *armée* often assumed the appearance of a punitive expedition against an entire populace suspected of having hoped for a Spanish victory. In such cases, the repression was directed less against a specific social category than against a way of speaking, a foreign patois, against members of a nation who had shown themselves unworthy of liberty. In such cases the revolutionary force served the interests, not of any 'communalist' policy, but of unity, indivisibility and Jacobin centralisation.

In the final analysis the social range of those arrested was so diverse that it is impossible to see the arrest warrant as any kind of instrument in the struggle of poor against rich, sans-culottes against *égoïstes*, urban artisans against big farmers, men of the law and financiers. If such categories often figured in warrants, the reason was usually political rather than social. Federalism in the departments had largely been a movement of the *grands bourgeois*, not involving the people. The exceptions were Lyon, the Yonne, the Isère, the Calvados, and, to a certain extent, Bordeaux – places where the movement benefited from a certain degree of popular adhesion, to such an extent that it was sometimes able to use the most authentically popular Sectionary institutions against the centralisation of Paris. In Bordeaux, however, those Sections with a predominantly sans-culotte population seem to have remained outside the movement, even at the height of the crisis, and such non-involvement paid off when the machinery of repression was installed. The repression then, insofar as it was directed against the framework of Federalism, tended to affect mainly the *honnêtes gens*.

But when it was a question of armed rebels fighting against the Republic, repression also caught in its net the former royal bodyguard, the small seigneur, the man of the law, the lady of quality returned from emigration, the *chefs de bande*, and a whole range of dependent menials: servants, day-labourers driven by poverty from their home villages and recruited into the royalist ranks for the same reason (certainly the case in the Lozère), former soldiers of élite regiments, deserters, *paysannes* become canteen women, and finally professional bandits, thugs and *chauffeurs*. The last-mentioned category in particular, coming from the seedy underworld of urban slumland, were politically ultra-conservative, remaining attached to the Ancien Regime with its outmoded concepts of honour and courage, even its dreadfully cruel and slow system of justice. The armies of crime had the same troops as those of Christ and the King, sometimes also the same leaders, for royalism had its plebeian element, and crime was part and parcel of the old France. In terms of political intent, therefore, such arrests made no distinction between social categories among the country populace.

Indeed the political repression was above all directed against two categories: the country populace as a whole, and the women in particular. Arrests were rarely numerous in the towns, Nantes and Bordeaux being the exceptions – though even here many of the prisoners actually came from the surrounding countryside. As the instrument of municipal policy, the revolutionary battalion had no quarrel with the townspeople, and most of those shut up in the *maisons d'arrêt* in the *chefs-lieux* had been arrested in the countryside. Besides, suspects, by very definition, were more numerous in the villages than in the towns; those with good reason to fear the revolutionary policy tended to retire to their country homes, or quite simply take to the fields by joining the nearest *bande*, and former Federalist authorities, as with deserters and refractory priests, fled the towns. Every malcontent in the country could count on widespread complicity, even from the established authorities, from the municipalities, indeed even from the village *comités*, whose sole *raison d'être* seems to have been to placate their fellow citizens and to protect them from the effects of the *lois d'exception*. In the country, it was the detested and isolated sans-culotte, who, even in the Year II, risked death. The revolutionary forces should be seen as the arms of a body whose brain was the urban *comité*, arms which extended urban repressive action and surveillance to the most inaccessible villages. The urban soldier left his town, not without trepidation, to embark upon perilous mountain paths, and plunge into the *bocage* with its treacherous hedges, regions where it was unpleasant to live as a *révolutionnaire*, pursuing the *ennemi de l'intérieur*, an enemy who assumed the very colour of the countryside and was largely invisible.

The repressive action of the *armées*, especially in terms of arrest, was directed as much against the women as against their husbands and sons, for in the country in particular it was they who represented one of the greatest threats to the regime. It was they who kept the flame of the Catholic faith alight, they who flocked to clandestine masses, they who appealed to the vanity of the men and pushed them into taking up the struggle against the 'atheists'. They were the most effective recruiting agents for the *bande à Charrier* and its like, and served the counter-revolution just as effectively as the beautiful marquises and pretty courtesans in Paris, who urged their lovers to emigrate.[66] The anti-feminism of the sans-culottes was un-doubtedly due in part to the reputation women had for excessive attach-ment to Catholicism. But the country women were themselves responsible for attracting the attention of the repressive authorities, for in their bond with the refractory priests and their services to the irregular forces (even to the point of feeding them), they sustained the disorders which threatened internal peace and disrupted communications between the towns. Some imperilled the total mobilisation of the resources of the nation by harbouring deserters or bringing them food in their hideouts. Others took up arms at the side of their menfolk, to fire upon the *bleus*, which was the case with most of the *paysannes* who later found themselves on the way to Le Gouffay prison, then to the barges. The fury of the Marats was directed particularly against their female prisoners, women and young girls, nobles and peasants alike, whom they insulted and manhandled in every con-ceivable way, dragging them along by their hair, before sending them to the bottom of the Loire. The anti-feminism of some of those responsible for the repression caused them to single out women, those 'fanatical', 'frivolous' creatures,[67] as the main prey for their battalions. They also spent their time thinking up new, spectacular ways of conquering feminine 'égoïsme'.[68] Lack of statistics prevents an exact calculation of the proportion of women among those arrested by the *armées*. But in Nantes at least there were almost as many women as men among the prison population and the victims of the *noyades* and *mitraillades*.

It is impossible to calculate the number of arrests made by the battalions and companies. The local authorities, hostile to the *armées*, tended to exaggerate the numbers in order to make the popular forces seem more odious. But we do possess some fragmentary statistics for certain areas. In Nantes, some 400 to 500 were arrested by the Marats. In the Allier we know of about 50 persons arrested by the battalion, though this figure must fall far short of the actual number of victims. In the Year III, Fouché was to be accused of having terrorised 'les habitants les plus intéressants' of the Nièvre, but no one knew the precise number of arrests. In the Corbigny district, the *commissaires civils*, led by Chaix and assisted by his accurate information on the wealth of his compatriots, arrested no more than a dozen priests and farmers.[69] It has been claimed – though on what authority we know not – that in the Loire Javogues's *armée* arrested more than 300 people, a figure which does not seem excessive for a department where many Lyonnais took refuge and where Federalism had considerable support. The presence of the Military Commission of Feurs must also have helped increase the volume of arrests.[70] In the Aveyron, the Lot *armée*, and the other battalions accompanying it, arrested at least 400 suspects – the figure cited for those detained in the prison of Rodez in Brumaire and Frimaire[71] – to which must be added the numbers incarcerated at Villefranche, Sévérac, Najac, Laissac, Saint-Geniez and other administrative centres of the repression in this department, a factor which spared them from being called before the Military Commission. The figure for the Aveyron, however, must surely have reached 1,000, perhaps even more. This was the area where those *grands moyens* were fully employed – too fully, in fact, if we believe General Marbot, writing in the Thermidorean period and claiming that Charrier had only an insignificant force of some 60 men.[72] Such calculations, however, take no account of the widespread complicity which a very small band of determined men might enjoy in this *pays*.

Elsewhere, events unfolded in a much less dramatic fashion – a case of finding the ringleaders rather than punishing an entire population. In Grenade, for example, despite the numbers involved, and the threatening tone of proclamations by the *commissaires civils* and the officers from Toulouse, not more than 10 people were arrested. Even in the district of Toulouse arrests were isolated occurrences, one or two per commune, with most communes unaffected by this repression at artisan level.[73] We are less well informed on the Ariège, where the existence of a military tribunal, sitting at Pamiers, and the energy of the young Vadier, the public prosecutor, must have produced numerous arrests, particularly among the priests and the faithful of the Saint-Girons district.[74] We have counted some 30 arrests in Agen and its environs. Most were on economic charges and did not have serious consequences for the victims – at the most a few weeks in prison. Figures show about the same number for Montauban and Montpellier and its surrounding region.[75] In the Basses-Alpes, the company arrested three persons in Digne itself, while eight arrests took place at Sisteron – thanks, no doubt, to the presence of an active *société populaire*, which unhesitatingly ordered arrests on its own account and seemed to have had the *comité de surveillance* firmly in its control.[76]

So how many of these lacemakers of Prudhomme's account were arrested in the Haute-Loire? Prudhomme does not tell us, preferring, like many hostile historians, the kind of vagueness which permits the imagination to ignore all obstacles and see the repression as unlimited. We are not told, for instance, how many victims Schneider and his zealous *commissaires* claimed in the terrible hunts through the communes and districts of Haguenau, Sélestat and Strasbourg. We are only told about the harshness of their methods, the horrors and atrocities of which they were guilty, the summary executions of victims in front of their farms and families.[77] Nor is there any information on the weight of a terror which sent thousands of inhabitants fleeing to the Palatinate. As for the *armée* of the North, we know of no arrests made by it. Certainly the denunciations made by Dufresse's sans-culottes must have led to some arrests, but these were products of individual initiative (see below, pp. 411–14). In Bordeaux, the Military Commission had several hundred persons arrested, accused of having taken part in the Federalist movement. Some of these arrests were made by the revolutionary battalion, which was likewise sent into the districts of Lesparre and Libourne to arrest former Federalist officials and escort them to Bordeaux.

But in the Gironde, thanks to the energy of the *comité de surveillance* and the ferocity of Lacombe, the repression did not need the battalion's assistance and arrests continued at the same level after its disbandment.[78] Here too the existence of an *armée révolutionnaire* scarcely affected the tempo of the arrests and the Terror.

IV   Les grands moyens: *the exceptional operations*

Normal operations for the revolutionary detachments consisted of delivering warrants, escorting suspects to the *maisons d'arrêt* in the *chefs-lieux*, carrying out frequently extensive domiciliary visits in the urban Sections, inspecting *auberges*, scrutinising passports, searching for foreigners, deserters and fugitives from the Federalist departments, sometimes also policing the prisons, guarding those under house arrest, mounting guard at the door of the *comités* – in short assisting the *comités de surveillance* with their daily tasks. This was the administrative repression, so mundane that public opinion retained little memory of the departmental and communal *armées* which put it into effect; people simply became accustomed to them, as they did to nearly every aspect of such an exceptional system as the Terror. Seven-eighths of the activities of these small companies consequently escaped the notice of the chroniclers and journalists; they were more interested in the big game than in these artisans employed in revolutionary policing, and it is significant that while in Paris the soldiers of Ronsin were hunted out with unusual ferocity, in the departments the Thermidorean authorities did not consider the members of the companies sufficiently important even to have them included in lists of those to be disarmed or arrested.

But there were also multi-sided operations, such as those undertaken in the Nièvre and the Allier, assuming many different aspects: repression (arrests), political purification (the purging of local authorities), levelling (*taxes révolutionnaires*, distribution of surpluses), assisting the sans-culottes, civic sermonising. Such missions, following the model of those led by Chaix and Commerçon in the Corbigny district, or Parent in the district of Clamecy, went far beyond the bounds of pure repression, and we shall return to the activities of these Chaixs, Vauquoys, Picots and Villers when we look at the political action of the communal forces: dechristianisation and pillage, real or imaginary. In the present context, however, it must be stressed that arrests played a very secondary role in the operations and in the activities generally of these egalitarian *commissaires*. Chaix was criticised mainly for his propaganda in favour of the *loi agraire*, his violent sorties against the bourgeoisie, his slurs on religion and the *représentants*; but although he often brandished the threat of arrest, he made few in reality. Likewise Baby and Picot, in the Ariège, preferred words to action. Many threats were made, but few people were arrested. The multiple-type operation was terror on a small scale, noisy, but relatively anodyne.

Of the many activities of the Parisian *armée*, it was its (still debatable) participation in the Lyon *mitraillades* which contemporary opinion remembered best. A similar distortion of the work of the departmental *armées* earned them a sanguinary reputation which few merited. In Robespierrist and Thermidorean literature, *compagnie révolutionnaire* was translated as *noyades, frères* as *noyeurs, mitrailleurs* and, after the Year III, as *égorgeurs*. The Compagnie Marat, despite its very different character from that of all the other *armées révolutionnaires*, despite its uniqueness, its independence, its autonomy of action, was taken by contemporary writers as the prototypical instrument of a pitiless repression. Indeed, the main factor distinguishing this tiny company from all the others was its exclusive concentration on repression. The Marats did not evangelise the countryside, they did not preach equality of wealth or attack religion – or if they did, they did so in the style of le Père Ubu, equalising wealth by emptying the pockets of prisoners, dechristianising by drowning priests in sinister baptisms, evangelising the peasants by insults and blows from their rifle butts before throwing them into the water. The Marats saw the repression through all its stages, conducting the victims from mansions and furnished lodgings alike, through the prisons of Le Gouffay or Sainte-Claire, and finally to the barges on the Loire. The company had free access to the prisons as well as to individuals' homes, a privilege which they used extensively to maltreat prisoners and to help themselves to the jewellery of rich Nantaises and the noblewomen of the surrounding country. They shared, with the *comité révolutionnaire*, with the Vincent-la-Montagne *société*, with the garrison officers, with Carrier, responsibility for the repression at Nantes; they were participants rather than instruments and it is this factor which above all else distinguishes them from other *révolutionnaires* in the departments. They were a corps of killers, terrorising the Nantais in a thousand different ways, arresting them for the way they looked, breaking down doors, imposing and lifting sequestrations at will. They were, for a time, the uncontested masters of the repression in its most violent of forms.

The Marats were convinced, as were the Nantes sans-culottes, that the suspects shut up in Le Gouffay, in Sainte-Claire and in the other prisons of the town were preparing a general break-out to coincide with a major offensive by brigands from outside. Letters sent to the prisoners from their friends and relatives, and intercepted by the *comité révolutionnaire*, seemed to confirm such, perhaps not entirely groundless, fears and they were communicated to Carrier and his colleagues by the Nantes *révolutionnaires* as soon as they arrived.[79] This general fear of a prison plot, far more than the atrocities committed by brigands on volunteers from Nantes who fell into their hands, was the starting-point for the *noyades* and *mitraillades* which soaked this town in blood and the reason why its populace sanctioned them. The Marats did not act in isolation; they could count on support from the militants of the *comité* and *société*, as well as that of the republican garrison officers. According to some witnesses, they were even helped in the massacres by a troop of mulattos raised by the *comité révolutionnaire* and proving just as enthusiastic in disposing of suspects as the Marats.[80] Carrier later admitted to having condoned such measures because of his 'conviction... that a civil war can only be terminated by the destruction of one of the two parties...'. A prison plot, the Vendéan atrocities, a civil war – the Marats had any number of arguments with which to convince the soldiers of the necessity for such action. But their commanders, leaving nothing to chance, further stimulated the resolution and ferocity of the men with copious supplies of drink. Many witnesses claimed that the soldiers were already drunk before they left the Le Gouffay prison on the evening of the first *noyade*. Forget, governor of the Sainte-Claire prison, was to claim that 'Goulin gave 50 livres to the *cabaret* to supply the Marat company with drink at the time of the Le Gouffay *noyade*'. And Laquère, his counterpart in the Le Gouffay prison, added: 'the Marat company called for drink, and tried to see who would be the most skilful in tying the prisoners together'. An escapee from the *noyade*, Tintelin, for his part declared that Grandmaison and the soldiers were already drunk when they arrived at the Le Gouffay prison with the lists in their hands; and Maigniet, a member of the company or the *comité*, 'said he had signed the order for the *noyade*, but his name wasn't on it. They were all drunk...'.[81]

Thus initiated, the expedition took off in an atmosphere of gaiety, amidst coarse jokes and drunken cries. 'On the night of 24 to 25 Frimaire', declared Laquère, 'two from the Marat company demanded 155 prisoners and took aside 128, placing two coils of rope on the table. "Where are you taking them?" "To Belle-Isle to build a much-needed fort." Then they left, two hours later [at 10.30 in the evening] 30 to 40 from the Marat company arrived and asked for the 128 – "I need an authorisation from the established authorities" – two left, went to the *comité*, I think, and brought back a list of 155 prisoners...'. The accuracy of this statement was confirmed by Durossier, clerk to the company: 'I was called out one day with the company by the captain, in the evening we went down to the prison with a list, had the prisoners tied two by two and sorted into groups, the last of which I led away to the pit in the port...'. Here is how Poupon, who survived that terrible night, described the conditions in which the transfer took place: 'During the night of 24 Frimaire the Marat company brought ropes, Duçon and Joly did the tying. Durossier worked through the night, the list in his hand...they seized prisoners by the hair, by the ears, punching them with their fists, smashing their faces with musket butts, tearing their hair out... Joly at least spoke truthfully...he himself did not do too much harm...'. Some other escapees did not share this opinion of the copper-caster, a leading figure in the company, whom they claimed had acted in a particularly revolting manner: 'Joly treated the prisoners like a butcher's dog harassing herds of cattle', giving those he was tying up blows with the flat of his sabre, claimed other witnesses. 'I had to do all I could', was Joly's reply when questioned.[82]

Who issued the order for the transfer of these prisoners? It surely cannot have been subalterns like Joly and Durossier. Batelier, *commissaire* to the criminal tribunal of Nantes, attributed it to the commander of the company, Captain Fleury, who 'gave the order as night was falling to go to Le Gouffé [*sic*], the prisoners were brought down, tied two by two, made to embark and pushed out into the middle [of the river]....'.[83] Phélippes, in his printed account, held the members of the *comité* responsible for the order: 'On 24 Frimaire, Goulin, Grandmaison and another member of the *comité* arrived at the *maison de justice*, followed by Joly and other members of their [*sic*] *armée révolutionnaire*. They drank and ate and called for the 160 prisoners on their proscription list to be brought up...only 129 could be found... Goulin and the *armée révolutionnaire* then took the 129 victims, tied up...and threw them into the terrible waves of the Loire'.[84] But these versions were of little interest to the judges of the revolutionary tribunal, who listened instead with undisguised satisfaction – as did the public and the *jeunesse dorée* crowding and pushing behind the barriers – to the testimony of a former adjutant, Richard, who had been expelled from the company by Carrier himself for corruption. Richard knew what was expected of him, 'it was the *représentant* who issued the order, and the Marat company which implemented it', he declared amidst the applause of his hearers.[85]

The active participation of the members of the company in the *noyades* is unquestionable and many admitted as much. Crespin declared 'that he had only carried out orders, in climbing on board the boat'; Coron said 'that he had taken part, but had saved one of the unfortunates whose pleadings he listened to, recognising him as innocent'. Ducourt admitted to having been on a barge three-quarters of a league out from Nantes, and Leroy saw Grand-maison and Joly on one of the boats stripping priests of their possessions. Boussy just had time to jump on board a small boat as the barge on which he had climbed went down, a trap having been opened in its hold.[86] Other soldiers described the atrocities which followed: as the barges slowly sank into the frozen waters of the Loire, the unfortunate prisoners, still tied in twos, climbed on one another's shoulders, trying to grab hold of the boats carrying the soldiers; but the soldiers slashed at their hands with sabres and prevented them from boarding. Most were carried off by the current; but some reached the banks, where the more humane Marats brought them help and assisted their escape, while swearing them to silence on the terrible happenings from which they were fleeing. Some members of the company, called as witnesses in Carrier's trial a year later, broke down when recalling the scenes they had witnessed.

The tribunal, however, did not deal harshly with the Marats for their participation in the *noyades* (and the *mitraillades*). In its eyes they were simply tools, who had in any case helped to establish the culpability of Carrier and his associates – for the most part garrison officers and members of the *comité*.[87] On 26 Frimaire Year III, Naud (armourer), Charretier (shopkeeper), Ducourt (wigmaker), Caron (ex-*procureur*), Boussy (parasol-seller), Boulay (shoemaker), Gauthier (cutler) and Crespin, or Crepin (wig-maker) were found guilty of participation in the *noyade* of 24 Frimaire Year II, but as they had acted 'without malice', and on the orders of superiors, they were acquitted. Joly, Durossier and Richard, however, were dealt with more severely, undoubtedly because of their role in choosing the victims, their apparent premeditation, and – on the evidence of escapees – their exceptional brutality during the transfer of victims to the port.[88]

The affair of the *noyades* was undoubtedly the most remarkable operation carried out by this small company and the reason for its notoriety. However it would be wrong to see the Marats as professional executioners, constantly employed in drownings and shootings. The *noyades* was an exceptional episode in the history of the repression; even in Nantes the revolutionary soldiers were largely employed, as elsewhere, in serving arrest warrants,[89] making domiciliary visits, imposing and lifting seals on property; and the Marats were to be talked about more for their acts of pillage than for their participation in the *noyades*.

The *noyades* were the outcome of fear and panic. The repression in Nantes took place amidst very special circumstances, and this exceptional situation had given rise to a revolutionary company which bore as much resemblance to the real thing as a caricature does to a faithful portrait. The Marats were probably no more brutal than sans-culottes in other towns, but the personal danger which they experienced daily, in a besieged town and amidst a populace which was hostile to the regime of the Year II, made these small shopkeepers and artisans ferocious. It was only in the Year III, when they recalled those horrific scenes, that some broke down in sobs; nor should we doubt their sincerity on that occasion any more than express astonishment at their brutal joy a year before, as they pushed women, children and old men under the water. 'The phenomenon of the terror', Pierre Paganel, former proconsul in the South-West, was to write later, 'will be viewed by future observers with astonishment and horror – a notable reminder to moderate governments of the importance of protecting the people from the vice of fear, a deadly poison polluting the nation, destroying all noble senti-ment, all generous passions...'.[90]

The expedition to the Morbihan created less stir than the activities of the Marats at Nantes. The *armée* of Le Batteux shot only a dozen at the very most; and even if Redon's troop was sufficiently cruel to force the victims to dig their own graves, the toll was nothing like that of the *noyades* and the massacres in the neighbouring department. This invasion of a peaceable department by an armed force from the Ille-et-Vilaine is of interest for other reasons apart from the horror which such a departure from republican civility must inspire in us: it is, above all, another demonstration of the key role played by these 'hommes de liaison' in the development of major repressive initiatives. It required the presence of one (Le Batteux) to initiate the operation and the fortuitous intervention of another (Jullien) to bring it to an end. Le Batteux was the *délégué* of Carrier; Jullien, who chanced to be in the Morbihan when Redon's troop arrived, was the emissary of the Committee of Public Safety, and, more particularly, of the Robespierrist clan. The Morbihan affair was the embodiment – in the persons of these two men – of the conflict which had finally come into the open between the anarchic and decentralised ultra-revolutionary repression and the conciliatory policy of central government. It was perhaps symbolic that the thundering entrance into the town of Vannes of this *délégué* of Carrier at the head of his '*armée*' should have coincided with the promulgation of the law of 14 Frimaire. The arrest of Le Batteux sealed the final condemnation of these *grands moyens*, this anarchistic and violent policy of repression. Jullien recognised this; he did not condemn the soldiers of Le Batteux – they were, he said, good republicans, whose sole crime was to have defended the regime with excessive zeal – but he was unrelenting against their commander, the Redon postmaster, the appointed representative of ultra-revolutionary authority in all its irresponsibility and inconsistency. To underline his disgrace, Le Batteux was, for the moment, sent to prison in the *chef-lieu*, while his soldiers were sent home, if not with the full honours of war, at least with certificates of patriotism.

In the last days of Brumaire trouble broke out in the canton of Noyal-Muzillac. The Morbihan authorities, on the advice of Jullien, took immediate steps to end this nascent insurrection, which had been fomented by refractory priests and threatened to spread to the extremely Catholic countryside. No effort was spared, and Jullien promised to send 2,000 men from the *armée révolutionnaire* (Parisian?).[91] The intervention of the troops sent from Vannes and Lorient, however, sufficed to restore calm by the first *décade* of Frimaire.[92]

It was then that Carrier intervened from Nantes, having been informed of the events by the Morbihan authorities some days earlier. On 4 Frimaire he ordered Le Batteux 'to take the 5th battalion of the Bas-Rhin into the different cantons of the department of Morbihan...at Redon he is to raise all the forces which the commune can spare...citizen Le Batteux is authorised to take every measure to ensure subsistences to every citizen and to recruit reinforcements from every commune. He will put to death all those forming *rassemblements* to revolt against the Republic...'.[93] On 9 Frimaire Carrier informed the Committee of Public Safety of these measures: '...I have told the Convention of the counter-revolutionary troubles which have erupted in the Morbihan; as soon as the news reached me, I sent extraordinary couriers to Lorient, to Saint-Brieuc and to the patriot communes of the Morbihan' (but he was careful not to alert the authorities of Vannes, however 'patriote' they might be) 'to urge them to rise *en masse* and fall upon these new brigands...'.[94] Finally, on the 11th, he wrote again to his *délégué*: 'I have written to Avril [adjutant-general] inviting him to consult with you. I have provisionally given him command of the Republic's troops in the Morbihan, and you must co-ordinate measures with no one but him...'.[95] By this date Le Batteux's troops had passed through Noyal-Muzillac and were pressing on towards Vannes and the coast.

'All seemed peaceful', Mancel, a former administrator of the department of Morbihan, was to write in the Year III, when the case against Carrier was being prepared, 'then various people told us that someone called Le Batteux from Redon had entered the department at the head of an *armée révolutionnaire*. The department...was astonished that Le Batteux had not informed us of his powers and of the march of his army.... Then several individuals told it that Le Batteux had taken his army to Noyal-Muzillac, where he had found some country people gathered in a church and had eight of them shot.... These eight unfortunates were shot when, on the arrival of the army, they came forward to leave the church.... Le Batteux levied contributions from the communes through which he passed...'; he likewise had an employee of the Noyal-Muzillac customs shot.[96] At his trial Le Batteux did not deny these summary executions (10 or 11 in number), even if his recollection of them was hazy; but in defence he argued that the toll was far below that of Carrier – he had shot only the leaders of the insurrection and spared the rank and file (the *piétaille*).[97] Besides, he added, the indignation of Mancel was somewhat manufactured, since, on 26 Frimaire Year II – the very time of these events – he had signed a certificate of good conduct for Le Batteux in his capacity as a member of the Commission Militaire of the Morbihan.[98]

On 20 Frimaire, at the head of an army of 350 men, according to some, 600 according to others, Avril and Le Batteux arrived at the gates of Vannes. 'Finally', wrote Mancel in the Year III,

> the roll of drums announced the arrival of Le Batteux and his *armée révolutionnaire*. At the same time we received a letter designed to inspire terror from the *représentant* Carrier, then at Nantes.... He treated us like scoundrels and threatened us with national vengeance.... He [Le Batteux] accused us of planning to march against him and his army [the National Guard of Vannes] and to use the cannon to prevent his entrance into the town. This was a downright lie.... He told me that he was a *délégué* from the *représentant* Carrier.... I did not think that I could refuse to recognise his powers, even though I had never encountered such unlimited and arbitrary ones.... From the time of the arrival of the *armée révolutionnaire* the cannon were trained on the *maison de détention*. That evening Le Batteux was at the *société populaire*. Citizen Mouquet, an apothecary from Lorient, and a *délégué* from the Commission des Subsistances just arrived from Paris, announced that he had been present at the session of 14 Frimaire when the *armée révolutionnaire* had been suppressed. After the session, Le Batteux took his escort to the home of Mouquet's mother, called him out, showered him with invective, dragged him to prison, slapped him in the face and had him put in chains. However, citizen Mouquet was released on the request of the department. The law

of 14 Frimaire became public. General Avril, who commanded the *armée révolutionnaire*, wrote telling us that he would return his troops to camp. Le Batteux presented himself before the department on the same day... he complained loudly about the spinelessness of General Avril in leaving so abruptly, I replied that I could see nothing to reproach in a general who obeyed the law....[99]

The essentials of this account were confirmed by Jullien, then at Lorient. On the 22nd he told the Lorient *société* about 'the arbitrary violence with which the patriot Mouquet was incarcerated and put in chains in Vannes by *commissaires* whom he regarded as anti-revolutionary; he announced the order which he had issued for the release of the republican Mouquet; the *société* was indignant at news of this imprisonment.... Renaud put forward the motion to dispatch a courier to inform the Committee of Public Safety of the tyrannical conduct of these supposed revolutionary *commissaires*... but Jullien said that the courier had already left and that soon these *commissaires* would no longer be able to violate liberty...'.[100] Two days later the issue of the *affaire* Mouquet was again raised and

the acts of violence and imprisonment to which [Jullien] had been exposed by these *malveillans* seeking to destroy the Republic by oppressing patriots and to overthrow the Revolution by the Revolution. He [Jullien] distinguished the *Armée révolutionnaire* at Vannes from its commander; the *armée*, he said, was useful in the Morbihan and was composed almost entirely of excellent patriots, excellent sans-culottes, firm supporters of liberty, with whom the inhabitants of Lorient would be delighted to associate if they came to their town. He had quite a different opinion of its commander, the man called Le Batteux, to whom could be attached the meaningful term of *ultra-revolutionary*.... In consequence he put forward the motion that the *société*...should write immediately to citizen Carrier asking him to withdraw the powers so dangerously delegated to a man who, far from deserving his confidence, could not be left in possession of such power without imperilling the public good. The motion was supported from all sides and one member also denounced Avril as an equally dangerous leader....[101]

The leaders of the two groups addressed themselves to their respective masters, Le Batteux complaining to Carrier of 'harassment' by the emissary of the Committee of Public Safety, Avril venting his discontent with Jullien and the Vannes authorities after his return to the Ille-et-Vilaine. Jullien, for his part, wrote on 26 Frimaire to Tréhouard, the *représentant en mission* to the Breton departments: 'I leave Lorient this evening for Vannes to dissolve the *armée révolutionnaire*, some actions by it having been denounced to us, and to gather positive and detailed information on the conduct of its commanders...'.[102] Tréhouard ordered the arrest of Le Batteux; but on 4 Nivôse, his order, described as 'impudent', was countermanded by Carrier, who called the oppressed and 'brave republican' to Nantes.[103]

Le Batteux does not seem to have remained long with his protector at

Nantes, for in Nivôse he was back in Redon where he escaped an attempted assassination. Having resumed his functions as postmaster, he seems to have experienced no further upsets, despite the many denunciations by the Morbihan authorities. But in Germinal Year II, at the time of the great offensive against so-called 'hébertistes' in the departments, he received threatening letters, and on 11 Floréal, when the ultra-revolutionaries had clearly fallen from grace, he was interrogated by the Redon *comité* about 'excessively revolutionary words spoken in the *société populaire*...'. After Thermidor, things grew worse for this former protégé of Carrier. On 10 Vendémiaire Year III, the *comité de surveillance* placed two sentries on guard at his house, and on the 28th he was transferred to prison in the *chef-lieu*, Rennes. On 18 Frimaire he was sent to Paris to appear before the revolutionary tribunal, and a few days later (the 23rd) he was cited as witness no. 299 in the trial of his former master, when he cowardly hid his own guilt behind orders issued by the *représentant*. After giving details of the summary executions, he also admitted burning a chapel in the commune of Questembert. At the same session his former enemy Jullien gave details on the punitive expedition of the previous year: 'the department of the Morbihan', he told his audience, 'wrote to me that Le Batteux and Avril, agents of Carrier, were burning and pillaging everything there. I informed Tréhouard. From the documents I also learned that they had not only killed but robbed, and made their unfortunate victims dig a grave into which they threw them right away...'.

In Nivôse the case of Le Batteux was again raised in his native town, where, on the 7th, the Redon *comité* had his wife arrested on charges of having organised a campaign in his favour among the former terrorists. Le Batteux in fact still had many supporters, not only among the artisans, the former members of the *société populaire*, but also among the garrison soldiers; indeed the *honnêtes gens* were so terrified when Bouvard, their commander, proclaimed that the former cook would soon return to Redon 'white as snow', that they demanded his transfer. In Paris Le Batteux was finally brought up for judgement on 28 Floréal, but he was sent by the revolutionary tribunal, along with the acquitted members of the Nantes *comité révolutionnaire*, to answer charges of murder, pillage and abuse of powers before the criminal tribunal of Angers. We do not know the outcome of this second trial, but the penalty must have been mild, for Le Batteux was able to return to Redon, where he died around 1805.[104] As for Avril, far from experiencing any persecution at the hands of the Thermidorean authorities, he was rewarded with the confirmation of his grade as *général de brigade* in Ventôse Year III, 'for having defended the route from La Vilaine and prevented the enemy from penetrating into the Morbihan after his defeat at Le Mans...'.[105]

Le Batteux had certainly made things worse for himself by his high-handed treatment of Mouquet, a Jacobin who had the confidence of Robespierrist circles in Paris and Lorient;[106] he would have done better attacking someone of less importance. The Redon cook was in any case a hot-headed man, the victim above all of that extraordinary administrative imbroglio which permitted rival *représentants en mission* in the same groups of departments to argue about the direction of repressive operations. Le Batteux had the unfortunate honour of being Carrier's man. His enemy, Jullien, was likewise a supporter of *grands moyens*; indeed, with the Redon *armée* forced back into its department of origin, this emissary of Robespierre recommended the use of the *armée révolutionnaire* in the Morbihan to search for refractory priests and former nobles, going even as far as to claim a partial counter-revolution in the department. But Jullien was thinking of the Parisian *armée*, and he carried through the disbandment of Avril's and Le Batteux's tiny *armée* according to the law of 14 Frimaire with obvious satisfaction. It was not Le Batteux's repressive action or the executions he ordered which Jullien held against him, so much as his tendency to act outside the established hierarchy of power. Had he not 'invaded' a department without informing the Morbihan authorities of his orders and plans? Had he not acted under a so-called 'delegation' from Carrier? These were procedures which the government man could not tolerate, they had ultra-revolutionary undertones and were 'patriotically counter-revolutionary'. Jullien and Mouquet supported the use of the political force against reputedly disaffected rural areas; but they wanted it to be under the control of the established authorities and respectful of established hierarchies. Le Batteux respected neither. His condemnation resembled that of Vauquoy; their adversaries sought to discredit these two ultra-revolutionaries by depicting them as pillagers. But their real crime was to have acted autonomously in their repression. The expedition to the Morbihan accordingly closes the period of the anarchic repression carried out by forces outside the control of central authority. The Committee of Public Safety henceforth used its own instruments in a repression which proved to be much more brutal and accounted for many more victims than that which had gone before.

The great expedition to the Aveyron, having already preoccupied the chroniclers of the Years II and III, attracted more attention from the historians than almost all the other operations of the departmental *armées*. They were struck by the large numbers deployed to implement orders calling for pitiless severity, by the pillaging which accompanied the 'promenades' of the Lot *armée*, and by the spectacular brutality employed by Viton and the *commissaires civils* in the exercise of their functions.

Above all else, this expedition was spectacular; that was the desired effect. In notes prepared for the Committee of Public Safety, Taillefer wrote on 9 October: '...At present the *armée révolutionnaire* of the Lot is dispersed, operating against a counter-revolutionary force formed in the Aveyron... but as soon as circumstances require, it will be ready to crush all rebellion and can be increased to around 3,000 men'.[107]

As with so many other operations, the origin of this 'invasion' of a poor department by a clutch of ravenous soldiers lay in an appeal from the local sans-culotte minority. 'It is more than likely', wrote the four leading Thermidoreans and members of the *société populaire* of Rodez – Bô, Monseignat, Arssaud and Mazars – charged with preparing a report on those responsible for this affair, 'that we owe the irruption of the *armée révolutionnaire* under the brigand Viton to this lying denunciation and to the deceitful manœuvres of the ex-Capuchin [Chabot] and his agents.... Everyone knows that a *rassemblement* of 60 to 80 brigands[108] was the pretext; but no one doubts that the real motive was to bring terror to the department.... They pretended to believe that they did not have enough strength in the *armée révolutionnaire*, and called in also the National Guard of the Lot...'. According to these investigators – in themselves suspect because it was in their interest to blacken their fellow countrymen, whose real crime was to have been republicans and to have alerted Taillefer and the Committee of General Security to the dangers which the *rassemblements* of Charrier's men held for internal peace – the arrival of the *armée révolutionnaire* permitted a local minority to seize control in Rodez. Who were these militants? The names figuring most prominently in the denunciations were Cabrol (a shopkeeper), Prompt, Lagasquie (a doctor), Paroissès (a former clerk in naval supply), Azémar (an apothecary) and his brother, an administrator of the district of Rodez in 1793. Cabrol replied to the charges in print in Messidor Year III: 'Cabrol in no way provoked the irruption of the *armée révolutionnaire* into the Aveyron, and never approved of the vexations it committed, regardless of the perfidious insinuation that he was one of those who recommended the devastation of the forests and the violation of property...'.[109] Nevertheless, the *armée révolutionnaire* did find allies among the sans-culottes of Rodez (where it respected property), as it was to do also in Villefranche-de-Rouergue, Saint-Geniez and in other communes. So the appeal does appear to have come from inside.

The events of this expedition belong to another chapter, since they involve pillage, abuse of powers and rape, rather than policing duties carried out by an instrument of revolutionary terror. The indictment drawn up against Viton with painstaking care by the public prosecutor, Bô, spoke of a vulgar pillager rather than a terrifying figure with blood on his hands, and we have already seen how the meagre results of this expedition scarcely justified such a deployment of forces and certainly did not live up to the expectations of its organisers, who had spoken so lightly of putting the inaccessible 'bands' of Charrier out of action at a stroke. Few brigands were arrested in the course of this expedition and nearly all the *chefs* who had gone to ground during the stay of the *armée révolutionnaire* simply resumed their activities after its departure. In this respect the grandiloquent address sent to the Convention in Frimaire by the *armée*, on its return to Cahors and Aurillac, presented an incredibly optimistic picture of the results accomplished.[110] By this date many *chefs* had already resumed the armed struggle, necessitating further intervention by armed troops as early as Frimaire Year II – this time from the first requisition, the *armées révolutionnaires* having terminated their service.[111] A year later, in Pluviôse Year III, the royalist *bandes* were no longer disturbed in a department which they largely 'administered'. Even the roads were no longer safe, the bandits attacking diligences and government couriers: the officials of the Year II (the collaborators of Viton) were found hanging in front of their farm doors, as were many farmers who had acquired *biens nationaux*, and constitutional priests.[112] The armed peasants and gentlemen of the royalist *bandes* continued to exercise a much more effective and bloody terror over this unfortunate, poor and ravaged department than that of the incompetent Viton and the humane soldier, Marbot. In the final analysis, the main result of the passage of Viton's soldiers through the Aveyron was to add famine to the many other ills from which this troubled region was already suffering.

The most striking aspect of these grand expeditions is their uselessness. The *noyades*, by suppressing a core of future opposition at one stroke, may perhaps have spared Nantes a prison plot – this of course is pure conjecture, though it was sufficient, in *sans-culotte* opinion, to justify recourse to such horrors. In the Morbihan, by contrast, calm had been restored everywhere before Le Batteux's troops arrived, the National Guard from Vannes and Lorient proving sufficient for the task. The Aveyron suffered as much from the incursion of the revolutionary soldiers as from the, by then much reduced, activities of the *bande à Charrier*; while in this department royalist banditry was to assume infinitely greater proportions in the Year III than in the autumn of 1793. It is, of course, easy to judge events in retrospect; but even at the time, authoritative voices – not only those of departmental authorities, always anxious to spare their constituents the passage of political troops – were raised against such a costly and politically dangerous recourse to punitive expeditions. In the summer of 1793 Charrier could count on the support of only a few determined partisans among the Catholic peasantry in the hills of the Aveyron and the Lozère; but after the passage of Viton's soldiers he could be sure of attracting many farmers and even simple day-labourers forced to flee to the *maquis* and await the chance to avenge themselves on the terrorist minority – the apothecaries, doctors, shopkeepers, clerks, artisans and men of the law of Rodez, Villefranche, Saint-Geniez – who had called the 'hordes' from the Lot and the Cantal into the *pays*. It was a particularly inept form of revolutionary proselytising.

Inept and above all ineffective. In such bandit country, devoid of major roads, it would have required troops experienced in guerrilla warfare and commanded by generals who had fought in America or in the Indies to achieve military success. What could a Parisian wigmaker be expected to achieve – even if seconded by Marbot and by Lamarque – or a group of officers, most of whom had come straight from the National Guard of Cahors? To employ such political forces on real military expeditions was to misconstrue the aims of their creators and the conditions of their recruitment. These troops were only good for accompanying guillotines and justiciary commissions, for serving warrants, making domiciliary visits, or shooting a few peasants coming out of high mass. It was too much to ask them to fight against ferocious bandits, expertly commanded by former royal body guards who knew the terrain and enjoyed the semi-complicity of the villagers. Such methods were as inefficient as they were unjustified, they were remedies more deadly than the illness. Viton and his acolytes helped install royalism for a long time to come in this mountainous back country and in the hearts of these poor and ferocious peasants. The real bandits escaped with ease; the weight of repression fell rather upon the villagers.

The same negative outcome can be seen elsewhere. In the Ariège the intervention of the Toulouse *armée* gained new recruits for the royalists and for Charles IV, after the dechristianising excesses committed by the *commissaires civils* and by the officers. If not many people were arrested, an unfortunate Pyreneean shepherd was killed when cannon fuses were lit to frighten the frontier population, and, as in the Aveyron, a few houses were burnt. Perhaps the arrival of the *armée* nipped a religious revolt in the bud, as young Vadier seemed to believe; but this is pure speculation. In the Haute-Garonne, at Grenade, the detachment did not succeed in 'regenerating' a town of which the Toulouse *patriotes* despaired. The failure of this expedition is evidenced by the order brought by Paganel on 2 Pluviôse Year II for the transfer of the *chef-lieu* of the district from Grenade to Beaumont, and in the dispatch of a new detachment – this time from the National Guard – to Grenade, 'a commune which today more than ever is pulling in the opposite direction to the Revolution...In this commune the aristocracy is so entrenched that the *armée révolutionnaire* and the *commissaires civils*...in a mission of 41 days, could not defeat it...'.[113] It was scarcely a victory bulletin.

The *représentants* and *commissaires civils* who imposed military duties beyond their capabilities on these civilian formations, did a real disservice both to the *armées révolutionnaires*, as instruments of the repression, and to the revolutionary cause itself. The failure of such expeditions made republican opinion forget the very real services of these companies in policing the prisons and watching suspects, and the formations, too costly in any case, thus came to appear entirely useless. More serious still, the resort to methods of force, but without sufficient means, simply won new partisans for the counter-revolution, without terrorising the hesitant. The most concrete result of the Aveyron expedition was to supply future Thermidorean propaganda with one of its favourite themes.

V   Individual activities

Lacking the political experience gained by most of the Parisian soldiers – notably the cannoneers – in their home Sections, the departmental *révolutionnaires* were far less formidable denunciators than their brothers from the capital. In the terrible list of denunciators in Lyon – published at Lausanne in

1795 and supplying the perfect manual for the royalist assassin in Lyon during the Thermidorean period – only two or three names from the Nièvre and Allier battalions can be found alongside those of hundreds of Lyonnais.[114] Generally these ignorant soldiers did little more than denounce those who spoke unfavourably of their formations and, like the Parisians, they were touchy on points of honour, and were quick to take offence if called informers or murderers.[115]

Their officers, in their frequent denunciations of both individuals and groups, showed signs of a more active revolutionary orthodoxy. Fleury, commander of the La Montagne battalion at Troyes, 'after replying... heatedly' during a stormy meeting with the General Council of the commune on the eve of his departure, 'added, that since he had been in Troyes he could scarcely believe that they were at the height of the Revolution...'. 'This same armed force', the administrators of the Ervy district would later state, 'was quick to punish anyone who dared make the smallest criticism.' Another member of the battalion was to tell one inhabitant 'that since the town was in counter-revolution, more troops would arrive to surround it and pacify it, just like Lyon...'.[116] The entire stay of the battalion in Troyes was marked by such incidents, by denunciations and counter-denunciations, rendered all the more bitter and personal by the officers' violent support of the sans-culotte mayor – a shady figure, constantly at odds with his compatriots and more particularly with the Sections. But denunciation as a weapon could just as easily be used against these officers as by them; it was a hazard of their trade. The unfortunate Adhémar, commander of the detachment of the Lille *armée* stationed at Cambrai, had this bitter experience, the town population missing no opportunity to malign his *armée*. 'It reached the point where yesterday evening', this overtaxed officer informed his superior, 'it was claimed that the *armée révolutionnaire* was in no way revolutionary but counter-revolutionary. It was proposed to send an address denouncing it to the Convention, it was, they said, composed of nobles – I myself was named as one – indeed they invent something new every day...'.[117] Nearly all the formations had to defend themselves against attacks of this nature; the denunciators soon became the denounced, and when they were not accused of being nobles, then their probity was being questioned.

It was the political personalities, the notables, above all the former Federalists who figured most often in denunciations made by the members of the companies to the *comités de surveillance* and the *sociétés populaires*. In Bordeaux the revolutionary general, d'Arnaud, set an example by 'urging his general staff to sign an address to Barère, demanding the heads of the deputies Picqué, Lacrampe, Gertoux and Dupont de Barrège for their support of the *journées* of 31 May, 1 and 2 June...'. Nor were the career soldiers outdone in this respect by the civilians, except in the case of the former monk, Peyrend-d'Herval, who also became an important political figure in the same place, and whose attempt to blacken the ex-minister,

Servan, in letters to his friend Vincent, became a real passion.[118] In Bordeaux also, a cavalier denounced a noblewoman, mother of an émigré, to the *comité*, while the accusation brought by a fusilier against Duranthon, former Minister of Justice, caused the latter to be summoned before the departmental *comité de surveillance*. A third soldier from the Bordeaux battalion delivered a written denunciation to this *comité* against Tyssadié, the former mayor of Montauban, who had taken refuge in the city.[119] In all of these cases the consequences for the denounced would have been serious because of the existence of the terrible Commission Militaire in Bordeaux. The members of this battalion seem to have been particularly zealous denouncers, doubtless because of the Federalist past of so many Bordelais.

Elsewhere, the *révolutionnaires* rarely denounced, and when they did, as at Agen or Montpellier, it was usually to reveal the existence of hidden stores or infractions of the Maximum. At Entrevaux, the commander of the revolutionary company denounced a municipal officer of the Federalist period for having furnished General Letandière with a false certificate of ill health.[120]

It is difficult to reach even an approximate figure for the individual denunciations made by members of the departmental companies. It is easier for Paris, because of the voluminous daily correspondence reaching Fouquier-Tinville, with its thousands of denunciations, signed and unsigned alike. In the departments such a readily available source is lacking, and we have to be content with the official denunciations made publicly at sessions of the *sociétés populaires* or before the *comités de surveillance*. The denunciator (more particularly the denunciatrix) dislikes publicity. Moreover, in the Year III, many booklets containing such denunciations were withdrawn from the archives of former *comités* by those seeking to destroy compromising evidence which might expose them to individual vengeance – a wise move in view of the fate of the Lyon *mathevons*. From official evidence alone, therefore, we can see that the departmental *révolutionnaires* rarely took the initiative in making individual denunciations, except in matters of economic crime, and in general adhered to their role as instruments of revolutionary policing in the service of the *comités*. But this relative leniency is hardly a tribute to their goodness of heart, for denunciation presupposes a certain political consciousness lacking in most of these poor wretches. There is too a less honourable explanation for such unexpected moderation among these political soldiers; in some areas their silence was a marketable commodity, purchased by victims threatened with arrest. The Marats of Nantes were certainly capable of this, and we know of a number of officers in Viton's entourage exchanging denunciations for certain 'favours'. But transactions of this nature were purposely left unrecorded; there is no evidence, and we can only proffer hypotheses. For the rest, the departmental *révolutionnaires* scarcely measured up to the calls for constant vigilance issued by the *comités* and *sociétés* at the time of their enrolment.

Most *commissaires civils* and some revolutionary officers had already had experience in repressive administration and summary justice before their enrolment in the new formations, the *représentants* preferring men who had already proved themselves as members of the *comités de surveillance* or the extraordinary commissions. Thus Taillefer placed his secretary Viton, who had sat on the military commission of Montauban, at the head of the Lot *armée*. Nor was Vauquoy a novice at repression; as secretary of the Jacobins, he had denounced Marie-Antoinette because of the suspicious company she kept. Le Batteux won favour with Carrier by drawing his attention to the suspects in Redon. At the time of the formation of the Loire *armée*, Javogues and Bassal appointed Civeton, a local shopkeeper, to command the Roanne company. Civeton had already been delegated by Dorfeuille, in August 1793, to arrest suspects in the district; in October, Javogues gave him full powers to arrest, dismiss and purge.[121] Several commanders of the Toulouse *armée* were already specialists, having been judges or prosecutors with the criminal tribunal.[122] It was owing to this experience no doubt that in the Lot the governing Council of the *armée révolutionnaire* shared the duties of the *comité de surveillance* of Cahors, sitting with it and jointly ordering repressive measures.[123] This, however, was an exceptional case.

Some soldiers were given repressive or judicial roles after their enrolment. Caussade, a soldier in the Agen company, was simultaneously a member of the *comité*. But the authorities, on hearing of this situation, eventually forced him to opt for one or the other – plurality of offices being formally forbidden. Ducos, from the same town, a member of the *comité de dénonces* of the *société populaire*, resigned on entering the company.[124] But the resignations were only temporary, and when the company was disbanded these soldiers resumed their repressive offices. In Lyon the *représentants* appointed 6 soldiers from the Nièvre and Allier battalions as adjoints to the 32 *comités révolutionnaires* of the Sections.[125] All the repressive institutions were interdependent, and the lines of division between a company, a *comité de surveillance*, a *comité de dénonces* of a *société populaire*, and a revolutionary commission of justice were often difficult to trace. All were in the service of the Terror; but the 'aristocrats of repression' were the *commissaires civils*, the popular judges, some officers and former *délégués* of the *représentants*. If repressive functions were confided to simple soldiers, those soldiers were nevertheless denied the right to judge and arrest on their own authority. At most the revolutionary soldier might aspire to be appointed a juror by a commission of justice, or an adjoint by a *comité révolutionnaire*; he was not considered fit to administer justice on his own account. In this respect the departmental companies were less democratic, less egalitarian than the *armée révolutionnaire* of Paris.

Comités and companies were tributaries of each other. In certain distant departments – the Hautes- and Basses-Alpes, for example – they were created at the same time; when the company disappeared the *comité*'s channels of action were seriously curtailed. In small towns, the terrain of the communal companies, the *comité* was the brain, the company but the arm of repressive activity. That was the normal relationship between the two institutions. But it did not exclude conflict; in Bordeaux the battalion criticised the orders of the *comité*, which quickly put the insolent and overbearing officers in their place. In Nantes there were constant disputes between the company and the *comité*, with the latter emerging the victor by appealing to Carrier. The Montauban *comité* complained of Viton's insolence in failing to keep it informed of his operations, and in the Aveyron the so-called general sometimes acted without consulting the local *comités*. These, however, were exceptional incidents produced by exceptional situations. The usual activity of a company in the service of the repression was that of the small companies of the Basses-Alpes, of Agen, of Montpellier, of Marmande. Company, *comité*, *comité de dénonces*, these were three faces of one institution dedicated to repression. But the repression did not abate with the disappearance of the companies; and where their presence had contributed to its acceleration, it was thanks not to them but to the *commissaires civils*, the real masters of the anarchic Terror.

As instruments of the great Terror, the *armées* and companies were quite ineffective, failing even to put an end to serious troubles. It is even questionable whether the *noyades* – the horror of which rubbed off on all the revolutionary forces – saved Nantes from a plot which may have existed only in the imagination of the sans-culottes. The passage of Viton's *armée* through the Aveyron was just another episode in the long and sorrowful history of civil war in this *pays*; and yet it lingered in peasant memory for a very long time, because of the depredations committed and the insolence and conceit of Viton. As time passed the revolutionary companies assumed a more terrifying aspect in written memoirs, particularly those of the country people. It was, however, a retrospective reputation which was scarcely merited, for it was their disorder and anarchy of which contemporaries disapproved, rather than their terrorist action.

CHAPTER 5

The Political Action of the *Armées révolutionnaires*

The first concern of the Parisian soldiers on detachment in the country was to establish contact with the local *société populaire*. Ronsin's *armée* was a political body; the *révolutionnaires* had their cartouches like real soldiers, but their true passport was the *diplôme de sociétaire*. The political action of this *armée* was carried out in association with the *société*. The Parisians' goal was to find allies in the country. It was not simply a case of preferring revolutionary institutions (*sociétés* and *comités*) on principle; the resort to the local *société* was a practical necessity imposed by the hostility of most municipalities towards the outsiders.

The Parisian *armée* consequently served as a bridge between the Sectionary movement in the capital and the *sociétés populaires* in the departments. The *révolutionnaires* diffused ideas dear to the Parisian sans-culottes through the small towns. But at the same time they contributed to the hardening of Parisian opinion against the rural population by keeping their Sections minutely informed of every incident during their stay in the country. They in turn experienced the effects of local conflicts and personal quarrels; innocent of village ways and anxious always to explain things in terms of a struggle between *petits* and *gros*, they were easily deceived and sometimes served the ends of unscrupulous demagogues. The political life of small towns was often more complex, more impenetrable than that of the Parisian Sections, and twenty miles from Paris political niceties had a quite different meaning.

The political influence of the departmental *armées* was all but conterminous with the personal role of the *commissaires civils* and, more rarely, of the officers, for most of the soldiers were apolitical, simple instruments in the hands of their leaders. In the eyes of the *commissaires*, the most effective political action was the arrest of a 'malveillant' – repression being the political weapon *par excellence* of these forces. To a lesser extent one might say the same of the action of the Parisian *armée*; for example, when the *gros bonnets* of a village were arrested, the political balance was entirely changed, usually to the benefit of the sans-culottes. The immediate result of the intervention of the Parisian *armée* at Jagny or at Trouville was the expulsion of the moderates from the municipalities and their replacement by artisans and day-labourers. Political action properly speaking – co-operation with the rural *sociétés*, founding new *sociétés*, giving political advice, egalitarian

416

sermonising – was only secondary. In the final analysis, the most potent argument of the *commissaire civil* and the Parisian officer was the arrest warrant. The *révolutionnaires* were police agents, repressors – and, at times, executioners – before they were political missionaries.

As we have seen, egalitarian measures such as the levy of *taxes révolutionnaires* were marginal means used by the *commissaires civils* to pay for the war effort; but although it may be going too far to attribute class consciousness to men who came from different social backgrounds, personal convictions did play a part. Several *commissaires* claimed that the *armées révolutionnaires* were working for the poor, and for someone like Chaix this was not mere verbosity. In the countryside things went further than in the towns – thanks to the great repressive expeditions – and here and there one can detect faint traces of an unrecognised revolution committed to the eradication of poverty and the equalisation of wealth. To the bourgeois, such aberrations prefigured a *dissolution générale*, and the *commissaires* were anarchists because they sought to destroy everything, to overturn everything. This too was the theory of the Revolutionary Government, whose agents treated the *commissaires civils* as anarchists.

The political action of certain *commissaires* seems also to represent the transposition to the department and the village of that direct democracy which, according to Albert Soboul, was the vaguely perceived aim of the militant *sectionnaires*. The doctrine which endowed the popular *sociétés* with representative and sovereign powers does in fact find an echo among the Parisian soldiers, and even more among the *commissaires civils*. 'The *sociétés populaires* are sovereign, they are above the law', proclaimed the Parisians. It was not quite a *dissolution générale*, but it was certainly an attempt to establish a new power, a kind of Parlement des Saints, composed of *sociétaires* united in huge federations. If most Parisian soldiers exhibited a respect for the Convention that was religious in its intensity, there is a noticeable anti-parliamentarianism among the most restless and imprudent of the 'hommes de liaison', which manifested itself in a personal hostility towards the *représentants*.

According to Jaurès, this system – if it was one – had a name: Hébertism; and a goal: military dictatorship. Following this thesis, the *armées révolutionnaires* were the means by which Hébertism would assume power by force. The evidence was that the officers and *commissaires* favoured the dissemination of the *Père Duchesne*; they were consequently Hébertists and conspirators. We will see just how fallacious is the identification of a certain ultra-revolutionary policy with the existence of an organised party. As for dictatorship, it would be extremely difficult to fathom the intentions of these hot-tempered men who spoke so readily, in fiery sermons, of the need for a new *journée*, a great purifying burst. The mistake they made was to have talked too much.

The political action of the *armées révolutionnaires* did not form one homogeneous whole. The Parisian *armée* remained subject to the Convention, even if it sometimes opposed the local authorities. But under the direction of the *commissaires* the action of the battalions and companies in the departments was much more violent and anarchical. The real stronghold of *ultracisme* was the departmental company and the *armée* of Ronsin suffered from the reputation gained by the formations in the Centre and in the Midi, because moderate and Jacobin opinion looked on all the *armées* as part of one whole. In reality the only trait they had in common was their support for the *sociétés populaires*. The difference was largely one of degree; the most spectacular interventions of the *commissaires civils* were a caricature of ideas barely outlined by the Parisian *sectionnaires*.

I   *The Parisian* armée *in the politics of the Sections*

The *armée* of Ronsin played no political role in Paris itself. Under the command of Hanriot, it remained in a state of debilitating inaction at the École Militaire and at Vincennes, taking scarcely any part in the arrests ordered by the *comités révolutionnaires*. The National Guard sufficed for repressive duties, and any political action took place outside the detachment of 300 or 400 men who remained behind in their town of origin. It is true that the *armée* was the subject of bitter political disputes between the various currents of Parisian opinion throughout its existence, but these struggles concerned the entire institution, not the detachment, the rear guard whose existence was scarcely noticed except at the time of the so-called 'military plot' of Ventôse. Individually, by their drinking binges and pranks in the *cabarets*, the *révolutionnaires* attracted the attention of the *comités révolutionnaires* and Jacobin or sans-culotte opinion, which was fairly intolerant of these 'costly idlers'. But this will be dealt with later, in the chapter on brawls and indiscipline.

The presence of the Parisian *révolutionnaires* caused two political incidents within the Sections: one at the very beginning of the existence of the *armée*, the other after its disbandment, when the companies of cannoneers returned home. The company of the Réunion Section was at the bottom of a series of conflicts pitting the members of the *comité révolutionnaire* against the general assembly. It was a complicated affair: the captain of the company complained to the general assembly about the poor quality of the shoes which were issued to his fusiliers. The shoes had been made by the shoemaker members of the *comité révolutionnaire* who, feeling themselves under fire, launched a violent attack on the officer and the assembly for having accepted these complaints and aired them in a way which the *comité* considered insulting. The affair dragged on for three months, involving some fairly sordid personal matters, but most of all raising the issue of the fundamental opposition between a *comité révolutionnaire*, the instrument of central government, firmly under the control of the Committee of General Security, and a popular assembly which sought rather to free itself from government tutelage.[1] The company, the innocent pretext for the dispute, was to pay dearly for the audacity of its captain by incurring the lasting hatred of the *comité* members. When the unfortunate fusiliers asked the *comité* to help them find work on their return to Paris, they were rudely dismissed and showered with insults.[2]

The *comités révolutionnaires*, as the instruments of the Jacobin dictatorship, do not seem to have been particularly well disposed towards the companies, even though they had been directly associated with their levy and organisation, and had issued orders for their future political action. In the Boisgirault–Thunot affair, the Panthéon-Français *comité* supported the Compiègne authorities, and when the Laon prisoners escaped and took refuge in Paris, the Bondy *comité* had them picked up for transfer back to Laon. We cannot of course derive any concrete conclusions from single episodes, particularly when there are other examples, such as that of the Bonne-Nouvelle Section, of good relations between *comité* and company – in that case, Réaume sending daily reports of the activities of the fusiliers on detachment in Lyon. But when they got into difficulty with the local authorities, the officers and soldiers preferred to address themselves to the assembly or to the *société populaire*. Thunot wrote initially from his Compiègne prison to the Société des Défenseurs de la République, of which he was a member.[3]

The second example of direct intervention by the Parisian *armée* in the political struggles of the Sections was in Germinal, in the Brutus Section, where the assembly was the battlefield of a ferocious conflict between rival factions. On this occasion the leaders of one of the factions came up with the idea of using the presence of the company physically to pressurise their opponents.[4] In the departments we will encounter many such examples of the *révolutionnaires* appearing under arms in the *sociétés*.

On the whole, however, the role of the companies in the capital was confined to that of representing the *armée* at the many fêtes which served the dual function of pastime and encouragement in the life of the good sans-culottes of the Sections. It was a purely symbolic role, the fusiliers or cannoneers taking their places docilely in the cortège behind the councillors, the *sociétaires*, the venerable old men and the young maidens, at a fête to inaugurate the busts of the Martyrs de la Liberté, or to celebrate the recapture of Toulon.[5]

With the exception, therefore, of the quarrels in the rue de Choiseul, which were important because of their part in the political crisis of spring 1794, and in the hardening of part of Sectionary opinion against the entire *armée*, the *armée révolutionnaire* had very little political influence in Paris. Nevertheless, the many letters from the soldiers to their Sections did contribute to the mounting distrust felt by sans-culotte opinion in Paris for the peasants in general and the yeoman farmer and grain merchant in particular. These letters were read and applauded at the general assembly and the Sectionary *société*, while the *comités révolutionnaires* received numerous reports from the officers – some of whom were also *com-*

missaires – concerning the ill will of the country people and the inhabitants of Lyon and other towns in which detachments were garrisoned. This correspondence was an important element in the formation of Sectionary opinion, the *révolutionnaires* providing it with a window on to the bourgs and the villages. If some extreme Sections could still call, in Ventôse, for *grandes mesures* against recalcitrant *paysans* and fanatical *paysannes*, and once again for the establishment of roving commissions of justice, it was because of complaints received from their 'frères' of the detachments, concerning their own inaction in the face of blatant economic fraud and the moderantism of *les gros* who still ruled the roost in the bourgs and villages. Faced with such a bleak picture, the Parisian sans-culottes felt even more isolated, and this in turn sharpened their desire for repression and their anger at a government which seemed criminally indulgent towards the farmers and the men of the law.

II *From the Parisian Section to the rural* société populaire: *the political role of the Parisians in the departments*

The *révolutionnaires* were political animals – most being members of the Sectionary *sociétés*, or , more rarely, of the Cordeliers, the Jacobins, or clubs such as the Société des Défenseurs de la République. Their first action on arriving in a commune was to present themselves to the local *société* in order to lodge with its committee their *diplômes* as Parisian *sociétaires*.[6] The *sociétés* in turn were eager, in varying degrees, to accept them as members, giving them the honours of the session (one had to be wary of the touchiness of these Parisian shopkeepers).[7] The external harmony between the detachments and the local *sociétés* was further illustrated by the participation of the former in fêtes, as noted above. In some communes the Parisians served on the committees organising these fêtes; in others they organised their own, and invited the municipal officers and even some Parisian personalities to attend. In Versailles, for example, the *révolutionnaires* informed the General Council of the commune of Versailles that they were organising a fête at their barracks in honour of the martyrs of liberty, when a tree of Liberty would be planted, followed 'by a frugal and fraternal repast. They further announced that deputies from the National Convention, some members of the revolutionary tribunal and a deputation from the Jacobin Society in Paris would be attending...'. It was an invitation which the *représentants* advised the municipality to accept.[8] On leaving a particular *pays* for another posting, the soldiers took away, not only their *diplômes* as Parisian *sociétaires*, but also one from the local *société populaire*.[9] Not everybody could be a Jacobin or a Cordelier, but since *civisme* was such a valuable commodity, it did no harm to accumulate certificates for a rainy day – and *diplômes* from *sociétés* affiliated to the Jacobins were considered superior. Such stockpiling was not simply a political decision of the *révolutionnaire*; it was a measure of prudence.

The *sociétés populaires* were the principal terrain of political action by the *révolutionnaires*; as individuals they used the *société* as a platform on which to voice their own particular brand of political philosophy; collectively, the *société* served as a support in conflicts with the municipalities, the district directories, and sometimes with the *comités de surveillance*. In order to act politically the *révolutionnaires* had first to establish themselves as a party within the popular assemblies. In this effort they started with many advantages: they had force at their disposal, they enjoyed prestige as Parisians and as experts in revolution, and since, however ignorant they might be, their social and political consciousness was much more highly developed than ·that of the sans-culottes of the small towns and the countryside, they were consulted as advisers and protectors by ordinary *patriotes* and ultra-revolutionary minorities alike. Their political intervention thus took the following forms: maintenance of an armed presence at sessions of the assembly, with its implied threat held over the entire gathering; colonisation of the committees and the important positions on behalf of the military; co-operation with local militants; arbitration in village disputes when called upon to act as redressers of wrongs.

Let us take first intimidation in its most brutal form. The Parisians had no hesitation in using force or the threat of it to see motions passed, devised by themselves but running counter to the political and religious sentiments of most of the *sociétaires*. In a small *société* with no more than a hundred members – and only in the larger towns were the numbers greater – the persuasiveness of an argument backed up by armed men was considerable, particularly in view of the assiduity of the soldiers at the sessions. In communes like Noyon, Provins, Laon, Honfleur and Le Havre, the detachments consisted of several hundred men. With such numbers of armed men at the sessions, it was easy to dominate the debate, and in the event of opposition they would shout and brandish their swords. Better still, a Parisian *commissaire* (an 'homme de liaison') attending a session could deploy the soldiers like a ballet-master, having them intervene at set times in support of a motion or one of the proscription lists which so terrified the moderate *sociétaires*. At Lagny, Ballardelle could manipulate the *société* at will by appearing with 'his' fusiliers and cavaliers;[10] while at Noyon a triumvirate of terrorists, consisting of the revolutionary captain, Gasson, and two local sans-culottes, Hennon and Decaisne, were able to dominate the political and administrative life of the little town by introducing the soldiers into the *société*. When Gasson demanded the resignation of the entire municipality on a paltry matter – a silly affair of requisition orders which still bore the fleur-de-lis heading – 'the bulk of his detachment attended the *société* that day…Every member of the *société*…maintaining a solemn silence…the motion was approved, such being the terror inspired by the detachment of the *armée révolutionnaire*…'.[11] In small towns in particular the *sociétaires* did not have the courage to protest against such procedures. In Le Havre, on the other hand, when the soldiers, still carrying their swords, arrived in the chamber, they were promptly called to order by the president and required to leave their swords at the entrance.[12] In Lyon, despite the presence of several hundred Parisians, the local sans-culottes never permitted these outsiders totally to dominate the *société*. In the large communes, there were always enough sans-culotte militants to put the troublesome soldiers in their place when they tried to use force of arms to push through an unpopular motion. But in the country, the small *sociétés* were powerless against such massive interventions. The republicans were right to denounce these procedures as savouring of military government.

The Parisians also had less brutal means of intervention at their disposal, those of 'colonising' the offices of the local *sociétés*. We have seen how at Lyon the *révolutionnaires* at times controlled the presidency and vice-presidency of the *société*, the presidency of the *comité des dénonces* – a position of considerable strategic importance – and that of the *comité de présentation*, which even gave them power to decide the order of the day, to prevent their enemies from speaking, to threaten them with exclusion or worse (for some of these soldiers were also popular judges or members of *comités révolutionnaires* in the Sections), and to supervise the choice of new candidates.[13] Such pronounced colonisation of the Lyon *société* by the Parisians, however, was eventually their undoing, for it provoked such a vigorous counter-offensive by the sans-culottes of Lyon that the outcome was the demilitarisation of the *société* altogether. In Caen too the revolutionary cannoneers and the other garrison soldiers controlled the *société populaire* – which had been shunned by most Caennais in any case.[14] Ballardelle seems to have been vice-president of the Lagny *société* during most of his period as Ministry *commissaire*,[15] and in Noyon Gasson ensured his control of the *société* by placing his soldiers in leading positions on its committee.[16] In Provins the cannoneers admitted to the *société* were appointed *commissaires* to convey the wishes of the *société* to the *comité de surveillance*; in Honfleur, a Parisian officer, member of a Sectionary *société*, also became a member of the correspondence committee of the local *société*.[17] In the L'Isle-Adam *société*, fusiliers who became members of the *comité de présentation* used the position to put aside candidatures which they considered politically undesirable.[18] These last three cases were rather different from the others, the Parisians having secured seats through the support of the majority of *sociétaires*. One of the Versailles *sociétés* so feared such domination by outsiders that it banned the *révolutionnaires* from its sessions altogether, which provoked quite an outburst from the latter.[19] But generally speaking the soldiers were automatically admitted in the small communes; the result was a monopolisation of places by men who were politically better instructed and informed than most of the locals, who, even in the Parisian region, might go for weeks without seeing a newspaper.[20] The Parisians were their talking newspaper.

The principal reason for intervention by the *révolutionnaires* lay precisely in the political ignorance of the country people and the small-town sans-culottes. In Le Havre the restless and politically well-informed *sociétaires*[21] could doubtless do without the opinions of these political soldiers. But at the other side of the estuary, the tiny *société populaire* of Honfleur constantly sought advice from Donville, garrison commander and head of the revolutionary detachment. In Provins the fusiliers lectured the *société populaire* on the numbers of priests and men of the law among its members; they would have to be expelled.[22] In Vernon they protested against the presence of women. Everywhere they vigorously supported proposals for the removal of all remnants of feudalism, at the same time requiring *citoyennes* to wear the national cockade, and crosses to be covered with the tricolour flag.[23] Indeed such was the respect for the political opinion of the Parisians, that at Melun the *comité* and *société* consulted the detachment captain, Dumany, on interpreting the laws and applying repressive measures. The Parisians were so conscious of the importance of their role as advisers that sometimes, when they arrived in a village without a *société populaire*, they pressured the inhabitants into forming one; without a *société*, they claimed, no commune could be republican and patriotic. At Brie the foundation of the *société* at the time of the detachment's arrival cannot have been pure coincidence.[24] Likewise, in the Pays de Caux, when the rural *sociétés* were forcibly closed down by moderate municipalities composed of large farmers, the soldiers on tour in the region intervened to have them re-opened.[25] The *révolutionnaires* were protectors, as well as advisers, to these popular assemblies.

They were also their censors, and the letters sent by them to their Sections were a further means of exerting pressure on the local authorities and the small *sociétés*. Unfavourable reports could cause considerable trouble for the inhabitants, since such letters had been behind several missions entrusted to *commissaires* by the Committee of General Security. If the Parisians instructed the country people on the political events in Paris by transmitting the principal watchwords of the sans-culotte movement, they also kept the Parisian Sections informed on the political life of the departments. It was therefore advisable to make the men welcome, as a proof of the patriotism and good will of the inhabitants. On 17 Brumaire, the soldiers, who had just arrived in Montereau, were addressed by a member of its *société*; he 'said that he was pleased to see the members of the *armée révolutionnaire* in the hall of the assembly, and asked it to show its satisfaction at having them within its midst. . . . One of the members of the *armée révolutionnaire*, citizen Adrit, from the Harmonie *société* in Paris, replied . . . that he would immediately inform his Section of the republican sentiments he had found in the Montereau *société*. . . '.[26] The correspondence kept by some of the Sectionary *sociétés* contains an abundance of such testimonials, sent by the soldiers, to the patriotism, or lack of it, of the inhabitants and authorities of the departments.

Politically, however, the *révolutionnaires* could do little without the support of at least a few local personalities, and if their intervention had any political effect it usually took the form of co-operation between these *étrangers* and the sans-culotte minorities of the *pays*. Such was the pattern at

Noyon, at Jagny, at Provins (where the Parisians found allies among the so-called 'atheists' of the *sociétés populaires*), and at Presles, where the mayor, national agent and members of its *comité de surveillance* were *sociétaires* who had been in touch for some time with Clémence and Marchand and other Jacobins and Cordeliers. In the neighbouring commune of Taverny, the shoemaker Etienne Brings, a member of the local *comité* and formerly an inhabitant of the Contrat-Social Section – with whose *comité* and *société* he frequently corresponded – used the detachment to put a stop to the activities of the 'moderate' party, composed of the curé and the large farmers;[27] and in Jagny similar collaboration occurred between the Parisians and the terrible Madame Pruneau. In Trouville it was the fishermen's wives and the popular element of the little port who called upon the assistance of the Parisians against the mayor, whom they accused of starving the poor.[28] During their tour in Vermenton, the Parisians were won round by another domineering woman, an innkeeper calling herself 'Mère Duchesne', and in Avallon they were assisted in their political and anti-religious actions by some local artisans.[29] In general this kind of co-operation worked to the advantage of the sans-culotte minorities and against the groups of moderates: farmers, men of the law, priests and women. But the Parisians were politically naïve, and had difficulty making impartial judgements on issues complicated by personal conflicts and long-standing village disputes. Without possessing any clear class consciousness, the Parisians naturally sought allies among those of similar social standing. But this was not always the case, and the *armée révolutionnaire* was a double-edged weapon which could just as easily be used against *patriotes* as against suspects. It was simply an instrument, and, as we have seen, the repression carried out by this *armée* was not always revolutionary, even if it was always political. In Viarmes, the detachment served as the instrument of the former municipality, disguised as a *comité de surveillance*, against an over-zealous, over-revolutionary mayor, whom they successfully removed.[30]

Were these repeated efforts at close association with the *sociétés populaires*, rather than with the other authorities, simply an effort to find reliable allies where they could be expected to be most numerous; or did this attachment to the *sociétés* reveal a genuine political doctrine, a revolutionary conception of popular sovereignty? From the interventions of some Parisians in the course of their operations, one might be tempted to think that they did contemplate the establishment of a new political system, a kind of direct democracy, based on the *sociétés* throughout the country as small sovereign diets. Take for instance the remarkable events in Avallon, which began with the usual formalities; at the session of 14 November, 'a member of the *armée révolutionnaire* asked if he might fraternise with our *société*. The *société populaire*, applauding the zeal of this brave defender of the *patrie*, ordered the president to bestow the fraternal embrace on him in the name of all his brothers in arms, and at that moment a great number of volunteers appeared at the rostrum and received the fraternal accolade from the president and secretary to repeated cries of "Vive la République".[31] The following day

> a member of the *armée révolutionnaire* and of the Jacobins of Paris said that he had learnt from a sentence imposed by the *juge de paix* of the canton, that citizens Rémond and Foulon had been condemned to imprisonment for having used certain words in a public place; that this condemnation had all the appearances of the tyranny and arbitrariness of the Ancien Regime; that *in a revolution and when terror was the order of the day, one could dispense with the law and take measures appropriate to the occasion*, and he asked the *société populaire* to depute two of its members to visit the *juge de paix* in order to reverse the action taken against these two individuals and for the *comité de surveillance* to authorise them to act as they saw fit.... After listening to this document, a member asked for Rémond and Foulon to be released, since the entire proceedings were vague and nothing had been proved against them. A member commented on the possible consequences of such a relaxation, saying that they had been condemned by the law and that no one could put himself above the law. On this objection the *armée révolutionnaire* rose *en masse* and said: 'the *sociétés populaires* are sovereign and have the power to release Rémond and Foulon' on their own authority, and we demand that this be discussed immediately....

Somewhat perturbed, but nevertheless giving in to this overwhelming pressure, the *société* ordered the release of the two *patriotes*, upon which the *armée révolutionnaire* rushed to the *maison de détention* in a body and effected the release under the very nose of the *juge de paix*. In subsequent sessions, the *révolutionnaires* dictated a series of measures which the *société* – cowed, though sovereign, whether it wanted to be or not – promptly carried out. The other authorities of the little town were equally docile, longing for the departure of these stormy democrats.[32]

Not content with proclaiming a doctrine of popular sovereignty which put in question that of the Convention, the *révolutionnaires* had gone a stage further and exercised sovereign powers in the name of the *société populaire*, most of all in their interruption of the course of justice. It was the only occasion on which the Parisians expressed in such precise terms this idea of a *démocratie directe*, based on the *sociétés* and exercising supreme power in the place of the regular authorities and of the Convention. Certainly we must not attach too much importance to words spoken in the heat of debate and in the surcharged atmosphere of a collective assembly (in Avallon the *révolutionnaires* were conscious of their strength, and under leaders such as Lefranc and Fauveau, could risk anything). But there are other examples of such abuse of power, which the Parisian officers and soldiers sought to justify by invoking a *droit révolutionnaire*, superior to the law, and a hierarchy of power quite apart from the municipalities, the districts and the established authorities. In Noyon, the *société*, encouraged by Gasson, exercised a sovereign authority, ordering the replacement of the municipality and even obliging the members of the *comité de surveillance* to carry certificates stamped by itself.[33]

Even more revealing is the doctrine outlined by Chaumont to justify the arrest by his soldiers of the mayor of Chaourse, a public official, in the exercise of his duties. Was the *armée révolutionnaire*, he asked, not entitled to act sovereignly when confronted by a counter-revolutionary situation, and did this instrument of the Terror not have the power to decide upon the seriousness of that situation? 'It will hardly be denied', wrote Chaumont, 'that the commander of a revolutionary detachment can, in certain counter-revolutionary situations, summon a person to appear before him and make decisions about handing him, if necessary, over to the police, or permitting him to return home. . . . *In times of revolution in particular*, it would paralyse surveillance by every authority' (to hold them, that is, to the strict letter of the law). In conclusion he declared 'that the conduct of Captain Chaumont and Lieutenant Martin, both good patriots, was more in *the real spirit of the Revolution* than that of the mayor of Chaourse. . . .'.[34] Chaumont had expressed in a nutshell the real aim of this *armée révolutionnaire*: and that was to act *révolutionnairement*. Chaumont considered himself to be acting *in the spirit of the Revolution*, even if not according to the letter of its law. The mayor was clearly acting within its law, but he was not very patriotic in his conduct, he had hindered the implementation of revolutionary measures, and in the judgement of the Paris jeweller he had not acted *in the spirit of the Revolution*.

Other Parisian officers, though they did not proclaim the doctrine quite so openly, nevertheless exercised sovereign powers of justice in the arrest and liberation of individuals on their own authority. Lemaire had members of the Montesquiou family arrested when he was on detachment in the Coulommiers region; but, more astute than the imprudent Chaumont, he took the precaution of informing the Committee of General Security, which ratified his action. In Pontoise, the officer, at the head of his detachment, burst into the headquarters of the *comité de surveillance*, demanding the return of the list of suspects and the arrest of Boileau.[35]

What conclusion can we draw from these examples? Did the members of the Parisian *armée* contemplate the overthrow of the Revolutionary Government, the dissolution of the Convention and its replacement by some new authority, either in the form of a military government or in the dispersal of power to the communes throughout France: a free association of thousands of sovereign *sociétés populaires*? Contemporary opinion hostile to the *armées* opted for the former, one witness at the trial of Chaumont declaring that a Parisian officer during his stay in the commune of Ebouleau, in the canton of Liesse, had said that 'Paris would dissolve the law and the National Convention and would take over authority as the one sole power. . .'.[36] In Ventôse–Germinal, when the case against the Hébertists was being prepared, the revolutionary tribunal also gathered statements attributed to the revolutionary soldiers, suggesting that they secretly desired a violent coup and even that they were about to mount one. We will deal with that accusation in our discussion of the famous *complot militaire*.[37] The present writer believes that all this was merely hot air, words spoken in the heat of discussion to which little importance can be attached, even though they were conveniently remembered after the *armée* had disappeared. The very violence of the remarks is indicative of the absence of any deep-seated plan. The *révolutionnaires* were much given to verbosity, particularly when crossed. Above all they wanted to impress their audience, which sometimes caused them to speak out against the Parisian *commissaires* and the rival instruments of the Terror, as well as against the royalists and the *modérés*.

Some historians have preferred the second hypothesis, seeing the Parisian *armée* as an instrument of 'communalist' anarchy and Polish-style decentralisation. This thesis has some foundation when applied to certain departmental formations. But despite its many conflicts with the municipalities and the districts, and its close links with the sans-culottes, the *armée* of Ronsin remained an instrument of the Revolutionary Government, particularly of the Committee of General Security, which directed all repressive activities – its principal duty. The words of the soldiers at Avallon and the arguments of Chaumont are of interest as manifestations of a particular state of mind, rather than as enunciations of some new doctrine of popular sovereignty. The *révolutionnaires* became more and more frustrated at their powerlessness and developed an aversion for the local authorities whom they saw as obstacles to the progress of the revolutionary movement. If they preferred to address themselves to the *sociétés populaires*, whose administrative importance they sought to enhance at the expense of the established authorities, it was less the execution of some full-blown plan for establishing a counter-power than a search for allies in regions where the majority of the population was bitterly hostile to them. As *sectionnaires*, the Parisians had a certain political consciousness, and on detachment they sought to spread to the departments those institutions which had allowed the Parisian Sectionary movement to develop and reach a limited autonomy. For them it was a case both of political preference and sheer good sense; they recognised well enough – or if they did not when they left Paris, they soon did when sent on mission – that municipalities composed of *les gros*, of men of the law and farmers, would try to hinder the execution of grand revolutionary measures. One can hardly attribute to class consciousness their greater confidence in *sociétés* and *comités de surveillance*, composed of artisans and shopkeepers like themselves, than in municipalities which, more often than not, were dominated by the very people they detested most.[38] Above all the *société* provided them with the best means of intervention in local affairs, while offering a platform for the development of their ideas as *sectionnaires*.

Into simple preferences the historians read a political programme: that of Hébertism, with the *révolutionnaires* as the instrument of the Hébertist group in the Cordeliers and the War Ministry. But this is highly unlikely, and we have already seen that the *révolutionnaires*, members of the Sectionary *sociétés* in the capital, or even more of non-Sectionary *sociétés* such as the Harmonie-Sociale and the Défenseurs de la République, were rarely Cordeliers and even more rarely Jacobins. The Cordeliers remained the preserve of the officers of the general staff; the ordinary soldier never reached such exalted heights, and complaints against their officers, which they naïvely addressed to the club, were received unfavourably. Some leaders of the Parisian *armée* were undoubtedly personal friends of Vincent and Hébert – Gasson, who gave rise to so much scandal in Noyon, was a personality of the Marat Section, and was perhaps connected with Momoro. One of the *commissaires* responsible for the operations of the detachments in the Oise, Decuve, was to be accused by the inhabitants of Chaumont of having defended 'Père Duchesne' at the time of his arrest.[39] But this did not make Decuve a Hébertist; a number of sincere patriots had difficulty accepting the official version of the guilt of the former popular idol. Otherwise no soldier raised his voice in Hébert's favour; most were silent too about the fates of the other leading personalities of the regime, and we know of only one who expressed any pronounced Robespierrist sentiments.[40] The Parisian soldiers belonged to no Hébertist group whatsoever; but they read the *Père Duchesne*, and they helped increase its circulation in the *sociétés* of towns through which they passed, as well as that of other Parisian newspapers such as the *Journal de la Montagne* and the *Journal Universel*, likewise recommended by them.

Later, in the context of the excesses of the anti-religious campaign, the *représentants* or the local authorities spoke of Hébertist cores in the *sociétés populaires* of Provins, Fontainebleau, Brie-Comte-Robert, Lagny and Taverny, all localities in which the detachments were billeted and where the soldiers were in touch with the *sociétaires*. But too much importance must not be attached to accusations which sought to establish a connection between atheism and Hébertism, and which identified every ultra-revolutionary with the Cordeliers. Undoubtedly the presence of the *révolutionnaires* in these *sociétés* encouraged zealous minorities and contributed to a certain revolutionary exaggeration, notably in religious matters. But it is an error in perspective to try to link every village demagogue or energetic revolutionary with some imaginary party in Paris.[41]

In the final analysis, the political was less important than the repressive and economic action of the Parisian *armée*, and it was rather through police measures that it sometimes modified the political balance in the communes of the Parisian region. Arrests, dismissals and *scrutins épuratoires* had more durable political effects than the advice lavished on their country 'frères' by the Parisians. The *armée* left its mark on the political life of the tiny communes through the brutal fact of its force, the threat of arrests, and through the more important political episodes: Villeblevin, Vermenton, Jagny, Livry, Montcornet, Noyon, Trouville, which were dictated by repressive considerations rather than by the desire to convert. The political impact of these operations was a secondary, even unforeseen, consequence. Nor was it always a clear-cut struggle between *gros* and *petits*, between *modérés* and *patriotes*; the intervention of the *révolutionnaires* tended to redress the political balance in favour of the sans-culotte minorities, but most of these conflicts reflected subtle personal disputes rather than precise political and social divisions. The Parisians thought they were intervening on behalf of oppressed sans-culottes, but they were easily led astray and unable to penetrate the complexity of such village quarrels.

That, however, in no way lessens the importance of the role played by the detachments within the *sociétés populaires*. The *révolutionnaires* dominated the political life of Caen and of Lyon for several months, and installed themselves as masters, with the complicity of their local allies, in Noyon and in several other small communes. The presence of the Parisians gave a powerful thrust to the development of political life in the countryside; as 'hommes de liaison', they translated into the simple everyday language of the country people the essence of Sectionary propaganda. By their encouragement, they helped the popular assemblies towards a sense of their own importance and strength. To say that they helped to familiarise the country people with the idea of *démocratie directe* and of popular sovereignty is to go too far; but if the *société* began to occupy a preponderant position in the political, social and administrative life of the countryside during that autumn and winter, much of the credit goes to the *révolutionnaires*. The *sociétés* through which they passed were among the most energetic in the region, and after their departure the debates became less lively, as if the *sociétaires* no longer had the strength or the intelligence to continue the political struggle in the absence of the Parisian Sectionaries.

III   *Direct democracy and primitive egalitarianism: the* commissaires civils *in the country*

'The public interest seemed threatened with a general dissolution.' This is how the Thermidorean administration of a district in the Nièvre described the mission carried out in the department during the previous year by *commissaires civils*, at the head of revolutionary companies or battalions.[42] For once the authorities of the Year III were not exaggerating in the charges drawn up against the men and the institutions of the Great Terror. The experience of anarchy was particularly violent in a department where the most ardent members of the revolutionary movement were virtually free to act as they pleased, like oriental satraps,[43] knowing no law, no restraint. A 'general dissolution' did at first glance seem to have been the aim of these violent individuals, who, accompanied by armed men, took great delight in attacking all the authorities, all the powers, preaching the destruction of established society, denouncing the ownerships of large property, and heralding the advent of the *République des pauvres* and the end of the *tyrannie des riches*. Nor was it mere verbiage, for these men exercised sovereign power, levying taxes on some, removing them from others, usurping judicial power to revoke judgements made by the criminal tribunals, assuming the title of representatives of the people at the same time as ridiculing them.

Above all these 'hommes de liaison' were men in a hurry. Time was short. They sought to move quicker than external events, overturning and changing things all at once, even the everyday customs of the country people. They worked quickly, violently, taking advantage of the atmosphere of urgency which favoured major innovation. This sense of hurry, which they brought to all revolutionary action, disturbed their contemporaries, including moderate republicans, as much as the dangerous doctrines which they espoused, and an air of enthusiasm, of anarchy, suffused their missions. What was the reason for such haste by these *commissaires* for whom the violent word, the brutal gesture seemed to have replaced any theory or plan? Their victims, as well as most of the established authorities, were to conclude that their goal was to overturn everything.

This indeed was how things looked. But if we open the file of a Chaix, a Vauquoy or a Villers, we will also discover traces of a doctrine, however primitive and poorly expressed, and the reflection of a sincere egalitarianism. There are elements common to the various missions carried out by the *commissaires* in the departments, besides those of disorder and violence. In the first place, they all addressed themselves to the sans-culotte minorities, by leaning upon the popular *sociétés* as the principal instrument of their action. All took up the defence of the interests of the poor and denounced the bourgeois, the 'fanatiques'. All had the trappings, the emblems, the clothing of the ultra-revolutionary, calling themselves *délégués du peuple*, after the example set by the proconsuls, at the same time assuming Roman or Greek names: in the Nièvre we find names like Manlius, Bias, Diogène, Misobasile and Erostrate jostling one another in the village squares, alongside those of Tell and Axenstrom. The names of tyrannicides were also in fashion and the *révolutionnaires* were nothing if not fashionable.

Take the case of Chaix, a *juge de paix* from the canton of Lormes in the district of Corbigny, who at this stage called himself 'Marat' Chaix. The deeds and gestures of this man between September 1793 and Frimaire to Nivôse Year II were not peculiar to him, rather he united in himself all the traits, all the 'crimes' of the *ultra-révolutionnaire*: [44] social anarchy, abuse of power, bringing the national representative bodies into disrepute. Chaix is a perfect example of the local personality, taken over by the new ideas and searching for allies among the village poor against *les gros*, the men of the law and the farmers. Excluded from municipal office, he fell back upon the *société populaire* and the *comité de surveillance*, seeking to pack them with his supporters and attending the sessions himself in order to impose his views. Chaix was also presented with a situation favourable to revolutionary action: the commune of Lormes suffered near-permanent food shortages, caused by the ill will of farmers in the surrounding countryside, while the municipality had seen to it that the main burden of taxation during 1791–2 fell on the less well-off artisans of the small town. Chaix thus had a perfect situation to exploit against the big landowners and their friends and protectors within the municipality. He also knew how to play upon another, equally sensitive note – the long-standing hatred between Lormes, *chef-lieu* of the canton, and Corbigny, *chef-lieu* of the district – by representing the directory as in the hands of the big forest owners, who were particularly powerful in this grain-short district.[45] Chaix thus enjoyed the support of a powerful group of artisans with a vested interest in seeing the Maximum and the grain requisitions in favour of the town market implemented in all their rigour, despite opposition from the municipality and the district. In the canton of Lormes all the ingredients existed for a social struggle between sans-culottes and large landowners.

Chaix also had friends in high places. He was in correspondence with Fouché from the time of his arrival in the department, and wrote to him again in the Year III.[46] He knew he could count on the support of a *représentant* who recommended wide-ranging action to his *commissaires* against *les riches* and *les fanatiques*. Just as the revolutionary personalities of villages in the districts of Gonesse and Pontoise were able to catch the ear of the *comités révolutionnaires* and the Sectionary *sociétés* in Paris, so Chaix, during his many visits to Nevers, made contact with the *commissaires civils* of the revolutionary battalion, Henriot, Enfert, Commerçon and others; he had no difficulty representing Lormes to them as entirely under the thumb of the *modérés*, its market abandoned, the Maximum scarcely applied, and he called for a visit from the battalion. The *commissaires* of Nevers could hardly ignore this appeal from their 'frère', who was to share their detention in the prison of the *chef-lieu* during the Thermidorean reaction.

And their channel of action? – for the *commissaires* and Parisian officers it was, above all else, the control of the *société populaire*. 'The said Chaix formed a party of at least 20 followers, which supported everything he said in every session and [he] called them his sans-culottes.' He was accused of using every means to slander the established authorities and of 'influencing the *société populaire* of Lormes in such a way that it became a channel for his vengeance and for his own interest…'.

Did Chaix belong to any party? The *comité* of Corbigny, instructed to draw up the case against him after Thermidor, concluded: 'He was, in a word, the Robespierre of our district, he only liked disorder'. Poor Chaix scarcely deserved this, and with far more justification called himself the 'victim of Robespierre' after Thermidor; he had in fact been arrested on 17 Floréal Year II, at the height of the Robespierrist dictatorship, for abuse of power and for levying *taxes révolutionnaires*, and only regained his freedom on 22 Thermidor as a result of the *journée* of the 9th.[47] As for his political programme, it seems to have been that of those Parisian *commissaires* and soldiers who proclaimed popular sovereignty through the medium of the *sociétés populaires*. Had he not preached disobedience to the established authorities in the words: 'There will be an insurrection in all the *sociétés populaires*, a 10 August is necessary, we must shake off the yoke...'? The crime of *lèse-député* should also be added, for he denounced Jourdan, *représentant* from the Nièvre in the Convention.

'He called himself a great patriot and protector of the poor'. Appointed judge to the district tribunal, Chaix spoke on the subject of his future colleagues: 'I will teach them to judge revolutionarily, they will find it easy with me, I will teach them how to judge in three days, and with me the poor will always win out...'. After *justice populaire* came *loi agraire*. He was also accused of having said 'that the goods of the rich must be shared out to help those whom he called his sans-culottes', 'that all the buggers of bourgeois in Lormes were aristocrats and *égoïstes*', 'that the former bourgeois ought to...help those he [Chaix] called his sans-culottes...they even ought to share their goods with them', 'that he would prefer to be a dog on all fours than to be bourgeois, because of their ill will in not wanting to give grain'. Chaix himself seems to have been conscious of the reality of this social struggle, claiming in the Year III to have been held in horror by the *honnêtes gens*, his principal victims.[48] To him the *armée révolutionnaire* was simply an instrument in this conflict. Having called in a detachment, under the leadership of Paumier and Enfert, which arrived in Lormes at nine in the evening, Chaix sought to assure the *société*: 'my sans-culottes, you need have no fear, the *armée révolutionnaire* has come to impoverish the rich, and enrich the poor...'.

Chaix, to begin with simply a personality in the *société populaire* of Lormes, usurped supreme power by placing himself at the head of 'several citizens of Lormes...armed with sabres, pikes, lances, guns, pistols and batons'; he was heard on one of his promenades 'arrogantly calling upon several citizens [in the commune of Jourland] to respect the *délégué du peuple*...'.[49] The 'delegate of the people', that was he, 'Marat' Chaix, since Fouché had apparently granted him some vague powers. But if a delegate could thus dispose of the armed force, the sovereignty of the Convention would recede and fritter away to nothing; and Chaix was simply a *délégué*, not even a *commissaire civil*. That is why he could be accused of abuse of power.

Chaix was not alone. The Nièvre had many others who preached the same egalitarianism, who also had it in for the rich, and who, even more than Chaix, usurped judicial power. 'Perfidious and counter-revolutionary insinuations by anarchists, spreading through all the districts, promising a carve-up of the major properties, particularly the wooded land, and preaching insurrection against the rich or those said to be such, are the reason for the non-execution of all lease clauses...', ran the statement of the *commissaire national* with the Corbigny tribunal in the Year III.[50] At the same period an inhabitant of Decize was to speak of '*commissaires* calling them-selves *révolutionnaires*. . . men fraudulently assuming the capacity of *délégués* of the *représentants*. . . who have vilified *bons citoyens* under the banal label of "riches", or "égoïstes". . . '.[51]

In other departments *commissaires civils* outlined similar doctrines; witnesses spoke of hearing Sadet and Théret, members of the Commission Temporaire, declaring to the *société* of Crémieu 'that they had all paid tithes and they should now make the rich cough up the last penny of what they had taken. . . that they no longer needed the rich and that it was time the poor took their places and slept on feathers and mattresses. . .'.[52] The Bourgoin *société* attributed similar words to the two *commissaires* and to their colleague, Vauquoy: 'They openly preached the *loi agraire*, the insurrection of the poor against the landowners, whom they called scoundrels, brigands; . . . Sadet said that their goods were the patrimony of the sans-culottes, that the reign of the landowners had lasted too long and that the turn of the sans-culottes had finally arrived. . .'.[53] At Saint-Marcel, in the same department of the Isère, the locksmith, Contamin, after arresting a rich farmer, announced 'that it was high time these buggers were taken up and their goods distributed to the poor, that in other times one had to go to them cap in hand and they would scarcely give you a scrap of bread and a glass of wine'. Going then to the temple of Reason, he preached the equality of wealth: 'Until now, he said, the people have been deceived; he who has not should be able to enter without fear the house of him who has, for we must have equality of wealth. . .'. In a similar vein he declared to the *société* of Morestel that 'for a long time the rich had profited from their wealth, but today everyone was equal, all wealth should be held in common, the rich had always occupied the first positions and today all the poor should do so. . .'.[54] In Moulins the former canon Grimaud was accused of having held that 'equality consists in taking from where there is too much, and in giving to where there is not enough. . .'. His colleague and friend, Boissay, cried out to the poor people of the town: 'Brave sans-culottes who want for everything, throw yourselves on the rich, the merchants, the financiers, the *notaires*, etc., let them also eat black bread and onion soup. . .'.[55]

We must not, of course, attribute too much importance to such expressions of a primitive egalitarianism, partially provoked by the economic mobilisation for the revolutionary war. But many of the *commissaires* did consider it their moral duty to combat the extreme poverty produced by inequality, and the repetition of such appeals testifies to the diffusion of Rousseauistic ideas in certain circles. Moreover, Vauquoy, Sadet, Théret and Contamin were not content simply to preach about the coming reign of the poor and the reversal of the social order; at the head of the small *armée* of Crémieu, composed of these very poor, they took excess linen, sheets and blankets from the cupboards of the rich farmers and distributed them to their soldiers or to the poor of the villages.[56] This, it is true, was still a war measure, recommended by Fouché in the orders to his *commissaires civils* in the Nièvre and in the Allier. It is nevertheless of interest to see that the egalitarians sometimes practised what they preached. Contamin, the future *panthéoniste* and protégé of Félix Lepeletier, was a rural egalitarian of the purest kind, while the fan-maker, Théret, was later to be shot at the camp of Grenelle.

The experience of the Crémieu *armée* was made possible by repressive circumstances and by the economy of war – the pretext for Contamin's 'promenades' being the collection of silverware and precious metals. But other *commissaires* went even further in their efforts to equalise wealth and put an end to the poverty which shocked these egalitarian moralists. Thus Villers, sent on mission to Epernay by the Châlons *société*, wrote on 10 Frimaire telling its members of the measures projected by himself and his colleagues: 'We have already done several things since our arrival in this town, of which you will hear later. . . . For the moment I am happy to inform you that at Epernay there is going to be no more poor, no more *maison de charité*, but rather a *maison de partage de famille*, in which every *frère* will receive a share . . .'. This measure had been passed by the *société*, and, as in other places, was to be financed by a voluntary subscription which was never entirely voluntary, the well-off preferring to purchase tranquillity by ostentatious donations.[57] Elsewhere they were happy with purely symbolic measures, recalling, as one great historian of the Revolution recognised, the basic elements of Catholic charity.[58] In Cahors, the poor were invited to a civic repast, at which they were served by the rich, and this 'touching demonstration' was organised by the *commissaires civils* and by the revolutionary officers.[59] It was a completely harmless way of affirming social equality; once the feast was over, everyone returned to their normal rank and the established order of things was restored.

Did such 'doctrines' penetrate the revolutionary *armée* itself? Undoubtedly the soldiers of Crémieu were well pleased with the material profits of their 'promenades', during which their *chef* distributed shirts and handkerchiefs taken from the rich. Any soldier would espouse this kind of doctrine. The Lille soldiers were to cry out against the rich and the merchants. But these prejudices against *les gros* did not necessarily involve a precise class consciousness; rather they reveal an instinctive desire for revenge against the economically privileged. Since the Revolution had reversed the old order, it was the turn of the oppressed of yesterday to take the place of the 'magnificent', and like them to sleep in feather beds. Hence the somewhat childish insistence in popular petitions and addresses, as well as in the sermons of the *commissaires* on paying tribute to the externals of equality: no more bowing or kissing of hands, no more 'my master' or uncovering of the head – hats and caps would remain in place, and the Lille soldiers carried this further by keeping their pipes in their mouths (pipes being egalitarian and popular at this period); everyone was equal, the people were sovereign. In the countryside, where everyone knew each other and spied upon each other, this desire to turn things upside-down went further than in the towns (though even here there were women who wanted to mark the new order of things by adopting the high style of living of *les grands* of yesterday).[60] The popular armies gave the new order a more practical expression in the country than in the towns, which were more policed, and dominated still by a National Guard partly composed of bourgeois. Few *révolutionnaires*, however, came anywhere near even the very basic egalitarianism of the Lillois. Those from the Lot thought only of their pay; in general this visceral egalitarian feeling was confined to the *commissaires* and the officers, the soldiers instead thinking of themselves as privileged and seeking to derive the maximum profit from their position as élite troops of the new regime. This was quite the reverse of egalitarianism.

Though vague and very basic, the desire for social justice nevertheless contributed to the immense popularity of some *commissaires* among the poor of the villages and the small towns. Some, like Chaix, even had their own party, composed of poor folk who were entirely devoted to them.[61] To the *honnêtes gens* this was yet another crime, and the *commissaires* were accused of being demagogues and anarchists, rousing the 'ignorant populace' to commit 'excesses harmful to public tranquillity' and 'all manner of vexations against peaceable and patriotic citizens...'. In the great Thermidorean petition prepared by the *patriotes* against Chaix, the social reasons for the animosity of the signatories come through quite clearly.[62] In Moulins, the hatters' assistants, the Brillantais metal-casters, the cutlery workers and other former soldiers of the battalion of the Allier (which was particularly popular in composition) were to show their gratitude towards the *commissaires* of the Year II in a series of demonstrations which rocked the town in spring 1795. These protests, which the *représentants* on the spot attributed to the evil influence of Fouché, were perhaps the finest homage of the poor to the efforts made on their behalf by the former protégés of this proconsul.

Other aspects of the political activity of Chaix can also be found in the words and actions of his colleagues, the *commissaires civils* and officers of the departmental forces. They were not as explicit about popular sovereignty based on the *sociétés* as the Parisians, but they evinced the same preference for the *sociétés*. In the Ariège, Picot-Belloc formed *sociétés* to speed the process of political proselytisation; in the district of Gien, Rousseau told his superior, Laplanche, whose *délégué* he was, that their formation was the surest way of regenerating public spirit.[63] The *sociétés* were above all to be used in the struggle against Catholicism; but they were also important in the political work of the *commissaires*, who consulted them on every matter of personnel, and assigned to them the task of purging and replacing authorities considered too timorous, too indulgent. Sometimes they went even further and voiced the doctrine of *démocratie directe*. Thus Louis Giroux, a Reims trader and a former *commissaire civil*, was to be accused 'of having sought the dissolution of the Sectionary assemblies and of having announced...that the *sociétés populaires* represented the people,...'.[64] At Moulins, Grimaud – again – was heard proclaiming 'that it was the people and the *société* who were sovereign...';[65] while General Dufresse, after his purge of the *société* and municipality of Dunkerque, informed the Lille *société*: 'Things are now as they ought to be in this town, it is the people who govern the people...'.[66] But these are isolated cases, and it would be foolish to claim that officers and *commissaires* everywhere held theories of the sovereignty of the *sociétés*. Generally their intervention took the simple, if symbolic, form of participating in the fêtes organised by the *sociétés* and designed to establish in the eyes of the populace, particularly the rich, the union and fraternity of the sans-culottes. It was also a way of giving their measures the semblance of popular support.[67]

The practice, which was more frequent the further one moved away from Paris, of powers being delegated by *représentants* to secondary agents, left the door open to all kinds of abuse and provided the initial step in the alienation of authority from the Convention and the tribunals. Most of the *délégués* probably felt, in all sincerity, that they had the right to usurp the functions of legislator and judge. But others were less scrupulous, taking advantage of their privileged position and using this argument to justify blatant abuse. 'I am the delegate of the *représentant du peuple*', Vauquoy was to say;[68] 'I am therefore the same as a *représentant du peuple*'. And this former secretary of the Jacobins and *petit commis* of the Ferme Générale acted according to this formula, arresting, releasing, levying taxes, confis-cating and distributing goods. By guillotining him the Revolutionary Government was merely restoring things to their rightful place. Vauquoy paid the price for all his *délégués*, who, during the active period of the revolutionary forces, had multiplied this usurpation of powers, to the detriment of the established authorities and even the Convention itself.

Fouché was particularly generous in his distribution of *délégations*, and the activities of his *commissaires* in the districts of the Nièvre posed many judicial problems for the Thermidorean authorities. In Vendémiaire Year II, Henriot, Grangier and Pauper arrived in the district of Moulins-la-République (Moulins-Engilbert), in possession of extensive powers. Their first action was, of course, to present themselves to the *société populaire* of the *chef-lieu*: 'They introduced themselves as invested with every power, they assisted at the sessions of the *société populaire*, they asked the people if they had recovered their communal rights...', and on being told that the poor labourers were being prosecuted for crimes committed in the national forests, they 'ordered that all such prosecutions be quashed...'. The national agent of the district queried the right of the *commissaires* 'to interrupt the course of justice', and pointed to Fouché's orders empowering Grangier and his colleagues to 'purify' the established authorities in the district. 'Everything which they have done beyond their powers', the agent concluded in good legal terms, 'is null and void as coming from unauthorised personnel. The *commissaires* of Fouché were simply *délégués*, representatives, and a representative cannot exceed the limits of his mandate. The mandates given to the *commissaires* did not authorise them...to release delinquents from the fines which they had incurred... In blocking such fines, were they not throwing away public funds?'[69]

Worse still, the *commissaires* also exercised a kind of *droit de grâce* in ordering the release of two *notaires* of Lizy, awaiting sentence on charges of misappropriation of funds. They were due for sentencing before the criminal tribunal of Nevers, when the *armée révolutionnaire* arrived in Moulins-la-République. They presented a petition to the commanders of this *armée*, who acquitted one and released the other, ordering him to pay 500 livres to the complainant and suspending him from practice as a *notaire* for ten years. This, declared the agent Chapsal, with good reason, 'was to usurp the powers of the Convention, a sovereign body with sole entitlement to use the prerogative of sovereign power...', and the tribunals and the police commission instructed him to initiate prosecution procedures against the *commissaires* 'for usurping sovereign authority by interrupting the course of justice...'. 'The crime in question', continued Chapsal, 'must be considered as a usurpation of the power of the Convention'. We know nothing of the reasoning of the *commissaires* in this case. No doubt they would have justified their actions, as Chaumont had, by invoking *droit révolutionnaire*, and on the first occasion they probably wanted to help the poor sans-culottes exposed to the anger of the *honnêtes gens* and to the justice of the rich. Their appropriation of judicial powers was further aggravated in the eyes of the authorities by their announcement of the liberation of the two *notaires* at a session of the *société populaire*, thus transforming it into a court of appeal.[70]

The *commissaires civils*, like the officers of the *armée*, belonged to no political party; they were not representatives in the departments of militant Hébertism, devoted to the triumph of a particular group and the realisation of a definite programme. Certain *commissaires* had personal contacts with the War Ministry (at least half depended on it administratively), and with the Cordeliers. Others appear to have been connected with Robespierrist or Dantonist circles.[71] But too much importance should not be attached to professions of friendship, attached as postscripts to official letters, particularly when they were addressed to top officials like Sijas or Vincent. It certainly does not prove the existence of some vast political network throughout France, with a few men at its head controlling the threads of correspondence. There were, it is true, versions of the *Père Duchesne* just about everywhere: in the Nord, in the Midi, in the Centre, in Lyon, and doubtless elsewhere.[72] But this simply testifies to the immense popularity of Hébert's newspaper. It is not proof of a party organised around the person who stood in for Chaumette. It would be more accurate to claim that a Fouché party existed in the Centre and in Lyon (in the Year III it was openly called 'Collot's party'), of which the battalions of the Nièvre and the

Allier, and the detachment from the Parisian *armée* in Lyon, were the instruments for intervention in the Lyonnais and the Dauphiné. The recall of Fouché was a political event of national importance and had immediate consequences (particularly in Moulins) for Grimaud and all those close to the *représentant*.[73] But Fouché, like Collot, was not in league with Hébert, and he was quickly dropped by the two proconsuls when he became compromising. The departmental *armées* served no precise party, even if they were the instruments of execution of a particular policy: that of *exagération*.

The *commissaires civils* on their tours of duty gave political advice to the rural *sociétés*; like the Parisians they were instructors in Revolution and one of their essential functions was to recommend patriotic newspapers to the *sociétaires*. Thus the *commissaires civils*, Grimaud and Griveau, passing through Cérilly with a detachment of the battalion from the Allier, on being asked to recommend certain newspapers, 'listed the *Journal des Hommes Libres ou le Républicain*, the *Journal de la Montagne*, the *Anti-Fédéraliste* and the *Feuille villageoise...*'.[74] It was hardly a *hébertiste* selection; quite the contrary, for at this period – Brumaire Year II – the *Journal de la Montagne* had already become the channel of virulent propaganda by its editor, the Dantonist Jean-Charles Laveaux, against Vincent and the War Ministry, and they had not mentioned the *Père Duchesne*. Elsewhere, it is true, the *commissaires* did recommend it, and in Lyon the members of the Commission Temporaire even produced a paper in its style and with its title. But Grimaud and Griveau can hardly be called Dantonists for having publicised the *Journal de la Montagne*, and the *commissaires*, asked for advice on newspapers by the local *sociétés*, simply recommended those considered patriotic, with little thought for their affiliations, supposed or real. In any event, it is highly unlikely that men such as Grimaud would have been informed of the differences between the various coteries in Paris; to them, Jacobins and Cordeliers were equally recommendable. One had to be a Parisian, like Vauquoy, to understand the various subtleties and actively to campaign on behalf of the Cordeliers against the rival society.[75] In the departments the ambition of every little *société populaire* was to secure republican respectability through affiliation with the Jacobins. It was only in the area around the capital, at Vaugirard, Versailles, Issy or Vitry, that the influence of the Cordeliers was sufficiently strong for it to figure in requests for affiliation, and in any case those requests were made in the absence of the *armée révolutionnaire* and its *commissaires*. The *commissaires civils* from the departments and the revolutionary officers were not emissaries or agents of any so-called 'groupe hébertiste', for the simple reason that they did not know one existed.

The scattering of individual forces and the creation of numerous virtually private armies posed dangers of quite a different order. There was no chance that they would come under the control of some Parisian group, or that they would lend support to some national counter-power in the form of a federation of all the *sociétés populaires* of the Republic. The Légion des Montagnards might have constituted such a force if it had continued to be recruited exclusively from among the *sociétaires*. But recruitment dragged to such an extent that the threat was quickly removed, and its organisers were obliged to take recruits from the soldiers of the first requisition. The Légion soon lost its exclusive and political character as 'child' of the *sociétés populaires* and became just another *armée* like all the rest. Far from contributing to the development of some *pouvoir militaire* on a national scale, the proliferation of tiny companies and battalions actually increased the erosion of central authority and accelerated the move towards decentralisation by placing armed force at the disposal of the smallest administrative units. The battalions were in the service of a district, or more often of a commune, not of the Republic. It was a misnomer to call the 350-strong force raised at Moulins the 'Armée révolutionnaire de l'Allier', for it was exclusively *moulinoise* in its composition, and even more so in the use to which it was put. One could say the same of nearly all the other so-called departmental forces, with the exception of those of the North and of the Moselle.

With communes thus in possession of their own armed force, we have arrived at the logical outcome of the 'municipalisation' of institutions, the administrative 'communalism' which was one of the most deep-seated tendencies of the popular movement in France. That is not the same as saying that these forces were in the service of the municipalities. On the contrary, they became instruments of a *société populaire* or a *comité de surveillance* rather than of the established authorities. Even if the *sociétés* tried to organise themselves into regional assemblies, they remained staunchly communalist, devoted to purely local interests; what concerned the average *sociétaire* most was the construction of a new road, the repair of a bridge, and above all the supply of the local market. A *comité de surveillance* was undoubtedly more subject to national influences, since it depended on the Committee of General Security for police operations. But the *comités de surveillance* of the departments were far more independent than the *comités révolutionnaires* in the capital, and in many small communes they were simply an extension of the *sociétés*, members frequently being municipal officers or their near relatives, and that regardless of the law prohibiting the accumulation of positions.

These *armées* contributed nothing to the formation of a *pouvoir militaire*, and even though some *commissaires* held anti-parliamentary sympathies, scorning the deputies and dreaming of new elections according to the Constitution of 1793, or of a new *journée populaire*, the tiny battalions and companies would have been little help. There is no incidence of two *armées révolutionnaires* merging on the orders of an individual, and it was only on the express orders of the *représentants* at Lyon that the battalions from the Nièvre and the Allier joined the 7th battalion of the Parisian *armée* – even then they maintained separate commands and autonomous companies. An *armée révolutionnaire* might unwillingly have become the instrument of *one société, one* commune, but not of a *mouvement communaliste* or a group of *sociétés*.

The former possibility was where the real danger lay. *Gouvernement militaire* consisted of Caesarism by the *chef-lieu* of the canton. At Dax, in the Landes, two brothers, the Despérieuxs, used the small company to maintain their personal empire in the *société* and to dominate the *comité* and municipality. But their tyranny was fragile and survived only because of the isolation of the small town and their lack of communication with the garrison troops and 'outsiders' from surrounding communes. Their reign lasted several months, but it was brought to an abrupt end by the arrival of the *représentant*.[76] In Lassay a handful of men allowed themselves the luxury of a personal guard, which accompanied them as they walked through the streets, beating up 'fanatiques' and their own personal enemies.[77] Small towns, *chefs-lieux* of cantons or districts – these were the chosen territory of the *système militaire*. But such abuse was rare and difficult to implement, for the *révolutionnaires* were civilians who remained in close contact with the other inhabitants. Moreover, like the *sociétés populaires* themselves, the companies were provisional institutions, created by an exceptional situation. Personal tyrannies depending on part-time soldiers could have little durability.

The political interventions of the *armées révolutionnaires* were of less importance than their repressive action; it was through the latter that the detachments sometimes temporarily altered the political balance of a small town or village. But these *coups de force* were limited in their effects, and once the soldiers had left, the sans-culotte minorities sooner or later found themselves again facing rural hostility.

On an individual level the Parisians, as 'hommes de liaison', familiarised the sans-culottes of the departments with the ideas of the Parisian Sections. But it was as a body that the Parisian *armée* gave the rural and small-town *sociétés* the means to dominate. It was from the co-operation between the detachments and the *sociétés* that a popular power developed, which, in exceptional circumstances, came to rival that of the regular authorities.

The *armées* simply gave more weight to the eloquence of the *commissaires civils*, encouraging village *partageux* and revolutionary minorities in the country to abandon their prudent silence. Their passage unleashed brief bursts of egalitarianism, which were verbal rather than dangerous. The *honnêtes gens* escaped with but a moment of fear; but that fear was ferocious and the allies of the *commissaires* were to pay dearly for moments of panic caused by the detachments among *les gros*. More than anything, the existence of the *armées* increased the violence of the moderate reaction long before Thermidor.

But they did not reinforce the authority of any political party, and if they made any contribution to the political history of the Terror, it was rather to strengthen the vague desire of the country populace for a genuine popular sovereignty, decentralised and communalist. That is what was meant by 'le peuple armé par le peuple'. Even the *armée* of Ronsin, the *armée* of the Convention, was, above all, that of Paris; and the *armées révolutionnaires* as institutions were so dear to the sans-culottes of the Year II because they put force at the service of the commune, the very antithesis of revolutionary government.

CHAPTER 6

The *Armées révolutionnaires* and Dechristianisation

The departmental *armées* were ill served by the dechristianising campaign in its violent and military form, for they were held responsible for an anti-religious policy based on force. The Parisian *armée*, even though it managed to stand back from the affair, also suffered from the crisis of confidence produced in both the public and the government , and the force was put under much closer scrutiny following certain excesses for which it was blamed. The peasants in particular did not hesitate to hold the political *armées* and the men who led them responsible for a policy which they detested. Rural opinion in fact saw that policy as an attempt to uproot Catholicism, to abandon the neutrality which the state had imposed in matters of religion and to replace Christianity with other religions: of Reason or *la Patrie*. The government, or the Committee of Public Safety at least, had no real understanding of the precise nature of events taking place far away in obscure communes, and was quick to rail against formations which they saw as seed-beds of military atheism.

We will leave government reaction to forced dechristianisation to another chapter, except to say that it proved fatal to the existence of the departmental *armées* and to the position of the *commissaire civil*. Here we will attempt to estimate the role of the Parisian and departmental *armées* in the development of a complex movement which went beyond the simple destruction of religious objects and a childish, if spectacular, iconoclasm, to the forced closure of churches, the struggle against rural customs and the attempted establishment of a kind of military atheism. Those responsible fought on several fronts simultaneously; their attack on the Sunday was fitting work for *révolutionnaires*, since nothing could be more revolutionary than a desire to change custom and habit. Aulard was right to see the new calendar as the most sensational innovation of the entire revolutionary period; dechristianisation sought to change profoundly the personal lives of every French man and woman, and the women in particular were to revolt against such an attack on their customs and their personal beliefs. We have already seen how dechristianisation could affect the mobilisation of the resources of the nation and the maintenance of order in the interior. It is important to keep in mind the chronology of this movement, for some excesses were provoked initially by the disorders stirred up by country

442

women at the time of the removal of the church bells. The *révolutionnaires* had no monopoly on violence and the supporters of Catholicism were very often the first to resort to force. Religion was a sensitive issue, and the revolutionary regime could not let refractory clergy fish in troubled waters. Revolt or the threat of revolt brought repression, and repression brought excesses of all kinds. In this domain both parties acted amidst disorder and violence.

In the eyes of history, as in those of rural opinion at the time, the *révolutionnaires* have, till now, shouldered almost total responsibility for inspiring and executing the anti-religious policy. Historians have been only too ready to use the epithets *hébertiste*, *exagérée*, even 'counter-revolutionary', to describe it. In their eyes it was a matter of demagogic excess and was morally and politically suspect. The royalists had a particular interest in turning the countryside away from an urban and atheistical Revolution, and they had a tendency to paint things blacker than they were. According to their reasoning, when the dechristianisers were not agents of Calonne or the baron de Batz, they were adventurers who 'took down crosses to avert attention from their own misdeeds'. At very best they were madmen, witless men, who had turned the Catholic populace of the countryside against the Revolution. What could be more impolitic, more shocking, than to attempt thus to 'teach philosophy at the point of a bayonet'! The debate continues. But contemporaries firmly labelled the *armées* and their leaders as agents of an atheistic, violent and militaristic *hébertisme* – yet again that all-encompassing political tag, which explains nothing and subtly mixes up parties and groups.

Such biased and simplistic explanations must be avoided. The *armées révolutionnaires* were convenient scapegoats, and if their half-baked attack on religion was the pretext for their dissolution, it does not necessarily follow that they alone were responsible for it. But it is difficult to get at the truth in a subject arousing such passion. What precisely was meant by dechristiani-sation? What were the origins of a movement which existed long before the Revolution? Answers to these questions might allow us to assess the importance of the participation of the *armées révolutionnaires* in one of the most baffling and least understood phenomena of the period of the Great Terror. Dechristianisation struck the departments rather than Paris and the *plat pays* was more affected by its brutalities than the towns. 'The Terror in the village' above all meant dechristianisation.

I *General aspects of the problem*

The campaign of forced dechristianisation which was unleashed in nearly every department during the autumn and winter of 1793 (and even more in spring 1794) has been the subject of heated debate among historians of different outlooks. Where did such a movement come from, a movement which did not stop at the separation of Church and State and the confinement of religion to private practice, but went on to attack religion itself by the enforced closure of the churches and the prohibition of religious services even within those edifices? Can we reach far back into the history of the French people to a long-standing trend towards dechristianisation, slowly evolving behind prudent and apparent orthodoxy, revealing itself in a sharp decline in the fulfilment of the Easter duty and in religious observance generally, and bursting forth on the proclamation of religious toleration? And can we see all this as a proof of positive dechristianisation, or simply the manifestation of a growing indifference? Aulard considered the movement, with its unexpected and violent change of direction, as a manifestation of the revolutionary war effort, an aspect of national defence. His is an hypothesis which still commands credence.

When we move from the obscure origins of the movement to its participants, just as many questions await us. Are we talking about a mass movement in which the revolutionary élite of sans-culottes, if not the entire urban *petit peuple*, willingly participated? Or was it a case of dubious elements seeking to widen the gulf between town and country by attacking the most entrenched customs of the peasants, and thus to weaken the revolutionary regime by ensuring their almost unanimous hatred of it? In other words, were the dechristianisers patriots, though imprudent and over-zealous ones, or were they genuine counter-revolutionaries?[1]

Finally, can we separate this movement – which, in its violence and the implacable opposition it aroused in some regions, complicated the task of central government in supplying the towns and the armies – from the struggle against hoarding, the application of the Maximum, and the very unpopular laws on recruitment? Had dechristianisation – the 'legal', repressive kind – not been forced upon authorities anxious to maintain order and to accelerate the mobilisation of the nation's economic resources, by opposition, in some cases armed, from the inhabitants of certain cantons to the removal of bells and silver? How far was the government's desire to maintain the rhythm of war production outstripped by subordinates who, not content with 'legal', economic dechristianisation, proceeded totally to dismantle religion itself?

The process of truly revolutionary dechristianisation – with its forced closure of churches, its prohibition of religious practice, the obligatory abjuration and the marriage sometimes required of former priests – went far beyond the intentions of a government which was always careful to respect freedom of religion. What part did the *armées révolutionnaires* play in the process? Were they agents of a considered policy against religion, like that which Fouché was accused of following, and which the authorities, Robespierrist and Thermidorean alike, termed atheist and Hébertist? Did the *armées* take the initiative in such a policy, or were they merely instruments of a zealous minority, which took advantage of repressive circumstances to extirpate religion?

Many of these questions go beyond the limits of a study devoted solely to the *armées révolutionnaires*, and we must content ourselves with an account of their participation in the movement against religion in the regions where they saw action. It is an aspect of the problem which has attracted little historical attention, except where the question is posed but no answer attempted. Thus Georges Lefebvre writes, in his work on the Revolutionary Government: 'Dechristianisation was already under way in a number of communes around Paris. Who had taken the initiative? The question deserves study. It is very likely that the *armée révolutionnaire* operating in the Parisian countryside played some part; it must have aroused and sustained the zeal of the local sans-culottes...'. Commenting then on the action of the *armées révolutionnaires* in the departments, he again puts forward the hypothesis of an active initiative on their part: 'At the outset it was the same as around Paris and in Paris itself: the *armées révolutionnaires*, composed of determined sans-culottes, closed the churches...'.[2] In these two phrases the great historian of the French Revolution evokes the two principal means of action employed by the *armées* during their missions in the countryside: brutal and direct intervention, with little concern for the opinion of the authorities, and revolutionary propaganda, principally in the form of moral and physical assistance to the sans-culotte minorities in the country. It is this latter aspect which another historian, Marcel Aubert, also singles out in his studies of the Revolution in Douai. After mentioning the first resignations of priests on 25 Brumaire, the author adds: 'Some days later, the central committee of the Douai National Guard, excited perhaps at the prospect of the arrival of the *armée révolutionnaire*, denounced the obscene and deceitful practices of the priests and asked the Convention to adopt an anti-religious policy...'.[3]

Most local historians, particularly those of the Church, have something to say on the dechristianising activities of the *armées révolutionnaires*, emphasising the destructiveness and persecution involved. Canon Bridoux, in his religious history of the Seine-et-Marne, simply enumerates the arrests of priests by the Parisian detachments and mentions the dissolute behaviour of the garrison in the cafés of Melun.[4] It is natural that such historians, seeking to describe the sufferings of the Church and the misfortunes of the clergy, should single out the negative, but spectacular, aspects of such activities, with no attempt to ascertain the respective responsibility of the detachments, the *comités de surveillance, sociétés populaires, représentants* and their *délégués*.

The extreme variety of anti-religious action and the motives behind it defy simple explanations. Take first the personal attitude of the officers and soldiers towards religion – difficult to determine, for these men spoke little of theology. In the first place we need to distinguish between popular anti-clericalism and the political hatred of the urban sans-culottes for the refractory priest, the enemy *par excellence* of the regime. A distinction should also be made between the simple taste for destruction (iconoclasm was above all a military phenomenon) and the drunken blasphemy which characterised the sermons of certain *commissaires*, officers or soldiers. Finally, there was an element of fear: the political soldiers felt insecure among religious enthusiasts who believed in *lettres d'or*, in prophetesses and sorceresses, who consigned the republican soldiers to some kind of counter-revolutionary Saint Bartholomew's Day. In the *révolutionnaires'* hatred for the Chouans in particular, the instinct for self-preservation and the desire to avenge their murdered comrades were as strong as any anticlericalism. As for attributing dechristianisation to the influence of the Enlightenment, the *révolutionnaires* have nothing to say on the subject, and some even condemned the *philosophes* as enemies of the Revolution. But for years the almanach-sellers had carried scabrous, immoral and anti-religious verses from the boutiques of the Palais-Royal into the heart of the countryside. They were doubtless as familiar as the imagery of Chartres to the few country folk who could read,[5] and were certainly so to the town-dwellers who made up the revolutionary battalions.

If the personal views of the *révolutionnaires* are largely unfathomable, however, the other question posed by Lefebvre – concerning the role of the *armées* in dechristianising initiatives in the countryside – is easier to answer. Here we must distinguish between operations in which the detachments were simply instruments of higher authorities, and those where intervention was spontaneous. It was the second variety which dominated the case compiled by the Committee of Public Safety against these men and their institutions, which had thus escaped from its authority.

Dechristianisation had its purely destructive side, but it had positive aspects as well. Under the first heading can be ranged the iconoclasm, the removal of religious objects, and the abolition of the priesthood; the sermonising, civic fêtes, the imposition of the *décadi*, and the establishment of the cult of Reason came later. Certainly the imposition of the *décadi* was only the positive side of the struggle against Sunday observance, and it is difficult to establish a line of demarcation between the puerility and idiotic destructiveness of iconoclasm and the organisation of blasphemous ceremonies in aid of propaganda. Even the closure of churches may simply have been the last in a series of measures to restore public order, or the civic fêtes simply another means of combating Sundays – the *révolutionnaires* considering boredom and idleness the best allies of Catholicism in the countryside.[6]

We must try also to draw a map of this movement, which spread from commune to commune along the great military roads or into the country surrounding the big towns. This will help us to analyse the diffusion of a movement which was urban in origin, will highlight perhaps certain regional tendencies, and help single out any Protestant influences.

It is equally important to establish the chronology of 'legal' dechristianisation, and its development into an actively anti-religious movement after the forced closure of the churches. This last was undoubtedly the high point of a movement which developed over four months, from September to December 1793. (See the Chronological Table of Forced Dechristianisation,

Appendix B.) But closer analysis will show that the most violent operations, involving the active participation of the revolutionary battalions, were concentrated in the period Vendémiaire–Brumaire, and that
there was a certain relaxation before the promulgation of the law of 14
Frimaire.[7]

The Parisians had a respite of four months after this law. Did they take
note of the warning given in Nivôse about their spontaneous interventions
against religion? After that the intentions of the government were perfectly
clear; if the *révolutionnaires* continued their violent action against religion in
Pluviôse and Ventôse, we can be sure that they sealed the fate of the Parisian
armée. Some of the most violent operations did occur in Ventôse, in the final
days of Ronsin's *armée*, and in the very fief of Robert Lindet, the Eure.

The aims of this chapter are, therefore, to situate the problem, by defining
the various aspects of dechristianisation; to identify the dechristianisers; and
to assess the role of the *armées révolutionnaires* in the execution of measures
which, more than any other operation of the Terror, shocked the country
people and caused them to identify the Great Terror exclusively with its
anti-religious aspects.

II   *The revolutionary soldier and religion*

The savage pleasure shown by the revolutionary soldiers in their organisation of blasphemous demonstrations, the enthusiasm with which they
applied pickaxes and hammers to holy statues, and declared their hatred of
the deceitful and outmoded priest, were tokens of their personal support for
the attack on Catholicism and its adherents. Dechristianisation in its
primitively violent form was a manifestation of the popular mentality.

It is, however, difficult to establish the causes of this enthusiasm – of
which there are abundant examples – or to determine the personal outlook
of these soldiers on Christianity. The *révolutionnaires* were neither philoso-
phers nor theologians and had little concern for literature; their enthusiasm
seems rather to have come from a very widespread anticlericalism and a
marked hostility to the Catholic religion. Anticlericalism, a hatred of
priests, anti-Catholicism, condemnation of a religion which the urban
sans-culottes identified as the backbone of the Ancien Regime – such were
the main characteristics of the soldiers' attitude (and the urban sans-culottes
in general) towards religion.[8] These were political judgements; a Catholic, a
'fanatique', could not be a good republican, being by definition an enemy of
the Republic and an accomplice of the Ancien Regime.[9] On their arrival in
the canton of Pont-de-l'Arche, two personalities of the Parisian *armée*,
Halm and his adjutant, Bernard, protested to the established authorities:
'What, saints? Crosses? You surely cannot be revolutionaries...'.[10] Two
cannoneers from the Luxembourg Section, camped at Alençon, were
equally dissatisfied with the attitudes of the local inhabitants, who remained
attached to their priests and hindered the removal of bells and silver; this to

the Parisians was proof of their *incivisme*: 'All our complaints against the inhabitants of this place', they wrote on 16 Nivôse, 'boil down to one thing – fanaticism. The churches here remain open and it was only with great difficulty that we have managed to remove their silver and copper. It was only after considerable debate that they allowed it to leave for Paris . . . . The countryside is not enlightened, the priests still have considerable influence there . . .'.[11] Similar complaints came from a Parisian soldier on detachment from the *société* of L'Isle-Adam to Jouy-le-Peuple;[12] while the soldiers sent by Gaulthier into the rural communes of the district of Compiègne denounced the priests 'who are attempting to form a treacherous coalition to hamper the progress of the Revolution'. The curé of Francières they considered particularly dangerous; 'recognising that fanaticism is a wick needing but a spark' to set it off, they complained that this cleric was trying to rouse his flock against the Parisian soldiers by telling them that 'the *armée révolutionnaire* would tear down the saints and take the ornaments from the churches . . .'.[13]

The Parisians in fact were anticlerical as much out of fear as conviction. The unease of these urban sans-culottes is understandable, isolated as they were in a hostile countryside, charged with unpopular missions which exposed them to angry crowds that gathered when they tried to remove bells and silver, or even more when they arrested a priest. It is not surprising in such circumstances that the soldiers should have associated their own security with the defence of the regime, and called for measures of force against a Catholic religion which seemed a pretext for crowds to gather and for disturbances. Their fears seemed all the more justified when most of the churches in a particular canton had been closed; huge crowds of peasants would then converge on the one last church remaining open, and the discontent of an entire population, already excited, was thereby channelled into a single commune. The soldiers on garrison in L'Isle-Adam were all too well aware of the dangers of such a situation, and the disturbances in Fourqueux, in Nanterre and in the 'Vendée briarde' all arose from the existence of communes still practising religion in regions where most of the churches had been closed. The Parisians had a vested interest in preventing disturbances, believing that they themselves would be the principal victims.

Political considerations were also behind their hatred of priests and religion, for even if that hatred can be traced back to pre-revolutionary times, it was exacerbated by the peculiar circumstances of the summer and autumn of 1793. Marcellin and Paillardelle advised the *comité de surveillance* during their stay in Joigny, 'to remove from their soil all the enemies of the Revolution, to destroy all traces of fanaticism and feudalism . . .'.[14] Some soldiers of the Vernon detachment in the small neighbouring commune of Saint-Pierre-lès-Bitry, attacked the curé as 'little better than an aristocrat'.[15] The soldiers had been provoked into revealing a conviction which was deeply felt by most *révolutionnaires*, that Catholicism and counter-revolution were one and the same thing, and that the partisans of religion had deliberately chosen the enemy camp.[16] One could not be both *patriote* and *catholique*, and the exercise of religion, since it implied a political choice – apart from the fact that it was the root cause of all the disorders and discontent – could not be considered a private matter.

Political considerations would not have been so strong with the Parisian *révolutionnaires* – and likewise with the soldiers of the first requisition for the urban battalions – had the attachment of the *petit peuple* of Paris and of the other major towns to religion not experienced a lengthy period of erosion. It would be going too far to claim that a religious indifference similar to that on the upper levels of French society in the eighteenth century was also developing in popular circles. But it is important to remember that religious practice in the towns, and, with more reason, in the countryside, was still compulsory, and one should not lay too much store by the apparent participation of the people in the major religious feast days. Easter duty, like baptism and marriage in church, was obligatory, and when the Revolution removed such constraints, many regions, like the Parisis and the Pays de France, experienced a sometimes quite remarkable drop in the number of those practising – which seems to suggest that even in certain rural circles, religious practice had become a matter of orthodoxy and social conformity.[17] It is impossible to gauge the extent of popular dechristianisation in the closing years of the century, but the anti-Catholic movement did not arise solely out of the political and economic circumstances of the Revolution. The Revolution had simply polarised certain currents in popular opinion, which beneath apparent orthodoxy already contained the elements of a virulent anticlericalism, hostile alike to all forms of Christianity and to Judaism, and which would find expression in the most revolutionary aspect of this movement, the forced closure of the churches.

In urban circles the priest was clearly a detested figure long before 1789. What the future sans-culotte criticised most in the priest was his laziness and a licentiousness which offended the sans-culotte husband's manly pride.[18] The lower clergy of the Ancien Regime were undoubtedly morally upright. But even here one might find the flirtatious curé, frivolous and seductive, painted, perfumed and glittering. It was of him and the ravages he could cause in the hearts of his female parishioners that the sans-culottes were thinking in anticlerical outbursts which were those of cuckolded husbands.[19] Listen to one Parisian lieutenant who tried to prevent mass being said on a Sunday morning in Ventôse Year II, in a village through which he was passing, only to be thrown into prison by the rural authorities: 'You have destroyed many weeds', he wrote from his prison in Arcis-sur-Aube to the Gardes-Françaises Section on 3 Germinal, 'but others remain to imperil the fruits of our efforts. . .it is those rascally priests who still lord it over our towns and villages, who turn the heads of our wives and our children. . .it is these priests who are the real root of the evil. . . . It is my opinion that all such people should be put under arrest. . .made to work from morning till night under a harsh commander, and after that they might leave our wives alone and cease leading them astray in the confessional'.[20] The letter of this lieutenant – who had been so furious at finding mass still celebrated in a commune in Champagne in spring 1794 that he threatened to call in the *armée révolutionnaire* and a guillotine – illustrates the beliefs held by many urban sans-culottes and soldiers, and indeed by some commanders. Mazuel, for instance, told his troop in Beauvais: 'It is fanaticism and superstition which we will be fighting against; lying priests, whose dogma is false-hood..., whose empire is founded on the credulity of women...these are the enemy...'.[21] In *Le Grand Voyage du Cousin du Père Duchesne* – a news-paper modelled on that of Hébert, and published in Lyon by the Parisian *révolutionnaires* and the local sans-culottes – Millet and Bonnerot, members of the Commission Temporaire, criticised the inhabitants of Trévoux for their attachment to the priests, whom the two *commissaires* accused of continuing their domination over feeble minds: 'What, you useless buggers, you have not ceased deceiving husbands, seducing their wives and producing bastards? ...No more priests, in God's name, let us be brothers..., no more liars, no more idlers...'.[22]

It was the priest as an idler and destroyer of the household, who gained ascendancy over women through the confessional, that the soldiers and their leaders attacked more than the priest as magician and upholder of the old order. The *révolutionnaire* was no theologian, even if he talked of 'superstition',[23] and the real reason for his prejudice against the confessional was the power he felt it gave the priest over his womenfolk. Such prejudices at times came near to misogyny and there are many examples of this in the expressions of the sans-culottes, the *commissaires* and the *représentants en mission*. This anti-feminism was fortified by the frequently furious opposi-tion from the village women which they encountered on their iconoclastic missions – more than one *révolutionnaire* had to take to his legs to escape their fury. But most of all the soldiers held a grudge against women because of the way they let themselves be seduced by these lying and lazy priests. At Bec du Tarn, Hugueny, a Toulouse *commissaire civil*, 'thundered against fanaticism, and in particular against women, who were more easily seduced by it; he said that the Revolution had been made by men, and the women should not be allowed to make it backtrack...'.[24] Dartigoëyte, *représentant en mission* in the Gers, gave vent to similar feelings in his tirade against the *dévotes* of Mirande: 'And you, you bloody bitches, you are their whores [the priests'], particularly those who attend their bloody masses and listen to their mumbo-jumbo'; but he also had a word for the '*jean-foutres* of hus-bands who are naïve enough to accompany them [and who] simply show what cuckolds they are by doing so...'.[25]

Enlightenment thinking seems to have played no part in the development of this anticlericalism and anti-Catholicism among the urban *petit peuple*. Thunot, a joiner of the faubourg Saint-Marceau and an officer in the Finistère company, caused an uproar in the Compiègne *société* by 'shame-lessly exclaiming that the *philosophes* had destroyed the Revolution...'.

At the same *société* some Parisian soldiers interrupted one speaker in the middle of a long discourse on civil society, accusing him 'of dealing with "abstract" and "theological" questions', which they felt made him no more than 'the mouthpiece of a refractory priest'.[26]

Nor did atheism hold any more attraction for the *révolutionnaires* than theology, and if they can be credited with any thought on the matter, it translated itself into action: an incontestable delight in the destruction of the baubles of fanaticism. 'So I put on a chasuble, I don't think I committed any sacrilege by that, yes indeed, it was with satisfaction that I saw the baubles of superstition transformed into ingots in the republican crucible', explained the Parisian *limonadier*, Delacroix, in the Year III; he was a former revolutionary captain who had been denounced to the authorities of his Section for having organised blasphemous processions in the small communes of the Gonesse district while commanding a detachment of cannoneers from the Bon-Conseil Section.[27] It was a testimonial of personal satisfaction all the more credible in that it was made during the Thermidorean reaction, when iconoclasm and blasphemy were no longer acceptable.

There are many examples of sans-culotte support for anti-religious activities at their most basic level, and iconoclasm was as popular in the world of the shopkeeper and the artisan as it was among certain Jacobins. The 'republican crucible', the needs of arms manufactories, these were probably no more than pretexts to give these destructive country outings a patriotic respectability. One has only to look at the ribald humour with which the sans-culottes and Jacobins described such operations in the departments in their correspondence with their Sections, to recognise this. Thus Le Rolle, a member of the Luxembourg *société sectionnaire* and manager of an arms manufactory at Clermont-Ferrand, described with satisfaction the visit by his workers, his 'Vulcans' as he called these filers and metal-casters, to the town's cathedral: 'There, with terrible, vigorous blows, they swooped on Saint Peter, smashed Saints Paul, Luke and Matthew...all the angels and archangels, Raphael himself, the winged fowl of the celestial band, the beautiful Mary, who bore three children while remaining a virgin, and her babe-in-arms...'.[28] Listen too to the words of another Parisian from the sans-culotte milieu, a wine-seller like Delacroix, who wrote from Marseille to his Section: 'Today I came across a crowned virgin with a box for alms at a street corner; down with crowns, no more alms for your lazy courtesans, let them work, and you, you wooden hussy, away with you, we'll have no more superstition, and our triumph will be assured...'.[29]

The iconoclasts revelled in their work and enjoyed scandalising the *bonnes gens*. 'The religious of this region do not like me', wrote another Parisian *commissaire*, from Lorient, 'but what do I care, for I maintain, with Voltaire, that priests are men whom Circe changed into swine and who must be given back their human form, and besides, next to war, plague and famine, a priest is the thing to be feared most...'.[30] It was an iconoclastic, an anti-clerical humour, unsurpassed even by that of certain journalists in 1900, and which we hear again from the mouths of *représentants en mission*, and even from that of a member of the Committee of Public Safety, Prieur de la Marne; on his way through Lorient, he asked the *société* to ensure that the 'apostles' which it sent into the countryside tried 'to emulate the sneaking, hypocritical tone, the angelic voice, the seraphic glance of the good priests...'.[31] But such humour had something forced, something suspect about it; as with the lewd language of the *Père Duchesne*, it was a way of manifesting revolutionary conformism, with the maximum of ostentation and the minimum of effort.[32] We will return again to this aspect of dechristianisation, the product of a certain revolutionary one-upmanship.

Ronsin's soldiers manifested their anticlericalism in a much more dangerous way, making frequent denunciations to their officers and the local authorities against priests accused of having used words hostile to the government and most of all of having tried to 'fanatiser' the country people by saying mass. They took their example from on high, Maubant, the most representative figure of the Parisian *armée*, having denounced Gravier, the vicar-general of Saint-Roch, to the Committee of General Security on 7 September, just before he joined the general staff.[33] On mission, the soldiers denounced the priests and those accused of having used fanatical words or of having raised mobs to prevent the withdrawal of religious objects.[34]

Finally, anticlericalism and iconoclasm were just one more aspect of Parisian and *révolutionnaire* mistrust of the peasantry. The work of the iconoclast was no joy-ride, and many a foolish *révolutionnaire* spent an anxious few minutes in the hands of country men and women infuriated by the removal of their bells.[35] The country people knew how to avenge themselves on the village sans-culottes, auxiliaries of the Parisians, whom they considered traitors to the rural community, allies of the towns and of the godless men. If the *révolutionnaires* on the whole remained immune from this vengeance, the rural iconoclasts experienced all manner of ill treatment in the Year III at the hands of religious supporters. Their chief crime had been that of going over to the side of the town. The *révolutionnaires* were fully aware of the hostility which surrounded them during their missions to rural communes. The most absurd rumours were spread about them being Huguenots and emissaries of the Protestants said to be in the Convention,[36] and false stories circulated designed to spread alarm among the town-dwellers, who were almost as credulous as the country people, with their faith in prophecies and '*lettres d'or* written by God'.[37]

Iconoclasm had the *auberge* as its point of departure. Canon Bridoux affirms that the great destructive operations in the Seine-et-Marne under Meltier, a former priest, were organised amidst blasphemous singing at the *auberge* – headquarters for the *révolutionnaires*, where the Parisians and Melunois terrorists concocted their plans.[38] In Vermenton, the Parisians received information against the former curé and his supporters at 'Mère Duchesne's *auberge* on the main road. It even looks as if the *commissaires civils* and the officers deliberately brought their troops to the *auberges*, as the most favourable launching-pad for destructive attacks on churches, statues and wayside crosses.

The much-advertised drunkenness of the Parisian soldiers was partly a manifestation of group psychology. The iconoclastic aspect of dechristianisation was also an activity of crowds. We have, it is true, encountered some incidents of soldiers foolish enough to act on their own, as individual dechristianisers, and who suffered the consequences. But in general iconoclasm was a group activity. The most voluble in the group set the tone and their comrades quickly followed their lead, so as not to appear 'tiède', or, worse, as favouring Catholicism. In this respect, the military iconoclasm of the political and conscripted soldiers alike bears the hallmark of that same desire to conform which lay behind the massacres and popular brutality in general. The Parisian artisans went from café to café during the entire *journée* of 2 September 1792 carrying the head and intestines of the princesse de Lamballe – the symbol of a detested (and defeated) regime. In like manner the crowd avenged itself on a regime of which it was no longer afraid when it attacked holy statues and emblems of feudalism. Some were to claim that these *révolutionnaires* were direct descendants of those who so violently destroyed the temple of Charenton, and some, like Taine, would speak of popular bestiality and cowardliness. It is indeed true that even at the close of the century the *petit peuple* of Paris enjoyed a reputation for violence, partly inspired no doubt by the example of the nobility. Dechristianisation was just one more manifestation of the violence of collective crowd action.

There was also the element of one-upmanship. Dechristianisation was the favourite outlet for revolutionary demagoguery; it was open to everyone and a former canon or a marquis might use it as a way of recouping a misspent past, of 'recovering his republican virginity',[39] to use a contemporary phrase, by thundering against religion and gaining fairly lamentable victories over opponents made of wood and stone. Others, however, feared the supernatural consequences of such a challenge to divine wrath, and the country people were not the only ones to predict terrible punishments for these godless men. But one had to move with the tide, particularly if one was a member of an élite corps which was expected to set an example of orthodoxy.[40]

Iconoclasm, moreover, was a way of displaying their strength and making the civilian population sit up and take note. Certainly they could hardly have found a more effective means of terrorising domestic enemies, of showing them the vigour of these indomitable *sectionnaires*, than a feat of arms of this kind. Indeed, most of the more spectacular operations took place as the detachments were arriving in a locality, and were clearly designed to shake the people out of their apathy as quickly as possible and with the greatest *éclat*. There was a large element of the theatrical, of visual propaganda in everything the *armées révolutionnaires* did, and nothing was more spectacular than a holocaust of religious images, a republican *auto-da-*

fé. Some dechristianisers carried the spectacle a stage further by calling upon divine vengeance: 'If there is a God, let him strike me down here and now, in front of you all', declared Vauquoy, as he noisily gulped *vin de pays* from a ciborium used in the mass and smacked his lips before the horrified peasantry of a village in the Isère. Nor was he the only *commissaire* or revolutionary officer to act in this manner. Many *révolutionnaires* challenged God and the saints, in a clumsy and – because of its extreme and shocking nature – impolitic effort to convince the poor people that their images were but wood and plaster, and that the time of miracles and mysteries was past.[41] Iconoclasm also had its educative side; the Parisians did not simply act out of demagoguery or pride in their position as enlightened town-dwellers. Dechristianisation was a spectacular schooling in demystification.

Anticlericalism and popular iconoclasm, therefore, had many sources, ranging from political opposition to Catholicism and to the clergy as allies of the monarchy, to more personal concerns such as the desire to avenge years of sermons and obligatory penance, and anti-feminism, fear, hatred of the peasantry, violence and drunkenness. Urban popular circles may also have been touched by certain philosophic trends. It can of course be argued that, given the immense value of the objects taken from the churches, and however much the *révolutionnaires* scorned these 'baubles of fanaticism', their iconoclasm was nothing less than pillage in disguise. However, one does not destroy what one hopes to sell or steal; and as for the religious objects made of precious metals, these were sent off to the Convention amidst flourishes of noisy patriotism. Pillage will be discussed in another chapter; dechristianisation itself owed nothing to the desire for booty.

All the members of the *armées révolutionnaires* were not enemies of Catholicism and christianity. But all did share the sans-culotte prejudice against Judaism and the Jews, particularly detested by the *petit peuple* of the towns as money-lenders, *étrangers* and idlers who did not work with their hands;[42] yet we know of no antisemitic initiatives taken by the formations, whose own ranks, in Bordeaux at least, contained a significant proportion of those of Jewish origin. There were persons described as 'fanatiques' even within the Parisian *armée*, just as there were some authentic counter-revolutionaries.[43] The departmental *armées* contained an even higher number of religious supporters, for the selection process there was less rigorous than for the Paris forces, the composition more humble, and the most deprived from the towns and countryside were more attached to the Catholic religion than the élite of the *sans-culotterie*. In the Lot *armée* the 'fanatiques' were numerous enough to occasion considerable disquiet among the revolutionary authorities of Cahors.[44] Dechristianisation and iconoclasm seem largely to have been carried out by the more politically conscious among the *révolutionnaires*: the soldiers from Paris, Lille, the Nièvre and the Allier distinguished themselves more in this area than those of the two large *armées* (partly rural in composition) of the Midi.

It would likewise be wrong to allow the *armées révolutionnaires* a mono-poly of iconoclasm, anticlericalism, and that revolutionary dechristianisation which went beyond church closures to the attempted replacement of Catho-licism by a new religion. Anticlericalism was rife throughout the regular army in the Year II, and the Le Havre region was to be dechristianised by the Gravilliers and Montargis battalions.[45] The *armées révolutionnaires*, as armies of the interior, simply had more opportunity to put the policy into practice than those who fought at the frontiers. Even so, the troops march-ing towards the Rhine, the Alps, or the Lys were just as active as the poli-tical soldiers in smashing statues and proclaiming against Catholicism. If the map of iconoclasm largely followed the major routes, the reason was the intervention by battalions of the regular army – the *armées révolutionnaires*, with the exception of that from Paris, tended to operate in the *plat pays* bordering the great arteries of communication. A complete study of icono-clastic action would require a detailed examination of movement orders for the urban formations during the entire period from July 1793 to Prairial Year II, for this military dechristianisation continued long after the dis-appearance of the revolutionary forces and into the reign of the Robespier-rist Supreme Being.

The personal attitudes of the soldiers were conditioned, then, by a deep-seated anticlericalism, by a somewhat childish iconoclasm, as well as by strong political prejudices against Catholicism and by the fear of rural dis-turbances. On rare occasions the soldiers might go beyond such negative sentiments to a timid sketch of some positive system comprising patriotic considerations and religious sentiment – a kind of 'patriotic religion', hazy in outline, confused in doctrine. For the most politically informed sans-culottes, it was a case of replacing Christianity, compromised in the fall of the monarchy, with a religion of *la Patrie*, the martyrs of Liberty, and the new patriotic saints. Lagarde, for instance, the *commissaire civil* in the Avey-ron, proposed organising a series of fêtes to be called 'The Triumph of the Poor', 'The Triumph of Reason', 'The Triumph of Virtue', and so on.[46]

One of those who went furthest in this direction was the German draw-ing master, Mathias Halm, whose wife was entrusted with the education and upbringing of a 'fille de la Nation', Suzanne Lepeletier, only child of Lepeletier de Saint-Fargeau. Thus the Halms became high priests of the new temple consecrated to the memory of the republican martyrs.[47] Already in the Year II, Halm had distinguished himself during his service in the *armée révolutionnaire* by his brutal and destructive interventions against the Catholic religion, particularly during his mission in the Eure. At Vernon the Parisian cannoneers presented themselves to the *société populaire* on 22 Brumaire and asked 'that all stone statues of apostles and other saints be removed from the front and sides of the church'. It was a relatively normal request following the law on the removal of external symbols of religion; but they then proposed 'that the same stone should be used to build a pyramid in honour of Lepeletier and Marat, that in consequence commissioners should go straight away to the General Council and request that stone masons be appointed to commence work the following day . . .'. The *société* immediately sent this proposal to the municipality.[48] The cannoneers, who were from the Marat Section, were in fact organising a symbolic act: they were planning to make 'the vile remnants of superstition' serve the glory of the new religion. The proposal was not particularly original, for similar pyramids or mounds were being raised almost everywhere, often on the initiative of the 'hommes de liaison' from Paris and from the other major towns.[49] But on the part of the cannoneers it represented a revolutionary consciousness which went beyond the simple bounds of iconoclasm. At Montcornet, two Parisian soldiers went even further, demanding that a notice be placed on the front of the church proclaiming the building dedicated to the cult of Reason.[50] The Parisian *révolutionnaires* enthusiastically took part in *fêtes patriotiques* in their cantonments to celebrate the consecration of former churches to the cults of Reason or the *Patrie*. Here, once again, it was a matter of revolutionary conformism rather than an expression of some doctrinaire adhesion to atheism.[51]

In the final analysis, it is impossible to pronounce with any real confidence on the personal and political motives propelling men from such different backgrounds into the anti-religious movement. That the movement lent a certain impetus to the exaggeration of attitudes and doctrines, and to a peculiar form of verbal demagogy, is undeniable, and it is not surprising to find a Dolle or a Vauquoy among the leaders responsible for it. However, one must not read too much into their admittedly compromising presence: for every Dolle there were ten honest *commissaires*, who were perfectly sincere in their hatred of the clergy and of Catholicism. But how can we explain the presence of so many former ecclesiastics in a movement where they were often the first to take action against their gods?[52] It was a question which many contemporaries also asked, and the brothers Robespierre, along with Gateau and Jullien, cast doubt on the revolutionary convictions of all the dechristianisers by pointing to a certain 'colonisation' of the movement by former priests, and by attributing political motives to the phenomenon. But that was going too far; these men had the right to revolt against a vocation which in many cases had been forced upon them, and if they took *ouvrières* or good republican sans-culottes as wives, it was usually because they wanted a wife rather than a manifestation of revolutionary conformism or some kind of political belief.[53] They were also educated men, possessing the ability to speak and the habit of command, and their talents recommended them to positions of leadership in the eyes of the departments. One senses a considerable reluctance among Robespierrists and supporters of the Supreme Being to recognise the joy with which many priests and monks, former Oratorian or Minim doctrinarians, adopted a lay state which enabled them to marry; they were judged as if they had no right to free themselves from their former yoke. It is also downright dishonesty to use the foreignness of the main dechristianisers in Alsace as proof that dechristianisation was somehow part of a conspiracy by Pitt and Coburg.[54] The main crime of the dechristianisers – if it can be called a crime – was their imprudence and thoughtlessness in proclaiming ideas which could not fail to shock three-quarters of the rural populace.[55] But they were no statesmen, and dechristianisation was above all an outgrowth of passions rather than a political statement.

Besides, the dechristianisers came as we have said from a wide social background. The most clear-sighted of the leaders were undoubtedly well-informed men, but the *armées révolutionnaires* included representatives of every element of the *petit peuple* in the towns, and even members of the rural proletariat. Almost every commune had its own enemies of religion and the revolutionary soldier tended automatically to adhere to such groups. If he proclaimed against priests, it was because he did not like them; if he created havoc, it was because he enjoyed doing so. There is no need to look for mysterious watchwords (of which there is no trace). The presence of a vigorously anti-Catholic *représentant* in a department would undoubtedly have changed things; but this is not the only explanation. In France of the Year II there were thousands of people, from every milieu, a restless and vociferous minority, who took advantage of the situation to do what they had probably long wanted to do in any case. Dechristianisation gave them immense personal satisfaction.

III   *Spontaneous dechristianisation and regular operations: the example of the Parisian* armée

Georges Lefebvre has questioned the notion that the Parisian *armée* was the principal initiator of measures taken against the Catholic religion in the communes of the Parisian region and in the other departments in which it was active. It is this question – whether the Parisian *armée* was engine or instrument in the campaign of dechristianisation – to which we must now turn. The campaign took three forms: spontaneous operations undertaken by the soldiers or the officers on their own authority; operations under proper commanders, mostly repressive, and at times assuming the proportions of proper military expeditions (when the *armée* was supposed to be simply a policing instrument under the control of higher authorities); and, in between these two, the detachments acting as stimuli, propagating ideas, encouraging others. Sometimes the very presence of a detachment was enough to give local zealots and village dechristianisers the courage, and above all the strength, for a major attack on religion. Sometimes those minorities were able to use the mere threat of the arrival of the *révolution-naires* to attain their ends.[56] The action often took the form also of co-operation between the *révolutionnaires* and the sans-culotte minorities of the area, the latter taking advantage of the presence of the Parisians forcibly to shut the churches and to destroy religious symbols. In such cases the task was shared equally and it is impossible to assign responsibility for the initiative. At Avallon the local artisans led the Parisians to the church of Saint-Lazare and to other churches in the canton; at L'Isle-Adam, the *sociétaires* had the detachment accompany them on their mission to preach *la morale civique* in the communes of Nesles and Labbeville – one of the 'apostles' explaining on this occasion 'that he could only go there in the company of the revolutionary soldiers, for such was the fanaticism of these communes that he would not be well received...'.[57]

A more striking example of the kind of encouragement which the presence of a detachment afforded to elements hostile to religion comes from the village of Croix, in the district of Compiègne: on 2 Frimaire the mayor announced to the *procureur-syndic* of the district,

> that it was the duty of all the established authorities to destroy...error, falsehood, magic spells, pride, fanaticism, superstition and religious prejudices, the single source of the misfortunes of many people, a multitude of excellent creatures having been the blood-stained victims of the barbarous cruelty of the Roman papist clergy. In view of which we have required the former curé to give up all ornaments and silver.... Before doing so he struck each vase three times with a hammer to deconsecrate it, as he put it, before we laid hands on it. After this theatrical farce, the municipal officers called on me to seize the keys.... I therefore invite you to send a deputation from the *armée révolutionnaire* immediately to receive and take away everything of any use to our dear and much-loved Republic of France.... Hurry, for the remaining fanatics will continue to slander us until the operation is completed. I have also required the schoolmaster to use no book in his school but those decreed by the Convention. [Signed] DUPAIN *fils*.[58]

There can be no doubt about the origin of the initiative in this village. But the brave Dupain recognised that the task of the village dechristianiser was a dangerous one and he would need the protection of the armed force against the threatening attitude of the villagers. Finally, in Noyon, the dechristianising movement developed out of the close collaboration between two local sans-culottes (Hennon, *procureur-syndic* of the district, and Decaisne, a clerk in the same administration and a leading personality in the *société*) and the commander of the revolutionary company, Gasson, a young Bordeaux man, as ardent and imprudent a dechristianiser as the two Picards.[59]

This then was the kind of alliance between rural minorities and townsmen which sometimes created favourable conditions for intervention by the *armées révolutionnaires* in religious matters. If they acted without either internal support in the communes or the assent of the Paris authorities, the results of their action proved fleeting and they were severely cautioned. This is what happened to Lefebvre, captain of the detachment sent to Viarmes, in the district of Gonesse, when he embarked on dechristianising activities on his own initiative. Alerted by the municipality of the tiny commune, the Committee of Public Safety demanded an explanation from headquarters in the rue de Choiseuil. Grammont in turn wrote a letter to the offending officer on 21 Nivôse, outlining government attitudes towards measures of force against religion: 'I cannot disguise my annoyance that your detachment has become mixed up in religious matters. Since the National Convention has decreed freedom to all religions, it is not for us, created to lend force to the law, to adopt measures contrary to it. I instruct you therefore to be more circumspect in future and to confine yourself to your duties...'.[60] We do not know whether this recall to order had the desired effect in the case of the Viarmes detachment, but other Parisian detachments continued to carry out anti-religious expeditions at will until the *armée* ceased to exist.

These operations, however, were isolated cases, spectacular rather than important. The *révolutionnaires* were sometimes victims of a reputation for violence and ferocity which had been specifically manufactured to terrify the country people. In iconoclastic actions it was always the Parisians wielding their pickaxes who were seen, while the real initiators, the *commissaires* from the towns or the zealots from the country, remained in the background, in the *auberge* or at the *comité de surveillance*. The Committee of Public Safety was kept informed by the local authorities – with increasing frequency from Brumaire onwards – of the church closures and the military action of the Parisians against religion. But these reports said nothing of the collusion of certain local personalities. The *armée révolutionnaire* was a perfect scapegoat; the rural municipalities took advantage of the soldiers' verbal indiscretion to attribute every violent deed to them, so that by Nivôse, the Committee was automatically holding the *armée* responsible for any and every act of violence committed against religion. But the *armée* did not bear sole responsibility for forced dechristianisation, even in areas where it was active; rather it was paying the consequences of some spectacular actions which occurred in the first weeks of its existence.

Two operations in particular were responsible for this reputation: the mission under Clémence and Marchand into the district of Gonesse, and the sizeable detachment sent from Paris to Lyon in Brumaire. The former is of less interest, since the *armée* was little more than the instrument of the two *commissaires civils*. But during their journey to Lyon, the *révolutionnaires* were free to act as they pleased. In Montereau, Sens and Joigny, the officers simply sermonised and encouraged the local authorities to destroy religious emblems; but in Auxerre the soldiers took things into their own hands and were assisted by a sans-culotte minority which included some future Babouvists. This 'furie d'Auxerre' is well documented because of a journal kept by a citizen of Auxerre: a man of the law, in easy circumstances, he was no great supporter of the Revolution and was frightened by the violent acts committed by the Parisians in his town.[61]

'Several detachments of this *armée révolutionnaire*', he writes,

set off for the departments of the Midi, some 3,000 men passing through Auxerre. The first units arrived in Auxerre on 11 November [21 Brumaire], the feast of Saint Martin, with mounted cannon, wagons, flags, banners and drums. They were met at the Saint-Siméon gate by a patrol from the Auxerre guard, lodged, and their expenses met largely by the citizens of the town, and they left the following morning. The second force arrived at Auxerre on the 13th, and were greeted in like manner. This detachment had committed along the way all kinds of frenzied excesses against religious objects, battering down church doors, smashing altars, flinging down statues and images of saints. When they arrived at the chapel of Sainte-Marguérite, they carried out similar horrors, seizing a copper crucifix from the altar and one of them, mounted on a cart, derisively holding it out upside-down for passers-by to spit upon. At some distance from the chapel, they encountered a quarryman...and forced him to spit upon the crucifix.[62] On his refusal, one of the soldiers cut off part of his nose with a blow of his sabre; he had to be cared for in the Hôtel-Dieu.

'They continued their hostilities after arriving in the town', the journal continues,

mutilating and overturning all the stone and plaster crosses they encountered, and climbing upon towers and roofs of the churches to remove the exterior crosses and statues. In the evening, with the help of four horses and ropes, they tore away a beautiful cross installed in the middle of the cour de Saint-Pierre, on which the emblems of the Passion had been sculpted, a monument worthy of the piety of our ancestors, who had raised it at great expense.[63] If they were unable to vent their full fury on the churches of Saint-Etienne and Saint-Germain, it was because they did not have time. The precaution had been taken of hiding the superb paintings which decorated the nave of the former, the profanation carried out there was the work of the Auxerre iconoclasts. They then divided up into different bands and continued on their way the following day, using side routes so that the small towns, bourgs and villages of the region would also experience their fury. They found imitators among the young libertines of Auxerre, who fanned out through the neighbouring parishes, demolishing crosses, images and statues; nothing escaped their rage, they had no respect for the antiquity of the monuments, the most touching images only irritated them, in less than a week every external mark of Christianity had disappeared from the Auxerre area and from the neighbouring parishes.

The third detachment of the *armée révolutionnaire* to pass through Auxerre arrived on the 17th. It was received and welcomed like the other two. It it did not behave with the same indecency, it was because the second detachment left nothing more for it to do.[64]

The most memorable moment in this passage of the three detachments through Auxerre, however, came on 25 Brumaire just as the third detachment was leaving. On that day the churches of Saint-Eusèbe, Saint-Pierre-en-Vallée and Sainte-Madeleine were forcibly closed. Who had issued the order? From accounts given after the event, it would be difficult, without accepting some extraordinary coincidence, not to conclude that the initiative had come from the *armée révolutionnaire*.[65] Only one church remained open in the town, that of Saint-Etienne, and efforts made later by the *révolutionnaires* to close it were to raise the threat of crowd violence during Nivôse.[66] On 25 Brumaire also the General Council of the commune ordered the *commissaires* to go and examine the pictures and statues inside Saint-Etienne,[67] doubtless to have them taken away for safekeeping in the event of some new fit of iconoclastic fury by the Parisians. As for the bells, they had already been removed from all the churches on 7 Brumaire, two weeks prior to the passage of the detachments.

Finally, on 26 Brumaire, the day after the departure of the last detachment of the *armée*, Maure wrote ordering the General Council to finish off the work which had been initiated amidst such disorder and violence by the Parisians. He reminded them of government policy on the freedom of religion and the neutrality of the State towards the private practice of the Catholic religion: 'The Constitution, Citizens, guarantees the free practice of Religions and this wise provision requires all external signs of any religion whatsoever to be kept inside the place where the religion is exercised. I invite you to remove the remainder of those [objects] which were overturned by some soldiers from the *armée révolutionnaire* and to dispose decently of those which still remain within the commune of Auxerre.'[68] As for the forced closure of the churches, the prudent *représentant* said nothing, but acted more effectively by protesting to the Committee of Public Safety about the excesses committed in the department by the Parisian soldiers. But what had been done was done; and for Maure it was doubtless a matter of preventing a recurrence of such violence, and sparing his fellow citizens, who were peaceable people, the shocking spectacle of new destruction.

Thus, even in a town as tranquil as Auxerre, the Parisians embarked on a mania of destruction, and their example was followed by a clutch of sansculottes and young madcaps in the town. They had been able to force the closure of nearly every church in Auxerre with the co-operation of its *société*, which finished off the work after their departure by consecrating the cathedral to the cult of Reason.[69] Nor did the Parisians stop there; before continuing their journey, they also devastated the churches of the small communes around Auxerre.

The journey down to Lyon was punctuated by more incidents of the destruction of crosses and statues, the forced closure of churches, and the arrest of priests and *fanatiques*. In Vermenton the Parisians arrested the supporters of the curé Legry; in Avallon, their passage produced the same scenes as at Auxerre: churches devastated and locked up, crosses turned upside-down, and the extension of similar activities into the surrounding villages. In Cluny they launched a widespread attack on religion and a supposed nucleus of fanaticism, under the direction of the very active *société populaire* of Mâcon.[70] The march from Paris to Lyon in fact marked an important point in the history of the Parisian *armée*. Never had so many *révolutionnaires* been deployed together – more than 2,000 cannoneers, fusiliers and cavaliers – never had the Parisians felt so strong, so conscious of the importance of the task awaiting them at Lyon. Leaving Paris for the first time, their heads still buzzing with the praise, the instructions of the revolutionary *comités* and Sectionary *sociétés*, and commanded by officers like Lefranc and Fauveau, these *révolutionnaires* were easily convinced that they carried the destiny of the Revolution and the regime upon their shoulders. The 'furie d'Auxerre', and similar actions elsewhere, bore the stamp of their enthusiasm, and it was the violence and anarchy which characterised this, the first major sortie by the new army, which so frightened the local authorities and Montagnard *représentants* like Maure. They had certainly achieved their aim of striking *un grand coup* at the very outset. But they would never again be given such leeway and the memory of this first 'promenade' was to weigh heavily on all future action. The higher authorities had learnt their lesson; in future the detachments would be prevented from embarking on any spontaneous action on a large scale.

Finally, the progress to Lyon is a good illustration of the way in which geographical conditions frequently imposed precise limits on the map of dechristianisation, the campaign largely following the major military routes leading from Paris to the frontiers. Enforced dechristianisation and iconoclasm were, on the whole, carried out by soldiers. The stopping places and communes situated along the routes were naturally the first to experience the assault of these *hommes sans dieu*,[71] But unlike the units of the first requisition, the Parisian *armée* would also break into small detachments and spread out into the countryside around the towns in which they had stopped. It was in such out-of-the-way places, until then relatively untouched by the propaganda of the urban militants, that the sudden action of the Parisians often raised the most intense opposition.

The 'furie d'Auxerre' was to provide the model for other spontaneous action by the soldiers of Ronsin against religion and its emblems. But in no other place would such operations reach the same level of importance. At Ognolles, in the Oise, 'when the *Armée révolutionnaire* came to devastate our former church, they scattered the vestments'; at Parnes, in the Chaumont district, the cavaliers took sabres to a picture suspended above the main altar. In the village of Mée, near Melun, a small detachment closed up the church and took away its keys and effects without waiting for orders from the Melun *comité*.[72] The former parish priest of Saint-Martin-le-Vieux, near Honfleur, was to state in the Year XII that he had been 'forced to abandon his parish after seeing his church devastated by the *armée révolutionnaire*'[73] – characteristic of the kind of spontaneous dechristianisation or iconoclasm which preceded the forcible de-priesting of a parish. At Pont-de-l'Arche, acting under orders from the celebrated Halm, the Parisians destroyed all the churches, and they were to be accused of provoking a civil war in the Louviers district by their violent actions against religion. Finally, in the neighbouring district of Evreux, at Saint-Pierre-lès-Bitry, 'the captain and *commissaires* ordered the soldiers to devastate the church and to burn the books.'[74] After the notorious Gonesse affair, the *révolutionnaires* even searched private houses, reproaching a doctor, Saillant, for having a Bible in his possession: 'they called it a horrible crime, questioned him; asked if it was not because he loved God; I love the Republic [he replied] and all her laws. . .'.[75] Clearly one could not love both God *and* the Republic in the eyes of these sans-culottes from the Observatoire Section.

Generally the *révolutionnaires* confined their attack to inanimate objects, breaking statues, slashing pictures. But sometimes their anticlericalism assumed a personal aspect in the form of insults and attacks on priests and their supporters. In the district of Noyon, particularly in the canton of Lassigny, which became a refuge for refractory priests, they mistreated the priests whom they had been sent to arrest; and at Pont-de-l'Arche, Halm's soldiers provoked a riot in front of the church when they tried to thrash the *procureur-syndic* for attempting to retain the curé. In the communes of the La Tour-du-Pin district, detachments led by roving members of the Commission Temporaire mistreated the curés and vicars and ransacked the presbyteries.[76] But these occasions seem to have been rare; the arrest of their curé was an event of major importance for these people, and they tended to exaggerate the brutalities committed by the Parisians, and to embroider accounts of arrests to the point of creating positive myths in which the *révolutionnaires* were agents of Satan and the arrested priests martyrs.

However, the sans-culotte soldiers do not appear to have used wanton brutality in the implementation of arrest warrants, and the above examples are of interest mainly as manifestations of the anticlerical and anti-christian prejudices of the *révolutionnaires*. But individual and spontaneous action scarcely marked an important stage in the anti-religious movement, and apart from the unusual circumstances in Auxerre, such intervention by the Parisians was spectacular rather than effective, an irritant to the supporters of religion rather than a lasting achievement. Ronsin's soldiers were only birds of passage; as soon as they had gone, the faithful reopened the churches and replaced the crosses. Individual action by the soldiers could only achieve negative, destructive effects, rather than anything positive. It was poorly co-ordinated, limited by and dependent on the whims of the officers and the sobriety or drunkenness of the soldiers. They in turn were conscious of their helplessness in the face of the religious conviction of the country people,[77] and it was yet another factor fuelling their hatred and mistrust of the rural population. Individual action by the *révolutionnaires* was worthless except as an example. The few successes either came from local support by the village atheists, or were larger-scale measures such as the deployment of real military expeditions to tackle widespread religious disturbances. By itself the *armée révolutionnaire* amounted to little; it was only successful in the hands of higher authorities, *commissaires* or others using it to implement some carefully-thought-out policy. Under the leadership of a Ballardelle at Lagny, a Bachod at Chaumont, a Gaulthier at Compiègne, or a Hennon in the environs of Noyon, on the other hand, the *armée* might become a powerful instrument of dechristianisation, *déprêtrisation* and repression. It is to these regulated operations that we will now turn.

The operations of September–October 1793 in the district of Gonesse were only remotely related to dechristianisation, since they were dictated largely by considerations of public order. The two Committees, always concerned about any threats to the peace of a region so vital to the supply of Paris and to the security of military communications, had been over-receptive to the alarms of some local sans-culottes who had depicted the Pays de France as being on the verge of a 'fanatical' uprising. They had therefore given full powers to their *commissaires*, Clémence and Marchand, to arrest refractory priests and suspects, and, above all, to remove church bells.[78] The bells were accordingly removed, and their delivery, along with other religious objects taken from the churches of the district, was to be the occasion for considerable ceremonial at the bar of the Convention. But the *armée révolutionnaire* was the docile instrument of the two 'hommes de liaison' throughout the affair, which was also the case elsewhere in this troublesome district. At Jagny and Luzarches – communes in which the presence of the detachments coincided with the beginnings of dechristianisation – the initiative was taken by the local sans-culottes, while responsibility for the violent actions against religion at Livry belonged to Preslin and to the *commissaires* of the Observatoire Section. In the district of Pontoise the *comité de surveillance* used the detachments to put an end to the religious troubles, caused in the rural communes by the removal of their bells.[79] In the famous affair of Fourqueux, a strong detachment was sent against the population of this tiny commune which had risen to defend its curé, a much-loved figure. On this occasion a repressive military expedition was ordered by the two Committees, which in turn were responding to warnings from the *comité de surveillance* of the Montagne-Bon-Air district about the need for brutal and swift intervention. In this case the *armée révolutionnaire* was simply a political gendarmerie, acting under orders from the Revolutionary Government and the sans-culotte authorities of the region.[80]

Between 22 and 24 Frimaire, a far more important insurrection occurred in the district of Rozoy (in the heart of the Brie region) and spread rapidly through the canton of La Ferté-Gaucher. In this bourg the tocsin sounded for the first time on the 22nd. The following morning, a large force of peasants from the surrounding villages (chiefly the canton of Mauperthuis, which gave the affair [p. 325] its name) entered the town, manhandled the municipal officers and restored the religious objects, to cries of 'Long live the Catholic religion! Down with the Jacobins! We will have our curés! We want mass on Sundays and feast days!'. The insurgents then moved against the *société*, sacking its meeting room – one of them saying that the Jacobins 'were the reason why the Virgin and the saints were weeping in the churches' – and demanding a list of *sociétaires* who had acted in the same fashion in the other communes.[81] The riot, which quickly subsided but which involved several thousand armed peasants, poor folk for the most part, had taken the authorities by surprise. The *représentant* Morisson arrived in La Ferté on the 24th at the head of a large force of National Guard and gendarmes from every district in the Seine-et-Marne. In Paris the Committee, alerted by couriers dispatched by the national agent, Vincent, ordered the Minister of War to arrange for the immediate dispatch 'of all available forces from the *armée révolutionnaire* to restore public tranquillity in Coulommiers and its environs...and to make secure the stores of supplies for Paris situated there...'.[82] Three hundred revolutionary fusiliers left Paris that very day, the 24th, to be joined en route at Claye by a company of cannoneers, by the 2nd revolutionary squadron, and by six pieces of artillery – a force of 500 *révolutionnaires* in all.[83] The restaurateur, Lemaire, was appointed commander and was recommended by the Committee to use 'surveillance and republican severity'.

Lemaire and his soldiers showed considerable zeal in the execution of their repressive tasks under the orders of the *représentants*, disarming the unfortunate and misled peasants, effecting over 300 arrests, and conducting the *fanatiques* to prison.[84] But with the exception of their commander, who exceeded his brief by making arrests on his own authority, the soldiers participating in this, the most important expedition in the history of the *armée révolutionnaire* – in terms of numbers deployed – after that of Lyon, were content to carry out orders issued by the *représentants* and by the *comités de surveillance*. In this affair the *armée révolutionnaire* played a purely passive part. It had not been responsible for provoking this popular Catholic uprising, which was due rather to the imprudence of the Coulommiers *comité* in trying to force through dechristianisation by decree, ordering all the communes in the district of Rozoy 'under pain of death...to make the priests give up their letters [of ordination], cease functioning, close their churches, stop practising religion and teaching school'. 'This order', added Maure, 'as illegal as it was impolitic, angered the people in the country...'.[85] The revolt of Mauperthuis was a popular uprising; the intervention of the Parisian *armée* against it belongs to the history of the repression.

In the district of Nemours, a Parisian detachment was called in to help suppress some minor disturbances which had erupted in the environs of Château-Landon, following orders by the *comité de surveillance* for the removal of bells and religious objects. The commander of this detachment observed: 'that a spirit of fanaticism reigned in this commune, which demanded all the attention of the established authorities, that the *décadi* were not at all observed and Sundays alone celebrated, that the office was even rung out with full force'.[86] In the district of Melun, the detachments confined themselves to a repressive role, implementing summonses issued by Meltier against the former priests. It is more difficult to assess the role of these men as preachers of the new religion, but it is worth noting that the *société populaire* of Brie-Comte-Robert – denounced in Germinal as a haven of atheism – was only founded on 3 October 1793, shortly before the arrival of the revolutionary detachment. Did the Parisians contribute by their presence at its sessions to its reputed atheism, surprising in a small-town *société?*[87] In Provins too the members of the *société* were denounced as supporters of atheism, though here again it is difficult to trace any connection between its development and the presence of the *révolutionnaires*.[88]

In the Aisne – with the exception of the affair of Chaourse, a typical example of spontaneous action – the zeal of the *révolutionnaires* was confined to ensuring that the laws on the removal of external signs of religion were observed; they forced the Laon municipality, for example, to place a tricolour on the tower of the cathedral and to remove all emblems reminiscent of Catholicism from funeral processions. In the districts of Chauny and Château-Thierry, the *armée* acted under orders from the *comités de surveillance* against refractory priests, and the schoolmasters who continued to say mass in the place of the arrested priests.[89]

In Paris itself, and in the two rural districts which together with the capital made up the department, the *armée révolutionnaire* seems to have had no part in any dechristianising activities, and the movement in this department never reached the same proportions as in those further away.[90] But even in the Norman departments, the Eure excepted, the Parisians played no part in initiating measures against the priests and the practice of religion. In Honfleur and its environs, the detachments were content to execute measures passed by the *comité de surveillance* against refractory priests and their supporters, and in the small port action was confined to the arrest of the *soeurs de charité* of the former *hôpital*. It was only in the Isère, in the Loire and in the area around Lyon – where the operations led by the *commissaires* took a more violent turn – that the actions of the *armée* went any further.[91] In the final analysis, except in regions where the *commissaires civils* could revolutionise at will, the dechristianising of the Parisian *armée* was confined to acting as an instrument in the hands of the *comités de surveillance* or the local zealots, implementing the laws against the external signs of religion and making repeated, though futile, attempts to apply the *décadi*. The Parisian *armée* was not a particularly formidable instrument in this forced dechristianisation which so distressed the government. The few cases of individual excess do not justify the reputation it acquired as the *grand moteur de l'athéisme*.

IV   *The departmental* armées *and the campaign against religion*

Some of the small departmental *armées* were far more vigorous than Ronsin's forces as instruments of forced dechristianisation, with its accompanying verbal and physical assaults on the supporters of religion. The anti-religious campaign, imposed militarily and taking the revolutionary form of church closures and blasphemous sermons, was essentially a phenomenon of the departments, particularly those furthest removed from Paris. The map of forced dechristianisation also corresponds with that of *exagération*; both were the particular preserves of the *commissaires civils*, who, more than anyone else, stamped the movement with real anti-christian passion and the violence of their own temperaments.

In some regions, dechristianisation was even the main, if not the exclusive, activity of the departmental battalions and it is scarcely surprising that this aspect should so firmly have imprinted itself upon the consciousness of the country people. In the Nord, the Morbihan, the Loiret, the Allier, the Nièvre, the Isère, the Drôme, the Toulouse region and the Ariège, the activities of the *armées* were almost entirely taken up with the open struggle against religion, Catholic and Protestant alike. 'Mixed operations' – of which the 'promenades' of Chaix, of Commerçon and of Henriot in the Nièvre are the most characteristic – were directed against the partisans of religion and against religion itself. What were Chaix's intentions in his 'promenades'? In the first instance, to get the village curés to abdicate their duties and surrender their letters of ordination to him, and if persuasion and threats did not work, he added arrest to his arguments. After that he sought the closure of the churches, having raided them first, and threatened the inhabitants with the vengeful return of the companies, assisted by a guillotine, if they attempted to restore religion once his back was turned. In the Loiret, Parmentier, one of the *commissaires civils* appointed by Laplanche, used the same methods to persuade those who had renounced the priesthood to take wives and thereby consummate their rupture with the Church, and he offered all kinds of political guarantees to those who did so. The forced closure of churches and the marriage of former priests were the two principal means by which these *commissaires* sought to destroy the Catholic religion in the departments of the Centre, the chosen ground of revolutionary dechristianisation. They would have preferred some semblance of local adhesion – that was the aim of the addresses prepared for the *sociétés populaires*, of which another *commissaire*, Picot-Belloc, made so much use in his appearances before the tiny Ariège *sociétés* – but failing this, they went ahead anyway. The very presence of the armed force was a token of the arbitrary and violent character of the movement.

In the Nord, the prime dechristianiser was the *représentant*, Châles, former canon of the cathedral at Chartres. From his sickbed in Lille, he sent forth curses against the priests and fanaticism in his paper, *Le Révolutionnaire*, aimed at the country people of the department who were deeply attached to religion.[92] Châles found in the high command of the Lille garrison, officers who were enthusiastic and already experienced dechristianisers: Dufresse, Nivet, Target and Calmet-Beauvoisins had already turned their hand to dechristianisation in October 1792, when in command of the garrison at Brussels. Nor were they much concerned about the feelings of the people in the towns through which they passed; they were convinced that Belgium had been lost by the *fanatisme* of its peasantry, and were delighted at the opportunity to avenge this attachment to their priests by the *défanatisation* of the Walloons and Flemings on French soil. In Frimaire Dufresse took a detachment to Dunkerque, and on the 13th appeared before the *société* in his general's uniform and at the head of his soldiers bedecked in *bonnets rouges*. A somewhat partial witness described the scene: 'The subject dominating this session was that of the abjuration of all religion, it was proposed to open a register! the general said: "What! you are afraid that people won't sign this register of abjuration, well! those who will not sign will do so in a *maison d'arrêt*".[93] The intervention of Dufresse had the desired effect and on the 22nd the actor general informed the *société révolutionnaire* at Lille of the success of his operations in the port: 'The churches are now closed, but we are not planning to raise a temple of Reason'.[94] The success, however, was one of propaganda only; Dufresse was a man for whom talk took the place of action, and if the intervention by himself and the *armée* temporarily ended the exercise of religion in Dunkerque and Bailleul, it failed to impress the authorities of Douai and Cambrai. In Douai the National Guard had anticipated the action of the *armée révolutionnaire* by bringing pressure to bear on the *société*, while in Cambrai the battalion was totally powerless.[95] Despite the sabre-rattling by Dufresse, the Lille *armée* proved a pretty ineffective instrument of dechristianisation in the department, and any success in the field was the work of the local militants.[96]

In the Aube and the Loiret the companies carried out a much more active campaign against Catholicism and Protestantism. But as in the Nord, the soldiers were simply instruments of the militants of Troyes and Orléans. In the Aube all action occurred under the direction of the national *commissaire*, Alexandre Rousselin, friend of Danton and agent of the Committee of Public Safety. Rousselin selected his aides from among the *sociétaires* of Troyes, several of whom were former priests and monks.[97] Fleury, commander of the La Montagne battalion, was a very secondary figure supplying Rousselin and his associates with the force required for the violent action unleashed against religion and its adherents in the district of Ervy, and more particularly in the Pays d'Othe.[98] As usual the pretext was supplied by some very minor disturbances, which were nevertheless baptised a 'petite Vendée'.

In the Loiret Laplanche's *commissaires* directed everything; the companies served as escorts. Parmentier surrounded himself with the brigades from Neuville, Malesherbes and Boiscommun when he set out on a mission which was both repressive and educative: 'I ordered all the curés to marry...some twenty promised to marry within two months, and I have authority to find wives for them'.[99] In the area around Montargis, the members of the *société populaire* went out with armed patrols, instilling the cult of Reason and respect for the *décadi* into the country people.[100]

In the Marne the *commissaires civils* likewise took the initiative; they even acted without any armed force, pressurising the *sociétés* into issuing orders for the closure of churches. The mission carried out by Villers, *commissaire* from the Châlons *société* at Epernay, is characteristic of the methods used by these 'hommes de liaison', who, rather than employ the *révolutionnaires* immediately, preferred to keep them in reserve as a final argument if 'persuasion' did not produce the desired effect. This department was exceptional in that the *commissaires civils* secured the necessary orders to close churches on the simple threat of force.[101] Perhaps Villers and his companions were cleverer and more eloquent than their colleagues in other departments.

In the Morbihan and the Bas-Rhin, in contrast, no attempt was made to give dechristianisation a semblance of popular consent. Everything was carried out with the greatest violence, with revolting and often bloody brutality. In the Morbihan, Le Batteux arrived with his *armée* one Sunday as the congregation was emerging from high mass. Not content with simply closing the church, he had eight of the faithful (accused of having caused disorders) shot in the churchyard. The march of his *armée* from Redon to Vannes had all the appearance of a punitive expedition in enemy territory and simply fortified Breton Catholicism by giving it a new martyrology. Le Batteux's excuse was that in this region the use of force had followed rather than preceded disorder – religious disturbances having erupted in the neighbouring districts of the Ille-et-Vilaine; dechristianisation in this civil war zone took the form of republican defence.[102] It was the same in the Bas-Rhin; Schneider and his acolytes – German priests and Prussian deserters – were sincere, but over-zealous and imprudent, revolutionaries. The insanely violent dechristianisation which they unleashed in the districts of Strasbourg, Sélestat and Haguenau, spread panic through the profoundly Catholic villages of Alsace, sending a portion of the inhabitants to seek refuge in the Palatinate. 'Detachments from the *armée révolutionnaire* behaved horribly... having attempted unsuccessfully to carry out the most audacious enterprise, well calculated to inflame the hopes of the scoundrels who rejoiced in our misfortunes and swallowed our blood, I mean the sudden and total destruction of all forms of religion which the robust stomach of the Revolution has happily digested...', wrote Saint-Just's secretary to Vincent.[103]

As we move towards the centre, and even more, to the south of the Loire, we find dechristianising measures accompanied by atheistical sermonising and a positive campaign on the part of the *commissaires civils*, and occasionally of the revolutionary officers, to replace Catholicism with the cults of Reason and civic religion. In the canton of Lormes, Chaix was said to have proclaimed 'that God was too old, that he was an aristocrat and that it was necessary to change him for another'. Arriving in Bazoches on the day of the *décadi*, which also happened to be a Sunday, he mounted the pulpit at the end of mass and preached the doctrine of atheism: 'You are going to hear the truth spoken for the first time from this platform... you have been persuaded that there is a god, a hell and a paradise, don't believe it, it is all the invention of the church party, you have not seen them, neither have I, it is sanctimonious rubbish, get rid of it, you no longer need it...'. And Chaix followed up his words with action. Wherever he went he used the threat of calling in his detachment to force the priests to hand over their letters of ordination. Insistence did not always succeed, and a lengthy correspondence, in which threats were mingled with appeals to patriotism, was necessary to bring Granet, the parish priest of Bazoches, to heel. The latter relented in an effort to spare his flock the rage of the *commissaire* and the return of a revolutionary detachment.[104]

Chaix's doggedness in his efforts to secure that priest's letters of ordination shows that he did not feel himself authorised to impose *déprêtrisation*. Parent likewise, in the Clamecy district, tried to secure the 'voluntary' withdrawal of the priests from their duties: 'Citizens', he wrote in his circular letter of 18 Brumaire, 'the Revolution no longer permits old errors to impede the progress of reason.... I expect you on your own good faith to renounce your former doctrine and help me to disabuse our fellow citizens of those errors which less fortunate times made them accept as truth. People have spoken ill of me to you; but I assure you that I hate deceit and hypocrisy and I will do everything in my power to help those former priests who seek to preach truth and republican doctrine...'. His methods appear to have been successful, for the moment at least, since he informed Fouché on the 20th: 'Already have the churches of the *chef-lieu* been converted into republican temples; already have the riches which sustained superstition and the idolatry of precious metals been deposited in the national treasury; already have the dark confessionals, from which the priest, hunched like a spider at the back of his web, poured into the souls of his flock the poison of error and intolerance, provided sentinel boxes for our brave volunteers....'.[105]

In the Gironde also the *commissaires civils* of the Bordeaux *armée* were accused of preaching militant, and militaristic, atheism. Even in Bordeaux, Peyrend-d'Herval attempted to launch the movement in the national club by having a letter from Paris read, describing in detail the civic fête celebrated in the temple of Reason, formerly Notre-Dame. The intention of this friend of Vincent and Hébert was clearly to urge the Bordeaux sans-culottes to follow the example set by the dechristianisers in Paris. In the same *société*, Dufrêne, another Parisian and Ministry *commissaire*, was likewise accused of having preached atheism.[106]

The importance of these 'hommes de liaison' – Parisian *commissaires* or former revolutionary *commissaires* of the region – as advisers in dechristianisation and promoters of the cult of Reason, is even more clearly illustrated in the minutes of the *société* of Violès in the Vaucluse. At its 19 Ventôse session, 'one member said that they should organise a fête for the rest-day of the *décade*, another said that they should follow the example of the commune of Orange, and Esprit Espagneu [the *commissaire*] was asked what Orange planned; he answered that C. Nicolau [*sic*] told him that they were going to affix a memorial to liberty on the church door and place a goddess on the altar...'. This Nicolaud, a printer in Orange, was the same who had commanded a revolutionary company in the rural communes of the district; in this department too, then, the *commissaires civils* were assuming responsibility for the organisation of the new cult.[107]

Some of the former *commissaires* even had the courage to boast about having publicly defended atheism, when they found themselves the objects of Thermidorean proscription as terrorists and dechristianisers. In Germinal Year III, Socrate Damour, a former *commissaire* from Nevers, made a profession of materialist faith: 'As to the materialism which I am accused of having taught', he wrote to the *Comité de législation*, 'I answer that my lessons on the errors of human knowledge were taken from Locke, Condillac, and Helvétius, which were approved by the *représentant* Fouché, and those on morals from Helvétius and Jean-Jacques'.[108] Damour, like the former theatrical prompter, Peyrend-d'Herval, and the printer Nicolaud, fancied himself a man of letters; though unlike most dechristianisers, he does seem to have read the *philosophes*. But atheistic propaganda was not the monopoly of journalists, actors and printers, it also had more humble disciples, and village artisans, urban sans-culottes and soldiers, as well as better-educated men, made up the bulk of the dechristianisers in the Midi. In the Year III also, Sabatier, formerly mayor of La Réole and its health officer, was accused of 'fanning the flames of fanaticism and discord by proclaiming that neither God nor the Virgin existed, of having helped bring about the ruin of the parish church, overturning altars, crushing underfoot images which had been venerated for centuries...'.[109] Sabatier too had been a *commissaire civil* with a revolutionary battalion which he used against the 'faithful'.

In the Isère and the Ariège the atheistic *commissaires* were even more imprudent, taking a kind of savage joy in totally uprooting customs and shocking a peasantry, still attached to religion and respectful of the saints, with their excesses. On his way through Biol, witnesses described Vauquoy as drinking wine from a chalice and remarking: 'They say it is a sin even to touch a chalice and here am I drinking from one...'.[110] Behind such shocking gestures, there also seems to have been some kind of desire to recall the simplicity of the first christians. '...Jesus was a sans-culotte', wrote Parent to the mayor of Asnan on 25 Brumaire, 'and never drank from chalices or silver cups'.[111]

At Andressin, in the Ariège, Picot-Belloc, at the head of his detachment, and Allard, *commissaire civil*, 'attacked religion...in a brusque and revolting manner. On arrival in the communes, particularly the frontier communes, they entered the churches with their armed force...and preached before a simple and ignorant people that there was no god, no devil, no heaven or hell, that Jesus Christ was a *jean-foutre* who had the pox and his mother was a whore; that they had to exterminate the priests, burn their saints, shut up their churches and bring their bells down with cannon shot...'. At Seix, Picot, who no doubt had acquired solid anti-religious convictions during his long residence in Spain before the Revolution, also sermonised the *société*, 'saying that Jesus Christ was a bastard, a useless bugger, a man with no power, who, by consorting with the Magdalene, had hit the jackpot, that the Virgin was a whore, Christ a bastard and Saint Joseph a bloody cuckold, adding that if there was a bloody God, he only had to show his power by crushing him...'.[112] Nor did Picot only employ this lewd imagery to shock the dumbfounded Pyreneean peasants; he also issued pamphlets and songs in the same mould as vehicles for his impertinent attacks on the christian religion.[113] Remember too the language used by Dartigoëyte in the Gers against *fanatiques* and *dévôtes*.

Certain republicans shied away from this kind of propaganda, which in assaulting the religious sentiments of the peasants threatened to push them into appealing to Charles IV of Spain against these godless men. 'In the effort to bend the bow, one can break it', wrote the *société* of Saint-Girons to the Convention, denouncing this crusade by the *commissaires civils* and the friends of Vadier. 'If the people have always professed the Catholic religion, like their fathers before them, and today they hear the apostles of the Revolution trying to persuade them that all religion is based on fable, or on inept absurdities, is it not natural that, shocked at such a doctrine, they will be led to rebel against a new system which seems to be forcing them to renounce their religion and their religious beliefs?' [114] This is not the place to take up the question of the political consequences of forced dechristianisation, except to say that an old religion firmly grounded in popular tradition could not have been uprooted without the use of violence; the French peasantry was not open to arguments based on philosophy or on reason. Picot and his like adopted a deliberately violent and vulgar tone – it was instruction through shock. One might of course object than any novel measure which threatened to provoke serious opposition among a conservative people was impolitic, especially in time of war. But that would mean condemning the entire revolutionary movement, with its spontaneity and its anarchy. Moreover it would be wrong to doubt the sincerity and patriotism of these *commissaires civils*; they were imprudent, yes, but their convictions were deep-seated, and their careers provide abundant proof of courage and sincerity in their anti-religious principles.[115]

Commissaires civils of the Chaix–Picot mould were not the only militant atheists active in the departments that winter. They had many imitators among the *commissaires* of the Ministries, 'apôtres' among the urban *sociétés*, and those village atheists – clogmakers, shoemakers, blacksmiths – who preached Reason to their peril in the tiny communes of the *plat pays*. But these were all minorities, and what distinguished the *commissaires civils* from the others was their disposal of armed force, giving them the power to put their preachings into practice – to close churches, get priests to hand over letters of ordination, under threat of arrest and the guillotine, oblige people to abandon old customs and to work on Sundays. The sermons of Picot and his colleagues would have been mere curiosities of revolutionary violence, exercises in the style of the *Père Duchesne*, had they not been accompanied by the apparatus of force. Dechristianisation by very definition was a minority movement. It progressed militarily, or it did not progress at all. Herein lies the importance of the revolutionary companies; as instruments of energetic men, they made it possible to implement measures which were contrary to the wishes of the majority of people in the country areas.

Atheism was military not only because many atheists were officers or soldiers[116] – and atheism was to remain a powerful force for a long time in the armies of the Revolution and the Empire – but even more because it could only impose its views through force and compulsion.

The military aspect of dechristianisation was most apparent in the great anti-religious expeditions conducted by the revolutionary forces. The classic operation was that carried out at Grenade by the battalions from Toulouse and Beaumont. The Toulouse soldiers were particularly eager to see the new laws on the *décadi* applied and, according to one of the *commissaires*, 'on Sunday 20 Brumaire the *armée révolutionnaire* took action against the customary holiday; there was a dangerous gathering of women from Grenade and of people from the country; to disperse them the *commissaires civils* had cannon brought up and troops on horseback dispersed the crowd without hurting anyone. Two girls had their white ribbons torn off, that was all...'.[117] Ballardelle too was acting militarily when he sought to stop the young people of Lagny dancing on Sundays instead of working, by threatening them with his Parisian soldiers.

The final military operation took place in the district of Valence, in Ventôse, under the leadership of 'apôtres' and with the assistance of a small *armée* composed of sans-culottes of the *chef-lieu*. The inhabitants of some villages in the canton of Peyrus had formed themselves into communal assemblies to demand the reopening of the churches, which had been closed in this district since Brumaire, due to the active vigilance of the *société* of Valence (an offensive in which Protestants suffered as much as Catholics).[118] In some communes, in Pluviôse, the peasants had forced the constitutional priests who had abdicated their duties to celebrate mass, baptisms, marriages and burials. It was precisely at this time that other regions were also beginning to experience the consequences of Robespierrist policy in the countryside, in mounting demands for the reopening of churches and even the restoration of bells.[119] 'Fanaticism is raising its head once more', wrote Jorelle, War Ministry *commissaire* at Montpellier, to a friend in Paris, 13 Nivôse Year II; '...[Robespierre] may have delayed its downfall, but as soon as the question was raised in the Convention, the progress of Reason halted, several communes sought to reopen their churches, others went so far as to demand the restoration of their silver, which had been deposited with the district...'.[120]

Having learnt of the troubles in the communes of Peyrus, Barbières, Alexan and Besayes, the *société* on 6 Ventôse invited the district of Valence 'to take prompt repressive and revolutionary measures to bring terror to these fanaticised communes in which patriots are oppressed'.[121] At this session, the national agent for the district, Claude Payan, and Figuet (member of the *comité de surveillance* and brother of the Babouvist architect) promised the *société* that they would go at once to these villages, and asked it to choose 'apôtres' to accompany them. These 'apôtres', the two revolutionary officials, and a small force made up of sans-culottes from Valence – they had the sense not to call it a *compagnie révolutionnaire*, even though it acted as one [122] – left the *chef-lieu* on the 7th, passing through Chabreuil the following day, then through Peyrus, which had been the scene of Protestant and Catholic disturbances alike, the former demanding the release of their pastor, the latter obliging their curé to reopen the church. On the 9th they passed through Saint-Vincent and Barbières, preaching *la morale civique* wherever they went and terminating their journey at Charpey, Besayes and Alexan. On 11 Ventôse, in the account of their mission sent to Barbières, Payan and Figuet declared: 'we had considerable difficulty in assembling the members of the Council of the commune and most of those of the *comité de surveillance*. We quickly recognised the depth of their ignorance, some could scarcely sign their names, others were quite illiterate, needing someone else to write for them, in this case the curé who was almost as ill educated as themselves . . .'.[123]

This tiny expedition, interesting because of its late date, ended in the arrests of several ringleaders – accused of heading the gatherings in Peyrus and in other mountain communes – in the closure of churches and temples, and in the destruction of images, pictures, Bibles and crosses. It is of further interest to the historian of the anti-christian movement because it was directed as much against Protestant *fanatiques*, who were numerous in this region, as against Catholics; because it was led by a central figure of the Robespierrrist clan, Payan; and because, in the person of Figuet, it links dechristianisation with Babouvism. It was also the last incidence of a political and urban armed force being used in an anti-religious expedition.

The general map of the activities of the revolutionary forces does not at all correspond to that of their dechristianising action. In certain important areas in which these *armées* were raised, no religious initiative whatever can be attributed to them. The decisive factor seems to have been the presence of the *représentant* hostile to religion. In the final analysis, dechristianisation was an affair of the proconsuls; it was pursued mainly in the Loiret, the Nièvre and the Allier, the Bas-Rhin, the Loire, the Nord, the Morbihan, the Haute-Garonne, the Gironde, the Ariège and the Isère, and those responsible were Laplanche, Fouché, Mallarmé, Javogues, Châles, Carrier, Dartigoëyte and Baudot, Isabeau and Tallien, Vadier, Collot, Albitte[124] – above all, Fouché. He was the protector of that crowd of *commissaires* who swarmed over the two departments of the Centre, and we have seen how Damour took his inspiration from Fouché in the matter. Likewise, Le Batteux acted under the influence of Carrier, and the *commissaires* in the Ariège derived strength from the open support of Vadier and his son.

But this map does not take in certain of the regions which experienced the most spectacular expeditions. In the Lot, the Aveyron and the Lozère, the theatre of Viton's excesses, there is no sign of any dechristianising activities, and though the 'General' was reproached for the destruction and pillage of valuable paintings, they came from the château of Sévérac rather than any church. It is true that Viton's soldiers arrested some priests, and 'taxed' some people for having attended clandestine masses,[125] but these were cases of repression rather than dechristianisation. In the neighbouring departments of the Lot and Lot-et-Garonne, the *commissaires* were accused of using the companies to accelerate the removal of church bells,[126] but there is no mention of iconoclasm. In Montpellier, the Basses-Alpes and the Bouches-du-Rhône, there is no sign of any anti-religious activity by the many revolutionary forces in these areas.[127] Even in the Nord, the work of the Lille *armée* was short-lived, spectacular rather than effective. Only half the departments which harboured active companies witnessed revolutionary dechristianisation – the forced closure of churches, *déprêtrisation* and the conversion of churches into temples of Reason. In every area the *révolutionnaires* were the instruments for the removal of religious objects, but it was only in the Nièvre and the Allier, the Loiret, the Ariège, the Haute-Garonne, the Morbihan (doubtless also in the Finistère), in one district of the Mayenne (Lassay), in the Bas-Rhin, in perhaps two districts of the Haut-Rhin, in several communes of the Marne, the Haute-Marne, the Nord, the Mont-Blanc, the Bouches-du-Rhône and the Vaucluse, that the existence of these *armées* truly accelerated and facilitated the execution of the most spectacular measures in the anti-religious campaign.[128]

In these departments, *commissaires civils*, who had the confidence of the all-powerful proconsuls, used the armed force in the service of their own philosophic ideas. Elsewhere the *armées* were only involved in actions against religion as part of their policing and repressive roles – the arrest of refractory priests, the maintenance of order, the application of the *décadi* being interconnected. With the exception of the Nièvre and the Allier – scene of the *grande déchristianisation* – the movement was just as active, just as violent and brutal in departments with no revolutionary battalions or companies. All depended on the attitude of the *représentants* and their *commissaires*, and in the absence of sans-culotte companies, they could always find the necessary armed force among the newly requisitioned troops, the cavalry, and even sometimes among the urban National Guard. The nature of the armed force was of little importance, and sometimes particularly energetic *commissaires* were able to achieve their ends by the power of speech alone, or through local complicity.

What then was the particular contribution of the departmental *armées* to the various forms of dechristianisation? 'The *armées révolutionnaires*, composed of determined sans-culottes, closed the churches', writes Lefebvre.[129] No doubt they did close churches in certain regions. Yet the *armées* were not always composed of 'determined sans-culottes', and they rarely closed churches on their own initiative, acting rather as the instruments of more important figures the like of Grimaud, Vauquoy, Chaix, Commerçon, Pauper, Allard, Picot and Calmet-Beauvoisins, and behind them of the *représentants* who cloaked such abuses of power with their authority. Un-

doubtedly the individual attitudes of the soldiers and officers greatly facilitated their task. When it was a matter of going to the frontiers, sailing up
and down the Channel in a fishing boat, or exposing themselves to peasant
wrath by collecting *taxes*, the *révolutionnaires* were unreliable agents. But
where iconoclasm and dechristianisation were concerned, no one objected
and the anti-religious programme was assisted by the personal support of
most of these political soldiers.

One must also distinguish between rural dechristianisation and the corresponding movement in the major towns, where there were sufficient
numbers in the garrison and in the popular *sociétés* to conduct the enterprise
without any help from the revolutionary companies and battalions.[130] In
Lille, in Toulouse, in Montpellier, as in Moulins, Nevers and Troyes, the
revolutionary forces were not involved in dechristianisation,[131] and in Paris
Ronsin's *armée* had no part in it. Indeed it was probably only in Strasbourg,
a suspect town, and Lyon, the *ville infâme*, that the *révolutionnaires* were
called upon to invigorate a faltering anti-religious campaign; there, as in the
country, dechristianisation was the work of 'outsiders'. As for the assault
experienced by the localities bordering on the great military roads, that was
carried out by the troops of the line and by soldiers in transit. No, the field
of operation of the *révolutionnaires* was the *plat pays*, the remote countryside
where the faithful still attended mass, where crosses still remained in place,
people still got married in church, and the former curé, now clerk to the
municipality, still wielded the same moral influence over his flock by
supplying his own interpretations of the laws and orders. This was the
sleepy world in which men of the law, former seigneurial agents, friends of
the curé and large farmers still dominated affairs by excluding from the
municipality (it was more difficult to keep them out of the *sociétés populaires*
and the *comités de surveillance*), the rural artisans and proletariat; it was these
last who were to turn the sudden eruption into the area of the *commissaires*
civils and the revolutionary companies into a social struggle between *gros*
and *petits*. Each village had its 'enragé', and the rural atheist was the ally of
the urban sans-culotte. In the departments. as around Paris, the urban
revolutionaries were often called in by village minorities, who would pay
for their temerity in the Year III with their lives or their tranquillity. To
succeed, the movement had to come from outside and be assisted by force.

This explains the most spectacular aspect of rural dechristianisation, the
effort to shake off the weight of custom by organising blasphemous
processions. One had to strike with speed and with force. An afternoon, an
evening, punctuated by visits to the *auberge*, was sufficient to destroy everything. More than the recruitment, the requisitions, the Maximum, the billeting, it was the iconoclasm, the 'sermons' and the closure of the churches
which represented the revolutionary system, the new spirit from the town,
in the eyes of the peasants. In every age the peasant had been obliged to
provide lodging, grain and fodder for the military; but iconoclasm was a
novelty unheard of since the Wars of Religion.

But the rural dechristianisation, made possible by the intervention of the revolutionary companies, was as short-lived as it was destructive.[132] There were not enough *révolutionnaires* to place garrisons everywhere; they had to be content with passing through a commune, destroying the external signs of religion, and removing those of use to the war economy. But the real work had still to be done: that of breaking with secular custom, substituting the *décadi* for Sundays and civic religion for Christianity, tasks which did not lend themselves to force and which were beyond the range of the revolutionary operations. The soldiers recognised the fragility of their accomplishments; everywhere they saw looks of hatred and they departed with the threat: 'We'll be back', but they rarely were. At most they left behind a new municipality, a purged *comité*, a *société* from which the moderates had been expelled. But such precautions were insufficient. Once the detachment had gone, the commune would call a general assembly, which would vote overwhelmingly for the reopening of the church. In some communes the arrests had decapitated the *parti des gros*; but the women remained, and they were proof against the observance of the *décadi*. The soldiers were conscious of their weakness, and the violent deeds, the presbyteries and farms burnt, the women scolded and insulted, were just so many tokens of their ineffectiveness. Every 'promenade' assumed an aspect of revenge. Iconoclasm was itself an avowal of powerlessness and failure.

There was no systematic dechristianisation, save in the removal of bells and silver and the destruction of the external signs of religion in accordance with government orders. Dechristianisation in its most violent form was an act of anarchy, and the dechristianisers were indeed, as Augustin Robespierre wrote, *anarchistes*. Everything was done amidst disorder, according to the whim of some *représentant* or the inspiration of some *commissaire civil*, and on the excuse of local disturbances, deliberately exaggerated by the townspeople. In one canton everything might be destroyed and all the churches closed, while the neighbouring *pays* retained its crosses and filled churches. Anarchy increased the danger of disturbances, and the enormous crowds attracted to communes where mass was still celebrated rapidly assumed the aspect of seditious gatherings.[133] The dechristianisers themselves had no clear idea of where they were going. Yes, they wanted churches closed and priests dismissed. But even though naïve and impolitic, they saw themselves working for the future. 'Superstition' belonged to a former, a detested regime; if the Revolution was really to penetrate the rural mentality and the customs of the peasants. it had to give them new gods: Reason, the cult of the martyrs, the religion of *la Patrie*. The dechristianisers agreed on the need to replace Catholicism with a new religion, but not on the form it should take. The most optimistic were simple atheists; others, still dominated by the Catholic mentality, by the custom of great feast days and the collective and controlled rituals of the Church, wanted to impose a new religion as exclusive and as universal as the old one. The atheists were individualists and anarchists, agreeable men who found themselves in the vanguard of a spontaneous revolutionary movement; but the proponents of a *réligion civique* were simply Catholics in disguise, or more likely disciples of Jean-Jacques, men with a religious mentality who distrusted the individual. The genuine dechristianisers were the most authentic revolutionaries, the most pure, the most courageous to emerge from the optimistic and naïve era of the anarchic Terror.

Enforced and military dechristianisation had important and immediate political consequences. Central government became anxious about the numerous excesses which the local authorities claimed were being committed by the *révolutionnaires*. The Committee of Public Safety opened a special dossier devoted to the supposed misdeeds of the *armées révolutionnaires*, of which the most common were attacks on the freedom of religion and on religious beliefs. Certain members of the Committee, including Robespierre and Saint-Just, tried to attribute a movement which was essentially anarchic, uneven, individualistic and artisanal, to some concerted manoeuvre by a determined political group of *exagérés* in the service of Machiavellian royalism. In support of this improbable theory of *malveillance* and *ultracisme*, Robespierre and his friends called into question the probity and sincerity of the main dechristianisers (and above all the atheists), representing them as tarnished characters, with dubious pasts. If they were of popular origin, that was considered a crime: they were hired hands, vulgar wigmakers and thankless cooks; if they were wealthy young men, or former nobles, then their revolutionary principles were open to question.

All these arguments were used by Robespierre's correspondents – among them his brother Augustin, Gateau and Jullien – to blacken the *exagérés*. The government espoused the thesis of 'exaggeration', with varying degrees of sincerity, to compromise politically a movement which had profound popular support in the towns and to cast suspicion on the moral honesty of the dechristianisers. The 'virtuous' men, the correspondents of Robespierre, these popes of the new morality, had the conceit to judge from the heights of their own infallibility the private convictions of those who had distinguished themselves by their anticlerical ardour. Châles, the courageous *révolutionnaire*, they had the presumption to accuse of having fled the field of battle; not surprisingly, the former canon was to speak out against these monopolisers of virtue, with their corner on clear consciences, on the night of 9 Thermidor. Le Batteux they reproached for having been a cook with the monks, Picot, for having worked in Spain. Every fact was mobilised to support the thesis of collusion between dechristianisation and counter-revolution.

Certainly, the possibility of such collusion cannot be altogether excluded. There was a form of ultra-revolutionary royalism, employing specialists in excess; and dechristianisation did provide a perfect opportunity for stirring up trouble and rousing the peasants against the regime. Every movement has its paid agents, its adventurers, its shady characters. But from what we know of the dechristianising *représentants*, the *commissaires civils*, the officers and soldiers, such a thesis, applied to the entire movement, is as implausible as it is unjust. These men were revolutionary patriots and nothing could have turned them into agents for the counter-revolution. If they sometimes lacked good sense and political judgement, that was no crime; revolutions are not made by supporters of compromise or by government men.

As for the government claim that forced dechristianisation was the first step towards a military atheism, who knows? – or towards military government itself? The government strove to lay the entire responsibility for iconoclasm and the closure of churches at the door of the *armées révolutionnaires*, and closed its eyes to the fact that all the troops of the Republic participated. To have recognised this fact would have undermined the government position, for this would have been to admit to a popular element in the anti-religious movement. There is scarcely any mention, in the official version of events, of the role of troops in transit, while that of the revolutionary battalions is considerably exaggerated. But government calculations proved to be accurate, for their interpretation was quickly accepted by rural opinion. Thus did the dechristianisers become the objects of vile slander and the *armées révolutionnaires* the victims of a developing myth, even though they had had no monopoly on military dechristianisation. The importance of the change of direction in Ventôse-Germinal lies in the political sphere, in the desire of the government to renounce its main instrument. The disbandment of the Parisian *armée* was above all symbolic, and the news was greeted with *Te Deums* in some communes. Dechristianisation continued, but its most frightening instrument had gone.

CHAPTER 7

'*Armées* of Crime': Thefts, Pillage, Brawls and Indiscipline

The best means of destroying the credit of a revolutionary institution with its orginal supporters was to cast doubt on the probity of its members. The instruments of the Terror had to be pure, or else they were worthless. Necessarily unpopular, the *armées révolutionnaires* – formed, as the *Père Duchesne* said, not 'to cast pearls' but to cut off heads and police the countryside – had to be incorruptible, and what was more important, had to have that reputation everywhere. They were to be feared by *malveillants* and respected by *patriotes*. Their honesty was to be the touchstone of their effectiveness. As things turned out, however, they were despised as much as they were detested by the *malveillants*, and a portion of sans-culotte opinion turned away from them in disgust.

What a coup thus to have whittled away the prestige of an institution in which the sans-culottes had placed such store! From the moment of their formation – sometimes even before it – the *armées* were the object of a campaign of denigration. The campaign had political motives and was conducted by the leaders of the new *modérantisme*, who sought to cast doubt on the whole system of the Terror by attacking its élite force. The most assiduous denouncers were the proponents of 'la pause', those who feared the Terror because they had been involved in shady dealings and had guilty consciences. It was the old story of the poacher turned gamekeeper.

However, despite the many temptations, the *révolutionnaires* on the whole were personally upright. The crime tally of the Parisian *armée* was, as we have seen, slim. Occasional pillage did not make men criminals, and pillagers were often honest men in civilian life, pillage being one of the occupational traits of military life, along with venereal disease, scabies and drunkenness. The soldier was a pillager the way the second-hand clothes dealer was a receiver of stolen goods, the Auvergnat a café-owner or a coal-miner, the Savoyard a commission man,[1] and these occasional soldiers in the *armées révolutionnaires* were no innocents.

The myth, however, was as important as the reality. Opinion was soon influenced by the arguments of people like Fabre or Bourdon de l'Oise; the militant *sectionnares* themselves fell victim to the propaganda and considered their comrades guilty of some kind of treason. The *révolutionnaires* appeared unworthy and ungrateful: unworthy of the confidence placed in them by their Sections, ungrateful because, to ensure their moral and political virtue, they had been showered with privileges. Between Brumaire and Pluviôse a portion of Sectionary opinion began to turn against the political soldiers, depriving the Parisian *armée* of its natural allies.

The *honnêtes gens* already supported the thesis that the *révolutionnaires* could be nothing other than robbers and brutes. Bourgeois opinion had other grievances against the companies; they were pure trouble-makers whose presence in a commune always provoked disturbances. The *armées révolutionnaires*, they declared, were forces of disorder.

Far from redoubling their cautiousness in the face of such hostile attention, the soldiers sealed their own fates by their indiscipline and their shameless demands, so contrary to the egalitarian spirit of the sans-culottes. In the tranquil villages they caused nightly disturbances as they left the *auberges*, and there were constant petty squabbles about everything and anything between the pseudo-soldiers and their pseudo-officers. Their high pay had already set them apart from other soldiers; but demands for extra pay to cover travel and guard duty alienated certain *comités de surveillance*, shocked by such sharp practice on the part of republican soldiers. Finally, the *révolutionnaires* constantly invoked their terms of engagement, refusing to march against Chouans, rebelling when garrison commanders wanted to use them for military operations. The *patriotes* considered such protests proof of a cowardliness and selfishness unworthy of republicans. The privileged should never draw attention to themselves; but these pampered soldiers did everything to attract notice.

The *révolutionnaires* thus succeeded in mobilising a wide range of opinion against themselves: moderates and some Jacobins, *honnêtes gens* and sans-culottes were repulsed by their weaknesses and by their many demands. After their disbandment they became scapegoats for the anarchic Terror; anarchy became synonymous with pillage, and the trial of Vauquoy, just before Thermidor, effectively became that likewise of all the same companies. In Floréal Year II the Aisne judges tried to convict Chaumont of having pocketed the *taxes* levied during his operations as a way of recovering his 'campaign' expenses; but since he had returned the money obtained in this fashion when such *taxes* were declared illegal, they had reluctantly to abandon the charge against him. He was, however, condemned that same month for abusing his powers. The proceedings against Vauquoy went more smoothly; Fouquier-Tinville sought to establish a direct connection between *ultracisme* and pillage. Vauquoy was an *anarchiste* and a rogue; he was not 'virtuous'. In the Aveyron the public prosecutor, Bô, was preparing a case against Viton as early as Nivôse Year II, trying to find proof of the acts of pillage attributed to the wigmaker general and his officers. In Paris the polemics surrounding the supposed misappropriations by Clémence and Marchand in Marly-la-Ville continued to fuel café gossip long after the death of Fabre. Thus, even before Thermidor, the term 'armée révolutionnaire' had become synonymous with theft. The Robespierrist judges kept alive the confusion in people's minds between real and false *armées révolutionnaires*, and rural opinion was happy to go along with it.

After Thermidor, those chiefly responsible for the anarchic Terror found it to their advantage to blame the *armées* for everything, thereby diverting the anger of the *honnêtes gens* on to their former subordinates. No one would think of prosecuting a Fouché; in vain did the officers accused of dilapidations and abuse of powers invoke the orders issued by the *représentants*. The Thermidorean judges were sincere when they proclaimed the return to legality and condemned all revolutionary action as prejudicial to property. But their aims went beyond a desire to defend property and traditional rights. All the cases heard during the Year III were propagandist, and the downfall of the former terrorist personnel was attributed to their own vice.

The Thermidorean prosecutions are, however, our main source of evidence for the morality of the *armées révolutionnaires*. While we possess some pleas and justificatory memorials by officers and *commissaires*, they are rarities and carry little weight beside the enormous mass of evidence collected for the prosecution. One is obliged therefore to judge the *armées* according to the evidence of their accusers, in whose interest it was to blacken them as much as possible. It is important to remember the bias in these accounts, taken from the stormy days of the Thermidorean reaction, when examining the misdeeds attributed to the revolutionary companies.

I   *The trial of the* armées révolutionnaires *by public opinion: the origins of a legend*

The adversaries of the *armée révolutionnaire*, having lost the first round of the contest with the *journées* of 4–5 September and the official creation of a new instrument of the Terror, were not yet defeated. Since the Parisian *armée* was to be formed, they adopted the new tactic of questioning the probity of its leaders and soldiers, and of undermining its moral authority in advance. It was a clever move; Sectionary opinion would never tolerate the idea of tarnished men – men capable of being bought – being entrusted with the 'noble task' of applying the great revolutionary laws or of brandishing the Terror's 'blade of justice' over the heads of *les malveillants*. In the chronology of attacks repeated in the press and at the bar of the Convention during Brumaire, Frimaire, Nivôse and Pluviôse, one can trace a carefully organised campaign with precise political aims.

In the last days of October, detachments from the Parisian National Guard, under the command of a certain Burlot, made off with furniture, foodstuffs and livestock from some farms in Thieux, a village situated in the district of Meaux. The victims complained to the Convention, blaming the *armée révolutionnaire*. The Parisians had been astute enough to claim that they were members of Ronsin's *armée*, a tactic adopted by many brigands who formed themselves into bands and attacked farms and diligences during that autumn and winter. When the *armée révolutionnaire* was called to task in the Convention by Bourdon de l'Oise, Ronsin set the record straight in a letter to the Interior Minister, defending the honour of his *armée* as still intact. 'Citizen Minister', he wrote on 2 Brumaire,

> the detachments sent into the area around Paris up to the 1st of this month were in no way part of the *armée révolutionnaire*, which was only finally organised on the 30th day of the 1st month [i.e. Vendémiaire, or 21 October]. The men making up these detachments left under orders from General Hanriot and had been recruited in haste from the Parisian National Guard and from the troops of the first requisition; nearly all said they were from the *armée révolutionnaire*, though at that time it had no general, no chief, no general staff, not even any officers. It is therefore to the general of the Parisian armed force [Hanriot] that you must go for information on those responsible for the excesses committed on the farm of citizen Gibert....

The revolutionary officer added: 'You can count on my zeal to suppress similar excesses. I am confident that the citizens in the various detachments of the *armée révolutionnaire* which left yesterday to replace the first units, will act as true patriots and adhere to the orders and strict instructions which I have issued to each commander concerning the respect owed to property...'.[2] This promise was adhered to faithfully and the hopes expressed in it were not entirely vain.

The protestations of Ronsin seem to have had little effect, for the newspapers continued to hold his *armée* responsible for the incidents at Thieux. In Brumaire the campaign intensified, with the accusations made by Bourdon de l'Oise, by Fabre and Maillard – all three specialists in questions of morality – against Clémence and Marchand, *commissaires civils*, called to task for taking furniture and jewels from the house of an émigré in Marly-la-Ville, in the district of Gonesse. This affair, and its many ramifications, continued to feed the moderate press and the Thermidorean papers with anti-*révolutionnaire* ammunition for the entire life-span of the Parisian *armée* and during the whole of the Year III.[3]

But it was only in the third *décade* of Frimaire that the grand offensive unfolded. Ronsin's denials achieved nothing. The Thieux affair was still being exploited and other misdeeds were being attributed to the Parisian *armée*. On the 24th, in the Convention, 'Lecointre [of Versailles] recalled that in the first days of Brumaire, several denunciations had been made against an armed force calling itself *révolutionnaire*. The communes of Thieux, of Tully and many more in the district of Meaux had been victims of its unpunished brigandage. The same infamous deeds were committed in the commune of Corbeil. On the 9th of last month [Brumaire] a detachment of this supposed armed force, composed of 25 men as a kind of vanguard, wearing the national uniform, armed with sabres and pistols, entered the home of citizen Gilbon, a farmer of Saint-Gery near Corbeil, at seven o'clock in the evening...'.[4] Lecointre had left an air of doubt hovering over the real *armée révolutionnaire* by holding back the fact that in this case, as in the other, it was a pseudo-*armée*, one of the groups of brigands active in the wooded areas around Paris, which had been responsible.

Lecointre's efforts were seconded by Fabre, who led the attempts at denigration with a smear campaign against the chiefs in the rue de Choiseul. On 28 Frimaire, Ronsin having been arrested the evening before, Fabre directed his attack at Paillardelle: 'At the head of the *armées révolutionnaires*', he proclaimed to the Convention, 'were government *commissaires*....'[5] One, among others, had been the valet of the principal counter-revolutionaries in Marseille and was married to a Spaniard; he lived on the revenue from his wife's property in Spain...'.[6] This was pure calumny, for poor Paillardelle had lost his entire fortune at Cadiz, having refused to take the oath required by Charles IV of all French nationals. But that would not have concerned someone like Fabre.

Moreover, his efforts were rewarded with some success, for the *Journal d'Audoin*, though having little affection for Fabre and his friends, meekly reported the news of the arrest of Ronsin and his colleagues without comment.[7] More significantly, on 1 Nivôse, the *Sans-Culotte Observateur* (formerly *Feuille de Paris*), while indicating that it considered the accusations against the *armée* the product of a campaign intended to discredit *all* the revolutionary institutions, nevertheless called for that 'pause' so cherished by theorists and moderates, and did not entirely discount the charges of pillage so obviously put about by those determined to sully the reputation of these politically privileged men. The editor was right to urge the *révolutionnaires* to greater prudence in the face of such hostile scrutiny, but his reservations surprise somewhat. 'Soldiers', he declares,

> you are being denounced from all sides.... Are these denunciations not aimed at the entire system of arrests, *taxes* on the rich, indeed all the great measures of public safety and at the central Revolutionary Government itself...? Or are you really the guilty ones? Look carefully into your own consciences and answer me with the same frankness which has moved me to tell you of these denunciations. What! will citizens injured by you dare to complain? Is there no one to bring their grievances before the tribunal of public opinion, before the bar of the Convention...? And you, soldiers, think of your reputation and do nothing, say nothing which might support the claims of the counter-revolutionaries. It is not only that complaints have been made against you publicly on two occasions now, but that they were of such an atrocious nature that your brothers in Paris cannot bring themselves to believe you are guilty of them, blaming them instead on brigands acting in your name and wearing your uniform. Try at all times to show by your conduct that you are worthy of this conclusion, and incredulity will be the reaction of all good citizens when you are accused of brigandage....[8]

One thing is certain; the farmers were not afraid of denouncing even the smallest act of pillage. The fear inspired in the countryside by the name *armée révolutionnaire* was not enough to deter hostile critics, and it is quite wrong to claim that the victims had to wait until the Year III to abandon their discreet silence and call the terrible *révolutionnaires* to task. Far from silencing its detractors, the Parisian *armée* was in fact exposed to constant denunciations throughout its existence.

Given the dimensions of the campaign – whose real aim the editor of the *Sans-Culotte Observateur* had indeed perceived – the chiefs in the rue de Choiseul could do little more than defend and explain themselves. In a letter to Jourdeuil of 14 Nivôse, Grammont outlined the complaints of the officers in the field that 'they had not received their brevets; they observe that when they are on detachment, they are asked for their authorisation, and in its absence they are often taken for the groups of brigands which have been infesting the Paris environs under the name *armée révolutionnaire...*'. The following day he conveyed to Léonard Bourdon a copy of a letter he had just sent to the editor of the *Journal du Soir*, following an article which had appeared in that paper on 27 Frimaire in which the *armée révolutionnaire* had been unjustly accused. 'I beseech you to make the Convention aware of the extent to which the *armée révolutionnaire* is exposed to the schemes of *malveillants* in its various cantonments since the arrest of its general-in-chief.... It is vital, both to destroy the unfavourable image which might attach to my brothers in arms from brigands calling themselves the *armée révolutionnaire*, and the harmful impression created by the arrest of Ronsin, that the Convention declares that the *armée révolutionnaire* has done nothing to show itself unworthy in the public view...'.[9]

The Parisian *armée* was not the only one under attack. Léonard Bourdon had a brother, Denis, who was *commissaire des guerres* at Lille. The campaign spread to that town and the morality of the Lille *armée* was in turn attacked in the *Courrier de l'Egalité*. Number 57 of the *Journal de la Montagne*, dated 20 Nivôse, contained a letter from young Calmet-Beauvoisins to the editor of the *Courrier*: 'In your paper of 9 Nivôse', wrote the former adjutant-general, 'you had the gall to say...that the "*armée* calling itself *révolutionnaire*" had left behind wherever it went, notably in Bailleul, Cassel and Dunkerque, nothing but traces of the most frightful brigandage, that the soldiers of this *armée* had forcibly removed gold and silver jewellery and gold crosses from the women.... As for the *armée* which you dismiss as "calling itself *révolutionnaire*", it is made up of the most determined patriots.... It is totally false to say that they are capable of the brigandage which you so cravenly accuse them of.... The audacity of your calumny crumbles beneath the walls of Cassel and Dunkerque, where no soldier of the *armée révolutionnaire* has ever set foot...'.[10] There is certainly more than pure coincidence in the date of the attacks on the Lille *armée*, so close to that of the campaign in Paris against Ronsin's.

In the capital, with Ronsin still in prison, the detractors of his *armée* scored yet more points in Pluviôse. The most advanced Sections were beginning to be influenced and, on 5 Pluviôse, the general assembly of the

Sans-Culottes Section passed a motion which represented the final stage in this insidious campaign: 'The general assembly, considering that the *armée* as useful as that which is called *révolutionnaire* should be composed of citizens known for their purity of conduct, and not of *malveillants* who seek and bring nothing but trouble and fear to the countryside...has decided to invite our brothers in the other [Paris] Sections, to undertake a second *scrutin épuratoire* of the members of the *armée révolutionnaire* from their arrondissement in order to exclude all bad citizens....'.[11] Several Sections approved of this motion, the Bon-Conseil Section adopting it on the 14th, with the observation: 'We consider this of the first necessity. We must always remind ourselves...that if, having honoured these men with our confidence, they abuse it, we must not hesitate to punish them without distinction...'.[12] On the 10th both the Contrat-Social and the Révolutionnaire Sections passed a motion of censure against the general staff in the rue de Choiseul: 'men who are not aristocrats, or patriots, simply utter scoundrels...'.[13]

By this date the campaign in the press was completely submerged in the increasingly bitter political conflict between the Indulgents and the so-called 'parti de la Guerre'. On 14 Pluviôse Ronsin was released from prison; ten days later Grammont was replaced on the general staff by Maubant. These two events changed the balance of the situation; with its general cleared, the *armée* he commanded was restored to respectability. The local authorities, conscious of the change in atmosphere, returned the accusations of pillage and banditry made by the farmers against the detachments to their files, to await a more suitable occasion for using them. In Paris the intensity of the press campaign seemed to diminish, and for nearly a month there was scarcely a mention of depredations committed by the detachments in the countryside. At the same time, the dismissal of Grammont and the removal of the gamblers and womanisers from the general staff deprived the opponents of the *armée* of one of their best arguments. Grammont had always been an object of scandal, and his presence in the rue de Choiseul had worried such sincere supporters of terrorist measures as the Cordelier, Henry, who wrote on 12 Pluviôse to Bouchotte, denouncing the actors of the 'bande aux Grammont'.[14]

The second arrest of Ronsin was the welcome signal for certain local authorities to reopen their files and to unleash a particularly dangerous campaign against the detachments. On this occasion the municipalities successfully destroyed the reputation of the *révolutionnaires* in sans-culotte circles by accusing them of having trafficked in primary foodstuffs and of being the first to infringe the laws of the Maximum, which they had been charged with implementing. The *armée* could still find friends among the *petit peuple* of Paris, who were not taken in by such self-interested accusations, designed above all to divert attention from the failings and complicity of the municipalities in the matter. The sans-culottes asked themselves if there was not in fact something suspect about this sudden zeal on the part of the local authorities. But in Jacobin circles, and no doubt among some militant sans-culottes, people began to see the *armée révolutionnaire* as having outlived its usefulness, and as compromised, its weaknesses perhaps having actually aggravated the shortages experienced in the Paris markets. Accordingly, they severed their links with it, expressing no regret, and the farmers made no attempt to conceal their joy. As the municipalities of the communes in which detachments were stationed were reopening their files, in the last days of Ventôse and the first of Germinal, the *Journal des Jacobins de Reims* of 24 Ventôse printed a vigorous attack by a local *sociétaire* on the 'bandes à la Cartouche' which, under the orders of the national agent of the district, were supposed to be ravaging and desolating the surrounding countryside. 'Formerly', said this Jacobin, 'tax officials might give arbitrary orders, but at least they were applied with mildness; this new method resembles that of Cartouche, when he forced contributions from the villages through which he passed...'.[15] Foretastes of the denunciations of the Year III against the 'buveurs de sang' and 'hordes dévastatrices' were already appearing in print.

Under the Thermidorean reaction, the former *armées* and their leaders became the favourite whipping boy of the journalists of the *honnêtes gens*. The *Anti-Terroriste*, the paper of the Toulouse *jeunesse dorée*, hounded the *commissaires* and officers of the Haute-Garonne *armée*. In its issue for 17 Floréal Year III, it reproduced a letter from Montané accusing the *armée* of Beaumont, under the orders of Blanchard, of having pillaged the house of Ginestre, a *notaire*; on 18 Thermidor, it was the turn of Gélas and Barateau to be treated as thieves.[16] The campaign in Toulouse had echoes in Paris, Fréron's paper publishing a letter in its issue of 13 Nivôse Year III from a Toulouse Thermidorean who signed himself 'A Pedlar': 'A figure known for his pillaging, theft and judicial murder', wrote the paper's informant, 'is in charge of local administration [the person in question was mayor of Toulouse at this stage], of the *société populaire*, and is daily becoming more dangerous.... He has already succeeded, as commander of the *armée révolutionnaire*, known for its brigandage, in procuring national property according to the custom; his name is Barateau and is worthy of your attention...'.[17] On 13 Messidor, the *Anti-Terroriste* accused the former *commissaires civils* of the La Réole detachment – one of them the former mayor of the commune – of having pillaged the château and taken the effects from individuals' homes.[18]

Following in the footsteps of the Thermidorean papers, the departmental administrations made up for the necessary discretion of the previous year, and piled on the denunciations against the former personnel of the *armées révolutionnaires*. According to the administration of the Nièvre, the '*commissaires* calling themselves *révolutionnaires*' had 'pillaged and devastated public and private property', and their commanders had 'insolently frittered away...enormous sums extorted from honest citizens, regaling their protégés at the local *auberge*'.[19] Yet again, in this department, 'the *armées révolutionnaires* just took what they wanted and gave no receipts...'.[20] In the canton of Lormes, Chaix's soldiers were accused of having stolen *assignats* from the priest in charge of the chapel of Vésigneux.[21] On 5 Ventôse Year III the *comité* of Orange heard the complaints of some inhabitants of Vivans, from whom a revolutionary company had taken arms in October 1793 – 'the day of justice', observed the *comité* on this occasion, '[has] replaced the days of brigandage and thievery, when associations of evil men gave themselves over to all manner of excess...'. Having thus proclaimed the return to legality, the *comité* then turned to the chiefs of 'this band of perverse and immoral men', who had taken arms from the people. What in the Year II had been deemed a measure of revolutionary policing, in Thermidorean vocabulary had become an act of pillage. There is no finer example of the gulf separating the Thermidorean conception of the sanctity of property and the exigencies of a revolutionary situation which, among other public-order measures, required the disarming of suspects.[22] According to the Thermidorean *comité* of Orange almost every terrorist measure was simple theft if it involved the confiscation of private belongings.

The lesser agents of the terrorist system, members of the companies or former *commissaires*, thus vilified by the press and dragged through the mud by the local administration, were particularly angered by the imputations made against their personal honour. 'We are the men of 14 July and 10 August', was the dignified protest of the ex-terrorists of the commune of Tonneins-la-Montagne, in the Garonne valley, 'and although, in carrying out to the letter the revolutionary laws and decisions of your colleagues on mission, which held in check all manner of evil-doers, we never spilt or caused to spill one drop of blood, or damaged or caused to be damaged any property, we are nevertheless booed and hissed in the streets, insulted in our houses, proscribed, looked upon and treated as "Brigands". Brigands! No, we are artisans, who have lost our children in the service of the *patrie*...'.[23] It is not difficult to understand the indignation of these men who, on the whole, had simply implemented with scrupulous zeal measures ordered by the proconsuls or by the other higher authorities. They were indignant both at the unjust calumnies and at the immunity of 'les grands' who had been responsible for the Terror. The term 'brigand' in fact had changed sides. Reserved in the Year II for Chouans and royalist rebels in the interior, it had become in the mouths of the Thermidoreans – with the term 'buveur de sang' – the semi-official, indeed almost the required, description for former terrorists.

The authorities of the Year III were not only pursuing political goals in thus seeking to deprive the instruments of terrorist policy of their honour; the Thermidoreans never quite forgave these 'artisans' their modest origins. In the eyes of the *honnêtes gens*, who felt they had some God-given, some kind of hereditary right to power, who considered the Revolution made for their benefit alone, it was intolerable that locksmiths, blacksmiths, cooks and shopkeepers could dispose of armed force, could act with sovereignty, replacing public officials better educated than themselves, levying *taxes* and disturbing the propertied. It was above all quite intolerable to think that such vile and base creatures could act out of patriotism, proving their honesty and disinterestedness. This is what was as inadmissable to the Thermidoreans as it would be to Taine.[24] It was therefore imperative to prove the venality of these people, imperative for the peace of mind of the bourgeois of the Year III who claimed, as the ruling class, an exclusive right to power. It was not simply a matter of vengeance; the unworthiness and unsuitability of the common people for positions of command must also be demonstrated.

But there was another difficulty; not every *commissaire* or soldier, as we have seen, was an artisan, an employee or a wage-earner; some were proprietors, men of the law, important figures with good educations. These were the greatest criminals, traitors to their station in life, they above all must be stripped of honour. For them was reserved a different explanation for their actions; they were ferocious men, eager for vengeance, cruel, undoubtedly unbalanced, certainly bad fathers, bad husbands, bad sons. The Thermidoreans, like the sans-culottes before them, claimed to have a kind of monopoly on family virtue. The essence of Thermidorean, of bourgeois thinking, was that a man without property could not possibly be honest; exposed to great temptation while executing a police mission, he could not but succumb (the Thermidoreans certainly did so when placed in such a position, and they judged the sans-culottes by their own standards); it followed that property alone conferred the moral worth required for the exercise of public office. The Thermidoreans put the morality of the *révolutionnaires* on trial because they were poor; they strove to prove the acts of banditry attributed to the *armées révolutionnaires* because they were popular *armées*.

II   *Pillagers and pillage*

Like all armies, the *armées révolutionnaires* had their share of pillagers. A Dolle, a Viton, a Joly were godsends to Thermidorean propaganda; but the judges of the Year III had to content themselves with rather slim dossiers. What is most striking, in soldiers exposed to such great temptations, is how honest they were in general. Considerable damage was inflicted on the sequestrated property of the great merchants of Lyon; but it was the local guards who were responsible,[25] and we know of only one Parisian soldier prosecuted for pillage during his stay in the richest town in France – he had an expensive mistress in Paris![26] The reality is far removed from the legend, and even the evidence derived solely from Thermidorean trials is insufficient to support the insinuations and accusations of the press campaign of autumn 1793 to winter 1795, designed to show the revolutionary forces as 'armées du crime'. Indeed, judging by the testimony of a Girondin man of the law detained in the Paris prisons, professional criminals tended rather to be royalists and counter-revolutionaries.[27] Certainly no milieu was more traditionalist, more conservative, more respectful of established hierarchies and suspicious of egalitarianism and innovation than that of hereditary, professional crime. The term 'brigand' was used in several different contexts; but it was more appropriate when applied to the royalist bands already active in the mountains of the Aveyron and the Lozère in the Year II, than to the poor wine-growers sent from Cahors to chase them from their dens. Crime, on the whole, was royalist, and the criminal like the prostitute continued to feed on the aristocrat, as the louse on the peasant.

If we examine closely the charges of pillage and abuse of powers brought against the officers, the *commissaires civils* and the members of the revolutionary forces, before the criminal tribunals, they seem to fall into five principal categories. The main charge – and one can understand this, given that many Thermidoreans had themselves fallen victim to it – was that of having levied revolutionary *taxes*. The second was that of having distributed the produce – or some of it – to the poor and to members of the companies; the third, of having taken silverware and precious metals, currency and hidden savings from individuals; the fourth, of having pillaged foodstuffs (the number of bottles, turkeys, chickens and rabbits being reproduced in detail). Fifth and last, they were accused of trafficking in arrest warrants or blackmailing victims with the threat of arrest. These formed the essence of the case for the prosecution. There were other charges, special cases: the Marats were accused of having elicited favours from prisoners by promising their release, or of having taken watches and jewels or removed the seals on furniture during their visits to prisons or the houses of the rich arms dealers of the île Feydeau. These soldiers were also to be accused of having robbed the dead, the ultimate dishonour – witnesses at Carrier's trial declared that certain Marats had divided up among themselves the clothes of the victims of the *noyades*. Accusations of this nature were, however, rare, even in the Year III, and the Nantes artisans seem to have been unusually depraved. Soldiers from other formations were sometimes accused of petty larceny – usually of wine and food – and, more rarely, of the theft of wallets and watches. But these crimes were dealt with extremely harshly at the time, by the *commissaires militaires* or the disciplinary councils on which revolutionary officers sat – the latter defending the honour of their battalions by showing rigorous severity towards delinquents. The tally of crime by individual soldiers (pp. 154–5) was not sensational, no more than 50 cases in the Parisian *armée*, for example, three-quarters of which involved theft of foodstuffs.

No, it was the abuse of powers and extortion for personal profit, rather than criminal offences, of which the battalions and companies were most frequently accused. The levy of revolutionary *taxes* and the collection of precious metals were war measures, ordered by the *représentants* or the Committee of Public Safety itself; in obeying superiors' orders and remitting the proceeds to the Convention or to the *représentants*, the *révolutionnaires* felt they had acquitted themselves well towards the Republic, and were sincerely indignant at being accused, sometimes more than a year after the fact, of theft and misappropriation, the charges seeming all the more unjust when they knew in their consciences that they had been scrupulous in their returns.

As for the gastronomic pillage, that was indeed theft, but theft committed by soldiers, and even if such acts seemed particularly shocking because they were perpetrated by French soldiers against French peasants, the *armées* were fighting against 'the enemies of the interior'; they could not live off conquered territory as other armies did, and their victims were the big farmers and the priests. Moreover, the pillage of foodstuffs was an integral part of the conflict between town and country, and in the eyes of the *révolutionnaires*, what they took was a sort of supplementary *taxe* on 'incivisme'.

Except for the theft of foodstuffs, we have been concerned so far with administrative crimes – the administrative status of the *armées révolutionnaires* was in itself so ambiguous that it encouraged abuse, disorder and violence. But the final charge, that of trafficking in arrests and orders of release, was indeed a patent abuse of power, and even a form of fraud, involving as it did the exploitation of police powers vested in the detachments for the soldiers' own personal profit. This kind of fraud, practised on a large scale by the *armée* of the Lot and the Cantal, and by the company of Nantes, was particularly repugnant. It was also dangerous, since it threatened to compromise the functioning of the Terror by diverting it from its real goals. If arrests were made for profit, the need for political surveillance would count for nothing. It was only the rich who were held to this kind of ransom: when the detachment arrived in a commune the *commissaires* or officers would ask the *comité de surveillance* for a list of the most wealthy inhabitants, who would then form the clientele of this indecent trading – so many livres, in specie, so many louis d'or per release or undelivered warrant. These payments were often pocketed by those concerned and did not find their way into the national Treasury, or figure in the accounts sent by the detachment commanders to the *comités de surveillance* or to the *représentants*. The net result was that the soldiers arrested – or made a show of arresting – only the rich inhabitants of a particular locality. But the richest were not always the most suspect – although they often were – and good republicans were sometimes penalised in consequence, whose only error was to have provoked the jealousy of the modest artisans or poor labourers who were members of the *comités de surveillance*. This kind of abuse was not prevalent in all the *armées révolutionnaires*. The Parisian *armée*, which was under strict supervision from the *comités* or the *commissaires* of the Committee of General Security, could not have acted in this manner, even had it wished to do so. It was the same with most of the communal companies; they were mere agents of the *comités*, executing warrants received from

them. The most favourable opportunities for such abuse were furnished by
the great repressive expeditions and even more by prison duties.

Finally, there was another abuse which, if not exactly a crime, nevertheless, because of its pettiness and indelicacy, was one of the main grievances
of the country people against the political soldiers. This was the tendency of
the soldiers to ensure that they were paid extra for any 'journey' they made
away from their station to execute a warrant, even to the point of making
their victims defray the costs of being arrested. There was nothing new
about this. The *révolutionnaires* were rarely innovators; like all sans-culottes
they were firmly attached to traditional ways, and simply turned to their
own account the Ancien Regime practice whereby the royal police recouped
from its recipient the costs of serving a summons. As we have seen, there
were large numbers of former soldiers in the ranks of some *armées* and they
brought with them the practices of the old military police. In this sense the
armées scarcely deserved the epithet 'révolutionnaires', which set them apart
from other military forces; as one great historian of the French Revolution
put it, the action of the political soldiers of the Year II was simply an extension of certain authoritarian tendencies prevailing under the monarchy.[28]

The mercenary bent of the soldiers manifested itself in another iniquit-
ous practice, likewise inherited from the Ancien Regime, of making
prisoners defray the costs of their imprisonment. Prison duty was therefore
particularly popular with the most self-serving and the poorest of the *révolutionnaires*, and the authorities of the Year II even considered it a way of
compensating the relatives of soldiers at the front and poor and worthy
sans-culottes. The soldiers attached to *maisons de détention* had other ways of
turning their duties to profit, making the relatives of prisoners, often well
off, pay for any concessions allowed them. These prison guards were
always the most corrupt, the most detested and the most despised of the
political soldiers, and the *révolutionnaires* attached to the prisons at Aix-en-
Provence, Digne, Sedan and Nantes were no exception in this respect, and
fully merited the contempt of patriots and the hatred of their victims.

Lastly, and a further legacy from the Ancien Regime, were those
specialists in falsifying travel costs, grades,[29] or requisition orders – the
anarchy of military administration in the Year II supplying a congenial
atmosphere for these quasi-professional criminals, who found in the *armée* a
perfect arena in which to exercise their talents. The somewhat illicit *armées*
had their fair share of Vidocqs.

We have already mentioned the importance of distinguishing between
myth and reality. In the first category must be placed certain simplifications, coloured by the terminology of the Thermidoreans and the press
campaign of autumn 1793 and spring 1794. The *armées révolutionnaires*
cannot be treated like ordinary gangs of criminals; their members were
not necessarily debauchees and thieves.[30] The myth derived in part from
the very ambiguity surrounding the existence of the popular *armées* –
Thermidorean and peasant opinion never permitting these soldiers the

ultimate excuse of obedience owed to higher authorities. We must accept as reality the pillaging by the soldiers and their leaders – always making a distinction, however, between collective extortion and individual abuse. With the exception of the few concrete examples with which we shall open our account, the bad reputation of these forces appears to owe a good deal to their idleness, to the greedy demands of their soldiers and their indecent rates of pay. If they rendered a disservice to the revolutionary regime, it was less through pillage than by their debasement of the Terror to the level of vulgar bargaining.

The leaders of the Parisian *armée* were men of integrity. Ronsin died poor, leaving his widow a small annuity, a few theatrical books and the wardrobe of a general of the Republic. The Grammonts left debts, poorly kept accounts, mistresses in tears, as well as some outstanding credit which they had been unable to redeem; in the world of actors one lent money generously, but repaid it parsimoniously. Mazuel's tastes were undoubtedly too grand for a sans-culotte, but, apart from his hotel bill, he left nothing behind. The trials of the Hébertists reveal more than anything the modesty of the spoils of the principal defendants. It is clearly more difficult to pronounce on the case of Parein, for this astute general survived all these political catastrophes; and if, as he claimed, he tended cows as a child, at his death he left a sizeable fortune and had succeeded in marrying his daughter off to a *notaire* from Sarcelles.[31] Did Parein enrich himself by his service with the *armée révolutionnaire*, particularly in Lyon where its dreadful duties would have furnished him many an occasion for reaching well-rewarded accommodations with prisoners? We do not know; but royalist historians of Lyon during the Thermidorean period never questioned his probity. It is possible that his fortune came from a later period, when he began to draw a salary from the secret funds of Fouché, by then Minister of Police, to whom he rendered considerable service. As for Boulanger, the inventory of his belongings, drawn up shortly after Thermidor, shows that the former jeweller's assistant from Liège was almost as poor in 1794 as he had been when he first arrived in Paris at the age of eighteen.[32] Houssaye and Collard were rogues; but they did not stay long in an 'armée de purs', its well-deserved title. Doré, who abandoned his men at Pont-l'Evêque, was a gambler, the archetypal bad officer – but not a thief.

The author of the *Dictionnaire des Jacobins vivans* questions Dufresse's probity.[33] He was indeed one of the men who enriched themselves during the Revolution; but as with many soldiers, his fortune dated mostly from the period following the reconquest of Belgium, when pillage and embezzlement were rife. At his trial in the Year III, Dufresse was accused of extortion and the abuse of powers, but neither the general of the Lille *armée* nor the officers of his general staff were accused on this occasion of pillage or embezzlement. We have already noted the attack made by a Toulouse paper on certain members of the Haute-Garonne *armée*; but once again the

Thermidorean case against Blanchard, Hugueney and their colleagues placed the accent on the abuse of powers, the arbitrary arrests, and the destruction carried out by the soldiers under their orders. With the exception of some objects taken from the house of a Beaumont *notaire*, no charge of theft was made by the Thermidorean judges against this *armée* and its leaders. But not all the *armées* can be given a clean bill of morality, and detailed dossiers exist on the activities of three of the most reprehensible: the *armées* of the Lot and the Cantal, and the Compagnie Marat of Nantes. The honesty of the companies of the Haute-Loire, the Ardennes and the Bas-Rhin is likewise suspect. But the most substantial case is that against the *armée* of the Lot.

Bô, public prosecutor of the Aveyron department, whose brother sat in the Convention, was a good jurist and a leading bourgeois. He had no sympathy with the Terror, or with its instruments; disorder, violence and anarchy were anathema to him. It was he who prepared the case heard at Rodez against Viton and his officers, with meticulous care and not a little desire for vengeance. But such was the hatred which the extravagant behaviour and insolence of the young wigmaker general inspired in this man of order, that he somewhat overstated his case. The departmental *armées* were not short on adventurers; these ranged from the major-league pillager to the shameful petty thief. Viton belonged in the first category; this satrap from the Aveyron was not only a pillager but an uncontrollable philanderer. 'General Viton requisitioned and delegated the power to requisition; following his example, all the officers and soldiers of the [Lot] *armée* requisitioned everything that fell into their hands. Such was the depravity of these corrupt men, that they were seen to drag off girls whom they claimed to have put under requisition....'.[34] The testimony, being Thermidorean, is somewhat suspect. The documents are less so, and the evidence compiled against Viton and his officers is overwhelming. The prosecution, drawn up almost with tender care by Bô, comprises six main charges arranged in the following order:

- theft of furniture and effects belonging to the nation, from the château-fortress of Sévérac, sequestrated property of the duchesse de Biron, an émigré;
- violence against individuals to extort from them the location of caches of silver and precious objects;
- atrocities committed against individuals, on orders from Viton, with a view to terrorising the inhabitants of certain communes in the Aveyron;
- wanton burning of houses on the orders of Viton;
- requisition of grain, foodstuffs, personal effects and girls, on the orders of Viton, on behalf of his *armée*;
- forced contributions, imposed by individuals with no legal mandate, on citizens, under threat of arrest or of the guillotine.[35]

A wide spread of accusations, encompassing all of those made by the Thermidoreans against the former revolutionary forces, and cleverly grouping common-law crimes with revolutionary extortions. In Bô's eyes *taxes révolutionnaires* were as much an attack on property as pure theft for personal gain. But when we examine the dossier against Viton, prepared over an entire year – between Frimaire Year II, when his *armée* had already left the Aveyron, and Frimaire-Nivôse Year III, when witnesses appearing before the *comité* of Sévérac, or the examining judges of Rodez and Cahors, had re-found their tongues – we have to admit that the two categories of accusation were supported by a number of testimonies, which were in fundamental agreement. It would be difficult to see Viton as a victim of the political justice of the Year III. Besides, this young man went to great pains to evade the many warrants issued against him, by taking refuge in the undergrowth of military administration, the best cover for men of his kind. Most of the crimes were committed in the districts of Sévérac, Rodez and Villefranche (the most important thefts occurring in the château of Sévérac); but Viton and his officers were also accused of theft and of extorting contributions in the Lot. The château affair, according to many witnesses from Sévérac, involved the removal of paintings, fine furnishings and antique tapestries by the soldiers of the Lot *armée* under orders from their 'general' and two other officers, captains Lacroix (from Cahors) and Orliac (from Moissac). The aggravating circumstance, affirmed by all the witnesses, was that the operation had taken place in the presence of Viton and the two officers, and the objects removed were then taken off in the direction of Rodez in carriages belonging to the three officers.

The quest for details on the Sévérac affair was hindered for over a year, until Frimaire Year III, by the silence of the witnesses 'held back by terror'. According to the most important of these witnesses, Joseph Durand, receiver for the district of Sévérac, most of the paintings were taken by Orliac. But the concierge of the château claimed that Lacroix had demanded the keys, and when he found several *révolutionnaires* about to remove the paintings, he went to warn Orliac, then commander of the fort, who, far from preventing the pillage when he arrived in the reception hall, actually threatened this witness with his sabre. According to Ricard, a cutler, Orliac himself took a large antique chandelier from the bedroom of the one-time duchesse, declaring that it would be used to light the premises of the *société populaire* at Figeac; he also took sundry other items, including a rhinoceros tusk 'fifteen feet long' and an old pistol. Orliac clearly had a mania for souvenirs. The deeds attributed to Lacroix were more serious, more base; he left Sévérac with a horse (requisitioned?) loaded with bed linen and clothes. 'In their eagerness these officers', observed another witness, 'went so far as to remove the covers from the armchairs and the horsehair with which they were stuffed...'. These men from the Lot general staff did not do things by halves. As for Viton himself, the witnesses formally declared that he had participated in the thefts: Vernhet, a weaver, saw him in the main room of the château rolling up 'a magnificent picture' representing the martyrdom of Saint Sebastian and Saint Fabian, a masterpiece which would figure once again when the case against the young wig-maker and his colleagues was heard by the criminal tribunal of Cahors.[36]

The main witnesses then moved on to the question of requisitions of grain and foodstuffs. According to Viton, these requisitions had been made against his orders by undisciplined soldiers from his *armée*. The people of the commune of Coussergues were of a different opinion: 'chickens...were sent in large numbers to General Viton, then at Sévérac...'.[37] But more serious charges were also made against him, some inhabitants of the Lot claiming that he took personal effects from the home of Decourt in Moissac, declaring: 'That is how one treats and how one must treat aristo-crats, *égoïstes* and *modérés*...'.[38] Theft had thus become an instrument of egalitarian policy. We must not attach too much importance to the words of this young hothead, always the first to condemn himself by his rash speech, for Viton was a poor paymaster and *égoïstes* and *modérés* were not the only ones to suffer from his offhandedness. Six months later, the caterers of Cahors were still demanding payment for the feasts hosted by the young general in Frimaire.[39] As for Orliac, the citizens of Castelnau in the Lot rightly accused him of having pocketed spoons and forks during a search made in that commune.[40]

Commanded by officers like this, the *révolutionnaires* from the Lot and the Aveyron had little reason to behave themselves and most of the depreda-tion attributed to them was committed in the presence of their officers. A mason from Sévérac described the Lot soldiers mounted on ladders to take down the silk tapestries from one of the banqueting halls of the château, while their officers directed operations from below.[41] More significant is the testimony of a member of the *comité de surveillance* at Villefranche, who on 19 Brumaire Year II, at a time when the *comités* were still in the hands of the sans-culottes, 'stated that the soldiers going to the *armée révolutionnaire* or coming back from it, committed many acts against the patriots, that it was unfair to leave them at the mercy of these soldiers, and that to prevent errors of this kind it was imperative to give good sans-culottes some sort of protection conceived in the following terms: "Republicans, respect the person and property of ★★★★★★ , sans-culotte, who lives in this house...".' The Rodez authorities had similar placards placed on the shops of *sociétaires* and patriots.[42] Such precautions speak volumes; they were also an implicit invitation to the *révolutionnaires* not to respect the houses and property of those without such anti-theft devices. It is not surprising that contempo-raries should have likened Viton's *armée* to a swarm of grasshoppers which had descended on one of the most deprived departments of the Republic.[43] The only excuse for the soldiers in Cahors was that this was a war zone, and Taillefer had advised them, before their departure, to use extreme severity. The Lot soldiers acted as if they were in conquered territory, as their brothers in Belgium, or in Italy after the Year III.

As for their victims, they could no longer tell whether these operations were carried out by real or by false *armées révolutionnaires*. During that autumn and winter the whole area, from the Lot to the mountains of the Lozère, was handed over to armed forces, and even if the men were not always *révolutionnaires* – the soldiers from the Mont-Blanc and the Vaucluse conscripts were guilty of various robberies in the Sévérac district in November 1793, all the more unfortunate since that was the principal scene of simultaneous 'campaigns' by Viton[44] – the unfortunate inhabitants of these poor regions were subjected to the same brutal pressure. The practice of blackmail through threat of arrest assumed such proportions in this former 'bandit country' that some particularly well-off inhabitants of the Lot and the Aveyron had to pay the price of their liberty twice, sometimes three times over, and to multiply their patriotic contributions – having already bought their liberty from Viton's *armée*, they had to do so again from a battalion of regular recruits.

We possess a number of accounts of the disarray thus caused to these unfortunates. Listen, for example, to the experience of the former mayor of Cahors, an old man of seventy-three detained in the Bon Pasteur, who wrote on 30 Frimaire Year II to the *comité* of the *chef-lieu*:

> Citizen Louis Dufourt Léobard had lived in peace as a good republican citizen, and was recognised as such... and had donated 2,000 livres to his country about two months previously, when, on 15 September last, a young man, his sword drawn, and at the head of 30 fusiliers armed with guns and bayonets, entered his house and brusquely demanded a sum of 2,000 livres, threatening to take him to prison if he refused; in vain did citizen Dufourt tell him that he had already made a gift of such a sum to the nation...[he] went and searched out 2,000 l. in *assignats*, the young officer took them and retired; citizen Dufourt went into his garden to relieve his sorrow, hoping that he would be left in peace after the sacrifice of 4,000 l.; but half an hour later the same officer, at the head of the same detachment, appeared at the garden gate, his sword in hand, and ordered him to follow him...he was shut up in the Bon Pasteur and has been detained there ever since....[45]

On 15 September the revolutionary forces were already in action in the Lot, but in this case we do not know whether it was the act of an astute bandit or a revolutionary officer. Whichever it was, Dufourt lost 4,000 livres in the purchase of a liberty which he did not retain.

Now let us turn to Viton's soldiers' traffic in liberty in the Villefranche-d'Aveyron district. On 21 Brumaire, Miret, a captain in the *armée révolutionnaire* of the Lot, signed the following statement:

> Today M. Peyroudit, arrested yesterday and detained in the *maison d'arrêt* of the château of Vareins, sent word to me that his health was not up to a journey to Najac, and offered me 3,000 l., which I refused, finding the sum too modest in relation to his fortune, on my response he asked for an interview with me, when we agreed that the cost of his liberation would

be 4,000 l., a pair of fattened cattle, two sacks of wheat and a barrel of mature wine and some poultry to feed the brigade, the 4,000 l. to be brought tomorrow, I spent the rest of my day in correspondence or in gathering further information.

The following day Miret wrote in his diary: 'Received from M. Peyroudit the sum of 4,000 l. in fulfilment of the agreement we made on the 21st of this month...in return for which I ordered the guard, placed on his door by the municipality of Sainte-Grégoire, to be lifted...'.[46]

In the Cantal also the *commissaires* and officers practised the same kind of carefully administered and accounted-for pillage. Fougère Delthil, Taillefer's *commissaire* in the department, and the members of the *comité* of Aurillac had the detachments march into the different districts. 'The detachments', we read in a famous Thermidorean pamphlet, 'stripped citizens of their money, furniture, everything metal and their jewels. Then they had to pay the heavy costs of the detachment's mission, then a contribution, and even all that was not always enough to avoid arrest'.[47] But 'Delthil had already revoked several arrest warrants in return for some pecuniary sacrifice for the benefit of the nation'; the 'sacrifice' in some cases reached the tidy sum of 21,000 livres.[48] Witnesses in the Year III were to claim that in other parts of the same department, Delthil's soldiers took jewels from them, earrings, crosses, watches, and even a metal shaving mug.[49] It would be interesting to discover the destination of all these objects. Delthil and his subordinates claimed in their defence that they were simply carrying out the orders of the Committee of Public Safety for the collection of precious metals. Here we find ourselves in an administrative twilight zone in which it is difficult to distinguish between simple pillage and the economic terror. The witnesses referred to in the Thermidorean pamphlet never accused Delthil and his subordinate, Brutus Valette, of having derived any personal profit from the confiscations; they seem to have been honest, if violent, republicans, whereas Viton and his officers were both violent and dishonest.

Apart from the *armée* of Viton, the most notorious example of pillage and abuse of powers – to say nothing of rape and arson – is that of the small 'bande à Vauquoy', operating in those districts of the Isère nearest Lyon. The events of this expedition, which was to supply Robespierrist propaganda with its most effective weapon against ultra-revolutionary policies, are examined elsewhere.[50] But Vauquoy himself was no pillager; he derived no personal profit from the revolutionary *dîmes* (tithes) he collected, and returned precise inventories of everything confiscated in the La Tour-du-Pin district.[51] It is true that he was arrested after accusations by the officers of the Parisian *armée* that he had authorised the lifting of sequestrations, and had sent the effects of victims of the guillotine in Lyon to his wife to defray the costs (over a thousand livres) of a feast held in a Crémieu *auberge*. But he was only detained for two days in prison and those charges were not included in the indictment drawn up against him by Fouquier-Tinville. For Vauquoy and his emulator, Dorzat, the *dîme révolutionnaire*, the confiscations and the distribution of the 'surpluses' found in the cupboards of the farmers, were all part of a good joke played on the rich; the former secretary of the Jacobins mocked his soldiers when they complained of finding nothing in their searches of the houses of rich farmers: 'You stupid buggers, when I go into a house I find plenty; you, you don't know how to search...'.[52] Vauquoy was to be guillotined for abusing his powers and for having slandered the nation's legislators, but not for acts of pillage.

Those around him, however, had little to recommend them. Dolle is indefensible; he had every vice.[53] In his hands the company from Crémieu and the Parisian detachments in the Isère became instruments for terrorising his debtors and settling accounts with his personal enemies, who had been guilty of reporting his previous depredations.[54] The presence of Dolle, a kind of *commissaire* with ill-defined powers, but claiming a 'delegation' from Fouché and Collot, compromised the dragoons from Crémieu and the Parisian soldiers, by lending an air of scandal to all the repressive operations undertaken in the district of La Tour-du-Pin.

The Compagnie Marat was the principal victim of the kind of legend which was building up around former terrorist institutions from the Year III onwards. If Carrier served as an alibi for all his colleagues, those great proconsuls who had been just as merciless as himself, the small company from Nantes was likewise to pay for the violence of all the revolutionary formations of the Year II. The trial of Carrier in effect turned a spotlight on the *comité révolutionnaire* and on this company. They were presented to Thermidorean opinion as the chosen instruments of a bloody debauchery, and the Marats, alone among the former *révolutionnaires*, were exposed to the terrible publicity of a major political trial in Paris, before a howling public and with a group of journalists instructed to discover the slightest bit of evidence which might blacken their characters and present them as murderers and savages. No other *armée* underwent such scrutiny. The Thermidoreans had chosen their Medusa's head well, for none of the former popular forces was so indefensible. Most of the Marats seemed to have been involved in the *noyades* and some had carried their zeal to the point of slashing at those unfortunates who tried to hang on to the barges. But the Thermidoreans, and the historians taking their cue from them, not content at thus highlighting the cruelty of these artisans from Nantes, tried also to destroy them entirely by casting doubt on their probity. 'In order to quicken the pace of these murders', wrote a historian of the Restoration, 'Carrier surrounded himself with cutthroats, making them his bodyguards and calling them the "compagnie Marat"...'.[55]

At Nantes the revolutionary institutions were not united. In the summer of 1794 the members of its *comité révolutionnaire* appeared before the revolutionary tribunal in Paris charged with abuse of powers, extortion and misappropriation. In their defence they cited orders from Carrier and blamed the members of the company. Thus on 11 Messidor Year II, Chaux, a member of the *comité*, testified: 'They [the Marats] had offices, and books in which their operations had to be listed. But, whether it was one of them or some evil individuals outside their ranks, profiting from the trouble and terror which the arrests had caused...to make a number of extortions, the *comité*...protested to Carrier [and] demanded the withdrawal of the powers given [to the company]...the *Réprésentant* hastened to accede to the protests of the *comité* and the powers were restricted.... The result was the arrest of one member of this company, who is still in detention, and the removal of several others'. Chaux added, somewhat hypocritically: 'I do not wish to accuse the members of this company, for we all considered them brave and upright, but I must tell the truth for the sake of the *comité révolutionnaire*...'.[56]

The charge drawn up against Carrier on 17 Vendémiaire Year III is more specific. 'To carry out so many crimes', it reads, 'it was necessary to bring together the most immoral of men; a revolutionary company was formed; it was filled with the most abject subjects...it was this company which was the instrument of all the crimes of the *comité*...'.[57] The accusations against individual members of the company were put with greater precision in the testimony of those who had been prisoners in Nantes, or who had escaped from the terrible barges. 'Where were we told to leave our effects, our arms and our wallets?' asked one witness. '... With the Marat company'. He added, 'Did the Marat company have the right to take away our goods? There were two periods before its suppression when the company acted without orders...'.[58] Other witnesses also accused this small 'armée', singling out two or three members as the most guilty. Most agreed in accusing Richard, the former hat merchant, and Joly, a copper-smelter, of having stripped the priests of their clothes and crowded them on to the barges before pushing them into the waters of the Loire. Joly was also accused of having taken watches and wallets from the pockets of those detained, during his visits to the prisons. Richard, who was denounced from all quarters at the time of these operations, had in fact been expelled from the company and arrested on orders from the *comité* and from Carrier; but it was he whom detractors singled out as representative of the entire company. 'Other companies were guilty of malpractice', Naud, the quartermaster, was to state at the trial in the Year III, 'but it was always us [who were accused of it]. We were ashamed to belong to the Marat company. We expelled thieves from it...'. Durossier, clerk of the company and a former cargo-broker in Santo Domingo, was also charged with having abused his position in the prisons to obtain jewels and gold crosses from the prisoners.[59]

These were the dubious elements among the Marats. The other members were only criticised for their brutality and their gastronomic pillaging – the soldiers using some of the money extorted from rich prisoners to buy wine, notably before their sinister operations in the Loire estuary. The real crimes committed by the Marats were no different from those commonly attributed to prison warders and policemen, and in the guarding of prisons and the inspection of suspects' houses which made up the bulk of their duties, the Marats bore a greater resemblance to these two groups than to soldiers. Extortion was indeed widespread at Nantes. But the Marats did not possess a monopoly on this; they shared responsibility with the garrison troops, just as they shared responsibility for the massacres and the *noyades* with the soldiers commanded by O'Sullivan and the mulatto troops. The Thermidorean authorities, however, were loathe to incriminate the troops of the line and the career soldiers, many of whom were still serving in the region (when they were not pillaging the Belgian provinces with the complicity of the *représentants*). The honour of the army could not be put in doubt; the Thermidorean regime depended upon it for protection against the double menace of a royalist coup and a popular uprising. The Compagnie Marat on the other hand no longer existed, several of its former members were in prison, and no one in the Year III would have been foolhardy enough to come to the defence of a terrorist institution accused of having participated in the *noyades*.

Robespierrist and Thermidorean opinion and the jurists of the Year III further criticised the *révolutionnaires* for the violence and brutality with which they carried out their duties. Not only did they steal, they stole without any respect for propriety. It was this of which the Reims newspaper was most critical in the conduct of the district *procureur* and his troops, while Maure denounced a young soldier for 'violence unworthy of a defender of liberty'.[60] The *révolutionnaires* in fact brought a violence to their operations which was truly military. In their visits to the prisons, they tore flesh from prisoners' ears and fingers, in their efforts to remove rings and earrings, and showered obscenities on the women, whom they feared as much as detested – for in the area around Nantes in particular, the comrades of these Marats had been tortured, even mutilated, by peasant women stirred up by the wives of the *seigneurs*. The *commissaires* of Viton pretended to bury alive the old women of the canton of Najac, to make them reveal the secret hiding places of their valuables.[61] Elsewhere the soldiers resorted to the tried old method of slowly burning the soles of the feet of farmers who had shown no alacrity in co-operating with the economic war effort.[62]

These methods caused a scandal among republicans, who considered them unworthy of free men. And yet the *représentants* had recommended the greatest severity to their agents, while the two Committees incessantly urged patriots to abandon all 'criminal indulgence' towards internal enemies. Pity itself seemed to be a counter-revolutionary crime. But once the missions had been accomplished, the Committee of Public Safety revised its opinion, and turned against the instruments which had taken its advice too literally. To charge the revolutionary companies with violence, cruelty and torture, while treating them as instruments of organised banditry, was the best way of releasing the Revolutionary Government itself from blame, and whitewashing the most extreme of the *Conventionnels*. The *armées*, then, were to pay for the brutality of the entire terrorist programme, just as they had paid for the extortions committed by the *représentants* and their *délégués*. The former *commissaires civils* and revolutionary officers had no chance of changing their allegiance when the Terror went out of fashion, as Boisset, Fouché, Tallien and other repentant terrorists had done. In condemning them, one could also condemn the policy of which they had been execu- tants, with little danger to oneself. Deprived of their commands, they were now ordinary individuals, who no longer instilled fear and who were subject to the justice of the criminal tribunals.

III   *The 'forces of disorder': mutinies and brawls*

To the country people, the *armées révolutionnaires* represented the 'forces of disorder'. These soldiers from the town came to their homes, ransacking their cupboards, upsetting their habits, taking away their treasures, insult- ing and scolding their wives, drinking their wine, eating their chickens, preaching the reversal of the established order by announcing the death of God and the advent of an egalitarian society. The officers seemed to have no control over these terrifying-looking savages, who destroyed religious objects and artistic monuments which the peasants scarcely appreciated, but which they knew to have been of considerable value. Howling and shouting, the *révolutionnaires* smashed doors which blocked their way, and having installed themselves in well-furnished and well-stocked houses, they caused unintentional fires by dropping ash from their pipes or trying to warm themselves by fires made from the furniture. It was the very epitome of disorder.

The peasants' opinion was shared by the inhabitants of the bourgs and towns. The political soldiers respected nothing, sacking their billets, getting drunk in the cafés, picking quarrels with the local people. In garrison towns the spectacle was particularly dramatic; hardly a night went by without riots and brawls between the *révolutionnaires* and the conscripted troops. In the ports and fortified places, when local commanders tried to use the Parisian soldiers for garrison duty, guard duty or defence of the coasts, they mu- tinied, invoking the terms of their engagement. The generals and officers of the general staff agreed with the municipal authorities' description of the soldiers as dirty, undisciplined, arrogant, aggressive, impossible good-for- nothings.

This reputation was not unmerited. The *révolutionnaire*, particularly if he was from Paris, had little respect for his officer; subordination was too reminiscent of the Ancien Regime. The officer was constantly at the mercy of men who, having elected him to the position, could remove him by denouncing him. Parisian *comités*, local *sociétés* and *représentants* alike fell victim to such denunciations. One officer might be accused of being drunk, of frequenting aristocrats, or of having a weakness for the Federalists; another of betraying the sans-culottes by coming to an arrangement with the big farmers; yet another, of a harshness reminiscent of the Ancien Regime army and of acting unworthily towards his 'frères', his 'equals in rights'; another spent his night in gambling and debauchery. The officer was thus in constant danger of finding himself back again in the ranks. Whereas discipline rests on inequality and respect, the *armées révolutionnaires* were democratic and egalitarian.

Considering themselves political veterans, the Parisians seem to have been the most difficult to control; they accepted military constraints with ill grace, claiming the right to question every order and to judge the political and moral conduct of their officers. Barracks advocates and naturally anti-authoritarian, they were forever insisting on the terms of their engagement. Physically, they seemed to want to demonstrate, like certain christians, that filth and purity somehow went together. Their terrifying appearance, on which so many hostile witnesses dwelt, was above all due to their slovenliness. Like the Rochefort sailors who measured their revolutionary convictions by the length of their whiskers,[63] the soldiers of Paris and Lille spread the sloppy, unbuttoned image of the perfect sans-culotte throughout France.

Représentants, municipalities and *comités* alike lost patience with the indiscipline and the eternal complaints of the revolutionary soldiers.[64] The Committee of Public Safety reminded Grammont that the armed forces had to obey orders, and a decree passed by the Convention placed the Parisian *armée* under military law by subordinating it to the military command.[65] The interpretation of the decree was a source of much contention, and in the Norman departments some fusiliers and cannoneers refused to obey orders from the local military commanders and from the commander of the Côtes de Cherbourg Army when they were assigned to coastal defence or to the war against the Chouans.[66] The cannoneers, better educated and with a more acute political awareness than most *révolutionnaires*, seem to have taken the initiative in both these cases of mutiny. In Lyon too it was the cannoneers who first demanded to return to Paris, when they felt that their service in France's second town was not consonant with their own concerns as sans-culotte *sectionnaires*.[67] In contrast, the detachment of fusiliers sent from Alençon to Domfront obeyed without protest the orders of the Domfront commander when he sent them to repel an invasion of Chouans. Indeed in the last days of the Parisian *armée* several witnesses commented on its improved discipline and its greater readiness to submit to military requirements.[68] If the revolutionary forces had remained under arms a little longer, they might have acquired the military virtues of obedience and tactical skill. But this would have posed other problems for a republican government, notably that of maintaining what were essentially provisional armies.

The political soldiers were detested by other military men because of their high pay. Moreover, the conscripted troops, the hussars and the dragoons, considered them cowards, taking refuge in *armées* in the interior and hiding from the real dangers of war behind their noisy patriotism and ostentatious political orthodoxy – a judgement borne out by the fact that many young men of conscription age had joined the ranks of the popular armies.[69] In a country such as France, with an old military tradition and where people remained very much attached to archaic conceptions of honour and martial fervour, there could have been no more effective way of discrediting this corps than to cast aspersions on its bravery. Nor were the regular soldiers content simply to claim that the hateful *politiques* were cowards; they also tried to demonstrate it by pursuing the unfortunate *révolutionnaires* through the streets of the garrison towns, striking them with their sabres, and making them the objects of ridicule and scorn from the inhabitants. In garrison towns where the Parisian *armée* was stationed – Compiègne, Vernon, Noyon, Rozay, Le Havre, Versailles, Provins – there were sometimes brawls for several nights running, with the Parisians invariably emerging the losers. In Lyon a full-scale battle occurred, involving several thousand soldiers, and lasting many days.[70] The *représentants* and the patriot authorities were disturbed at the frequency of such disorders, which they attributed, perhaps with good reason, to a ploy by *malveillants* to render the political *armées* ineffective by rousing the military against them and by exacerbating the disorders.[71] The moderates and *anti-révolutionnaires* made no attempt to disguise their satisfaction at such incidents; in Lyon in particular the population rejoiced in the rout of the Parisian fusiliers and cannoneers, those guardians of the guillotine, those executioners' aides, who had flanked the scene of the *mitraillades*.

Sometimes the *révolutionnaires* themselves were responsible for disorders. In Pluviôse the indiscipline of the fusilier detachments under Halm and Buard, left unoccupied in the Ecole Militaire, was displayed in a drunken, sword-brandishing pursuit of one another through the Petite Pologne and Gros Caillou quartiers, to the scandal of the general assembly of the Invalides Section which complained bitterly of the conduct of these idle wretches.[72] Parisian opinion was already accustomed to such events after the incidents provoked by Mazuel in Frimaire at the Opéra Comique. The result was that many Parisians considered the term 'revolutionary soldier' synonymous with 'trouble-maker', while the sans-culottes were angered by the insolent behaviour of these privileged men of leisure. In Versailles too the cavalrymen were the first to attack officers and members of the Versailles National Guard.[73] Finally, in Vernon, on the eve of their departure, the fusiliers from the Halm detachment attacked and seriously wounded a volunteer of the Ardennes battalion whom they accused of having spoken ill of the *armée révolutionnaire*.[74] But in general the aggressors were the line troops, sometimes incited by locals seeking revenge for the arrogance of the *étrangers*. This, however, did not prevent the local authorities taking the side of the 'défenseurs de la patrie' against the political soldiers, who almost everywhere were held responsible for troubles of which they were the principal victims. Several municipalities, having been sardonic witnesses of these disorders, had the gall to invoke them as pretexts for the removal of the revolutionary companies. The privileged soldiers had few defenders, and no one mourned the passing of an institution which had been nothing but an encouragement to riot, disturbance and disorder.[75]

The *révolutionnaires* further added to their poor reputation by their destructiveness, and the buildings they had occupied retained the scars of their visit. The people of Provins justly complained of the damage caused by these burdensome, rude and ever dissatisfied Parisians.[76] In Le Havre and Honfleur, they kept themselves warm in the dank convents and monasteries by burning the balustrades and wainscoting.[77] Unable to obtain the keys to the Collège at Toulouse from the municipality, the *armée révolutionnaire* broke down the main door and forcibly occupied the premises.[78] The scene created by their searches, particularly in presbyteries and in the houses of émigrés, was one of utter desolation: dishes smashed, cupboards emptied, curtains torn down, tables and chairs overturned.[79] If Carrier recommended pseudo-accidental fire as a means of forced dechristianisation, most of the fires caused by the detachments were indeed accidental, normally the outcome of excessive drinking.[80] In the Pyrenees the Toulousains destroyed several houses by setting off a cannon which they did not know how to use.[81] Clumsiness counted for as much as destructiveness, and in the Aveyron it was the inadequate watch maintained by Viton's soldiers over their bivouacking which caused the fires in the forests and wheat fields.[82] No doubt most of the destruction was accidental. But it helped turn opinion against these political soldiers who were privileged and whose lives were not at risk fighting the enemy on the frontiers.

The reputation of the *armées révolutionnaires* had been lost at a very early stage in the eyes of a portion of republican opinion, and in Nivôse and Germinal the disappearance of institutions which seemed to have departed from the strict code of Jacobin purity was accepted without regret. This development was not entirely fortuitous; detractors had easily sullied the *armées'* reputation early on by casting doubt on the personal probity of these overprivileged soldiers, and then by inflating every misdemeanour committed by them. The reputation of the Parisian *armée* had sunk so low because some fusiliers had sent pots of lard and jam to their wives in Paris, and the Sections had learnt of it. To arouse the envy of other soldiers, and disturb the entrenched egalitarianism of sans-culotte opinion, the adversaries of these special armies had only to emphasise their privileged status. Their enemies also appealed to those who liked order, by underlining the apparently wanton destructiveness of these sloppy soldiers – the newspapers scarcely mentioned the damage caused by other soldiers. But the real coup scored by this campaign was its success in representing the political soldiers as cowards, and their brawls delivered the *coup de grâce* to the prestige of these somewhat clownish soldiers.

But why wage such a campaign against men scarcely worthy of all the attention? The fact was that the campaign against the *armées révolutionnaires* represented a major success for the opponents of the Terror. Discredit just one of the instruments of a system in which every element was connected, and the system itself would fall into disrepute. When the attack against the Parisian *armée* was at its height in Ventôse-Germinal of the Year II, the more astute sans-culottes recognised that it was the Sectionary *comités* and the entire system of the Terror which was under attack.

The reality was less dramatic. The *armées révolutionnaires* were not entirely innocent, but neither were they forces of rapine. They were relatively pure, but not entirely so. Their ranks contained some notable pillagers, and many small offenders. These were the shadowy areas, but it was that shadow which remained behind. The sham *armées révolutionnaires* were the real 'bandes à la Cartouche'. But it was asking too much of the victims to make that distinction. One stole for the nation, the other for themselves; the farmer knew only that he had been robbed, and some newspapers deliberately sustained the confusion.

The *armées révolutionnaires* were good beasts of burden. The great terrorist proconsuls tried to clear themselves before Thermidorean opinion by heaping blame upon these subordinate instruments, although peasant opinion recognised the true culprits. For its part, the Revolutionary Government, having decided to reassure the country people by changing its policy, found it convenient to direct the passions provoked by its brutal and egalitarian war economy towards institutions of which it no longer had any need. The legend of the *armées* served the purposes of those men of delicate consciences, the leaders of the Terror, as it did the *honnêtes gens* for whom 'revolution' simply meant 'theft' and 'rape'.[83] It is not difficult to understand the sense of frustrated anger felt by these *révolutionnaires* when they were deprived of their honour, having already – in many cases – lost their liberty.

Conclusion

The balance-sheet of revolutionary action

We have been examining the work of more than 30 *armées révolutionnaires*, differing from each other in numbers, composition and, above all, in their means of action. Did an *armée* such as that of the Lot, which numbered thousands, and a small town company of some 50 or 60 men have any traits in common? Some battalions were the docile instruments of a *comité de surveillance* or a district municipality; others, though they were rare, were more autonomous, carrying out the wishes of a political clique within the *société populairé*, or those of their own leaders, sincere though impetuous revolutionaries. Among the latter, prudent men rubbed shoulders with the violent and the hotheaded; there were men who respected order and legality, obedient functionaries eager to serve whatever regime was in power, as well as highly disciplined career soldiers. But there were also some total scoundrels and a handful of sanguinary brutes.

All these forces had the qualifying term *révolutionnaire* in common; but it was a qualification devalued by the sham *armées*. The real *armées* were *révolutionnaire* by virtue of their composition, their command and their egalitarian organisation; but in their action their originality is less apparent. There was nothing original in the use of military force against domestic enemies, whether they were peasants defaulting on requisitions, deserters from the front hiding with their relatives, or religious or political heretics. Authoritarianism was already a tradition under the old monarchy, and Pierre Caron has correctly noted that Louis XIV's and Napoleon's use of garrisons did not make them revolutionaries for all that. Carlyle's association of these bizarre *armées* with the *dragonnades* and the terrible soldiers of Colonel Kirk was not a product of the literary imagination. In France, as in England, the armed forces, the 'standing armies' were designed as much to combat the enemy within as the enemy without. The Ancien Regime had had its dragoons, its mercenaries, its repressive armies. Only the face of the heretic had changed.

It is just as difficult to find a common denominator in the action of the new armies. In one place their action may have been gentle, in another violent; in one department their presence may have altered nothing in the tone of the Terror, while in the neighbouring one they may have been the chief suppliers of victims to the popular commissions. In one commune the *révolutionnaires* were sent to guard old men too ill to endure the rigours of imprisonment; in another near by, they shot the old and killed women and children with their swords.

The extortions, the brutalities committed by the detachments figure so prominently in Thermidorean pamphlets, prosecution briefs and local histories, that it is easy to fall into the simplistic overstatement of Thermidorean language, which depicted 'the whole of France [as] given over to pillage, vandalism and rapine'. Such a picture is entirely wrong. Violent operations were the exception, and taken together the incidents affected only a quarter of the entire country. This may seem an impressionistic statement, for the *révolutionnaires* operated within the Belgian and Rhine provinces, on the Atlantic coast, in the Centre, in the Lyon region, on the Spanish frontier, in a large part of Languedoc and in the areas bordering the Swiss cantons and Piedmont. However, entire departments were spared, and even in the interior of those affected most districts never experienced any large-scale egalitarian initiatives.

What were the reasons for this geographic scattering? The distribution of detachments from Ronsin's *armée* was almost exclusively dictated by the supply map for the capital. The repressive operations in Lyon, the Finistère, the Loire-Inférieure and the Maine-et-Loire were secondary, and appeared as such to the soldiers themselves, who protested against being sent to such destinations as contrary to the terms of their engagement. The distribution of the other armed forces was dictated by events which for the most part had little to do with the requirements of urban supply. The most important were the search for those who had escaped from the siege of Lyon into neighbouring departments (the Loire, Ain, Isère, Saône-et-Loire, Mont-Blanc, Haute-Loire, Puy-de-Dôme, Ardèche, Drôme); the treason of Toulon, involving repressive action along the coasts, in the Alps and in the Rhône valley; the suppression of Bordeaux Federalism (repression extending into most of the communes in the Garonne valley); the religious uprisings in the Pyrenees; and finally the counter-revolutionary troubles in the bandit country of the Aveyron and the Lozère. The operations in the Morbihan and in Nantes occurred in a war zone; those of the North and the East were in response to military supply requirements. These were the major lines of action. But the decisive element was the presence in a department or district of an energetic proconsul or a rural *enragé*. The Nièvre and the Allier were peaceful departments, and yet because of Fouché they became the major field of operations of *ultracisme*. The great repression was also one of the best schools for innovatory measures. The Commission Temporaire – veritable Sanhedrin of the Terror – sent its shocks through a whole group of departments encircling Lyon. There were certainly village egalitarians such as Contamin throughout the French countryside, but other locksmiths and shoemakers lacked the encouragement of a great repressive commission near by.

The scattering of the detachments was one of the main causes for the ineffectiveness of the tiny companies in the sector of economic and anti-religious activity. In terms of urban supply, small-scale operations could achieve little; the detachments would have needed to extend their operations over a wider area corresponding to the natural supply zones. Only one *armée*, that of the East, had any real success in this respect, for it was allowed to operate in half a dozen departments which together made up the supply zone for the huge Rhine and Moselle Armies. But all the *armées*, even the smallest, helped implement the Maximum on grain and contributed to the supply of precious metals for war needs. In anti-religious operations, the scattering of forces aggravated the dangers which the *armées révolutionnaires* had been instructed to combat; the detachments failed to close all the churches in a district, and discontent and disorder became polarised around those remaining. The piecemeal attack on Catholicism simply created many new places of pilgrimage. Finally, the dispersion of the troops in tiny companies raised serious political problems; the communal company became the instrument of popular decentralisation, and in the hands of anarchic communalism it threatened the unity of the Republic.

Révolutionnaire action was therefore dispersed, scattered, variable, and frequently communalist. The effectiveness of the *armées* suffered; but it is difficult to say whether they failed or succeeded in the missions assigned to them, since we do not know how things would have turned out if they had not been there. It is also necessary to know the real intentions of those who used them most readily. Fouché for instance referred to revolutionary defence and the war effort when addressing himself to his *commissaires*, but it is probable that he had ulterior motives and it is a fact that he used his battalions to accelerate the anti-religious measures so close to his heart. We must content ourselves with half-answers, given the reticence of those responsible, the ambiguous administrative status of these *armées*, local conditions and the numbers deployed. One *armée* which successfully supplied the market of a large town with bread had no political influence; another which contributed directly to the acceleration of repressive measures was economically ineffective. *Révolutionnaire* action varied in effectiveness, as in violence, from one region to another.

Paris and the armies on the frontiers were well served by the *armées révolutionnaires*, for they made a considerable contribution to the supply of markets and the implementation of requisitions. Where a large unit was involved, the capital, an army, a large port, a departmental *chef-lieu*, the intervention by the *armées* was relatively successful and there was a noticeable improvement in terms of *arrivages* for the markets. One has only to recall the situation in the Year III to establish a favourable comparison with the winter and spring of 1794. By that summer the situation of the urban markets had worsened appreciably, and in the case of Paris and Versailles, dramatically. This was due partly to seasonal conditions in the sale and movement of grain, but the situation was aggravated by the lack of availability of any instrument of constraint. The success of the *armées* in this context compensates for the indignation aroused in the countryside by the resort to force. In the scale of urgent necessities the supply of the towns and the armies had to be placed ahead of the interests of the peasants and their rural allies, and the interests of the town were irreconcilable with those of the country.

The Parisian *armée* was above all an instrument of the Terror: and as an instrument it was docile, controlled at all times by the repressive authorities. Its assistance perhaps facilitated the execution of the great policing and surveillance measures. But if it had never existed the Terror would have followed the same pitiless course, and the task of serving summonses would simply have fallen to the gendarmerie. It was as the executant of the Committee of General Security and its innumerable agents that the *armée* of Ronsin rendered the greatest service to revolutionary policing, particularly in matters of arrest. When it came to pure repression – *fusillades, mitraillades, noyades* – the troops of the line were more competent. As for the communal companies, most were little more than super-gendarmes in the service of the *comités de surveillance*. The Compagnie Marat was almost alone in undertaking independent repressive action and it did not hold a monopoly on atrocities. Contemporaries were particularly impressed by this aspect of the activities of the political armies, and they were depicted as suppliers of the guillotine. But the terror they spread derived less from the number of arrests made by the detachments, still less from the atrocities committed by them, than from their way of acting, violently, spectacularly, chaotically. Empty threats, however, were the very worst kind of politics.

Political life in the small communes did not lend itself easily to grand frescoes and elegant and ordered syntheses; it was dominated rather by bitter, mysterious conflicts, the causes of which escape us just as they did the *étrangers*, the soldiers and *commissaires* from the towns. The political action of the *armées révolutionnaires* defies all definition; certainly it favoured the pretensions of the *sociétés populaires*, sometimes it permitted sans-culotte minorities to seize municipal power. Above all the presence of these political soldiers accelerated the execution of great measures of social egalitarianism. As social levellers the *révolutionnaires* were unsurpassed.

The assistance given to the dechristianisers was also an important aspect of their activities. Dechristianisation was a movement at once popular, authoritarian and militaristic; but the *révolutionnaires* had no monopoly on anticlerical convictions or on iconoclastic violence. The garrison troops closed churches with as much effectiveness as the so-called 'sicaires', the hired assassins, of atheism. The latter had a more visible role, however, and they were to pay dearly for the spectacular character of their *promenades*. The members of the government in particular were persuaded that the *révolutionnaires* alone were responsible for this attempt at 'preaching philosophy with guns in their hands'.

The popular armies were not forces of rapine. But their innocence – always relative – mattered little, because of the reputation created for them from the outset. Public opinion thought of them as such; that was what mattered. Moreover, their wantonly destructive violence, the disorder of their interventions, their all-too-visible indiscipline, sealed their fate with many republicans who, while accepting the necessity of the Terror, required it to proceed in an orderly fashion.

In short, the action of the *armées révolutionnaires* was above all spectacular and short-lived. This verbal violence, external and superficial, a violence of threatening words and dramatic gestures, was a sort of cut-price Terror, more economical, perhaps more humane, than the resort to *grands moyens*. Besides, the *armées révolutionnaires* lacked such *grands moyens*. But their verbal violence was to be the downfall of the popular armies, public opinion taking them not for what they were (and in truth that did not amount to much), but for what they pretended to be: terrifying institutions, cruel, pitiless, knowing neither law, restraint, nor pity. By placing the accent on the anarchic violence of these methods, the leaders of the Revolutionary Government pulled off a political coup of the first order, convincing moderate opinion that violence was the sole preserve of these former democratic forces and their most famous political protectors. Hébertism equalled violence; it was a magic formula, all the more credible in that for years Hébert had earned his living through daily doses of such verbal violence, incitement to murder, and cries of hatred. If a *parti hébertiste* did not exist, there was nevertheless a 'club of violence', a group of *excités*, and despite their reduced effectiveness and limited action, the *armées révolution-naires* did not go unnoticed.

There were two principal reasons for their relative ineffectiveness, one external to the institution, the other central to its existence. The first lay with the government, which never gave the *armées* the necessary means to attain concrete success in any quarter. Moreover, it left their administrative status vague for so long that their provisional and temporary character was simply accentuated. Secondly, there was a fundamental contradiction between a certain military authoritarianism, dear to all convinced revo-lutionaries, and the egalitarian and civil nature of these political soldiers. The *révolutionnaires* wanted to use force against all kinds of *malveillants*, who seemed to them to be impeding the progress of the Revolution; but they were unwilling to submit to even the minimum of discipline and organisation which would have given these measures some effectiveness. These soldiers were free men, not military personnel; they could not be counted upon to carry out mundane jobs, or the kind of exhausting and dangerous tasks which were the lot of career soldiers. These were soldiers who thought, reasoned and disputed – in a word, bad soldiers. Their obedience was a political act, one of free consent. At times they could be very effective, particularly in matters which affected them directly: the execution of the Maximum and the supply of the markets. But this again involved an element of choice. Their ineffectiveness in most other areas – an ineffectiveness which was sometimes to their credit – derived once again from this, perhaps insurmountable, contradiction between the desire to ensure the democratic and popular character of this armed force, and the necessity of producing a minimum of cohesion by subjecting the soldiers to constraints and to a level of discipline which was unacceptable to a truly free man. The contradiction left only two choices: anarchy or blind obedience. The *armées révolutionnaires* showed themselves to be anarchical forces, in the best and worst senses of the word. Many of the civilian commanders, and no doubt some of the soldiers too, were true democrats, hostile to all government and established institutions, who saw these formations as the physical means of smashing the authorities and destroying the existing order. But there was also that other anarchy, made up of blind violence, disorder and sometimes cruelty. How were such opposed aims to be reconciled?

The Terror in the village was as complex as life itself. It was an affair of men; it is therefore complicated and difficult to define, and its contradictions and hidden motives are further clouded by the labels current in the revolutionary vocabulary – and they were only labels. Was the Terror ineffective because its means were insufficient? Would it have been enough to 'package' it for popular consumption? Or was it preordained to fail, however great the means, by the very fact that it was impossible to make war on the entire rural population, a few minorities excepted? We must leave these questions and rest content with conclusions which are almost entirely negative and always imprecise, avoiding the temptation to impose a false sense of unity and simplicity on a subject which has neither. I have tried to let the actors speak for themselves and to recount the train of events, which, because of their many ramifications, defy simplistic and logical interpretations. Let the reader draw his own conclusions. I have simply tried to illustrate life as it was.

BOOK THREE

The Liquidation of the Popular Armies:
Frimaire–Germinal Year II

Preamble

The law of the 14 Frimaire, altering the very structure of the Revolutionary Government, marked the main turning-point in the history of the Terror in the departments. The anarchic Terror, spontaneous, revolutionary, was replaced almost overnight by an administered Terror, under the direction of agents of the central government. As the new year 1794 opened, everything was brought to an end: the *commissaires civils* returned to the wilderness of the large towns, some to seek new employment, others under arrest, the instruments of their policy having disappeared without trace, save in the hatred and long memories of the country people. For another four months the Parisian *armée* remained the only political army in activity and the chosen target of the moderate campaign. The 'picnic in the country' had been ended, save for the Parisians who continued to 'revolutionise' in some localities. Elsewhere, there was no more 'revolutionising'. The Terror itself continued, but it was a policed Terror.

Frimaire and Germinal were the two landmarks in government policy towards the *armées révolutionnaires*. Before Frimaire the government had no precise policy on the subject. In Book Three, therefore, the focus of our attention shifts from the activities of the detachments to Paris, to the governmental Committees and to public opinion. From Frimaire onwards the history of the *armées révolutionnaires* becomes merged with the general political history of the Revolution, the attention of the various political groups focusing on the Parisian *armée*, both in Paris itself and in several large departmental towns. The Committee of Public Safety intervened for the first time in Frimaire, and in Germinal it abolished the Parisian *armée*. In the period between these two events, the *armée révolutionnaire* and its leaders were under constant scrutiny. What prompted the government to formulate – at last – such a positive and immediate policy? What was the position of the Parisian *armée* in Jacobin and Sectionary opinion during that winter and spring? To answer these questions we must alter our range of vision and look closely at government decision-making.

Once the government had finally settled its policy on the departmental and communal *armées* (doubtless as a result of the anti-religious and fiscal initiatives of some *commissaires civils* at the head of their *bandes*), it had little difficulty bringing to a close this experiment in anarchy, which had served

515

its purpose in propelling the revolutionary movement forward. The announcement of the law of 14 Frimaire was welcomed by the local authorities; but the institutions and the men directly affected also proved remarkably eager to comply with the terms. Most of the *révolutionnaires* in the departments, on the advice of the *commissaires* or their officers, proceeded to disarm themselves, and very few took up the option afforded them by the law of transferring to the line troops. There were undoubtedly a few cases of resistance, easily put down, and in certain localities the connivance of the *représentants* allowed some to get round the law. But after Nivôse, the Parisian *armée*, augmented by a 7th battalion made up of elements from the former departmental forces of the Nièvre, the Allier and the Saône-et-Loire, was the only institution remaining with a right to call itself an 'armée révolutionnaire'. However, some revolutionary battalions and companies continued their activities by divesting themselves of the proscribed title and assuming that of 'garde soldée' or 'compagnie des sans-culottes'. The imprecise and fantastic titles of the ultra-revolutionary institutions – an essential condition of their spectacular initiatives in the departments furthest away from Paris – facilitated this unfortunate transformation. But most of the departmental *armées* disappeared entirely or suffered the fate of the Légion des Montagnards and were absorbed into the troops of the line – another form of depoliticisation.

The turn-about of Frimaire was the cue for a general political reaction. The popular armies were not the only institutions affected. The entire repressive machinery was dismantled, and with the instruments of the anarchic Terror disarmed in many departments, the next stage was the pursuit of the men who had shown most energy in the employment of those means. The administrative reform and the restoration of power to central government was followed in Nivôse and Pluviôse by the first wave of arrests. It was then that the term 'ultra-révolutionnaires' began to be heard, in the North, in the West, in the South-West, in Lyon and in Moulins; and these 'ultras', *commissaires civils*, roving agents of the great commissions of justice, *commissaires* of the Ministries, 'apôtres' of the urban *sociétés*, gave way to national agents, local men, former district administrators in particular, appointed by central government and responsible to the two Committees. Centralisation was the trend; the entire Republic was put into a hierarchical strait-jacket, powers were strictly defined and there was no room for revolutionary fantasies. There was no more talk of a counter-power, of direct democracy, or of *taxes révolutionnaires*. The Committees reigned supreme, their dictates obeyed everywhere. It was enough for them to *want* to govern, to be able to do so throughout France. In the absence of government, the country had been given over to the anarchic and often impolitic ideas of local revolutionaries. From September to December they had revolutionised at will. But after December the Committees governed, and the anarchy disappeared as if by a miracle. It needed no more than a *décade*, even a few days, to turn a region which had been prey to all kinds of revolutionary extravagances into a calm, controlled district. People were still afraid, the Terror became even more ferocious and infinitely more effective, but everything was done in an orderly fashion. The anarchic and spectacular repression was condemned.

The leaders of the Parisian *armée* were not unhappy with a measure which assured the *armée* they commanded a position as élite corps of the regime and a monopoly of political force. Some even applauded the disappearance of *armées* which they considered compromising. Had not the law of 14 Frimaire ensured the Parisian *armée*, the '*armée* of the Convention', a choice place in the new system? And did not the disappearance of the other *armées* enhance its importance as the only one remaining? Certainly the more prudent and astute of the chiefs in the rue de Choiseul sought to ensure their own futures by conspicuous obedience to the government. Doubtless they hoped to escape the fate of the other popular institutions. But they were deceiving themselves, for all the agencies of the Terror were interlocked, the anarchic Terror of the autumn and winter forming part of a unified system and a particular way of thinking. The law of 14 Frimaire not only terminated the material existence of the departmental *armées*, it also represented a condemnation of the very principle of political armies and the use of force against the farmers, 'Frenchmen just like ourselves'. After Nivôse, the days of the Parisian *armée* were numbered.

The Indulgents, themselves the *pourris*, the corrupt, were the first to recognise the about-face of Frimaire, and they tried to turn it to their advantage. They did not even wait until the end of that month to launch their first offensive against the leaders of the Parisian *armée*, and against their protector, Collot-d'Herbois. With the arrest of Ronsin and Vincent the political crisis was taking shape. It was not simply an attack on individuals; the politics of repression was also at stake, and Collot rushed back to Paris to defend his men and his decisions. To the offensive mounted by the *pourris* was added that of the Lyon Jacobins who had come to Paris and captured the ear of Robespierre. The pretext for this double offensive was a letter sent from Lyon by Ronsin to the Cordeliers, in which he had boasted of the effects of the *mitraillades*. The Parisian *armée* itself was therefore put on trial as the instrument of the executions, and in Pluviôse it was already receiving a bad press in Lyon and Paris. This was the moment chosen by rival groups within the general staff to air their personal quarrels, and all Paris reverberated with their cries and mutual accusations. Just as the *armée* was being dissected by the press, its command was torn by bitter quarrels.

Ronsin's triumphant release from prison brought about a reversal of the political situation in the middle of Pluviôse. The 'outraged patriot' sought vengeance, and spoke of a 'new 2 September' and an acceleration of the repression. But in the departments the detachments of his *armée* were in difficulties with the municipalities and districts, the latter encouraged by the law of 14 Frimaire. Ronsin's arrest at the end of Frimaire had been taken as the signal for a government-approved witch-hunt against his subordinates.

In Paris the general staff were airing in public their sordid quarrels; in the departments the detachments were the butt of the now open hostility of the local authorities. The *armée* was no longer imposing, no longer an object of fear, but a simple irritant. And yet the Parisian troops continued to 'revolutionise', some of their most spectacular operations occurring in Ventôse – in several cases with the approval of the Committee of General Security and its agents. As long as the two Committees remained at odds with each other, the *armée* of Ronsin still had an important role to play in policing the departments.

In Ventôse Ronsin's verbal imprudence played into the hands of his enemies. When a general spoke of insurrection, he ran the risk of being taken literally, and this is exactly what happened. The Committees believed, or pretended to believe, in his insurrectionary intentions. For a month the general raged and one section of opinion attributed his fury to the frustrated ambition of a man whose path to power was blocked by the Convention and the Revolutionary Government. The Committees moved quickly against this blusterer who spouted forth inflammatory declarations without any sense of plan or direction. Public opinion, already marshalled by Robespierrist conformism, accepted unquestioningly the thesis of a military plot, with Ronsin, a sincere and courageous republican, consecrated as the new Cromwell, and his army the instrument of a new Pride's Purge.

Ronsin's fellow officers quickly abandoned the compromising general-in-chief in an attempt to save the *armée révolutionnaire*. In the belief that the *armée* could survive its unworthy chief as an essential cog in the system of the Terror, the general staff called the detachments to order, going even further than the Committee of Public Safety in recommending total obedience to the demands of the municipalities, and increasing their contacts with Collot, their mentor within the Government. It was a futile effort; his colleagues on the Committees had already decided on the dissolution of this political army, which, half-believing their own propaganda, they feared. But they moved cautiously, in stages, waiting until all the detachments were out of the Paris region before announcing the disbanding of the *armée*. They did not even allow the companies to return with their arms to their Sections, and the *révolutionnaires* had to undergo the bitter humiliation of being disarmed outside Paris, often by jubilant local authorities.

Calm prevailed, however, and the Parisians proved to be far more submissive than the *révolutionnaires* in the departments when the law of 14 Frimaire was announced. No doubt they were afraid of being treated as outlaws – which was the threat held out to them if they did not surrender their arms. But in their alacrity to abide by the decree, conformism was mixed with fear. The Convention had created the Parisian *armée* – 'we are your children', they proclaimed, 'you need us no longer, we will cease to exist'. The Convention had spoken; the *armée* which had belonged to it, the force which had, it was claimed, been preparing for a *coup d'état*, was scattered to the winds, and as ordinary individuals the ex-*révolutionnaires* returned, unarmed, to Paris, to prostrate themselves before the Assembly. Thereafter, oblivion, the search for employment, the return to the counter and the workshop. The popular army had been a reality. Other regimes would use armed force against the peasants, but they would keep well clear of arming the people themselves.

The *armées révolutionnaires* had been one of the most characteristic institutions of the anarchic Terror, and it was natural that they should undergo the same proscription as the *comités de surveillance* and extraordinary commissions during the Thermidorean period. The former political soldiers were hounded both in Paris and in the departments, and many suffered a second disarming in 1795. In most cases their only crime was to have belonged to a popular army. The persecution hardened the real militants, and elements from the former *armées* were to be found in every republican plot that arose during the years between 1795 and 1816.

CHAPTER 1

The Law of 14 Frimaire
and the End of the Departmental and Communal *Armées*
(Frimaire-Nivôse Year II)

I   *The Committee of Public Safety decides on a policy*
(28 Brumaire – 14 Frimaire)

The law of 14 Frimaire on the organisation of revolutionary government
came with lightning suddenness, destroying the hopes of the *sociétés
populaires* in the departments and the sans-culottes for the creation of a great
national and popular *armée révolutionnaire*. The promulgation of the law
interrupted the organisation of some 20 forces, destined in consequence
never to see the light of day. Sans-culottes, *commissaires civils*, *représentants en
mission* and their *délégués* were all taken by surprise – the Committee of
Public Safety having omitted to inform the *représentants* of its deliberations.
Only a privileged few had wind of what was being planned; for everyone
else, the proconsuls along with the mass of the populace, the *armées révolutionnaires* were fast becoming permanent fixtures of the new regime.

Had the Committee of Public Safety planned the announcement as a
surprise, fearing that any 'leaks' might give ambitious chiefs or undisciplined *commissaires civils* the time to organise resistance? Or had it acted in a
fit of anger, provoked by the anti-religious excesses of the revolutionary
forces? Was the famous law, with its condemnation of the essentials of
revolutionary politics as they had operated since the previous September,
the work of the entire Committee or only of its moderates – Carnot, Lindet,
Prieur de la Côte-d'Or, Barère – who on several occasions had publicly
displayed their hostility to the employment of special forces? What was the
attitude of Robespierre and his friends? Had the Committee of General
Security been consulted?

The fact that the Committee itself deliberately shrouded its policy
towards the departmental *armées* in mystery makes these questions all the
more difficult to answer. A certain hostility in principle had been revealed as
early as 30 September, but no one seems to have paid any attention. By 28
Brumaire, however, the Committee had already made its decision; only the
date of liquidation remained to be decided. It was undoubtedly the
advanced state of organisation of the group of *armées* in the East and the
Alps in the first two weeks of Frimaire that precipitated the decision. But
the Committee was careful not to inform more than a handful of
représentants of its intentions.

But why Frimaire? Letters from the Committee to its proconsuls show that it was the departmental *armées'* brutal implementation of the policy against Catholicism which destroyed them in its eyes. No one had condemned such action more roundly than the Robespierre brothers, and it is likely that by Frimaire Maximilien shared with his brother Augustin and with Saint-Just their belief that these special forces were prejudicial to the unity of the Republic.[1] There was no doubt a confusion of motives among the members of the Committee, but it was the excesses of dechristianisation which led Robespierre to take up the position at which Carnot, Lindet and Prieur had arrived for quite different reasons. With Collot still in Lyon, it is doubtful whether the departmental *armées* found any defenders within the Committee in the last days of Brumaire. It was Billaud-Varennes who was charged by his colleagues with drafting the law of 14 Frimaire; but there is nothing to suggest that they did not approve of the proposals contained in his draft decree of 28 Brumaire, which was to serve as the model for the final law. It was a collective decision. We still have to determine, however, why normally cautious men acted so precipitately in the first days of Frimaire. In the absence of minutes of Committee discussions, we must resort to the few insights furnished by its correspondence with the *représentants en mission*.

On 14 Brumaire, Maure, on mission in his native department, wrote from Auxerre to the Committee complaining of the impolitic zeal of a revolutionary cavalier who, on his way through Coulanges, 'forced the inhabitants to pull down the crosses'. Maure observed on this occasion that 'reforms carried through by force and terror are not as durable as those produced by instruction'. He was echoing the fears of the Committee itself. Some days later (20 Brumaire), he again complained to the Committee, this time about violent acts committed at Auxerre by a member of the Parisian *armée* (a bogus adjutant-general).[2] About the same time the Committee received the account of the affair of Vermenton, in a letter from the municipality, with accompanying observations from Maure.[3] The Committee carefully noted these letters and opened a register devoted to the misdeeds of the *armées révolutionnaires*. In the meantime, Maure, forewarned by Garnier de Troyes, became anxious about the order he had just issued for the formation of a departmental *armée* of the Yonne, and on 25 Brumaire he expressed his doubts to the Committee: 'I have written to you about the composition [of this *armée*] and submitted it for the approval of the Convention. Its silence I took as authorisation; however, Garnier, by an order which he has not shown me, has stopped me from going ahead. If this force, established through zeal, is contrary to the good of my country, speak, and it will not be assembled'.[4] Maure was inviting the Committee, in no uncertain terms, to break a silence which had perplexed many a *représentant*.[5]

The Committee needed little coaxing, and on 4 Frimaire in two letters, one to Maure, the other to Paganel, it finally defined its policy towards the departmental *armées*, announcing the forthcoming decree which would terminate their existence. Article 10 of the draft presented by Billaud on 28 Brumaire read: 'No armed force, no tax, no loan, forced or voluntary, may be raised except by decree...'.[6] The Committee ordered Maure 'to repress the ill-considered enthusiasm of the revolutionary force in trying to preach philosophy with weapons in its hands', pointing out that, 'it is through reason that the downfall of Catholicism will be brought about...'.[7] It also considered the proliferation of departmental forces as an invitation to a Federalist revival, particularly in the departments affected by the movement during the summer. 'The Committee feels obliged to point out that the revolutionary force, which is useful so long as it is under the hand and the eye of the *représentant*, can become extremely dangerous and turn against liberty when left to its own devices.... You might then see this departmental force supporting the unholy designs of the Federalists.... On your departure [from the Yonne] you will dissolve the *armée révolutionnaire* formed by the department in which you are. This measure will also be carried out by the other *représentants* in each of the departments through which they pass...'.[8] And that was not all. The Committee went on to condemn the very principle of revolutionary forces: 'The true revolutionary force is opinion; its lever is in your hands.... You have at your disposal the National Guard; you only need to purge it'. Carnot had already given similar advice to a deputation from Le Havre. And then, at the end of the letter to Maure, comes the announcement of the law of 14 Frimaire: 'You will be supported by a decree which the Convention is about to pass...'. On receipt of this letter, 7 Frimaire, Maure issued an order halting preparations for the Yonne *armée*.[9] The Committee had at last broken its silence, and on the 4th it sent a similar letter to Paganel.[10] The departmental *armées* were finally condemned.

The Committee was to find other reasons to congratulate itself over this decision in a letter of 9 Frimaire addressed to it from Caen by the *représentant* Laplanche. Though a supporter and creator of the popular *armées*, the former monk complained of the indiscipline of the detachment from the Parisian *armée* at Caen.[11] His letter reached the Committee on the 12th or 13th, by which date the Lille 'counter-revolution' was already decided. *La Sentinelle*, the Arras paper which enjoyed the confidence of Robespierre, led a campaign against the *armée révolutionnaire* of the North from the outset of its activities, while the *sociétaires* of Cambrai and Douai invoked the intentions of the Committee to oppose the formation of revolutionary companies in these towns. The *représentants*, Hentz and the detestable Florent Guiot, sent to the Nord to spy on Châles and Isoré, had their instructions from the Committee, from Robespierre in particular. Guiot wrote from Arras on 21 Frimaire, before learning of the decree: 'You instructed us to watch the movements of the *armée révolutionnaire*; we have not lost sight of this and look forward to the moment when we can dispense with this institution, which can do a hundred times more evil than good...'.[12] The counter-revolution which took place the following day (22 Frimaire) in the Lille *société populaire* was premeditated and was above all the responsibility of Robespierre.[13]

Despite the biased claims of Barère, Prieur de la Côte-d'Or, Lindet and Carnot, that they alone were responsible for the decree, it looks as if Robespierre fully shared their views on the popular armies. Saint-Just for his part sent the *révolutionnaire*, Schneider, to the scaffold, while the younger Jullien denounced the misdeeds of Le Batteux and his *armée* in the Morbihan to Robespierre. However much Saint-Just complained about the effects of this law,[14] he was just as much responsible for it as his colleagues, with the exception of Collot-d'Herbois and Jeanbon Saint-André. The law of 14 Frimaire was the outcome of a collective decision, the origins of which can be traced to Carnot's hostility in principle to armies of the interior, the unshakeable opposition of Lindet and Prieur de la Côte-d'Or to the use of force against the peasants, and above all to the examples of forced dechristianisation which ran counter to Robespierre's metaphysical ideas. As for the fears of a 'new Federalism', these were mere pretexts; it is more likely that these government men, faced with the assemblies of the *sociétés populaires* and the activities of *commissaires civils* and *délégués*, feared a threat from the left, backed by armed force. Finally, the secrecy in which they prepared the law shows their fear of disturbances by the revolutionary forces. They had convinced themselves that administrative anarchy and the multiplication of individual forces could pave the way for a military government and Caesarism.

If the attitude of the Committee of Public Safety was not formulated until the closing days of Brumaire, that of the Committee of General Security remains one of the great unknowns of the political history of the period. It is certain, however, that the departmental *armées* had more friends in this, the older of the two Committees, and Amar, Vadier, Rühl and Bayle often spoke in favour of a policy of forced dechristianisation. Bayle had even called for the raising of a revolutionary force in the Bouches-du-Rhône, and Vadier was no stranger to the famous expedition of the Ariège.[15] On 4 Frimaire, Paré, the Interior Minister, tried to enlist the support of this Committee by sending on to it the letter of Garnier de Troyes concerning the *armée* of the Yonne;[16] but there is no indication that his own prejudices against the departmental *armées* were shared. Did the Committee of General Security play as much of a part in the preparation of this law as its rival Committee? Or was it presented with a ready-made decision which it could hardly oppose? These are among the many questions which must remain unanswered until an exhaustive history is written on this mysterious, relatively unknown, but immensely powerful Committee.[17] It is probable, however, that the police Committee was unenthusiastic about the disappearance of the popular forces which it had helped to create in several departments, and which had been among the most violent instruments of a policy supported by several of its members. The Committee of General

Security compensated by using the Parisian *armée* on a number of police missions during its last four months of existence. It would be an exaggeration to speak of disagreement between the two Committees – though it was already in evidence by this date – but the preparation of the law of 14 Frimaire appears to have been the collective work of the Committee of Public Safety, and of it alone.

II   *The law of 14 Frimaire and the condemnation of the popular institutions*

Article 18, Section III (Competence of the established authorities) read: 'Every *armée révolutionnaire* other than that established by the Convention, and common to the whole Republic, is disbanded by the present decree and it is required of all citizens belonging to these military institutions to disperse within 24 hours of the publication of this decree, on pain of being regarded as outlaws, and treated as such'. Article 19 of the same Section re-established the subordination of military power to the civil authorities, in other words to the districts and municipalities: 'It is expressly forbidden to any armed force, whatever its institution or denomination, and to all those in command, to undertake acts which belong exclusively to the regular civil authorities, and this order will be executed according to the procedures set out in the decrees'. Article 20, adopting the terms of the order of 28 Brumaire, dealt with the possibility of raising new revolutionary forces in the future, as well as the whole area of 'revolutionary fiscality' which had produced some of the most characteristic initiatives of the popular armies during their short life-span: 'No armed force, no tax, no loan, forced or voluntary, may be raised except by decree. Revolutionary *taxes* levied by the representatives of the people cannot be collected without the approval of the Convention, unless in enemy or rebel territory'.

All the *armées révolutionnaires*, apart from that of Paris, were to be dissolved, the '*taxes* on the rich' abandoned, and the powers of the *représentants en mission* seriously curtailed. But the law also attacked all those institutions which had allowed the revolutionary movement to take off in the departments in the face of opposition from the local authorities. Article 12 forbade delegation of powers by the *représentants du peuple*; article 13 put the agents of the Executive Council under the control of the Committee of Public Safety, and article 14 deprived those agents of all autonomy of action by subordinating them to the *représentants*. Article 15 was designed to prevent 'invasions' of neighbouring departments by agents from the extraordinary Commissions, with the itinerant *commissaires* and *délégués* from the Commission Temporaire of Lyon particularly in mind. Article 16 sought to deprive the *sociétés populaires* of any possibility of setting themselves up as a sovereign authority by holding general assemblies and reunions, and article 17 also covered the special commissions, the departmental *comités* and the military commissions – the institutions with 'tendencies towards Federalism'. The Committee wanted to prevent gatherings such as those of

Valence, Avignon and Marseille, which had given rise to the Légion des Montagnards, to deprive the *sociétés populaires* of all possibility of concerted action and to reduce them to the level of 'yes men' in the service of official propaganda. Henceforth, policing would be the exclusive preserve of the *comités de surveillance*, which in turn would be under the strict supervision of the Committee of General Security, the municipalities and the districts.

Nothing had been overlooked in the dismantling of the entire revolutionary network. The *armées révolutionnaires* were condemned, the 'hommes de liaison' – *délégués* of the *représentants*, *commissaires* from the special commissions, *commissaires civils* – deprived of every means of making their action effective. The *sociétés populaires* saw themselves reduced to the level of simple auxiliaries of the *comités de surveillance*. They could send insipid congratulatory addresses to Robespierre, raise subscriptions for clothing the volunteers or equipping the 'Jacobin cavaliers', or watch over the production of saltpetre; but were they to try to discuss problems of government, or to broach 'dangerous' subjects such as subsistences, they would be quickly put in their place. Everything was subordinated to the territorial unity of the district, in other words to authorities favouring the interests of the country people, their electors. The armed force could no longer take any initiative, make any arrest or domiciliary visit, without the authorisation of the established authorities. The Parisian *armée* had been given a stay of execution, but it was deprived of all opportunities for autonomous action against religion. The real essence of the law did not become apparent until 18 Frimaire, with the publication of the decree on the freedom of religion, article 1 of which forbade 'all violence or threats contrary to the freedom of religion'. The law of 14 Frimaire prepared the way for that of the 18th, which sought to prevent any return to a policy of forced dechristianisation, and both affirmed the Supreme Being and the official return to Catholicism.

Saint-Just was quite right when he declared that the law of 14 Frimaire was the total opposite of *révolutionnaire*. It was in effect the negation of revolutionary action and held up to condemnation what the sans-culottes meant by the words 'to revolutionise'. If people continued none the less 'to revolutionise' it was because the law took some time to reach village halls, and local zealots still had several weeks in which to repress *égoïstes*, *fanatiques* and the *tièdes*, to raise more *taxes révolutionnaires* and to conduct a frontal attack on religion at the time of the great feast of Christmas (5 Nivôse).

The Committee of Public Safety had thus separated itself from the ultra-revolutionary movement in the departments, by taking a stand against all the major initiatives of the men from the towns and the militants of the urban *sociétés populaires*. The law was masterly; it proscribed all 'parallel hierarchies', regulated the 'hommes de liaison' and disavowed the excessive action of certain *représentants*: Javogues, Châles, Carrier, Taillefer (recalled to Paris on 25 Brumaire), and Dartigoëyte, to mention only the most prominent.

The political nature of the law was demonstrated more crudely still, in the days following its promulgation throughout the whole of France, by the proscription of the militant personnel of the urban *sociétés*. It also heralded social appeasement in its abandonment of the economic programme of the 'hommes de liaison', that egalitarian war economy which consisted of making the rich pay for the war in the interior. The farmers and the rich merchants no longer had anything to fear. The *armées*, and the *commissaires* who had led them, were alike condemned.

The principle of revolutionary legality was abandoned for that of juridical legality; extraordinary tribunals gave way to the civil and criminal tribunals of the department and the district, and revolutionary justice – popular justice – intended above all to protect the regime and to punish its many enemies, was replaced by traditional justice based on the defence of property. One of the consequences of the publication of the law was to set in motion procedures against the detachments and their leaders for acts of pillage and dilapidation, and preparations for these trials began as early as Nivôse.

In short, the law of 14 Frimaire established the dictatorship of the Committee of Public Safety by seeking to compromise, under the all-encompassing term *fédéralisme*, the great administrative initiatives which had flared through the entire countryside since September and brought the urbanised Parisian Revolution into the furthest corners of the nation. Revolutionary vigilance and the will to punish would henceforth be administrative matters, reserved to professionals, to the national agents and to the *comités de surveillance*, and under strict supervision from the agents of the two Committees.

The dissolution of the departmental and communal *armées* was thus part of a whole series of measures launched against all the revolutionary institutions and all the 'hommes de liaison'. The law, in fact, was an entire programme. Contemporaries were not mistaken about the direction in which the Committee of Public Safety wanted government policy to move; district administrators, farmers and men of order were jubilant. Energetic Montagnards like Reynaud, Javogues, Châles, Taillefer and Baudot expressed their fears about a return to *modérantisme*, following publication of the decree, but saw themselves henceforth deprived of the means of checking it.[18] The law of 14 Frimaire undoubtedly increased central control considerably, but we must also examine the way in which this accession of power was used by the Committee and its agents: certainly not to implement the economic measures of September, but to reassure property owners and believers, to put an end to the revolutionary anarchy of the September–Frimaire period, and to give France a centralised administrative framework.

III   *The disbanding in the departments*

The Committee had feared resistance on the part of the military leaders or the *révolutionnaires*, under orders to disband, deliver up their arms to the civil authorities or the *commissaires des guerres*, and either return to their homes or be incorporated into the armies of the Republic; but events were to show the groundlessness of such fears. Almost everywhere the process was carried out quickly and in an orderly fashion. A few *commissaires civils*, officers, and ordinary soldiers greeted news of the law with incredulity, so convinced were they of the good will of the Committees towards them. Were they not the appointed defenders of the regime? And who would benefit from the disappearance of an instrument of the Terror which struck fear into *les malveillants*? On first hearing of the law, the officers and soldiers in some areas refused to credit a measure which was greeted with such obvious delight by the enemies of the Revolution. It was, they said to reassure themselves, a falsehood spread by all who wanted to do harm to revolutionary action and its executants. Throughout their existence the *armées révolutionnaires* had been the objects of similar false reports: in the Lot the massacre of the *révolutionnaires* had been announced; in the Centre, the volunteers had been 'worked upon' by claims that the *armées* were destined to fight at Toulon or sail for England; and everywhere real volunteers were confused with false *armées révolutionnaires*. This, they felt, was just another such report, and from the joyous expressions on the faces of the *honnêtes gens*, the *commissaires civils* were convinced that they were once again victims of rumours spread by the country people.

But evidence to the contrary soon arrived, as the rumour was succeeded by the official statement in the *Bulletin de la Convention* and the papers from the capital. Generally the local authorities had to take no special measures to ensure disarmament; the soldiers relinquished their arms voluntarily, after proclaiming their respect for the Convention and their submission to the laws – there was no sign of any disposition to resist. Some chiefs grumbled quietly. As for the men, if they were unhappy at losing such well-paid employment, or disappointed at the Committee's apparent lack of confidence in them, they nevertheless submitted without voicing their innermost thoughts.

If a *décade*, sometimes two, went by before the measures of disarmament were fully implemented, the reason lay in the time it took for the law to reach every town, and indeed for it to be fully understood by the local authorities.[19] Some of the latter hesitated to implement it before checking on its precise meaning, or taking the precaution of writing to the higher authorities and the *représentants* to query what precisely was meant by 'revolutionary armed forces'. In the Midi in particular, such a variety of titles had been used that it was difficult to know one way or the other, while the case of the *comité de surveillance* of the village near Lyon which confused the Commission Temporaire in Lyon with the Committee of General Security in Paris, was not unique. The law of 14 Frimaire, a true *loi du gouvernement*, posed many problems in interpretation. There is nothing surprising about the need of the small-town municipalities and *comités* to seek advice. The delays in execution were therefore caused by slowness of communication, ignorance among the local authorities, and the very imprecision of a law which had turned departmental administration upside-down, rather than any bad faith among those directly affected by its terms.

The first disbandment orders were issued on 20 and 21 Frimaire: one to an *armée* near Paris, the other to that from Redon, on mission in the Morbihan, to which an agent from the Committee of Public Safety brought the dispatches from the capital. A dozen other orders followed in the closing days of Frimaire. In the South-West the process of disbandment was spread over 1–15 Nivôse, the Clamecy company was not dismantled until the end of the month, and that of Dax not till the end of Pluviôse. The Basses-Alpes companies were still active throughout Nivôse, but they had changed their name, if not their character. The battalions of the Nièvre, the Allier, the Loire and the Saône-et-Loire (Mâcon company) received preferential treatment, certain elements being attached to the Parisian *armée* as its 7th battalion, with the result that the Moulins soldiers, having been disbanded at their home base, then found themselves recalled to the revolutionary standard to rejoin the garrison in Lyon. The time lapse between the date of the decree and its implementation, traced in the Chronological Table of Orders for Disbandment (see the References, p. 735)[20], is explained by the fact that the revolutionary forces were particularly numerous in the regions furthest removed from Paris: the South-West, the South-East and in the relatively inaccessible Alpine departments and the Massif Central.

The list of orders for disbandment is incomplete. We have no precise information as to the dates and conditions of the disbanding of several companies in the southern departments. The registers of the *comités* and *sociétés populaires*, so voluble on the formation of these forces, are silent on their disappearance, and one is reduced at times to pure conjecture. In general, there is no further mention of their activities after a particular date; the silence is total. Thus in the Basses-Alpes, the numerous companies in the department disappear from the registers after the second *décade* of Nivôse. Were they disbanded? Nothing could be less certain. It seems rather that in certain Basses-Alpes towns, they continued under different names, following Javogues's method in the Loire. In Digne, for example, the 'compagnie révolutionnaire' was still making domiciliary visits on 6 Nivôse; but on the 9th we have the first mention of a 'compagnie des sans-culottes de cette ville' carrying out the same duties.[21] The commander of the company underwent a similar metamorphosis, from 'commandant de la compagnie révolutionnaire' (6 Nivôse) to 'commandant de la compagnie des sans-culottes' (9 Nivôse), and finishing up with the more banal title of 'commandant chargé de la garde des détenus' (22 Nivôse). Neither the man nor the function had changed, only the title. In the Hautes-Alpes it is probable that the law was circumvented in the same manner, while the various paid companies of the Bouches-du-Rhône seem to have remained active until Pluviôse.[22]

With these exceptions, and the very many companies whose fate is unknown, the law was implemented elsewhere before the end of Nivôse.

The delay separating the publication of the decree and its execution, particularly in the South-West, allowed several detachments to continue 'revolutionising' until Christmas and into the New Year. The Toulouse *armée* for example was still throwing its weight around and living it up in the countryside of the Haute-Garonne during the first half of Nivôse. But around the 15th all the detachments were assembled at Toulouse, some were disarmed, others were incorporated into the conscripted troops and sent to Perpignan to rejoin the Army of the Pyrénées-Orientales.[23] If there was a certain wavering, some hesitation on the part of the officers and soldiers and local authorities, the reason was their uncertainty about how to interpret the decree. Thus the companies of Montauban, Agen, and Villeneuve-sur-Lot wondered if they were really revolutionary forces; perhaps they were not, but in order to accede to the wishes of the Convention, and to avoid being treated as bandits outside the law, they preferred to comply with the decree and proceeded to disarm themselves.

The actual process of disbanding was entrusted to the *comités de surveillance* and the local authorities, with assistance, if required, from the garrison commanders, the *commissaires des guerres* and the garrison troops. But in general the established authorities managed without military help, such was the submissiveness of the former *révolutionnaires* to the decrees of the Convention. In Toulouse it was the district which supervised the operation. As for the *représentants*, their role was confined to that of advising the authorities on the terms of the law, and issuing the orders which were then implemented by the municipalities, the *comités* and the districts.

IV   *Attitude of the* représentants, *the* commissaires civils *and the military leaders*

For the former *révolutionnaires*, the chief concern was to prove their submissiveness to the Convention. Great was the anxiety of the officers and men of the Loire *armée*, torn between their desire to conform with the decree – for had their disbandment not been proclaimed to the roll of the drum at Roanne? – and their fear of displeasing the terrible Javogues, who had ordered them to remain under arms. Whom should they obey? In their perplexity, these cautious soldiers wrote to the Committee of Public Safety through the intermediary of the district. Soldiers capable of a *coup d'état*, or of fostering the personal ambitions of their chiefs, would not have acted in this way.

So much for the visible reaction of these *révolutionnaires*. But what did they really think of a decree which restored them to the mediocre obscurity of civilian life after several weeks of political glory? 'The disbandment was carried out amidst the greatest calm and the soldiers of this *armée* seemed to want it as much as the people themselves', wrote Hentz and Guiot to the Committee after the dissolution of the *armée révolutionnaire* of the North. Boisset, on the other hand, told of the discontent of the former members of the revolutionary battalion of the Hérault, thus deprived of their daily wage of 2 livres.[24] The two accounts were not entirely contradictory: many soldiers were happy to return to civilian life, their businesses threatened by an extended absence. But those who had nothing to return to lamented the loss of a congenial diversion and the high pay of privileged service. Most of all their vanity was hurt – the most important element in the performance of these part-time soldiers. Boisset was right in his observations.

The attitude of the *représentants* varied according to their political convictions and their temperament. That of Boisset was characteristic of the weather-vanes – of which, unfortunately, there were many – who followed the prevailing winds and were anxious to fulfil the desires of the Committee. Having been enthusiastic supporters of the use of force, they suddenly rediscovered the merits of persuasion. But the true Montagnards recognised at once the real essence of the decree: the condemnation of all revolutionary methods. Javogues and Fouché were astute enough to find in the terms of the decree itself – the article relative to areas in a state of rebellion[25] – the means of retaining the instruments of constraint they considered necessary for the pursuit of an energetic policy against farmers and Catholics. Whereas Prost chose this occasion to request the dispatch of a detachment into the Jura, Reynaud wrote that, as a result of the law, all his 'measures carried through in good faith were wiped away'. Even Boisset, the future *massacreur* of the Midi, went so far as to write: 'This battalion has saved Montpellier, its disbandment will cause the utmost harm...'.[26] Lacoste and the energetic Baudot – whom the Dantonist historian Hamel described as 'the archetypal Hébertist' – wrote of the Rhine *armée* that 'the law on the organisation of the revolutionary government is obstructing all our operations.... These obstacles are largely due to the removal of the revolutionary *commissaires*. Gaubert [*sic*] will inform you of the inertia in all our affairs since the arrival of this decree...'.[27] The Montagnard deputies complained of their powerlessness in the face of the ill will and immobilism of the established authorities. Deprived of *délégués*, *commissaires civils*, extraordinary commissions and revolutionary forces, they were left without weapons to combat the collusion of the district administrators with the farmers. Châles recalled with good reason at the beginning of Pluviôse that 'each time we tried to implement repressive or revolutionary laws, the batteries of *égoïsme* and aristocracy were trained on us'.[28] One can, in effect, gauge the 'patriotism' of a *Conventionnel* according to the way in which he greeted the law of 14 Frimaire.

In contrast to these complaints from Montagnards such as Javogues, Baudot, Châles and Reynaud, were the cries of satisfaction from moderate deputies, *pourris*, reactionaries and Robespierrists. For Hentz and Guiot the decree represented a personal victory over Châles, and for the dubious Gouly, the disavowal of the measures adopted by Javogues; the dark-skinned Creole returned to Bourg amidst cries of gratitude from suspects and aristocrats.[29] It was a triumph for Fabre d'Eglantine, who, a week later, extracted a decree from the Convention placing Ronsin and Vincent under arrest, along with the former *commissaires civils* of the *armée révolutionnaire* in the Haute-Garonne; also for Bourdon de l'Oise, Legendre, Lecointre, Delacroix, and Louchet, who had never ceased their attacks on the *armées révolutionnaires*, and who now profited from a favourable political atmosphere to wage a campaign against the command of the only surviving political force. Within the Convention the decree had the enthusiastic support of the *pourris* and the future Thermidoreans; while in the departments the Montagnard *Conventionnels*, future martyrs of Prairial, expressed their anxiety at the sudden upsurge of rural *égoïsme* and the recrudescence of Catholicism. The same alignment of supporters and opponents of the *armées révolutionnaires* would appear again in the autumn debate.[30]

The reaction of certain *commissaires*, on receipt of the decree, was even more violent than that of Javogues and Baudot; for if the *représentants* were being attacked in their powers as proconsuls, the *commissaires* were attacked on a personal level, since the new law, by terminating their command, terminated their positions also. When Le Batteux arrived in Lorient at the head of his *armée*, and was told by the *société* of the promulgation of the decree, his fury was as great as his incredulity. A year later, at Carrier's trial, the younger Jullien stated: 'Mouquet was arrested and slapped in the face by Le Batteux for having said that a decree had suppressed the *armées révolutionnaires*'. For Le Batteux this could only have been a false rumour spread by *malveillants*: 'I was told that he [Mouquet] had spoken against the *armée révolutionnaire*', he later explained to the court.[31] The former Redon postmaster, lately promoted to the important position of *commissaire civil* and right-hand man of the *représentant* at Nantes, was politically naïve; he could not believe that central government had abandoned these chosen instruments of the Terror and left the men who had shouldered such responsibilities to the anger of the country and the mercy of the districts. Le Batteux in particular had blood on his hands after shooting the people coming out of mass; the disbanding of his *armée* and termination of his mission exposed him to the possibility of criminal proceedings. His anger was the measure of his fear.

Adhémar, commander of the detachment of the Lille *armée* in Cambrai, also reacted to the first rumours of the decree with incredulity. On 21 Frimaire he wrote to his chief: 'I am still having to combat the most unfavourable impressions which the *malveillants* continue to spread about us'. But this career soldier showed himself to be a good deal more shrewd than Le Batteux by adding: 'I have already overcome these by observing to those who have spoken to me [of the dissolution] that when that happened we would submit readily, since it would undoubtedly have been ordered in the interests of the Republic...'.[32] There were some protests and much dismay among the members of the Toulouse command at the sudden termination of their proconsulates, and many were anxious, with good reason, about their own futures.[33] But incidents such as that at Lorient were rare; the public temper was considerably roused against these political soldiers and still more against their chiefs – Jullien was not the only one to make a distinction in the last days of Frimaire between the soldiers, 'patriots', 'good sans-culottes', and the leaders, 'men of ambition', 'ultra-revolutionaries' – and the government's view that these individual armies were a danger to the regime was widely espoused. Nearly all the military chiefs, however, and many of the *commissaires*, reacted with the docility of Baldy, second in command of the Allier *armée*, of Gobert and Delteil, *commissaires* with the *armée* of the East. The decree was undoubtedly a rude awakening for all the *commissaires*, particularly the *civils*; but many continued to enjoy the favour of the *représentants*, who kept them in their entourage[34] or had them re-deployed in normal administrative positions, in judicial posts, or more often in the many branches of military supply. But for some the disbanding of the departmental *armées* unleashed an offensive from the moderates and opened a period of persecution which was to continue until the great turning-point of Ventôse–Germinal. From the end of Frimaire, a campaign was mounted to discredit the most energetic Montagnards, by attacking them through their *délégués* and their confidants. The attacks had common characteristics, suggesting a full-scale campaign rather than a series of isolated incidents unconnected with each other.

V *The initial political reaction in the departments and the arrest of the 'hommes de liaison' (21 Frimaire–14 Ventôse)*

The disbanding of the departmental *armées* was but one in a whole series of measures against the revolutionary institutions and the largely Cordelier personnel of the 'hommes de liaison'. The political significance of the about-turn in Frimaire emerges from the number of arrests in the different regions which removed from the *sociétés populaires* and from active revolutionary life the most zealous *sociétaires*. This organised and calculated repression took the form in some towns of a veritable counter-revolution, which prefigured the crisis of Ventôse–Germinal. In some towns the political reversals assumed national importance because of direct involvement by the Committee of Public Safety. This was the case in Lille, Lorient, Toulouse, in the Loire, Ariège, Aveyron, Nièvre (at Clamecy), Bas-Rhin, Haute-Saône and the Jura. In Lille and Vannes the intervention of the Committee came directly, through the agents and confidants of the Robespierrist clan. Elsewhere it was a case of the *représentants* or the local authorities taking advantage of the insight into government intentions provided by the 14 Frimaire decree, to attack directly the 'hommes de liaison' and *délégués*, and through the latter the Montagnards in the departments. This campaign was the revenge of the country people on the agents of the economic policy and the forced dechristianisation of the winter.

The most important operation of the campaign was that of Lille. This mini-counter-revolution started on 22 Frimaire, the day on which Florent Guiot and Hentz presented themselves, incognito, to the *société révolutionnaire*. The following day the disbandment process commenced at Lille, as at Douai and Cambrai. Within the *société* the 'coup d'état' effected by the two *représentants*, in close contact with Le Bon and Robespierre, re-established a moderate majority of notables and merchants in place of the group which had run the *société* since October, and which was made up of some sans-culottes from the town and soldiers of the garrison, mostly Parisian *sectionnaires* from the Panthéon-Français Section, Cordeliers and friends of Vincent and Ronsin.[35] The coup was the product of mature planning, for the very day after the pronunciamento of Hentz and Florent Guiot, a printed pamphlet appeared in Lille which was a tissue of lies against Dufresse, against the garrison command and against the sans-culottes in the *société*. Its author was the *commissaire des guerres* in Lille, Denis Bourdon, brother of Léonard Bourdon.[36] The same day (the 23rd), Lavalette, Dufresse, Nivet, Target, some of the other garrison officers and a small group of Lille sans-culottes – members of the administrative council of the *armée révolutionnaire*, notables, municipal officers and members of the committee of the *société* – were arrested on orders from the two *représentants* and conducted to the citadel where they were kept in secret until 6 Nivôse.[37]

From 23 Frimaire denunciations flowed, not only against Dufresse and the leaders of the popular party, but also against Châles, whom they dared not arrest: they had to be content with denouncing him to the Committee and showering him with every conceivable slander. They even went as far as accusing him of cowardice and questioning his revolutionary patriotism by stressing his former position as canon at the cathedral of Chartres. Through Châles, as through the leaders of 'his' *armée*, the *représentants* and the moderates of Lille sought to get at the dechristianisers and the men who were not afraid to apply the Maximum. In the first days of Nivôse, when the *société*, purged of its popular elements, was able to devote itself entirely to the work of denunciation, the words which recur most often are 'ultra-revolutionaries', 'dilapidators', 'atheists' and 'dictators' – they even went so far as to accuse poor Dufresse, the play-actor general, of having sought to establish a 'military dictatorship' at Lille, an accusation which would be used against the Hébertists in Ventôse–Germinal. For the Committee of Public Safety, which had sent Hentz and Florent Guiot to Lille to destroy Châles, the Lille purge was a trial run for the attack on the Hébertists.

In Lille itself the purge had important consequences. Thereafter the rich merchants and manufacturers had nothing to fear, either from the *petit peuple* or the garrison, alike expelled from positions of command in the *société*, the *comité révolutionnaire* and the municipality, all of which experienced purges in the first half of Nivôse.[38] The victims of the proscription were to be transferred to Paris after Thermidor, and some were not released until Vendémiaire Year IV.[39] Others gained their freedom at the fall of

Robespierre, the person principally responsible for the coup of Nivôse. It was not a simple case of settling scores, nor of the proscription of a few fanatics, but of the systematic repression of a group identified with the *armée révolutionnaire* and with the Lille *société* – some of the victims were accused of having 'acted on behalf of the *armée révolutionnaire*'.[40] In other words, following the publication of the law of 14 Frimaire, not only was the *armée* itself dissolved, but the very fact of having been involved with it or defended it became a cause for suspicion in the Lille of Frimaire Year II. This tactic of proscribing an entire institution was a foretaste of the tactics of the Year III, when certain categories of persons were persecuted for having belonged to the most characteristic institutions of the terrorist period. Politically, therefore, the Lille affair represented not simply the triumph of reaction, the expulsion of popular elements from positions of authority and the condemnation of dechristianisers, it also exposed everyone who had been involved in any way with the *armée révolutionnaire* of the North – victim of a systematic campaign of denigration – to the accusation of 'exagération'.

The Morbihan affair also opened with the condemnation of the 'ultra-revolutionaries' in an effort to reassure the local authorities, the Catholics and the propertied. Le Batteux's order to shoot those villagers at Sunday worship who had been accused of promoting 'fanatical' disturbances, was what was most held against him. But it was on Carrier's recommendation to adopt the greatest severity that Le Batteux had acted, and the affair resolved itself into a conflict between the two *représentants* operating in the same region, the moderate Tréhouard and the energetic Carrier. Tréhouard had Le Batteux arrested on 26 Frimaire. Carrier immediately issued an angry counter-order for his release and recall to Nantes, near himself. As at Lille, it was the *représentant*, Carrier, and dechristianisation that critics wanted to get at through the persons and practices of Le Batteux, Avril and their *armée*. But this time proscription was confined to the leaders; the soldiers, their instruments, were sent back to Redon, with a brevet of patriotism.

In Bordeaux also the disbandment of the battalion coincided with a moderate offensive against the *exagérés*. Things were not quite on the same scale here as in Lille and Vannes, but the political consequences of the application of the decree were no less evident. On 30 Frimaire the *comité de surveillance* of Bordeaux ordered the arrest of one of the Parisian soldiers – the *bêtes noires* here, as at Lille, of the local authorities. This was Augé, adjutant-general, friend and correspondent of Vincent, Sijas, the War Ministry and the Cordeliers. He was accused of having 'tried to sow division between the different battalions making up the *armée révolution-naire*' – in other words, he had defended the revolutionary troops when they were attacked by those of the garrison; of having 'composed and sung songs against the representatives of the people'; of having 'openly preached atheism in a manner capable of arousing the people'; and finally of having 'constantly sought to intrigue' during his stays in La Teste, La Réole, Royan and Bordeaux.[41] The 'crimes' attributed to Augé, who liked to proclaim himself 'the Ronsin of the West', were the same as those the ultra-revolutionaries were being accused of elsewhere in this period: atheistical preaching, supported by force and with counter-revolutionary intentions, and most of all the attempt 'to bring the national representation into disrepute'. Like Vauquoy, Viton and Baby, Augé was accused of having spoken ill of the *représentants* – but only of the moderate *représentants*, and no one accused Denis Bourdon of such a crime when he attacked Châles. The accusations made against Augé, the friend of Vincent, prepared the way for the trial of the Hébertists, and when news of the arrest of the Cordeliers arrived in Bordeaux, the national club decided to denounce Augé – still in detention – to the Committee of General Security.[42]

In the Ariège, the announcement of the decree raised the hopes of the clerical faction of Saint-Girons, which took advantage of the occasion to launch an offensive in the grand manner, sending letters to the Committee of Public Safety, the Convention and the local *représentants*, against the revolutionary battalion of Pamiers, and against the men who had brought it, along with a Toulouse detachment, into the region: Allard, Baby, Picot-Belloc, and behind them, the Vadiers, father and son. This manœuvre was entirely successful, and on 27 Frimaire, Fabre d'Eglantine extracted from the Convention an indictment against Allard and Picot-Belloc. On 6 Nivôse both requested a hearing from the Committee of General Security. Picot was released towards the end of the month, in compliance with an order from Chaudron-Rousseau, a supporter of the departmental *armées*; but he was arrested once more in Germinal, when the 'conspiracy' was uncovered.[43]

If the arrest of Viton in Nivôse cannot be ascribed to political motives,[44] that of Vauquoy was certainly part of the general attack on revolutionary politics. Vauquoy was first arrested in Nivôse; but the preparation of a case against him did not begin until after the Hébertist affair, which was interpreted as a favourable omen by the authorities of the La Tour-du-Pin district. We will return to this affair in the context of the disbandment of the Parisian *armée*.

In the East two cases were directly connected with this overall offensive. In the Marne, during a mission to Epernay, where he had been sent by the parent *société* of Châlons, Villers, *commissaire civil* of the *armée révolutionnaire*, was arrested by the *comité de surveillance*, on orders from the *représentant* Massieu, around 2 Nivôse. He had distinguished himself the previous week by a major dechristianising offensive, and once again the date shows that the decree had something to do with his arrest – though in this case Villers could not be held because of pressure from the Châlons *société*.[45]

Troyes at this time was the scene of a real political crisis. Invoking the law of 14 Frimaire, the Sections of the town, followed by the municipality, mounted a general attack against the battalion from the Montagne Section that was stationed in the town and regarded as an *armée révolutionnaire*; against the *commissaire civil*, Alexandre Rousselin, who, with the Troyes *commissaires*, had used this *armée* to suppress religious disturbances which had erupted in the Pays d'Othe; and finally against the sans-culotte mayor of the town, the shoemaker, Gachet, whipping boy for all the *honnêtes gens* of Troyes. The operation opened on 1 Nivôse with an attack by the 6th Section on Rousselin.[46] On the 2nd, other Sections, with the General Council, joined the 6th in demanding the removal of the Bataillon de la Montagne[47] – a demand which was renewed, with as little success, on the 7th.[48] The issue at stake was the control of the armed force. Thanks to the presence of the Bataillon de la Montagne, which was entirely devoted to Rousselin, and to the compliance of Gachet, the National Guard was powerless. The Sections protested against this dictatorship and pretended to see it as the precursor of a violent coup. The Sections were not unanimous, however, and some refused to take part in the offensive. But were these Sections sans-culotte? Certainly it was the rich Sections which demanded the head of the mayor and the removal of his protectors, Rousselin and the battalion – the law of 14 Frimaire providing the required excuse.

The plan of campaign was simple; it consisted of proving that the battalion was in reality an *armée révolutionnaire*. It was still under arms on 1 Nivôse, when the opposition proclaimed an infraction of the law and demanded its disbandment. The commander of the battalion was adamant – it was his departure they really wanted, for then the only remaining force, the National Guard, would be in their control – and in the face of firmness on the part of the battalion and the defection of certain Sections, including the 8th, the manœuvre was cut short. In Rousselin, the moderates of Troyes were up against no mean opponent; he was no ordinary Ministry *commissaire*, but a *commissaire* of the Committee of Public Safety, like Marcellin and Paillardelle. No, his turn came only in Prairial, when he was accused of surrounding himself with a praetorian guard.[49] As for the battalion, it remained in Troyes for the whole of Pluviôse and in Ventôse was in action in the district of Ervy.[50] The mayor, Gachet, was removed and arrested at the same time as Rousselin; but he still had supporters in the town and in Messidor the authorities were again complaining of Hébertist intrigue.[51]

It was, then, a typical moderate offensive triggered off by the announcement of the law. The date of the first Sectionary demonstrations leaves us in no doubt about this, particularly when the steps taken by the Sections on 30 Frimaire and 1 Nivôse followed immediately upon the repressive 'promenade' of the *commissaires civils* and the *armée révolutionnaire* to the Ervy district on the 25, 26 and 27 Frimaire.[52]

There were other victims of a reaction which, in certain departments, extended from the end of Frimaire right through to Pluviôse and Ventôse. In the Loire, Javogues may have managed to keep his *armée révolutionnaire* in being, but his two *délégués*, Jean-Marie Lapalus and the adjutant-general

Duret – incorrectly described on the occasion as 'commander-in-chief of the *armée révolutionnaire* of the Loire'[53] – fell victim to his enemies, and like Vauquoy, paid with their lives for their revolutionary zeal and violence, which the farmers of Le Forez termed pillage and rape. They were victims of the hatred inspired in Couthon and the Loire moderates by their hotheaded master. It is significant that the campaign against them was mounted by the moderate *société* of Roanne, while that of Charlieu, far from following its example, compromised itself by coming to the assistance of Lapalus, whom it considered to have been a victim of intrigue. To remove the stigma attaching to this *société*, which had been a leader in the original campaign for the formation of *armées révolutionnaires*, an internal revolution was arranged to rid it of Javogues's supporters, leaving the field free for the moderates, most of whom had suffered personally at the hands of Lapalus.[54]

Lapalus was an agent of the Committee of General Security, but this time the police Committee could do nothing to save its subordinate from the fury of the moderates. However, when a Parisian Section tried, on orders from the police authorities, to arrest two members of the Clamecy *comité de surveillance*, on an official mission in Paris under orders from the Committee of General Security, the Committee bared its teeth and had the two men liberated, after a stiff rebuke to the Halle-au-Bled *comité* and the person standing in for Fouquier-Tinville. This time the manœuvre of the moderates, supported by the *Conventionnel* Lefiot, proved abortive: the Committee of General Security felt itself under attack because Tenaille and Pilavoine had been acting under its orders. From then on, however, the two Committees were directly affected by the reaction, particularly the police Committee whose agents in the departments were among those caught up in the wave of proscription. The Clamecy affair, which occurred at the end of Pluviôse, was another product of the reaction to the policy of forced dechristianisation, for Pilavoine and Tenaille had been associated with the national agent of the Clamecy district in hunting down the *fanatiques* of their arrondissement, with the assistance of the *armée révolutionnaire* which they had created.[55]

Finally, on 14 Ventôse, only twelve days away from the arrest of the Hébertists, the political reaction manifested itself in the Vaucluse with the arrest, in the middle of one of its sessions, of three members of the Avignon *société populaire* known to be supporters of terrorist measures. A fourth, and undoubtedly the most important, included in the order – Barjavel, public prosecutor of the department – had been warned by friends, and escaped persecution by the *représentant*, whom he had denounced for favouring the release of Federalists, of whom there were many in this ultra-royalist department. An attack on Barjavel was a frontal assault on the Vaucluse *sociétés*, which lost no time in rounding on their oppressors and mounting a campaign on Barjavel's behalf.[56] In the middle of this outburst news arrived of the fall of the Hébertists, and the occasion was exploited by Rovère retrospectively to label the public prosecutor and his supporters as Hébertists. Thanks to the intervention of Maignet, however, Barjavel was released in Germinal.[57] What were the charges brought against this energetic revolutionary? Barjavel was charged with 'bringing the national representation', in the person of Rovère, 'into disrepute', and committing various excesses, notably the removal of religious objects, during a mission to Malamort.[58] The case against him was identical with that made out against all the zealous agents of the Terror during the reaction which followed 14 Frimaire. Here again the attack was abortive; but as in the cases of Tenaille, Pilavoine and Parent, Barjavel was again proscribed during the Thermidorean period, when his persecutor, Rovère, finally triumphed.[59]

It was not the downfall of the Hébertists, therefore, which had inaugurated a policy of appeasement. Rather, that policy had dated from Frimaire, and found its inspiration in the very clauses of the decree. Its implementation in the various regions opened the way to persecution of those who were most compromised, having led the revolutionary companies in their implementation of the anti-religious policy and the levying of *taxes* on the rich. Through their subordinates – *délégués, commissaires civils,* members of the central *comités* – those carrying on the campaign hoped to get at the most violent, the most anti-Catholic of the proconsuls, the Fouchés, the Javogues and their like. In the departments, as in Paris, the 'pause' preceded rather than followed the arrest of the Cordeliers. The campaign was conducted largely by moderates: farmers, men of the law, administrators, judges of the criminal and civil tribunals, as well as some *représentants*, future Thermidoreans on the whole, but in a few notorious cases, Robespierrists as well. The campaign would not have assumed such proportions if its leaders had not been encouraged, covertly and sometimes overtly, by the Committee of Public Safety and its agents, who were the first to represent the violent men, the chiefs of terrorist policy, as anarchists and ultra-revolutionaries. They were of course a little of both, but the fact that from Nivôse onwards criminal accusations were being made against them as such is a striking indication of the new standards and the progress of reaction even in the thinking of government agents and in public opinion.

That this reaction did not assume truly national proportions was due to the fact that the departmental *sociétés populaires* were still a powerful force in political life – witness the successful campaign by the Avignon *société* on behalf of its imprisoned *frères* – and were still dominated by sans-culottes. But in the Loire and the Nord, this was no longer the case, internal revolutions during Nivôse and Pluviôse having brought the moderates to the fore. The Committee of General Security also helped to restrain this new *modérantisme*, which was attacking not only its subordinates but some of its own members, who were enthusiastic dechristianisers. The development had already produced a conflict with the rival Committee, the behind-the-scenes conductor of this campaign against the 'hommes de liaison', *hommes sans dieu*. The Hébertist affair injected new life into a movement which, until Ventôse, had been limited to a few scattered departments.

VI   *The 'merger', re-engagements or return to civilian life*

The only *armées* to escape the common fate were those of the Nièvre, the Allier, the Loire and the Saône-et-Loire, retained under arms or re-engaged to form the 7th battalion of the Parisian *armée*. The Toulouse *armée*, after being assembled in the town, left it on 14 Nivôse for Perpignan.[60] But in the time intervening, many soldiers had taken advantage of the opportunity to return to their homes and had invoked the terms of their engagement. The number of those re-enlisting in the 10th Bataillon de la Montagne – the name given to the former revolutionary companies – must have been far below the expectations of Paganel and the authorities, to judge from the complaints of this *représentant* and the district of Toulouse about the 'want of patriotism' of the former revolutionary soldiers, who after all were simply following the example set by their leaders. These showed little enthusiasm, after their discharge, to resume service, this time in a real army destined to combat the Spanish invader. Their lukewarm response was the subject of an animated discussion at the 16 Nivôse session of the Toulouse *société*, when several members, including Boyer, a wigmaker, and Goux, a cook, had their names struck off for refusing to go with the *armée révolution-naire* to Perpignan. On this occasion Paganel denounced the former chiefs of the general staff, notably Gélas, already dismissed from the *société* (though readmitted later after his own account of the situation). Some days after this Gélas and Hugueny complained of the slanders being made against them, and towards the end of the month Gélas and Delport travelled to Perpig-nan.[61] Picot remained in Toulouse after his liberation. Thus only about a quarter of the former *armée*, officers and soldiers, re-engaged in the Pyrénées-Orientales Army. The merger had been an almost total failure.

For the officers, however, the possibility of re-engagement was extreme-ly advantageous, because it allowed those who were simple civilians to retain the fantastic ranks they had acquired in the political armies when they transferred to a regular army. For the career soldiers, the advantages were even more evident. The case of the young Calmet-Beauvoisins, former adjoint to the adjutant-generals of the Lille *armée*, is typical. Having success-fully evaded the disgrace which engulfed the general staff of Dufresse, this rich young man protested against his dispatch to the Côtes de Cherbourg Army; he was hoping, he wrote, to go with the son of the *représentant* Beauvais 'to revolutionise the Midi', under the direction of the *représentants* Milhaud and Soubrany, who knew his talents and his patriotism.[62] This young man knew how to get ahead through useful connections.

Calmet was not alone of his kind. The officers of the Légion de la Montagne, elevated to their rank by the *sociétés populaires*, took advantage of their engagement in the Légion to keep the same high rank in the regular army. Even someone like Viton put his service in the revolutionary forces to good use, and although he remained an adjutant-general, he profited from his contacts in military circles to secure a place in the administration of military transport.[63]

Most officers, however, returned to civilian life. Take the case of the battalion from the Allier. Although some cavalry officers, former hussars or dragoons, rejoined regiments of light cavalry, the commander and second in command returned to their civilian trades in Moulins, while de Goy, an officer in the battalion of the neighbouring Nièvre, returned to his printer's and stationer's.[64] The commander of the ephemeral *armée* of Besançon, the wigmaker Charles Millet, remained in his home town, while Le Batteux returned to his postmastership in Redon.[65] When his company was dissolved in Ventôse, Civeton, bourgeois from Roanne, returned home.[66] In Lille, all the civilians in the *armée*, spinners and operatives for the most part, went back to their workshops, while the young men of conscription age were obliged to return to the battalions of Lille and the Somme. But their case was exceptional.

Generally speaking, therefore, the efforts of the *représentants* and the established authorities to further the transition of these political soldiers to regular military life, through the kind of 'merger' which permitted the former Toulouse *armée* to be absorbed into the Army of the Pyrénées-Orientales, had derisory results. We have no precise figures for the total number of re-engagements, but every account emphasises its smallness and complains of the 'want of patriotism' and the 'cowardice' of the former *révolutionnaires*. Such accusations were unjust, for most of these men had responded to an emergency call, with no thought of a military career or of serving far from home. As soon as the Convention announced that it no longer had need of these institutions, established in response to an exceptional situation, the men had every right to consider their debt to the Republic paid, particularly since they were scarcely honoured at the time of their disbandment. Had they not *sauvé la chose publique* at a time of danger? The Convention itself had said so. These men were not soldiers; they were neither the right age – the *armées* of the North and the Haute-Garonne were exceptions – nor of the right temperament.

The most important effect of the law of 14 Frimaire was undoubtedly that it removed the armed force from the control of the *représentants en mission* and transferred it to the local authorities which in turn were under the control of central government. The main victims of the decree, the proconsuls, could no longer surround themselves with élite guards. The decree marked the return of the National Guard and the authorities who directed it: the municipalities and districts.

The execution of the decree was thus accompanied by a reaction which, in the departments, preceded and possibly went beyond the intentions of the Committee of Public Safety. If the Parisian *armée* had been given a reprieve, its eventual demise was pre-ordained by the logic of events. The municipalities would in future be given support in high places if they came into conflict with the detachments, since all armed force was now subject to their authority.

The speed with which the decree was executed – notwithstanding the slowness of communications, the imprecision in the wording of certain articles, the sabotage by certain *représentants* – is proof of the effectiveness of the Revolutionary Government. When it wanted to govern, it could do so; when the Committee of Public Safety spoke, everyone listened. Outside the Convention, outside the Committee, that is, there was no salvation. The unpardonable error of the Hébertists – it was a political error – and of all those who believed in a 'parallel hierarchy', was to have underestimated the magnetic power of the Convention. The *armées révolutionnaires* themselves were in the service of the law; outside the law, they were nothing but 'armed bands'. In practice, at the end of 1793, there was no power capable of competing with the Revolutionary Government.

The law of 14 Frimaire represented, in spite of everything, the triumphant affirmation of the supremacy of civil over military power. In the hands of a few violent and ambitious *commissaires*, the *armées révolutionnaires*, 'special' armies, might have constituted a real danger to the Republic. The experiment had barely started when it was abruptly terminated by the decree. But who can say what might have happened if the chiefs had had time to get used to command and had developed a taste for power? The Parisian *armée* very quickly became convinced that it had a monopoly on revolutionary patriotism, and within little more than two months it was acting in the most off-hand manner towards municipalities 'guilty' of having crossed its wishes. It had acquired an 'esprit de corps', an *esprit militaire*, to such a degree that these simple soldiers equated every criticism of themselves with counter-revolution. Nothing was more typically military than this claim to be above the criticism of ordinary civilians, this refusal to be controlled by civil authority. The departmental *armées* had not had long enough to develop this kind of mentality, to develop a sense of their own strength and homogeneity. But it was only a question of time. The Committee of Public Safety, and the many democrats who feared the development of a 'military power', had exaggerated the danger; but their fears were more premature than ill founded. In Frimaire–Nivôse Year II, the special armed forces constituted no danger to the civil regime. But if they had remained in existence for six months, a year, if the *révolutionnaires* had had time to become accustomed to their special status as political soldiers, or to missions which would have increased the gulf between them and their fellow citizens, now their victims, then one might have witnessed the development, in half the departments, of an 'esprit militaire', a formidable instrument in the hands of a few chiefs, which even the more powerful of the Committees would have been unable to control.

The decree of 14 Frimaire was only one in a series of measures of appeasement; but it put an end also to the development of a sense of political autonomy among the *armées révolutionnaires*, which, from serving the *sociétés populaires* and sincere revolutionaries, would undoubtedly have finished up as an aim in itself. Such fears were reasonable enough; in acquiring permanent status, the *armées révolutionnaires* would have attained a professional effectiveness, which would at the same time have separated them from the popular milieus out of which they had first emerged. Disbanded in Frimaire, they were easily re-absorbed by the *petit peuple*. The ineffectiveness which, as we have seen, seriously limited the range of their activities, was at the same time a guarantee of their loyalty to the regime. These fears, though somewhat premature, nevertheless explain both the decree of 14 Frimaire and the injustices to which it gave rise, notably the proscription of the 'hommes de liaison', victims of the fear they had inspired, when at the head of their *bandes*, in the country people and the government men. After Frimaire they could no longer 'revolutionise'; but anarchy itself could open the way for a military regime. This danger was now definitely laid to rest. Therein lies the chief merit of the decree of 14 Frimaire.

CHAPTER 2

The Parisian *Armée* in Difficulty
(Nivôse-Ventôse Year II)

After 14 Frimaire, the political battles in Paris took shape, each side struggling for dominance. Between 27 Frimaire and 14 Pluviôse *modérantisme*
triumphed, then receded, in the capital and in the departments, the fate of
Ronsin becoming the barometer of the political climate in these stormy
months. The Revolutionary Government had yet to speak its mind; the
Committee of Public Safety proclaimed freedom of religion by making a
dogma of state neutrality in matters of religion, but the Committee of
General Security did nothing to moderate its encouragement of the dechristianising initiatives of its many agents. That was not the only subject in
dispute between the two heads of the revolutionary eagle. The government
seemed to be searching for a policy, and in the meantime it tacked between
several. If it was turning away increasingly from the popular movement –
and these months witnessed the gradual asphyxiation of the institutions
most dear to the sans-culottes – the Committee of Public Safety was still
capable of sudden bursts of repressive energy.

The repression was the subject of impassioned debates in the assemblies,
the clubs and the cafés. In Paris the campaign of the Indulgents intensified,
and had already scored a considerable success in casting doubt on the
probity of the Parisian *armée*. The campaign gained adherents among the
Jacobins and was given a valuable boost by the emissaries from Lyon, come
to Paris to plead the cause of the nation's second city. But the repression
was not yet condemned definitively and the supporters of strong measures
were still conducting major repressive operations in the Paris region in
Ventôse. The sans-culottes still had faith in the *grands moyens*. True, they
criticised the revolutionary general staff as frivolous and intriguing, but in
Ventôse they were still demanding a summary and mobile justice, favourite
panacea of the *sectionnaires* in the face of economic difficulties. When, in
Pluviôse, a detachment left Paris for Le Havre, the *petit peuple* gave it a
handsome send-off, its punitive will and revolutionary enthusiasm in no
way blunted by the government policy of wait-and-see. Indeed observers
were astonished by the continuing popularity of the *révolutionnaires* in the
Sections.

However, the opponents of repression were notching up points. The excesses committed in Lyon had caused a change of heart among the Paris Jacobins. The delegates from Lyon denounced Collot, Fouché, the extraordinary commissions, and the commanders of the garrison to the Committee of Public Safety, representing Lyon as the outpost of a military Hébertism every bit as dangerous as the Hébertism thundering in the Cour des Miracles – as the garrison of *ultracisme*, a rendezvous for the violent, the hard-liners, the hotheaded. The Committee showed signs of anxiety; but the enemy was already in position. In Nivôse and Pluviôse the struggle between the Lyon Jacobins and the Cordeliers or Parisian *sectionnaires* became more bitter. The Lyon sans-culottes denounced the 'colonisation' of the proud commune by *étrangers*, thus cleverly appealing to local particularism. In Lyon as in Paris, the sans-culotte movement supported decentralisation, and in the great town on the Rhône centralisation had assumed a bloody and militaristic aspect. Those responsible for the repression were thus faced with an alliance taking shape between the sans-culottes and Jacobins of Lyon and the Robespierrists in Paris.

The Committee of Public Safety, having rid itself of the departmental *armées*, went on to reduce the powers and privileges of the central, Parisian one. Everything was subordinated to the war effort; there was to be no more 'revolutionising' at will. The duties of the companies were whittled down to searching out men suitable for work in the arms manufactories. The Committee, however, had not yet condemned outright this much-criticised *armée*; its policy was more subtle. Rather than condemn publicly an institution which still enjoyed considerable support in popular, and even in government, circles, the Committee strove to reduce the *armée*'s powers of intervention by progressively dispersing the detachments, breaking up the cohesion of the companies, and assigning the detachments to military tasks. At the same time it reassured the municipalities of its total support for complaints against the initiatives of the revolutionary officers.

The Revolutionary Government, however, remained divided. Whereas the Committee of Public Safety used the detachments for garrison duty in the West and along the Channel, and to break strikes organised by transport and naval workers, the Committee of General Security entrusted important repressive and political missions in the Paris region to companies commanded by *commissaires* from the Paris *comités*. The repressive missions of Ventôse were, in their violence, a response to the desire expressed by the most advanced Sections for *grandes mésures*.

But something had changed. Even the chiefs of the *armée révolutionnaire* sensed it and were already on the defensive; they were no longer sure they had the confidence of Government and felt that a part of their public support was slipping away. Consequently they tried to moderate the zeal of their soldiers, and the tone of the officers' correspondence in Nivôse and Pluviôse was very different from that of the good days of Brumaire. The *armée révolutionnaire* was at the centre of the political debate which had Paris and Lyon in thrall. Such attention was dangerous, and with their utility as instruments of the Terror being so openly debated, their effectiveness was already considerably diminished. They were no longer *terribles*.

The Parisian *armée* was ill prepared for the crisis that was impending and that everyone expected. In the face of its critics it presented a public spectacle of internal dissension: the general staff was riven by political factions, each recommending a different policy and conducting their under-handed struggles on the public stage of Paris. The clans went in search of allies outside the rue de Choiseul, on the boulevards and in the Committees themselves; the Dantonists were their clientele, the Grammonts ingratiating themselves with Hérault. The young Mazuel, in open conflict both with the head of the general staff and his colleagues, and disowned by Ronsin, tried to enlist the support of the Minister and bombarded his Montpellier pro-tectors, Cambon and Aigoin, with letters. Maubant, pressurised from all sides, sought advice from Collot and Léonard Bourdon. The command seemed to be breaking up through the rivalries of the different groups. Hanriot took advantage of all this further to increase his own autonomy – the commander-general also had friends in the rue de Choiseul. Jaurès was never more accurate than in his statement that the headquarters in the rue de Choiseul had begun to resemble a Polish diet. Anarchic in many of its activities, the *armée* was displaying to the whole of Paris the sorry spectacle of its Byzantine conflicts. On the eve of the battle, its command was being eaten away.

I   *The* armée révolutionnaire *and the political struggles in Paris (Nivôse–Pluviôse)*

The 14 Frimaire decree had made an exception in the case of the Parisian *armée*, renamed the 'armée révolutionnaire nationale'. At first sight, the disappearance of the other revolutionary forces, the anarchy and disorder of which had reflected on the central *armée*, seemed to reinforce the position of Ronsin's *armée* – henceforth the only one of its kind, the decree seemingly confirming its legal, its official, status, and raising it to the level of a per-manent institution of the new regime. Ronsin and his colleagues foresaw a bright future for the *armée* – the recruitment of the 'armée de la Convention' throughout the entire Republic perhaps. Ronsin also viewed the decree as an occasion for demanding an increase in the number of effectives. The special armies had been condemned, but the government still favoured methods of compulsion, and in any event the execution of the economic laws still required the use of force. The disbanded *armées* would have to be replaced. This no doubt was the reasoning which led Ronsin to seek Collot's support in his approach to the Committee of Public Safety.

Ronsin's illusions seem to have been communicated to the officers and men of the *armée*. The announcement and promulgation of the decree pro-duced no relaxation in the activities of the detachments in the countryside. Nivôse witnessed particularly violent action against religion; Pluviôse and

Ventôse were months of considerable revolutionary activity. In Ventôse the detachment in the La Campagne district carried out a repressive operation in the grand manner. That same month, the detachments in the Eure and the Yonne made life difficult for the municipalities and *les gros*. This was not the behaviour of an *armée* which knew its days were numbered.

If the soldiers seemed unaware of the political drama in which they were one of the principal pawns, or rather, indifferent to the fate of a commander whom they did not know or recognise as a fellow sans-culotte, they were the only ones to be unconcerned. It was not difficult to see that the condemnation of the communal *armées* was a death sentence for the Parisian *armée* as well. If the general staff momentarily shared the illusions of Ronsin and his soldiers, they soon changed their stance to a defensive one. Parisian opinion was quick to sense the direction of events, and on 28 Frimaire, the day following the arrest of Ronsin, some groups had already dethroned the *armée* from its position as the national political force, by calling it 'the army of the Commune'.[1] The description was inaccurate; but it marked the politicisation of an institution which till then was supposed to have been serving the Republic. In Paris in particular, after 27 Frimaire, the conflict over the *armée révolutionnaire* and the daily debates in the cafés and on the boulevards concerning the severity of the repression, were the main themes in the political crisis. The *citras* and *ultras*, Philippotins and Cordeliers, were at odds over the Parisian *armée* and the policy it had applied, and with which it was, sometimes unjustifiably, identified. The *citras* scored an initial success in the decree of 27 Frimaire – directed not only against Ronsin, but even more against the former leaders of the Toulouse *armée* – and in the Lille *coup de force* which restored the moderates to control of the *société populaire* and municipality. The moderates could claim victories in three of the most important communes in the Republic. At the same time, as the public saw it, the 14 Frimaire decree brought about the first signs of a 'normalisation' of revolutionary administration, with the abatement of a repression which had been the main responsibility of the extraordinary institutions. A general offensive was soon to be unleashed against the men and the institutions of the revolutionary movement. But for the moment the Sections joined to block the new *modérantisme*, and from the end of Frimaire to the middle of Pluviôse its progress was slow. There was a genuine upsurge of popular feeling in support of the imprisoned leaders, and if the soldiers – cavaliers excepted – remained indifferent to the fate of their general, the militant *sectionnaires* in Paris, more aware of the issues at stake, did not. The campaign on behalf of Ronsin and Vincent succeeded in winning over the Convention and the Committees; the two men were released on 14 Pluviôse, and were paraded triumphantly round the Sectionary assemblies.[2] But their victory was not total: Vincent was not accepted into the Jacobins, and Ronsin vainly demanded the heads of his persecutors.

From 27 Frimaire to 23 Ventôse, when Ronsin was arrested for the second time, the *armée révolutionnaire* was constantly at the centre of political debate. Attention had turned away from the detachments, stagnating in demoralising inactivity in remote corners of the countryside or locked in remorseless struggles with the municipalities and districts, to focus on the political scene in Paris. It is this 'political' phase in the history of the *armée révolutionnaire* which is best known, because this phase and the idea of a military plot associated with it, has attracted most attention from the historians.[3] There is no need to retrace here the outlines of a struggle which took place in the Sections and the clubs, and whose importance has been meticulously described by Albert Soboul. Let us simply examine the evolution of opinion concerning the *armée révolutionnaire* and establish the chronology of events.

The kind of sustained attention it was receiving did the revolutionary institution no good whatsoever; with every action by the detachments and their chiefs subjected to minute scrutiny, imperfections and unsuspected weaknesses were quickly revealed. These made unsavoury news. The period opened badly, where Parisian opinion was concerned, with one of the many escapades at which the young Mazuel was a master. On 20 Frimaire he provoked a scuffle at the Opéra-Comique, striking the actors and insulting the stage manager whom he accused of a want of respect towards his cavalrymen.[4] The *chef d'escadron* cooled his heels in detention. But Parisian opinion was growing weary of such escapades, particularly when provoked by a young man who, instead of fighting on the frontiers, spent his time in gilded idleness at the *auberge* of the Cadran Bleu, in front of the château of Versailles, or in the foyers of Parisian theatres. A week later, according to a witness clearly hostile to the entire *armée*, public opinion looked to its forthcoming dissolution, following the arrest of Ronsin. At the same time murmurs against the general revived.[5]

The real tenor of public opinion is more difficult to establish. Observers reporting to Franqueville noted in particular the criticisms of the members of the general staff. This was probably a fair statement of the facts, the sans-culottes turning away, sickened by the scenes in the rue de Choiseul. But at the same time they remained confident in the *armée* and in measures of force. On 28 Frimaire one observer wrote: 'The people seem to want the *armée révolutionnaire* to visit the tanners and curriers, for rumour has it that there is no more leather to be had since the Maximum. They are convinced that there are hoarders of this merchandise in Pontoise and Saint-Germain-en-Laye, and that in other places too one can find pits filled with leather'.[6]

Some days later the attacks on the *armée* became more specific; through Ronsin, it was his protector, Collot, recently returned from Lyon to defend his work, who was being attacked. 'It is not surprising, it is said, that Collot-d'Herbois is coming to the defence of former general Ronsin, for the latter, in the Lyon affair, simply acted as subordinate agent to the *représentant* Collot...'.[7] The *armée révolutionnaire* was of interest to those supporters of 'la pause' only in so far as it led them to *les grands* responsible for the repression. But the *armée* too could still call on protectors in high places. On 2 Nivôse the revolutionary cavaliers on detachment in Versailles cancelled a projected civic fête, as a discreet way of expressing their sorrow at the sufferings of their chief. On the 3rd, however, they wrote to Fouquier-Tinville telling him that the fête would take place as planned, on 5 Nivôse, and both he and the *représentants en mission* in the Seine-et-Oise appear to have accepted the invitation.[8] The *armée* was still a respectable institution if it could count on the presence of Fouquier.

The enemies of the Terror also used other methods; in Nivôse they multiplied their insinuations concerning the probity of the Parisian soldiers – this was what occasioned Grammont's approach to Léonard Bourdon on 15 Nivôse. The following day the head of the general staff tried to end the rumours about the poor composition of the cavalry by requiring the squadron commanders to expel ex-nobles, priests and deserters.[9] These recommendations had little effect, but they show that the general staff was already being forced on to the defensive. The success of the moderates was also beginning to worry the Revolutionary Government, for the Indulgent press was attacking the general staff without distinction, and even Boulanger was accused of having spoken ill of the Convention and the deputies – a charge against which he defended himself at the Jacobins on 18 Nivôse. But Boulanger was a sacred figure; this time the adversaries of the Terror had gone too far, and Robespierre intervened in favour of his friend and protégé.[10] Thereafter the second-in-command of the *armée* was spared, but the general staff was still in the line of fire and on 19 Nivôse an observer noted, not without satisfaction: 'We are assured that the *armée révolutionnaire* has in it a large number of bad characters, as lacking in principle as in patriotism...'.[11] A week later, 28 Nivôse, just as public interest in the minutiae of the *armée révolutionnaire* was fading, Mazuel, never long out of the headlines, revived attention by creating a scene in a café in the Montagne Section. Once more he found himself in prison, where, unhappily, he remained but a few hours.[12] Moreover, he was attracting emulators: on 2 Pluviôse the Invalides Section protested about the undisciplined conduct of the detachments billeted in the Ecole Militaire. To relieve their boredom, the *révolutionnaires* had been fighting among themselves and pursuing passers-by in the street.

The *armée* also had the confidence of the *petit peuple*. On 7 Pluviôse the police agent, Bacon, wrote in his report: 'Towards midday, a detachment of the *armée révolutionnaire* left for Le Havre-Marat, this detachment was accompanied by women and children as far as the Saint-Laurent gate. After drinking the health of the Republic and the Mountain, fraternal kisses were exchanged. The volunteers drank to their wives and friends and promised not to return until their enemies were destroyed...'. Dugard for his part noted: 'A division of the *armée révolutionnaire* left today for Le Havre. The appearance and stature of those who composed it were rightly admired...'. The following day the sans-culottes expressed their satisfaction at the object of this expedition: 'Someone has received a letter from Rouen', reported

Monic, 'this letter stated that it was urgent and necessary to send a detachment from the *armée révolutionnaire* to this town to help the sans-culottes by enforcing the laws against the cupidity of all the large merchants...'.[13] Rouen, thanks largely to the *Père Duchesne*, enjoyed a very bad reputation with the Parisian sans-culottes, who were further influenced against the Norman capital by delegations from the Le Havre *société populaire*.[14]

The release of Ronsin on 14 Pluviôse concentrated attention on his *armée* more than ever and aggravated rather than appeased passions. The debate over the repression and its instruments took on a more violent tone. On the whole, Sectionary opinion remained faithful to the *armée* – even though it was criticised at the 10 Pluviôse session of the Révolutionnaire Section[15] – and on the 14th the *comité* of the l'Unité Section transmitted an invitation from its general assembly to the detachment stationed at the Ecole Militaire, to attend its civic fête on the 20th. It was a token of its confidence in the *armée*.[16] Two days later criticisms were growing concerning one of Ronsin's aides-de-camp.[17] Finally, on the 19th, the agent, Letassey, reported a major debate between supporters and opponents of measures of constraint:

> Quantities of flour are still being transported to the former Capuchins in the Marais, yet the stores are only kept stocked by force, everyone speaks of this; but many ask why the *armée révolutionnaire* is not doing its job; others reply that it is because they are obliged to take their orders from the local authorities, most of them moderates who favour the former suppliers, farmers and others, particularly in the Paris region and 20 leagues beyond; another says: 'we know that, because it is happening close to Pontoise, and the soldiers who were there were recalled'; 'indeed', says another, 'what use can they be if they do not know from whom their authority comes; their orders should come from the executive power, and through it from the Convention, then things would be better...'.[18]

Two days later a report from Jarousseau sounded another warning: he had heard 'many complaints from different groups about the *armée révolutionnaire* in the countryside. It was said that they grabbed up everything at their price and that they would be better off at the frontiers, that the National Guard and *comités révolutionnaires* could perform the service just as well as they did...'.[19]

But the sans-culottes were far from thinking likewise and were still convinced of the value of punitive methods to deal with the ill will of the farmers. Carron, *commissaire* from the Droits-de-l'Homme Section, charged with the prevention of hoarding, and a friend of Descombes, told his Section on 21 Pluviôse 'that knavery prevailed in matters of subsistences and primary foodstuffs.... "if [he said] we republicans do not decide to march in three columns with the *armée révolutionnaire* and a guillotine as back-up, to ensure that this great city of Paris gets everything that is coming to it, then all is lost"...'. This classic statement of sans-culotte thinking was received with 'loud applause' and the assembly decided that 'at the first session, this subject would be made the order of the day'. On the same day Monic noted similar feelings about the farmers. 'The citizens on guard with me spoke of the roguery of the big farmers in the environs of Melun and Coulommiers, their native towns. They said that the big farmers there were all counter-revolutionaries and that the local authorities were little better...'. And so, on 23 Pluviôse as news spread of Ronsin's second arrest,[20] opinion still favoured the idea of massive intervention by the *armée révolutionnaire*, with a popular commission and a guillotine in train. In Ventôse the advanced Sections – Observatoire, Finistère, l'Unité, Théâtre-Français – were still echoing Carron's complaints.[21]

To judge from these fragmentary and sometimes tendentious reports – one senses that the spy *commissaires* were opposed not only to the men of the Cordeliers and the rue de Choiseul, but even more to their chosen institutions – what most damaged the *armée révolutionnaire* in Parisian opinion was its inactivity. No one wanted to pay for an army which did nothing. But the sans-culottes were still convinced that only force could resolve the subsistence problem and they remained extremely attached to this instrument of the economic Terror. As for the general staff, unfortunately it constituted the most visible part of an *armée* whose soldiers were normally absent from Paris on detachment. No doubt the more astute sans-culottes made a distinction between the general staff and the *armée* itself. But the adversaries of the institution found their most convincing arguments in the behaviour of the young men gathered around Grammont, the impossible Mazuel and the cavalrymen on detachment at Versailles. In Pluviôse the general staff was as torn by struggles between the opposing clans as before, each side appealing to public opinion through printed notices. Mazuel, for his part, refused to leave Versailles to resume his post in Lyon, and pressed the Minister to rid him of his colleague, Payot, who, as a former officer in the gendarmerie, had sinned by trying to bring order and discipline to the revolutionary cavalry. All Paris reverberated with the dispute between the former silk-embroiderer from the Croix-Rousse and Payot, the obstinate Ardennais.[22] At this moment of crisis, then, the chiefs of the Parisian *armée* were divided and their disputes and debauched idleness were making the entire *armée* appear foolish and useless. The men in the rue de Choiseul inspired neither respect nor fear. The Parisian *armée révolutionnaire* was rotting from the top.

II   *The Lyonnais against the 'étrangers'*

The change of direction in high places after the law of 14 Frimaire is more noticeable in Lyon than anywhere else. The arrest of Ronsin, who had spoken so ferociously of the town and sung the praises of the Lyon massacres in a bloodthirsty notice issued on his return to Paris, was considered by the Lyonnais a victory for their city. To them Ronsin was 'l' homme des Brotteaux' as much as Collot and Parein; his arrest, they said, must surely have been due to the horror which his murderous apologia had aroused in Parisian opinion. Between Nivôse and Ventôse, Lyon, like Paris, was torn by the struggle between moderate Jacobins, *hommes d'Etat*, and proponents of out-and-out repression. Lyon – what was left of it – became the capital of military *ultracisme*, more terrifying than the thundering violence of the *Père Duchesne* in Paris, for it had at its disposal the entire machinery of repression, the armed force, the entire administration of a town doomed to extinction, and in addition the monopoly of the newspapers. In Commune-Affranchie there were two *Pères Duchesne* and no *Vieux Cordelier*. This kind of Hébertist colonialism – the *étrangers* governing Lyon possessed the mentality of colonial functionaries, for whom no word was too scornful to describe the stupidity of the 'native'[23] – recruited its support from among the 'ultras' of the Cordeliers, the War Ministry, the *sociétés* of Nevers and Moulins, and a few Lyonnais renegades such as the journalist Dorfeuille, editor, as 'Damame', of the Lyon *Père Duchesne*, who was to pay with his life for the company he kept during this period.[24]

But against this military and *étranger* tide of opinion, the Lyon Jacobins, such as the mayor, Bertrand, the national agent, Achard,[25] the militant sans-culottes like Revol, Castaing, Candi,[26] and the painter Martinetcourt,[27] reacted vigorously. The *étrangers* had the support of Fouché and Collot, but the Lyon Jacobins took the opportunity provided by the funeral of Chalier to travel to Paris and bypass the *représentants* in a direct appeal to the Jacobins, their mother society, and to the Committee of Public Safety. They warned of the dangers of a purely anti-Lyon policy, through which the industry and talents of the population of this great town would be lost to France. In practical terms, Gravier, Bertrand, Candi and Castaing demanded the return of Couthon, who had won the respect of all Lyonnais by his opposition to the excesses and initiatives of men like Collot and Javogues. It was the beginning of Nivôse when these emissaries arrived in Paris.

In Lyon the Parisians had established at the outset a *modus vivendi*, and even a working arrangement, with the former friends of Chalier who had survived the 29th May. The situation of the town in Frimaire was so disastrous that it needed all the good will available to get essential public services moving again. Thus the architect, Lefranc, captain of the Tuileries cannoneers, divided his time between his military and repressive duties and his concerns as the member of the municipality in charge of public works. The sans-culottes of the *société* had the same opinion of the farmers as their Parisian brothers, and looked to the detachments to combat infractions of the Maximum and apply requisitions in favour of the large town. Between a Martinetcourt, a Candi, a Chédeaux and a Parisian sans-culotte, there was no disagreement on the necessity of measures of force against the country people. But this collaboration and unanimity of political outlook between sans-culottes of similar background did not long withstand the much more powerful pull of Lyon particularism, cut to the quick by the sight of this colonisation by *étrangers*. It is significant that the revolt against the Parisian and Nivernais soldiers had its beginnings in the *société populaire*, whose Lyonnais members were finding it increasingly difficult to accept the military stranglehold of its committee. Their leader in this was a Lyon artisan, the painter Martinetcourt.

In the affair of the Parisian fusilier Arnaud, the Lyon *sociétaires* saw their chance to attack Maubant who, as an officer under the Ancien Regime, had been a hard taskmaster towards his men. The affair preoccupied the *société* during the second half of Nivôse and the first days of Pluviôse. Through Maubant, Martinetcourt and his friends wanted to get at Parein and the Commission des Sept, the Commission Temporaire, and Fouché. The *représentant* and the Commissions frowned upon such manifestations of independence on the part of the 'occupied', and Fouché himself went to the *société* and threatened it with dissolution if it did not stop its campaign against the Parisians. The Lyonnais element in the *société*, however, was un-moved, and the rupture between it and the revolutionary general staff was complete when, on 7 Pluviôse, the Parisian officers came and announced that they would no longer assist at its sessions. On the 19th Lefranc, a member of the General Council, resigned; but it had been done in a fit of temper, and the same day Bertrand and his Lyon colleagues invited him back. Peace was re-established between the stormy architect and the patriots of Lyon; it was a lasting peace, and both sides found themselves among the minority of republicans who fought courageously against the progress of reaction through the dark years of 1795–9. But the rupture between Parein, the Commissions and the general staff on the one hand, and the *société populaire* and municipality of Lyon on the other was final, and neither side would lay down its arms. Fouché was to have the *société* closed and Martinetcourt arrested at the time of the Hébertist affair, but the Lyonnais experienced a sweet revenge in the recall of this *représentant* and the arrest of his favourite protégé, the Nivernais Duvicquet, secretary of the *société* and a spy for the *étrangers*.[28]

The *armée révolutionnaire* was caught up in this conflict. The Lyonnais of course detested these 'outsider' soldiers, who had come to them as repressors and avengers of a republican unity endangered by Rhône particularism. But, as in Paris, the *armée* itself was not united; the men of the detachment complained bitterly of the harshness of their officers and the Military Commission, and found defenders among the locals. As in the capital, the young officers regaled the public with the spectacle of their quarrels; the 1st squadron was divided into two rival clans which sought support from within headquarters and from the Ministry.[29] At the time of the scuffles, no doubt partly provoked by the populace, and with the detachment hard-pressed by the troops of the line, unity was momentarily restored, and in Ventôse the *représentants* finally imposed a truce. Harmony between *révolutionnaires* and Lyonnais was officially re-established for the great Fête de la Fraternité which took place at Les Brotteaux on 20 Ventôse. This 'reconciliation' in the middle of that sinister plain was no doubt designed to show the population that the time of *la grande pénitence* was passed; but it was not enough to make the Lyonnais forget the sorrowful and humiliating past.[30] A week later, when news reached Lyon of the arrest of the Hébertists, the attack on the *étrangers* was renewed, and in Floréal the *représentant*, Reverchon, rewarded the principal leaders of the offensive for their zeal in serving the Revolutionary Government.[31]

This conflict was simply the Lyon extension of the triangular conflict to which Paris was subjected at the same period. Through the presence of Parein and Boissay, as ambassadors of Hébertism, Lyon had become the Cordelier capital. But thanks to Bertrand, Achard and Gravier, the large city sided, in defence of its particularism, with Robespierre and Couthon. Following Ronsin's notice, printed by the Cordeliers on 20 or 22 Frimaire, the *armée révolutionnaire* became identified in the Lyonnais mind with the repression – which was unjust, for the *mitrailleurs* had been mostly troops from the first requisition. But that did not matter; to the population of Lyon the Parisian *armée* represented the plaine des Brotteaux, the place des Terreaux, and the terrible Commission.

But there was more. To the internal quarrels which divided the general staff and made the cavalry an object of ridicule, to the scuffles which made the unfortunate Parisians look foolish, to the political struggle between the *étrangers* and the Lyon Jacobins, was added a bitter personal conflict between Declaye, the garrison commander, and Maubant, commander of the detachment. Both were intransigent by nature; there was no political difference between them, the Liégeois Declaye being as much opposed to the Lyonnais as Parein and Maubant, but both wanted to be in charge, and that was the sum total of the quarrel. Maubant invoked the autonomy of the *armée révolutionnaire* and both appealed to Collot, Fouché and the Minister.[32] Bouchotte, Billaud-Varenne and Robespierre were irritated by these stupid quarrels. The *armée révolutionnaire* had become quite impossible; everywhere it went it provoked conflicts of authority, which the Minister and the Committee of Public Safety had to spend time and tact in resolving, when they had already quite enough to occupy them. The correspondence of the Committee is full of vengeful letters from the two soldiers, equally violent, equally bad-tempered.

As if all this was not enough already, to crown its misfortune the Parisian *armée* suffered the presence, in Lyon and Villefranche, of a young featherbrain from Rouen, Edouard Dobigny, aide-de-camp to Parein, who, in between extended bouts of drunkenness – he was stationed for some time in the Beaujolais capital – found little better to do with his time than to become engaged to the daughter of a noble. The imprudent Norman then began demanding the liberation of half the former aristocrats of Villefranche, and waging war on the municipality, the *société populaire*, the district, and the *comité de surveillance*, whom he cursed in the streets as he stumbled out of the *auberge.* So at a time when the *armée* in Lyon was being blamed for the entire repression, in Villefranche an officer from its general staff was both slandering the regular authorities – and in his drunkenness Dobigny did not forget the Convention – and showing himself a champion of clemency, in demanding the release of several notorious *émigrés*, returned to France. What a windfall for Robespierrist propaganda, which tried to show it as the meeting of extremes, the *ultras* and *citras* being in reality united in opposing the Revolutionary Government. Dobigny, under the influence of true love and Beaujolais, would not listen to the counsels of prudence from his superiors; he was becoming compromising. Dispatched to Paris in the middle of Pluviôse, he convinced the credulous Ronsin of his good intentions and had himself sent back to Villefranche. It was not long before he supplied his many enemies with new ammunition, proclaiming in the streets on 14 Ventôse that Villefranche was a town in counter-revolution. He was again sent to Paris after these incidents and had the misfortune to arrive just as his protector Ronsin was about to be arrested. He was kept over for a later trial, from which he had the good fortune to emerge with no more than a prison sentence. Dobigny was simply a giddy young man, 'without an ounce of political sense', as Parein put it, who had fallen in love with a young noblewoman. His affair was trivial; but that did not keep it from adding to the discredit which this Lyon detachment, so remarkable for incidents and quarrels, was acquiring in official circles in Paris.[33]

The excesses committed by that other giddy young man, Vauquoy, in the La Tour-du-Pin district in Frimaire and Nivôse, could only indirectly be charged to the Parisian *armée* – Vauquoy's main employment was with the Crémieu company. But the victims of such operations did not distinguish between the different revolutionary forces which harassed them, and in Pluviôse protests from the municipalities of La Tour-du-Pin began to flow into the Committee of Public Safety, the Convention and the *Comité de législation.*[34]

The detachment at Lyon represented a third of the effective force of the Parisian *armée.* Its importance inspired fear not only among the Lyonnais, but also among certain Parisian authorities who suspected its general staff of having political ambitions. The conduct of people like Dobigny and Vauquoy gave such fears substance, for both had spoken against the Convention and the *représentants.* Through the Indulgents press these fears, though perfectly illusory, were communicated to part of Parisian opinion, which found proof in Ronsin's efforts to gather the maximum number of soldiers from his *armée* in Lyon.[35] They also found suspect the persistent demands of the cannoneers in Lyon, after Nivôse, for a return to Paris. The most unfavourable interpretation was placed on the commanders' every action, and it was concluded that Ronsin was building up an outpost of Hébertism in the Lyon garrison. Lyon, in any case, was the capital of the kind of extraordinary administration which was condemned by the law of 14 Frimaire. It was the only major commune in which the established

authorities had not yet recovered their prerogatives. On the other hand, that
the cannoneers were demanding to be returned home gave rise to the opposite interpretation, namely, that the *ultras* were trying to group their forces
in Paris. Under both hypotheses the Lyon detachment was at the centre of
popular speculation – for public opinion was always hypersensitive about
any troop movement. The fault lay with the officers. In Lyon the general
staff dabbled in politics. In Paris and Versailles, a succession of officers,
designated either to take command of the 1st squadron or to succeed
Maubant (Mazuel, Payot, Vézien, Bertrand) had all preferred to remain
near Paris; Lyon had no attractions for them. But in the public mind these
officers had remained behind in Paris to plot.[36]

In these months the *armée révolutionnaire* became such a hot political
subject that even purely technical orders attracted the most sinister interpretations. The ground had been well prepared for the belief in a 'military
plot' by the polemical campaign of the Indulgents press on the subject of
the Lyon detachment's participation in the repression. Lyon itself was consumed by the decisive conflict between two systems of government, between the extraordinary Commissions, so dear to the 'hommes de liaison',
and the regular authorities. If the Cordeliers were weak in Paris, in Lyon
they were in force; but the Revolutionary Government and the Jacobins had
also positioned their men, and could count on Bertrand, Gravier, Castaing
and Candi to counter the influence of the Boissays and the Pareins. Political
events in Lyon and Paris were closely intertwined in these crucial months.

III   *The Committees and the Parisian* armée: *revolutionary government and the problem of authority*

The law of 14 Frimaire upheld the regularly established authorities, and
condemned the principle of extraordinary revolutionary authority, of
which only the great Lyon Commissions remained along with an already
suspect Parisian *armée*, which at least some people expected quickly to
disappear. Confusion persisted concerning the administrative competence
of this political force. The law on revolutionary government had clearly
defined the new hierarchy of powers, but its interpretation was still a matter
of dispute and an entirely theoretical definition could not resolve the
practical problems which personal and administrative rivalries were
producing daily when the detachments operated in the country. Since its
formation the Parisian *armée* had been the victim of its ill-defined status.
Ronsin was to say that it had been castrated at birth and that the very
principle of its creation as a revolutionary force had been vitiated when the
Committee instructed it to obey the orders of the municipalities. How right
he was. Nor were the municipalities and districts the only bodies with
authority over the detachments. In every department there were authorities,
not regularly constituted but which issued orders to everyone in the name
of Paris or the *armées*. What were the limits of power of the detachments

themselves? Who were the officers to obey in cases of conflict between the municipal authorities and the Parisian *commissaires*? If they encountered opposition from the municipalities which threatened to compromise the aims of their mission, could they use force and overrule local objections by invoking the superior interests of Paris and the armies, or the safety of the revolutionary regime itself?

The problem was dramatically illustrated in Nivôse, when the detachments in several localities used coercion against the municipalities in executing orders from the *commissaires* of the various Parisian authorities. In the face of complaints from the districts and municipalities of arbitrary use of power, *coups de force*, the development of military government, the Committee of Public Safety was obliged to intervene and define, once again, the relationship between the political force and local administration. At the beginning of Nivôse the attitude of the Committee hardened; the *armée révolutionnaire*, it proclaimed, must at all times and in all circumstances defer to the local authorities – municipalities, districts, *comités de surveillance*. But the confusion remained. In Montcornet, for example, the detachment was under the orders of Gênois, *commissaire* of the Commission des Subsistances in Paris; if it obeyed him it risked coming into conflict with the municipalities of the canton, and this is what did, in fact, happen. Yet Gênois, acting in the name of central authority, had extensive powers over an entire district. If, in the interests of Paris, he ordered the *armée* to use constraint against recalcitrant municipalities, should the officers obey him?

Elsewhere the detachments operated under orders from the *commissaires* of the Committee of General Security, some of whom had little time for local objections and susceptibilities. Besides, the Committee accorded a considerable degree of autonomy to those who served it, trusting to their good sense and energy to resolve problems at the source. It was understood that men charged with the execution of major surveillance measures on which the safety of the regime depended, would not be required to remain within the strict limits of their written orders. They were to decide for themselves and, if necessary, act *révolutionnairement*. One Longueville-Clémentière was to treat the officers of the Noyon municipality with utter contempt.

How, then, did the Committee of Public Safety approach the question of administrative competence? On three occasions it issued statements on this subject, condemning any attempt by the detachments to act independently of the local authorities or to take administrative initiatives themselves. The *armée* was not allowed to act *révolutionnairement*, even if faced with a situation demanding exceptional and brutal action. The armed forces, even if *révolutionnaire*, stated the Committee in its first warning of 10 Frimaire, 'have no right to take direct and spontaneous action against the established authorities and the populace...'.[37] On 21 Nivôse, through Grammont, it again insisted on the supremacy of the existing authorities: 'It [the *armée révolutionnaire*] must undertake nothing without precise, written orders from the regular authorities...'.[38] The Committee emphasised 'the regular authorities'; there was no mention of the other authorities on whose orders most of the detachments actually operated. If the Committee felt obliged, a third time, to reiterate this doctrine through Maubant, it was because the detachments had ignored its warnings and acted as sovereign authorities towards the municipalities. In the meantime the Pontoise and Montereau affairs had occurred, and in Pluviôse too the Committee learnt of the case prepared by the Laon authorities against the detachment from the Bondy Section. On 28 Ventôse Maubant felt obliged to remind one detachment commander that 'the armed force...should and must confine itself to protecting the execution of the laws, and not become involved in administrative functions...'.[39]

So much for doctrine. But there was also a series of apparently unrelated measures designed to diminish the effectiveness of one of the last instruments of the Terror. The Parisian *armée* in effect was isolated; on 9 Pluviôse the Convention passed a decree, no doubt inspired by Carnot, suppressing Legions, forbidding the use of the title, and obliging corps bearing such titles to exchange them for regiment numbers. The measure was the culmination of that tendency, apparent in government policy since Frimaire, to proscribe special armies and reduce the autonomy of privileged corps which, in response to the great popular surge of September 1793, had developed throughout France alongside the revolutionary forces. This decree no doubt had in mind the Légion des Montagnards, with all its popular associations; 'la fille des sociétés populaires' could scarcely retain its autonomy when the Committee of Public Safety was preparing to reduce that of the *sociétés* themselves. But the decree also affected the German Legion and the corps of Belgian refugees, which, even more than the *armées révolutionnaires*, had aroused the opposition of the local authorities by their insubordination.[40] The condemnation of the foreign legions was also implicit in the increasingly nationalistic turn of official policy since the winter. The disbandment of the German Legion was a warning to Cloots and to the supporters of an international revolutionary crusade. The Légion des Montagnards, deprived of its title and its autonomy, was reorganised into a demi-brigade of light infantry and incorporated into the line army.[41] The new law left the Parisian *armée* in a position of visible and vulnerable isolation.

Another indication of the hardening of Committee policy was a series of reminders to the generals of armed corps and military divisions that the Parisian *armée* was subject, like all troops, to the laws and to military discipline, and was to obey orders from the garrison commander and any other competent military authority. In Lyon, the detachment was annexed to the Army of the Alps, and, alike with the other garrison soldiers, placed under the command of General Dumas, father of the writer.[42] This subordination, it is true, was only theoretical, the detachment remaining under the effective control of the *représentants* and the great extraordinary commissions, but Maubant had to take orders from Declaye, and the Parisian *armée* figured in the orders of the day issued by the garrison commander. In the Normandy departments, all the detachments were placed under orders from General Vialle, commander-in-chief of the Côtes de Cherbourg Army. In Pluviôse the mutinous cannoneers, in garrison at Caen, had to submit to normal garrison service, Florenval ordering them to undertake guard duty like all the other soldiers there; and at Le Havre, General Beaufort had the detachments following his every order.[43] In Honfleur, it is true, the Parisian *armée* retained its autonomy by virtue of an administrative compromise: Donville, its commander, was also the garrison commander, roles on this occasion having been reversed, and all the troops, even the National Guard and those of the first requisition, coming under the orders of a revolutionary officer. But the military authorities knew their man; Donville was an old soldier, with many years' service behind him, and in no way a political soldier.[44] In Domfort and Alençon the detachments were under orders from the garrison commander. In Brest the cannoneers were responsible to the general commanding the Côtes de Brest Army.[45] In the Aisne the Parisians came under the authority of the general commanding the army in transit; while some detachments were at the disposition of the *représentants* with the Army of the Nord.[46] In Paris itself, the commander of the armed forces took advantage of Ronsin's arrest in Pluviôse to make further encroachments on the autonomy of the *armée révolutionnaire* by having the National Guard arrest *révolutionnaires* on leave in the capital or who had deserted. Grammont, then Maubant, protested in vain that discipline was a matter for headquarters in the rue de Choiseul alone; Hanriot insisted that he had responsibility for all troops in Paris.[47]

Movement orders for the revolutionary detachments during Nivôse and Pluviôse provide another indication of the intentions of the Committee of Public Safety, particularly a wish to depoliticise them. Indeed in stepping up the dispatch of political troops to the West – i.e., to the war zones – the Committee was effecting a disguised merger, for in the West, more than anywhere else, the Parisians would have to be organised into regular formations. But we must not overstate the case; it would be wrong to see in such orders a desire by the Committee to reduce the number of *révolutionnaires* within reach of Paris to the bare minimum. On the contrary, on 29 Ventôse there were still 973 men from the revolutionary detachments within 10 leagues of the capital; and if we add the detachments from the Aisne and the Oise, the cavaliers at Coulommiers, and the fusiliers and cannoneers in the Eure and the Seine-Inférieure, we reach a total of some 2,000 *révolutionnaires* remaining in the Paris region[48] – almost the same number as at the time of Ronsin's arrest in Frimaire. The only important movements to take place in Pluviôse were the dispatch of two cannoneer companies to Chartres and three to Brest, and a force of 476 fusiliers to Le Havre.[49] During this period none of the 27 companies of cannoneers attached to the Parisian *armée* returned to the capital. Two squadrons, long destined for Brest, were kept in total inactivity at Versailles. But at the same time no detachment was brought into Paris, despite the protests of Ronsin on the subject.[50] In short, the Committee during this period tended to give the detachments military destinations, to replace troops which had been on detachment for some time.

More revealing still was its progressive division of detachments into frequently ridiculously small units. Few companies were left intact; squadrons and battalions were scattered through as many as a dozen different localities. In Lyon no battalion had its full complement, and most companies had left men dotted over the Paris region. A good example of this is the fusilier company from the Chalier Section, which on 11 Ventôse had 38 men on detachment at Soissons, 6 at Noyon, 12 at Château-Thierry, 16 at Caen.[51] The result of such fragmentation was that the *révolutionnaires* found themselves at a disadvantage with the local authorities. There was little need solemnly to proclaim the supremacy of the civil over the military power, when the latter was represented by a mere clutch of five or six men. It is important to remember when examining the complaints of the municipalities, ever ready to denounce military arbitrariness, that the *révolutionnaires* were rarely in force in a given *pays*. At the same time the companies lost their *esprit de corps* when they lost their homogeneity, and when the men from a Parisian Section were dispersed through several departments, it was as difficult to maintain any close liaison within the company as it was between it and the Sectionary authorities. This is why Ronsin frequently demanded the regrouping of companies and battalions for the good of the service. The Committee refused, no doubt from systematic distrust. But it must also be recognised that service in the country in itself required such splinterisation. Those responsible for the supply of Paris called for detachments in even the tiniest hamlet.

There was, of course, another solution: an increase in the numbers of the Parisian *armée*. Ronsin repeatedly demanded this and was undeterred by the repeated refusal of the Committee. On 29 Pluviôse he proposed incorporating in the artillery the Réunion company; on 14 Ventôse he suggested adding a further 2,000 men to cover losses through leave, and the return to the arms manufactories of metal-workers from the companies. The Committee on the contrary continued to whittle away at the Parisian *armée*, in Pluviôse requiring the detachment commanders to supply lists of iron-workers, clockmakers, goldsmiths, shoemakers, printers and engravers in their companies. On 26 Pluviôse Ronsin informed the Committee that all the lists had been sent,[52] and at the beginning of Ventôse the process of returning the men to the manufactories commenced, to the corresponding detriment of the service. At the same time these departures, at increasingly more frequent intervals, provoked a sense of insecurity and discontent within the ranks. Those remaining felt abandoned, belonging to an institution which had already been disinherited. These measures were a clear demonstration of the Committee's rejection of purely revolutionary ends in favour of the war effort, and the *armée révolutionnaire* figured less and less among its concerns as it devoted itself entirely to its military programme.

Very different was the attitude of the Committee of General Security. The campaign in Paris and Lyon against the repression and its instruments in no way impeded the repressive activity of the detachments; on the contrary, the agents of the Committee of General Security, particularly the *commissaires* of the *comités révolutionnaires*, seemed to resort more readily to the detachments in Pluviôse and Ventôse than in previous months when the repressive machine was less furtive. Pluviôse and Ventôse saw the most energetic sans-culottes at the peak of their activity, men like Dumoustier, Goust, Petit-Drouet, Moroy, the men involved in the expeditions to Villeblevin, Livry, Vernon and Pont-de-l'Arche. The *armée révolutionnaire* was still in favour with Jagot and his colleagues, and they quickly called to account those authorities who questioned the competence of the *comités de surveillance* and the *commissaires* of the Committee. The latter was unable to reconcile the needs of revolutionary surveillance with the Committee of Public Safety's unceasing apologia for local autonomy. There was accordingly a fundamental disagreement between the two Committees which placed the *armée révolutionnaire* in considerable jeopardy; for, as always in such cases, the object of the dispute was to pay the price for the reconciliation.

The Montcornet affair, and doubtless others of the same nature, certainly played a part in the Committee of Public Safety's growing support for local autonomy. The incidents at Montcornet and Chaourse illustrate with particular clarity the problems of regular authorities co-existing with revolutionary administrations. The viewpoint of Chaumont, on the one hand, and that of the municipalities of the canton on the other, were so fundamentally opposed as to defy any real possibility of reconciliation. For the former, and those carrying out his orders, the interests of Paris and the *armées* were uppermost – that is, what was understood by the 'marche de la Révolution' – while the district and municipality of this little corner of the Thiérarche sought to spare their fellow citizens (and electors) material sacrifice and coercion, and invoked the hierarchy of powers to justify their stance. In this the law was on their side.

There is no need to repeat all the details of this complex operation, which combined all the economic, repressive, political and anti-religious aspects characteristic of the activities of the Parisian *armée* in the country. Only the administrative aspect of Chaumont's initiatives need detain us here, for they were the real heart of the matter.[53] The mission of the detachment to the canton of Montcornet originated in an order of 25 Frimaire from Gênois, *commissaire* for Parisian supplies in the Aisne. The mission was a typical one: surveillance and acceleration of requisitions. But Gênois attached certain recommendations to his order: 'they [the Parisian soldiers] should show fraternity towards the farmers with whom they are lodged, aiding the good, keeping an eye on the wicked [*les méchans*]...'. And what if the 'méchants' should be municipal officers, public functionaries? The *commissaire* thought of that, for he instructed the detachments to correspond regularly with him, informing him 'of any obstacle encountered in the conduct of their mission so that the appropriate measures might be taken...'. Before their departure, Gênois seems to have imparted to Chaumont and his companions the poor impression he had of the authorities of this canton, who were extremely laggardly in fulfilling requisitions, and were thought by all the *commissaires* to be ill disposed towards Paris. Before leaving Laon, Chaumont recognised that he was going to have trouble with the authorities, who, at the very least, aided and abetted the delays, and he had been warned to keep an eye on *les méchants* and *les égoïstes*.

On 2 Nivôse, shortly after their arrival in the cantons, two soldiers from the Bondy company provoked a small disturbance by an extremely foolish and decidedly illegal attempt to interrupt the celebration of mass and consecrate a church to the cult of Reason. The populace of the village (Chaourse), roused by the women, mobbed the two Parisians, and the immediate relatives of the mayor of the commune, Fournier, were among the most violent of the attackers. The detachment captain learnt of these events on the 3rd, from other soldiers who had observed them from afar, and had eventually succeeded in rescuing their comrades from the furious crowd. They spoke of 'attempted murder', and of the aggressors, who were known to the mayor, having been set at liberty. They implied that this public official was unwilling to prosecute the guilty parties.

Chaumont acted as any good officer would have done. His first concern was the security of his men, and if they ran the danger of being assassinated in the course of their duty, then the local authorities would be held responsible. Angry, and having been forewarned about these village authorities, he went alone to the mayor to demand an explanation. The mayor, having promised to come to meet him in the *chef-lieu*, had not kept his word. 'Chaumont, afraid of being manhandled by the Thiérarchiens, as the two soldiers had been, took it upon himself to go in force [to Chaourse] with some 40 men. But it was to forestall rather than to incur trouble. He also went alone, with Béranger [second lieutenant] to the mayor's house.... The mayor was alone. He [Chaumont] invited him to come as promised. The mayor, who was plotting something, put on his sash of office, came to Chaumont's, drank a bottle of wine with him, explained what had happened in terms designed to play down the crime committed by his fellow citizens and his relatives, whom he was careful not to denounce, claiming on the contrary that no one knew the culprits, and withdrew calmly, Chaumont having treated him with complete openness and politeness...'. Such was the captain's version and its main thrust is confirmed (although the details differ) in the mayor's account. But

Fournier's emphasis was on the use of violence against a public official in the exercise of his duties (that was why he donned his sash before joining Chaumont). 'This day [5 Nivôse], around midday', wrote Fournier in a formal report drawn up about the incident, 'citizen Martin, "so-called" lieutenant of the *armée révolutionnaire*, accompanied by citizen Béranger and others wearing the National Guard uniform and under arms, required the citizen mayor to follow them in the name of the law, which he obeyed in fear of trouble, knowing however of no offence against the law, and he was taken to Montcornet'. Having arrived at the *auberge* of the Soleil d'Or, where Chaumont awaited him, 'the captain said to Martin: "this is not what I ordered", to which Martin replied: "that is what you wrote..."'. The captain said to the plaintiff: "have a seat and we'll drink a bottle" to which he consented and they drank several bottles, after which he returned home, the plaintiff observing [this Thiérarche peasant was much craftier than the jeweller Chaumont] that when he was required to follow the escort, he had put on his sash of office, and thus decorated had asked citizen Martin to show him the law or warrant authorising him to take him from his residence, the response was always the same: "come with us or we will return in force..."'. The plaintiff demanded...if he should have been led like a common criminal at the head of an armed troop...'. Doubtless there had been some misunderstanding between Chaumont and Martin, the latter, who was not very intelligent – he was only a market porter – having perhaps exceeded his chief's instructions by threatening the mayor. But an armed force *had* been present, and Chaumont *had* used force against this official, even if Fournier's claim to have been 'seized' is somewhat exaggerated.

The day after these declarations, 6 Nivôse, the Laon municipality developed its offensive against the detachment in a letter to the Commission des Subsistances. 'We cannot hide from you the fact that their stay in the cantons of Montcornet and Rozoy has already given rise to complaints, which a *commissaire* has been sent to investigate...'. On the 7th the president of the district wrote to the *comités* of Chaourse and Montcornet: 'I have just been informed that some kind of disturbance has occurred in Chaourse between the citizens of the *armée révolutionnaire* and those of the said commune'; he asked for a detailed report on the incident and urged them to take immediate steps to prevent such abuses. Clearly the district had already reached a verdict on the affair in its invitation to the two *comités* – simultaneously judges and litigants – to supply evidence against the detachment. It was an invitation to which they responded with some zeal, for the district president had already compiled a dossier, extremely unfavourable to the detachment, by 13 Nivôse, when he wrote to the Committee of General Security and the public prosecutor of the department about 'the seizure of the mayor of Chaourse, though wearing his sash of office, and his transportation to Montcornet...'. The district official observed on this occasion 'that not only had an armed force sent into a commune no right to exercise any authority over municipal officers, but its members ought actually to obey any orders issued to them by the said municipal officers; there is not a good republican who will not tremble at the account of what happened in the commune of Chaourse; 50 men arrived in that commune, bringing, not fraternity, but the most rigorous and most cruel despotism. . . '.[54]

This bitter attack by the Laon authorities is in no way surprising. The town of Laon was already in the bad books of the suppliers of Paris, and its authorities clearly considered attacking the *armée révolutionnaire*, on whatever pretext, to be its best means of defence. Nor did the district rest content with having raised the issue of the 'seizure', but went on to accuse the detachment of having levied arbitrary *taxes* on the farmers of the canton of Montcornet. Furthermore, news of Ronsin's arrest had a greater impact on this department than elsewhere; he was a native of Soissons and had family in Laon itself[55] and friends and enemies throughout the region. In Pluviôse, therefore, the district returned to the charge – having received first-hand accounts from the various authorities of Montcornet, and additional details about the *coup de force* committed by Chaumont – and on the 21st its president communicated the completed dossier to the public prosecutor of the criminal tribunal. The investigation started there. But once Ronsin was freed, the local authorities were careful not to expose themselves to a possible reversal of the situation, and the investigation proceeded without publicity. Chaumont himself returned to Laon and remained undisturbed until 28 Ventôse, the day after news of Ronsin's second arrest was received in the town. The arrest was confirmed on 11 Germinal and the indictment drawn up over 23–4 Germinal. A month later, 23 Floréal, it was the turn of Chaumont and Martin to be indicted, the former 'accused of having issued orders for the conduct of the mayor of Chaourse to Montcornet, and having done so maliciously and deliberately', the latter 'for having, by virtue of these orders, taken the said mayor from his home, despite the fact that he was wearing the distinctive badges of his office, and had him transported from the commune of Chaourse to that of Montcornet, surrounded by an escort of 40–50 men from the *armée révolutionnaire*, and for having done so maliciously and deliberately. . . '.[56] As a result 'according to article 19 of section III, heading 1 of Part Two of the penal code', the tribunal condemned the two officers to six years' hard labour and to exposure for four hours in the public square of Laon, bearing placards telling of their misdeeds against the public official. The following day the two Parisians lodged an appeal with the Court of Appeals; but it was rejected on 2 Thermidor.

In his appeal Chaumont tried to show that the mayor had come to him of his own free will and that their discussion had been calm. As a soldier, he demanded to appear before a military court. He also tried to justify his conduct towards the mayor in terms of public safety and defence of the regime; what he was saying in fact was that he had acted 'in the spirit of the

Revolution'. (Cf. above, p. 426.) In Floréal, the Committee of Public Safety, despite its title, was deaf to the force of such an argument. True, it had dithered throughout the winter before deciding in favour of municipal autonomy and proclaiming the 'normalisation' of institutions. In the autumn it had leaned towards force, recommending to the detachment commanders the utmost severity towards the *méchants* and the *égoïstes*, whether or not they were municipal officers or district administrators (which they often were). But in the spring the accent was on juridical legality and respect for the established authorities. The two unfortunate officers had been victims of the Committee's equivocation, which left them in ignorance concerning the real intentions of the government; for what could a jeweller and a market porter know of such things? It is clear that Chaumont felt he had acted correctly, having been given a mandate to bypass opposition from village mayors in virtue of his revolutionary mission on behalf of the Commune of Paris. The affair had arisen out of the fundamental contradiction between the demands of revolutionary action and the respect for the forms of legality, and it could not have occurred at a more unfavourable moment for the captain.

The Laon municipality was not the only one to recognise a change in the political climate in Nivôse and a return to administrative 'normalisation'. The reprimands, the trivial harassments which the Committee had visited on the detachments since the law of 14 Frimaire, were echoed in the countryside. In Nivôse and Pluviôse, there were renewed complaints from the municipalities in the Paris supply zone about the insolence and high-handedness of the officers and soldiers of the *armée révolutionnaire* towards them. The first complaints were lodged at the beginning of Nivôse, became more numerous in the second half and positively flowed in the first two *décades* of Pluviôse. But after the 20th they ceased almost entirely, and only began again more than a month later, in the closing days of Ventôse, when news of the arrest of the Hébertists reached every commune in the Paris region. In only one locality were there any complaints against a detachment in the second *décade* of Ventôse. Now the dates of Ronsin's first detention were 27 Frimaire to 14 Pluviôse, and it does look as if the local authorities chose their moment for developing the campaign against an *armée* which, to judge from events in Paris, was losing ground. Certainly the delay of several weeks before some municipalities and districts complained of incidents long past supports such a hypothesis. Moreover, after 14 Pluviôse, one of the authorities which had complained most about the detachments began to back-track and adopt a more conciliatory attitude towards the Parisians.[57]

There was then a direct connection between the hardening of attitude by the Committee of Public Safety towards the Parisian *armée* after 14 Frimaire, and the first offensive by the local authorities. One is tempted indeed to draw an even closer connection between the two; for had not the

Committee itself inspired such complaints by insisting, in its letters to the municipalities, on the subordination of the detachments, and on the fact that the *armée révolutionnaire* was not an autonomous force? Certainly the repetition of such complaints from opponents of the *armée* was used to good effect by Lindet, Carnot and Barère to influence their colleagues within the Committee who still supported methods of constraint; while the very number of such accusations became an annoyance to everyone on the Committee, and caused them to ask whether an *armée* which provoked such discontent in the country should continue in existence.

On the Parisian scene the *armée* entered a difficult period in Nivôse. The causes were political: the campaign of the Indulgents further discredited the general staff and put in doubt the disinterestedness of the officers and soldiers. The chiefs in the rue de Choiseul added to their own difficulties by their ridiculous and petty personal squabbles. Events in Lyon aggravated the loss of confidence in the *armée* on the part of Jacobin opinion, by identifying the institution itself with a pitiless repression which had already become an object of horror. The spotlight trained upon the *armée* as a result of the debate between Indulgents and 'ultras' did it no good whatsoever.

The municipal authorities, aware of the 'politicisation' of the debate for and against the *armée révolutionnaire*, lost nothing by waiting – country people are patient by nature. With the detention of Ronsin they again found courage and the voice to denounce the acts of insubordination, the abuse of power and the extortions by officers and soldiers. The Committee of Public Safety opened the way for the enemies of the terrorist institutions by its favourable reception of the Lyonnais and its insistence, in letters to the municipalities, on the supremacy of the civil power. It refused Ronsin the reinforcements he asked for, and opposed the return to the capital of detachments whose presence was no longer needed in the places where they had been stationed. At the same time, it whittled away at the already meagre strength of the detachments to man the arms manufactories. In Nivôse and Pluviôse the Committee was totally preoccupied with its military programme. In Pluviôse and Ventôse it had recourse once again to the detachments to suppress the combinations among workers in the shipyards and those manning the waterways transport. The *armée révolutionnaire* was tolerated only in the degree to which it was useful in the war effort, notably as a means of forcing workers to accept the Maximum on wage rates.

These difficulties at the centre, in Paris, did not affect every detachment as yet, and some continued in Pluviôse and Ventôse to carry out frequently spectacular operations. They still had the full support of the Committee of General Security and its many agents, and it was not until the very eve of its abolition that the repressive activity of the Parisian *armée* underwent any curtailment.

A final decision, therefore, had not yet been made on the fate of the *armée*, and if some were already looking to its disbandment after Frimaire, they were to be disappointed. Indeed, by insisting on the subordination of the detachments to local authority, the Committee seemed even to be envisaging a new period of activity for them according to different principles. The *armée* was weaker, but it still had its fervent supporters in the more advanced Sections of the capital. The *révolutionnaires*, for their part, had lost much of their earlier enthusiasm, and the demobilisation of certain categories of artisans had made those remaining more impatient to return home. The *armée* itself was becoming militarised and the career soldiers who commanded certain detachments were trying to make them into disciplined forces. In Lyon and in Normandy the *révolutionnaires* were having to abandon their political games – the discussions in the *auberge* and in the club, the *parties de campagne* in the homes of rich farmers – for military exercises and guard duty. This only served further to increase the discontent of men who had not enlisted to learn how to drill. The Parisian *armée*, then, approached the great political crisis of Ventôse–Germinal in a state of considerable weakness, undermined by internal discontent, public indifference and rivalries at the top. By the end of Ventôse, its only remaining defenders were a tiny group of militant *sectionnaires*, who were themselves compromised in the débâcle within the popular movement.

CHAPTER 3

The 'Military Plot' of Ventôse and the Disbandment of the Parisian *Armée* (14 Ventôse–6 Floréal Year II)

The political climate, which had been stormy since the New Year, suddenly darkened in the spring of 1794. The largely political crisis, anticipated throughout the previous month, was deliberately provoked by the Revolutionary Government. It had to act more quickly than an increasingly threatening opposition, which for a *décade* had been making public declarations about popular oppression and using the explosive word 'insurrection'. The government had to strike before this opposition, still only political, could find backing among the *petit peuple*. Yes, the people in the Sections were discontented at the catastrophic cut in meat rations and *arrivages* of dairy produce. But bread was plentiful, and housewives could queue at the bakeries and buy it at prices set by the Maximum. The economic climate was not conducive to the hatching of a popular *journée* provoked by shortages. The government was actually able to utilise popular discontent as an additional weapon against the political opposition, which it accused of having caused an artificial shortage in secondary foodstuffs.

In the middle of Ventôse Fouquier-Tinville was called before the two Committees, sitting together in plenary session, as they did during all the great crises of the regime. The agreement between the two heads of the revolutionary eagle announced the condemnation of all 'ultras', atheists, egalitarians and men of violence, and the public prosecutor was given full scope to prepare a convincing indictment against those whose heads were to fall. The object was to isolate them completely from the militant *sectionnaires* and the *petit peuple*. It took only five days for Fouquier, a zealous official with an enormous capacity for work and a creative imagination, to stock his arsenal. On 23 Ventôse Ronsin, Hébert, Momoro and 15 others were arrested and charged with involvement in a foreign plot against the Revolutionary Government.

According to the charges there had been a 'plot' – or rather several 'plots' – which sought to replace the two Committees and the Convention by a military dictatorship. The leader of this 'conspiracy' was Ronsin, christened the 'new Cromwell'; his chosen instrument was the *armée révolutionnaire*, kept for some time in 'shameful inactivity' within reach of Paris. Ronsin and his principal military accomplices planned to bring the revolutionary troops cantoned at Versailles and in the fort of Vincennes back to Paris, where they would seize the powder magazines and the arsenals and capture the 24 members of the Revolutionary Government. In the event of complications, the 'conspirators' planned to set up a stronghold on the Ile Saint-Louis and to withdraw to Vincennes. Once the 'military plot' had succeeded, they would install a military dictator and France would be given over to widespread massacre. But these were only the practical elements of a vast conspiracy which also relied on food shortages and a prison plot as psychological accessories. The presence of foreigners and bankers among the conspirators shows that the proposed change in regime was in response to orders from abroad. The dictatorship was to be purely temporary, preparing the way for a restored monarchy by destroying the *patriotes* and creating a *pacte de famine* of which the people would be the victim.

Fouquier and his masters had brought together all the elements most calculated to disturb the *petit peuple*: a military plot, a foreign plot, a *pacte de famine*, a prison conspiracy – all taken from long-established popular mythology. Best of all, Versailles and the fort of Vincennes were to be the assembly points for this 'coup against Paris'. The government had calculated well; Sectionary opinion credited the reality of a military plot, just as the *petit peuple* always believed in sinister projects of this kind. Instinctively mistrustful of those in high places, the people of Paris were always ready to accept the idea of a 'conspiracy' as the cause of all their troubles. Hébert in particular found himself execrated by his most faithful readers for having betrayed them. As for Ronsin, his manner of speech was always so violent that public opinion had no difficulty accepting the image of him as an apprentice dictator, presented to them by Fouquier. The government had pulled off a magnificent propaganda operation, depriving its enemies on the left of all popular support. Indeed its success was almost too complete, for the peripheral Sections of Paris and the communes on the outskirts were seized by a general panic, and people saw foreigners and evil-looking men with whiskers at every corner. Popular opinion reasoned that, since the 'conspirators' had caused an artificial shortage, abundance would return after they were executed. But abundance did not return; the government had gone over the top in its gamble on such a sensitive issue.

The suppression of the *armée révolutionnaire* went ahead smoothly, despite government fears of resistance from Ronsin's soldiers. Popular opinion, taken in by Fouquier, did not at first grasp the real implications of a measure which left the farmers free to cheat on the Maximum, in complicity with the districts. The Committees had also taken a considerable risk in bringing down the leading demagogues, for now it would be difficult to contain the advance of *modérantisme*. Murmurs began against Marat. In the departments news of the 'plot' sent a shock wave through the most varied communes, from the periphery of Paris to the Comtat, the Alps and the Pyrenees, as, between 23 Ventôse and 22 Germinal, the most energetic dechristianisers and 'apôtres' of egalitarian politics were proscribed as accomplices of

Ronsin. The municipalities, pretending to take seriously government warnings about 'ramifications of the plot in the departments', trumpeted their vengeance against the 'étrangers', the emissaries of Paris and the large towns.

Undoubtedly many of the 'internal revolutions' which occurred within the *sociétés populaires* and *comités* in Floréal and Prairial were simply a case of settling scores between rival clans – nothing could be easier than to sink a rival by calling him a Hébertist. But the reaction in the departments was genuine. In condemning the *armée révolutionnaire* the government had also condemned an entire policy. Military *ultracisme* was essentially a departmental phenomenon, and in towns like Lyon, Toulouse, Lille, Bayonne, as well as in the small communes, popular opinion grasped the full import of this official abandonment of *les grandes mesures* much more quickly than it did in Paris. There it took the terrible Year III, with its train of misery, famine, suicides and cold, to bring home to the people in the Sections the defeat which they had suffered in Germinal Year II when the popular army was disarmed. It was then that many former *révolutionnaires* acquired once again a collective consciousness. But this time the government no longer needed to deceive the people with myths; it simply called in the army and disarmed the Sectionary artillery. After Prairial Year III, the history of the former *armées révolutionnaires* becomes intertwined with that of the survival of terrorist cadres and with republican martyrology.

I *The political crisis of 14–23 Ventôse*

In the first half of Ventôse, there was a rush of events in Paris. In addition to the political crisis, there was greater than normal agitation in the Sections about the eternal problem of subsistences. Can we accept Albert Soboul's argument that an economic crisis, aggravating popular disquiet, was creating a climate conducive to another *journée*?[1] The subsistence-crisis factor should not be exaggerated, for the Parisian markets had been in a state of permanent crisis since the autumn. True, there had been a marked drop in *arrivages* of supplies such as meat, vegetables, eggs and firewood since the beginning of Pluviôse, and during this month, and more particularly in the first days of Ventôse, popular complaint assumed a sharper tone and there was talk of a crisis in meat supplies. Meat, in fact, was unobtainable in the butchers' shops; but the rich managed to procure it by sending their servants or hired hands into communes on the periphery to meet graziers going to the markets of Poissy and Sceaux; trading seems to have been particularly heavy at Montrouge, Belleville, Charenton and Ivry.[2] The language used by queuing housewives provides the best barometer of popular anger. In Ventôse the women were complaining more than normal. The deterioration in *arrivages*, partly seasonal, was sufficiently acute to give a new urgency to demands, echoed since October in the Sections, for the use of force against the farmers. In the middle of the month of Ventôse, the advanced Sections, alerted by complaints from the detachments of their inaction, their powerlessness in the face of the immunity enjoyed by the farmers, called out again for the famous popular commissions and mobile guillotines. But the shortages complained of were in non-essential supplies; Paris was not about to run out of bread. And up to now, the people had never revolted for foodstuffs other than bread; a shortage of meat, which they consumed in tiny quantities, posed no danger to the regime.

Whether the food crisis was real or artificial, the Committee of Public Safety seemed in fear of a popular *journée*, which would be all the more dangerous if it coincided with an already explosive political situation. Popular opinion certainly expected some change, and a 'new 2 September' was being spoken of. The punitive will of the people had revived. The Committee in any event had decided to strike, and made its plans before 16 Ventôse; it would put an end to the increasingly vociferous opposition within the Cordeliers and from the Marat Section by drawing up a case against the leaders of the supposed *parti hébertiste*. When, on the 16th, the Committee ordered Fouquier-Tinville, in the name of the two Committees jointly, to gather information in the communes on the periphery of Paris about the attempts of *malveillants* to interrupt the *arrivages* of staple foodstuffs, the stage had been set, the fate of the leading Cordeliers was already decided on high, and the affair had simply to run its course. Fouquier lost no time. The only thing left to be decided was who was to have the honour of occupying the green chair of judgement and who would be excluded from the holocaust in preparation. In the event the Committees had to restrain the appetite of the public prosecutor, who was not only proceeding with undue haste – though he had been advised to do so, for the Committees were in a hurry to strike before the threatened *journée* erupted – but was also trying to include Jacobin personalities still in favour in his terrible honours list.[3]

Since 15 Pluviôse Ronsin and Vincent had been trying to turn the Sections' campaign for their release into a personal triumph. Increasingly irritated by the impunity enjoyed by their enemies among the Indulgents, and at their own powerlessness, they were imprudent enough to accuse Robespierre of protecting the *pourris* and accommodating avowed counter-revolutionaries. Ronsin, in his official role as head of the *armée révolutionnaire*, had given his critics little ammunition, corresponding regularly with the Committee on all current issues – including the movements of his troops – and reminding the detachments of the strict obedience owed to the local authorities; but Ronsin the private man, the Cordelier, made numerous violent statements, flinging about the dangerous word 'insurrection' with cheerful abandon. Vincent and Ronsin were indeed men of violence – Marat alone came anywhere near them – and bitingly ambitious,[4] as members of a group whose future was blocked, access to the higher reaches of government being almost entirely closed to them. Within the Committee of Public Safety they could count on Collot alone, and he was not the sort to let himself be compromised by the irresponsible.[5] In the Convention they had scarcely any supporters; the Jacobins remained hostile, and, to Vincent, completely closed. They had access to minor organisations only: the Cordeliers, the War Ministry,[6] the Marat Section assembly and *comité*, and some *sociétés* in the Sections. In the state of play existing in spring 1794, they found their way still barred by the Committee of Public Safety, the Convention and the Jacobins, as well as the local authorities. If their opinions were to triumph, they needed to take power, arrange new elections to bring more of their supporters into the Convention, apply the Constitution and organise the Ministries. But how could the Revolutionary Government be brought down in the face of opposition from the Committees, most of the Convention and the Jacobins? Political means offered little chance of success. Nor was recourse to the Sections a viable option, since, apart from the Marat Section, they had no extensive following within the popular institutions – or indeed in Paris itself; their disciples were scattered all over France in the vast machinery of military administration – and, as Albert Soboul has shown, their strictly political aims bore no relation to the mainly economic demands coming from the Sections in Ventôse.[7]

There remained the resort to force, to a *coup d'état*, to dictatorship. Ronsin was not alone in considering this. In Paris and in the departments, there had been talk since the beginning of the month of the need for a violent coup to revive the Convention, or render it powerless, but above all to give a new impetus to *grandes mesures*. On two occasions, 4 and 18 Ventôse, Erimanthe Lambin, an employee of the department of Paris, wrote to his brother, a clerk in the military administration at Châlons-sur-Marne, indicating the necessity for a new insurrection, announcing the imminent creation of six *commissions populaires* to deal swiftly with suspects, and an acceleration of revolutionary justice.[8] Such ideas did not arise spontaneously in the mind of someone in such a junior position; Lambin was an assiduous member of the Cordeliers. A resort to force seemed all the more realistic when the force was there, at hand, with Ronsin in command of the *armée révolutionnaire*. When a political general starts talking of insurrection, even though by that he only means drawing attention to the rights of the oppressed, there is good reason for thinking that his intentions are not entirely theoretical. But for the head of an army to speak flippantly of insurrection is political suicide, and Ronsin was an inveterate candidate for suicide.

From the middle of Pluviôse, those familiar with the political scene in Paris expected some violent coup. Interior Ministry agents paid particular attention to the sessions of the Cordeliers and the general assemblies in Sections where Hébert and his friends were supposed to have a following, and were the first to remark upon a kind of civil war being waged between the Cordeliers and the Jacobins. Public opinion, even among the sans-culottes, and a part of the *armée révolutionnaire* were prepared to accept the official version of events, believing in Ronsin's dictatorial ambitions and his intention of carrying out a *coup d'état* against the Revolutionary Government and installing a *système militaire*.[9] When Ronsin, Vincent, Momoro, Hébert and their so-called 'accomplices' were arrested on the night of 23–4 Ventôse, by *commissaires* from the *comités révolutionnaires* of their Sections, serving warrants from the Committee of General Security – Ronsin was arrested in his apartment on the boulevard Montmartre, not far from the offices in the rue de Choiseul, Faubourg-Montmartre Section – public opinion accepted it with no apparent surprise, and did nothing. At that moment the Hébertists were lost. They were guilty because the Committees had said so; the very fact of their imprisonment proved it.

II   *The 'new Cromwell': Ronsin the dictator*

Fouquier's thesis of a military plot rested on Ronsin. As general of the *armée révolutionnaire*, he had force at his disposal and had already had a long career in military administration, in which he had placed many of his people. He had a 'clientele', he was 'party leader'. In the 'military plot' thesis the general's personality dominated events. But what were his secret intentions? The truth was he had none; there wasn't even the outline of a plan and no indication of any military preparations. There was no sign of a movement of revolutionary forces towards Paris during Pluviôse and Ventôse; the *armée*'s every move was given full publicity by Ronsin himself, and the few regroupings which he tried to effect at this stage, after seeking authorisation from the Committee of Public Safety, were designed to restore cohesion to certain Sectionary companies which had been scattered over several localities. Lastly, he did try to augment the garrison in Lyon; but this was hardly the best way of preparing a coup in Paris. Nor did the indictment stress this point; Fouquier was content to mention some hunting parties and pleasure trips by the general and his officers into the Paris countryside to sustain the thesis of a maturing *coup de force*.

But what did Ronsin himself want? Dictatorship? Supreme power? It was said of him, that he had wanted to imitate Cromwell, and that through reading David Hume's *History of England* – in English, no less – he became enamoured of this figure and had said that if he could be in Cromwell's position for only 24 hours, he would do great things.[10] Rubbish! The Cromwell story is absurd. The sans-culottes had an extremely poor opinion of the Lord Protector; he was thought of as simply a military dictator, a tyrant whose power rested on the army, and Ronsin himself was to state at his trial 'that he had always regarded Cromwell as the oppressor of his country . . .'. All the *révolutionnaires* dreaded military power, and Jacobins and Cordeliers were at one on this. Cromwell was given a bad press in the Year II and had no place in the historical pantheon of revolutionaries, reserved for figures like William Tell and Algernon Sidney.[11]

To make of this revolutionary general a 'new Cromwell' was to flatter him: Ronsin was not the stuff of dictators. He had no precise aim, no sense of direction. He was not even the best politician among the Cordeliers; that honour belongs rather to the printer Momoro.[12] Ronsin was certainly no fool, and, on occasion, even displayed a certain tactical skill; his discourse of 17 Ventôse to the Cordeliers was not an exaggerated declaration of war, as most of his earlier contributions had been, but a sincere attempt by a simple man, and above all a revolutionary patriot, to re-establish unity between Jacobins and Cordeliers in a common effort to halt the disturbing progress of *modérantisme*. 'Take care, citizens', he said on this occasion, 'lest from the debris of these two factions [of Brissot and Philippe Egalité] another, more disastrous one of ambitious and dominating men does not arise. The people must always stand firm, terror should be the order of the day, and all the great revolutionary measures outlined in the different reports made in the name of the Committee of Public Safety carried through.... Let us rally round the brave Montagnards, who, in the Committees of Public Safety and General Security, have foiled so many intrigues, prevented so many plots...'.[13] These were not the words of a conspirator, of a man preparing to overturn the Revolutionary Government and take its place. Albert Soboul's conclusions regarding the apprentice dictator are far more plausible than those of Jaurès and the other historians who have subscribed to the 'plot' theory. Ronsin's discourse on 17 Ventôse Soboul describes as a 'real effort to rise above the bitterness and construct an effective popular policy...'.[14]

But his appeal was not listened to, and he saw clearly that the government had no wish to subscribe to this popular programme designed to 'accelerate the progress of the revolutionary machine' and stop that of the Indulgents. Thereafter the general gave free rein to his anger. He may have lacked the ambition, but he had the temperament and the violence for a dictator. He was anti-parliamentarian and spoke with as much scorn as his friend Vincent of those 'robed mannequins', the representatives of the people; his distrust of the deputies was akin to that felt by the militant *sectionnaires* for the 'mandataires infidèles'.[15] There were several Ronsins; but which was the real one? The one who spoke like a truly political man, anxious to maintain unity among the patriots, in his appeal of 17 Ventôse? Or the one who, at those grand dinners in the banker de Kock's house at Passy, gave free rein to his anger when he spoke out against the Convention and the Committees? The private man was unbelievably imprudent, and in these crucial days of Ventôse it was increasingly difficult to distinguish the private from the public man. Ronsin was one of those people who destroy themselves by talking too much. Seen thus among his friends – though the Passy dinners were also attended by jurors of the revolutionary tribunal, by faithful agents of the government, *and* by Fouquier-Tinville – Ronsin appeared impatient, disrespectful of forms and authority, and to hold certain rather simplistic political views, notably on the effectiveness of an intensified terror against the moderates. At some stage in Ventôse, having become convinced that the Jacobins were in league with the Indulgents to bring about the destruction of the Revolution, he began to entertain the possibility of a *coup de force* to safeguard it.

This coup might indeed have come off if Ronsin had put his mind to it and had been given sufficient time. But he did little more than talk about it. At de Kock's he spoke in support of the Constitution of 1793. Even if he did not seek power for himself, he was certainly a supporter of strong government; and the Committee of Public Safety was not that. Perhaps he envisaged some sort of military government, based on parallel hierarchies among the great extraordinary commissions, and composed of *commissaires civils* and 'hommes de liaison'. Ronsin applauded *grands moyens*, but he made the grave mistake of never clarifying what he meant by these words, leaving his enemies in the government in total freedom to supply their own interpretation, that he was preparing a massacre. Vagueness in a conspirator is as dangerous as loquaciousness. What is certain is that he wanted to continue to 'revolutionise', to make life impossible for hoarders and moderates through a reinforced Terror, possibly plunging France into a bloodbath. Ronsin and his friends talked a lot about such things at the dinners, and even more in the prisons, where their visits used to spread terror among the inmates; for these jack-in-boots walked about with lists in their hands, proclaiming that they would release imprisoned patriots, but holding out the threat of new massacres to the others.[16] Violence was in the air at that time; the *société populaire* of Tonneins, in the Garonne valley, which had been a fief of the dechristianising movement, was outlining an entire plan for a military dictatorship under a *Grand Juge*.[17]

Ronsin then had inclinations, but as yet no plans. However, according to several witnesses, the Parisian *armée*, in existence for some six months, was learning how to manoeuvre and was holding itself in readiness for all eventualities.[18] It might have seemed to Ronsin, as it did to the Committee, that this political *armée* was becoming militarised. For the Committee it was a matter of clipping its wings while there was still time. Ronsin for his part allowed himself to be taken before he had planned anything; the most obliging of conspirators, on the very eve of his 'coup' – his last 'situation report' is dated 20 Ventôse[19] – he was revealing all his dispositions, particularly the incredible weakness of his means of intervention, to the government he was trying to topple.

According to the indictment drawn up by Fouquier against the Hébertists, Ronsin was to have grouped around Paris the revolutionary troops brought in from their cantonments, so as to have them on hand to attack strategic points in the city under cover of 'mock patrols'.[20] If so, the general went about things in a most unusual way, for his orders after Nivôse produced quite the opposite result. Not one cannoneer remained in Paris at the beginning of the month of Ventôse, and the nearest company was at Coulommiers. In the absence of artillery, how was he to effect his coup? On 4 Ventôse he proposed to Bouchotte the dispatch to Saumur of the three squadrons of cavalry then on detachment in Beauvais and

Coulommiers, and their replacement by the squadrons left at Versailles; on his orders, two squadrons left Beauvais on 6 Ventôse, and if the others remained in place, it was not the fault of the general. In reality he had nothing to hide because he had nothing prepared.[21] Instead of plotting, he talked and he hunted. But, always the good loser, on his way to the guillotine he was to admit that he regretted his inactivity during these crucial days. Around 15 Ventôse, he went hunting with Boulanger and some aides-de-camp in the Bois d'Arcy.[22] On the 20th he went again with Boulanger, the deputy Ludot, and a group of young officers to the fort of Vincennes to investigate the living conditions of his men, and to receive complaints from the sans-culottes of the commune against the *commissaire aux accaparements*, before 'eating a fish stew' on the Rapée.[23]

The dossier on Ronsin's part in this 'military plot' is so thin that one is left wondering why Fouquier and his superiors insisted on according this general the principal role in such a theoretical conspiracy. There were many other generals just as violent, just as hotheaded, and certainly more ambitious. There was Parein; but Parein was in Lyon, so he would not do. There was Boulanger, who had accompanied his chief on the outings to the Bois d'Arcy and to Vincennes; but he would not do either. He did have a role in the 'plot'; but it was that of an informer, warning his friend Le Bas, a member of the Committee of General Security, of the impending arrival of Boissay in Paris to take part in the 'conspiracy'.[24] As for Hanriot, he too was taboo, having his protectors in the Committee of Public Safety. Another general then? In the Year II generals lolling in the capital were disquieting, and, like the troops of the line, they were rarely permitted to linger. The absence from Paris of generals and troops simply focused attention all the more on the most insignificant acts and words of Ronsin and his general staff.

Once the idea of Ronsin being at the head of a military conspiracy was accepted, everything else fell into place, all his actions since his release in Pluviôse apparently supporting this thesis. On the other hand many of his actions are difficult to explain if the idea of a conspiracy is dismissed entirely. Why, for instance, should he have thought of visiting the prisons with Mazuel? With Ronsin one blunder, one gratuitous gesture or foolish word, was followed by another, and another. That is how a man with no precise aim, and with few ideas, but who wanted change and perhaps had some thought of effecting it, could pass for the leader of a conspiracy. Ronsin was the key to all the thinking behind the indictment. Fouquier had chosen his man well, for this violent and foolish Picard had already done much to bring about his own downfall.

III   *The 'accomplices' of the general*

As early as 23 Ventôse the Revolutionary Government was insisting that the plot had ramifications in the departments, and repeatedly urging vigilance on the municipalities and the *comités de surveillance*. Already, on the 16th, it had indicated to Fouquier its belief that the affair was not purely Parisian when it asked him to send rogatory commissions out to some 30 communes on the periphery.[25] All the chiefs of the revolutionary general staff were suspected of complicity, and in the departments the calls to vigilance found a ready response in municipalities where revolutionary detachments were stationed. Ronsin by himself did not amount to much; if he was showered with attention, it was because of his generalship of the *armée révolutionnaire*. He needed 'accomplices' who shared his ambitions, and instruments to realise them. Nor was opinion slow to find both in the most unlikely places. Indeed such was the network of relationships and dangerous friendships discovered for him, that one might have thought Ronsin a truly important figure.

The 'accomplices' of Ronsin were of two types: firstly, those suspect because of their positions on the revolutionary general staff – the Parisian *armée* having been the instrument of the supposed ambitions of its general; secondly, his personal friends, and above all a host of people who owed their places at every level of the extensive military establishment to him. Certain 'accomplices' in the latter category had worked under Ronsin when he was chief *commissaire* at Liège, and two were relatives, his cousin and his father-in-law. Government had again excelled in the choice of lesser characters in the drama, for the revolutionary general staff was so far discredited in its eyes that public opinion was ready to accept the news – unlikely as it seemed – that the Grammonts, protégés of Hérault and sworn enemies of Ronsin, were deeply involved in the conspiracy.[26] The third figure in this 'supporting cast' was Mazuel, who, like his chief, had been incautious in his speech during those critical days of the second *décade* of Ventôse; witnesses were to tell the revolutionary tribunal that they had heard him declare his intention of transferring the revolutionary squadrons from Versailles to the Ecole Militaire and Vincennes.[27] His own officers toed the official line by reporting his conversations, just as Halm and Vézien were to testify against Ronsin. Such testimony was particularly damaging to the two men, for if the revolutionary officers were ready to subscribe to the idea of such a conspiracy led by Ronsin and Mazuel, the public, strangers to the various internal struggles in the general staff, could not but see that as further proof of the guilt of those in charge of the *armée*. A fourth 'accomplice', the adjutant-general, Berthaud, was arrested on 24 Ventôse, on a warrant issued by the Committee of General Security.[28] We do not know the nature of the charges against this former second-in-command of the Tuileries Section, but the date of his arrest, the day following that of his chief, suggests that in the eyes of the Committee he was in some way connected with the 'plot'.

On 26 Ventôse, at the same time as Mazuel was arrested, a young cavalry officer, Bourgeois, son of a *Conventionnel*, was taken along with his coachman and two young women, come to sweeten the stay at Versailles of the handsome *chef d'escadron*; all were suspected of involvement in the 'conspiracy'. Finally, on 29 Ventôse, Berger, adjoint to the adjutants-general, was arrested, accused of having been sent by Ronsin to Laon and Noyon to warn the important detachments there of the impending coup.[29] Berger, who seems to have been Ronsin's favourite factotum, where visits to the detachments were concerned – the general rarely left Paris himself, except for those hunting parties in the surrounding countryside – had indeed just returned to Paris from Laon, where he had gone to implement the orders of the Committee of Public Safety on the demobilisation of iron-workers among the *révolutionnaires*.

Mazuel was an important catch, and Fouquier assigned him a double role. As the second leader in the 'military plot', he was said to have refused to rejoin his squadron in Lyon, to be on hand to supervise the preparations in the Paris region. Likewise he was supposed to have accompanied Ronsin on his visits to Sainte-Pélagie and to the Luxembourg in Pluviôse to help draw up the 'lists' of prisoners for a new 2 September.

These men had other 'accomplices' in the rue de Choiseul and among the detachment commanders around Paris, and above all in Lyon. Without an extensive network of accomplices the movements required to concentrate troops in Paris could not have been achieved. As early as 24 Ventôse it was being said that the 'conspiracy' had ramifications in Lyon; Boissay was preparing to come to Paris for a 'secret rendezvous', a sort of conspiratorial council of war, which was to have taken place around 20 Ventôse, but which had been deferred to a later date to allow the 'conspirators' to perfect their plans. The Committee had beaten them to it.[30] Parein was to defend himself against such charges in a letter to Payan the following month: 'I have heard from citizen Reverchon...that the Committee of General Security...had certain suspicions about me relating to Ronsin...based on my friendship with him.... I knew Ronsin, it is true, but it was because I considered him a good citizen. If he was a traitor, must I also share his guilt even though my intentions have always been of the purest? For almost a year, I was absent from Paris.... Called to Paris as *général de brigade* of the *armée révolutionnaire*, I left it after a fortnight for Commune-Affranchie...'. The cunning general added, at the end of his letter: 'See Nicolas...tell him to speak on my behalf to the virtuous Robespierre...'.[31] In the event, Parein and Boissay were saved because of their absence from Paris. Fouquier needed 'accomplices' who could be used in the trial of Ronsin.

If the commanders of the detachments in Lyon knew of the plans of the 'conspirators', it is scarcely likely that Ronsin could have hidden his intentions from his close collaborators in the rue de Choiseul, with whom he worked every day. From the time of his arrest, all the members of the general staff, suspected of complicity, were themselves threatened with arrest. Writing to the Committee of Public Safety on 30 Ventôse, Maubant alluded to these suspicions: '...One of them [the conspirators] commanded this army. The crimes of the commander, and the disorders of several detachments, has placed every member of this body in an unfavourable

light which causes us extreme distress. We are well aware that the members
of the general staff have not escaped suspicion...'. Maubant also feared for
himself, for the *comité révolutionnaire* of his Section was taking advantage of
this favourable opportunity to settle an old score.[32] Even the faithful
Boulanger, who had denounced Volland and Boissay as 'accomplices' of the
general, was for a while menaced by a campaign which ranged so widely
that it threatened to engulf the entire corps and escape from the control of
the Committees.

The reaction of the Committees was to lend their support to the Liège
general and the new head of the general staff. These two, Boulanger and
Maubant, still believed that by separating themselves from those most
compromised with Ronsin, they could save the *armée* and retain its
command. On 29 Ventôse, Boulanger, with full support from Robespierre,
arranged for some *révolutionnaires* from the Paris detachment to file in front
of the Jacobins in a carefully staged operation. The *révolutionnaires* loudly
proclaimed their attachment to the Convention and the Committees, and
one carried his zeal to the point of offering to reveal the names of other
'traitors'.[33] The same day Maubant supplied the Committee with information on the political affiliations of his entire personnel, and in the
days which followed he performed all manner of small services for the
Revolutionary Government, and required total obedience to the established
authorities from the detachment commanders.[34] His zeal paid off; Allais,
Benoît and the other protégés of these two men within the general staff
were cleared, while Robespierre stood surety for the patriotism of the entire
corps. Finally, apart from the adjoints of Grammont and Mazuel's entourage, only Boissay was arrested, and since his arrest did not take place until
22 Germinal, in Lyon, he was spared the fate of his compatriot Hébert.[35]

The proscription of Ronsin's 'accomplices' extended far beyond the
narrow circle of the revolutionary general staff. The Committee of General
Security and the offices of the revolutionary tribunal were swamped with
denunciations from every quarter against military and civilian personalities
who were accused of having known of Ronsin's 'criminal intentions', even
of having advanced them in the departments. The *armée révolutionnaire* alone
would not have been up to such a task, and the Committees were the first to
recognise that most of the officers and soldiers were patriotic republicans
who would never have lent themselves to the dark designs of someone
wanting to proclaim himself 'Lieutenant General'. On the other hand the
presence alongside the political generals of career soldiers, holding posts of
command in the real armies, gave the 'plot' theory a more convincing
aspect.

Three adjutants-general were among those denounced as friends and
accomplices of Ronsin: Leclercq, Valframbert and Colette. Leclercq was
doubly suspect, being a first cousin of the general, and owing his
appointment as adjutant-general to him. He had, in addition, returned to
Paris just as news broke of the conspiracy. But because of his services to the

Laon authorities, he was only detained for a few days.[36] Valframbert, adjutant-general on the staff of the Army of the West at Rennes, and former commander-in-chief of the Le Mans National Guard, was less fortunate. He was denounced on 11 Germinal by the soldiers of his general headquarters for having said to his adjoint, Bucquet, on 23 Ventôse, the very day of Ronsin's arrest, 'that there was a bunch of scoundrels in the Convention and that he would like to see it reduced to 40 members...'.[37] This was an offence under the general category of 'bringing the national representation into disrepute', and Valframbert remained in prison for a long time, a victim of his personal prejudices, though he escaped the fate of his so-called chief. Colette falls into the same category; another adjutant-general to the Army of the West, stationed at Caen, he was known for his relations with the Cordeliers, of which he was a member, and with the War Ministry – he had even been mooted as a member of the general staff of the *armée révolutionnaire* when it was newly formed – and he was a friend of Vincent, with whom he corresponded frequently. He was denounced on 19 Germinal for having advocated insurrection to a session of the Jacobins (of Caen?) in the middle of Ventôse. This he denied, but his associations were against him; he was arrested in Germinal and also seems to have spent a long time in prison.[38]

On 1 Germinal Loiseau, *représentant en mission* in the Eure, wrote to Fouquier, denouncing one Le Duc, an employee in the military remount bureau at Le Bec-Hélouin, as a friend and correspondent of Ronsin and the Grammonts. Suspicion had fallen on him, as on Leclercq, because he had made a trip to Paris – doubtless to 'receive orders' – on the eve of the discovery of the 'conspiracy'.[39] Ronsin also had agents nearer the capital and a host of accusations, mainly from the *comité de surveillance* of Gentilly, implicated a picturesque and somewhat demagogic *révolutionnaire*, Julien Leroy, called 'Eglator', bursar of the *maison nationale* at Bicêtre, along with Vassard, commander of the armed force attached to this establishment. Both had received many visits from Ronsin and the officers of his general staff. Leroy was a long-standing friend of Ronsin, whose literary talents – debatable at best – he admired sufficiently to borrow his forename, Eglator, from one of the general's patriotic plays. He had made the Bicêtre a veritable fief of the Cordeliers – so it was yet another stronghold of the conspirators, with Versailles, Vincennes, Vaugirard, Meudon, Issy, Clamart, Bicêtre, forming a Hébertist fortified circle around Paris. Choisy and Bercy would also be added to the list. The Cordelier chiefs, and Momoro in particular, had in fact a fair number of supporters in the tiny *sociétés* of these communes.[40] The Committee showed considerable interest in the denunciations against Leroy, and he took his place in the 'plot' as Ronsin's emissary in the fortified town which dominated the southern approaches to Paris, Vassard ensuring him control of the armed force. Worse still, the two men took shelter behind the poor, lodged in this *maison nationale*, trying, according to one witness, to make them 'their creatures' by placing them in all the positions of control in the establishment. Eglator did not recover his liberty until 12 Fructidor, when he proclaimed himself the 'victim of the Triumvirs'.[41]

Volland too, a confidant and perhaps an associate of Ronsin, was assigned an important role. This draper and manufacturer, a native of Châteauroux, with a workshop on the quai and offices in the Observatoire Section, was a man in comfortable circumstances, far removed from those of the sans-culottes. Ronsin and he had done business together and he also knew Mazuel and the Grammonts. But his accuser, Boulanger, made more serious charges against him; in Pluviôse, during a visit to Châteauroux, he had appeared before the *société* and boasted of powerful connections in Paris, claiming even to have power to make and unmake generals, whom he could place at will on the general staff of the *armée révolutionnaire*. He further prejudiced his case by denouncing the priests who, according to him, still dominated the Châteauroux *société*. He was arrested by the *comité* of his Section, and on 15 Germinal committed suicide by throwing himself from the window of his house, a victim more than anything of his own boastfulness and desire to dazzle the people of his home town.[42]

Another personal friend of Ronsin, and like him a violent and hotheaded man, was his former aide-de-camp in the Vendée, Musquinet Saint-Félix – a noble with a troubled past, brother of the famous mayor of Ingouville, near Le Havre, who had been imprisoned for shady dealings under the monarchy.[43] Saint-Félix and the actor Fusil, also attached to Ronsin's general staff in the Vendée, accompanied the general to Lyon. Fusil remained there and became a member of the Commission Temporaire, but Saint-Félix returned to Paris with his friend. On 1 Ventôse the Committee of General Security issued a warrant against him; he was arrested on the 2nd by the *comité* of the Fontaine-de-Grenelle Section, interrogated on the 3rd, but allowed to remain under house arrest at his home in the rue du Bac. His papers contained nothing compromising and the seals were removed on the 10th. But he came under renewed scrutiny with Ronsin's arrest, and on 25 Ventôse his Section *comité* wrote to the Committee of General Security: 'We have just learnt from the guards on Saint-Félix, placed under arrest on orders from the Committee...that citizen Ronsain [*sic*],...had come to see him during these last few days and that at the time when the seals were lifted...citizen Mazuel was found with him.... The said Saint-Félix is very violent, very hot-tempered, he insulted his guards and extended his invective to the members of our *comité*. We invite you to let us know what we should do about him...'. Here then was another member of Ronsin's 'party of violent men'. The Committee considered Saint-Félix sufficiently important to send all the documents about him to Fouquier on 27 Ventôse. But he was more fortunate than Volland; although mentioned several times in connection with the supposed 'prison plot' at the time of the Hébertist trials, he remained under house arrest, and was liberated in Pluviôse Year III, claiming, like Leroy, to have been a victim of Robespierre. His favourable treatment was undoubtedly due to Héron, to whom he had furnished information.[44] His brother was not so lucky; he was condemned to death and guillotined on 26 Ventôse, two days after the arrest of the Cordelier chiefs, with whom he had had regular contacts.[45]

On 21 Floréal the Committee of General Security had another Vendée associate of Ronsin's arrested, Lachevardière, a member of the Jacobins and from the department of Paris. At the time of his arrest he was writing a pamphlet entitled 'The Crimes of the English Government', which was to attract considerable publicity and in which he exclaimed: 'Woe betide the audacious imitator of Cromwell'. The phrase was taken from his discourse to the Jacobins on 1 Pluviôse, and there is no indication that he was thinking of Ronsin, even if he claimed as much in Floréal. On the other hand, at the general assembly of the Lepeletier Section on 24 Ventôse he had warned the people against the schemes of ambitious conspirators.[46] Why then did this Jacobin, this government man, figure in the delayed proscription of the Cordeliers in Floréal and Prairial? The simple answer seems to have been his service with Ronsin in the Vendée in July 1793. His case belongs in the category of automatic arrests of those who had worked, however long ago, with Ronsin and the other personalities.

The same principle governed the arrests by the *Comité* of the Contrat-Social Section on 4 Germinal, and the transfer to La Force, of Laurent Lequesne – a former official in the bureau of military clothing and Ronsin's brother-in-law – and Prudent Prangey, both denounced by the *représentant* Piory on 3 Germinal for theft from that bureau the preceding day. 'I have been thinking about this theft of 200,000 livres', Piory told the Committee. 'Might it not have been committed in order to facilitate, through corruption, the escape of the traitor Ronsin? I submit this idea to the Committee of General Security.... The Conspirators had many friends in the bureau of military clothing...'.[47] So this is how the conspiracy was funded; Piory had supplied the only missing piece in the myth created for popular consumption, of a plot in which the leading culprit makes good his escape.

On 9 Germinal the Gravilliers *comité* arrested Jacques Lablée, administrator of military supplies. He had put the seal on his own conviction of fleeing from his home on 22 Ventôse – proof positive of his complicity, in the eyes of the Committee. From his hiding place he wrote to it on 3 Germinal: 'It is being insinuated that I am connected with the plans of Ronsin because I called to thank him on one occasion.... I knew nothing of his secret, nor that of any faction...'.[48] The Committee thought otherwise; Lablée had sinned because of his indebtedness to Ronsin for his position, and in the complicated edifice of the 'plot', the administrations of military supply and clothing were added to the revolutionary general staff and the adjutants-general in the West.

Lachevardière, Prangey, Lequesne and Lablée managed to emerge from these dangerous liaisons relatively unscathed. The first was released on 7

Fructidor, Prangey and Lequesne on 22 Thermidor and Lablée on the 30th. Nicolas-Louis Lasalle was much less fortunate. A navigator and second officer from Boulogne-sur-Mer, he had come to Paris in Ventôse to request active service with the navy, only to find himself accused – for what reason we know not – of complicity with Ronsin, whom he claimed not to know. The unfortunate man was condemned to death on 24 Germinal by the revolutionary tribunal.[49] Did Fouquier want to show that the 'military plot' was also a naval one?

Ronsin and the Cordelier group had many correspondents in Lille, and although they had been removed from command positions by the *coup de force* of Florent Guiot and Duhem on 22 Frimaire – the military commanders being arrested at the same time – they still had determined supporters in the *société révolutionnaire*, and at the 23 Pluviôse session they organised a congratulatory address to the Jacobins on the liberation of the 'two oppressed patriots'.[50] The atmosphere in which the news of Ronsin's second arrest and conviction was received was just as heated; violent quarrels broke out anew in Frimaire–Nivôse; Hébertism having been proscribed there first, three months in advance of Paris, Lille now felt the effects of the definitive condemnation of a group of men who had been closely associated with the affairs of the commune. The address of 23 Pluviôse had been issued in the name of the entire *société*, which thereby assumed collective responsibility. That, however, was not the view of the *comité de surveillance*, forewarned perhaps by Duhem, as vindictive as ever. Its members tried to identify those responsible for the move, and, at the 5 Germinal session, they specifically accused Butelle – *sociétaire* and former lieutenant of artillery in the *armée révolutionnaire* – of having pressurised the *société* into applauding the liberation of the two 'traitors'. The *société*, however, was satisfied by Butelle's explanation on this occasion. His turn was to come after Thermidor, when he was arrested, this time as a supporter of Lavalette and Robespierre.[51]

As a measure of appeasement the *société* decided to forget the unfortunate address. But Duhem was intent on profiting from such a splendid opportunity to continue his personal vendetta against the Montagnard Châles, and his protégés in Lille. The following day, 6 Germinal, the *société* received a 'letter from Duhem, pointing out to the *société* that the relations between Ronsin and Lavalette were there for everyone to see . . .'.[52] But the efforts of the *représentant* proved fruitless. Lavalette was not just another Colette; he was a soldier and a friend of Ronsin, as was Colette, but he was also the confidant of Robespierre, and the exploitation of the business of 'Ronsin's accomplices' was cut short in the capital of the Nord.

There were also repercussions at the other end of France. On 3 Germinal the head of the general staff of the Toulouse garrison ordered the arrest of the *commissaire des guerres*, Picot-Belloc.[53] The arrest on this date of a famous personality from a departmental *armée* cannot have been unconnected with events in Paris. The reverberations were felt in Bordeaux also: on 1

Germinal, at the national club, a letter was read from two of its members, on mission in Paris, announcing the discovery of the 'intrigue'; 'one member demanded that the *société* write to the Committee of General Security to denounce Augé', adjutant-general, who had been under arrest since 30 Frimaire.[54]

The episodes at Lille, Toulouse and Bordeaux serve to emphasise the links between the first wave of proscription against certain ultra-revolutionary personnel, arising from the law of 14 Frimaire, and the second wave arising from the Parisian plot, which revived the repressive spirit of the moderate authorities, in power after Frimaire–Nivôse. Since then they had been looking for an opportunity finally to settle the score with the 'hommes de liaison', the Cordelier soldiers, and the former *commissaires civils* or emissaries from the War Ministry.

IV *Public reaction to the 'plot': the soldiers and Parisian* sectionnaires *(24 Ventôse–7 Germinal)*

The government's thesis scored an immediate success. The *petit peuple* in the Sections did not doubt it: ambitious men had betrayed the confidence of the people and conspired with the foreigner against the unity of the Republic. Fouquier and the Committees even knew how to play upon Parisian pride and big-city contempt for these 'provincials', up from the departments, eager for advancement, and attempting to seize position and power by storm.[55] The thesis had an element of truth, since the real strength of Hébertism lay in the departments. As always on such occasions, the addresses of the popular assemblies echoed Fouquier's indictment in calling for swift and exemplary justice against the 'traitors'. This eagerness to accept the official line was not simply a matter of prudent orthodoxy (though it would have been dangerous not to be loud in expressing one's joy, in view of government vigilance); it also derived from popular credulity and mistrust, ready to accept conspiracy as an explanation for every difficulty. It is of little importance whether Ronsin, Mazuel and their friends were conspirators or not – we will probably never know the truth – the important fact was that the great mass of the Parisian populace believed them capable of it.

Popular credulity on this occasion cannot be doubted. Granted that the congratulatory addresses sent to the Convention and the Committees are unreliable sources; they were simply stylistic exercises telling the Government what it wanted to hear. But there is a second, more authentic source shedding some light on the reception of news of the 'conspiracy' by the *révolutionnaires* and the *petit peuple*. This second source is all the more valuable in that it reveals the sometimes important divergence between the expression of popular opinion and its reality. The unanimity, the linguistic uniformity of the addresses makes them suspect; the voice of truth expresses itself diversely.

There were in fact people who did not believe all that was being said about the leading Cordeliers, and who had the courage to express their indignation at what they considered a scandalously got-up case. In his report of 3 Germinal, the spy, Latour-Lamontagne, noted: 'Some rejoiced at seeing this affair brought to such a speedy conclusion. Others complained that it had not been adequately discussed...'.[56] On 26 Ventôse Chéneaux, interim president of the Cordeliers, received a letter from a Liège refugee, H. Q. Demancy, who, less credulous than the Parisian sans-culottes, was angered at the way in which the chiefs of the supposed conspiracy were condemned without a hearing and held responsible for the shortages.[57] A very few Cordeliers also protested at the travesty which passed for the trial of the Hébertists. But fear imposed silence, and most of those in the club followed the example of Sandoz, a member of the Administrative Council of the *armée révolutionnaire*, who presided over the Cordeliers during the *Semaine de Cendres* after the arrest of Chéneaux, and who sent address after address to the Convention and the Committees denouncing the former 'ringleaders'.[58]

There was no regret in Ronsin's *armée* for the fall of a chief who was not popular, and who was unknown to most of the detachments. 'The Paris cannoneers declared that they would take pleasure in conducting their general to the guillotine, that he had never shown his patriotism save under the influence of copious wine', noted Charmont on 1 Germinal;[59] to other *révolutionnaires*, Ronsin and his like were bad commanders, who had never taken the trouble to visit the detachments, and maintained them in a state of 'culpable inactivity'.[60] The fusiliers of the Finistère Section had written to the Lazowski *société fraternelle* on 16 Ventôse, expressing their belief that Grammont was quite capable of such a plot;[61] and certain revolutionary cavaliers, NCOs among them, were supposed to have had the indecency to attend, on horseback, the execution of their chief on 4 Germinal in the place de la Révolution, much to the scandal of onlookers.[62] Yet such accounts of rejection by the *révolutionnaires* are in conflict with the words attributed to Ancar, spoken to Bourgeois on the way to the guillotine and overheard by a sergeant of the gendarmerie: 'I see no trace of the *armée révolutionnaire*, this crowd of people is unbelievable...'.[63] Did he expect some last-minute intervention by the *armée*? – an empty hope when the victim was but a few steps from death. Yet what else could the *armée révolutionnaire* have done on 4 Germinal but follow the tide and shower with insults the leaders whom they didn't much like anyway.

The soldiers had no reason to doubt the guilt of Ronsin, and were all the more angry at their former chief, become conspirator, since he had involved the entire *armée* in his disgrace. One of the soldiers in the delegation to the Jacobins, on 29 Ventôse, 'announced that he had just received the order to leave Paris; he thought that people were afraid of the soldiers of the *armée révolutionnaire*...', and as proof of his innocence, he offered to denounce other 'traitors' in the corps.[64] 'The traitors Ronsin, Grammont and Mazuel wanted to involve us in their treason', a former cavalier would later write; 'we were innocently at our post in the Vendée destroying rebels, and it was in Nantes that we suffered the hardships which the villainous counter-revolutionaries had brought on us...'.[65] One fusilier sergeant, who had the misfortune to arrive in Paris on 28 Ventôse, in the middle of the crisis, to be arrested as an 'accomplice' of the general and to spend several months in prison, was likewise indignant: 'General Ronsin and his agents may have been scoundrels', he wrote on 29 Floréal, 'but the soldiers should not be made his victims. I never laid eyes on this character, nor spoke with him...'.[66] Another *révolutionnaire*, a sergeant known as 'Bamboche', though of the most dubious character, a swindler, thief and bone-setter all rolled into one, was even more piously indignant, in a petition sent from his prison in Lyon, 17 Floréal, to the Convention: 'We ask to be brought once more before any court you choose...there the villainy of these intriguers and their behaviour, causing nothing but harm to the true sans-culottes, will be exposed...along with their vile plots on which I sent a memorial to the Convention dated 6 Germinal...'.[67] As in every other revolutionary crisis, those who felt most threatened were the ones who denounced most and revealed most to prove their own patriotism. And why shouldn't Bamboche blame Ronsin for his own misfortunes, for officers who could send such a great patriot to the prison of Roanne, when all he had wanted to do was alert the Convention to the 'threads of the conspiracy', must surely be great criminals themselves.

Besides, the *révolutionnaires* were past masters at denunciation, thanks to their missions in the departments. For them denunciation was the most important of political acts, and in Lyon and elsewhere they did not hesitate to make full use of it, as often against their officers, whom they denounced for conduct unbecoming republicans, as against the inhabitants, some of whom they sent to the guillotine. It was easy enough, then, to go a stage further and denounce their own chiefs, Boulanger, Halm, Vézien, as traitors to *la patrie*. Pérony set them an example, by giving evidence against Ronsin and Mazuel before the tribunal, and by writing to Fouquier. Sensing also perhaps that their days as privileged political soldiers were numbered, and that they would soon be returned to the obscurity and anonymity of life in their quartiers, the *révolutionnaires* sought to use to the full the only political weapon remaining to them.

Listen, finally, to the words of a more sincere witness to the personal feelings of the *révolutionnaires* on the fate of their former leaders. 'It is with all possible regret', wrote the fusiliers of the Temple company to the assembly of their Section, probably in the second half of Germinal (the letter is undated), 'that we have seen the *trayson* [sic] of our chiefs', but (the letter went on in illiterate though eloquent French) 'les malheureux naurait pas trouvez de secour par mie nous pour servire leur infâme projet car il ny en a pas un de nous qui n'est frémie d'orreur en aprenant lorrible conspiration...Nous somme ravie d'apprendre que le glaive de la loix a frappée c'est monstre, du courage et lon détruira jusquaux dernier...'. If some of their officers still dared to question the official version, by taking a more measured attitude to Ronsin's guilt, most of his soldiers would certainly have subscribed to the feelings expressed by the Temple fusiliers.[68]

As for opinion in Paris, it was so taken in by the official line that it was still awaiting some 'great event', some coup, not only in the days between Ronsin's arrest on 23 Ventôse and his execution on 4 Germinal, but throughout almost the entire latter month. As always when Paris was in the grip of a political crisis, the most fantastic rumours circulated freely. On 27 Ventôse the *comité révolutionnaire* of the l'Homme-Armé Section 'ordered one François Carterait, wine merchant, calling himself a brigadier in the gendarmerie...to be brought to the Conciergerie for having said that he was the bearer of an order to cut the moustaches of the cannoneers and others, which appeared to us extremely suspect in view of the present critical situation...'.[69] On 8 Germinal, four days after the execution of Ronsin, there were new fears of a coup by the *moustachus*: 'A crowd of men with moustaches, great swords and fur hats has been gathering for some days', reported one of Fouquier's agents. 'Their gestures have a mysterious air, above all a way of pointing or directing their eyes as if they had designs on certain people...'.[70] On 29 Ventôse Lafosse, head of the *bureau de surveillance* of the Commune of Paris – Lafosse was himself a dubious character who perished shortly afterwards, condemned to death in Germinal by the revolutionary tribunal following a mysterious *guerre des polices*, which decimated the ranks of the rival police forces in Paris – warned Fouquier of new coups in preparation: 'It has been reported to us that yesterday [28 Ventôse], in a group gathered near the Temple, some individuals were saying: "On the next day of the *décade* [30 Ventôse], we must rescue Hébert at whatever cost, force must be answered by force...'.[71]

Such was the force of these rumours that they found credit even among the judges of the revolutionary tribunal, though one would have thought those talented myth-makers immune to popular credulity. In the last days of Ventôse the tribunal, 'after having heard a report of the charges, and above all in consideration of public safety', found it 'indispensable to take measures of security with regard to *General Hanriot and his principal accomplices*...we instruct the public prosecutor and Dumas, vice-president, to present this declaration to the Committee of Public Safety and explain the reasons behind it...'.[72] On this occasion the Committee of Public Safety itself intervened to limit the range of a proscription which threatened to engulf figures still in favour. It cannot have acted too soon, for already in Paris – and the departments would quickly follow suit – there were rumours that Marat was involved in the coup.[73] Worse still, at the end of the month, two former revolutionary officers – Thunot and Boisgirault – denounced Bonin, a printer from the Panthéon Section, for claiming to have heard it said in an *auberge* 'that soon the head of Robespierre would roll through the window [the guillotine]'. Bonin was to pay with his life for his prophecies, condemned to death by the revolutionary tribunal on 5 Floréal, a delayed victim of the denunciatory zeal of these two former revolutionary officers.[74]

The thesis of Fouquier and Billaud-Varenne had been all too readily accepted, and the problem now facing the Committees was to limit the effects of a *peur* which threatened even those with well-established revolutionary reputations, and which was strongest in the Sections on the outskirts of Paris – Invalides, Finistère, Fontaine-de-Grenelle, Bondy – and the disturbed communes of the department of Paris. With public opinion overexcited by incessant official calls to vigilance, old fears were revived of evil-looking men, foreigners, men with moustaches and those affecting the outward appearances of Hébertism. The Invalides Section watched with excessive anxiety the transport of cannon along the Seine from the château of Meudon to the arsenal of Meulan. The *sectionnaires* were convinced that a military coup was in preparation against the people of Paris. The same Section experienced anxieties about the comings and goings of Austrian prisoners-of-war. In both cases it was a matter of entirely normal movements, but the panic was such that the Committee of Public Safety felt obliged, through its *comité de guerre*, to reassure the public with posters explaining its motives.[75] The authorities had acted out the 'plot' thesis so well that it soon took on a life of its own and became more and more uncontrollable. The *petit peuple* were long accustomed to explain everything in terms of *malveillance*, and had no reason to look on the shortage of meat and dairy produce in any different way. There was a 'complot de la viande'. What would the government do to suppress it? In the Lombards Section, when on 20 Germinal some sans-culotte artisans dared to suggest that the rations system favoured the butchers and their wealthy clients, the response of the Committee was extremely brutal. It ordered the arrest of the ringleaders and forbade any further talk about subsistences.[76] The Hébertists were good scapegoats, and long after their deaths Ronsin and Mazuel continued to be used in Fouquier's various concoctions. But they could not be made to fit every case: the idea of a 'military plot' could be trotted out only once, while that of a 'plot to starve Paris' could be used only if conditions improved after the 'guilty' were punished. In Floréal there was still no sign of improvement; so what had been the point of guillotining the conspirators?

But the Committee cared little for Sectionary opinion, now powerless, and the 'military plot' thesis allowed it to isolate the Cordelier chiefs from the mass of the sans-culottes and from their own troops. The eagerness of the *révolutionnaires* to side with the official line emphasises the immense prestige which the Convention still enjoyed with the *petit peuple*, and, in contrast, the feebleness of the so-called 'parti de la Guerre': a clutch of ambitious men, a general staff without any troops, officers without an army, conspirators without a plot, Cordeliers isolated from the Sections. The Committee easily achieved its immediate aim: to remove all possibility of a popular *journée* on behalf of the Hébertists by cutting the ground from under their feet, and presenting them to public opinion in extremely compromising terms as small-time Cromwells, amateur conspirators, who would have subjected the people to military government.[77] The *armée révolutionnaire* paid the price of this massive campaign of deception; but it was not the only victim, and the people were to draw the lesson that no one could be trusted, when their idols, their *marchands de fourneaux*, turned out to be nothing but ambitious traitors. Marat himself, being dead, became suspect; the popularity of Robespierre seemed forced, something required by his position as the new pope of revolutionary infallibility, rather than freely given. The 'plot' operation may have paid off in the short term, but ultimately it intensified sans-culotte mistrust of government men, and helped isolate the Revolutionary Government itself. Every observer noted the satisfaction of the *honnêtes gens* on receiving news of the sentencing of Ronsin and his accomplices; they had good reason to be pleased, for they were the real beneficiaries of this devaluation of great revolutionary reputations.

V   The repercussions of the 'plot' in the departments (23 Ventôse–22 Germinal)

By insisting on the many ramifications of the 'plot' in the departments, the Revolutionary Government gave a lead to the municipalities and districts, which did not need a second invitation to launch a massive offensive against the Parisian detachments and those local men, traitors to their communes, who had helped them. The municipalities which had been most hostile to the interests of Paris were naturally the first to respond to this call to arms; theirs was an easy role to play, a chance to assuage their pent-up thirst for vengeance while defending *la patrie*. The hour of revenge had struck, and was observed with remarkable synchronisation. When letters from Paris arrived in the communes of the capital's supply zone, on 24, 25, 26, 27, or 28 Ventôse, the authorities at once grasped the significance of the events and took immediate steps to depict the Parisian officers and soldiers as accomplices of the principal conspirators. The first arrests occurred the very day the news was received, and such was the zeal of some municipalities that they proceeded to disarm the soldiers immediately, even before orders to this effect were issued by the Committee. News of the 'plot' sent shock waves through the whole of France, reaching the communes furthest removed from the capital between 4 and 10 Germinal, and continuing to cause anxiety throughout that month. We shall be looking here at the chain reaction set off by news of the 'military plot', without going into the far more extensive campaign carried out at the same time against the *Père Duchesne*, which was solemnly burnt by many *sociétés populaires* in ceremonies of purification.[78]

In communes with detachments the municipalities took measures to prevent the soldiers rallying to help the 'conspirators'. But news of the 'plot' also gave rise to a series of inquiries designed to implicate the detachment commanders in the 'criminal plans' of Ronsin. Officers from the general staff in the rue de Choiseul, 'emissaries from Ronsin', had visited the detachments between 1 and 23 Ventôse: Berger had gone to Noyon and Laon, Halm to Vernon, Vézien to Saint-Germain and Montereau, Folleville and another adjoint also to Montereau, where the latter remained. All this coming and going, largely caused by the demobilisation of the iron-workers, took on in retrospect a highly suspect appearance. The officers, said the municipalities, had come in reality to communicate 'secret orders' from the leader for the accomplishment of some great insurrectional plan. The notables heard knives being sharpened and the *révolutionnaires* sealed their own fate by talking in the *auberges* of a great and dreadful coup, the revolutionary Last Judgement. To get a better picture of this conspiratorial web, the municipalities and *comités de surveillance* had the correspondence of the soldiers with their Sections and their families intercepted and scrutinised. Many communes doubled the patrols on the town gates, while *commissaires* from the *comités* made scrupulous searches of the *auberges* at which travellers stopped. Recent arrivals from Paris were closely interrogated. The extent of this chain reaction might at first seem surprising; but Hébertism, or *ultracisme*, was above all a departmental phenomenon and the crisis of Ventôse-Germinal had consequences more far-reaching in garrison towns, towns on major routes, and market centres, than in Paris itself.

The local authorities were afraid, and many sincerely so. But there was also considerable hypocrisy and calculation behind their vigilance. Some *comités* proved adept at exploiting the careless talk of the *révolutionnaires*, taking words out of context to fit Fouquier's ready-made scheme of a widespread network of connivance and complicity. In any case, the *révolutionnaires* lost out: if they spoke, it was to threaten the municipalities with terrible reprisals; if they did not speak, their silence was taken for complicity, and whether they kept quiet or not their intrigues proved that they were accomplices in the 'plot'.

The communes nearest to Paris, Versailles and Vincennes, were the first to feel the effects of the 'plot'. In Versailles rumours were rife, and as early as 26 Ventôse the municipality introduced extra precautions, arranging night patrols, doubling the guard on all the gates and public buildings, watching all *étrangers*, and checking the inns, *cabarets*, cafés, dance-halls and other public places. The same day it told the *représentant*, Crassous, of its fears about the presence in the commune of revolutionary squadrons; which it suspected of complicity with their chief, Mazuel.[79] Two days later, on the 28th, Crassous wrote telling the Committee of General Security of the rumours circulating in the town, and of the fears of the municipality and the district directory about a possible move on the part of the cavaliers.[80] Their fears were groundless; as early as 27 Ventôse, the day after Mazuel's arrest, his fellow officers and the cavaliers were quick to disavow Ronsin and the young *chef d'escadron* in an address to the Convention congratulating it on its vigilance. The address carried the signatures of Bresch, *chef d'escadron*, Pérony, captain and a witness at the trial of the Hébertists – it was he who 'uncovered' the plan of Mazuel to move units of the cavalry from Versailles to Vincennes – and Blanchet, lieutenant, and friend and confidant of Mazuel.[81] One can never be too careful.

As for Vincennes, it was in a state of full alert from 23 Ventôse, the very day of the arrests of the Hébertists. At its session on that day, the General Council became interested in the visit made by Ronsin three days earlier to the château. On that occasion a local butcher had denounced the *commissaire aux accaparements* for having permitted infractions of the Maximum on meat. On the 26th the members of the municipality claimed that the general had distributed money to various inhabitants at the time of his visit, doubtless for the purpose of enlisting support. They also discussed a memorial presented to the Cordeliers by some inhabitants calling themselves 'les sans-culottes de la commune de Vincennes', and would return to the matter on the 27th and 28th. Then on the 29th the municipality became alarmed again at word that the night guard, doubled since the 23rd, had fallen asleep at their post on the town gates. Once again an alarm was raised about 'plots', and the importance of increased vigilance urged at a time when the Republic was again exposed to 'coups' by 'conspirators'. A single visit from Ronsin, therefore, on 20 Ventôse, had been enough to throw the commune into an uproar and for suspicions of complicity to be attached to a group of inhabitants whose only crime was to have taken advantage of the general's visit to express their grievances against a public official. In addition, after 9 Nivôse, when beds in the château were requisitioned, the municipality repeatedly queried their destination.[82] Living in the shadow of the terrible fort, and left in ignorance of prospective troop movements, the commune tended to latch on to the most trivial pieces of evidence.

The *peur* extended to the neighbouring commune of Montreuil, whose municipality received a deputation from the *société populaire* at its 28 Ventôse session. 'The speaker voiced their feelings that, in view of the new conspiracy lately discovered, each commune should redouble its vigilance at this time to defeat the blackest of plots...and finished by demanding, in the name of the said *société*, the establishment of a night patrol', of 15 men, which was immediately ordered.[83] There can be no more remarkable homage to the success of government propaganda than these security measures taken by small towns in the shadow of Paris. Every great crisis had the same immediate effects on these villages on the periphery of the capital city. On 9 Thermidor and 2–3 Prairial Year III, the municipalities at the gates of Paris would take similar precautions, to prevent the gangrene spreading from the capital.

The municipalities which had been most backward in the supply of Paris were the first to respond to the government's call for accusations. In contrast, revolutionary municipalities such as that of Ecouis demanded the retention of the detachments, despite the disgrace of their chief.

The worst incidents took place at Vernon and Laon. At Vernon on the 27th, on receipt of news of the 'plot', a fight broke out between some Parisian soldiers and a volunteer from the Ardennes battalion, who was badly roughed up by the political soldiers defending the honour of their *armée* (see above, p. 504). It was a banal affair, the kind of thing which occurs daily in any garrison town. But on the very same day, the municipality, district directory and *société populaire* used the brawl as a pretext to mount an attack on the detachment, particularly on its captain, Dumont. At its session on that day, the directory accused Dumont of having instigated the 'attempted murder' and claimed as proof of his guilt the 'precipitous flight' – better to call it a hasty departure – of the Vernon detachment as soon as news of the 'conspiracy' broke. Accordingly, it passed the following resolution:

> The directory...considering on the basis of information received...that the conduct of the *armée révolutionnaire* appears more than suspect and *could be related to the machinations hatched in secret to upset public tranquillity and cause civil war in the commune of Vernon*, since it appears from eye-witness accounts that the commander mustered his forces at a time of the most perfect public tranquillity; that he had them armed without any orders from the established authorities, and told them: 'friends, we must conquer or die...', the sudden flight of these revolutionary soldiers from the walls of Vernon when they saw that the administration had not fallen into their trap is sufficient proof of their hostile intentions...it follows that this troop had a plan and it would be interesting to know its extent.

This the directory sent to the Minister of War and the Committee of Public Safety.[84]

What was the true story? Doubtless, after the brawl and having received news of the 'conspiracy', Dumont, knowing full well the ill will of the Vernon authorities, may have feared some kind of Saint Bartholomew episode with the *révolutionnaires* as victims. There is no other way of explaining the defence measures, those dramatic words and then that hasty departure which seemed an admission of complicity. The detachment moved on to Mantes, stopping only at Houdan, from which it wrote to the Minister and to the Committee for further marching orders.[85] Dumont had lost his head and played straight into the hands of the municipality, which at a single stroke was rid of a detested presence. Two days later, 29 Ventôse, the municipality received a deputation from the *société populaire* which demanded 'that the general council take measures to prevent the return of that *armée* which fled Vernon and which could cause further trouble in the town...'.[86]

All that remained now was to develop the thesis concerning the 'ramifications' of the conspiracy. On 1 Germinal, in a speech to the *sociéte populaire*, one member exonerated the *révolutionnaires*. 'The general of the *armée révolutionnaire*, and one of those involved with him', he said, '...misled those commanding under his orders [this on Dumont's behalf]. God forbid that any of the soldiers of this *armée*, nearly all family men and republicans, should have been the accomplices of their chief...'.[87] This did not prevent the national agent, in a speech of 3 Germinal, from implicating the soldiers and their captain: 'This conspiracy, *the ramifications of which extend throughout the republic*, was hatched in secret, within the very prisons. In Evreux, in Vernon, the prisoners enjoy considerable freedom and unlimited communication, the public officials appointed to guard them and to implement the laws seemingly protecting them. In Vernon some soldiers from the *armée révolutionnaire* and their captain, *who was waiting for the signal to return to Paris*, have just assassinated under your very eyes a volunteer from the 3rd Ardennes battalion; a member of the *comité de surveillance* of this town [i.e. Patin], closely linked with these revolutionary soldiers, their defender and protégé, partook of a sumptuous meal at the prison; and at what a time, good god! – a time when civil and military officials, traitors to the republic, are hatching...their infamous plots...'.[88]

The reaction of the Vernon authorities was typical. News of the 'plot' was the signal for a general attack on the entire detachment, which the authorities claimed to be implicated with its general, and even more for a settling of scores with the sans-culotte minority which had set itself apart from the community by co-operating with the *révolutionnaires*.

In Laon the authorities had compiled a particularly full dossier, which they intended to exploit to the full. In Berger they had a 'personal emissary' of the general, they had uncovered the secret of correspondence carried on between members of the detachment and the Parisian Sections, and they had the makings of a criminal case against certain officers. The aim of the authorities is revealed in a decision taken at the session of the General Council on 27 Ventôse, when news of Ronsin's arrest reached Laon; it was designed to throw suspicion of complicity on the entire *armée*, and on the Laon detachment in particular. 'The General Council, considering that one of the principal leaders of the conspiracy...appears to be Ronsin, general of the *armée révolutionnaire*, and that it is probable, if he is guilty, that he has accomplices and agents among the officers subordinate to him,...has decided...as a measure of general security that *commissaires* chosen from among its members should go at once to every officer of the *armée révolutionnaire* to examine their papers'. Two days later, Berger, Chaumont and Martin were placed under arrest. The first had been frank enough to admit, at the time of his interrogation on the 27th, 'that he was strongly attached to Ronsin, whom he would like to think innocent', and he was suspected by the municipality 'of having been sent to Laon for reasons connected with the conspiracy'.[89] The tables were now turned on the soldiers. On 29 Ventôse the municipality issued a proclamation to the inhabitants inviting denunciations against members of the detachment, and in the days which followed the Parisians had to endure jeers and mistreatment at the hands of the Laonnois.

It was on the initiative of the Laon municipality that Gasson, commander of the Noyon detachment, was interrogated by the Noyon *comité* ten days later, on 8 Germinal. The *comité* was particularly interested in his relations with Berger, asking him if he 'had not seen him lately in Noyon'. Gasson replied that he did not know Berger, had never corresponded with Ronsin, and had never denounced the commune of Noyon. On 11 Germinal, the *comité* interrogated Desgal, a sergeant in Gasson's company, about his chief and his relations with Berger, but with no more success; they had to wait until Fructidor to bring his auxiliaries in the commune to trial.[90] In Noyon the exploitation of the coup came to a dead end; Gasson returned peacefully to Paris, and there was no further talk of Berger.

In Beauvais the news of the conspiracy was exploited above all by the aristocrats and moderates, who did so with such indecent relish that the national agent, in a communication of 7 Germinal, felt obliged to recall them to some sense of decorum. In Chantilly, the *comité* had Grossin, captain of a company of fusiliers, arrested on 10 Germinal; but his arrest was quite unconnected with the 'plot', for the officer had been denounced by his own soldiers.[91] In this department of the Oise it was above all the Compiègne authorities who sought to profit from the 'plot' to avenge themselves on a detachment whose presence they had always found offensive. At its 4 Germinal session, the *comité de surveillance* declared itself 'eager to respond to the vigorous measures of general security taken by the intrepid Mountain in the Convention to discover and dismantle the crimes against liberty and the ambitious plots of the Conspiracy of Vincent, Momoro, Hébert and Ronsin etc.' Feeling it 'its duty to act quickly with respect to the detachment of the *armée révolutionnaire* cantoned in this commune and suspected of complicity in the conspiracy, or rather of having been involved and of having supported their scoundrel of a leader, Ronsin', the *comité*, 'determined to seek out and break every last thread of the scheme which may have been hatched by the officers and second officers of this detachment', ordered two *commissaires* to examine the papers of all the Parisian officers. We must conclude that the *comité*'s hopes of finding anything were thwarted, for there were no arrests in Compiègne.[92]

In the Seine-et-Marne, the Lagny authorities led the offensive, this time against the Parisian *commissaire*, Ballardelle, accused of being an accomplice of Ronsin and of having been in on the secret of the preparations for the 'coup'. The president of the *comité* claimed that Ballardelle, on hearing the news of the arrest of Ronsin and Hébert, on 28 Ventôse, had said: 'My friend, we would be done for if the plot had not been discovered, for the Conspiracy was to have been carried out on the day of the *décade* [30 Ventôse]. . .'.[93] It was a perfect excuse for the Lagny *comité* to avenge itself on an agent over-zealous in the interests of Parisian supply, and a *sectionnaire* who on several occasions had denounced the commune for hindering *arrivages* and the movement of foodstuffs.

On 28 Ventôse, the municipality of Provins was content simply to ask the officers of the detachment for a list of the chiefs to whom they had written during that month. When the chiefs did not reply, the municipality attributed the silence to their desire to maintain the strictest secrecy in preparing their insurrection, and took no further action against the detachment. On 9 Germinal, somewhat tardily, it decided to arm *les bons citoyens*.[94]

At Brie-Comte-Robert the events in Paris provoked a violent onslaught against the 'ultras'. On 28 Ventôse the *société populaire* decided to take the usual precautions: 'citizen Thibault added that at a time when a major conspiracy against our liberty, possibly with extensive ramifications, had erupted, we ought to ask whether some of the agents in charge of troop movements might not have been in touch with the conspirators now exposed, and have assisted their designs by indicating false routes to the defenders of *la patrie*, causing them to scatter and thus be rendered ineffective. . .'. It was decided to communicate this far-fetched idea to the Committee of Public Safety (yet another 'plot'), but despite its vivid imagination, the Brie *société* did not take any action against the detachment, which in this commune had been on good terms with the local authorities. On the other hand, one *sociétaire*, a rich farmer, took advantage of the opportunity to denounce the *exagérés* of the locality, attacking alike supporters of the *loi agraire* and proponents of atheism: 'We must refute these diatribes', he declared on 28 Ventôse, 'these ridiculous attacks on the rich, this affectation of sans-culotte speech. . .'.[95]

The *comité* of Rozoy-en-Brie had one of the soldiers of the detachment arrested on 7 Germinal – a poor illiterate drunk, accused of using royalist language, who tried to kill himself by throwing himself into a well the day of his arrest. He was sent to Paris and condemned to death by the revolutionary tribunal on 8 Floréal.[96] A similar incident took place in Coulommiers, where the *comité* accused the colour-bearer of the detachment of using language hostile to the Convention; he also 'tried to disturb the tranquillity of the patriots by saying that in a few days everything would be changed in Coulommiers and the *honnêtes gens* would be taken care of. . .'. The *comité* considered this soldier, who had expressed feelings unusual for a *révolutionnaire*, to have known of the plans for an insurrection, and he was arrested on 1 Germinal and sent off to Paris.[97]

The directory of the district of Nemours accepted the official conspiracy thesis and urged the municipalities and *comités* under its authority to greater vigilance;[98] but it took no action against the detachment, which it did not suspect of involvement with the conspirators. At Montereau, the *société populaire* decided, at its session of 29 Ventôse, to denounce to Fouquier the soldier Noël. He had been responsible for most of the differences between the municipality and the detachment under Chamault; but he was also denounced by his fellow soldiers, and the affair had no connection with the 'conspiracy'. It is true that on 2 Germinal the municipality accused the detachment of having illicitly traded in eggs and butter.[99] But despite a number of incidents which had occurred during the stay of the detachment in Montereau, the authorities made no attempt to use the crisis as an excuse for attacking the *armée* itself.

In the plot theory, Ronsin and Mazuel were not the only figures implicated. Fouquier was also interested in a journey made between 12 and 19 Ventôse by young Vincent, secretary-general of the War Ministry, to Neufchelles, a village in the district of Meaux (now in the Oise). Since it was a mission on behalf of the Executive Council – Vincent's passport supports this – could the journey not have had some connection with preparations for the 'plot'? It would be difficult to see how; nevertheless, the Meaux *comité* decided, at the height of the crisis, to open a dossier for the receipt of information on Vincent's journey to Meaux two weeks earlier.[100] One essential element was missing, however: at the time of Vincent's journey there was no revolutionary detachment in the Meaux district, nor at Neufchelles, the nearest being that of Dammartin.

Finally, in Fontainebleau, the scene of violent conflict between the municipal officers, the *comité*, and the militants in the *société populaire* – former priests and servants, whom the authorities later claimed had adhered to 'Hébert's system' – news of the 'plot' provoked one of the most characteristic reactions of this kind of popular *peur*: fear of the foreigner, especially the Englishman, the agent of Pitt. The Fontainebleau *comité* was worried, as they were in the communes around Paris, about the comings and goings of the Prussian officers, prisoners-of-war, who were left in almost total freedom. On 16 Ventôse, 'in view of the movements in the Capital and the arrests made on orders from the Committee of Public Safety, in view also of the report made by a member, of a supper given by an Englishman at the *auberge* Sirène, for Prussian officers in custody in this commune, which has seemed extraordinary to us, the *comité* fearing that some traitors have escaped the vigilance of the Commune of Paris, and wanting to know everything that is happening in this place, has decided: 1st, that two of its members should visit the *auberges* daily...as well as those responsible for the coach stages, so as to take cognizance of all persons arriving and departing...'.[101] We do not know what became of the scandalous English diner.

Thus, although most of the Seine-et-Marne authorities accepted to the letter the official account of a 'plot', they did not implicate the detachments, but confined themselves to watching foreigners, taking normal precautions, and, here and there, mounting an offensive against the local *exagérés*. Only at Lagny did the authorities exploit the situation to accuse Ballardelle. How can we explain this lenience, which was in marked contrast to the attitude of the municipalities of the Oise, the Aisne, the Eure, and, as we shall see, the Seine-et-Oise? One is tempted to see in it an element of revolutionary patriotism, noticeably absent with the authorities of Vernon, Noyon, Pontoise and Laon.

In the Seine-et-Oise, the authorities followed the example of Versailles in their use of the 'plot' as a pretext for action against the revolutionary soldiers. In Etampes, Pontoise, Beaumont, Asnières, and in the district of Gonesse, all hell was let loose against the unfortunate Parisians, the 'accomplices' of their general. The Etampes affair is particularly interesting. The arrest of two soldiers from the detachment, Dumas and Barbe, artisans of the faubourg, and their 'translation' before the revolutionary tribunal as accomplices of Ronsin, was conceived by the municipality and the *comité* as a cover-up for a much more serious affair: the arrest of the mayor, Clarton, on 30 Ventôse, by agents of the Committee of General Security, for having impeded supplies to Paris. The manœuvre was simple: to disguise the responsibility of the mayor by pointing to real conspirators in the town who had spoken of the imminence of a 'coup' in the eventful week preceding its discovery. Happily, the unfortunate soldiers were to be acquitted by the tribunal in Floréal.[102]

In Pontoise and Beaumont the *révolutionnaires* were attacked mainly on the economic front and accused of trafficking in various goods, but the Beaumont *comité* also took up the statement of a serving-girl, claiming to have heard one of the soldiers use subversive words. 'We know', he was supposed to have said in a conversation at the inn where the girl Merlin worked, 'that some people would like to send us to the frontiers, however that is not what we were enlisted for, we are not supposed to go further than 10 or 30 leagues from Paris, and if they want to send us to the frontiers, we have 8,400 in our regiment, all of like mind, we will return to Paris and bombard it...'. This was wine-talk, and even the revolutionary tribunal chose not to attach too much importance to it.[103] The Beaumont *société* also bared its teeth, writing on 1 Germinal to the district of Pontoise: 'On receiving the news of the contemplated assault on liberty and the involvement of the *armée révolutionnaire* – a detachment of which is stationed in this town, and its conduct is not above reproach – the *société* thinks it its duty to inform you that it has just appointed a commission to investigate...'. The commission, however, only managed to uncover some minor offences connected with the traffic in eggs and butter by the Parisian soldiers. Finally, on 4 Germinal, the *comité de surveillance* of the district told of 'rumours that some volunteers from the *armée révolutionnaire* have been speaking of their intention to use their arms if anyone picked a quarrel with them...'. It seems to have been an affair similar to that involving the soldier Billoré, which had no sequel, and the hefty dossier sent by the national agent in the district to Fouquier spoke only of the 'artificial shortage'.[104]

The calm of country life continued to be ruffled for several months by the shock waves caused by the crisis of Ventôse. Between Ventôse and Messidor the effects were still being felt in the West, the Alps, in Alsace, in the Pyrenees, on the Swiss frontier and in the former Comtat. In all these regions the *exagérés*, and those accused of supporting the system of Ronsin and Hébert, were being hunted. It was a national phenomenon.

It was a long time before calm returned to the communes on the periphery of Paris. In Ventôse the inhabitants of Bercy denounced their national agent, Thiboust, as an atheist and a supporter of the 'conspirators'.[105] There were said to be Hébertists too at Neuilly and at Passy, scene of the lively dinner parties at de Kock's.[106] On 24 Prairial the tribunal condemned to death the national agent and a municipal officer of Belleville as 'accomplices of Hébert' and as having sought to starve Paris.[107] In Messidor, Rousseville, agent of the Committee of Public Safety and a spy of the Revolutionary Government in the communes of the *banlieue* – of which he had considerable experience, having been a vicar in Bagnolet – reported information against Lenoir, national agent of the commune of Choisy, denounced by its inhabitants as an agent of the 'conspirators'.[108] Under cover of the pursuit of ultra-revolutionaries, many old hatreds and animosities were satisfied. Most of those pursued were victims of their energetic application of revolutionary measures; only a handful had known Ronsin, who frequently visited the bowers of Passy.

In the Vaucluse, when the news from Paris arrived, there was much talk of the dangers to the regime, and on 5 Germinal the *société populaire* of Puyméras decided to draw up 'an address to the National Convention, asking it to form a special guard of 400 men to guarantee the safety of our esteemed representatives'.[109] In the Mont-Blanc, in Germinal, a gendarme described as being from Turin revealed the existence of a nucleus of Hébertists in the *société populaire* of Carouge, on the frontier with the Republic of Geneva. It was an indirect means of getting at Marino, a member of the Commission Temporaire, who had installed his own followers in the *société*.[110] In the Bas-Rhin, 'the Conspiracy hatched in Paris against the national representation and the security of the prisons had dangerous ramifications reaching as far as Strasbourg', according to the indefatigable Rousseville, who denounced Schneider's men in a report to Elie Lacoste of 22 Germinal.[111] All those denounced by him, Jüng, Voegt, Massé and Edelmann, were condemned to death on 29 Messidor. In Germinal too, the former national agent of the Le Mans district, Bazin, was translated to Paris, accused by the local *société* of having sided with the '40 sols', of having spoken against the Convention, and of being an 'agent of the conspiracy'.[112] On 7 Prairial a member of the Tarbes *société* denounced some intriguers who 'have created an imaginary conspiracy in the department; they pretended that the conspiracy of Hébert had links with the department'; and on the 12th it was claimed that the intriguers 'tried to give some foundation to this fiction by saying that the Hébertists had gone against their consciences in the matter of religious opinions and had used the two powerful forces of fanaticism and food shortages to bring about civil war...'.[113] Fouquier clearly had many imitators. Finally, in Messidor, a Hébertist clique was discovered within the Gap *comité de surveillance*.[114] At the same time the pace of arrests of 'hommes de liaison' accelerated; ministerial *commissaires* and former *commissaires civils* lost their liberty and their positions, and the proscription extended as far as Nice, Bayonne and many other fortified towns.[115] The Committee of Public Safety had succeeded in imposing its version of a 'military plot' on the entire Republic.

VI   *Removal of the detachments from the Paris region*
     (28 Ventôse–10 Germinal)

There were few arrests of revolutionary officers and soldiers, even at the height of the crisis; no more than 40 during Ventôse, Germinal and Floréal, and barely more than 50 during the whole period from Ronsin's arrest to 9 Thermidor.[116] They were mainly of detachment commanders and officers, and only rarely the soldiers themselves, as if to demonstrate the validity of Billaud-Varenne's argument that the men had no part in their leaders' crimes, and that the *armée révolutionnaire* as a corps deserved well of the country. There were individual cases: the old drunkard, Mouret, accused of wanting to set fire to the commune of Asnières, near Royaumont; the sergeant, Guillaume, who had the misfortune to arrive in Paris from Laon at the height of the crisis; and a further handful arrested in Paris or in their cantonments, for reasons unconnected with the 'conspiracy' – indiscipline, larceny or personal misconduct.[117] The arrests were not levelled against the *armée* as a body. Some detachment commanders were sacrificed to the anger of the country people – the Committee of Public Safety allowing the local authorities free rein. But such arrests were not sufficiently numerous to indicate any hostility in principle in high places towards the Parisian *armée*, and there was nothing automatic about them.

However, on 28 Ventôse, the Committee gave its official sanction to the many accusations against the popular army as the instrument of the 'plot', in a measure penalising the entire corps and prefiguring its disbandment. This was the decision to send all the *révolutionnaires* in Paris, or within six leagues of it – the cannoneers excepted – to distant cantonments in the West. The next day, the 29th, the Committee sent the following order to the divisional heads of the War Ministry: 'Send immediate orders to the various detachments of the *armée révolutionnaire* within a radius of six leagues of Paris and in Paris itself, cavalry, infantry and artillery, to leave within 24 hours and go to Laval, Fougères, Ernée and Lapellérine. The orders should be taken to the various detachments either by courier or by the gendarmes...'.[118] The same day, in execution of these orders, Jourdeuil issued movement orders to the 252 fusiliers still at the Ecole Militaire, to leave the next day, the 30th, for Ernée and Lapellérine, in the Mayenne. The 5th and 6th squadrons left Versailles the same day for their new cantonments, the 5th to Laval, where they were to arrive 8 Germinal, and the 6th to Fougères, to arrive on the 9th. These orders were executed with little difficulty and by 1 Germinal no *révolutionnaires* were left in Paris, beyond a few fusiliers in civvies, attempting to avoid the departure order. On 3 Germinal Maubant asked Hanriot to have the *comités révolutionnaires* in the Sections arrest these lingerers and send them immediately to Ernée.[119] A more privileged 'deserter' was the *chef de bataillon*, Halm, who had commanded the *révolutionnaires* left in the Ecole Militaire, and had evaded the order to leave for the Mayenne by having himself called as a principal witness in the trial of Ronsin.[120]

Paris and Versailles were easily rid of revolutionary troops, but the orders did not arrive everywhere in time: in Vernon, Pontoise and Beaumont, the detachment commanders anticipated them as soon as news of Ronsin's arrest reached their cantonments, and they left on their own authority, intending to return to Paris under arms, and to surrender those arms to their Sections.[121] This is precisely what the Committee of Public Safety sought to avoid, but the displacement orders had been issued in such a rush, that for several days there was considerable indecision and disorder in the movements of these 'abandoned' detachments.

The detachment at Vernon, as we have seen, left the town for Mantes on the 27th, before the Vernon authorities could satisfy their thirst for vengeance against Dumont and his men. On the 28th Bouchotte ordered the 5th Division 'to send orders to a detachment...which is said to have left Vernon for Paris without authorisation, to remain where it is at the time of receipt of this order from me, and to wait there for further orders'. 'The commander of the detachment', the Minister added threateningly, 'should explain the motives which caused him to leave Vernon. Send a courier...'. On learning that the detachment had halted at Mantes, on 2 Germinal Bouchotte sent a second order, by courier, instructing Dumont to return to the Vendée. The order was repeated on the 4th, when he was told to leave Mantes on the 9th for Doué, near Saumur.[122] By then the detachment of 110 men under Dumont had been joined by another from Les Andelys, under Daviel; it was assigned the same destination, and both detachments left Mantes on 9 Germinal. Then came the decree of the 7th, disbanding the *armée révolutionnaire*; since these men were fusiliers, they were not needed in the Vendée, and Bouchotte tried to stop them en route. Thinking that they would pass through Chartres on the 11th, Bouchotte asked Jourdeuil on 10 Germinal to send couriers to that town. But news of their disbandment had already reached the two detachments, and on the 9th, the same day on which they left Mantes for Doué, Dumont stopped at Houdan. From there he wrote to the Minister: 'having seen in the newspapers that the *armée révolutionnaire* has been disbanded, I request guidance on what action to take', and he gave notice of their planned stopping points: the 11th at Chartres, the 12th at Bonneval. His eagerness to comply with the orders of the Committee could not have been more marked. Contact having been re-established, both detachments were stopped on 11 Germinal at Chartres.[123]

The example of the detachments at Vernon and Les Andelys was repeated by those at Beaumont and Pontoise, which also anticipated the Minister's orders of 29 Ventôse by several days, and left their cantonments for Paris, taking their arms and baggage, in protest at the many vexations they had had to endure at the hands of the local authorities. Their conduct appeared all the more dangerous when other companies on detachment in the department, and likewise anxious to return under arms to their Sections, threatened to follow suit.[124] Eventually, the Beaumont and Pontoise detachments, commanded by Captain Loude, were disarmed at Versailles.

The removal order appears not to have reached the cannoneers, even though the artillery was also mentioned in the order of the 28th. The nearest company was that at Coulommiers; it remained in the Brie region after 15 Germinal, along with the companies at Soissons and Chantilly, but several cannoneers, notably from the Champs-Elysées company, returned to Paris at this time; they had been granted their discharge for personal reasons.[125]

Everywhere else the movements were carried through with little difficulty. Few troops were directly affected: two squadrons at Versailles, the detachment at the Ecole Militaire, those at Vernon, Beaumont, Pontoise and Les Andelys, ordered to Chartres or to the Mayenne and the West – a total of some 600 cavaliers and fusiliers at most. The detachment at Coulommiers – infantry and cavalry – remained in place; as did that at Brie-Comte-Robert, and the remnants of the companies in the Gonesse district;[126] the detachments cantoned in the Oise, at Etampes, and the handful of men left, since Brumaire, at Auteuil did not move either.[127]

The other movements involved detachments already outside the six-league radius of Paris; but these too were sent to the West. The Finistère company left Honfleur on 9 Germinal, arriving at Alençon on the 16th. It had left behind four of its men and an officer in prison, and its captain, Doré, and the lieutenant, Martin, left it en route and went directly to Paris.[128] As for the cavalry, the 4th squadron, under the command of Fischer, had already reached Nantes in the first half of Ventôse; the 3rd, under Delgas, had been in service in Saumur since Pluviôse, and the 1st in Lyon since Frimaire;[129] only the two squadrons at Versailles were affected by the order of 28 Ventôse.

VII   *The disbanding of the infantry and cavalry: the decree of 7 Germinal*
(*7 Germinal–6 Floréal*)

(i)   THE DECREE OF 7 GERMINAL

At its session of 7 Germinal, three days after the execution of Ronsin and his fellow accused, and when the Parisian troops were en route to their new cantonments in the Mayenne and the Vendée, the Convention, 'after hearing the report from its Committee of Public Safety', decreed:

Article I

The *armée révolutionnaire* is disbanded; the volunteers who compose it and who wish to return to their homes should return the horses, arms and military equipment furnished them by the Republic. They will be given marching orders at once for their return to their places of residence: their wages and salaries will nevertheless be paid until 1 Floréal.

Article II

Those who wish to continue in service will be incorporated individually and according to their wishes into existing infantry and cavalry regiments in the various armies of the Republic.

Article III

This will not affect the Parisian artillery attached to the *armée révolutionnaire* or its present duties; it will remain under requisition for special service, though the provisional Executive Council will not be able to make use of any part without a special order from the Committee of Public Safety.

Also on the 7th, the Committee of Public Safety issued the following order:

Article I

The Minister of War shall take immediate steps to carry out the law passed today . . . proclaiming the disbandment of the *armée révolutionnaire*.

Article II

In consequence he will bring together from these detachments as many as possible of their former cadres, to receive by incorporation the volunteers from this army who wish to continue their service.

Article III

He will also take from the nearest available corps the detachments necessary to replace those of the *armée révolutionnaire* thus dispersed, and will see to it that there is no gap in the service performed by either.[130]

Bouchotte received the order that same day, but it does not look as if the Convention's decree was communicated to him at the same time, for he added a note, in his small handwriting, to his copy of the order: 'send for a copy of the law from the proceedings of the Convention; see that the detachments of the *armée révolutionnaire* are replaced so that military service does not suffer any ill effects; arrange for the placement of those who wish to remain in the service . . .'.[131]

The task of implementing both decree and accompanying order was confided to the Executive Council, which in practice meant Bouchotte. But the Committee and the Convention distrusted the Council almost as much as the *armée* it had just disbanded, and the days of this puppet 'Government' were numbered. The execution of the law of 7 Germinal was to be the final act of citizen Bouchotte's ministerial life. His successor, Pille, a safe military man, would carry out the remaining provisions of the law and the order concerning the payment of wages owed to the former *révolutionnaires*, and the continued service of those young men of the age of the first requisition. Bouchotte did not even have the right to move the companies of cannoneers without prior permission from the Committee.

The decree and order were drawn up so hurriedly that they omitted to say anything about how the disbandment was to be carried out. Were the detachments to be disarmed where they were? Were they to surrender their arms to the local authorities or to the garrison commanders and the *commissaires des guerres*? For several days doubts persisted concerning this matter, each one interpreting the law in his own best interests. The Executive Council, however, laid out precise rules to be followed, in an *Instruction* sent to every division of the War Ministry on 9 Germinal, two days after the decree. But such was the lack of co-ordination between the Ministry and the general staff, that four days later Maubant still knew nothing of it. The *Instruction* stated that the disbandment of the troops was to be carried out by the military authorities, who would disarm them on the spot, and deposit their arms with the municipalities. Then the garrison commander, or the *commissaire des guerres*, as the case may be, would invite those men not of conscription age to take advantage of the provisions of the law permitting them to continue in service with the regular army; those who were of conscription age were to be directed to the regular corps nearest their place of disbandment. Finally, the Council was to draw up a list of Parisian cannoneers who were to remain under requisition and send it to the Committee of Public Safety.[132] The latter clearly sought to control all the movements of the former revolutionary artillery.

These arrangements were perfectly clear; they were not too unfavourable to the *révolutionnaires*, who, seeing themselves thus spared the ultimate humiliation of being disarmed by the civil authorities, the municipalities and districts, hurried to surrender their arms, and the operation was completed. In most localities, it was the *commissaires des guerres* who carried out the disarmament; in important military posts, like Lyon, Nantes, Le Havre, Saumur and Alençon, the *révolutionnaires* had the luxury of the presence of a garrison commander or a general. But it took time for these arrangements to be made known, and between 9 and 13 Germinal the local authorities acted as they saw fit. The disarmament commenced amidst the greatest disorder, to such an extent that the Executive Council, which was supposed to report every detail of the process to the Committee,[133] was unable to control the actions of the detachments and the municipalities. The immediate result was that young men of conscription age succeeded in being demobilised and then disappeared into the towns; likewise arms disappeared. The fault lay with the Committee of Public Safety, which, in its haste to rid itself of the popular army, had omitted to take account of all the conditions governing its disbandment.

Whatever precautions were adopted, however, in the final analysis the successful execution of these measures depended upon the good will and co-operation of the Parisian officers and soldiers themselves. Except in fortified places and garrison towns where the *révolutionnaires* were flanked by regular troops, the Parisians were generally the only armed force present in the communes, outside the local National Guard. It would have been easy for them to resist the orders of the municipalities and to have set out with their arms for Paris, even if there was little chance of them arriving. Having a monopoly of armed force in the country areas, the *révolutionnaires* had the power to resist the orders of the Convention and the municipalities. Resistance was certainly a practical possibility; but the Parisians were 'soldiers of the Convention'.

(ii) REACTION OF THE *RÉVOLUTIONNAIRES* TO THE DECREE

If the political soldiers were disappointed with a decree which confirmed official disapproval of them, they showed no sign of it, and their addresses to the Convention reveal the most touching resignation and submission. The delegation of 40 soldiers which presented the flags of the Lyon detachment to the Convention, spoke of 'the respectful emotions we feel in finding ourselves amidst our representatives, amidst our fathers! yes, we are your children, you formed us into an *armée révolutionnaire*, and we marched with enthusiasm, you disbanded us and we obeyed with respect...'.[134] This was in Floréal. But the same sentiments, worthy of the first-class funeral promised by the Convention to the *armée révolutionnaire*, can be found even in the addresses of Germinal. Thus the fusiliers of the Temple Section declared: 'the Convention in its wisdom considered it time for our disbandment, we received the news without complaint.... We have but one regret, it is that the arms which were entrusted to us have not served to destroy any enemy to the public good; let them be restored to us when the time is judged right and we will act according to your wishes, we will show that true sans-culottes know how to obey...'.[135] Was this naïveté or calculation, this hope by the Temple fusiliers for a revival of their army once Ronsin was forgotten?

Chef de bataillon Buard had a good political head and was more acute in his observations. Recognising that the *armée* was finished, he tried for a glowing finale that would secure the future for himself and his subordinates. 'A true republican', he declared on 18 Germinal during the disbandment ceremonies at Le Havre, 'cannot display his respect for the laws in any better way than by submitting to them.... I would have liked nothing better than to return this flag [that of the 1st battalion] to the National Convention, from whom I received it. I and my brothers in arms can only regret that we did not have the chance to bear it to victory on the field of honour...'.[136] Pious words, meaning nothing; for all the fusiliers of this detachment, without exception, opted to return to civilian life. In Alençon the garrison commander informed his chief on 23 Germinal: 'We disbanded and disarmed the detachment of the *armée révolutionnaire*...there were tears and sorrow, but they soon got over it...'. Nor was that the end of the matter, for the company from the Sans-Culottes Section also went to the lengths of securing promises from the municipality, district, *commissaire des guerres* and garrison commander in Alençon, to write to the Minister and the Committee of Public Safety, testifying to its good conduct during its stay in the town.[137] In the same way the detachment in Lyon obtained an attestation of good conduct before it left, signed by Reverchon, Delaporte and Méaulle, Boissay and Parein. The deputation of 40 charged with taking the flag from Lyon, and returning through the Bourbonnais – there was no question of going through Avallon and Auxerre again – also gathered good-conduct certificates from all the municipalities of the communes through which they passed: Roanne, Varenne-sur-Allier, Saint-Pierre-le-Moûtier, Nevers, La Charité, Cosne, Bonny-sur-Loire, Gien, Montargis, Nemours, Melun.[138] One could never take too many precautions, especially when one had participated in the repression in Lyon. The municipalities were generous, playing their part in this false atmosphere of good will, which cost them nothing. In their triumph they could afford such gestures to old enemies who could no longer hurt them. Perhaps too there was, in these expressions of fraternity by the authorities, an element of relief that the disarmament process had gone ahead with such ease.

Such were the official, the collective feelings of the soldiers. On a personal level, and considering the circumstances, most soldiers had but one desire: to remain anonymous. It was not a time to expand on the ingratitude of governments. A few were sufficiently courageous to express their regret about the probable consequences of the new economic policy towards the farmers. On 9 Germinal, the police agent Perrière noted in his report: 'Today members of the *armée révolutionnaire* were heard to say that every day they watched the peasants piling up butter and eggs but bringing none to the town; but if they tried to make any complaint about this, they were put in prison...'. Even more revealing are the words, quoted in the same report, of one man, undoubtedly a former revolutionary officer: 'I do not know what will come of all this; the *comités révolutionnaires* were complained about, and they became suspect; the *armées révolutionnaires* were complained about, and they have been dissolved; it seems as though everything which bears the name *révolutionnaire* is under attack...'.[139] Such indeed had been the intention.

Government agents noted, with satisfaction, the favourable reaction of the boulevards and the cafés to news of the decree. 'The decree suppressing the *armée révolutionnaire* has been generally well received, announces Leharivel; everyone is talking about it in rapturous terms, saying: the Convention has pulled the tree up by its roots, for no one denies the fact that this destructive corps was created by the faction which has just paid for its sins...'. Charmont's account is full of similar remarks about the former 'armée des Coquins'. Soulet claimed that every patriot was happy about the disbanding of the *armée révolutionnaire*; Rollin, that 'the decree disbanding the *armée révolutionnaire* is applauded from all sides...it is said that the shortage of eggs being experienced is largely due to their brigandage...'. Even the Cordeliers club took the most conformist of lines; 'the announcement of the decree disbanding the *armée révolutionnaire* was showered with applause', wrote Boucheseiche, who had just come from this *conseil de rats*. According to Charmont, the return of the *révolutionnaires* to Paris was dreaded: 'People would like to see them incorporated into the armies of the Republic, but they should not be allowed to return to Paris where they might cause trouble...'. But according to Hanriot, Parisians were just as much afraid of these 'brigands' being incorporated into the armies.

This unanimity of support for the official line – the *armée* as the creation and instrument of the 'faction', its soldiers' brigandage having caused the food shortage – is somewhat suspect. Orthodox opinion simply reflected government propaganda; while the militant *sectionnaires*, who were hunted down in Germinal, were afraid of expressing their regret at the condemnation of their favourite institution. The comments of some less conformist observers, however, show that public reaction was not quite so cut and dried. Some regretted the freedom of action now guaranteed to the farmers, others would have liked to retain the *armée* after purging its command. Le Breton, in his report of 8 Germinal, told of the immense satisfaction of the peasants in the environs of Paris who 'proclaimed that their troubles were over, since the intention of the general [Ronsin] had been to increase this army to 100,000 men...'. 'I was in a café in the market', wrote Letassey the same day, 'and heard many citizens discussing the disbanding of the *armée révolutionnaire*. Some said it should have been purged but retained, others that it was better to disband it, for they feared that it might have proved to be the hired band of the conspirators...'. 'In groups of people and in the cafés the decree...is welcomed', wrote Monic. 'Everyone accepts that the institution was a good thing, but that the intriguers in this *armée* sought ends contrary to the public good...'. In the eyes of Paris, then, the *armée* had been the victim of its command.

On 9 Germinal the debate was expanded to include opinions on all the organisations involved in the repression of Lyon. Soulet reported that 'it is even being said that the *représentants* of the people in that town supported this *armée* and had the popular club closed...'. The following day the attack became more specific, focusing first on Fouché, then on his commissions. 'It is being said in several places', declared Béraud, 'that the Commission Temporaire in Lyon was a tool of the Hébertist conspiracy, that many patriots were guillotined, and even some who refused to take part in their plots...'.[140]

In disbanding the Parisian *armée* the government had opened the floodgates to a whole range of moderate opinions. It was the logical outcome of the great debate in Paris and Lyon concerning the Repression, its instruments, and its men. One could not condemn the *armée*

révolutionnaire and spare the Commission Temporaire; the institutions of the
anarchic Terror were of a piece. Along with the Cordeliers leaders, the
armée révolutionnaire and its Moulins and Nièvre companies, went also all the
other organs of the repression in Lyon, and Grimaud found himself bitterly
attacked by the *société* on his return to Moulins.[141] Fouché himself felt
threatened. The exultant moderates could scarcely contain their joy and
sought to push their advantage even further.

(iii) IMPLEMENTATION OF THE MEASURES OF DISBANDMENT (9–27 GERMINAL)
The decree of 7 Germinal was published in the *Bulletin des Lois* and in the
Parisian papers, which reached the various places where the detachments
were stationed on the 9th and in the days following. The *Instruction* of the
9th, however, did not arrive until several days later, and some
municipalities went ahead with the disarmament on receipt of the *Bulletin*.
In Laon, as early as the 9th, the General Council ordered the garrison
commander to disarm those 'individuals making up the *armée révolutionnaire*'.[142] The decree, however, had not been officially promulgated; the
Council was obliged to postpone the measure and the Laon detachments
were only finally disarmed ten days later. The imprecision of the decree
encouraged other communes to follow this example. 'The *armée révolutionnaire* being disbanded', wrote Maubant to the Committee on the 13th, 'I
await orders on how to proceed. I hear that some communes, simply on
reading the *Bulletin*, have already disbanded the different detachments
stationed in their arrondissements. That of Noyon has disbanded the
detachment stationed there, collected its arms...and issued marching
orders to each of the volunteers...'.[143] This example, however, does not
seem to have been generally followed, and elsewhere the municipalities and
districts waited for orders from the *commissaires des guerres* or the garrison
commanders responsible for the disbandment, before proceeding. Most
communes carried through the process between 11 and 18 Germinal, and
some not until the 20th or 22nd. The first soldiers had returned to their
Sections before the end of the month. At the beginning of Floréal, on
receipt of new instructions from the Commission responsible for army
movements, the municipalities began a hunt for former *révolutionnaires* of
conscription age who had taken refuge in out-of-the-way communes of the
plat pays.

    The first commune to implement the decree – if we except Noyon, for
which we have no precise date – was that of Compiègne: the municipalities
least well-disposed towards the *armée* were clearly the most impatient. On
the 9th the *Bulletin* was read out to the *société* and the decree applauded. The
comité expressed similar satisfaction; 'since the rule of law has been
re-established, these measures should be executed vigorously', and it
decided to write to Ferrand, the *commissaire des guerres*, 'inviting him to
accelerate the departure of the soldiers of the detachment from the *armée
révolutionnaire* stationed here, provided they surrender their arms and effects

beforehand...'. Two days later the *comité*, 'considering it its duty [an agreeable duty] to have this decree read out to the detachment cantoned here, in order officially to inform it of the decree, so that it may then be put into effect', ordered that the detachment 'be assembled today, at four o'clock in the afternoon, on the place de la Loi, to hear the decree and then file in front of the established authorities, to present themselves before the District Court and deliver up their arms and equipment....'.[144]

In the district of Rozoy, the disbandment was being spoken of as completed by 12 Germinal, and by the 13th people in Rozoy itself were already referring to the 'former *armée révolutionnaire*'.[145] On the 15th the detachment commanders were still in doubt as to what interpretation should be placed on the decree. Should the cannoneers be included, for example, and their cannon returned to Paris? Lemaire, who commanded all the revolutionary troops at Coulommiers, was perplexed and wrote to Hanriot, who in turn got on to Bouchotte. 'I invite you to reply immediately about this matter', wrote Hanriot, 'so that I can communicate your intentions to citizen Lemaire, who fears that news of the disbandment of the *armée révolutionnaire* may cause trouble in his detachment...'. Bouchotte responded swiftly to this mention of possible resistance by the soldiers – the only reference to such a possibility at this time. 'Act immediately', he noted in the margin of this letter; 'the cannon must stay with the cannoneers, they are not included in the decree, and they cannot be moved except by a decision from the Committee of Public Safety ...'.[146] It took an entire week to clarify the position on the artillery with the detachment commanders. The day after Hanriot wrote, 16 Germinal, the Coulommiers authorities proceeded to disarm the squadron and fusilier company making up Lemaire's detachment. On the same day Dumany's detachment in Melun was disarmed.[147] The La Ferté-Gaucher detachment was disarmed on the 23rd by the *commissaire des guerres*, Charlot, who then proceeded to Faremoutiers on the 25th.[148] It was the last operation of its kind in the Brie region.

In Lyon the fusiliers and cavaliers were disarmed at a grand ceremony held at Les Brotteaux on 15 Germinal.[149] That same day Bartélémy, *commissaire des guerres* in the Eure-et-Loire, disbanded the detachment at Chartres.[150] On the 18th it was the turn of the detachments at Le Havre, Chantilly and Viarmes, and of Laon on the 20th.[151] In Alençon the interim commander had to await the arrival on the 23rd of the 33rd gendarme division before disarming the detachment; the Parisians left the town the following day.[152] On 26 Germinal the 6th squadron, which had just been disbanded at Fougères, sent an address to the Convention requesting permission to retain its flag.[153] On the 25th Barbier, *commissaire des guerres* in the Seine-et-Oise, announced that all the detachments in the department had been disbanded. On 15 Germinal the *représentants*, Prieur de la Marne, Hentz and Francastel, on mission to the Army of the West, issued an order concerning the incorporation of cavaliers of conscription age into that force, and the squadrons commanded by Fischer and Blanquet were disbanded at Nantes some days later.[154] Everything had gone through by 26 Germinal, calmly and with the minimum of disturbance.

Despite having served six months, the *révolutionnaires* at the time of their disbandment had all the bearing of civilians, which they had never entirely lost, and to which state they were being returned, this time for good. The fears in some quarters about possible 'militarisation' of this political army appear to have been quite illusory, seen in the light of the main preoccupations of these former soldiers of Ronsin at the time of their demobilisation. They wanted to ease their return to civilian life by obtaining testimonials from all the authorities, military and civil alike, under whose orders they had served. Nor did they show any inclination to take up the offer held out by the decree, of re-engagement in the regular army at the same grade. On 20 Germinal, Renard, commander of the Laon garrison, told the Committee that of 360 fusiliers just disbanded he could not find one who wished to continue in the service. In Lyon too nearly all the fusiliers opted to return to their Sections. Nor could one volunteer be found among the 400-plus disbanded at Le Havre, despite the fine words of Buard.[155] This repugnance to signing up seems to have been shared by all the fusiliers. True, some did attempt, unsuccessfully on the whole, to join the companies of cannoneers on their return to Paris;[156] but this was not so much a re-engagement as the continuation of a largely political service. Candidates for the post of 'Jacobin cavalier' were few, as we have seen, and came mostly from the revolutionary squadrons of cavalry rather than the infantry. (See p. 152, n. 163.) The former *révolutionnaire* had no vocation for the military life, and with his service in a political force completed, he returned to his modest position in civilian life, ready for another kind of political combat in Paris.

The young men of conscription age, who had been able to ensconce themselves in comfortable service with the *armée révolutionnaire*, were in no rush to find their way into the regular army. The number of deserters and draft-dodgers seems to have been high, for the Commission du Mouvement, which replaced the War Ministry, sent a circular on 10 Floréal to all administrations, ordering an intensification of effort to discover Ronsin's former soldiers.[157] Two days later, 12 Floréal, the Convention issued a new decree, recalling the terms of that of 7 Germinal and ordering all authorities to make the young recalcitrants rejoin without delay.[158] The district of Noyon replied that there was no soldier of this category in its sphere of jurisdiction; but the very day of the decree the *comité* of the Lombards Section arrested a twenty-one-year-old, demobbed from the *armée révolutionnaire* and claiming to have been conscripted for arms manufacture.[159] On 26 Floréal the district of Meaux sent the gendarmerie after several former *révolutionnaires* in the commune of Armentières, near Lizy-sur-Ourcq.[160] And in the commune of Fosseuse, in the district of

Chaumont, were two ex-fusiliers who still had not re-joined the regular army ten months later, in Pluviôse Year III.[161]

It was around 27 Germinal when the final *révolutionnaires* left their places of cantonment,[162] and already on the 26th the Chalier Section was according aid to two former *révolutionnaires* who could not pay their way home. Its *comité* wrote on the 27th, asking the municipality of Soissons to verify the certificates of good conduct it had given to the detachment.[163] On 24 Germinal the Chantilly *comité* issued a passport to Vallantin, captain of the Guillaume-Tell Section's cannoneers, who had resigned his commission in order to return to his Parisian business, and on the same day the *comité* was notified by a former fusilier of his intention of establishing himself in Chantilly.[164] On 26 Germinal the Droits-de-l'Homme Section's company of cannoneers was replaced at Laon by the company from the Lepeletier Section; on the 30th some soldiers from the Lyon detachment presented themselves to the Moulins *société populaire* in order to take up their places.[165] On 13 Floréal the fusiliers from the Tuileries Section, back from Lyon, had their certificates attested by the *comité*.[166] And finally, on 19 Floréal, a former cavalier took up lodgings at the *auberge* of the Cadran Bleu, former headquarters of the unfortunate Mazuel.[167]

The revolutionary infantry was no more. Disbanded without difficulty, its members were now second-class citizens, seeking obscurity, but as former soldiers of Ronsin, already suspect in the eyes of the *comités révolutionnaires*. Those who took this semi-disgrace badly, provoking disturbances in the cafés and picking quarrels with those who spoke ill of the former *armée*, were treated harshly by the *commissaires de police* in the Sections; opinion had turned against them. Some political officers, like Réaume, Tolède, Langlois, Constant and Renault, were more fortunate, returning to their places on the *comités révolutionnaires* and in the Sectionary institutions;[168] as Sectionary officials they had nothing to fear from the reaction which began as early as Floréal and Prairial. Fortunate too were the former military men, some of whom found employment at the Ecole Militaire, the Camp des Sablons, the Invalides, in the general command or in military supply.[169] The ordinary fusiliers returned to their trades, or sought work in the powder and saltpetre stores, in the arms manufactories or in the prisons.

There was no question of these former soldiers forming an old-boy network. All that remained of the political *armée* in Floréal were a few officials helping the *commissaire des guerres*, Martin, in his task of going through the accounts and inventorying the returned clothing and effects.[170] We have to wait until the proscriptions of the Year III and the conspiracies of the Years IV and IX, to find any retrospective *esprit de corps* among the former revolutionary fusiliers, who found themselves proscribed as such.[171]

The dispersion of the former revolutionary cavalry was likewise almost total. Most of the *chefs d'escadron* managed to retain the ranks they had held in the political army, in virtue of a decision which Gossuin persuaded the Committee to adopt on 17 Prairial.[172] The former cavaliers disappeared into the conscripted regiments or back into civilian life; few took part in any political activity in the years which followed.[173] The cavalry was not a corps of the political élite like the artillery and the infantry.

The *journée* of 9 Thermidor brought about the downfall of several personalities from the former revolutionary general staff who had been saved by Robespierre in Germinal, and had found employment in the general command of the armed forces of Paris, under the orders of General Hanriot. Boulanger, who had been an effective auxiliary of the police surveillance bureau and of Fouquier-Tinville during the summer, had rendered the Robespierrists important services, and shared the fate of his protectors. He was guillotined on 11 Thermidor.[174] His aide-de-camp, Benoît, summoned before the Committee of General Security, committed suicide the following day, profiting from the momentary inattention of his guards.[175] Maubant owed his escape from the holocaust which engulfed the rest of Hanriot's general staff to his fortuitous absence from Paris on the 9th, having been sent by the Committee of General Security on a mission to Meaux, with his two adjoints, Allais and Martin. He was arrested there on the 15th, at the request of the *comité* of his Section, still out for his blood; but on the 28th, at Fouché's behest, he was released by the Committee of General Security. From this time on we lose sight of this soldier, an experienced and wily politician, save for a request from him to the Directory in the Year VI for military employment in the interior, accompanied by a warm recommendation from Bailleux, president of the Council of Five Hundred.[176]

(iv)   THE FATE OF THE FORMER REVOLUTIONARY ARTILLERY
        (GERMINAL YEAR II – PRAIRIAL YEAR III)

The revolutionary artillery, shorn of its name and indistinguishable from the 20 or so other Sectionary companies,[177] remained under colours, and even retained a certain homogeneity and *esprit de corps* which was to serve it well in Thermidor, as in Germinal and Prairial Year III. The former revolutionary cannoneers were conscious of their strength and political importance, and the Thermidorean authorities had reason to fear them, since it was to them that Babeuf and his friends looked in drawing up lists of men to be counted on. Certain of these companies were served, moreover, by the presence at their head or in their ranks of militant *sectionnaires* like Lefranc, captain of the Tuileries company, Dauphinot, who commanded that of the Bon-Conseil Section, Potemont, captain of the Montreuil company, Eude and Sormois, captain and sergeant of the Droits-de-l'Homme company, the Monvoisins, officers of the Luxembourg company, Fontaine, a cannoneer from the Arcis Section.

The 13 companies garrisoning Lyon were still there at the time of the events of Ventôse–Germinal: Tuileries, Gardes-Françaises, Halle-au-Bled, Marchés, Faubourg-Montmartre, Bondy, Temple, Popincourt, Montreuil, Homme-Armé, Indivisibilité, Arsenal, Fontaine-de-Grenelle. The can-noneers from the Tuileries and the Gardes-Françaises in particular played an important role in the repressive administration, occupying two-thirds of the positions as adjoints to the 32 *comités révolutionnaires* of the Lyon Sections.[178] The Cité, Brutus and Marat companies were still in service at Brest during Germinal.[179] That from the Bon-Conseil was at Honfleur with the Contrat-Social company in Germinal, having moved there from the Gonesse district.[180] The company from the Gravilliers Section was serving in the Gonesse district, those from Guillaume-Tell and the Maison-Commune in the Aisne, and the Luxembourg company was still in Alençon at the time of the crisis.[181] We do not know the Sections of origin of the companies left at Coulommiers when the revolutionary infantry was being disbanded.

What became of the companies from the former revolutionary artillery between Germinal and Thermidor? Did they return to Paris, as they had a right to expect, or were they kept far from the capital? The question is not purely academic, since it has a bearing on governmental policy towards this force of militants. Several historians have broached the problem: General Herlaut claimed that between Floréal and Thermidor, Carnot, distrustful of these political troops, sent as many as possible away from the Paris region, without replacing them with companies already on detachment. It was a matter of political calculation, he says, Carnot seeking at all costs to prevent a concentration of this artillery in Paris, aware as he was of its political importance, and having acquired experience of repressive administration during his missions to the *armée révolutionnaire*. According to Herlaut, Carnot was afraid of furnishing his enemies in the Committee, and in the Commune, with a formidable weapon, by authorising the return to Paris of the 26 or 27 companies which had served under Ronsin.[182] But Herlaut's analysis of movement orders for the period makes no distinction between the former revolutionary companies and the 20 or so other companies remaining outside the Parisian *armée*. It would be interesting to know whether Carnot did want to penalise the former, as more dangerous and more advanced than the latter. According to the findings of Marcel Reinhard, which agree with my own, rather more companies returned to Paris than left it, 17 as against 15.[183] And among those 17 can be found most of the companies which had formerly served in the *armée révolutionnaire*. The Tuileries company left Lyon at the beginning of Floréal; but its stay in Paris was brief and it went to Besançon in Prairial or Messidor.[184] The Indivisibilité, Faubourg-Montmartre, Fontaine-de-Grenelle and Bondy companies set out for Paris on 8 Prairial, and all 13 of the companies detached to Lyon were back in Paris by Messidor.[185] In Messidor also the three companies from the Cité, Marat and Brutus Sections were replaced in Brest by that from the Poissonnière Section.[186] Shortly after the crisis of Germinal, the Guillaume-Tell and Maison-Commune companies on detachment in the Aisne were replaced by that from the Lepeletier Section, and returned to Paris,[187] Dauphinot, who commanded the Bon-Conseil company, also returned from Honfleur in Floréal, while the Luxembourg company left Alençon for Paris in Floréal or Prairial.[188] We know nothing of the movements of the Contrat-Social company which spent the winter at Granville.[189] Elements from the Panthéon-Français and Fraternité companies were kept on at Chartres and Le Havre after the disbandment of the revolutionary infantry.[190]

There is, therefore, no question of these companies from the former revolutionary artillery having been treated with disfavour during these months, and requests to return home were not dismissed by the Committee and the Commission des Mouvements. The Commission readily acceded to such a request from three companies in garrison at Brest; and if they had to wait until Messidor before leaving, it was because of Pille's difficulty in finding replacements rather than any inherent mistrust. Nor did the companies which had never formed part of the *armée révolutionnaire* remain behind in Paris while their comrades were sent to distant parts; several of them were sent to the Armies of the Nord and the Alps while Ronsin's *armée* was still in existence. And, like the former fusiliers, most of the revolutionary cannoneers found their way back to Paris eventually.

After Thermidor things were quite different. It is interesting to note that on the night of 9 Thermidor, of the 16 companies which went to the place de Grève on orders from Fontaine, responding to an appeal from the Commune, 7 – from the Arcis, Marchés, Sans-Culottes, Popincourt, Bon-Conseil, Luxembourg and Droits-de-l'Homme Sections – belonged to the former revolutionary artillery.[191] It was another proof of the personal influence of certain militants – whether officers or simple cannoneers – within the companies. His brother being a member of the General Council of the Commune (he was guillotined on 11 Thermidor), Eude, captain of the Droits-de-l'Homme company, no doubt dragged his men along to defend the Commune.[192] The Luxembourg, Arcis and Popincourt companies were particularly frowned upon by the Thermidorean authorities as having several notorious militants at their head or in their ranks.

Only four of the former revolutionary companies gave their support to the Convention: Gardes-Françaises, Gravilliers, Guillaume-Tell and Faubourg-Montmartre. If later, during the *journées* of Prairial, the Gardes-Françaises and Guillaume-Tell companies again supported the Convention with their cannon, that of the Faubourg-Montmartre showed itself particularly fiercely opposed to the Thermidorean authorities. What caused this turn-about? Undoubtedly the personal influence enjoyed in this Section by Léonard Bourdon was largely responsible; he turned the company and the Section against the Commune, but found himself proscribed in Germinal Year III.[193] At least three former revolutionary companies took no part whatever in the events of this dramatic night, for they were out of Paris: those of the l'Homme-Armé – sent to Alençon shortly after their return from Lyon, the Champs-Elysées,[194] and the Tuileries. Like the cannoneers from the l'Homme-Armé, Lefranc and his men wrote to the Convention, in Fructidor from their cantonment in Besançon, congratulating it on having uncovered the intrigues of the 'triumvirs'; this company from the Tuileries was in such favour that shortly afterwards it was assigned to the defence of the Convention. On 22 Frimaire Year III it again left Paris, to join the Sambre-et-Meuse Army, and once more was spared the necessity of making a painful choice at the time of the events of Prairial.[195]

In the course of the Year III, individual members of the former revolutionary cannoneers distinguished themselves as among the most courageous critics of the new order, and during the last of the great popular *journées* their intervention was to be decisive. On 23 Frimaire Year III, a former revolutionary cannoneer, Faroux, acted as spokesman to the Convention for his co-workers in the arms manufactories of the Sans-Culottes Section.[196] The former revolutionary artillery did not play a major part in the *journée* of 12 Germinal, even though Vaneck seems to have succeeded in bringing part of the company from the Cité with him, a company indeed which contained several seasoned militant *sectionnaires*.[197] But the day after this indecisive *journée* the cannoneers from the Faubourg-du-Nord company mutinied in support of Léonard Bourdon, and a police report from the end of that month described the company as 'largely composed of workers, . . . all of like mind and forming a stubborn coalition; they speak with one voice and their will is always preponderant. . .'.[198]

On 1 Prairial a former cannoneer from the Montreuil Section – the twenty-three-year-old engraver Lîme, whose company had been with the revolutionary detachment at Lyon in the autumn of 1793 – placed himself at the head of an armed force from the Quinze-Vingts Section and brought part of his old company into the riot. His intervention had a considerable impact on the events of that *journée* in the faubourg, and the authorities recognised as much in condemning him to death on 18 Prairial. Two other former *révolutionnaires* from the Lyon detachment were ringleaders in the Popincourt company, the cannoneer officer, Potemont, and the fusilier Vafflard, a courageous soldier, later to have an equally glorious career in the Army of Italy. In the Convention, it was another cannoneer – perhaps from the Arsenal Section – who climbed on to a chair and read out the 'Insurrection du Peuple'.[199] The following day, the cannoneers of the Halle-au-Bled Section, in revolt against their officers, brought their cannon over to the insurgents of the Montreuil Section and fraternised with the people from the faubourgs – an action which resulted in the disarmament and arrest of every member of the company, in the days following the defeat of the sans-culottes.[200] The cannoneers of the Faubourg-du-Nord Section also seem to have decided in favour of the insurrection, while those of the Fontaine-de-Grenelle Section, following the example of the Halle-au-Bled mutineers, wanted to go to the assistance of their brothers of the faubourg.[201] On 5 Prairial a former cannoneer from the Brest detachment, the shoemaker Etienne Chefson, was arrested for having tried to rouse the Poissonnière Section during the two previous *journées*; on the same day, public opinion, always quick to see the former cannoneer officers as unrepentant terrorists, accused Denis Dauphinot, former commander of the Bon-Conseil company, of having had similar intentions.[202] These men were probably as much the victims of the Thermidorean authorities' systematic distrust of the revolutionary cannoneers after Frimaire, as of their own verbal imprudence in proclaiming their hatred for the Convention of the Year III. Often it was enough to have commanded a company to be the object of all kinds of accusations, and if, in Prairial, many other cannoneers were denounced for having taken part in the insurrection, it was more often because of their past than any active intervention in the *journées*. Theirs was, moreover, such a well-established reputation that in the Arsenal Section, when measures were taken to disarm the 'buveurs de sang', the entire company of cannoneers was involved, as if to underline its collective responsibility, while former fusiliers were dealt with individually.[203]

A legend had already developed around the former artillery, and it was to grow steadily as the years went by. However, far from participating as a body in the insurrection of the Year III, most companies approached the *journées* in some disarray, torn between their officers, who wanted above all to obey the orders of the Convention, and the ordinary soldiers, who, out of political conviction and for reasons of social solidarity, wanted to join with the troops of the faubourg. If, in the faubourg itself, the insurrection was actually sparked off by some former revolutionary officers and soldiers, cannoneers and fusiliers alike – Potemont, Foucault, Placet and Laurent[204] – elsewhere it was the cannoneers who supplied the decisive element. As in Thermidor, the Sections in the west of Paris remained faithful to the Convention, with the Lepeletier and Brutus companies joining the Gardes-Françaises and Guillaume-Tell ones. The autonomy of the Sections undoubtedly favoured this dispersion, and prevented the Parisian artillery from acting coherently as a united body. On 9 Thermidor, in the absence of any overall direction, many cannoneer companies spent the night drifting aimlessly, torn between the contradictory wishes of their officers and the *commissaires* from the Sections. In Germinal Year III there was a total absence of superior command. In the *journées* of Prairial some of the officers and cannoneers of the three companies of the faubourg undoubtedly supplied rather better, more centralised direction to the insurgents, but they were poorly seconded by companies from the other Sections. In the Sections of the centre and the left bank, the companies were preoccupied with minor internal revolutions, the officers wanting to obey the Convention, some of the cannoneers trying instead to bring their cannon to the assistance of the *faubouriens*. Disorder and doubt abounded, and in the end each company tended to take the political line of the Section to which it belonged. This was true even for companies like those of the Lepeletier, Champs-Elysées, Gardes-Françaises, Guillaume-Tell and Brutus Sections, which had been part of the *armée révolutionnaire* in the Year II and which, in the Year III – the Champs-Elysées excepted – became defenders of order and fired upon the insurgent populace.

The Thermidorean government, like that of the Year II, was the victim of its own myths. During four days of rioting which very nearly toppled the regime of *honnêtes gens*, the revolutionary artillery had shown itself an unreliable force, easily led astray and made to change sides by the first determined agitator. This time the Convention decided to end, once and for all, the nightmare of the people in arms, by suppressing the companies of cannoneers which, composed as they were of shopkeepers and artisans, were unsuited to the defence of a government of *nouveaux riches*. In their place would be ranged the cohorts of the *jeunesse dorée*, a hand-picked National Guard, and a Legion of police to act as rampart for the new regime (but which in its turn was to fall under democratic influences). After a stay of execution of 14 months, the former revolutionary artillery underwent the same fate suffered by the infantry and cavalry in Germinal Year II. The institutional history of the Parisian *armée révolutionnaire* was brought to a close in Prairial Year III, with the disarming of the faubourg and the collective proscription of the former cannoneers of the *armée révolutionnaire* along with the members of the *comités révolutionnaires* of the Year II.[205]

The decree of 7 Germinal Year II was not the outcome of a hasty decision; on the contrary, everything indicates minute preparation. The Committee of Public Safety proceeded prudently, in stages, first ridding itself of the chiefs, whose impatient and unassuaged ambitions posed considerable dangers. Then it was the turn of the detachments, and three days after the execution of Ronsin any possible 'mouvements' on the part of his *armée* were forestalled by its dissolution. Apart from a few minor incidents, largely caused by the impatience of the municipalities to disarm the detested soldiers, the disbanding was an orderly and calm process. The eagerness of the detachments to comply with the law was touching.

Was the 'military plot' simply a pretext by the government to eliminate an army which had ceased to be useful and become a burden? Did the Committee really believe its own myths? Were they in fact myths? There was indeed expectation in certain circles, not only in Paris, of a coup or 'mouvement' on 30 Ventôse or 10 Germinal. There is no agreement on the date, but all accounts claim that it was to have taken place on the *jour de la décade*, as if the *décadi* had some magic quality suited to great catastrophes and decisive *journées*. The *jour de la décade* had replaced those tumultuous and so often sanguinary Mondays of village riots under the Ancien Regime.[206] The Committee had perhaps simply beaten its adversaries to the post. We could speculate forever without reaching any final conclusion. We will never know the secret thoughts, barely even formulated perhaps, of the unfortunate Ronsin and his *enfant terrible*, Mazuel.

But the 'plot' had served government interests well. The people believed in it, or pretended to do so, and there can be no doubt that the governmental version had all the necessary ingredients to gain popular adhesion. At a stroke the reputation of the entire Parisian *armée* was destroyed by the suspicion of complicity with an ambitious general who sought to become a French Cromwell. The importance of popular credulity is most strikingly displayed in the fact that the 'plot' permitted the government to suppress an institution so close to the hearts of the people in the Sections, without incurring the accusation of *modérantisme*. And yet the ease with which the process of disbandment was effected showed the absurdity of the official thesis. But the proof had come too late, and in any event the *armée* had become an anachronism, with the soldiers themselves as eager to return to their homes as the government was to have them disarmed. An army has served its time when its members can think of nothing but regaining the anonymity of their hearths and the comfortable obscurity of their shops.

The *révolutionnaires* had come a long way from their enthusiasm of the autumn; inactivity, wear and tear, the absence of wives, worries about businesses left idle, and about the future, the lassitude – all had sapped the energy of men who for the most part were not the stuff of which revolutionaries or martyrs are made. Daily living asserted its claims. When, in addition, they were told they had been duped, that traitors had taken over the high command and wanted to use them for their dubious enterprises, they began to fear for themselves. Might it not be said that they too, by association, were traitors, apprentice rebels? They asked only to be left in obscurity, and in the general *sauve-qui-peut* they thought simply of returning to civilian life under the least objectionable terms possible. It was only among the cannoneers, spurred on no doubt by hunger, that most persuasive of popular tribunes, that the creeping indifference was kept at bay for more than a year by a certain *esprit de corps*. But when, in the summer of 1795, some cannoneers rose and turned their cannon on the Convention and on troops near to mutiny and ready to fraternise with a populace whose anger and poverty they shared, it was too late. The insurgents lacked any unity of command and any clear idea of ends to be achieved. Some wanted little more than bread and the Maximum, others had political aims, some even longed for Robespierre and the Commune of the Year II. The struggle, however, had already been lost in Germinal Year II, when an army, which might have been the army of the *petit peuple* and was never that of Ronsin, had let itself be disarmed with indifference and sickening expressions of orthodoxy and loyalty.

The *armée révolutionnaire* in fact had the same secret defects as all great revolutionary institutions; its prolonged existence imposed too much strain, required too many sacrifices from men whose preoccupations were of a more human, more banal nature than that of being always in the breech, lying in wait for the enemies of the interior. They quickly tired of 'revolutionising'. Revolutionary regimes are by nature weak, because they are not normal, they upset personal habits and overturn the normally immutable pattern of a man's daily routine. It was already something of a miracle to have kept together in a body for eight months and to have imposed some sort of discipline on men who, in the last analysis, were more attracted by women and the gaming table than by night marches, by tumultuous sessions of *sociétés populaires*, and even by the extraordinary feasting at some *parties de campagne*. How sweet it was to return to normal life, to the anonymity of the large towns, to the domestic obscurity of a seventh-floor dwelling.

Epilogue
1796–1816

The Parisian *armée*, and, to a lesser extent, those of the departments, were destined for a certain notoriety, a sort of posthumous existence, long after their final disappearance as a corps in 1794 and in Prairial Year III. The former *révolutionnaires* in Paris, the officers and *commissaires civils* of the departmental *armées*, continued to be looked upon with fear by the governments which, from 1795 to 1814, tyrannised the French and the satellite peoples in turn. Political proscription, misfortune and economic ruin brought to the surface of the anonymous waters of quartier life the purest, the most committed and the most courageous of those recruited by the *armées*; a new ardour was aroused, as much by the police as by conviction. Cadres of the former popular forces made their contribution to each of the many crises occurring between 1795 and 1800, and in the prisons as in the cafés, ex-*révolutionnaires* from Paris and from the departments joined forces in trying to infuse some energy into the pale reflections of the *grand soleil de 93*. A former Parisian soldier, the restaurateur Cardinaux, even supplied the setting for many of these reunions. There was a progressive closing of former terrorist ranks, which considerably eased the task of the police, for at any given moment they knew where to find these men who, isolated from the mass of the people, tended to gather every day for mutual encouragement. Unanimity was returning to the terrorist ranks, which were swelled in Paris by the arrival of many 'hommes de liaison' and 'exagérés' from the departments, fleeing the terrible massacres of the Year III in the Midi and the activities of the 'Jesuses' and 'Jéhus'. Men who in the Year II, the *belle époque* of the *armées révolutionnaires*, would not have known each other, even though revolutionising with equal zeal, were coming together some years later in dark little cafés on the streets leading up to the half-finished Panthéon, or in the undergrowth of warehouses and alleyways of the Petite Pologne, the Gros Caillou, the village-like streets of Vaugirard or the labyrinths of the faubourgs Saint-Martin, Saint-Denis and Montmartre. Each crisis produced a rendezvous, each proscription a list of associates, each police swoop the poetic names, like passwords almost, of an *auberge*, an old street or a quartier: Soleil d'Or, Cadran Bleu, Veau d'Or,

619

Panier Fleuri, Bal Cardinaux, Abbaye aux Bois, Blancs Manteaux, Pré-aux-Clercs, Marmousets, Traversière, Nicaise. There was a weird poetry in the abortive plots, the coups uncovered by an increasingly experienced police, the explosive devices – unbelievable devices, patiently put together by versatile craftsmen at the back of some courtyard or in a furnished room, bizarre, touching objects, tied together with strips of metal and string, and hidden under the bed to await the dawn of the glorious day when tyrants were to die. This poetry, so marvellously urban, even in the romanticism and country earthiness of its symbols, was that of popular Paris in the closing years of the century, violent, generous, ingenious and naïve.

The journalist, Lebois, was the first to try to rally the survivors of Germinal and Prairial, as early as Brumaire Year III, and on the list of subscribers to his paper, *L'Ami du Peuple*, were the names of Halm and Réaume, from the Parisian *armée*, Figuet, from the ephemeral *armée* of Valence, Baby, former *commissaire* in the Ariège, and Dufresse, commander of the Lille *armée*. The subscription list to Babeuf's paper is virtually an inventory of terrorist high society: among former *révolutionnaires* and those closely involved in the operations of the Parisian *armée* were Réaume (subscriber no. 10), Tolède (15), Combas (90), Corchand (119), Boissay (162), Lefranc (170), Sandoz (196), Ronsin's widow, Annette Lequesne (246 – she was to marry General Turreau about this time), the *commissaire des guerres*, Paris (276). Mouly, former *commissaire civil* in the Aveyron, Contamin, Allard, and Baby, again, were among the subscribers in the departments.[1]

Most of these men, and many others, either too poor or too uneducated to subscribe to these papers, reappear on the lists drawn up by Babeuf and his companions in preparation for their absurd conspiracy. Babeuf and his friends deserved the attention of Cochon's police and of the historians, both so obligingly and abundantly informed on the surviving forces of the republican opposition – even if the Babouvists, as optimistic as they were inept, considerably exaggerated the number of supporters at their disposition. The lists of 'men capable of commanding', of *patriotes sûrs*, of 'democratic cannoneers', gave an important place to the former officers and soldiers of the Parisian *armée*, some of whom were destined for top posts in the nebulous administration of these foolhardy conspirators. Uppermost in their minds were the cannoneers, particularly those who had taken part in the Lyon Repression or in the defence of the faubourg during the *journées* of Prairial. These were the men on whom the 'Equals' counted to take command of the popular forces, to recruit new adherents in their Sections, or to administer the new Commune. The table in the References (see p. 749),[2] extracted from Babeuf's lists, includes only the names of those from the former *armée* whom we can identify for certain, though their number must have been much greater, for the *armée révolutionnaire*, along with the *comités* in the Sections, was the principal recruiting ground for

Babeuf and his friends, just as it was to supply the police of the Directory with their main source of cannon fodder.

Among the others who had figured in the designs of the Babouvists was Paris, former *commissaire des guerres* in Ronsin's *armée*; he was likewise destined for high office, that of ordnance *commissaire* for the armed force of Paris, under the command of Massard.[3] In the departments the Equals also indicated men whom they could trust, and it is no surprise to find Baby's name mentioned for the Ariège. But most of their departmental agents were Jacobins the like of Mouquet, a pharmacist in Vannes and an orthodox Robespierrist, rather than former ultra-revolutionaries like the cook, Le Batteux, who, despite his participation in the political opposition in the prisons in Germinal Year III,[4] was not honoured by a mention in the lists.

Lefranc's important part in the Equals' scheme was to bribe the officers commanding the artillery depot at Vincennes. But with his usual lack of prudence, he told all to the adjutant-general, Valory, whom he was trying to enlist in the plot, as well as to his chief, the general, Vachot. Valory let the talkative architect ramble on; he was soon in possession of all the military plans of the conspirators and alerted the authorities. On 19 Floréal they issued warrants against Lefranc, Paris, Parein and Coulon, former secretary of the Military Commission in Lyon.[5] Parein managed to conceal himself with a woman from the markets; Paris took refuge at Bercy. Lefranc, not surprisingly, was taken.

The police, admirably well informed, were quick to act. Even before these preparations they had become interested in the former *révo-lutionnaires*, and a report sent to Cochon on 25 Frimaire Year IV had mentioned Buard and Lemaire, both from the Butte-des-Moulins Section, as having founded a new political club at the hôtel de Noailles.[6] In Floréal, when the conspiracy had been exposed, the police mounted another search for Parein, at the same time initiating a hunt for Corchand, Louis (or 'Brutus'),[7] Vafflard,[8] Ladreux, Fontaine, 'Eglator' and Boissay,[9] Sandoz ('a very dangerous scoundrel'), Baby,[10] and Paris.[11] Most were arrested, but Parein and Paris could not be traced, and Louis, who was arrested, was released thanks to a deal – Barras was still looking out for his protégé.

Police investigations were extended into the departments and the annexed territories, attention focusing on the members of the Commission Temporaire, the former *commissaires civils* of the Nièvre and the Allier *armées*, the more fortunate of whom recovered their liberty in Vendémiaire Year IV.[12] One informer, living in Clermont-Ferrand, wrote to a divisional chief in the Ministry of Police on 30 Floréal, telling of suspicious gatherings which had taken place on the 22nd and 23rd at the time of Fouché's journey.[13] Brunière, who had taken refuge in Paris, was strictly watched by the police as a dangerous man, simply because he was poor and courageous.[14] Lecanu, from Rouen and a member of the Commission Temporaire, was likewise put under surveillance, as were those members of the *comité de surveillance* of Le Havre, who in the Year II had requested the dispatch of a revolutionary detachment into the Seine-Inférieure.[15] With Paris having become the capital of terrorism in the Year IV, the police had their hands full.

The rendezvous for the disastrous affair of the camp of Grenelle was the *auberge* of the Soleil d'Or in the rue de Vaugirard. There and in the area around the camp, the police and General Foissac-Latour's troops arrested three former officers of the Parisian *armée*, Eude, Sandoz and Réaume, as well as Baby, Théret (a member of the Commission Temporaire and a *commissaire* with the revolutionary detachments in the Isère), Bertrand, former mayor of Lyon, the sculptor Hennequin, and many more terrorist personalities from Paris and from the departments. The authorities had mounted a real ambush, and in his report General Foissac-Latour placed particular emphasis on the presence of so many persons who had belonged to the *armées révolutionnaires*.[16] The general knew what price they would have to pay. Sandoz, Théret, Baby and Bertrand were to be condemned to death and shot on the plaine de Grenelle in the first days of the Year V. Eude was condemned to be transported, but the judgement was contested and he managed to disappear momentarily into the army, only to have his case resurrected in the Year IX. Réaume, detained and interrogated for ten days, regained his liberty.[17]

Agents' reports in Prairial and Messidor Year VII were to focus particularly on the daily walks in the Tuileries of the still talkative Lefranc, along with Boissay and Vilain d'Aubigny – persecution was uniting former Cordeliers and Jacobins.[18] We hear nothing more of Paris at this stage; like many of the terrorist military men, he was prudent, and had found a refuge as *commissaire des guerres* with the Army of Italy. The former *révolutionnaire* from the Jura was shielded from the proscriptions of the Year IX, and died of fever at Capodistria in 1806.[19]

On 20 Brumaire Year VIII, several known terrorists were condemned to be transported to Guyana, among them Corchand, Figuet, the former *commissaires civils*, Clémence and Marchand – both figuring in this kind of proscription for the first time since their arrest in the Year III – and Mourgoin, former *commissaire civil* in the departments of the East, and a great supporter of the *armées révolutionnaires* – whose name also appeared for the first time in the lists established by the political police.[20] This time they escaped with a few days' detention and increased surveillance; but the police would remember them.

It was a year later that the explosive device went off – unfortunately a few seconds too late – in the rue Nicaise, just as the First Consul was passing; and it brought on the final and most important swoop by Fouché's police on erstwhile terrorist personalities. The First Consul personally ordered Fouché to conduct a vast man-hunt throughout France for the 'exclusifs', many of whom had been former collaborators of the Minister in the Nièvre, in the Allier and in Lyon. In the list of deportees drawn up by the Sénatus-Consulte on 14 Nivôse Year IX, there were several former *révolutionnaires*: Brabant,[21] Cardinaux, Corchand, Fontaine, Derval,[22] Lefranc,[23] Louis or 'Brutus', René Joly (who figured on the list as much for being a so-called 'septembriseur' as an officer of Ronsin's *armée*),[24] Marcellin (former *commissaire civil* of this *armée*), and Charles Sormois. Marcellin, alerted by friends in the police – he was himself a former inspector, dismissed in the Year VI or VII – managed to hide himself in Paris, and was not arrested until three years later, 15 Nivôse Year XII. But he avoided deportation, thanks perhaps to Fouché's intervention, and instead of sharing the fate of his unfortunate companions, he was able to establish himself in Bordeaux, the object still of special surveillance, though this too was finally lifted in 1806.[25]

The government also deported at this time others who had been associated in some way with the activities of the *armées révolutionnaires*: the engraver Petit-Drouet, former member of the *comité révolutionnaire* of the Panthéon-Français Section ('he went on mission at the time of the *armée révolutionnaire* to requisition grain', says a police note of 16 Nivôse Year IX, meant for the Minister),[26] the inevitable 'Eglator', the printer Goulart, from the Observatoire Section (charged with having made several missions with the revolutionary detachments),[27] the former adjutant-general Colette (Ronsin's 'accomplice' in Germinal Year II), recalled after having served under Augereau in Italy.[28] Most of these men, members of a terrorist 'nucleus' which shrank with each new proscription, had appeared on all the lists since Prairial Year III, and some had even been victims of the first witch-hunt during the crisis of Ventôse–Germinal Year II.

Nor was that the end of the matter; the deportations were accompanied by a number of arrests in Paris and in the departments, and by orders of internal banishment. Among those arrested in the capital we recognise Eude and Pudepièce (who died in prison). A search was again made for Boissay, and again was unsuccessful (perhaps the police did not want to find him); some years later this former ordnance officer and friend of Fouché was restored to grace with the imperial regime and appointed judge on the Alençon tribunal.[29] At the same time a search was mounted for the starch-maker, Massé, the former *chef de bataillon*, Vézien, the locksmith Contamin,[30] the officers Potemont, Langlois and Petit, the soldier Vafflard,[31] the former *commissaires*, Rognon (Finistère – his colleague Moroy would be deported) and Dumoustier (Observatoire), who had been denounced by spies or police officers. The police found them for the most part without difficulty, having been watching them constantly for five years. The former militants, far from being secret conspirators, had been living openly, known to all in their quartiers. For several more months during the Years X and XI, police agents followed their every movement with exemplary patience; they were hauled up regularly before the Ministry for intensive interrogation, and several, including the locksmith, Berger (was he Ronsin's former aide-de-camp?), were banished from Paris and the Paris region.[32]

As in the Year IV, the police were particularly interested in the refugees who had come up to Paris from the Midi, and the former terrorists of the Centre, still resident in Nevers and Moulins, or in hiding in the environs of those places. A secret note of 8 Nivôse indicated the presence in Paris of a group of terrorists from Avignon, Marseille and Montpellier, all of course living in the hôtel des Languedociens. Of one of them, Tinelle, the writer noted: 'This man, corrupted by debauchery and the habit of murder, having served in the *armée révolutionnaire* [of the Hérault], sees nothing but pillage and civil war in the project of the insurgents . . .'. He was arrested that same evening, a man who was doubly suspect for having called the First Consul 'a little Cromwell'.[33] Brunière was himself denounced once more in this period for having taken part in the clandestine gatherings of Italian republicans at Mâcon.[34] The terrorist cadres were about to be internationalised.

Nor were the former *commissaires civils* and the officers of the Toulouse *armée* (already under surveillance for several years) overlooked. Hugueny, elected president of the municipal commission of the canton of Beaumont in Germinal Year VI, was dismissed in Vendémiaire Year VII, after an unfavourable report by François de Neufchâteau. Guillaume Barateau, who had remained in military service after the dissolution of the Toulouse *armée*, was suspended in Fructidor Year VIII. On 29 Nivôse Year IX Fouché took things in hand and wrote to the prefect of the Haute-Garonne, instructing him to arrest Hugueny and Descombels without delay; they were imprisoned on 19 Pluviôse. In Brumaire Year X, Hugueny, now released, was placed under surveillance by the municipal authorities of Beaumont. Delport had been a member of the Toulouse bar since the Year IV; the leader of the republican opposition, which was extremely strong in this region, was Hugues Destrem.[35]

The deportees, who had set sail from Rochefort in dreadful conditions,[36] were distributed between Mahé, Cayenne and Guadeloupe; a few privileged ones were interned on the île d'Oléron. On arrival at Mahé the tiny group of militants were extremely badly received by their compatriots, the white colonists, who were soon accusing them of trying to rouse the black slaves against their white masters. The French on the island, who were shortly to welcome the English with open arms, made life so impossible for the deportees that the Marine authorities were obliged to send most of them into the territory of the king of Anjouan, along with several blacks suspected of having been 'contaminated' by the principles of Lefranc and his companions.[37] On Anjouan the deportees nominated General Rossignol, Vaneck, Corchand, Lefèvre and Lefranc as their 'ambassadors' to the king, 'their education placing them in a special class . . .' – the final homage to the exceptional qualities of these men. Nearly all were to die of fever, Lefranc, Sormois and Vauversin alone escaping, the former two to Zanzibar, where Lefranc began to prosper through giving medical advice to the Sultan.[38] As for those sent to Cayenne and Guadeloupe, some

15 survived, all the others dying without ever seeing France again.

In 1804 Lefranc and Sormois disembarked from an English brig – they had been taken prisoner by the English – at Morlaix, in a state of utter destitution and racked by malaria.[39] Lefranc went on to Brest from Morlaix, and tried to draw on funds still owed him by the government for some unpaid work. This unwise move simply drew the attention of the police, and he was accused of many things, including that of being 'the spy of the cabinet of Saint James'. He was shut up in the château – where the maritime prefect showed more compassion than the French on Mahé by supplying him with clothing and assistance – and then transferred to Bordeaux. There he fell ill, and was cared for and became infatuated with a former nun, whom he called 'Mademoiselle Irène'. But he was not allowed to stay near his loved one, having been again denounced and sent to reside, under surveillance, at Lunel, where this follower of Jean-Jacques was extremely critical of the easy living of its inhabitants. In 1813 he obtained permission to return to Bordeaux; there he became engaged to his 'Sainte-Irène' and was on the point of marrying her when he was again thrown into prison and sent to Angoulême. Only under the First Restoration was he permitted to return to Bordeaux; but too late, his fiancée died shortly afterwards. Lefranc prudently lay low during the Hundred Days. An eternal optimist, he hoped for better things under the Second Restoration: '...I have at last made port after many storms', he wrote in 1816. 'I have nothing more to fear from the dark and damp of prisons, for there is now a protecting government, a King, who is the father of all his subjects....' But he was not to be allowed to escape from his terrorist past and his fate of eternal proscription quite so easily.[40]

As for Sormois, he went from Morlaix directly to Paris. The Minister of Police still considered such men dangerous, and he too was sent under surveillance to Lunel, where he found work with the city toll-collecting service. In 1811 or 1812 he tried to regain favour by grandiose declarations of imperial orthodoxy: 'a man raised in the camps since the age of seventeen', he wrote, 'cannot be the enemy of heroes who have put an end to the discord which was tearing his country...'.[41]

In the meantime, in 1810, Chastel, former commander of the Légion des Montagnards, after a stormy political and military career, found himself accused of the attempted murder of the count-general Dupas, whom he had struck with his sword in the *auberge* of La Couronne in Geneva. But on 19 January 1811 he was acquitted by a Geneva jury, despite loud protests from Dupas and the French authorities, who claimed that he had formed a party among the democrats of the town.[42]

In February 1812 Parein was again under scrutiny, and after having obtained unlimited leave in the Year VIII, to be near Fouché in Paris,[43] he was, like so many former terrorist soldiers, dismissed in the Year IX. In 1812 the former president of the Commission des Sept was compromised by Fouché's disgrace and sent by the duc de Feltre to reside, under surveillance, at Caen.[44] That same year, at the time of the Malet affair, one of the main conspirators – the Batavian refugee, Josué Steenhouwer, a former cadet in the Dutch navy, who had served in Mazuel's cavalry – was condemned to death and shot along with the general from the Jura.[45] In 1813, as the internal situation in France worsened, the militant terrorists were subjected to even stricter surveillance, and several leading personalities, former police agents or members of the *comités révolutionnaires*, were banished from Paris.[46]

In 1814, Sormois, forgetting his admiration for the 'hero' of national unity, prostrated himself at the 'foot of the throne', and his example was followed by Chastel and Mutelé. The fall of Bonaparte was seen as a personal deliverance by many former terrorists. Viton and the baron-general Dufresse went even further and tried to prove to the new authorities that they had always been royalist by conviction.[47] Such a turn-around was not permitted to Parein, who had been too much compromised in the previous regime. Installed at Le Mesnil-Aubry, he became the subject of extremely unfavourable reports from the gendarme officers, who pointed to his 'detestable' opinions and his 'plebeian' associations. For another 15 years the gendarmerie remained preoccupied with this sworn enemy of the Bourbons.[48]

After 1815 the political police seemed to be less concerned with the deeds and actions of the former cadres of militant terrorism, rendered inoffensive by ruin, age and repeated proscription. Doubtless the few survivors were too old and too destitute to warrant the costs of a surveillance which might be turned to better effect against a rejuvenated opposition employing new methods. The survivors of terrorism had never been professional conspirators. But in 1816 Lefranc, the historian of the sufferings of his unfortunate fellow deportees, was the object of attention for the last time. Accused of involvement in the affair of the 'Patriots', he was sent with 95 others, almost all from a different generation and different backgrounds, to the fort of Mont Saint-Michel. In that damp cell the door was closed once and for all on his tempestuous career.[49] This final proscription seems to have laid to earth the spectre of the *armée révolutionnaire* for good. When, in 1830, Eude, old and almost blind, tried to seek favour with the new dynasty, no one, not even among the police, remembered him.[50]

The persistence of this police persecution against the same tiny group of men allows us to examine from a new angle those who made up the former popular *armées*, and to distinguish the convinced militants from the revolutionaries through circumstance. In the Year II the young Calmet-Beauvoisins had affected all the external signs of sans-culottism; but on 12 Germinal Year III he took up arms to defend the Convention and was ready to fire on the people.[51] Other revolutionary personalities likewise settled their differences with the regime, Duvicquet becoming a teacher at the lycée Napoléon, Boissay a judge of the Alençon tribunal, the former *commissaire civil* Gobert entering the Conseil des Anciens, and marrying his daughter to the prefect of the Moselle.[52] These men had more luck, or less conviction, than men like Lefranc, Corchand, Chastel, Brunière, Louis, Baby or Sandoz. We must not, however, be too ready to pass judgement on either one group or the other. Many who figured repeatedly in the police proscriptions had not chosen voluntarily the difficult and costly existence of the militant. Often the role was imposed upon them, by the continual detention, the regular police interrogations, the terrible threat of deportation constantly held over them. Such methodical persecution simply created the militants whom the police were supposed to combat. Cardinaux – and he cannot have been the only one – merely asked to be let live in peace, with his wife and children, to manage his business and remain on good terms with the people of his populous quartier (he seems to have been particularly popular with the workers on the Panthéon building site), without taking any part in politics. But he was a prisoner in his café, and a café-owner can scarcely hold himself aloof from his regular clientele. He therefore found himself sent to the islands along with those for whom he had poured drinks in the six years before. He was one of the victims. Others, no doubt, were better served by violent temperaments and by truly revolutionary convictions.

There was a further stimulus to the courage and sacrifice of this handful of men, most of whom were married or had women they lived with – and that was the firmness and courage of these women. There is never enough emphasis placed upon the preponderant role of women, not only in the popular disturbances of the Year III, but also in the movements of republican opposition during the Years IV to IX. The police recognised it, and were just as harsh on the wives, companions and widows of the militants as on the men themselves. The widows of Babeuf, Sijas and Chaumette were constantly watched, and often imprisoned. Ronsin's widow read democratic newspapers and Parein, in the Year IV, found sanctuary with a market porteress. And if Marcellin managed to evade police searches for three years, it was because of the devotion of his laundress wife, who was arrested along with him.[53] How many instances do we have of wives being the cause of their husbands' revolutionary vocation, spurring them to action, treating them as cowards when they wanted to abandon it – few men could resist such arguments. The *armées révolutionnaires* were alone in this period in not having any female soldiers, disguised as men, in their ranks – the exploits of such women with the regular armies supplying a favourite subject for the *Soirées des Campagnes* and other works from the revolutionary press. Their absence from the *armées* and from the political life of the Sections in the Year II was due to the anti-feminism of the sans-culottes. They were likewise excluded from every other institution of the Terror, and were to find a better outlet for their energy and enthusiasm in the great bread riots of the Year III and in the conspiracies of the years of proscription.[54]

Married or single, men like Lefranc, Corchand, Rossignol and Baby sought martyrdom – these were the classic *révolutionnaires*. But one also had to live; Boissay, Parein, Gobert and their like were neither traitors nor renegades because they made their peace with the new regimes, they were simply luckier than most of their former comrades. Boissay and Parein were under the protection of Fouché, and were spared police persecution for a considerable time. There was nothing dishonourable about that; many other former *révolutionnaires* had sought similar favour, with less success, from the all-powerful Minister of Police, and even the unfortunate Marcellin wrote to him from his prison in the hope of having the deportation order against him revoked. Fouché may indeed have been watching over him also, for unlike most of his colleagues, Marcellin remained in France.[55] Marcellin was himself a former police agent, and in the world of the informer and the informed-upon the line of demarcation was sufficiently unclear for a certain element of connivance to exist between old terrorists and new police agents. Nor was that all; Parein and Gobert were rich men and a whole world separated this comfortable proprietor of Le Mesnil-Aubry and the tanner on the outskirts of Metz from the miserable and tattered inhabitants of the Abbaye-aux-Bois and the rue des Blancs-Manteaux. Those implicated in the Chevalier affair, Marcellin, Gombaut and their companions, were half-naked and in rags. The police were right to say that someone like Brunière was dangerous because he was poor. But the poor could not afford the luxury of numerous imprisonments.

We should not therefore sit in judgement on these men, some of whom, a rare few, became militants by choice; most did so through the simple force of events; some, the more fortunate, the more realistic, managed to compose their differences with the authorities and be pardoned for having belonged momentarily to one of the most characteristic institutions of the Terror. We have simply tried to show how they reacted, each in his own way, to a persecution directed less against them as individuals, than against the shadow cast by an egalitarian and popular army.

CHRONOLOGY

Events of Years I and II

1792

September 21		Abolition of monarchy

1793

January	21	Execution of Louis XVI
February		Formation of First Coalition against France
March	9	Creation of Committee of General Security; beginning of system of *représentants en mission* (*Conventionnels* sent on mission to the departments and the armies)
	10	Decree setting up the revolutionary tribunal; revolt erupts in the Vendée
	18	French defeat at Neerwinden
	21	Establishment of *comités de surveillance* (also known as *comités révolutionnaires*)
April	5	Defection of Dumouriez to the Austrians
	6	Creation of Committee of Public Safety
April–September		Campaign for formation of *armées révolutionnaires*
May	4	First 'Maximum' on grain prices
	29–30	Revolt of Lyon
May 31–June 2		Fall of the Girondins
June	4	June decree on *armée révolutionnaire* (never fully implemented)
	6	Federalist outbreaks in Bordeaux and Marseille
	24	Constitution of the Year I (1793)
July	13	Assassination of Marat
	26	Hoarding made a capital offence
	27	Robespierre enters Committee of Public Safety
August	23	*Levée en masse* decreed
	29	Surrender of Toulon to the British

September 2   News arrives in Paris of treason of Toulon
          4–5   *Journée*: uprising of Parisian sans-culottes
           5   'Terror' adopted as order of the day; creation of
                        Parisian *armée révolutionnaire*
          17   Law of Suspects

YEAR II

1793
September 29   Law of general Maximum on prices and wages
September–December   Organisation of the departmental *armées révolution-
                        naires*
October (10 Vendémiaire–10 Brumaire)
           5   Adoption of Revolutionary Calendar
           9   Lyon (in Federalist hands since May) recaptured
          10   Declaration of 'revolutionary' (i.e. emergency)
                        government until peace
          16   Execution of Marie-Antoinette
         24–31   Trial and execution of Girondins
November (11 Brumaire–10 Frimaire)
          10   Festival of Reason in Nôtre-Dame
November–May 1794   Dechristianising campaign
December (11 Frimaire–11 Nivôse)
           4   Law of 14 Frimaire on Revolutionary Govern-
                        ment—end of the 'anarchic' Terror
          4–5   Mass shootings of 'suspects' in Lyon
December 11–March 1 1794 Reaction against the departmental *armées
                        révolutionnaires*
December–January 1794 Mass executions (including the infamous *noyades*)
                        in the Vendée
1794
March (11 Ventôse–11 Germinal)
         13–14   Arrest of Hébertists (including Ronsin)
         18–30   Removal of detachments of the *armée révolution-
                        naire* from Paris
          24   Execution of Hébertists (Hébert, Vincent,
                        Momoro, Ronsin, Cloots)
          28   Decree disbanding *armée révolutionnaire*
March 31–April 5   Arrest and execution of Dantonists
July (13 Messidor–13 Thermidor)
         27–28   *Coup d'état* of 9 Thermidor: fall and execution of
                        Robespierre

REFERENCES
APPENDICES
INDEX

List of Abbreviations
and short forms used
in References

Sources of unpublished material   *abbreviated as*

Archives Administratives de la Guerre (Fort de Vincennes)   AAG
Archives Historiques de la Guerre (Fort de Vincennes)   AHG
Archives Nationales   AN
Archives de la Préfecture de Police   APP
British Library (London)   BL
Bibliothèque Nationale   BN
Bibliothèque Victor-Cousin   BV-C
Bibliothèque Historique de la Ville de Paris (Archives révolutionnaires)
John Rylands Library, University of Manchester

A full account of the archival material drawn on, with a complete list of the departmental and communal archives consulted, appears in vol. II of the French edition of *Les Armées révolutionnaires*, pp. 895–951.

Published sources frequently referred to

F.-A. Aulard, *Recueil des actes du Comité de salut public*, vols. I, VI–XVII
(1892–1906)   Aulard

P.-J.-B. Buchez and P.-C. Roux, *Histoire parlementaire de la Révolution française*, 29 vols. (1836)   Buchez and Roux

L.-M. Prudhomme, *Histoire générale et impartiale des erreurs, des fautes et des crimes commis pendant la Révolution française*, 10 vols. (1797)   Prudhomme

A.-M. Soboul, *Les sans-culottes parisiens en l'an II. Histoire politique et sociale des sections de Paris: 2 juin 1793–9 thermidor an II* (La Roche-sur-Yon, 1958)   Soboul

Other sources referred to by short forms are given in full at the first citation. The place of publication is Paris unless otherwise indicated. RCC = R. C. Cobb.

Periodicals frequently referred to

Annales historiques de la Révolution française   A.h.R.f.

Révolution française   R. F.

A full list of published sources is at pp. 953–9 of the French edition, vol. II.

Cross-references to book and chapter of the present work are abbreviated throughout as, e.g., I. 3, sect. III, p. 125, that is, Book One, chapter 3, section III, page 125.

References

Introduction

1 *Un Allemand en France sous la Terreur. Souvenirs de Frédéric-Christian Laukhard, Professeur d'Université saxon et sans-culotte français (1792–1794)*, trans. W. Bauer (1915), 268. This curious work was pointed out to me by Jean Dautry.

2 A.-M. Soboul, *Les sans-culottes parisiens en l'an II. Histoire politique et sociale des sections de Paris: 2 juin 1793–9 thermidor an II* (La Roche-sur-Yon, 1958), 877.

3 J. Godechot, *Les institutions de la France sous la Révolution et l'Empire* (1951), 301–3.

4 Gén. Herlaut, *Ronsin, le général rouge* (1957).

5 For Parein, see E. Herriot, *Lyon n'est plus*, III: *La répression* (1937); E. Querneau-Lamérie, *La Commission Parein–Félix* (Angers, 1912); and R. C. Cobb, 'Note sur la répression contre le personnel sans-culotte de 1795 à 1801', *A.h.R.f.*, jan.-mars 1954.

6 On the Grammonts, see J. Hérissay, *Le monde des théâtres pendant la Révolution* (1922), 30, 87, 97, 188–92, 223, 226, 227–30 – a hostile commentator. For Dufresse, see E. Leleu, 'Le général Dufresse et l'armée révolutionnaire du Nord', *Revue du Nord*, VI (1920), 102–26; Gén. Herlaut, 'Le général-baron Dufresse', *Revue du Nord*, août 1927; Hérissay, op. cit., 228–30; *Mémoires et notes de Choudieu*, préf. V. Barrucaud (ré-éd. 1897), 188–9; and P. Caron, *Les massacres de septembre* (1935), 226 (4).

7 R. C. Cobb, 'Robespierre und der general Boulanger: Nationalgarde und Revolutions-armee', in *Maximilien Robespierre 1758–1794* (Berlin, 1958), 255–86.

8 M. Dommanget, 'Mazuel et l'hébertisme', *Annales révolutionnaires*, 1922–3, and R. C. Cobb, 'Le "complot militaire" de ventôse an II', in *Mémoires de la Fédération des Sociétés historiques de Paris et de l'Ile de France*, VII (1956), 221–50.

9 See P. Gérard's excellent article, 'L' armée révolutionnaire de la Haute-Garonne', *A.h.R.f.*, no. 155 (jan.-mars 1959); L. Dubreuil, *Le district de Redon pendant la Révolution* (Rennes, 1903); P. Cavard, *Vienne la Patriote* (Vienne, 1955), and D. Fischer, 'L'armée révolutionnaire du Bas-Rhin', in *Curiosités d'Alsace*, I (1861–2), 430; also F. C. Heitz, *Les sociétés politiques de Strasbourg* (Strasbourg, 1863), 286, and R. Paquet, *Dictionnaire biographique de l'ancien département de la Moselle* (1887), for the *commissaires civils* to the *armées* of the Bas-Rhin and the Moselle respectively.

10 H. Calvet, *Un instrument de la Terreur à Paris: le Comité de Salut public ou de Surveillance du département de Paris (8 juin 1793–21 messidor an II)* (1941).

11 A. Thiers, *Histoire de la Révolution* (1834 edn.), III. 188, 386: Abbé A. Guillon de Montléon, *Mémoires pour servir à l'histoire de la ville de Lyon pendant la Révolution* (1824), II. 440.

12 H. Taine, *Les origines de la France contemporaine. La Révolution* (1885 edn.), III: *Le gouvernement révolutionnaire*, 99.

13 Taine, op. cit., III. 99, 100, 105; D. Guérin, *La lutte des classes sous la Première République: bourgeois et 'bras-nus'* (1946), esp. I. 186, 189.

14 L. Blanc, *Histoire de la Révolution* (1858), X. 247; Maréchal Gouvion Saint-Cyr, *Mémoires sur les campagnes des armées du Rhin et du Rhin-et-Moselle* (Toulouse, 1829), I. 137.

15 Laukhard, 265, 267; Soboul, 877.

16 Taine, op. cit., 100; A.-E. Borély, *Histoire de la ville du Havre* (Le Havre, 1884), II. 140; *Les mémoires de Bertrand Barère* (1842), 370.

17 Taine, op. cit., VIII, ii. 100.

18 A. Hadengue, *Les gardes rouges de l'an II: l'armée révolutionnaire et le parti hébertiste* (1930).

19 Cf., e.g., M. Cabet, *Histoire populaire de la Révolution française* (1840), and J. Jaurès, *Histoire socialiste de la Révolution française*, VIII: *Le gouvernement révolutionnaire* (1922). Buchez and

Roux stand apart in this matter and, characteristically, are more just even than later historians; see P.-J.-B. Buchez and P.-C. Roux, *Histoire parlementaire de la Révolution française* (1836), xxix. 4. They rise above the moral judgement and, with Kropotkin, are virtually the only historians of the 19th century to stress the economic role of the *armées révolutionnaires*.

20 P. Kropotkin, *La Grande Révolution* (1909), 659. Kropotkin recognises the central problem posed by the creation of the Parisian *armée révolutionnaire*, and its policy of 'provisioning [Paris] by force'. The Revolutionary Government could have placated at least a part of the rural populace, associating it more closely with the course of the revolution through the sale of national land in small plots. By not doing so and by treating that population as hostile to the interests of the capital and therefore to the revolution, it re-fortified rural animosity towards Paris and exposed the new *armée* to rural hatred.

21 J. Charrier, *L'Histoire religieuse du département de la Nièvre pendant la Révolution* (Nevers, 1925); Canon Bridoux, *L'Histoire religieuse du département de la Seine-et-Marne pendant la Révolution* (Melun, 1954); E. Sol, *La Révolution en Quercy* (1926–32). Sol's work and E. Dubois's, *La Révolution dans le département de l'Ain* (Bourg, 1931–5), are the best local French studies to have been written in recent years. L. Chaumont, *Recherches sur la persécution religieuse dans le département de Saône-et-Loire pendant la Révolution* (Châlon, 1903), is an exaggerated account.

22 G. Tridon, *Les Hébertistes* (Paris–Bruxelles, 1871); and see E. Leleu, 'Le général Dufresse et l'armée révolutionnaire du Nord'.

23 A. Mathiez, *La vie chère et le mouvement social sous la Terreur* (1927), 421.

24 G. Lefebvre, *La Révolution française* (1951), 359. In my conversations with Lefebvre, this great historian of the Revolution put forward the hypothesis that the measures taken by the *représentants* were part and parcel of the government's preoccupation with public order, particularly the policy of distancing dangerous elements from the towns.

25 C. Pichois and J. Dautry, *Le conventionnel Chasles et ses idées démocratiques* (Aix-en-Provence, 1958).

26 A. Duboul, *L'armée révolutionnaire de Toulouse* (Toulouse, 1891); see also M. Albert, *Le féderalisme dans la Haute-Garonne* (1932), 206–13, and P. Gérard, 'L'armée révolutionnaire de la Haute-Garonne'.

27 Gén. Herlaut, 'Le général-baron Dufresse', and 'Les armées révolutionnaires de Versailles et de Saint-Germain', *Revue de l'hist. de Versailles et de Seine-et-Oise*, xxi (1919–20).

28 A. Gernoux, *La compagnie Marat de Nantes* (Nantes, 1933): see also G. Martin, *Carrier et sa mission à Nantes* (1924).

29 D. Fischer, 'L'armée révolutionnaire du Bas-Rhin', 430; E. Dard, *Hérault de Séchelles* (1907).

30 M. Reinhard, 'Note sur Carnot et l'armée révolutionnaire', *Bull. de la Soc. d'Hist. moderne*, juin 1952.

31 A. Montier, *Robert Lindet* (1899). Lindet vies with Barère for the merit of having forced his colleagues on the Committee to disband the Parisian *armée*; like Barère, he dreaded an institution which had all the appearances of a 'gouvernement militaire' in embryo.

32 See below, I. 1, n. 5. Mathiez, always ready to defend his hero, says that Robespierre turned against the *armée* because it had not lived up to expectations as an instrument of government economic policy, but had become instead an instrument of ambition in the hands of Ronsin and Mazuel (A. Mathiez, 'Robespierre terroriste', *Etudes sur Robespierre* [re-ed. 1958], 70).

33 R. C. Cobb, *L'armée révolutionnaire parisienne à Lyon et dans la région lyonnaise* (Lyon, 1952) and 'Les armées révolutionnaires des départements du Midi', Cahier no. 1 de l'Assoc. Marc Bloch de Toulouse (Toulouse, 1955); in *Annales de Normandie*: 'La campagne pour l'envoi de l'armée révolutionnaire dans la Seine-Inférieure' (août 1952), 'La mission de Siblot au Havre-Marat' (mai 1953), and 'L'armée révolutionnaire au Havre-Marat et dans le district de Montivilliers: pluviôse-germinal an II' (oct.-déc. 1953); 'L'armée révolutionnaire dans le district de Pontoise', *A.h.R.f.*, no. 119 (sept. 1950); 'L'armée révolutionnaire parisienne: composition sociale et politique', *Bull. de la Soc. d'Hist. moderne*, juin 1952; and 'L'armée révolutionnaire parisienne dans le département de l'Aisne', *Revue du Nord*, nos. 132–4 (oct. 1951–juin 1952).

34 R. C. Cobb, 'Le "complot militaire" de ventôse an II'; 'Jaubert et le procès des hébertistes',

A.h.R.f., no. 147 (avril–juin 1957); 'Robespierre und der general Boulanger'.
35 RCC, 'Note sur la répression contre le personnel sans-culotte de 1795 à 1801'.
36 For the use of this source, see A. Corvisier, 'Un problème social de l'Ancien Régime. La composition de l'armée', *L'Actualité de l'Histoire*, no. 22 (fév. 1958).
37 Notably *L'Anti-Terroriste*.
38 On the lacunae in this collective documentation, conformist and impersonal, see R. C. Cobb, 'Quelques aspects de la mentalité révolutionnaire; avril 1793–thermidor an II', *Revue d'Hist. moderne et contemporaine*, no. 2 (avril–juin 1959).

BOOK ONE

Chapter 1

1 For the Brussels Legion see RCC, 'Les armées révolutionnaires des départements du Midi', 7–8, and Bibl. royale (Coll. van Hulthem 27 154, Rés. préc.), Société des amis de la liberté et de l'égalité de Bruxelles (sessions of 16 Dec [1792] onwards).
2 RCC, 'Les armées révolutionnaires du Midi', 20.
3 Soboul, 11.
4 Buchez and Roux, xxv. 272. This address is cited by Gén. Herlaut in his article, 'La levée d'une armée révolutionnaire à Paris au 31 mai', *A.h.R.f.*, no. 129 (1952).
5 G. Lefebvre et al., eds., *Discours de Robespierre* (1958), IV. 492; and id. 515 and 552–3 for his addresses of 12 May and 12 June. On six occasions Robespierre made such representations to the Jacobins: 3 Apr, 8 and 12 May, 12 June, and 27 and 28 Sept 1793.
6 *Bulletin de la Convention*, session of 27 Apr 1793.
7 Arch. Hérault, L 5500 (*société populaire* of Montpellier, session of 10 Apr).
8 Arch. Rhône, 2 L 10 (Dept. of Lyon to municipality of Vaise), and *Délibérations du Conseil général de la commune de Lyon* (Lyon, 1905 edn.) – session of 9 Apr.
9 Arch. Rhône, 34 L 1 (Bellecordière Section, session of the *société populaire*, 4 May), and 34 L 3 (*société* of the commune of La Croix-Rousse).
10 Buchez and Roux, XXVII. 420.
11 BN, MSS Nouv. acq. fr. 8608 (159).
12 *Délibérations du Conseil général de la commune de Lyon* (1889–1902 edn.), Buchez and Roux, XXVII. 420, and Arch. Rhône, 1 L 98 (Département).
13 Arch. Rhône, 1 L 98 (Département), 34 L 1 (*société* of the Bellecordière Section), 34 L 3 (*société* of the commune of La Croix-Rousse); and *Délibérations*, op.cit.
14 Arch. Rhône, 1 L 98 (Département) (session of 3 May).
15 Arch. Indre, L 1582 (*société républicaine* of Châteauroux, sessions of 12 May and 16 Sept 1793).
16 Arch. Haute-Vienne, L 489 (Bellac district, session of 20 May 1793).
17 Soboul, 36-89.
18 Soboul, 36. I have been unable to discover this petition (AN, C 335 [1860]), nor that of 18 May which also appears in Soboul.
19 Soboul, 25: '... On 18 May, the five Sections of Gravilliers, the Marchés, the Contrat-Social, the Lombards and Bon-Conseil united in an oath *to support the oppressed sans-culottes*...'. In June, the Marchés Section will again be found at the head of a group of Sections agitating for the immediate organisation of the *armée*.
20 BV-C, MSS 118 (21). On 27 Apr, the petition from the Hérault was read at the bar of the Convention, and after a favourable reception, the Assembly ordered the Committee of Public Safety to draw up a report on the project – hence the reference in the Marchés petition, pretending to see the promise of a decree in this order.
21 AN, BB 3 80; also Gén. Herlaut, 'La levée d'une armée révolutionnaire à Paris au 31 mai'.
22 AN, F 7★ 2520 (Panthéon *comité*, sessions of 1 and 4 June), and BB 3 80, for the letter of 4 June to the department; F 7★ 2517 (Finistère *comité*, session of 9 June); F 7★ 2514 (Observatoire *comité*).
23 BN, MSS Nouv. acq. fr. 8606 (224), Mail Section to the 47 other Sections.
24 AN, F 7 4704 d 2 (Féline), and Soboul, 46. The *comité révolutionnaire* of the Réunion Section was to denounce Féline's conduct to the Committee of General Security.
25 AN, F 7 4710 d 1 (Fossey) and F 7 4745 d 4 (Huet). Huet added: '...about a month later the Convention decreed the organisation of this *armée*; at first I applauded it, because things had

become so much worse through the insatiable greed of the hoarders...' – an interesting observation on the change of climate between June and September, when economic motives superseded all others.

26 AN, W 36 (2319) (Jacquemier affair).
27 BN, MSS Nouv. acq. fr. 2664 (220), 'La section des Piques aux 47 autres sections' (printed), undated.
28 AN, F 7 4774 84 d 5 (Pyron). Pyron also referred to his role in the second petition sent by the Section on 12 July, and claimed that the Committee of Public Safety and the Convention had followed its recommendations in the decree which disbanded the *armée révolutionnaire*. Germinal in fact marked the triumph of Pyron and the other moderates.
29 These are the dates given by Soboul, 46; see AN, F 7 4775 9 d 3 (Sade).
30 BV-C, MSS 120 (132-169) (Droits-de-l'Homme Section); AN, F 7 4710 d 1 (Fossey).
31 APP, A A/266 (153) (Invalides Section). And see Soboul, 47.
32 AN, F 7 4474 d 3 (Pyron). Pyron claims that the address and petition were well received by the Convention. The petition is not to be found in series C in the AN.
33 On this see Soboul, 92-150.
34 See P. Tartat, *Avallon au dix-huitième siècle,* II: *La Révolution* (Auxerre, 1953), 71–3.
35 Arch. Mantes, D3 8 (*société* of Mantes, session of 24 June 1793).
36 On this subject see P. Libois, *Les représentants du peuple Prost et Lejeune dans le Jura en l'an II* (Lons-le-Saunier, 1936).
37 Arch. Gironde, 11 L 27 (Club national de Bordeaux).
38 E. Sol, *La Révolution en Quercy*, III. The *armée* of the Lot was certainly the first to become active, even if its creation did not date from May, as claimed by Canon Sol (Arch. Lot, L 72 and L 389). The *armée* in the neighbouring Cantal was formed only on 9 Oct (Arch. Cantal, L 684), while in the Aveyron an *armée* was already active on 17 Sept (Arch. Aveyron, 72 L 4).
39 This social antagonism is epitomised in the petition of the Nesle municipality to the Commission des Subsistances in Sept 1793 (AN, F 11 407, Subsistances, Somme, 1793-1815). The petition claimed that although the Somme was one of the richest departments in the Republic, particularly in grain, nevertheless it was threatened with famine because of 'le monopole le plus inouï'. The big farmers were refusing to bring their grain to market at the price fixed by the Maximum, and since they dominated many municipal authorities, their speculation was given free rein. To combat the 'arrogant farmer who insults the misery of the poor', the Nesle petition proposed that national or departmental Legions, recruited from among the working population, should implement those measures designed to bring grain to the markets.
40 Arch. Drôme, L 1086 (*société* of Valence, sessions of 24–6 June), assembly of 42 *sociétés* from the departments of the Midi.
41 AN, C 272 (672), *société* of Mâcon to the Convention, 14 Sept 1793, mentioning the earlier petition of 15 Aug. See also Soboul, 161. The proposal was taken up again by Royer in the Cordeliers on 1 Sept.
42 For this assembly at Valence, see Arch. Drôme, L 1086 (*société* of Valence), Arch. Bouches-du-Rhône, L 2076 (*société* of Marseille), AHG, B3 7 (Armies of the Midi), AAG, Cl. gén. 1655 (Gourgonnier). The Valence delegate at this assembly, the carpenter François Allier, was to demand the creation of an *armée révolutionnaire* for the Drôme at the session of 13 Frimaire.
43 Other *sociétés* of towns not situated in the South, like Lille, Grenoble, Châlons-sur-Marne, Paray-le-Monial, La Clayette, etc., also supported this Legion, and it does indeed appear to have been recruited from all over the Republic (Arch. Châlons, I 199, Arch. Nord, L 10226, Arch. Saône-et-Loire, IV L 10 and 26, Arch. Grenoble, DD 77, etc.).
44 See RCC, 'La campagne pour l'envoi de l'armée révolutionnaire dans la Seine-Inférieure', and E. Lockroy, ed., *Une mission en Vendée: 1793 (d'après les notes de Jullien* (1893), 14; and for the Gap assembly, see Arch. Hautes-Alpes, L 1512.
45 See Soboul, 570–6.
46 Buchez and Roux, XXIX. 16–17, and Soboul, 161.
47 Soboul, 162. And see RCC, 'Les armées révolutionnaires du Midi', 5.
48 Buchez and Roux, XXIX. 41.
49 id., XXIX. 28.
50 Soboul, 168.
51 See Buchez and Roux, XXIX. 37–8, for Chaumette's similar arguments before the

Convention.

52 Soboul, 174–5. For Mathiez and Hadengue see above Intro., pp. 6–7, 11.

53 AN, C 271 (668) (17), Châlon *société* to the Convention, 6–7 Sept, signed by 49 members.

54 AN, C 272 (672) (2), *société* of Le Puy to the Convention, 9 Sept. Among the 24 signatures is that of Charles-Robert Levoyer, a government *commissaire*.

55 Arch. Bouches-du-Rhône, L 881 (district of Arles).

56 AN, C 271 (669) (12), *société* of Tours to the Convention; Arch. Seine-Maritime, L 5644 (*société* of Le Havre-Marat).

57 AN, C 275 (709) (37), *société* of Toulon-sur-Arroux to the Convention, 18 Sept.

58 AN, C 276 (715–16) (11), *société* of Arc-sur-Tille to the Convention, 29 Sept. The enthusiasm of many rural areas for the *armée révolutionnaire* during this period was undoubtedly partially inspired by the desire of such 'workers and yeomen' to find paid work during the long winter months.

59 Arch. Versailles, D I 186 (13th Section, session of 19 Sept). This decision escaped Gén. Herlaut in his article 'Les armées révolutionnaires de Versailles et de Saint-Germain', where he has the campaign starting much later, on 5 Brumaire Year II.

60 Arch. Versailles, I² 1236 (Vertu Sociale *société*, 23 Sept 1793).

61 AN, F 11 407 (Subsistances, Somme).

62 AN, C 275 (703–4) (18), commune of Sourdon to the Convention, 26 Sept; C 275 (707–8) (15), Pierre Blondel to the Convention, 18 Sept; C 276 (714) (22), 3rd Cantal battalion to the Convention, undated, but Oct 1793.

63 AHG, B2 26 (Army of the Moselle, corres.), Mourgoin to Bouchotte, 10 Oct 1793; AN, F 7 4774 d 3 (Mourgoin), Mourgoin to Bouchotte, 15 Oct 1793.

64 Among such supporters, several agents of the Committee of Public Safety were also to be found: Rousselin, Marcellin, Paillardelle and Vauquoy – they would later become *commissaires civils* with the *armées*. In general, however, the secondary agents of the Committee, particularly those in the confidence of Robespierre, shared his reservations concerning these popular armies.

65 BN, L 2c 2583, *Journal de l'armée des côtes de Cherbourg* (*société* of Caen, sessions of 13 and 19 Sept). 'Public spirit is weak in this town', wrote Lindberg, a Cordelier and a volunteer in the Bonnet-Rouge battalion, 'and as a result, the *société populaire* is completely dominated by Parisian soldiers and volunteers...' (AN, F 7 4774 10 d 3 [Lecreps]).

66 BN, L 2c 2583 (*société* of Caen), session of 6 Oct.

67 AN, C 276 (714) (8), *société* of Sarlat to the Convention, 4 Oct, and C 276 (715–16) (15), *société* of Conches to the Convention.

68 J.J. Derché, *Journal*, op. cit., 5 Brumaire.

69 AN, C 276 (717–18) (32), *société* of Varennes to the Convention, 4 Oct – a *société* under the control of Drouet.

70 Arch. Seine-Maritime, L 5696 (*société* of Rouen), session of 2 Oct; RCC, 'La campagne pour l'envoi de l'armée révolutionnaire dans le Seine-Inférieure'.

71 Arch. Lille, 18'229 (*société* of Lille), discourse of Decrosne, n.d. Brumaire; AHG, B2 27 (Armée de la Moselle), public notice of 14 Brumaire announcing the creation of the Moselle *armée révolutionnaire*; AN, T 492 I (Séquestres, Carrier papers); Arch. Haute-Marne, L 2014 (*société* of Chaumont), session of 15 Brumaire; Arch. Châlons, 1* 199 (*société* of Châlons); Arch. Troyes, D* 24 (General Council, reg. corres.): letter from the municipality to the department of the Aube, 12 Oct 1793.

72 Arch. Loire, L 399* (*société* of Charlieu), session of 13 Brumaire; Arch. Saône-et-Loire, IV L 10 (*société* of La Clayette), and IV L 26 (*société* of Paray-le-Monial), session of 26 Brumaire; AHG, B5*20 (Army of the Côtes de Cherbourg), for Lisieux; Arch. Seine-et-Oise, IR 529, petition of the Vertu Sociale *société* to the department, 19 Brumaire; Arch. Saint-Germain, D 15 (General Council), session of 29 Brumaire; Arch. Cantal, L 684 (*comité* of Aurillac, 9 Oct); Arch. Basses-Pyrénées, 25 L I (*société* of Monein), and 27 L I (*société* of Morlaas).

73 Arch. Basses-Alpes, L*852 (*société* of La Mure), L*857 (*société* of Senez), L*859 (*société* of Thorame), L*756 (*comité* of Digne), L*778 (*comité* of Manosque).

74 AN, D III 292(2) (4) (Comité de législation, Vaucluse), Avignon: Barjavel to the Committee of Public Safety, 25 Frimaire; see also Arch. Vaucluse, L VI 12 (*société* of Vaison-la-Romaine).

75 On the situation of the Amiens market, supplying a population of 70,000, from the district as well as the town, see Arch. Amiens, I D 10 7; on Toulouse, supplying more than

150,000, see AN, F*20 16 (Haute-Garonne); on Lille, id., F*20 18 (Nord) – outside of Paris, the district Lille had to supply was the next most populous (239,000) in France; for Bordeaux, supplying approx. 150,000, see id., F*20 16 (Gironde). Rouen supplied some 120,000.

76 This has been well illustrated by Gaston-Martin, *Carrier et sa mission à Nantes*, 159. It would be interesting to know the social origin of those who spoke out so openly in favour of the *armées*. From later events, it seems that most were sans-culottes. In the proscription lists for the Year III in Clermont-Ferrand, for example, we find a café-owner, two tailors, a printer and binder, and one with no trade. For this information I am grateful to M. Soanen, archivist and librarian of Thiers.

77 Robespierre, who until 12 June supported the campaign personally, is the exception. The only member of the Committee to remain unswervingly hostile to the *armées* was Robert Lindet, who saw in them the prospect of a military government. See A. Montier, *Robert Lindet*.

78 See AN, F 7 4435 d 6(4) (papers of Collot-d'Herbois), Collot to Robespierre, 3 Frimaire.

Chapter 2

1 AN, W I a 164, public notice, 'Mazuel à ses concitoyens'... (Nivôse Year II).

2 AHG, Xp 12 kf (Volontaires nationaux), '*Chefs d'escadron* of the new levy'.

3 Arch. Seine-et-Oise, IV Q L 186 (Séquestres, Mazuel papers). On 23 Aug the officers of the 2nd company of the 1st squadron were elected: Guignard (1st lieut.), Séran (first 2nd lieut.), Hurault (second 2nd lieut.), Dumond (squadron sgt.). Hurault was the only Parisian; Séran was a friend of Mazuel's from Montpellier.

4 Buchez and Roux, xxix, 41–6 and AHG, B5 75 (Armée révolutionnaire).

5 *Mémoires de B. Barère*, ii. 370.

6 AHG, B 5 75 (*Ordre du Ministre* and *Ordre du jour*, 6 Sept).

7 AHG, B 5 75 and Xp 12 kf (Volontaires nationaux). Most of the enrolment lists were not drawn up by the Sections until the latter half of Sept.

8 *Journal de la Montagne*, no. 100 (Jacobins, session of 8 Sept).

9 AN, AF II 203B (1712) (Committee of Public Safety, Military Affairs). This text, drafted by Carnot, differs from that in Buchez and Roux, xxix. 46 in only one detail: Carnot had set the age-limits at 18 to 40. The decree, on Bouchotte's recommendation, set them at 25 to 40 (AHG, B 5 75, report of the 5th Division, 20 Oct 1793).

10 AN, F 7 4742 d 4 (Hérault). Hérault was also the creator of the Haut-Rhin *armée révolutionnaire*. See E. Dard, *Hérault de Séchelles*, 307. Hérault was connected with both Grammonts on the general staff of the *armée*.

11 M. Reinhard, 'Note sur Carnot et l'armée révolutionnaire', 9. See also RCC, 'L'armée révolutionnaire au Havre-Marat'.

12 The following Sections supplied companies of cannoneers to the revolutionary artillery:

1 Tuileries	19 Arcis	32 Maison-Commune
2 Champs-Elysées	20 Faubourg-Montmartre	33 Indivisibilité
6 Lepeletier	22 Bondy	34 Arsenal
9 Gardes-Françaises	23 Temple	36 Cité
10 Halle-au-Bled	24 Popincourt	39 Fontaine-de-
12 Guillaume-Tell	25 Montreuil	Grenelle
13 Brutus	27 Gravilliers	41 Marat
14 Bonne-Nouvelle	28 Faubourg-du-Nord	43 Luxembourg
16 Bon-Conseil	30 Homme-Armé	47 Sans-Culottes
17 Marchés	31 Droits-de-l'Homme	48 Finistère

Cannoneers from the République, Contrat-Social, Fraternité, Chalier and Panthéon-Français Sections were to be found also in the artillery detachments. See below, III. 3, sect. vii (iv).

13 AHG, B 5 75, Jourdeuil to the *commissaire-ordonnateur* of the Rhine Army. On the recruitment in the South see RCC, 'Les armées révolutionnaires du Midi', 77.

14 Arch. Seine, DL IV I (*société* of Sceaux), session of 7 Frimaire. See below, I. 3, p. 143.

15 *Mémoires de B. Barère*, ii. 370; also AHG, B 5 75, order of 3 Brumaire.

16 AHG, B 5 75, Ronsin to the Minister, 15 Brumaire; see also id., the Committee to Grammont, 10 Frimaire (letter signed by Carnot and Billaud-Varenne, in the former's hand), and the Committee's reply to the Luzarches municipality.

17 AN, W Ia 94 (Tribunaux révolutionnaires, Antoine Descombes papers), Champeaux and Dumez to Descombes, 18 Sept 1793.
18 AHG, B 5 75, report from the Minister, 3 Nivôse.
19 F.-A. Aulard, *La société des Jacobins* (1889–97), VI.
20 On 3 Oct, the *commissaire des guerres*, Paris, complained to Bouchotte of the difficulties of keeping to the age-limit for recruits as set out in the laws, and the impossibility of proceeding without further guidelines: '. . . if this *armée* is not to be a mere scarecrow it must be composed of *hommes solides* . . .' (AHG, B 5 75). The Sections too were confused about the age-limit of recruits and general enrolment procedures, and the process was often suspended until the Committee of Public Safety had made concrete recommendations (see AN, F 7 4774 71 d 1, also 2 d 4 [Mercier]).
21 For these elections see AHG, Xv 42–5 (Volontaires nationaux); Arch. Seine, D 4 AZ 124 (Arcis, Faubourg-du-Nord and Quinze-Vingts Sections); and *Journal de Paris*, particularly no. 270 for 27 Sept: '[the] *commissaire* [Paris] . . . announced that a list of 1,200 citizens who have put their names down for the *armée* was sent today for the *scrutin épuratoire* and that there were three times as many yet again to be thus sorted through . . .'. The Commune was not responsible for this delay, and it was not a question of slow enrolment – quite the contrary. Volunteers were enrolling in large numbers, but there were not enough uniforms or arms for them. Paris complained on 4 Oct of having seen a company depart with pikes, and Hanriot promised both clothing and weapons for them by the following day (*Journal*, nos. 272 and 279).
22 AN, AF II 5 (27) (Conseil éxécutif).
23 A. Guillon de Montléon, *Mémoires pour servir à l'histoire de Lyon*, II. 440.
24 AN, AF II 203B (1712).
25 F.-A. Aulard, *La société des Jacobins*, VI. 536–7, Council session of 17 Sept. In AN, AF II 5 (24) (Conseil éxécutif), there is a more complete list, indicating also the kind of backing some candidates received. Thus we learn that Maubant and Boulanger were recommended by Hanriot, Delorme by the Paris Commune, Cordier by the Jacobins. In addition this list contains the names of the adjutants-major (wrongly referred to in Aulard as adjutants-general), i.e. Thomasset, Gondrecourt, Du Hommier and Tolède, as well as Hary, Vézien, Lemois, Gachet, Guinot and Sevrai, who do not appear on Aulard's list. Tolède is described as 'having served the Revolution since 1789'. All the adjutants-major were recommended by the Jacobins. The list published in Buchez and Roux, XXIX, 152–3, corresponds to that in Aulard and is much less complete than this MS list. Halm's case was raised at the Jacobins on 13 Pluviôse (*Journal de la Montagne*, no. 82): 'Mathias Halm . . . being a native of Coblenz [*sic*], Saintex observed that all foreigners should, with ex-nobles, be excluded from the Society . . . Momoro spoke up . . . Halm, an elector of '91, had fought the club of Sainte-Chapelle; for 18 years he had been married in France; hence by the law of the land he was French'. Following a glowing report on Halm's patriotism, on what he had done to support the Revolution, on the way he had risked his life to denounce Lafayette, his admission was called for.
26 Buchez and Roux, XXIX, 153.
27 AN, AF II 203B (1712), order of 1 Oct; also AHG, B5 75. Buard's name was omitted after the Jacobins' *scrutin épuratoire* because of an oversight; see RCC, 'La mission de Siblot au Havre-Marat'.
28 AAG, Cl. gén. 1666 (Grammont), 765 (Collard-Dutrône), and 1843 (Houssaye); AN, AF II 6 (34) (Conseil éxécutif), session of 29 Pluviôse.
29 AHG (*reg. d'ordre*), Ronsin to Audouin, 3 Ventôse.
30 See AAG (*reg. des brevets*; Teinturier, Benoît, Piette, Pagès, Krems); Cl. gén. 765 (Collard-Dutrône); AN, F 7 4774 96 d 1 (Rocher), F 7 4578 d 2 (Allais) and AN, W1a 146 (tribunaux révolutionnaires) for Gaillard. Also see *Almanach national* for the Year II under heading 'Armée révolutionnaire parisienne, État-major', which gives a fairly complete list of aides-de-camp and adjoints; and RCC, *L'armée révolutionnaire à Lyon*, for Dobigny.
31 AHG (*reg. d'ordre*), and Cl. gén. 2964 (Payot). See Arch. Seine-et-Oise, N Q 187 (Gury); Arch. Loire-Inférieure, L 550 Nantes (Fischer), and RCC, *L'armée révolutionnaire à Lyon*.
32 AN, F 7 4774 63 d 2 (Parent), report from the *comité révolutionnaire* of the Arcis Section, 28 Sept 1793.
33 AHG (*reg. d'ordre*), Ronsin to Bouchotte, 11 Ventôse, and AAG (*reg. des brevets*).
34 RCC, *L'armée révolutionnaire à Lyon*.
35 AN, AF II 58 (70). The order is in Robespierre's hand. The Committee of General Security had no permanent *commissaires* attached to the *armée révolutionnaire*. For Boissay's

adjoint, Rayot, see RCC, *L'Armée révolutionnaire à Lyon*.

36 For Sandoz see below, I. 3, p. 106, and AN, W 1a 74.

37 AAG (Officiers de santé), dossiers Pascal and Poisson, and AHG (*reg. d'ordre*).

38 AAG, Cl. gén., Gén. de div. 128 (Ronsin).

39 Buchez and Roux, XXXII. 58, 'Note against Ronsin in the hand of Baudin from the Ardennes'.

40 On Ronsin's mission to Belgium, see S. Tassier, *La Belgique sous l'occupation française* (Brussels, 1932). Ronsin was author of a *Rapport de la Bataille de Jemappes*, in which he praised Dumouriez (AN, H 1449).

41 Gén. Herlaut, *Ronsin, le général rouge*. See also J. Hérissay, *Le monde des théâtres pendant la Révolution*, 188–92: '...Ronsin strutted around with his sinister general staff of stage puppets, Grammont, Robert, Parein, Momoro, Saint-Félix, Hazard...'. Saint-Félix, with the actor Fusil, would later sit on the Commission Temporaire (see R. C. Cobb, 'La Commission Temporaire de Commune-Affranchie', *Cahiers d'Histoire*, no. 1 [1957], and 'Robespierre und der general Boulanger').

42 AHG, B* 1211 (Army of the Côtes de La Rochelle, corres.).

43 Buchez and Roux, XXXII, 55–6; see also Hérissay, *Le monde des théâtres*, 192.

44 Arch. Seine, DQ 10 436. Ronsin's wife, whom he married in June 1793, brought him a dowry of 10,000 livres – seemingly the sum total of his wealth. She managed eventually to win back his furniture and library in the boulevard Montmartre. See AN, Wla 159 on Ronsin's son. What became of this unfortunate child, an infant abandoned by his parents and adopted by Ronsin when serving in the Army of the Côtes de La Rochelle and whom he had planned to make a republican and defender of liberty? Was he eventually adopted by General Turreau, who married his colleague's widow? Unfortunately we know nothing further about the child.

45 AAG, Cl. gén., Gén. de brig. 201 (Boulanger), and RCC, 'Robespierre und Boulanger'; AN, F 7* 4796 (Halle-au-Bled Section, reg. of *Cartes rouges*); BL, F 826 (9) (Place-Louis XIV Section – active citizens, *c.* 1790); F.-A. Aulard, *La société des Jacobins*, I xxxviii (printed list of Jacobins membership, 21 Dec 1790).

46 Buchez and Roux, XXXVI. 132, and see entry for Boulanger in G. Six, *Dictionnaire biographique des généraux et amiraux de la Révolution et de l'Empire 1792–1814* (1913). F.-A. Aulard, *La société des Jacobins*, VI. 192. Boulanger was elected to the position of commander-general by the Commune in its session of 15 May. His candidacy was supported by Desfieux (see RCC, 'Robespierre und Boulanger').

47 AAG, Gén. de brig. 201.

48 BN, L 2 C 2583, *Journal de l'armée des côtes de Cherbourg* (*société* of Caen, sessions Sept–Oct 1793).

49 AN, F 7 4611 (Boulanger). At the time of his arrest at his dwelling, 59, rue Saint-Honoré, after 9 Thermidor, four sword-canes and a blunderbuss were confiscated. Apart from such implements of war, his only worldly goods were clothes and furniture. He was a bachelor and lodged with his niece.

50 AN, W 434 (976) and RCC, 'Robespierre and Boulanger'.

51 Arch. Mesnil-Aubry (reg. deliberations, General Council of the commune and État-civil).

52 AN, T 514 1 (Séquestres, Osselin), list of Vainqueurs de la Bastille.

53 AN, F 7 4774 63 d 1 (Parein) and AAG, Gén. de brig. 349 (Parein). On these missions see P. Caron, *La Première Terreur (1792)*, I: *Les missions du Conseil éxécutif provisoire et de la commune de Paris* (1950), 17, 28, 35n., 36, 39, 56n., 61, 66, 67, 99, 105, 109, 127, 133, 195.

54 E. Quernau-Lamérie, *La Commission Parein-Félix*.

55 RCC, *L'armée révolutionnaire à Lyon*, 14.

56 RCC, 'Note sur la répression contre le personnel sans-culotte'; Arch. Mesnil-Aubry, État-civil (year 1831).

57 Parein also had literary pretensions, being the author of several plays; *La Prise de la Bastille* was staged in the first years of the Revolution (see J. Hérissay, *Le monde des théâtres*, 188). See Buchez and Roux, XXX. 426 for his role on the Commission: '... He was small, with a characterless face and blotched complexion and always wore his hat cocked at an angle, in a way guaranteed to arouse fear.... Parein was reputed to be a cruel enemy of the priests...'.

58 *Nouvelle biographie générale* (Didot, 1862 edn.), under Nourry (Guillaume). See also J. Hérissay, *Le monde des théâtres*. Michaud, *Biographie universelle* (1857) repeats the anecdote of Grammont bringing his son to the execution of his patroness, the Queen, and having

him dip his handkerchief in her blood after she was guillotined. On his rise in the *garde bourgeoise*, see Hérissay, op. cit., 30, citing a pamphlet, *Les comédiens commandants...* (BL, F 370 5).

59 AN, T 1632 (Séquestres), inventory of Grammont papers (father and son, *condamnés*), 3, rue des Petits-Pères, Guillaume-Tell Section, 12 Ventôse Year III. Grammont has had a bad press with historians. Hérissay never forgave him his career as a *révolutionnaire* after having been a well-known Court actor; the republican historians for their part have always held his theatrical career, a profession 'peu sérieuse', against him, considering it to have reflected badly on the dignity of the new *armée*.

60 AAG, Cl. gén. 1843 (Houssaye).

61 AN, W 369 (823) (91) (*comité* of the Lombards Section, 15 Germinal). Houssaye was living in furnished rooms, Maison de Molière, rue aux Ours; see also id., bill of indictment, 1 Prairial.

62 F. Braesch, *La commune du 10 août* (1911), 344, n. 2, and AAG, Cl. gén. 765 (Collard-Dutrône).

63 AAG, Cl. gén. 765 (Collard-Dutrône); AN, F 7 4607 d 4 (Bonnard). On 28 Apr 1793, Collard-Dutrône and Nicolas Bonnard, an artillery lieutenant in the Army of the Nord, were brought in for questioning by the *comité* of the Mail Section – Bonnard had come to Paris without permission; Collard claimed to be there waiting for a brevet from the Minister, and in the meantime was living off the proceeds of the sale of some watches and jewels. He explained the Dutrône part of his name as coming from the name of the land in the Caen region belonging to his father. A woman dressed as a man, and living in the same hotel, was also under suspicion. Bonnard said she was the wife or mistress of Collard. The *comité* was still suspicious and asked if Collard had been Dumouriez's aide-de-camp, which Bonnard denied. The two were eventually released. But the incident shows that by this date Collard was already suspected by the Sectionary authorities, and that suspicion was increased by his account of the jewel sales, which suggested he was disposing of stolen goods. See also AN, W 390 (905) (Tribunaux révolutionnaires: prosecution brief by Fouquier-Tinville, 1 Messidor Year II).

64 AN, W 390 (905), *comité* of the Lombards Section, 12 Nivôse Year II, interrogation of Collard; also AN, T 1611 (Séquestres), Collard-Dutrône, inventory, 11 Pluviôse Year III.

65 AN, W1a 147; also APP, AA/15(404), order of the departmental *comité de surveillance* to the keeper of the Conciergerie, 12 Nivôse Year II, to receive Collard, 'adjoint of adjutant-general Hussey [*sic*] accused of being a counter-revolutionary'; AN, W 390 (905).

66 AAG (Casemates), reg. Régiment de Chartres-Infanterie, 253.

67 AN, F 7 4774 39 d 1 (Maubant), and AAG, Cl. gén. 2594 (Maubant).

68 See A. Goodwin, 'The Underworld of the French Revolutionary Terror', *Memoirs and Proceedings of the Manchester Literary and Philosophical Society*, xcvi (1954-5).

69 AN, F 7 4774 39 d 1 (Maubant).

70 On the Bourdons and Constant, see RCC, 'La mission de Siblot au Havre-Marat'; AN, F 7 4652 d 3 (Constant); and AAG, Cl. gén. 794 (Constant).

71 AN, F 7* 2471 (Tuileries Section, reg. of the *comité*).

72 Renault described Theurel as 'mon supérieur'; see RCC, *L'armée révolutionnaire à Lyon*, 29.

73 For the visits of Berger and Dorchy, see RCC, 'L'armée révolutionnaire dans l'Aisne'.

74 RCC, 'La mission de Siblot au Havre-Marat', and 'L'armée révolutionnaire...dans le district de Montivilliers'.

75 See AN, W 1a 124, F 7 4620 d 3 (Buard) and AAG, Cl. gén. 533 (Buard).

76 AN, F 7 4774 15 d 3 (Lemaire), Lemaire to the Committee of General Security, 6 and 19 Messidor Year III, also id., *comité civil* of the Butte-des-Moulins Section to the Committee of General Security, 19 Messidor Year III.

77 On Donville, see Arch. Saint-Denis, I D* 1 5, General Council of the commune of Saint-Denis; AAG, Cl. gén. 1112 (Donville).

78 AN, F 7* 2509, Fontaine-de-Grenelle Section, reg. of general assembly, Messidor Year II; also F 7 4277, list of subscribers to *L'Ami du Peuple*, Brumaire Year III; AAG, Cl. gén. 1768 (Halm); and AN, F 7 4738 for his earlier life.

79 AN, F 7* 2509, id., session of 4 Prairial Year III. Halm was accused on this date of having threatened Raffet's supporters in the summer of 1793, of having been a friend of Raisson, and of having 'dechristianised' the Eure. He was undoubtedly one of the principal terrorists of his Section.

80 AHG, B 12* 77, Bouchotte's notes.

81 AAG, Pensions militaires 413 (Theurel). In March 1817, Theurel, then living in Metz, received an annual pension of 12,000 francs as a captain with 32 years of service. His rank as *chef de bataillon* was not recognised. For his letter to Joguet from Lyon, see AN, F 7 4750 (Joguet). He signed it '*Vale et me aura*, THEUREL'.

82 AAG, Casemates (reg. Chartres-Infanterie); AN, BB 3★ 83, Lubin to the Committee of General Security, 1 Thermidor Year II. Vézien was made a member of the Invalides *comité* on 2 Thermidor.

83 APP, A A/281 (Machine Infernale). Richard, one-time aide-de-camp to Santerre, escaped from the Fenestrelle prison in the Year VIII. After 9 Thermidor Vézien disappeared from Paris, reappearing only on 18 Fructidor Year V. In the Year IX the police believed him to be living in the Louvre Section.

84 AAG, Cl. gén. 3742 (Thomasset); also AN, T 514 1 (Séquestres).

85 AN, AF II 11 (5).

86 AN, F 7 477 4 90 d 1 (Renault). See also RCC, *L'armée révolutionnaire à Lyon*, 26, 29.

87 AN, F 7 4775 31 d 3 (Tolède).

88 AAG, Cl. gén. 1149 (Ducastel).

89 AN, AF II 5 (Conseil éxécutif). Bernard was the only member of the general staff living in the faubourg Saint-Antoine.

90 The aides-de-camp and adjoints were also used to serve arrest warrants made out against officers and men by the Parisian authorities; see, e.g., APP, A A/15.

91 AN, W 191, spy report of 16 Pluviôse, and F 7 4578 d 2 (Allais). Jean-François Allais was 25 when he was appointed to the general staff, and had only just escaped the first requisition.

92 AN, F 7 4774 96 d 1 (Rocher) and W 191 (spy reports). On the *affaire de l'affiche* see also AHG (*reg. d'ordre*).

93 AN, W1a 146–7 (papers of Edouard Dobigny, Tribunaux révolutionnaires).

94 B. Combes de Patris, *Procès-verbaux de la société populaire de Rodez* (vol. III of the *Archives historiques du Rouergue* [Rodez, 1912]), 475n. AN, T 514 1 (Fonds Osselin), list of Vainqueurs de la Bastille.

95 P. Caron, *Les missions du Conseil éxécutif provisoire et de la Commune de Paris*, 66–7; and F. Braesch, *La Commune du 10 Août*, 183, n. 1. Corchand was named with the group of 29 Aug 1792.

96 AN, F 7 4653 d 3 (Corchand); AAG, Cl. gén. 801 (Corchand).

97 Buchez and Roux, xxx. 426.

98 RCC, 'Note sur la répression contre le personnel sans-culotte'.

99 RCC, *L'armée révolutionnaire à Lyon*, 22; and AHG (*reg. des brevets* [aides-de-camp]).

100 Benoît does not figure in P. Caron's work on the first Terror, cited above, n. 53.

101 AAG, Cl. gén. 766 (Colette). Colette would later be hunted as an 'accomplice' of Ronsin in his 'military plot'.

102 AN, F 7 4594 d 4 (Benoît); also AAG, Cl. gén. 245 (Benoît).

103 AAG, Cl. gén. 1971 (Krems); for Piette see AHG (reg. aides-de-camp).

104 AHG, B5 75, the Cordelier, Henry, to Bouchotte, 12 Pluviôse Year II.

105 RCC, *L'armée révolutionnaire à Lyon*, 22; J. Hérissay, *Le monde des théâtres*, 223. Grasset had such a bad reputation in Lyon as a womaniser and a gambler that Maubant had him recalled to Paris to save the detachment's reputation from sinking entirely in the eyes of the Lyonnais. See also AN, F 7 4775 38 d 3 (Vallière) and 44 d 2 (Vertheuil).

106 AHG, B5 75 (cf. n. 104); in his letter to Bouchotte, Henry expressed an opinion common among the sans-culottes when he said 'the general headquarters is a real brothel always full of prostitutes'.

107 AHG (*reg. d'ordre*, armée révolutionnaire) for Berger, and (reg. aides-de-camp, 1793–4) for Puech.

108 AHG, B5 75 and RCC, *L'armée révolutionnaire à Lyon*, 17, 22, 23, 91, 95.

109 On Dobigny see RCC, *L'armée révolutionnaire à Lyon*, 23, 64–72; and Arch. Rouen, Y9 (General Council of the commune). He is not to be confused with Vilain d'Aubigny, the adjoint of a Division in the War Office, as Louis Jacob does in his 'Robespierre et Vilain d'Aubigny', *A.h.R.f.*, no. 119 (juillet-sept. 1950).

110 AAG, Cl. gén. 2964 (Payot). Payot was formerly *procureur-général* to the duchy of Mazarin.

111 AAG, Cl. gén. 178 (Bastien) and 1755 (Gury); also AHG, roll of the Royal-Piedmont regiment (Casemates).

112 AAG, Cl. gén. 549 (Bussy) and 496 (Bresch).

113 AAG, Cl. gén. 384 (Blanquet).

114 Arch. Seine-et-Oise, IV Q 187 (Mazuel papers).

115 RCC, *L'armée révolutionnaire à Lyon*, 26, 42, 77, 91.

116 AHG, Xp 12 kf (Volontaires nationaux); Arch. Loire-Inférieure, L 550; and Arch. Seine-et-Oise, IV Q 186–7.

117 On 12 Oct Ronsin wrote to all the *chefs d'escadron*, ordering them to correspond directly with headquarters and not through Mazuel. On 10 Pluviôse, in the face of Mazuel's continued intervention in his colleagues' affairs, Grammont wrote to him: 'I am concerned, Citizen, that you have to be reminded of the circular sent by the general-in-chief on 12 October…I enclose an extract, urging you to conform to it and to confine yourself to your own duties.'

118 Arch. Seine-et-Oise, IV Q 186–7; also RCC, 'Le "complot militaire" de ventôse an II'.

119 Mazuel's personal papers contain many affectionate notes from Aigoin. See also AN, WIa 164, the public notice 'Mazuel à ses concitoyens', Nivôse Year II, which speaks of his persecution in Montpellier because he professed Jacobin principles; he attached a warmly worded testimonial to his patriotism from Aigoin.

120 F. Braesch, *La commune du 10 août*, 948, 951, 952, 956, 1058.

121 A. Troux, *Le département de la Meurthe sous la Révolution* (Nancy, 1936).

122 AN, WIa 164, Mazuel to his fellow citizens.

123 Arch. Seine-et-Oise, IV Q 187, Roujon to Mazuel, 6 Frimaire Year II.

124 Arch. Seine-et-Oise, IV Q 187.

125 AHG (*reg. d'ordre*, armée révolutionnaire).

126 Arch. Seine-et-Oise, IV Q 187, letter from the officers of the 4th squadron at Beauvais to Mazuel, 28 Nivôse: 'we learnt of your arrest, comrade, with as much pain as the news of your release brought us pleasure. Good republicans, true sans-culottes will continue to exist as long as the Republic does….'

127 In his passport, issued 24 July 1793, for his return to the Vendée, Mazuel is described as 5 feet 5 inches, hair chestnut, nose long and large, eyes brown, mouth middling, chin round and dimpled.

128 Arch. Seine-et-Oise, IV Q 187, Vincent to Mazuel, 15 Sept 1793. He concluded: 'Je t'embrasse. VINCENT'. Between Vincent and Mazuel there was not only a meeting of ideas and temperaments, but also ties of genuine affection.

129 *Journal de la Montagne*, no. 106.

130 Arch. Seine-et-Oise, IV Q 186.

131 Mazuel's papers are preserved in two cartons, IV Q 186 and 187 (Séquestres) Arch. Seine-et-Oise. I am grateful to the archivist, M. Lions, for having indicated this invaluable source to me. For A. Mathiez's life of the *révolutionnaire*, see also RCC, 'Le "complot militaire" de ventôse an II'.

132 AN, F 7 4774 37 d 3 (Mary); E. Querneau-Lamérie, *La Commission Parein-Félix*, 6.

133 RCC, 'La Commission Temporaire de Commune-Affranchie'.

134 AN, AF II 58 and F 7 474 61 d 3 (Paillardelle); and see *Journal de la Montagne*, no. 14 (4th ser.), session of the Jacobins, 5 Brumaire Year III.

135 On this subject see. H. Calvet, *Un instrument de la Terreur à Paris*. Clémence and Marchand were sent on mission to the Gonesse district and the districts bordering the Oise.

136 AAG, Cl. gén. 365 (Boissay). Boissay was an expert at using his friendships to political advantage. In April he described himself to Bouchotte as 'Recommended by Hébert…, my close friend, supported by Audoin, your adjoint, I was nominated by Pache, your friend…a Cordelier since the inauguration of their excellent society, I am known and connected…notably to Vincent, your secretary-general…'.

137 On the revolutionary life of Boissay see RCC, *L'armée révolutionnaire à Lyon*, 7, 8, 17–19, 20–1, 24, 36, 76, 85, 88, 90–1, 92–3, 96–8.

138 AAG, Cl. gén. 2933 (Paris). Paris was accused of having said to the Thionville *société*, in May 1793, that taxation should be imposed by physical force if it could not be done otherwise, thereby ranging the soldiers against 'les négociants de la ville et les gens de la campagne' – an interesting quarrel which drew a dividing line between the sans-culottes and the farmers and merchants in matters of taxation. In this conflict the Minister decided in favour of Paris and against the municipality.

139 AN, F 7 4713 d 1 (Gachet). The Saint-Florentin *comité* apologised to Gachet for this confusion. See also F 7 4713 d 1 (Fromant); F 7 4774 37 d 2 (Martin); and AAG, Cl. gén.

3258 (Rayot).

140 AN, F 7 4767 d 2 (Lassagne). Was there an administrative Council to decide disputes concerning the entire *armée*? This seems likely, for Sandoz called himself 'a member of the administrative Council of the *armée révolutionnaire*'. But we have found no other references to a body which, in any case, would have come together only in exceptional circumstances – and which may never have met at all.

Chapter 3

1 Of the 9 officers on whom we have such information, Lefranc was 31, Simon 43, Delacroix 52, Vallantin 38, Poupart 37, Hardy 37, Coppin 47, Suicre 34; Eude, at 25, is out of step with the rest of the group.

2 Among 15 cannoneer officers, there were 2 former soldiers (Diacre and Hardy); 1 building contractor, 1 clockmaker, 1 toymaker, 1 in the shoemaking business, a clerk, a 'worker' and a farmer. Most were also family men.

3 AN, F 10 450 (Agriculture, workers requisitioned for the harvest, by Section, Thermidor Year II).

4 AAG, Cl. gén. 1308 (Eude) and AHG, Xv f 45. Eude was condemned to transportation at the beginning of Year V, after his arrest in the camp de Grenelle affair. But the judgement was quashed and in the Year VII he was appointed captain in the 2nd auxiliary battalion of the Côte d'Or. In Brumaire Year IX he was serving in the line infantry, 23rd demi-brigade, Army of the Rhine, but was suspended by the Consular decision of 1 Brumaire and was back in Paris by the 5th in his old trade as a clockmaker. He was arrested again with his former sergeant-major, Sormois, during the events of Nivôse Year IX, and there is no further trace of him until Aug 1810 when he was again in service as captain in charge of outfitting draft-dodgers in the 5th depot at Blaye (Gironde). On 22 Nov 1811 he was appointed commander of the 30th battalion of Spanish prisoners-of-war, and the following year was made commander of seven of these battalions on the Helder. Appointed adjoint in 1813 to the general staff of Mayer, brigadier, he was sent to Naarden to negotiate the surrender of the Helder forts. On his return to France he re-established himself in his old trade in Bordeaux; having vainly sought another command, from 1816 to 1819 he received a retirement pension of 600 francs. In 1828 he went to live in Sens, and the 1830 revolution revived his hopes of returning to service as a garrison commander. But his requests went unanswered, despite his professions of loyalty to the new dynasty, and he was obliged to take up his old trade, in 1831 establishing himself once again, aged 64, in Paris (342, rue Saint-Jacques).

5 AN, F 7 4774 12 d 5 (Lefranc).

6 See *Journal de la Montagne*, nos. 144 and 163.

7 AN, F 7 6276 (Lefranc to Bonaparte, 1 Frimaire Year XII). He was also suspected of having received assistance from the British government and made several statements against the French authorities during his captivity in England – accusations which he denied (id., note to the Grand Judge, sent from Brest, 24 Frimaire Year XII).

8 Soboul, 831–2. See also AN, WIa 138 (denunciation of the terrorists of the l'Unité Section); WIa 138, W 554 (*commission militaire* of the Temple Section); F 7 4276 and 4277 (Babeuf affair) and see below, Epilogue.

9 AHG, Xv 45 (4th co. 2nd bn.): Courmaceul capt., Coppin lieut., Turpin 2nd lieut.

10 AN, F 7 4653 d 1 (Coppin). Coppin was arrested 14 Pluviôse Year II on orders from the *comité* for having said to the *société* 'that we were 50 cannoneers who would not rest until the law was enforced'.

11 AN, F 7 4662 d 5 (Dauphinot), F 7 4666 d 2 (Delacroix), and AHG, Xv 45.

12 AN, F 7 4646 d 3 (Chevalier); F 7 4774 42 d 3 (Mera).

13 AAG, Cl. gén. 3822 (Vallantin); AN, F 7 4775 23 d 3 (Suicre).

14 AN, F 7 4774 81 d 4 (Poupart).

15 APP, A A/274 (Machine Infernale). In Babeuf's lists Potemont is mentioned as 'good in action, like his company'.

16 BN, MSS Nouv. acq. fr. 2705 (1 33) – the Monvoisins were members of the Luxembourg Section *société*. APP, A A/272 (Chevalier-Desforges affair); and see also AN, F 7 4779 (*comité révolutionnaire* of the l'Unité Section) and F 7 4428 for the brothers' arrest after the *journées* of Prairial Year II, and the liberation of the eldest by order of the Committee of General Security, 27 Vendémiaire Year IV.

17 APP, A A/276 (167) (Machine Infernale).
18 AN, F 7 4774 47 d 1 (Mirau) and C 203 (1099) (Petitions) (List of signatories of the *société*).
19 AAG, Cl. gén. 1778 (Hardy); and for Diacre, AHG, Xv 43 (Volontaires nationaux). There are other cannoneer officers of whom we know only the name and Section: Heno, capt., Popincourt co.; Preslot, capt., Champs-Elysées co.; Vincent, capt.; Danneu, lieut.; Charbonnaux, 2nd lieut., 4th co. 3rd bn.; Dupont, capt.; Calippe, lieut., and Gentler, 2nd lieut., l'Indivisibilité co.; Houlier, lieut., and Sanson, 2nd lieut., Faubourg-du-Nord co.; Guérin, capt., 1st co. 3rd bn. These men have left no trace save for their signatures on addresses of congratulations to the Convention, or their names on election lists (AN, C 299 [1951] and AHG, Xv 45 [Cannoneers]).
20 *Journal de la Montagne*, no. 163 (3rd ser.) (Jacobins, session 17 Vendémiaire Year III).
21 AHG (*reg. des brevets*, 1793 – Year II).
22 Simon, 54; Réaume, 44; Bouveron, 40; Briois, 42: Carteron, 39; Chamot, 44; Dumany, 51; Gasson, 24; Huel, between 47 and 50; Langlois, 32; Macquart, 34; Edme, 40; Belhomme, Devic, Desjardins, Guénin, Laboria, Pépin, Thévenot and Gayrand, between 38 and 45; Martin, 48; Chaumont, 36; Pudepièce, 60; Joly and Fauveau, 27.
23   1 Tuileries (Bourgoin, capt.)
      2 Champs-Elysées (Gary, id.)
      4 Montagne (Grossin, id.)
      6 Lepeletier (Carteron, id.)
      7 Mont-Blanc (Garnier, id., and Vitau)
      8 Muséum (Dumany, id.)
      9 Gardes-Françaises (Collin, id., Keller)
     10 Halle-au-Bled (Lecourtier, id.)
     11 Contrat-Social (Henry, id., and Lallemant)
     12 Guillaume-Tell (Hébert, id.)
     14 Bonne-Nouvelle (Réaume and Simon)
     15 Amis-de-la-Patrie (Soulet, capt., and Villedieu)
     17 Marchés (Langlois)
     19 Arcis (Chaussepied, capt.)
     20 Faubourg-Montmartre (Chamot, id., and Martin)
     21 Poissonnière (Queneuille, id.)
     22 Bondy (Chaumont, capt., and Martin)
     24 Popincourt (Dagorno, id.; Desjardins)
     26 Quinze-Vingts (Dufour)
     28 Faubourg-du-Nord (Constant)
     29 Réunion (Coste, capt.)
     30 Homme-Armé (Huel and Pudepièce)
     31 Droits-de-l'Homme (Fouques, capt., and Charbonnier)
     32 Maison-Commune (Deslauriers, id., and Thévenin)
     33 Indivisibilité (Loude, id., and Briois)
     34 Arsenal (Joly)
     38 Invalides (Fauveau, capt.; Heusé)
     40 Unité (Ruide, id.)
     41 Marat (Gasson)
     43 Mutius-Scévola (Du Mans, capt.)
     44 Chalier (Surbled, id.)
24 AHG (*reg. d'ordre*), Maubant to Chuine, 22 Ventôse Year II, also *reg. des brevets*, 1793 – Year II, and RCC, *L'armée révolutionnaire à Lyon*.
25 AN, F 7* 2478, reg. Lepeletier *comité*; J. Durieux, *Les Vainqueurs de la Bastille* (1911), and AHG, *reg. des brevets*.
26 AN, F 7 4634 d 3 (Carteron), list of his activities under orders of Hanriot and Maillard (25 Floréal Year II): '1. at Saint-Germain-en-Laye, case of a conspirator enrolling for the Vendée. 2. at the Palais Infernal when it was blocked. 3. at the Hôtel l'Intendant du Prince Louis, near Clignancourt. 4. rue Saint-Marc, with Maillard. 5. at the Moulin Joli, with Marino, as ordered by General Hanriot and his aides-de-camp. 6. seeking la Tour du Pin. . . . 7. in the Sans-Culottes Section, with the aides-de-camp, not having been able to find the scoundrel. 8. rue Traversière-Saint-Honoré, three conspirators from Lille. 9. at Argenteuil, arrest of a chevalier and former deputy. . . . 10. at the château de la Barre with the scoundrel la Barthe, intendant of Monsieur. . . with an administrator of the

department.... 11. at Mesnil-Simon's for the arrest of Pigasse, who was selling a summons order...I was sent the following day to Livry by Galquet [sic] president of the Committee [of General Security] to bring Richemain in to testify against Dossonville and Pigasse. On my return I was shot at in the Bondy forest and my only recompense was 25 livres to pay for the carriage. Carteron, rue Helvétius...'.

27 AN, WIa 184 and W 389 (904) (Pigasse, Mesnil-Simon et Burlandeux affair). Burlandeux, against whom Carteron testified, was condemned to death by the revolutionary tribunal on 29 Prairial Year II. It was a ramification of the Batz conspiracy; for this last, see A. de Lestapis, 'Un grand corrupteur: le duc du Châtelet', *A.h.R.f.*, nos. 131, 133, 138 (1953–5). Carteron therefore was moving in the most dubious police circles, occupied by Marino, Lafosse and Dossonville. At the same time he was in the service of Hanriot, and yet it seems that he was not bothered after Thermidor, though he undoubtedly continued 'to render service'.

28 AAG, Cl. gén. 1549 (Gasson) and Arch. Oise, reg. Noyon *comité de surveillance*.

29 AN, F 7 4774 16 d 3 (Lenoir), denunciation of the Marchés Section terrorists, 30 Germinal Year III. See also APP, AA/272 (26) (Chevalier-Desforges affair): interrogation of Bonjour, ex-agent of the Committee of General Security, 14 Nivôse Year IX. The police spy accused Langlois of wanting to liquidate the informer Tyraud. The same day a police note said he intended going to the fort at Vincennes to capture the cannon and corrupt the troops. The former revolutionary officer seems to have been a man of action and was already referred to as such on Babeuf's lists for the Marchés Section (AN, F 7 4277).

30 AN, F 7 4689 d 5 (Dumany) and AAG, Cl. gén. 1121 (Dumany).

31 AHG, Xv 45 (Volontaires nationaux – Chamot capt., Masson lieut., Goyot 2nd lieut.), also (Casemates) reg. Chartres-Infanterie, 253. AN, W 554 (camp de Grenelle affair – list of those arrested).

32 AHG, *reg. des brevets*, Xv 45, for Loude; AAG, Cl. gén 1280 (Edme). See also RCC, 'L'armée révolutionnaire dans le district de Pontoise'.

33 RCC, *L'armée révolutionnaire à Lyon*, 91; AAG (Casemates) reg. Chartres-Infanterie, 253 – Macquart joined the same Godeau company in which Maubant was serving in 1781.

34 AN, F 7 4765 d 2 (Ruide); AHG, *reg. des brevets*; and BL, F 826* (membership list of the l'Unité *société*).

35 AAG, *reg. des brevets* and RCC, *L'armée révolutionnaire à Lyon*. The other military men among the infantry officers were Belhomme (Perche-Infanterie 1773–8), Devic (49th régiment d'infanterie 1774–90), Desjardins (Bassigny 1769–77), Fouques (Chasseurs des Pyrénées 1779–87), Gayrand (Vexin 1773–81), Guénin (régiment du Roi 1772–7), Laboria (Gardes-Françaises 1778–82), Pépin (Conty-Infanterie 1777–85), Poisson (Normandie-Infanterie 1757–75), Thévenot (Gardes-Françaises 1778–86), Tramblay (Régiment Royal...) (AAG, *reg. des brevets*, 1793–Year II).

36 AN, F 7 6272; also F 7 4633 d 3 (Cardinaux), F 7 4771 d 1 (Lebois), F 7 4276 (Babeuf affair), F 7 6267 (Chevalier affair), F 7 6271–6276 (déportés, Year IX) and APP, A A/272-283 (Machine Infernale). In the Year IX Cardinaux wrote reminding Fouché of the services rendered by him, and claiming to have been recommended by Parein.

37 AN, F 7 4644 d 1 (Chaumont) and D III 5 (298–365) (Comité de législation, Aisne, Laon, criminal tribunal of the department) – trial of Chaumont and Martin; also RCC, 'L'armée révolutionnaire dans l'Aisne'.

38 RCC, 'Quelques aspects de la mentalité révolutionnaire'.

39 AN, F 7 4774 88 d 2 (Réaume), F 7 4278 (Babeuf affair), W 554–5 (camp de Grenelle affair). He is listed as 'Réum' in the *Dictionnaire des Jacobins vivans* (Hamburg, 1799), 152, with the comment, '...one of the *frères* sent to Lyon to organise massacre and pillage'. The royalist author cites Réaume's letter to the Bonne-Nouvelle *société* or *comité*, and accuses him, incorrectly, of having participated in the *noyades* in the Vendée – he was thus assured a place in the terrorist pantheon. Réaume, with the full force of his militant terrorism, dominated the other officers in his company, of which the lieutenant (Jacques Simon, born 1739) was a journeyman mason, son of another journeyman mason (AHG, Xv 45 (4th co. 2nd bn.).

40 AHG, Xv 45 (4th co. 2nd bn.): Colin [sic], capt.; Keller, lieut.; Vicq, 2nd lieut. AN, F 7 4710 d 4 (Fouques).

41 AN, F 7 4741 d 3 (Henry), and RCC, *L'armée révolutionnaire à Lyon*.

42 AN, F 7* 2517 (*comité* of the Finistère Section, session of 4 Floréal Year II).

43 AN, F 7 4734 d 2 (Grossin); see also F 7 4764 d 4 (Lapierre). Lapierre, member of the *société*

républicaine, Montagne Section, wrote on 16 Ventôse reproaching Grossin for his supposed indulgence towards the farmers: 'remember...that we have declared war on all those blood-suckers of the people, on all *égoïstes*, all aristocrats...the soldiers you command complain of your conduct towards these people; they think you have forgotten that you are a sans-culotte.' Grossin replied on the 20th denying the charges: 'No, I have not forgotten...that I have the honour of being a sans-culotte.' Among the former terrorists banished from Paris in 1813, there was a Grossin, a shoemaker, who in April 1813 was living in Tours (AN, F 7 6586).

44 AN, WIa 147.
45 RCC, 'La mission de Siblot au Havre-Marat'.
46 Arch. Seine, D 4 AZ 124, for Dufour; AN, F 7 4774 16 d 3 (Lenoir) (List of terrorists of the Muséum Section) for Leconte.
47 APP, A A/274 (321); the captain of the l'Homme-Armé company was Jarle, the lieutenant, Moutin. See also id. (Machine Infernale), Pudepièce, defence evidence, 11 Nivôse Year IX.
48 AN, AA 56 (1521) (trial of the Septembriseurs, 23 Floréal Year IV; the massacres at La Force).
49 AN, F 7* 2520 (reg. Panthéon-Français Section *comité*, session 19 June 1793; also denunciation by Thunot, 14 Sept 1793), and F 7* 2517 (reg. Finistère Section *comité*). See also AN, W 416 (953) (Hû affair), denunciation made by Thunot against the *juge de paix* of the Panthéon-Français Section. For other denunciations made by this decidedly zealous militant, see AN, F 7 4775 30 d 1, and Arch. Seine-et-Marne, L 854 (Provins *comité*).
50 APP, AA/22 (146) (Committee of General Security), warrant for arrest of Fauveau, 7 Prairial Year II; AN, F 7 4703 d 3 (Fauveau).
51 AN, F 7 4774 10 d 2 (Lecourtier).
52 Arch. Seine, D4 AZ 124, for Chaussepied; id., D4 AZ 876, for Du Mans; Arch. Honfleur, 1 63 (*société populaire*), for Edmond.
53 AN, F 7 4776 (*comité de surveillance*, 3rd arrondissement), *déclaration de domicile* of Queneuille, 23 Frimaire Year III.
54 AN, F 7 4777 (*comité révolutionnaire*, Champs-Elysées, 4 Floréal Year II), and F 7* 2474 (stamp of the *comité* on Gary's *certificat de civisme*, dated 28 Prairial Year II).
55 AN, F 7* 2471 (reg. Tuileries *comité*), session of 23 Vendémiaire, when Bourgoin resigned from the armed force to take up his command of the fusilier company – proof of the importance attached to this new army by the *sectionnaires*.
56 AN, F 7* 2495 (reg. Réunion *comité révolutionnaire*), and F 7* 2511 (reg. Chalier *comité révolutionnaire*).
57 Villedieu (Jean), lieutenant, was received as a member of the *société sectionnaire*, 23 Ventôse Year II (BN, Nouv. acq. fr. 2690 [142]). Among the former terrorists from this Amis-de-la-Patrie Section, disarmed by order of the general assembly on 5 Prairial Year III, it is worth noting one, 'Wolff, member of the military commission of Nantes', who may have been with the revolutionary detachment sent to that town (see AN, F 7 4774 53 d 3 [Mothrée]).
58 AHG (*reg. d'ordre*), 22 Ventôse Year II.
59 AN, WIa 344 (671), Borcsat to the Committee of General Security, 10 Germinal Year II. 'Baladin [wandering actor] des Brotteaux [the plaine des Brotteaux where the mass shootings of the Lyonnais took place]' is a take-off on the title of a play in which Mazuel had once acted in Lyon, his home town.
60 A sample of the ages of these officers will give some idea of the remarkable contrast between the cavalry and the other corps: Richard 21, Steenhouwer 30, Bourgeois 22, Lépine 23, Seran 36, Roman 21, Péré 33, Pérony 32, Menu 57, Machard 46.
61 Arch. Seine-et-Oise, IV Q 186 (Mazuel papers).
62 id., IV Q 187 (Mazuel papers); and Arch. Oise (reg. Chaumont district).
63 AN, F 7 4774, 59 d 4 (Orhand); and AHG (*reg. d'ordre*), 28 Pluviôse.
64 Arch. Seine-et-Oise, IV Q 186. Steenhouwer would be shot in 1812 as accomplice to General Malet at the assassination of General Hulin. AN, F 7 6499 (Malet affair). See also below, Epilogue.
65 General Goguet, former commander of the garrison in Brussels in 1792, assassinated 1793, was a native of Montpellier.
66 Arch. Seine-et-Oise, IV Q 186 (Lamotte to Mazuel, 10 Nivôse Year II).
67 For Bourgeois, see AN, W 185 and W 355 (Tribunaux révolutionnaires), and RCC, 'Le

"complot militaire" de ventôse an II'; for Lépine, see Arch. Seine-et-Oise, IV Q 186.

68 AN, WIa 151, Borcsat to Fouquier-Tinville, 26 Pluviôse Year II; and WIa 344 (671). Borcsat was imprisoned in La Force on 31 Aug 1793, 'accused of having used counter-revolutionary language...'. On 22 Germinal Jagot wrote in his favour to Fouquier-Tinville; he was interrogated and acquitted the following day, 'since there is no proof against him and he appears to have been arrested simply as a result of the infamous Mazuel's despotic wrath...'.

69 Arch. Rhône, 31 L 170 (comité de surveillance, Lyon), letter from the Montpellier comité, 27 Ventôse Year III; and Arch. Seine-et-Oise, IV Q 186, letter Séran to Mazuel, Aug 1793.

70 AAG, Cl. gén. 2989 (Péré).

71 AN, F 7 4774 42 d 2 (Menu). He was rearmed 1 Vendémiaire Year IV. In a petition of Messidor Year II to the Convention, Menu provided additional information about his life, claiming to have served his country since the age of 17, first with the Aquitaine regiment in Hanover; then, after 1764, as quartermaster, sergeant-major and finally adjutant with the Ile de France regiment. After 1787 he claimed to have fought for the Revolution in the capture of the Bastille (though he is not on the lists of Vainqueurs), at Vincennes, at Versailles 5 Oct, at the Champ de Mars against Lafayette, in the journées of 20 June and 10 Aug – in sum, in every combat where liberty was at stake. 'A founding member of the first société populaire of the Republic [though he was not a Jacobin], I am well known, if I may say so myself, as a zealous republican...'. (AN, AA 74 (1372)). Quite a list of revolutionary achievements, if they can be believed.

72 AN, F 7 4775 18 d 4 (Sijas).

73 AN, F 7 4774 98 d 1 (Roman).

74 Arch. Seine-et-Oise, IV Q 187.

75 Arch. Seine-et Oise, IV Q 186–7; and Arch. Mantes, D 38 (société populaire, Mantes, session of 11 July 1793).

76 AN, F 7 4774 67 d 5 (Pérony), and W 355 (739). On leaving the cavalry, the artisan Pérony found employment in a workshop in the Quinze-Vingts Section.

77 Arch. Seine-et-Oise, IV Q 187, undated letter.

78 AHG (reg. d'ordre), 10 Germinal Year II.

79 AN, F 7 4668 d 1 (Delgas). Delgas was connected with the rich foreign banker de Kock, who played Maecenas to the Bonne-Nouvelle Section, not for any political reason, simply to remain on the good side of the Sectionary authorities. But since his house at Passy thereby became a rendezvous for Hébert, Ronsin, and the officers of the revolutionary cavalry, the banker fell victim to his own hospitality when Fouquier took the opportunity to label him 'Hébertist' (AN, WIa 116 and 117).

80 Arch. Seine-et-Oise, IV Q 187.

81 AN, F 7 4774 28 (Machard), F 7* 2741 (Tuileries comité révolutionnaire); Arch. Seine-et-Oise, IV Q 187, letters from Blanchet and from Paul, vice-president of the Tuileries société, to Mazuel, 13 and 23 Brumaire Year II respectively.

82 AHG (reg. d'ordre), Rigaud to Durand, commander 6th squadron, 5 Ventôse Year II.

83 Louis-Dominique Cartouche (?1693–1721), a famous French bandit.

84 The very name révolutionnaire was designed to inspire terror, and if the Parisian armée was called armée révolutionnaire rather than armée centrale it was for 'terrorist' reasons. On 2 Sept, when a petition presented to the Convention demanding the formation of an armée révolutionnaire was discussed at the Jacobins, one citizen observed that 'the word révolutionnaire is not appropriate to the body we wish to establish, and the army should be called armée centrale...'. Royer (author of the petition) disputed this opinion: 'the word révolutionnaire makes the aristocrats tremble, and should be adopted...' (Journal de la Montagne, no. 95, 5 Sept 1793).

85 A. Fray-Fournier, Les archives révolutionnaires de la Haute-Vienne: procès-verbaux de la société des Jacobins de Limoges (Limoges, 1908), 100. See also the biography of Dumoustier ('Moustache') in the counter-revolutionary Dictionnaire des Jacobins vivans; and see R. C. Cobb, 'The Revolutionary Mentality in France', History, Oct 1957.

86 L.-M. Prudhomme, Histoire générale et impartiale des erreurs, des fautes et des crimes commis pendant la Révolution française (1797), v. 489.

87 See AN, F 7* 2478 (Lepeletier comité, session of 23 Vendémiaire), for a list of fusiliers of that Section, aged 53, 45, 40, 36 (2), 35, 33, 31, 30, 28 (2) and 27; also F 7* 2517 (Finistère comité, 4 Floréal Year II) – the fusiliers of the Finistère company were aged 47, 38 and 33.

88 AHG, B5 75, Paris to Bouchotte, 3 Oct 1793. There were also some youths: a 16-year-old

cannoneer from the Amis-de-la-Patrie Section (AN, F 7 4774 75 d 2 [Pigeon]), the 17-year-old Jean-Louis Gourgot, accepted into the Champs-Elysées cannoneers (id. F 7 4777, Champs-Elysées *comité*). But such cases are rare; the Parisian *armée* was rather a corps of veterans, and in the departments where such youths were recruited, it was into special corps, frequently called *bataillons de l'espérance*, which were entirely separate from the revolutionary forces.

89 AHG (*reg. d'ordre*), Maubant to Donville, 7 Germinal Year II, also his letter to Lefebvre, 2 Germinal.

90 AN, F 7 4774 52 d 2 (Moroy).

91 Laukhard, 267–8.

92 AN, F 7 4574 29 d 1 (Magnard) and F 7 4594 d 1 (Benoist); Arch. Oise (district of Compiègne, reg. deliberations).

93 Antoine Mouret, a 50-year-old carpenter from the Gravilliers Section, on detachment in Viarmes, had spent the night drinking in the former abbey of Royaumont at the end of Ventôse; he then argued with the people of Asnières, a village which he claimed to be populated with aristocrats, and which ought to be burnt. The net result was that he found himself accused of being an incendiary, implicated in the Hébertist plot, and dragged from prison to prison, scarcely knowing what had happened to him. (AN, WIa 195 and F 7 4774 54 d 2 [Mouret].)

94 It is difficult to discover if free unions were common among the sans-culottes. Soboul (649) thinks that sans-culottes did indeed live with companions in an unmarried state. In support of this opinion the case of Chomel, sergeant in the revolutionary cavalry, can be cited: 'Married in 1779 in Lyon, my wife left me in 1784. I remained alone until 1788', from which time he lived with another woman, whom he wanted to marry in Pluviôse Year II. (Arch. Seine-et-Oise, IV Q 187.) For a contrary opinion see *Les Révolutions de Paris*, no. 213 (7 Brumaire), where Prudhomme talks of 'this phalanx of good republicans, most of them family men', and no. 215 (23 Brumaire): 'The women...may not...always have praised the stern and uncultivated ways of the sans-culottes.... But they reaped the benefit in that regular marriages were the norm among them...'.

95 AHG (*reg. d'ordre*), Boissay to Bouchotte, 18 Ventôse Year II.

96 AN, F 7 4774 II d 1 (Ledoux), Réunion *comité* to Grammont, 24 Frimaire Year II.

97 APP, A A/60 (Arcis) (commissaire de police), complaint of Bardoux, 9 Brumaire Year II. See also AN, F 7 4666 d 4 (Delamare): this cannoneer in the Bon-Conseil company was accused in Prairial Year III of having 'repeatedly put forward sanguinary motions, and proclaimed against the merchants and *honnêtes gens*, calling for...a permanent guillotine...'.

98 Laukhard, 267. See also the letter addressed by the Finistère detachment in Pont-l'Evêque to their Section, 16 Ventôse, claiming that the rich of the countryside were in league with those of the town, and that 'only the poor sans-culottes have difficulty supplying their needs...' (AN, BB 3 71). The condemnation of Grammont in this letter is indicative of the same puritan hostility to luxury: 'We want family men to lead us, at least they would see the need of securing bread for their children; instead most of those imposed on us seek only luxuries, while their brothers cannot even find the basic necessities of life...'.

99 Arch. Vaucluse, I VI 12 (*société* of Vaison), 5 Sept 1793. Twelfth commandment: 'Never inform unjustly, but watch out for the enemies of liberty, and never be afraid of denouncing conspirators, by your silence you would be as guilty as they are...' (cited in RCC, 'Quelques aspects de la mentalité révolutionnaire').

100 Arch. Rhône, 42 L 149 (Commission Temporaire, Fanchette Mayet).

101 The denounced man claimed to be afflicted with a kind of nervous tic in his tongue (Arch. Eure, 235 L 89*, *comité* of Vernon).

102 AN, F 7 4583 d 6 (Avenel).

103 Arch. Vernon, D 1/7 (General Council, session of 1 Frimaire Year II).

104 Laukhard, 267. Signs of the same sentiment can be found in Collot's address to the Jacobins, 29 Ventôse: 'I know these good Parisian cannoneers, they are above reproach.... In Commune-Affranchie, I heard them say that they were the striking force of the nation, and that their weapons would only be turned against its enemies...' (*Journal de la Montagne*, no. 129 [2 Germinal Year II]).

105 AHG (*reg. d'ordre*), Maubant to the commander of the detachment at Provins, 22 Ventôse Year II. This kind of independent spirit was peculiar to the cannoneers and fusiliers. The cavalrymen were at one and the same time more servile towards their officers and more

arrogant towards civilians. Cochet, a cavalier in the 2nd squadron, accused of having threatened a sergeant, declared himself 'as innocent as a new-born babe... you can be sure that a former servant with 13 years of service knows his place too well to make such threats...' (Arch. Seine-et-Oise, IV Q 187). This was the flunkey rather than the sans-culotte speaking, and in that Cochet was representative of a good portion of the cavalry.

106 When Parein, just returned from the Vendée, appeared before the Jacobins on 18 Vendémiaire, he declared: 'My colleague Boulanger asks you for a guillotine, I ask for a *second*, and I promise you that the aristocrats and the hoarders will soon be reduced to nothing'. Momoro declared that Parein had already guillotined many aristocrats in the Vendée – which was in fact untrue, for in Parein's time the Commission Parein-Félix was relatively mild (*Journal de la Montagne*, no. 131 [11 Oct 1793]). Boulanger, the most 'governmental' of the commanders, did not rest there: at the Jacobins on 13 Brumaire, he 'used the occasion of some new betrayals to demand a *mouvement révolutionnaire* to crush all aristocrats, all those who were against the revolution'. Was this not simply another way of demanding legalised massacres? The *société* disregarded it (*Journal de la Montagne*, no. 157). Thus did the commanders, even more than the soldiers, who were a little more humane, rival each other in revolutionary brutality.

107 RCC, 'L'armée révolutionnaire parisienne: composition sociale et politique'. This incident was pointed out to me by my friend, Pierre Tartat, historian of Avallon, who was kind enough to let me see the relevant extract from the communal archives.

108 AN, F 7 4774 83 d 2 (Prévost).

109 AN, BB3 75, Gillet to the commanders of the detachment at Luzarches, 30 Sept 1793.

110 AN, F 7 4610 d 4 (Boudringuin). After the disbandment of the *armée*, Boudringuin was employed with Colin, a master locksmith, working on the large artillery. Arrested 12 Messidor, for having caused a disturbance among the soldiers, he excused himself by claiming that he had been drinking.

111 On 3 Aug 1793 the Gravilliers *comité* pointed to 'gatherings of locksmiths, nail-makers, etc.', meeting every two weeks in one of the *auberges* of the Section, who had enrolled in several of the corps, even those of the line troops (AN, BB3 73). On a chance enrolment, see id., F 7 4596 d 8 (Berthonier).

112 AN, F 7 4739 d 3 (Haumann).

113 AN, F 7★ 2472 (Tuileries *comité*, session of 13 Floréal Year II), and F 7 4596 d 2 (Berny).

114 AN, F 7 4739 d 3 (Hauplond).

115 AN, W 471.

116 AN, F 7 4688 d 4 (Deltufo). Deltufo, printer to the Convention, had agreed to employ this young man, Barrau, under his disguise as an apprentice printer. Barrau's father had powerful friends.

117 AN, F 7 4758 d 2 (Lafrété). See also F 7 4699 d 2 (Duvivier): Siméon Duvivier, native of Passais, Domfront district, aged 24 and a clerk in a business concern, joined the cavalry, and when arrested by the Poissonnière *comité* for having evaded conscription, boasted of having purchased an exemption for 100 *écus*. His parents, fortunately for them, had abandoned him 'because of his libertinage', and he was described by the *comité* as a 'Muscadin [who] associated with scarcely anyone but women'. He had worked in the office of the artillery's banker, Bouret de Vézelay.

118 AN, WIa 389 (904). Guéthenoc was condemned to death among the *Chemises rouges*.

119 Arch. Seine-et-Oise, IV Q 45 (Séquestres, Guillaume de Baudelaire); I am indebted to M. Arnaud de Lestapis for having drawn my attention to this dossier. See also AHG (*reg. d'ordre*).

120 AN, F 7 4587 d 5 (Barré).

121 AN, WIa 140.

122 AN, F 7★ 2473 (Champs-Elysées *comité révolutionnaire*, session of 30 Brumaire Year II).

123 AN, F 7 4639 d 1 (Chandèze).

124 AN, F 7 4774 30 d 4 (Maillet). Maillet remained in prison until 2 Fructidor Year II.

125 AN, F 7 4767 d 2 (Lassagne). For this continued surveillance from the centre see also id., F 7 4777 (reg. Champs-Elysées *comité révolutionnaire*). On 10 Frimaire a cannoneer sergeant, the 32-year-old Bernard from Chaumont-en-Bassigny, was denounced for having an unsigned certificate (he had picked it up in the corridors of the War Ministry). He had also left his post to go to a *cabaret*. This would not be the last occasion on which he was taken to task for insufficient papers or misbehaviour.

126 Arch. Seine, D L IV 1 (*société populaire* of Sceaux, sessions of 25 Brumaire and 7 Frimaire), in which it was observed that '*sociétaires* [were] for the most part farmers...'. Arch. Sèvres, Reg. P (*société populaire* of Sèvres). AN, F 7 4784 (*comité de surveillance* of Franciade, Saint-Denis).

127 AN, F 10 450 (Agriculture), list of workers by Section, requisitioned for harvest work, Messidor–Thermidor Year II.

128 Arch. Montereau, D 15 (General Council), session of 13 Frimaire Year II. See also AN, F 7 4637 d 2 (Chabot). Antoine Chabot, a native of Clermont-Ferrand, lately arrived from Marseille, was accepted by Paris, on the personal recommendation of Ronsin, into the La Montagne company, 17 Oct 1793.

129 RCC, 'Les armées révolutionnaires du Midi'. See also AN, F 10 450 (Agriculture, workers requisitioned for harvest work). Among the former *révolutionnaires*, it is worth noting Jacques Jouves, born in Puy-de-Dôme; Bizet, a 40-year-old casual labourer; Fougerot, a 32-year-old day-labourer; Doublé, a 35-year-old water-carrier, and Henry, a day-labourer. All were seasonal workers, like Loque, an almanach-seller and pedlar in the Eure, aged 46, who had been a journeyman founder for 18 years (AN, F 7 4774 25 d 4 [Loque]). See also Arch. Versailles, D 1 24 (General Council, session of 27 Brumaire Year II), concerning the brawls after which the cavalrymen Delorme, Lemaître, Francq, Bath, Cerval were arrested. They were all from the Mur-de-Barrez district in the Aveyron, 'speaking Auvergne patois' and scarcely understanding French, according to the claims of the Versailles municipality. The final cavalier arrested on this occasion was Pierre Pez of Issoudun.

130 AHG (*reg. d'ordre*), Maubant to the Committee, 23 and 24 Ventôse). Note, however, a contrary opinion in a letter from the Panthéon–Français cannoneer company to Bouchotte, 28 Vendémiaire Year II, stating that it was '...composed mostly of workers and fathers of large families, that none had yet been clothed or equipped...the pay of 40 sols...is grossly inadequate to defray their expenses...' (AHG, Xv 45, Volontaires nationaux, cannoneers of Paris). But this is undoubtedly a case of contradiction, for the word 'worker' (*ouvrier*) could be applied to an independent shopkeeper as well as to a small artisan. See also Arch. Rhône, 1 L 215 (Département).

131 AHG (*reg. d'ordre*), Ronsin to the Soissons detachment commander, 14 Ventôse Year II.

132 Arch. Seine-et-Oise, IV Q 187, Orhand to Mazuel.

133 *Journal de la Montagne* (1st ser.), no. 119 (session of the Jacobins, 25 Sept 1793). '...Mazuel proclaimed that several citizens in his corps were water-carriers, with no means of subsistence other than the pay they receive from the nation, the pay for a cavalryman is 16 sous 4 deniers, and their usefulness cannot be achieved with greater economy, for it is impossible to live on less...'.

134 RCC, 'L'armée révolutionnaire au Havre-Marat et dans le district de Montivilliers', and BN, MSS Nouv. acq. fr. 2708 (134), Luxembourg *société*.

135 AN, F 7 4741 d 3 (Henry). 'As Jacobins in this company we are constantly called *clubbists* and denied access to interesting papers...a complete cabal has been formed...against us by the command...' (undated letter from four fusiliers to the Contrat-Social *comité*, Year II).

136 RCC, *L'armée révolutionnaire à Lyon*, 39–43 (the Maubant-Arnaud affair).

137 On the lack of political consciousness of those in certain sectors of domestic service, and their attachment to the old order of things, see the strange claims of Pierre Millart, a 21-year-old wigmaker from Versailles, enrolled in the 3rd revolutionary squadron, and accused of having referred to the Parisian *armée* as an army of brigands. In his defence Millart claimed 'that he could not be entirely patriotic; for as a wigmaker he had little experience of such and had attended only people who were not themselves patriots and became angry when called citizens...' (Arch. Seine-et-Oise, IV Q 186, interrogation of Millart, 15 Brumaire Year II). Men like Millart were not true royalists, but as prisoners of their ignorance and their clientele, it was difficult for them to opt for the Revolution. The sans-culottes were right to distrust hairdressers, wigmakers and former servants, the rank and file *par excellence* of the counter-revolution.

138 AN, W 394 (914) (Potel); and see Soboul, 516, 663, 853–4, 961–3. AN, F 7 4768 d 4 (Laurent). BN, MSS Nouv. acq. fr. 2713 (108) (Pont-Neuf Section – its *société* was founded 20 Feb 1792), and AN, BB3 80.

139 AN, AF II 102 (750), decision of Tréhouard and Laignelot, 17 Pluviôse; AN, BB3 48 (Brest revolutionary tribunal); and Arch. Finistère, 66 L1 (reg. tribunal). At the end of the

Year III the three former jurors were sent to Brest and incarcerated in the château, where they remained until Brumaire Year IV. For Combas in the Year IV see AN, F 7 4278. At this time he lived at 145, rue des Fourreurs.

140 AN, F 7 4774 26 d 3 (Louis) (Dufils capt., Wicht lieut.). Louis was arrested for the first time in Frimaire Year II on the order of the République *comité*. The cannoneers of his Section claimed him back on the 7th of that month, and in Nivôse, the Lepeletier *comité* wrote to that of the République: 'our *comité* has no complaint against him, . . . on the contrary he is known as a good republican and revolutionary. . .'. He regained his liberty in Pluviôse, when this *comité* spoke of him as being 'on mission by order of the Executive Council'. His dossier (id.) carries the words: 'Louis, called Brutus senior, ex-President of the Military Commission of Marseille'. See also Arch. Bouches-du-Rhône, L 3128 (Commission Militaire). Brutus acquired a particular reputation for brutality; see C. Lourde, *Histoire de la Révolution à Marseille et en Provence depuis 1789 jusqu'au Consulat* (Marseille, 1838), III. 352.

141 For Louis's later career see AN, F 7 4278 (Babeuf affair). A police note dated '2e jour complémentaire an VIII' mentions his meetings with a group of enemies of the Police Minister in a café at 25, rue de Rohan, the previous Ventôse (AN, F 7 6276, Police d'Etat). And see APP, A A/273 (Machine Infernale), also AN, F 7 6271.

142 APP, A A/275 (232) (Machine Infernale).

143 APP, A A/273 (542) (Machine Infernale).

144 APP, A A/70 (Arsenal Section – disarming of terrorists).

145 AN, F 7 4277 (list of 'men capable of commanding').

146 AN, F 7 4277 and F 7 4615 (Brabant).

147 APP, A A/282 (398) (Machine Infernale), Charles Sormois to le comte Beugnot, director-general of the royal police, 5 Sept 1814. Sormois was not the only member of the Eude company to have a bone to pick with the authorities of the Year III, his friend, Pierre-François Duclos, being arrested at the same time as he and liberated only on 29 Vendémiaire Year IV. Duclos was a militant *sectionnaire*, a wigmaker's assistant aged 24, born in Rouen, who moved to Paris in 1791, where he married the sister of his employer and took over his shop. A member of the *comité* of the Droits-de-l'Homme Section, he resigned in Sept 1793 to stay in the cannoneers. But after the company was attached to the *armée révolutionnaire*, he left it to remain in Paris. He was appointed to the *comité de bienfaisance*, 15 Ventôse, presided over the general assembly of the Section on the night of 9 Thermidor and went to the Hôtel de Ville where he saw the younger Robespierre (AN, F 7 4684 d 3 [Duclos]). Like Potel, his spell of service in the Parisian *armée* was extremely brief.

148 AN, F 15 3270 (Secours publics – those wounded in the *journée* of 10 Aug). AHG (*reg. d'ordre*), Maubant to the Committee of Public Safety, 3 Germinal Year II: '. . . The enemies of the *armée révolutionnaire* should be reminded that it is composed of the men of the revolutionary *journées* who paid with their blood for the affair of the Champ de Mars . . .'.

149 AN, A A 55 (1521), trial of the Septembriseurs, 23 Floréal Year IV.

150 Arch. Seine-et-Oise, IV Q 187 (Mazuel papers).

151 *Journal de la Montagne*, no. 157 (Jacobins, session of 13 Brumaire). Massé and his friend Créton were both members of the club. See also RCC, 'Robespierre und Boulanger', 284.

152 Arch. Saint-Denis, 1 D 13 (General Council, session of 16 Brumaire), in which Massé and Créton were denounced as organisers of a conspiracy to turn the *sociétés populaires* and the Paris Sections against the Commune, the citizens of Paris against those of Franciade. This is a particularly interesting accusation, for the communes on the outskirts of Paris, like those of the departments, attacked the militant minority in particular, which in turn sought support from the Paris Sections. Appeals from the periphery were often the origin of missions by the *armée révolutionnaire* into the departments bordering Paris, and even more into the Yonne. Local militants of Massé's kind consequently played a major role in the activities of the *armée*. The Parisian *sociétés* and revolutionary *comités*, naturally suspicious of the outlying municipalities, eagerly took up such accusations and used them as an excuse to intervene arbitrarily in the affairs of the rural communes.

153 AN, F 7 4784 (Franciade *comité de surveillance*).

154 Arch. Saint-Denis, I D 14 (General Council, session of 4 Prairial Year III): '. . . Massé is recognised as having been the intimate friend of Collot-d'Herbois and aide-de-camp to Hanriot. . . . We have reason to believe that the troubles which have erupted in this

commune were the result of suggestions by the said Massé and Creton...'. As early as 29 Germinal Year II, the municipality had refused them *certificats de civisme*.

155 See APP, A A/281 (294) (Machine Infernale) for the note of the Year IX. If the numerous denunciations of the Franciade inhabitants are to be believed, Massé was even a former servant, *valet de chambre* of Gouy-d'Arcy, and had killed two horses with sabre blows (AN, F 7★ 2, reg. Committee of General Security, 1438).

156 AN, F 7 4751 d 4 (Jourdan), and RCC, 'La mission de Siblot au Havre-Marat', 179–80. Questioned about this mission at the Jacobins session, 9–10 Thermidor, Jourdan claimed to know nothing about it, which was probably true. The *Journal de la Montagne* , no. 57 (20 Nivôse), cites a discourse by one Mathieu Jouve Jourdan (former general of the Vaucluse *armée révolutionnaire*) at the bar of the Convention, 11 Nivôse. Was this not perhaps the brother of the drum-major, of whom he had been so proud in 1793 and the Year II?

157 AN, F 7 4644 d 1 (Chaufourier) and F 7 4714 d 3 (Faroux). See also R. C. Cobb and George Rudé, 'Le dernier mouvement populaire de la Révolution à Paris. Les journées de germinal et de prairial an III', *Revue Historique*, oct.–déc. 1955.

158 Laurent Grison, a cannoneer of the Montagne Section and a ladies' hairdresser, was expelled from the *armée* in Pluviôse for 'counter-revolutionary words'. Vasseur, former servant of Caron, president of the Parlement of Paris, was accused of having said a king was necessary, and condemned to death by the revolutionary tribunal on 3 Prairial Year II. He had been a fusilier in the Fontaine-de-Grenelle Section. Savoye, a former soldier and carter, was denounced by the Rozoy-en-Brie *comité* for royalist words, and condemned to death by the same tribunal on 8 Floréal Year II. Billoré, a 26-year-old wine merchant of the Lombards Section, accused by his comrades of having used royalist and defeatist words, was more fortunate. He did not appear before the tribunal until after Thermidor and was acquitted 12 Fructidor Year II. (AN, F 7 4733 d 4 [Grison], W 354 [734] [Savoye], W 370 [832] [Vasseur], W 442 [62] [Billoré], W 147 [Groslay].) For Groslay see also RCC, *L'armée révolutionnaire à Lyon*. And see Arch. Seine-et-Oise, IV Q 187 (Hugo to Mazuel, 27 Nivôse Year II), for the cavalryman Hugo, arrested on orders from the Mont-Blanc Section and suspected of being the accomplice of Achille Duchâtelet; we do not know his fate.

159 See R.C. Cobb, 'Quelques conséquences sociales de la Révolution dans un milieu urbain, d'après des documents de la société révolutionnaire de Lille (floréal-messidor an II)', *Revue d'Histoire économique et sociale*, XXXIV, no. 3 (1956), and 'Les armées révolutionnaires du Midi'.

160 AN, F 7 4714 d 1 (Galand).

161 AN, F 7 4698 d 1 (Duser). See also AN, F 7 4707 d 3 (Finet), Finet to the Bon-Conseil Section general assembly, 20 Floréal Year II. The assembly returned his request to the *comité révolutionnaire* with a favourable report.

162 AN, F 7 4738 D 1 (Hachet); F 7 4714 d 1 (Gaillard); F 7 4584 d 2 (Bacot).

163 Gilbert Laprat, a hatter's assistant, sought to move from the fusiliers to the cannoneers after the disbanding rather than return to his trade (Arch. Allier, L 851, Moulins *comité*). There were also some former fusiliers who sought to have themselves adopted by the *sociétés* as Jacobin cavalrymen in Floréal and Messidor, when Robespierrist conformism required this of the *sociétés*; see, e.g., the case of Morin, an iron-worker (Arch. Allier, L 901★, Moulins *société*), who was returned to his workshop as a requisitioned worker; or the more fortunate cases of Hubert, a former soldier, and Braille, son of a Versailles tapestry-worker, who after leaving the *armée* had themselves accepted as cavaliers by the Sèvres *société* (Arch. Sèvres, *société*, 1st reg.; Arch. Versailles, 1 2 1237, Vertu Sociale *société*).

164 AHG, Xv 45 (Dupuis's wife to the Committee of Public Safety, 12 Pluviôse Year III).

165 AN, F 7 4775 32 d 5 (Floquet). On Haumann, see id., F 7 4733 d 4, also p. 139, and on Dourlans, id., F 7 4681 d 1, also p. 141.

166 AN, W 174 for Ferrant; F 7 4769 d 4 (Lavigne); W 139, 159 and 168 (tribunaux révolutionnaires) for Guillaume.

167 Arch. Seine-et-Oise, 42 L 44 (trial of the Montfort band) and AN, D 11 1282 (437) (Comité de législation, Seine-et-Oise [Versailles]). Son of a weaver of Flavigny, Nicolas at first moved from fair to fair, from Metz to Toul, Lunéville to Reims. His business as a second-hand dealer saw him established – if such a word can be used for a man so difficult to track down – in the rue de Verneuil, Paris, around 1790. He married six weeks before his arrest, and was described in the 'Notice' to the public prosecutor as going under

various names and trades. This 'chef de bande' at the time of his arrest had invented a new mode of assassination, with a sledge-hammer made from fire supports. His predecessor as 'chef de bande' had been a former soldier, Bidault, who had deserted 17 July 1789 and lived off theft and crime thereafter. He was killed in an attack on a farm near Pontchâtrain, 15 Frimaire Year II, and his corpse was described as 'clothed in a sky-blue coat, with waistcoat and trousers striped blue and white, and a pistol with the barrel empty in his left hand...'. The other members of the troupe were poor devils like the rabbit-skin dealer, Nicolas Lelièvre, a 40-year-old Parisian serving with military transport at the time of the attack; Guillaume Le Normand, a calico and muslin dealer, aged 41, and a native of Mortagne; Nicolas Rochaux, a second-hand dealer from Paris, aged 26; François-Xavier Gohier, a former servant, then a tailor established in Paris, aged 31; François Le Blanc, a Versailles locksmith, aged 38; Louis Bûché, a rabbit-skin dealer and tiler, aged 40; Jean-Jacques Loy, called 'Vaudry', a horse dealer living in Paris, aged 24; Jean Langlois, a baker's assistant working in Versailles, aged 32; Toussaint Chambellan, a grocer-haberdasher, living at Versailles, aged 33; Germain Garçon, livestock dealer from the Beauce, aged 39; and Antoine Vidalin, who hired out horses, from the Auvergne, aged 33. All of these men had changed trades and homes frequently, and had only been in Paris a short period. Two at least were deserters. This was 'l'armée du crime'.

168 RCC, *L'armée révolutionnaire à Lyon*, 9–10.
169 See the case of Lassagne (AN, F 7 4767 d 2 [Lassagne]). On free unions see above, n. 94.
170 AN, F 7 4627 d 4 (Busserole). He was to be freed by a decision of the Committee of General Security, 21 Vendémiaire Year IV (AN, F 7 4428 d 7 [57]).
171 AN, W 307 (383) (Beauchant).
172 See, e.g., the case of the brothers Poupart (AN, F 7 4774 81 d 4).
173 To take but a few examples: Poupart, sgt.-major of the Montagne Section fusiliers – damage caused at Château-Thierry; Lacroix, sgt. – theft of church silver; Jacquemain, sgt. – imprisoned at Versailles for theft; Grenier, sgt., claimed expenses for false stops (AN, F 7 4774 81 d 4 [Poupart], F 7 4756 d 3 [Lacroix], F 7 4732 d 4 [Grenier]; Arch. Rhône, 42 L 2 [Commission Militaire]; AHG [*reg. d'ordre*]; Arch. Seine-et-Oise, IV Q 186–7).
174 The fusilier Choquet was accused of having stolen 250 eggs in the Provins area. Blondel, another fusilier, had sold military effects, and Artaud, a cavalier, former captain in a battalion of line troops, had stolen the volunteers' advance pay. (AN, F 7 4648 d 2 [Choquet], F 7 4581 d 5 [Artaud], F 7 4603 d 8 [Blondel], D 111 216, D 111 124.) The cavalier Rabot was something of an eclectic, practicing thaumaturgy and inventing explosive devices at his home the rue des Prouvaires (AN, D 111 216, Rabot to the Convention, 17 Floréal Year II).
175 RCC, *L'armée révolutionnaire à Lyon*, 78.
176 Certain trades do not fit easily into a rigid classification. In what group would we place toymakers or boxmakers, for instance? The former belong in some ways with the luxury trades, since they manufactured mainly ivory pieces (crucifixes, chessboards, draughts boards) and boxwood articles. Contemporary dictionaries did indeed describe them as 'turners in ebony and luxury goods'. Such objects, however, were also much sought after by the ordinary people, and the Auvergne and Aveyron pedlars who sold their wares throughout France and at the Spanish fairs specialised in these articles. The trade must certainly have declined after the emigration, but it also had a popular clientele, and it would be incorrect to classify such men with the artisans of the luxury trades, the economic victims of the Revolution. As for the boxmakers, they were little more than packers, makers of cases and boxes, objects for daily use, and belonging therefore to the wood trades rather than the luxury trade.
177 See AN, F 7 4577–4775 for the individual dossiers on the Parisian *armée* held by the Committee of General Security (listed in Cobb, *Les armées révolutionnaires*, vol. II [1963], Notes bibliographiques, pp. 937–42).
178 AN, F 7 4648 d 1 (Chompré). Chompré, a cannoneer with the Lepeletier Section, was a locksmith, owning both a shop and a workshop employing four workers. He was denounced by his Section for refusing to return his effects on leaving the *armée*, conduct which the *comité révolutionnaire* found reprehensible in someone they considered as 'well off'.
179 See, e.g., the decision taken by the Réunion *comité révolutionnaire*, 5 Nivôse (AN, F 7 2494) that '... citizens presenting themselves for the *armée révolutionnaire* ... should enrol only in

their own Sections, and be supported by two citizens when they have resided less than six months in that Section...'. While not entirely precluding entry to the population of the lodging-houses, it certainly rendered it much more difficult for them. Such precautions also took in deserters who had found refuge in Paris and sought to enlist in the new corps in Sections where they were unknown. (See, e.g., the case of Hocquart, 25, from the Mail Section, who sought to enlist in the Panthéon company; AN, F 7★ 2530, Panthéon *comité*). See also the observations of the Réunion Section *comité révolutionnaire*, 27 Vendémiaire, on the election of the hatter's assistant, Etienne Buisson, as fusilier captain; according to the *commissaire de police* he was unworthy to serve in the *armée*, '...since the said Buisson was someone who had done nothing for the Revolution, had been in possession of a *carte de citoyen* for no more than three months, was certainly a hatter's assistant, but had not worked for more than one month in the past six because no manufacturer would entrust him with merchandise, lives and has always lived in furnished accommodation and has no fixed abode...'. The *comité* therefore decided to quash his election and the decision was approved by the assembled company. (AN, F 7 4627 d 1 [Buisson].) A certain Faucheux was rejected by the Bondy Section for similar reasons (AN, F 7 4703 d 2 [Faucheux], the Bondy *comité révolutionnaire* to the Faubourg-Montmartre *comité*, 26 Vendémiaire Year II).

180 Arch. Rhône, 1 L 215 (Département, effective number of troops, 20–1 Pluviôse): 2nd bn. – 206 active out of 262 (13 in hospital, 3 on leave, 39 detached on other duties, 1 only in prison); 5th bn. – 426 active out of 476 (21 in hospital, 4 on leave, 20 detached, 5 in prison); 6th bn. – 208 active out of 238 (14 in hospital, 2 on leave, 10 detached, 4 in prison); 7th bn., composed of soldiers from the Allier, Nièvre, and Loire, 339 active out of 366 (11 in hospital, 3 on leave, 11 detached, 2 in prison). For the entire infantry, 1,179 were active out of a total of 1,342, 59 of those absent being in hospital; for the cannoneers, 574 active out of 627 (18 in hospital, 10 on leave, 25 detached, none in prison at this time); for the cavalry, 142 active out of 165 (5 in hospital, 18 detached, none in prison). The sick were more numerous in the infantry and artillery than in the cavalry, composed, as we have seen, of younger men. These figures are the official ones, but if 'individual' absences and desertions are added, the numbers of absentees would be greatly increased.

181 Peligoux, a cannoneer in the Bon-Conseil company and a dealer in used wood, impudently told his *comité* that when his officers refused his request to return to Paris to put his shop in order, so that his business could be continued by his wife and children, he took leave himself and would return to his company at Alençon when his business was completed. (AN, F 7 4774 65 d 4 [Peligoux]). Leroux, a toymaker from the Gravilliers Section, having enrolled in the artillery 'without sufficient reflection', demanded his discharge, grew impatient, and took it himself in Frimaire (id., F 7 4774 d 19).

Chapter 4

1 Arch. Var, I L 2001 (Lorgues *comité*, session of 1 Frimaire – letter from the commander of the 2nd Var battalion). See also AN, F 7 4701 d 2 (Escudier), *général de brigade* André Labarre to Escudier, 21 Oct, and Arch. Bouches-du-Rhône, L 2028 (Aix *société des anti-politiques*).

2 AN, AF II 107 (972), decision of Tallien etc., 27 Vendémiaire. On 1 Oct Bouchotte ordered that the 'armée révolutionnaire de l'Ouest' should no longer use the name 'révolutionnaire' (AHG, B 13 306 [Ordres du Ministre]).

3 The fantastic names of the many companies in the Midi pose a real problem when compiling a list of all the revolutionary forces functioning in the departments. The fateful adjective 'révolutionnaire' was even used for the Grand Armies laying siege to Toulon and Bordeaux, even though there was nothing 'révolutionnaire' about them, since they were composed of conscripted troops. Likewise historians have erred in giving credit to these make-believe *armées*, describing Brune, for instance, as 'commander of an *armée révolutionnaire*' (according to the anonymous author of a royalist work), or Dutertre as 'adjutant-general employed with the *armée révolutionnaire*', and Fion as 'ex-general of the *armée révolutionnaire*' (*Dictionnaire des Jacobins vivans*, 47, 54). It was the same for the small as for the large *armées*, the *bataillon des anti-politiques* of Aix adopting the adjective 'révolutionnaire', only to drop it some weeks later and thereby remain on foot for a long time after 14 Frimaire. The Basses-Alpes battalions did likewise, and the Montauban *comité* could not decide whether its battalion was 'révolutionnaire', or simply some kind of National Guard. Elsewhere we have 'gardes soldées' or 'bataillons de sans-culottes' who

were in reality *armées révolutionnaires*, even if they did not carry the name. Verbal inflation, popular in the Midi, further complicates the problem of enumeration. In October the adjective was fashionable, designed 'to strike terror into the *malveillant*' and to augment the importance of the artisans and shopkeepers, members of the National Guard. We have thus excluded some *armées* carrying the title 'révolutionnaire', while retaining others possessing all the attributes, if not the title itself.

4 The presence of soldiers, even if unarmed, was an impediment to the liberty of the *sociétés populaires*, correctly fearing the threat of 'pouvoir militaire'. On 27 Frimaire a Gap *sociétaire* raised the question of whether a soldier should be allowed to vote. He accepted the right of resident soldiers, or those garrisoned there, to do so, but a battalion simply passing through might thus dominate the deliberations of the *société* (Arch. Hautes-Alpes, L 939, *société* of Gap). The problem became a real one in Gap, where the soldiers in the garrison proved much more formidable than those passing through.

5 BL, F★ 49 (4), *Acte d'accusation contre Jean-Baptiste Boucher dit Vive l'Amour, ci-devant commandant de l'armée révolutionnaire du Mont-Dieu, Vassant et Boucher le jeune.* (Sedan [?], Year III). See also Canon J. Leflon, *Nicolas Philibert, évêque constitutionnel des Ardennes* (Mézières, 1954).

6 AN, F 7 4635 d 1 (Castet).

7 Standard Jacobin opinion found its expression in Laveaux's 'Observations', published in his paper, 22 Sept: 'An *armée révolutionnaire* in each department, or formed by citizens joining together from several departments, would be dangerous; it would resemble too closely the departmental forces, and the Federalists would do their utmost to direct it and corrupt it. But might we not augment the Paris *armée révolutionnaire* by adding good sans-culottes from the departments and dividing this *armée* into several sections, which would traverse the departments accompanied by a revolutionary tribunal and two *représentants du peuple* rigorously to enforce the laws everywhere?' (*Journal de la Montagne*, no. 112.)

8 For the enrolment, organisation and training of this Légion, see AHG, Xk 10 (Légions et corps francs), report of the general staff of the Légion, 20–2 Frimaire Year II.

9 Arch. Hautes-Alpes, L 1512, popular assembly of the Hautes-Alpes and neighbouring departments (printed: Allier, Gap).

10 AN, AF II 186 (1538), Paganel to the Committee of Public Safety, 15 Frimaire Year II. See below, III. 1, 'The Law of 14 Frimaire'.

11 The 'armée révolutionnaire de l'Est', should not be confused with the 'Force révolutionnaire des départements de l'Est', the title given by Bassal to the group of *armées* planned by him in the departments of Burgundy and Franche-Comté. (AN, AF II 112 [836], order of Bassal, undated, printed poster entitled *Armée révolutionnaire*, article VIII: 'Each division of the revolutionary force will carry a tricolour flag, with the device on one side, *Force révolutionnaire des départements de l'Est*, and on the other *Guerre aux châteaux, paix aux chaumières*'.)

12 See R. Paquet, *Dictionnaire biographique de la Moselle*, for the text of this order dated 24 Vendémiaire Year II: 'Article I. An *armée révolutionnaire*, taken from the two Armies of the Rhine and Moselle, or the garrisons, will be established'.

13 AN, AF II 124 (946), order of the *représentants* with the Army of the Alps, 9 Brumaire Year II, and (949), order of Simond and Dumas, Chambéry, 9 Brumaire Year II.

14 See AN, AF II 124 (946), and AF II 114 (859) for the order of Javogues and Bassal, 20 Oct 1793, authorising the enrolment of a battalion, composed of 12 companies, each of 100 men, which would carry a tricolour flag with the device *Force révolutionnaire du Département de la Loire* on one side, *Guerre aux châteaux, paix aux chaumières* on the other.

15 For the text of this order, see AN, AF II 112 (836); J. Sauzay, *Histoire de la persécution révolutionnaire dans le département du Doubs* (Besançon, 1867–73), IV. 303; and Arch. Haute-Saône, L 1363 (*société* of Jussey, session of 15 Frimaire). The notice does not give the date of the order, nor is it given by Sauzay, but it undoubtedly post-dated 18 Brumaire, when Bassal announced the measure as imminent at a session of the Besançon *société populaire* (Sauzay, loc. cit.).

16 AN, AF II 124 (946), order of 9 Brumaire. '. . . Experience has shown only too clearly the personal considerations, the local interests, the manoeuvring which come to the fore in matters of subsistence . . . and we must beware that this armed force, having assessed the resources of the locality, might then do all in its power to prevent them leaving it . . . from that moment a system of isolation and Federalism would prevail, harmful to the public

interest...such dangers might be avoided by appointing outsiders to preside over the operations in each department...then the great national interest of augmenting the means by which we can procure food supplies for everyone according to his needs would prevail...'.

17 See R. Paquet, *Dictionnaire biographique de la Moselle*, for the text of the order. See also AN, AF II 95 (699), the *représentants* Richaud and Soubrany, dated from Metz 24 Sept to the Côte-d'Or administrators: '...we cannot stress too much the state of penury of [the Moselle Army], and the urgency of enforcing requisitions in the different districts of your arrondissement; the army is living from hand to mouth, and this a month after the harvest should have rescued us from such shortages...'. And see Arch. Côte-d'Or, L 1306, Dijon district, for the printed notice of the two *commissaires civils* of this *armée*.

18 Arch. Marne, L 427 (Département), session of 14 Brumaire at which the department asked Bassal if his order concerned the enrolment of a revolutionary battalion in the Marne, or simply the dispatch of a Marne detachment to join that forming at Metz.

19 Arch. Haute-Marne, L 1014 (*société* of Chaumont, sessions of 30 Brumaire and 2 Frimaire). For the Chaumont *sociétaires* it was a matter of 'augmenting the nucleus of the Bas-Rhin *armée révolutionnaire*'. In the Mont-Blanc, a departmental official told the Thonon *société* on 26 Brumaire of his mission to form a company from those sans-culottes of the district who wished to fly to the aid of 'our brothers at Strasbourg'. Simultaneously the Thonon *société* was organising a revolutionary battalion, while at Chaumont on 15, 18, 30 Brumaire, 1 and 2 Frimaire, the *société* demanded the prompt enrolment of a Haute-Marne *armée* (F. Mugnier, *La société populaire ou club des Jacobins de Thonon, 1793–1795* [1898], and Arch. Haute-Marne, L 2014).

20 According to Sauzay, and M. J. Meynier, *La Révolution à Ornans* (Besançon, 1896), the Doubs *armée* was never organised because of 'public reprobation' (Sauzay, *Histoire de la persécution révolutionnaire dans le Doubs*, IV. 305). But the commander of the Besançon battalion would be discussed in the Year III, which suggests that in this town, at least, the revolutionary force saw some activity. See below, I. 5.

21 A *commissaire* of Charolles, delegate of its *société*, told the Paray *société* on 29 Brumaire that 'this [departmental] *armée* is intended to bring the grain from the barns, where the *malveillants* are hoarding it, and have threshed that which, through culpable negligence, remains in the sheaves...' – a programme certainly calculated to recommend itself to the *sociétaires* far more than that of helping supply distant armies (Arch. Saône-et-Loire, 4 L 26, *société* of Paray-le-Monial).

22 See, e.g., Arch. Creuse, L 734 (*société* of Guéret, session of 2 Frimaire), and Arch. Lozère, L 532 (*société* of Mende), where both resisted the formation of an *armée révolutionnaire* because the administrative authorities were already implementing the laws on subsistences. Such cases, however, were extremely rare and might perhaps be explained by a reversal of the majority within these *sociétés*. The Chaumont *société* also changed its mind on 2 Frimaire (Arch. Haute-Marne, L 2014).

23 '...The Légion...was authorised the 11 [Brumaire] following by the *représentants du peuple*...' (AHG, Xk 10, 'Observations...').

24 For the attitude of the Committee of Public Safety, see below, III. 1. In Brumaire the Committee had not yet formulated any policy towards those institutions which were being formed quite apart from it. On 25 Brumaire, however, it recalled Taillefer to Paris – a move which reflected a hardening of attitude towards zealous *révolutionnaires* (AN, AF II 152 [1230]).

25 AN, AF II 136 (1058), order of Hérault, 24 Brumaire. See also *Instructions pour les commissaires civils destinés à diriger les mouvements de la Force révolutionnaire*, 12 pp. (2 Frimaire). On 7 Frimaire Hérault sent word to his colleagues: 'I have created all the instruments of action and terror...a revolutionary force [the word 'armée' crossed out] circulating at the same time throughout the department and directed by *commissaires civils*...' (AN, AF II 152 [1230]). And see E. Dard, *Hérault de Séchelles*, 307.

26 According to Prudhomme, v. 474, 'Under the proconsulate of Faure, Jean-Baptiste Lacoste, Reynaud...*armées révolutionnaires*, commanded by individuals acting under the name of Marat, brought desolation and ravage...'. But did this *armée* really exist? We do not know, for there is no mention of it in the correspondence of the Puy *société* (Arch. Haute-Loire, L 860), or in its register of deliberations (E. Gautheron, 'Un club des Jacobins de Province: La société populaire du Puy [-en-Velay], 1790–1795', *Bull. hist...publié par la Soc. académique du Puy et de la Haute-Loire*, XXIII [1938]).

27 AN, T 492 1 (Séquestres, Carrier); Arch. Ille-et-Vilaine, L 1295 and L 1302 (district of Redon); Arch. Morbihan, L 1001 (*société* of Lorient); AN, F 7 4422 (*comité* of Nantes), AA 42 pl. 4d 1321b (Le Batteux's plea), W 499 (his trial), Wla 493 (trial of Carrier); Arch. Loire-Inf., L 1054 (district of Nantes), and L 1323 (*comité* of Nantes); AAG, Gén. de. div. (Avril), and E. Lockroy, ed., *Une Mission en Vendée*.

28 AN, AF II 186 (1540), Gouly to the Committee of Public Safety, 23 Frimaire. Javogues likewise engaged in conflict with Couthon, a man as formidable as the dubious Gouly, and he wrote to his friend Collot, 16 Pluviôse Year II, complaining of the 'moderantism' of Couthon and his colleagues in the Committee of Public Safety, and boasting that he had raised 200 cavalry horses in the Loire for the *armée révolutionnaire* without needing to contact 'Couthon's committees [*sic*] of public safety...' (AN, AF II 114 [861]).

29 C. Pichois and J. Dautry, *Le conventionnel Chasles et ses idées démocratiques*, 53, 54, 60, 61.

30 AN, AF II 169 (13388), Baudot and Chaudron-Rousseau to the Committee, 17 Oct 1793: 'Our Perpignan colleagues disapprove equally of our *armées révolutionnaires*, our *comités révolutionnaires*, and all our revolutionary actions...'. See also P. Gérard, 'L'armée révolutionnaire de la Haute-Garonne', 6.

31 AN, F 7 4394 d 1, Garnier to Paré, 18 Brumaire Year II: 'The Tonnerre district informs me of an order of the Yonne department setting up an *armée révolutionnaire* to be raised on its territory. We must beware of such a measure which is against all political rules...'. (I wish to thank Professor A. Goodwin for providing me with the text of this letter.) See also Arch. Yonne, L 157 (Département), Maure's order of 7 Frimaire Year II, and F.-A. Aulard, *Recueil des actes du Comité de salut public* (1892–1906), VIII. 675 (letter from the Committee of Public Safety to Maure, 4 Frimaire). For Maure's first letter, see Arch. Yonne, L 22 (Département).

32 AN, D III 180 (8) (Comité de législation, Nièvre, Moulins-Engilbert), district session, 27 Frimaire Year III. See also the address of the Nevers communal authorities at Merlino, 25 Thermidor Year III: 'There is a general outcry...against this imperious despot [Fouché]...[for his] creation of an *armée révolutionnaire*, savage attendants constantly at his beck and call...' (AN, D III 181 [1] [Nevers]). All this went back, in effect, to the order of 30 Sept.

33 See AN, F 7★ 2 (Committee of General Security, reg. corres.), for the *société populaire* of Orléans (917), under date of 24 Frimaire Year II, denouncing Laplanche 'for having misled by using a praetorian guard'.

34 AN, D III 355 (Comité de législation), denunciations against the *représentants en mission*, 13 Prairial Year III: Ozun, administrator of the Hautes-Pyrénées department, to the Convention, accusing Monestier of urging the Tarbes *société* to massacre the prisoners, of having slavishly imitated Hébert, of having taken a guillotine into the departments of the Haute- and Basses-Pyrénées, 'of having formed a small salaried *armée révolutionnaire* at Tarbes, admission to which was gained by enumeration of misdeeds...'. As early as Prairial the preceding year, Monestier had found himself accused of 'Hébertism' by an administrator of the Tarbes district for his praise of the *Père Duchesne* (Arch. Hautes-Pyrénées, L 1186 bis, *société* of Tarbes, sessions from 7 Prairial Year II onwards).

35 See AN, F 7 4422, *comité révolutionnaire* of Nantes, 15 Nivôse Year II, claiming paternity of this famous Marat company, a fact confirmed by Phélippes in a printed address of 21 Thermidor Year II. Carrier accepted responsibility to spare his subordinates, the real culprits. In fact, in Sept 1793, shortly after his arrival, he asked for a detachment of the Parisian *armée* to be sent into the region. On the 27th he wrote that 'the project is already half completed, will it meet with the approval of the Committee...?' It was a question asked by many *représentants*. (AN, T★492 1, Séquestres, Carrier.) Gaston-Martin, *Carrier et sa mission à Nantes*, attributes the initiative for the company's creation to Carrier. But his role seems rather to have been one of 'legalising' a measure already implemented by the *société* or *comité*, and most likely the latter, since it exercised a tight control over the company once it went into action.

36 Arch. Lille, 18′229 (*société révolutionnaire* of Lille). This 'project' bore the signatures of Dufresse, president of the *société*, Decrosne, president of the *comité de surveillance*, Favart, *général de division* and garrison commander, Lavalette, and Defferrez, artillery captain in the Panthéon-Français company, all Parisians. Article 5 declared that the plan would be submitted to the *représentants*. The first order by the *société* was dated 2 Brumaire, and on 13 Brumaire the *représentants* announced the measures which had been taken in a letter to Bouchotte (AHG, B 1 22 [Army of the Nord]).

37 *Châles à la société révolutionnaire de Lille* (1 Pluviôse Year II), 45. On Dufresse, see Gén. Herlaut, 'Le général-baron Dufresse', 177. On 18 Ventôse Year III, the revolutionary tribunal interrogated Dufresse about his involvement in drafting rules for the *armée révolutionnaire*. Dufresse denied any involvement, and attributed responsibility to Isoré and Châles; the latter on this occasion courageously accepted responsibility. (AN, W 498 [535], trial of Dufresse.) Decrosne, or Crosne, was an important personality of the Muséum Section in Paris. A former priest, 'a republican by nature and proven patriot since 14 July 1789...I was three times president of my Section. A member of the commune on 10 August, all my colleagues, from Hébert, Martin and Chaumette on down, will do me the justice of testifying that I founded with them the Club des hommes du 10 août, rue Saint-Denis.... I was responsible for regenerating the *société populaire* of Lille.... I am known to the deputies, Hentz, Grégoire, Couturier, David (most of all), Laignelot, Bentabole, Levasseur, etc...' (AHG, B 1 22, Decrosne to the Committee of Public Safety, 30 Brumaire Year II). Decrosne was still a member of the Cordeliers and had contacts in the War Ministry. He was the 'homme de liaison' *par excellence.*

38 RCC, 'Les armées révolutionnaires du Midi', 7.

39 AHG, B 1 20 (Army of the Nord), order of Châles and Isoré, 13 Brumaire. Those charged with the organisation of this *armée* were Dufresse, Favart, Nivet (one of the organisers of the Légion des Sans-Culottes of Brussels), Songis, Nartez (*chef de brigade*), Crosne, Target (who fulfilled functions similar to those of Nivet at Brussels), Vaillant (ordnance officer), Agut, Beauvoisin, Defferrez, Desjardins (mayor of Lille), Dubrusle (municipal officer), Marichalle (deputy), Cambray (municipal officer), Florent (*sociétaire*), Wattiers (*procureur* of the commune), Delahaye-Marracy (notable), Bidaux, Nicolay, Isnardy and Fleur. Most of these members of the administrative council also awarded themselves places in the new *armée.*

40 Arch. Loire, L 399 (*société* of Charlieu, session of 13 Brumaire), at which citizens Garnier (president) and Cucherat were directed to travel to Marcigny and request the prompt establishment of an *armée révolutionnaire* to accelerate the supply of the Charlieu market. The order of Bassal and Javogues, dated 20 Oct, preceded this request; but was it the first time it had been made? Certainly Javogues was not alone in demanding such a force in this department.

41 Taillefer, though incontestably the creator of the *armée révolutionnaire* of the Cantal, also worked through an intermediary. In the Lot, Viton was charged with all the organisational details; in the Cantal it was Fougère Delthil the younger, *commissaire* of the Lot, delegated by Taillefer to Cantal (Arch. Cantal, L 684, *comité* of Aurillac, session of 9 Oct – at which he ordered the *comité* to establish an *armée révolutionnaire*). A list of candidates was presented to Delthil two days later. For the Thermidoreans it was Delthil and the Aurillac *comité* who were responsible for creating the Cantal *armée* (see AN, F 7 4555, *La Révolution du Cantal* [n.d. Year III], also AN, D III 39 [20] [178], *Dominique Mirande, procureur-syndic du district du Mauriac, aux amis de la justice* [Aurillac, Year III], stating that Taillefer had delegated Delthil to Cantal, with immense powers). The origin of the Lot *armée* is less clear and Taillefer, writing to the Committee of Public Safety from Gourdon on 29 Sept, remarked: 'Thus, without having decreed it, I found myself with an *armée* which was already *révolutionnaire* in character...' (AN, AF II 169 [1387]). In fact it was a force made up of troops from the first requisition and it was not the only such force in this department to be called 'armée révolutionnaire'. That formed at Cahors, seemingly at the request of the *comité de surveillance*, was certainly Taillefer's creation.

42 AN, F 7 4563 (reg. Moissac *comité de surveillance*). This *armée* was formed on 27 Vendémiaire on the initiative of Feyt, *procureur* of the commune, which was scarcely an irregularity since he was also a member of the *comité*. See also AN, AF II 186 (1544), Paganel to the Committee, 23 Nivôse. The creation of the Moissac *armée* provoked a conflict between the *représentant* and Taillefer.

43 Arch. Tarn-et-Garonne, L 224, Montauban *comité* to Baudot, 21 Sept, and L 221, its sessions of 27 Sept and 1 Oct.

44 Arch. Hautes-Alpes, L 1512 (Gap *assemblée populaire*). Beauchamp gave his approval to the initiative of the assembly on 24 Brumaire. In the neighbouring department it was the members of the Marseille assembly who took the initiative: Allier, of Valence, Collet and Reybaud of Marseille, Goutier of Mondragon (Arch. Basses-Alpes, L 778, Manosque *comité*, 23 Oct session). It is true that these men exercised an authority delegated by the *représentants* at Marseille, Pomme, Charbonnier and d'Herbez-Latour, who, by an order of

8 Oct, sent them into the departments 'to discover exactly what is happening, to sound out public opinion...and have suspects arrested...' (T. Gautier, *La période révolutionnaire dans les Hautes-Alpes* [Gap, 1895], 27). But were they also instructed to create battalions? At Gap and Digne such units were formed on the initiative of the *délégués*. At Briançon the *société populaire* claimed responsibility, and though it is unclear whether its initiative preceded or succeeded Beauchamp's order, in this department each district seems to have followed its own initiative.

45 Arch. Hérault, L 5591 (Montpellier *société*, 14 Oct session), and RCC, 'Les armées révolutionnaires du Midi', 25. For Valence, see AHG, Xk 10 (Légion de la Montagne): 'The formation of a legion composed of members of the *sociétés populaires* was proposed at Valence at the beginning of September o.s. by the deputies of 71 *sociétés*.... The proposal was accepted unanimously and submitted to citizen Boisset...who approved its enrolment...'.

46 At Pau, Monestier simply executed a decision already taken by the local *société* as early as 25 Sept. See J. Annat. *La période révolutionnaire dans les Basses-Pyrénées: les sociétés populaires* (Pau, 1940), 164. Arch. Basses-Pyrénées, 27 L 1 (Morlaas *société*, session of 19 Vendémiaire Year II), at which the decision was taken to ask the *représentants* with the Pyrénées-Occidentales Army for the establishment of 'a company of 80 paid men to form part of the departmental *armée révolutionnaire*...'.

47 A. Fray-Fournier, *La société des Jacobins de Limoges*. The battalion was created by the *société*, reorganised by the *comité de surveillance*, and finally 'legalised' by Brival and Lanot, who forbade the recruitment of the 45 cavaliers which the Limoges *comité* had intended as an addition. See AN, AF II 146A (1170), order of Lanot and Brival, 5 Brumaire, also instructing the *comité* to seek final approval from the Committee of Public Safety, and to take volunteers from every canton according to its population. This was attaching almost unrealisable conditions, which is probably what the *représentants* intended. Nevertheless, the Limoges *armée* did in fact materialise.

48 See I. 3, p. 147. In the absence of registers of the deliberations of the Auxerre *société*, it is impossible to pronounce on this matter.

49 See AHG, B2 26–27 (Army of the Moselle). The order creating this *armée* is dated 24 Vendémiaire and signed by Mallarmé, Guyardin, Milhaud, Ruamps, Borie, Lacoste, Ehrmann, Richaud and Soubrany. Article 20 appointed as *commissaires civils*, Dominique-François Gobert the younger and Antoine Delteil, agent of the Executive Council, to the Moselle Army, Schneider and Elvert, mayor of Saverne, to the Bas-Rhin Army (see R. Paquet, *Dictionnaire biographique de la Moselle*). Gobert and Delteil were already operating, 10 Brumaire (Arch. Metz, 1 D 113, session of the General Council), and sending their first reports to the Minister and the *représentants* by the 23rd. In Prairial Year III the Thermidorean authorities in the Moselle denounced Delattre, ex-president of the criminal tribunal, for having demanded an *armée révolutionnaire* with guillotines and for having formed, with Lacoste and Gobert, a revolutionary tribunal at Strasbourg (AN, D III 174 d 2 [539], Comité de législation, Moselle, Metz, 1–4 Prairial Year III). In fact it is difficult to disentangle the roles of the *représentants* from those of the local terrorists on whom they depended, in the establishment of the institutions of the Terror, particularly in the departments of the East. Schneider certainly advised the *représentants* at Strasbourg and it is probable that the Metz Jacobins, supported by Parisians like Delteil and Mourgoin, did likewise in the Moselle. Their presence clearly reduces the personal responsibility of the *représentants*, and the Thermidorean authorities were to single out only certain *représentants*, notably Mallarmé, whom they considered the terrorist *par excellence*. See the anonymous drawing sent to Mallarmé, *La ville de Thionville reconnaissante*, depicting a guillotine in action, at the Musée de l'Histoire de France (AN).

50 M. J. Meynier, *La Révolution à Ornans*, 81. Sauzay, *La persécution révolutionnaire dans le Doubs*, IV. 303, is of the same opinion.

51 At Bordeaux, Isabeau and Tallien were seconded – and perhaps even pushed on – by an 'homme de liaison', the *commissaire des guerres*, Peyrend-d'Herval, a Parisian Jacobin, and if not its creator, certainly the principal organiser of the Bordeaux *armée* (Arch. Gironde, II L 27 and II L 68). At Moulins Boissay fulfilled the same role. However, although the Grenoble company was officially the work of Gaston, the local *société* had already requested its formation (Arch. Grenoble, LL 9, letters of 16–18 Brumaire, General Council).

52 Arch. Doubs, L 2360 (Ornans *société*, session of 18 Brumaire) and Arch. Hautes-Alpes, L

1512. See also AN, W 498 (535) (trial of Dufresse), Adhémar, at Cambrai, to Dufresse, 12 Frimaire. He had reproached the Douai *sociétaires* for their misplaced anxieties, telling them 'that it was the patriotism and zeal of the Lille *société* which had led to the formation of the *armée révolutionnaire*, rather than an order from the Committee of Public Safety, which nevertheless had approved it [?]'. One member protested 'that they could not act without the approval of the Convention, which had expressly forbidden the formation of departmental forces, that the order of the *représentants* concerned the town of Lille only [which was untrue, for it envisaged the creation of an *armée révolutionnaire* of the North]...'. Although the old Parlement town of Douai was not entirely sincere in all this, nevertheless, the anxieties of the *sociétaires* reflected the doubts of many sans-culottes about the legality of such measures – hence the demand for an appeal to the Convention or to the Committee. At Versailles too the Vertu-Sociale *comité* wanted to seek the approval of the Convention and the Committee (Arch. Versailles, D 1 186 [13th Section] and 1/2 1236 [Vertu-Sociale]).

53 The company at Serres was in action by the end of the month, 25 Sept (Arch. Hautes-Alpes, L 1506, Serres *comité*).

54 RCC, 'La campagne pour l'envoi de l'Armée révolutionnaire dans la Seine-Inférieure'. Lenud, national agent for the Yvetot commune, was one of the leading compaigners in this department, accompanying the delegation to Paris, calling Legendre and Louchet to account, and accusing them of laxness in the pursuit of hoarders. His intervention in the Jacobins, 26 Brumaire, was to unleash a lively debate between Hébert and Legendre and Lacroix.

55 On Chambon see RCC, 'Les armées révolutionnaires du Midi', 53, n. 25. This 'homme de liaison', a native of Boulou, had been a member of the first commission of popular justice established in Lyon after the siege.

56 The formation of the *armée* at Perpignan was decided on 28 Brumaire, two days after the arrival of Hardy. On 4 Frimaire the *société* elected him to the general staff, on the 7th Gaston and Fabre dismissed him, but the agitation of the *société* for the enrolment of the *armée* continued until 14 Frimaire, when the *représentants* changed their minds and authorised the measure.

57 Arch. Versailles, D 1 24 (General Council of the commune, session of 27 Brumaire Year II). At this session Delacroix called upon Ronsin and the other revolutionary officers to explain the disputes which had occurred between the revolutionary soldiers and the Versailles National Guard. But Delacroix does not seem actually to have opposed the projects outlined in favour of a Versailles *armée* (Arch. Versailles, D 1 51, 1st Section). In Ventôse Crassous was anxious to adopt the governmental version of events and affected a belief in the 'military plot' idea, with Versailles as its centre. Levasseur, on the other hand, always favoured the *armées révolutionnaires*, and on several occasions used Parisian detachments for the execution of repressive missions in the Gonesse district. (See below, II. 3.)

58 The *représentants* were not the only ones to oppose the formation of the new *armées*. When, on 23 Frimaire, Gobert and Delteil, *commissaires civils* with the Moselle Army, learnt of the Meurthe decision (5 Brumaire) for the establishment of a departmental force to levy requisitions, they wrote from Sarreguemines to condemn a measure which they considered illegal. If the department required such a force, they wrote, it had simply to request the dispatch of a detachment from the Moselle Army. The two *commissaires* had no desire for competition from a 'rival' army outside their control. (A. Troux, *Le département de la Meurthe sous la Révolution*, II. 147.)

59 The best proof of the positive influence of the *représentants* is the example of Javogues, who always discounted the need for confirmation by 'Couthon's Committee', and on his personal initiative succeeded, first of all in circumventing the law of 14 Frimaire by maintaining his Loire *armée* under arms, then by increasing its size in Pluviôse, two months after the official dissolution of all the departmental *armées*. (See AN, AF II 114 [861], order of Javogues, 6 Nivôse.) In his 16 Pluviôse letter to Collot, Javogues even broached the possibility of forming a great national *armée*, which might be increased to over 12,000 'if the interest of the Republic required it...' (id., 368).

60 On 7 Brumaire, when the 1st Section of Versailles was examining candidates for the new *armée*, 'citizen Bourniset demanded to be one of the first judges, if they decided to establish a tribunal to follow the *armée révolutionnaire*...' (Arch. Versailles, D 1 51, 1st Section). Many militant sans-culottes shared this ambition to secure a position as people's judge

with the *armées révolutionnaires*.

61 The companies of Orange, Moissac, Nantes, Valence, Manosque, Digne and Sisteron were raised by the *comités de surveillance* alone or in agreement with the *sociétés*.

62 AN, F 7 4394 d 2 (papers found at the house of Vincent; order of Saint-Just and Le Bas, 24 Frimaire).

63 Arch. Hautes-Alpes L 939 (*société* of Gap, sessions of 2 and 3 Frimaire). At the first, 'Brutus' complained that the revolutionary force was not being organised (it was only decreed 24 Brumaire), and the following day he was one of 'a deputation to the municipality to invite it to call the National Guard together the next day apropos the formation of the revolutionary guard...'. It was the same in many other places: a *société* in a hurry, growing impatient; a municipality, prudent, uncertain, anxious above all to gain time.

64 Arch. Ain, 9 L 5 (district of Trévoux), session of the directory, 6 Frimaire, complaining that the *sociétés populaires* had not yet sent in their lists of patriots to form an *armée révolutionnaire*, although they had been sent the order a fortnight before. The order concerned the dispatch of *commissaires* to the *sociétés* to accelerate these measures. One must therefore distinguish between the urban and the village *sociétés* – though the delays by the latter were the product of ignorance rather than ill will. (See complaint by the Serres directory 8 Frimaire, e.g., in Arch. Hautes-Alpes, L 1350). To find one's way through such disorder, one would have had to be an experienced bureaucrat; the *sociétaires* were completely out of their depth.

65 Among the 'étrangers' who played such an important part in the creation of these *armées*, and frequently also in their activities, we should note Rousselin, *commissaire* of the Committee of Public Safety at Troyes, and, with the mayor of this town, Gachet, the real creator of the small Troyes *armée*, called the 'bataillon de la Montagne'; Hardy, Ministry *commissaire* at Perpignan, creator of the Pyrénées-Orientales *armée*; Decrosne, Ministry *commissaire* at Lille, organiser and recruiter of the Lille *armée*; Delteil, Ministry *commissaire* at Metz, one of the *commissaires civils* to the Moselle Army; Peyrend-d'Herval, *commissaire des guerres* and secretary of the military commission of Bordeaux, the moving force behind the Bordeaux battalion; Boissay, *commissaire des guerres* at Moulins; Alfonce, employed with military supply at Châlons-sur-Marne, *commissaire civil* with the Marne Army; Chartrey, *commissaire des guerres* at Montpellier; Pierre Seigneur, *commissaire des guerres* at Nevers; Vauquoy and Théret, members of the Commission Temporaire of Lyon, creators of the little Crémieu *armée*; Mourgoin, Ministry *commissaire* at Sarrelouis. All these men were Parisians; nearly all were Jacobins or Cordeliers. In addition there were the 'hommes de liaison', natives of other large towns: Picot-Belloc, native of Toulouse and *commissaire des guerres* there; Reybaud from Marseille and Allier from the Drôme, delegates from the Marseille assembly to the Hautes- and Basses-Alpes; the Catalan, Chambon, *commissaire des guerres* at Perpignan.

66 Among the 'local *révolutionnaires*' it is worth noting the members of the *comités de surveillance* of Nevers and Moulins, future *commissaires* with the two battalions; Lapalus and Duret, in the Loire, agents of Javogues; Delthil, *délégué* of Taillefer in the Cantal; the locksmith Contamin at Crémieu; Barjaval, public prosecutor of the Vaucluse; LeBatteux, postmaster of Redon; Civeton, officer in the Roanne National Guard; Marc Dolle, a shady character from La Guillotière; the Doubs terrorists, notably the bailiff Gouvernet, the public prosecutor Rambour, the wine-grower and member of the Ornans *comité*, Etévenon, and the wigmaker Duprey; Bon, a stone-cutter; Robert; and most of all the Clermont-Ferrand artisans who had been so vociferous in their demand for the formation of an *armée* in the Puy-de-Dôme. We will encounter these men once more when we discuss the composition and activities of the departmental *armées*. They can be found in every locality where *armées* were formed, initially noisily demanding their formation and the execution of sweeping measures; then it was often the same men who 'revolutionised', as *commissaires civils*, at the head of these forces. Without the help of these men, the campaign would never have been as widespread as it was.

67 The order of the Gap assembly, 24 Brumaire, refers repeatedly to candidates for the *armée* being chosen 'from the bosom of the popular societies' (Arch. Hautes-Alpes, L 1512). The Ain declared that: 'The *armée révolutionnaire* will be composed of noted republicans, appointed by the departmental administrators from lists sent to them by the popular societies...' (Arch. Ain, 5 L 30, directory of the Montluel district to the Pérouges *société*, 2 Frimaire). The Lille *armée* too was to be made up of patriots from the *société* (Arch. Lille,

18' 229, *société révolutionnaire* of Lille). In the Doubs the Ornans *comité* was to draw up an initial list which would then be presented to the *société* 'where each candidate will be discussed individually to see if he is worthy to hold a position in this glorious troop' (Arch. Doubs, L 2360, *société* of Ornans, 18 Brumaire). See also AN, AF II 114 (859) and Arch. Saône-et-Loire, 4 L 26, *société* of Paray, for similar procedures elsewhere; and P. Gérard, 'L'armée révolutionnaire de la Haute-Garonne', 7–8, commenting on the strictly political character of the Toulouse *armée*, whose men and officers were recommended by the Toulouse Jacobins. At Vienne, the municipality confided the task of recruiting to the *société populaire* (Arch. Vienne, reg. meetings of the municipality, session of 24 Frimaire). At Grenoble the national agent of the commune wrote, 28 Brumaire, asking the *société* to place '100 good sans-culottes' at the disposition of the municipality the following day (Arch. Grenoble, LL 19, General Council, reg. corres.).

Bassal was the inventor of the system of 'core' groups, or nuclei. His order spoke of all the *sociétés* in an arrondissement forming a company, appointing 12 of the most ardent patriots, who would then choose a 13th, the 13th choosing a 14th, and so on until the company had reached 100; '...the companies thus formed would still be subjected to the scrutiny of the popular *sociétés*...' (Sauzay, *La persécution révolutionnaire dans le Doubs*, IV. 305). On receipt of Bassal's order, citizen Vallet (of the Dijon *société*) demanded that 12 candidates be chosen immediately, 'family men, aged over 30', and so indeed they were (Arch. Côte-d'Or, L IV B 9/1, *société* of Dijon, session of 8 Frimaire). On the same day in the Nuits *société*, a member proposed that, in accordance with Vallet's proclamation, 'the *sociétés populaires* of the arrondissement should be invited to join with this *société* right away to organise the inscription for and formation of the four companies of the *armée révolutionnaire* determined by the Côte-d'Or department...' (id., L IV B 14 bis/2). The same process was followed in the Jura (Arch. Jura, 1st reg. Salins *société*). In this department it was the *sociétés* which started sorting out candidates, while the final word rested with the *comités de surveillance* (id., reg. *comité révolutionnaire* of the lower Section of Salins, session of 5 Frimaire). The Lons-le-Saunier *société* ordered, 13 Frimaire, 'that all the *sociétés populaires* of the district be written to' about the formation of such 'core' groups (id., *société* of Lons, only reg.). At Jussey and Gray, all the *sociétés* sent one or two members to the *chefs-lieux* to form such 'cores' – five, one per district, were created, to form the basis of five companies of 100 men each (Arch. Haute-Saône, L 1365, *société* of Jussey, and 361 L 1, *société* of Gray).

68 The order of Javogues and Bassal, 20 Oct, setting up the Loire *armée révolutionnaire*, makes no mention of the *sociétés* (AN, AF II 114 [859]). That of Couthon and his colleagues states: 'This *armée* is to be composed of noted Republicans; they will be nominated by the Departmental Administrators, from lists sent to them by the *sociétés populaires*...' (AN, AF II 124 [946]).

69 Paganel's order of 24 Vendémiaire concerning the formation of the Agen company states that the *comité de surveillance* should form a company composed of 25 sans-culottes (Arch. Lot-et-Garonne, 1st reg., Agen *comité*, session of 25 Vendémiaire). Within two days the company was activated. At Montauban too the *comité* reserved to itself all the details of organisation of the revolutionary battalion (Arch. Tarn-et-Garonne, L 221, *comité* of Montauban, sessions of 27 Sept, 1, 2, 6, 10, 13, 15 and 16 Oct, 8 and 10 Brumaire). Fouché's order of 2 Oct concerning the enrolment of the Allier and Nièvre battalions, assigned the choice of candidates to the Moulins and Nevers *comités de surveillance* (AN, AF II 169 [1387]) – in Moulins there was no question of participation by the *société* in the organising process which followed (Arch. Allier, L 850, Moulins *comité de surveillance*). At Cahors (Arch. Lot, L 389, *comité* of Cahors) and Aurillac likewise, the *comités* took charge of the organisation, and in the case of the latter *comité* its members were also to be the chiefs of the departmental *armée*: Hébrard, president of the tribunal, Milhaud and Boudier, district administrators, Valette the elder, from Salers, former district administrator (Arch. Cantal, L 684, *comité* of Aurillac, and AN, F 7 4555, Cantal, arrests, Boudier dossier). In the Basses-Alpes at Digne, Manosque and Sisteron, the *comités* took full charge; in the Puy-de-Dôme, the Riom *comité* proposed to that of Clermont the formation of a revolutionary battalion (Arch. Puy-de-Dôme, L 6 127, *comité* of Clermont, session of 2 Brumaire).

70 We must distinguish, however, between the *comités de surveillance* officially established by order of the *représentants*, and the *comités révolutionnaires*, formed by the *sociétés* and with no legal backing. But the authorities in the countryside and in the small towns were ignorant

of such subtleties and allowed the latter to assume the functions of a legal *comité*. At Orpierre in the Hautes-Alpes, the *comité* even assumed the title 'comité de surveillance de la société républicaine d'Orpierre'. Nearly all the *comités* of this department fell into this category (Arch. Hautes-Alpes, L 1052, *comité* of Orpierre). Indeed in many small towns and bourgs, two *comités*, the legal and illegal, operated – a sign of the administrative anarchy of the period, and an example as well of the interference of prying *sociétés* in every aspect of local administration. It was also as much a product of ignorance on the part of the local authorities, as of a deliberate plan by the *sociétés* to capture the important police functions which belonged to the *comités de surveillance*. At the 4 Frimaire session of the Orpierre *société*, for example, the president of the *comité* proposed visiting the *auberges* to examine passports, and although one member raised doubts about the authority of the *comité*, it continued to function (Arch. Hautes-Alpes, L 1502). Similar cases can be cited for Montbrison (Arch. Loire, L 432, *comité* of Montbrison, session of 27 Frimaire), and Ecully, Lyon-Campagne district (Arch. Rhône, 32 L 28, *comité* of Ecully). Such cases illustrate the difficulties surrounding the implementation of the law at the lower levels. It was because of such ignorance that the *armées révolutionnaires* proliferated, and the administrative anarchy is the reason why it is so difficult to define with any clarity the responsibility of the different authorities for these new *armées*.

71 AN, AF II 107 (792), order of Tallien and Isabeau, Baudot, Chaudron-Rousseau, 27 Vendémiaire, Article III.

72 Arch. Gironde, 11 L 67–8–9 (*comité de surveillance* of the Bordeaux district). One hundred and sixty underwent the *scrutin épuratoire* of the Bordeaux national club. But this accounted for only half the effective number, the others no doubt being spared the club *scrutin* because they had already passed that of the Sections. Indeed, the lists presented by the Sections did not correspond with the 'scrutinised' list of the club (Arch. Gironde, 11 L 27, Club national).

73 Arch. Gironde, 11 L 9 (general assembly of the 10 Août Section, session of 22 Oct), 11 L 8 (Franklin Section assembly); Arch. Bordeaux, 1 64 (general assembly of the Bon-Accord Section, session of 21 Brumaire), and 1 67 (assembly of the Parfaite-Union Section, session of 23 Oct). In all these cases lists were presented by streets. We do not know if lodging-house inhabitants were excluded, but such a method can only have favoured the resident citizen.

74 Arch. Lille, 18′ 338, enrolment reg. for the 1st Section. In his plan of organisation, Decrosne had foreseen close co-operation between the *société* and the Sections (Arch. Lille, 18′ 229, *société révolutionnaire*, discourse by Decrosne, Brumaire).

75 Arch. Lille, 18′ 338, loc. cit. For example, many candidates were recommended by the Rossignol brothers, manufacturers of the rue de la Vignette and *sociétaires*, and by Auger and Richard, also *sociétaires*, in the 2nd Section (id. 18′ 339, also 18′ 222 for submission of lists to the *comité de surveillance*).

76 Arch. Versailles, D 1 51 (general assembly of the 1st Section); D 1 186 (13th Section); D 1 59 (4th Section); D 1 184 bis (10th); D 1 52 (2nd); D 1 53–4 (4th); D 1 184 (9th). The *scrutins* took place in the Versailles Sections, 7–12 Brumaire.

77 Arch. Allier, L 850 (*comité de surveillance*, Moulins, session of 1 Oct); the *comité* appointed *commissaires* to go on to elections in the Paris, Egalité, Liberté, Bas-Allier, Haut-Allier and Ville Sections. Arch. Jura (reg. of the Salins, Arbois, and Lons-le-Saunier *comités*).

78 Arch. Hautes-Alpes, L 939 (*société populaire* of Gap). In the Briançon district the municipalities made the choice; in Saint-Verant the general assembly of the commune actually elected, rather than simply recommended, two candidates. The district objected to this method because it involved no detailed scrutiny by the municipality (Arch. Hautes-Alpes, L 1082, district of Briançon).

79 AN, F 7 4422 (*comité révolutionnaire* of Nantes) and W 493 (479), trial of Carrier; Arch. Landes, L 783 (*comité* of Dax, session of 30 Pluviôse).

80 Arch. Côte-d'Or, L IVb 14/1–2 (*société populaire* of Nuits-Saint-Georges, session of 20 Frimaire). The mayor of Nuits presented himself as one of the candidates for the 'nucleus'. In the Jura and particularly in the Lons district, the communes chose mainly notables and municipal officers for this group (Arch. Jura, reg. *société populaire* of Lons). At Ornans, one of the principal centres of terrorism in the Doubs, the wine-grower Etévenon, a member of the *comité de surveillance*, put himself forward as a candidate (Arch. Doubs, L 2360, *comité* of Ornans, session of 21 Brumaire). See also J. Meynier, *La Révolution à Ornans*, 81.

81 See, e.g., the collective order of 9 Brumaire (AN, AF II 124 [946]). See also (id.) the order of Simond and Dumas setting up the Mont-Blanc *armée*. The *représentants* did not take into account the *sociétés populaires*, and the enthusiasm – or self-interest – of the sans-culottes. See Arch. Hautes-Alpes, L 1082, for Briançon.

82 See, e.g., on the subject of the commander-in-chief of the Toulouse *armée*, *L'Anti-Terroriste*, no. 51 (18 Thermidor Year III). This paper of the *jeunesse dorée* in Toulouse reserved its main criticisms for the *commissaires civils* of this *armée*.

83 See, e.g., the order of Javogues and Bassal, 20 Oct (AN, AF II 114 [859]), Article IV: 'This revolutionary force will be subject to the demands of the administrative bodies and the municipalities'. The order of Couthon and his colleagues, 9 Brumaire, gave full powers to the *commissaires civils*, of whom there were to be two per department (AF II 124 [846]). Simond and Dumas, on the other hand, opted for the local authorities (AF II 124 [946]). Hérault favoured the predominance of the *commissaire civil* (AF II 136 [1058], order of 24 Brumaire). Article XII of the order from the *représentants* with the Rhine and Moselle Armies entrusted the direction of operations and the right to request the armed force to the *commissaires civils*.

84 Arch. Haute-Saône, L 1365 (*société* of Jussey, session of 23 Frimaire). Projean, charged with the enrolment of the departmental *armée*, announced the dispatch of 1,000 livres to pay the 12-man 'nucleus'. See also Arch. Haute-Saône, 361 L 1 (*société* of Gray, session of 10 Nivôse). In the Mont-Blanc, on the other hand, where the process was slower, no payment had been made to the members of the 'nucleus' (Arch. Savoie, L 1771, Chambéry district, session of 13 Nivôse).

85 Arch. Doubs, L 2358 (*société* of Montbéliard, session of 17 Frimaire), when a subscription was opened which produced 224 livres. In Gap one *sociétaire* offered a gun to arm a volunteer of the *armée* (Arch. Hautes-Alpes, L 939, *société* of Gap, session of 2 Frimaire). At Thonon, Joseph Davet, and another *sociétaire*, offered to pay 100 francs quarterly for the upkeep of four soldiers (*société* of Thonon, session of 19 Frimaire; F. Mugnier, *La société des Jacobins de Thonon*). Such gifts were also one way of manifesting revolutionary conformism. Those *sociétés* which had contributed to the upkeep of the families of *révolutionnaires* were also those which later gave such spectacular backing to the Jacobin cavaliers, and during the summer their names were found heading the subscription lists for the construction of the ship, *Le Vengeur*. Prosperous *sociétaires* found in this a way of justifying wealth which might otherwise have been in conflict with the egalitarian spirit of the sans-culottes.

86 This was already posing serious problems for the poorer and more rural districts, that of Serres, e.g., complaining that even a requisition of arms in the neighbourhood would produce only hunting guns (Arch. Hautes-Alpes, L 1082, district of Serres, corres.).

87 These were Griois, Picot-Belloc and the younger Gau. However, *commissaires des guerres* had been intended for other *armées*; see, e.g., Javogues's order, Article VII (AN, AF II 114 [859]).

88 In the Nièvre, e.g., the enrolment of the revolutionary battalion was the concern of Pierre Seigneur, *commissaire des guerres* at Nevers, a soldier who had been a *commissaire des guerres* before the Revolution (AAG, Cl. gén. 3565 [Seigneur] and Arch. Nièvre [corres. reg. for the Clamecy district] – he is also described as 'commander of the Nevers *armée révolutionnaire*'). He was a member of the Nevers *comité* in April 1793. At Moulins it was Boissay, *commissaire des guerres*, who undertook all the details of organisation of the battalion. In the Haute-Saône, it was the former soldier, Projean, with the rank of lieut.-col. in the *armée révolutionnaire*, who took charge of the organisational details (Arch. Haute-Saône, 261 L 1, *société* of Gray).

89 See, e.g., Chaix, *juge de paix* of the canton of Lormes, Corbigny district (Arch. Nièvre, reg. *comité* of Corbigny, session of 14 Vendémiaire Year III). He was accused of having led 'seditious armed bands, sometimes under the name "Marat" Chaix, once under the title of representative of the people'. See also AN, D III 180 (Comité de législation, Nièvre, Moulins-Engilbert), district session of 27 Frimaire Year III.

90 AN, D III 179 (1) (68) (Comité de législation, Nièvre, Decize). Similar complaints were made by the departmental administrators of the Finistère, who wrote to the *représentant*, Bréard, on 17 Frimaire claiming that *he* was responsible for their powerlessness, or rather the multitude of *délégués* and *commissaires* claiming to act in his name and to possess full powers (AN, AF II 102 [748]).

91 Vauquoy, Théret, Marcellin, Fusil, Marino, Bonnerot, Delan, Sadet, in the area around

Lyon, in the Ain, Isère, Loire and perhaps in the Drôme and Ardèche. See RCC, 'La Commission Temporaire de Commune-Affranchie', App. no. 1, 52–3.

92 Peyrend-d'Herval, *commissaire des guerres* at La Réole, then Bordeaux, and the driving force behind its revolutionary battalion, was also president of the *comité de surveillance* of the Bordeaux district, and secretary of the Commission Militaire. See P. Bécamps, *J. B. M. Lacombe, président de la Commission militaire de Bordeaux* (Bordeaux, 1953).

93 Lémare, president of the Commission Départemental, was the principal organiser of the ephemeral *armée* of the Jura. (See Arch. Jura, reg. Orgelet *comité*, Lémare to the Orgelet district, 21 Brumaire, and P. Libois, *Les représentants Prost et Lejeune dans le Jura*.)

94 Archimbaud, captain in the Loire *armée révolutionnaire* (Saint-Rambert company), sat on the Feurs Commission Militaire, along with Fusil, Lefranc and Marcellin (Arch. Loire, 42 L 163 and L 432, *comité* of Montbrison).

95 The members of this Commission 'Civile-Révolutionnaire' – Lagarde, the doctor Lagasquie and Cléophas Périer – also held simultaneous positions as *commissaires civils* with the Lot *armée*. See below, I. 5, also P. Caron, 'La Commission civile révolutionnaire et de surveillance de l'Aveyron (brumaire–frimaire an II)', *R. F.*, LXXXIV (1931), 336.

96 Grimaud, Delan and Desmazures – members of the Moulins *comité de surveillance*, established by Fouché – as *commissaires civils*, took detachments of the revolutionary battalion into the districts of the Allier, before going to Lyon (Arch. Allier, L 850–2, Moulins *comité de surveillance*). In the Nièvre, the *commissaires civils* appointed by Fouché were nearly all members of the different revolutionary administrations in Nevers. Bompois, a proprietor, Seigneur, *commissaire des guerres* and organiser of this *armée*, and Bureau were members of the *comité de surveillance*, along with two officers of the *armée*, the printer-stationer de Goy, and Pauper (Arch. Nièvre, 20 L 7, *comité* of Nevers, session of 16 Apr 1793). Commerçon, an ex-monk, was a *juge de paix*. Henriot, Bidault, Paumier, Grangier, and the *aubergiste* Gautherot, also *commissaires civils* with this *armée*, seem to have been members of the district or the department. Only one, Chaix, was not from Nevers, being a *juge de paix* in the canton of Lormes (AN, D III 177–81, Comité de législation, Nièvre; F 7 3683 3, Police générale, Nièvre, Year IV; and Arch. Nièvre (great reg. district of Corbigny). For both departments, see below, I. 5.

97 This is neatly summarised in the Lyon petition of May 1793: 'The time has come to put a stop to everything which the people consider unjust...' (Arch. Rhône, 1 L 98 [Département]).

98 The most typical orders listing motives are those of Couthon and his colleagues, those of Bassal, Simond and Dumas, and those of Javogues. Bassal fixed 11 goals for his *armée*: '1, implementation of the Maximum; 2, demolition of châteaux; 3, control of prisoners; 4, pursuit of suspects; 5, searches for arms; 6, taking down of church bells and searches in sacristies for gold and silver objects; 7, search for hidden provisions, hoarders, speculators and those undermining the value of the *assignats*; 8, surveillance of all roads and exits to foreign countries; 9, searches for horses, carriages and fancy harness; 10, establishment and encouragement of *sociétés populaires*; 11, surveillance of Sunday observance, superstitious signs and practices abolished by the Convention...' (Sauzay, *La persécution révolutionnaire dans le Doubs*, IV. 304). See AN, AF II 112 (836), which contains a 12th, 'the search for soldiers of all ranks in the countryside and scrutiny of their papers'. See also AN, AF II 124 (949) and 136 (1058) for the orders of Simond and Dumas, Javogues and Bassal, and Hérault. Hérault also brings to the attention of the *commissaires civils* 'Jews, plague of the country', fishermen and boatmen on the Rhine, guilty of maintaining contact with those on the other bank, smugglers, deserters, foreigners and observers of Sunday. Finally, in its 6 Frimaire session, the Trévoux district summarised all the motives: 'The effect of these *armées révolutionnaires* should be to hasten the progress of the Revolution, so necessary to the triumph of liberty and equality.... It must also undermine aristocratic and priestly intrigues by punishing the plotters, and ensure the supply of the markets by facilitating the circulation of grain, forcing the *égoïste* to think of others, putting an end to hoarding, and finally ensuring the implementation of the Maximum, the scourge of all speculators...' (Arch. Ain, 9 L 5, district of Trévoux).

99 BN, L 41 b 4947 (general assembly of the Saint-Paterne church, session of 9 Sept). See also the outline of a communal *armée* at Orléans (Arch. Orléans, D 23 E).

100 This affair would be invoked at the time of the small Lille counter-revolution, 22–3 Frimaire Year II, and during the proceedings against Dufresse before the revolutionary tribunal in Paris, Year III (AN, W 498 [535]). The statement of charges, 20 Ventôse Year

III, blamed Dufresse for creating an ensign destined 'to inspire a spirit of carnage, anarchy and brigandage in all who joined this corps...' (AN, W 25). On either side of the engraving of a guillotine on wheels were the words: 'The People are tired of Traitors; Terror and the Guillotine are the order of the day' (AN, W 498 [535]). Photographs of the cartouche and seal are reproduced in Gén. Herlaut's article, 'Le général-baron Dufresse'. The national agent of the Bergues district wrote of Dufresse and his officers: 'These scoundrels spoke of nothing but the guillotine...' – undoubtedly a case of wanting 'to strike terror' in order to avoid using it. (See Châles's address to the country people, AHG, B 1 22, Le Révolutionnaire of 18 Brumaire.) None of this was malicious, but Châles's threats, the 'terrifying' discourse of Dufresse, and the paper guillotine supplied abundant ammunition to the Thermidorean judges. Dufresse, however, was acquitted; his guillotine carried no weight.

101 At a session of the Thonon société one member tried to show how useful the arrival of a guillotine would be, which 'with the revolutionary battalion would succeed in annihilating this monstrous horde of Aristocrats and royalists...it has been decided that the société should write to thank the departmental administration for sending us this exterminating Angel...' (F. Mugnier, La société des Jacobins de Thonon, Thonon société, session of 16 Brumaire). See also the petition for an accompanying guillotine from the 13th Versailles Section, Article 5 (Arch. Seine-et-Oise, L 1R 159). 'The revolutionary blade is suspended over the heads of the malveillants', Gobert and Delteil announced in their address to the country people, 14 Brumaire (AHG, B 2 27, Army of the Moselle). In many orders, the enrolment of a revolutionary battalion and the dispatch of a guillotine were announced together, but usually it amounted to no more than a threat – it was moral, rather than active, terrorism.

102 Arch. Seine-et-Oise, L 1R 529 (armée révolutionnaire, petition from the 13th Section, 13–16 Brumaire).

103 id. See also Châles's notice in Le Révolutionnaire (AHG, B 1 22, Army of the Nord).

104 AN, W1 a 493 (479), trial of Carrier. For Jullien's letter, see E. Lockroy, ed., Une mission en Vendée, 153.

105 AN, AF II 185 (1531 and 1533), Paganel to the Committee, 5 Brumaire, and his order of 7 Brumaire.

106 In other orders the emphasis was on economic functions. Reynaud, on mission to Le Puy, declared that an armée révolutionnaire was 'necessary to discover grain and have it circulated inside the Republic' (AN, AF II 186 [1538], Reynaud to the Committee, 14 Frimaire). In the Bas-Rhin, Mallarmé announced the creation of an armée of 1,000 men, with a tribunal and guillotine in its train, destined 'primarily to strike against the égoïstes who...hide or spoil subsistences'; Schneider told the people of Strasbourg that with the armée révolutionnaire 'le glaive exterminateur' would be suspended over the heads of the speculator and the 'égoïste': 'shops would re-open...supplies return to the markets, the Maximum would be strictly applied'. The Sélestat comité complained to the commissaire civil that the Maximum was not being applied: 'Come with your brothers to help us, you will find abundant material for the guillotine...' (Arch. Bas-Rhin, 50 L 6, comité of Sélestat, 23 Brumaire).

The same threats against the country people can be found in the address of the two commissaires civils with the Moselle Army: 'Citizens, you have given your brothers in the towns much to complain of since the law of the Maximum was passed; when you came to them they sold their goods to you at prices fixed by the law and since then the markets have remained empty. Woe betide those who do not hasten to bring their town brothers those gifts of which nature has made them custodians. The armée révolutionnaire will go through all the villages and treat the selfish monsters as enemies of the patrie, just like the Austrians and the Prussians...' (AHG, B 2 27 [Armée révolutionnaire]). Maure, trying to justify himself to Garnier, declared that the object behind his creation of the Yonne armée was 'to ensure food supplies, since their circulation had been hindered...' (Arch. Yonne, L 157, Maure to the department, 7 Frimaire). See also Arch. Savoie, L 1771 (Chambéry district), order of 7 Nivôse; Arch. Evreux, D3, explanation by the municipality, 2 Oct; and Arch. Hautes-Alpes, L 1082 (Briançon district, 5 Frimaire), for the expression of similar sentiments.

107 AAG, Cl. gén. 365 (Boissay), Fouché's printed address to the Moulins comité – cited in RCC, L' armée révolutionnaire à Lyon, 19.

108 'The said Contamin climbed on to the altar...and made it known that he wanted to

impose a tithe before leaving the commune, but it would be the reverse of former tithes, for in houses where he found 100 shirts, he would only take 90...' (Arch. Rhône, 1 Q 637, Séquestres; also RCC, *L'armée révolutionnaire à Lyon*, 59). See also the remarks attributed to Vauquoy during his missions to the Isère (AN, W 523, trial of Vauquoy). See below, II. 5, also the printed address sent by Chastel, commander of the Légion de la Montagne, to the *sociétés populaires*, 17 Brumaire: 'Depart – a Jacobin army will set out to enlighten our camps and terrorise the enemy ranks; it will thwart the plots of the treacherous, and unmask the intriguer; it will bring understanding to those whom ineptitude or ambition has led astray; it will be on the lookout for scoundrels profiting from war to better themselves.... You, Jacobins, are our only hope! No Muscadins! No aristocrats! No rich! *Just as ground that nourishes gold produces neither grass nor plants, so the rich are sterile, fathering only crime*. Sans-Culottes! Sans-Culottes! These are the real defenders of equality...' (AHG, Xk 10). Behind this cry of indignation against the rich lay a programme of repressive action identical with that outlined for many other revolutionary companies.

109 R. Paquet, *Dictionnaire biographique de la Moselle*. Article X of this order stated: 'The special function of this *provisional* [our italics] army concerns the supply of the Rhine and Moselle Armies...'. The order of Couthon and his colleagues saw the other part of the *armée* ensuring the threshing of grain and that supplies reached the stores of the Alps Army (AN, AF II 124 [946]).

110 RCC, 'Les armées révolutionnaires du Midi', and AHG, B 4 10 (Gen. Muller to Bouchotte, 1 Frimaire). 'The *représentants*...have just issued an order for the creation of an *armée révolutionnaire* to suppress some troubles in the neighbouring departments and to ensure the regular supply of the army [Pyrénées-Occidentales].'

111 AHG, B 1 22 (Army of the Nord), address from the Brétecque municipality, 13 Brumaire.

112 id., order of Châles and Isoré, 13 Brumaire. See also J. Annat, *La période révolutionnaire dans les Basses-Pyrénées*, 164. The goal which the *société* set for the battalion was 'to wipe out the evil race of priests', a sentiment echoed also in the Monestier order, assigning the battalion the task of 'defanaticising the communes...at the same time ensuring that all trace of royalism and feudalism is destroyed for good'.

113 Arch. Landes, L 783 (Dax *comité*, session of 30 Pluviôse).

114 BL, F★ 49 (4), statement of charges against Boucher et al.

115 Arch. Seine-et-Oise, L 1R 429; Arch. Landes, L 783.

116 Arch. Bouches-du-Rhône, L 2029 (Aix *société*, session of 2 Pluviôse). In the Jura the Salins *comité* sought guarantees that their men would be permitted to remain at home provided they turned out when required (Arch. Jura, 1st reg., Salins *comité*, session of 12 Brumaire).

117 Arch. Ain, 2 L 43 (Bourg district, session of 4 Frimaire).

118 'We do not want rich farmers, bourgeois, merchants, priests, corrupt or roguish fellows in this *armée*; what we need are sans–culottes, disinterested, fearless, and, if possible, enlightened' (Arch. Jura, Orgelet *comité*, Lémare's circular of 21 Brumaire).

119 The Briançon district asked for 'men who unite good will and rectitude with the qualities of a true and good republican...' (Arch. Hautes-Alpes, L 1082).

120 RCC, *L'armée révolutionnaire à Lyon*, 57 – 'since there are no true sans-culottes among the bourgeoisie', Vauquoy explained, they had been obliged 'to form this small *armée* from poor sans-culottes...'.

121 Arch. Bouches-du-Rhône, L 1813 (Marseille *comité*, interrogation of Mollé, 24 Germinal Year III). Mollé, a 39-year-old shoemaker and former *commissaire* of the *comité* of the Liberté Section (Terreaux) in Lyon, who had fled the massacres, travelled without a passport to Lyon, and gone into hiding, was asked if he had ever worked at his trade whilst occupying the aforesaid position. 'Yes,' he replied, 'I worked for a short time in the morning and again in the evening...'. Most members of the revolutionary companies expected likewise to be only half-time *révolutionnaires*.

122 Arch. Nièvre (Corbigny *comité*, great reg.).

123 Arch. Allier, L 851 (Moulins *comité*, sessions of 5 Frimaire, 23 Nivôse and 6 Pluviôse Year III). Nightly meetings were said to be taking place, designed to incite former revolutionary guards to revolt, and the *comité* was concerned to learn that several former soldiers had retained their pistols. Verd was eventually accused of having said that 'if the *armée révolutionnaire* still existed and those dismissed still held their positions, then wheat would not cost so much...'. On the riot itself see below, III. 1.

124 The accusation that *représentants* or local terrorists had threatened the populace with the

dispatch of the *armée révolutionnaire* was a common one, particularly in the Year III. But even as early as Ventôse Year II, an anonymous inhabitant of Gers denounced Dartigoëyte to the Committee of General Security, accusing him of having appointed Montagnie, a Protestant, as *commissaire civil* in the canton of Mauvezin 'in order to propagate...the terrifying idea of an *armée révolutionnaire* having been formed to punish every faithful Catholic priest with death...' (AN F 7 4662, Dartigoëyte). Likewise in the Aude, Sabatier, a doctor and member of the former *comité de surveillance* of Montréal, was denounced for having terrorised the town with the announcement of an *armée révolutionnaire* and a guillotine (Arch. Aude, L 2136, *comité* of Carcassonne, session of 27 Ventôse Year III). In both instances it was simply a case of threatening to use such a force, for none existed in these departments. See also Mirande's remarks on Taillefer: 'His arrival [in the Lot and Cantal] was preceded by terror and the most absurd rumours. It was said that he was dragging after him a guillotine capable of cutting off seven heads at a time, some called him *Iron arm*, others *Iron-breaker*...' (AN, D III 39 [20] [178], Comité de législation, Cantal, Mauriac, *Dominique Mirande...aux amis de la justice*).

125 See Bassal's order (Sauzay, *La persécution révolutionnaire dans le Doubs*, IV. 304), Article 10: 'the establishment and encouragement of *sociétés populaires*'.

126 AN, AF II 124 (946), order of the *réprésentants* at Lyon, 9 Brumaire – Article 11.

127 The necessity to act quickly was stressed by the *représentants* in their orders. Those in Lyon ordered, on 9 Brumaire, that 'an *armée révolutionnaire*...should be formed within two weeks from today...', revealing thereby either excessive confidence or an excessive sense of optimism. The Saône-et-Loire department witnessed a similar attempt to instil zeal into the districts and the *sociétés*: 'The republican *sociétés* will submit lists...to the departmental directories, four days from the receipt of this order'. In the Haut-Rhin, Hérault ordered the *commissaires civils* 'to check...if the order of the *représentant* concerning the *armée révolutionnaire* had been dispatched and publicised as required by its terms...' (AN, AF II 124 [946], AF II 114 and AF II 136 [1058]).

128 BN, L 41 b 4974; AHG, Xk 10 (Légions); Arch. Indre, L 1582 (*société* of Châteauroux).

129 Take the case of the Légion de la Montagne: its creation dated from the beginning of Sept, its organisation commenced on the 9th, and Avignon was named as the point of assembly for the 25th. But the general assembly of *sociétés populaires* in the Midi, meeting at Marseille, wanted that commune named instead of Avignon, and the ordnance officer, Chauvet, appointed a provisional commander and opened a registration office. The Légion was authorised by the *représentants du peuple* on 11 Brumaire: 'The notice printed...has been circulated to the 86 *procureurs-syndics* in the departments, with an invitation...to have them distributed to all the *sociétés populaires* of their departments. Another circular has been drawn up and sent to all the communes of several departments, by which means volunteers arrive daily in Marseille. The Légion would have been complete now if we had been able to admit others besides those citizens possessed of testimonials to their *civisme* from the *sociétés* or the General Councils of the communes.

'The Administrative Council hopes that the energy of its correspondence with the *procureurs-syndics*, the mayors and municipal officers of the communes and the *sociétés populaires* will soon see the organisation of this Légion, from among the many robust young men under 18, and equally vigorous married men whom the Law does not need.... We can assure you that all those already under arms are genuine sans-culottes, intrepid Jacobins, Montagnards determined to spill the last drop of their blood...' (AHG, Xk 10). By this date the Légion had only 416 officers and men out of a projected total of 2,191, which was never reached. In Vendémiaire Year III, when the Légion was bivouacking on the heights of Villarosa, it was composed of 1,151 officers and men, 556 of whom were present under arms.

130 Arch. Côte-d'Or, Livb 9/1 (*société* of Dijon, session of 8 Frimaire). At Dijon the nucleus was formed on 13 Frimaire (Livb 14 bis/2 [*société* of Nuits, session of 8 Frimaire]). On the 14th the *société* received a request for inscription from a man of 60 (Livb 14/1–2 [*société* of Montbard, session of 20 Frimaire]). On this occasion the *société* invited non-members to join the formation, after having received 42 requests from the *sociétaires* of Montbard and from other *sociétés* in the canton. The directory of the Dijon district only commenced activity on 12 Frimaire, though they had written to Vattel, the *commissaire* for the formation of the *armée*, on the 9th of their eagerness to distribute his order 'to the *sociétés populaires* and the principal places of our arrondissement...' (Arch. Côte-d'Or, L 1529).

131 Arch. Haute-Saône, 361 L 1 (*société* of Gray, session of 21 Brumaire). At Gray, the names

of those forming the nucleus were received on 17 Frimaire. The *société* sent the lists of volunteers to Projean on 19 Frimaire, and on the 27th it learnt of 'the dissolution of *armées révolutionnaires* not ordered by the Convention...' (L 1363 [*société* of Jussey, session of 19 Brumaire]). At Jussey, the nucleus had not yet been appointed on 20 Frimaire. It was formed on the 21st and dissolved on the 24th, following receipt of the *Bulletin*.

132 Arch. Saône-et-Loire, IV L II (*comité* of Cluny, session of 10 Frimaire), when the presence of 'a soldier from the *armée révolutionnaire* of Mâcon' was announced, and IV L 26 (*société* of Paray, session of 29 Brumaire). Further inscriptions were received at the 7 Frimaire session. IV L 10 (*comité* of La Clayette, session of 26 Brumaire).

133 Arch. Ain, 9 L 5 (district of Trévoux, session of 6 Frimaire).

134 Arch. Ain, 2 L 43 (district of Bourg, *société* of Ceyziriat, sessions of 4 and 11 Frimaire). Such slow organisation was a fact of life with subordinate administrations in particular: municipalities, *comités*, even districts. The departments moved quickly to implement the collective order of 9 Brumaire, 13 Brumaire in the Loire, 14th in the Isère, Haute-Saône and the Rhône (AN, AF II 111 (830), AF II 114 (859), AF II 137 (1061) and AF II 138 (1073).

135 Arch. Ain, 5 L 30 (district of Montluel, session of 2 Frimaire).

136 F. Mugnier, *La société des Jacobins de Thonon* (sessions of the Thonon *société*). Arch. Savoie, L 1769 (district of Chambéry, sessions of 19, 26, 28 Brumaire; 5, 6, 15 and 26 Frimaire).

137 The first Isère proclamation is dated 15 Brumaire, which the order of 23 Brumaire simply expanded on. On 9 Frimaire, Marceau, *commissaire civil* of the *armée révolutionnaire* of the Grenoble district, put in a brief appearance at the municipality of Vienne (Arch. Vienne, reg. municipality).

138 Arch. Vienne (reg. sittings of the Vienne municipality, 30 Aug 1793 – 24 Frimaire Year II, fol. 92). 'The municipality announced today to the roll of drums, the opening of a register at the *société populaire* for citizens wishing to serve in the Revolutionary Battalion. Good citizens were therefore invited to come along...'. Canon Pierre Cavard, the historian of Vienne, had the kindness to tell me of this extract, for which I am deeply grateful.

139 Arch. Grenoble, LL 19, the national agent of the commune of Grenoble to the commander of the National Guard, 16 Brumaire.

140 Arch. Grenoble, LL 19, the municipality to the president of the *société populaire*, 28 Brumaire. Arch. Isère, L 870 (*comité de surveillance* of Grenoble, session of 12 Frimaire). The company was still in activity on 15, 16 and 23 Frimaire.

141 Arch. Basses-Alpes, L 752 (*comité* of Digne), L 778 (*comité* of Manosque), L 806 (*comité* of Oraison), L 821 (*comité* of Sisteron), L 848 (*société* of Digne), L 852 (*société* of La Mure).

142 Arch. Hautes-Alpes, L 1512 and 939 (*société* of Gap), L 1506 (*comité* of Serres, session of 25 Frimaire). The Briançon district directory also insisted on the necessity of moving quickly, writing on 5 Frimaire to the municipalities to remind them that they had to have their candidates, 'with their arms in good order, here by Sunday at the latest, so that the company can be organised and put into action...' (Arch. Hautes-Alpes, L 1082). On the 8th the Serres district reported delays, but its company was in action by the end of the month (id., L 1350).

143 Arch. Nièvre (district of Clamecy, reg. deliberations, session of 6 Sept); the lieut.-col. of the Nièvre revolutionary legion presented himself with a commission dated 21 Aug for the organisation of the legion from volunteers and deserters from the new requisition.

144 RCC, *L'armée révolutionnaire à Lyon*, 19.

145 Arch. Allier, L 850 (*comité de surveillance* of Moulins, sessions of 1, 2, 3 and 5 Oct). These first missions took place on 8, 10 and 11 Oct, and the *comité* was able to report proudly to Fouché: 'The *armée révolutionnaire* goes out every day, yesterday we sent a detachment of 50 men to Burges-les-Bains...' (id., L 833, *comité* of Moulins, corres. reg.). On 17 Oct Grimaud took a detachment to Cérilly. On the elections in the Sections see also Arch. Allier, L 893 (*armée révolutionnaire*, bureau militaire, session of 3 Oct). At this session the members of two companies were appointed, and the following day, 4 Oct, some members of the general staff. On the 6th, 86 citizens were registered and a further 24 on the 9th. The cannoneers underwent the *scrutin* on 21 Vendémiaire, the cavalry on the 30th. Elections went ahead at Nevers with equal rapidity (Arch. Nièvre, 20 L 7, *comité* of Nevers).

146 At Lille speed was of the essence, for a number of young soldiers conscripted from the Somme were being incorporated into the companies, as well as the Lille artisans and inhabitants. On the delays caused by the authorities of Cambrai and Douai, see AN,

W 498 (535) (trial of Dufresse, Adhémar to Dufresse, 23 Frimaire); see also his letter of 12 Frimaire.

147 AHG, B2 27 (Army of the Moselle, Delteil to the Minister, from Metz, 22 Brumaire). As early as 16 Brumaire the General Council of the Metz commune invited the *commissaires civils* to send a detachment to protect the market area (Arch. Metz, ID 1 13, General Council, session of 16 Brumaire).

148 AN, W1a 493 (479) (trial of Carrier), order of Carrier and Francastel, 9 Brumaire, and F 7 4422 (*comité révolutionnaire* of Nantes, *Mémoire justificatif du comité fait par P. Chaux, membre*, 15 Messidor Year II). In a letter of 22 Brumaire to the *comité*, Carrier declared the company operational (id., T 492 1).

149 AN, D 111 91 d2 (61) (Comité de législation, Haute-Garonne, Toulouse).

150 The Cahors *comité* dealt with the enrolment of the *armée* in its session of 19 Sept; it was in action by 7 Oct (Arch. Lot, L 389, *comité* of Cahors). Likewise the Aurillac *comité* put a detachment of the Cantal *armée* into action (14 Oct) only five days after first discussing its enrolment (9 Oct) (Arch. Cantal, L 684, *comité* of Aurillac).

151 Arch. Lot, L 389 (*comité* of Cahors, session of 5 Frimaire). The record for speed must go to the small company of Agen, 25 strong: its enrolment was ordered by Paganel on 24 Vendémiaire, a list opened by the *comité* on the 25th and filled the same day, and it was in action by the 27th. But then such a small company experienced few administrative problems (Arch. Lot-et-Garonne, Agen *comité*, 1st reg.). The Montauban battalion, with 500 men, was raised almost as quickly. The battalion was initiated on 27 Sept, immediately on receipt of Baudot's order (of the 22nd); elections took place 1–10 October, and the battalion was in action by the 13th (Arch. Tarn-et-Garonne, L 221, *comité* of Montauban). Indeed Baudot's order seems to have been inspired by a letter from this *comité* on 21 Sept (id., L 224).

152 AHG, B4 31 (Army of the Pyrénées-Orientales), B4★ 41 (*ordres du jour*, garrison of Toulouse) and Arch. Tarn-et-Garonne, L 224 (Montauban *comité* to the Toulouse *comité*, 18 Frimaire, concerning a volunteer from the 8th Dordogne battalion).

153 As early as 23 Oct, Pierre-Antoine Descombes, charged by Article XXVIII of Bassal and Javogues's order with the enrolment of the Loire *armée*, took up his duties at Saint-Etienne (J.-B. Galley, *Saint-Etienne et son district pendant la Révolution* [Saint-Etienne, 1903–4], II. 36). On the Roanne circular see AN, F 7 4648 d 4 (Civeton).

154 Arch. Loire, 42 L 157 (municipality of Bonnet-la-Montagne to the Montbrison *comité*, 16 Brumaire); id., L 432 (Montbrison *comité*). On 7 Frimaire, the *comité* instructed the 'commander of the revolutionary force' to arrest a noble.

155 Arch. Loire, L 399 (Charlieu *societé*, session of 10 Frimaire).

156 Arch. Loire, 42 L 163 (Capt. Archimbaud, writing from Saint-Rambert, to the Military Commission of Feurs, 12 Frimaire).

157 AN, F 7 4648 d 4 (Civeton). The companies mentioned in the disbanding process of 13 Ventôse were those of Ferréol (Commune-d'Armes), Montagne (Saint-Chamond), Châtain (Rive-de-Gier), Revolier (Commune-d'Armes), Martin (Montbrison), Civeton (Roanne), Archimbaud (Saint-Rambert), the commune of Sury-la-Chaux. See J.-B. Galley, *Saint-Etienne et son district pendant la Révolution*, II. 551.

158 The execution of Bassal's order was, however, confided to energetic *révolutionnaires* and zealous officials: Robert, municipal officer of Besançon, for the Doubs *armée*; Vallet, department administrator, for that of the Côte-d'Or; Gouvernet, a bailiff, that of the Jura; Projean, lieut.-col., that of the Haute-Saône; Convers, *procureur* for the commune of Bourg, for the Ain *armée*; and Melge, of Porrentruy, that of the Mont-Terrible (AN, AF II 112 [836]). As we have seen, these men wasted no time taking up their duties, and on many occasions they sought to increase the zeal of lower administrative bodies.

159 The collective order of 9 Brumaire made an exception: article XIV read: 'pay will be the same as that of other volunteers, but made in *assignats* rather than in kind...' (AN, AF II 124 [946]). Simond's order of the same date is less clear, article VII declaring that in matters of pay, administration, etc., the battalion would be subject to the National Convention's decrees for the organisation of the national volunteers (AN, AF II 124 [949]).

160 See the order of Javogues and Bassal, article X – pay to be taken from sequestrated property (AN, AF II 114 [859]). See also the order of Bassal at Besançon, XXI, saying the same thing (AN, AF II 112 [836]).

161 Arch. Allier, L 850 (Moulins *comité*, session of 17 Frimaire). 'One of the members said that

following Fouché's order...of 5 Vendémiaire...an *armée révolutionnaire* was to be formed...the pay would be 3 livres per day and would be taken out of funds supplied by the rich ...'; the *comités de surveillance* of the Gannat, Cusset, Val-Libre, Montmarault, Cérilly and Montluçon districts had to pay 50,000 livres each, out of the 'revolutionary *taxes*', and within the week, into the charities fund of the central committee. By 3 Pluviôse the *comité* was complaining of the enormous expense of paying for the detachment at Lyon, and proposed writing to Fouché 'to ask him to find means of reducing this expense...'.

162 On 9 Ventôse the Moulins *comité*, claiming that such exorbitant pay (3 livres per day) diverted funds from the poor, ordered that in future the 290 wives of those *révolutionnaires* on detachment to Lyon would receive only 30 sols per day. On the 12th the *comité* learnt that these women had written, calling upon their husbands to return because their wives were not paid enough, and ordered that the authors of these letters be found out. (Arch. Allier, L 850, Moulins *comité*, sessions of 9, 11 and 12 Ventôse.) The *société* condemned the women for being 'too concerned with their own interests' to be content with the same assistance afforded the families of 'our brothers, the brave volunteers' (id., L 901, Moulins *société*, session of 10 Ventôse). On 4 Pluviôse the *comité* complained to Fouché that pay amounted to 30,600 livres per month – 'an enormous expenditure'. All told, the Moulins authorities had to pay out 200,328 livres for the upkeep of the soldiers and their wives between October and Frimaire (Arch. Allier, L 894). It was indeed a luxury army.

163 Arch. Allier L 850 (Moulins *comité*, session of 21 Vendémiaire). It was ordered that the soldiers should receive an extra allowance of 50 sols per day, when they had to travel more than three leagues and were obliged to take lodging.

164 Monestier's order of 27 Pluviôse complained of the 'exorbitant pay of 30 sols for each fusilier', and the cost of 60,000–70,000 livres per year for the armed force of Dax (Arch. Landes, L 783, *comité* of Dax, session of 30 Pluviôse).

165 Boisset wrote to the Committee on 9 Nivôse: 'At Montpellier, the law suppressing the revolutionary battalions caused discontent amongst their members. They were individual despots, and were so no longer; they had 40 sols per day and now had nothing. They had reason to protest...' (AN, AF II 186 [1543]).

166 See Monestier's observations to this effect (Arch. Landes, L 783). On 16 Nivôse the Moulins *comité* demanded the return of its soldiers from Lyon, for work equipping and clothing the volunteers (Arch. Allier, L 850). On 1 Pluviôse it forbade the departure of shoemakers to the detachment, and on 8 Ventôse it received a complaint from the hatmaker, Bernard, that his work for the army 'could not be carried out for want of workers, most of whom had left with the *armée révolutionnaire* for Commune-Affranchie...'. On 18 Ventôse an order of Fouché was announced liberating Moulins iron-workers from the *armée* – Moulins had an iron foundry run by Brillantais, and in this commune the creation of an *armée révolutionnaire* had a particularly disastrous effect on war production.

167 The district of Serres, in a letter to Beauchamp, pin-pointed exactly one of the main weaknesses of the *armées révolutionnaires*: 'it is difficult to believe that this army, operating so close to its home base, will be as effective as expected...' (Arch. Hautes-Alpes, L 1350, district of Serres). Even the prospect of service within reach of their homes deterred some candidates, and at Briançon two farmers from Saint-Véran, elected to the company, declared 'that they could not accept this honour, as they had large families, still young, who would be reduced to beggary if they left...' (id., L 1082, district of Briançon).

168 Arch. Allier, L 850 (Moulins *comité*, session of 7 Oct), ordering such a proclamation, after Denis Barnier Tournengeot, a slate roofer, was 'accused of having said that the soldiers of the *armée révolutionnaire* would not earn an écu for staying at home, that they would be sent hither and thither at first and then to the Vendée...of having said further that they would pay him 6 livres per day for not enrolling, and that he would bet two corsets [!] that they would be sent to the Vendée'. The *comité* issued a warrant against this 'defeatist'. But despite these precautions the rumours continued, and Boitin, a tailor, was denounced by the commander of the National Guard for having said to Martinant, a wigmaker, 'that he had acted unwisely in enrolling in the *armée révolutionnaire*, not knowing where it would take him, Lyon first, then Toulon and perhaps to England, and saying other things designed to deter citizens from enrolling in the revolutionary guard...' (Arch. Allier, L 850). The same rumours were rife at Nevers, where on 6 Frimaire the *comité* received a denunciation against one inhabitant for having said 'that the revolutionary guard was

meant for the department and not for Lyon...' (Arch. Nièvre, 20 L 7, Nevers *comité*, session of 6 Frimaire).

169 Arch. Versailles, D1 184^b (Vertu-Sociale *societé*, session of 8 Brumaire); AN, AF II 169 (1387), Fouché's order of 2 Oct 1793.

170 Arch. Ain, 5 L 30 (reg. Montluel district directory), the district to the Pérouges *societé*, 2 Frimaire; Arch. Cote-d'Or, L IVb 9/1 (Dijon *societé*, session of 8 Frimaire). Arch. Hautes-Alpes, L 1082; Arch. Yonne, L 803 (district of Avallon, list of citizens enrolled for the *armée révolutionnaire*).

171 Arch. Jura (reg. Salins *comité de surveillance*, session of 9 Frimaire); Arch. Haute-Garonne, L 4553 (Toulouse *societé*, session of 26 Frimaire).

172 Arch. Lille, 18′ 339 (reg. 2nd Section for the *armée révolutionnaire*, 14 Brumaire). Arch. Côte-d'Or, L IVb 14 b/2 (Nuits-Saint-Georges *société*, session of 14 Frimaire); the man was permitted to enter a company of veterans. Arch. Versailles, D1 51 (1st Section, session of 7 Brumaire); a 57-year-old was also rejected on health grounds.

173 Arch. Lille, 18′ 340 (6th Section, *armée révolutionnaire*). The shoemaker Delobel was 50, Voermans, a Belgian tailor, 67, Laumondé, a grocer, 58.

174 Arch. Versailles, D1 51, 54, 186 (Sections). In addition, 7 candidates were between 25 and 29, 3 were only 17, and only 2 were the age of the first requisition.

175 Arch. Haute-Saône, L 1363 (Jussey *société*, session of 19 Brumaire); the man was Pierre Rigoulet. Arch. Indre, L 1582 (Châteauroux *société*, session of 16 Sept).

176 AN, W1a 493 (trial of Carrier), list of members of the Marat company, and APP, A A/269 (notes of Topino-Lebrun). We have the ages of 28 members of this company. See below, l. 5.

177 AHG, Xk 10 (Légions and corps francs). The Légion de la Montagne, headquarters claimed, had 'many young men, strong, robust, below the age of 18, and married men, equally vigorous, which the law does not require...'.

178 Arch. Lille, 18′ 338, 18′ 339, 18′ 340 (1st, 2nd and 6th Sections): Joseph Dumont, 17, son of an innkeeper; Aimable Dumont, 17, son of a master cooper; Joseph Loyez, 17, a volunteer in the 1st Lille battalion, etc. Arch. Versailles, D1 51, 54, 186 (Versailles Sections).

179 E. Leleu, 'Le général Dufresse et l'armée révolutionnaire du Nord'. On 18 Brumaire Isoré decided to permit such recruiting because the projected 1,000 could not be achieved. By this means, young soldiers found their way into the *armée*. See also AN, W25 (1511), deposition of J. Bâcle, 1 Nivôse Year II: '...I said to him [Lavalette] that I found it strange to see only volunteers from the different corps, that it was robbing Peter to pay Paul...', and Arch. Lille, 18′ 340 (6th Section).

180 Over 40 volunteers of the Somme battalion, and 126 soldiers in all joined the companies of the 1st, 2nd and 6th Sections (Arch. Lille, 18′ 338 – 18′ 340).

181 Arch. Lille, 18′ 229 (*société révolutionnaire* of Lille, *Réflexions de Denis Bourdon, commissaire des guerres, à la société populaire* [Lille, printed 25 Frimaire Year II]).

182 AN, W 25 (1511), deposition of Bâcle.

183 RCC, 'Les armées révolutionnaires du Midi', 32.

184 Arch. Lot, L 415 (Gourdon *comité*, session of 12 Brumaire). 'The young men [deserters from the *armée révolutionnaire*] were unable to hide themselves because all males between the ages of 18 and 25 were conscripted throughout the Republic'; also AN, AF II 116 (877), order of the Lot department, 20 Brumaire, provisionally suspending the call-up of young men between 18 and 25 for the first requisition, since many were already in service with the Lozère *armée révolutionnaire*, some even as officers.

185 See P. Gérard, 'L'armée révolutionnaire de la Haute-Garonne', and RCC, 'Les armées révolutionnaires du Midi'.

186 AN, D III 132 (Comité de législation), Martin, *juge de paix* of Cahors, to the Committee, 27 Germinal Year III. He spoke of 'labourers, artisans, farmers, wine-growers of recognised probity, torn from their hearths in the first days of the wine harvest... forced...to abandon their wives and children without support'.

187 Orders creating the large *armées* did try to subject them to military discipline; see, e.g., article XVII of Javogues's order and article XXIII stipulating military exercises once a week (AN, AF II 114 [859]). See also article VII of Simond's order.

188 Martin, *juge de paix* of Cahors, spoke in the Year III of 15,000 having been in the Lot *armée* (AN, D III 132, Comité de législation, Cahors), cited in RCC, 'Les armées révolutionnaires du Midi', 45. The younger Gau wrote from Gourdon to the Toulouse

société on 20 Sept: '...Our *armée* is composed of 3,000 infantry, 200 cavalry...' (*Journal révolutionnaire de Toulouse*, no. 111 [3 Oct 1793]). If we add the Cantal *armée*, which joined that of the Lot in the Aveyron, the total number would have fallen not far short of 5,000 men.

189 The Haute-Saône contingent – 500, in 5 companies (Arch. Haute-Saône, L 1363, Jussey *société*, session of 15 Frimaire); the Doubs – 600 (Sauzay, *La persécution révolutionnaire dans le Doubs*, IV. 304); the Jura –300, 50 men per district (P. Libois, *Les représentants Prost et Lejeune dans le Jura*, 7). The departments of the Côte-d'Or and the Ain had the right to 400 men each (see Appendix A, Table 1). We do not know if the Mont-Terrible contingent was 100.

190 The order of Couthon and his colleagues authorised the enrolment of 10 *armées* of 1,000 men each in the departments of the Ain, Jura, Côte-d'Or, Haute-Saône and Saône-et-Loire (AN, AF II 114 [859]), the Rhône, Loire, Isère, Mont-Blanc and Drôme (AN, AF II 124 [946]).

191 R. Paquet, *Dictionnaire biographique de la Moselle*.

192 AN, F 7 4648 d 4 (Civeton).

193 See P. Gérard, 'L' armée révolutionnaire de la Haute-Garonne', for the numbers in the Toulouse *armée*; and Appendix A, Table 1, for those of Redon.

194 *Le Père Duchesne*, no. 344: '...the only way of establishing the Maximum is to send strong detachments into every department...'.

195 See, e.g., the observant comments of the contemporary English historian, William Playfair (whose hostility to the Revolution in no way clouded his judgement), in *The History of Jacobinism. Its Crimes, Cruelties and Perfidies* (London, 1795), 613: 'The Revolutionary army...was intended to enforce obedience...; but so great was the dismay which these rigorous measures had occasioned, that force was not necessary, a few soldiers, who were at the command of the commissaries, were sufficient to exact the most absolute obedience in the hardest of cases...'.

196 Another characteristic common to nearly all the *armées* – except the large forces formed just behind the frontiers – was their democratic and egalitarian qualities. The order of Javogues and Bassal on 20 Oct stated that the officers could only wear woollen epaulettes, that their uniforms should be the same as those of the men, and that they should also eat with the men. With the exception of the order of Simond and Dumas, stating that the commander-in-chief should himself appoint his officers, in concert with the districts, all orders envisaged the election of officers by their men. Everything was done to prevent the 'militarisation' of these armies, and the net effect of such provisions was reduce the authority of the officer and raise that of the *commissaire civil* accordingly.

197 See, e.g., Sauzay, *La persécution révolutionnaire dans le Doubs*, IV. 305: 'This monstrous creation, in which the odious and the ridiculous seemed to reach their apogee, was the triumph of the clubs. Never had their subversive authority been so solemnly recognised, nor honoured with such *éclat*'.

198 Arch. Rhône, 42 L 19 (Commission révolutionnaire), municipality of Saint-Rambert to the department, 27 Frimaire).

199 Arch. Rhône, 33 L 29 (Denicé *comité*, session of 23 Frimaire).

200 *Journal de la Montagne*, no. 23 (25 Frimaire). See above, p. 153, for the exploits of the 'bande à Nicolas', a bogus revolutionary army operating around Montfort-l'Amaury; see also below, II. 7.

201 AN, D III 282 (437) (Comité de législation, Versailles). See also Prudhomme in *Les Révolutions de Paris*, no. 219 (27 Frimaire Year II), under the heading 'Derniers et vains efforts des ennemis de la république': '...no sooner had a revolutionary army of 6,000 men been decreed for Paris than brigands took the name and uniform and went through the departments kidnapping, pillaging, assassinating and raping, thus compromising in such a horrible manner the good intentions of the legislator, and causing him to be cursed and despised...'.

202 AHG, B2 27 (Army of the Moselle, printed notice dated 23 Brumaire).

203 AN, F7 4394 d2 (papers found at Vincent's residence: Gateau to Vincent). Gateau was referring to the soldiers of Schneider's army.

204 W. Playfair, *History of Jacobinism*, 614: 'These miseries of the people were not a little augmented by numbers of false commissaries, who committed the same excesses as the true; and as nobody dared ask a commissary to shew his powers, those vexations went on almost without either discovery or punishment...'.

205 Playfair, op. cit., 612, also recognised the administrative problem posed by the proliferation of *commissaires* with enormous powers, even if, like the Thermidorean witnesses, he likened these men to outright bandits: 'Besides the clubs which were so numerous, and which were centers of reunion everywhere for the robbers, there were estimated to have been about 50,000 [!] agents of one sort or another, going about like roaring lions, seeking whom they might devour. Barère complained in the convention, that besides these regular and good agents, there were men in red bonnets, with pantaloons and long sabres, who collected the taxes, and put the money received in their pockets. He supposed these tax gatherers to be Hébertists.... The frogs and locusts sent amongst the Egyptians were not near so terrible, and they could not be much more numerous, than the patriotic banditti who desolated France.'

Chapter 5

1 AN, W 498 (535), trial of Dufresse. Candidates, wrote the Briançon district in a letter of 13 Frimaire, should 'unite the qualities of good will and rectitude with that of good republicans...' (Arch. Hautes-Alpes, L 1082, district of Briançon, corres.).

2 Arch. Châlons, I 199 (Châlons *société*), letter from the Vitry *société*, 4 Nivôse Year II.

3 See I. 4, pp. 173 and 179 on the role of Decrosne and the Lille *société* in recruitment for the *armée révolutionnaire* of the North; see also the circular of Lémare cited above: 'Neither rich farmers, nor bourgeois, nor priests, nor venal men, nor rogues...'.

4 On the Rossignols see Arch. Lille, 18' 338 (*armée révolutionnaire*, 1st Section); for Dorez, see E. Leleu, 'Le général Dufresse et l'armée révolutionnaire du Nord'; Arch. Lille, 18' 081 (General Council of the Lille commune) for Cuigniez, and Arch. Lille, 18' 338 for Menteur.

5 AAG, Cl. gén. 570 (Calmet-Beauvoisins). We will return to this young man, a perfect weathervane.

6 AAG, Cl. gén. 937 (Defferrez).

7 AAG, Cl. gén. 9 (Adhémar) and 13 (Agut); Arch. Nord, L 10227 (Lille *société*) for d'Hollande and Christol; AAG, Cl. gén. 485 (Braëmt) and 1792 (Griois).

8 In Brumaire Benoît, who was called Louis, assumed the forename Fargeau.

9 Arch. Bordeaux, I 64 (Bon-Accord Section).

10 Arch. Bordeaux, I 66–7 (Parfaite-Union Section).

11 Arch. Nièvre, 20 L 7 (Nevers *comité*).

12 AN, F 7 4648 d 4 (Civeton).

13 Arch. Allier, L 900–1 (Moulins *société*).

14 At Toulouse the high command was entirely supplied by *sociétaires* from Toulouse and Beaumont; and so close and personal were the links between the *société* and the Toulouse *armée* that in Nivôse, when the *représentants* criticised the lack of patriotism of Gélas and the other military chiefs who hung back from re-engaging in the Pyrénées-Orientales Army, the *société* felt that its own reputation was being called into question. See P. Gérard, 'L'armée révolutionnaire de la Haute-Garonne', and below, III. 1.

15 See RCC, 'Les armées révolutionnaires du Midi'.

16 Arch. Marne, L 2561 (Châlons *société,* Terrorists), reg. Sainte-Ménehould *comité de surveillance*; and AN, D § 1, 6 (mission of Albert in the Marne, Year III).

17 Arch. Nièvre (great reg. Corbigny *comité de surveillance*).

18 See I. 4, n. 68. For Pontarlier, see Sauzay, *La persécution révolutionnaire dans le Doubs*, IV. 305.

19 J. Mandoul, 'Le club des Jacobins de Carcassonne', *R.F.*, XXV (1893), 241.

20 Prudhomme, v. 478.

21 AN, AF II 124 (collective order of 9 Brumaire); AF II 136 (1058), *Instructions données aux commissaires civils de l'armée révolutionnaire du Haut-Rhin*, 2 Frimaire Year II.

22 P. Gérard, 'L'armée révolutionnaire de la Haute-Garonne', 22.

23 W. Playfair, *History of Jacobinism*, 612.

24 H. Riouffe, *Mémoires d'un détenu pour servir à l'histoire de la tyrannie de Robespierre* (Year III), 30.

25 W. Playfair, *History of Jacobinism*, 612.

26 See, e.g. AN, D III 181(1) (139), the director of the *jury d'accusation* of the Nièvre to the Comité de législation, 20 Vendémiaire Year IV; Arch. Vaucluse, L VI 4, Orange *comité*; and AN, D § 1, 6 (Terrorists, Marne).

27 Here is a list of *commissaires civils* with the departmental *armées* – those whose names we know – which, while not exhaustive, serves to demonstrate the scale of the phenomenon:

Moselle	Gobert and Delteil, Dosda, Remoissenet, Arnoule, Ladoucette
Bas-Rhin	Schneider and Elvert Taffin and Wolf (circulating judges)
Haut-Rhin	Moget, Crevat, Berger and Lavie
Marne	Alfonce, Belpêche, Depoix, Gambert, Leclerc, Lemaître, Tessier and Villers
Loiret	Parmentier, Pignon and Rousseau
Morbihan	Le Batteux
Aube	Rousselin
Nièvre	Bompois, Bonnerot, Bureau, Commerçon, Chaix, Dumont, Enfer, the brothers Gautherot, Grangier, Gobet, Henriot, Guyon, Lelong, Pauper, Richard, Millet, Sadet, Seigneur, Vilain
Allier	Agar, Delan, Desmazures, Grimaud, Griveau, Marcillat, Perrotin, Roland, Thiriot, Tortel, Verd
Jura	Lémare, Riqueur
Doubs	Millet
Isère	Vauquoy, Dolle, Menu and Pierrey
Puy-de-Dôme	Ribeyroux (?) – a problematic case
Haute-Loire	Galavelle (?) – a problematic case
Gironde	Peyrend-d'Herval, Sabatier, Labernade
Haute-Garonne and Ariège	Allard, Blanchard, Baby, Descombels, Dirat, Brobrisse, Groussac, Hugueny, Lapujade, Monestier, Picot-Belloc, Picquié, Resnier
Lot	Viton, Lagasquie, Lagarde, Martel, Duprat (?)
Aveyron	Mouly, Poux, Verdier, Lagarde, Périer
Cantal	Delthil, Salsac, Vallette, Alary
Lozère	Martin
Aude	Lacroix
Lot-et-Garonne	Jouan (?) – a problematic case
Hérault	Bancal, Chauvet, Langlade
Drôme	Allier, Figuet
Vaucluse	Nicolaud

28 See, e.g., H. Riouffe, *Les Souvenirs d'un Jeune Prisonnier ou Mémoires sur les Prisons de la Force et du Plessis* (Year III), 6, referring to 'a swarm of young, black-haired and foul-smelling officials...'. Riouffe describes the 'chef de la bande' who accompanied them as 'a man with black, crinkly, Jacobite hair, a bilious countenance, heavy jaw, enormous paunch and the mysterious air of a satellite of Renoir and Sartine...'.

29 AN, D § 1, 6 (Marne, Terrorists); H. Riouffe, *Mémoires d'un détenu*, 26.

30 Arch. Saône-et-Loire, L IV 10 (Salornay *comité* to that of La Clayette, Messidor Year III).

31 *Mémoires d'un détenu*, 21: 'It was for this reason that the French were abandoned...', Riouffe observes.

32 Prudhomme, VI. 110: 'Toulon and Marseille...have in all ages been the refuge of brigands fleeing the justice of neighbouring states, Catalonia, Corsica, Italy, Turkey and Barbary.... This class of men, living constantly in the shadow of crime, would gladly embrace every convulsive movement...'.

33 See RCC, 'Quelques aspects de la mentalité révolutionnaire'.

34 AN, D § l, 6 (Marne, Terrorists); AN, F 7 4444 d 5.

35 See, e.g., article VI of the collective order of 9 Brumaire stipulating that *commissaires* should be strangers to the departments to which they were to be sent (AN, AF II 124).

36 AN, F 7 4444 d 5.

37 See E. Hamel, 'Euloge Schneider', *R.F.*, XXXIV (1898).

38 See Prudhomme, VI. 517: 'For centuries a slow, hidden fire smouldered within the sect, and the revolution was the product of a resentment...which had come down to individuals from their ancestors...'.

39 See RCC, 'Les débuts de la déchristianisation à Dieppe: note sur les origines du

mouvement déchristianisateur en province', *A.h.R.f.*, avril-juin 1956, for examples of such accusations in the Nièvre and Gers.

40 Duprat, a Swiss pastor in Montauban, was to be denounced in Messidor Year III by the Montauban *société*, as a *taxateur* and enemy of the rich (AN, D III 70 d 36, petition from the *société* to the Convention, 5 Messidor Year III). But it is impossible to discover if he was the *commissaire* with the revolutionary company of this town. Undoubtedly some of the Montpellier *commissaires* were Protestants, but we can say nothing definite in their case either. Jouan, mayor of Tonneins, a *société* personality and member of the *comité de surveillance*, who headed the Tonneins revolutionary company in some repressive operations, was probably a Protestant (Arch. Lot-et-Garonne, great reg. Tonneins *société*, and AN, F 7 3681 d 11, denunciations against the terrorists of Tonneins, 11 Brumaire Year III).

41 From the ARTISAN AND SMALL-BUSINESS world: Gautherot, *aubergiste* of Nevers; Laporte, an innkeeper, of Moulins; Sadet, a *bouquiniste* and bookseller of Nevers; Richard, a joiner of Nevers; the other Gautherot, a shopkeeper of Nevers; Depoix, a ropemaker of Châlons-sur-Marne; Lemaître, a carpenter of Châlons; Belpêche, a herbalist of Sézanne; Pierrey, a hatter of Bourgoin (Isère); Verdier, a shopkeeper of Villefranche-d'Aveyron; Remoissenet, a master hatter of Metz; Dosda, a furrier of Metz; Nicolaud, a printer, of Orange; Labernade, a blacksmith, of La Réole; Allier, a joiner, of Valence; Riqueur, a saddler, of Lons-le Saunier (16 in all).

42 MEN OF THE LAW: Rolland, of Moulins; Perrotin, ex-presidial judge of Moulins; Gélas, former *feudiste*, then a geometer and surveyor, employed in the departmental administration of the Haute-Garonne; Choix, *juge de paix* of the canton of Lormes, district of Corbigny; Hugueny, ex-*procureur* of Toulouse; Blanchard, former clerk, of Toulouse; Descombels, former attorney, of Toulouse; Brobrisse, clerk of the Toulouse tribunal; Lapujade, former clerk of the Toulouse criminal tribunal; Massiac, a clerk of Rieux (Haute-Garonne); Mouly, *juge de paix* of Villefranche-d'Aveyron; Salsac, valuer and *notaire*, of Aurillac; Valette, ex-*procureur* of Aurillac; Alary, former solicitor, of Aurillac; Galavelle, *juge de paix* of the canton of Rozières (Haute-Loire); Martin, *notaire*, of Mende; Bancal, president of the criminal tribunal of the Montpellier district (17 in all).

43 PROPERTY-OWNERS AND 'BOURGEOIS': Bureau, Bompois and Bonnerot, property-owners, of Nevers; Desmazures, former actor, property-owner, of Moulins; Ladoucette, property-owner, of Metz; Verd, former *gabelle* (salt tax) assistant, acquirer of national land, man of the law and property-owner, of Moulins; Thiriot, bourgeois, of Moulins; Figuet, architect, of Valence; Pauper, property-owner, of Nevers; Groussac, mayor of Toulouse, merchant; Baby, merchant and property-owner, a bankrupt (?) of Tarascon (Ariège); Gobert, man of the law and master tanner, of Moulin-lès-Metz; Dolle, former merchant of Grenoble, a gambler, bankrupt, speculator, château-owner and acquirer of national land, of La Guillotière and the château of Saint-Ondras (Isère); Allard, substitute deputy to the Convention and manufacturer of Montesquieu-Volvestre (Ariège); Tortel, a tannery-owner of Moulins (15 in all).

44 DOMESTIC SERVANTS: Le Batteux, a cook, then postmaster, of Redon; Tessier, dancing-master and former valet, of Châlons-sur-Marne; Millet, a wigmaker, of Besançon (3 in all).

45 FORMER ECCLESIASTICS: Commerçon, a former Franciscan monk, of Nevers; Grimaud, a former theology teacher at the *collège* of Clermont-Ferrand, a canon of the cathedral in Moulins; Agar, ex-lay brother of Moulins; Marcillat, a former curé of Jaligny (Allier); Delport, former constitutional curé of Beaumont (Haute-Garonne); Schneider, a German and former priest; Wolff and Taffin, German priests; Peyrend-d'Herval, a former *charitain* monk of Clermont-Ferrand, *commissaire des guerres* at La Réole, then at Bordeaux; Gambert, ex-curé of Sainte-Ménéhould; Leclerc, former curate of Sainte-Ménéhould; Menu, former curé of La Guillotière (12 in all).

46 EMPLOYEES: Vauquoy, a former clerk with the Ferme Générale, later secretary of the Society of Jacobins in Paris, then *commissaire* with the War Ministry; Alfonce, employed in military supply at Châlons (2 in all).

47 FARMERS: Dirat, a farmer at Cox (Haute-Garonne); Monestier, a farmer at Merville (Haute-Garonne); Picquié, a farmer in the Toulouse region (3 in all).

48 MILITARY MEN: Seigneur, *commissaire des guerres* at Nevers; Picot-Belloc, a former Garde-du Roi (?), son of Capitoul, one-time merchant in Spain, then *commissaire des guerres*; Resnier, adjutant-general (3 in all).

49 MEDICAL MEN: Delan, a surgeon, mayor of Moulins; Gayon, a surgeon, of Nevers; Sabatier, a health officer, mayor of La Réole; Arnoule, a doctor, of Metz; Lagasquie, a doctor, of Cahors (5 in all).

50 There was in addition one *maître de pension*: Jouans, from Tonneins, bringing the exact total of *commissaires civils* whose professions are known to 77.

51 J. Charrier, *L'histoire réligieuse de la Nièvre*..., refers to the *commissaires* of Nevers as 'des déclassés', undoubtedly because they were bourgeois and men of the law.

52 Arch. Marne, L 2561, AN, D 51 6 and AAG (Dossiers des Officiers d'Administration, Alfonce).

53 AAG, Cl. gén. 3037 (Peyrend-d'Herval). He was a friend of Ronsin and Vincent and, contrary to Prudhomme's claims, v. 444, he belonged to Cordelier circles.

54 Picot-Belloc's cousin, Picot-Bazus, baron de Bazus, one time Garde du Roi, was arrested as a former noble in Nivôse Year II (AAG, Gén. de div. 245, Picot-Bazus).

55 AAG, Pensions militaires, 175 (Picot-Belloc).

56 BL, F 957 (22), *Avis au public, par le citoyen Baru* (n.d., Year V).

57 AN, D III 174 d 2 (539) (General Council of the commune of Metz, list of terrorists to be disarmed, 1-4 Prairial Year III): '*Gobert le jeune*, rue de la Haie, a great, a very great terrorist, who flaunted the rank, orders and decorations of the *chevaliers* of the Terror...'. See also R. Paquet, *Dictionnaire biographique de la Moselle*, 1435. Gobert carried out a mission in Ventôse Year II, with Ladoucette, in Alsace and Germany.

58 Arch. Ille-et-Vilaine, L 1302 (Redon district) and AN, AA 42 pl. 4 d 1321b (84), *Mémoire justificatif et instructif pour le citoyen Le Batteux, aubergiste à Redon et ci-devant Directeur des Postes de la même commune* (Rennes [?], Year III).

59 On Grimaud see F. Mège, *Pascal Grimaud: Histoire d'un prêtre révolutionnaire* (Clermont-Ferrand, 1882), a work kindly pointed out to me by M. Soanen, municipal archivist of Thiers. There is a copy in the John Rylands Library, Manchester.

60 On Dolle see Arch. Grenoble, LL 19, and see also below, II. 6.

61 AHG, B★ 12 11 and Arch. Orléans, D 23E. Vauquoy obtained from Bouchotte an order for a mission, dated 15 Aug 1793, as national *commissaire* for assembling the Valenciennes garrison. The mission was terminated on 18 Sept, when he was arrested by the garrison commander of Orléans, Charles Hesse.

62 AN, F 7 4444, and see RCC, 'Les armées révolutionnaires du Midi', 77.

63 For Lagasquie, see Arch. Lot, L 92 (Département) and L 389 (Cahors *comité*). Another *commissaire* active with the Lot and Cantal *armées*, Gérard Alary, seems to have been a man of some wealth before the Revolution: he was a solicitor in Aurillac (AN, D III 38 (5) (56).

64 The age-range of a sampling of *commissaires civils*:

Grimaud	58	Descombels	25
Lemaître	51	Agar	24
Hugueny	50	Viton	21
Allard	49		
Gobert	45		
Commerçon	45		
Perrotin	41		
Picot-Belloc	40		
Resnier	38		
Delan	37		
Vilain	36		
Baby	35		
Sadet	35		
Verd	35		
Alary	35		
Dirat	35		
Vauquoy	34		
Menu	32		
Pierrey	30		
Bonnerot	30		
Richard	28		
Guyon	28		

65 Prudhomme, v. 434.

66 AN, F 7 3683 3, letter from the president of the Nièvre tribunal, 2 Ventôse Year IV.

67 See Arch. Allier, L 900 (*société populaire* of Moulins), and RCC, 'La Commission Temporaire de Commune-Affranchie'.

68 E. Hamel, 'Euloge Schneider'.

69 RCC, 'Les armées révolutionnaires du Midi.'

70 RCC, 'Quelques aspects de la mentalité révolutionnaire'. In reality, most of the *commissaires civils* were well educated, and there were many men of the law and former ecclesiastics, many of whom had been *collège* instructors before embarking on the civic and revolutionary evangelisation of the countryside.

71 P. Gérard, 'L'armée révolutionnaire de la Haute-Garonne'.

72 The *commissaires civils* were not brutes and it is difficult to accept the accusations of atrocities sometimes made against them. Prudhomme complacently reproduces (v. 147) an unlikely story spread in Nantes, about a certain Héron, commander or *commissaire* of the Marat company, which had him 'never appearing in the streets of Nantes without human ears or genitals in his hat...'. Such savage habits were not those of the *révolutionnaires*.

73 For the Metz 'band' see L. Bultingaire, *Le club des Jacobins de Metz* (Metz, 1906), 72. See also AN, D III 174 d 2 (539). Gobert's acolyte was the doctor, Arnoule, member of the revolutionary commission. 'He always used intoxication as an excuse. Can we thus leave arms in the hands of a man made ferocious by wine...?', asked the General Council of the Metz commune at its session of 4 Prairial Year III.

74 AN, W 532 (Tribunaux révolutionnaires, Vauquoy), and RCC, *L'armée révolutionnaire à Lyon*, 58–9.

75 Arch. Nièvre (great reg. Corbigny *comité de surveillance*), deposition of Granet, ex-Capuchin friar, 29 Frimaire Year III.

76 AN, F 7 4444.

77 Arch. Morbihan, L 2001 (Lorient *société populaire*, session of 22 Frimaire Year II).

78 Baby subscribed to the newspapers of Babeuf and Lebois and figured also on the list of 'men capable of commanding'. Mouly, Allard, Contamin subscribed likewise to Babeuf's paper. Guyon and Grimaud were accused by the police of being accomplices of Babeuf. As for Sadet, he died in the prison of La Tour-du-Pin, following ill treatment. See on this subject RCC, 'La Commission Temporaire de Commune-Affranchie'.

79 Dufresse is the only military commander of a departmental *armée* to figure in the *Dictionnaire des Jacobins vivans*, though the author wrongly cites as revolutionary officers other military men such as the Belgian general Fion, and the infamous pillager, Dutertre, Hébert's compatriot (pp. 47 and 54).

80 Prudhomme cites the supposed commander of the Marat battalion and the generals of the Bordeaux *armée révolutionnaire*, which he confuses with that commanded by Brune: 'The *armée révolutionnaire* organised at La Réole had as generals Brune and Janet, one the friend of Danton, the other his nephew...' (v. 433). Prudhomme is not the only historian to attribute Dantonist tendencies to the *armées révolutionnaires* and to their commanders in particular. The same accusation was made against Rousselin and the commanders of the Troyes *armée* and had as much foundation in fact as the charges of Hébertism against certain officers: Danton was friendly with some leading figures in the *armées* as well as with some of their organisers, like Hérault.

81 At the time of his appointment to the Lille command, Adhémar, who enrolled in Apr 1792, was a lieutenant in the 21st battalion of light infantry. He married at Lille in Pluviôse Year II, took up service again with the garrisons of the Nord, and died of his wounds at Landau, 11 July 1796. At this time his wife was on the list of indigents in the 5th arrondissement of Paris. (AAG, Cl. gén. 9 [Adhémar].)

82 Born Oct 1757 at Verneuil, Agut served in the Boulogne regiment from 1781 to 1789, then in the Gardes-Françaises. In 1789 he enlisted in the paid National Guard of Paris and in 1792 entered the 30th gendarme division. After the dissolution of the *armée* he rejoined the gendarmerie, and in 1820, signing himself 'Agut of Betesta', he wrote to the maréchal de Latour-Maubourg and to the duc de Tarente requesting the Légion d'Honneur (calling himself then 'retired captain of the general staff [?] and member of the Bordeaux Royal Academy of Sciences'. (AAG, Cl. gén. 13 [Agut].)

83 AAG, Cl. gén. 570 (Calmet-Beauvoisins).

84 AAG, Cl. gén. 587 (Capron). Born 10 Sept 1769, he was appointed 2nd lieut. to the 15th infantry regiment in May 1793.

85 AAG, Cl. gén. 937 (Defferrez). He was a native of Lille and was married there in 1772. In the Year IV he was appointed head of the Bureau des Plans of the Sambre-et-Meuse army. He died at Mainz in the same epidemic that killed Jeanbon Saint-André.

86 Born 1764 at Besançon, Jean-Baptiste Griois belonged to a family of highly placed officials – his father was paymaster-general of the Doubs, Jura and Haute-Saône in the Year IV. The son studied for a time at the École des Ponts et Chaussées, then entered the War Treasury and in Aug 1789 was provisional commander of the bourgeois militia in the Saint-Gervais district of Paris. In 1793, living then in the Bon-Conseil Section, he was appointed Ministry *commissaire* in the Nord, to arrange military supply. Having fulfilled his duties zealously he was appointed provisional *commissaire des guerres* in Lille in Sept 1793, and was there appointed by the *société révolutionnaire* as *commissaire* in charge of the organisation and clothing of the *armée révolutionnaire*. In Pluviôse Year II he was transferred to Beauvais and in Germinal oversaw the disbanding of the Parisian detachments in that town. Thereafter he served as a high-ranking official in succeeding regimes, suffered temporary disgrace in the Year IV after being denounced for his royalist sympathies, and retired in the Year X. In Nov 1814, he was director of contributions and surveys in the Seine-Inférieure and wrote from Rouen to the Interior Minister soliciting the Légion d'Honneur, remarking that his father 'had served for 40 years as first secretary to the Intendant and sub-delegate of the province of Franche-Comté', that his elder brother had been killed in 1793 at Wissembourg, serving in the army of Condé, and that his younger brother, a Chevalier de Saint-Louis, was in charge of artillery at Mézières. His monarchism was well rewarded, for he was still employed in Rouen in 1824, and was decorated with the cross of Saint-Louis. Griois was undoubtedly the only authentic royalist on the general staff of an *armée révolutionnaire*, though his former commander, Dufresse, would also succeed in profiting from the Restoration. Service in an *armée révolutionnaire* sometimes had unexpected consequences. (AAG, Cl. gén. 1692 [Griois].)

87 For Dorez see E. Leleu, 'Le général Dufresse et l'armée révolutionnaire du Nord', and RCC, 'Quelques conséquences sociales de la Révolution dans un milieu urbain'. After his spell in the *armée révolutionnaire*, Dorez, an unemployed launderer, was appointed police commissioner through the support of the *société révolutionnaire*. Nicolas d'Hollande, having served in the army since 1783, found himself without work on 9 Nivôse Year II. 'This citizen is worthy of a position', declared the report from the 5th Division of the War Ministry (AHG, B 12★ 17). On the *journée* of 12 Germinal Year III, he fired on the people in defence of the Thermidorean authorities. In the Year V he was adjutant in the 2nd battalion, 1st demi-brigade of the Légion de Police; on its disbandment, he was retired. (AAG, Cl. gén. 1075 [d'Hollande].)

88 Butelle, a lieutenant in the *armée révolutionnaire*, was, like Defferrez, a member of the Panthéon-Français company of cannoneers. This so-called Hébertist was arrested at the end of Frimaire with Defferrez and the other leaders of the *société* (Arch. Lille, 18′ 229). Christol, captain of a company of *révolutionnaires*, was a sergeant in the 31st gendarmerie division, garrisoned at Lille (Arch. Lille, 18′ 338); Blondeau and Bourdet were officers in a company of cannoneers formed at Lille (Arch. Nord, L 10224); the younger Mille was a captain of the 2nd Lille battalion (Arch. Lille, 18′ 338); Lebreton and Pinard were captains in the Lille formations of the first requisition (Arch. Nord, L 10224); Target, a Parisian soldier, served in Brussels under Lavalette, was one of the founders of the Society of Jacobins there, and, in Frimaire, when appointed to the general staff of the *armée révolutionnaire*, was *chef de brigade* of the 13th cavalry regiment. He was also one of the leaders of the so-called Hébertist party of Lille (AAG, Cl. gén. 3680 [Target]).

89 AAG, Cl. gén. 483 (Braëmt). There was another Braëmt, member of the *société* (Arch. Lille, 18′ 229). On Buisine, see RCC, 'Quelques conséquences sociales…dans un milieu urbain'. Dubrusle, quartermaster in the *armée révolutionnaire*, was another of the rare civilians in the officer corps; he was a Lille shopkeeper (Arch. Lille, 18′ 339).

90 RCC, 'Les armées révolutionnaires du Midi', 49–52.

91 AAG, Gén. div. 772 (Avril). Born at Loudun in 1753, Avril spent long years on garrison duty in the Ile de France, where on the eve of the Revolution, he commanded a colonial regiment. His father had been *procureur* in the royal courts of Loudun.

92 Petit commanded the 7th battalion of the Légion du Centre, serving under the orders of Brune (Arch. Bordeaux, D 104). It was he who commanded the revolutionary battalion of Bordeaux. For his lieutenants, see AAG, Cl. gén. 2063 (Lamarque), and 2675 (Mialhe).

93 *L'Anti-Terroriste*, no. 51 (18 Thermidor Year III) and P. Gérard, 'L'armée révolutionnaire de la Haute-Garonne', 8 (42). Bonnafous served eight years in the Régiment de Foix. During the Revolution he commanded the National Guard of the Castelsarrasin district.

94 A. Duboul, *L'armée révolutionnaire de Toulouse*, 44; RCC, 'Les armées révolutionnaires du Midi', 30–1; P. Gérard, 'L'armée révolutionnaire de la Haute-Garonne', 8 (41). Barateau owned a house in the rue de la Madeleine in Toulouse.

95 The *Anti-Terroriste* journalist saw Gélas as the most important person in this *armée*, though he was content with the position of adjutant-general: '...This man was everywhere; he said he had more powers than the *commissaires civils*, than the National Convention itself; he insulted, molested, threatened everyone' (no. 51). See also RCC, 'Les armées révolutionnaires du Midi', 31; AN, F 7 4721 d 1 (Gélas); Arch. Haute-Garonne, L 4258 (district of Toulouse); and P. Gérard, 'L'armée révolutionnaire de la Haute-Garonne', 8 (43), also 11 (59) on Delport. The *Anti-Terroriste* attributed the worst motives to Delport. In fact this former priest was entirely devoted to the republican cause, for which he made considerable sacrifices. Another officer of the Toulouse *armée*, Guillaume Barbe, captain of a company sent to the Ariège, seems also to have been a career soldier (see P. Gérard, *art. cit.*, 21 [127]).

96 AAG, Cl. gén. 700 (Chauvet).

97 E. Hamel, 'Euloge Schneider', and D. Fischer, 'L'armée révolutionnaire du Bas-Rhin', 430. In 1802, 2nd gendarme officer Pfersdorf was charged with the kidnapping of the duc d'Enghien. See also AN, F 7 4568 d 6.

98 AAG, Cl. gén. 530 (Brunière). In Lyon he was nominated to the Commission des Sept, which exposed him to proscription by the Thermidorean authorities of Nevers; he was arrested at the same time as the other members and was detained until the Year IV. (AN, D XL III, petition of those detained at Nevers to the Convention, 16 Vendémiaire Year IV.) In the Year VII he was a lieutenant in the gendarmerie. He was a political militant whose name figures both in Babeuf's lists and on those of the police who considered him as dangerous as he was poor: 'Brunière...aged 42, rue des Marmousets, no. 24, a hairdresser's, has lately had frequent contact with Laignelot, was of the Panthéon and one of the clubs which succeeded it. He is a former judge of the revolutionary tribunal of Lyon, against his will, he assures us, and he saved many who appeared before it [a fact confirmed by Montléon and those detained, who paid tribute to his moderation and kindness].... He is poor; his faults come from that poverty.... He does not fear death' (AN, F 7 4276) – a perfect testimony to revolutionary conviction. Brunière belonged to the category of purist militants.

99 AAG, Cl. gén. 549 (Bussière). Born at Nevers in 1766, Pierre Bussière enlisted in 1783 in an infantry regiment, leaving in 1787 with the grade of corporal. He then joined a Nièvre volunteer battalion, fighting in the campaigns of 1792 and 1793 with the Army of the Rhine. After leaving the *armée révolutionnaire*, he also fought in the campaigns of the Years III, IV, V, VI, VIII and IX with the Armies of the West (that of Year VII in Italy). He received a retirement pension in Prairial Year XI. He was accused of various acts of pillage during his stay in the district of Clamecy in Frimaire Year II (Arch. Nièvre, L reg. 7 and 20 L 7).

100 AAG, Cl. gén. 3565 (Seigneur). Pierre Seigneur, born at Pontoise, 10 Aug 1740, was a noble, his grandfather, a Pontoise merchant, having bought the office of *secrétaire du roi*. In 1757, he enlisted in the regiment of La Tour-du-Pin, becoming ensign-lieut. in 1758. He was a *commissaire des guerres* right through from 1771 to 1796, apart from a brief interlude in Ventôse Year II, when he was suspended and arrested as an ex-noble by the *représentant* Lefiot. On this occasion he was supported by all the Nevers authorities, who spoke for his revolutionary patriotism, and he was reinstated after a favourable testimonial from Fouché. He is frequently referred to as 'commander-in-chief of the *Légion révolutionnaire*'; but although, as *commissaire des guerres*, he was in charge of its organisation, his role was never as important as that of Boissay in the neighbouring department. (See Arch. Nièvre, L reg. 7, corres. Clamecy district). See also the pamphlet *Noël Pointe...aux habitants de Nevers* (Nevers, Floréal Year II) in the John Rylands Library, Manchester, p. 69, on Seigneur's arrest in the Year II.

101 Arch. Nièvre (reg. delib., Clamecy, 8, session of 6 Sept 1793).

102 Arch. Nièvre, 8 L 8 (Nevers district).
103 id., 20 L 7 (*comité de surveillance*, Nevers).
104 Arch. Allier, L 850 (*comité de surveillance*, Moulins).
105 id., L 852 (*comité* of Moulins) and L 900 (*société* of Moulins).
106 Arch. Troyes, D 38 (8th Section) and Arch. Aube, Lm 4c3 352 (Terrorists).
107 AN, F 7 4648 d 4 (Civeton). Civeton was arrested as a terrorist after Thermidor. His
     activity as conveyor and executor of Javogues's warrants was particularly condemned.
     He was freed on 20 Vendémiaire Year IV. J.-B. Galley, *Saint-Etienne et son district...*,
     II. 551, cites the names of other officers of this *armée*: Ferréol, who commanded the Saint-
     Etienne company; Montagne, commanding that of Saint-Chamond; Châtain, captain
     of the Rive-de-Gier company; Revolier, of Saint-Etienne, and Martin, of Mont-
     brison. According to Galley (II. 37), Descombes, commander of this *armée*, was
     commissaire-général, charged by Javogues and Bassal with its enrolment. He was, like his
     second-in-command, Escoffier, an inhabitant of Saint-Etienne. Escomel, of Saint-
     Chamond, the quartermaster, was to be prosecuted in Prairial Year II for
     misappropriation of funds. Galley also lists Elie Egalon, from Polignais; Mourgès,
     captain; Thivet, adjutant-major, though we know no more of these than we do of the
     mysterious Descombes.
108 See Arch. Loire, L 434 (Saint-Bonnet-le-Château *comité*), LL 432 (Montbrison *comité*),
     L 416 (Saint-Germain-Laval *comité*) and L 184 (Roanne district).
109 Padiolleau is called 'commander' by Gaston-Martin, *Carrier et sa mission à Nantes*.
     Prudhomme speaks of one Héron or d'Héron as leading the company, and attributes to
     him (n. 72 above) a certain original taste in clothes.
110 On the Naud brothers see Arch. Loire-Inf., L 1054 and L 98, and AN, Wla 493 (479).
     They were both arrested on 25 Prairial Year II on an order from Bô and Bourbotte.
111 AN, Wla 493 (479) for Richard. And see *Dictionnaire des Jacobins vivans*, 76: 'Jolly [*sic*]
     (Jean-Baptiste), copper-caster'. In the same work is a reference to another officer of this
     company, Robin (whom we have been unable to identify).
112 AN, Wla 493 (479).
113 Arch. Gironde, II L 27 (Club national) and II L 67–8 (*comité de surveillance*, Bordeaux).
114 On Contamin, see RCC, *L'armée révolutionnaire à Lyon*.
115 Sauvaire, commander of the Entrevaux company, was an officer of the National Guard of
     this small town (Arch. Basses-Alpes, L 756). Ailhaud, officer of the Oraison company,
     Braissaud, lieutenant, and Revast, 2nd lieutenant, were farmers of Oraison, elected at a
     general assembly of the commune (id., L 806) – they were all members of the town *comité*.
     Rolland, lieutenant of the Sisteron company, was an officer of the National Guard (id.,
     L 821). Colomb, elected captain of the Senez company, was a farmer of that commune
     (id., L 857). Finally, Coupier, who commanded the sans-culottes of Manosque, was an
     officer of the town's National Guard (id., L 778).
116 *Journal de la Montagne*, no. 57 (20 Nivôse Year II), giving an account of a speech by
     Mathieu-Jouve Jourdan, '*ci-devant* general of the *armée révolutionnaire* of the Vaucluse', to
     the Convention on 11 Nivôse (he was then squadron leader of the departmental
     gendarmerie). On the printer Nicolaud of Orange, see above, nn. 27 and 41.
117 See RCC, 'Les armées révolutionnaires du Midi'.
118 Viton served for 18 months in the Lorraine-Infanterie regiment, Jan 1791–Sept 1792.
     Adjutant of Brune, Ministry *commissaire*, in Sept–Oct 1792, he entered the Régiment de la
     Reine as a lieutenant in Oct, and left, apparently without leave, in Feb 1793, when he gave
     himself the somewhat fantastic title: '*aide-commissaire-générale* of the Ministries'. His
     military experience was correspondingly slight. (AAG, Cl. gén. 3944 [Viton].)
119 Pierre Orliac (or Orlhac), '*chef de division*' of the Lot *armée révolutionnaire*, was naval
     commissaire civil at Cahors; Louis Lacroix, captain in the Lot *armée*, and Fournier,
     commander of one of the detachments sent to the Séverac region, came from the Cahors
     National Guard (Arch. Aveyron, 77 L 1). The younger Gau, quartermaster general of this
     armée, was the son of a Toulouse merchant (RCC, 'Les armées révolutionnaires du Midi',
     44). Miret, captain of a company active at Villefranche, and Cassagnes, commander of a
     detachment in that town, were both from Cahors; while Valette, commander of the
     Cantal *armée*, was the brother of a man of the law in Salers (Arch. Cantal, L 684).
120 For the Bouches-du-Rhône companies see RCC, 'Les armées révolutionnaires du Midi';
     and Arch. Landes, L 783, for the Dax affair. At Agen the officers were likewise local
     personalities; the second-in-command, Joseph Saussade, was a member of the *comité de*

surveillance, though he had to abandon his command. The younger Secondat, the lieutenant, was a well-off young man, whose father had retired with the rank of lieutenant-colonel. The son was content to serve out his career in Agen with this peaceful and unremarkable little company (Arch. Lot-et-Garonne, reg. 1, Agen *comité de surveillance*).

121 None of the officers of the Lille *armée* could be considered political militants, most imitating young Calmet-Beauvoisins, an archetypal military weathervane, who had the gall to announce himself to Pille as 'a victim of Vincent', when it had been Vincent who recommended him to the War Ministry. In Germinal Year III he took part in the Thermidorean repression of the Parisian proletariat. Of all the officers of the Nièvre and Allier battalions, only Brunière claimed in Years III and IV to be a convinced republican, and like all the militant terrorists in the departments, this former member of the Revolutionary Commission in Lyon returned to Paris and took part in the Panthéon reunions after his liberation in the Year IV. Of the Toulouse officers, Bonnafous fell into total obscurity after demobilisation. Barateau continued in political life, but Delport alone showed any convinced republican and anti-Catholic principles. As for Gélas, the *Anti-Terroriste* picture of him as a mere conformist seems to have been totally accurate, and he does not figure in the small group of Toulouse *révolutionnaires* clustered around Destrem, Allard and the former mayor, Groussac. Contamin, creator and commander of the Crémieu army, was a born militant, the epitome of those 'enragés de village' who were the best auxiliaries of the 'hommes de liaison', and still figured in police reports in the Year X. In the Loire, Civeton, captain of the Roanne company, was sufficiently 'political' to be persecuted by the Thermidoreans, but disappears after his release at the beginning of the Year IV. As for the officers of the Marat company of Nantes, Robin, Joly and the sugar refiner Gaillon, their inclusion in the *Dictionnaire des Jacobins vivans* was due to their participation in the *noyades* rather than to their political militancy. The officers of the other *armées révolutionnaires* either fade from view or follow relatively uneventful careers after their demobilisation – with the exception of the Légion de la Montagne, whose command contained several authentic revolutionaries: Chastel, who became one of the militants of the revolutionary opposition under the Directory, was later a protégé of Brune in Italy, and finally in 1810 was accused of having taken part in a terrorist plot in Geneva; and Gourgonnier, who also found refuge in Italy during the difficult years (see RCC, 'Les armées révolutionnaires du Midi').

122 On the curious military and political career of general-baron Dufresse, see AAG, Cl. gén. 386 (Dufresse), E. Leleu, 'Le général Dufresse et l'armée révolutionnaire du Nord', Gén. Herlaut, 'Le général-baron Dufresse', and J. Hérissay, *Le monde des théâtres pendant la Révolution*; see also AN, F 7 4771 d 1 (René-François Lebois), containing Dufresse's defence, Year III, and W 498 (534) (his trial).

123 On Viton see AN, F 7 4775 49 d 2 (Viton); AAG, Cl. gén. 3944 (Viton); Arch. Tarn-et-Garonne, L 224 (Montauban *comité*); and RCC, 'Les armées révolutionnaires du Midi', 40–4, where his adventurous life after the Revolution, and his efforts to confirm his rank of *chef de brigade* in 1814, are described.

124 Arch. Lille, 18′ 229 (Lille *société révolutionnaire*); *Réflexions de Denis Bourdon*. According to the *société* the woman with Dufresse was a former prostitute called Aimée.

125 Arch. Lille, 18′ 229 (Lille *société*). There are many myths about Dufresse, this figure whose only crime was to have been too visible. He seems, however, to have been a courageous man, more ridiculous than wicked, and full of his own importance. But he was no imbecile, and, like many career soldiers, showed a remarkable gift for political sycophancy. His portrait in the royalist *Dictionnaire des Jacobins vivans* is as unflattering as it was inaccurate: 'At Lille he became enamoured of Mme Guillotine and had the portrait of this charmer engraved on his seal.... When he was imprisoned after 9 Thermidor, his courage did not desert him, and to avenge his oppression he sang hymns all day long to his beloved Marat. This republican and former wigmaker [he was in fact an actor and merchant] now possesses horses, carriages and country houses, and cries: *thieves*! The fashion now is for thieves to shout "thieves" in order to direct public attention away from themselves'.

126 Arch. Tarn-et-Garonne, L 224.

127 See below, II. 7. On his debts, see the letter of the Cahors *comité* to Viton, 5 Prairial Year II: 'Your obstinate silence...has forced the sans-culotte, Cazals, to protest to the *comité*. This matter shocked us.... The debt is such that someone in your position must pay it'.

And the *comité* signed off with brutal insistence: '*Salut*, justice, probity and fraternity'(!). The letter was effective, producing a contribution towards his drinking debts (Arch. Lot, L 406, Cahors *comité*, corres. reg.). Viton left other debts behind in Rodez and Paris.

128 Prudhomme, v. 147, 178, 286, 300.

129 H. Riouffe, *Mémoires d'un détenu*, 21.

130 E. Leleu, 'Le général Dufresse et l'armée révolutionnaire du Nord', 109.

131 See Arch. Allier, L 850–2, 878 and 900 (*comité de surveillance* and *société populaire* of Moulins).

132 'Service' occupations in the departmental *armées*:

Armée	Wigmakers	Domestic servants	Cooks	Supernumeraries	Total of professions listed overall
North	2	1	1	8	230
Versailles	1	1	1	8	–
Saint-Germain	1				
Nantes	4				28
Avallon		6 (farm)			37
Allier	1				–
Toulouse	1	1	1		94
Bordeaux	1				37
Nièvre	1				–
Salins	1				17
Cahors	1				–
Agen	1				25

Of course, since these figures are merely samples, they have no statistical value, except in the case of Lille (North), for which more complete figures exist. It is therefore certain that wigmakers and servants were more numerous in reality. But in the existing state of documentation, servants are clearly outnumbered by artisans, small traders and workers.

133 AN, F 7 4774 d 58 (Nutin). Jacques-Denis Nutin is a curious figure, in whom criminality mingles with militant revolutionism. An active member of the Vertu-Sociale *société* of Versailles – of the two Versailles *sociétés* it was the more closely linked with Cordeliers or War Ministry circles – Nutin carried out several missions in the Versailles district in the Year II as 'apostle' of this *société*, with all the violence generally used by 'hommes de liaison'. On hearing of the dissolution of his *société*, which was considered ultra-revolutionary, Nutin wrote to the Versailles *comité*: 'Our club is destroyed...I don't give a damn; I will make up for it by going into the villages...and amusing myself with the peasants, who will be delighted to have me. I will bring those bloody farmers and wine-growers to heel, and make them pay up.... My reign will last a long time, because I am a sans-culotte, first and foremost'. In fact that reign ended on 12 Thermidor Year XII, when he was guillotined in the public square of Montreuil, condemned for having murdered his sister-in-law at Bonnelles, on the preceding 12 Ventôse.

134 Tinette, a member of the Nevers battalion, claimed to be a pottery turner and to have sustained great losses when his merchandise was confiscated by the toll collectors in 1789, while in transit by water through the Auvergne. He was then forced to sell his business and property to pay his creditors. The Nevers district rewarded his patriotism by assuming his debts and awarding him an indemnity of 1,200 livres (Arch. Nièvre, 8 L 4).

135 René Naud, quartermaster of the Marat company of Nantes, a former merchant, aged 43, had fitted out an 18-gun ship before the Revolution, which seems to have ruined him. Durossier, secretary to the company, aged 50, was a former broker for cargoes from Santo Domingo; the 29-year-old merchant, Jomard, had also suffered losses (APP, A/A 269).

136 Two members at least of the Bordeaux battalion came from the world of international commerce: Castera, member of the Bon-Accord Section company, sent to Copenhagen in Floréal Year II to contact the Danish shipowners about transporting grain to Bordeaux; and Laurent Albert, captain, who in Germinal requested a passport for Lübeck – where he had relatives – because of the almost complete cessation of his business (Arch. Bordeaux, F 21 and D 107). The two were not, however, bankrupts.

137 Arch Allier, L 850 (Moulins *comité*, session of 30 Vendémiaire Year II). The principal culprit here was the soldier Lavigne. We will examine later the many complaints of drunkenness among the revolutionary soldiers in the departments (see below, II. 7). As for their moral conduct, though pillaging was common, sexual crimes were rare; Goulin, member of the Nantes *comité*, was a real monster who claimed to have slept with 16- and

17-year-old prisoners by promising to do favours for their parents.

138 Arch. Hautes-Alpes, L 1082 (Briançon district). The average age of the Marat company was 42; it was 47 at Versailles – an army of old men. At Lille, on the other hand, a third of the *armée* was made up of young men of the age of the first requisition, and according to the figures presented by Gérard, even if incomplete, a third of the Toulouse *armée* was also made up of young men of this age. But they were exceptions; the Marat and Versailles forces were more typical, and men of ripe years were deliberately recruited into the *armées révolutionnaires*.

139 AHG, B 1 22 (Army of the Nord), Nivet to Bouchotte, 12 Brumaire Year II.

140 A few personalities in the Lille *société* did remain content with subordinate positions: the sculptor, Cuigniez; Degroux, cotton manufacturer; Certail, second-hand clothes dealer of the rue des Malades; Montagne, a shopkeeper; Richard, a joiner; Dewal, a powder manufacturer; Hudlo, a wine merchant; Laumondé, a grocer; Laleu, a *sacéteur;* Salmon, son of a rich doctor. But many such *sociétaires* were influential figures in their Sections, they secured good positions for themselves in the companies in which they had enrolled their friends, protégés, neighbours and employees. (Arch. Lille, 18′ 338–40.)

141 See RCC, *L'armée révolutionnaire à Lyon*, for the important place accorded to the Nièvre and Allier battalions by the *représentants* and the Commission Temporaire, in administering the repression in Lyon, notably as *commissaires* attached to the 32 *comités révolutionnaires* in the Sections. Only the Parisian soldiers enjoyed such confidence with those responsible for the repression.

142 Arch. Lot, L 391 (Cahors *comité*).

143 How better to erase past errors than by becoming staunch patriots and orthodox revolutionaries – as one member declared at the general assembly of the Bon-Accord Section on 29 Vendémiaire: 'let us prove our sincere regeneration by going this instant to sign the register of the *armée révolutionnaire...*' (Arch. Bordeaux, I 64). In such circumstances, it would have been inadvisable not to be a candidate. Even then the risks were great, since the candidate had to undergo the *scrutin épuratoire*, in which his past errors might be revealed. But indulgence was necessary in Bordeaux, and one's candidacy was in itself taken as a sign of the desire to have one's past sins forgiven.

144 Occupations of the Lille *armée* (1st, 2nd and 6th Sections):

Soldiers of conscription age		Iron trade	5
(80 from the Lille battalions,		master cooper	1
46 from those of the Somme)	126	blacksmith	1
Textile and clothing trades	40	tinsmith	1
machinists	14	wheelwright	1
spinners	4	plumber	1
carders	2	Domestic service	5
weavers	2	wigmakers	2
cotton workers	3	cook	1
stocking-makers	2	servant	1
second-hand clothes dealers		floor polisher	1
(notably the rich Buisine,		Luxury and literary trades	4
a prominent figure in his		sculptors	2
société, who had done		porcelain-painter	1
well in business since 1789)	3	'botanist'	1
master tailors	3	Employees	2
tailors	2	(military transport)	
launderers	2	Various artisans	15
draper	1	joiners	5
sacéteur	1	shoemakers	3
guersonnier	1	ropemaker	1
Food trade	7	market-stall keeper	1
wine merchants	2	furrier	1
cabaret-keepers	2	measurer	1
brewer	1	town crier	1
grocer	1	Rural occupations	5
baker	1	day-labourers	
		(all of them from Wazemmes or	
		from the faubourg des Malades)	5

There were also 5 Belgians, tailors and other artisans, whose names were removed from the roll, probably because they were foreigners and subjects of the Emperor.

145 Arch. Versailles, D 1 51 (1st Section): at Saint-Germain, candidates accepted included a café-owner, a jeweller, a wigmaker, a perfumer, a sacristan and a cabinet-maker (Arch. Saint-Germain, D 1 15); Arch. Versailles, D 1 186 (13th Section); id., D 1 59 (4th Section).

146 For the composition of the Vertu-Sociale *société* see Arch. Versailles, D 1 184bis (list of members). Among these will be found 2 master joiners, an architect and building contractor, a master locksmith, a lodger, a bourgeois, a teacher, a tobacconist, 2 sailors, a baker, an innkeeper, a roofer, a timber merchant, a painter, a wigmaker, a master tailor, a day-labourer – i.e. the whole spectrum of membership of a *société* which also called itself 'Société des Sans-Culottes'.

147 Among the candidates of the 4th Section were a wine merchant, a master carpenter, a bookseller, 2 master shoemakers, a wheelwright, a mattress-maker, a second-hand clothes dealer, an instrument-maker, a pottery merchant, an embroiderer, a cooper, a·furniture dealer, a haberdasher etc. (Arch. Versailles, D 1 59, 4th Section).

148 Arch. Versailles, D 1 51 and D 1 62. Javon was in fact commissioned to build a workshop in Paris, place des Invalides.

149 Arch. Versailles, D 1 59 (4th Section), and D 1 51 (1st Section).

150 Arch. Saint-Germain, D 1 15.

151 Leclosmesnil, of the 10th Section, asked to be released, as he had found another position. Denis resigned, to devote all his time to his locksmith's business (Arch. Versailles, D 1 51). In the 4th Section nearly all the businessmen and master artisans resigned, for fear of having to serve outside Versailles.

152 Arch. Versailles, 1 2 1217 (list of members of the Société des Amis de la Liberté). In Frimaire Year III it included 33 coachmen and grooms, 28 wigmakers, 7 chair-porters, 3 dancing masters, 23 tailors, 10 painters and engravers, 10 tapestry-makers. The *limonade* group had 20 members, mostly day-labourers, and the artisanal and business element was less important than in the rival *société*. The first *société*, that of the Jacobins, was situated nearer the Château, in a quartier where servants and stable hands were particularly numerous, which undoubtedly explains the preponderance of domestic help and those in the luxury trades. But in the Versailles *armée*, only 10 out of the 50 whose employment is known, came from the world of domestic service. This *armée* was consequently far from being an 'army of valets'.

153 Arch. Allier, L 850 and L 900 (*comité* and *société* of Moulins). There were some very poor people in this *armée*: Gosse, who termed himself a shopkeeper, asked to retain his uniform on leaving the *armée*, while at the time of the departure of 110 men for Lyon, the *comité* had to supply most of the soldiers with shoes.

154 Arch. Allier, L 900.

155 Arch. Nièvre, 20 L 7 (Nevers *comité*, 3 Brumaire). Also included were a shoemaker, a glazier, a joiner and a surgeon (Arch. Nièvre, 8 L 4, district of Nevers).

156 Arch. Côte-d'Or, L IV b 9/l (Dijon *société*).

157 Arch. Doubs, L 2358 (Montbéliard *société*). All the members of this company seem to have been Lutheran Protestants.

158 Arch. Jura, 1st reg. (Salins *société*, 2 Floréal Year II). This company was composed of 3 veterans, 2 tanners, a weaver, a baker, a wigmaker, a tailor, a joiner, a gardener, a café-owner, a wine-grower, a stocking-maker, and a journeyman. It was the Versailles *armée* at a lower echelon.

159 Arch. Jura, 1st reg. (Salins *société*, session of 2 Floréal Year II).

160 Arch. Lot-et-Garonne, great reg. (Agen *comité de surveillance*).

161 AN, AF II 107 (796). See also Prudhomme, v. 432; RCC, 'Les armées révolutionnaires du Midi', 44; and AN, D III 132 (Comité de législation).

162 Part of the Lot *armée* was enrolled in the towns of the Gourdon district (Arch. Lot, L 415) and on 16 Sept the Montpézat *société* decided to raise a company (Arch. Lot, L 92, Département). On 30 Vendémiaire that of Castelnaud took a similar decision (Arch. Lot, L 389).

163 Companies were raised at Peyruis, La Mure, Senez and Thorame (Arch. Basses-Alpes, L 809 [1st ser.], L 852, 857 and 859). See also Arch. Hautes-Alpes, L 1082 (Briançon district), where two farmers were exempted by the district because of their large families, who would starve without them. Service in a revolutionary force could thus be a luxury as well as a privilege. It was certainly no army of the unemployed.

164 Arch. Côte-d'Or, L IV 14 (Montbard *société*); Arch. Haute-Saône, L 1163 (Jussey *société*).
165 Arch. Doubs, L 2358 (Montbéliard *société*) and Arch. Jura (1st reg., Salins *société*).
166 Arch. Yonne, L 83 (Avallon district). In Avallon itself, 2 shopkeepers, a solicitor, a turner and a toymaker enrolled. At Sauvigny, the candidate was a yeoman farmer of 27, but elsewhere in the district the rural proletariat joined in numbers: at Censoir, 5 casual labourers out of 6 candidates; in the Vézelay canton, 2 servants and a wine-grower out of 9; in that of Joux, 2 casual labourers out of 6 (1 butcher); in that of L'Isle, 2 casual labourers, a weaver, a mason, a quarryman, and a wine-grower; in Montréal, a wine-grower and a weaver out of 5; in Guillon, 4 casual labourers, a servant and a yeoman farmer; and finally in the district of Quarrée-les-Tombes, 3 servants, a casual labourer, a boot-maker and a yeoman farmer.
167 AN, F 7 4422 (*comité révolutionnaire* of Nantes); Prudhomme, vi. 286; AN, F 7 4422.
168 The details below come from the notes taken by Topino-Lebrun at the trial of Carrier (APP, A A/269):

1 Boulay (Jean), 26, shoemaker, born at Le Mans.
2 Boussy (Jean), 45, parasol-seller, born at Chassaigne (Puy-de-Dôme).
3 Bouvier (Edouard), 30, carpenter.
4 Charretier (Julien), 32, shopkeeper, born at Nantes.
5 Coron (François), 40, former *procureur*.
6 Cousin (Julien), 35, cooper, born at Nantes, brother-in-law of Vic, member of the *comité révolutionnaire* there.
7 Crépin (Nicolas), 38, wigmaker and café-owner, born at Nantes.
8 Dubreuil (Joseph), 40, jeweller.
9 Ducourt (Paul), 37, wigmaker, born at Poitiers.
10 Durossier (Jean-François), 50, former broker for the Santo Domingo trade, secretary of the company.
11 Fleury, captain, commander of the company.
12 Gauthier (Jean), 41, cutler, born at Nantes.
13 Giret (Claude), 39, painter.
14 Guyot (Jacques), 27, nail-maker.
15 Jomard (Nicolas), 29, shopkeeper, established at Montlhéry in the Year III.
16 Joly (Jean-Baptiste), 50, copper-caster, member of the Nantes *comité révolutionnaire*.
17 Lebrun (Privat), 38, dyer, a volunteer returned from the Vendée.
18 Mony (Pierre), 31, roofer.
19 Naud (René), called Naud the older, 43, an arms dealer before the Revolution, which ruined his business. But it is uncertain whether he was actually a bankrupt. Quartermaster of the Marat company, appointed by Carrier and living on the quai des Gardes-françaises. His brother, Louis Naud, was a member of the Nantes *comité révolutionnaire*.
20 Petit (Julien), 32, cooper.
21 Pinatel (Joseph), 41, wigmaker.
22 Poulet (Joseph), shoemaker.
23 Prou (Jean), 39, nail-maker and member of the Nantes *comité révolutionnaire* – it is uncertain whether he was also a member of the company.
24 Richard (Jean-Claude), 33, hatter, born at Dijon, adjutant of the company.
25 Sauvage (Jacques), 44, cooper.
26 Sequinet (René), 39, joiner.
27 Varin (François), 34, wigmaker.
28 Viaut (Louis), 27, nail-maker.

169 See APP, A A/269, AN, F 7 4422 and Wla 493 (479).
170 Arch. Gironde, 11 L 27 (Club national).
171 Members of the Bordeaux battalion:

1 National club:
Brun (Jean-Baptiste), *notaire*
Barrié (Pierre), gendarmerie sergeant
Barbet (Jean), mason
Bourgade (François), tailor
Capdeville, painter

Cazamayor, schoolmaster
Dussau *fils*, tailor
Delbos (Pierre), shoemaker
Fournier (Jean), upholsterer
Gautier (Jacques), merchant
Guérin (Pierre), rope-maker

Lafon (Ambroise), plasterer
Lys (Jacques), merchant
Léon (Mardoché), dealer in silver
Mathieu (Sulpice), hatter
Rénaud (Bernard), saddler
Roumilliac (Joseph), stone-cutter
Segant, mason
Verd (Jean-Baptiste), wigmaker
2 List for the Bon-Accord Section:
Aran, semi-official defense counsel

3 List for the Parfaite-Union Section:
Prosper, wagoner
Simon, joiner
4 List for the Franklin Section:
Bourgade, tailor
Delbos, shoemaker
Lafon, plasterer
Roumilliac, stone-cutter
Segant, mason
Verd, wigmaker

Arch. Gironde, 11 L 27; Arch. Bordeaux, 1 64 (Bon-Accord), 1 66–7 (Parfaite-Union); Arch. Gironde, 11 L 9 (10 Août), 11 L 8 (Franklin).

172 Note, e.g., 10 Août Section: Mardoché Moléna, Benjamin Bar Abraham, Aaron Molina, Abraham Soria, Salomon Fernandès, Joseph Cardoze, David Gonastalla, Daniel Bar Abraham and Moise Bar Mardoché [native of Polneau (*sic*)] (Arch. Gironde, 11 L 9). In this Section Jews accounted for the majority of those inscribed. Among those admitted by the Bon-Accord Section were: Moise Faranco D'Almeyda, Baruch, Coblentz (member of the Sectionary bureau) (Arch. Bordeaux, 1 64). Among those accepted by the club also note: Louis Fraich, Mardoché Gazère, Pierre Idnano, Mardoché Léon, Mola, Pierre Marialla, B. Rodrigue, F. Saul, Antoine Tarsi and J. Terrodo (Arch. Gironde, 11 L 27). The Jewish community therefore played a full part in the enrolment process.

173 Arch. Bordeaux, D 104 (General Council); Arch. Gironde, 11 L9 (10 Août Section).
174 Arch. Bordeaux, 1 64 (Bon-Accord).
175 See list at end of P. Gérard, 'L'armée révolutionnaire de la Haute-Garonne'.
176 RCC, 'Les armées révolutionnaires du Midi'.
177 The word 'worker' is here used in the 18th-century sense; the Dax company was composed largely of apprentice shoemakers and apprentices to other such traders, in small workshops under masters.
178 T. Carlyle, *The French Revolution* (1837 edn.), III. 260, paints a picturesque and impressionistic portrait of the *révolutionnaire* from a distance of 50 years: 'in red nightcap, in tricolor waistcoat [!], in black-shag trousers, black-shag spencer, with enormous moustachioes, enormous sabre...'. At Brest he has Jeanbon Saint-André surrounded 'with an Army of Red Nightcaps'.

BOOK TWO

Chapter 1
1 Arch. Eure, 143 L 1 (Pont-Châlier district to the Committee, 10 Germinal).
2 AN, F 7 4443 d 6 (Oise), order from Isoré, 2 Ventôse.
3 In the zone that supplied Paris, the country people claimed that the requisitioned grain was destined for the Vendée or the Austrians; in Haute-Normandie the farmers of the Seine valley refused to send grain to Honfleur and to the coastal towns, on the pretext that it would be sent to England; in the East the excuse was fear of exportation to the Austrian Low Countries, while throughout the Garonne and Saône valleys all movement of supplies by river was stopped on the pretext that they were destined for Bordeaux, the Federalist town, or Lyon, then under siege.
4 Boucher d'Argis wrote, 5 Brumaire: 'The formation of an *armée révolutionnaire* seems a wise and useful move to protect requisitioned grain against pillage...along the various routes to Paris...'(AN, F 7 3299 d 3).

5

TABLE A
Distribution of Grain Stores Supplying Paris

1st arrondissement:
Longjumeau
Montlhéry
Arpajon
Etampes
Orléans[a]

Montargis[a]
Pithiviers[a]
Malesherbes[a]
Chartres
Gaillardon
Dourdan

Epernon
Dreux
Houdan
Rambouillet
Chevreuse
Montfort-l'Amaury
Versailles
2nd arrondissement:
Saint-Germain-en-Laye
Meulan
Maule
Mantes
Rosny
Vernon[b]
Evreux[b]
Louviers[b]
Les Andelys[b]
Rouen[c]
Gournay
Gisors
Beauvais
Chaumont-en-Vexin
Magny-en-Vexin
L'Isle-Adam
Pontoise
Montmorency
3rd arrondissement:
Beaumont
Senlis

Clermont-sur-Oise
Compiègne
Noyon
Coucy-le-Château
Soissons
Crécy
Villers-Cotterêts
La Ferté-Milon
Château-Thierry
Meaux
Dammartin-en-Goële
Gonesse
4th arrondissement:
Choisy-sur-Seine
Corbeil
Melun
Fontainebleau
Nemours
Pont-sur-Yonne[d]
Sens[d]
Nogent-sur-Seine[e]
Provins
Rozoy-en-Brie
Coulommiers
Lagny
Brie-Comte-Robert

AN, F10 261 (*Subsistances*, Paris) – the same arrondissements were used in Pluviôse Year II as collection points for grain and seed.

[a]Transferred to the requisition area for the Army of the West and the town of Orléans.
[b]Transferred to the requisition area for the two rural districts of the Paris department: Franciade (Saint-Denis) and Bourg-l'Egalité (Bourg-la-Reine).
[c]To Rouen ought to be added the ports of Le Havre and Honfleur: they too had stores for Paris, as had the town of Amiens, and the ports of Calais, Aire and Dunkerque, where Baltic grain bought for Paris was stored.
[d]Wood stores for Paris.
[e]Withdrawn from the list of stores for Paris, since the Aube was not in its requisition area.

6 Etampes, Chartres, Dreux, Houdan, Chevreuse, Montfort, Versailles, Saint-Germain, Meulan, Maule, Vernon, Evreux, Louviers, Les Andelys, Beauvais, Chaumont (Oise), Magny, L'Isle-Adam, Pontoise, Montmorency, Choisy, Corbeil, Melun, Fontainebleau, Nemours, Provins, Rozoy, Coulommiers, Lagny, Brie, Beaumont, Senlis, Clermont, Compiègne, Noyon, Chaumont (Haute-Marne), Coucy, Soissons, Château-Thierry, Dammartin, Gonesse.
7 Pont-sur-Yonne, Sens, Gournay, Gisors, Villers-Cotterêts, Rouen.
8   TABLE B
Movement of Troops Deployed round Paris
to escort the convoys of grain and flour,
from 20 Floréal Year III

Andelys (Les)[a]
Angerville
Arpajon
Artenay
Beaumont
Beauvais
Bondy
Bourget (Le)

Breteuil
Brie-Comte-Robert
Chantilly
Charenton
Chartres
Chaumont-en-Vexin
Chevreuse
Claye

Clermont-sur-Oise

Compiègne

Corbeil

Coulommiers

Creil

Crépy-en-Valois[b]

Dammartin

Dormans

Dourdan

Dreux

Egalité-sur-Marne[c]

Ecouen

Epernay

Ecouis

Etampes

Evreux

Ferté-Gaucher (La)

Ferté-Milon (La)

Ferté-sur-Marne (La)[d]

Fismes

Fontainebleau

Franciade (Saint-Denis)

Franconville

Gaillon

Gisors

Gonesse

Houdan

Lagny

Laon

L'Isle-Adam

Longjumeau

Louvres

Luzarches

Magny-en-Vexin

Mantes

Meaux

Melun

Meulan

Milly

Montdidier

Montereau

Montfort-l'Amaury

Montmirail

Nangis

Nanteuil-le-Haudouin

Nemours

Noyon

Poissy

Pont-de-l'Arche

Pont-Maxence[e]

Pontoise

Pont-sur-Yonne

Provins

Rambouillet

Reims

Rozoy-en-Brie

Rouen

Roye[f]

Saint-Brice

Saint-Germain-en-Laye

Saint-Just-en-Chaussée

Senlis

Sens

Sézanne[g]

Soissons

Tournan-en-Brie

Vaudreuil

Vernon

Versailles

Villeneuve-Saint-Georges

Villeneuve
 (près Montereau)

Villeneuve-la-Guyard[h]

Villers-Cotterêts.

AHG, B13 200 (Army of the Interior – movements reg., Floréal Year III).

[a] Italics denotes communes in which the *armée révolutionnaire* was garrisoned in the Year II.

[b] The district of Crépy, which was rich in grain, figured prominently on Isoré's requisition list; but such was the zeal of its administrators that the Parisian authorities did not feel it necessary to send any revolutionary detachment there.

[c] Revolutionary name of Château-Thierry. There was a Parisian garrison in this district throughout the life-span of the *armée révolutionnaire*.

[d] Revolutionary name of La Ferté-Allais.

[e] Revolutionary name of Pont-Saint-Maxence.

[f] There was talk of sending a Parisian detachment to Roye, but it is uncertain whether one was actually sent.

[g] The town and district of Sézanne, though not included in the Paris requisition area, played an important role in supplying it with wood and an entire army of harvest workers for the cornfields of the Pays de France.

[h] This commune was visited briefly, as were several others in the district of Sens, by a detachment during the final mission carried out by the Parisian *armée*.

9 G. Rudé, 'La taxation populaire de mai 1775 à Paris et dans la région parisienne', *A.h.R.f.*, avril-juin 1956; R. C. Cobb, 'Les disettes de l'an II et de l'an III dans le district de Mantes et la vallée de la Basse-Seine', *Mémoires Paris et Ile-de-France*, III (1954).

10 R. C. Cobb, 'Le mouvement revendicatif parmi les bateliers de l'Oise et de la Marne au cours de l'hiver 1793–1794', *Revue d'Histoire économique et sociale*, XXXII, no. 4 (1954).

11 This route to the Nord, so important for the transport of foreign grain landed at Dunkerque, Calais, Aire and at the ports of the Somme, of Dutch and Belgian grain

requisitioned for the French departments after their re-conquest, and for the transport of troops, was the scene of many disorders in the Year III, and even more in the Year IV, the year of famine and unrestrained banditry. A report of 30 Brumaire Year IV indicates the same danger spots for stoppages and pillage – with soldiers in transit figuring among the many culprits. The report also points to the poor state of the roads and the shortage of workers to make repairs (AN, F 7 3683 5, Nord). The problem, then, was not confined to the Year II. In 1792 grain travelling south from Dunkerque had already provoked disturbances along the Dunkerque-Saint-Omer canal, as well as in the hunger-stricken area of Amiens.

12 AN, F66 221 (*Subsistances*, Seine-et-Oise), deliberations of the Gonesse district, 11 Sept 1793. See also L. Noël, 'Le pain de Gonesse', and 'La crise des subsistances dans le district de Gonesse pendant la Révolution', *Bull. de la Soc. hist. du Raincy et des environs*, nos. 13 and 14 (nov. 1942, mars 1944). The cantons producing grain in this district were those of Gonesse, Louvres, Ecouen; those deficient in grain were Livry, Montmorency and Luzarches. Gonesse itself had two windmills and two water mills, and a concentration of large farms (18 over 3,400 acres, while Garches and some other places had only 2).

13 Arch. Montrouge, reg. 1 (General Council, session of 15 Pluviôse Year III). The mayor observed on this occasion that there were a considerable number of drivers at the town's *auberge*, as well as 40 workers from citizen Bry's quarry. Gentilly also had a bad reputation with the Paris authorities for stoppages – its main trade, according to its municipality, was '...selling meat and wine and attracting crowds of people...' (Arch. Gentilly, 1 D 1/1, General Council, session of 2 Floréal Year II).

14 Arch. Etampes, D 1 1 (General Council, session of 15 Germinal) and Arch. Eure-et-Loire, L 133 (district of Janville, session of 11 Oct).

15 R. C. Cobb, 'Problèmes de subsistances: la question des arrivages', *Bull. de la Soc. d'Hist. moderne*, avril-juin 1954. Shortly after the arrest of the Hébertists and the disbanding of the *armée révolutionnaire*, the Montrouge municipality – much criticised by the Paris authorities for holding up the *arrivages* – issued an order on 30 Germinal for nightly patrols to protect goods travelling to Paris (Arch. Montrouge, reg. 1, General Council). Longjumeau, on the same route, had a similar reputation for stoppages (Arch. Sceaux, reg. 4). See also Arch. Moret, reg. IV (session of 18 Frimaire), on the volume of traffic passing through Moret and Loing.

16 RCC, 'Le "complot militaire" de ventôse an II'.

17 Arch. Eure-et-Loire, L 71 (district of Châteaudun, session of 25 Brumaire).

18 See RCC, 'Le "complot militaire"'; and see also below, III. 3.

19 Arch. Montereau, D 1 5 (General Council, session of 29 Nivôse). 'Facilities for transports, 6 to 8 high tides per *décade*...finally, good major roads when transport by water becomes impossible because of ice or low water' – such were the virtues of maintaining the grain store for the commune of Paris at Montereau, as the municipality told the Commission des Subsistances when a move to Beaulieu was mooted.

20 Arch. Seine-et-Marne, L 587 (district of Nemours); Arch. Nemours, D 2 (General Council, session of 13 Sept) and Arch. Pithiviers, great reg. (session of 29 Aug). See also Arch. Moret, reg. IV (municipality) and great reg. (*société populaire*). On 30 Sept one member of the municipality spoke of Moret's 'extreme penury in subsistences', and in Frimaire, when the municipality claimed that the farmers of the canton could no longer provision its market, the district of Nemours suppressed it entirely, despite protests from the municipality and *société* of Moret that a market had existed there since Ancien Regime days.

21 Arch. Aube, Lg 6 8 (district of Nogent to the Commission, 6 Ventôse).

22 See J. Bellanger, *Les Jacobins peints par eux-mêmes. Histoire de la société populaire et montagnarde de Provins* (1908), for the steps taken by the *société* of Provins to have a canal built between there and Bray.

23 Arch. Poissy, D 6 (General Council, session of 14 Nivôse): '...The considerable livestock market held there every Thursday (o.s) attracts around 1,500 outsiders and a large number of dogs each week, who have to find their food at Poissy...'.

24 The intensity of the river traffic between Pont-de-l'Arche and Paris can be seen in the number of boats passing through Le Pecq and the importance of their cargoes. See, e.g., Arch. Le Pecq, D1 2 (reg. General Council of the commune), sessions of 4 Ventôse and 10 Prairial Year II. Another commune which had a bad reputation for frequent stoppages and its turbulent river populace was Choisy-le-Roi, an important port for the unloading of wood from the Yonne and the Morvan, and wine from Burgundy; its municipality was

severely criticised by the Commission des Subsistances in Floréal (Arch. Choisy, D 5, General Council, sessions of 15 Germinal and 1 Floréal).

25 Arch. Luzarches, reg. 1 (session of 6 Frimaire Year II). The authorities complained that the commune was not prosperous enough to support the '150 to 300 soldiers passing through every day...the different detachments of the *armée révolutionnaire*...occupying the best lodgings', and asked that the detachment be sent elsewhere, to Mesnil-Aubry for instance, where most of the inhabitants were innkeepers and well-off farmers; a request which was granted.

26 AN, F 11 278a (*Subsistances*), deliberations of the commune of Jouy-le-Châtel, 26 Thermidor Year II; Arch. Rozoy, D 4 (General Council of the commune), session of 21 Ventôse.

27 Arch. Montargis, D 1n 2 (General Council of the commune), session of 4 Nivôse Year II, concerning the disbanding of the local revolutionary company. We have found no trace in the registers of the municipality of the Parisian *armée révolutionnaire* passing through.

28 Arch. Seine-et-Oise, 2Lk 7 (district of Etampes), session of 27 Nivôse; and Arch. Etampes, D1 (General Council), session of 20 Vendémiaire Year II.

29 See R. C. Cobb, 'L'armée révolutionnaire au Havre-Marat', and 'Problèmes des subsistances en l'an II et en l'an III: l'exemple d'un petit port normand: Honfleur', *Mémoires du Congrès des Sociétés savants de Rouen* (1958).

30 AN, F 7* 2509 (General assembly, Fontaine-de-Grenelle Section, 6 and 7 Prairial Year III), and A. E. Sorel, *Pont-de-l'Arche pendant la Révolution* (Evreux-Rouen, 1919), 88–9.

31 Arch. Eure, 60* L 10–12 (district of Les Andelys); Arch. Vernon, D 1/6 and 7 (General Council) and 8 (commune of Vernonnet, deliberations); also Arch. Eure, 99L 11–12 (district of Evreux).

32 Arch. Meulan, reg. A (General Council); Arch. Poissy, D 5 (General Council) and Arch. Seine-et-Oise, 2 Lk 17 (district of Montagne-Bon-Air); Arch. Sèvres, P (reg. 1, *société populaire*).

33 RCC, 'L'armée révolutionnaire dans le district de Pontoise'.

34 RCC, 'L'armée révolutionnaire dans l'Aisne', and Arch. Oise, reg. of deliberations, districts of Noyon and Compiègne.

35

TABLE C

Situation of the *armée révolutionnaire* on 20 Ventôse

Places of cantonment	Numbers	
Infantry:		
La Ferté-Gaucher	42	
Honfleur	234	
Chauny	134	
Soissons	247	
Noyon	119	
Château-Thierry	133	
Compiègne	114	
Provins	107	
Laon	380	
Melun	87	
Brie-la-Ville (Brie-Comte-Robert)	42	
Vernon	102	
Pontoise	220	
Chantilly	99	
Montereau	55	
Coulommiers[a]	267	
Etampes	53	
Viarmes	25	
Meulan	43	
Le Havre	375	
Paris[b]	252	
Lyon	1,145	
	4,474	total infantry

Artillery:

Commune-Affranchie (Lyon)	13	companies (51 men in each)
Brest	4	
Coulommiers	2	
Chartres	2	
Honfleur	1	
Laon	1	
half at Soissons, half at Chantilly	4	
	24	companies (1,200 men)

Cavalry:

Commune-Affranchie (Lyon)	1st	squadrons (170 men in each)
Coulommiers	2nd	
Saumur	3rd	
Beauvais	4th	
Versailles (being equipped)	5th	
Versailles (being equipped)	6th	
	6	squadrons (1,020 men)

Grand total: 6,694 men

AHG, B 5 75 (Armée révolutionnaire).

---

[a] The size of the contingent due to the repression of the religious revolt ('la Vendée briarde') and not because of concern for the *arrivages*.
[b] In the Ecole Militaire, awaiting a posting.

36 E. Créveaux, *Le ravitaillement de Paris par le département de l'Aisne pendant la Révolution* (1936).
37 AN, AF II 58 (423) (99) (Marcellin and Paillardelle).
38 Arch. Rhône, 3 L 64 (district of Lyon-Campagne), sessions of 4 Frimaire and 19 Ventôse, in which the administration resorted to the garrison to protect *arrivages* for Saint-Just, Vaise and La Mulatière.
39 RCC, 'L'armée révolutionnaire dans l'Aisne'.
40 See E. Driault, 'Un agent national à Alençon pendant la Terreur', *R.F.* (1893), and RCC, 'Problèmes des subsistances...Honfleur'.
41 Arch. Eure, 60* L 11 (district of Les Andelys), district of Franciade to the district of Les Andelys, 2 Frimaire Year II.
42 Arch. Eure, 60* L 10 (district of Les Andelys), session of 28 Aug 1793; id., 99* L 11 (district of Evreux, session of 29 Pluviôse).
43 Arch. Eure, 60* L 10 (district of Les Andelys, sessions of 28 Aug and 1 Brumaire) and L 13 (3, 5, 11, 16 and 17 Ventôse).
44 Arch. Oise, reg. copies of letters (*comité de surveillance* of Compiègne), *comité* to the mayor of Paris, 5 Frimaire.
45 Arch. Oise, L (Compiègne) P 4e (district of Compiègne). The district considered the conduct of Gaulthier 'anarchic' and 'despotic', and decided to send two *commissaires* to Paris to demand his recall.
46 AN, W 1 94 (Descombes papers) – a very full account of the mission of Descombes and Geoffroy to the Provins district on behalf of the Commission des Subsistances; and F 7 4584 d 7 (Ballardelle).
47 Arch. Louvres, great reg. (General assembly, 8 Sept).
48 RCC, 'L'armée révolutionnaire dans le district de Pontoise'.
49 Arch. Oise, reg. (*comité* of Compiègne), account of a visit made to the farm of Desmoulins, 3 Frimaire Year II. A year later the mayor of Montrouge stated that the commune had been without grain for four days because there were no threshers, and he called on all citizens who could perform the task to present themselves within 24 hours (Arch. Montrouge, reg. 1).
50 The *armée* was no longer involved, that is, in the task of surveillance of threshing. The difficulties caused by the shortage of threshers, however, persisted, particularly in the district of Meaux, where the authorities continued to complain about this matter right up

to the great crisis of summer 1794. Sometimes the shortage of threshers was simply a pretext used by some rural municipalities for not sending their quotas to the Parisian grain stores. This, according to the Meaux district, was certainly the case with the neighbouring municipality of Saint-Soupplets (Arch. Seine-et-Marne, L 524, district of Meaux), and many village municipalities even went as far as encouraging the threshers in their demands. But the main difficulty was indeed caused by the threshers themselves, and in Messidor the directory of Meaux denounced them for starting threshing, then abandoning it for better-paid employment and leaving the crop to perish (id.; see also L 512–13).

51 River traffic was undoubtedly interrupted for six to eight weeks, particularly during Nivôse. There is no sign of combinations in Brumaire–Frimaire, when traffic again started to move after the drought of the summer (see Prudhomme, *Révolutions de Paris*, no. 213).

52 RCC, 'Le mouvement revendicatif parmi les bateliers de l'Oise et de la Marne'.

53 Arch. Provins, great reg. (session of 3 Ventôse).

54 Arch. Le Pecq, 1 D 3 (General Council, sessions of 4, 24 and 25 Ventôse and 10 Prairial).

55 RCC, 'La mission de Siblot au Havre-Marat', and N. Hampson, *La Marine de l'an II. Mobilisation de la Flotte de l'Océan* (1959).

56 G. Rudé and A. Soboul, 'Le maximum des salaires et le 9 Thermidor', *A.h.R.f.*, jan.–mars 1954.

57 Arch. Seine-et-Oise, IV Q 186 (Mazuel papers).

58 Arch. Eure, 99★ L 11 (district of Evreux, 24 Germinal), attributing the marked decline in 'versements' to the withdrawal of the *commissaires*, which '...proves quite clearly that it is fear rather than love of *la Patrie* which produces action from the farmers...'.

59 BN, MSS Nouv. acq. fr. 2720 (letter from Lemaître, 25 Sept).

60 AN, F 7 4774 53 d 4 (Mouchain).

61 Arch. Rhône, 42 L 149 (Commission Temporaire), denunciation by three cannoneers, 27 Ventôse.

62 AN, Wla 159, and RCC, 'L'armée révolutionnaire à Pontoise'.

63 Arch. Seine, D 4 AZ 698 (Sans-Culottes Section company, based at Alençon, to their Section); AN, Wla 76 (Hébertist affair).

64 AN, F 7★ 4 (Committee of General Security, reg. letters received, 24 Ventôse); 'Jouy' was almost certainly Jouy-en-Josas, where there was a detachment.

65 AN, F 11 218 (*Subsistances*, Seine-et-Oise). The Section appointed two *commissaires* to inform the Interior Minister of this. The accusation seems to have had some foundation, for a similar complaint was made by the Minister in a letter to the mayor of Paris, 10 Brumaire.

66 AN, F 7 4439 1 1 (mission of Mailhe in the Yonne, Year III).

67 Arch. Calvados (reg. Honfleur *comité de surveillance*), denunciation by Captain Petit, 26 Ventôse.

68 See, on this subject, RCC, 'Quelques aspects de la mentalité révolutionnaire'.

69 AN, Wla 18 (tribunaux révolutionnaires, Chavessey affair). Chavessey, a café-owner in the faubourg Saint-Germain, and a member of the *comité révolutionnaire* of his Section, was a *commissaire* of the Committee of General Security in the districts of Saint-Germain-en-Laye.

70 Arch. Rozoy-en-Brie, D 3 (General Council, session of 12 Nivôse).

71 AHG, B 4 10 (Armies of the Midi), Hardy and Robert to the Minister.

72 Arch. Yonne, L 1124 (Joigny *comité de surveillance*), session of 20 Brumaire.

73 Arch. Yonne, L 22 (Département), session of 28 Brumaire, on a petition from the commune of Vermenton, asking for a detachment of the *armée révolutionnaire* to implement requisitions on the communes of the canton in favour of the Vermenton market.

74 Arch. Avallon, I 2 23 9 (*société populaire*, session of 15 Nov), and P. Tartat, *Avallon au dix-huitième siècle*: II, *la Révolution*.

75 Arch. Saône-et-Loire, IV L 11 (Cluny *comité*, session of 7 Frimaire). The sans-culottes of Cluny denounced their mayor to the detachment as having three farms, and a fourth which he had just sold, which meant his granaries were well stocked. For Mâcon, see id. (Passage des Troupes, unclassified).

76 Arch. Coll. Deschamps (private) (reg. *société* of Sennecey-le-Grand, session of 27 Brumaire). On the arrival of the detachment, the *société* presented it with 'a paper banner bearing the words "Unity, Indivisibility of the Republic, Equality, Liberty" on one side, and "The Sans-Culottes of Sennecey to the *Armée Révolutionnaire*" on the other, and the

banner, pike and *bonnet rouge* were accepted amidst loud applause...'.
77 AHG, B 5 75 (Armée révolutionnaire), for Tonnerre; Arch. Troyes, D 3 (General Council, session of 27 Sept).
78 Arch. Meulan, 1 A (reg. General Council, session of 24 Frimaire).
79 Arch. Calvados, (reg. *comité de surveillance* of Lisieux, session of 6 Pluviôse); and see RCC, 'L'armée révolutionnaire au Havre-Marat et dans le district de Montivilliers'.
80 Arch. Eure, 236* L 10 (*société* of Ecouis). At its session of 5 Germinal this *société* demanded the return of the detachment.
81 Arch. Honfleur, 1 62 (*société* of Honfleur).
82 RCC, 'L'armée révolutionnaire au Havre-Marat'.
83 Cited in RCC, 'La campagne pour l'envoi de l'armée révolutionnaire dans la Seine-Inférieure'. Similar sentiments were expressed in the paper of Prudhomme, *Les Revolutions de Paris*, no. 213 (7 Brumaire), just as the *armée révolutionnaire* was about to go into action: 'Only the ill-willed will fear it; the good citizen already welcomes it. The poor family man in his sad little cottage already looks to raising his children without the fear of going short. The hoarders, on the other hand, the *égoïstes*, the wicked rich, the farmer of bad faith..., tremble at the approach of this phalanx of good republicans.... The wicked realise that there can be no republic without the sans-culottes...'.
84 Arch. Oise (great reg. of the district of Chaumont, sessions of 15 and 18 Brumaire).
85 Arch. Oise (district of Noyon, reg. of corres.).
86 Arch. Oise (*société* of Compiègne, reg. of deliberations). For the fears among the *honnêtes gens* caused by news of the arrival of the *armée révolutionnaire*, see also *Mémorial d'un citoyen d'Auxerre*, unpub., which M. Henri Forestier, archivist of the Yonne, kindly brought to my attention. Page 245 tells of the alarm which spread through the town in Oct 1793, at news of the passage of a revolutionary detachment through Auxerre. The 'clubbists' placed republican signs outside their houses, and very soon most of the inhabitants did likewise, 'thinking the sign would preserve them from persecution...'. In the towns of the Midi too the *sociétaires* affixed notices to their shops proclaiming 'This house belongs to a sans-culotte patriot', so that they would escape the *taxes révolutionnaires* imposed on the rich. Another example of the terror which the *armée* inspired among moderates and 'fanatiques' was the prosecution in the Year III of the former bishop of Sidon for having a cache of gold and silver in his home. He claimed to have hidden it for fear that it would be removed by the *armée révolutionnaire*, and was acquitted by the district; 'considering the alarm caused in every soul at that time by the passage of the *Armée révolutionnaire*...' it felt his precautions justified (Arch. Yonne, L 893, directory of the district of Sens, 4 Pluviôse Year III).
87 The municipality of Laon launched its first offensive against the detachment on receipt of the news of Ronsin's arrest. So long as the *armée révolutionnaire* appeared to have the confidence of the Committees, the *représentants* and the other higher authorities, the municipalities acted prudently.
88 Among the municipalities expressing satisfaction were Le Havre, Alençon, Lyon, Saint-Germain (Arch. Saint-Germain, D 1 15, session of 27 Frimaire), Soissons, Chauny (see RCC, 'L'armée révolutionnaire dans l'Aisne'), Chantilly (AN, F 7 4649 d 2, Clémence), Jagny, Marly-la-Ville, Senlis, Chatenay (id.), Luzarches (Arch. Luzarches, great reg.), Melun (Arch. Seine-et-Marne, L 553, district of Melun) – most stating that the detachments had ensured supplies to their markets and the application of the Maximum.
89 See, e.g., the protests of the municipality of Saint-Germain-en-Laye against a report of Delacroix and Musset, suggesting that a revolutionary force was being established in the commune because of 'a disposition to insurrection' (Arch. Saint-Germain, D 1 15, session of 24 Frimaire).
90 See AHG (*reg. d'ordre*), Grammont to Jourdeuil, 3 Pluviôse; also Arch. Etampes, D 1 (General Council), session of 1 Pluviôse.
91 On 27 Ventôse a member of the district directory told the *société* of Mantes that the order on subsistences would be executed at once, and the *armée* would not be needed (Arch. Mantes, D 3 9, *société populaire*).
92 See RCC, 'La disette dans le district de Mantes', and AHG (*reg. d'ordre*), Grammont to Léonard Bourdon, 15 Nivôse.
93 AN, F 7 4775 30 d 1 (Thunot), report by Captain Thunot on the situation in Compiègne, 28 Pluviôse. It was also Thunot who denounced the farmers of the district of Provins (Arch. Seine-et-Marne, L 854, *comité* of Provins, session of 8 Oct).
94 See Arch. Rozoy, D 3 (General Council, session of 3 Nivôse); RCC, 'L'armée

révolutionnaire dans le district de Pontoise'; and Arch. Montereau, D 1 5 and P 2 (General Council and *société populaire*).

95 Arch. Etampes, D 1 (General Council). The detachment denounced the mayor, Clarton, as having prevented the departure of grain convoys to Paris.

96 See below, II. 5, for the Ballardelle affair. The reluctance of certain municipalities to let precious supplies go, dates from the time of the first Maximum, long before the *armée révolutionnaire* had been activated; the authorities of Lagny had been denounced in July by the Paris bakers, well before Ballardelle did so (AN, F 7 4693 d 3 [Dupetit-Manieux]).

97 On the affairs of Presles and Taverny, see RCC, 'L'armée révolutionnaire dans le district de Pontoise'.

98 Arch. Seine-et-Oise (reg. *société populaire* of L'Isle-Adam, session of 4ᵉ *jour sans-culottide*) – the pupils also gathered beechnuts.

99 See Arch. Mantes, D 3 8 (*société populaire*, session of 20 May 1793) for an example of this, and there were many more.

100 RCC, 'Les disettes...dans le district de Mantes et la vallée de la Basse-Seine'.

101 See RCC, 'Problèmes de subsistances: la question des arrivages'.

102 The difficulties in supplying the markets with secondary foodstuffs were described at length by the *comité de surveillance* of Brie-Comte-Robert at its session of 29 Brumaire Year II. The shortage of butter and eggs it attributed to farmers converting milk into cheese for greater profit, and to the direct sale of foodstuffs in the *auberges* or en route before they could be brought to the main market (Arch. Seine-et-Marne, L 887).

103 AN, AF II 58 (423) (97) (Marcellin and Paillardelle), proceedings of the commune of Mions, 23 Frimaire Year II, and Saint-Priest, 24 Frimaire.

104 See RCC, 'L'armée révolutionnaire dans l'Aisne'.

105 The officer commanding the detachment in Provins received 210 livres in 'taxes' from M. Laboullay, 8–9 Oct 1793 (48 for the 2 *commissaires*, 24 for the officer, 12 for the sergeant, and 120 for 10 fusiliers (Arch. Seine-et-Marne, L 857, *comité de surveillance* of Provins). The *révolutionnaires*, however, had not invented this practice; it was already recognised as a kind of *droit de course* by the soldiers and the *maréchaussée* of the Ancien Regime, and the Parisian soldiers, as a kind of political gendarmerie, regarded themselves as heirs to the latter.

106 Arch. Eure, 99* L 11 (district of Evreux, 29 Pluviôse and subsequent meetings).

107 Arch. Vernon, D 1/7 (General Council, session of 2 Floréal).

108 Arch. Eure, 60*L 11 (district of Les Andelys, session of 1 Brumaire).

109 Arch. Oise, (district of Noyon, *subsistances*). It was of course in the interests of each district to hide its resources. But some resources one could not hide, and the district of Meaux had to admit to abundant supplies of wheat in the Year II (Arch. Seine-et-Marne, L 524, district of Meaux, weekly report, Pluviôse Year II), just as that of Provins had to admit to a surplus capable of supplying Paris in the crisis of spring Year III (id., L 609, district of Provins, Ventôse–Germinal Year III). La Goële was likewise well stocked with wheat, while Argenteuil was not (Arch. Argenteuil, 1 D 5, General Council, session of 3 Pluviôse Year II). Similar imbalances occurred in the Oise, as Isoré recognised well enough (Arch. Oise, district of Grandvilliers, reg. 2, 20 Ventôse; district of Breteuil, reg. 2, session of 8 Sept 1793; district of Noyon, subsistances). To judge from the requisition list for Paris (2,000 sacks of flour per week to come from the Oise), the most abundantly supplied districts were Crépy-en-Valois, followed by Noyon and Clermont, though this was hotly denied by the Noyon directory (Arch. Oise, reg. *comptes décadaires*, 1–10 Vendémiaire Year III).

110 Arch. Brie-Comte-Robert, reg. D (General Council, session of 23 Ventôse).

111 A. de Lestapis, 'Gentilshommes charretiers', *Revue des Deux Mondes*, 1 sept. 1953, and RCC, 'Le "complot militaire" de ventôse an II'.

112 The *armée* was used, e.g., to ensure that the carriers of Brie worked 9 out of 10 days, after the national agent of Brie had complained about them refusing to work on Sundays, on the pretext that they could not work 9 consecutive days without rest (Arch. Seine-et-Marne, L 566, district of Melun).

113 See RCC, 'L'armée révolutionnaire dans l'Aisne', and, on Pontoise and Etampes, 'Les disettes dans le district de Mantes'.

114 RCC, 'Les disettes dans le district de Mantes'.

115 RCC, 'Le mouvement revendicatif parmi les bateliers de l'Oise...'.

116 Arch. Honfleur, D 10 (General Council, sessions of 8, 19, 21 Pluviôse). The municipality announced the arrival of the detachment and required the farmers of the canton (circular of

8 Pluviôse) to supply the market every Tuesday, Thursday and Saturday; one farm particularly was to be watched to prevent clandestine buying.

117 For the environs of Lyon, see Arch. Rhône, 3 L 64 (district of La Campagne, session of 4 Frimaire), the district to the garrison commander, and RCC, *L'armée révolutionnaire à Lyon*.

118 The municipality of Montereau ordered such visits after finding out that no butter, eggs or wine had reached the market since the beginning of the month and there was no more oil being sold (Arch. Montereau, D 1 5 [General Council, session of 21 Brumaire]).

119 See Arch. Oise, L 109, Chantilly *comité* to the municipality, 12 Brumaire. On 8 Brumaire the Pierrefonds *comité de surveillance* passed resolutions to ensure that the town's daily market met at 6 a.m. in the summer and 8 a.m. in the winter; that nothing should be sold before these hours, that each trader should bring sufficient quantities of foodstuffs to market each day; that none should be sold from door to door until the market was finished; that anyone stopping traders en route and buying for themselves to the detriment of others would suffer the severest penalty; and that bran and oats could not be sold in private houses, only at market (Arch. Oise, reg. Pierrefonds *comité de surveillance*, session of 8 Brumaire Year II).

120 Arch. Yonne, L 1124 (*comité* of Joigny); Arch. Avallon, I 2 23 11 (Police).

121 On 11 Frimaire the mayor of Vernon was requested to ask the captain and lieutenant of the detachment their motives in transporting religious objects from the surrounding villages to Vernon's Maison Commune (Arch. Vernon, D 1/7).

122 In Attichy, canton *chef-lieu* in the Noyon district, the *commissaires* from the Noyon *comité* and the Parisians arrived at the home of Collar at 3 a.m. In that of Méra, *aubergiste*, they 'searched through my cupboards, drawers, beds, even that of one of my children, two years old, still sound asleep'. The search of Thorin's home took place at 2 a.m.; a cache of 1,200 livres was found in the garden '600 of which was for his daughters' dowry' (Arch. Oise, *Juge de paix* of Attichy, Frimaire Year II).

123 Arch. Rhône, 1 L 212 'Received from c[aptain] Jean Tolède...from a discovery of silverware...at Tolosan's house'.

124 Arch. Seine-et-Oise, 2 Lk 17 (district of Saint-Germain).

125 Another economic duty of the *armée révolutionnaire*, associated with the war effort, was the surveillance of shoemakers under requisition to shoe the troops (Arch. Oise, district of Compiègne, 3 Nivôse).

126 See Arch. Seine-et-Marne, L 554 (district of Melun). On 26 Ventôse a group of *révolutionnaires* was ordered to accompany citizen Joubert, instructed by the administration to make domiciliary visits in the area around Fontainebleau in order to discover any devastation of the national forests. Indeed the detachment in this district was fairly constantly employed in the discovery of forestry offences and the seizure of wood in offending households.

127 Arch. Oise (regs. of the Compiègne, Breteuil and Grandvilliers districts).

128 Arch. Seine-et-Oise (reg. of deliberations, L'Isle-Adam *société populaire*).

129 RCC, 'L'armée révolutionnaire au Havre-Marat'.

130 RCC, 'L'armée révolutionnaire dans l'Aisne'.

131 Arch. Vincennes, 1 D 3 (General Council, sessions of 23 and 26 Ventôse).

132 There are innumerable examples of individual *révolutionnaires* denouncing traders for selling goods above the price fixed by the Maximum; see, e.g., Arch. Avallon, I 2 23 9 (Avallon *société populaire*, session of 16 Nov), Arch. Brie-Comte-Robert, D 1 (reg. General Council, 11 Pluviôse), Arch. Rhône, 32 L 10 (district of Lyon-Campagne, 17 Pluviôse), Arch. Seine-et-Oise (reg. of the L'Isle-Adam *société populaire*, 5 Nivôse). One fusilier, Noël, denounced a merchant to the municipality of Montereau for not declaring six casks of wine – in fact he seems to have wanted to buy the wine for his own use (Arch. Montereau, D 1 5, General Council, 24 Frimaire). A wine-grower of Clairoix, denounced by Amoureux, sergeant-major of the Compiègne detachment, and told to bring forth his wine, replied: 'I have some, and it is not for sale at the price of the Maximum...bugger the Maximum...those who made the Maximum made it so that they could take what belonged to the country people...' – a cry from the heart, which shows what the country people thought of this detested law (Arch. Oise, reg. Compiègne *comité de surveillance*); see also id., L 4, (reg. Noyon *comité de surveillance*).

Caches of silver and precious objects were also reported – and sometimes discovered – by the *révolutionnaires*; see, e.g., Arch. Oise (reg. Compiègne *comité de surveillance*), denunciation made by three fusiliers of the Thunot detachment, 4 Frimaire Year II. The total value of specie seized by the detachment in the area around Compiègne came to 27,233 livres (17,570 in gold). Some of the caches – in these times of shortage – were also of a more banal nature: on 21 Brumaire, the soldier, Wilhelm, from the Brie detachment, reported to the *comité* of this town that he had information from a citizen, who wished to remain anonymous, that there was a hidden store containing soap and other goods belonging to the grocer Anceaux; upon which the *comité* took itself to Anceaux's house, accompanied by Wilhelm and some fusiliers, but found nothing. The denouncer, Bridoux, brought before them, claimed he had the information from one Dubois, and the *comité* had both of them arrested. (Arch. Seine-et-Marne, L 887, Brie-Comte-Robert, *comité de surveillance*, session of 21 Brumaire Year II.) A similar report was made about a hidden store at Chantilly; as at Brie, a detachment was sent to search, with the same result (Arch. Oise, L 109, Chantilly *comité de surveillance*, session of 1 Frimaire).

133 The case of Provins is of particular interest, as one of the largest producers of wheat in the Paris region, whose authorities were constantly charged with *mauvaise volonté* from Aug 1793 onwards. Indeed the accusation against the detachment was the municipality's response to a complaint by the Commission des Subsistances, 23 Ventôse, that the municipality had forbidden the departure of foodstuffs for Paris. (AN, W 81 and Wla 94.) The municipality of Beaumont produced a similar counter-attack on the detachment in the first days of Germinal. See RCC, 'L'armée révolutionnaire dans le district de Pontoise'.

134 The so-called subsistence crisis of Ventôse–Germinal was above all one of meat, dairy produce and vegetables. Bread supplies to Paris were assured. See below, III. 3, on this crisis, also the observations of the directory of the Meaux district on the extreme shortage of oats (Arch. Seine-et-Marne, L 524, *comptes décadaires*, Ventôse-Floréal Year II).

135 AN, Wla 94 (Descombes papers, Champeaux and Dumez to Descombes, 18 Sept).

136 See RCC, 'Problèmes de subsistances; la question des arrivages'.

137 At the Ivry municipality session of 12 Fructidor Year II, the national agent asked permission to send an armed force to search wagons reported to be bringing cereals to Paris to sell at excessive prices (Arch. Ivry, D 1, General Council). On the resort to force in the Year III see R. C. Cobb, 'Politique et subsistances en l'an III: l'exemple du Havre', *Annales de Normandie*, mai 1955.

Chapter 2

1 Arch. Hautes-Alpes, L 1082 (district of Briançon to the municipalities under its authority, 5 Frimaire): 'A revolutionary company...designed solely to execute the laws issued by the Convention, notably that fixing the Maximum, and rigorously to combat all hoarders...'.

2 Audouin, in the *Journal Universel*, no. 1406 (30 sept).

3 Arch. Basses-Pyrénées, 27 L1 (*société populaire* of Morlaas, session of 8 Floréal). A member proposed excluding citizens who did not work every day from the distribution of grain, because 'a citizen who did not work was undoubtedly a *Monsieur* with a private income and should not be allowed to eat the bread intended for the labouring poor who sweat 9 days to earn the wherewithal to live for 10...'.

4 See, e.g., Arch. Vaucluse, L VI 13 (*société* of Vaison, session of 6 Pluviôse): 'one member observed that the *armée révolutionnaire* had arrived at Orange and since it would see that the laws of the Maximum were observed wherever it went, they would soon see the end of all *égoïstes* and hoarders...'.

5 The authorities were only too well aware of the explosive nature of the problem of shortages, and just as the Committee of Public Safety ordered the assemblies in the Paris Sections to allow no further public discussion on subsistences, so the *représentants en mission* proposed silence as the best remedy. Thus Dartigoëyte, on mission in the Gers, intervened in the *société* of Auch, when the question of grain supplies was raised, claiming 'that it was best not to speak about subsistences, even favourably. He observed that ill-disposed persons had already raised fears about subsistences...' (Arch. Gers, L 694, *société* of Auch). This was an easy solution, and one supported by the government, permitting it both to silence popular discontent, and to protect its own agents. Nor was their analysis of the situation entirely unfounded, for as soon as the subject was raised, it attracted all kinds of myths, the *sociétaires* became excited and their alarm contributed to popular disquiet. See also Arch. Allier, L 901★ (*société* of Moulins, session of 6 Floréal Year II), for an example of this kind of clamp-down on discussion about subsistences.

6 See complaints about ravages by wolves in the canton of Carluces and the Clamecy district, 8 and 27 Frimaire (Arch. Nièvre, L, reg. 7, correspondence of the district of Clamecy). The tables were sometimes turned, however, and in the same district a butcher was prosecuted during the crisis of the Year III for having sold wolf as hare (id., session of 14 Pluviôse Year III).

7 For Arles, see RCC, *L'armée révolutionnaire parisienne à Lyon et dans la région lyonnaise*; and see Arch. Haute-Saône, 55 L 3 (district of Gray, session of 25 Brumaire).

8 RCC, *L'armée révolutionnaire à Lyon.*

9 See, e.g., Arch. Lot-et-Garonne (reg. 1, deliberations of the *société* of Tonneins-la-Montagne, session of 4 Germinal), in which the entire assembly agreed to escort the 50 barges waiting to carry subsistences from Bordeaux up river. The grain had been brought to Bordeaux in the American vessel the *Fame*, out of Philadelphia.

10 R. Mayer, 'L'agence de Montpellier', *Revue du commerce, de l'industrie...des Alpes-Maritimes* (1945). Many communes in the Vaucluse sent *commissaires* to Marseille and Nice, in the hope of buying grain from Italy, Greece, Dalmatia or the Maghreb, and throughout this region ships entering Marseille from Tunis and Genoa were watched with anguished attention. See Arch. Vaucluse, L VI 12 (*société* of Vaison-la-Romaine, session of 22 Pluviôse Year II), at which a letter was read announcing just such an arrival at Nice.

11 RCC, 'Les armées révolutionnaires du Midi', 15.

12 *Journal Universel*, no. 1442, 15 Brumaire Year II.

13 Arch. Cantal, L 691 (*comité de surveillance* of Saint-Flour); Arch. Basses-Pyrénées, 27 L 1 (*société* of Morlaas, session of 3 Floréal Year II).

14 Arch. Sceaux, reg. 4 (General Council of the commune, session of 21 Ventôse Year II), general assembly of the retailers of Sceaux.

15 Arch. Sceaux, reg. 4, id.

16 Arch. Gironde, 4 L 50 (district of Bordeaux). At its session of 6 Ventôse, the district of Bordeaux insisted on the necessity of bringing in grain, either by sea from the United States, or along the Dordogne and the Garonne, the shortage of horses and transports rendering supply by road impracticable.

17 See Arch. Metz, 1 D 1 15 (General Council, session of 18 Germinal), for the navigation facilities offered by the Moselle.

18 The municipality of Châlons wrote, with some exaggeration, 2 Prairial Year III: 'It is the busiest route of the Republic, whether for Paris, or the armies of the Nord, Sambre-et-Meuse, Moselle or Haut- and Bas-Rhin etc. Numerous military convoys pass through daily...'. (Arch. Châlons, D★ 22.)

19 Arch. Nièvre, 8 L 8 (district of Nevers). On 19 Fructidor Year II this district complained that low waters in the Loire had prevented any markets being held until then. See also RCC, 'Problèmes des subsistances en l'an II et en l'an III'.

20 L. Dermigny, *Naissance et croissance d'un port. Sète de 1666 à 1880* (Sète, 1955).

21 Restif de la Bretonne, *Les Nuits de Paris ou le spectateur nocturne* (ré-éd. 1960), 151, 252.

22 *Journal Universel*, no. 1442, 15 Brumaire Year II.

23 RCC, 'Quelques aspects de la crise de l'an III en France et dans les provinces belges', unpub. paper [1961] delivered to the Anglo-French Congress, Cambridge.

24 See the report made to the *société populaire* of Grenoble, 28 Pluviôse Year II, by the *commissaire-ordonnateur*, Bersonnet, stating that for the past 50 years the French troops had been fed on bread composed of 2/3 wheat, 1/3 rye; but whereas previously France would only have had to feed 300,000 men at most, in the Year II there were some 1,500,000 men under arms, and perhaps another 2 million to feed in the towns (including the rich, the beggars, the children and the old) – which gives some idea of the enormity of the task facing those responsible for supplying the large towns and the armies. (Arch. Grenoble, LL 77, *société* of Grenoble, corres.)

25 AN, F 7 4551 (Hautes-Alpes, arrests), district of Forcalquier to the Committee of General Security, 8 Ventôse Year II. In the Haute-Saône the *commissaires* overseeing requisitions for the Army of the Rhine described how at Autoreille they were surrounded by the entire populace, claiming that they would rather be guillotined than see the grain go; 'we did everything to reassure them and calm their fears...saying that if supplies to the armies were held up...our enemies might take advantage by seeking to destroy our liberty, to which they replied they did not give a damn, and they would eat all the bread they wanted...' (Arch. Haute-Saône, 32 L 4, district of Lure [*subsistances*], letter of 9 Germinal Year II). Such scenes, reflecting the fear of going short and the lack of patriotism among

the country people, were repeated in every department at the time of the Maximum and the major requisitions.

26 See, e.g., Arch. Chalon-sur-Saône (reg. 2, General Council, session of 6 Floréal Year II); also AN, F 11 372 (Commission des Subsistances), General Council of the commune of Puymirol, session of 15 Brumaire Year III. The Moissac *comité de surveillance* scrutinised the cargo certificates of every carrier taking grain down river to Bordeaux, and each day there were instances of delays until the real destination of the cargo could be checked with its point of departure (AN, F 7 4563, Moissac *comité de surveillance*, session of 2 Brumaire Year II). The correspondence of the municipality of Bordeaux with the Moissac authorities highlights the obstacles hindering requisitions in favour of the large town from the surrounding departments. Bordeaux sent *commissaires* into the Haute-Garonne and the Lot-et-Garonne to try to combat such prejudices, and connived at the extensive clandestine traffic on the Garonne. (Arch. Bordeaux, D 106, General Council [*subsistances*], also Arch. Gironde 11 L 27, Club national.) For similar accusations concerning supplies to Lyon, see Arch. Côte-d'Or, L 1330 and L 1343 (district of Beaune), and L 1973 (district of Saint-Jean-de-Losne); also Arch. Haute-Saône, 56 L 2 (district of Gray), Silvy, subsistences agent for the Army of the Rhine, to the district, 11 Pluviôse Year II.

27 From Toulouse we have an example of the kind of vexations experienced by the farmers who came to the official markets and causing them to prefer selling to middlemen waiting for them along the roads. 'A farmer arrives at the market place; instantly he is surrounded by 20 or 30 hungry purchasers, who throw themselves upon his produce before he has time to display it...' (*Journal révolutionnaire de Toulouse*, no. lxxi, 'Situation de Toulouse', 10 Prairial Year II).

28 The district of Gray and the authorities of the Haute-Saône were in the unenviable position of being exposed to all kinds of concurrent requisitions in favour of the Armies of the Rhine and the Alps, and the town of Lyon. The department was not rich in grain and Gray owed its importance solely to its position as a river port, at which grain was loaded for shipment. (Arch. Haute-Saône, 55 L 4, district of Gray, session of 29 Brumaire Year II.) For the Ain, see RCC, *L'armée révolutionnaire parisienne à Lyon et dans la région lyonnaise*, 43–50.

29 Arch. Lot, L 405 (*comité* of Montauban to Bô, 7 Floreal).

30 See, e.g., Arch. Vaucluse, L VI 13 (*société* of Cheval-Blanc, session of 16 Ventôse), when the two neighbouring communes agreed to exchange wood for grain. The communes of the Ardèche exchanged their chestnuts for grain from the Drôme (see RCC, 'Les armées révolutionnaires du Midi'), those of the Nièvre their wine for corn from the Cher (Arch. Nièvre, 8 L 8, district of Nevers, session of 3 Messidor Year II), and those of the Rhône their wine for grain from the Isère (Arch. Rhône, 34 L 28★, *société populaire* of Montagny, session of 10 Pluviôse Year II).

31 On the Beaumont–Grenade rivalry, see A. Duboul, *L'armée révolutionnaire de Toulouse*, also P. Gérard, 'L'armée révolutionnaire de la Haute-Garonne'.

32 The Aveyron too was short of grain: see J. Viguier, 'Le directoire du district de Cahors et la question des grains de 1790 à l'an III', *R.F.*, XVII (1889), 20–39; Arch. Lot, L 72 (département), Lagasquie, national agent of the Cahors district, to Bô, 14 Pluviôse Year II, proclaiming that the district faced immediate famine if supplies were not forthcoming, and id., L 405, *comité* of Montauban to Bô, 7 Floréal, with the same story. See also Arch. Cantal, L 684, 689 and 690, and Arch. Aveyron, 72 L 4, for complaints from various communes and districts in these afflicted departments about their inability to feed their inhabitants, even in normal times. During the summer and the terrible winter of the Year III, the situation in these three departments was tragic.

33 Arch. Aube, Ld 73 (district of Troyes).

34 AHG, B2 27, printed notice of 14 Brumaire Year II: *Les commissaires civils...aux habitants des campagnes*.

35 Arch. Loire, L 396 (Charlieu *comité*, session of 15 Brumaire). The Charlieu *société* had a poor opinion of the Vougy people, complaining 'that most country people do not treat other citizens as brothers' (id., L 400).

36 Arch. Aube, L 4 30bis (*comité* of the 1st Section of Troyes).

37 Arch. Basses-Pyrénées, 25 L 1 (*société* of Monein).

38 Arch. Aveyron, 72 L 4 (*comité* of Saint-Geniez).

39 See, e.g., Arch. Gers, L 949 (*société* of Auch, session of 24 Prairial Year II). '...The cause

[of the shortage] lies in the shameful monopolising by the *aubergistes*... who buy up goods at high prices and during the night... so that tables at the *auberges* are abundantly and sumptuously supplied... with meals costing 4 l. and 100 s.... while the sick poor are deprived of basic necessities...'.

40 Every district in the Loire had often to draw provisions from distant areas: the most populous, that of Commune d'Armes (Saint-Etienne), was also the one which produced least grain and in 1793, like Lyon and the communes of the Rhône, it looked to the Saône-et-Loire, the Côte-d'Or and to the departments of Lorraine, Franche-Comté and Burgundy for supplies (Arch. Loire, L 155, district of Saint-Etienne). The three districts of the Rhône (Lyon, Lyon-Campagne and Villefranche) were largely given over to vines and produced little grain. Supplies had to come from outside, as well as from abroad. In the Moselle it was the Metz district which experienced most difficulty (Arch. Metz, 1D1 13); while the Allier complained of shortages because of requisitions made on behalf of the Army of the Alps (Arch. Allier, L 850, *comité* of Moulins, session of 9 Brumaire Year II).

According to the Commission des Subsistances (AN, F 11 274 Pl. 4), the districts of the South, deficient in grain and permitted to take supplies from the national stores, were: Marseille, Salon, the Ardèche and Lozère departments, Le Vignan, Villeneuve-sur-Lot, Barjols, Béziers, the Var and Alpes-Maritimes departments, Libourne, Nîmes, Alès, and Grasse. The plain of Arles seems to have been their principal internal source of supply (Arch. Saint-Tropez, reg. 1, session of 12 Aug 1793). According to Haller, agent for the stores at Nice, grain from Genoa was also needed to supply Toulon, the Hérault, the Gard 'and above all unfortunate Aveyron' (Arch. Marseille, 1 D 12, General Council, 12 Germinal Year II) – no doubt an accurate estimate of the hierarchy of needs in these regions.

41 Always taking into account the tendency of most communal authorities to exaggerate, the situation of Moulins seems to have been particularly tragic and the municipality spoke, on 11 Germinal, of having to harvest unripe corn for bread, such was the shortage being experienced there (Arch. Allier, L 852).

42 See, e.g., Arch. Orléans, D 23 E (General Council, session of 4 Sept); Arch. Grenoble, LL 19, municipality of Grenoble to the Commission des Subsistances, 1 Pluviôse Year II; Arch. Haute-Vienne, L 402 (district of Limoges), session of 26 Vendémiaire Year II.

43 Arch. Loire, L 434 (*comité* of Bonnet-la-Montagne) and L 396 and 399 (*comité* and *société* of Charlieu).

44 Arch. Loire, 42 L 127 (Commission de Feurs), municipality of Saint-Bonnet to the *comité* of Montbrison, 16 Brumaire Year II.

45 Arch. Loire, L 396 (*comité* of Charlieu, session of 25 Vendémiaire).

46 Arch. Basses-Pyrénées, 25 L 1 (*société* of Monein, session of 7 Nov 1793).

47 This was all the more true considering the apparent abundance of the 1793 harvest. The district of Gray, always well informed in matters of production and distribution of grain, claimed (at its 11 Frimaire session) that even a mediocre harvest would produce at least one-fifth more than was needed for the whole of France (even without foreign purchases); '... and yet evil men still try to cause disquiet' (Arch. Haute-Saône, 55 L 4). The *comité* of Bonnet-la-Montagne (Saint-Bonnet-le-Château) in the Loire expressed its surprise that even after such an abundant harvest the granaries were so poorly supplied (Arch. Loire, L 434, *comité* of Bonnet-la-Montagne).

48 However, 'la malveillance' was not always pure myth. Dartigoëyte denounced to the Auch *société* 'a former baron from Verduzan with an income of 40,000 livres, who sought to starve people by letting 20 sacks of corn rot in a dunghill...' (Arch. Gers, L 694, *société* of Auch, session of 25 Germinal Year II).

49 In all the frontier areas, the authorities attached great importance to 'la malveillance' and to exportations abroad; see Arch. Savoie, L 1770 (district of Chambéry), 19 Frimaire. A month later the Thonon *comité* complained of barges passing daily through to Switzerland and demanded an inventory of grain in the cantons of Evian and Abondance to prevent its export to Valais (Arch. Haute-Savoie, 5 L 13bis, 24 Messidor). See also Arch. Basses-Alpes, L 756, Digne *comité* to the district, 2 Frimaire Year II, with a similar complaint about export abroad; and see I. 4, n. 98, for the role of the *armées révolutionnaires* in the prevention of export and contraband.

50 The dependence of the wage-earner on the application of the Maximum is underlined in a debate which took place, 3 Vendémiaire Year III, in the *comité de surveillance* of Murat: 'One member observed that since the terms of the Maximum had been displayed in the

commune, essential supplies could no longer be had; cooking oil, so essential to the lacemakers and all the inhabitants, seems to have disappeared, all the shopkeepers proclaiming that they had none, while intimating vaguely that it could be had for 100 sols a *livre*, and the same with soap, for as much as 12 livres a *livre*, and since such commodities are indispensable, citizens are obliged to buy them, whatever the price, so that those who have no wealth but what they earn by their toil are reduced to misery, and those who have country produce to sell...do not wish to do so at the price of the Maximum because they too are obliged to buy all their necessities at prices which bear no relation to the Maximum...' (Arch. Cantal, L 689, *comité* of Murat).

51 On 5 Frimaire, Parent, *procureur syndic* of the Clamecy district, urged those employed at Pressures: 'work for the Republic, and you work for your family...'. But in Pluviôse the district administration supported their demands for a wage increase 'owing to their patriotism...'. (Arch. Nièvre, reg. delib. 8, Clamecy). On 13 Brumaire the municipality of Cosne put an end to the seamen's practice of demanding the exclusive right to load and unload merchandise with the words: '...all privileges due to former laws or former practice are abolished...' (Arch. Cosne, reg. 5, General Council).

52 Arch. Allier, L 850–2 (*comité* of Moulins, 4 Brumaire). The revolutionary authorities everywhere had problems with threshers demanding high wages and food allowances; see Arch. Loire, L 434 (*comité* of Saint-Bonnet) and Arch. Hautes-Alpes, L 1178, reg. corres., district of Gap, 13 Frimaire Year II).

53 Arch. Metz, 1 D 1 14 (General Council of the commune of Metz).

54 Arch. Châlons, 1* 99 (*société* of Châlons) and Arch. Marne, L 427 (*département*; *commissaires civils*, communication of 28 Brumaire).

55 RCC, 'Les armées révolutionnaires du Midi'.

56 AHG, B2 27 (Army of the Moselle).

57 AHG, B2 27 (circular to departments).

58 AHG, B2 28 (Moselle Army, Mourgoin to Bouchotte). He added: 'Now that they [the *armées*] are suppressed, things are no longer the same, and only revolutionary measures will force the selfish to act'.

59 AHG, B1 20 (Army of the Nord), Dufresse to the Committee of Public Safety, 4 Oct 1793. It is clear that this *armée* was destined solely to assist military rather than civilian supply, except in applying the Maximum (AN, W 498 [535], Lavalette to his friend Dufresse).

60 Châles issued a notice, for the eyes of the merchants and shopkeepers of Lille, in which he assigned precise economic duties to this *armée*: 'You will see [it]...penetrating your storehouses, whisking away those essential supplies amassed by you, and restoring joy and abundance to the markets...' (AHG, B1 22). The cattle they took to the military stores at Lille (id., B1 20). At Dunkerque the arrival of the *armée* saw a renewed effort to apply the Maximum (Arch. Lille, 18′ 229, *société révolutionnaire*).

61 Prudhomme, v. 506; also Aulard, VIII. 70: Mallarmé and his colleagues at Strasbourg to the Committee of Public Safety, 6 Brumaire. The Bas-Rhin was particularly noted for its non-execution of the Maximum (Arch. Bas-Rhin, 50 L 6, *comité* of Sélestat; also AN, D III 355, Comité de législation, Bas-Rhin).

62 Arch. Grenoble, LL 19 (municipality to the *société*, 28 Brumaire).

63 See, e.g., Arch. Aveyron, 77 L1 (*comité* of Sévérac), interrogation of Gibelin, 7 Frimaire Year III, on a cache of jewels etc. found at this landowner's – which included his son, a deserter from the army.

64 Arch. Nièvre (great reg., *comité* of Corbigny).

65 Arch. Cantal, L 687 (*comité* of Aurillac), declaration of Capelle, a landowner of Clavières, 5 Frimaire Year III. For the later observation see *La Révolution du Cantal* (Aurillac, 6 brumaire an III).

66 Arch. Lot, L 389 (*comité de surveillance* of Cahors, session of 24 Brumaire).

67 Arch. Nièvre, L reg. 7 (district of Clamecy, corres., 27 Frimaire), and great reg. (*comité* of Corbigny).

68 Arch. Allier, L 850, 853, 878 (*comité* of Moulins).

69 Arch. Aube, Ld 4 5 (district of Ervy, session of 25 Frimaire).

70 RCC, 'Les armées révolutionnaires du Midi'.

71 RCC, *L'armée révolutionnaire parisienne à Lyon et dans la région lyonnaise*.

72 AN, F 7 3681[9] (Terrorists), denunciations made in Prairial Year III against the terrorists of Marmande and La Réole.

73 See, e.g., Arch. Nièvre, reg. delib. 8 (district of Clamecy, session of 11 Brumaire), on the opposition of the peasants of Entrains to the requisition of horses, necessitating the intervention of a revolutionary detachment.

74 AN, D III 180 (8) 19 (Comité de législation, Nièvre, Moulins-Engilbert), district session, 27 Frimaire Year III.

75 See B. Combes de Patris, *Procès-verbaux de la société populaire de Rodez*, 198, session of 3 Floréal Year III.

76 Arch. Metz, 1D1 13 (General Council of the commune, sessions of 10 and 16 Brumaire).

77 APP, AA/269 (notes of Topino-Lebrun).

78 See RCC, 'Les armées révolutionnaires du Midi', esp. p. 60, and P. Gérard, 'L'armée révolutionnaire de la Haute-Garonne'.

79 Arch. Allier, L 853 and 878 (Moulins *comité*). The Moulins authorities also used the detachment to police the market and to combat retailers.

80 Arch. Allier, L 850 (Moulins *comité*).

81 Arch. Loire, L 432 (Montbrison *comité*), L 434 (*comité* of Bonnet-la-Montagne); Arch. Grenoble, LL 19 (General Council).

82 RCC, 'Les armées révolutionnaires du Midi', 60, 70–1.

83 See in particular, Arch. Basses-Alpes, L 756 (Digne *comité* to the district, 6 Frimaire).

84 See E. Gautheron, 'Un club des Jacobins...: La société populaire du Puy [-en-Velay]'; also Prudhomme, v. 474–8.

85 Arch. Gironde, 11 L 27 (Club national) and Arch. Bordeaux, D 104 (General Council).

86 Arch. Lot-et-Garonne, reg. 1 (Agen *comité*), sessions of 25 and 27 Vendémiaire.

87 See Arch. Lot-et-Garonne, reg. 2 (Agen *société populaire*), session of 6 Brumaire Year III. Certain members of the former company were accused of abusing their powers to impose fines on the *aubergistes*, then pocketing the proceeds without informing the authorities.

88 AN, D III 178 (71) (Comité de législation, Nièvre, Corbigny).

89 Arch. Vaucluse, L VI 25 (Courthézon *société*).

90 Arch. Hautes-Alpes, L 1507 (Saint-Bonnet *comité*), report of the 2nd *décade* of Messidor Year II). See also AN, D III 30 (6) (Comité de législation, Aubagne), observations by Delon, showing that the Maximum on grain was effective in the Bouches-du-Rhône.

91 This was true even though the quantity and quality of taxed bread was, according to the farm workers, inferior to that received by the privileged Parisians: 'It is impossible to persuade the people of our canton', wrote the small *société* of Vauvillers to the Haute-Saône department, 19 Germinal, '...that a *livre* of bread is enough, their stomachs do not reason, they digest some two *livres* at least...' (Arch. Haute-Saône, 32 L 4, département, *subsistances*).

92 Wine was considered a primary necessity by the worker and had the added advantage of enabling him to avoid the often contaminated water of that period. Indeed requisitions of wine for the army were considered as important as those of bread. See complaints about the want of wine in Arch. Vaucluse, L VI 13 (*société* of Cheval-Blanc, session of 9 Floréal Year II).

93 See P. Gérard, 'L'armée révolutionnaire de la Haute-Garonne'; also RCC, 'Les armées révolutionnaires du Midi', 85, n. 2. The *Journal révolutionnaire de Toulouse*, no. xviii (4 Frimaire), when the *armée* had been in activity for a month, spoke of the abundance in the town. But this situation did not survive the dissolution of the *armée*; issues of 9 Nivôse (xxviii) and 7 Pluviôse (xxxvi) speak of growing alarm about subsistences, and although Montauban reported continuing abundance in Toulouse, 7 Floréal, the former town was trying to establish its urgent need over that of Toulouse and its claims are unreliable (Arch. Lot, L 405, Montauban *comité* to Bô).

94 Aulard, viii. 70, Mallarmé to the Committee of Public Safety, 6 Brumaire.

95 Arch. Grenoble, LL 19 (General Council, 28 Brumaire); for Puy-de-Dôme see AN, AF II 186 (1541) (Reynaud to the Committee, 28 Frimaire).

96 AHG, B2 28 (Moselle Army), Mourgoin to Bouchotte, 4 Nivôse.

97 Arch. Aveyron, 80 L 1 (Villefranche *comité*, sessions of 22 and 29 Brumaire). See also AAG, personnel, Gén. de div. 237 (Marbot), Marbot to the Committee, 24 Messidor Year III: '...Above all I need to restrain the *Armée révolutionnaire*, which, like a torrent, threatens to devastate the regions...'. See also B. Combes de Patris, *Procès-verbaux de la société populaire de Rodez*. Every commentator agrees that the arrival of this great *armée* caused a kind of famine in the dreadfully poor region.

98 Arch. Haute-Saône, 55L3 (district of Gray). For Vaise see RCC, *L'armée révolutionnaire à*

Lyon and 'Le "complot militaire" de ventôse an II'.

99 The commune of Aix-en-Provence, complaining about smaller communes supplying larger, and Marseille in particular, claimed that all communes were equal in a democratic republic (AN, D III 29 (2) (6), Comité de législation, petition from Aix, 16 Pluviôse Year III). Such equality, however, did not operate in subsistence matters, the large communes possessing all the means of reaching the *représentants* and central government with their complaints.

100 This multiplication of individual forces also had the disadvantage of aggravating the 'federalisation' of supply, by giving many small communes the means of pressurising their neighbours. In the Eure, the Cantal and the Allier there were complaints of communal forces invading neighbouring territory and carrying off subsistences (Arch. Allier, L 850, session of 12 Frimaire Year II). The law of 14 Frimaire put a stop to this proliferation of forces, which might otherwise have ended with the inhabitants of the poorer regions locked in bitter conflict over grain with those of supposedly rich regions. The only real solution would have been the creation of several large *armées* or a national one, and the Parisian sans-culottes were right to fear the consequences for supply policies of a multiplication of individual forces.

Chapter 3

1 V. Lombard de Langres, *Histoire des Jacobins depuis 1789 jusqu'à ce jour* (1820), ch. xxiii, 112. See also *Histoire de la Révolution française par deux amis de la liberté* (Year VII), XIII. 58.
2 *Journal Universel*, no. 1395.
3 RCC, *L'armée révolutionnaire à Lyon*, 7.
4 *Journal de l'armée des côtes de Cherbourg* (Caen *société*, session of 6 Oct).
5 Ibid., session of 13 Sept.
6 Dorfeuille, who was to be a victim of the Thermidorean massacres, wrote to a fellow actor and friend at the time of the September Massacres, 1792: '...Paris is a jungle at present, given over to 40,000 assassins...' (AN, F 7 4678 d 3, Dorfeuille).
7 AHG, B⁵ 20 (Côtes de Cherbourg Army) for Bouchotte's letter; Arch. Honfleur, D 10 (municipality, circular of 8 Pluviôse).
8 *Le Père Duchesne de Commune-Affranchie*, no. xxii, 'Grande Colère' (17 Pluviôse).
9 AN, F 7 4767 d 2 (Lassagne).
10 Prudhomme, v. 409.
11 Arch. Seine-et-Oise, IV Q 187 (Mazuel papers), letter from Fayet cited in RCC, 'Quelques aspects de la mentalité révolutionnaire'; id., Penelle and Colombel to Mazuel, 27 Frimaire.
12 AN, F 7 4774 16 d 3 (Lenoir), list of terrorists of the Marchés Section, 30 Germinal Year III. The man was Verter, of 28, rue du Chevalier du Guet.
13 RCC, *L'armée révolutionnaire à Lyon*. The two authors of the *Histoire de la Révolution français* of the Year VII – not normally inclined to treat the soldiers of 'this horrible militia' favourably – also cite (p. 631) an example of them intervening on behalf of the victims of two over-zealous *commissaires*, preventing them from taking suspects from a barge travelling from Paris to Sens. It was clearly a case of competition between two institutions of the Terror, rather than any leniency on the part of the soldiers, and they must have been delighted at the chance afforded to put the meddlesome *commissaires* in their place in front of the barge's passengers.
14 AN, F 7 4775 30 d 1 (Thunot).
15 AN, BB3 71, citizens of the Finistère company to Brigant, member of the Lazowski *société*, 16 Ventôse.
16 Arch. Oise (reg. *société* of Compiègne), session of 10 Pluviôse; and AN, F 7 4775 30 d 1 (Thunot), Thunot to the *comité* of the Panthéon-Français Section, 28 Pluviôse Year II.
17 AN, F 7 4774 29 d 2 (Magon-Labalue).
18 Michel Eude's *Paris pendant la Terreur* (1964) has helped bridge this gap. For a study of a single district in the Pas-de-Calais, see G. Sangnier, *La Terreur dans le district de Saint-Pol* (Blangermont, 1938).
19 Adjutant-general Régnier, garrison commander in Granville in the Year II, was to be accused by the Thermidorean authorities of the town in the Year III of having used the revolutionary cannoneers to make a number of arrests there (AN, F 7 4774 89 d 1 [Regnier]). They exonerated the former members of the *comité de surveillance* (AN, D III

143 [9] [7], Comité de législation, Manche, district of Avranches to the Committee, 12 Frimaire Year III). Here, as in many towns, the most active terrorists were the soldiers. See also R. du Coudray, *Granville et ses environs pendant la Révolution* (Granville, 1922), for the repressive activity of these soldiers.

20 See RCC, 'La mission de Siblot au Havre-Marat', and 'L'armée révolutionnaire au Havre-Marat et dans le district de Montivilliers'.

21 BL, 936 c 36, *Liste générale des dénonciateurs et des dénoncés, tant de la Ville de Lyon que des Communes voisines et de celles de divers Départements* (Lausanne, 1795). Among others, we find the names of the *révolutionnaires* Philippe Abat and André Jurlat, living in Villefranche; Pierre Grange, living in Vienne; Contamin, former national agent of Crémieu – i.e., only four in a list of hundreds accused of having been denouncers.

22 On the arrests made by the Paris detachments see: for BEAUVAIS: Arch. Oise (reg. Beauvais *comité*) and AN, Wla 138 (Fouquier-Tinville papers); for NOYON and the canton of ATTICHY: Arch. Oise (regs. Noyon *comité de surveillance* and district, papers of the Attichy *juge de paix*) and AN, F 7 4662 d 5 (D'Aumont), F 7★ 4 (reg. corres., Committee of General Security), Wla 37 (2382) and Wla 121 (Hennon affair); for COMPIÈGNE: Arch. Oise (reg. corres., Compiègne *comité*) and AN, Wla 113 and 135; for BRETEUIL and CHAUMONT: Arch. Oise (regs. *comité* and district of Chaumont) and Arch. Seine-et-Oise, IV Q 186 (Mazuel papers).

For the GONESSE district: AN, F 7 4649 d 2 (Clémence), F 7 4662 d 5 (Dauphinot), F 7 4730 d 1 (Goupy), BB3 81, F 7 4685 d 4 (Dufau), F 7 4693 d 1 (Dumoustier), F 7 4731 d 1 (Goust), F 7 4774 82 d 3 (Preslin), F 7 4774 99 d 4 (Roubaud); Arch. Seine-et-Oise, 2Lm Gonesse 37 (district of Gonesse, terrorists), 2 Lm Gonesse 28, 30 and 33. See also id., IV Q 148 (Séquestres, Lallemant); AN, F 7 4666 d 2 (Delacroix), F 7 4775 27 d 3 (Thibault), BB3 65 (petition of Oudaille); and Arch. Luzarches (reg. 1 municipality).

For the SEINE-ET-MARNE: Arch. Seine-et-Marne, L 588 (district of Montereau), L 854 (*comité* of Provins), L 827 (*comité* of Melun), L 796 (*comité* of Fontainebleau), L 885–6–7 (*comité* of Brie); Arch. Brie (reg. municipality and *société populaire*); Arch. Montereau, D 15 (reg. municipality), and P. (reg. *société*); Arch. Nemours (reg. municipality); Arch. Provins (id.); Arch. Lagny (id.). See also AN, F 7 4584 d 5 (Bailleul), F 7 4584 d 7 (Ballardelle), F 7 4774⁵⁰ d 2 (Montesquiou), W 332 (561 bis) (affair Mauperthuis), F 7 4774 15 d 3 (Lemaire); Arch. Rozoy (reg. municipality); and Arch. Seine-et-Marne, suppl. (reg. district of Rozoy-en-Brie).

For the EURE: Arch. Eure, 99 L★ 10 (district of Evreux) and 235 L★ 89 (*comité* of Vernon), 60 L★ 13 (district of les Andelys), and Arch. Vernon, D 1/6, 7 et 8 (reg. municipality). For HONFLEUR and its region: Arch. Calvados (reg. district of Pont-Chalier); Arch. Honfleur, reg. A (*comité de surveillance*, l'Ouest Section), I★ 62 (reg. *société populaire*); Arch. Trouville (reg. 1 municipality); Arch. Calvados (Trouville *comité de surveillance*) and (reg. Lisieux *comité de surveillance*). For the district of PONTOISE: RCC, 'L'armée révolutionnaire dans le district de Pontoise'.

For the department of PARIS: F 7★ 2 (*reg. d'ordre*, Committee of General Security), F 7 4781 (Auteuil *comité de surveillance*), F 7 4645 d 6 (Chévrier), F 7 4766 d 1 (Laroche), F 7 4775 33 d 2 (Tracy), Wla 149 (tribunaux révolutionnaires), F 7★ 2511 (*comité révolutionnaire*, Beaurepaire Section), W 391 (906) (tribunaux révolutionnaires), F 7 4647 d 1 (Chicheret), BB3 81 (*comité de surveillance*, department of Paris), and F 7 4774 86 d 2 (Radel).

For the district of SAINT-GERMAIN-EN-LAYE: AN, W1a 18 (883) Chavessey and Allain affair, F 7★ 2 (reg. corres., Committee of General Security); Arch. Meulan, 1A (reg. municipality); Arch. Poissy, D5 (reg. municipality). For the affair of Fourqueux, see below, II. 6. For LE HAVRE, see RCC, 'L'armée révolutionnaire au Havre-Marat et dans le district de Montivilliers'. For the YONNE, see pp. 344 ff. – on the Vermenton and Villeblevin affairs.

23 See AN, F 7 4567 (Oise, arrests).

24 RCC, 'L'armée révolutionnaire au Havre-Marat et dans le district de Montivilliers', and see AN, F 7 4699 d 1 (Duval); AN, F 7 4584 d 5 (Bailleul) and Arch. Seine-et-Marne, L 854 (Provins *comité*).

25 AN, F 7 4646 d 5 (Chéron): the operation was carried out by Jean Cordier, member of the Poissonnière Section *comité révolutionnaire*. For Potter, see Arch. Oise (reg. Compiègne *comité de surveillance*).

26 Arch. Loire, L 432 (Montbrison *comité de surveillance*, session of 13 Nivôse Year II).

27 AN, W 302 (342) (tribunaux révolutionnaires, Oudaille affair).
28 Arch. Oise (reg. Chantilly *comité de surveillance*).
29 See, e.g., the affairs of Tiphaine and Montesquiou, Arch. Seine-et-Oise, 2Lk Pontoise 11 (district of Pontoise), and AN, F 7 4774 67 d 2 (Montesquiou).
30 See RCC, 'L'armée révolutionnaire dans le district de Pontoise', for the disturbances in Cormeilles-en-Vexin and in other villages of the French Vexin.
31 Arch. Fourqueux (reg. 1, municipality) and AN, Wla 21 (1132) (tribunaux révolutionnaires, Ducastelier affair).
32 Deserters were arrested in the Lyon region, in the rural communes of the Pontoise district, in the villages of the Breteuil, Chaumont, Grandvilliers and Compiègne districts in the Oise, and in the different communes of the Seine-et-Marne, the Eure, the Orne, Calvados, the Loire, the Isère and the Drôme – see RCC, *'L'armée révolutionnaire à Lyon*, 'L'armée révolutionnaire dans le district de Pontoise', 'L'armée révolutionnaire dans l'Aisne'; Arch. Oise (regs. Breteuil, Chaumont, Grandvilliers and Compiègne *comités de surveillance*), Arch. Seine-et-Marne, L 885–6–7 (regs. Brie-Comte-Robert *comité*), Arch. Montereau, D 15 (reg. municipality), Arch. Eure, 235★ L 80 (Vernon *comité*), Arch. Orne, L 4879 (Alençon *comité de surveillance*), Arch. Calvados (*comité de surveillance*, Pont-Chalier district), Arch. Loire, L 432 (Montbrison *comité de surveillance*).
33 See in particular Arch. Oise (reg. Chaumont district, liasse 3), for the serious mutiny which erupted on 8 Brumaire within the battalion of the first requisition of the Chaumont district, requiring the intervention of a force of 170 *révolutionnaires*.
34 AHG (*reg. d'ordre*) and Arch. Oise (reg. Compiègne district).
35 RCC, 'L'armée révolutionnaire dans l'Aisne', and Arch. Eure, 235★ L 89 (Vernon *comité*).
36 Arch. Seine-et-Marne, L 827 (Melun *comité*) and L 885–6–7 (Brie-Comte-Robert *comité*); see also RCC, 'Politique et subsistances en l'an III: l'exemple du Havre'.
37 AN, W 391 (906) (tribunaux révolutionnaires), F 7 4775 27 d 3 (Thibault) and RCC, 'L'armée révolutionnaire dans le district de Pontoise'.
38 Arch. Seine-et-Oise, 2Lm Gonesse 37 (district of Gonesse, former terrorists) and IV Q 148 (Séquestres, Lallemant de Nantouillet).
39 See p. 333 n. 54, also AN, Wla 149 (Fouquier-Tinville papers), on a couple arrested 19 Frimaire in the faubourg Saint-Antoine for subversive words; W 391 (906) (Parquet) (reg. Neuilly-sur-Marne *comité de surveillance*), on a drunk who had called the *révolutionnaires* thieves and snitches; and AN, F 7 4647 d 1 (Chicheret).
40 AN, F 7 4774 82 d 3 (Preslin).
41 Arch. Seine-et-Oise, 2Lm Gonesse 29 (district of Gonesse), list of citizens of Luzarches whose *civisme* was doubtful, presented to the *représentant* Levasseur de la Sarthe, 16 Brumaire Year II.
42 Arch. Luzarches (reg. 1, General Council, session of 16 Oct 1793) and AN, F 7 4394 d 2 (papers found at Vincent's); Arch. Seine-et-Oise, 2Lm Gonesse 37 (Terrorists, district of Gonesse), denunciations made against Clémence and his supporters in Luzarches, Year III.
43 AN, F 7 4775 34 d 1 (Trenonay) and F 7 4775 27 d 3 (Thibault). The Trenonays, finally arrested 28 Sept 1793, were freed 13 Brumaire; Thibault was guillotined. See also Arch. Seine-et-Oise, 2Lm Gonesse 37 (Terrorists).
44 AN, F 7 4684 d 2 (Duchesne). For the text of the letter, 26 Germinal, that led to his arrest, see below, II. 5, n. 30.
45 AN, F 7 4666 d 2 (Delacroix).
46 E.g. of those arrested: Chapelle (gardener), Maindron (stone-cutter) and Cordier (apprentice locksmith) from Livry; Fourcy (wigmaker) and Bouly (carpenter) of Noyon; d'Hertizy (postmaster) of Luzarches; Thorigny (schoolmaster and former cantor) of Saint-Brice. The municipality of Marly-la-Ville, Hautin president, seems to have been comprised in equal parts of village artisans and small farmers; it was the same at Jagny.
47 RCC, 'L'armée révolutionnaire dans le district de Pontoise'.
48 Ibid.
49 AN, Wla 37 (2382) and 121 (tribunaux révolutionnaires, Hennon affair); also Arch. Oise (reg. Noyon district *comité de surveillance*). 'Marat' Hennon, national agent of the district, was a former surveyor; Decaisne was a former royal *procureur*.
50 AN, W 333 (561 bis) (tribunaux révolutionnaires, Mauperthuis affair), and F 7 3689 d 4 (La Ferté-Gaucher, municipality proceedings 23–26 Frimaire). 'You will see from the enclosed documents', wrote Vincent, national agent of Rozoy, to Fouquier, two months later, 'that most of these unfortunates were poor sans-culottes, led astray by priests and

malveillants…'. Among those condemned to death were Lecourt, *maréchal*, Proffit, yeoman farmer, Laval, ex-gamekeeper of Condé, O'Michenon the elder (the ringleader), yeoman farmer, Prunelle, former schoolmaster, Billcours, clog-maker, Montagne, a former curé; among those acquitted: Lecuyer and Dubois, weavers, Pinson, thresher, Dorgé, yeoman farmer, Cadine, *cabaretier*, Lerat, sawyer, Lombart, miller, Gaumy, carter, Nivert, ex-canon.

51 Arch. Loire, L 432 (Montbrison *comité de surveillance*, session of 13 Nivôse Year II).

52 See RCC, *L'armée révolutionnaire parisienne à Lyon et dans la région lyonnaise*, 43–50, 59–64. See also below, II. 5

53 BL, 936 c36, *Liste générale des dénonciateurs…*. Among the *mathevons* appearing in this sinister list, which served as a guide to the massacres of Floréal Year III, were Martinetcourt, former priest and painter from the Le Change Section; Claude Brunet, apprentice hatter, and the younger Lurin, silk-worker (both from the Gourgillon Section); Rey, stocking manufacturer, Bonrencontre Section; Guigne, locksmith, from the commune of Villefranche. See also Arch. Rhône, 34 L8 (*société* of Lyon), order of Reverchon and Dupuy, 14 Floréal Year II, forming the nucleus of a *société* purged of Hébertist elements. This 'nucleus' contained the names of most of the *mathevons* on the Thermidorean list.

54 Some cannoneers denounced Fanchette Mayet, aged 18, a serving-girl, and Perrier, a butcher; fusiliers denounced the woman Miou (Arch. Rhône, 42L 149 and 151).

55 See RCC, 'Quelques aspects de la mentalité révolutionnaire', and 'Politique et subsistances en l'an III: l'exemple du Havre'.

56 AN, F 7 4685 d 4 (Dufau) – an account of the Livry episode extremely hostile to the *révolutionnaires*.

57 AN, BB3 81 (department of Paris, *comité de surveillance*), order of the two Committees, 21 Sept 1793. See also p. 363.

58 AHG, B12 62 (reg. corres., War Ministry), order of the Committee of Public Safety, 24 Frimaire. The decision to deploy the armed force was taken as usual by the Committee of Public Safety. But the same day a decision concerning military intervention was taken by the two Committees in plenary session. It was Jagot, a member of the Committee of General Security, who issued the orders to the *commissaires* accompanying the armed force. See below, II. 6.

59 Arch. Seine-et-Oise, 2Lk II 58 (*comité de surveillance*, Montagne-Bon-Air district, Saint-Germain-en-Laye, session of 7 Nivôse Year II).

60 AN, AF II 58 (Committee of Public Safety, military affairs), order of 9 Brumaire Year II, in Carnot's hand. See RCC, *L'armée révolutionnaire à Lyon*, 6.

61 Aulard, x. 400, Committee of Public Safety to Siblot, 4 Pluviôse Year II, and Arch. Le Havre, D2 21 (General Council), Commission des neuf to the municipality, 4 Pluviôse Year II. See RCC, 'La mission de Siblot au Havre-Marat', on this subject.

62 Soboul, 374–88.

63 RCC, 'Les armées révolutionnaires du Midi', and see *Dictionnaire des Jacobins vivans*, 83, 'Lacombe'.

64 AN, F 7 4693 d 1 (Dumoustier).

65 AN, F 7 4774 52 d 2 (Moroy). See also below, Epilogue.

66 Arch. Eure, 235 L 35★ (Evreux *comité de surveillance*, session of 11 Ventôse Year II), 235 L 89★ (Vernon *comité de surveillance*, sessions of 6 Pluviôse and 3 Floréal Year II).

67 Arch. Seine-et-Marne, L 854 and 855–6 (Provins *comité*); AN, F 7 4649 (Clémence).

68 See below, pp. 349, and Epilogue, pp. 623.

69 On receipt 17 Brumaire of a petition in favour of the prisoner Obry, a former gamekeeper of Condé, the Creil *comité* replied that it had not sanctioned his arrest by the *armée révolutionnaire* and did not know the charge or source of the arrest warrant. At Plailly and Précy too the *comités* declared their ignorance of the reasons for the arrests made there (Arch. Oise, regs. *comités* of Creil, Plailly and Précy). On 1 Fructidor and 17 Vendémiaire Year III, the Committee of General Security ordered the release of several prisoners at Chantilly and Liancourt, 'arrested without cause by the *armée révolutionnaire…*' (AN, F 7 4567, Oise, arrests and releases).

70 Arch. Oise (reg. Chaumont *comité de surveillance*, liasse 3), *société populaire* of Chaumont, session of 20 Fructidor.

71 See *Le Peuple* (Lausanne-Geneva), 30 Jan 1961, for an account by Sylvain Goujon of my paper, 'Les institutions de la Terreur dans les Départements', delivered at Lausanne

University, 10 Jan 1961.

72 Arch. Eure, 99 L 11* (directory, Evreux district, sitting at Vernon, session of 3 Germinal Year II).

73 AN, F 7* 2 (reg. corres., Committee of General Security), letters received 8 Frimaire Year II. Mordant asked the *révolutionnaires*, at the 17 Frimaire session of the *société*, what charges they had against him, to which they replied none (Arch. Vernon, D1/14bis, reg. *société*). The initiative therefore seems to have been Halm's alone.

74 For Montereau, see, e.g., the arrest of the curé of Cannes (Arch. Montereau, D1* 5, General Council, session of 5 Pluviôse). For Nemours, Arch. Nemours, D2 (General Council, session of 7 Nivôse) and Arch. Seine-et-Marne, L 588 (Nemours district, session of 24 Nivôse).

75 Arch. Seine-et-Marne, L 827 (Melun *comité*) and L 885–7 (Brie-Comte Robert *comité*).

76 See RCC, *L'armée révolutionnaire à Lyon*, 33–5, for the attempt made by the *comités* of the Bon-Rencontre and Ovize Sections to get rid of the cannoneers attached to them as assistant *commissaires*.

77 RCC, 'L'armée révolutionnaire dans l'Aisne'. On 4 Prairial Year II, the Laon district denounced the town's *société populaire* and *comité de surveillance* to the Committee of General Security, as 'attached to the system of Hébert' and as 'seeking to bring the established authorities into disrepute by accusing the district of lacking in energy'. Throughout the previous months the *comité* had accused the district administrators of complicity with the large farmers in their opposition to the application of the economic laws.

78 AN, F 7 4775 30 d 1 (Thunot), Thunot to the Panthéon-Français Section, 28 Pluviôse Year II). See also p. 320, and Arch. Oise (reg. Compiègne *comité de surveillance*).

79 Arch. Honfleur, reg. A (*comité de surveillance*, Ouest Section). See also below, II. 5, n. 28.

80 Arch. Oise (reg. corres. Noyon, *comité de surveillance*). The detachment also liaised with the *comité* in the arrest of the former duc d'Aumont (AN, F 7 4662 d 5 [D'Aumont]).

81 Arch. Havre, D2 38 (reg. Le Havre municipality), General Council to the Committee of General Security, 18 Germinal Year II – letter cited in RCC, 'L'armée révolutionnaire au Havre-Marat', 302.

82 Arch. Loire, L 432 (Montbrison *comité*, session of 13 Nivôse). At this session Fusil and Lefranc expressed their intention of making domicilary visits throughout the commune and arresting 'all priests, foreigners, nobles and rich, after putting the following questions to them: 1. Who are you? What is your name? What do you do? What did you do during the siege of Lyon or when the Muscadins were at Montbrisé [Montbrison]? 2. Did you pay to support the siege? And at the slightest sign of vagueness in responding... women or men alike will be arrested...'. The *comité* were quick to agree and the visits took place between 8 p.m. and 4 a.m., but the returns were insignificant; only four persons were arrested, despite the extensive means deployed. See also Arch. Loire, L 416 (*comité de surveillance*, Saint-Germain-Laval), for Marcellin's activities in this commune.

83 In Fructidor Year II the Noyon authorities reproached Hennon for having given members of the *société* power to make arrests in the surrounding villages, helped by the detachment, without consulting the *comité de surveillance*. Hennon retorted that the *comité* was made up of moderates and he was therefore obliged to address the *patriotes* of the *société* instead. Arrests were carried out in Thiéscourt and several other communes of the canton of Attichy. (Arch. Oise, regs. district and *comité de surveillance* of Noyon, and AN, Wla 37 [2382] and Wla 121 [Hennon affair].) The detachment, however, was to prove a docile instrument of the legal *comité*, on whose orders it arrested the *commissaires* (15 Frimaire) under whose command it had marched only days before.

84 See RCC, 'Problèmes de subsistances: la question des arrivages'.

85 AHG, reg. d'ordre (Ronsin to Jourdeuil, 22 Ventôse Year II) and Arch. Oise, L IV (reg. Noyon *comité de surveillance*), interrogation of Gasson, 8 Germinal Year II.

86 AN, F 7 4775 30 d 1 (Thunot).

87 See below, pp. 358 and 363, for the powers given by the Committee of General Security to the *commissaires* of the Finistère Section in their mission to Villeblevin, or to Clémence and Marchand by the Committee of Public Safety.

88 At Noyon, too, the sans-culotte minorities were criticised for resorting to the *révolutionnaires* to have *patriotes* released who had been detained on warrants from the *juge de paix* (Arch. Oise, reg. Noyon *comité de surveillance*, deposition of the woman Verdelet, 11 Fructidor Year II). On Gasson and the municipality, see id., deposition of Moët, 16 Fructidor.

89 AHG, B5 75 (Armée révolutionnaire). For the text of the letter to Grammont, see below, III. 2, pp. 556–7.

90 Arch. Seine-et-Oise, 2Lm Pontoise 29 (district of Pontoise, *comité de surveillance*, session of 3 Frimaire Year II): '...they told us they had come to fraternise with us', wrote the *comité* about the invasion of its meeting place by the armed force, 'that they had just arrested several citizens and that we should keep a list of suspects, and that they would require us to communicate it to them, for they had powers higher than our own.... The *comité* observed that it needed time to deliberate, upon which the officers violently opposed any debate on the arrests...and one member who objected to this arbitrary expedition was himself threatened with arrest as a suspect; the *comité* finding itself overwhelmed by a large force decided to hand over the list of 24 citizens...'. (Cited in RCC, 'L'armée révolutionnaire dans le district de Pontoise'.)

91 RCC, 'L'armée révolutionnaire dans l'Aisne.'

92 On the Auteuil affair see AN, F 7★ 2 (*reg. d'ordre*, Committee of General Security, 13 Brumaire Year II), F 7 4781 (Auteuil *comité de surveillance*), F 7 4645 d 6 (Chévrier), F 7 4766 d 1 (Laroche), F 7 4775 33 d 2 (Tracy). The Auteuil *comité* claimed that they had signed the arrest warrants under pressure from Ronsin; but the soldiers guarding the prisoners had a different story, and claimed that it was not Ronsin who arrested them, but a *commissaire* from the Committee of Public Safety.

93 AN, F 7 4774 50 d 2 (Montesquiou), Lemaire to the Committee of General Security, 23 Nivôse Year II: 'On orders from the Committee of Public Safety, I went to Coulommiers... [and] was happy at being able to restore order and tranquillity, but I was surprised to find ...still at liberty a family which had done everything to destroy France.... I do not know whether I did right...but my intentions were entirely pure...'.

94 See A. E. Sorel, *Pont-de-l'Arche pendant la Révolution*, ch. xiii: 'L'armée révolutionnaire', 88–9.

95 Arch. Eure, 235 L 89★ (Vernon *comité de surveillance*).

96 Four members of the detachment – one an officer – remained in prison at Honfleur when the Parisians left for Alençon (Arch. Honfleur, reg. *emprisonnement*). A fifth member of the detachment was arrested at Alençon (Arch. Orne, L 4879, Alençon *comité de surveillance*, session of 30 Germinal). A dozen fusiliers were arrested at Laon (RCC, 'L'armée révolutionnaire dans l'Aisne'). Other arrests took place at Lyon, Provins, Etampes, Rozoy, Montereau, Pontoise, most on the request of the Parisian officers themselves. The charge was usually some sort of economic offence, minor theft or appropriation of military effects. See I. 3, p. 149.

97 The *armée* had been called into Livry by the supporters of Roubaud, former *juge de paix* and dragoon officer. He had appeared before the revolutionary tribunal of Paris and been acquitted in Pluviôse of the charge of misappropriation of funds, after a brilliant defence plea by his friend, Jean Preslin, protégé of Robespierre and Legendre. Roubaud then mounted a campaign against his denouncers and, thanks to his friends in the commune, the Observatoire Section *comité* obtained an order from the Committee of General Security for the dispatch of three *commissaires* accompanied by an imposing force and four cannon. Their first action was to call together the few sans-culottes, 'patriotes sûrs', pointed out to them by Preslin and Roubaud, and ask them to draw up a list of moderates and suspects. See AN, F 7 4685 d 4 (Dufau), for the tendentious version of these events published by Roubaud's enemies in their *Mémoire instructif sur les troubles de Livry et causes de l'arrestation de 25 Patriotes* (16 Vendémiaire Year III), carrying the signatures of some 20 men of the law and large farmers, as well as the Thermidorean mayor of Livry and the extremely moderate national agent of the Gonesse district, Valnet. See the well-documented but equally tendentious article by L. Noël, 'L'armée révolutionnaire à Livry', *Bull. de la Soc. hist. du Raincy et des environs*, nos. 1, 7, 16 (1929); and see also AN, Wla 195, F 7 4693 d 1 (Dumoustier), F 7 4731 d 1 (Goust), F 7 4774 82 d 3 (Preslin) and id. 94 d 1 (Roubaud), F 7 4775 9 d 5 (Saillant), and Arch. Seine-et-Loire, 2Lm Gonesse 36 (Terrorists, disarmaments ordered in the Year III). On the close relations between the sans-culottes of Livry and Dumoustier, see also AN, F 7 4686 d 1 (Dufrênois), letter from Livry, 4 Thermidor Year II.

98 At Mareil the initiative was taken by some village sans-culottes; all were to be disarmed in the Year III. At Saint-Brice the detachment was called in on the night of 6 Vendémiaire by the mayor, Thorigny, a schoolmaster, and by three members of the *comité de surveillance*. In the Year III the former mayor of Marly-la-Ville, Hautin, was denounced by the

Thermidorean authorities of the commune, who in Floréal Year III had re-established religious practice, re-opened the church, protected the most notorious royalists, and hunted down the men of the Year II. (Arch. Seine-et-Oise, 2Lm Gonesse, 37.)

99 See Arch. Trouville (reg. deliberations, commune of Trouville, Pluviôse Year II–1829, vol. I, extracts from which were passed to me by my friend George Rudé).

100 On this affair, which touches upon the history of the dechristianisation campaign, see below II. 6, p. 457, n. 56.

101 Arch. Yonne, L 22 (Département, session 28 Brumaire), petition from Vermenton requesting the presence of a detachment to implement requisitions in the communes of its canton in favour of its market; also L 761 (district of Auxerre, 6 Nivôse).

102 Bull. de la Société des Sciences de l'Yonne (1876), 166, note on Jacques-Laurent Legry.

103 Arch. Yonne, L 761 (district of Auxerre) and AN, F 7 4775 21 d 1 (Souflot).

104 AN, F 7 4439 1 (mission of Mailhe, communal assembly, 21 Floréal Year III).

105 Arch. Avallon, I 2 28 8 (société populaire) and G. Michon, Correspondence de Maximilien et d'Augustin Robespierre (1935).

106 AN, F 7 4439 1 (mission of Mailhe).

107 Arch. Yonne, L 208 (terrorists) and L 22 (Département); AN, F 7 4439 1 (mission of Mailhe). In Frimaire Year II Labrousse's relative, Martin Labrousse, was involved in a lawsuit with the municipality over a woodcutting offence (Arch. Yonne, L 761, district of Auxerre).

108 For the incidents in Auxerre, see below, II. 6, pp. 459–61. AN, F 7 4775 21 d 2 (Souflot) contains the receipt of this petition signed by Lefranc.

109 Arch. Yonne, L 23 (Département). Dathé sent three of his friends (Decourt, Roux and Maignan) to take the petition to the department.

110 AN, F 7 4775 21 d 2 (Souflot), 'Le 2ᵉ bataillon de l'armée révolutionnaire à Vermenton. Observations sur l'établissement de la société populaire de Vermenton', signed by Dathé.

111 Id. The Auxerre comité also denounced the Cravan municipality as being 'in coalition with the Curé to prevent the triumph of Reason'.

112 AN, F 7 4439 1 (mission of Mailhe). Labrousse was denounced, 21 Floréal Year III, for having accompanied Desmargot when he went to make the arrest.

113 AN, F 7 4775 21 d 2 (Souflot).

114 Arch. Yonne, L 208 and L 68 (terrorists).

115 AN, F 7 4439 d 1 (mission of Mailhe).

116 Bull. de la Soc. des Sciences hist. et naturelles de l'Yonne, xxx (1876), 166, article on J.-L. Legry.

117 R. C. Cobb, in A.h.R.f.: 'Note sur Guillaume Bouland, de la Section du Finistère', no. 118 (avril–mai 1950), and 'L'arrestation de Bouland en messidor an II', no. 121 (janv.–mars 1951).

118 At its session of 5 May 1793, the municipality stated that the commune had only 530 bichets (a bichet=approx. 22 livres) of corn and barley left to feed its inhabitants. 'We have been fortunate in the tranquillity of the citizens until now...but many citizens without much land, all under vine which produced so little last year, might abandon their small portions to become day-labourers, this however is the position in which most find themselves because of high prices and no relief...'. (Arch. Villeblevin, municipality, reg. 2.)

119 AN, F 7 4774 53 d 2 (Moroy): 'The denouncers had the appearance of oppressed workers...'.

120 I should like to thank Mme Lorillon, secretary of the mairie, for her help during my researches in the Villeblevin archives.

121 AN, F 7 4774 25 d 2 (Lombard).

122 Arch. Villeblevin, reg. 2 (sessions of 2 and 23 June, 5 July, 3 and 29 Aug, 27 and 29 Sept, 2 Oct 1793, 17, 23 and 24 Brumaire), and Arch. Yonne, L 891 (district of Sens, sessions of 21, 22, 24 and 25 Brumaire).

123 The first detachment passed through Sens on 23 Brumaire (see below, II. 5), and when the two commissaires enquired about the public spirit of the Sens comité and authorities, the latter were careful to say nothing of the affairs of Villeblevin.

124 To cite just one example, on 24 Brumaire the Sens district received a sharp reprimand from the department for its delay in raising a company for the departmental armée révolutionnaire, which every other district had already done (Arch. Yonne, L 903, district of Sens).

125 AN, F 7* 2517 (Finistère *comité*, session of 19 Nivôse Year II).
126 Was Fénin arrested a second time during this period? This we do not know; suffice it to say that the Lorillons and Lombard were particularly relentless in their persecution of the former mayor.
127 AN, F 7* 46 (reg. corres. Committee of General Security, 26 Nivôse and 27 Pluviôse Year II).
128 Arch. Villeblevin, reg. 2 (session of 5 Ventôse Year II).
129 AN, F 7 4774 25 d 2 (Lombard) and 53 d 2 (Moroy).
130 AN, F 7 4613 d 1 (Bourgoin). Lorillon had a strange conception of his duties as a national agent and his behaviour towards the sans-culottes was not that of a republican. Such attitudes gave the affair the appearance of a class conflict.
131 AN, F 7 4613 d 1 (Bourgoin).
132 Id. On one of the two occasions mentioned Fénin had been removed from office by the district of Sens, 25 June 1793 (Arch. Yonne, L 891).
133 AN, F 7 4774 25 d 4 (Lorillon), F 7 4774 53 d 2 (Moroy) and F 7 4613 d 1 (Bourgoin). As against the 2,550 livres collected in *taxes révolutionnaires*, the total cost of the expedition approached 2,400 livres. On 17 Frimaire Year III, the *Comité des finances* of the Convention denounced the *commissaires* for having levied a forced contribution, and on the 20th the affair was placed before the *comité de surveillance* of the 12th arrondissement.
134 AN, F 7 4774 25 d 4 (Lorillon).
135 Arch. Yonne, L 907 (district of Sens). In its weekly report of 20 Germinal, the directory returned to the charge, demanding the liberation of all the prisoners.
136 AN, F 7 4613 d 1 (Bourgoin).
137 The Villeblevin prisoners had studied the newspapers of the first days of Germinal, which gave a picturesque description of the external appearance of 'ultra-revolutionary Hébertism'. (The reference to *cabarets* was doubtless an allusion to the supporters of Fénin, who, like all good sans-culottes, spent much of their time in the cafés.)
138 AN, F 7 4613 d 1 (Bourgoin). Perhaps the line dividing Lombard's supporters from his opponents was one of age rather than social background. His most entrenched support came from elderly rich men, while Fénin's supporters were relatively young (Guillaume Rognon was even elected to the new municipality after the July days of 1830). In Villeblevin, the old men were both rich and moderate.
139 AN, F 7 4684 d 2 (Duchesne). Most of the denouncers were members of the municipality and *comité de surveillance*, ousted by the coup of Brumaire Year II; they charged Duchesne with having trafficked in silver, acted arbitrarily as mayor, and formed 'monarchical cabals with the priests and seigneurs'.
140 AN, F 7 4613 d 1 (Bourgoin).
141 Arch. Yonne, L 907 (district of Sens).
142 AN, F 7 4774 52 d 2 (Moroy).
143 Arch. Yonne, L 208 (Département, terrorists).
144 Arch. Villeblevin, reg. 2 (sessions of 15 Thermidor Year III and July 1830).
145 AN, BB3 81 (*comité de surveillance*, department of Paris, session of 21 Sept 1793).
146 There was, in addition, a complicated business of fruit picked from trees bordering communal paths. The opponents of Mme Pruneau (headed by the farmer of the former seigneur of Jagny) claimed that she had persuaded the non-propertied of the commune that the trees belonged to them, whereas they themselves claimed they belonged to the property bordering the river. The district directory (taking the latter's part) called the offending municipality to appear before it; but the municipal officers refused, and instead took their case to Paris. (AN, F 7 4649 d 2 [Clémence], petition of Louis de Vouges and other inhabitants of Jagny to the Convention, 29 Vendémiaire Year II.)
147 AN, F 7 4649 d 2 (Clémence).
148 AN, F 7 4730 d 1 (Goupy), report of Mothrée and Vuable and petition of the inhabitants of Jagny to the Convention, 22 Brumaire Year II.
149 AN, F 7 4649 d 2 (Clémence) and 4730 d 1 (Goupy).
150 On the activities of Crassous in this district, see Arch. Seine-et-Oise, 2Lm (Gonesse 28, 29, 30 and 37), arrests etc.
151 Arch. Seine-et-Oise, 2Lm (Gonesse 23), district directory to the Committee of General Security, undated, Year II.
152 See above p. 266, for the complaints of Gaulthier and Thunot against the authorities of this town.

153 For the case of Thunot and Boisgirault in Compiègne see Arch. Oise, regs. (*comité de surveillance* of Compiègne), corres. session of 26 Nivôse; district corres., letters to the Committee of Public Safety, 26 Nivôse, and to the two Committees, 11 Pluviôse; *société populaire*, sessions 10, 13 and 20 Pluviôse Year II.

154 AHG (*reg. d'ordre*), Ronsin to the municipality of Compiègne, 23 Pluviôse Year II.

155 AN, F 7 4775 30 d 1 (Thunot).

156 *Histoire de la Révolution française par deux amis de la liberté*, XIII. 53, 62: '. . . We assume that when they set out for the environs of Paris, before going to shoot down the Lyonnais, they received specific orders from Chaumette or some other such revolutionary to leave no signs of Catholicism remaining along their route . . .'.

157 RCC, *L'armée révolutionnaire à Lyon*, 28–9.

158 AN, F 7 4774 84 d 1 (Prou), cited in RCC, *L'armée révolutionnaire à Lyon*, 28.

159 AN, F 7 4774 90 d 2 (Renault), and see RCC, op. cit., 29.

160 AN, F 7 4774 88 d 2 (Réaume), and id.

161 AN, F 7 4774 12 d 5 (Lefranc).

162 Arch. Rhône, 1 L 215 (Département, military affairs, garrison at Commune-Affranchie, 20–1 Pluviôse).

163 A. Guillon de Montléon, *Mémoires. . . de la ville de Lyon . . .*, III.

164 *Le Courrier Républicain*, no. 452, cited in Maton de la Varenne, *Les Crimes de Marat et des autres égorgeurs* (Year III).

165 Prudhomme, v. 53.

166 *Histoire de la Révolution. . . par deux amis de la liberté*, XIII. 256.

167 RCC, *L'armée révolutionnaire à Lyon*, 30.

168 Arch. Rhône, 3 L 64 (district of La Campagne to the garrison commander at Lyon, 19 Ventôse Year II). The Parisians did not have a monopoly on repression in Lyon and its region; besides the soldiers from the Nièvre and the Allier, they were seconded by the battalions of conscripts from the Puy-de-Dôme and the Ardèche. The Auvergnats, who seem to have taken special pleasure in humiliating and terrorising the Lyonnais, were particularly detested. The *comité* of Francheville had everyone in the neighbouring communes arrested who could not give proof of good citizenship (Arch. Rhône, 32 L 30, *comité* of Francheville to the Committee of General Security, 26 Pluviôse Year II).

169 Arch. Loire, L 432 (*comité* of Montbrison, session of 13 Nivôse) and Arch. Ain, 2 L 27 (district of Bourg, national agent to Gouly, 20 Nivôse). See also AN, D III 355 (Comité de législation), 'Dénonciation des citoyens de Bourg contre Javogues', 23 Floréal Year III.

170 See RCC, *L'armée révolutionnaire à Lyon*, 30–5, 108–9.

171 Arch. Seine-et-Oise, IV Q 186, Fayet to Mazuel, 2 Pluviôse Year II.

172 AN, AF II 139 (1077) (12), order of Javogues, 13 Frimaire Year II. He also formed a *commission populaire* at Bourg, '. . . three assassins chosen from his army to pass judgement' (AN, D III 355, denunciation against Javogues, 23 Floréal Year III). See also id., AF II 84 (620), observations of the deputies from the Ain to the Committee of Public Safety, undated, Year II.

173 Arch. Finistère, 66 L1 (reg. Brest tribunal), and AN, AF II 102 (750), order of Tréhouard and Laignelot, 17 Pluviôse Year II. The three jurors were Fourrier, lieutenant, Combas, sergeant-major, and Dessirier, corporal. Dessirier was attached to the *comité de surveillance* by an order of Jeanbon Saint-André, 25 Ventôse Year II.

174 R. du Coudray, *Granville et ses environs pendant la Révolution*, 351; for Saumur, see E. Quernau–Lamérie, *La Commission Parein-Félix*.

175 We know of 9: Constant (Faubourg-du-Nord), Langlois (Marchés), Laurent (Quinze-Vingts), Martin (Réunion), Tolède (Faubourg-du-Nord), Renault (Halle-au-Bled), Potet (Contrat-Social), Cardinaux (Panthéon-Français), Sandoz (l'Unité).

Chapter 4

1 Restif de la Bretonne, *Les Nuits de Paris*.

2 AAG, Cl. gén. 683 (Chartrey), Chartrey to Sijas, 27 Brumaire Year II, cited in RCC, 'Les armées révolutionnaires du Midi', 21.

3 H. Affre, *Tableau sommaire de la Terreur dans l'Aveyron* (Rodez, 1886), 56.

4 Arch. Lot, L 415 (Gourdon *comité*), sessions of 9, 10, 12, 14 and 16 Brumaire Year II. The young man in the check shirt too 'had even heard in one town [Rodez] that there had been several deaths caused by poisoned flour . . .'.

5 See RCC, 'Les armées révolutionnaires du Midi', 26.
6 AHG, B2 27 (Moselle Army).
7 APP, A A/269 (notes of Topino-Lebrun for the session, 24 Frimaire Year III, of the revolutionary tribunal in Paris).
8 APP, A A/269 (trial of Carrier). The other *représentant*, warned at the same time, was doubtless Francastel, who accompanied Carrier to Nantes.
9 AN, AA 42 pl. 4 d. 132lb (84), *Mémoire justificatif et instructif pour le C. Le Batteux, aubergiste à Redon*. . . . See also Prudhomme, VI. 298: '. . . Le Batteux. . . had eight people shot as they left a church at Noyal-Muzillac, as well as a captain of a revenue cutter, before which he had their graves dug at their feet. . .'.
10 APP, A A/269 (deposition of Carrier, 9 Frimaire Year III). He added, not without humility: 'I was perhaps wrong. . .but such were the times. . .'.
11 AN, Wla 125 (tribunaux révolutionnaires, affair of Poux and Verdier), orders from the district of Villefranche-de-Rouergue to its *commissaires civils*.
12 AHG, B4 33★ (*reg. d'ordres du jour* and corres. from the garrison of Toulouse), the commander to Gen. Marbot, 8 Brumaire Year II.
13 AAG, Gén. div. 237 (Marbot), Cart to Bouchotte, 4 Brumaire Year II.
14 AN, F 7 4775 49 d 2 (Viton).
15 AN, Wla 125 (*mémoire* of Verdier, Year III).
16 AN, F 7 4554 1 (Aveyron, arrests), Périer and Lagarde to the Committee of Public Safety, 15 Frimaire Year II.
17 The pretext for this military intervention were the disturbances which had erupted in the Saint-Chély district at the beginning of the winter. But according to Allard, secretary to the *représentant*, Châteauneuf-Randon, the troubles were not counter-revolutionary, but had been provoked by poverty: 'The fact is that a host of poor people from the Saint-Chély district, forced to leave their localities to search for food elsewhere,. . .have appeared in the area around us, gathering at night in small groups, without arms or horses, to take away whatever small amounts of grain they can find. . .' (Arch. Lozère, L 354, district of Saint-Chély, *subsistances*). Poverty had indeed played a part in these troubles, by recruiting the rural proletariat into them. But they only became dangerous when given political content by priests and royalist *gentilshommes*. These incursions of poor labourers from one department into another were common in the autumn of 1793, but elsewhere they did not assume the character of an armed revolt. Despite the efforts of the Mende *société* to spare this department a visit from the *armée révolutionnaire*, such a force was in operation at Saint-Chély and Le Malzieu from Vendémiaire onwards (Arch. Lozère, L 532, *société* of Mende, session of 5 Brumaire; L 355, district of Saint-Chély; and AN, D III 139, Comité de législation, Mende).
18 Carrier was born at Aurillac, Taillefer in the Lot.
19 BN, L 41b 4947 (general assembly of Saint-Paterne); BL, F 49, *Tableau des crimes de Javogues dans le département de la Loire* (Saint-Etienne [?], Year III).
20 AN, W 25 (1511), national agent for the district of Bergues to the public prosecutor, 20 Nivôse Year III.
21 Arch. Allier, L 878 (*société* of Moulins), declaration of Cornichon.
22 Arch. Nièvre (great reg., *comité* of Corbigny).
23 APP, A A/269 (78th witness), words attributed to Pierre Jolly [*sic*].
24 Id.
25 APP, A A/269 (196th witness).
26 AN, F 7 3681 9 (reports on the mission of Viton to Moissac).
27 Restif de la Bretonne, *Les Nuits de Paris. Suite des Nuits*. Restif, a political weather-vane, sensitive to the direction of opinion, has many pages on the strength of the desire among the *petit peuple* of Paris for the total elimination of the refractory clergy.
28 See Abbé H. Brun, *Manosque révolutionnaire* (Digne, 1911).
29 Arch. Basses-Alpes, L 752 (reg. *comité* of Digne), L 765 (*comité* of Entrevaux), L 778 (*comité* of Manosque), L 821 (*comité* of Sisteron); the same strict control existed in the Hautes-Alpes (Arch. Hautes-Alpes, L 1506, *comité* of Serres; L 1178, corres. district of Gap, 1st *décade* of Frimaire).
30 Arch. Lot-et-Garonne (reg. 1, Agen *comité de surveillance*).
31 Arch. Hérault, L 5748 (reg. Montpellier *comité de surveillance*) and L 5500–2 (regs. *société populaire*); Arch. Gironde, 11 L 69 (reg. Bordeaux *comité de surveillance*).
32 See, e.g., Arch. Lot, L 415 (Gourdon *comité de surveillance*), sessions of 13 Brumaire, 10

and 24 Frimaire.

33 AN, F 7 3681 9 (doss. Viton, affair of Moissac), and F 7 4563 (Moissac *comité de surveillance*).

34 Arch. Lot, L 72 (Département), Thérèse Brugier to Bô, Pluviôse Year II. The revolutionary officers and the Cahors *comité* jointly decided arrests on 7 and 9 Oct, 25 Vendémiaire and 24 Brumaire (Arch. Lot, L 389, reg. Cahors *comité de surveillance*; also L 412, Figeac *comité*).

35 Arch. Lot, 72 L 4 (Saint-Geniez *comité de surveillance*). In the commune of Coussergues, near Sévérac, it was the municipality which authorised the captain of the detachment to make requisitions and arrests and to levy *taxes révolutionnaires* (id., 77 L 1 [Sévérac *comité*]).

36 Arch. Lot, 80 L 1 (Villefranche *comité*), session of 19 Brumaire Year II. What happened at Saint-Geniez was not, strictly speaking, a case of arbitrary arrests, for when the captain of the Lot detachment denounced certain individuals the *comité* hastily entered into his views and issued the necessary warrants (id., 72 1 4 [Saint-Geniez *comite1*]).

37 See I. 4; also AN, Wla 493 (479) and APP, A A/269, order of Carrier and Francastel, 9 Brumaire, giving every member of the company the power of surveillance of all suspects.

38 AN, F 7 4422 (*comité révolutionnaire* of Nantes), deposition of Chaux, 15 Messidor Year II.

39 APP, A A/269 (deposition of Durossier, member of the Marat company).

40 Arch. Morbihan, L 2001 (*société populaire* of Lorient). For the details of this affair, see below, pp. 405–8.

41 APP, A A/269.

42 G. Martin, *Carrier et sa mission à Nantes*.

43 AN, F 7 4422, deposition of Chaux, op. cit.

44 G. Martin, *Carrier et sa mission à Nantes*.

45 For the affair of Vaugrenant, e.g., see RCC, *L'armée révolutionnaire à Lyon*; for the activities of the revolutionary forces in the Rhône and the Ain, see pp. 332–3.

46 R. Delachenal, *Histoire de Crémieu* (Grenoble, 1889), 398. Contamin's father was also a master locksmith.

47 A similar case occurred at Nevers: Arch. Nièvre, 20 L 7 (Nevers *comité de surveillance*, session of 3 Brumaire Year II), denunciation against Taurau, a carter, for having said in an *auberge* that 'the revolutionary guard was a pack of scoundrels, vermin, to be pissed on and that [the carters] could go about their business better if they buggered off...'.

48 Arch. Allier, L 850 (Moulins *comité de surveillance*). Responsibility for the operation seems to have lain with Verd and Delan, who had written to the Commission Temporaire recommending that this Moulinois group be shot. See also AN, D III 10 (305) (Comité de législation, Moulins), for the case against the former members of the Moulins *comité*, 15 Vendémiaire Year IV.

49 Arch. Allier, L 850 (Moulins *comité*) and L 878, *société populaire* of Montmarault to that of Moulins, 25 Brumaire Year III. The origins of this operation were typical of so many others: Grimaud and Boissay, at the head of 50 *révolutionnaires*, were called in by a local, Faynaud, 'an oppressed sans-culotte', who had denounced the moderates and their accomplices among the village authorities to the Moulins *comité*. For the accusation of Verd, see id., L 901★ (reg. *société* of Moulins), session of 22 Floréal Year II.

50 BN, L 41b 4947 (general assembly, church of Saint-Paterne), session of 23 Vendémiaire Year II.

51 AN, D III 178 (53) and 179 (17) (Comité de législation, Nièvre, Corbigny), 179 (1) (Decize), 181 (187) (Nevers), 180 (8) (19) (Moulins-Engilbert). See also Arch. Nièvre, L Reg. 7 (reg. corres., district of Clamecy), district administrators to the *représentant* Legendre, 5 Nivôse Year II.

52 See Arch. Nièvre (great reg. Corbigny *comité de surveillance*); also see below, II. 5, on the political and social action of the battalions. In the Year III the Decize authorities were to denounce the *commissaires* who came into the district for having 'used the terms "rich", "selfish", "Muscadin" to slander good citizens...' (AN, D III 179 [1] [Decize]).

53 Arch. Aveyron, 77 L 1 (Saint-Geniez *comité de surveillance*).

54 AN, D III 29 (3) (22) (Comité de législation, Aveyron, Rodez). The same day the Commission sent Caplat before the departmental criminal tribunal to answer the charge of 'acts of brigandage'.

55 H. Affre, *Tableau sommaire de la Terreur dans l'Aveyron*, 40, 42.

56 Arch. Aveyron, 77 L 1 (Saint-Geniez *comité de surveillance*).

57 Arch. Cantal, L 684 (Aurillac *comité de surveillance*), session of 14 Oct. The measure was

suggested by Fougère Delthil, Taillefer's *délégué* in the Cantal, who attended this session.

58 Arch. Cantal, L 684 (Aurillac *comité*), session of 11 Brumaire, also sessions of 14 Oct, 1, 17 and 27 Brumaire, and 13 Frimaire.

59 See in AN, D III 39 (20) (178), the Thermidorean pamphlet *Dominique Mirande...aux amis de la Justice*, also in F 7 4555 (Boudier), *La Révolution du Cantal*. Carrier's main correspondents were the brothers Boudier, one of whom had been appointed to the *comité* by Delthil, 9 Oct (Arch. Cantal, L 684).

60 On 13 Frimaire the *comité* ordered the battalion to make a complete search of the homes of the prisoners (Arch. Cantal, L 684 [Aurillac *comité*]). See id., session of 11 Brumaire, for the deployment to the Aveyron.

61 Arch. Lot, L 415 (*comité* of Gourdon), sessions of 9 Brumaire, 10 and 27 Frimaire; L 412 (*comité* of Figeac); L 92 (Département); L 389 and L 407 (*comité* of Cahors), Dufourt Léobard to the *comité*, 30 Frimaire. For the affair of the country notables, see below, II. 7.

62 Arch. Basses-Alpes, L 752 (*comité* of Digne), L 765 (*comité* of Entrevaux), L 778 (*comité* of Manosque), L 821 (*comité* of Sisteron).

63 Arch. Hérault, L 5748 (*comité* of Montpellier), Arch. Lot, L 405 (*comité* of Montauban), Arch. Lot-et-Garonne (reg. 1, Agen *comité de surveillance*).

64 Prudhomme, v. 476.

65 Arch. Vaucluse, L VI 17(2) (*société populaire* of Méthanis), session of 20 Prairial Year II.

66 Restif, *Nuits de Paris*, 212, after overhearing a conversation between two lovers on the terrace of the Tuileries, observed: 'I recognised then that it was the women who made the men emigrate, and it was they who were most opposed to the Revolution...'.

67 See Prudhomme in *Les Révolutions de Paris*, no. 214 (15 Brumaire Year II), 'Origine, définition, moeurs, usages et vertus des sans-culottes', on the influence of the women over their sans-culotte husbands. On the natural counter-revolutionary spirit of women, see also Restif, *Les Nuits de Paris*.

68 At Sévérac, with Valette, Viton had women whipped who had not revealed their caches or who had given refuge to 'brigands' (AN, Wla 34 [2092]). Verdier too used the whip to discover the hideouts of refractory priests in the canton of Najac. One woman, who had harboured a priest, he even threatened to burn on a pyre if she did not inform, but seeing her determination he simply admonished her for her fanaticism (AN, Wla 125). See also H. Affre, *Tableau sommaire de la Terreur dans l'Aveyron*, 80, the account of Jean-Joseph and Rose Bastide (brother and sister) of Laissac: 'After pillaging the house, [Viton] had the informant [Rose] brought...into the farmyard [and] announced that he was going to cut off her head if she did not reveal where her grandfather had hidden his money. She said she knew nothing of it; the savage Viton ordered her to lie on the ground, her head on a block, and ordered his minions to cut off her head with an axe which he had sharpened in front of her.... The axe was raised. She thought she was lost. But Viton wanted her écus, not her life, and after repeating the exercise four times, he saw that the informant had no knowledge of the money and had her taken off to prison'.

69 Arch. Nièvre (great reg. *comité* of Corbigny). It is noticeable that *commissaires civils* who were strangers to the district were less hard on the farmers and priests than Chaix, a local, who knew his victims. In this district the bark of Fouché's *commissaires* was worse than their bite, and most of the arrests were not upheld.

70 See R. C. Cobb, 'Un comité révolutionnaire du Forez: le comité de surveillance de Bonnet-la-Montagne (Saint-Bonnet-le-Château) (Loire)', *A.h.R.f.*, no. 149 (1958).

71 H. Affre, *Tableau sommaire de la Terreur dans l'Aveyron*, 53.

72 AAG, Gén. de div. 237 (Marbot), letter of Messidor Year III. By this date it was in Marbot's interest to minimise Charrier's role in order to defend himself from accusations of being a ferocious terrorist, and to shift blame instead on to Viton for showing a severity out of all proportion to the crimes.

73 For Grenade, see P. Gérard, 'L'armée révolutionnaire de la Haute-Garonne', also II. 2 and 6; for Toulouse, see RCC, 'Les armées révolutionnaires du Midi', 82, and *Journal révolutionnaire de Toulouse*, no. xiv, 20 Nov 1793.

74 The work of the Hon. Mrs Cunnack (Alice Wemyss), *Les Protestants du Mas-d'Azil: histoire d'une résistance 1680–1830* (Toulouse, 1961), has important additional information on the progress of the Terror in this department.

75 Arch. Tarn-et-Garonne (great reg. *comité* of Agen). For Montauban and Montpellier see RCC, 'Les armées révolutionnaires du Midi', 59–60.

76 Arch. Basses-Alpes, L 752 (Digne *comité de surveillance*, sessions of 11 Brumaire, 7, 12, 22

Frimaire and 9 Nivôse); L 821 (*comité* of Sisteron), sessions of 12 Brumaire, when the *comité* ordered the company to arrest Fauchier, a 'federalist' locksmith; of 16 Brumaire, when it offered the help of the company to the Hautes-Alpes authorities, 'to purge the department of aristocracy...'; and 13 Brumaire, when it ordered the arrest of one Giraud, of Sisteron, who had just been released by the *représentants*.

77 AN, F 7 4880 d 2 (Doss) and F 7 4775 53 d 3 (Zimmermann), and D III 355 (denounced *représentants*, Milhaud). See also Prudhomme, v. 506–7.

78 P. Bécamps, *J. B. M. Lacombe*, and Arch. Gironde, 11 L 69 (Bordeaux *comité de surveillance*).

79 See Carrier's declaration to the session of 24 Frimaire Year III (APP, A A/269).

80 Prudhomme, vi. 302.

81 This and the following account of the expedition is taken from APP, A A/269 (session of 24 Frimaire Year III).

82 Joly was accorded his place in the terrorist pantheon of the *Dictionnaire des Jacobins vivans*, 76–7: '...Pregnant women, infirm old men, wounded soldiers, infants at the breast, all were massacred without pity by Jolly [*sic*] and the *comité* of which he was part, to avenge, it was said, not the Republic, but the blood of S. Marat'.

83 APP, A A/269.

84 AN, F 7 4422 (*comité révolutionnaire* of Nantes), printed leaflet: *Phélippes dit Tronjolly à la Convention* (Nantes [?], 12 Thermidor Year II).

85 There was a series of clashes between the members of the *comité* and those of the company during Carrier's trial, each seeking to shift responsibility for the *noyades* on to the other. Listen to Chaux, on one side, claiming that 'we were pushed by the company which was electrified by Carrier', or Duçon and Charretier, members of the company, protesting on the contrary to have acted only on orders from the *comité*. Responsibility was undoubtedly shared by the *comité*, the officers of the company, the garrison commanders and Carrier himself, though it is impossible to state precisely which of the four first put forward the idea of emptying the prisons and drowning the inmates in the Loire. But this did not concern the Thermidorean judges, who were simply seeking to establish the guilt of Carrier.

86 On this see the testimony of the 64th witness, Alifet, a ship's carpenter, that Richard had come for carpenters on the night of 15–16 Frimaire to work throughout the night; 'il faut faire une baignade...', he had said, and the following day it was decided 'that a hole should be made, covered by a plank which would be held in place by a cord that could easily be cut...'. This testimony seems to show that Richard, and doubtless other members of the company, officers and NCOs, had participated in the detailed and premeditated preparation of this mass murder.

87 Arch. Loire-Inférieure, L 1323. On 29 Vendémiaire a witness named Robin, aide-de-camp to Lamberty, Charles, adjutant-major with the Nantes garrison, and O'Sullivan, garrison commander at Paimboeuf, as having assisted in the *noyades*.

88 AN, Wla 493 (479) (tribunaux révolutionnaires, Carrier affair, sentence delivered).

89 AN, F 7 4774 35 d 2 (Marie), Pierre-Jean Marie, to the Committee of General Security, 19 Prairial Year II.

90 P. Paganel, *Essai historique et critique sur la Révolution française* (1815), II. 315.

91 Arch. Morbihan, L 2001 (*société populaire* of Lorient), session of 12 Frimaire Year II. See also AN, T★ 492, *société populaire* of Redon (mouthpiece of Le Batteux) to Carrier, requesting 'une force imposante'. Already, 26 Brumaire, the Redon National Guard had been sent against a small force of brigands operating in the area around Lohéac (Arch. Ille-et-Vilaine, L 1295, district of Redon). Jullien himself recognised the need for armed intervention against 'brigands' and 'fanatiques': '...A section of the *armée révolutionnaire* is needed [in the Morbihan]', he wrote to the Committee of Public Safety, 29 Frimaire, 'to lay hold of all the former priests and nobles disseminated throughout the countryside where risings occur daily and give the appearance of a partial counter-revolution...' (E. Lockroy, ed., *Une Mission en Vendée*, 153).

92 AN, Wla 493 (497), Yves Mancel to the Convention, 18 Vendémiaire Year III.

93 AN, AA 42 pl. 4 d 132 lb (84), *Mémoire justificatif et instructif pour le C. Le Batteux, aubergiste à Redon...*'.

94 AN, T★ 492 1 (Séquestres, Carrier papers).

95 AN, AA 42 pl. 4, op. cit.

96 AN, Wla 493 (497), Mancel to the Convention.

97 L. Dubreuil, *Le district de Redon pendant la Révolution*, 135–42.

98 AN, AA 42 pl. 4 id.

99 AN, Wla 493 (479).

100 Arch. Morbihan, L 2001 (*société populaire* of Lorient), session of 22 Frimaire Year II.

101 id., session of 24 Frimaire.

102 AN, T★ 492 (Séquestres, Carrier papers), Avril to Carrier, 27 Frimaire Year II; E. Lockroy, ed., *Une Mission en Vendée*, 145; Jullien to Tréhouard, 26 Frimaire Year II.

103 Arch. Ille-et-Vilaine, L 1302 (district of Redon), Boursault to Fouquier-Tinville, 22 Vendémiaire Year III.

104 For Le Batteux's subsequent career and the events of Redon, see Arch. Ille-et-Vilaine, L 1302 (district of Redon, reg. corres.); AN, F 7 4562 (Ille-et-Vilaine, arrests, decision of the Committee of General Security, 24 Vendémiaire Year III), W 499(552) (tribunaux révolutionnaires, Le Batteux affair), W1a 493 (479) (Carrier affair); APP, A A/269 (notes of Topino-Lebrun); L. Dubreuil, *Le district de Redon*. Following representations from the Redon district, the military authority transferred Bouvard, garrison commander, to Lorient.

105 AAG, Gén. de div. 772 (Avril). He received his commission as *général de brigade*, 21 Ventôse Year III.

106 Secret reports of the Year IV represent Mouquet as 'babouviste', 'exclusif' and 'robespierriste'. At this time he was chief pharmacist to the Army of the West; but like many former terrorists he had taken refuge in Paris. The Minister of Police asked for his expulsion from Paris along with two other Lorentais, 11 Floréal Year IV (AN, F 7 6611, Morbihan, dossier 'Partisans de Robespierre and Babeuf'). In the Year IX his name was again mentioned in association with the 'Machine infernale' affair, as 'Mouquet...agent de Carrier'. Justifiably, he hotly denied the charge of having been one of Carrier's agents; he was released after interrogation by Desmarest (APP, A A/274 [273], Machine Infernale).

107 AN, AF II 185 (1572). See also I. 4, p. 199, n. 188.

108 The figure of 60 to 80 is less than one-tenth of the actual figure for the *rassemblements* in the Aveyron.

109 B. Combes de Patris, *Procès-verbaux de la société populaire de Rodez*, session of 3 Floréal Year III, and 'Réponse de Cabrol jeune'.

110 AN, C 285 (829) (Petitions), the *armée révolutionnaire* of the Lot and the Cantal to the Convention, Frimaire Year II. They claimed to have scotched a counter-revolutionary explosion and to have overwhelmed the *bandes* of Charrier, but that a plot still existed in the attempts to slander the *armée*, and they requested permission to carry the inscription 'Convention Nationale' and 'A Marat' on their banner. The younger Delthil also blew the trumpet of victory rather too soon (AN, AF II 92 [684], his letter to the Convention, 11 Brumaire Year II).

111 Arch. Aveyron, 77 L 1 (Sévérac *comité*), session of 2–3 Nivôse Year III.

112 The national *commissaire* attached to the tribunal of the Sévérac district wrote on 17 Messidor Year III to the *Comité de législation* that the Aveyron and Lozère were fast becoming another Vendée: 'Royalists, émigrés and all kinds of scoundrels...move about openly...they are organised in companies, they intimidate, pillage and murder honest and virtuous men, on the excuse that they are terrorists...' (AN, D III 29 (3) (22), Comité de législation, Aveyron, Sévérac). His claims were in no way exaggerated and were fully sustained from other quarters (Arch. Aveyron, 77 L 1, session of 22 Brumaire Year III, and 72 L 4, Saint-Geniez *comité*, sessions of 15 and 22 Frimaire Year III). The same situation existed in the Cantal (Arch. Cantal, L 691, *comité* of Saint-Flour, session of 7 Nivôse Year III, and AN, F 7 3662, Cantal, *commissaire provisoire* of the Directory in the Cantal to the Interior Minister, 30 Frimaire Year IV).

113 AN, D III 91 (2) (61) (Comité de législation, Toulouse).

114 *Liste générale des dénonciateurs et des dénoncés, tant de la Ville de Lyon...*; and see pp. 321–2.

115 See Arch. Nord, L 10265 (Lille *comité de surveillance*, session of 28 Brumaire Year II), three soldiers of the Lille *armée* denouncing a soldier of the first requisition for 'anti-republican words' in accusing them of 'doing the work of executioners'. See Arch. Allier, L 850 (reg. Moulins *comité de surveillance*), session of 1 Frimaire, and Arch. Hérault, L 5748 (Montpellier *comité*), session of 3 Frimaire, for similar denunciations.

116 Arch. Troyes, D 4 (General Council of the commune), session of 7 Nivôse Year II; Arch. Aube, Lm4c 3 (352) (Terrorists, Floréal Year III) and L4 36 (4th Section), session of 21

Prairial Year II.

117 AN, W 498 (535) (tribunaux révolutionnaires), Adhémar to Dufresse, 23 Frimaire Year II.
118 AAG, Gén. de brig. 501 (d'Arnaud), report to the Directory, 5 Thermidor Year VI; and
     id., Cl. gén. 3037 (Peyrend-d'Herval).
119 Arch. Gironde, 11 L 69 (Bordeaux *comité de surveillance*).
120 Arch. Basses-Alpes, L 765 (Entrevaux *comité*), session of 3 Nivôse Year II.
121 AN, F 7 4648 d 4 (Civeton). See also p. 211.
122 P. Gérard, 'L'armée révolutionnaire de la Haute-Garonne'.
123 Arch. Lot, L 389 (reg. Cahors *comité de surveillance*).
124 Arch. Lot-et-Garonne (reg. Agen *comité*), session of 6 Brumaire Year II.
125 See RCC, *L'armée révolutionnaire à Lyon*, 108–9.

Chapter 5

1 See Soboul, 374–88, on this subject.
2 For this complicated affair, see AN, F 7 4774 26 d 4 (Louvet-Dubois) and F 7★ 2495 (reg.
   comité révolutionnaire, Réunion). See also below, III. 3.
3 AN, F 7 4775 30 d 1 (Thunot).
4 AN, F 7 4646 d 3 (Chevalier), Chevalier to the Committee of General Security, 22
   Germinal Year II. See also Soboul, 834–7. The *révolutionnaires* may not have had much
   political sense and were easily manipulated, but in affairs of this kind, involving a struggle
   to the death between *modérés* and sans-culottes, they knew on which side their friends were
   placed and took the part of the sans-culottes.
5 *Journal Universel*, 11 Nivôse, carrying a report on the fête celebrating the recapture of
   Toulon.
6 RCC, 'L'armée révolutionnaire au Havre-Marat et dans le district de Montivilliers'.
7 The banquets, the festivities organised by the Sennecey-le-Grand *société* to greet the
   Parisians (Arch. Coll. Deschamps, reg. *société* of Sennecey) were exceptional; but every
   société in towns through which they passed accorded them the honours of the session. See
   RCC, 'L'armée révolutionnaire dans l'Aisne'.
8 Arch. Versailles, D 1 24 (General Council, commune of Versailles, session of 1 Nivôse)
   and I 2 1236 (Vertu-Sociale *société*), session of 2 Nivôse, in which Mazuel's cavaliers
   received the accolade of the president. The Parisian detachments took part in processions
   and fêtes at Meulan, 10 Frimaire and 9 Nivôse; at Ecouis, 30 Nivôse, 10 Pluviôse and 5
   Ventôse; at Provins, 16 Frimaire; at Pontoise, 20 Pluviôse; at Vernon, 29 Pluviôse; at
   Honfleur, 30 Pluviôse; at Nemours, 10 Nivôse; at Marolles, near Montereau, 9 Ventôse; at
   Lyon, 20 Ventôse (Arch. Meulan, reg. la; Arch. Eure, 236 L 10★ [Ecouis *société*]; Arch.
   Provins [great reg., General Council]; Arch. Pontoise, 1 Da 9 [General Council]; Arch.
   Vernon, D1 1/7; AN, AF II 92 [678]; Arch. Nemours, reg. 2 [General Council]; Arch.
   Montereau, P2 [reg. *société*]). In several communes the Parisians helped organise fêtes to
   celebrate republican unity, e.g., the grand fête at Les Brotteaux to show the restored
   harmony between the Parisians and the Lyon Jacobins (see the *Père Duchesne* of Millet and
   Dorfeuille).
9 On arrival at Le Havre, the Parisians deposited their *diplômes* from the tiny *société* of
   Viarmes (RCC, 'L'armée révolutionnaire au Havre-Marat').
10 AN, F 7 4584 d 7 (Ballardelle).
11 Arch. Oise, L IV (Noyon *comité*, Ventôse Year III).
12 RCC, 'L'armée révolutionnaire au Havre-Marat et dans le district de Montivilliers'.
13 RCC, *L'armée révolutionnaire à Lyon*.
14 *Journal de l'armée des Côtes de Cherbourg*, of J. J. Derché (nos. Frimaire-Nivôse).
15 AN, F 7 4584 d 7 (Ballardelle).
16 Arch. Oise. L IV (Noyon *comité*, Ventôse Year III): '...When the ringleaders of our
    society took it upon themselves to have inquisitorial visits made in the communes of the
    district...we quickly repudiated them.... It is to the glory of our *pays* that among these
    sanguinary manipulators and wreckers of the *société*...there were many outsiders
    [*étrangers*]...'.
17 Arch. Seine-et-Marne, L 854 (Provins *comité*, session of 2 Brumaire Year II); Arch.
    Honfleur, I★ 62 (reg. *société populaire*).
18 Arch. Seine-et-Oise (reg. *société* of L'Isle-Adam).
19 This was the supposedly Hébertist Vertu-Sociale *société*. On 29 Brumaire a membership

card was refused to a *révolutionnaire* who was a member of the Cordeliers. Later the *révolutionnaires* seem to have been admitted. (Arch. Versailles, D 1 284bis, reg. Vertu-Sociale *société*.)

20 'One would think we were 200 leagues from Paris', wrote Captain Guerrier from Rozoy-en-Brie to the *société* of his Contrat-Social Section, 'so rarely does one see the public print...' (AN, F 7 4753 d 2 [Guerrier]).

21 Captains of neutral ships were frequently admitted to the *société* of Le Havre, while correspondents of the Havre arms dealers at Lübeck and Copenhagen kept the *sociétaires* informed of political and military events (see RCC, 'Politique et subsistances en l'an III: l'exemple du Havre').

22 For Honfleur see above, II. 3. And see J. Bellanger, *Les Jacobins peints par eux-mêmes. Histoire de la société...de Provins* – session of 4 Brumaire.

23 Arch. Vernon, L1/14bis (Vernon *société*), session of 29 Pluviôse; Arch. Poissy, D 6 (General Council), session of 11 Frimaire Year II; Arch. Montereau, P 2 (reg. *société*), session of 27 Frimaire. On the anti-feminism of the *révolutionnaires*, see below, II. 6.

24 For Melun see above, II. 3. And see Arch. Brie-Comte-Robert (reg. 2, *société populaire*); the *société* was founded 2 Oct 1793.

25 RCC, 'L'armée révolutionnaire au Havre-Marat et dans le district de Montivilliers'. The small *société* of Saint-Pierre-des-Authils, near Vernon, was thus re-established by the intervention of a detachment (Arch. Eure, 99 L 11★, district of Evreux, session of 19 Pluviôse Year II).

26 Arch. Montereau, P 2 (reg. *société*, session of 17 Brumaire). The Harmonie *société*, which was not *sectionnaire*, was based in the Arsenal Section. See Soboul, 1085–6.

27 For Provins, see below, II. 6. On events at Presles and Taverny, see RCC, 'L'armée révolutionnaire dans le district de Pontoise'.

28 Because of these accusations the mayor dissolved the *société*, made several arrests, and refused to reveal what grain purchases had been made for the commune. The women showed Petit the poor-quality bread supplied by the mayor, who had told them to go eat unripe corn. (Arch. Calvados, Trouville *comité de surveillance*, liasse 3, and Arch. Honfleur, I★ 62, reg. *société populaire*, session of 6 Germinal.)

29 For Vermenton, see II. 3, sect. III [i]. On Avallon, see Arch. Yonne, L 208 (Terrorists). The artisans were Laureau, a notable, the elder Bertrand, and Somin, a cooper.

30 See AN, F 7 4684 d 2 (Duchesne). Duchesne the younger, agent of the Committee of General Security, to the Committee, 26 Germinal Year II, protesting on behalf of his father, the imprisoned mayor: '...my father has many enemies, because he had some counter-revolutionaries...arrested for stirring up protest over the dispatch of former church silver by the municipality to the Convention...the *comité de surveillance* is the former municipality which has not yet handed over its accounts to the new one...they are all relatives and it is they who are protecting Travant [the industrialist Travenet, who had acquired the former abbey of Royaumont and transformed it into a spinning mill, and whom the younger Duchesne had been sent to arrest]...they even sent the captain of the *armée révolutionnaire*...to arrest me at my father's house.... They meet in the home of a man who has made his fortune since the Revolution, buying up the furniture and effects of the former Condé...'.

31 Arch. Avallon, 1 2 23 9 (reg. *société* of Avallon). This document was pointed out to me by my friend Pierre Tartrat, the historian of Avallon.

32 Id. In subsequent sessions the soldiers stepped up their interventions, denouncing the district and municipality for not making the relief payments due to the families of volunteers, demanding mattresses and blankets for troops on the march, and calling out for 'the destruction of tyrants', as if they had personal responsibility for the conduct of the war and the smooth operation of the revolutionary system – an arrogant pose which quickly alienated the local authorities.

33 Arch. Oise, L IV (Noyon *comité*).

34 AN, D III 5 (298–365) (Comité de législation, Aisne, Laon), *Procès contre Adrien-Josse Chaumont et Nicolas Martin*, etc.

35 See RCC, 'L'armée révolutionnaire dans le district de Pontoise'; see also II. 3, n. 90 and (for Lemaire) n. 93.

36 AN, D III 5 (298–365), pièce 344.

37 See below, III. 3. Two hostile historians, writing in the Year VII, fully accepted the official version of events which saw Ronsin's *armée* as planning to bring down the

government and replace it with a military dictatorship: '...the government committees', wrote the 'deux amis de la liberté', 'fearing that the *septembriseurs* would become formidable in the hands of a clever man, suppressed the *armée révolutionnaire*...' (*Histoire de la Révolution française*, 145).

38 'Nearly all the rich detest the *armée*, notably the cannoneers from Paris, whereas all the sans-culottes love us and are loved in return', wrote Guerrier, captain of the Contrat-Social cannoneers, from Rozoy-en-Brie (AN, F 7 4735 d 2 [Guerrier]). Such was the simplistic judgement of the Parisians on the conflicts witnessed by them in the tiny communes. Their enemies were *les gros*; those who welcomed them were ex-officio sans-culottes.

39 Arch. Oise (Chaumont *comité de surveillance*), opinion of Véron on Decuve, 26 Germinal Year II. When news arrived in Chaumont of the arrest of 'Père Duchesne' 'the *société*...expressed its surprise and indignation at having been duped by this scoundrel...but Decuve did not share this opinion. He rushed to the rostrum...proclaiming his astonishment that they were so quick to condemn Hébert and shouting at the top of his voice: "The Aristocrats are laughing behind your backs at seeing a Patriot thus imprisoned, but imprisonment does not always mean that one is guilty..."'.

40 Arch. Seine-et-Marne, L 885 (Brie-Comte-Robert *comité*), session of 11 Pluviôse. The soldier Capucin was arrested for 'bringing the national representation into disrepute' by calling the *représentant*, Dubouchet, 'un sacré coquin' who had put aristocrats in the place of patriots, 'but Robespierre would come to Brie to reverse this...and restore them to their place...'.

41 It is regrettable that, like so many other historians, Louis Jacob in his biography of 1960, *Hébert, le Père Duchesne, chef des sans-culottes* – the title alone speaks volumes – should have failed to tackle the problem of *hébertisme* as a rallying point, and a way of thinking for many ultra-revolutionaries in the departments.

42 AN, D III 180 (8) (19) (Comité de législation, Moulins-la-République district directory), session of 27 Frimaire Year III.

43 So the Montauban *comité* referred to Viton; see I. 5, p. 231.

44 '*Ultra-révolutionnaire*' was a title which Chaix himself accepted as a compliment; but for the young Jullien, factotum of the Robespierres, it was a term of abuse. See Arch. Nièvre (great reg. Corbigny *comité*), deposition of Sadon, 23 Frimaire Year II.

45 Even in Ventôse Year III, the people of Lormes were complaining that they could not get the surrounding communes and the rich of the district to supply their market, 'and that the district was entirely silent on the matter...' (Arch. Nièvre, id.) The entire district, however, was poor in grain (AN, D III 178 [47] [Comité de législation, Corbigny]). See also Arch. Nièvre (great reg. Corbigny *comité*), deposition of Sadon, and id., session of 14 Vendémiaire Year III, for the accusation that Chaix was trying to set the two communes against each other.

46 Id., session of the Corbigny *comité*, 17 Nivôse Year III.

47 AN, D III 179 (17) (Comité de législation, Nièvre, Nevers) – Chaix, from his prison to the Committee of General Security, 19 Thermidor Year II. On his arrest in the Year II, see AN, D III 178 (72) (Comité de législation, Nièvre, Corbigny).

48 AN, D III 178, Chaix to the Comité de législation, Nièvre, Corbigny, 21 Floréal Year III.

49 For all the foregoing on Chaix, see Arch. Nièvre (great reg. Corbigny *comité*), depositions of Vendémiaire to Nivôse Year III, and AN, D III 178 (71) (comité de législation, Nièvre, Corbigny).

50 AN, D III 178 (47) (Comité de législation, Corbigny district).

51 AN, D III 179 (1) (Comité de législation, Decize).

52 Arch. Isère, L 937 (Crémieu *société*, session of 5 Fructidor Year II).

53 Arch. Isère, L 936 (Bourgoin *société*, session of 27 Thermidor Year II).

54 AN, W. 523 (Dolle affair).

55 For Grimaud, see RCC, 'La Commission Temporaire', 34. Boissay's outburst (Arch. Allier, L 902 [*société* of Moulins]), session of 15 Floréal Year III) was a Thermidorean accusation, it is true, and too much store cannot therefore be set by it.

56 RCC, *L'armée révolutionnaire parisienne à Lyon et dans la région lyonnaise*, 57–64.

57 Arch. Châlons, I 199* (*société* of Châlons, corres.).

58 P. Caron, 'La Commission civile-révolutionnaire et de surveillance de l'Aveyron', 336. Lagarde, *commissaire civil*, organised a number of fêtes, one of which was called 'Le

Triomphe du Pauvre'.

59 The doctor Lagasquie, friend and colleague of Marat, organised a 'fête des sans-culottes' at Cahors, 30 Vendémiaire, to be paid for by 'aristocrats' and 'égoïstes' (Arch. Lot, L 389, *comité* of Cahors). At Saint-Geniez, in the Aveyron, the officers of the Lot *armée* and the *commissaires* organised a 'fête des pauvres', at which the poor would receive a pound of bread, a quarter of cheese and a *demi* of wine, to be paid for and served by the rich (Arch. Aveyron. 72 L 4, *comité* of Saint-Geniez).

60 Soboul, 466–7. See also Restif, *Les nuits de Paris*, 253: '...I see the women of Paris...boat-women, embittered by suffering and who, like animals, live only for the present and have the same envy for the better-dressed grocer's wife as the *bourgeoise* has for the wife of the lawyer or councillor, or the latter for that of the financier or noble! The woman of the people has no higher aspiration than that of bringing the grocer's wife down to her own level...'.

61 The Thermidorean authorities denounced one of Chaix's supporters, the mason, Gros, for having said 'that it was Chaix who fed the poor', and an anonymous friend warned Chaix to hide when the Thermidorean hunt against him was launched: 'I know you are a good republican, that is why you will always find brothers wherever you are' (Arch. Nièvre, great reg. *comité* of Corbigny, depositions against Chaix and inventory of his papers).

62 The accusations are from Arch. Nièvre (great reg. Corbigny *comité*). Chaix's accusers were Sadet, a health officer; Chapuis, *juge de paix*;) Leflot, a judge at the district tribunal; Granet and Hasseler, priests; Mathé, Robé and Tardy, propertied farmers; Clémendot, usher at the district tribunal; Maréchal, a teacher; Hainoux, a hatter. They were not sans-culottes, unlike his supporters – or those accused of being such: Louis Gros, a mason, Jacques Marotte, a wigmaker, and Jean Guillaumot, a shoemaker (id., depositions of Vendémiaire-Frimaire Year II against Chaix).

63 For the Ariège see below, II. 6; on Gien, see BN, L41 b 4947 (assembly of Sainte-Paterne).

64 Arch. Marne, L 371 (Reims district), 27 Floréal Year III, reasons for disarming former terrorists.

65 Arch. Allier, L 850 (*comité* of Moulins), session of 17 Floréal Year II. Grimaud's denunciation coincided with the great offensive by Forestier and the Robespierrists against Fouché, and the very fact of having proclaimed the sovereignty of the *sociétés populaires* marked the culprit out as a supporter of Hébertism.

66 Arch. Lille, 18′ 229 (*société révolutionnaire*, corres.).

67 AHG, B2 27 (Moselle Army), Gobert and Delteil to Bouchotte, 23 Brumaire. The Moulins *comité* recommended that its *commissaires*, leaving for Bourbon-l' Archambault, give a civic banquet shortly after their arrival (Arch. Allier, L 850, 10 Oct). See also, on fraternal banquets, id., L 878, *société* of Montmarault to that of Moulins, 25 Brumaire Year III.

68 RCC, *L'armée révolutionnaire parisienne à Lyon et dans la région lyonnais*, 64, n. 212.

69 AN, D III 180 (8) (19) (Comité de législation, Nièvre, Moulins-Engilbert), session of the directory, 27 Frimaire Year III.

70 AN, D III 181(1) (118), (Comité de législation, Nièvre, Nevers); letter of Chapsal, national agent, to the Comité de législation, 6 Ventôse Year III.

71 See I. 5, p. 220 for War Ministry and Cordelier contacts. Rousselin had close links with Danton. Griois, *commissaire des guerres* to the Lille *armée*, was a friend of Pereyra (see AN, W 498 [535] [Dufresse to Lavalette, 4 Frimaire], and L. Lemaire, *Les Jacobins à Dunkerque* [Dunkerque, 1913], 389). The officers of the Lille *armée* were linked with Lavalette, himself a protégé of Robespierre. The young Calmet-Beauvoisins sought protectors in all political circles, Jacobin and Cordelier alike.

72 See, e.g., Arch. Nord, L 10224 (Lille *société*, session of 11 Frimaire), for the *Père Duchesne de l'armée du Nord*, and Arch. Rhône, 34 L 29★ (reg. *société populaire* of Condrieu, session of 20 Frimaire Year II).

73 RCC, 'La Commission Temporaire'.

74 Arch. Allier, L 853 (Moulins *comité*).

75 According to the *société* of Bourgoin, Vauquoy's political programme consisted of: '...Preaching the *loi agraire*, proclaiming atheism, holding up the Jacobins of Paris to ridicule, an affiliation to the Cordeliers to be chosen in preference, threatening...to march against the National Convention etc....' (AN, W 166 [tribunaux révolutionnaires], and RCC, *L'armée révolutionnaire parisienne à Lyon*, 62).

76 Arch. Landes, L 783, *comité* of Dax, session of 30 Pluviôse Year II).

77 AN, F 7 4635 d 2 (Castet). The head of this troop, the national agent of the district, Saint-Martin (he too called himself 'Marat'), is represented as parading the streets with his 'armed satellites', insulting the female inhabitants. '...One woman appeared better dressed than the others, he insulted her...and had the impudence to order his men to lift the women's skirts to see if they had white petticoats...'. That was carrying the egalitarian spirit too far. Eighty-year-old spinsters who had asked for help were refused it and '...reproached for their sterility...'. The denouncer concluded: 'It was absolutely the Hébertist system put into operation...'.

Chapter 6

1 Robespierrist historians tend to espouse the theory of their idol and his brother, according to which the dechristianisers were a clutch of Parisian adventurers, mostly foreigners, some of them Jews, all bankrupts, *pourris*, former subjects of the Emperor, doubtful characters in other words, enjoying no respect in popular circles. The tone was set by Augustin Robespierre, describing them as people 'without morals, without virtue, who attack crosses so that no one will look into their own crimes'. They were, he continued, *exagérés*, anarchists, who 'think that the revolutionary system gives them the right to do anything regardless of the authorities...even the Government itself...'. (G. Michon, *Correspondance*, letters of Augustin to his brother, 6 and 16 Germinal Year II.) The prime example of a Robespierrist historian insinuating that the dechristiansiers were *étrangers* and Jews is that of M. Dommanget, 'Robespierre et les cultes', *Annales révolutionnaires* (1924), 192–216.

  Soboul is less dogmatic, recognising the spontaneity of the movement and its popular roots (317). On the other hand, he considers forced church-closures to have gone against the views of the majority of the *petit peuple*, pointing to the hostility of the workers to the suppression of Sunday and the imposition of the *décadi*, which obliged them to work a nine-day week (319). Departmental records support this point. However, they also reveal the strength of popular anti-Catholicism, and Soboul's evidence on the resistance to dechristianisation in certain popular circles (311) seems inadequate. Nor can one support his claim as to the hostility of the Committee of Public Safety towards the movement, for Jeanbon Saint-André, Prieur and Collot favoured dechristianising initiatives when on mission in the Breton and Lyonnais departments.

2 G. Lefebvre, *Le Gouvernement révolutionnaire* (Cours de Sorbonne, Paris, 1947), 182. He is thinking in the first instance of certain initiatives taken in Brumaire, by the communes in the district of Corbeil.

3 M. Aubert, 'La Révolution à Douai', *A.h.R.f.*, no. 87 (1938), 202–23.

4 Canon Bridoux, *Histoire réligieuse de la Seine-et-Marne pendant la Révolution*, II. 45, 153, 187.

5 See, e.g., Arch. Vaucluse, L VI 9 (*société populaire* of Violès), session of 6 Ventôse Year II: '...The *comité de surveillance* had difficulty in organising itself...the *société* being so small and composed of mostly illiterate voters, it looked as if a committee of 12 members could not be formed...there were only 130 inhabitants in this town, mostly illiterate and ignorant...and those with a little more education were members of the municipality...'.

6 See Arch. Seine-et-Marne, L 566 (district of Melun, report to the Committee of General Security, 13 Pluviôse; also Arch. Aude, L 2136 (Carcassonne *comité de surveillance*), 3 Pluviôse Year III: '...[the people] are poor and in general have no other distraction besides the Catholic religion...'.

7 However, enforced closures proceeded slowly, and in distant departments, like the Vaucluse, the *sociétés* were still trying to convert churches into Temples of Reason as late as Messidor. See, e.g., Arch. Vaucluse, L VI 5, 10, 12, 14, 16–17 and 27; also Arch. Saône-et-Loire, IV L 10, and Gautheron, 'La société populaire du Puy-en-Velay'.

8 A member of the Darney *société*, in the Vosges, said 'that they should separate religious and civil institutions...that royal despotism was based on religion and sustained by filling people's souls with the terrors of superstition...' (Arch. Vosges, reg. *comité* of Darney). See also Arch. Basses-Pyrénées, 27 LI (*société* of Morlaas, 12 Ventôse), for the expression of similar ideas.

9 See Arch. Vaucluse, L VI 18 (*société* of Puyméras, session of 23 Germinal).

10 AN, F 7★ 2509 (reg. general assembly of the Fontaine-de-Grenelle Section, 7 Prairial Year III).

11 BN, MSS Nouv. acq. fr. 2705 (383) (*société* of the Luxembourg Section).
12 Arch. Seine-et-Oise (reg. *société* of L'Isle-Adam).
13 Arch. Oise (Compiègne *comité de surveillance*, reg.). However, the *comité* recommended clemency, considering the curé an ' *honnête homme...et non incivique...*'.
14 Arch. Yonne, L 1124 (reg. Joigny *comité*, session of 21 Brumaire Year II). The two authors of the *Histoire de la Révolution française*, published in the Year VII, recognised this dualism, the soldiers attacking crosses and fleur-de-lis alike as odious emblems of the old regime.
15 Arch. Eure, 99★ L 11 (district of Evreux), proceedings of the Saint-Pierre-lès-Bitry municipality, 17 Frimaire Year II.
16 This sentiment is behind the word 'aristo-catalino-crate', found in many revolutionary documents of the period. A good example of the very real alliance existing in the Côtes-du-Nord between refractory priests, deserters, criminals and rebels is in the *comité* of Port-Brieuc's letter to Carrier of 1 Oct, which speaks of '...bandits...and deserters who find a welcome in the homes of the *aristo-catalino-crates...*' (Arch. Côtes-du-Nord, L 197).
17 See, e.g., H. Labroue, 'La société populaire de La Garde-Freinet (Var)', *R.F.* LIV (1908), 145.
18 Doubtless there was also a certain popular Jansenism behind all this. See H. Forestier, 'Les campagnes de l'Auxerrois et la déchristianisation, d'après la correspondance d'Edme-Antoine Rathier, agent national du district d'Auxerre (pluviôse an II – germinal an III)', *Annales de Bourgogne*, XIX (197), 185–206.
19 Restif, *Nuits de Paris*, cites numerous examples of such masculine anticlericalism.
20 AN, F 7 4582 d 2 (Aubertot).
21 Arch. Seine-et-Oise, IV Q 186 (Mazuel papers).
22 *Le Grand Voyage...*, no. of 17 Ventôse Year II (holdings in the BN).
23 Superstition, however, was a real problem for the *révolutionnaires*, because of the existence throughout the countryside of sorcerers and fortune-tellers, who could spread terror through an entire canton by predicting catastrophes. In one Vaucluse village, the *société populaire* was told by one of its members, the baker, Michel Guérin, that he had found in the book of Nostradamus everything that had happened since the Revolution, and that everything it predicted had come about: 'the president showed that it was an absurdity to believe in Nostradamus and that if our brothers had gone to the frontiers with their pockets full of Nostradamus [rather than arms]...it would not have prevented our enemies from swarming over the Republic...', and the superstitious baker was expelled, for 'this would simply be setting up new priests in another form'. (Arch. Vaucluse, L VI 28, *société* of Malaurène, session of 7 Thermidor Year II.)
24 AN, D III 91 (2) (61) (discourse of Hugueny, 23 Frimaire Year II). The *révolutionnaires* of the Marat Section, on detachment at Vernon, objected to women participating in the sessions of the *société populaire* (Arch. Vernon, D 1/14bis, session of 23 Brumaire Year II). At Etrepagny, in the same department, one woman, a poor cotton-spinner, Mme Courbet, a widow of 33, responded to the motion that someone should sing a patriotic hymn by singing instead a song violently attacking forced dechristianisation, which she claimed to have composed herself, and which she sang in various houses to earn a few *assignats* to support her blind mother:

> The Convention has decreed
> that our beloved religion
> by which we assembled
> to pray to our divine master, must go

> With bleeding hearts we watch
> our altars destroyed
> God will open the eyes
> of all these faithful souls

> Our dead are taken to their graves
> without a prayer
> They are buried like Huguenots
> to rot in the earth...

The following day she was brought before the *comité de surveillance* which tried to discover who was behind this illiterate woman – but their efforts were in vain. (Arch. Eure, 64L 4, *comité de surveillance* of Etrepagny.) See also Arch. Rhône, 34 L 29★ (*société* of Condrieu, session of 20 Frimaire Year II) – the women attending demanded the reopening of their church so that they could practice their religion; and Arch. Nièvre, L 7 (reg. corres., district of Clamecy, Parent to the municipality of Tannay, 1 Nivôse Year II, revealing the anti-feminism of this national agent.

25 AN, F 7 4662 d 1 (Dartigoëyte).
26 Arch. Oise (reg. *société* of Compiègne, sessions of 10 Pluviôse Year II and 3 Frimaire Year II).
27 AN, F 7 4666 d 2 (Delacroix).
28 BN, MSS Nouv. acq. fr. 2705 (364), Le Rolle to the Luxembourg *société*.
29 BN, MSS Nouv. acq. fr. 2705 (359), Prière to the Luxembourg *société*, 24 Brumaire Year II.
30 BN, MSS Nouv, acq. fr. 2713 (60), Bonneval, called 'Marat', to the Société des Hommes-Libres.
31 Arch. Morbihan, L 2001 (Lorient *société*, session of 17 Brumaire Year II).
32 It was also a way of shocking the devout. A member of the Auch *société* (Gers) '. . .washed down 60 hosts with a bottle of white wine' at a civic reception (Arch. Gers, L 694, Auch *société*, session of 14 Frimaire Year II). This was dechristianisation *à la sauce Gasconne*!
33 AN, F 7 4732 d 3 (Gravier).
34 Thus a member of the Brie-Comte-Robert detachment denounced the mayor of Grisy for having proclaimed New Year's Day and Epiphany as obligatory holidays (Arch. Seine-et-Marne, L 885, *comité* of Brie-Comte-Robert, session of 23 Nivôse Year II).
35 Aulard, VIII. 237, cites the case of a cavalryman from the Nièvre battalion who was almost torn to pieces by the crowd, after he had forced the people of Coulange-sur-Yonne to take down their crosses.
36 See Arch. Nièvre (reg. corres., Clamecy district, administrators of the district to the *représentant* Legendre, 5 Nivôse Year II); see also RCC, 'Les débuts de la déchristianisation à Dieppe'.
37 In the Lot all kinds of absurd rumours circulated about the fate of the *révolutionnaires* from Cahors sent into the Aveyron. In the same region the populace was being stirred with reports 'that no crucifixes, crosses or ciboriums would be left anywhere. . .that we would have to pay one and a half pounds of bread in tax. . .that priests who went out wearing soutanes would be shut away. . .' (Arch. Lot, L 415, *comité* of Gourdon).
38 Canon Bridoux, *L'histoire réligieuse du département de la Seine-et-Marne*, II. 45.
39 See below, II. 7, p. 499, n. 53, for the case of Marc Dolle. There was a similar case in the Hautes-Alpes, that of the revolutionary mayor of Orpierre, Taxis de Clermont-Dupoët, a former noble of Romans, who had himself renamed 'Publicola' in the Year II. Like the unfortunate Musquinet Lapagne, mayor of Ingouville, also an ex-noble and energetic dechristianiser, Publicola was a victim of the Robespierrist climate of Floréal to Messidor. (Arch. Hautes-Alpes, L 1502, *comité* of Orpierre.)
40 Members of *sociétés populaires* felt compelled to conform to avoid accusations of 'fanatisme' or 'modérantisme', and decisions on the closure of churches were rarely taken in an atmosphere of free discussion. See, e.g., Arch. Basses-Pyrénées, 27 L 1 (*société* of Morlaas, session of 20 Pluviôse). The Somme proved far more resistant to church closures, and there were a number of disturbances (Arch. Somme, L^c 2076, district of Montdidier; also L^h 3072, *société* of Saint-Valéry-sur-Somme, Frimaire). The Sèvres *société* was more liberal, refusing permission to a member to take down crosses in the course of a journey he was about to make, on the grounds that '. . .the *sociétés populaires* are not regular authorities, they do not have the right to give orders, only to offer fraternal advice to the magistrates of the people. . .' (Arch. Sèvres, reg. 1, *société*, 25 Brumaire).
41 But if they could not count on miracles to destroy these rash iconoclasts, the faithful could use natural means to remarkable effect: e.g., the case of Pressagny-le-Val, district of Evreux, where the villagers put gunpowder in wooden figures taken from the church for burning (Arch. Eure, 6414, *société* of Pressagny-le-Val, Ventôse Year II).
42 See RCC, 'Quelques aspects de la mentalité révolutionnaire'.
43 Two corporals of the detachment at Montereau were denounced as fanatics (Arch. Montereau, P2, reg. *société*, 9 Ventôse). A leaflet heralding the apparition of the Virgin Mary was found on Grenier, a sergeant in the revolutionary cavalry, when he was arrested by the Mont-Blanc Section. He would be condemned to death by the revolutionary tribunal in Paris. (AN, F 7 4732 d 4 [Grenier], report of arrest, 9 Brumaire.)

44 Arch. Lot, L 389 (Cahors *comité*, session of 5 Frimaire Year II).
45 See RCC, 'L'armée révolutionnaire au Havre-Marat'.
46 See P. Caron, 'La Commission Civile-Révolutionnaire et de Surveillance de l'Aveyron', 336. Similarly, the *société* of Epinal proposed the following toasts for a *banquet frugal* to celebrate, on 10 Thermidor, the fête of liberty and equality: 'the French People', 'Liberty and Equality', 'the National Convention', 'the Defenders of the *Patrie*', etc... (Arch. Vosges, reg. 9, *société* of Epinal, session of 18 Messidor Year II). See also A. Soboul's very stimulating article: 'Sentiments réligieux et cultes populaires sous la Révolution: saints patriotes et martyrs de la liberté', *A.h.R.f.* (1957), 193.
47 See P. Dally, 'Suzanne Lepeletier, fille de la Nation', *R.F.*, LXII (1912).
48 Arch. Vernon, D 1/bis (*société* of Vernon, session of 22 Brumaire).
49 See Arch. Vaucluse, L VI 30 (*société* of Valréas, session of 10 Pluviôse Year II).
50 The imprudent soldiers were almost torn to pieces by an enormous crowd of villagers which gathered in the church square; see below, III, 2, on this incident.
51 The presence of the *armée* at such fêtes was a way of visibly sealing the alliance between them and the *sociétés*. See, e.g., the account of the inauguration of the Temple of Reason at Ecouis, which terminated with the burning of the Pope in effigy and a civic banquet and ball (Arch. Eure, 236 L* 10, *société* of Ecouis, session of 30 Nivôse).
52 See, e.g., AN, D III 30 (2) (Comité de législation, Bouches-du-Rhône, Arles), deputies of Arles to the Convention, Ventôse Year III, listing the names of those heading the ultra-revolutionary faction of the previous year: Famin Lardenol and Ripert, former priests; Paris, formerly vicar-general to the bishop of Angoulême; Paris senior, writer for the paper *Le Père Duchesne du Midi;* Couston and Jaquet, former abbés; Antoine Pignard, sailor, etc.
53 There was also a simpler reason for former priests', eagerness to abandon a vocation condemned by a sector of public opinion: they had to earn a living, and as educated men they were often ambitious. See the *Journal révolutionnaire de Toulouse*, no. xxii, 18 Frimaire: 'This abandonment has set them on the road to a political career. Civilian and military employment is now the sole object of their ambitious cupidity'.
54 Rather the dechristianisation was a manifestation of revolutionary patriotism and even of xenophobia, particularly when directed against Piedmontese or Spaniards. See Arch. Vaucluse, L VI 27 (*société* of Châteauneuf-du-Pape), session of 25 Fructidor. E. Le Gallo, 'Les Jacobins de Cognac', *R. F.*, XLVII (1904), 429, claims dechristianisation was considered 'a measure of national defence' by the Cognac Jacobins.
55 This indeed was the conclusion of the *représentant*, Maure, more charitable than the Robespierrists (AN, W. 332 [561bis], Maure to Fouquier-Tinville, 26 Pluviôse).
56 This is exactly what happened in Epone, district of Mantes, where two sans-culottes so terrorised the municipality with false stories of what the *armée révolutionnaire* was doing close by in Meulan, that they secured orders banning religion, closing the church and forbidding work on the *décadi*, and went on to smash the altar and statues. When the *procureur* overturned the orders in response to public protest, the sans-culottes represented the commune as in the grip of a *révolte fanatique* and caused the district to send in a detachment of *révolutionnaires*. In this case, however, they accepted majority opinion in the commune and left without intervening in the quarrel. See AN, F 7 4742 d 4 (Hérault).
57 Arch. Yonne, L 208 (district of Avallon, Terrorists), denunciation against Nicolas Bertrand, roofer, 30 Prairial Year III; Arch. Seine-et-Oise (reg. *société* of L'Isle-Adam, session of 7 Nivôse Year II).
58 Arch. Oise (reg. district of Compiègne), Dupain to the *procureur-syndic*, 2 Frimaire Year II.
59 'It is I who have destroyed fanaticism in the district of Noyon,' wrote Hennon, 27 Prairial Year II. '...I am detested by the majority of the inhabitants of Noyon, but by the few patriots I am revered...' (AN, W 37 [2383] and W 159).
60 AHG, *reg. d'ordre*, Grammont to Lefebvre, 21 Nivôse. The affair was complicated by personal conflicts between the members of the Viarmes municipality and those of the *comité de surveillance*, and Lefebvre seems to have had some local support. Certainly, in Germinal Year II, the small detachment left behind there was ordered by the *comité* to arrest the mayor on charges of atheism and anti-religious provocation (AN, F 7 4684 d 2 [Duchesne]).
61 The extracts which follow from this *Mémorial d'un citoyen d'Auxerre* were kindly sent to me by M. Henri Forestier, head archivist of the Yonne.
62 At this point the author notes: 'thus did they repeat the insults of the Jews against J.C. at

the time of his passion...For christians to participate in such excesses was final proof of the hardening of their hearts!'

63 One senses that the author of the *Mémorial* was as shocked by the futile destruction of valuable objects as by the blasphemous and iconoclastic aspect of these events.

64 *Mémorial*, 42–5. (For the dechristianising activity of the Parisian *armée révolutionnaire* in the Yonne, see also *L'Histoire de la Révolution française par deux Amis de la Liberté*, vol. XIII, in which the authors emphasise the iconoclastic role of the *révolutionnaires* [70] and the moderating role of Maure [65].)

65 Arch. Auxerre, P 5 (General Council of the commune of Auxerre, session of 25 Brumaire Year II).

66 On this occasion (Sunday, 12 Nivôse) the Auxerre *révolutionnaires* were buffeted by a crowd largely composed of women. On 15 Nivôse the parishioners of the three closed churches invaded the town hall, insulted the members of the General Council, and demanded the reopening of the churches.

67 Arch. Auxerre, P 5. The report of the two *commissaires* on the same day declared: '...most of the statues...are in bad taste and have no merit as works of art...the Council...should choose *commissaires* from among connoisseurs and artists to judge what objects are worth retaining...'.

68 Arch. Auxerre, P 5 (Maure to the General Council of the commune, 25 Brumaire Year II).

69 H. Forestier, in 'Les campagnes de l'Auxerrois...', states that the cathedral was consecrated to Reason on 10 Nivôse Year II.

70 L. Chaumont, *Recherches sur la persécution réligieuse dans le département de Saône-et-Loire...*, 84–6: '...All the paintings, wooden statues, papers and deeds of the abbey were piled up in the public square and burnt in an *auto-da-fé* by these stupid iconoclasts, to the howls of the populace...'. See also Lorrain, *Histoire de l'abbaye de Cluny*, 276–7.

71 See Arch. Drôme, L 924* (reg. corres., district of Valence, report of 29 Nivôse).

72 Arch. Oise (regs. *comité* of Ognolles and district of Chaumont); Arch. Seine-et-Marne, L 827 (*comité* of Melun, session of 25 Frimaire).

73 AN, AF IV 1915 (E.B. Morin to Mgr. Caprara, 16 Frimaire Year XII). This priest married in Oct 1794. I am deeply grateful to Robert Dauvergne, who kindly pointed out this document to me.

74 See AN, F 7* 2509 (general assembly of the Fontaine-de-Grenelle Section, Prairial Year III). In the Louviers district, disturbances occurred at the time of the marriage of the parish priest of Ailly. The district sent 12 *révolutionnaires*, one of the many occasions on which the Parisian *armée* was called in to help married priests, who were singled out for vengeance by the *campagnards* (Arch. Eure, 120 L 5, district of Louviers, 27 Frimaire). The detachment from Louviers was also at the centre of disturbances when they attempted to remove the curé, Dubusc, from Pont-de-l'Arche (A.E. Sorel, *Pont-de-l'Arche pendant la Révolution*, 88–9). For Saint-Pierre-lès-Bitry, see Arch. Eure, 235 L 89* (Vernon *comité de surveillance*).

75 AN, F 7 4775 9 d 5 (Saillant), notes of 9 Ventôse and 17 Floréal Year II. The doctor's book was the New Testament.

76 Arch. Oise (Justice de Paix, canton of Lassigny); and see A.E. Sorel, *Pont-de-l'Arche pendant la Révolution*, and RCC, *L'armée révolutionnaire à Lyon*.

77 See H. Forestier, 'Les campagnes de l'Auxerrois...', 187.

78 AN, BB 3 65 (Oct 1793), *armée révolutionnaire*, communes which surrendered their bells at Luzarches.

79 RCC, 'L'armée révolutionnaire dans le district de Pontoise'.

80 The curé of Fourqueux, Adrien-Louis Ducastelier, who was executed 25 Prairial Year II, was much esteemed by his parishioners. He was also a *patriote*, supported the events of the Revolution, and was appointed constitutional priest of Fourqueux on 26 Nov 1792, when he delivered an address against tyranny (see J.T. Thénard, 'L'élection du curé de Fourqueux', *R.F.*, XI [1882], 522). On 5 Nivôse Year II, an attempt to arrest him on the orders of the two *repésentants*, Delacroix and Musset, was beaten off by a crowd of several hundred; another attempt was made on the 7th backed up by a large force of gendarmes, National Guard and 40 *révolutionnaires*. The municipal authorities were arrested and the people disarmed; but the curé had fled, leaving behind a curious letter for his flock, urging them to 'Love your country, the revolution, and religion divested of all fanaticism...'. For details of the affair see AN, Wla 21 (tribunaux révolutionnaires, Ducastelier); Arch. Fourqueux (reg. 1, municipality, deliberations); Arch. Seine-et-Oise, 2 Lk 58 (Saint-Germain *comité de surveillance*); Arch. Mantes, D3 8 (reg. *société populaire*).

81 The *sociétaires*, as originators of the measures against religion, were the particular object of the Briard peasants' hatred. The national agent, Vincent, writing to Fouquier-Tinville two months later, described the insurgents as: '...mostly poor sans-culottes, led astray by priests and *malveillans*...' (Arch. Seine-et-Marne, reg. supplémentaire, district of Rozoy, and AN W 332 [561bis], Mauperthuis affair).

82 AHG, B★ 12 62 (reg. corres., 5th Division, order of the Committee, 24 Frimaire). The city of Paris had important stores at La Ferté-Gaucher, Rozoy, Jouy-le-Châtel and Coulommiers. Any troubles in the Brie endangered the supply of the capital, which explains the swiftness of the Committee's intervention.

83 AHG, B5 75 (Armée révolutionnaire), Grammont to Jourdeuil, 25 Frimaire Year II.

84 Arch. Seine-et-Oise, IV Q 187 (Mazuel papers), letter of Chomel, 4 Pluviôse, on detachment in La Ferté-Gaucher; also AN, F 7 4774 50 d 2 (Montesquiou), Lemaire to the Committee of General Security, 12 Nivôse.

85 AN, W 332 (561 bis) and F 7 3689 4. The rioters for the most part were very poor people and of the 500 arrested most were threshers, day-labourers, pit-sawyers, weavers, blacksmiths, clog-makers, from the rural proletariat, along with a few yeomen farmers, former priests and schoolmasters, and gamekeepers.

86 Arch. Seine-et-Marne, L 577 (district of Nemours, session of 24 Nivôse Year II).

87 Arch. Brie-Comte-Robert (reg. *société populaire*). Among the 'atheists' of this commune we find Favret, the former mayor, and Giot, both *commissaires aux subsistances* (Arch. Seine-et-Marne, L 566, district of Melun).

88 Arch. Seine-et-Marne, L 854 (Provins *comité*). At Montereau the *société* took the initiative in the dechristianisation campaign, while the detachment took no part in religious matters (Arch. Montereau, P 2, reg. *société*).

89 See RCC, 'L'armée révolutionnaire dans l'Aisne', and J. Rollet, 'Les procès-verbaux de la Société populaire du Château-Thierry en l'an II de la République', *Annales de la Soc. hist. et archéologique de Château-Thierry* (1881).

90 In Nivôse Year II there were masses at Christmas and on Epiphany in a number of communes (AN, F 7 4781–5, *comités de surveillance* in the communes of the department of Paris); it was the National Guard from the Finistère Section which was sent to quell disturbances at Ivry and Choisy. See also AN, D III 232–3 d 8 (Comité de législation, department of Paris, Bercy), denunciation addressed to the Committee of General Security, Ventôse Year II, for an account of a discussion hostile to the dechristianisers at the general assembly of the commune of Bercy.

91 See II.3 for Honfleur, and see RCC, *L'armée révolutionnaire à Lyon*.

92 See C. Pichois and J. Dautry, *Le conventionnel Chasles et ses idées démocratiques*.

93 AN, W 498 (535), trial of Dufresse, deposition of 30 Brumaire.

94 Arch. Lille, 18′ 229 (Lille *société*).

95 See M. Aubert, 'La Révolution à Douai', and AN, W 498 (535), Adhémar to Dufresse, 23 Frimaire Year II.

96 In his newspaper of 26 Brumaire, Châles congratulated the citizens of Armentières on having expelled their priests and he invited the Lillois to follow their example (AHG, B 1 22, Army of the Nord, *Le Révolutionnaire*).

97 Arch. Aube, Lm4c 3/352: Bourdon, *commissaire civil* in the district of Ervy, was former vicar of Saint-Pantoléon of Troyes.

98 AN, F 7 4421 (mission of Rousselin in the Aube), report by the *commissaire* Regnault on the disturbances at Saint-Mard-sur-Othe.

99 BN, L 41b 4947 (general assembly of Saint-Paterne, session of 23 Vendémiaire), report of Parmentier, *délégué* of Laplanche in the districts of Neuville and Boiscommun. His colleague Pignon, at Châtillon-sur-Loire, used the *sociétés populaires* to accelerate dechristianisation.

100 Arch. Montargis, Dln2 (General Council, session of 30 Ventôse Year II).

101 Arch. Châlons, I. 199★ (*société populaire* of Châlons-sur-Marne), Villers, *commissaire civil* at Epernay, to the *société*, 10 Frimaire Year II. However the apparent compliance was suspect, and as early as 5 Nivôse we learn of plans by the village women to hear midnight mass in the churches.

102 AN, W 493 (479), Mancel to the Convention, 18 Vendémiaire Year III; and see II. 4, n 9.

103 Arch. Bas-Rhin, 50 L 7 (Strasbourg *comité*) and AN, F 7 4394 (papers found at Vincent's), Gateau to Vincent, 30 Frimaire Year II. In the Year III the departmental administration, describing these events, put it this way: '...the *armée révolutionnaire* went through the country, attacking innocent and guilty alike' (AN, D III 212 d 11). One Eisinger, 'prêtre

étranger', was denounced in particular for having 'publicly preached atheism' (Arch. Bas-Rhin, id.).

104 Arch. Nièvre (great reg. *comité de surveillance* of Corbigny, session of 23 Frimaire Year III), deposition of Hainaux, and id. (session of 29 Frimaire Year III), deposition of Granet, ex-Capuchin and head priest at the church of Bazoches. In the neighbouring district of Clamecy, the national agent, Parent, acted likewise, taking the precaution of surrounding himself with the revolutionary guard of Clamecy. On 10 Brumaire he reported to Fouché: 'Today...I joined with our brave sans-culottes of the *armée révolutionnaire* and the deputies of the three *sociétés* of Vézelay, Varzy and Clamecy; and without a priest, we celebrated the marriage of a sans-culotte couple with full republican festivity and solemnity. A huge crowd applauded this new form of ceremony...' (Arch. Nièvre, reg. corres.).

105 Arch. Nièvre (reg. corres., district of Clamecy), Parent to Fouché, 20 Brumaire Year II; also his circular to the priests of the district, 18 Brumaire.

106 Arch. Gironde, 11 L 27 (Club national, sessions of 9 and 28 Brumaire).

107 Arch. Vaucluse, L VI 9 (*société* of Violès, session of 19 Ventôse). Despite the desire to conform, so evident in the *commissaire* Espagneu, and the patronage of a *révolutionnaire* as important as Nicolaud, the supporters of religion carried the session. On Nicolaud, see I. 5, nn. 27 and 41, and Arch. Vaucluse, L VI 4 (*comité* of Orange, session of 5 Ventôse Year III). There can be no doubt that the introduction of the cult of Reason was the product of a carefully organised campaign by the *révolutionnaires* of Orange and Avignon, rather than of any kind of spontaneous movement by the local *sociétés*. Most of the orders date from Ventôse and Germinal, which suggests a co-ordinated effort.

108 AN, D III 181 (1) (209) (Comité de législation, Nevers), Damour to the Committee, 11 Germinal Year III.

109 *L'Anti-Terroriste*, no. 41, 13 Messidor Year III.

110 AN, W 523 (Vauquoy affair).

111 Arch. Nièvre (reg. corres., district of Clamecy). This resembles the propaganda of the *Père Duchesne* about the 'sans-culotte Jesus'. It is scarcely surprising that the peasants of the Morvan should have treated Parent and his like as Huguenots.

112 AN, F 7 4444 d 5 (address of the *société* of Saint-Girons, Nivôse Year II). Picot was at Seix 21 Oct.

113 See BN, Ye 20078 and *Journal Révolutionnaire de Toulouse*, no. xxx (16 Nivôse Year II), for some of Picot's publications. The commune of Mas-d'Azil, which had a very old Protestant community, had already been singled out for anti-religious measures – the Convention chastising the department, 23 Brumaire, for having reversed the municipality's measures suppressing religion and closing the churches (Lefebvre, *Le Gouvernement révolutionnaire*, 156). See also A. Wemyss (Mrs Cunnack), *Les Protestants du Mas-d'Azil*.

114 AN, F 7 4444 d 5. This opinion on the ill effects of forced dechristianisation is very clearly expressed in a letter from an inhabitant of Anduze (Gard), to the Committee of General Security, 25 Pluviôse Year II: '...I think the ultra-revolutionary patriots more dangerous than the aristocrats; at Saint-Jean-du-Gard, they are trying to force the people to observe the *décade* and work on Sundays, they ripped and burnt the Huguenot minister's vestments. All this has caused turmoil and I fear now that this most patriotic of areas might become the most fanatical, because your wise decrees on religion have not been respected and things have been carried too far.... The passage of time would have done more than bayonets to deter the Protestants from going to their mass...' (AN, F 7 4609 d 2, Borie).

115 Delport, e.g., died in 1819, refusing the sacraments, faithful to his anti-christian principles. (This information is from an unpublished study, 'Le capitaine "Sans-Quartier": Pierre Delport, curé de Beaumont', by Col. Bernard, who was kind enough to send it to me, along with his notes on the revolutionary personalities of Beaumont and Castelsarrasin.)

116 See, e.g., Arch. Haute-Savoie, 5 L 13 (Thonon *comité*, reg. corres.), letter of 8 Nivôse to the Committee of Public Safety – soldiers cantoned in the town having to be removed after 'committing indecencies in the church, during office and even the Christmas mass...'. See also Arch. Seine-et-Oise (reg. Sarcelles *comité*), 30 Ventôse: 'the *société populaire*...was told that citizen Marthon, a quarryman, had pissed in the Temple of Reason...'.

117 AN, D III 91 (2) (61) (Comité de législation, Haute-Garonne), note of Delport and

Blanchard, Floréal Year III.
118 Chuard, a Protestant minister of Peyrus, arrested as a *fanatique* in Ventôse, gathered together a group of some thousand faithful. See Arch. Drôme, L 1064 (*comité de surveillance* of Valence) and RCC, 'Les débuts de la déchristianisation à Dieppe'.
119 Arch. Nièvre (reg. corres., district of Clamecy), district to Legendre, 5 Nivôse Year II.
120 AN, F 7 4694 (Duperon). See also Arch. Aude, L 393 (*comité* of Carcassonne, session of 1 Germinal), demands for the churches to be reopened; and see Arch. Loire, L 400★ (*société* of Charlieu, session of 20 Floréal), Arch. Vaucluse, L VI 13 (*sociéte* of Cheval-Blanc, session of 14 Germinal) and L VI 12 (*société* of Vaison, 12 Messidor – the *cabarets* crowded on Sundays, despite the law obliging people to work), Arch. Vosges (reg. 9, *société* of Epinal, session of 10 Fructidor), and Arch. Eure, 235 L 7★ (*comité* of Beuzeville, reg. corres., session of 21 Ventôse), for the widespread return to Sunday observance after the condemnation of the Hébertists.
121 Arch. Drôme, L 924 (*société* of Valence, session of 6 Ventôse).
122 In the Year III, the Thermidorean authorities accused Figuet – Payan having been guillotined with the Robespierrists – of having 'sought to spread consternation through the surrounding communes...by marching with a *compagnie révolutionnaire* [and] smashing, burning or stealing everything inside the churches...'(Arch. Drôme, L 942, district of Valence, and AN, F 7 4707 d 2 [Figuet]).
123 Arch. Drôme, L 924 (district of Valence, session of 11 Ventôse Year II). At Peyrus Payan's 'sermons' had persuaded the people to reconsecrate the church to the cult of Reason. What is astonishing is that this Payan was to become a member of the intimate circle around Robespierre, despite his energetic actions in support of Reason.
124 See Aulard, x. 23, Carrier to the Committee, 12 Nivôse: 'As for Brittany...a deputy...should take 1200–1500 cavalry on a revolutionary tour...starting with the large towns...then the country areas, burning all the churches by carefully planned accidents...'. Le Batteux was right to invoke Carrier's orders in Year III, when prosecuted for the shootings at Noyal-Muzillac. For Albitte, see the entry in *Dictionnaire des Jacobins vivans*, 9.
125 Arch. Aveyron, 80 L 1 (Villefranche *comité*, 20 Brumaire).
126 AN, F 7 3681 9 (Lot-et-Garonne).
127 Note, however, the incident in which 26 inhabitants of the commune of Mallemort appeared before the Bouches-du-Rhône criminal tribunal in the Year III, accused '...of having insulted and ill-treated those who wore slightly better clothes on Sundays than on other days'. They had, it was claimed, devastated the churches, burnt statues and ornaments, and brandished their sabres at those who did not share their views (AN, D III 30 [19] [4], Comité de législation, Bouches-du-Rhône, Mallemort, letter from the departmental criminal tribunal, 24 Fructidor Year III). If this was not the action of an *armée révolutionnaire*, properly speaking, it was certainly violent and iconoclastic dechristianisation by force.
128 Summary of areas witnessing forced dechristianisation by the departmental *armées*:
   Allier (all districts)
   Ariège (districts of Pamiers and of Saint-Girons)
   Aube (district of Ervy)
   Bouches-du-Rhône (Mallemort?) ('private' *armée*)
   Drôme (canton of Peyrus)
   Haute-Garonne (districts of Toulouse and of Grenade)
   Isère (districts of La Tour-du-Pin and Vienne)
   Loiret (districts of Montargis, Malesherbes, Boiscommun)
   Lot-et-Garonne (district of Marmande)
   Marne (districts of Châlons, Epernay, Vitry-le-François)
   Haute-Marne (district of Joinville)
   Mayenne (district of Lassay) ('private' *armée*)
   Mont-Blanc (district of Thonon)
   Morbihan (canton of Noyal-Muzillac)
   Nièvre (all districts)
   Nord (Dunkerque, Bailleul)
   Bas-Rhin (districts of Strasbourg, Haguenau and Sélestat)
   Haut-Rhin (district of Colmar?)
   Vaucluse (district of Orange)

129 G. Lefebvre, *Le Gouvernement révolutionnaire*, 182.

130 In the Vaucluse the *sociétés populaires* of Châteauneuf, Jonquières, Piolenc, Méthanis, Oppède and Malaurène took the decision to close the churches without resorting to outsiders or to force. The same was true for certain towns in the Saône-et-Loire and the Somme.

131 See the *Journal révolutionnaire de Toulouse*, 'Situation de Toulouse' for 18 Frimaire Year II (no. xxii), reporting that most of the Catholic priests in the town had ceased their functions. And see Arch. Hérault, L 5502 and 5503 (*société* of Montpellier, sessions of Frimaire–Pluviôse).

132 Arch. Nièvre (district of Clamecy, reg. corres.), national agent of the district to the Committee of General Security, 19 Germinal Year III: '...Nearly every commune has reopened its church and recalled its curé.... The temple of Clamecy now has all the trappings of Catholicism.... Crosses have been restored in several places in the district...'. However, this district was dechristianised far more systematically, with the assistance of the *armée révolutionnaire*, than most other districts of the Republic.

133 See Arch. Vaucluse, L VI 5 (*société* of Oppède, session of 12 Ventôse) and Arch. Saône-et-Loire, IV L 10 (*société* of La Clayette, session of 30 Nivôse), for examples of this.

Chapter 7

1 Restif, a keen observer of popular phenomena, depicts the Savoyards and Auvergnats as born criminals, and, with the coal-miners, 'the most dangerous of troublemakers, because of their natural brutishness and, given their poverty, their disregard of the consequences...'(*Les Nuits de Paris*, 17). 'I tremble', he adds, 'every time I see the lower orders of the people aroused...for I know with what hatred they regard the well-off...'(137, also 257). The Savoyards and Auvergnats sinned above all in not having a Parisian accent, in being too poor, in having *mauvaises mines* (the latter were dark and swarthy). Restif, a *bon bourgeois* of Paris, feared these *étrangers* who had no ties in the capital city.

2 AN, F 7 3689 4, Ronsin to Paré, 2 Brumaire Year II. The legend about the visit of the *armée révolutionnaire* to the Meaux region was to have a long life. It was echoed in the Abbé de L'Espinasse de Langeac, *Journal de l'anarchie, de la terreur et du despotisme* (1821); see II. 589, under '4 Sept 1793' (i.e., three days before the *armée* was created).

3 For this complicated affair, see Arch. Seine-et-Oise, 2 Lm 28 (district of Gonesse), IV Q 148 (Séquestres, Lallement de Nantouillet), dossier containing a complete inventory of the objects taken by the *commissaires* and the revolutionary officers. See also AN, F 7 4649 d 2 (Clémence), F 7 4774 34 d 3 (Marchand), Wla 191 (tribunaux révolutionnaires), Wla 194 (Maillard's attack). The relentlessness of the campaign by Goureau, *procureur* of the commune, and some big farmers of the Gonesse district against the two *commissaires* is a token of its political nature. It was the use of force and the *armée révolutionnaire* which was on trial. They returned to the charge in Vendémiaire Year III, trying to destroy the reputation of two terrorists who had been particularly energetic (AN, F 7 4649 d 2), but could not make the charge stick, and instead turned upon the lesser participants, the members of the municipality and *comité* of Marly-la-Ville, the artisans and day-labourers who had collaborated with these *étrangers* (Arch. Seine-et-Oise, 2 Lm 37). In reality, all the evidence suggests that Clémence and Marchand had acted honestly in their execution of a difficult mission and had given a precise account of the gold and silver taken from Lallement. Indeed, in Brumaire they were congratulated by the Convention for their zeal. At most they were guilty of taking food for their soldiers (for which they accepted full responsibility). The affair is worth attention if only because for more than a year it was the principal focus of moderate attack on the Parisian *armée*.

4 *Journal de la Montagne*, no. 32 (25 Frimaire).

5 Fabre's charge was not accurate. Paillardelle was *commissaire* of the Committee of Public Safety.

6 *Journal Universel*, no. 1489 (29 Frimaire). On the 28th evidence against Buard, *chef de bataillon*, was sent to Franqueville (AN, Wla 124). The coincidence of dates indicates a concerted campaign.

7 *Journal Universel*, no. 1489.

8 Bib. hist. de la Ville de Paris, R.F. divers. The success of the campaign against the *révolutionnaires* was such that Hébert intervened to defend the honour of the Parisian *armée*

and to denounce the actions of the false *armées* (see *Père Duchesne* no. 344, also Prudhomme's *Révolutions de Paris*, no. 352 (27 Frimaire).

9 AHG (*reg. d'ordre*) for Grammont's two letters, of 14 and 15 Nivôse. See also below, III. 2.

10 *Journal de la Montagne*, no. 57 (20 Nivôse Year II). Despite Calmet's claim, Dufresse did take a detachment to Dunkerque (see pp. 467–8).

11 Bib. hist. de la Ville de Paris, Acloque Club (extract from deliberations of the Sans-Culottes Section, session of 5 Pluviôse Year II).

12 Id. (general assembly of the Bon-Conseil Section, session of 14 Pluviôse).

13 AN, Wla 191 (Bacon's report). It was in Pluviôse too that the fireman, Rocher, former aide-de-camp to Ronsin, launched his personal campaign against his old chief by posting notices all over Paris accusing Ronsin and his wife of stealing cutlery. The notice can scarcely have added to the prestige of the general staff, and one can just imagine Parisian opinion laughing at such indecent quarrels. See AN, Wla 191, and F 7 4774 86 d l (Rocher), Dugard's report of 29 Pluviôse.

14 AHG, B5 75.

15 AN, AD XXa 337, Coll. Rondonneau, *Journal des Jacobins de Reims*, no. 14 (session of the *société*, 24 Ventôse Year II).

16 *L'Anti-Terroriste*, no. 25 bis (17 Floréal) and no. 51 (18 Thermidor Year III).

17 *L'Orateur du Peuple*, 13 Nivôse Year III.

18 *L'Anti-Terroriste*, no. 41 (13 Messidor Year III).

19 AN, D III 179 (1) (Comité de législation, Nièvre, Decize). See also Arch. Nièvre (district of Clamecy, reg. deliberations, session of 9 Pluviôse Year III), listing those accused of various offences. The district put their property under sequestration and their trial took place during Messidor Year II.

20 AN, D III 180 (8) (19) (Comité de législation, Nièvre, Moulins-Engilbert).

21 Arch. Nièvre (great reg. Corbigny *comité de surveillance*). See also Arch. Saône-et-Loire, IV L 3 (Autun *comité*), national agent to the district *comités*, 2nd *décade*, Brumaire Year III.

22 Arch. Vaucluse, L VI 4 (Orange *comité*, session of 5 Ventôse Year III).

23 AN, D XL III (Committee of General Security, 'Les Patriotes de Tonneins à la Convention', 17 Sept 1795).

24 We meet with the same idea in Prudhomme, v. 432, when he comments that the revolutionary battalion of the Gironde was composed of peasants 'who were stimulated by hopes of pillage. They were commanded by Jacobins and thieves...'; also in the 'deux amis de la liberté' in their *Histoire de la Révolution française* of the Year VII, XIII. 53, 62.

25 AN, F 7 4436 A pl. 4 (233), Laporte to Couthon, 24 Germinal Year II.

26 This was Armé, Bonne-Nouvelle Section, enrolled as a fusilier in the Halle-au-Bled company, appointed clerk-secretary to the Commission des Sept on arrival at Lyon. He sent substantial parcels to his mistress, Mme Villot, who was denounced by her neighbours in the Brutus Section for such a rapid and visible improvement in her circumstances. Armé was arrested, brought to Paris 12 Thermidor, but was spared an appearance before the revolutionary tribunal by the crisis of Thermidor. In Vendémiaire Year III, a number of Lyonnais testified to his humanity. It is probable that he had used his position to sell pardons. (RCC, *L'armée révolutionnaire à Lyon*, 37.)

27 H. Riouffe, *Mémoires d'un détenu*, 44–7, refers to his fellow prisoners, the professional criminals, in the Conciergerie as '...nearly all aristocrats... They have considerable contempt for *les révolutionnaires*, as they call those arrested on political charges...'.

28 See P. Caron, in *R.F.*, vol. LXXXIV (1931), 86–8, on Antoine Hadengue's book on the *armées révolutionnaires*: 'Blinded by the similarity which he sees between the Bolsheviks of 1930 and the Hébertists of the Year II, he cannot see the authoritarianism behind the... violence of the *armée révolutionnaire*, which had nothing specifically communist about it. Was Louis XIV communist when he mobilised his dragoons, or Napoleon when he billeted garrisons on the families of fleeing conscripts? In this respect as in many others, and because practices change less quickly than ideas, the French Revolution, far from pointing to the future, was a prisoner of the past ...'.

29 See Aulard IX. 46, also RCC, *L'armée révolutionnaire à Lyon*, 279.

30 The myth, however, was strong enough to cross the Channel and find its way into Carlyle's *The French Revolution*, vol. III: 'Ronsin, they say, admitted in candid moments, that his troops were the elixir of the Rascality of the Earth. One sees them drawn up in market places, travel-splashed, rough-bearded, in *carmagnole complète*...Pipe in cheek, sabre on thigh...Such things have been; and may again be. Charles [the] Second sent out

his Highland Host over the Western Scotch Whigs; Jamaica Planters got Dogs from the Spanish Main to hunt their Maroons with. France too is bescoured with a Devil's Pack, the baying of which, at this distance of half a century, still sounds in the mind's ear...' – a vivid picture of the archetypal bandit. Carlyle based his account on Buchez and Roux, in turn drawn from the Hébertist trials and the words attributed to Ronsin. So Fouquier-Tinville has claimed another victim.

31 AN, F 7 4436 A pl. 4 (254), Parein to Payan, 22 Germinal Year II, trying to sans-culottise his past by claiming his father had been a poor butcher – in fact he was a saddler, and does not seem to have been particularly poor. On the fortune of Parein, see I. 2, p. 68.

32 See I. 2, pp. 65–6, and RCC, 'Robespierre und Boulanger'.

33 *Dictionnaire des Jacobins vivans,* 40–1. But then this royalist author thought all the *armées révolutionnaires* destined for robbery and murder.

34 B. Combes de Patris, *Procès-verbaux de la société populaire de Rodez: société* of Rodez, session of 3 Floréal Year III.

35 AN, Wla 34 (2092) (tribunaux révolutionnaires), Bô to Fouquier-Tinville, 11 Floréal Year II. The crime of levying *taxes révolutionnaires* and distributing the proceeds to the poor, of which Viton was accused, was not confined to revolutionary officers and *commissaires*. The most characteristic example of this comes from the municipality of Heyrieux, a small commune in the district of Vienne, whose national agent was to be guillotined under the Robespierrist dictatorship for abuse of powers, atheism, etc. (AN, W 454 [143b]). Among those listed by the municipality in Nivôse as liable for *taxes révolutionnaires* we find: 'Louis Gillet – lack of concern for the public good, taxed 4 pairs of men's clogs; the wife of Michel Bouvard – *égoïste* and *fanatique*, taxed a good ham; Mme Richard and her eldest daughter – fanatics and aristocrats, taxed, the mother, clothes for 3 women, the daughter, 1 chemise, 1 skirt, 1 headdress, 1 kerchief...'. It seems that the authorities of this commune took their example from the activities of Vauquoy and Contamin in the neighbouring district.

36 Arch. Aveyron, 77 L 1* (Sévérac *comité*), depositions of Durand, Hérail, Ricard and Vernhet, 15–20 Frimaire Year III.

37 Id., deposition of an inhabitant of Coussergues, 7 Pluviôse Year III.

38 AN, F 7 3681 9 (Lot), interrogation of Autefage, of Moissac, 27 Nivôse Year III.

39 Arch. Lot, L 406 (Cahors *comité*, 5 Prairial Year II).

40 Arch. Lot, L 391 (Cahors *comité*, 11 Frimaire Year III).

41 Arch. Aveyron, 77 L 1* (Sévérac *comité*), deposition of Fabre, 21 Frimaire Year III.

42 Arch. Aveyron, 80 L 1 (Villefranche *comité*), session of 19 Brumaire Year II, and see B. Combes de Patris, *Procès-verbaux de la société populaire de Rodez*.

43 RCC, 'Les armées révolutionnaires du Midi', 28.

44 Arch. Aveyron, 77 L 1 (Sévérac *comité*).

45 Arch. Lot, L 407 (Cahors *comité*).

46 Arch. Aveyron, 80 L 1 (Villefranche *comité*, proceedings of 27 Brumaire Year II). See also Prudhomme, v. 476 ('Crimes committed in the Haute-Loire during the proconsulate of Faure, Jean-Baptiste Lacoste, Reynaud...'): 'their order of payment was conceived in these terms: "It is required of M***, in virtue of the powers vested in me, to pay the sum of *** within 24 hours, failing which the sum will be doubled and 50 volunteers placed at discretion with him for several days"'.

47 *La Révolution du Cantal*.

48 AN, D III 39 (20) (178) (Comité de législation, Cantal). *Dominique Mirande...aux amis de la justice*, 30.

49 Arch. Cantal, L 685 (Aurillac *comité*), deposition of Capelle, 5 Frimaire Year III. The shaving mug is from *La Révolution du Cantal*.

50 RCC, *L'armée révolutionnaire à Lyon*, 57–62.

51 Arch. Rhône, 1 Q 138–8 (Séquestres) – register containing a daily tally of sums collected during Vauquoy's operations in the Isère. Most of the officers and *commissaires* were equally scrupulous in compiling their accounts, and the authorities of the Year II were quick to call them to order for not submitting such reports. Thus a complaint from the former curé of Asnois caused the directory of the Clamecy district to mount an enquiry into the confiscations made by Bussière, commander of the Nièvre revolutionary guard stationed at Clamecy. See I. 5, n. 99.

52 AN, W 523 (tribunaux révolutionnaires, Vauquoy affair), deposition made before the committee of La Tour-du-Pin, 8–9 Germinal Year II). See also p. 434.

53 See Arch. Grenoble, LL 19 (General Council of the commune of Grenoble to the

Commission Temporaire, 4 Pluviôse Year II). The municipality of Grenoble painted an unflattering picture of this adventurer, gambler and sometime swindler: 'the elder Dolle, whom everyone saw with the utmost surprise at the head of an *armée révolutionnaire* in the district of La Tour-du-Pin...was a merchant from Grenoble, with an unearned income of some 25,000-30,000 1., which at no time did he put at the service of morality or of humanity, but entirely dissipated in debauchery and villainy'. The statement goes on to tell how Dolle somehow got himself accepted into a *société* of sans-culottes in Grenoble, was then (as we have seen) implicated in Federalism, moved to Paris, where he set up a gaming house which was to be the ruin of many young men (including Virieu, former *seigneur* of Favergues, whom Dolle managed to strip entirely of his château and land, situated in the district of La Tour-du-Pin). 'It is said that his civic mission in the district...had no object other than vengeance against the administrators and farmers who blocked his enjoyment of such ill-gotten gains....' Having recouped his fortune in Paris, he settled at La Guillotière, where his many talents soon made him the darling of the poor patriots. When he again took refuge in the capital at the time of the prosecutions of 1794, he was arrested, but claimed to be too ill to answer charges in Grenoble. See AN, F 7 4554² (arrests, Bouches-du-Rhône, order of the Committee of General Security, 19 Germinal Year III).

54 Dolle arrested the farmers of Les Abrets, where he was proprietor of the château of Saint-Ondras. His principal enemy was Fugier, administrator of the district of La Tour, who denounced him in the Year II (AN, F 7 4678 d 3 [Dolle]). See also AN, W 523 (tribunaux révolutionnaires), and RCC, *L'armée révolutionnaire à Lyon*, 113–14, App. E.

55 V. Lombard de Langres, *Histoire des Jacobins depuis 1789 jusqu'à ce jour*, 147. See also I. 5, p. 231.

56 AN, F 7 4422 (*comité révolutionnaire* of Nantes), deposition of Chaix, 11 Messidor Year II.

57 AN, Wla 493 (tribunaux révolutionnaires, trial of Carrier), bill of indictment, 17 Vendémiaire Year III.

58 APP, A A/269 (notes of Topino-Lebrun on the hearings at Carrier's trial).

59 APP, A A/269. Richard and Joly were to take pride of place in the 'gallery of crime' of Thermidorean iconography.

60 *Journal des Jacobins de Reims*, session of 24 Ventôse Year II; and Aulard, IX. 46, Maure to the Committee, 20 Brumaire Year II. See also Arch. Nièvre (district of Clamecy, reg., session of 23 Prairial Year II), for a description of the arrests of the wives of those condemned.

61 AN, Wla 125 (papers of Fouquier-Tinville), memorial of Verdier.

62 AN, Wla 34 (2092) and D III 27 (35) (Comité de législation, Lot, Cahors), Dehaussé, inhabitant of Najac, to the Committee of Public Safety, 20 Messidor Year III.

63 AN, D III 45ᵃ (54) (515) (2) (Comité de législation, Charente Inférieure, Rochefort), the naval officers to the Convention, 5 Thermidor Year III.

64 Aulard, XI. 699, Maure writing from Melun, 24 Ventôse Year II, also AHG, B5 75, Musset and Delacroix writing from Versailles, 28 Brumaire, all complaining of indiscipline and insubordination. However, see Aulard, VIII. 255, for praise by the same *représentants* of the detachment at Mantes; but this was a company of fusiliers, who were more disciplined than the cavaliers.

65 AHG, B5 75, Committee to Grammont, 10 Frimaire Year III, and id. (*reg. d'ordre*), 11 Ventôse. See also I. 2.

66 See RCC, 'L'armée révolutionnaire au Havre-Marat et dans le district de Montivilliers'; also Aulard, IX. 46, on the mutiny of 200 cannoneers on detachment at Caen.

67 See RCC, *L'armée révolutionnaire à Lyon*.

68 AN, F 7 4767 d 2 (Lassagne), Réaume's letters to the Bonne-Nouvelle *comité révolutionnaire*. See also below, III. 3.

69 Florent Guiot wrote on 21 Frimaire to the Committee : 'It seems to me that this *armée* [*révolutionnaire* of Lille] is being treated like a spoilt child where clothing and equipment are concerned, while our troops stationed at our outposts lack clothes' (Aulard, IX. 330). Over a third of the Lille *armée* was made up of young men from the conscripted battalions of Lille and the Somme (see I. 5).

70 See RCC, *L'armée révolutionnaire à Lyon*, 79–84

71 See, e.g., the *Père Duchesne de Commune-Affranchie*, no. xv (20 Nivôse), in which Damame says as much.

72 AHG (*reg. d'ordre*), Grammont to Buard, 2 Pluviôse. Shortly afterwards the detachment was sent to Le Havre and calm returned to the quartier.

73 See RCC, 'Le "complot militaire" de ventôse an II'.

74 Arch. Vernon. Dl 14 (General Council, session of 25 Ventôse).
75 Laukhard, 290.
76 Arch. Provins (great reg. General Council), session of 3 Pluviôse Year II. The municipality of Rozoy made similar complaints (Arch. Rozoy, D 3, session of 3 Nivôse).
77 RCC, 'L'armée révolutionnaire au Havre-Marat'.
78 Arch. Haute-Garonne, L 4258★ (district of Toulouse, 24 Brumaire).
79 Arch. Nièvre (great reg. Corbigny *comité*).
80 Arch. Oise (*juge de paix,* canton of Attichy, district of Noyon).
81 RCC, 'Les armées révolutionnaires du Midi'.
82 B. Combes de Patris, *Procès-verbaux de la société populaire de Rodez.* See also Prudhomme, v. 478.
83 See, e.g., the far-fetched description of Dumoustier in the *Dictionnaire des Jacobins vivans,* 44–5, and of the expedition to Livry: 'Nothing was spared...in the attempt to sans-culottise these unfortunate agriculturalists, theft, rape, vexations of all kinds were employed by this scoundrel and several others of the same band...' (see above, II. 3, on the operation) – and yet Dumoustier, an artisan from the Observatoire Section, seems to have been a perfectly honest man.

BOOK THREE

Chapter 1
1 See the journal of Robespierre, under heading '17 frimaire. Guerre-Nord'. Robespierre was undoubtedly concerned about the 'fanatisme' provoked in the country by the dechristianising activities of the *armée* of the North and its like.
2 Aulard, VIII: Maure to the Committee, 14 Brumaire and 20 Brumaire (331).
3 AN, AF II 152 (1227). On 28 Brumaire, Parein and Boissay wrote to the Vermenton municipality: 'We were dismayed to hear of the disorders committed in your commune by scoundrels following the second column of the *armée révolutionnaire*...we hope that you will be able to forget these insults you have suffered and which the main body of the *armée* had no part in'.
4 Aulard, VIII, Maure to the Committee, 25 Brumaire.
5 See also AN, AF II 186 (1541), Reynaud, from Le Puy, to the Committee, 28 Frimaire, chiding it for its lack of response to his requests for advice.
6 Aulard, VIII, draft order, 28 Brumaire.
7 See also Prieur's rough draft for a letter to Maure, 8 Frimaire: 'You have created an *armée révolutionnaire,* it is a perfidious institution and should be dissolved instantly. The strength of a representative of the people lies in public opinion. It is following in the train of the despots to resort to bayonets...' (AN, AF II 152 [1228]). These lines are scored out and the letter was probably never sent.
8 Similar fears were expressed by the Committee in a letter to Laurent, 8 Frimaire (AN, AF II 152 [1228]).
9 Aulard, VIII. 676, Committee to Maure, 4 Frimaire; Arch. Yonne, L 157, order of Maure, 7 Frimaire.
10 Aulard, VIII. 676, Committee to Paganel, 4 Frimaire: '...An *armée révolutionnaire*...taken over by astute leaders, could become a force of terror and be turned against liberty itself...'.
11 id. IX. 46, Laplanche to the Committee, 9 Frimaire.
12 Aulard, IX. 330, Guiot to the Committee, 21 Frimaire.
13 See C. Pichois and J. Dautry, *Le conventionnel Chasles et ses idées démocratiques.*
14 'You have destroyed the revolutionary government that I legislated for some months ago', Saint-Just wrote to Billaud. 'As soon as the decree was *written,* the government ceased to be *revolutionary*: it consisted in this single word...'. But Saint-Just took no account of this during his mission in Alsace. See G. Bouchard, *Prieur de la Côte-d'Or* (1945), 447.
15 See AN, AF II 186 (1450), Boisset to the Committee, 22 Frimaire, and, on the Ariège, RCC, 'Les armées révolutionnaires du Midi', 12, 15, 35, 79.
16 AN, F 7 4394 1, Paré to the Committee of General Security, 4 Frimaire. Like the Committee of Public Safety, Paré was mistaken about the order setting up an *armée* in the Yonne: it came not from the department, but from Maure. This letter was communicated to me by Prof. Albert Goodwin.
17 See, however, M. Eude, *Paris pendant la Terreur.*
18 '...I fear that the suspension [of his *délégués*] will breathe life again into *égoïsme*', wrote

Solon Reynaud on 28 Frimaire, 'for without revolutionary measures, I doubt if the necessary grain will be forthcoming...' (AN, AF II 186 [1541]). See also the observations of the national agent for the Clamecy district on the disastrous effects of the decree for freedom of religion: 'Reason and its apostles had triumphed everywhere...over error, when the law of 18 Frimaire was issued...then the *malveillans* regrouped, recalled the people of the countryside to their former practices and rekindled religious zeal by appealing principally to the women...' (Arch. Nièvre, L reg. 7, district of Clamecy, the national agent to the *représentant* Legendre, 5 Nivôse Year II).

19 The *comité* of Orpierre (Hautes-Alpes) only learnt of the law of 14 Frimaire at their session of 14 Nivôse. Even then they were obliged to apply to the department for further advice on its terms (Arch. Hautes-Alpes, L 1502, *comité* of Orpierre, session of 14 Nivôse). A letter of 22 Frimaire took until 23 Nivôse to reach Ribiers in the same department (id., L 1503, *comité* of Ribiers).

20   Chronological Table of Orders for the Disbandment of the
                      Departmental and Communal *Armées révolutionnaires*

21 Frimaire: detachment of the Lille *armée* at Cambrai, letter from Adhémar, its commander[a]
22 Frimaire: announcement of the decree in the Lille *société*[b]
23 Frimaire: disbandment of the Douai and Cambrai detachments[c]
25 Frimaire: order from the Moulins *comité de surveillance* disbanding the Allier revolutionary battalion[d]
——— order of Bassal for the disbandment of the Jura *armée*[e]
26 Frimaire: order of the Isère department for the disbandment of the Grenoble company[f]
——— letter of Tréhouard about the disbandment of the Redon *armée*[g]
——— letter of the *commissaires civils*, Gobert and Delteil, on the disbanding of the *armée révolutionnaire* of the East[h]
——— order of the district of Toulouse to disarm the Haute-Garonne *armée*[i]
27 Frimaire: circular letter of Projean about disbanding the Doubs *armée*[j]
28 Frimaire: letter of Boisset announcing the disbandment of the revolutionary battalion of the Hérault[k]
——— order from the Toulouse garrison commander for the assembly at Toulouse of all those making up the detachment sent to Grenade[l]
 2 Nivôse: request of the 2nd Troyes Section for the disbandment of the Bataillon de la Montagne[m]
 3 Nivôse: order of the Bordeaux *comité de surveillance* for the disbandment of the revolutionary battalion of the Gironde[n]
——— order of the Montargis *comité de surveillance* for the dissolution of the revolutionary companies of the Loiret[o]
 6 Nivôse: order of Javogues and Girard retaining the Loire *armée* under arms[p]
 7 Nivôse: order of the Montauban *comité de surveillance* announcing the dissolution of the revolutionary battalion[q]
 8 Nivôse: letter from the Roanne district concerning Javogues's order[r]
14 Nivôse: order of the Agen *comité de surveillance* dissolving the Agen company[s]
14–15 Nivôse: order of the district of Villeneuve-sur-Lot on the disarmament of the revolutionary company of the town[t]
20 Nivôse: order of Fouché, Albitte and Laporte, attaching the revolutionary forces of the Allier, the Nièvre, the Loire and the Saône-et-Loire, then at Commune-Affranchie, to the Parisian *armée révolutionnaire*[u]
26 Nivôse: order of Lefiot dissolving the revolutionary guard of the Clamecy district[v]
 3 Pluviôse: order of the Moulins *comité* for the assembly and dispatch to Lyon of part of the Allier *bataillon révolutionnaire*[w]
——— order of the Charlieu *société populaire* maintaining the Loire *armée* under arms[x]
16 Pluviôse: letter of Javogues to Collot-d'Herbois on his efforts to re-establish a national *armée révolutionnaire*[y]
27 Pluviôse: order of Monestier (Puy-de-Dôme) and Pinet dissolving the *garde soldée* of Dax[z]
13 Ventôse: disbandment of the six companies composing the Loire *armée révolutionnaire*[aa]
28 [?] Ventôse: disbandment of the detachment of the Allier *armée* at Lyon[bb]

a AN, W. 498 (535) (Dufresse affair), Adhémar to Dufresse, 21 Frimaire.
b See III.1, sect. v.

c Arch. Nord, L 10224 (*société* of Lille, session of 24 Frimaire). See also Aulard, IX. 527, letter from Hentz and Guiot, 29 Frimaire.

d Arch. Allier, L 850 (*comité* of Moulins, session of 25 Frimaire).

e Arch. Jura, liasse 'Représentants', Bassal's order of 25 Frimaire – though Bassal, and some other *représentants*, were under the illusion that the companies would be retained in the end.

f AN, D III 117 (24) (Comité de législation, Isère, Grenoble), departmental order, 26 Frimaire.

g Aulard, IX. 450, Tréhouard to the Committee, 26 Frimaire.

h Arch. Metz, 121 13 (General Council, session of 26 Frimaire).

i Arch. Haute-Garonne, L 4258 (district of Toulouse, session of 26 Frimaire).

j Arch. Doubs, L 2358 (*société* of Montbeliard, session of 27 Frimaire).

k AN, AF II 186 (1540), Boisset to the Committee. On 22 Frimaire he had written to the Committee for permission to keep his company under arms, but prudently withdrew his request on the 28th with the comment, '. . .there must be no half-measures. . .'. See RCC, 'Les armées révolutionnaires du Midi' on this subject.

l AHG, B⁴ 31★ (Toulouse garrison, *ordres du jour*).

m Arch. Aube, Lm 4c3 and Arch. Troyes, D3 and D38 (session of 2 Nivôse). The Section demanded the departure of this 'so-called revolutionary' force within 24 hours. On 7 Nivôse, the battalion still not gone, the General Council decided to denounce this non-compliance with the law to the public prosecutor. On this affair see pp. 535–6.

n Arch. Gironde, II L 69 (session of the *comité*, 3 Nivôse).

o Arch. Montargis, D 1 n2 (General Council of the commune, 3 Nivôse Year II).

p AN, AF II 114 (861) (5): Article I of the order retaining the 1,200 men under arms, according to Article XX of the law, making an exception in cases of 'pays rebelles' until the restoration of order; Article II forbidding use of the term 'armée révolutionnaire' to describe it, '. . .it will be considered a National Guard for the detention of conspirators. . .'. This ploy, by which Javogues was able to keep his *armée* in being until Ventôse, was to be condemned in the Thermidorean pamphlet *Tableau des Crimes de Javogues* (BL, F. 49), 11. That same day, 6 Nivôse, the *représentant* Prost, equally out of touch with governmental policy, wrote to the Committee: '. . .An *armée révolutionnaire* is needed in the Jura more than anywhere else, to obtain through terror what is unattainable through Reason. . .' (AN, AF II 186 [1543] [22]).

q Arch. Tarn-et-Garonne, L 221 (*comité* of Montauban, session of 7 Nivôse).

r AN, AF II 186 (1543), district of Roanne to the Committee, 8 Nivôse Year II. The district communicated the confusion of the officers and soldiers about whether to follow the law of 14 Frimaire or Javogues's order of 6 Nivôse, and through the district they asked the Committee for advice, preferring to obey the decree rather than Javogues's order.

s Arch. Lot-et-Garonne (reg. corres., *comité* of Agen).

t F. de Mazet, *La Révolution à Villeneuve-sur-Lot* (Villeneuve, 1894), 139, citing the order of the district disarming a company of 40 men, 'even though they were not an *armée révolutionnaire*'.

u AN, AF II 138 (1075) (7), order of Fouché, Albitte and Laporte. These detachments, in all 366 men, became the 7th battalion of the Parisian *armée* (Arch. Rhône, 1 L 215, Département, state of the garrison, 20–1 Pluviôse Year II).

v AN, F7 4774 12 d 4 (Lefiot), printed report on his mission in the Nièvre. He arrived 21 Nivôse and on the 23rd received complaints about *taxes révolutionnaires* raised in the Clamecy district by the district vice-president, Diogène Tenaille. Lefiot complained bitterly of this administration to the Committee, accusing it of failing to comply with the law of 14 Frimaire by retaining a paid revolutionary guard (Aulard, x. 253). On 26 Nivôse he ordered the authority purged, and the law of 14 Frimaire applied. See also Arch. Nièvre, L. reg. 7 (district of Clamecy, reg. correspondence), showing the revolutionary battalion of the Nièvre, and the special guard formed at Clamecy, still an existence on 28 Frimaire.

w Arch. Allier, L 850 and L 852 (*comité* of Moulins, sessions of 1 and 3 Pluviôse). The detachment composed of 161 men left for Lyon on the 3rd.

x Arch. Loire, L. 400 (*société* of Charlieu, session of 3 Pluviôse).

y AN, AF II 114 (861), Javogues to Collot-d'Herbois, 16 Pluviôse: '. . . I have attached 800 infantry to the *armée révolutionnaire* and the numbers could be augmented. . .to over 12,000 if the interest of the Republic required it. . .'. Javogues was totally out of phase with political changes and was quickly made aware of the fact. On the 22nd he wrote in a bitter tone to his friend Collot: 'The fate of the patriots is sorrowful, everywhere they are harassed and persecuted, everywhere the people are dying of hunger and the rich fully supported in the Convention. . .'. See III. 1, sect. IV.

z Arch. Landes, L 783 (Dax *comité*, session of 30 Pluviôse). The *garde révolutionnaire* of Pau was still in existence 13 Ventôse. See J. Annat, *La période révolutionnaire dans les Basses-Pyrénées*.

aa RCC, *L'armée révolutionnaire à Lyon*, 110.

bb Arch. Allier, L 901 (Moulins *société*, session of 30 Ventôse).

21 Arch. Basses-Alpes, L 752 (Digne *comité*, sessions of 6, 9, 15, and 22 Nivôse).

22 See RCC, 'Les armées révolutionnaires du Midi', 71, and Arch. Hautes-Alpes, L 1506 (*comité* of Serres, session of 25 Frimaire).

23 The order to leave for Perpignan on 13 Nivôse was given by the commander of the Toulouse garrison. See RCC, 'Les armées révolutionnaires du Midi,' 82.

24 Aulard, IX. 527, Hentz and Guiot to the Committee, 29 Frimaire; AN, AF II 186 (1543), Boisset to the Committee, 9 Nivôse, also commenting that the Hérault *révolutionnaires* 'are individual despots', as another reason for their dissatisfaction with the decree.

25 Section III, article 20: 'No armed force, no tax, no loan, forced or voluntary, may be raised except by decree...unless in enemy or rebel territory'.

26 AN, AF II 186 (1541), Reynaud, from Le Puy, to the Committee, 22 Frimaire Year II; id. (1540), Boisset, from Montpellier, to the Committee, 22 Frimaire Year II.

27 Aulard, x. 345, Lacoste and Baudot to the Committee, beginning of Pluviôse. On Baudot, see E. Hamel, 'Euloge Schneider', 435. 'Gaubert' was the master tanner from Metz, Gobert, *commissaire civil* with the *armée révolutionnaire* of the East.

28 *Châles à la société révolutionnaire de Lille.*

29 AN, AF II 186 (1540) Gouly, from Bourg, to the Committee, 23 Frimaire.

30 See I. 4 for the division among the *représentants* between supporters and opponents of the *armées révolutionnaires*.

31 APP, A A/269, depositions of Jullien, 14 Frimaire Year III, and id. Le Batteux. For Mouquet, see II. 6.

32 AN, W 498 (535), trial of Dufresse.

33 *L'Anti-Terroriste*, no. 51, 18 Thermidor Year III.

34 See Aulard, x. 559: Albitte writing from Bourg, 11 Pluviôse, on his aides 'the patriots Dorfeuille, Millet, Vauquoy, Bonnerot, Dazolle and Soubireau, in whose zeal I take much pride...'.

35 See RCC, 'Quelques conséquences sociales de la Révolution dans un milieu urbain...', concerning the victims of this purge.

36 *Réflexions de Denis Bourdon, commissaire des guerres, à la société populaire* (25 Frimaire Year II).

37 Arch. Lille, 18′ 229 (*société révolutionnaire* of Lille, order of Hentz and Florent Guiot, 6 Nivôse Year II).

38 Arch. Lille, 18′ 222 (*société, représentants*) and AN, W 25 (1511) (Dufresse affair, depositions to the Lille *comité*).

39 Arch. Lille, 18′ 222 (order of Florent Guiot, 29 Thermidor Year II), and AN, F7 4566 d 8 (Committee of General Security, arrests) (Nord).

40 Arch. Lille, 18′ 229 (*société révolutionnaire*), deposition of Bernard against Fleur, municipal officer, 26 Frimaire Year II.

41 Arch. Gironde, II L 69 (Bordeaux *comité*, session of 30 Frimaire).

42 Arch. Gironde, II L 27 (national club, session of 1 Germinal).

43 AN, F 7★ 4. (Committee of General Security, reg. corres.), and F 7★ 3 (id.). Gohier sent a copy of Picot's order of release to the Committee, 3 Pluviôse. For his re-arrest. see AHG, B 4 41★ (*reg. d'ordre*, état major, Toulouse garrison, 3 Germinal).

44 See RCC, 'Les armées révolutionnaires du Midi', and AN, F 7★ 4, 3 Pluviôse, Viton demanding his release from La Force.

45 Arch. Châlons, 1★ 199 (Châlons *société*, corres.), Villers to the *société*, 5 Nivôse Year II. Massieu threw the order for his arrest into the fire.

46 AN, W 426 (tribunaux révolutionnaires, Rousselin affair).

47 Arch. Troyes, D 38 (6th Section, session of 2 Nivôse). Not all the Sections followed the example of the 6th. The 8th refused, with the comment 'that it did not regard this portion of the army as *révolutionnaire*, but as republicans and friends...'.

48 Arch. Troyes, D 4 (General Council, session of 7 Nivôse). On this occasion there was an extremely violent dispute between Fleury, the battalion commander, and the municipality, terminating with the General Council ordering 'that the non-dissolution of this force, under the terms of the law, be denounced to the public prosecutor...'.

49 See Arch. Aube, L4 35 and 36 (*comité* of Troyes, sessions of 10 and 21 Prairial) – witnesses stated that Rousselin was always surrounded by members of the former *comité révolutionnaire*, the mayor Gachet, and officers of the Bataillon de la Montagne 'which arrived in the town using the name *armée révolutionnaire*', claiming the town to be in a state of counter-revolution and threatening another Lyon.

50 Arch. Aube, Ld 5 4 (district of Ervy, session of 11 Ventôse Year II).

51 Arch. Aube, L4 50 (district of Troyes, session of 3 Messidor Year II). On 14 Floréal the *comité* of Troyes received a letter damning Gachet from the Clermont-sur-Oise *comité*: 'This man who has nothing, not even a sou...a member of the central committee which levied 1,700,000 livres in *taxes révolutionnaires*...and did everything to push our town into insurrection...was a clerk in the stamp office in Paris from which he was dismissed for

dishonesty...'. Gachet, then, possessing nothing, was suspect to the 'honnêtes gens' and he was never forgiven either his severity towards the rich or his sans-culotte origins.

52 Arch. Aube, Ld 5 4 (district of Ervy).

53 AN, Wla 193 (Lapalus and Duret affair). Duret was called this by the Seure (Loire) *comité de surveillance*, 25 Oct. In reality he was adjutant-general of the *armée* of the Alps.

54 Arch. Loire, L 400 (Charlieu *société*). On 6 and 22 Pluviôse the *société* had expressed its confidence in Lapalus, only changing its opinion on 7 Floréal. By the 20th the reaction was in full swing, and the victims of Lapalus released from prison. The *société* of La Clayette likewise hailed as *patriotes* those arrested by Lapalus (Arch. Saône-et-Loire, IV L 9, *société* of La Clayette).

55 AN, F 7 4775 26 d 2 (Tenaille) and Wla 163. One of the two, Diogène Tenaille, aged 29, was asked by the Halle-au-Bled *comité* if he was a relative of Fouché – his Clamecy accusers in effect trying to get at the proconsul through one of his most enthusiastic subordinates. In Pluviôse Year III Tenaille and Manlius Pilavoine were tried, and were still in prison in Thermidor Year III (Arch. Nièvre, L reg. delib. 13 of the district of Clamecy, sessions of 9 Pluviôse and 23 Prairial Year III). The principal dechristianiser of the Clamecy district was Bias Parent, national agent in the Year II.

56 Arch. Vaucluse, L VI 17 (*société* of Méthanis, session of 29 Ventôse) and L VI 18 (*société* of Puyméras, session of 26 Ventôse). The Avignon *société* sent an address to this effect to its affiliates, and many other *sociétés* followed its example in the last days of Ventôse and the first of Germinal (Arch. Vaucluse, L VI 16).

57 AN, Wla 170, *Barjavel, accusateur public près le tribunal criminel du Vaucluse, à la Convention national* (Avignon [?], 17 Germinal Year II).

58 Arch. Vaucluse, L VI, 1st ser., I (*comité* of Avignon, session of 22 Ventôse Year III).

59 The Piolenc *société* was still making efforts on behalf of Barjavel in Fructidor Year II (Arch. Vaucluse, L VI 16, session of 24 Fructidor Year II). For further information on this Avignon terrorist, see P. Vaillandet, 'Le Conventionnel Rovère et les Montagnards du Midi, 1793-1794', *Mémoires de l'Institut historique de Provence* (Marseille, 1931), 39–62. Barjavel was to be condemned and executed at Avignon on 8 Messidor Year III, victim above all of Rovère, and his past as an active terrorist.

60 AHG, B4 1 (Toulouse garrison, *ordres du jour*).

61 Arch. Haute-Garonne, L 4553 (*société* of Toulouse, sessions of 16, 22 and 24 Nivôse). On the 24th, Gélas 'emerged victoriously' from the experience. See also *Journal révolutionnaire de Toulouse*, no. xlvi (account of session of the *société*, 12 Ventôse). Gélas was still in Perpignan on this date. However, at the beginning of the Year III, he and all the other members of the old general staff were back in Toulouse working in the civil administration. The service of these former *chefs* in the real army seems to have lasted no more than two to three months at the most.

62 AN, F 7 4394 2 (papers found at Vincent's), letter from Calmet-Beauvoisins, 24 Pluviôse.

63 RCC, 'Les armées révolutionnaires du Midi', 42, 68–70.

64 Arch. Nièvre, 8 L 8 (district of Nevers, session of 17 Germinal). On this date de Goy was appointed a member of the judgement jury of the district tribunal. On the other hand, Thureau, lieutenant of the cannoneers of this battalion, and a career artillery officer, rejoined the Army of the Nord in Pluviôse (id., session of 11 Pluviôse).

65 Arch. Doubs, L 2354 (*société* of Besançon, list of exclusions, Frimaire Year III); L. Dubreuil, *Le district de Redon pendant la Révolution*.

66 AN, F 7 4648 d 4 (Civeton) – he retained his officer's rank in the Roanne National Guard, was arrested after Thermidor and only regained his liberty on 20 Vendémiaire Year IV (id., F 7 4709 d 3 [Fontenelle], and RCC, *L'armée révolutionnaire à Lyon*, App. C: 'Note sur l'armée révolutionnaire de la Loire', 110).

Chapter 2

1 AN, Wla 124 (situation of Paris, 28 Frimaire).

2 On the development of this campaign see Soboul, 332–59

3 See Soboul; Gén Herlaut, *Ronsin, le général rouge*, 180–201, and his *Le colonel Bouchotte. Ministre de la Guerre en l'an II* (1946); also D. Guérin, *La lutte des classes sous la Première République*.

4 Arch. Seine-et-Oise, IV Q 186 (Mazuel papers), Mazuel's report on the Opéra-Comique incident, 20 Frimaire Year II.

5 AN, Wla 124 (report of 27 Frimaire).
6 id., (report of 28 Frimaire).
7 id. (report of 2 Nivôse).
8 AN, Wla 170 (Fouquier-Tinville papers), the cavaliers at Versailles to Fouquier, 2 and 3 Nivôse.
9 AHG (reg. d'ordre), Grammont to Bourdon, 15 and 16 Nivôse.
10 Journal de la Montagne, no. 57 (session of the Jacobins, 18 Nivôse). It was at this session that Robespierre spoke in Boulanger's favour. See also RCC, 'Robespierre und Boulanger'.
11 AN, Wla 124 (report of 19 Nivôse).
12 Arch. Seine-et-Oise, IV Q 186. The same day, 28 Nivôse, the officers of the 4th squadron congratulated Mazuel on his release. During this period Ronsin was never free from criticism. See AN, Wla 124 (report of 17 Nivôse).
13 AN, Wla 191, reports of Bacon, Dugard (both 7 Pluviôse) and Monic (8 Pluviôse). See also RCC, 'La mission de Siblot au Havre-Marat'. The letter of 11 Pluviôse from Marque, commissaire of the Halle-au-Bled Section, sent to Rouen to arrest a merchant there, spoke of the extreme shortage of provisions, the contempt of the merchants for the Maximum, for the Revolution itself and the people, and the disappointment of the sans-culottes that the detachment bound for Le Havre had simply passed through their town (AN, F 7 4775 2 d 3 [Roussel]).
14 See RCC, 'La campagne pour l'envoi de l'armée révolutionnaire dans la Seine-Inférieure'.
15 AN, Wla 191, report from Bacon (10 Pluviôse). See II. 7. On 13 Pluviôse a movement to expel Halm as a foreigner developed in the Jacobins. But some spoke out so warmly in his favour that the session turned into a triumph for the drawing master (Journal de la Montagne, no. 82 [15 Pluviôse]).
16 AHG (reg. d'ordre), Grammont to Vézien, 14 Pluviôse.
17 AN, Wla 191, report from Monic (16 Pluviôse). On the aide-de-camp, Allais, see above, I.2.
18 AN, Wla 191, report from Letassey, 19 Pluviôse; see also Charmont's report, 11 Pluviôse.
19 id., report from Jarousseau, 20 Pluviôse. This statement is reminiscent of the proposals made by the Compiègne société.
20 See AN, Wla 191, report from Rollin (24 Pluviôse), and the reports from Bacon and Monic (20 Pluviôse), for the foregoing. On Carron, see also Soboul, 403 and n. 278.
21 See RCC, 'Note sur Guillaume Boulland, de la section du Finistère,' and Soboul, 689.
22 On the conflicts within the general staff, see RCC, L'armée révolutionnaire à Lyon, 89–92; Arch. Seine-et-Oise, IV Q 186–7 (Mazuel papers). Grammont criticised Payot for staying in Paris rather than rejoining his regiment in Coulommiers and claimed that he was the Committee of Public Safety's man within the general staff.
23 See RCC, 'Quelques aspects de la mentalité révolutionnaire'.
24 R. Fuoc, La réaction thermidorienne à Lyon, 1795 (Lyon, 1957), 132, and L. Trénard, Lyon, de l'Encyclopédie au Préromantisme (1938), I. 353.
25 On Achard see Dr J. Rousset, Les thèses medicales soutenues à Lyon aux 17e et 18e siècles et le Collège royal de chirurgie de 1774 à 1792 (Lyon, 1950). I should like to thank Dr Rousset for the wealth of information which he was kind enough to supply on the Lyon personnel of the Year II and indeed on the history of Lyon in general.
26 Castaing and Candi were part of a deputation sent from Lyon to Paris in Frimaire to plead the cause of the town and ask for an abatement of the repression (AN, F 7 4639 d 1 [Changeux] and F 7 4632 d 3 [Candi]). See also E. Herriot, Lyon n'est plus, vol. III: La répression, 242.
27 The name of Martinetcourt figures in the terrible Liste générale des dénonciateurs...de la Ville de Lyon, which was to be the manual for the assassins of Floréal Year III. See also R. Fuoc, La réaction thermidorienne à Lyon.
28 RCC, L'armée révolutionnaire à Lyon, 39–53, 118.
29 id., 72–8, 85–8, and Arch. Seine-et-Marne, IV Q 186 (Mazuel papers), Gignard to Mazuel, Pluviôse–Ventôse.
30 Père Duchesne, no. xxix (23 Ventôse): '...I was extremely amused yesterday', wrote Damame, 'to see soldiers, magistrates, officers, mingling pell-mell with the people at the fête de l'égalité...'.
31 An order of Reverchon, 14 Floréal, listed as members of the regenerated société and 'former friends of Chalier and Gaillard': Bertrand (braid-maker), Fillion (comb-maker), Thonion (stockinger), Ferenz (draughtsman), Revol (printer), Fillion (gold-drawer), Ragot (joiner),

Verrat (silk-worker), Revol (manufacturer), Mayousse, Philix, Rivière (silk-workers), Côte (gas-worker), Duplanud (manufacturer), Miraillier (merchant), Ruffard fils (vinegar-maker), Brouet (shoemaker), Siniard (hatmaker), Baud (shoemaker), Milet (teacher), Madinier (silk-worker), Ferrière (haberdasher), Laroche and Rivière (silk-workers), Laurent (gas-worker), Auzanne (carpet-maker), Dutelle, Poupée and Thévenet (silk-workers), Sinjean (belt-maker), Pilot (postal administrator), Assadat (gas-worker), Léon (silk-worker) (Arch. Rhône, 34 L 8, Société des Jacobins de Lyon). There was, in other words, no difference socially between the militant *sectionnaires* of Lyon and those of Paris; the conflict was an intra-sans-culotte one, local patriotism taking precedence over class solidarity.

32 RCC, *L'armée révolutionnaire à Lyon*, 83–4. See also the articles of my friend Gén. R. Willems, 'Nicolas Declaye, patriote liégeois, général français sous la Terreur', *Carnets de 'La Fourragère'* (Brussels), juin et sept. 1953.

33 AHG (*reg. d'ordre*), Parein to the Committee, 24 Ventôse. See also RCC, *L'armée révolutionnaire à Lyon*, 64–70.

34 id., 57–64.

35 AHG (*reg. d'ordre*), Ronsin to the Committee, 14 Ventôse Year II, requesting permission to bring several companies of the 5th battalion to Paris (a total of 229 men) prior to sending them to Lyon.

36 See RCC, *L'armée révolutionnaire à Lyon*, 89–92.

37 AHG, B 5 75, Committee to Ronsin, 10 Frimaire; see I.2, pp. 52–3.

38 AHG (*reg. d'ordre*), Grammont to Lefebvre, 21 Nivôse.

39 id., Maubant to the Chauny detachment commander, 28 Ventôse.

40 See the complaints of the municipality of Amiens against the Belgian corps garrisoned in the town (Arch. Amiens, 1 D 10 8, General Council, session of 9 Nivôse). Some Belgian patrols had arrested several inhabitants of Amiens.

41 AHG, Xk 10 (Corps particuliers, Légion de la Montagne), administrative council of the Legion to the Commission du Mouvement des Troupes, 8 Vendémiaire Year II.

42 AHG, B3★ 106 (Army of the Alps).

43 AHG, B5★ 91 (Army of the Côtes de Cherbourg). On Le Havre, see RCC, 'L'armée révolutionnaire au Havre-Marat'.

44 Arch. Honfleur, D 10★ (General Council).

45 AHG, B5★ 21 (Army of the Côtes de Cherbourg); Arch. Orne, L 4879 (*comité de surveillance* of Alençon). For Brest, see Arch. Finistère, B 1 62 (military affairs, département).

46 RCC, 'L'armée révolutionnaire dans l'Aisne'.

47 AHG (*reg. d'ordre*), Hanriot confirming arrests made by the Tuileries and Temple *comités*, 12 and 26 Nivôse.

48 On 29 Ventôse, 250 soldiers remained in Paris, 203 at Pontoise, 340 at Versailles, 42 at Brie-Comte-Robert, 60 at Meulan, 53 at Etampes, 25 at Viarmes (AHG [*reg. d'ordre*]). For a tally of other forces in the Paris region, see id., B5 75.

49 AHG (*reg. d'ordre*), Grammont to Jourdeuil, 3 Pluviôse. For Le Havre, see RCC, 'La mission de Siblot au Havre-Marat'.

50 See AHG (*reg. d'ordre*, Nivôse-Ventôse). On 6 and 14 Ventôse Ronsin requested the return of the detachments at Pont-de-l'Arche and Compiègne respectively.

51 AHG (*reg. d'ordre*), Chalier company, 11 Ventôse).

52 id., letters of Ronsin to the Committee, 26 and 29 Pluviôse, 14 Ventôse.

53 The full dossier on this important affair of Montcornet and Chaourse is in AN, D III 5 (298–355), Comité de législation, Aisne, Laon, under the title 'Procès contre Adrien Josse Chaumont et Nicolas Martin...'

54 Arch. Aisne, L 1645★ (district of Laon), and RCC, 'L'armée révolutionnaire dans le département de l'Aisne'.

55 The brothers Leclercq, one an artillery officer in the Army of the Nord, the other a hatter in Laon. Ronsin had wanted to appoint the first man adjutant-general to the *armée révolutionnaire* (see I.2, and Arch. Laon, reg. 7).

56 AN, D III 5 (298–355), P^{ce} 1.

57 The Committee, the Minister and the *armée* general headquarters were bombarded with complaints from municipalities and districts (Rozoy, Laon, Chantilly, Provins, Montereau, Franciade [Saint-Denis], Compiègne), 3 Nivôse – 21 Pluviôse, denouncing the soldiers and officers for indiscipline, insubordination, drunkenness, denuding the *pays* of supplies, etc. Then silence. Ronsin was free again. The complaints started up again on 12 Ventôse, with

the 1st Section of Pontoise denouncing the economic crimes which had been committed by the soldiers.

Chapter 3

1 Soboul, 721.
2 RCC, 'Problèmes de subsistances: la question des arrivages', and 'Le "complot militaire" de ventôse an II'.
3 On Fouquier and the Committees, see RCC, 'Le "complot militaire"...', and Arch. Seine-et-Oise, 2 Lm 92 (Sèvres *comité*, session of 21 Ventôse).
4 Even Damame saw crude ambition motivating Ronsin. See the *Père Duchesne de Commune-Affranchie*, no. xxxiii (2 Germinal).
5 Collot was content simply to defend the corps, particularly the cannoneers who had been in Lyon, condemning the 'ambitious', the 'traitors' who had taken over the command of this 'army of patriots' (*Journal de la Montagne*, no. 129 [2 Germinal], reporting the session of the Jacobins of 29 Ventôse). Collot defended the *armée* out of necessity and to defend himself. He had no need to defend Ronsin.
6 Gén. Herlaut, *Le colonel Bouchotte, Ministre de la Guerre en l'an II*.
7 Soboul, 757.
8 AN, W 345 (676), denunciations against Lambin to the *comité* of the Chalier Section, 28 Ventôse.
9 One report of 19 Ventôse even provided precise details of the Hébertists' so-called 'project' to take over government and govern the Republic the way they wanted; Hébert – who had long wanted rid of the Minister, Paré – taking over the Interior Ministry, Vincent, Marine, and Ronsin, War (AN, 112, report of Bérard). Witnesses at the trial spoke of a secret rendezvous between Vincent and Ronsin, in the hôtel de Rohan, cour du Commerce, on 17 Ventôse, in which they discussed their plans for the coup (AN, Wla 77).
10 RCC, 'Jaubert et le procès des hébertistes'. For a long time it was accepted opinion that Ronsin sought to follow the example of Cromwell and place France under military rule. See, e.g., a police report of 3 Nivôse Year III (Le Breton), AN, F 7 3688 3 (2).
11 RCC, 'Quelques aspects de la mentalité révolutionnaire'.
12 Soboul, 786.
13 AN, Wla 193, printed discourse of Ronsin to the Cordeliers.
14 Soboul, 738. On 16 Ventôse the Cordelier chiefs were abandoned by Collot. Ronsin's call of the 17th was an attempt to compensate for the wrong moves committed at the session of the 14th, and his effort might have been successful had he been master of his 'group'. But Vincent, much more hotheaded than the revolutionary general, compromised any chance of reconciliation between Cordeliers and Jacobins by his actions of 19 Ventôse. By that date, in any case, the government had decided to move against its political opponents in the War Ministry and the Cordeliers. The fate of the alliance was sealed more than anything else by the impossible character of the young Vincent.
15 Soboul, 505.
16 See RCC, 'Jaubert et le procès des hébertistes'.
17 AN, F 7 4438 d 1 (32), letter addressed to Pache, 6 Germinal, signed 'your *apôtre zélé* B.G.N'. The popular insistence on the municipalisation of institutions is also echoed in this letter. See also AN, Wla 175, Venès (delegate from the Tonneins *société* to Paris), to the two Committees, 1 Germinal Year II, offering information on 'the ramifications and appendages of the abominable conspiracy which you have so happily uncovered...'.
18 *Père Duchesne de Commune-Affranchie*, no. xxviii (18 Ventôse).
19 AHG, B5 75 (Armée révolutionnaire), situation report, 20 Ventôse.
20 *Procès instruit et jugé au Tribunal révolutionnaire contre J.-R. Hébert...*, & ca. (1794), 154. The deposition of Halm to the tribunal, 28 Ventôse (AN, Wla 77 [7] [379], seems to have been the origin of these accusations.
21 Perhaps Ronsin had written compromising letters to the cavalry commanders, for after the arrest of Mazuel at Versailles, Boulanger was to search through his belongings, seemingly wanting to carry off his papers. See the statement made by the *aubergiste*, Verdelet, before the *comité* of Versailles, 27 Ventôse, in RCC, 'Le "complot militaire"...'.
22 Arch. Seine-et-Oise, 2Lm 91 (district of Versailles, Bois d'Arcy *comité de surveillance*, session of 28 Germinal).

23 Arch. Vincennes, reg. 4 (General Council); AN, F 7 4746 d 1 (Huguenin).
24 RCC, *L'armée révolutionnaire à Lyon*, 97, and AAG, Cl. gén. 365 (Boissay). Boulanger's
    note to Le Bas was dated 13 Germinal, and led to a warrant for Boissay's arrest the
    following day. He was arrested in Lyon 21 Germinal, and remained in detention there
    until 22 Thermidor. In Nivôse Year III, he depicted himself as having been a victim of
    Robespierre, adding that he was 'on the way to the revolutionary tribunal when the Head
    of the Tyrant fell...' (AN, W 56 [3438]).
25 Fouquier sought information from Antony, Arcueil, Arpajon, Asnières, Belleville, Bercy,
    Bourg-la-Reine, Chanteloup, Chantilly, Charenton, Clichy, Colombes, *Creil, Dammartin,
    Ecouen, Etampes, Franciade,* Gennevilliers, *Gonesse,* Linas, *Marly,* Le Mesnil-Amelot,
    Montlhéry, Nanterre, *Nanteuil, Passy, Poissy, Pont-Saint-Maxence, Provins, Roissy,
    Saint-Germain, Senlis, Sèvres, Versailles, Villeneuve-sous-Dammartin* and *Vitry.* (Those
    places in italics had detachments of the Parisian *armée* stationed in them.)
26 The Grammonts were, however, under arrest after 5 Ventôse and can have had no part in
    the 'plot', which was not yet spoken of at that time (APP, A A/16 [301], arrest warrants).
27 Mazuel was not arrested until 26 Ventôse, at Versailles. See RCC, 'Le "complot
    militaire"...'.
28 AN, F 7 ★ 2471 (Tuileries Section, *comité révolutionnaire*).
29 On Bourgeois, see RCC, 'Le "complot militaire"...'. And see AN, F 7 4595 d 1 (Berger)
    and APP, A A/18 (arrests).
30 RCC, *L'armée révolutionnaire à Lyon,* 90
31 AN, F 7 4436 A, pl. 4, P^{ce} 254, Parein to Payan, 22 Germinal.
32 AHG (*reg. d'ordre*), Maubant to the Committee, 29 Ventôse. And see RCC, *L'armée
    révolutionnaire à Lyon,* 90.
33 *Journal de la Montagne,* no. 129 (session of the Jacobins, 29 Ventôse). After the
    révolutionnaires' demonstration of loyalty, Robespierre declared: 'No one should be
    surprised at the feelings expressed by the soldiers of the *armée révolutionnaire.* The
    defenders of the *patrie,* coming from the very heart of the people, will be the eternal
    models of patriotism...'.
34 AHG (*reg. d'ordre*), Maubant to the Committee, 29 Ventôse, and to the commanders of the
    detachments at Noyon, Provins, Vernon, Compiègne and Chauny, 29 and 30 Ventôse, 3,
    5, 6 and 7 Germinal.
35 RCC, *L'armée révolutionnaire à Lyon,* 98.
36 RCC, 'L'armée révolutionnaire dans l'Aisne'.
37 AN, Wla 27 (tribunaux révolutionnaires, Valframbert). An anonymous informant also
    denounced the general, Huché, as an accomplice of Ronsin, with whom he had served in
    the Vendée. 'What can one say', the person wrote to the Committee of Public Safety, 15
    Messidor,'...about this inconceivable appointment of the scoundrel Huché...who owes
    his political existence to the traitor Ronsin and is dripping still with the blood of patriots
    whom he had sacrificed before his very eyes...?' (AN, F 7 4634 d 2 [Carrier]).
38 AN, Wla 121 (tribunaux révolutionnaires, Colette).
39 AN, Wla 81 (tribunaux révolutionnaires, Loiseau to Fouquier, 1 Germinal).
40 See RCC, 'Le "complot militaire"...'.
41 AN, Wla 27 (Gentilly *comité de surveillance,* sessions of 5 and 7 Germinal). Ronsin went
    several times to the Bicêtre in Pluviôse. Vassard was released on 26 Germinal and restored
    to office on the order of the Committee of General Security (AN, F 7 4775 50, Wafflard –
    as he was sometimes referred to). For Eglator's release, see Arch. Gentilly, 1D 1/1
    (General Council, session of 12 Fructidor).
42 RCC, 'Robespierre und Boulanger', and AN, F 7 4775 49 (Volland), T 920 (Séquestres);
    Arch. Indre, L 1538 (*société* of Châteauroux, session of 24 Pluviôse Year II) and Arch.
    Seine-et-Oise, IV Q 186 (Mazuel papers). Volland may have carried out missions in Lyon
    on Ronsin's behalf, which would have made him even more suspect. In a note of 13
    Germinal Boulanger called the attention of Le Bas to Volland, and his associations with
    Ronsin.
43 On Musquinet Lapagne, mayor of Ingouville, see RCC, 'La campagne pour l'envoi de
    l'armée révolutionnaire dans la Seine-Inférieure', and 'La mission de Siblot au Havre-
    Marat'.
44 AN, F 7 4775 10 d 4 (Saint-Félix), F 7 4775 1 d 4 (Musquinet), and Wla 25 (1479) (*comité
    révolutionnaire,* Fontaine-de-Grenelle Section, to the Committee of General Security, 25
    Ventôse Year II). In Ventôse Saint-Félix issued a printed account of his life under the
    Revolution. He had been sent on mission in 1790 to Arpajon and into the district of

Gonesse to secure supplies for Paris, and was arrested with Momoro, Brune, and
Buirette-Verrières after the Champ de Mars affair. In 1793 he was sent on mission to the
Vendée, where he denounced the duc de Biron, and where he was accused of having
preached the *loi agraire*. Saint-Félix went with Ronsin to Ville-Affranchie and spent the 11
months up to 13 Pluviôse Year III under house arrest. For further details on him, see E.
Querneau-Lamérie, *La Commission Parein-Félix*.

45 AN, Wla (tribunaux révolutionnaires).
46 AN, F 7 4775 d 4 (Lachevardière), Lachevardière to the Committee of General Security,
Messidor Year II.
47 AN, F 7 4774 82 d 2 (Prangey). Prangey was charged and brought before the
revolutionary tribunal on 21 Germinal. He was acquitted.
48 AN, F 7 4754 d 2 (Lablée); also F 7 4774 37 d 3 (Mary). The latter, employed like Lablée in
military supply, was denounced as an associate of Ronsin by a *révolutionnaire*, Floquet,
husband of Mary's mistress; but he was released on 30 Frimaire Year III. Pierre Casimir
Bayard, another employee in the military administration, was denounced the next year as
a cousin of Ronsin and an extremist; he was arrested, 13 Thermidor Year III, but was
released provisionally, 12 Fructidor Year III, on the intercession of the police, for whom
he was working (AN, F 7 4589 d 8).
49 AN, Wla 147 (Lasalle to Fouquier, 22 Germinal).
50 Arch. Lille, 18′ 229 (*société* of Lille to the Jacobins, 23 Pluviôse): 'Long live the Mountain!
intrigue and calumny have been defeated! truth, liberty are triumphant! Ronsin and
Vincent have been restored to the Republic, whiter, purer, if that were possible, than
before their arrest.... The people of Lille are truly grateful. With Vincent and Ronsin they
were slandered, with them they have triumphed. [Signed] COMMITTEE OF
CORRESPONDENCE'.
51 See Arch. Nord, L 10224 (*société révolutionnaire*, session of 5 Germinal) for the accusation
against Butelle. And see AN, F 7 4566 d 8 (Nord, arrests). Butelle was still in prison in
Vendémiaire Year IV.
52 C. Pichois and J. Dautry, *Le conventionnel Chasles et ses idées démocratiques*. And see Arch.
Nord, L 10228 (*société* of Lille, session of 6 Germinal).
53 AHG, B 4 41* (*reg. d'ordre*, état-major, Toulouse garrison, 3 Germinal). The arrest of
Picot was ordered by the *représentant* Chaudron-Rousseau.
54 Arch. Gironde, 11 L 27 (Club national, session of 1 Germinal). See also III. 1.
55 'We have but one further desire', wrote Hanriot in his report of 5 Germinal; 'it is that
citizens...be on guard against intriguers coming from the departments to obtain top
positions, people like Mazuel, former shoemaker from Lyon and now, through intrigue,
dispenser of favours in the bureaus of the War Ministry...' (AN, Wla 174).
56 AN, Wla 174 (report of 3 Germinal).
57 AN, W 345 (676) (tribunaux révolutionnaires, Chéneaux affair).
58 BV-C, MSS 117 (47–52) (sessions of the Cordeliers). Sandoz presided over the club from
2 Germinal, after the arrest of Chéneaux, and throughout the entire *grande pénitence* of
Germinal.
59 AN, Wla 174 (report of 1 Germinal).
60 See also *Acte d'accusation contre Jean-Baptiste Boucher...*, 21, making the same accusation.
61 AN, BB 71.
62 AN, Wla 174 (Héron's report, 4 Germinal).
63 AN, Wla 140 (report made by a gendarme to the tribunals, 5 Germinal, on the behaviour
of the condemned the preceding day).
64 *Journal de la Montagne*, no. 129 (2 Germinal), account of the session of the Jacobins, 29
Ventôse.
65 AN, F 7 4774 42 d 2 (Menu, letter dated 22 Messidor Year II).
66 AN, Wla 136 (Sergeant Guillaume, prisoner, to Fouquier, 29 Floréal Year II).
67 AN, D III 216 (Comité de législation, Rhône, Lyon), petition of Sergeant Rabot, called
'Bamboche', to the president of the Convention, 17 Floréal Year II. The prisoners were
always eager to make 'discoveries', hoping to attract favourable attention from the
authorities, and perhaps get a chance to plead their own case.
68 BN, MSS Nouv. acq. fr. 2690 (130) (General assembly of the Temple Section, undated,
Germinal). Masson, lieutenant of the Finistère company of fusiliers, was accused of having
said 'that Ronsin was cleared...' (AN, F 7 2517*, *comité* of the Finistère Section, session of
4 Floréal).
69 AN, F 7 * 2496 (reg. *comité* of the l'Homme-Armé Section).

70 AN, W 345 (676) (Mengaud to Fouquier, 8 Germinal).
71 AN, Wla 149 (report by Lafosse, 29 Ventôse). Rumours were already circulating on 15 Ventôse, when the police administration felt it necessary to warn the Sections 'of treacherous manoeuvres by the enemies of the public good to make the people believe that they are about to be disarmed...' (APP, A A/266 [209], Pont-Neuf Section). On the existence within the police administration itself of a certain exaggerated Hébertism, see BN, MSS Nouv. acq. fr. 2720 (209), *Renseignements sur des administrateurs de police de Paris, donnés le dix germinal* (Year II, by Baude), note on Menessier and Fiquet.
72 AN, Wla 149.
73 Soboul, 820. And see RCC, 'L'armée révolutionnaire au Havre-Marat'.
74 AN, F 7 4607 d 3 (Bonin) and W 351 (719) (tribunaux révolutionnaires, Bonin).
75 AN, F 7 4668 d 2 (Delmotte), report from the *comité*, Invalides Section, 28 Ventôse. On this 'fear' see also RCC, 'Le "complot militaire"...'.
76 AN, F 7 4667 d 1, F 7 4774 23 d 2 and 95 d 1, F 7 4775 11 d 2 and 25 d 2, also the account of this affair in A.-M. Soboul and W. Markov, *Die Sansculotten von Paris* (Berlin-Est, 1957).
77 Bellechasse wrote to Carnot, 18 Messidor: '...I have no hesitation in stating...that if these dangerous *armées* had been established throughout the Republic...before long they would have been dictating the laws through force...'.
78 See RCC, 'L'armée révolutionnaire dans l'Aisne'.
79 Arch. Versailles, D 1178 (General Council, session of 26 Ventôse). The commune was seized by a kind of panic and the municipality felt obliged to intervene to put an end to it (AN, F 7 3689 7). Other towns in the district of Versailles were also affected (Arch. Seine-et-Oise, 2Lm 91, district of Versailles, *comité* of Rocquencourt).
80 AN, F 7★ 4 (Crassous to the Committee of General Security, 28 Ventôse).
81 AN, C 299 (1347) (petitions and addresses).
82 Arch. Vincennes, reg. 4 (General Council, sessions of 23, 26, 27, 28 and 29 Ventôse and 9 Nivôse).
83 Arch. Montreuil, reg. 2 (session of the municipality, 28 Ventôse).
84 Arch. Eure, 99 L II (directory of the district of Evreux, meeting in Vernon, session of 27 Ventôse).
85 See AHG, B5 75, and RCC, 'Les disettes...dans le district de Mantes'.
86 Arch. Vernon, D 1/7 (session of the Council, 29 Ventôse).
87 Arch. Vernon, D 1/14 bis (reg. *société populaire*, session of 1 Germinal).
88 Arch. Eure, 99 L 11 (directory of the district of Evreux, session of 3 Germinal). Gisors too took precautions on news of the 'plot', ordering domiciliary visits, and guards to be placed on suspects' houses, though little came of these measures (Arch. Eure, 235 L 47, reg. *comité de surveillance* of Gisors, session of 27 Ventôse). It was otherwise in Ecouis, where there was a particularly active group of sans-culottes in the *société*; on news of Ronsin's execution they actually requested the return of the revolutionary detachment (Arch. Eure, 236 L 10, *société populaire* of Ecouis, session of 5 Germinal).
89 RCC, 'L'armée révolutionnaire dans l'Aisne'.
90 Arch. Oise, L IV (Noyon *comité*).
91 Arch. Oise, L IV (Beauvais *comité*), Girard to the *comité*, 7 Germinal; L 109 (Chantilly *comité*).
92 Arch. Oise (reg. *comité* of Compiègne, session of 4 Germinal).
93 AN, F 7 4594 d 7 (Ballardelle), deposition of Soyer, 1 Germinal. Ballardelle had already spoken of an imminent 'coup' on 20 Ventôse.
94 Arch. Provins, reg. D (General Council).
95 Arch. Brie-Comte-Robert (reg. 2, *société*, session of 28 Ventôse).
96 AN, Wla 354 (734) (tribunaux révolutionnaires).
97 AN, Wla 26 (Coulommiers *comité* to Fouquier, 3 Germinal).
98 Arch. Seine-et-Marne, L 588 (district of Nemours, session of 1 Germinal): 'One member said that the new conspiracy which had just been discovered required the most active vigilance on the part of the authorities, the Convention having announced that it had extensive ramifications, it was essential to watch all those who, like the conspirators, hid behind the mask of patriotism...'. This was a thinly disguised invitation to denounce the *exagérés*, who would have been numerous in this department.
99 Arch. Montereau, P2 (reg. *société*, session of 2 Germinal), and D1 5 (General Council, session of 2 Germinal).
100 Arch. Seine-et-Marne, L 821 (*comité* of Meaux, session of 2 Germinal), '...to discover if

there are any citizens in this commune who may have been implicated in this conspiracy...'. On the journey of Vincent, see AN, F 7 4645 (Chéneaux), his passport, and RCC, 'L'armée révolutionnaire dans le district de Pontoise'.

101 See RCC, 'Le "complot militaire"...', and Arch. Seine-et-Marne, L 794 (Fontainebleau *comité*, sessions of 21 Pluviôse Year III [the claim about 'Hébert's system'] and 26 Ventôse Year II).

102 For the arrest of the mayor, see Arch. Etampes, D1 (General Council, session of 30 Ventôse). The two soldiers, Dumas and Barbe, were arrested by the Etampes *comité*, 29 Ventôse, which wrote to Fouquier the same day accusing them, (1) of seeking to rouse the people of the commune, (2) of trying to discourage the farmers by saying that all their horses were to be taken, (3) of being accomplices in the conspiracy, by saying, around 20 Ventôse, 'that in 10 days' time there would be a new system' (AN, W 345 [676]). (Ballardelle was himself accused of having announced the coup for 10 Germinal.) Dumas, in a letter to his wife, 17 Germinal, described how he was brought before the Committee of General Security, denied knowing Ronsin, and claimed that his comment about a new system in 10 days had in mind the new Maximum, which was to come into force around 10 Germinal (AN, Wla 146).

103 AN, Wla 442(62) (Billoré affair), deposition of the girl, Merlin, 16 Germinal. The soldier in question was acquitted, 12 Fructidor Year II.

104 Arch. Seine-et-Oise, 2Lm 30 and 133 (district of Pontoise). See also, on the subject of shortages, RCC, 'L'armée révolutionnaire dans le district de Pontoise'.

105 AN, D III 232–3 d 8 (13) (Comité de législation, Bercy).

106 RCC, 'Le "complot militaire"...'; see also AN, Wla 116 (Degesne, lieutenant at Passy, to Fouquier, 24 Ventôse Year II).

107 AN, W 385 (895) (Sibillot affair).

108 AN, F 7 4775 2 d 5 (Rousseville).

109 Arch. Vaucluse, L VI 18 (*société* of Puyméras, session of 5 Germinal).

110 AN, Wla 133, the gendarme Mouthon to Fouquier, 21 Germinal. For Marino, see RCC, 'La Commission Temporaire de Commune-Affranchie'.

111 AN, W 421 (956) (Jüng affair).

112 AN, W 356 (744) (Bazin affair). The charge drawn up against him on 9 Floréal declared '...that like Hébert, Ronsin and the others, he said that the Convention was old and worn-out, that power was abused and kept in the same hands, that the *représentants* had become despots, their immense power was a crime against the people...'. '40 sols': a reference to the poor sans-culottes subsidised to attend sectional assemblies.

113 Arch. Hautes-Pyrénées, L 1186 bis (*société* of Tarbes).

114 AN, F 7 4774 75 d 5 (Pinet).

115 On the arrests see RCC, 'Les armées révolutionnaires du Midi', 83–4.

116 *Ventôse–Germinal:* some 35 revolutionary officers and soldiers were arrested (11 in Paris, 7 at Laon, 4 at Honfleur, 2 each in the communes of Etampes, Versailles, Lyon, Sèvres, Pontoise, and 1 each in those of Montargis, Alençon and Rozoy-en-Brie). *Floréal–Messidor:* 8 former *révolutionnaires* were arrested, 7 for criminal offences, 1 for taking part in a combination of tobacco-grinders.

117 See, in AN: F 7 4774 54 d 2 (Mouret); Wla 136, for Guillaume; and e.g., F 7 4774 75 d 3 (Pilleul). Pilleul was arrested 4 Germinal by the *comité révolutionnaire* of the Réunion Section for having caused a riot by insulting an agent of the Committee of Public Safety. There were several cases of this nature, products above all of the extreme nervousness of the Parisian soldiers in the days of Ventôse–Germinal, when they were constantly exposed to the hostility and suspicion of the local authorities, the country populace and the Parisian *comités révolutionnaires*.

118 AHG, B 12 20 (orders of the Minister).

119 AHG, B 5 75 (Armée révolutionnaire), and (*reg. d'ordre*): Maubant wrote to Halm, 29 Ventôse (the troops were to assemble on the Champ de Mars), 'You should recommend...to this detachment the greatest exactitude in service, decency in their behaviour towards the citizens with whom they are lodged and in the towns through which they pass...tell them...that it is time the *armée révolutionnaire* set an example of civic and social virtues. If you encounter resistance, punish'.

120 AHG (*reg. d'ordre*), Maubant to Sijas, 1 Germinal. Halm was allowed to remain in Paris. His deposition against Ronsin figured in the case for the prosecution before the revolutionary tribunal.

121 RCC, 'L'armée révolutionnaire dans le district de Pontoise'.
122 AHG, B 12 20 (orders of the Minister) and B 5 75 (Armée révolutionnaire); and see Arch.
    Seine-et-Oise, 2Lm5, letter from the district of Mantes to Jourdeuil, 4 Germinal Year II,
    demanding the removal of the detachment, which it clearly feared.
123 AHG, B 5 75 (Armée révolutionnaire).
124 See RCC, 'L'armée révolutionnaire dans le district de Pontoise'. On 25 Germinal, Barbier,
    commissaire des guerres at Versailles, wrote to Jourdeuil: 'The great desire of this troop is to
    be able to return their arms to their Sections, and some have already manifested this desire,
    thinking they have the same right as the 3rd company, 5th battalion, under Captain
    Loude, which was allowed to leave without condition...' (AHG, B5 75).
125 AN, F 7★ 2473 (*comité* of the Champs-Elysées Section, session of 27 Ventôse); also AHG,
    B5 75.
126 Arch. Coulommiers, reg. 2 (General Council, 16 Germinal); Arch. Brie-Comte-Robert,
    D1 (General Council); for the Gonesse companies, see RCC, 'La mission de Siblot au
    Havre-Marat'.
127 Arch. Oise (regs. *comités* of Noyon, Compiègne and Chantilly); Arch. Etampes, D 1
    (General Council); AN, F 7 4781 (*comité de surveillance* of Auteuil to the Committee of
    General Security, 4 Germinal).
128 Arch. Honfleur, D 10 (General Council) and AHG, B5 21 (Army of the Ouest, temporary
    commander of the Alençon garrison to the head of the general staff, 23 Germinal); and see
    AN, F 7★ 2517 (reg. *comité* of the Finistère Section, session of 4 Floréal).
129 On the cavalry squadrons, see Arch. Loire-Inférieure, L 550 d 5 (military affairs); AHG,
    B5 75; and RCC, *L'armée révolutionnaire à Lyon*, 26.
130 AHG, B5 75 (Armée révolutionnaire), decree and order, the latter signed in the register:
    Carnot, C.A. Prieur, Billaud-Varenne, Collot-d'Herbois, B. Barère, Saint-Just, Couthon,
    R. Lindet. By this date, 7 Germinal, the Parisian *armée* was the only revolutionary force
    still under arms. The Loire, Nièvre and Allier companies, attached to the Parisian
    detachment in Lyon after the law of 14 Frimaire, were already disbanded at the beginning
    of Germinal; that of the Loire around 6 Ventôse (AN, F 7 4648 d 4 [Civeton], Arch. Loire,
    L 432, *comité* of Montbrison, session of 19 Ventôse); that of the Allier, before 5 Germinal
    (Arch. Allier, L 850, *comité* of Moulins, session of 5 Germinal, and L 901, *société* of
    Moulins, session of 30 Ventôse).
131 AHG, B5 75.
132 Id.
133 AN, AF II 6 (36) (Committee of Public Safety, military affairs). The Committee asked the
    Council on 23 Germinal where the decree had been implemented. The Council submitted
    its final report, 28 Germinal, when the operation had been completed everywhere.
134 AN, C 303 (1105) (Petitions). This petition was presented at the 6 Floréal session.
135 BN, MSS Nouv. acq. fr. 2690 (130) (Temple Section).
136 AN, F 7 4620 d 3 (Buard).
137 AHG, B5 21 (Army of the Côtes de Cherbourg); Arch. Seine, D4 AZ 698 (Sans-Culottes
    Section).
138 The attestation, dated 20 Germinal, stated that 'The members of the said *armée*, while on
    garrison at Commune-Affranchie, have behaved as good republicans, maintained good
    military discipline and at all times have been subject to the laws...'. For this and the other
    good-conduct notes, see AN, C 303 (1105).
139 AN, Wla 174 (report of 9 Germinal).
140 For all the foregoing see the various reports, 7–10 Germinal, in AN, Wla 174.
141 RCC, 'La Commission Temporaire de Commune-Affranchie'. Grimaud was excluded
    from the Moulins *société* on 16 Floréal.
142 RCC, 'L'armée révolutionnaire dans l'Aisne'.
143 AHG (*reg. d'ordre*), Maubant to the Committee, 13 Germinal, and Arch. Oise (district of
    Noyon, liasse 1, *Subsistances*), Commission to the district, 10 Floréal, complaining that
    because several detachments had been disbanded before formal instructions had reached
    the agents, some men in the age group of the first requisition had been sent home rather
    than incorporated into the nearest army.
144 Arch. Oise (reg. *société* of Compiègne), session of 9 Germinal, and id. (reg. *comité* of
    Compiègne), sessions of 9 and 11 Germinal.
145 Arch. Seine-et-Marne (Coulommiers, Supplément), municipality of Boissy to the
    Coulommiers *comité*, 12 Germinal.

146 AHG, B5 75, Hanriot to Bouchotte, 15 Germinal.
147 Arch. Coulommiers, reg. 2 (General Council, session of 16 Germinal); Arch. Seine-et-Marne, L 554 (district of Melun, session of 16 Germinal).
148 AHG, B5 75 (Armée révolutionnaire) and AN, F 7 4610 d 4 (certificate of disbandment, Mont-l'Egalité [Faremoutiers]).
149 RCC, *L'armée révolutionnaire à Lyon.*
150 AHG, B5 75.
151 RCC, 'L'armée révolutionnaire au Havre-Marat...', 315; AHG, B5 75 and 21; Arch. Oise (reg. *comité* of Chantilly).
152 AHG, B5 75.
153 AN, AF II 26.
154 Arch. Loire-Inférieure, L 550 d 5 (military affairs), Guillot, *commissaire des guerres* at Nantes, to the president of the department, 20 Floréal Year II. See also AAG, Cl. gén. 384 (Blanquet).
155 See RCC, *L'armée révolutionnaire à Lyon*, 92, and articles cited above on the *armée* in Havre-Marat and the Aisne.
156 AN, H 2121 (Bureau de Ville, Lavergne).
157 Arch. Oise (district of Noyon, corres.).
158 Arch. Seine-et-Marne, L 513 (district of Meaux, session of 26 Floréal).
159 Arch. Oise (district of Noyon, corres.), *comité* to the Commission, 6 Floréal; AN, F 7★ 2485 (reg. Lombards Section *comité*, session of 13 Floréal).
160 Arch. Seine-et-Marne, L 513 (district of Meaux, session of 26 Floréal).
161 Arch. Oise (*comité* of Chaumont, liasse 4), national agent of the commune of Fosseuse to the *comité*, 6 Pluviôse Year III.
162 Arch. Oise (reg. *comité* of Compiègne), 27 Germinal, visa on the certificate of Ferrant, fusilier.
163 AN, F 7★ 2511 (Chalier Section *comité*, sessions of 26 and 27 Germinal).
164 Arch. Oise, L 109 (Chantilly *comité*, session of 24 Germinal).
165 AHG, B5 75; Arch. Allier, L 901★ (*société* of Moulins, session of 30 Germinal).
166 AN, F 7★ 2472 (reg. Tuileries Section *comité*, session of 13 Floréal).
167 Arch. Versailles, I² 1237 (reg. security, police bureau of the municipality, session of 19 Floréal).
168 Seven former members of the Parisian *armée* returned to their positions on the *comités révolutionnaires* in the Sections at this period. See RCC, 'L'armée révolutionnaire parisienne: composition sociale et politique'.
169 Dumany was employed at the Invalides, Carteron at the Ecole Militaire, Grossin and Lemaire at the Ecole de Mars and Camp des Sablons, Maubant, Boulanger and several adjoints in the general command, Boissay and Rayot in military supply. See I.2 and 3.
170 AN, F 4774 37 d 2 (Martin).
171 See the Epilogue below, on the officers or fusiliers Vafflard, Langlois, Keller, Pudepièce, Mirau, Bourdin, Placet, Petit, Fouques, Corchand, Berger etc.
172 AN, AF II 23 (comité militaire, session of 17 Prairial), which permitted the cavalry officers 'to return to the positions they had left for the *armée révolutionnaire*...provided they could produce certificates of good conduct'.
173 Menu was one of the few cavalry officers to be denounced as a terrorist in the Year III; see I.3, n. 71. As for Delgas, he was viewed so favourably by the Thermidorean authorities that they recommended him in Brumaire Year III as a member of one of the new arrondissement *comités de surveillance*; see I.3, n.79.
174 Boulanger was a notable personality of the Halle-au-Bled Section, and on 29 Floréal he appeared before the Jacobins to announce that the *société* of that Section had dissolved itself, asserting that it had always acted on the best principles and denounced conspirators and traitors (*Journal de la Montagne*, no. 22 [29 Floréal]). He was thus assisting the government offensive against the Sectionary *sociétés*. In Prairial he denounced the famous Teresa Cabarrus (Aulard, VI. 414), also the young Edouard Dobigny, if the latter is to be believed (AN, Wla 186). He also acted as a spy for Fouquier-Tinville, with whom he had very close relations (see, e.g., AN, Wla 111, Boulanger to Fouquier, 20 Messidor Year II). For his execution see AN, W 434 (976).
175 AN, F 7 4594 d 4 (Benoît).
176 AN, F 7 4774 39 d 1 (Maubant) and F 7 4637 d 3 (Chaguignée), bulletin of the Faubourg-du-Nord Section *comité* for the first *décade* of Thermidor. Maubant had been

recommended to Hanriot by Boulanger, on 26 Floréal, and the former secured his attachment to the 17th military division. For his request of the Year VI, see AAG, Cl. gén. 2594 (Maubant).

177 On the number and identity of the cannoneer companies attached to the *armée révolutionnaire*, see I.2, n.12.

178 RCC, *L'armée révolutionnaire à Lyon*, App. B, 108–9.

179 Arch. Finistère, 8 L 63 (military affairs).

180 AHG, B5 21 and 91 (Army of the Côtes de Cherbourg).

181 RCC, 'L'armée révolutionnaire dans l'Aisne'.

182 Gén. Herlaut, 'Carnot et les compagnies de canonniers des sections de Paris au 9 Thermidor', *A.h.R.f.*, no. 123 (1951).

183 M. Reinhard, 'Note sur Carnot et l'armée révolutionnaire'; these calculations are based on AHG, B5 75, BX 13 203, 204; AN, C 298, 299, 308 (addresses and petitions from the companies to the Convention).

184 *Journal de la Montagne*, no. 144 (session of the Jacobins, 3rd sans-culottide, Year II), and AN, F 7 4741 12 d 5 (Lefranc).

185 AHG, Xv 43 (national volunteers, cannoneers). On 16 Messidor the 13 cannoneer companies donated a day's pay (amounting to 1759 1. 3s. in *assignats*) to the war effort (extract from the *Bulletin de la Convention* in AN, F 7 4741 12 d 5).

186 Arch. Finistère, 8 L 63 (military affairs). The three cannoneer companies had been on service in Brest for eight months.

187 RCC, 'L'armée révolutionnaire dans l'Aisne'.

188 AN, F 7 4663 d 5 (Dauphinot), and BN, MSS Nouv. acq. fr. 2705 (383) (Luxembourg Section *société*).

189 AN, F 7 4774 89 d 1 (Resnier).

190 AN, C 305 (1148) (Addresses and petitions), 8 Prairial, petition from elements of the two companies at Le Havre to the Convention. For those left at Chartres, see AHG, B5 75.

191 Soboul, 1003–5. See also AN, F 7 4775 18 d 2 (Servais).

192 P. Sainte-Claire Deville, *La Commune de l'an II* (1946), 365–6.

193 K. Tønnesson, *La defaite des sans-culottes. Mouvement populaire et réaction bourgeoise en l'an III* (Oslo, 1959), 353–4

194 BN, MSS Nouv. acq. fr. 8607 (72) (l'Homme-Armé Section), l'Homme-Armé cannoneers at Alençon to the Convention, 13 Thermidor Year II, congratulating the Convention on its action. For the Champs-Elysées company see AHG, Xv 45 (national volunteers, cannonneers).

195 *Journal de la Montagne*, no. 144 (2nd ser.). See Lefranc's description of the hopes inspired in him by Robespierre's downfall, in his 1816 publication prepared in collaboration with Sormois, the only other survivor of the 71 deported to the Seychelles in the Year IX, *Les infortunes de plusieurs victimes de Napoléon Bonaparte ou Tableau des malheurs des 71 Français déportés sans jugement aux îles Séchelles, à l'occasion de la machine infernale du 3 nivôse an IX, Par l'un des deux seules victimes qui aient survéçu à la déportation*, 11: '...The calm which followed so many storms after the death of Robespierre, seemed to reanimate all kinds of hopes. ...I admit that I saw in this republic which succeeded the monarchy the happiness of France...I thought that liberty could be nurtured by a people enlightened by the experience of the past...'. For the Tuileries company in the Year III, see AN, F 7 4741 12 d 5 (Lefranc).

196 AN, F 7 4702 d 3 (Faroux). See also RCC and G. Rudé, 'Le dernier mouvement populaire de la Révolution a Paris'.

197 K. Tønnesson, *La défaite des sans-culottes*, 189.

198 RCC and G. Rudé, 'Le dernier mouvement populaire de la Révolution à Paris', and AN, F 7 4593 d 8 (Benezy) on the Faubourg-du-Nord cannoneers. See also AN, F 7 4686 d 4 (Dulac), denunciation of 17 Germinal against Paris, former *commissaire des guerres*, who, along with Keller and Langlois, former fusilier officers, was accused of having tried to bring their Sections on to the side of the rioters; and F 7 4774 16 d 3 (Lenoir, list of terrorists of the Marchés Section). The name of Paris appears again, with Dumoustier, both from the Observatoire Section, among those accused of having shown their joy, in prison, at news of the *journées* of 12–13 Germinal (AN, Wla 172).

199 K. Tønnesson, *La défaite des sans-culottes*, 266, 269, 271-2. For Potement and Vafflard see RCC, *L'armée révolutionnaire à Lyon*, 102.

200 RCC and G. Rude, 'Le dernier mouvement populaire de la Révolution à Paris'; K.

Tønnesson, *La défaite des sans-culottes*, 302; RCC, 'Robespierre und Boulanger' and Bib. hist. de la Ville de Paris (reg. *comité civil*, Halle-au-Bled Section, session of 12 Prairial Year III); it was also the Section of Boulanger and Dufresse (AN, W 498 [535]).

201 RCC and G. Rudé, 'Le dernier mouvement populaire de la Révolution à Paris', and AN, F 7 4747 d 1 (Isambert); see also K. Tønnesson, *La défaite des sans-culottes, 302.*

202 RCC and G. Rudé, 'Le dernier mouvement populaire de la Révolution à Paris'; also AN, F 7 4646 d 1 (Chefson) and F 7 4662 d 5 (Dauphinot).

203 RCC, 'Note sur la répression contre le personnel sans-culotte...'; RCC and G. Rudé, 'Le dernier mouvement populaire de la Révolution à Paris'; K. Tønnesson, *Le défaite des sans-culottes*, 338. See also AN, F 7 4703 d 3 (Fauveau), on the arrest of Pierre Fauveau 'former captain in the *armée révolutionnaire*', 6 Prairial Year III, accused of being one of the terrorist ringleaders of the Invalides Section. In the Luxembourg Section, as in the Arsenal and Halle-au-Bled Sections, the former members of the *armée révolutionnaire* suffered collective discrimination; see BN, MSS Nouv. acq. fr. 2704 (168) (Luxembourg Section), Le Boeuf to the *comité* of 12 of the Section, 22 Prairial.

204 RCC and G. Rudé, 'Le dernier mouvement populaire de la Révolution à Paris'. Potemont was a cannoneer, Foucault and Placet were former fusilier officers. On Placet, see RCC, *L'armée révolutionnaire à Lyon*, 93; and for Jean Laurent, a marble-cutter, member of the Quinze-Vingts company, and *commissaire* of the *comité révolutionnaire* of this Section, see AN, F 7 4768 d 4 (Laurent).

205 In the departments also the members of the former revolutionary forces were the object of automatic discriminatory measures; see II. 5 and AN, F 7 4411 b (Besançon, terrorists). At the same time, after Prairial, and sometimes after Frimaire Year III, local authorities had terrorists in their own communes, those responsible for having called in the revolutionary detachments, Parisian or other, disarmed and even arrested. See RCC, 'Politique et subsistances en l'an III: l'exemple du Havre', and 'L'armée révolutionnaire au Havre-Marat'. That someone had 'called upon the *armée révolutionnaire*' or threatened his fellow citizens with it, was one of the most common justifications for having that person disarmed or arrested, and the grudge against such people was very often greater than that against the revolutionary officers and soldiers, who were considered simply the instruments of notorious terrorists.

206 G. Lefebvre, 'Foules révolutionnaires', reprinted in *Etudes* (ré-éd. 1954).

Epilogue

1 AN, F 7 4771 d 1 (Lebois) and F 7 4278 (Babeuf affair, subscribers to the *Tribun du Peuple*). On Halm see also P. Dally,' 'Suzanne Lepeletier'. Boissay was employed at the Commission des Subsistances of Paris during the Thermidorean period; see RCC, *L'armée révolutionnaire à Lyon, 97.*

2 Babeuf's list of 'patriots and men capable of commanding' (see AN, F 7 4277 [Babeuf affair]), includes the following former *révolutionnaires* from the Paris Sections:

   (1) *Tuileries:* Lefranc (destined to play an important role militarily, and to have had a political post on the General Council of a new Commune).[a]
   (4) *Butte-des-Moulins:* Corchand (former aide-de-camp to Parein).
   (9) *Gardes-Françaises:* Colin (fusilier officer, having been on detachment to Lyon); Keller (id. to Laon)[b]
   (10) *Halle-au-Bled:* Ladreux (cannoneer).
   (13) *Brutus:* Mirau (former fusilier officer).
   (17) *Marchés*: Langlois (fusilier officer, on detachment to Laon);[c] Crosnier (cannoneer).
   (19) *Arcis:* Fontaine (cannoneer; he was to have been a recruiting agent); Henry (fusilier, to have been part of the General Council).
   (20) *Faubourg-Montmartre:* Berger (former aide-de-camp to Ronsin).

(a) Lefranc was recommended to Babeuf, 13 Germinal Year IV. A note of 20 Floréal described him as '...in charge of the upkeep of the Feuillans building which contains a sizeable deposit of guns; ...he will facilitate its capture by the People...'.

(b) Keller was accused of having taken part in the movements of 12 Germinal Year III (AN, F 7 4774 16 d 3 [Lenoir]).

(c) A member of the *comité révolutionnaire* of the Marchés Section on leaving the *armée révolutionnaire*, Langlois was doubly suspect in the eyes of the Thermidorean authorities, who accused him of taking part in the *journée* of 12 Germinal. See also AN, F 7 4774 16 d 3 (Lenoir).

(23) *Temple*: Fiquet (from Valence).

(25) *Montreuil*: Potemont (cannoneer officer – the note on him states: 'speaks for the entire company').

(26) *Quinze-Vingts*: Placet (former fusilier officer, having been to Lyon – the note on him states: 'captain for all the faubourg Saint-Antoine').[d]

(27) *Gravilliers*: Petit (former fusilier officer)[e].

(31) *Droits-de-l'Homme*: Brabant (cannoneer, intended for the General Council); Fouques (fusilier officer).

(34) *Arsenal*: Petit (cannoneer).[f]

(40) *Unité*: Sandoz (cannoneer officer, former member of the Administrative Council of the *armée révolutionnaire*).

(42) *Bonnet-Rouge*: Lecerf (cannoneer).

(43) *Luxembourg*: The brothers Monvoisin (captain and second lieutenant in the cannoneers); Sormois (a cannoneer sergeant).

(46) *Observatoire*: Dumoutier (member of the *comité révolutionnaire; commissaire* who took the detachment to Livry).

(48) *Finistère*: Bourdin (former fusilier, chosen because he knew many workers in the ateliers); [g] Moroy, Rognon (former members of the *comité révolutionnaire, commissaires* who took the detachment to Villeblevin; Moroy in particular held an extremely important place in the plans of the conspirators).

(d) On Placet, see also Arch. Seine, D 4 AZ 124. On 19 Floréal Year IV he was designated commander of the faubourg.

(e) Petit figures on a list of 'patriots eligible for employment'; Babeuf singled him out to represent his Section at the General Council of the Commune.

(f) This Petit had commanded the company of cannoneers of the Bon-Conseil Section. The Section had him arrested as a former terrorist, 6 Prairial Year III. He then resettled in the Arsenal Section.

(g) The name of Bourdin appears in a note of Moroy, 1 Floréal Year IV, finding this gas-fitter of the rue Mouffetard, having been 'in the *armée révolutionnaire*, capable of acting as a soldier and sitting on the civil committee...' – the fact that these *patriotes* had been 'in the *armée révolutionnaire*' or even more importantly, had been members of the Sectionary committees, was considered as significant by Babeuf's agents as by the police.

3 The office of *commissaire* to the National Treasury in the Revolutionary Government which the Equals intended forming was likewise reserved for Paris. Imprisoned in the Orties after the *journée* of 12 Germinal Year III, he was already well known to the police, having been denounced by a fellow prisoner for approving of the *journée*. He was released 26 Vendémiaire Year IV (AN, F 7 4686 d 4 [Dulac] and AAG, Cl. gén. 293 [Paris]).

4 See K. Tønnesson, *La défaite des sans-culottes*, 372, 375. Le Batteux was imprisoned at Le Plessis in Germinal Year III, at the same time as Brutus Magnier, Varlet, Charles Germain and his former persecutor, the arch-Robespierrist, Jullien. Paris seems also to have been imprisoned there at the same time – one of the many examples of former enemies coming together in adversity.

5 AN, F 7 4655 d 1 (Coulon) and F 7 4276. In his *Les Infortunes*..., of 1816, 11-12, poor Lefranc gave his involvement a retrospective gloss: 'My natural frankness carried me perhaps beyond the limits of prudence...but my heart was so filled with enthusiasm for the system of liberty, with such anger at the manner in which it was being abused...by those vile plebeians who were sacrificing everything to their own sordid interest. Vengeance was not long in coming. Babeuf was one of the vilest agents of the Terror; but the directory, viler still, allotted me a role in a supposed conspiracy which it had closely followed in order to foil it, and I was sent before the high court of Vendôme....Restored to liberty, I have distanced myself from men and events. I did not have the gifts necessary to suppress or destroy revolutionary power.... I shut myself away in my own nullity...'. This indeed was retrospective modesty.

6 Aulard, II. 520.

7 'The two Rossignols, Parein and Corchand are among the warmest supporters of Babeuf', declared an anonymous informant, undated report. 'Louis, called Brutus, an employee of Barras, is in on their secret.'

8 On 24 Floréal one informant wrote of Vafflard as among the agents going around the workshops of the faubourg; 'he came out of the *armée révolutionnaire*'. (See also AN, F 7 4736 d 2 [Guillaume].)

9 On 16 Messidor the Minister received a report about an 'itinerant club' meeting on the terrace of the Tuileries and frequented by Boissay and 'Eglator'.

10 On Sandoz, see AN, F 7 4276, also I.3. On Baby see AN, F 7 4584 d 1 (Baby).

11 'Pierre-François Paris, aged 36 to 37, medium height, cropped hair, dark, pock-marked skin, large black eyes, wearing a blue coat, laced boots and a round hat, one of the conspirators on the run, stayed six months rue de Richelieu...since 21 Floréal he and his wife hiding at Bercy...either in the big château [also indicated as the hiding-place of Jourdan, former drum-major of the *armée révolutionnaire*] or the beautiful house adjoining...'.

12 See RCC, 'La Commission Temporaire de Commune-Affranchie'.

13 Those at the gatherings were Verd, Delan, Perrotin, Laporte, Desmazures, Léger (AN, F 7 4276).

14 Id., '...Rue des Marmousets, no. 24, *chez* a wigmaker, has lately had frequent meetings with Laignelet, has been a member of the Panthéon and of one of the clubs which succeeded it...'.

15 AN, F 7 4774 8 d 3 (Lecanu) and RCC, 'La Commission Temporaire...', also RCC, 'Politique et subsistances en l'an III: l'exemple du Havre'.

16 See RCC, 'Note sur la répression contre le personnel sans-culotte de 1795 à 1801'. See also BL, F 1124 (12), *Liste officielle des 132 prisonniers faits au camp de Grenelle*, F 51★ (2, 3 and 5) (*Jugements*), F 576 (14) (*Réflexions générales sur la police*, by Limodin).

17 AN, W 554 and 555 (Military Commission of the Temple). See also G. Javogues, 'L'affaire du camp de Grenelle', 'Le procès de Claude Javogues', and 'L'arrestation de Claude Javogues', *Annales révolutionnaires* (1925, 1926, 1928).

18 Aulard, v. 582.

19 AAG, Cl. gén. 293 (Paris). But if Paris had succeeded in eluding the attention of the police, he did not escape the vigilance of the author of the *Dictionnaire des Jacobins vivans*, 130–1: 'This unimportant *révolutionnaire* was no stranger to the massacres in the prisons; he was one of the most hardened denunciators in the Sections, and did not forget to look after himself when sent to Mainz in an exchange of prisoners...'.

20 J. Destrem, *Les déportations du Consulat et de l'Empire* (1885).

21 Jacques Brabant, or Bréban, was at this time secretary to the Cité division of the Commissariat of Police. He died on Anjouan, 13 Floréal Year X (Destrem, 333).

22 Corchand died in Zanzibar, according to Lefranc, Fontaine in the Seychelles, and Derval, or Duval, at Sinnamary, 9 Feb 1809 (Destrem, 125, 130, 389).

23 Lefranc wrote in 1816: '...Many arrests were made, terror spread throughout Paris...several old moustached *révolutionnaires* remembered that I had thanked the gods for the catastrophe of 9 Thermidor; they mingled with the satellites of the prefect Dubois and I was arrested..... I told them that my liaisons in Paris were confined to my relations with my workers and my clients...' (*Les infortunes...*).

24 Louis died at sea in 1809 or 1810 (Destrem, 444–5 and APP, A A/280 [128]); Joly, discharged officer, also died at sea in the Year XII (Destrem, 416).

25 Marcellin was appointed *juge de paix* to the Invalides division, 5 Floréal Year VI (Arch. Seine, D 11 I 1 Carton 51). In Nivôse Year IX he was described as 'inspector of police, dismissed'. On his arrest in the Year XII, see APP, A A/273 (148); he described himself in his interrogation of 5 Nivôse as '...37 years of age, native of Paris, formerly a peace officer, now a haberdasher...'. A note of Brumaire Year IX mentioned him as 'a fanatical terrorist, accomplice to the conspirators [in the Chevalier affair]...keeping them informed of every resolution made against them by the Ministry of Police...he warned Destrem about the day when the First Consul was to have been assassinated at the Opéra...he had charge of the correspondence from the terrorists of the Midi to Destrem...'. See also Destrem, 447.

26 APP, A A/276 (223) (Machine Infernale).

27 'Eglator' was banished to Nantes in the Year X and was refused permission by the police to return to Paris in 1810; Goulart died at Cayenne, 4 Thermidor Year XIV (Destrem, 437, 404). The latter, like Dumoustier, figures in the *Dictionnaire des Jacobins vivans*, 62–3.

28 Colette was arrested in Paris, 14 Nivôse Year IX, deported first to the île d'Oléron, then to Cayenne, where he died in 1807 or 1808 (Destrem, 360, and APP, A A/283). Even Augereau figured in the royalist works of this period, *Le fléau des tyrans et des septembriseurs, ou réflexions sur la Révolution française, par un vrai patriote de 89* [i.e. Danican] (Lausanne, 1797), accusing him of being a deserter before finding favour with the army of Santerre, and marvelling at such an illiterate becoming one of France's best generals.

29 AAG Cl. gén. 365 (Boissay). He was to be dismissed in 1815 and remained without employment until his death.

30 After having been detained in the Year II, Contamin took refuge after Thermidor in Lyon, where he referred to himself as 'victim of Robespierre'. Like so many former terrorists he returned to Paris and was living in the Cité division in the Year IX. Information received 17 Nivôse from a medical student, Michu, stated that after the Grenelle affair Contamin lay hidden for a long time in the sewers; he had received help from Félix Lepeletier, and the informant had it from 'a reliable relative' of the terrorist that, 'far from having changed his opinion, he said he would prefer to stab his children rather than let them live under the regime of Bonaparte'. But Contamin was not disturbed in Nivôse; for the former ultra-revolutionary of Crémieu, the intrepid egalitarian, had sunk to the level of a police informer. Twice he gave voluntary information about the preparation of the first *machine infernale*, that of the rue des Blancs-Manteaux, his declaration of 18 Brumaire Year IX leading to the arrest of the locksmith Decrept. Contamin's excuse was his poverty, his lack of employment and the needs of his family. (APP, A A/272 [Chevalier affair] and A A/282 [350] [Machine Infernale].) We cannot, of course, expect too much of these poor men, persecuted at every moment and constantly near starvation. Lepeletier had ways of making opposition politics pay; but the unemployed locksmith's first priority was to stay alive, and to the honour of the former terrorists it must be said that his is the only case of this kind which we have encountered.

31 Vafflard had been invalided out of the Army of Italy, severely wounded but covered in glory. At the time of the rue Nicaise bomb he was living in the nighbouring rue de Malte. He was interrogated about his relations with Gombaut-Lachaise, 10 Pluviôse Year IX, but released immediately (APP, A A/275 [395]).

32 AN, F 7 6586 (banishment orders). An order of 17 Nivôse Year IX banished Berger from the Parisian region (Destrem, 12). One cannot but be struck by the similarity (surely not accidental) between the names appearing on the list of the Sénatus-Consulte and those in the *Dictionnaire des Jacobins vivans*.

33 AN, F 7 6276 (Machine Infernale).

34 APP, A A/272 (Chevalier affair).

35 See Col. Bernard, 'Le capitaine "Sans-Quartier": Pierre Delport, curé de Beaumont'; RCC, 'Les armées révolutionnaires du Midi', 30–2; and AAG, Cl. gén. 138 (Barateau). Delport died in 1819 refusing the sacaments.

36 En route, they were insulted by the populace, roused against them by government propaganda. In Saumur they were jostled by some cavaliers, with one of whom Lefranc, with his usual violence, came to blows (*Les infortunes*, 31).

37 In his 1816 work Lefranc expressed his horror at the way in which blacks were treated. En route for the Seychelles 'the sight of the Barbary coast had a sorrowful effect on us.... In the eighteenth century all the laws of humanity are being violated, all the rights of peoples are trodden under foot in the name of Mahomet and the Koran!...' (*Les infortunes*, 37). Later he writes of the Congolese: '.... It seems as if nature has degraded these people. They are without intelligence, without imagination...they have no idea of sociability.... This no doubt is why the Europeans think they can buy and sell them like animals. Might it not be better to educate and civilise them than to turn them into vile, unfortunate slaves? ... Sufferers ourselves at the hands of despotism, we were even more aware of the misfortune of men condemned like us to misery.... Their fate was so similar to our own! ...Only the colour of our skins separates us...' (45–6).

38 On Anjouan, after the death of most of his companions in an epidemic, Lefranc gained permission of the king to erect a monument to their memory, 'an obelisk supported by 32 columns...carrying their 31 names and a legend telling of their proscription under the tyranny of Bonaparte...'. Lefranc was so impressed with his work that he used the plan as frontispiece to his 1816 book; the king too was impressed and commissioned him to build a palace. Later, on Zanzibar, he became nostalgic for his own country (*Les infortunes*, 67–8, 127). Some of the deportees remained on Mahé, and in 1809 we hear of Cardinaux exercising his old trade of innkeeper (Destrem, 271, 341).

39 Before reaching Europe, Lefranc and Sormois had travelled via Oibo and Mozambique, where they had met two other deportees, the brothers Linage; they went on to Sainte-Hélène, then experiencing a smallpox epidemic, which gave Lefranc the opportunity to boast of the merits of the new vaccine. At Saint-Thomas, the former architect took a job as a cook on board the *Maria*, out of Antwerp. He then went on to Batavia, was made

prisoner by the English, and brought before the naval governor of Portsmouth who required him to remain in England. But Lefranc (who recounts all this in *Les infortunes*) insisted on returning to France, and the governor found the necessary means.

40 Lefranc, *Les infortunes, passim.*

41 Destrem, 271; AN, F 7 6276 (Machine Infernale) and Lefranc, *Les infortunes.*

42 On 26 Thermidor Year V, Chastel caused a scandal at Chambéry during the fête of 10 August, by praising the Revolutionary Government in the presence of General Kellermann and the authorities, shouting out amidst indignant protests 'that it was only after 9 Thermidor that anarchy and counter-revolution began their progress...'. Dismissed after this incident, he was restored to active service in the Year VI with the Army of Italy, under the orders of Brune. Made head of the Army of Naples general staff, Frimaire Year VII, he was pensioned off, 13 Prairial Year IX, in the proscription following the rue Nicaise affair, and went to live in Geneva (AAG, Cl. gén. 687 [Chastel], and Cl. gén. 187.

43 Parein was appointed to Dijon, *chef-lieu* of the 18th military division, early in the Year VI. He moved on to Mâcon, Chalon and Autun. He was denounced in Germinal Year VI for 'arbitrary acts', dismissed and recalled to Paris, where he took up residence with a caterer in the rue Nicaise! In the Year VII the Directory restored him to active service with the Army of Italy, and he seems to have been attached to the Ministry of Police by Fouché in the Year VIII. Nor was Parein forgotten by Prudhomme (vol. VI, published 1797, p.41).

44 See AAG, Cl. gén., Gén. de brig. 349 (Parein), the duc de Rovigo to the duc de Feltre, 1 Feb 1812. Gourgonnier, formerly provisional commander of the Légion de la Montagne, was removed about the same time (AAG, Cl. gén. 1655 [Gourgonnier]).

45 AN, F 7 6499 (Malet affair). See also E.Guillon, *Les complots militaires sous le Consulat et l'Empire* (1894), 188.

46 AN, F 7 6586 (banishment orders). In 1812 Corchand and Cardinaux tried to return to Paris, but their requests were rejected by the imperial authorities.

47 APP, A A/282, Sormois to count Beugnot, 4 Sept 1814. Sormois had always been extremely anxious to enter into the opinions of whatever men were in power; see APP, A A/273. For Mutelé, Chastel and Viton, see AAG, Cl. gén., 2825, 687 and 3944 respectively, and Gén. Herlaut, 'Le général baron Dufresse', for Dufresse.

48 See AAG, Gén. de brig. 349 (Parein), the colonel of the royal gendarmerie to the duc de Feltre, 2 Nov 1815, listing the charges against Parein, including his association with the events in Lyon, his connection with Fouché, and his opposition to the restoration of the monarchy. On 6 Nov 1815, the Minister of War instructed the commander of the 1st military division to have Parein closely watched. He died at Le Mesnil-Aubry in 1831.

49 APP, A A/333 to 336 (affair of the Patriots). My friend Jean Dautry drew my attention to this document – one of the many occasions on which I have been in his debt for his kindness and advice.

Lefranc was not the only former *révolutionnaire* to attract the attention of the Restoration police: several Lille *révolutionnaires*, notably Buisine, were named in a police note of 18–19 Apr 1816 (AN, F 7 3028, surveillance and arrests, 1815–16); and see p. 209 on Buisine. A number of former members of the *comités révolutionnaires* in the Paris Sections – Dautancourt, L'Honoré, Pio, Florentin, and many more – as well as noted militant *sectionnaires* like Lindberg, also attracted police attention because of their revolutionary past (id.).

50 AAG, Cl. gén. 1308 (Eude).

51 AAG, Cl. gén. 570 (Calmet-Beauvoisins).

52 For Duvicquet see RCC, 'La Commission Temporaire...'; and see p. 623 (Boissay) and I.5 (Gobert).

53 Marcellin's wife, Geneviève Cartaut, was accused by the police of having warned the inhabitants of the Abbaye-au-Bois, rue de Sèvres, of their imminent arrest (APP, A A/272).

54 My friend Vladimir Dedijer, historian of the Yugoslav partisan movement, has always stressed the extremely important role of women soldiers in that movement, in discussions I have had with him.

55 On the occasion of writing to Fouché Marcellin referred to 'the interest which the Minister...has shown in him on many occasions...'. The senator Cabanis intervened on his behalf on several occasions (APP, A A/273). See also Destrem, 447.

APPENDIX A

1 GENERAL TABLE OF DEPARTMENTAL AND COMMUNAL *ARMÉES*

1 L'armée révolutionnaire du Nord [armée of the North]: Lille, Douai, Cambrai, Bailleul – effective: c.500 (of a projected total of 1,000)

2 L'armée révolutionnaire de l'Est [armée of the East] ('armée révolutionnaire de la Moselle'): Longwy, Metz, Thionville, Sarreguemines, Sarrelouis – effective: 1,000

3 L'armée révolutionnaire du Bas-Rhin: Strasbourg, Haguenau, Sélestat – effective: 1,000

4 L'armée révolutionnaire du Haut-Rhin: Colmar, Belfort – effective: 1,000 (?)

5 La compagnie révolutionnaire d'Evreux: Evreux, Conches

6 Le bataillon révolutionnaire du Finistère (?): Brest

7 L'armée révolutionnaire de Redon: Vannes, Roche-Sauveur – effective: 500 to 600

8 La 'compagnie Marat' de Nantes: Nantes and environs – effective: 60 (?)

9 Le 'bataillon de la Montagne' ('armée révolutionnaire de Troyes'): Troyes, Ervy – effective: 400 (?)

10 La 'cavalerie de la force publique du Cher': Bourges, Aubigny, Vierzon – effective: 62

11 L'armée révolutionnaire de la Marne (?): Châlons, Reims, Sézanne, Epernay

12 Le bataillon révolutionnaire de l'Indre-et-Loire: Tours – effective: 1,000

13 Les compagnies révolutionnaires du Loiret: Orléans, Montargis, Beaugency, Neuville, Gien, Boiscommun – effective: 400 (?)

14 Le bataillon révolutionnaire de la Nièvre: Nevers, Château-Chinon, Cosne, Corbigny, Moulins-Engilbert, Clamecy, Lyon and environs, Saône-et-Loire, Loire, Ain, Isère – effective: 300–350

15 La compagnie révolutionnaire du district de Clamecy: Clamecy and environs – effective: 80

16 Le bataillon révolutionnaire de l'Allier: districts of the Allier, Lyon, Saône-et-Loire, Loire, Ain, Isère – effective: 350

17 L'armée révolutionnaire de la Loire: districts of the Loire, Lyon – effective: 1,200

18 Le bataillon révolutionnaire de Saône-et-Loire: Mâcon and Bourg district (Ain) – effective: 175

19 Le bataillon révolutionnaire du Puy-de-Dôme

20 La compagnie révolutionnaire de la Haute-Loire

21 L' 'armée révolutionnaire' de Crémieu: district of La Tour-du-Pin (Isère) – effective: 32

22 La compagnie révolutionnaire de Grenoble: Grenoble and environs – effective: 100

23 La compagnie révolutionnaire de Limoges: Limoges and environs – effective: 200

24 Le bataillon révolutionnaire de Bordeaux: Bordeaux and district, districts of Libourne and Lesparre – effective: 500 (?)

25 Le bataillon révolutionnaire du Lot-et-Garonne: Agen, Tonneins, Marmande, Villeneuve-sur-Lot, Nérac – effective: c. 150

26 La compagnie révolutionnaire de Montauban: Montauban and environs – effective: 500

27 La 'gendarmerie révolutionnaire' de Castelsarrasin: Castelsarrasin

28 La 'gendarmerie révolutionnaire' de Moissac: district of Lauzerte

29 L'armée révolutionnaire du Lot: Cahors, Gourdon, Aveyron, Lozère – effective: 3,200

30 L'armée révolutionnaire du Cantal: Aurillac, Murat, Saint-Flour, Aveyron, Lozère – effective: 1,000

31 L'armée révolutionnaire de l'Aveyron: Aveyron.

32 L'armée révolutionnaire de la Haute-Garonne ('armée révolutionnaire toulousaine' and

'compagnie révolutionnaire de Beaumont'): Toulouse, Beaumont-Grenade, Muret, Saint-Gaudens, and, in the Ariège: Pamiers, Saint-Girons, Foix – effective: 750

33 Le bataillon révolutionnaire de l'Ariège ('compagnie révolutionnaire de Pamiers'): Pamiers, Foix, Saint-Girons – effective: 250

34 La 'garde soldée de Dax': Dax et environs

35 L'armée révolutionnaire des Basses-Pyrénées: Pau and environs

36 L'armée révolutionnaire des Hautes-Pyrénées: Tarbes and environs

37 Le bataillon révolutionnaire du Tarn (?): Castres? Aveyron?

38 Le bataillon révolutionnaire de Montpellier: Montpellier, Lunel – effective: 500

39 La 'compagnie révolutionnaire' de Sète (?): Sète and environs

40 La Légion de la Montagne ('Légion des Montagnards, fille des sociétés populaires'): Drôme, Vaucluse, Bouches-du-Rhône, Var, armées of the Pyrénées-Orientales – effective: 2,200 (as projected); 1,151 already by Vendémiaire Year II

41 La 'compagnie montagnarde' d'Orange: Orange and environs

42 La 'compagnie révolutionnaire' de Valence: Valence and environs

43 Le 'bataillon des sans-culottes révolutionnaires' d'Aix-en-Provence: Aix, centre for Toulon

44 Le 'bataillon des sans-culottes' de Marseille: Marseille and environs

45 La 'compagnie révolutionnaire' de Lambesc: Lambesc – effective: 60

46 La 'compagnie révolutionnaire' d'Auriol: Auriol – effective: 50

47 La compagnie révolutionnaire de Digne: Digne and district – total for all *compagnies révolutionnaires* of the Basses-Alpes: 1,000

48 La compagnie révolutionnaire de Castellane: Castellane

49 La compagnie révolutionnaire d'Entrevaux: Entrevaux

50 La compagnie révolutionnaire de La Mure: La Mure

51 La compagnie révolutionnaire de Manosque: Manosque

52 La compagnie révolutionnaire d'Oraison: Oraison

53 La compagnie révolutionnaire de Sisteron: Sisteron

54 La compagnie révolutionnaire de Senez: Senez

55 La compagnie révolutionnaire de Thorame: Thorame

56 L'armée révolutionnaire des Hautes-Alpes: Gap, Embrun, Briançon and Serres – effective: 200 (4 companies of 50 men each)

2 LIST OF DEPARTMENTS WITH ACTIVE *ARMÉES*

*Ain (Paris, Mâcon, Nièvre and Allier *armées*)

 Aisne (Paris *armée*)

*Allier (*bataillon révolutionnaire* of the Allier)

*Alpes (Basses-) (*compagnies révolutionnaires* of the Basses-Alpes)

*Alpes (Hautes-) (*bataillon révolutionnaire* of the Hautes-Alpes)

*Ariège (*bataillon révolutionnaire* of Pamiers, Toulouse *armée*)

*Aube ('bataillon de la Montagne')

*Aveyron (Lot, Cantal, Tarn and Aveyron *armées*; *bataillon* of Montpellier, Toulouse *armée*).

*Bec-d'Ambès (Gironde) (*bataillon* of Bordeaux, *armée* of Lesparre)

*Bouches-du-Rhône (Légion de la Montagne, *bataillons* of Marseille, Aix, Lambesc, Auriol)

 Calvados (Paris *armée*)

*Cantal (*armée révolutionnaire* of Cantal)

*Cher ('cavalerie de la force publique')

*Côte d'Or (Paris *armée*, in passage only)

*Drôme (Paris *armée*, *compagnie* of Valence, Légion de la Montagne)

*Eure (Paris *armée*, *compagnie* of Evreux)

 Eure-et-Loir (Paris *armée*)

*Finistère (Paris *armée* – cannoneers, and *bataillon révolutionnaire* of the Finistère [?])

*Garonne (Haute-) (Toulouse *armée*; *compagnie* of Beaumont, 'armée' of Castelsarrasin)

*Hérault (*bataillon* of Montpellier, *compagnie* of Sète [?])

*Ille-et-Vilaine (*armée* of Redon)

*Indre-et-Loire (Paris *armée* and *bataillon révolutionnaire* of Tours)

---

*indicates departments which saw departmental and communal *armées* in action

*Isère (Paris *armée*, *compagnie* of Grenoble, 'armée' of Crémieu, *armées* of the Nièvre and Allier)
*Landes ('garde soldée de Dax')
*Loire (Paris *armée*, *armée révolutionnaire* of the Loire)
*Loire (Haute-) (*bataillon révolutionnaire*)
*Loire-Inférieure (Paris *armée*, 'compagnie Marat' of Nantes)
*Loiret (Paris *armée*, *compagnies révolutionnaires* of the Loiret)
*Lot (*armée révolutionnaire* of the Lot, *compagnie* of Montauban, *gendarmerie révolutionnaire* of
    Moissac)
*Lot-et-Garonne (*compagnies révolutionnaires* of the Lot-et-Garonne)
*Lozère (*armées* of the Lot and Aveyron) (*bataillon* of Montpellier)
 Maine-et-Loire (Paris *armée* – squadrons)
 Manche (Paris *armée* – cannoneers)
*Marne (*armée révolutionnaire* of the Marne)
*Morbihan (*armée* of Redon)
*Moselle (*armée révolutionnaire* of the East)
*Nièvre (*bataillon révolutionnaire* of the Nièvre, *compagnie révolutionnaire* of the district of
    Clamecy)
*Nord (*armée révolutionnaire* of Lille [the North])
 Oise (Paris *armée*)
 Orne (Paris *armée*)
 Paris (Paris *armée*)
*Puy-de-Dôme (Paris *armée* [?], *bataillon révolutionnaire* of Clermont?)
*Pyrénées (Basses-) (*compagnie révolutionnaire* of Pau)
*Pyrénées (Hautes-) (*compagnie révolutionnaire* of Tarbes)
*Rhin (Bas-) (*armée révolutionnaire* of the Bas-Rhin)
*Rhin (Haut-) (*armée révolutionnaire* of the Haut-Rhin)
*Rhône (Paris *armée*, *bataillons* of the Loire, the Nièvre and the Allier)
*Saône-et-Loire (Paris *armée*, *bataillon révolutionnaire* of Mâcon)
 Sarthe (Paris *armée*)
 Seine-et-Oise (Paris *armée*)
 Seine-Inférieure (Paris *armée*)
 Seine-et-Marne (Paris *armée*)
*Tarn (*bataillon révolutionnaire* of Castres [?])
*Vaucluse (Paris *armée*, 'compagnie montagnarde' of Orange, Légion de la Montagne)
*Vienne (Haute-) (*bataillon révolutionnaire* of Limoges)
 Yonne (Paris *armée*)

3   CHRONOLOGICAL TABLE OF ORDERS CONCERNING
THE DEPARTMENTAL *ARMÉES*

August 1793
21 Aug: commission to raise a *légion révolutionnaire* in the Nièvre department.[1]

September 1793
7–10 Sept: general assembly of 71 *sociétés populaires* in the Midi meeting at Valence (decision to
    set up a Légion de la Montagne).[2]
9 Sept: order of Laplanche for the creation of *compagnies révolutionnaires* of the Loiret.[3]
13 Sept: order of Taillefer and the *comité militaire* of Montauban for creation of an *armée
    révolutionnaire* of the Lot.[4]
13 Sept: order of the *société populaire* of Largentière (Ardèche) for the creation of a paid guard.[5]

---

1 First executed in the Clamecy district as early as 6 Sept, when the lieutenant-colonel of that region
   presented his commission to its directory.
2 Organisation of the Légion commenced at Valence and Marseille in Oct. In Brumaire and Pluviôse
   especially, volunteers were recruited from all over France.
3 Companies were activated at Montargis and Neuville at the end of Sept.
4 The origin of Viton's powers. The *armée* was active in the Gourdon district in Sept.
5 Does not appear to have been executed.

16 Sept: order of the *société* of Châteauroux for the creation of an *armée révolutionnaire* of the Indre.[6]

19 Sept: order of the *comité* of Cahors for the formation of a *bataillon révolutionnaire*.[7]

20 Sept: resolution of the *société* of Limoges in favour of the enrolment of an *armée révolutionnaire* of the Haute-Vienne.[8]

21 Sept: resolution of the *société des anti-politiques* of Aix in favour of the enrolment of a *bataillon des sans-culottes* for the town of Aix.[9]

21 Sept: first order of the *représentants* of Toulouse for the formation of an *armée toulousaine*.

22 Sept: resolution of the *société* of Valence in favour of the enrolment of an *armée révolutionnaire* for the Drôme.[10]

22 Sept: order of the *représentants* for the enrolment of a *bataillon révolutionnaire* for Montauban.[11]

25 Sept: order of the *représentants* for the formation of an *armée* for the district of Lesparre.

30 Sept: order of Fouché for the enrolment of *bataillons révolutionnaires* for the Nièvre and Allier.[12]

30 Sept: order of the War Minister for the creation of an *armée révolutionnaire* de l'Ouest.[13]

October 1793

2 Oct: order of municipality of Evreux for the enrolment of an unpaid battalion, to be called *bataillon révolutionnaire*.[14]

2 Oct: resolution of the *société* of Rouen in favour of the formation of an *armée révolutionnaire* of the Seine-Inférieure.[15]

4 Oct: letter of Taillefer to his *délégué* in Cantal for the formation of an *armée révolutionnaire* of the Cantal.[16]

5 Oct: supposed date of formation of the 'compagnie de la Montagne' in the district of Orange.[17]

9 Oct: order of the *comité* of Aurillac for the enrolment of an *armée révolutionnaire* of the Cantal.[18]

9 Oct: order of the *représentants* of Toulouse for the formation of an *armée révolutionnaire* of the Haute-Garonne.[19]

10 Oct: order of the *société* of Morlaas demanding the formation of a *compagnie révolutionnaire* of 80 men.[20]

11 Oct: order of the *représentants* of Toulouse for the creation of an *armée* in the district of Pamiers.[21]

12 Oct: order of the same for the creation of an *armée révolutionnaire* in the Lot-et-Garonne.[22]

12 Oct: order of the municipality of Troyes demanding the formation of an *armée révolutionnaire troyenne*.[23]

14 Oct: resolution of the *société* of Montpellier in favour of raising a *bataillon révolutionnaire* of Montpellier.[24]

---

6 Again not executed; there was no Indre *armée*, though it is possible that the Parisian *armée* passed through the department.

7 A company subsequently incorporated into the Lot *armée*.

8 The *représentents* of the Haute-Vienne were to prevent the execution of this order, though it was confirmed by them on 5 Brumaire.

9 Enrolment was to commence at the beginning of Oct.

10 Not executed.

11 Commenced execution on 27 Sept.

12 On 1 Oct the Moulins *comité* opened an enrolment register.

13 Not executed. It was rather a real army, wrongly labelled 'revolutionary'.

14 Swiftly executed.

15 Not executed, despite a district-wide campaign.

16 An order which was executed fairly rapidly.

17 According to evidence for Year II, the 'company' would have been formed at this time.

18 Swiftly executed.

19 This *armée* was reorganised in Brumaire.

20 Nothing came of this order at Morlaas.

21 Swiftly executed.

22 Eventually executed.

23 Not executed.

24 An order confirmed by Boisset on 1 Brumaire. The battalion was organised in the first days of Brumaire.

24 Vendémiaire: order of Mallarmé and others for the formation of an *armée révolutionnaire* of the Moselle.[25]

17 Oct: order of the *société* of Senez opening an enrolment register for the *compagnie révolutionnaire*.[26]

27 Vendémiaire: order of Tallien and Isabeau for the formation of a *bataillon révolutionnaire* of Bordeaux.[27]

27 Vendémiaire: order of Taillefer and the *comité* of Moissac for the formation of the *gendarmerie révolutionnaire* of Moissac.[28]

20 Oct: order of the *société* of Thorame for the same.[29]

20 Oct: order of Mallarmé for the formation of an *armée révolutionnaire* of the Bas-Rhin.[30]

21 Oct: order of Javogues and Bassal for the creation of an *armée révolutionnaire* of the Loire.[31]

24 Oct: order of the *comité* of Manosque for the formation of a *compagnie révolutionnaire*.[32]

(?) Oct: order of the district of Pau on the formation of a paid sans-culotte guard at Pau.[33]

Brumaire Year II

1 Brumaire: order of the *société* of La Mure for the formation of a *compagnie révolutionnaire*.[34]

2 Brumaire: order of the *société révolutionnaire* of Lille on the formation of an *armée révolutionnaire du Nord*.[35]

5 Brumaire: order of Paganel on the reorganisation of the *armée révolutionnaire* of the Haute-Garonne.[36]

5 Brumaire: order of the *société* of Mende on the formation of a *bataillon révolutionnaire* in the Lozère.[37]

5 Brumaire: order of Brival and Lanot on the reorganisation of the *armée révolutionnaire* of the Haute-Vienne.[38]

5 Brumaire: order of the department of the Cher for the formation of a *cavalerie d'ordre public*.[39]

5 Brumaire: second order of the *société* of Rouen.[40]

5 Brumaire: order of the department of the Meurthe for the formation of an *armée révolutionnaire* of the Meurthe.[41]

5 Brumaire: order of the district of Versailles on the formation of the *armée révolutionnaire* of Seine-et-Oise.[42]

7 Brumaire: order of Maure for the formation of an *armée* of the Yonne.[43]

9 Brumaire: collective order of the *représentants* to the Army of the Alps for the creation of *bataillons* for the Côte-d'Or, Haute-Saône, Doubs, Jura, Ain, Mont-Blanc, Mont-Terrible, Saône-et-Loire and Isère.[44]

9 Brumaire: order of Simond and Dumas for the formation of an *armée révolutionnaire* for the Mont-Blanc.

---

25 This *armée* was ready to march on 14 Brumaire.
26 On this date the Digne company was already activated.
27 Parts of this battalion were active in Brumaire, but its organisation dragged on into Nivôse.
28 Swiftly executed.
29 Swiftly executed.
30 This *armée* was ready to leave on 24 Oct. It was put into action on 5 Brumaire.
31 Slowly executed; the general review of this *armée* took place only on 15 Frimaire.
32 By this date, several companies were on foot in the Basses-Alpes, notably at Digne and Sisteron.
33 Swiftly executed at Pau, where the company was in action by Brumaire. In the other districts of the Basses-Pyrénées, things proceeded more slowly, and the order was not executed at all in Morlaas and Monein.
34 We do not know if this company was raised.
35 Confirmed by the order of the *représentants* on 5 Brumaire.
36 This order increased the number of effectives of this *armée* – already activated – by extending enrolment to the entire region of La Place.
37 Nothing came of this order.
38 This order was subject to authorisation by the Committee of Public Safety as far as the cavalry and artillery were concerned. The fusiliers were organised.
39 Incompletely executed.
40 No sequel.
41 Not executed.
42 In Brumaire the Versailles Sections drew up enrolment lists, but the *armée* was never activated.
43 Execution of the order commenced immediately, and by 24 Brumaire, lists had been completed in the Avallon district.
44 Commencement of execution everywhere, and at Mâcon and Besançon companies activated.

13 Brumaire: order of Châles and Isoré confirming that of 5 Brumaire on the formation of the *armée du Nord*.[45]

14 Brumaire: order of the department of the Marne on the enrolment of a *force départementale*.[46]

14 Brumaire: order of the *commissaires civils* of the *armée de l'Est*, executing that of the *représentants* of 24 Vendémiaire and announcing that the *armée* was being activated.[47]

15 Brumaire: order of the *société populaire* of Chaumont concerning the formation of an *armée révolutionnaire* of the Haute-Marne.[48]

16 Brumaire: order of the *représentants* at Tours for the formation of the *armée révolutionnaire* of the Indre-et-Loire.[49]

16 Brumaire: order of the Mont-Blanc department on the formation of the departmental *armée*.[50]

17 Brumaire: order of the *représentants* at Marseille for the formation of the *compagnie* of Lambesc.[51]

18 Brumaire: order of the *société populaire* of Ornans on the organisation and recruitment of the Doubs *armée*, in execution of the collective order of 9 Brumaire.[52]

20 Brumaire: order of the Gray district on the enrolment of the *armée* of the Haute-Saône, in execution of the 9 Brumaire order.[53]

20 Brumaire: order of the *société* of Valence to demand the formation of an *armée* for the Drôme.[54]

21 Brumaire: circular of Lémare, of the *commission départemental* of the Jura, on the enrolment of the *armée* of this department (in execution of the order of 9 Brumaire).[55]

23 Brumaire: order of the Annecy district on the formation of the *armée* of the Mont-Blanc (in execution of the order of 9 Brumaire).[56]

24 Brumaire: order of the *assemblée populaire* of the *sociétés* united at Gap for the formation of an *armée révolutionnaire* of the Hautes-Alpes; order confirmed by the *représentant* Beauchamp.[57]

24 Brumaire: order of the *comité* of Digne for the formation of a *bataillon révolutionnaire* (a company existed there after October).[58]

24 Brumaire: order of Hérault for the formation of the *armée révolutionnaire* of the Haut-Rhin.

26 Brumaire: order of the *société* of Thonon for the raising of a company (in execution of the order of Simond and Dumas, 9 Brumaire).[59]

26 Brumaire: order of the *comité* of La Clayette for the organisation of the battalion (in execution of the order of 9 Brumaire).[60]

27 Brumaire: order of the *comité* of Oraison announcing the activation of the company.[61]

28 Brumaire: order of the municipality of Grenoble on the formation of a Grenoble company.[62]

28 Brumaire: order of the *société* of Perpignan for the formation of an *armée révolutionnaire* of the Pyrénées-Orientales.

---

45 Swiftly executed – the Lille *armée* was in action by the end of Brumaire.
46 We do not know if this order was executed. *Commissaires civils* were active in this department at the head of revolutionary forces. But were they those of the Marne?
47 By this date the *armée* was already active.
48 Commencement of execution; but this *armée* was not activated.
49 No information about the execution of this order.
50 Commencement of execution; enrolment lists drawn up.
51 Order executed. The company was already active in Pluviôse.
52 Commencement of execution; enrolment lists drawn up.
53 Execution of order begun, interrupted by the law of 14 Frimaire.
54 No issue. But there was talk again of a revolutionary army in Ventôse.
55 Enrolment procedures began at once and continued until the last *décade* of Frimaire.
56 District lists were prepared and material bought to make uniforms, but things went no further.
57 The National Guard came together for the election of men and officers on 3–4 Frimaire. The battalion was activated at Serres on 25 Frimaire.
58 The companies were already active. We do not know if organisation at battalion level was completed, but the companies were still in service at the beginning of Nivôse.
59 Not executed.
60 Not executed.
61 This company was already active.
62 Swiftly executed, this company being activated around 12 Frimaire. The order concerned a municipal *armée*. The departmental *armée* never saw the light of day, and at Vienne enrolment lists were not opened until 14 Frimaire.

29 Brumaire: order of the *société* of Paray for the organisation of the battalion (in execution of the order of 9 Brumaire).[63]

29 Brumaire: order of the municipality of Saint-Germain for the formation of a battalion in this district (in execution of the order of the Versailles district, 5 Brumaire).[64]

Frimaire Year II

1 Frimaire: order of the *représentants* for the enrolment of an *armée* in the Basses-Pyrénées.[65]

2 Frimaire: resolution of the *société* of Guéret in favour of the formation of an *armée révolutionnaire* in the Creuse.[66]

3 Frimaire: order of the *société populaire* of Gap to accelerate enrolment of the departmental *armée* (in execution of the order of 24 Brumaire).[67]

4 Frimaire: order of Fabre and Gaston for the formation of an *armée* in the Pyrénées-Orientales.[68]

8 Frimaire: orders of the *sociétés* of Dijon and Nuits on the formation of the *armée* of the Côte-d'Or (in execution of the order of 9 Brumaire).[69]

11 Frimaire: order of Vauquoy, member of the Commission Temporaire, for the formation of the *armée* of Crémieu.[70]

11 Frimaire: order of Carrier appointing Le Batteux to the command of the armed force at Redon.[71]

12 Frimaire: order of the Lorient *société* about the *armée*.[72]

14 Frimaire: order of the *représentants* at Brest for the formation of a company in the Finistère.[73]

16 Frimaire: order of the *société* of Montbéliard on the enrolment of the *armée* of the Doubs (in execution of the order of 9 Brumaire).[74]

19 Frimaire: order of the *société* of Monein to demand the formation of a company in the district.[75]

20 Frimaire: order of the *société* of Montbard about the organisation of the *armée* of the Côte-d'Or (in execution of the order of 9 Brumaire).[76]

25 Frimaire: letter of Barjavel, public prosecutor in the Vaucluse, about the raising of a force in this department.[77]

---

63 Enrolment was still in progress in the last *décade* of Frimaire.

64 Enrolment commenced the same day, but, as at Versailles, little progress was made.

65 No issue, though Pau was to have a paid guard.

66 No issue; the *société* declared against the enrolment.

67 The company was activated at the end of the month.

68 Enrolment was still in progress when the law of 14 Frimaire reached Perpignan.

69 Lists were still being drawn up when the law of 14 Frimaire was promulgated in the Côte d'Or.

70 This order was annulled on 16 Frimaire by the Commission Temporaire, but the Crémieu *armée* was to remain in action until 8 Nivôse.

71 Redon's *armée* had already been enrolled by this date and it was activated the day after this order.

72 This was the date on which the *société* learnt of the arrival of the *armée* in the Morbihan.

73 Date of Jeanbon Saint-André's order. We do not know whether this order was partially or fully executed.

74 Proceedings did not get beyond the enrolment stage – itself delayed by the unification of the territory with France.

75 This order had no more success than the earlier moves of the *société* in favour of a municipal company. It appears then that no company existed in this department besides the paid guard of Pau.

76 Proceedings were still at the stage of the enrolment of volunteers when the law of 14 Frimaire was promulgated in the Côte-d'Or.

77 The request of Barjavel, renewed on 14 Nivôse, seems to have resulted in the dispatch of a detachment of the Parisian *armée* in Pluviôse.

APPENDIX B

CHRONOLOGICAL TABLE OF FORCED DECHRISTIANISATION*
(INTERVENTION BY THE *ARMÉES RÉVOLUTIONNAIRES*)

September–October 1793:

20 Sept–15 Oct	District of Gonesse (repression, arrests, iconoclasm, closures, removal of bells and silver: Parisian *armée*)
(22 Sept)	(commune of Jagny)
10–11 Oct	Allier: Bourbon-l'Archambault (arrests, sermons, closurés: Allier battalion)
13 Oct	Loiret: Boiscommun (sermons, *deprêtrisations*: companies from the Loiret).
21 Oct	Ariège: Seix (sermons, iconoclasm, closures: Haute-Garonne battalion)

Brumaire Year II:

20 Brumaire	Nièvre (district of Clamecy) (closure)
20 Brumaire	Haute-Garonne: Grenade (closures: Haute-Garonne *armée*)
20–22 Brumaire	Yonne: Sens
21–23 Brumaire	Joigny
22–25 Brumaire	Auxerre
25–27 Brumaire	Vermenton
27–29 Brumaire	Avallon and environs
	(iconoclasm, sermons, closures, arrests, passage of the Parisian *armée*)
22 Brumaire	Eure: Vernon (iconoclasm, closure: Parisian *armée*)
25–30 Brumaire	Nièvre: district of Corbigny (closures, iconoclasm, etc.: Nièvre battalion)
26 Brumaire and after	Nièvre: districts of Decize and Moulins-Engilbert (id.)
28 Brumaire	Aisne: Laon (iconoclasm, closures: Parisian *armée*)
end of Brumaire	Allier: Montmarault and district (closure, arrests, iconoclasm: Allier battalion)
Brumaire (no date)	Oise: Beauvais (closure, sermons: Parisian cavalry)

Frimaire:

2 Frimaire	Oise: Croix (closure, iconoclasm: Parisian *armée*)
7–15 Frimaire	Saône-et-Loire: Cluny and environs (id.)
8 Frimaire	Marne: Vitry-le-François (closures, sermons, cult of Reason: *commissaires civils* of the Marne *armée*)
10 Frimaire	Marne: Epernay (id.)
10–15 Frimaire	Morbihan: Noyal-Muzillac, Questembert (closures, shootings, burnings of churches: Redon battalion)
11 Frimaire	Oise: Noyon (iconoclasm, closure: Parisian *armée*)

761

12 Frimaire–8 Nivôse	Isère: district of La Tour-du-Pin (closures, iconoclasm, burnings, atheistic sermons, etc.: Crémieu *armée* and Parisian *armée*)
(14 Frimaire	(Jons and Jonage
19–20 Frimaire	Jons
23–25 Frimaire	Biols
27 Frimaire	Bizonnes
26–29 Frimaire	Morestel
26–27 Frimaire	Brangues
29 Frimaire	Biols
30 Frimaire	Flachères
1 Nivôse	Eydoches
3 Nivôse	Le Gaz
5 Nivôse)	Les Abrets)
13 Frimaire	Nord: Dunkerque (closures, sermons: Lille *armée*)
17 Frimaire	Oise: Saint-Pierre (iconoclasm, closures: Parisian *armée*)
20 Frimaire	Seine-et-Marne: Provins (celebration of Reason: Parisian *armée*)
24–27 Frimaire	Seine-et-Marne: district of Rozoy (the 'Vendée briarde': Parisian *armée*)
25 Frimaire	Seine-et-Marne: Le Mée (closures: Parisian *armée*)
27 Frimaire	Eure: district of Louviers (Ailly) (repression, closures: Parisian *armée*)
25–27 Frimaire	Seine-et-Oise: district of Mantes (Epone) (closure, etc., on threat of the arrival of the Parisian *armée*)
30 Frimaire	Ariège: Le Mas-d'Azil (sermons, cult of Reason: *commissaires civils* of the Toulouse *armée*)
15–18 Frimaire	Bas-Rhin (arrests, shootings, burnings, closures, sermons: Strasbourg *armée*)

Nivôse:

2 Nivôse	Aisne: Chaourse, canton of Montcornet (attempted closure, cult of Reason: Parisian *armée*).
7 Nivôse	Seine-et-Oise: Fourqueux (arrests, closure: Parisian *armée*)
7 Nivôse	Seine-et-Marne: Nemours (iconoclasm: Parisian *armée*)
10 Nivôse	Seine-et-Oise: Saint-Germain (proposed ban on religious observance: Parisian *armée*)
17 Nivôse	Seine-et-Oise: district of Pontoise (Nesles) (closure, repression: Parisian *armée*)
20 Nivôse	Eure: Ecouis (cult of Reason: Parisian *armée*)
21 Nivôse	Seine-et-Oise: Cormeilles-en-Vexin (repression: Parisian *armée*)
22 Nivôse	Seine-et-Oise: Presles (arrests, closure: Parisian *armée*)
23 Nivôse	Seine-et-Marne: Brie-Comte-Robert (repression of religious disturbances, arrests: Parisian *armée*)
24 Nivôse	Seine-et-Marne: Château-Landon (closure, bells removed, etc.: Parisian *armée*)
30 Nivôse	Saône-et-Loire: La Clayette (closure): but uncertainty about presence of a Parisian detachment

Pluviôse:

5 Pluviôse	Seine-et-Marne: Cannes (arrests: Parisian *armée*)

Ventôse:

4–9 Ventôse	Seine-et-Oise: Livry (repression, iconoclasm, closure: Parisian *armée*)
6–9 Ventôse	Drôme: district of Valence (repression, closure: Valence battalion)
11 Ventôse	Calvados: Honfleur (repression: Parisian *armée*)

16 Ventôse	Calvados: Villerville (repression, closure: Parisian *armée*)
16–18 Ventôse	Eure: Pont-de-l'Arche (repression, closure, iconoclasm: Parisian *armée*)
19 Ventôse	Calvados: Trouville (repression) (id.)
19 Ventôse	Vaucluse: Violès (closure: intervention by the *commissaire civil* of Orange)
19–22 Ventôse	Yonne: Villeblevin (repression: Parisian *armée*)
Ventôse (no date)	Calvados: Saint-Martin-Le-Vieux (closure and iconoclasm: Parisian *armée*)

---

*This table is incomplete because we do not know the dates of several important operations such as those in the Aube, Loire, Ariège, Finistère and Orne. Nevertheless a calendar of dechristianisation can be compiled: *Sept to Oct*: removal of bells and silver, iconoclasm and repression of disturbances.

Brumaire to early Nivôse: atheistic propaganda added – movement reaches peak – installation of the cult of Reason and the campaign against Sunday – positive dechristianisation.

early Frimaire: protests from local authorities begin to flood in to the Committee of Public Safety – decree of 14 Frimaire intervenes – anti-religious activity continues 10–20 days longer in certain departments, before the law is known to the local authorities.

Nivôse: sees a crescendo of activity by the *armées révolutionnaires* in the dechristianising campaign, because of disturbances provoked by the celebration of masses at Christmas, and on the feast of Saint Sylvestre and Epiphany. Punitive expeditions mounted by the *comités de surveillance* and the Committee of General Security encourage spontaneous action by the Parisians, closures of churches and attempts to impose the cult of Reason, in association with sans-culotte minorities – which provoke a sharp warning to the Viarmes detachment (21 Nivôse) not to interfere in religious affairs and to respect religious freedom.

Pluviôse: a calmer month, though difficult for the *armée révolutionnaire*: its commander in prison till the 14th, and the attitude of local authorities, knowing of political events in Paris, hardening towards the detachments.

Ventôse: with the rehabilitation of Ronsin and Vincent, violent revolutionary activity is renewed: start of the expedition to Livry, the 'new Vendée', according to the *commissaires* leading it; sacking of churches by soldiers around Honfleur, and arrests of religious supporters in the coastal towns (fear of English agents caused particular concern about public opinion in these areas – though here it was less a question of dechristianising than of maintaining a position already attained, and of resisting the efforts of the women to reopen the churches). Ventôse closes with the celebrated expedition of Villeblevin, following a long conflict between a minority of sans-culottes (installed in the *mairie*) and a group of notables (supported by the majority of the inhabitants), over the suppression of the confraternities. The same month sees Halm's soldiers treating the canton of Pont-de-l'Arche like conquered territory.

Thus, in the zone of activity of the Parisian *armée*, forced dechristianisation continued to the end, despite the law of 18 Frimaire on religious freedom, and the warning of 21 Nivôse. But even elsewhere, in the Vaucluse for instance, sans-culotte minorities were able to close churches and install the cult of Reason without armed assistance, showing once more that the *armées* were not always responsible for initiating the process of dechristianisation.

APPENDIX C

Year II	1793–4
1 Vendémiaire	22 Sept 1793
10	1 Oct 1793
20	11
1 Brumaire	22
10	31
20	10 Nov 1793
1 Frimaire	21
10	30
20	10 Dec 1793
1 Nivôse	2
10	30
20	9 Jan 1794
1 Pluviôse	20
10	29
20	8 Feb 1794
1 Ventôse	19
10	28
20	10 Mar 1794
1 Germinal	21
10	30
20	9 Apr 1794
1 Floréal	20
10	29
20	9 May 1794
1 Prairial	20
10	29
20	8 June 1794
1 Messidor	19
10	28
20	8 July 1794
1 Thermidor	19
10	28
20	7 Aug 1794
1 Fructidor	18
10	27
20	6 Sept 1794
1er jour complémentaire	17
5e	21

INDEX OF NAMES

Officers and men of the *armées révolutionnaires* are identified as '*rév.*' (= *révolutionnaire*), with their rank, when known, and the *armée* in which they were enrolled in brackets; (P) = Parisian *armée*. Place-names are in small capitals. Bold-face references indicate substantial treatment in the text.